The 1988 Media Guide

A Critical Review of the Print Media's Recent Coverage Of the World Political Economy

Jude Wanniski
Editor

Peter A. Signorelli
Managing Editor
Patricia Koyce
Associate Editor

Polyconomics, Inc., Morristown, N.J.

LIBRARY OF CONTRESS CATALOG CARD NUMBER: 87-092220

ISBN: 0-938081-01-2

88   89   90   91   10   8   7   6   5   4   3   2   1

TABLE OF CONTENTS

MediaGuide

The 1988 Media Guide

INTRODUCTION

This third annual edition of the *MediaGuide* covers the work of journalists in an extremely demanding and complex news year, by far the most difficult of the years since we began our evaluations in 1985. The great global stock market crash of October put an incredible exclamation point to a year of dizzying swirls in the world political economy, led by the decline of the Reagan Administration from a giddy peak in '86, evidence of at least the beginnings of dramatic changes in the Soviet Union and Eastern Europe, and the emergence of the AIDS epidemic as a pressing fact on the world's political agenda.

In an absolute sense, the print media seemed more productive during the year, simply because so much more was demanded of it. At the same time, there was no discernible decline in reporting objectivity and fairness and we were rather pleased at the high levels generally maintained in these areas, although there were notable lapses now and then. The clear trend away from advocacy journalism in the 1980s continued. In the face of great temptations to engage directly in the bitter political debates and struggles of the year, most editors and reporters showed admirable restraint. Our scattered complaints are noted elsewhere in the guide.

Given the assignment of covering the swift changes and intricate and myriad variables at work on the planet, the press corps should have done a better job on substance. Too often we waited for a newspaper or periodical, any one at all, to offer reports, analysis or commentary where there seemed gaping holes in the total coverage of events and trends. Where we use the word "timely" in this book, in commenting on a journalist's specific story or column, it means we were pleased on this point. "Ah, we've been waiting for this." More than in previous years, our readers were left mildly dissatisfied in rather important areas and we were simply left wondering.

Many of the holes were in foreign correspondence. We have less of a feel for the Chinese economy and its political evolution this year. We have a satisfactory feel for the cultural reform developments in the Soviet Union, but have gotten less than we'd like on the internal economic debate. Coverage of Third World debt has been exhaustive, from New York and Washington banking and political angles. But Third World economic development coverage remains unsatisfactory, with some notable exceptions in South America and sub-Sahara Africa.

The decline of the Reagan Administration involved a series of separate stories. Some — like the Iran-Contra hearings — were covered thoroughly. Others — like the failed Supreme Court nomination of Judge Bork — had several missing pieces, which is why the average citizen wound up with such a distorted view of the Judge that even his opponents would not recognize him. There were gaps in the struggle over economic policies — taxes, trade and international money, but relatively fewer than we might have expected. The biggest was the failure of the financial press to probe the reasons why the massive dollar devaluation of the previous two years had not decreased the U.S. trade deficit, as the devaluationists had predicted. If the trade deficit was linked to the October Wall Street Crash, as was widely reported, we think the print media's lapse contributed to the crash in a not insignificant way. In general, we believe the greatest failings of the press in 1987 were those of omission. In a year where resources and expertise were stretched thin by so many big, complex events, we can to a degree understand why.

When we set out three years ago to produce the *1986 MediaGuide*, a kind of *Michelin Guide* to the national print media, we knew the easy part would be to evaluate the work of the top reporters and rate them the way Michelin rates the restaurants of Europe. The hard part would be to win the acceptance of the news media itself, in the way the chefs and hoteliers of France accept as authoritative the observations of Michelin. It is only very recently that the print media has begun writing about itself, and it has finally grown out of its early self-consciousness. Every major newspaper has a full-time reporter covering the other newspapers and periodicals, not only the business news of the communications industry, but also the politics of the profession. It has been a healthy and necessary development that accommodates to the times.

Criticism is essential for excellence in any endeavor, for journalism as in the culinary arts. But criticism becomes of greater importance when the endeavor becomes more complex, more sophisticated. It's hard to imagine the need for a *MediaGuide* in the meat-and-potatoes world of news that we had prior to, say, the 1950s, when reporters with college degrees, especially in journalism, were objects of curiosity and gentle ridicule in most of the nation's newsrooms. Now, the demands of the computer age and the increasing number of political debates that are rooted in technological change require journalistic cadres of great expertise. The continuing political and financial integration of the world, with the United States at the center, puts even greater burdens on the communications industry. The burden is especially great on the national print media, the primary processors of news that feed the electronics media.

There has been no systematic attempt to critique the print media, except from ideological vantage points. The watchdog organizations and newsletters like Accuracy in Media or Newswatch are financed, generally by conservative money, to spot error and bias and make public complaint. The concept behind the *MediaGuide* is to look for excellence, to elevate the best we can find in reporting and commentary, and point out what we feel are the shortcomings of those who aspire to excellence. Although it may be too much to ask, we hope that even the most negative of our observations are viewed as honest, constructive criticism. At the outset, we believed it would take several editions before the profession would come to accept our professionalism, and that this, the third edition, would be the most important in this regard. There's certainly no question that the *MediaGuide* had achieved some recognition in its first two years. Journalists love to read about themselves, and by all accounts they have been devouring the book, but they have not quite accepted it yet, we are quick to admit.

The Washington Post did mention the 1987 guide in a few paragraphs within days of publication. *The Washington Times* ran a lengthy news account, noting the publication "is sure to be greeted by the snorts and cries of the wounded, just like last year." *The New York Times* ran a respectful book review July 12, by the dean of the University of Missouri School of Journalism: "(The book) is briskly self-confident but not supercilious, one that makes some provocative and penetrating comments about many of the nation's top journalists, papers and magazines."

However, for the second year, neither of the Dow Jones publications, *The Wall Street Journal* or *Barron's*, mentioned the guide — nor did *BusinessWeek*, *Fortune*, or *Forbes*. Both *Time* and *Newsweek* have press sections, but neither had even a discouraging word to say about us. *The American Spectator* did run a lengthy scathing review in its September issue. It called the guide "a real clunker" and insisted the world does not need such a book, but this was one of the high spots of the year on press attention. Without a doubt, more than any other book, the *1987 MediaGuide* was avidly read by more national journalists than in the previous year. But for the most part they kept it to themselves.

This 1988 edition, like the third point of a triangle, is important because it gives dimension to the *MediaGuide*. Those who thought they saw a tilt to the first editions, in one direction or another, should now see more method than tilt. We are serious about wringing out any ideological bias, and while our method may leave some doubts over one or two years, it should work to remove those doubts in this third year and beyond. At the same time, those who thought they were unfairly rated in the first two years may feel better this time. Even if the rating has not improved, they know it would be hard for us to be unfair to the same person three years running, with reviews coming in from so many different readers in that span.

We now have about 50 people involved in the project, paid and volunteer "news gourmets." In 1987, we logged more than 4,500 reviews of stories and articles by about 1,300 journalists and estimate our readers consumed more than 100,000 bylined pieces before choosing those they reviewed. We selected half the number of journalists, about 650, for this year's guide. Most of those journalists eliminated were cut because of insufficient samplings.

The guide is limited to the "national press" newspapers and periodicals that are readily available to national policymakers in Washington, D.C. and New York City, the political, financial and communication centers of the nation. We consider the great newspaper chains — Gannett, Newhouse, Scripps-Howard, Hearst, Knight-Ridder, etc. — clusters of regional papers, because they are without outlets in the opinion centers and because they are clearly directed at regional audiences. This year, for the first time, we include the *Los Angeles Times* in the national press category, although it does not have an outlet in New York or Washington. Our resources permitted us to expand coverage, and our editors concluded that *LAT*'s foreign service is so competitive we had to subscribe.

There are several thousand journalists who work for the national newspapers and periodicals, but we consider only those whose work bears on national matters. Of these, we select those whose work stands out on a regular basis, either because of excellence or prominence or both. Unlike the *Michelin Guide*, which only recognizes excellence, the *MediaGuide* takes note of journalists who have had unsatisfactory years. Those who have two consecutive subpar years are dropped from the guide, although they can always get back in. As a rule, we focus on the 1987 product of individual journalists, and there is no reason in our method why a rating can't rise from unsatisfactory to extraordinary, or *vice versa*, year over year.

Our criteria are described in detail in the rating section, but generally we are looking first for objective reporters and subjective commentators. We also want depth of information or analysis, accuracy, compactness and lively writing. Because there are so many variables involved, the rating process is as intangible as that which goes into a dining guide. There is an acceptable level of bias in a reporter, for example, if he or she is exceptional on other counts. "Objective" reporting in and of itself means as little to a news gourmet as the caloric count means to a food gourmet. For columnists, objectivity is as much a negative as blandness is in a dessert; we read columnists and commentators for sharp, even pungent, well-shaped points of view, "liberal" or "conservative."

The *MediaGuide* does not pretend to be comprehensive. It isn't possible for the Polyconomics staff and the part-time readers to consume everything. We do look more carefully at pieces that are prominently displayed, but because so much is sifted even in the back pages, we believe we cover representative samplings of a reporter's work. Routine dispatches are usually not reviewed. By rotating the newspapers and periodicals on a monthly basis, we get cross-checks that we hope winnow out individual biases that may creep into our reviews.

Many of the journalists who didn't "make the cut" this year for the rating section are included in the separate biographical section — a kind of "who's who" in the print media that includes editors of regional newspapers and many periodicals that are not normally reviewed. More than 1,000 entries are listed this year, up from 700 in 1987. We continue to hear from editors who have used the *MediaGuide* as a source of information on the talent pool.

Harry H. Crosby, the former director of The Writing Center at Harvard, provided an unsolicited but greatly appreciated critique of last year's *MediaGuide*: "In purpose and content your book gets highest marks," but it has "the format of a novel, not a reference work." To correct this, an important change in the new edition is a cross-reference in the index. It is not as complete as we expect it to become in future editions, but we believe it will be useful to librarians, students and even future historians. The information explosion growing out of the dramatic evolution in the power of computers is limited by any abstracting on quality. A student doing a term paper, or a journalist or corporate affairs manager looking for background material, can now tap into the universe through electronic news retrieval, but there's nothing to guide them on the quality of material available in that universe. In the next decade, the utility of electronic news retrieval will be more evident, as will the need for this kind of quality guide. Our improved index is a step toward filling that need.

The *1988 MediaGuide*, which involved a much greater deployment of resources than in previous editions, could not have been published without the support of Repap Enterprises Corporation, Inc., of Montreal, and its founder and inspiration, George S. Petty, chairman and chief executive officer. Repap, which is "Paper" spelled backwards, is the largest producer of high-quality coated paper in Canada, paper used in the publication of many American magazines and on which the *1988 MediaGuide* is printed.

About Polyconomics

Polyconomics, Inc., was founded in 1978 by Jude Wanniski, formerly Associate Editor of *The Wall Street Journal*, to advise corporate and financial clients on the emerging "Supply-side economics," a phrase he coined in *Journal* editorials of the mid-70s. The company now advises more than a hundred of the nation's biggest institutional investors and industrial corporations on the financial markets and the impact of political decisions on the unfolding world political economy. Much of the staff time of Polyconomics, Inc., in Morristown, N.J., is spent reading the world press.

Wanniski's book, *The Way the World Works*, was published in 1978 to critical acclaim. Irving Kristol called it "The best economic primer since Adam Smith;" Arthur Laffer called it "the best book on economics ever written," and Representative Jack Kemp cited it as "The original manifesto of the modern supply-side movement." Wanniski is generally credited with discovering, in 1977, the triggering cause of the 1929 Wall Street Crash, a finding central to the revival of supply-side economic theory. The *1988 MediaGuide*, though, does not revolve around economics, although it is an important element in the continuing news flow.

As an editorial writer for the *Journal* from 1972 to 1978, Wanniski concentrated on domestic and global political economics and energy, an early leader in debunking "the energy crisis." He was named "Petroleum Writer of the Year" in 1976 for his energy editorials. Wanniski joined Dow Jones & Co. in 1965 as Washington columnist for *The National Observer*, and earlier worked for newspapers in Alaska, California and Nevada.

With Alan Reynolds as chief economist, Polyconomics has been cited by *Barron's*, *Bond Week*, and *The Wall Street Journal* for the accuracy of its forecasts. Reynolds had previously been chief international economist for the First National Bank of Chicago, and earlier had been economics editor of *National Review*.

Managing Editor of the *MediaGuide* is Peter A. Signorelli. Patricia M. Koyce is Associate Editor. Ronald deLaRosa, general manager of Polyconomics, was publisher of the *MediaGuide*. They were assisted by Alan Reynolds, John Passacantando, Alexandra Mackenzie, Barbara Haslam, and Donna White of the Polyconomics staff. About 50 friends, associates and volunteers — the *MediaGuide*'s "news gourmets" — who wish to remain anonymous, contributed to the project.

AN OVERVIEW OF THE PRINT MEDIA

1987 PRESS DEVELOPMENTS

Abe Rosenthal, Columnist

In the *1987 MediaGuide* we lamented the death of syndicated columnist Joseph Kraft, January 9, 1986, and listed "Joseph Kraft's Empty Chair" as one of the most important print media events of the year. "For at least 35 years there has been some one journalist in the symbolic chair Kraft occupied — the columnist "in the know" when it came to Establishment thinking. James Reston of the *NY Times* was the dominant figure in the 1950s and '60s in fulfilling this function, but Kraft began taking over in the Nixon years...[as] Reston began to wind down. Where is the new Reston-Kraft?"

The only possibility we could come up with was "the gentleman who has just bowed out at the *NY Times* in a puff of smoke: Abe Rosenthal." It seemed a natural. A.M. Rosenthal, 65, had retired as executive editor of the *Times* at the end of '86, but would remain as twice-a-week columnist. "This man, one of the Great Reporters and Newsmen of Our Time, could surely fill the Reston-Kraft chair for five, even ten years," we said. "At the top of the heap for 20 years, Abe is Mr. Lofty himself, with mainline ties to all elements of the Establishment. In 1987, if he's willing to exert himself that much, Rosenthal could amply fill the Kraft chair. We'll see."

The first troubling news was that Rosenthal had selected as the name for his Tuesday & Friday op-ed column, "On My Mind," which conveyed a picture of Abe skimming through the papers, gazing out the window, thinking a great thought, and assembling it into a column. For the first several months of the year, this is just what we got, hitting absolute zero with "Ecuador, Who Cares?" 2-12, about a fearless iguana. It was so bad that Jonathan Alter, *Newsweek*'s news-media correspondent, got it out of the closet in "Abe Speaks His Mind," 3-9, "He admits that the subtext of the iguana was about such fear. But he does not know that since becoming a columnist in January another emotion often rises inside colleagues, enemies, even friends. It's a premature response, perhaps, based on scrutiny of only a dozen or so columns. But it's there: embarrassment."

We had, of course, read every word of the columns, which some in the *Times*' newsroom began calling "Out of My Mind," and were beginning to get nervous, experiencing the same emotion. But Abe had never written an opinion column before, and we decided it would take six months of trial-and-error gargling before he found his "voice." The Alter column undoubtedly helped, because it underscored that he was becoming "prey to the worst occupational hazard of the columnist: insufficient reporting," quoting Seymour Hersh. "It's much more important to see what he finds out about stuff than what he thinks about it."

Maybe we were wrong. Maybe it is more important to find out what he's thinking than stuff he's finding out. Possibly, he either wasn't thinking hard enough about the right things, or wasn't composing his punditry with sufficient power. In any event, Abe found his voice, and it isn't Reston's and it isn't Kraft's, which still leaves that "chair" open. It remains more armchair punditry, but with ever deepening insights about topics that are more and more precisely on the margin. By this we mean the center of gravity of global events that shifts from moment to moment, a fulcrum against which Rosenthal can use his experience and wisdom to leverage national opinion.

We knew he'd be okay as soon as we read "A Question for Cuomo," 2-26, pure, unadulterated opinion on Mario's decision not to seek the presidential nomination, but with a question that knifes through to the heart of why Rosenthal feels frustrated with the decision, not because he's pro or con, but because Cuomo had removed his talent from this all-important democratic process by which we select our national leader. "I am not so 'understanding' about Mario Cuomo deciding that there were other things more important than trying to lead this nation. He had gone too far — not in the campaign, but in what he had said the country meant to him." Isn't the country important, Governor?

In "Here's a Strange Story," 3-5, he offers a sharp critique of Soviet "openness," his straight-shooting commentary on this theme taking up residence all year in an otherwise empty void, shunned by ideologues right and left. There's even a bit of beat reporting in "The Mother and the Judge," 4-5, on Baby M: "The Baby M case was a tragedy without villains until the very end, and then the judge stepped in." More in "The U.S. Case Against the Estonian," 4-24, on the Karl Linnas case, the most economical assembly of known information presented with fine balance. In his "Eight Steps For Life," 5-31, on AIDS, he's again at the margin, eloquently, "Some of these points are unpleasant to read or write, particularly those that may touch on civil liberties. Better now and minimally, rather than late, when, with fear, disregard for liberties may grow even faster than the spread of the disease."

There were flat columns, especially in the summer as he honeymooned around the world with his new bride, but even then we got some great ones, "Thatcher's Second Revolution," 7-9, and "Streets of Seoul," 7-23, with penetrating commentaries on the political economies of both countries. Back home, "They Should Have Quit," 8-4, zaps Weinberger and Shultz, straight shooting again against the politicized consensus. In December, two columns in the same week bowl us over, "For U.S. Intervention in Haiti," 12-1, which says what it says, and "Thank You, Mr. Gorbachev," 12-4, which unvarnishes Gorbachev's English, finally persuading us we have been barking up the wrong tree, that we really don't need another reporter, because there are plenty of them. We have needed another great mind, because we have so few. Rosenthal fills not the Kraft chair, which has been vacant for two years, but aspires to the Walter Lippmann chair, which has been vacant for more than twenty.

Competition From Abroad

Chrysler's Lee Iacocca once chided the U.S. business press for being so adamant about free trade. It was easy for the press to be free marketeers, he said, because it doesn't face any foreign competition. This may have been largely true at the time, but not any more. *The Economist* of London has been circulated in the U.S. for more than a century, of course, and since it began printing in the U.S. in 1981, it now sells more copies here (about 100,000) than in the U.K. However, it is Britain's equivalent to *The Wall Street Journal* that is becoming a genuine competitive threat to American business journalism, in a way that only became apparent to us this year.

The *Financial Times*, like the *Economist*, has always had a casual circulation in the U.S. business and financial community. Its influence was insignificant because of the delivery lag, at times a week or more. But since the newspaper set up shop in Belmar, New Jersey in 1985, it has doubled its North American circulation to around 14,000. That may not sound like much. In fact, it's a drop in the *Journal*'s bucket of 2 million, but there are already as many copies of the *Financial Times* in the U.S. as there are of *The European Wall Street Journal* in Europe. The *Financial Times* has by no means stopped penetrating its potential U.S. market. Publication is by satellite, and the distribution keeps getting broader and faster — timely enough, even by mail, thus ending its previous competitive disadvantage. It's, of course, available on the day of publication in the power centers, and this is really where the competition is being felt. As might be expected, nearly half of the U.S. readers are in the financial industries, but for the first time in '87, we began hearing industrialists at U.S. multinationals express a *preference* for the *FT* over the *Journal* or *Times*. American editors, especially those at foreign desks, have always looked at the *FT*, but now it is being read soon after it hits the desk.

Where we had dismissed the *Financial Times* as a serious competitor to *The Wall Street Journal*, seeing it solely as a supplement, it's now not that hard to see it gradually taking the toehold it has grabbed and pushing ahead in the elite audiences, biting into advertising dollars. At this stage, there is barely any news about the United States, which shares half a page with the rest of the American continent, and there is far more detail about British industry than U.S. readers want to see. Yet two things set *The Financial Times* ahead of any U.S. paper or magazine. One is extensive coverage of the whole world, complete with surveys on specific countries. The only comparable world coverage is in *The Economist*, which happens to be half owned by the same conglomerate.

We made the point last year that the U.S. press, including the pacesetting newspapers, still thinks of the rest of the world in a geopolitical sense, a collection of nation states. Because London was the center of global capital for two centuries, it developed a way of thinking about the world as an integrated political economy, a collection of *countries*. The foreign dispatches of the American press have a distinctly different feel, as if the audience simply wants to know about, say, South Korea's developments as they might affect the rest of the world. The *FT* more often will give us details on internal policy debates and the political factions that represent one side or the other of a debate. The *Wall Street Journal* has begun to do this a bit in its Asian coverage, but for Europe, especially, there's nothing comparable to the *FT*.

The second edge at the *FT* is related. The analysis and commentary on the *FT*'s editorial page on foreign affairs and international finance is superior to what we find in the U.S. press, even though it gives up the advantage of looking at the world from the centers of financial and political gravity, New York and Washington. The top U.S. financial writers all seem to have been politicized by comparison, identifying with one ideological faction or another, usually with a political faction as well. There may be just as much of this at the *FT* and we may not recognize it, being less attuned to ideological and partisan crosscurrents in London. At least we don't have to read with the same degree of defensiveness, discounting for known biases. It occurred to us in reading the *FT*'s special survey, "World Economy," 9-28, that neither *The New York Times* nor *The Wall Street Journal* could have assembled as sophisticated a section with their available talent. Too few of the U.S. financial writers think in terms of a world economy. The best at the *WSJ*, Peter Truell, was imported from London early in the year.

As far as consumers of news are concerned, competition is always welcome. As consumers of news ourselves, we not only appreciate the quality of product available in the *Financial Times*, but also the awareness that the U.S. news media is going to develop in positive ways by having this new kid from abroad on the block. The influence probably has been felt already.

Settling Down After Musical Chairs

Musical chairs among the staffs of the three newsweeklies abated sharply this year. Instead, the major shifts and changes in personnel were almost wholly at the top. The biggest ones occurred at *Time* magazine.

Henry Grunwald stepped down at year's end as editor in chief of *Time*, the company's out-at-65 policy leaving no choice. While Grunwald goes on to serve as U.S. ambassador to Austria, former managing editor Jason McManus takes over his position, with Henry Muller moving up to fill McManus's spot. Ray Cave, who was once in the running to succeed Grunwald, assumes "the second highest position," editorial director of *Time*. Only the fourth editor in chief in the magazine's history, McManus has been around for 28 years and was a longtime protege of Grunwald. It isn't so much a change of regimes, then, although there are some areas he may highlight more than his predecessor, business and finance likely.

Perhaps the more important personnel change was when Time, Inc. chairman J. Richard Munro tapped Nicholas J. Nicholas as new president. In the midst of cost-cutting and restructuring, the company had already laid off a few hundred people, a small number of them from the magazine this year. In a situation somewhat similar to that at the TV networks, head counts became an issue for cost-minded accountants. With Nicholas viewing Time, Inc. as "superb collection of franchises in key market positions," as *BusinessWeek* observed in "TIME's Nick & Dick Show," 8-3, "That is the talk of a manager of assets, not a journalist or builder of empires." No one, including McManus, doubts that further cuts might be necessary, but McManus may very well be able to balance corporate and editorial skills. So far, he intends to keep *Time*'s traditional format intact, and we'll really need another year to assess what these changes will produce at the weekly.

U.S.News was in the process of absorbing the new blood from outside this year, and a version of musical chairs went on inside the weekly, various shiftings in editors' turfs taking place. Managing editor Peter Bernstein, from *Fortune* (one of the few among the last two year's worth of recruits who didn't come aboard from *Newsweek*) now handles national news, and among the *cognescenti* is said to be the one on the way to the top. The ex-*Newsweek*ers realigned this year, with executive editor Mike Ruby withdrawing from national news to concentrate on international coverage; deputy managing editor Christopher Ma moved heavily into business and features, while the presidential campaigns were staked out by Mel Elfin. There's still some confusion at Mort's magazine as to who's in charge at various levels, but somehow it worked out well enough this year, as we assess elsewhere.

No major changes at *Newsweek*, of either personnel or direction, the magazine frolicking happily with its "boomers-grown-up" readership. Steve Smith's vision for *Newsweek* didn't alter this year, and the trend to trendiness continued. But the leap into that pond was always associated with producing big splashes of new ad revenue. It was a rough year for the three weeklies in those competitive waters, and *Newsweek*'s buoyant formula wasn't as leak proof as it thought. There is a new culture there, however, and its roots continued to deepen, as we outline in this year's evaluation. There was less a concern with what *Time* was doing, though certainly satisfaction with McManus's reaffirmation of the magazine's traditional goals, which gives *Newsweek* little competition for the audience it wants.

With the peaking of musical chairs and the switches back and forth between staffs of the three newsweeklies sharply slowing down this year, we got a better chance to see what else occurred there beyond frequent changes in the mastheads. On the whole, no real change, of course, at either *Time* or *Newsweek*, but from *U.S.News*, the best year it's had in a long time.

A New *New Yorker*?

The squawk of the town early this year was the major transition at the top of *The New Yorker* magazine. For 35 years, William Shawn reigned as editor of the magazine, cutting a deep impress. On behalf of the family that bought *NYer* in 1985, Sam Newhouse advised Shawn that his resignation would take place March 1, 1987, and that Robert Gottlieb would replace him. Gottlieb, president and editor in chief of the publishing house of Alfred A. Knopf, has been an intimate of the NY literary scene for years, but was considered an "outsider" at the *NYer* nonetheless.

Shawn and most of the staff at the magazine had assumed that an in-houser would succeed him. Shawn, in fact, favored managing editor for fiction, Charles McGrath. Immediately there was a storm of protest against an outsider coming as new editor. Petitions circulated, and a letter signed by 154 staffers and contributors was sent to Gottlieb, urging him to decline the offer. "It is our strange and powerfully held conviction that only an editor who has been a long-standing-member of the staff will have a reasonable chance of assuring our continuity, cohesion, and independence," the signatories advised. When Gottlieb affirmed he was coming aboard, some writers departed in a show of respectful devotion to Shawn, among them Jonathan Schell. From the outside, though, it seemed that finally a breath of fresh air might move through the magazine.

NYer's urbanity of the Harold Ross years had long since dried up. Since the '60s, when the magazine indulged shrill social commentary and traded its appreciation of the excellent for predictability and formula essays, it's been dull, inflexible, and without the authority it once commanded in literary culture. An ideological tone intruded where once an informed style of vigor, richness and variety reigned. Long-winded features replaced reflective essays and the emphasis on intellectual works diminished. After awhile the often-heard question became "Does anyone really read *The New Yorker* anymore?" Its cartoons are always skimmed, the movie, theater and restaurant reviews consulted, at times a Pauline Kael essay on cinema perused, but for the most part, the magazine graced coffee tables without being opened. This once-lively magazine simply became a drudge to read, conformity seeping from its pages.

Does Gottlieb's coming aboard represent a new breath of fresh air? With less than a year on the job, it's simply too soon to tell where *The New Yorker* will go. Gottlieb hasn't given a sense yet of his vision for the magazine, though hints of less politics and more cultural themes are there. Mimi Kramer, theater critic of *The New Criterion* appears regularly, and Renata Adler is intended to be a frequent contributor. "The Talk of the Town," the magazine's "editorial" is less estranged from relevant political events, a little more sprightly this year, but beyond the barest outlines of some changes, we wonder if editor Gottlieb recognizes the shift that has taken place at the magazine *vis a vis* a new readership.

Circulation is way up, largely the work of an aggressive publisher, Steve T. Florio, but the ads appearing in the weekly are increasingly geared toward a liberal gentry. Book ads are infrequent, for example, while ads for resort hotels, credit card agencies, and all the glossy accoutrements of the successful life abound. Staffers have always insisted there is a solid wall between the business side and writing side of the magazine. But ad revenue needs sometimes have a way of affecting what readership a magazine begins catering to. *The New Yorker* seemed to be addressing a readership along the lines of the *NYT*'s upper echelons of readers, a readership that's less demanding than the one of yore. George Steiner and C.V. Pritchard are still there to uphold the older tradition of excellence, but often swimming against the muddier currents that dominate. We still saw the exhausting, rather than exhaustive, essays appear, Doris Lessing's "A Reporter at Large" essay on Afghan refugees, 3-16, running 16,000 words. Elizabeth Drew's political column, "A Letter from Washington," was not up to last year's standards, too much preaching and editorializing, instead of the exhaustive reporting that previously distinguished her.

Some of this is a holdover from the Shawn era and Gottlieb seems intent on restoring some sprightliness to the magazine. We will wait to see what new talent he attracts, as a guide to his vision. This will take another year before we might tell if there is going to be a new *New Yorker*.

COVERING THE MICROCOSM

For many years, America's media has faithfully followed a new Parkinson's law: The more important the event, the less the coverage...and the greater the misunderstanding. Thus during this decade when racism in America was essentially overcome and the U.S. economy took a global lead in competitiveness, the media found racism and economic decline everywhere. Blending its blindnesses, the press during the 1980s entirely missed the dramatic upsurge in black incomes and employment created by our record economic boom, which it also mostly missed.

Although newsrooms were full of computer gear and scarcely a reporter set out on a story without a portable in hand, the computer revolution hardly touched the front pages of America's papers, where sexism among firemen and unemployment among steelworkers were perennial favorites. Watching television news features on homelessness and hunger and on the hollowing of America's heavy industries, an interplanetary observer might have assumed the U.S. was part of the Third World, technically retarded and blighted by debt. Indeed, many featured stories compared the U.S. with Mexico and Argentina as "the world's greatest debtor nations." Preoccupied with the "twin towers" of the trade and budgetary deficits, none of the establishment media pointed out the countervailing assets of a U.S. economic and technological renaissance. And none reported that our governmental debt was both smaller and growing more slowly than the average debts of the other leading industrial countries.

The key question in journalism is always what is the real news, as opposed to what happens to make the papers under Parkinson's law. This issue is especially acute in science and technology where fads (artificial intelligence, extraterrestrial life) and panics (acid rain, carcinogenic pancake mixes) typically overshadow the real work that changes the world.

In 1987, Parkinson seemed still in command in American journalism. From the Iran-Contra affair to the stock market crash of "Reaganomics," the press revelled in triviality and partisanship and mostly missed the epochal events in science and technology. *The New York Times* memorably emblazoned its front pages with stories of hunger among U.S. farmers ("suffering more today than during the Great Depression") and "America's Army of Non-Workers" (totally ignoring historic and global highs in U.S. employment).

In 1987, the U.S. continued to create jobs and launch new technical products at a world-leading pace. Meanwhile, the European economies actually lost employment and Japan suffered stagnation and turmoil after thirty years of leading the world in growth. In key technologies targeted by industrial policy, both Europe and Japan lost market share to the U.S. But the media continued to report depression in America — on its farms, in its factories, in its racially-afflicted cities, in Silicon Valley itself. Even *Scientific American*, for many years probably the best-edited publication in the language, began flaunting lugubrious pieces on hunger in America and "A New Surge of Inequality."

Nonetheless, despite ideological lapses, *The New York Times* in 1987 finally and irrefutably defied Parkinson. History will show that the year's most important events were the development of high-temperature superconductivity, the acceleration of progress in information technology, and the competitive breakthroughs of American computer and semiconductor companies. The *Times* led the world in covering these stories, regularly putting them on its front page. Moreover, the *Times'* example of excellence provoked an impressive catch-up effort by other papers. By the end of the year, there was reason to hope for a decisive long-term improvement by America's media in covering these frontiers of human progress.

The Technology Reporters

In any field governed by ideas, excellence is chiefly an attainment of individuals. Propelling the *Times'* achievement were the superb performances of a group of young reporters led by David Sanger and James Gleick. Throughout the year, Sanger was unequalled by any other

11

writer in the level of excellence and energy he brought to the treatment of developments in microelectronics and computers. Unique among America's technology reporters in the daily press, he often broke stories before the electronics industry media. Among scores of superb pieces, standouts include his 3-8 story on IBM's world-leading factory for commodity memory chips in Essex Junction, Vermont (written at a time most of the press was conceding leadership to Japan in this field); and his front-page scoop, 8-12, on the strange decision of the National Security Agency to create a supercomputer project in competition with the many private suppliers who have given the U.S. the world lead in the field.

Sanger's feats show that technical sophistication is not enough in covering the dramas of modern technology. It was his political and economic savvy that gave rare analytical depth to several probing stories on the Pentagon's efforts to impose export controls on U.S. and foreign computer manufacturers. Sanger revealed the obtuseness even of the generally applauded attack on Toshiba for allowing sale to Moscow of a milling machine used to reduce the audibility of Soviet submarines. He showed that Toshiba had already secured the resignations of everyone involved and was a crucial supplier to scores of U.S. companies, from IBM to Apple. Under a shared byline, Sanger disclosed the comedy of Pentagon efforts to stop IBM-West Germany from selling an outdated mainframe computer to a Soviet subsidiary in West Germany. While the U.S. government stalled IBM, Hitachi moved in and got the order through National Advanced Systems of Silicon Valley, the computer arm of National Semiconductor. In all these stories, Sanger pays careful attention to the arguments for export controls and then shows how in practice, they nearly always damage the U.S. more than the Soviet Union.

Focusing on the superconductivity story, the other young *Times* star, James Gleick, did not shine in such solitary splendor as Sanger. Contributing crucially to Gleick's feats was the grand old man of *The New York Times* science coverage, Walter Sullivan, who had written his first science scoop for the paper in 1946, revealing the phenomenon of "fallout" from the first atomic explosions.

As a former *Times* science editor (now in semi-retirement), Sullivan inspired Gleick and broke the superconductivity story on New Year's Eve 1986. Sullivan persuaded the *Times* to run the piece above the fold on the front page, "Two Groups Report a Breakthrough..." In the story, he asserted the "vast implications" of the development for electrical storage and transmission, superconductive magnets, and nuclear fusion, among other uses. After a subsequent front-page blast, "Four Labs Achieve New Gains in Conducting Electricity," 2-16, Sullivan passed the baton to Gleick. By that time, the paper was far in the lead over the rest of the American media, including most of the science and engineering publications. *Scientific American*, for example, was yet to address the story in depth and no news magazine or paper had recognized its importance.

Although the minimal temperature needed for superconductivity had risen from about 7 degrees Kelvin to around 40 degrees, the phenomenon could still be clearly demonstrated only with expensive and volatile liquid helium refrigerants. But with liquid helium, superconductivity was already routine in industry. Many editors took solace in assurances that it would be many years before the far cheaper and simpler liquid nitrogen could be used. And without the move to liquid nitrogen, there was really no big story.

"Plunging toward the impossible, scientists on three continents are racing to achieve one of the great dreams of science — an everyday material that carries electricity without the slightest loss of energy." So began Gleick's pioneering story leading off the "Science Times" of 3-10. By allowing electricity to circulate endlessly in a ring, exerting magnetic force but not losing power, superconductivity offers the closest thing to perpetual motion ever found by scientists. The claims were so improbable and so widely disbelieved in the field, that for several months no American laboratory had even tried to validate the original discovery at IBM in Zurich reported late in 1986. It was not until Japanese and Chinese researchers confirmed the IBM breakthrough that physicists across the country began to show acute interest. But skepticism was still dominant among scientists and engineers when Gleick began his epochal coverage.

In a relentless series of major articles, however, Gleick week-after-week singlehandedly developed this abstruse tale of high science into a rival for the exploits of Jessica Hahn and Donna Rice for the covers of major news magazines. With a pellucid style, leavened with humor and metaphor, and with a knack for clarifying obscure issues of science, Gleick made this subject his own crusade. As the temperature rose above the liquid nitrogen threshold, Gleick and the *Times* were vindicated. In the end he forced nearly every editor in America to give in and acknowledge the epochal dimensions of the story they had long overlooked.

A reporter chiefly known for lucid stories on the new theory of patterns discoverable in "chaos," Gleick boldly asserted the revolutionary portent of the new superconductivity discoveries. His confidence, partly inspired by Sullivan, contributed to the success of the now famous "Woodstock" meeting of the American Physical Society at the New York Hilton, when physicists jammed the aisles and hallways and stayed up all night debating the remarkable discoveries. Although this meeting occasioned a few further reports and comments in the press, no other paper committed major resource to cover it until five months after the first *Times* articles.

Except in a splendid editorial entitled "Super Discoveries," 3-30, *The Wall Street Journal* responded to the *Times* scoop chiefly by trying to discredit it. In early March, for example, Jerry Bishop reported that superconductivity research was running into fundamental limits in current carrying capacity which would not be overcome for "five years, if ever." The next day, Gleick reported that IBM researchers had already exceeded those limits in some applications.

The Washington Post also checked in with a four-part series in May that offered lively accounts from the laboratories. Boyce Rensberger was even more lucid and thorough on possible applications than the *Times*. Dale Russakoff, however, went into the *Post*'s manic-depressive mode of competitiveness analysis, quoting Frank Press: "Superconductivity has become the test case of whether the United States has a technological future." Russakoff also located the key problem as the "yawning federal deficit." (We also yawned).

Even when *The Wall Street Journal* got a good story, it usually botched its significance. Dennis Kneale went to IBM's Watson Laboratory to investigate the progress of the company's effort to create superconductive thin films that could be laid down as the metalization layer of wires on semiconductor chips. Kneale estimated that "it may take more than a decade to accomplish." Then he reported the comment of a researcher that at present only "one of three batches works out. For real production we'll need one for one." One in three, however, represents a production yield far above what most producers of gallium arsenide chips (the chief rival technology) can accomplish. It would seem that the technology is a lot closer than ten years away. The reader gets no idea from Kneale. He simply didn't know enough to get the story.

So it went, for most of the year. The climax of the tale came on 10-2, when in an article buried deep in the paper, *Wall Street Journal* reporter David Stipp at last transcended the *Journal*'s debunking mode and showed real insight into the potential of the technology. In a clear and authoritative article which did not shrink from technical detail, he told of several new breakthroughs. Toward the end of his piece, he described recent experiments at IBM and several other laboratories indicating that superconductive ceramics could transmit data 100 times faster than fiber optic cable. Why, the reader wondered, was this finding not emblazoned in the lead paragraph and on the front page? Was there something wrong with the experiments? Vastly exceeding all previous expectations, this arresting discovery seemed to show the kind of positive surprises that this technology offered. But neither Stipp, nor his editors, comprehended their own story.

Sure enough, the *Times* that same day did put this stunning finding in the first paragraph of a front-page story by Gleick. Unlike Stipp, Gleick identified the central effect of this development. Electronic superconductors transmitting a trillion bits/second (15 million phone

13

calls on one line) could connect directly to silicon chips. This would obviate the current rigamarole of converting telecom signals to light pulses and then back to electronic signals, as is required by fiber optics. The optical computer, long a dream of ambitious designers, is in theory suddenly obsolete.

Creating Science Journalists

This finding in October once again thoroughly vindicated the *Times* and its aggressive approach to science and technology coverage. Most newspapers and magazines shrink from serious science stories until they are already history. The *Times* is willing to treat science as news and even to make news in its coverage of science.

This approach, however, requires specialization. The *Times* could break this story chiefly because it had abandoned its usual assumption that any reporter can cover any subject. The *Times* dominated the superconductivity saga because Sullivan and Gleick knew what they were doing and remained unshaken by the doubt and disparagement that surround any new discovery. *The Wall Street Journal, Fortune, Time, Newsweek, The Economist*, and other publications always had space for disgruntled physicists who upheld the perennial dismissive banners of NIH (Not Invented Here). The *Times* kept its eye on what was happening in the laboratories and developed the science story of the decade.

The *Times*' lead in science coverage seems likely to last for a long time. Their weekly section, "Science Times," is developing a large stable of sophisticated reporters who will be ready to break the next major science story. Other publications seem to regard science as the opportunity for an occasional feature, offering a break from the more relevant issues of politics and economics. As time passes, however, it becomes increasingly clear that a mastery of science and technology will also be needed to comprehend the key issues of politics and economics.

For example, there is no doubt that Sanger's political and economic savvy improved his coverage of the export control issue, but it was his knowledge of computers that allowed him to see the futility of Pentagon policy. He knew that the IBM machines involved in the West German case were already obsolete. He could understand the meaning of the Toshiba milling machine case because he realized that the crucial innovations in most contemporary technology, including perhaps the huge milling device, can be reduced to a software program and transmitted over the telephone or bounced off satellites around the globe. He comprehended the fact, still unrecognized by the Pentagon, that information devices are fundamentally different from previous military technologies.

Similar sophistication is necessary for successful coverage of the other prime technology story of 1987, the fast breaking story of the computer industry. This is a field — central to any understanding of the U.S. economy and its financial dimensions — that *The Wall Street Journal* should stress. Yet surprisingly enough, for most of the year, the *Times* reporters regularly outperformed the *Journal* on the business news of computing.

Inherited from popular books and news magazines, the *Journal*'s debilitating disease is the concept of company culture. It allows reporters to ignore technology and write about atmospherics and personalities when they cover industry. For example, William M. Bulkeley is one of the smoothest *Journal* writers and in the fierce rivalry between Sun Microsystems and Apollo Computer, he was addressing one of the most dramatic and significant stories of the year. Why is it that in a world full of computer companies — including Digital Equipment and Hewlett-Packard, both oriented toward engineers — it took two recent start-ups to launch the two billion dollar market for engineering workstations?

Bulkeley, no doubt, got kudos from his editors for his front-page story on this struggle. Well written, crisp, anecdotal, entertaining, the piece effervesced for several hundred lines in the manner favored for the *Journal*'s front end. But it left the reader with a head full of bubbles, knowing little more about the two companies and their market than he did at the beginning. Eschewing both news and analysis, Bulkeley does a frothy counterpoint between the California culture of Sun (jeans, beer, and an April Fool's Day "tradition" of practical jokes) and the stuffy New England chill at Apollo (business suits and "scheduled meetings"!). He implies that the Apollo people work less hard and drink less beer, but doesn't explore the point or prove it. In any case, Sun folk wear suits most of the time, too, and by doing a sartorial "business culture" potboiler, Bulkeley missed a fascinating story on this exciting new dimension of the computer market invented and entirely dominated by American firms. Meanwhile, totally missed by Bulkeley but reported in the industry press, Sun during the previous week had won an estimated $280 million contract with the National Security Agency, beating out both Apollo and IBM for the sale of some 3,500 workstations and changing the real story into a question of how Sun has already won the battle. Clue: it wasn't with "Miller time."

Like most of the business press, the *Journal* made this error repeatedly in 1987. On July 16, for example, their most savvy computer writer, Brenton R. Schlender, did a story on Apple Computer based on the idea that the problem with Steve Jobs was his "one-man-team" leadership style. Jobs' problem was in fact a series of terrible decisions. By making better decisions, Scully retrieved the company.

Meanwhile, the *Journal* missed the real news at Apple: actual sales of its current computer line. The *Journal* should not simply pass on Apple's claim that "Macintosh is the nation's best-selling computer" without defining which model, against which set of compatible IBM products. Moreover, Schlender missed the provocative story reported in *The New York Times* the day before: Apple's urgent testimony to a House committee against the proposed ban on Toshiba products. The ban would be "devastating" to Apple, a spokesman said, because of Apple's dependence on Toshiba desktop printers (and memory chips as well). Once again, as in a Semiconductor Industry Association mission to Tokyo demanding more memory chip production, we discover that almost any punishment of Japan will hurt the U.S. more. The *Journal* should cover that story and leave the world of fashion to *Vogue*.

The *Times* was almost entirely devoid of business fashion stories, but Sanger, Andrew Pollack, Susan Rasky, and others offered a series of insightful stories about the changing technology. On November 8, for example, Pollack wrote an interesting and comprehensive story about Jobs' new firm, Next Inc. While offering acute observations on Jobs' management style, Pollack also addressed the technical challenges the company faced and provided a detailed technical description of the rumored new computer. Pollack's sophisticated understanding of semiconductor technology, gained during several years covering Silicon Valley, allowed him to discuss the implications of Jobs' choice of microprocessors from Motorola and speculate about the performance of the Next machine compared to other workstations.

The *Times*' strength is its ability to strike a balance between technical detail and accessibility. *Times* science stories are all generally intelligible to the layman. Moreover, they do not shrink from reasonably difficult concepts that make the story valuable to the sophisticated readers who are most likely to read it. The *Journal*, the *Post*, and the business magazines tend to make such an effort to eschew technical terms that their technology coverage becomes gibberish. In the *Journal*, discussing "tiny storage devices" without identifying Dynamic Random Access Memory chips (DRAMs) fails to educate the uninformed reader and mystifies the reader who knows that there are scores of different "tiny storage devices." The estimable Jerry E. Bishop of the *Journal* on 5-29 offered a long front-page story on new ballistics transistors which use special quantum effects to accelerate switching speeds. The story was so dogged in its avoidance of technical language, that for most of its considerable length the reader was given to understand that it was an account of the promise of gallium arsenide chips as a "silicon successor." Ballistics transistors, however, need not even use gallium arsenide. The article tried so hard to be readable by laymen that, in the end, it was incomprehensible to anyone capable of understanding its subject.

This was an epochal year for technology and for *The New York Times*. But the *Times*' lead is less awesome in technology business stories than in science. Because the *Times*' edge is based on the polished skills of a relatively small stable of talented writers, other papers could catch up by hiring experienced reporters from industry publications such as the *Electronic Engineering Times* or from local papers with technical expertise such as the *San Jose Mercury* or *The Boston Globe.*

Indeed, by autumn, other papers were beginning to make a challenge. The *Journal* began using Silicon Valley veteran Michael Malone on its op-ed page. On 9-3, *The Wall Street Journal* actually outdid the *Times* on a business and technology story. With Sanger temporarily off the computer beat writing a series on the aftermath of the space shuttle disaster, Richard Gibson not only got the story of supercomputer design star Steve Chen's departure from Cray Research the same day as the *Times'* Lawrence Fisher, but Gibson's story was better and more complete. Moreover the *Journal* ran it as the right hand lead on the front page while the *Times* buried Fisher's report.

The next day the *Journal* once again scooped the Times, this time with two stories, one on Seymour Cray and one on Steve Chen and his current plans. While Fisher wrote that Chen was "unavailable," Udayan Gupta of the *Journal* not only reached Chen but wrote an incisive article on his prospects for finance, which were treated as farfetched by Fisher (who presumably consulted only sources at Cray). Gupta pointed out that a new company headed by Chen would have access not only to the entire U.S. venture capital community and the supercomputer users in the U.S. government, but also to a variety of Japanese funding sources. Neither Fisher of the *Times* nor Gibson, however, mentioned Sanger's related piece on the government's supercomputer project that ran on the front page of the *Times* just a few days before.

The lesson is that like the computer business itself, the reporting of science and technology is based on information processing. Dominated by ideas rather than by manufacturing capital or financial power, the information industry leaves no one any time to rest on his laurels. The *Times* won decisively in 1987, but an enterprising editor following the *Times'* example might well displace that venerable institution over the next few years. The effort will certainly be worthwhile. The journals that master the intricacies of the information age will gain a crucial vantage on most of the key stories of the coming decade.

MAJOR STORIES OF 1987

AIDS: The Year of the Plague

AIDS, a major news story of 1987, is fast becoming the story of the decade. It has become the subject of hot debate within the Washington Beltway, and a subject of great confusion and controversy everywhere.

No division of the press was left untouched. Columnists and editorial writers argued policy and prevention while political reporters found themselves in the thick of things as AIDS became politicized. With Surgeon General C. Everett Koop's advocating condom use, Ronald Reagan urging abstinence, the President's Commission on AIDS and presidential candidates taking varying positions, the political correspondents were given a real workout in something generally beyond their ken.

As a political issue, AIDS has had a short half-life, as Michael Kinsley predicted in a bomb-dropping, conservative-blasting op-ed piece: "A year from now, no one will be talking much about AIDS anymore....something *else* will come along," *The New Republic*, "Time's Up," 7-27. Coverage waxed and waned throughout the year as publications found themselves printing medical AIDS reports on covers and front pages with alarming regularity. Business reporters tried to determine how AIDS is affecting the economic base; socio-political reporters counted the human cost.

The AIDS story is probably one of the most complex the press has ever encountered. It is a disease, medical emergency, domestic policy issue in the current administration and for the 1988 presidential campaign, an international health problem, financial worry, legal nightmare, business disaster, social revolution, sexual counterrevolution. And that's just for starters. On each side of the issue you find conservatives, liberals, Republicans, Democrats, the Surgeon General, the Secretary of Education, civil libertarians, evangelicals, doctors, and lawyers.

Among the daily press, *The New York Times* had consistently the best medical reporting on AIDS. Unfailingly superb coverage came from Lawrence Altman, who had several front-page AIDS stories. A medical doctor, Altman did a terrific question and answer piece, "Fact, Theory and Myth on the Spread of AIDS," 2-15. He effectively debunked the conservative hysteria about heterosexual transmission, citing Dr. Harold Jaffe, chief AIDS epidemiologist at the Center for Disease Control, who concluded there was no evidence of an epidemic heterosexual outbreak, but still advised caution, "AIDS Expert Sees No Sign of Heterosexual Outbreak," 6-5.

Jane E. Brody's "Myths About AIDS Danger and Hemophiliacs Assailed," 9-1, was a fascinating, eye-opening front-pager filled to the borders with understandable information on AIDS and hemophilia. Lindsay Gruson covered AIDS victims as patients, from the viewpoints of hospitals, doctors, administrators, and victims themselves, handling well the privacy issue, "Privacy of AIDS Patients: Fear Infringes on Sanctity," 7-30, and sounding the alarm on children with AIDS while reporting on a Philadelphia conference, "AIDS Toll in Children Is Called 'Deadly Crisis'," 4-9. But the *Times* was a day late in reporting the 8-18 announcement of MicroGeneSys Co.'s potential AIDS vaccine, in Lawrence M. Fisher's "Tiny Company Joins Front Ranks of AIDS Fight," 8-20.

We found that the *Times*' general coverage was also the best on AIDS. Jane Gross brought the AIDS issue home to Manhattan and the boroughs in some harrowing but important pieces. Two of her best: "An Ever-Widening Epidemic Tears at the City's Life and Spirit," 3-16, a vivid picture of how AIDS has changed New York City through interviews of victims, families, and neighbors in the areas most affected; and "AIDS Threat Brings New Turmoil for Gay Teenagers," 10-21, a grim portrait of lives of gay teens, who, with ever-present fear, are "hiding their maelstrom of feelings and pushed by loneliness into furtive, dangerous sexual encounters."

An important front-page piece by Tamar Lewin, one of the best we saw on AIDS and civil liberties, was "Rights of Citizens and Society Raise Legal Muddle on AIDS," 10-14, on quarantine and related issues, noting that Cuba already has a quarantined colony of AIDS victims outside Havana. Clyde Haberman reported on pending Japanese legislation to bar AIDS carriers "likely to spread the disease" from entering the country, "Japan Plans to Deny Visas to Aliens With AIDS Virus," 4-1. James Brooke, in Africa, had two terrific pieces on AIDS control, "AIDS Danger: Africa Seems of 2 Minds," 1-4, and AIDS transmission, "AIDS Is Now Spreading to Populous West Africa," 4-15. Francis Clines had a haunting piece, "Dutch Fear: AIDS Cases' Last Stop," 4-15, outlining government fears of an overflow of AIDS immigrants because of liberal Dutch attitudes toward euthanasia.

The *Times*' editorial and op-ed pages ran some pretty sensitive material, for which we commend them. "My Husband Has AIDS" by Susan Day (pseudonym) gave compelling insights. William Safire argued against the "slippery slope" of testing, "Failing the Tests," 6-4. A.M. Rosenthal had two AIDS columns: one noting the larger issues in the Ray family's being driven from Arcadia, "Our House In Arcadia," 9-1, and one unveiling an AIDS program, "Eight Steps for Life," 5-31. In the Arcadia piece Rosenthal stressed the need for "the social compact of compassion and self-interest between the sufferees and society that must be created to bridge the years, perhaps decades before a cure or vaccine is found. Until then we are all in Arcadia."

The *Times*' political reporters were dragged into the debates as well: Maureen Dowd, Gerald Boyd, Phil Boffey, even Paul Lewis at the U.N. had pieces relating to AIDS and possible government responses. Unfortunately, we found the *Times* to be skimpy on the business and financial effects of AIDS, such as rising insurance costs, although Steven Prokesch had a good piece on Levi-Strauss' pioneer employee AIDS program, "Employers Face Up to AIDS," 3-12.

Other papers and periodicals, while not matching the caliber of the *Times*, had shining moments in their reporting of the AIDS story.

The Washington Times had the most regular coverage, by dependable, understandable Joyce Price. Producing solid medical pieces she reported experts' fear of the disease's potential to spread among teens, since the formative years are a time of experimentation, with both sex and drugs, "AIDS Experts Fear Epidemic Among Teens," 3-11. This she followed up with a more personal "Students Haven't Changed Behavior Despite AIDS Fear," 9-3, which was an inconclusive (too small a sampling) but interesting behavioral survey of college students. She detailed the myth of the heterosexual epidemic early with loads of statistics and sources in a "AIDS Among Heterosexuals," 3-5/6, setting the stage for other whistle-blowers. Price also covered the President's AIDS Commission with "AIDS Commission Holds Hearing Amid Howls of Protest," 9-10, and "AIDS Policy Confused, Panel Member Charges," 9-11 and research with "Leading AIDS Scientist Sees No Cure in 'Anyone's Lifetime,'" 3-26 and "Researchers Suggest 'Manhattan Project' to Fight AIDS Virus," 9-2. Her best: "For Women, Too, AIDS Can Come As A Deadly Surprise," 9-22, on Washington women with AIDS. Cathryn Donohoe, a "Life!" reporter, ventured into the doctor's world, a stark landscape these days, in "Doctors and AIDS," 6-10, an eloquent portrait of doctors who treat AIDS patients as a career choice.

The Washington Times' "Commentary" pages also ran controversial material. John Lofton went against the grain, coming down on the side of the *parents* of Arcadia in the Ray family debate, "Scared by the 'Almost,'" 9-4, noting "experts" who said, among other things, Pearl Harbor could not be bombed by the Japanese, hot kisses destroy germs and comparing them to current "experts" who say "AIDS cannot be transmitted by casual contact." Richard Grenier also advocated cautious panic, because AIDS does not conform to conventional wisdom and is unprecedented medically, "Good Reason to Panic Over the AIDS Threat," 6-10, while Suzanne Fields advocated mandatory testing for marriage licenses, arguing that "women have always been vulnerable to men who lie, but lies in the past rarely came with a death sentence," "The Cruelest Lie of All," 6-9. Joe Sobran, in a guest appearance, put it all in perspective:

"I really don't see why abstaining from casual sex is supposed to be such an effort. After all, you have to make a rather complex effort to indulge in it" by going out to find a partner and a place and even "the most active lecher has to endure a certain amount of delay, frustration, obligatory social ritual. It isn't just a matter of direct satisfaction of an appetite" in favor of abstinence, "How Not to Fight AIDS," 3-19.

The Wall Street Journal concentrated mostly, as one would expect, on the business side of AIDS, although Roger Ricklefs had a couple of good pieces. The most powerful humanized the financial cost in a front-page leader "AIDS Victims Find That A Death Sentence Leads First to Poverty," 8-5. Marilyn Chase also took a terrifying front-page look at the same subject, somewhat more dispassionately, but still hauntingly, "In Lives and Dollars, The Epidemic's Toll Is Growing Inexorably," 5-18; and accompanied inside by "How Insurers Succeed in Limiting Their Losses Related to the Disease" and "Spread of AIDS Infection in U.S. May Be Slowing, Studies Indicate", quoting an AIDS victim: "I'm a medically indigent adult — MIA — missing in action." The *Journal* also had good coverage of MicroGeneSys, on time and on target, "FDA Clears Human Tests of Vaccine Against AIDS Made By MicroGeneSys," 8-18, by Marilyn Chase and Edward Sussman; and "U.S. Will Begin Human Clinical Tests of MicroGeneSys Inc.'s AIDS Vaccine," 8-19, by Edward Sussman. David Shribman of the Washington bureau gave AIDS a nod in "Divided Right: Conservatives Face A Bitter Struggle in Reshaping Movement," 4-29, citing the disease as a major quandary as far as policy goes. Surprisingly very little that we saw was on the op-ed pages, the *Journal* being more concerned with economic and foreign policies.

The Washington Post's coverage was certainly adequate. Michael Specter did a couple of pieces on AIDS research and control measures that were credible and reliable, "U.S., France Settle AIDS Study Feud," 4-1, and "Hospital AIDS Measures Debated," 7-28. Philip Hiltz handled the MicroGeneSys coverage, beating *The New York Times*, and in a photo finish with the *Journal*, "Testing of AIDS Vaccine Approved, Study of Human Inoculations Would Be First in U.S.," 8-18 and "Experimental AIDS Vaccine Showed Encouraging Animal Results," 8-19. Sharon Warren Walsh managed a piece on the upward turn in condom sales without so much as a smirk, "Condom Sales Take A Turn," 2-15.

The *Post*, forging ahead when other papers feared libel suits, later ran an Elizabeth Kastor piece on closet gays, precipitated by the death of NCPAC founder Terry Dolan, allegedly from AIDS, "The Cautious Closet of the Gay Conservative," 5-11, which created a storm of controversy. Pulitzer Prize winner Tony Dolan, now a Reagan speechwriter and brother of Terry, took a double-truck ad in *The Washington Times* to refute the story, a good deal of which dealt with Terry Dolan's alleged homosexuality, but never mentioned his supposed later rejection of it as a Christian. Demerits as well for "Rep. Stewart B. McKinney Dies of AIDS Complications," 5-8, by Michael Specter and Richard Pearson, for rumor-mongering that could not be denied by the party in question. McKinney's doctor said his patient, married with five children, had contracted AIDS through a blood transfusion during open heart surgury in 1979; but according to Specter, "knowledgeable sources on Capitol Hill and in the gay community said McKinney had had homosexual relationships. Homosexual men are at greatest risk for AIDS."

On the *Post*'s international pages, Blaine Harden had a bizarre piece, "Tribal Customs Worsen Spread of AIDS in Africa," 7-3, that told us of the "cleansing" custom and other traditions that help to spread the virus, which we saw nowhere else ("cleansing" is the tradition of a widow or widower sleeping with an in-law to dispel the dead spouse's spirit). Edward Cody's "Belgian AIDS Test Trigger Protests," 3-21, reported on the testing of African students and the rejection of the seropositives. The op-ed pages were refreshing, ringing with viewpoints: Bill Buckley, (having abandoned the tattoo idea), asking Harvard's Stephen Jay Gould in "What Can We *Do* About AIDS," 4-23; Colman McCarthy advising the Catholic Church that AIDS is a health crisis, not a moral issue, "Of Condoms and Condemnation," 3-1, and Nat Hentoff advocating testing, "AIDS: Mandatory Testing Would Help," 5-30.

The Christian Science Monitor's coverage of AIDS that we saw was sparse, excepting a piece by Robert M. Press on the World Health Organization's adoption of different AIDS strategies for different cultures, "Nations Step Up AIDS Education Campaign in Developing World," 1-14. Barry Siegel of the *Los Angeles Times* had a terrific, no-nonsense piece on testing, "How to Test for AIDS — A Dilemma," 9-20, and Dr. Kathleen Bailey of the Bureau of Intelligence and Research brought to our attention the Soviet claim that AIDS was created in a Pentagon experiment as a byproduct of germ warfare, "Soviets Sponsor Spread of Disinformation," 4-19. Even the *Financial Times* ran a winner on AIDS, something not generally within their editorial perimeters: David Fishlock's "Optimism Grows Within UK AIDS Research," 9-16, tells us the virus mutates five times as fast as any other infectious agent! But "there is an effective and simple vaccine which cures a similar disease in cats." Illuminating.

AIDS reporting in the periodicals was sometimes more sensationalist. *Newsweek* ran a black-and-white cover of photos of dead AIDS patients, "The Face of AIDS: A Year in the Epidemic," 8-10, which was supposed to touch us the way the Vietnam cover did, and inside ran page after page in a monthly blow-by-blow of photographs and epitaphs, some of which were less than sympathetic (Althea Flint, co-publisher of *Hustler* and wife of Larry, had under her name and photo: "A drug addict"). Also unsympathetic was the Aric Press admonition "caveat emptor" in "The Charge: AIDS Assault," 6-22, concerning AIDS and prostitution. *The Atlantic* ran two articles by Katie Leishmann which were just weird. The first, "Heterosexuals and AIDS: The Second Stage of the Epidemic," February, was a cover story that gave no evidence to support a heterosexual epidemic and interviewed lawyers and porno stars to get their views. Leishmann included such spacey analysis as "Whatever happens, people will never get enough of tales of the epidemic, any more than they will tales of American slavery or of Nazis and their captives: the subject is subliminally pornographic, at once appalling and erotic. There is a certain excitement in having a legitimate reason — even a responsibility — to discuss in public what nice people never discussed." The second, "AIDS and Insects," September, was equally strange, discussing the possibility of arthropod viral transmission, citing some maverick research, justifying such citation by noting "who's to say that a question that often goes disregarded isn't one that holds an answer everyone is looking for?"

The definitive article in this type of publication was Michael Fumento's "AIDS: Are Heterosexuals At Risk?" in the November issue of *Commentary*, scholarly and detailed.

Mostly, the periodicals offered better fare. *Newsweek* had a powerful cover story detailing the life of Celeste Carrion, a 9-year -old with AIDS, "Kids With AIDS," 9-7; Jane Bryant Quinn evaluated the problems of testing and insurance in "AIDS: Testing Insurance," 6-8: does a positive test mean automatic rejection of insurance for HIV patients? *U.S.News & World Report* carried a heartwrenching personal account of an AIDS sufferer who tried to return to his hometown and was treated like a leper, "AIDS: When Fear Takes Charge," 10-12.

Time's 2-16 cover, "The Big Chill: Fear of AIDS," comprised three separate articles "The Fear of AIDS," "'You Haven't Heard Anything Yet,'" and "In the Grip of the Scourge" plus a sidebar "Tracing A Killer." Thorough and comprehensive, *Time*'s articles, covered social mores, medical progress, insurance, the situation in Africa, and preventions for the future of AIDS, noting that a condom is not particularly effective in protecting pregnancy, so why should it be so for AIDS? Alessandra Stanley noted the Republican politicizing of AIDS in "AIDS Becomes A Political Issue," 3-23, quoting those advisers who would turn disease into a campaign issue.

Business Week ran a credible, comprehensive cover story about how AIDS is affecting the business world and how the business world is responding, "AIDS and Business," 3-23. Robert Bazell, science correspondent for NBC News, wrote a bleak piece for *The New Republic* on the devastation of Africa by AIDS, "The Plague," 6-1. We chuckled at Jeffrey Hart's "'Safe Sex' and the Presence of the Absence," *National Review*, 5-8, tastefully peppering the issue of the Dartmouth Safe Sex Kit with humor. In outlining what one finds in the kit and accompanying pamphlet, Hart notes, "I myself have never heard of some of these sexual practices, and I have lived in Paris."

Pulitzer Prize winner Charles Krauthammer callously asks "Why should AIDS be a privileged disease — federally protected, as it were — while other diseases, many of which cause suffering in many more Americans, are not?" and says the "gay-rights groups have turned AIDS into a political issue," in "AIDS: Why the Political Fuss," *The Detroit News*, 6-16. A very sour note, since AIDS is being transmitted heterosexually as well, although not as quickly. However, the press, on the whole did not respond to AIDS or report on it as specifically a gay issue. It really is no longer a gay issue. We heard about a recent business conference for young executives, where it took all of five minutes for the roundtable discussion group to turn from the economy to AIDS. AIDS is in everybody's mind, with effects that are still to be fathomed. We expect, unfortunately, to be watching this story for years, perhaps decades, to come.

The Great Crash of 1987

The most cataclysmic economic event of the century was the Wall Street stock market crash of 1929 and the market slide that continued in 1932, ushering in the global economic contraction we call the Great Depression, and ultimately, World War II. The Wall Street crash of October 19, 1987, Black Monday, was of an equal magnitude with the initial market decline in October, 1929. It was, of course, the most important story of the year as it resonated volcanically in markets around the world, but signaling what? A dramatic decline in the prospects for the world economy, we can say for sure, but from a very optimistic level to begin with. The story of the Crash and how it was reported by the press is a story of the unfolding world political economy in 1987, a seamless story of taxes and trade, money, debt and exchange rates, and the relative decline of the Reagan Administration.

At the outset of 1987 the central facts of the economy were these. A revolutionary tax reform had been enacted in 1986 and would take effect in stages, bringing the top marginal tax rate on income in the U.S. to 28% by 1988, the lowest in the industrial world. With the rest of the world holding on to high rates of taxation, global capital was flowing into the United States, resulting in an enormous trade deficit as the U.S imported goods and exported stocks, bonds and other productive assets. As in 1929, following a similar experience with U.S. tax rates declining throughout the 1920s, trade protectionist forces grew more politically vociferous. They pressed the Administration and the Congress to block the flow of imports through restrictive legislative barriers or through a devaluation of the dollar. The latter approach, which according to the prevailing economic theory, would make foreign goods more expensive and lead to fewer imports. The first important news account of the year was "Officials Say U.S. Seeks Bigger Drop for Weak Dollar," 1-25, by Peter T. Kilborn in *The New York Times*. The story became the first of many signaling the ambivalence of Treasury Secretary James Baker III on the dollar question as he heard arguments for and against devaluation.

The other central facts were these. The President was already seen to be in a weakened position because of the November 1986 revelations of arms sales to Iran and the diversion of proceeds to the Nicaraguan contras. The Democrats had regained control of the U.S. Senate in 1986 and were marshalling their forces against the "twin deficits," having taken over the traditional GOP role of trade protection and balanced budgets. The U.S. budget deficit had exceeded $220 billion in 1986 and was projected to come down, but not enough to meet the Gramm-Rudman targets legislated by Congress.

Forecasts at the outset of 1987 were for a weak economy with few surprises. Tax reform was supposed to hurt housing and business investment, inflation was supposed to stay tame, the falling dollar was expected to fix the trade deficit, and almost everyone had grown tired of crying wolf about the budget deficit. As late as July 20, Alfred Malabre, Jr. of *The Wall Street Journal* was writing about "just more of the same, slow persistent dull growth that has

21

become so boringly familiar of late" in his "In Its Unexciting Way, Expansion Nears Mark." The business press was hungry for something to write about.

An unexpected sharp upturn in the stock market provided some relief from the boredom, but it just didn't fit with the "consensus" forecast of a feeble economy. Leonard Silk of *The New York Times*, decided the forecasters were right and the markets were wrong, in "Fury in the Markets," 1-25. "Is this really a time for euphoria, as much of Wall Street believes," asked Silk, "or a time for desperation, as much of American industry and agriculture fears?" Silk concluded that the market simply rose because the dollar fell, not because the economy was picking up. The dollar couldn't keep falling without causing inflation, he reasoned, so the bull market could not continue. David Pauly and Rich Thomas of *Newsweek* took the cue, "Is The Fed Behind The Stock Boom?" 1-26, and argued that "Easy money may lead to bloated share prices." But Silk's colleague Robert Hershey had a prescient hunch, 2-13, about the upcoming "Louvre Accord" in Paris. The five major countries, said Hershey, "appear to be edging toward agreement on stabilizing their currencies." If stocks had merely risen because of a falling dollar, as Silk had argued, wouldn't stopping the dollar's fall now mean an end to the bull market?

The Louvre Accord of late February did indeed stop the dollar from falling. "New Dollar Accord an Encouraging Step," the *WSJ*'s Art Pine wrote, 3-9. While monetarists were also insisting money was too tight, stocks roared ahead. In February, the long campaign to drive chief of staff Donald Regan from the White House finally succeeded and former Sen. Howard Baker, Jr., not only a supporter of higher taxes to balance the budget, but also less committed to free trade, took over March 1. (Evans & Novak's column of 3-2 is aptly titled "Reagan's Surrender.") As the first consequence, in early April, the Administration slapped trade sanctions against the Japanese semiconductor industry, to show Congress it was getting tough. The dollar began to dip once again, and the Federal Reserve, ignoring the Louvre Accord, fed dollars into the system even as their value fell. The prices of stocks and bonds fell, too.

Next, the accounts were that a falling dollar was no longer good for the stock market, but was instead a disaster. *Newsweek* led off with "A Case of the Jitters," 5-4, in which Bill Powell and Rich Thomas complained that "the sinking dollar fans inflationary fears, driving up interest rates." The same issue also worried about "a Great Crash, a Depression, some kind of collapse...There's not much debate about the remedy. Nearly all economists agree that Washington should take steps to cut the budget deficit...pull in the national belt a bit." *BusinessWeek* immediately ran with this, even titling its lead story "Jitters," 5-11, and suggesting "the economy seems poised either to slide into recession or undergo a new round of inflation." As with *Newsweek*, there could be no middle ground between depression and inflation, and, as always, "not much debate." But the Louvre Accord was reaffirmed around new rates and the Federal Reserve complied, "Real Support for the Dollar, Finally," 5-4, by Randall W. Forsyth of *Barron's*.

On June 1, though, Fed Chairman Paul Volcker, a defender of stable exchange rates, submitted his resignation to the President. Alan Greenspan, a defender of floating exchange rates, was named his successor. *BusinessWeek*'s Blanca Riemer wrote in "What's in Store at the Fed," 6-15: "The Greenspan appointment marks the triumph of the GOP's old guard. With Howard Baker, Jr. heading the White House staff, James A. Baker III ensconced at the Treasury, and Greenspan on deck at the Fed, the Reagan Administration's revolutionary fervor has been supplanted by a cautious conservatism." The stock market hit its peak on August 25. The front page of the *NYT* of 8-23 reported "Reagan's Advisors See Shift in Focus," news that the Howard Baker team had decided to seek "compromise with Congress on several important domestic bills, such as...trade." Colin Millham warned in the *Financial Times*, "Dollar Set on Downward Trend Out of the Chaos," 8-24, that "the market is waiting to hear" a statement on dollar policy from Greenspan, who "will be very concerned not to send the currency into free fall with a few ill chosen words." Millham made the connection with trade policy, that with the U.S. trade numbers worsening, "the Democrat-led assembly now has further justification for overriding the veto," and "Japan may find further acceptance of a further depreciation of the dollar against the yen, as the lesser of two evils."

The U.S. economy nonetheless continued to perform well. Economic growth averaged 3.7 percent over the first three quarters, although *Business Week*, in "The Economy Isn't Sailing, It's Snailing," 8-17, by William B. Franklin and James C. Cooper, was still writing that the economy's "pace is decidedly slow — and chances are it will stay that way." The stock market rose from 2200 in late April to more than 2700 by late August. The periodic doomsday stories, and even the slow-growth forecasts, had to be put back on the shelf. Instead, a monster on the cover of *The Economist*, "Inflation's Return," 8-1, now proclaimed "an inflationary boom." In place of last year's stories about "losing jobs" to foreigners, or about all those low-paid "service jobs" on Wall Street, we now began to read about a "labor shortage" — too many jobs. A *Business Week* cover story, 8-10, covered "The Coming Labor Shortage," while a 9-14 *Wall Street Journal* story on "Workers Wanted" said good jobs were already going begging. *The New York Times*, 9-20, noted "the unemployment rate has already pierced the 6 percent threshold that for a decade was judged the flashpoint of rising inflation. At that moment, the government often tries to cool the economy by such means as raising taxes...or by raising interest rates."

The economy that the financial media consensus had agreed was on the verge of depression in May, and sluggish in August, was now said to be facing an overheated, inflationary boom by September. Both the depression stories and the boom stories were based almost entirely on some mixture of theories and opinions, with a bare minimum of factual information. One notable example was the widely hailed piece by Peter Peterson, a leader of the GOP "old guard," in *Atlantic*, 10-87. "The Morning After," simply asserted that the U.S. had "seven catastrophic years for U.S. manufacturers...and pink slips for one-to-two million domestic manufacturing workers each year." Manufacturing output was up 5.5% in the year ending in September, and a rousing 37% higher than in 1982. Employment in manufacturing was also up, not down, and productivity gains in that sector had averaged 4% a year since 1981, compared with 2.5% in Japan.

August marked the anniversary of the five-year bull market in stocks, with the Dow Jones index having more than tripled, to more than 2700 from 780. Yet as the economic expansion lengthened to a peacetime record, the financial press almost uniformly looked the other way. Behind the drive for "protection" of the strongest economy in the world came the work of two unabashedly socialist economists, Barry Bluestone and Bennett Harrison, "proving" that the expansion had mainly been in low-skilled and low-paying "McJobs." Their constantly massaged numbers were given magnification by Senator Lloyd Bentsen, chairman of the Joint Economic Committee, sponsor of the protectionist trade bill being urged by the AFL-CIO and parts of corporate America. By and large the press corps swallowed his hoax and perpetuated it throughout the year, an embarrassing blot. Only Robert J. Samuelson, writing in *Newsweek*, "The American Job Machine," 2-23, and Warren Brookes, writing in *The Washington Times*, "Sorry, Wrong Numbers on Jobs," 4-20, questioned the hoax and ridiculed it. In an incredible front-page leader, even the *WSJ* joined this parade, presenting the additional notion that the bull market itself was meaningless for most people, "Some of Rich Gained the Most While Millions Lost Jobs," 8-10, by Tim Metz. The stock market was no longer a meaningful indicator of anything, simply a product of the "Casino Society," to use *Business Week*'s snappy phrase.

U.S.News & World Report, on the other hand, was uniquely accurate *before* the crash, with a cover story, "The Bull Market: Time To Get Out?" 8-31 written at the very peak of the Dow. "Stocks don't seem like much of a deal any more," wrote Jack Egan and Daniel Wiener, and "given the worldwide and historic dimensions of this bull market, it's likelier to end with a bang than with a whimper." Indeed, the falling stock market suddenly restored the respectability of stock markets as a very meaningful indicator. The news in September and early October was mixed. Economic growth had brought the federal deficit down by $73 billion in the fiscal year ending September 30 compared to the previous year. Treasury Secretary Baker proposed at the IMF meeting in Washington a commodity-price indicator, including gold, to guide international exchange-rate policy, and the Louvre Accord still held together. But both West Germany and Japan resisted Treasury Secretary Baker's calls for economic expansion, the only positive way of cutting the U.S. trade deficit. But the *Financial Times'* Andrew Fisher, "Lambsdorff Attacks U.S. Over West German Economy," 9-29, reported that Otto Lambsdorff, economic spokesman for the junior partner of the Bonn coalition, was criticizing the U.S. "for not putting enough pressure on the West German Government to stimulate the economy." Soon thereafter the Bonn government announced it would *raise* withholding taxes on securities! At the same time, the Administration, which had two spending bill vetoes overridden in the summer, looked woefully weak as the President's Supreme Court nominee, Judge Bork, was rejected decisively by the Senate. The Wall Street slide in stocks and bonds continued. *Fortune*'s cover story, "Why Greenspan is Bullish," 10-26, appeared Monday, 10-12, noting that the Fed chief believes the U.S. dollar might have to fall by 3% a year indefinitely, which seemed to put him at odds with the Treasury and the Louvre Accord.

In *The Wall Street Journal*, 10-14, Monica Langley gave us the ominous news that "Tax Boosts Aimed at Wall Street, Rich, Agreed to by Democrats on House Panel," as a move to meet Gramm-Rudman budget targets. A few observers later noticed that takeover stocks, only one target of the House bill, were immediately hard hit. Also on October 14 the trade deficit for August was announced, somewhat higher than had been expected, and the market sank that day. It again sank the following afternoon when Secretary Baker revealed a dispute with the Bundesbank over monetary policy, Baker asserting it was the German central bank's responsibility to ease. He hinted at a news conference that he might be prepared to see the dollar sink rather than have the U.S. defend its rate with the Deutsch Mark. The Dow nosedived Friday the 16th by 100 points. On the weekend, Kilborn of the *NYT* reported "U.S. Said to Allow Decline of Dollar Against the Mark: An Abrupt Policy Shift," 10-18, quoting an unidentified official "that the Administration and the Federal Reserve would not interfere if market pressures start pushing the dollar down somewhat against the mark. They also said a decline of the dollar against the mark could be expected to bring a decline against many other currencies as well." This was the straw that broke the camel's back. The Administration had caved again to the protectionist forces of dollar devaluation, on a theory that had not worked before to reduce the trade deficit and would likely not work again.

Some newsmen somehow felt free to be rudely partisan. Walter Isaacson of *Time*, in "After The Fall," 11-2, described the President of the United States as follows: "As he shouted befuddled Hooverisms...or doddered precariously through his press conference, Reagan appeared embarrassingly irrelevant to a reality that he could scarcely comprehend." What was that reality? "Fortunes were conjured out of thin air," explains Isaacson, "by fresh-faced traders who created nothing more than paper gilded castles held aloft by red suspenders." "Panic Grips The Globe" by George Church, in the same issue, opined the market crashed because of "Reagan's long, obstinate resistance to tax increases." Again diverging from the pack, though, was Warren Brookes in *The Washington Times*, "Luring Securities Dealers Into Line?" 11-3: "One of the most remarkable aspects of the Great Crash episode is how quickly the 'conventional wisdom' developed that it was 'the budget deficit' that did it and the only way to stabilize the market was to raise taxes," arguing that securities lobbyists had been led to believe by "key Hill majority staffers that their own tax and regulatory future depends on how they support the Democrats tax-increase agenda."

The mass magazine that had been the most sanguine about the bull market continuing at the moment it was peaking, *BusinessWeek*, "Why The Bull Is Such A Long-Distance Runner," 8-24, by Jeffrey M. Laderman, was also the most hysterical after stock prices fell. After the crash, Edwin Diamond of *New York* reported in "Crash Reporting," 11-9, that "in a matter of days, the vision had turned apocalyptic: We were peering into the abyss...The market movement was also a movement event, fed by reports of its own activity as well as by news of presidential statements, trade reports, rumors of war, and fragments of gossip."

Kilborn of *The New York Times*, 11-8, whose 10-18 report triggered the Crash, now declared "the Reagan revolution, if it ever really began, has come and gone" in "Where The Revolution Went Awry." Had the revolution ended because stock prices were then merely double what they had been when President Reagan took office? No, said Kilborn, it was because the economy's "performance is no better than under President Carter." He also argued that tax "collections...grew four times faster under President Carter than under President Reagan" — a curious measure of economic success, and one that is quite untrue. Adjusted for inflation, real tax revenues grew very rapidly in 1983-87, but that was from higher profits, payrolls and capital gains, not from pushing the middle class into a 50% tax bracket.

Initial efforts to unravel the causes of the October crash were surprisingly thin. In *The Wall Street Journal*, George Melloan's "A Dollar Poker Game Aided the Market Plunge," 10-20, was written within hours of the Dow's 508-point collapse, and was the best instant analysis anywhere. The best wrap-up we saw was *The New York Times*, "Events That Changed Wall Street," 10-26, by James Sterngold, a long piece that assembled most of the elements with logical coherence. But very few newsmen questioned the idea that investors woke up one morning in October and suddenly noticed that the U.S. had a budget deficit. "Nearly every analyst," wrote *Newsweek*, "Averting A Crisis: What Can Be Done?" 11-9, "believes the perceived inability of U.S. policymakers to get the deficit down...contributed to the global financial panic." Yet markets turn on news, and the only news about the budget deficit was that it had just *fallen* by a third, to $148 billion, with tax revenues up $85 billion in a single year. Earlier in the year, Alfred Malabre, Jr., and Lindley Clark, Jr., of *The Wall Street Journal*, 2-2, had cited forecasts that the 1987 budget deficit would be $220 billion to $300 billion. Most of the financial press avoided asking how a federal deficit much smaller than expected could possibly have led to the Crash. *The New York Times* did give Robert Eisner of Northwestern University and Larry Kotlikoff of Boston University op-ed space to refute the notion that stock prices fell because of the budget, 11-15.

Fortune and *Forbes*, bi-weeklies, had time to reflect. Malcolm Forbes, Jr. was among the few to make sense of the overworked 1929 analogy, 11-16, noting that "the possibilities of protectionism, tax increases, rising interest rates and a weaker greenback did to equities what a similar combination did 58 years ago." *Fortune*'s Myron Magnet, "1987 Need Not Become 1929," 11-23, observed that those who make comparisons with 1929-32 "are clamoring to make similar mistakes," such as higher tariffs and taxes, quoting James Tobin of Yale: "A recession would not be confidence-building."

Other late reports on the crash also gained from the added reflection. Samuel Brittan, the distinguished columnist of the *Financial Times*, "Undoing Conventional Wisdom," 11-19, flatly declared that the budget deficit "did not trigger the crash," instead attributing the crash to the breakdown of efforts to support the dollar, and the widening gap between bond and equity yields. Robert Bartley, editor of *The Wall Street Journal*, wrote a masterful full-page article, 11-24, "1929 and All That," which convincingly blamed the crash on the House Ways and Means proposal to tax takeovers, the threat of a protectionist trade bill and the breakdown of international monetary cooperation, which raised the risk of a severe drop in the dollar. Robert Novak added a political dimension in "The Politics of the Crash," 11-20, in *National Review*.

But time for reflection did not help with "Behind Baker's Policy Shift," 11-8, as Hobart Rowen of *The Washington Post* asserts "with the benefit of hindsight, it becomes clear that the famous Louvre Accord designed to stabilize the dollar's exchange rate is a key cause of the crash of financial markets," never explaining why the crash came *after* Secretary Baker revealed he was prepared to cut loose from the Louvre Accord! One of the great puzzles of the year is how the devaluationists maintained their support of financial journalists like Rowen of the *Post*, Kilborn of the *Times*, and Murray and Mossberg of the *WSJ*. After two years of dollar devaluation, the trade deficit was as high as ever at year's end. We know of no effort in any corner of the financial press to rigorously examine the hypothesis, which was clearly at the center of the October cataclysm in one way or another. In that sense, the intramural debate on who did a better job of journalism in cleaning up after the Crash is of only minor interest.

All things considered, there were heroic efforts here and there in reporting on the rise and fall of the DJIA in 1987, but it was not a year that will go down as a high point of financial and economic journalism. We saw too much sensationalism and hysteria, emulation that led to sheep-like fads, minimal dissent from prevailing views, illogical and contradictory efforts to explain events, and the garbling or suppression of relevant facts and statistics. Will 1988 be any better? The central facts at the outset of the year are much the same as they were at 1987's start: A weakened President, a huge trade deficit, a protectionist trade bill waiting in the wings with powerful supporters in labor and business, and continued exhortations to devalue the dollar. We must hope the press can sufficiently untangle itself from the political forces at work here and communicate.

Gorbachev's Reforms

This was a year of significant changes in the USSR, with world attention focused on Gorbachev's policies of restructuring (*perestroika*) and openness or publicity (*glasnost*). Were these genuine reforms? How were they being implemented? These were the important questions facing the Moscow press corps. Getting them answered was no easy task, given the well-known problems of news-gathering in a totalitarian society, but as a whole the press did some of its best-ever reporting on the USSR.

There's a tremendous constraint that binds and limits news-gathering in the Soviet Union. Information always has to be re-weighed, reassessed, tested and examined against the context and demands of reporting from a country whose totalitarianism has endured for 70 years. This has always been apparent in reporting from that beat, and it wasn't hard to see who pushed against the constraints and who remained limited by them. That's why there have been certain reporters whose names stood out in this field as exemplary of the worst and the best of journalistic standards, from Walter Duranty to Harrison Salisbury of the *NYT*, for example. When they pushed hard against the constraints, as Andrew Nagorski of *Newsweek* did a few years ago, they became *persona non grata*. When they accommodated to the limits, they became candidates for the transmission of disinformation, handed "scoops" from high officials which events later revealed were pure and simple disinformation.

The press as a whole did well enough in 1986, giving us the outlines of the first stages of Mikhail Gorbachev's reform perspective — economic restructuring and some liberalization in cultural areas, all under the guidance and supervision of the CPSU. We also saw reported the stalling of the economic changes and the emergence of *glasnost* in that period. Coverage of *perestroika* dropped off, in part because the campaign itself hadn't progressed much as yet, but mainly because the "openness" or "publicity" phenomenon grabbed front-page attention.

It was clear from the reporting this year that Gorbachev's reform perspectives were far advanced beyond the mere anti-vodka campaign and exhortations for better work discipline initiated by his predecessor Yuri Andropov. The economic crisis within the Soviet Union necessitated more than that. The press was generally weak, however, in reporting verifiable information on Soviet economic growth. Don Oberdorfer of *The Washington Post*, for instance, gave front-page treatment to the CIA/DIA report that the Soviet economy had grown by 4% in "Soviet Economy Breaks Slump," 3-27, but without any testing of this or indication of how the numbers were arrived at. We know that the Soviets themselves had been looking at figures in the range of stagnation (1%), discarding from their own reports projections the CIA retained in theirs. Reporting here was insufficient, although there were some analytical pieces that touched on the issue, Seweryn Bialer's "Gorbachev's Moves," in *Foreign Affairs*, Spring, and "What's Happening in Moscow," a symposium appearing in *The National Interest*, Summer.

The press, though, did well in covering the problems the General Secretary was immediately running into, resistance from the Brezhnevian holdovers through all layers of the bureaucracy. Gorbachev's intentions of improving economic conditions by moving against the bureaucratic obstacles and by introducing pay rewards based on worker efficiency was indeed something new in the USSR. While not a basic structural change of the system, but an attempt to reform within it, the proposals were novel enough to threaten dislocation, social unrest and battle with a bureaucracy that enjoys special privileges from administering the unworkable system. We began getting a clearer picture that the changes underway were hardly mere cosmetics. Instead, a serious political struggle was taking place.

Paul Quinn-Judge, Moscow bureau chief for *The Christian Science Monitor*, produced a series of reports toward the end of 1986 and beginning of 1987 that were illuminating on Gorbachev's struggle with his opponents. "Gorbachev Ready to Take on Regional Bosses?" 12-19-86, "Soviet Ethnic Riots Reveal Policy Problems," 12-22-86, and "Cleaning Out the Soviet 'Mafias,'" 1-13, each added information to the growing perception that Gorbachev's reforms were running up against a combination of bureaucratic inertia and bureaucratic self-defense. *The New York Times* also explored this in "Demographics Put Strain on Soviet Ethnic Seams," 12-28-86, and "The Resistance to Gorbachev," 1-30-87, both by Bill Keller, new to Moscow. The treatment wasn't as informative as the *CSM*'s or that of the *WSJ*'s Mark D'Anastasio. Quinn-Judge, as a matter of fact, had touched a raw nerve with his reports, the *Monitor* earning a rebuke from the Soviets for reporting that opposition to Gorbachev existed at many levels.

Despite such important contributions from the *Monitor*, it was really *The New York Times* and *Financial Times* that covered the USSR best as a whole. Other press came up with important details and reports throughout the year, but none with the kind of comprehensiveness demonstrated by these two.

Gorbachev's efforts at economic reform had slowed in this period. *Glasnost* became the center of attention, the return from internal exile of Dr. Andrei Sakharov the major event early in the year. "There is more *glasnost*, more an openness in the press, in artistic works," Sakharov told *Newsweek*'s Joyce Barnathan in an interview 1-5, adding, however, that important as *glasnost* is for change, by itself it isn't enough. But what indeed was *glasnost*? We found that Henrik Bering-Jensen of *Insight* provided the best overall answer with "Gorbachev and Glasnost," 3-30, a three-part cover story assessing the reform. His report noted that it had become an important weapon in the hands of Gorbachev for use against his opponents in the Soviet bureaucracy. Gorbachev was successfully enlisting support from the Russian intellectual classes, a constituency he was relying on in his efforts to move against resistance to reform among the apparatchiks. With the *glasnost* campaign Soviet media began revealing aspects of Soviet history and life previously undiscussed.

The western press utilized the opportunities to examine aspects of Soviet society more deeply where little information had been forthcoming previously. The *Times* was especially perceptive here. Felicity Barringer in "Suddenly, A Soviet Veil is Lifted, Revealing Scenes of Bitter Youths," 2-16, reported the observations of Soviet social scientists on the lethargy and demoralization that had taken hold among the nation's youth: "A young man may well see the situation as hopeless...the young man may work well, but there is a line" beyond which there will be no reward for extra work. Bill Keller's "Russia's Restless Youth," 7-26, was one of the best of these reports, providing extraordinary glimpses of a disbelieving young generation "sanguine about Gorbachev's prospects" and showing "every inclination to abstain." The perceptions into *glasnost* were honed by Edward Mortimer, "Foreign Affairs" columnist of the *Financial Times*. In one of the year's ten-best political commentaries, "Parts That Glasnost Fails to Reach," 9-22, Mortimer meticulously examined where *glasnost* stood in relation to its extent so far and to its limits.

In addition to its internal use as a weapon against the anti-reformist opposition, *glasnost* served as a means of improving the Soviet image in the west. The press was resolute here in testing its promises and accomplishments. *Glasnost* "doesn't exist, and at best is a fraud," was the harsh assessment from Morris Abrams, "No Glasnost Seen for Soviet Jews," 7-10, in *The Washington Post*. Martin Sieff of *The Washington Times* had also entered a critical judgment, reporting that despite the release of Sakharov, the dissident movement was still severely persecuted in "Openness Policy Masks Repression," 2-17. And Bering-Jensen's *Insight* cover story, 3-30, had noted that in the era of *glasnost*, "dissidents have died in prison, which was not the case during the Brezhnev years." Felicity Barringer of the *NYT* provided reports that tested the application of *glasnost* to human rights questions. Barringer examined what had or hadn't changed on Jewish emigration since *glasnost*, finding no major alteration of policy in "No Easing of Exit-Visa Battles for Many in Soviet," 1-11. *NYT* columnist A.M. Rosenthal was sharply critical of any perspective that Gorbachev should get the benefit of the doubt about leading the USSR into a new era of political and personal freedom, producing sharp critiques in "Glasnost and the Church," 2-1, and "The Forgotten Prisoners," 4-23, among others. The *New York Review of Books* provided a quite different view, Arthur Hertzberg finding evidence of policy changes and prospects for better conditions for Soviet Jews in "Glasnost and the Jews," 10-22.

Glasnost itself, however, was continuing to undergo change, not quite developing a life of its own, but nonetheless pushing up against the limits imposed from the top. It was, as Keller of the *NYT* reported in "Reporter's Notebook: Searching For Outer Limit Of 'Glasnost,'" 8-13, evolving and maturing from sanctioned criticism of the last regime's shortcomings to the beginning of a political debate over the future of the Soviet system. The next step, he wrote, will be over who controls the debate. Philip Taubman of the *NYT* added important dimensions to the question in "Why Glasnost Drags," 5-28. No one in the press came up with a credible account of Gorbachev's long absence from public activity during this period, but Taubman noted that in the interim there was a loss of *glasnost*'s momentum. Opponents were moving into the open, *Pamyat*, for example, testing *glasnost* with a Russophile agenda laden with anti-Semitic overtones. Taubman also reported that critics of *glasnost* were citing the remarks of the number two Communist Party leader Yegor K. Ligachev as high-level support for their views. Celestine Bohlen of *The Washington Post* rounded out some of the picture on Ligachev, noting that he gives broad support to the economic and liberalization reform, but as ideological chief, intends to set the parameters of the debate and to draw back those conservatives alienated by the cultural reforms. Importantly, Bohlen drew attention to the fact that Viktor Chebrikov, head of the KGB, was engaging in public criticisms of the loosening of restraints on Soviet life.

We continued to be informed on the reality that Gorbachev still was not fully established in power. In his attempt to utilize the intelligentsia as a power constituency, he was limited by its marginal role, and by its tendency to go even further than the "reformist" leadership wished. "Dismantling the Stalin Myth: New Effort Under Gorbachev," 3-15 by Philip Taubman of the *NYT*, reported the fine line Gorbachev was walking on Stalin: "Mr. Gorbachev, apparently sensing the potential danger in a Khrushchev-style assault, has been careful to spread the blame for current problems and avoid direct attacks on Stalin." But it was clear in the press reports that Gorbachev is not fully established in power. Not one of the politburo's members at the beginning of the year had any long-standing links with the General Secretary. By midyear, press accounts seemed to indicate a stalling of his economic reforms. His January address to the Central Committee indicated he had to reorganize strategically, and the General Secretary put off many questions until the July meeting.

Patrick Cockburn of the *Financial Times* provided the best picture of the reformist agenda in "Gorbachev and the Committee," 6-24. On the eve of the Central Committee meeting, he reported, their disposition against piecemeal reform is unrestrained, but Gorbachev's "revolution from above" requires such upheaval that the "reformists'" agenda is viewed as revolutionary.

Both *The Washington Post* and *Los Angeles Times* added important readings on the "reformists'" agenda. Nikolai Shmelev, one of the bolder thinkers in the reform tendency, wrote in "It's a Long Road to a New Soviet Economy," *Post*, 6-28, that the introduction of competition in the restructuring reform would indeed promote in some instance lower wages, cuts in social spending, cut-backs in staff and work force, and the closing and disbanding of some enterprises. His palliative that restructuring is not a departure from socialism nor an abandonment of central planning, however, wasn't sufficient to overcome the tremendously adverse reaction this perspective evoked from the anti-reformists in the USSR. However, as William Eaton reported in "Gorbachev Economist Seeks Even Faster 'Leap Forward,'" *LAT*, 6-22, Gorbachev appeared to come out of the Central Committee meeting with enough support to begin price reforms. Gorbachev's economic adviser Abel G. Aganbegyan felt confident enough on that to argue that the state should move even faster on increasing prices for bread and meat, reducing and eliminating subsidies, and shutting down thousands of state enterprises that are running at a loss.

There was not, however, a comprehensive account of precisely what emerged from the Central Committee meeting or of what was occurring with *perestroika* at this point. The *Financial Times* came closest to that in an editorial, "Gorbachev's Reforms," 6-30, which gave the sense of a crucial shift from piecemeal economic change to radical reform of the entire Soviet economic system. While the press was more successful in its coverage of *glasnost*, it never really got in as deeply during the year with *perestroika*. With the stalemate between Gorbachev and the opposition at the beginning of the year, it seemed harder to get the satisfying details on restructuring. The *NYT* offered some information, as in Bill Keller's "Soviet Law Would Free Up Collectives," 2-8, but this was coverage of a proposed experiment in the industrial sector for an unprecedented loosening of centralization, and we never got a follow-up. "Does Moscow Mean It This Time?" 1-18, by Keller, was similar, providing some details on a new law permitting 49% U.S. ownership of joint ventures, but the report was limited to one trade official. One of the better reports came from Mark D'Anastasio of *The Wall Street Journal*, "Soviet Workers Resist Gorbachev Plan," 6-3, reporting on the lackluster reception the new reform proposals elicited from a skeptical, but also somewhat lethargic, work force.

After the July meeting, the press began giving better accounts of *perestroika*, though the material often emphasized the political struggle more than the economic content. "Gorbachev's Gamble," 7-19, by Philip Taubman, was exemplary. Excellent on the politics and factional lineups, it was thinner on economics, not really getting a grip on what is supposed to enable the reform to work. Keller's "Soviet Planning Big Labor Shift Out Of Industry," 7-4, an interview with a reform economist revealed plans for ending food and housing subsidies, and "Gorbachev Prepares the Ground for Raising Prices," *FT*, 10-8, by Patrick Cockburn, was an important update on the progress of that campaign.

D'Anastasio filled in with a very informative report on Soviet interest in China's economic reforms, "Soviets Now Hail China As a Source of Ideas For Reviving Socialism," 9-18, but it was clear that this was simply in the "ideas" stage. As Taubman noted in "Without Gorbachev, Glasnost Pauses," 10-4, there was still a lack of economic improvement and "Until benefits start to appear, all Mr. Gorbachev has to offer is a more interesting intellectual climate."

"Where Is Gorbanomics Leading?" *Fortune*, 9-28, by Richard I. Kirkland, Jr., a "quick report card on Gorbachev's first 1,000 days," provided a sharp assessment of his progress toward fundamental change and though it left us hungry for more analysis, seemed more satisfying than *BusinessWeek*'s cover story, "Reforming the Soviet Economy," 12-7, by Peter Galuszka, et al., though we did find new information in the latter on U.S.-Soviet joint ventures coming about. The *Los Angeles Times*' autumn series "Remaking the Revolution," was an impressive effort to produce a comprehensive picture of the reforms. The results were mixed, in some cases simply a cataloging of information, in others filling in with new detail areas where other reports were only sketchy. *The Washington Post*'s series in the spring,

"Communism: Can It Reform?" was less satisfying, although Jackson Diehl's "Hungary Leads in Reforms," 4-6, was outstanding, one of the year's ten-best foreign reports, far beyond the simple scanning of marketplaces and cataloging of information that characterized the rest of the series.

The *Post*, weak in Moscow (a situation being remedied in '88), was excellent on the winds of *glasnost* and *perestroika* in the East Bloc, Diehl covering that with insightful reports all year. The *NYT*'s Budapest bureau chief, Henry Kamm, also was resourceful and alert, filling out that picture in Hungary and Rumania and producing a blockbuster report on the changes taking place in what's sometimes called the USSR's 16th republic, Bulgaria, with "Economic Changes Stir in Bulgaria," 10-7. Leslie Colitt of the *Financial Times* did the best job on Czechoslovakia overall, though William Echikson of the *CSM* turned out some very insightful articles as well, "Winds of Reform Rustle Through Prague," 10-2, particularly well done. In these reports we found far more attention to details of actual economic changes taking place, more so than in the reporting from Moscow.

While the press did quite well in coverage of the cultural reforms, as a whole it didn't get as far with the economic. Hence a heavy emphasis on the statements and communiques from economists and officials, but less on examinations of concrete cases where *perestroika* is operating. Perhaps that was part of the story, that the campaign is still more words than deeds, as at least a number of assessments on Gorbachev's economics suggested. Nonetheless, it was an area where the coverage was still short of what we'd hoped for. An analytic by Bill Keller, "The Test of Gorbachev's Talents Has Just Begun," 12-13, gives an indication as to why the press corps lagged on solid coverage of Gorbachev's economic reforms. A "new economic law...takes effect Jan. 1," he reported; "60% of Soviet industry will be thrown into the deep end of Mr. Gorbachev's most critical economic changes to date." All the Moscow press corps knew this, which may account for their unfortunate lack of serious work on *perestroika* this year, they and everybody else waiting for Jan. 1, 1988, to roll around in the USSR.

Overall, however, the press corps deserves congratulations for its Soviet coverage this year, the best of them sometimes exceeding our expectations. There's a new crop of journalists that impressively met the demanding standards for news reporting from the USSR.

The Iran-Contra Affair

This was *the* big political story of the year, no other event quite testing the profession the way the Iran-Contra affair did. The U.S press was "scooped" on the two critical aspects of the story by revelations that came from outside the American Fourth Estate.

First, the small pro-Syrian Lebanese weekly, *Al Shiraa* "scooped" the U.S. media on the U.S. arms sales to Iran, revealing, 11-4-86, former NSC director Robert McFarlane's trip to Teheran. Then it was U.S. Attorney General Edwin Meese III who discovered and revealed the diversion of Iranian arms sales profits to the contras, 11-25-86. Passion and chagrin within the profession rose to a fever pitch over this, resulting in some disorientation. "Coverup," *Newsweek* asserted with the headline of its cover story, 3-2. The fact that the revelations had come from outside the American press seemed to confirm for some that there must be a bigger story, a deeper scandal that was being concealed. There's nothing at all wrong with this kind of healthy skepticism, but it was often translated into a tendency to slip into assertive editorializing that competed with straight reporting. Unsubstantiated speculation was reported as fact, policy interventions masqueraded as reportage, and a "judge-and-jury" bias competed with objective coverage and serious, non-speculative investigative work.

It was certainly the hardest story to follow, the search for evidence and facts turning into a search for "the truth" — something beyond the known facts and evidence. "This is the most fun we've had since Watergate," declared *The Washington Post*'s executive editor Benjamin Bradlee. "Simple honesty requires that journalists admit that this is the kind of episode we all live for. The adrenaline is flowing like Perrier," *The New Republic*'s Michael Kinsley wrote in "A Case for Glee," 12-86. *The Washington Post*'s Walter Pincus disclosed in a *Rolling Stone* interview, 5-21, that "All reporters want to have impact...And all reporters want to take down the government..." For some it seemed that finally the success of the Reagan Administration's roll was coming to an end, the whiff of scandal like the smell of blood in a pool of sharks. As the *Post*'s Lou Cannon observed to *Time* magazine 12-86, "people are finally listening to what's wrong with...[Reagan]."

Getting to the facts was the hardest job all year. It was the *Los Angeles Times* that did the best job on just straight, comprehensive reporting at the end of 1986, the efforts of Doyle McManus and Michael Wines solid. McManus' "Gipperdammerung," *Foreign Affairs*, Spring, was a balanced account of the "Contra" side of the affair prior to the testimony at the Congressional committees. The *Los Angeles Times* also produced an eight-page pull-out section, "The Iran Deception," 12-28-86, that at the time was the most comprehensive account. *The Washington Post* dominated with its coverage, at one point putting 28 reporters on the story, according to assistant managing editor Robert Kaiser. With exclusives, multiple stories in one issue, and frequent front-pagers, *The Washington Post* deployed energetically and widely, with *The New York Times* the runner-up. It was the *NYT* that best covered the Tower Commission report released 2-26 — 15 pages of transcript and analysis, 23 stories related to it. "This is a historic story and we're responsible for reporting as much of it as we can," executive editor Max Frankel said.

The issue quickly became the center of a power struggle, though, and it required extreme resourcefulness by the press to avoid being manipulated by the various players. The partisan divisions involved in the affair reflected the sharp differences between Democrats and Republicans and the two Houses of Congress; additionally, wide divergence over U.S. policy for Nicaragua and the role of the legislature vs. the executive in the formulation and conduct of foreign policy were parts of the story. Early in the year, *The Washington Post* editorialized against the bottling up of the Senate Intelligence Committee's report on the closed hearings it conducted into the affair. "Let's See the Report," it declared 1-7; sitting on it only feeds suspicion that the committee "came up with nothing showing that President Reagan knew of the diversion of Iran arms sales profits to the Nicaraguan resistance." *The Washington Times*' editorial "The War Is On," 1-7, charged that "the party of compassion wants to keep the report bottled up so that it can get on with the business of tanning Ronald Reagan's hide." Although the committee's report did indeed find no evidence of the President's knowledge of the diversion of funds, the issue was not buried, and a good part of the press pursued the search for the "smoking gun" that could prove otherwise.

"Scandal" became the term most solidly identified with the affair. On the whole, the media operated in that atmosphere, "Watergate" scenarios popping up in the various commentaries, and the quest for the "smoking gun" sending one journalist after another off on a search. This was a venture generally endorsed — and encouraged — by their editors, often with results that hurt press credibility as a whole.

The New York Times had some unfortunate experiences as a result of the frenzied scandal atmosphere. In a front-pager, "Lobbyist Said to Have Several Ties to White House," 12-16-86 authored by deputy Washington bureau chief R.W. Apple, Jr., the *Times* reported that there existed a plan to divert profits from the Iranian arms sales into congressional campaigns. Oliver North was reported as aware of the scheme. The *Times* had merely reproduced the unsubstantiated allegations of the *Lowell* (MA) *Sun* and no confirmation of the story was ever produced. Joel Brinkley authored a story, 2-15, that Oliver North's "Project Democracy" operations were the "secret side" of the National Endowment for Democracy, another "major scandal" that had no basis in fact. Fox Butterfield reported in a front-pager 6-18 that "congressional investigators" had testimony that would reveal financial connections between Gen. Richard Secord and Edwin Wilson, the ex-CIA official involved in illegal arms sales to Iran. The *Times*' transgressions stand out because it printed a front-page acknowledgment

31

of the misinformation in Butterfield's article, though there were others as well that ought to have been redressed. The *Times* alone in the news media paused to acknowledge error.

Elizabeth Drew of *The New Yorker* argued early that the search for a "smoking gun" was irrelevant, whether Reagan knew or didn't know about the diversion of funds a tertiary question, "Letter from Washington," 12-19-86. She maintained this point of view in subsequent reports all year, insisting that the real issues are the serious constitutional questions. Up until the testimony of Admiral John Poindexter, however, the majority of the media continued trying to discover the "smoking gun," the one piece of evidence that would tie Reagan into knowledge of the diversion of funds to the contras. In some cases, it seemed as if the press was creating its own evidence.

The Washington Post was the most zealous among the press, convinced such evidence had been deliberately concealed by the Administration. The *Post's* many newsbeats derived from this more intense deployment. The first word of allegations about a Swiss bank account that paid for a security system at North's Virginia home came in a page-one story, "Secord Fund Paid North Security Bill," 6-11, by Walter Pincus. The source for this was "congressional sources." Generally, most of the *Post* stories were based on "congressional" or "committee sources," always unidentified beyond that. Between May 1 and the July appearance of Colonel North before the committee, the front-page stories in the *Post* contained more than 60 references to unidentified sources. Revelations of secret wrongdoings about to come to light were the constant theme of these stories.

In "Poindexter Immunity Plan Set," 3-18, George Lardner Jr. and Walter Pincus of *The Washington Post* reported that at least "one source close to the President" said that Poindexter would "testify that he had 'direction and authority, directly or indirectly,' from Reagan and that the former national security advisor's testimony could undermine Reagan's claims of not having been aware that proceeds from the arms sales to Iran went to aid the Contras." In "Meese Didn't Ask Casey A Key Question," 4-19, Bob Woodward and Howard Kurtz reported that "Just hours before visiting Casey...Meese had read the 'smoking gun' memo, found in Lt. Col. Oliver L. North's White House files, that the $12 million from the Iran arms sales would be spent on the contras," but the Attorney General never pursued the issue with the CIA director. "Potential 'Smoking Gun' in Iran Scandal: Questions Center on Reagan and 'Undated Memo' Citing Diversion," was the 6-14 front-page story by Dan Morgan and Walter Pincus. Yet, the link to the President just wasn't there.

On the eve of Admiral Poindexter's testimony, Sen. Daniel Inouye (D-HA) alleged on national TV, 6-12, that the committee had discovered a memo that would prove that all along the President knew that profits from the Iranian arms sales had been used for the covert projects. This was the lead story on all three networks and in the national dailies, all of them running with it, none of them seeking to probe deeper and verify the allegation. Instead, it was the questioning the next day by committee members that brought forth Inouye's admission that he "had misread" the memo and that in fact it implied no such "smoking gun." The former NSC director testified, 6-15, that he'd never advised President Reagan of the plan to divert funds from Iranian arms sales to the contras. It seemed that the quest for the "smoking gun" was just about dead, only the testimony of Col. Oliver North remaining as the last possibility to produce it. The *Post* had "North Testifies All Actions Were Authorized. Reagan's Approval Sought in 5 Memos," 7-8, Walter Pincus and Dan Morgan reported. The report was not the link to Reagan the headline suggested. North's testimony blew the President's opponents out of the water and put an end to the search for the "smoking gun."

Max Frankel, executive editor of *The New York Times*, was correct to a degree that the *Post* was simply "shouting" louder than the *Times*, with its sourcing, headlines and play. The *Times* did produce material that impressed us and served its reputation well, at times with a whisper. Stephen Engelberg had a provocative "Memo Details How a Frustrated Reagan Pondered Ways to Get Aid to the Contras," 7-11, with a buried observation that told it all: "One month earlier, in the first week of April, Colonel North had drafted a memorandum for the President's approval that described using $12 million from the Iran arms sales to keep the contras alive until Congress approved more aid. If Mr. Reagan knew of this operation, it would seem unlikely he would be pressing Admiral Poindexter a month later for some other method to come up with funding for the contras." Case closed. As we detail in his entry, David Rosenbaum produced timely news analysis on the affair that helped restrain the pack.

The "Ollie" phenomenon dominated the media immediately after his testimony and some of the worst excesses of the press surfaced around this. It was as if everyone who had seen the Colonel testify on television somehow had been hoodwinked. Here came the "judge, jury, and executioner" material. *The Washington Post*'s assistant editor for "Outlook," Curt Suplee, wrote in "Ollie North and Our Search for a Hero," 7-19, "Oliver North a hero? It seems preposterous on the face of it, our public spasm of adulation for this self-professed liar and desk-chair martinet. By his own account, the former National Security Council staffer sold lethal weapons to a terrorist state, subverted an act of Congress, failed in most of his aims and then flaunted his actions before congressional committees. If this is 'heroism,' then words have lost their meanings." Suplee, however, *was* editorializing.

Time magazine's reporting on the Poindexter and North testimony went far beyond acceptable bounds, however. George J. Church's predisposition against Oliver North was apparent in his "Ollie's Turn," 7-13, the article containing a liberal mix of misinformation and disinformation. Richard Stengel set himself up as privy to the workings of North's mind, producing insupportable psychological conclusions in "True Belief Unhampered by Doubt," 7-13, which was not so much a profile of North, but a revelation of Stengel's biases. Jacob V. Lamar came as close as one could to saying that Ronald Reagan is guilty and Poindexter is lying to protect him in "The Admiral Takes the Hit," 7-27. Ed Magnuson's "The 'Fall Guy' Fights Back," 7-20, was surely the worst *Time* cover story of the year, the author functioning as judge and jury on North instead of reporting on the testimony. In general, *Time*'s correspondents couldn't detach their partisanship from their reports. *Newsweek* was a bit more restrained, observing in its cover story "Ollie Takes the Hill," 7-20: "In the end, the lesson of the Iran-Contra scandal will be that Ollie North's secret diplomacy is simply wrong for democracy: Rambo can be entertaining, but his place is in the movies."

The electronic media also pursued the North testimony along similar lines. For Dan Rather of CBS News, it was the "electrifying test of wills and test of skills," but the committee didn't get to the *real* questions. By this time, the *"real"* questions had become foreign policy mismanagement, the existence of an "outlaw government," and the role of the executive vs. the legislature in the conduct of foreign policy. The committee had "tried to break the spell," Tom Brokaw suggested. "Colonel North has acknowledged, of course, that he lied to Congress, that he mislead Congress, that he arranged false chronologies and rearranged documents." Yet his testimony did not result in a turning against the President many had anticipated. It was all "histrionics," was the anti-climatic pronouncement from public television commentators Judy Woodruff and Elizabeth Drew.

Among the themes that had been bouncing back and forth during the year, was the existence of the "shadow government." "Reagan Aides and the 'Secret' Government," 7-5, a page-one account in the *Miami Herald*, sketched the operations of a shadow government allegedly headed by Colonel North. The paper suggested the committee had information it would disclose on this operation. The paper's story was in fact based on a speculative staff memo written months ago when investigative strategies were being discussed by the committee. This alleged "shadow government" was also the theme of the articles on "The Reagan Junta," 1-29 and 10-22 by Theodore Draper in *The New York Review of Books*. Draper's initial essay could have been acceptable, although more assertive than investigative, but beating this dead horse in October seemed a waste of time.

The Wall Street Journal's editorials always proceeded from the conviction that the President was telling the truth and that the issue at hand was the political battle between the President and his opponents over foreign policy. The *Journal* defended this view every step of the way during the course of the affair in 1987, providing the best marginal and strategic analysis all year, "Boland Laws May Be The Real 'Crime'," 6-4, by assistant editorial page editor L. Gordon Crovitz was a rigorous examination of this question. Crovitz also authored "Crime, the Constitution & the Iran-Contra Affair," 10-87, which appeared in *Commentary* and was one of the best analytical essays on the subject.

The Washington Times seemed the best at watchdogging for misinformation on the story. For example, CBS News radio, AP wire service, and *The New York Times* all carried the story of a Greek newspaper that it had secret recordings of a promise by Robert McFarlane to supply billions of dollars worth of arms to Iran. *The Washington Times* exposed the charges as totally false, revealing the close ties of the Greek publication to the Soviet embassy in Athens. "How Press Stumbles on Facts of Iran-Contra Deals," 6-30, by George Archibald was also an important contribution, revealing the serious "mistakes of heart and head" that produced sloppy to irresponsible journalism in coverage of the affair.

The press was self-critical of its performance. "Why [did] the American news media...[miss] the biggest story of the Administration[?]," Eleanor Randolph of *The Washington Post* asked in "The Story the Press Didn't See," 11-30. Robert Pear of *The New York Times* had also probed into this question earlier with "Missing the Iran Arms Story: Did the Press Fail?" And *Editor & Publisher* had reported the sense of "failure" among members of the profession in "Missing the Big One," 7-11, quoting Joel Brinkley of *The New York Times* that the press' failure to jump on the activities of Oliver North earlier was a "scandal."

Some journalists had poked around the rumor circuit, coming close to unearthing the story. Syndicated columnists Jack Anderson and Dale Van Atta were reporting in a series of columns beginning 4-28-86 that the White House was involved in "behind-the-scenes negotiations with Iran over the American hostages held by pro-Iranian terrorists." Anderson's "Washington Merry-Go-Round" column produces many, many "leads" in a year that go absolutely nowhere, and the corps filed this one along with the others. Nathan Adams, a senior editor of *Readers' Digest* and the Hearst newspapers' foreign affairs editor, John P. Wallach, also had probed into secret negotiations between the U.S. and Iran and an Israeli connection with arms sales to Iran. These also took place prior to *Al Shiraa*'s revelations.

By the end of the year, there was only the release of the committee's report to cover, no new scandals to unearth, no last-minute miraculous discovery of new evidence of a "smoking gun," no critical, undisclosed information yet to be brought to the surface. Looking at the coverage of the committee's final report, one can get a good sense of who in the press accepted this and got on with the business of news reporting, and those who still bristled having to accept an end to the affair. With all the passionate partisanship involved in this story, *The Washington Post*'s "Reagan Was in Charge of Covering Up the Trail," 11-30, by David Hoffman was sloppy on keeping its distance from partisanship, presenting the majority report without qualifiers and without mention of the minority report. Perhaps it was just the last chance to get in a kick before the Iran-Contra story finally shut down. *The New York Times*, however, gave front-page treatment to the minority report of the Congressional Iran-Contra committee, "G.O.P. Iran Report Defends President," 11-17, by Philip Shenon, and David E. Rosenbaum's front-page wrap-up on the majority's Iran-Contra report, 11-19, was balanced and professional.

The Arms Control Summit

This was the year in which President Ronald Reagan, after six years of patience, finally saw the fruition of the zero-zero option on Euromissiles that he had presented to an incredulous world. He and Soviet General Secretary Mikhail Gorbachev concluded their agreements on intermediate range nuclear missiles (INF) in December. Progress on reductions in strategic missiles between the USSR and the U.S. stalled after the 1986 Reykjavik meeting when

Gorbachev, after dangling hopes of an agreement before the President, snatched them away when Reagan refused to bargain over the Strategic Defense Initiative. Still, the prospects for an INF treaty had not been foreclosed and the press did a good job overall following that story as it developed in 1987.

Running concurrently with the arms control discussions were the reforms in the USSR that Secretary General Gorbachev was attempting to implement. During the second week of December, the two stories seem to merge like a Marxian synthesis with the Washington summit, the signing of the INF agreement, and, Gorbachev's media blitz via television, newspapers, and a book (the Gorbachev volume was heralded by its publisher as "the book of the year by the statesman of the year"). Clearly the INF treaty and the ongoing negotiations over strategic arms and the President's Strategic Defense Initiative (SDI) would merit substantial treatment on their own. What was interesting about news coverage of the arms control story was the close identification of the arms issue with personality, and that personality was not Ronald Reagan. The association of Gorbachev, his internal reforms and political struggles, with the course of arms reductions was often highly speculative and sloppy, but it gave traditional approaches to the arms control story a compelling new angle. Unfortunately, there were instances where journalists got so caught up in the attractive figure of Gorbachev that the real issues and concerns about the INF Treaty were often blurred.

Some Soviet specialists, particularly those of the liberal-left variety (e.g., Stephen Cohen of Princeton and contributing editor for *The Nation* and Jerry Hough of Brookings, both frequent figures on the establishment op-ed circuit) argue that Gorbachev "needs" arms control in order to have greater resources for internal economic reforms. The idea that Gorbachev was pushing arms control for internal reasons became a staple of the coverage of arms control. This came across strongly in *The Christian Science Monitor*, both *Time* and *Newsweek*, and to a lesser degree in *The Washington Post* and *The New York Times*. *The Washington Times*, backed with the tenacious reporting of Bill Gertz, made an editorial decision to question this hypothesis, choosing to focus on continuities in Soviet military policy under Gorbachev. *The Wall Street Journal*, with a new Moscow bureau, was a lesser player, except for its op-ed pages.

On the American side, we were told that President Reagan also wanted an arms control treaty with the Soviets to polish his tarnished image. Lame duck status, a hangover from Reykjavik, the Iran-Contra scandal, the failed Bork nomination, the stock market crash, and other setbacks were headline news throughout the year, the arms control issue was, so the story went, pushed to the front burner.

Early in the year there was a flurry of news reports surrounding Gorbachev's acceptance of the zero option and on-site verification. James Markham, the *NYT*'s Bonn bureau chief at the time, reported 2-19 on subtle changes taking place in the Soviet negotiating stance, and on 3-4 broke the story of Soviet concessions on verification. *The Christian Science Monitor*'s Bonn bureau chief, Elizabeth Pond, got out ahead with "Soviet Said to Offer New 'Zero Option,'" 4-2, based on sources in Germany with access to Moscow officials. *The Monitor* also was on top of key INF negotiating points with Peter Grier's reporting, as in "Keeping Track of Scrapped Missiles," 3-3 and "Arms Agreement May Hinge on Converting Missiles," 3-25. *The Washington Post* was more sluggish, R. Jeffrey Smith reporting "Reagan Seen Complicating Arms Talk," 4-11, the President's unwillingness to put SDI on the bargaining table viewed as the impediment.

The administration, off-balance from scandal and the exodus of key officials such as Richard Perle, was unable to counter the growing impression that Gorbachev was advancing these proposals, rather than accepting American proposals. Gorbachev was winning the PR battle as Michael R. Gordon reported in *The New York Times*, "Soviet Leads U.S. in Arms Cut Image," 6-7.

One of the most interesting aspects of news coverage and commentary on this process was the way that it seemed to defy traditional line-ups on the issue. Syndicated columnist and *The*

New Republic senior editor Charles Krauthammer helped shed light on the matter of "strange bedfellows." In a column appearing in *The Washington Post*, "...A Strange Tag Team," 3-6, Krauthammer notes the "hardliners" want an INF treaty while the Eastern Establishment doesn't. "The coming war among Republicans over INF," however, "will not be between pro- and anti-arms controllers. It will be between the unilateralists and Atlanticists." (Krauthammer was referring specifically to *Foreign Affairs* editor William Hyland, as a spokesman for those who view the Atlantic Alliance as the U.S.'s paramount concern). Krauthammer, incidentally, predicted an INF treaty would be signed during the year.

In the early spring, much of the reporting focused on European reactions to the INF discussions, where divisions over policy were occuring. An interview by John Train in *The Wall Street Journal*, 4-13, with French General Pierre Gallois, one of the fathers of the *force de frappe*, revealed deep worries over Gorbachev's acceptance in principle of withdrawal of Soviet SS-20s along with America's European-based Pershing and Cruise missiles. In "Purpose of the Pershings," Gallois disputed that such a mutual move would bring the military balance back to 1979, where it was when the SS-20s were introduced. Gallois suggested the U.S. simply turn its Pershings over to the Europeans.

The anxiety the INF discussions were creating was summed up in an editorial in *The Economist*, "Achtung! Angst," 5-23, which explored the West German Chancellor's inability to make up his mind on the zero-zero option. UK Prime Minister Margaret Thatcher had journeyed to Moscow to meet with Gorbachev, but came away saying the talks "brought the two sides no closer to agreement on arms control issues," as reported by Karen DeYoung and Gary Lee of *The Washington Post* in "Thatcher: Arms Pact No Closer After Gorbachev Talks," 4-1. "Thatcher said that the West had to assure itself, through adequate verification procedures, that the Soviets would abide by an accord." An important feature at the time was the report by Daniel Marcus and Peter Adams, 4-6, in *Defense News*, that the French SPOT 1 remote sensing satellite had provided the "first public evidence" on the Soviet radar facility at Krasnoyarsk, long viewed as a Soviet violation of the ABM Treaty.

Defense News also covered the policy debates taking place among the allies. "NATO Defense Ministers Continue to Quarrel Over Zero-Zero," 5-18, and "Allies Face Tough Choices If Nuclear Umbrella Shuts," 6-8, both by Peter Adams provided solid readings on the issue. An additional reading on the Euro-jitters over INF came from David Morrison of the *National Journal*, "Trauma Over Treaty," 5-27. An important counterpoint was provided by Jim Hoagland of *The Washington Post*, who reported in "Mitterrand's Political Strategy," 5-22, that the French President was not attaching much significance to the debate raging within NATO over the Soviet proposal. During this period, however, the Administration was "currently being faulted for seeming to rush into an arms pact too hastily," Tim Carrington and Frederick Kempe of the *WSJ* reported, 4-10. Speaking for the Atlanticists, Henry Kissinger wrote "No Deal Is Better Than a Bad Deal," in a *Los Angeles Times* op-ed, 4-26, the position also taken by his former boss, Richard Nixon.

Editorially, "Take Yes for an Answer on Missiles," the *NYT* declared 4-22: "That these proposals are in his [Gorbachev's] country's interest does not make them, automatically, hostile to Western interests." There was still considerable uneasiness with the actual conclusion of an agreement between the U.S. and the Soviets, however. *Defense News* covered the criticism by the former NATO commander of what was viewed as an administration rush for an INF treaty in "Gen. Rogers vs. Reagan: A Crisis of Conscience," 7-6. Editorially, *The Washington Post* threw cold water on the *glasnost* glamour overshadowing the movement toward an agreement, pointing out in "And Dismantle the Radar," 9-11, that Soviet permission for an American inspection of Krasnoyarsk "...makes *glasnost* not the servant of treaty compliance but a substitute for treaty compliance. Krasnoyarsk is no less a violation for being acknowledged, finally, by Moscow...The radar should be dismantled."

By the summer, the momentum was clearly behind support for an INF agreement, particularly after West Germany found its way to resolve its divisions over the issue, best reported by the

NYT's Serge Schememann in "Kohl's Coup on Missiles," 8-28. *The Washington Post* and *Los Angeles Times* also carried important reports on Western Europe's attitude. The Europeans believe the treaty "may result in a small gain for the western alliance in the European nuclear balance," reported *The Washington Post*'s Bonn bureau chief, Robert J. McCartney in "NATO Advantages Seen in Treaty," 10-6. "Delighted With Missile Treaty, Allies Tell Shultz," 11-26, reported Robert C. Toth of the *Los Angeles Times*. Col. H.G. Summers, summed up the general Administration view in "For Once We're Bargaining Away a Disadvantage," *Los Angeles Times* 10-1, and in the fall, the arms control story really heated up, with the Administration declaring victory on INF. Robert C. Toth of the *Los Angeles Times* reported the breakthrough on the verification issue with the Soviets in "Accord Seen Near on Missile Plant Inspection," 11-19.

A discordant note came from Gorbachev with his 10-30 bombshell that he felt "uncomfortable" about going to Washington until he got some satisfaction on SDI. *Time* reported in "Stage Two for Star Wars," 9-28 that the administration "was preparing to accelerate" SDI, which was seen as a "major obstacle to arms control" by the Soviets. The *Monitor* also indulged in a similar critique, as with Elizabeth Pond's "Soviets Push Reagan to Reexamine What SDI Is Worth to Him," 10-26. Gorbachev advised in his interview with NBC's Tom Brokaw, 11-30, that SDI must not go forward. But an agreement appeared at hand, without the President having to cut any deals with the USSR on SDI, and Mr. Gorbachev came to Washington.

With the summit and the Treaty, much of the electronic media went overboard in admiration of Gorbachev and in equating arms control with "peace." Jonathan Alter of *Newsweek* had one of the best wrap-ups on the capital swoon over Gorbachev in "One-Liners and Party-Liners," 12-21. "Of course the notion that Gorbachev had 'beaten' Reagan doesn't bear real scrutiny; the Soviet leader has just signed away more than twice as many missiles as the president. But the 7,000 or so accredited journalists, only a small fraction of whom were in 'pools' that witnessed events in person, had to find some way to justify why they were not simply back home watching the whole thing on CNN and C-Span. As a result, the summit story, at least at first, became a hybrid of lifestyle and prizefight journalism, with Gorbachev the winner on points."

In the print media, the *NYT* supported the INF deal in its usual non-enthusiastic editorial manner, and its coverage was solid and focused on the substance of the treaty, the nuclear standoff, and the conventional situation in Europe. *The Washington Post* characteristically paid a lot of attention to minutiae and style, some of it very good, as in the three-part pre-summit series on Richard Perle, 11-23 to 11-25 by Sidney Blumenthal. Some of it was tangential, as in "Blessed Are the Peacemakers," on the White House dinner for Gorbachev. *The Washington Times* did a few stories about Soviet noncompliance with previous arms control treaties, specifically the ABM Treaty, which filled an otherwise large hole.

The conservative weekly, *Human Events*, was the forum all year for consistent criticism of tendencies toward "detente II." Importantly, *HE* featured coverage of complaints expressed by Gen. Alexander Haig, and Congressmen Jack Kemp and Jim Courter, among other conservatives. That information helped strengthen the President's hand at the summit, preventing it from going beyond what Reagan intended and in keeping any deal with SDI off the agenda.

It was *The Washington Times* which was left to be the party poopers, with two 12-2 headline stories on how the Soviets were withholding essential information on its missiles, "Potential for Cheating Rife in Treaty, Experts Caution," by Warren Strobel and Bill Gertz, and "'We Must Have That Data,' a Puzzled Shultz Declares," by Barry Schweid. The *WT* also gave prominence to responsible Treaty naysayers, such as the 12-7 Peter Almond story on former Gen. Bernard Rogers and his eloquent case against a new rush towards arms control.

Short of any "news era" of U.S.-Soviet relations, the President had finally gotten Soviet agreement on his zero-zero option, without abandoning SDI to Soviet demands for its curtailment, and without fracturing the Western Alliance. *New York Times* reporter Michael Gordon, writing in *Foreign Policy*, seemed begrudging in his assessment of the accord as neither a vindication of RR's overall approach to arms control nor a setback for NATO, "Dateline Washington: INF: A Hollow Victory?" *Foreign Policy*, Fall. Both *The Wall Street Journal* and *The New York Times* were more appropriately generous. "Last week's summit was a Soviet defeat thickly veiled as a victory," Zbigniew Brzezinski wrote in a *WSJ* op-ed," Summit Score: Reagan 3, Gorbachev 1," 12-15. "...for Mr. Gorbachev the summit was essentially a success of personal style, while for Mr. Reagan it was a victory of real substance." And "Ronald Reagan deserves great credit for seizing the opportunity, and those of us who have criticized him should be the first to say so," Anthony Lewis wrote in his *NYT* column, "What Is The Reality?" 12-10.

The best, most sober assessment overall came from Bill Keller of the *NYT* in "The Test of Gorbachev's Talents Has Just Begun," 12-13. Euphoria over Gorbachev had barely abated, but Keller noted that although "Gorbachev demonstrated that he has a way with Americans," he faces major problems with the Russians. "The most daunting problem facing Gorbachev is his ailing economy, and there it is not clear that the summit pays any immediate dividends. The central theme of Mr. Gorbachev's diplomatic ventures has been the need to free up money and brainpower — and his own energy — for economic and social restructuring. The arms agreement signed in Washington does not save any great deal of money, and he is unlikely to start raiding engineers from his military research centers as long as he sees the United States racing ahead with its own 'Star Wars' research. The Soviet leader's own attention will still be distracted by the array of arms issues left unresolved in Washington."

THE BEST STORIES & COLUMNS OF 1987

This is the second year the *MediaGuide* highlights individual efforts by ten print journalists in each of five categories: General, Business/Financial, Political, Foreign and Commentary. (Journalists are listed in alphabetical order.) This year we had more than 500 nominations for the 50 selections, the great majority by our readers who made nominations as they read throughout the year. We also asked editors of the newspapers and periodicals reviewed to submit material, if they liked, and almost all sent in their favorites on the chance we had missed them. Of the final 50, only three clearly came through submissions, most of the submissions already having been nominated as the year unfolded. Several of those submitted by editors as among their "best" had, in fact, been panned by some of our readers.

Of course, we can't certify that there were no better articles or columns. We're sure we missed many. But there are no other award citations we know of in American journalism where the judges have read as much as we have *at the time the material was published.* As a result, some of the pieces selected came through on timeliness; we remembered how important it was to get the material at the time, although other stories or columns later on might seem superior when set side-by-side. This year we have lengthened our comments on each of the 50 selections, to do justice to the excellence of the work cited.

General Reporting

1. **Gleick, James.** *The New York Times.* "Electricity Rushes Into a New Era of Discovery," 3-10. *The Economist* published "The Superconductor Comes in From the Cold," 2-21, an okay update that closed with the observation that "a small chance exists that scientists will achieve superconductivity at room temperatures. That would rival most technological breakthroughs of this century. But do not hold your breath." Gleick held nothing. "Plunging toward the impossible, scientists on three continents are racing to achieve one of the great dreams of science — an everyday material that carries electricity without the slightest loss of energy..." So begins this pioneering story, authoritatively breaking the major technical story of the decade, as "a series of new announcements around the United States have suddenly raised the prospect of a superconductor that could work at room temperature." It was bold journalism, both for Gleick and the *Times,* but vindication came 10 days later when the American Physical Society brought the breakthrough to the rest of the media, reported by Gleick as well in "Discoveries Bring a 'Woodstock' for Physics," 3-20. A Pulitzer if we ever saw one.

2. **Halevy, David** and **Livingstone, Neil C.** *The Washingtonian.* "The Ollie We Knew," 7-87. All roads in the Iran-Contra affair seemed to lead to Lt. Col. Oliver North at the National Security Council. Fortuitously, *Time* correspondent David Halevy had been meeting weekly with the otherwise little-known North since 1985, gathering material for a book on the contras. Teaming up with Livingstone, a consultant on terrorism and low-intensity warfare, the two produced the definitive profile of Ollie North. Unadorned by myth or second-guessing we learned "what he really did, and why he did it." We got every dimension of the man who "gave flesh and blood to the Reagan Doctrine and passion to the war against terrorism," and to his opponents was "the Svengali" of the contra movement. The story is dazzling with insights, not just about Ollie, but of the others caught up in those swirling currents. One incident stands out — the President turning to Ollie as the first students returning from Grenada deplaned and kissed the ground. North had worried they would criticize the President for an unnecessary military operation, but the President knew better. "You see, Ollie, you ought to have more faith in the American people," he said.

3. **Helmore, Kristin** and **Terry, Sara.** *The Christian Science Monitor.* "Children In Darkness," July series. A paralyzing global report on child abuse, the series, taken as a whole, represents one of the most important, albeit painful, things we read all year. Story after story of children enslaved in factories in India, Brazil, Burma, and youngsters selling themselves on the streets of Manila and Guatemala City, the series is relentless in its portrayal of childhood lost, the victims, the perpetrators, and those groups that are trying to help. But what we remember most are the faces of these children. "Kham Suk is 13 years old. She is a small child, with a delicate face. When she giggles, she sounds like any little girl at play. But Kham Suk doesn't have much time for fun. Three months ago, her mother walked her across the border from Burma into Thailand and sold her to a brothel for $80. Kham Suk's family desperately needed the money. Kham Suk is still paying the price: $4 a customer."

4. **Kotlowitz, Alex.** *The Wall Street Journal.* "Urban Trauma: Day-to-Day Violence Takes a Terrible Toll On Inner-City Youth," 10-27. What's it like, really like, to be a 12-year-old black kid living in a West Side Chicago public-housing project? Kotlowitz decided to find out, as best he could, and the *WSJ* readers were the better for it. Over a three-month stretch in the summer of '87, Kotlowitz got to know Lafeyette Walton, who was 12 on June 13, and with his nine-year-old cousin, Denise, was on his way to buy radio headphones with $8 he got as a birthday gift. "Suddenly, gunfire erupts nearby. The frightened children fall to the ground. 'Hold your head down,' snaps Lafeyette, covering Denise with her pink nylon jacket. As the shooting continues, the two crawl through the dirt toward home. When they finally make it inside, Lafeyette discovers that all but 50 cents of his birthday money had trickled from his pockets." And so it goes in a diary that carries through to late August, life up close, funny and sad, a powerful story.

5. **Kurtz, Howard.** *The Washington Post.* "Policy of Hospitalizing N.Y. Homeless Set Back," 11-13. The top of the *NYT* front page this same day told the story of how a judge had freed the first homeless street person hospitalized under New York Mayor Edward Koch's new policy of taking mentally ill people off the street. Later, we saw this account by *The Washington Post*'s New York correspondent and were astounded at the difference. In the *NYT*, the woman, Joyce Brown, was an abstraction, a generic bag lady, no doubt chosen to be first because A.M. Rosenthal of the *Times* had written a column about how he could see her from his East side apartment window. Kurtz's account makes it clear that Ms. Brown, a 40-year-old former New Jersey secretary, in the words of the judge, was articulate and displayed "a sense of humor, pride, a fierce independence of spirit, quick mental reflexes." And "While her 'mode of existence does not conform to conventional standards,' he said, 'she copes, she is fit, she survives.'" A psychiatrist reported "Her judgment is not great, but there's no law that says people can't live on the streets...The only time she gets angry is when these do-gooders try to force treatment on her." In his column of 11-27, Rosenthal fumed that Ms. Brown had been released from what Kurtz had said was a $600-a-night psychiatric unit at Bellvue.

6. **Mansfield, Stephanie.** *The Washington Post.* "Arianna's Grand Arrival," 2-17. A sparkling portrait done by the *Post*'s premier Style-section artist. Catch this first, breathless sentence: "She's written four books, one a best-selling biography of Maria Callas, sold her upcoming tome on Picasso for a TV mini-series, posed for Norman Parkinson in Town & Country, conquered Manhattan, Los Angeles and London society, dated Mort Zuckerman, Werner Erhard and Jerry Brown, and finally, in what was hailed as the Wedding of the Year, filled a Manhattan chapel last April with an armada of rich and famous friends to marry Texas oil heir Michael Huffington." Whew. We are, of course, prepared to dislike this jet-setter, but no, Mansfield has us fall for her too, her "dizzying ascent into the international jetset [is] not solely due to conventional assets like beauty and charm. It is largely due to her determination." Yes, Arianna is vibrant, witty, scintillating, fascinating. "At 36, she has everything she ever wanted. So why is Arianna Stassinopoulos Huffington crying? 'I feel in bloom,' she says over lunch in her thick Greek accent. 'I don't know if you cry out of joy...'

She pauses, catching a tear as it cascades down her peachy cheekbone. 'It's not sadness. It's more like gratitude...It's like Thank you, God.''' Double whew!

7. **Siegel, Barry.** *Los Angeles Times.* "How to Test for AIDS — A Dilemma," 9-20. No one knew this year what would stop AIDS — education, coercion, a combination of policies — but whatever prevails, the public health profession knows it must act. Siegel's article was selected out of the tons of AIDS stories we reviewed because it best addressed the policy questions within the profession on the frontlines in the battle against this plague. The divisions on how to contain its spread are professional ones, though the politics of AIDS aren't left out. "I don't think I can go about my business just wringing my hands and saying: 'There are no right answers. Oh, my gosh this is awful. There is no way to go.' Meanwhile the world is going right over you. You take the best shot at where you can go.'' This quote from a state health director sums up the thinking of the profession nationally. Siegel then proceeds to investigate and report what "the best shot" seems right now, and how the unresolved questions of mandatory vs. voluntary testing, quarantine, confidentiality, etc. are all constantly undergoing rethinking as the profession seeks to put a boundary around the plague. At the center of the critical debate, the article is one all policymakers need in their AIDS portfolio.

8. **Schlender, Brenton R.** and **Waldholz, Michael.** *The Wall Street Journal.* "Drug on Trial: Genentech's Missteps And FDA Policy Shift Led to TPA Setback," 6-16. There is no agency of the Federal Government harder to get information out of than the Food and Drug Administration, including the Federal Reserve. But Schlender and Waldholz barged into the breach with this superb story on the FDA, Genentech, and the Activase ruling. Vivid, informative, probing, we see Genentech's missteps in following the twists and turns of FDA policy as the upstart Office of Biologics struggled with the more prestigious Office of Drugs for control over the revolutionary blood-clot dissolver, called TPA. "In one publicized trial, results were so striking that the sponsoring National Heart, Lung and Blood Institute ordered the test curtailed because it couldn't in good conscience let half the subjects get the placebo...when TPA worked so well. Genentech officials began to believe that the FDA couldn't turn TPA down." But it did. And this story, getting into the workings of a bureaucracy that would be admired in the Kremlin, tells why, boiling our blood in the process.

8. **Tucker, William.** *National Review.* "Where Do The Homeless Come From?" 9-25. Myron Magnet of *Fortune* was Tucker's only real competition in reporting on this troubling urban phenomenon, "The Homeless," 11-23, a vivid, comprehensive report that was richly informative. But if he had read Tucker's earlier piece, his would have improved greatly. Tucker's reporting involved the statistical correlating of urban variables and the incidence of homelessness. Magnet dismissed the argument that rental housing could be the problem, the vacancy rate now the highest in 20 years at 7%, or 2.3 million units nationwide. Tucker studied 50 U.S. cities and found wide variations in the vacancy rates. In running statistical regressions on all reasonable variables, "rent control, with a correlation coefficient of .521, turns out to be the single most important factor for predicting homelessness. All by itself it accounts for 27 per cent of the variation among cities. The presence of rent control is associated with an increase in homelessness of *250 per cent*," and "*The nine rent-controlled cities have the nine lowest vacancy rates*," with none over 3.0 percent. The case may not be closed, but at least Tucker has opened it.

10. **Wermiel, Stephen.** *The Wall Street Journal.* "The Right Stuff?: Robert Bork Faces A Confirmation Battle For High-Court Post," 7-2. There were probably better profiles of Judge Bork written during the summer of 1987, a two-part series by Al Kamen and Dale Russakoff of *The Washington Post* coming to mind. But Wermiel wrote this front-pager the day Bork was selected by President Reagan and we read it with that knowledge, assuming much deeper portraits would be on the way. In November, in reviewing Wermiel's file for the *1988 MediaGuide*, we re-read "The Right Stuff?" and realized almost every salient fact we had

learned about Bork through the summer and weeks of Senate hearings, we had learned first there. "The president has picked a rare judicial — rather than a political — conservative, a judge committed to a narrow role for the courts rather than to the Reagan administration's political agenda." Wermiel reviewed those of Bork's opinions and writings which became the targets of the Judiciary Committee liberals, and he presented them clearly, fairly and with remarkably fine shadings. We were very impressed this second time around.

Business/Financial Reporting

1. **Epstein, Edward Jay.** *Manhattan, Inc.* "How Mike Milken Made A Billion Dollars and Changed the Face of American Capitalism," 9-87. Simply the best story of the year on the subject of Milken, Ivan Boesky, the Wall Street scandals and all that. While U.S. Attorney Rudolph Giuliani is cutting deals with Boesky if Boesky will rat on Milken, the "grand sorcerer of finance" who thought up junk bonds and got them flying for Drexel Burnham, and while *The Wall Street Journal* is pursuing Milken in its news pages, Epstein, acting on a wild rumor that Milken is an honest man, rolls up his sleeves and delivers this epic yarn. There's no better journalist to undertake such an effort. Epstein prefers to work on the largest of canvasses, on which folks like Boesky and Giuliani and Carl Icahn and Asher Adelman can be cut down to size. They are ordinary folks. But not Milken, a true financial genius who "Changed the Face of American Capitalism" *for the better* (in case you thought there was a smirk in the headline).

2. **Johnson, Robert.** *The Wall Street Journal.* "General Mills Risks Millions Starting Chain Of Italian Restaurants," 9-21. Definitely required reading, Exhibit A, in any Business/Journalism school. Johnson sets out to write a piece about a major food processing company opening a string of 58 Olive Garden restaurants, Italian style, and not only produces a fascinating story of the trials and errors of General Mills pumping $100 million into the effort, but along the way, almost subliminally, gives us the up-to-date poop on the entire generic restaurant industry. There is more information in this single front-page story about so many relevant management, marketing, and food industry topics, that we are compelled to read, from start to finish, whether we like it or not. Every time we're immersed in the fun of the Olive Garden story ("the menu includes an 'Italian Margarita' and a 'Venetian' chicken simmered in teriyaki sauce"), he hits us quickly with facts, "Food companies... are continuing to enter the market because of the long accelerating trend toward eating out. Restaurants' share of the total food market now is about $4 of every $10 spent, compared with $2.50 in 1955." Great job.

3. **Kirkland, Richard.** *Fortune.* "The Bright Future Of Service Exports," 6-8. An instantaneous "10 best," one of the few. We drank this in like a survivor who has crossed the Sahara. So much incredible nonsense was written in 1987 about the United States being so uncompetitive in almost everything in the world market that one day soon the USA would sink into the ooze. Then comes Kirkland and the *Fortune* of yore with this exciting article on the high value-added product in services the nation has that the world is clamoring for. We know it's true, but it's nice to see *Fortune* realizing that U.S. service exports will more than offset interest on the foreign debt!! "Across the globe, U.S. service companies are demonstrating some of the surprising ways that America can become competitive again. Last year they produced a world-beating $48 billion of service exports..." This is a rich, rich field to be mined, Marshall!!

4. **Mahar, Maggie.** *Barron's.* "Campus Rebellion: Professors Are Up In Arms About Their Retirement Funds," 8-17. "Everyone on Wall Street has heard of TIAA-CREF, the pension fund for college professors, though not everyone realizes how big it is: The Teachers Insurance and Annuity Association-College Retirement Equities Fund totals a cool $63 billion." So begins an astonishing tale of the rinky-dink management of this huge pension fund, which "all began in 1905 when Andrew Carnegie had a good idea." If this piece had run on the front page of the *NYT* or *WSJ*, instead of merely leading *Barron's*, it would have made big waves instead

42

of being one of the most thorough, enterprising, illuminating financial stories we saw all year. Mahar really makes it work by leading with a financial guru almost everyone knows, "Marty Zweig, the seer of the Zweig Forecast on Wall Street...though few realize that he was once Professor Zweig with a retirement fund in TIAA-CREF." And he doesn't have the foggiest idea what it's up to.

5. **Sanger, David E.** *The New York Times.* "A Peek at I.B.M.'s Trump Card," 3-8. At a time when much of the business press is engaged in bashing Big Blue (*Fortune*'s cover on "most admired companies" had IBM falling apart), Sanger demonstrates his unparalleled feel for technology issues in this, projecting the awesome power that IBM can unleash on the electronics industry. Getting into its Burlington, VT., semiconductor production facility — probably the world's largest and most advanced, was a real coup, missed by the entire industry press. With a sure hand rare in the mass media, Sanger discloses that IBM was producing megabit DRAMs on 8-inch wafers and had perfected its 4-megabit design, thus belying the scores of articles lamenting the American collapse in semiconductor memory technology. A great line: "The Burlington workers are, for the most part, sturdy New Englanders who, like the Japanese, measure their tenure in decades."

6. **Scardino, Albert.** *The New York Times.* "Building a Manhattan Empire," 4-18. We hear and read so much about Donald Trump, the commercial real estate developer, we sometimes forget there are others around, some of them even bigger than he. Indeed, Scardino has a way of making us realize just how big one of them is with one of the best business leads we can remember: "Olympia & York, the giant Toronto-based real estate company, came to New York 10 years ago to see the elephants and ended up buying the circus. Now the quietly effective Canadians, already the largest commercial landlord in New York, are negotiating to capture another mammoth chunk of the Manhattan market as well." This breathtaking story must have been told before, but until this piece came along, we hadn't the remotest idea how big Olympia & York had become, with 24 million square feet of office space in Manhattan valued at $8 billion, with plans, plans, plans to skyscrape some more. "'There have been two great real estate deals in the history of New York,'[says one state executive]. 'The first was when the Dutch bought the island of Manhattan. The second was when the Canadians bought the island again.'" A dazzling story.

7. **Sherman, Stratford P.** *Fortune.* "The Gambler Who Refused $2 Billion," 5-11. This is the best piece we've seen on the titanic Texaco-Pennzoil struggle, with Pennzoil's J. Hugh Liedtke at center stage in a white hat, Texaco's John K. McKinley and his successor as CEO, James W. Kinnear, in the wings, grumbling, in black. Sherman up front announces it's all a colossal waste of resources, through an imagined wise foreigner scratching his head over the crazy Americans. But then, he quotes a negotiating expert, "This is how we get into wars. This is how divorces occur. And it's simply how two giant corporations can go down the drain." Sherman tells us that "the man who turned down Texaco's $2 billion settlement offer, in mid-April still held out his hand for more. Asked by *Fortune* whether he is the greediest man in the world or simply in need of psychiatric help, Pennzoil's barrel-bellied chief executive chuckled and replied, in a voice so gravelly and deep you practically have to drill for it, 'Maybe both.'" Confident, colorful and authoritative, from A to Z.

8. **Stewart, James B.** and **Hertzberg, Daniel.** *The Wall Street Journal.* "The Wall Street Career Of Martin Siegel Was A Dream Gone Wrong," 2-17. The rags-to-riches-to-handcuffs story of a leading 38-year-old investment banker, by the best reporting team on Wall Street. Written like a grim fairy tale, it opens with Siegel, head of mergers and acquisitions at Drexel Burnham, subpoenaed, reduced to sobbing, his brilliant career over. Then the flashback to Siegel's 1980 meeting of Ivan F. Boesky, "awed by the vast wealth he saw Mr. Boesky amassing," the Boesky suburban estate dwarfing the house Siegel was planning, Boesky coming to play tennis at the Siegel home, arriving in his pink Rolls-Royce. Then the 1982 Bendix hostile bid for Martin

Marietta, "the takeover boom came of age," with Siegel in the middle of it all, developing a brilliant "Pac-man" defense for Martin Marietta, but needing somehow to juice the stock for it to succeed. "Mr. Siegel called Mr. Boesky and leaked the top secret plan, fully aware that he had just crossed the line of illegality." And then...but you all know the rest of this age-old story, never told better.

9. **Truell, Peter.** *The Wall Street Journal.* "Citicorp's Reed Takes Firm Stance on Third World Debt," 2-4. Truell, the *Journal*'s best reporter, moved from the London bureau to New York at the end of 1986. It was a great move by the editors as Truell lapped the field in covering the Third World debt crisis. This blockbuster, run on P.6, was the first interview that any reporter had managed with the elusive Reed on this incendiary subject. The piece foreshadowed Reed's decision in May to add $3 billion to loan loss reserves, shaking up global banking and angering Citicorp competitors, many weaker by comparison. Truell gets a few nuggets for quotes, illuminating Reed's fears, his motives in stacking up loan loss reserves and resisting discounts to Third World debtors. "In the past few months the 47-year-old head of the nation's largest bank has replaced the conciliatory approach initialed by his retired predecessor, Walter Wriston, with an uncompromising stand against easing further the terms for developing countries' debt settlements. 'It's a crummy world out there,'" says Reed.

10. **Weiner, Stephen B.** *Forbes.* "Is Leslie Wexner Riding for a Fall?" 4-6. It's hard to imagine a business publication other than *Forbes* running with this audacious, take-your-breath-away prediction that the high-flying retailing chain, The Limited Inc., could not stay aloft. And put it on the cover! The big reason the magazine could risk it is the airtight reporting and analysis that Weiner put into it. But even so. "No question: Leslie Wexner is the U.S.'s number one women's apparel merchant. His preeminence in the rag trade is without challenge and without precedent." The Limited has sales of $3.14 billion, 7% of the women's clothing market, 2,700 stores, triple the number in 1982. "'Trees really do grow to the sky,' Wexner is fond of saying." But then, "History shows that such inflated values usually end in big losses when it is finally realized that the growth of early years cannot be extended indefinitely. Will this case be different? There's little reason to think it will." What follows is a glowing, textbook report on a sure short. The stock, almost $50 at the time, inched to almost $53, skidding to $35 before the Crash and as low as $16 in November.

Political Reporting

1. **Blumenthal, Sid.** *The Washington Post.* "The Candidate From Kansas," 11-9. There were several fine profiles of Sen. Robert Dole in 1987, but this was the best. Blumenthal, the resident intellectual of the *Post*'s political team, sets Dole against the backdrop of his hometown, Russell, KS, observing that George Bush has a "Silver Spoon problem;" "Since Lincoln...the Republican Party has never nominated a candidate who could not claim a modest small-town origin, preferably in the Midwest. The contrast between Dole and Bush, in this regard, could not be sharper." We see Dole clearly here because Blumenthal takes him at face value: "Dole's difficulty in articulating his purpose as a 'vision' may be because his assumptions seem to him to be just common sense. Nothing reveals this more than the issue that lies at the center of his outlook: the deficit...he seems almost sympathetic to...Walter Mondale — who warned about the deficit and spoke of raising taxes to deal with it...'If I had been Mondale, I wouldn't have addressed it quite that way. But I think it was courageous'." Finally, the essence of the man gives way to the essence of his campaign: "People are willing to take the bitter medicine, but nobody wants to hold the spoon."

2. **Broder, David.** *The Washington Post.* "Gephardt's 'Greening:' An Eye On The Center," 8-31. There is a master at work here as Broder profiles young Gephardt in a way that the subject will come away feeling he has been treated with respect, and he has, but in fact at a deeper level, he has been peeled like an onion and reduced to something less than a dwarf. "In his

first six years in the House, Gephardt more than once defied the wishes of liberal lobbies. At various times, he opposed raising the minimum wage and increasing the mandatory retirement age, creating the Education Department, an independent Consumer Protection Agency, community mental health centers and shelters for battered women. He voted against extending the deadline for ratification of the Equal Rights Amendment and against a major expansion of the national park system. He has, at times, supported tuition tax credits and an antibusing amendment to the Constitution." All in defiance of the special interests!

3. **Brownstein, Ronald** *National Journal.* "Tangling Over Trade," 9-19. The GOP used to be the party of protectionism, the Democrats of free trade, gradually they've flipped sides. In approaching the political realignment aspects of the trade issue, Brownstein raises troubling questions for the Democrats in '88: [Their] "presidential hopefuls are seizing on the nation's trade deficit as a Republican sore spot, but a 'midnight in America' theme song might not catch on." No piece said it clearer: "There's little evidence that the public considers the nation's submerged trade account to be a crisis — or is even thinking much about it. The Democratic contenders' persistent focus on trade is defying a basic law of political gravity." Brownstein's splendid presentation and analysis suggests a dark political imperative that the Democratic Party cannot resist.

4. **Dionne, E.J. Jr.** *The New York Times Magazine.* "The Elusive Front Runner," 5-3. We had been waiting for the definitive piece on Gary Hart and Dionne provided it in this intelligent, careful portrait of the enigmatic, death-wishing candidate, whose candidacy was already doomed even as we read; *The Miami Herald* that same morning carried its first revelations about Donna Rice. Hart had told Dionne "'Follow me around. I don't care,' he says firmly, about the womanizing question. 'I'm serious. If anybody wants to put a tail on me, go ahead. They'd be very bored.'" Dionne's summation: "Gary Hart faces one of the most unusual dilemmas ever presented a Presidential candidate. He must prove that he is extraordinary enough — indeed 'different' enough — to bear the burdens of the Presidency. Yet he must also prove that he is really quite ordinary, not so different from the people he would lead. This is a game that is very hard to win. He is required to engage in forms of self-revelation not demanded of other candidates. Yet the very process of self-revelation makes him stand out."

5. **Edsall, Thomas Byrne.** *The New York Review of Books.* "The Political Impasse," 3-26. A sweeping reconnaissance of the national political picture that confronts the two political parties. This is the very best of its kind in 1987, by one of the most skilled of *The Washington Post*'s political writers. It treats dilemmas facing both parties, but Edsall clearly sees the most formidable problems facing the Democratic party, "which has only begun the painful process of accepting that it is no longer the permanent majority party in the country." And "In recent elections many working-class and lower-middle-class whites have chosen either not to vote or to vote for Republican presidential candidates. Cuomo's decision not to seek the nomination means that there is likely to be no Democratic competitor whose basic strategy is to mobilize such people." Coalition forces, demographics, the rise of the evangelicals, the economic issues, all are woven together masterfully in this "book review."

6. **McLeod, Don.** *Insight.* "George Bush: Front Runner," 10-19. A two-part cover story by McLeod in some ways reads as if it were commissioned by the Veep's campaign committee. The entire first page was an account of a heroic WWII experience of young George. Beginning the profile in this way, McLeod was a bit heroic himself. It had become conventional among political writers to *assume* that their readers suspect Bush is a "wimp" and to work their material in that general framework. The McLeod cover is the first portrait of Bush we remember that proceeded from the assumption that he may be the next President of the United States. It struck us as clear and refreshing as spring water dipped from a brook. The best line of all: "Blue ribbon, blue chip, blue blood. Maybe, the family says today, but not snobs, not elites and really not all that rich. The Bush men had this troubling habit of walking away before the big money came along."

7. **Roberts, Steven B.** *The New York Times*. "Reagan's Advisers See Shift in Focus," 8-23. One of the year's most important political developments as chief of staff Howard Baker, Jr. and his White House team, ensconced in their Santa Barbara summer quarters, decide the President is a lame duck and they may as well just relax and run out the clock. Roberts writes it up in this straight account and his editors are smart enough to put it atop page one. It becomes one of the most remarked on and cited news stories of '87. Citing the "political damage inflicted by the Iran-Contra affair," a senior aide is quoted: "One thing that came out of the Iran-Contra hearings was a very realistic analysis of what it means to deal with a Democratic Congress. It's going to be very difficult, more difficult than we anticipated. And with the election coming up, that will make it even tougher. I don't think anyone looks for huge legislative victories." And, says Roberts, "They also decided that the White House would be better off avoiding vetoes and reaching a compromise with Congress on several important domestic bills, such as those on trade, welfare and insurance for catastrophic illness." The Baker Administration formally began. The Wall Street slide began two days later.

8. **Romano, Lois.** *The Washington Post*. "The Rankling Puzzle of Pat Caddell," 11-18. The famed Democratic consultant and pollster is suddenly without a horse to ride, Senator Biden shot in the foot, and all of Washington is celebrating — including his closest friends, who Romano locates with a 10-foot pole. Quoting Robert Squier: "I've been his friend and I've been his enemy and takes less energy to be his enemy." Yes, this is gossipy, juicy, "Style" section political cackling, but Caddell has been a fixture of national politics for 15 years, and this marvelous, long relishment of his rise and fall reads as if written by a roamin' umpire. It ends by taking all the nastiness back, quoting a veteran observer of Democratic wars: "I think there is going to be a second coming of Pat Caddell."

9. **Schneider, William.** *The Atlantic*. "The Republicans In '88," 7-87. Perhaps the single best political piece of the year, "conversations with the candidates and an analysis of their candidacies," the magazine advises. This is a sure-footed climb along the craggy rocks and slippery slopes of the GOP contenders and the issues that separate them, and it establishes Schneider as the most important political analyst of them all. The close is symphonic: "The election will be closely fought and highly competitive, with the lead shifting from one candidate to the other. Ideologies on the left and the right will be unhappy with the choices and will bemoan the lack of clarity and coherence. The press will complain about the trivialization of the campaign. Pundits will ask whether it really makes any difference which candidate gets elected. Foreigners will criticize the lack of tone and rationality in American politics. And the voters, faced with a real contest, will have a wonderful time."

10. **Shribman, David.** *The Wall Street Journal*. "Robertson's Conversion From Rakishness to Faith Culminates in His Crusade for the White House," 10-6. Shribman in '87 did several long, chin-pulling, front-page political epics for the *WSJ*, but none of them impressed us as much as this back-page profile of GOP presidential contender Pat Robertson. This was the newsbeat on the Rev. Robertson's marriage ten weeks before his son was born, the information woven into the portrait so gracefully that it disarmed the entire political press corps. If Shribman would not seek to capitalize on it, putting it in context instead, who else would do so without looking cheap? The piece turned on this fleeting fact, but in a way elevated everything else Shribman wanted us to know about the man, and we read it all with respect.

Foreign Dispatch

1. **Bering-Jensen, Henrik.** *Insight*. "Gorbachev and Glasnost," 3-30. A key component of Gorbachev's attempts to improve the performance of the Soviet system, *glasnost* received constant attention all year. But it's Bering-Jensen's three-part cover story that you want to file away as the basic reference source on the topic. What is it, how does it work and for whom,

and does *glasnost* impede or assist perception of what is or isn't taking place at the foundations of the Soviet system? — he tackles it all. "Inside the USSR," we see it used as a weapon for propaganda and to get rid of bureaucrats and Brezhnevian opponents, but "the funny thing is...you never hear from the people under attack. What kind of *glasnost* is that?" As "A Cultural Offensive" the *glasnost* campaign has been most brilliantly conducted, the withdrawn educated class finding an outlet for protest other than emigration, defection or passivity. As "A Human Rights Offensive," Gorbachev "has recognized the power of the issue...for opening [the West's]...gates" to technology, credits, and trade. Yet, in the era of *glasnost*, "dissidents have died in prison, which was not the case during the Brezhnev years."

2. **Boustany, Nora.** *The Washington Post.* "Braving The Passage Of Death," 4-5. A harrowing portrait of life in a Palestinian refugee camp in Beirut. Boustany tells of the weekend she "slipped in clandestinely with a group of camp women for a 24-hour look at the conditions they endure," giving us nightmares. She describes the fighting between the Amal and Palestinian factions, political adversaries in the chaos of Lebanon; Shiite Muslim Amal fighters using the refugee camps as a "pressure point" to keep Palestinian guerrillas inside and under siege. Boustany takes us along the 200-yard run into the camp that must be covered daily for food, keeping us there overnight, talking to the denizens. "More intriguing than the risks taken outside the camps is the indomitable will to survive inside. 'We would have preferred to eat the flesh of our martyrs before giving in...We stopped thinking of the dead, only of the living,' said Shamiya Mohammed Musa, 55." Most telling and poignant is the quote from a young Palestinian woman Boustany uses as a lead: "Every mouthful of food that enters the camp is washed with blood." Kudos to this grand reporter for braving it herself.

3. **Cockburn, Patrick.** *Financial Times.* "Gorbachev and the Committee," 6-24. Nobody unravelled the story of *perestroika* this year, but no one came as close as Cockburn to getting us inside. Everyone's commentaries in both the West and the East reported that Gorbachev's economic reforms were failing to make headway in the USSR. By midyear, the battles between Soviet "conservatives" and "radicals" were well-known, but the balance of power was so close, not even Gorbachev knew how the chips would fall. On the eve of the critical Central Committee meeting in July, Cockburn presents the views of the reformist players, and we see for the first time, their bottom line is no mere piecemeal reform, but revolution indeed. Gorbachev's dilemma is starkly revealed. His "revolution from above" requires such upheaval throughout the Soviet system, that party and state sclerotics automatically clog the arteries as an act of self-defense. It only adds grist to the reformist charge that "Today we have an economy of shortages, totally unbalanced and unmanageable, and to be perfectly honest, virtually unplannable." A masterful weave of political-economic reporting and analysis that was more than the sum of its parts.

4. **Darlin, Damon.** *The Wall Street Journal.* "The Adjuster: Man Likely to Become Japan's Next Leader Lives to Compromise," 10-8. In fact, Noboru Takeshita, secretary general of the Liberal Democratic Party, was selected as Prime Minister, 10-20. Although the 63-year-old political figure had been in the news for several years, as a key supporter of Prime Minister Nakasone, this advance profile was his first real introduction to the U.S. business and political community. Darlin in March had misjudged Takeshita's chances of succeeding Nakasone in an otherwise prescient report, "Tax Uproar Threatens Japanese Premier," 3-19, so his subject is treated here with respect for his political skills, at bottom a consensus builder "...clever, cautious and quiet. His supporters say those are his great strengths, for he is able to forge compromise and get opposing sides headed in the right direction. Detractors say he lacks the independence, international stature and vision to guide the world's No.2 economic power in a period of rising tensions with the U.S. and Europe. The world is likely soon to have the chance to judge. For Mr. Takeshita seems about to emerge, like a brass rubbing, from the murky back-room political processes of Japan's ruling Liberal Democratic Party."

5. **Diehl, Jackson.** *The Washington Times.* "Hungary Leads in Reforms," 4-6. Of the *Post*'s noteworthy series, "Communism: Can It Reform?" only Diehl's contribution really sang with vigor and life, lifting curtains, iron or otherwise. "The dream of an economic system better than capitalism is dead." Indeed? But this is Diehl interviewing a state planning theorist in the East Bloc, who continues: "There is no third way, no model between Stalinism and capitalism that works well. The only reasons to stop short of returning to capitalism are pragmatic — and political." Diehl gives us the picture of Hungary's central problem — there is no middle course. For the mon_nt, farmers producing bounteously now make profits, small private businesses busy as bees keep retail trade and services from collapse, all squeezing the opening for market incentives as much as they can. But inevitably they bump up against a lumbering state-owned sector that bleeds the economy. Still, reform plans are afoot here as well, a version of common shares. And Diehl wryly asks of Hungary's planning chief, Janos Hoos, "if Hungary sells its workers shares in its state-owned industry, how will it then be a socialist rather than a capitalist country?" "That's the theoretical problem we have," conceded Hoos with a smile.

6. **Germani, Clara.** *The Christian Science Monitor.* "Drought And Famine Add To Haiti's Woes," 7-29. This was the only report we saw out of Haiti that added news of a two-year drought and widespread famine in the outlying regions to all the other economic miseries this pitiful nation has suffered these last two decades. Germani's report from "the thorny and dry moonscape of Plaine de l'Arbre" is written so matter-of-factly that it persuades us she isn't kidding, that in this poorest region of the poorest nation in the Western hemisphere, in our backyard, there is routine death by malnutrition. "crops refuse to sprout, and residents turn to tearing tree roots from the dusty earth to barter for a bit of food...Emerging from a knot of barefoot and half-clothed villagers who have spent the morning using their hand-made machetes on a stubborn tree root, young Adliner Pierre explains that existence on the Plain of the Tree has always been dry and meager. But in a macabre gauge of just how bad life is now, she adds that last year three of her children starved to death."

7. **Marsh, David.** *Financial Times.* "West Germany Pays the Price for D-Mark Policy," 1-8; "Wunder Turns to Whimper," 11-8. We relied on Marsh all this critical year for reports on West Germany's monetary and fiscal policies. These twins at either end of '87 show why, nominated as a pair for "10 Best." With Wall Street and Washington dithered by the U.S. trade deficit and Bonn reporting huge surpluses, the pressure was on Bonn for monetary and fiscal expansion. Marsh's January report, exquisite in detail, makes it seem probable, with France and Helmut Kohl's coalition partners joining the call for expansion by Bonn and West German industry complaining bitterly about the sharp rise of the D-Mark against the dollar. Of course, frustration with the stubbornness of the Finance Ministry and Bundesbank continued as they did not bow to pressures, internal or external, a clear contribution to the October Crash worldwide. Marsh's November report suggests a reason. "In rich, well-organized West Germany, the economic *Wunder* has turned into a whimper. Leisure, not industry, is in fashion." *Wunderblah.*

8. **Raines, Howell.** *The New York Times Magazine.* "Thatcher's Capitalist Revolution," 5-31. On the threshold of the British elections, 6-11, the *Times* London bureau chief gives us a keen sense of just where things stand at that very moment, but set against the sweep of Maggie Thatcher's vision of "an England free of socialism" and the force of her personality. Raines, whose coverage of the 1984 U.S. presidential race was brilliant, sees her coming third-term victory clearly, and she "is likely to lose only if she commits some huge — and uncharacteristic — political error..." So he disposes of her main adversary, Labor's Neil Kinnock, in a colorful opening anecdote that has him taking a verbal punch from the P.M. in a House of Commons debate: "Like a boxer sent reeling across the ring and into the ropes, he was finished for the day." The article, though, is not just color and anecdote but a layered cake of England today, its economy, its social crosscurrents, its place in the world, with Maggie at the center of it

all. Why, though, is she so widely respected but disliked? Raines quotes a western diplomat: "The British don't need to love their Prime Minister. They love their Queen."

9. **Rosett, Claudia.** *The Wall Street Journal.* "The Philippines' Dangerous Land Reform," 4-13. Land reform helped wreck the South Vietnam economy and send it down the tubes. It helped wreck the El Salvador economy, directly leading to the deaths of 60,000 citizens in crossfire killings over the U.S. planned reforms in the 70s. Now, practically every press report we get out of Manila on why Cory Aquino is in trouble lists as a given that she has dragged her feet on land reform. Which is why we were flabbergasted to read this report from Manila by Rosett, the editorial page editor of the *Asian Wall Street Journal.* Her opinion aside, it is the only dispatch we saw all year that tells us what's going on — details, costs, timetables. We learn the goal will be no estate larger than 17 acres and by 1992, the government will seize all land above that. The reform task force is aware, of course, that the post-reform small farms might be less productive than the same land today. "It doesn't matter," says an economist. "This is an exercise in democratization." It will take between 16,000 and 60,000 bureaucrats to administer the reform, "the state acting as broker, banker and regulator for life on the little farm." Editors! *She gives us information!*

10. **Temko, Ned.** *The Christian Science Monitor.* "Untangling a Web of Conflict," 5-18. Coverage of South Africa was so much better this year as a whole. Yet the routine, statistical approach to violence there was still much too constant, acquiring a grim sameness, no theme to provoke any response deeper than a wince. Temko, the best of this year's journalists on that beat, examines the "Battle of Guguletu Township," (one of the bloodiest, most controversial battles between South African police and black urban activists) in a way that brings to life all the realities of the multi-faced violence that's ripping apart their black communities. He answers no questions, but discovers beyond the black-and-white picture those gray areas where the changes on the margin are occurring. For the state, it was war, and from the state "In any war...there must be a loser and a winner." For older blacks, "the youngsters were different....You couldn't go talk to them." From the mothers of the dead, "I never really knew my son, saw inside him. The young people didn't talk to their parents about such things." Yet from another, "We see him as part of a struggle....we will win. We will try to punish those who killed him. We must not punish too much, but enough."

Commentary

1. **Bartley, Robert L.** *The Wall Street Journal.* "1929 and All That," 11-24. The Editor of the *Journal,* Bartley spent his 1985 summer vacation reading books on the Crash of '29 and the Great Depression, thinking this might come in handy someday. It did, of course, in October 1987, and while many commentators raised their voices in I-told-you-so Chicken Little hysteria, Bartley assembled his thoughts carefully into this squeaky tight analysis that relates the currency protectionism of the day as the modern equivalent of Smoot-Hawley's impact on 1929. His parallels and perspective on the Crash of '87 are stitched together with such careful logic that "the whole twin deficit crowd, who have been screaming that the market was wrong all during its ascent" are forced to confront the gaping holes in their linkages. This is not quite instant history; Bartley looks at what happened on October 19 through the prism of what we now know happened in '29. But it has to be dealt with by those who will write of the Crash.

2. **Buchanan, Patrick J.** *The Washington Post.* "You've Won, Mr. President; Now Pardon Ollie and John," 7-19. Not merely an essay, but a truly remarkable *document* by the President's former communications director, fit for citation in the history of the Reagan years. It is really not about pardons, but of the essence of the President's last 18 months. It opens: "Noon Wednesday, suddenly it was over; and everyone knew it. The coup d'etat had failed. Ronald Reagan would survive. One could see defeat etched in the faces of the network anchors and

correspondents...But it was all over. For once, Mary McGrory got it right. Ollie North had left the committee 'a smoking ruin' and the quarry, the President of the United States had escaped.'' At this moment, Buchanan saw, the White House could have gone off the defensive and ''on the attack,'' not only making the case for the contras, ''but against the Congress.'' In failing to bring down Reagan, the Democrats ''are retreating in disarray; and now is the time to let the jackal pack know what it means to strike a king.'' This call to arms was incandescent, but the President did not see it. Instead, the Baker White House decided the President had been crippled and threw in the towel.

3. **Grenier, Richard.** *The Washington Times.* ''A Little Glasnost At CBS,'' 6-29. When commentators on the right go after commentators on the left, they can almost never manage to contain their gorge. Except for the ''Point Man'' columnist for *The Washington Times.* Grenier is so engagingly playful when he sets out to media-bash that we can actually imagine Dan Rather, for example, howling at this particular bash, the funniest of the year. ''I am so mad. Ever since last week when CBS did its 'Seven Days in May,' investigating *glasnost* in the Soviet Union, I've been hearing people castigate poor Dan Rather for his obsequious, sycophantic, toadying smile when dealing with Soviet officials. This is deeply unfair. What they were seeing on Dan Rather's face was the warmth and natural love he feels for all humankind.'' How can it get funnier? It does. We can even see Gorby smile.

4. **Judis, John B.** *The New Republic.* ''Apocalypse Now and Then,'' 8-31. An up-and-coming *bona fide* political liberal, senior editor of *In These Times*, Judis had been studying the life and works of James Burnham when Burnham, ''a quiet, urbane man...died in Kent, Connecticut, a few weeks ago at the age of 82,'' how fortunate we were that Judis was poised to write, not a eulogy, but the first historical perspective of Burnham. ''Nobody was as important to the definition of modern American conservatism as James Burnham,'' this piece began. ''In a series of books published from 1947 to 1964, Burnham laid the foundations of conservative foreign policy. He provided not only a critique of the prevailing containment doctrine, but also an alternative of his own: the 'liberation' or 'rollback' of the Soviet empire.'' What a marvelous way to review conservative thinking on foreign policy and the East-West struggle over more than a half century than through the pilgrimage of James Burnham. And how relevant, how provocative the questions raised about that struggle today for American conservatives by this brilliant young leftist. How he has stirred the pot! *This is glasnost!*

5. **Kinsley, Michael.** *The New Republic.* ''Nice Young Man,'' 5-1. Here you are, Michael Kinsley, liberal editor of *TNR*, and the owner and publisher, a not so liberal Martin Peretz, just *loves* Albert Gore, that nice, young Democratic presidential hopeful who once voted to build a missile. But you do not care for Albert Gore. So you write this painfully accurate profile of Gore, who ''is an old person's idea of a young person.'' Yearning for a ''touch of madness'' a la Gary Hart ''as a desirable qualification for a presidential candidate,'' Kinsley promises that ''Sanity buffs will be increasingly attracted in the next few weeks to Senator Albert Gore Jr., a self-described 'raging moderate' who nevertheless does a good Hart-style generational-future routine. Thoughtful, sincere, responsible to a fault, handsome in a reassuringly unglamorous way, Gore is not the type who would ever change his name, alter his signature, or sail away on the Good Ship Monkey Business.'' When you finish the column, you feel like you need a drink.

6. **Lewis, Anthony.** *The New York Times.* ''A Question Of Judgment,'' 9-27. Lewis had celebrated Judge Robert Bork's defense of press freedom in an important 1984 U.S. Court of Appeals decision, ''Bork and the Press,'' 8-30. So he had his work cut out for him in drafting the intellectual case against Bork's confirmation to the Supreme Court. A Supreme Court reporter and cheerleader during the heyday of the Warren Court, Lewis produced a series of

masterful columns that gave respectability to the political assault against Bork. This was the most important of them because it left no loophole. He agrees with Nicholas Katzenbach, who suggested to the committee that they simply ask, "Is Judge Bork a man of judgment?...Is he a wise person?" Lewis then presents the argument that a person who discards abstract theories when they become inconvenient can not be a person of judgment. "There is something deeply troubling about a judge who seeks certainty in abstractions: who discovers a grand theory that will solve all the problems, then turns to another when the theory fails — as it must...Robert Bork's pursuit of theory has led him to profound misjudgments on great legal and moral issues, and to unconvincing changes. This is why this intelligent and engaging man should not sit on the Supreme Court."

7. **Morgan, Dan.** *The Washington Post.* "Falwell, Bakker and the Fundamentals," 3-29. Morgan, who has been writing a book about the progress of an Oklahoma evangelical family since the Great Depression, had to learn a lot about evangelicals in the process. In this richly informative "Outlook" feature, he shares that basic knowledge with us, all we wanted to know about evangelicals but were afraid to ask. The news peg begins: "Evangelist Jim Bakker's peccadillo may yet turn out to be the catalytic event that will bring together two wings of fundamentalism that have been at war since the beginning of the century. Indeed, the Rev. Jerry Falwell's effort to rescue Bakker's beleaguered PTL television ministry must be seen as a major religious event." Why? "He will have helped reconcile the two most antagonistic — and dynamic — wings of conservative American Protestantism: Pentecostals and non-Pentecostals within the fundamentalist movement. In 87 years, no one has been able to achieve that goal." We need to know about all this, so we read on, learn plenty and benefit enormously.

8. **Mortimer, Edward.** *Financial Times.* "Parts That Glasnost Fail To Reach," 9-22. Of course there is dramatic reform underway in the Soviet Union, but how far has it gone and what are its limits in the fall of 1987? Mortimer's commentary is at this margin, the best single piece to give us a rough sense of what is allowed in public discourse. No catalog, it gives representative anecdotes, quotes and observations to give a feel for the change. "A few years ago even the most dedicated anti-Soviet propagandist could hardly have produced more examples of the shortcomings of the Soviet system than I heard this month in an hour's conversation with [the] editor of *Moscovskaya Pravda*." But "there is no two-sided argument about the pros and cons of particular arms control agreements or weapons systems; nor about the correct way to respond to the much-denounced US naval presence in the Gulf, still less about how to achieve the now universally proclaimed objective of withdrawal from Afghanistan."

9. **Rosenthal, A.M.** *The New York Times.* "A Question For Cuomo," 2-26. When New York Gov. Mario Cuomo announced a few days earlier that he would not seek the Democratic presidential nomination, there was general astonishment among political observers, Cuomo seen as having an excellent chance at nomination and election. Cuomo's supporters were dismayed, the other candidates and their allies delighted, the political junkies irked at having such an interesting horse scratched from the big one. Only Rosenthal, the former executive editor of the *Times*, thought to ask the central question of Cuomo, one of a few Americans in the pool of leaders available to his fellow citizens. "What about the country?" [Is the decision] Best for the country, too? If the answer is yes... that is not only an answer that has to be accepted but respected. But if the answer from the Governor is no, I can't say it really is just best for the country, then we are all entitled to say the decision is disappointing."

10. **Wicker, Tom.** *The New York Times.* "A No-Trump Game," 11-26. A Thanksgiving column waiting to be written precisely as Wicker lays it out here. He invites "all good Democrats [to] give thanks today and hereafter that Donald Trump, the New York real estate tycoon, has rejected an invitation to play host to the 25th annual Democratic Congressional dinner next

year," an invitation extended by House Speaker Jim Wright, hat in hand, in Republican Trump's skyscraper office. The queasy tableau of this unnatural act, as presented in news accounts, gave sour stomachs to all Democrats and Republicans we know. It was, wrote Wicker, "another forlorn Democratic attempt to do what Democrats will never do: win the confidence of 'the business community'...which is solidly Republican, and if Heaven did not intend it that way, most businessmen would be hard to convince of it." Thank you, Tom.

PUBLICATIONS

THE PACESETTERS

The New York Times

In some extremely important and surprising ways *The New York Times* in 1987 added to its lustre as the world's greatest newspaper. In other ways, there were surprising disappointments in this, Max Frankel's first year as executive editor. Last year, we cited Frankel's appointment as one of the most important news developments of 1986, succeeding A.M. (Abe) Rosenthal, who had held the position since 1977 and was approaching the mandatory retirement age of 65. "This is big stuff, very big stuff," we observed. "The editor of the *Times*, like the sovereign pontiff, doesn't have actual firepower. But for those of us who believe the pen is mightier than the sword, the fellow at the top of the most important newspaper in the world is a big cheese indeed." Where most of the ruling establishment was wondering if Frankel would move the paper left of Rosenthal's more centrist design, we thought "the more interesting question is whether Frankel can maintain the quality of the *Times*, which is at its highest level in more than a generation." We thought the chances are he would not, only because "Abe's is such a hard act to follow, a hedgehog to Frankel's fox." But not by much, and of course we hoped we'd be proven wrong and the *Times* would get even better. In the first year of what will likely to be nine before Frankel himself retires, the net of pluses and minuses was about even, but with some hopeful signs on the horizon.

The Editorial Page

How ironic that in Frankel's first year as executive editor of the *Times*, after nine years as editor of the editorial page, the greatest single improvement was in the editorial columns. This is certainly no rebuke to Frankel, who ultimately gets credit for all the good in the *Times* and blame for all the bad. After all, the new editorial page editor, Jack Rosenthal, was Frankel's deputy and protege, who, in turn, brought Leslie H. Gelb from the Washington bureau to be his deputy. Where we had been skimming the *Times* editorials for years to see what was on their minds, now suddenly, at the turn of the year, we were reading them thoroughly, with interest and enthusiasm, finding them at the fulcrum of the great debates, attempting to persuade us of the correctness of their views, instead of setting forth positions to satisfy their already committed followers.

To be fair to Frankel, the editorial tone of his tenure had already been a welcome advance from the strident manifestos that were the daily fare under his predecessor, John B. Oakes. (This is it and if you don't like it, you're a dope.) The new team of Rosenthal and Gelb didn't begin their run with the burdens Frankel faced in 1977, when the Liberal Establishment watched like a hawk to see if he would do some *conservative* violence to the agenda! A year ago we expected the new team to shade the editorials a bit further left, but we did not expect their tone and energy to show such sharp improvement, which was the nice surprise. In 1987 we read more *Times* editorials from start to finish than we had in the three previous years combined. This advance is an important one to the liberal movement in America. Thus far, *The New Republic* has been in the lead, struggling to redefine liberalism in a way that once again will persuade the national electorate to turn power over to it. But *TNR* is a tugboat to the *Times*, the flagship of the embattled fleet.

Gelb's elevation was especially important in this regard because of his expertise on national security and strategic arms. His internationalist bent befits a man who began his career on Capitol Hill, as an aide to the late Senator Jacob Javits of New York. The Democratic liberal agenda has been steadily moving toward isolationist retreat for more than a decade, the natural result of a breakdown of liberal confidence in its agenda, just as the GOP retreated into an America-First isolationism in the 1930s. Where the *Times* had been harping at the Reagan Administration's maneuvers over strategic arms negotiations with the Soviets, in 1987 it engaged in focused, combative debate, scoring points where it could and acting as a vigorous, useful voice of the Loyal Opposition. "Defending Treaty From Star Wars," 3-18, was just such an effort, contesting the attempt to narrow the interpretation of the 1972 ABM treaty by citing the authoritative arguments of Senator Nunn. In "The Light and Darkness of Richard Perle," 3-16, the *Times*' chief intellectual adversary at the Pentagon is bid farewell on his departure: "Against the generally dim background of an Administration scarce on high-level talent and experience, this 'Prince of Darkness' has shown brightly. But his guiding light was mistrust, and in undermining more than he built he pressed a useful caution to sometimes harmful extremes."

In other areas of public policy as well, we noted several dozen impressive efforts during the year, including "Serving Notice on the Contras," 2-20, questioning their inherent vitality, and "Risks Worth Taking in Nicaragua," 8-19, pressing U.S. negotiations on the grounds that there is a split in the Sandinistas. "How to Revive Brazil's Miracle," 2-24, was unusually lively and informative. "End Rent Control," 5-12, was a stunning editorial switch, absolutely necessary to the complete revival of NYC; "A Bridge to the 21st Century," 8-23, was also stunning in a way, devoted to the decay of the Williamsburg Bridge, another sign of hope for the city when the lofty *Times* looks at the mess at its feet in its Sunday lead editorial!

Prior to 1987, the economic editorials had simply been lambasting Reaganomics while repeatedly calling for big boosts in gasoline taxes (which bites NYC least of any place in the U.S.). Now, even in the post-Crash editorials, there seemed a little more tentativeness and uncertainty in them. For years the paper has been urging the devaluation of the dollar as the solution to the trade deficit, *The Wall Street Journal* insisting that it won't, that currency changes don't change trade flows. The *Times* pressed ahead with editorials 4-3 and 4-10 on this line, but in "The Dollar's Down — Why Not the Deficit?" 4-28, the impatience of the editors with their economic counselors became evident, a sure sign of intellectual ferment behind the scenes. The trade editorials were vigorous, "What Mr. Gephardt Would Protect," 4-23, chides the Democrats generally, "The party that launched a half century of world trade expansion now threatens to take America back to tit-for-tat protectionism," and "The Senate Trashed Trade," 7-24, on trade-bill hypocrisy: "While most of the public posturing by Democrats and Republicans alike fixed on trade expansion, individual senators have diligently attended to protection for special interests." After the Crash, the *Times* lead editorial, 10-21, actually denounced House and Senate legislation aimed at "taxing the rich," as a possible cause, along with the trade bill hanging over the market, urging budget cuts and energy taxes.

The op-ed page also clearly strengthened during the year. Abe Rosenthal's new weekly column "On My Mind" got off to such a shaky start that *Newsweek* thought it worthy of public ridicule, "Abe Speaks His Mind," Jonathan Alter, 3-9, and it had us worried a bit, too. But he'd never written a column before, and clearly needed time to find his "voice." By trial and error, he seemed to find one of such sonority, relevance and wisdom that it has become a factor, perhaps even an influence. At the same time, William Safire, who had been dour and touchy in recent years, completed a major book project that was probably draining him. His column revived with a burst of energy, insight and its equanimity of yore. The liberal bookends, Anthony Lewis and Tom Wicker, also had vibrant years, pressing relentlessly against the Iran-Contra-weakened Lame Ducksville, which also seemed to cheer up Russell Baker, funnier than he has been for years. James Reston finally retired after one of the most illustrious careers in American journalism, putting to bed a column that had become very sleepy in recent years. Flora Lewis's Foreign Affairs column still shows up, nodding. The other material on the op-ed page has also continued to improve in its political range. There are now very few conservative arguments or ideas that can't be found at least occasionally on the page.

The Sunday *Times*

The Sunday paper is the most important of the week, because readers of the *Times* have the day to spend with it, browsing and brunching and because it has the biggest circulation. In 1987 the Sunday edition deteriorated further, so much so that there are weekends when we spend more time with the Saturday edition, a slender package of always interesting news features. The "Week in Review" section seems, more than ever, a collection of rewrites by unhappy staffers dragooned into squeezing their week's file into a short take. And "Arts and Leisure" still has the feel of an advertising supplement, where hardly is heard a discouraging word. But it is the magazine and business section that hurt most.

We have been especially critical of the Sunday magazine in recent years, finding fewer and fewer rewards there. We expect at least one solid, solid piece on domestic politics or foreign affairs and believe the *Times* readers as a whole expect nothing less, Sunday also being a day for such serious considerations by an informed citizenry. Our level of satisfaction in 1987 dropped to an all-time low. There were scattered winners, but there were no more than one in three issues that were adequate. "The Elusive Front Runner," 4-3, E.J. Dionne, Jr.'s cover on Gary Hart was among the best. "Thatcher's Capitalist Revolution," 5-31, by Howell Raines and "Russia's Restless Youth," by Bill Keller, 7-12, were winners. We'd even let "A Farewell to South Africa," 1-25, by Alan Cowell, in under the wire, after his undistinguished tour as Johannesburg bureau chief. But for the second year in a row, Seth Mydans, the Manila bureau chief, had a dreadful piece on the Philippines, "The Embattled Mrs. Aquino," 11-15, devoting several pages of pictures and text to proving she did not hide under her bed during a recent siege. Edward A. Gargan, who wrote a snooze of a swan song to his Africa beat in the 1986 magazine, 12-7, gave us "China's Cultural Crackdown," 7-12, on his new Beijing beat, with not a scrap of hard evidence about any sudden cultural crackdown in China, which is why he got a scoop!

Then there was "Alone Together, the Unromantic Generation," 4-5; "The Barbie Trial," 5-10; "Where are the Black Fans?" 5-17; "Why Your Family Doctor is a Group," 6-7; "Clustered For Leisure: The Changing Home," 6-28; and "The Ambivalent American Bachelor," 11-15. "Being Catholic in America," 8-23, by Joseph Berger, looked promising on the eve of the Pope's visit, but it also bombed. We were not happy at all with the magazine and took encouragement when late in the year, editor Edward Klein quit, replaced by James L. Greenfield, 63, a former Assistant Secretary of State in the LBJ era, obviously a caretaker.

The greatest disappointment with the Sunday edition, though, was with the business section, which we praised to the skies in the *1987 MediaGuide* as our favorite reading on Sunday. Even as the presses rolled, Sunday business editor Soma Golden was elevated to be national editor. She was replaced by Karen Arenson, an economics reporter. Almost instantly, the section plunged in relevance and readability, which baffled us, until we began to sense by March or April that Ms. Arenson has little interest in business. Her taste runs to the Great Society issues of the 1960s and the environmental, work safety, egalitarian issues of the 1970s. Here were great sweeping industrial and financial stories everywhere you looked, astonishing clashes over economic policies reverberating in Washington and around the globe, incredible business personalities involved in mind-boggling technological advances, and the Sunday *Times* biz leads gave us pieces on whether tall executives do better than short ones, 3-8; how black and Hispanic businessmen are still on the outside looking in, 7-3; and "Without the Playground, Mothers Meet at the Office," 7-19, all about corporate women, and some men, gathering to swap tips on managing parenthood. Then, in the same issue, 8-4, "Congress Takes up Labor's Cause" and "Rolling Stone Turns a Prosperous 20." It isn't that the *Times* doesn't have the reportorial talent. The weekday "Business Day," edited by Fred Andrews, is a superior business page that in most ways is competitive with *The Wall Street Journal* and in some ways beat the *WSJ* in coverage of the October market crash. The *Times* also has the three best technology reporters in journalism — David E. Sanger, James Gleick, and Andrew Pollack — but they rarely hit the Sunday edition. Soma Golden used to squeeze blockbusters out of the Washington bureau on the great policy struggles. Instead, we got touchy-feely stuff. The last straw was "America's Army of Non-Workers," 9-27, a weeper about all the people who aren't working because they aren't being offered meaningful employment at high enough wages, and it's all you-know-who's fault. Max?

The Washington Bureau

In the new scheme of things, Craig Whitney and Judith Miller took over from Bill Kovach and Howell Raines, as bureau chief and deputy. We heard complaints that they were letting the *Post* beat them on Iran-Contra, which was probably true day-to-day, but we thought the *Post* was often only louder, that the *Times* gave us better perspective. There was, though, the embarrassment of the wild goose chase following a "scoop" in *The Sun* of Lowell, Mass., about funds from Iranian arms sales going to GOP candidates, forcing the *Times* to a front-page confession of error. The *Post* was better on defense and national security, but that was to be expected with the elevation of Leslie Gelb from the bureau to the editorial page. White House coverage was superior and State Department slipped only because the peerless Bernard Gwertzman was named deputy foreign editor. The *WSJ* and *Post* edged the *Times* on some aspects of the Supreme Court coverage, but on points and split decisions.

The political coverage wasn't nearly as good as we expected and here it's likely that if Howell Raines were still around, instead of running the London bureau, he could have coaxed more out of the team with better deployment. Senator Dole was covered like a blanket, practically as if the bureau was betting its chips on him, the Veep getting a cool shoulder and nibbled at with anonymous quotes, as in "Issue for '88: Who Is George Bush?" 11-20, by Gerald M. Boyd. Meanwhile, we got much too little on Jesse Jackson and Pat Robertson as factors or candidates. Also, Kovach and Raines would not have approved of the harebrained idea of sending a *Times* questionnaire to all the political candidates, asking them to list their fetishes, amorous adventures, skeletons, etc. Especially after *NYT* columnists Rosenthal, Safire and Anthony Lewis had formed a united front in condemning Paul Taylor, *The Washington Post* reporter who tipped Gary Hart out of the race by asking "Did you ever commit adultery?" Maureen Dowd of the *Times* tipped Senator Biden out of the race with her report on Senator Biden's plagiarism of a Neil Kinnock speech. Bureau chief Whitney lavished praise on Dowd in *Time* for her dynamite reporting effort, but it then turned out the material was force-fed to her by John Sasso, campaign manager to Massachusetts Gov. Dukakis, which tipped Sasso out. It wasn't a boffo year for the political team.

Economic coverage from the bureau was also disappointing, but it was everywhere else too, with tons of stories in a wild, wild year, but not enough asking the right questions or looking into the dark, out-of-the-way corners. Peter T. Kilborn, the powerhouse Treasury reporter, irked us a number of times by seeming to make up Secretary Baker's mind for him on whether the dollar should stand or fall. His 10-18 piece will go into the history books as a footnote, the story that triggered the market crash, albeit in the same sense that a snowflake triggers an avalanche. We preferred the *WSJ* on budget, the *Post* on trade, but the *Times* on money and banks.

The *Times* Abroad

Joseph Lelyveld's first year as foreign editor reflects ups and downs from personnel shifts that were made before he took over, but he and Bernard Gwertzman, his deputy, can share in the credit for net improvement in the work of the foreign service.

The most exciting advance came in sub-Sahara Africa with the work of James Brooke, who leaped from one star to four, leaving the Metro section in 1986 to take the beat vacated by Edward A. Gargan, who went to Beijing. Brooke took on Africa the way we'd never seen it done before, engaging himself in the political economies of countries big and small as if it really means something to *Times* readers to know them the way they know New York State. With Sheila Rule out of Nairobi and John Battersby rescuing the Johannesburg bureau, the *Times* was on top overall in Africa.

But Gargan, as we suspected, has not been up to the complex China beat, a negative for the *NYT* unless they routinely send Nicholas Kristof out of Hong Kong to Beijing to deal with the economy, as he did in the spring. Young Kristof is a gem, sensing there was not a setback to China's economic reforms early in the year, as everyone else had reported. The Tokyo team of Clyde Haberman and Susan Chira seemed to be spread thin with double-duty in covering busy, busy Korea, keeping up but with no breakthroughs as they had in 1986. Manila is still very weak, although Barbara Crossette, ranging far and wide out of Bangkok, swung through Manila and produced solid reports. Crossette was a delight all year, outperforming the field in Indochina as well with sober, reliable assessments. Stephen Weisman improved in New Delhi, handling Rajiv Gandhi's political sweat, but is still weak on the economy and so-so on his Afghanistan tour.

The *Times* in Moscow was again great, a surprise because when Serge Schmemann moved to Bonn, replaced as Moscow chief by his deputy, Phil Taubman, a rookie was sent from the Washington bureau to fill out the staff. Bill Keller, who did not even make the cut in the *1987 MediaGuide*, was sparkling, immersed in Berlitz Russian and hit the ground running, the most aggressive digger on the *glasnost* scene. Taubman and his wife, Felicity Barringer, added to the bureau's stellar production.

European coverage showed a palpable improvement, the Paris bureau strengthened with James Markham, London stronger with Howell Raines, and the new Budapest bureau paying off immediately with veteran Henry Kamm producing a long string of richly informative dispatches out of Hungary, Romania and Czechoslovakia. Roberto Suro did not quite fill E.J. Dionne's shoes in the Rome bureau, but who could? Schmemann didn't get the hang of developing the critical economic news out of Germany, better on the NATO, East-West front. The Madrid and Athens bureaus produced in two dimensions, but Michael Kaufman in Warsaw did well again.

In the western hemisphere, moving Larry Rohter from the Metro beat to Mexico City proved another inspiration. Alan Riding had to work harder in Brazil against the *WSJ*'s new Rio bureau and chief Roger Cohen; he improved on economic detail, but Cohen still edged him. Shirley Christian covered the cone countries, doing the politics of Chile especially well, but no economics. The Central America coverage seemed to drag, almost always behind the curve, as if the bureau chiefs are awaiting assignments from New York instead of producing spontaneously, thereby trailing the *Washington Post* and the strong *Los Angeles Times* teams. John F. Burns, bounced out of Beijing in 1986, is the best we see out of Canada, along with Edith Terry of *Business Week*. Burns, as one of the best in the business, should be in Managua, at least.

Executive Editor: Max Frankel

Address: 229 West 43rd Street
New York, NY 10036
(212) 556-1234

Circulation: Sunday 1,589,290
Weekday 1,022,899

The Wall Street Journal

The *Journal* remains the best read of the national newspapers, with its circulation of nearly 2 million far ahead of *The New York Times* and *USA Today*. It is of course one of the most prestigious of all news publications, so thoroughly identified with affluence and understated good taste that it has become a ubiquitous prop in advertisements aimed at upscale audiences. Veterans of Dow Jones & Co., its publisher, believe this aspect of the paper was truly cemented into the American culture by Marilyn Monroe, in the 1950s film "Some Like It Hot," when she tells Tony Curtis she likes men who wear glasses, presuming they've had to "read all that tiny print in *The Wall Street Journal*."

There certainly was a lot of tiny print to read in the *Journal* in 1987, more than ever before, as the management continued to cram more and more newsprint and ink into it, pushing third sections at us from time to time, and stuffing it with special tabloid supplements bulging with advertising. This drive to bulk up the paper remains the central fact of the *Journal* as it has been for some years. In the greatest Bull Market since the Roaring Twenties, more and more readers grabbed for the tiny print and the *WSJ* was propelled into further expansion. But we doubt even the Great Crash of October slowed down the planning of a permanent third section, 80 pages a day down the line, and more tabs and supplements.

There is behind all this an imperative having nothing to do with greed. The *Journal* simply wants to be a Great Newspaper. It decided this long ago, around the time of Monroe's observation, and the push to expand is all part of it. The *Journal* wants to be a Great Newspaper like the *Times* is thought of as "Great," or as *The Times* of London was once considered great when London was the center of gravity on the planet. It has climbed to the top of the circulation peak, but it wrested that peak from the *New York Daily News,* which was okay at its top, but not great. The *Journal* knows it is not a Great Newspaper and knows the *Times* is, but it also knows it *has come very close!*

This was roughly in 1977 or '78, when the *NYT* was at its nadir after a long slide through the early '70s, its home base, the Big Apple staring bankruptcy in the face, the nation in the grips of "malaise," the *Times* editorial page waving white flags and the institution itself shrinking into self-doubt. The *Journal*, growing and confident and sure of itself, could smell greatness! All it would take is a bigger paper, more pages, more staff, some foreign bureaus, more advertising, more revenues, a bigger building, more foreign bureaus, even an Asian edition, even a European edition, more staff, more sections, more revenue, more, more, more.

After suggesting in the last two *MediaGuides* that the *Journal* was moving a bit too fast, we had hoped it would slow down. That it would allow the talent pool to develop, to fill all those pages and sections and tabs. We had even hoped that we would begin seeing a payoff in 1987, a payoff in quality that would match the expansion in newsprint and advertising tonnage that has taken place these several years. We had hoped, after chirping at the *WSJ* for two years, to be able to award garlands and praise and anticipations of greatness just around the corner.

This has not happened. The *Journal* in 1987 came out at about the same level as it did in '86, if anything a shade behind. There were of course parts of the paper improved, particularly its foreign coverage, and many individual journalists were much improved, but the net was about the same, almost entirely because of problems associated with growth. The good news is that the *Journal* is still *close* to being a Great Newspaper, closer than it was when it became impregnated with the imperative. But it's going to take a few more years.

The Front Page

The most important improvement of the paper in 1987 was on its front page. Not that we especially noticed much improvement of the raw material. But the presentation was much, much better. Gone are the soft, soft fluffy leads we groaned about last year, the "Snoopy leads'' (''It was a dark and stormy night,'') that devoted several paragraphs to setting the stage. We applaud the front-page editors for compressing these leads so that we can get to the gist of the stories before finishing our first cup of coffee. But not so tight that we think we are reading the wire services.

The column one and column six leaders are the twin pillars of the *WSJ*. Because of the traditional format of the paper, these are the only two serious pieces on P.1 that call *WSJ* readers to attention. We trust we will be rewarded. Because of the paper's format, the *Journal* editors have a special obligation to their readers, to offer two stories a day, ten per week, 500 per year, that are worth the time and attention of busy, busy people who are also being asked to confront second and third sections. As the critical entries of the *WSJ* reporters in this book clearly indicate, our readers find too high a proportion of leaders that do not belong on P.1. Not that they are unimportant. But not sufficiently rewarding. Too often we find leaders that should be column four features, light and amusing, or leads in the second section. This is clearly the expansion problem, with editors scraping in a too-small pool of quality material.

Which isn't to say this is a very small pool. As is also evident from the individual entries on *WSJ* reporters, most of the time the editors have provided us with rewarding leaders. We were especially pleased with the harvest of leaders that came from the regional bureaus in 1987, becoming familiar on P.1 with bylines we hadn't seen before, and looking for them thereafter: Alex Kotlowitz in Chicago, Jacob M. Schlesinger in Detroit, Paulette Thomas in Dallas, Betsy Morris in Atlanta, Robert Johnson in Chicago, Laura Landro in Los Angeles, to name a few. Some of them produced articles we cited as among the best in American journalism in '87. Stephen Wermiel, the Supreme Court reporter, produced a remarkable leader on Judge Bork the day after his nomination in May, which we did not fully appreciate until we read it again in November, long after the fight was over, and realized how much he had told us so early.

Covering Wall Street

The best personnel change we saw in '87 was the shift of banking reporter Peter Truell from London to New York. We noted last year that Truell was the only talent we saw at the *WSJ* able to compete on the geopolitical banking beat with the *Times* or *Washington Post*, but that he could only work at half speed in London. Truell was the brightest light of the New York bureau in '87, producing incandescent reports on the Brazilian, Mexican and other Third World debtors that were devoured by the creditor banks. He had no competition to speak of and was a great asset to the paper and the world of commerce. He should be sent to report on the Brazilian and other troubled economies in '88 as further service to the world and encouraged to write lofty leaders.

While Truell move higher in our esteem, James B. Stewart moved down. One of our four-star journalists in 1986, Stewart had been red hot in reporting on the merger and acquisition beat, burning up the track on the dealmakers, leaving his competitors eating dust. But in '87 he got ahead of himself and, we think, of the unwritten journalistic code, producing pieces that amounted to trial by press of Drexel Burnham's Michael Milkin, who, we hear by sources who wish to remain anonymous, is an honest man. Stewart, a lawyer by training, not a newsman, should not have been permitted by his editors to run so many unsourced stories implying crookedness, which is why we have only dropped him to three stars in '88. But since the anonymous *Journal* editor who passed on this material can't be docked, Stewart is now on his own for '88; we won't be as tolerant if he continues to use his powerful pen to prosecute.

In covering the October Crash, there was considerable debate across Manhattan on who covered it better, the *Journal* or the *Times*. We rather thought in this instance the print media was of less importance than the electronic media, because of the need for minute-by-minute information in the several days following the crash. Serious news gourmets stayed glued to Financial News Network or their Dow Jones and Reuter wires. The *Times* threw dozens of reporters into the breech and claimed a victory of volume over the *Journal*. But we saw no clear winner. The *Times*' James Sterngold had the best wrap-up of the events surrounding the Crash, 10-26, but the *WSJ* had the superior commentary. George Melloan's column of 10-20 was the best instant analysis we saw of the Crash; Bartley's "1929 and All That," 11-24, was the best single commentary we saw on it.

The *Journal* expansion not only put pressure on the reportorial pool, it strained management, too. It has always been rather amazing that the *WSJ* has blossomed as it has with a management team that grew up with pencils and notebooks as its basic work tools, not Ivy League MBAs. The expansion process has to slow a bit just to allow mid-management especially to catch its breath. We can't say for sure, but it is our hunch that the strain on management permitted R. Foster Winans to slip through the cracks. Winans was the "Heard on the Street" columnist who peddled advances on his column to Wall Streeters who used the news to make killings on specific stocks, an embarrassing blot on the *WSJ*'s escutcheon. In upholding his conviction on mail fraud statutes in November, the Supreme Court essentially wrote a private professional ethical code into public law. Becoming a Great Newspaper can be achieved, but it can't be hurried.

The Washington Bureau

The Washington Bureau is essential to the *Journal*'s objective of Greatness as a newspaper, which must be distinguished in its reportage of the business of the world's central government as well as its coverage of global finance, business and foreign affairs. The year was not a good one for the bureau, personnel problems nagging throughout. In two years, four of the strongest reporters cleared out of the bureau, Robert Merry, a seasoned political reporter, David Ignatius, their top diplomatic correspondent, Art Pine, a veteran covering international trade and finance, and Paul Blustein, a heavyweight on domestic monetary policy and government finance. There were replacements, as there always are, but the combined weight of loss was evident in the *Journal*'s catch-up coverage in each of these areas. Its coverage of the Iran-Contra affair was adequate. Its political coverage has still not recovered from Merry's departure, although David Shribman had a most promising year. Pine left just as he was beginning to run with the competition on international money, at times overtaking it; his replacement at a critical period is relatively green. Blustein should have been elevated, and when he wasn't, bolted for a choice portfolio at *The Washington Post*. The budget reporter, Jeffrey Birnbaum, and Wermiel at the Supreme Court are better than solid, and Alan Murray should get back up to speed in '88 on the Fed and economics. But there will still be a lot of huffing and puffing to keep pace in this big year.

The *Journal* is in good shape in Washington, though, compared to the licking it has been taking on technology at the hands of the *Times*. Who could have imagined 10 years ago that this would be the case? But the *Times*' decision to produce a weekly "Science Times" section several years ago forced it to produce a science staff, and it now runs circles around the entire print media. The *WSJ* has three promising talents we can see in the field, Brenton Schlender, David Stipp, and Michael Waldholz. But they would come in fourth, fifth and sixth in a contest with the top three at the *Times*. The weakness was most evident in the continuing newsbeats by the *Times* early in the year on the breathtaking superconductivity breakthroughs, made all the more evident as the *Journal*'s early response was to pooh-pooh the relevance of the discoveries, as if they weren't really left in the dust. This, too, could be rectified if the management committee resolves its indecision over the third section and gets serious about this critical sector of the business world.

The *Journal* Abroad

The foreign coverage of the paper was clearly a highlight for the *Journal* in '87. Even with the loss of Youssef Ibrahim to the *NYT* and Gerald Seib moving to Washington, foreign editor Karen Elliott House should be pleased with the overall performance of her crew — including the staffs of the Asian and European editions. In a year of enormous interest in the global economy and integrated world stock markets, on which the sun never sets, the *Journal* had the most inclination of all to treat economic developments in detail. This seems logical, but it wasn't necessarily the case in 1986, when we had to read the *Financial Times* and *Journal of Commerce* just to keep up.

Asia was the paper's greatest strength. With John F. Burns of the *NYT* gone from China, the *Journal*'s team of Vigor Fung doing grass roots and James R. Schiffman doing the peaks was dominant. And with the *FT*'s powerful Tokyo team of Jurek Martin and Carla Rapoport moved, the *Journal*'s Damon Darlin & Co. dominated Japan coverage. We got a steady stream of political, economic news and analysis out of the bureau in New Delhi, better reports out of Australia, continued steady reporting out of Manila, and Claudia Rosett, the Asian edition's new editorial page editor producing superb dispatches as she roamed the region.

The *NYT* and *FT* would have totally dominated news out of Moscow but for Mark D'Anastasio, the first chief of the new *WSJ* bureau, who strengthened as the year of *glasnost* unfolded, disappointing now and then by letting his opinion creep into news dispatches. A notable example being his report on the Gorbachev 70th anniversary speech, with scoffing read between the lines. In Europe, the material was not generally better than in '86, even with the attentiveness to economic news. The bureaus in London, Paris and Bonn are still not used to the new world economy. They still seem sluggish in peeling away the layers for detail on economic policy debates inside the European countries they cover.

In the *1987 MediaGuide* we urged the *Journal* to open a bureau in Rio and have it run by Roger Cohen, who had been covering Brazil out of Miami. It did, and it turned out to be a good idea. With Peter Truell doing the Brazil debt story from New York and Cohen on the ground in Rio and Sao Paulo, the *Journal* totally dominated the world press on the big international banking story of the year. Mary Williams Walsh had another solid year in Mexico. David Asman, who roams the region for the editorial page and his "Americas" column kept us up on fiscal, tax policies. The *Journal*'s Central America coverage continues weak, fourth behind the *Washington Post, Los Angeles Times*, and *New York Times*.

Elsewhere, *WSJ* foreign reporting was about at the same adequate levels as in '86, except for the hole in the Middle East. But that is the specialty of Ms. House, the foreign editor, who fills the hole quickly when we need to know what's up there.

The Editorial Page

The paper's editorial page was another plus for the year, completely out of the slump we detected in 1985. Reagan's lame-duck difficulties, the continuing great economic debate, the Crash in October, the struggles over the Supreme Court, SDI and INF and Gorbachev and *glasnost*, all got the editorial juices flowing. Editor Robert L. Bartley and his crew, mainly George Melloan and Dan Henninger, had to step lively as the new team uptown at the *Times* hit the ground running. The editorials are still be best around for informativeness and persuasiveness, rarely bothering with ideas less than Olympian. They frequently present news not seen in the news columns of the *Journal* or other papers and not infrequently present information that contradicts material presented elsewhere in the *Journal*. "Super Discoveries," 3-30, was a splendid editorial celebrating the superconductivity breakthroughs that the *WSJ* had been scooped on by the *Times*. The editorial page staff's grasp of domestic and international money and finance is several cuts above the Washington bureau's.

In "Your Turn, Mr. President," 4-1, we noted a classic, on RR's veto of the highway bill: "Mr. Reagan represents a particular threat to an establishment accustomed to two generations or so of power. Its adherents — among the Democrats, in the Congress, in the press, and in the permanent bureaucracy — want the Reagan presidency to be dismissed as one big mistake, to go back to the old habits and the old power constellations." In "Trade Bill Trumpery," 7-23, they observe "When Congressman Gephardt explains how to cause international commerce to obey his wishes, perhaps he can also tell us how to reorder the movement of the planets." And "a long string of non-germane riders in the Senate bill reflects the powerful impulse in this current Congress...to take over the conduct of foreign policy.'' All minor movements are seen against a broad canvas.

More Collective Journalism

One of the sources of difficulty the paper has not addressed is its continued movement toward collective journalism. The *Journal*'s legendary editor, the late Bernard Kilgore, had in the 1960s prohibited the use of multiple bylines on a story, believing a single journalist should take responsibility for each piece. Last year we rallied against "The Great Byline Inflation" that has crept into most publications, believing that collective journalism retards individual initiative and growth. Those reporters who like the system call it collegiality, but for the most part dual and multiple story efforts are collective crutches. The *Journal* in '87 sank deeper into this bog, especially in New York and Washington. The best talent we saw developing was in the regions and foreign bureaus where it is still usually every man for himself. At least some of those talents who have quit the paper in recent years cite a sense of frustrating bureaucracy, the layers likened to Time Inc.'s.

Even so, we have more of a sense that things are about to click at 200 Liberty Street, that all the grunting and groaning that has gone into the expansion will soon get the boulder to a higher plateau of excellence. As far as Greatness, who knows? Perhaps, like Sisyphus, the folks at Dow Jones are cursed to have the huge stone roll back at them every time they get near the top. But in journalism, at least, it's always worth the effort.

Editor: Robert L. Bartley

Managing Editor: Norman Pearlstine

Address: 200 Liberty Street
            New York, N.Y. 10281
            (212) 416-2000

Circulation: 1,961,846

The Washington Post

Of the three major newspapers, *The Washington Post* is the only one that showed definite improvement in 1987, so much so that even some of its harshest critics have acknowledged the advance. Because we look to the *Post* primarily for coverage of the federal government and national politics, some of this advance may have been an illusion, a gain that we may have noticed because of the relative decline of certain aspects of Washington coverage in the bureaus of *The New York Times* and *Wall Street Journal.* But we think most of the improvement is absolute and real. This involves not only a further movement toward objectivity in the news columns, but also better material, a higher quality of information. This is confirmed by our Washington readers, who read the *Post* either first or second to *The Washington Times*, telling us they didn't have to spend as much time with the New York papers in 1987 to feel sufficiently informed.

We have to admit this came as somewhat of a surprise. In the *1987 MediaGuide* we noted "a strong improvement" by the *Post* in overcoming a problem of advocacy in its news reporting that we had seen in the past. As the year began, with President Reagan on the Iran-Contra ropes and staring at his Lame Duck years, we wondered if the improvement would be maintained — or, if an institutional bias against the Reagan administration would be aroused to go for a Watergate-like "kill" and be felt in the rank and file of *Post* journalists. There certainly was such an attempt by the Loyal Opposition in Congress, probing for weakness at the White House and finding plenty of it. Admirably, the *Post* restrained the former tendencies that it used in this power struggle and kept its opinions to its editorial pages and columnists.

In the Iran-Contra investigation and hearings, the *Post* was clearly superior to the *Times* in its day-to-day handling of the material. There were assertions at the *Times,* from editor Max Frankel, that the *Post* was simply "louder," with bigger, blacker headlines atop front-page stories that were covered with less splash. There was a degree of truth to this, but this is a headline-writer problem. In the front page "Regan Says President Knew Of Cover Story," 7-31, the reporters don't quite say what the headline says, although there's no mention in the story that Regan said he didn't remember a cover story was ever necessary. Beyond the problem of how stories were displayed, the *Post* team seemed better managed and more productive. The fact that it didn't come up with any smoking guns after such aggressive pursuit should not be held against the team. The success of Dan Morgan and Walter Pincus working as a unit cut against our general dislike of double bylines; they genuinely worked at being an effective complementary team.

Defense and national security has always been a troublesome area for the *Post.* There is a natural inclination to view the world outside the Beltway as a vast military-industrial complex, trying to keep war scares going everywhere so that tax revenues which should be going to social programs can be diverted to building weapons. This isn't an entirely ridiculous assumption. In fact, it is part of the check-and-balance scheme of things that the *Post* should be institutionally suspicious of any motives that involve the interests of the American people, especially the taxpayers. The other fact of Washington is that the "special interests" that lobby the U.S. government include the governments of the rest of the world, through their embassies and the international financial institutions located in D.C. The *Post* hears the Soviet or Sandinista point of view through the USSR and Nicaraguan embassies directly, but mostly it is through U.S. government officials and members of Congress who have been lobbied by these governments in one way or another. Of course, the same is true of governments of the left and the right, and all this is to the good. The United Nations notwithstanding, Washington, D.C. is the political center of the world, where all voices can and should be heard.

Because the *Post* is *especially* centered in this mechanism, it is all the more important that its news, reporters and editors avoid taking sides *as much as possible* in these global debates. The defense and national security team at the *Post* in the last 20 years has frequently stepped past these bounds, taking sides by weighting stories and displaying them with a skew towards positions of the Liberal Establishment. As the entries within indicate, our readers in this area were more positive about the *Post's* national security and diplomatic reporting than they have been in recent years, although the *1987 MediaGuide* noted improvement last year. Some of this, we suspect, has been the presence of *The Washington Times*, which has its strongest reporting team in this area. Competition helps, but it may also be the *Post* is maturing, too — acting like the most important newspaper at the political center of the world, leaving the pamphleteering to others.

The Political Beat

In the *1987 MediaGuide*, we noted that the *Post* especially prides itself in its coverage of national political affairs, but that while it "has the deepest bench of political reporters in Creation...the *Post* did not score a clear knockout of *The New York Times* in 1986. Our readers were divided, giving it to the *Post* on points." In 1987, the readers were unanimous in citing the superior political coverage of the *Post*.

Some of this is the sheer commitment of manpower, space and resources by the *Post*. Those who appreciate political news at the margin cannot be fooled by having the volume turned up. The big gain at the *Post,* we thought, came in the work of David Broder, the dean of the political press corps. Two years ago we were ready to see Broder put out to pasture, getting from him undistinguished reports from the field in a non-election year, in between screeds against the federal deficits, which he knows little about. He picked up the pace in 1986 during the midterm elections, and we noted "his 1986 file was a pleasant, steadily productive surprise." In giving him the maximum rating in the *1988 MediaGuide*, we note his deep experience in national politics which, with hindsight, we realize counts a great deal in an environment as complex and fluid as the one leading into the 1988 elections. Most of the hot, young political reporters have only *read* about the last presidential race between non-incumbents in 1968 or the last that followed a full two-term presidency in 1960. We had expected the *Post's* Paul Taylor to vault into the lead in 1987, with E.J. Dionne, Jr. of the *Times* maybe eclipsing them all, but at times these young heaters seemed downright frustrated with the number of variables and the complexity of the work before them. Taylor, in fact, wrote an impassioned plea for political reform in "The Way We Choose Presidents Is Crazy and Getting Crazier," 3-29, arguing for less politics!

Meanwhile Broder and other old hands, like Jack Germond and Jules Witcover writing in the *National Journal*, kept their cool and plunged forward, knowing how unpredictable presidential politics can be. They know how ideology can come out of nowhere to change the chemistry of a campaign, taking the variables and complexities one at a time and finding a nexus that makes even small reports valuable communiques. Broder produced one of the best political pieces of the year with "Candidates Turn Corner Toward '88; GOP Hurdles Ahead For Bush," 9-8; with Taylor tagging along on the same post-Labor Day front page, "Democrats: A Formless Field," not bad either. Sidney Blumenthal, the *Post's* political intellectual, produced the best profile of Senator Dole, "The Candidate From Kansas," 11-9. Thomas B. Edsall, who seems underrated at the *Post*, but is second only to Broder, gave us "Dole's Transformation: Ideological Blur Characterizes Career," 3-9, almost as good in comparison, but eight months earlier.

The format of the *Post*, in addition to its commitment, clearly favors it in the coverage of presidential politics. As a "writer's paper" you can have an Edsall writing a Dole profile in the news section and a Blumenthal doing one in the Style section, from different angles, while yet another approach shows up in the Sunday "Outlook." The *NYT* can compete by producing regular snapshots of the various campaigns, as the newspaper of record, and in fact, dominated coverage in June and July, before the troops were pulled back to do Iran-Contra. The *WSJ's* back page has kept it in the competition, and it really produced the best reports on the days each of the candidates entered the race. The political teams at the *WSJ* and *NYT* each won plenty of games during 1987, but when we debate which of two *Post* profiles is the best of the year, we *know* who won the pennant.

The Opinion Pages

The *Post's* opinion pages have developed into the best total package around, despite our view that the unsigned editorials come in third behind the *WSJ* and the *NYT*. Editor Meg Greenfield produces the most *influential* editorials, the Beltway crowd looking to them for guidance and approval, but they don't have the range of the *Journal* or *Times*. Michael Barone is a heavyweight on politics, as is Stephen Rosenfeld on foreign affairs. The substantial debate on strategic arms and domestic and international economics and finance is between the *Times* and the *Journal*, with the *Post* kibitzing by comparison.

From our standpoint, the strength of the *Post* on commentary is its op-ed page and Sunday "Outlook." Both improved marginally in 1987 but both were already the best at what they did a year ago. The range of freelance op-ed features was a bit better at the other pacesetters on a day-to-day basis, but not when you add in Sunday's "Outlook," and the columnists at the *Post* are far and away the strongest. Evans & Novak had another in a long string of great years, Richard Cohen may have slipped a bit from a powerful 1986, but George Will and William Buckley, Jr. more than made up for this, both having their best seasons in several. Other eye magnets were the bylines of William Raspberry, Charles Krauthammer, Stephen Rosenfeld, Mark Shields, and Michael Kinsley. A rich, flavorful buffet of opinion, left and right, no better collection anywhere.

The Sunday "Outlook" section, edited by David Ignatius for the second year, is still a hit-or-miss product, but it improved steadily in 1987. We did two complete, stem-to-stern visits to "Outlook," the first on January 18, the second on August 9. We found the first unsatisfactory, among the most apolitical "Outlooks" we've ever seen, no piece strongly related to policy, with only columnist Mary McGrory and the editorial page worthwhile — except for an excerpt from a speech by a "Chinese Tom Paine" delivered in Shanghai two months earlier. Otherwise, a zero lead by a DC neurologist speculating on whether RR is senile or not. A tract on the savagery of Saudi justice ignored the fact that it is probably the most crime free society on earth. An okay piece on how U.S. lawyers have to protect our competitive ideas, hardly worth P.1 though. Another piece on "Semistics" belonged elsewhere, far elsewhere. A piece on Communist rebels using land mines in Salvador appeared. An appropriate "Time to Panic About Aids" article by Mickey Kaus computed on the cost of a medical holocaust. A back-pager debated whether DC hospitals should do heart transplants.

The second, "Outlook," 8-9, we found extremely interesting and entertaining. Richard Harwood on "Who Sets the Rules for the Press;" a striking piece on the death of a *Post* editorial assistant from AIDS, "A Death in the Family;" Mary McGrory on her new Mercedes; Broder on George Bush watching the Army-Navy game; an "Outposts" column that we found absorbing in spite of ourselves, about illusions ("There is no such thing as a batting slump in baseball"); an extraordinary editorial directed at Speaker Jim Wright, reminding him of his responsibilities in seeing that the Sandinistas do not cheat on their agreement; and a variety of other relevant and appropriate material for Sunday reading.

We read each issue of "Outlook," not always with rigor, but almost always finding a rich treat or two in addition to Mary McGrory, David Broder and George Will. One of the best pieces in "Outlook," was on "Falwell, Bakker and the Fundamentals," 3-29, by Dan Morgan. It treated the 87-year struggle between the two most antagonistic wings of conservative American Protestantism: The Pentecostals and the non-Pentecostals. The article taught us an enormous amount that we needed to know to even begin to understand the crosscurrents of politics and the evangelicals. "Outlook," along with the Sunday "Style" section, helped make the *Post* our Sunday paper of choice in 1987.

The Sunday magazine is abominable, an embarrassment after two years of trying to show something. We have not been happy with the *NYT* magazine either, but it's a wonderful treat compared to the *Post*'s. The Sunday business section of the *Post* has Hobart Rowen's column and more features of interest than in memory. We're expecting giant steps in '88 from the new business editor, Peter Behr, whom we admired when he was the paper's top business reporter. In getting Paul Blustein from the *WSJ*, Behr has a potential economic bigfoot to back up Rowen and to eventually succeed him.

The Foreign Service

The one area where the *Post* clearly slipped was in its foreign coverage, where it had the "single most impressive improvement for the *Post* in 1986," as we noted last year. Both years occurred under Michael Getler, the assistant managing editor for foreign affairs. However, a new foreign editor at the helm for all of 1987, William Drozdiak's first year on the job was coincident with the *Post*'s slide. In the stock market, we would call this a "correction," not nearly a crash, some of the slippage having to do with a single personnel change.

The most noticeable loss was in Paris, with the departure of Michael Dobbs to be Moscow bureau chief, replacing Gary Lee, who had not been up to the task of handling the momentous events of the second Russian Revolution. Dobbs spent his time studying Russian, it seems, and only now is heading to Moscow, with David Remnick as the No. 2 man, Remnick also spending the year with Berlitz. So all of Europe seemed to flatten out at the *Post*, excepting Jackson Diehl in Eastern Europe. In Paris, London, Rome, and Bonn the work is done, but we don't get as much as we'd like on France, England, Italy and Germany, the bureaus stressing NATO, East-West issues. In an ambitious five-part series "Communism: Can It Reform?" that ran April 5-9, only Diehl's contribution from Hungary, 4-6, was really outstanding; the efforts from Moscow, Beijing and Southeast Asia were routine; an overview from Jim Hoagland in Paris, a bit better.

Africa coverage also slipped a notch. Blaine Harden did less important work in sub-Sahara Africa than we thought in 1986, when he won our raves. William Claiborne, covering South Africa, had a hard time not filtering his reports through his ideological model. In Asia, we continued to follow Daniel Southerland in Beijing, his material somewhat better than the *NYT*, but not as rewarding as the various *WSJ* correspondents, Asian edition included. Manila was still solid. Tokyo had a new bureau chief, John Burgess ending a credit-worthy tour, so we will have to await performance there. Generally, the region was covered well. Getler's most successful move was in shifting William Branigan from Manila to Managua. Branigan was the standout Central America reporter of the year. He's backed by Julia Preston in San Salvador, who definitely has an ideological model, but is managing to keep it on the shelf while reporting. The *Post* continues to be weak on the inside economics of South America as a whole. If Dobbs can finally get us the big story out of the USSR in 1988, plus an adjustment here and there on assignments, Getler will be back in a bull market.

Executive Editor: Benjamin Bradlee

Address: 1150 15th Street, NW
          Washington, DC 20071
          (202) 334-6000

Circulation: Sunday 1,100,000
             Weekday 761,142

The Washington Times

The third most discussed deficit in the nation's capital, after the budget and trade deficits, is that of the city's second newspaper, *The Washington Times*, which continues to soak up colossal amounts of red ink. It was a bumpy year for the *Times* and its mercurial editor, Arnaud de Borchgrave, both editorially and financially. The best we can say of its valiant effort to swim upstream against the awesome power of *The Washington Post* is that it treaded water. The Unification Church of the Rev. Sun Myung Moon of South Korea, which founded the paper in 1982, has sunk close to $250 million into it and there is no end in sight to the losses. Annual advertising revenue is barely above $4 million compared to $475 million at the *Post*. The objective of the church was clearly to fill the political void left when the conservative *Washington Star* folded, not to make money, and it seems happy enough with the impact it has had. The owners, we hear, continue to push the editors toward a Sunday edition that would surely generate more stunning losses, but would fill that weekend political void.

It's not that easy, even with deep pockets. Journalistic talent at this highest level can't be produced with a cookie cutter, as even *The Wall Street Journal* learned in recent years when it decided to expand rapidly. For a publication in these big leagues, the available talent pool has already been stretched thin and has to be developed and coaxed out of the minors. It's even harder for the *Times* because of its ownership, prospective talent still having to mull offers from "the Moonie paper."

In this regard, the paper had a serious setback during the year when its editorial page editor, William Cheshire, resigned April 14 with four associates. Cheshire, who had not been getting along with de Borchgrave anyway, insisted that the editor had ordered him to alter an editorial critical of the South Korean government after talking it over with one of the Korean owners. As far as we can tell, the only way the Koreans attempt to influence the editorial product is through their hiring of the top editor, who must only be devotedly anti-communist. It is difficult to imagine Arnaud de Borchgrave acting as a conveyor belt for the Koreans' editorial views, and he calls the episode "the most absurd nonevent I've been a part of in 40 years." But he did read an editorial Cheshire had written. He did subsequently bring it up in discussion with a Korean executive at the paper to question a fact about the situation in Seoul. He did subsequently raise the question of fact with Cheshire, suggesting a recheck. When Cheshire protested this sign, to him, of interference, de Borchgrave did loudly advise him to go ahead and run the original, but it was too late. Cheshire, three editorial writers, and an editorial assistant walked out.

"A Black Eye for 'Moonie Paper,'" *The Boston Sunday Globe* headlined, 5-3, and so it was. It unraveled a good part of the independent image that we sensed had developed in the previous two years. The *1987 MediaGuide* had noted "Washington is forgetting the *Times* is a 'Moonie paper,' and is identifying it with de Borchgrave." No longer. Roger Mudd, a correspondent on the MacNeil-Lehrer News Hour, did a wicked number on the *Times* in a segment of the public television program, magnifying Cheshire's assertions, dismissing de Borchgrave's protestations, and essentially announcing the end of *Times* influence in Washington. It hurt and the memory lingers on.

The Opinion Pages

The silver lining in this cloud is that de Borchgrave, having to replace Cheshire, had to go on a talent hunt while he and the paper were under this cloud. The replacement had to be someone with standing and recognized talent or it would look like he was playing it safe. There were turndowns, but in retrospect he was lucky at that, finally persuading Tony Snow, deputy editor of *The Detroit News* editorial page, to take the job. Snow, the brilliant young protege of Tom Bray, the *News'* editorial page editor, whose mentor in turn was Robert L. Bartley, editor of *The Wall Street Journal* editorial page, seemed exactly the right choice. It was not only because Bray had imparted to him an international perspective similar to the *Journal*'s, but also because Snow had written in a city with a black mayor and a large black community, which has given the *Times'* editorials a dimension they never had with Cheshire.

Almost half the *Times* circulation, about a seventh of the *Post*'s 800,000, is among blacks in the District of Columbia, and the *Times* editors and reporters are rather proud of becoming known a bit as a "black paper." One of the reasons for its success in this area is the honesty of its Metro section and the commentary of its editorial page, in contrast to the patronizing of the *Post*, which shies from criticism of the mayor and City Hall. Managing editor Wesley Pruden has been aggressive in pursuing this opening the *Post* has left him and has been building a solid core of support in the black community. Snow's eagerness to move in this direction, with the confidence and experience he developed in Detroit, is readily apparent in his editorial page and we expect the pressure will tell at the *Post*, which is what competition is all about. Building a metropolitan newspaper from scratch against the *Post* would take a minimum of ten years anyway, but this is the way it has to proceed, probing and exploiting the *Post*'s weaknesses.

While the *Times'* editorials have sharply improved under Snow, fresher, brighter, more often on the margin, the "Commentary" section continues to suffer from the absence of any liberal viewpoints and has begun to seem tired. There are Warren Brookes, Richard Grenier and Suzanne Fields, all sparkling columnists whose work attracts us to the section. After this top tier of conservatives' there are second and third tiers of conservatives, and the chorus, lacking counterpoint, produces an overall monotone. One wonders, are the editors worried that the Koreans would not like to see genuine liberals, foreign-policy liberals on the page? Why the conservative spike?

The News Columns

The *Times*, with a staff of 230, half that of the *Post*, makes up some of the loss with youthful enthusiasm. The atmosphere at the *Times* is remarkably positive, an acceptance by the staff of the burden the paper carries with the Rev. Moon. If they can get enough into the paper that the *Post* is missing, they can force it into circulation increases. There is no sense of paranoia or defeatism, of the kind one finds in financially troubled papers. The paper gets enough big scoops to keep the opposition attentive, plus smaller newsbeats practically every day that provide a sense of competitiveness.

Youthful enthusiasm isn't enough. The national security reporters are strong; the foreign correspondents are competitive when they go one-on-one with the *Post*. These are de Borchgrave's principal areas of interest and he's been able to attract some seasoned journalists. The paper still does not have a political bigfoot that can run with the other major newspapers, and in Washington this is a major drawback, especially approaching the 1988 elections. There are competent professionals who can handle events, but nobody with the depth and experience to keep the *Times* close to the margin and, therefore, relevant in tracking and analyzing the 1988 elections.

In the same way, the *Times* does not have an economic heavyweight who can run with the pacesetting newspapers on global money, banking and finance, another critical area in Washington. Indeed, the best prospect at the *Times* for this assignment, Ralph Z. Hallow, was pulled off this beat two years ago to cover national politics, where he improves bit by bit, but without much chance of developing the skills, perspective and experience that goes with political bigfooting. So in these two areas that are by far the most important on the national desk, the *Times* is not really a factor.

The New Look

On May 17, 1987, the fifth anniversary of the *Times*, the newspaper came off the presses with a new design in six sections. There are mixed views among our readers on the new look. There are complaints it's gaudier, too colorful, a feel that approaches the *USA Today* McPaper. Others like it, especially the six divisions, making material easier to find. Over the years the newspaper has won a fistful of awards for graphics and presentation, but it still needs better editors and at least a few stronger reporters in key areas to keep from simply treading water.

In an impressive three-part series on the newspaper written by David Shaw of the *Los Angeles Times*, April 26-28, Shaw writes that *"Post* executives are probably delighted to have the *Washington Times* around; indeed, they might even be disappointed if, when Moon dies (he's 67), the other Unification Church officials and members whose businesses now subsidize the *Times* decide they no longer wish to provide subsidy. At present, the *Times* is not a serious rival for the *Post*, either commercially or journalistically, but its very presence both defuses criticism that the *Post* is a monopoly newspaper and discourages any other, potentially stronger competitor from entering the market. 'I'd be lying to you if I denied to you that that wasn't true,' concedes Nick Cannistraro, director of advertising for the *Post*."

A more respectful piece on the *Times* appeared in *The Washington Monthly*, 10-87: "Moonie Journalism: At *The Washington Times*, It's Better Than You Might Think," by Tom McNichol, which closes: "...the inroads the *Times* has managed to make in five years, despite an ownership which at every turn diverts attention from the product, can't be overlooked. To enjoy *The Washington Times*, it probably helps to be a conservative; to want the *Times* to stick around, one need only believe that two opinions are better than one."

Editor: Arnaud de Borchgrave

Address: 3600 New York Ave., NE
             Washington, DC 20002
             (202) 636-3000

Circulation: 91,508

MAJOR PERIODICALS

The American Spectator

There is more bumping and grinding of gears this year at the conservative monthly. Editor-in-Chief R. Emmett Tyrrell, now a city slicker, is no longer quite adequate grease for the vehicle. We'd hoped moving from Indiana to Washington would help clear the knocks and pings, but it hasn't yet, not completely. At least it's still on the highway, heading in the right direction.

Part of the time, four issues in '87, we get an excellent magazine, the columns witty and irreverent, the articles biting and timely. In these, Wladyslaw Pleszcyznski persuades us he is up to the job of managing editor. March, May, August and October were a pleasure this year. Otherwise the bag was mixed, the world all too often viewed with anger and irritation, instead of wicked amusement.

A central problem for the *Spectator* is Tyrrell's column, once the central asset. "The Continuing Crisis" columns are wildly erratic in quality; too often irritating and irrelevant, Tyrrell's great wit turned sour. He can still cruise as if out-of-control, an endearing quality, but goes flat trying too hard to outsnot up-and-coming satire mags like *Spy*, which also regularly falls flat, but is not quite as pretentious. We still look for Tyrrell's Menckenesque prose, which we do not disparage, but there is too much disappointment. Evidently we are not alone. *The Washington Post*, the main outlet for his weekly syndicated column, ran fewer than ten in 1987.

In almost every "Continuing Crisis" column, Tyrrell has something funny to say about AIDS, showing irritatingly bad judgment and proving it is not always better to laugh than to cry. And it's not just AIDS. The most tasteless lines of the year came from the November column: "In authentic news of veteran's affairs, Mr. S. Brian Willson, a Vietnam vet, reported his legs missing in action September 2 after he failed to derail an allegedly pro-contra munitions train in Concord, California. Later he was visited at his hospital bedside by Miss Rosario Murillo, the Sandinista Betty Grable and mother of President Daniel Ortega's children, while Jesse Jackson prayed aloud at the spot the limbs were first reported missing."

When Tyrrell does it right, he does it very right, delivering belly laughs: "Mrs. George Shultz gave personal and unimpeachable testimony that her husband, the Secretary of State, does indeed have a tiger (*Panthera tigris*) tattooed on his posterior. The adornment could not be closer to where conservatives and other public-spirited Americans would like to see an imprint of Ronald Reagan's shoe." And so we read on, buoyed by these sporadic displays of humor, hope springing eternal.

Fortunately, the *Spectator* has just about the best list of conservative contributors anywhere: Fred Barnes, Terry Eastland, Richard Brookhiser, Gordon Jackson, Ben Stein, and on into a cast of dozens. There is plenty to chew on in the monthly table of contents. Bright moments this year: P.J. O'Rourke's hilarious review of Jimmy and Rosalynn's book, *Everything to Gain: Making the Most of the Rest of Your Life* (August), calling Carter "a sort of Don Knotts of the undead;" Fred Barnes' shimmering "Washington Rules" (May) on what Don Regan did wrong (he broke the Washington establishment's cardinal rules of play); and David Brock's impressive "Democrat Policy Scandals" (August).

There are also some comfortable regulars, including Washington correspondent Tom Bethell. But we wonder if Bethell might just as well be the Vatican correspondent. He takes us on a delightful visit to Sidney Hook ("A Stroll With Sidney Hook," May), and gives a merry, haunting report on a secular humanists' conference ("Humanists and Heretics," November) in which he describes his reaction to two of the Catholic participants: "One would be inclined to call the Maguires heretics if it weren't so clear they would take it as a compliment." But a regular inside the Beltway column, which Bethell could do, ain't in sight.

Michael Ledeen handles the "Presswatch" column with aplomb, fearing no editor (except maybe his own). He meticulously chronicles the Toshiba-Kongsberg technology sale story revealed by *The Detroit News* ("Exposing the Disaster," July), not hesitating to indict other editors and journalists for an "inability...to recognize the crucial events of our time. It's easier to follow sexual politics or bash the politicians."

Assistant Managing Editor Andrew Ferguson is charming, disarming in his roving (mostly Washington, but sometimes venturing to San Francisco, Chicago) "Spectator" columns. His best line of the year came as a Chicago spectator: "In her [Chicago mayoral candidate Jane Byrne] gayer moments, she still makes Rosalynn Carter look like a drunken dance hall girl" ("Black Roots," April). But Ferguson's hatchet job against *The Washington Times*, "Can Buy Me Love: The Mooning of Conservative Washington," September, can only reflect Tyrrell's own unhappiness at being in the Capital and outshone by Moonshine.

There are other sour notes. Dave Shiflett is mean instead of wicked in "Plagues and the Common Life" (August), on AIDS: "'You remember Sidney Sheldon, Alexis?' 'Oh, yes. He was so very influential. I understand his work helped take out half of Southern California,'" and "AIDS could spay an entire generation of vixens." What's going on here?

The American Spectator remains worthwhile reading, at least a third of the time.

Editor: R. Emmett Tyrrell

Address: 1101 North Highland Street
            Arlington, VA 22210
            (703) 243-3733

Circulation: 37,445

The Atlantic

The Atlantic should congratulate itself for the excellent series on the 1988 presidential elections — "The New Shape of American Politics," 1-87, comprehensive on party shiftings; "A Consumers' Guide to the Democrats," 4-87, limning with both broad strokes and fine detail their aspiring presidential candidates; and one of the year's 10-best political pieces, "The Republicans in '88," 7-87. Authored by political analyst and *National Journal* contributor William Schneider, they were the strongest of *The Atlantic*'s features in 1987.

However, the magazine's editors may be inclined to think it was their economic features that make 1987 a memorable year. After all, two major features both practically predicted a stock market crash: first, Professor John Kenneth Galbraith on "the dynamics of speculation" in his essay "The 1929 Parallel," 1-87; then former U.S. Secretary of Commerce Peter G. Peterson on "the day of reckoning is at hand" in his (pre-Black Monday) October essay "The Morning After." Galbraith lamented the shortness of the public memory, but the professor's memory lapse was worse. He "forgot" the parallel of current protectionist legislation and the Smoot-Hawley bill, Hoover's tax hikes and the Democrats' push for the same, among other things. Peterson's essay was mammoth, incorporating every criticism of Reaganomics imaginable to buttress his "we consume too much, save too little" pleas for pain and sacrifice — as if by taxing consumption, we can assume people produce for some other reason than to consume.

The Atlantic dealt with several major issues in 1987. Noteworthy among them, the dilemmas of reform facing the Soviet leader in "What Gorbachev Is Up Against," a 6-87 cover story by Professor Paul Kennedy that concluded "the problem isn't *in* the system — it *is* the system." Also noteworthy was "The Key to Welfare Reform," by *U.S.News & World Report* associate editor David Whitman. Much lower down the scale, a very academic agenda for ending the cold war between "the superpowers" appeared in "How the Cold War Might End," 11-87, by Ohio University history professor John Lewis Gaddis. But Bruno Bettelheim's "The

Importance of Play," 3-87, was fascinating on the best tool for a child's integration into civilized life.

AIDS received cover story treatment, "Heterosexuals and AIDS," 2-87, by Katie Leishman, whose investigation of the disease's "second stage," i.e., transmission not related to homosexual behavior, was alarmist, ridden with factual and analytical errors. Leishman appeared again with "AIDS and Insects," 9-87, an investigation of arthropod transmission of the disease, asking "Who's to say that a question that often goes disregarded isn't one that holds an answer everyone is looking for?" despite the fact that "laboratory experiments point away from insect transmission."

We noticed a tendency to indulge alarmist features, there being a certain lawfulness in Peter Peterson appearing in the same journal as Katie Leishman.

The "Reports & Comments" column contained more satisfying material this year. Michael Massing's illuminating examination of disinvestment in South Africa, 2-87; Ya'ari Ehud's look into Lebanon, 6-87, for "Syria's most reliable instrument of terror"; and Justine de Lacy's "The Sexy Computer," 7-87, on Minitel, the "world's first electronic directory."

We were alternately pleased and disappointed with Washington editor James Fallows' features from East Asia. On Japan, "The Rice Plot," 1-87, did provide interesting detail and data, and "Playing by Different Rules," 9-87, was brilliant with insights into how Japan's reluctance to import keeps them poor and benefits the U.S. But there was something else going on with his reporting. Fallows presents Japanese culture as nearly inscrutable, threatening even, so different from western culture that it requires anthropological skills for "the outsider...[to] glimpse its soul's longings." In each of the essays on Japan there is his fundamental message: "deep cultural differences between Japan and the United States...explain Japan's success."

Editor: William Whitworth

Address: 8 Arlington Street
            Boston, MA 02116
            (617) 536-9500

Circulation: 450,000

Barron's

Barron's remains in a class by itself as the most important periodical for investors with a bottom-up approach. Lofty political analysis and sweeping industry surveys are left to others. The emphasis here is on providing solid analysis of many markets and plenty of raw statistical material. This assumes individual investors and money managers will pick and choose on their own from the broad weekend buffet of data. The buffet has been so popular for so long that editors Alan Abelson and Robert Bleiberg serve it up confidently, with rarely a change in the menu. Unlike the other business magazines, *Barron's* never seems as if it is looking over its shoulder at the competition, wondering what it has missed. As *Forbes* and *Fortune* raced to disclose the identity of the richest man in the world, *Barron's* was as comfortable as a tortoise in muttering: "We fervently do not want to know who the richest man in the world is, and, plainly, both magazines are heedlessly trespassing on our sacred right not to know."

The key to getting people to look forward to this weekly is a combination of clear writing, excellent Q&A interviews with truly intelligent market watchers (not the ubiquitous Wall Street hacks), Randall W. Forsyth's "Current Yield" column on the capital markets, and Abelson's front-page column, "Up and Down Wall Street." Floyd Norris' "The Trader" column is also one of the most popular features in the paper. The Q&A interviews, usually done by Kathryn M. Welling or Maggie Mahar, were important staples this year in watching the bull market unfold.

It was Welling who led off the year with "3600 on the Dow?" 5-5, a Q&A with Elliott Wave guru Bob Prechter: "I think this sideways consolidation between 1700 and 2000 of the past eight months has been, essentially, the second great correction separating three bull market waves — upward moves. The third and last wave is ahead of us. And in terms of Dow points, will turn out to be the most spectacular of all. That's the one I expect to carry us up into that 3600-plus area." Hmmm. Welling also did "How High Can This Bull Market Go?" 4-6, with Prechter still bullish, but Marty Zweig fretting: "When you get a market that's gone on for this long, and the P/Es have gotten up this high and everybody's speculating, it's hard to end it without a real blowoff, when everybody gets optimistic. So, as bad as my sentiment numbers are, they're probably going to get worse before this thing is over."

The cover story, "This Furry Creature Is A Mirage (It Says Here)," 9-7, pictures a bear sipping a drink under a beach umbrella. Maggie Mahar interviews four experts who expect a "Correction But No Crash," although Prechter remains convinced that the fifth wave will peak between 3600 and 3700: "I think we'll see a top before 1988." Hmmm. But there really is no attempt to present a *Barron's* crystal ball, and when the Crash hits, it's business as usual, a new round of Q&As. "Three Bulls and a Bear," 11-16, with interviews by Peter C. Du Bois, rounds up four panelists to survey the global stock market, only one of whom got out in time, the "other three panelists suffered big losses in their portfolios, yet still insist that the case for investing abroad is intact."

It's all pretty dry, but just the stuff institutional investors like to chew on. Abelson's column provides relief, reviewing the week's top stories with a dry wit and self-deprecating humor that has no bitter edge. A nervous pessimist as the bull market roared in 1987, he referred to himself as having membership in the "Royal Order of Worrywarts." After the Crash, he avoided an "I told you so," but in his 11-16 column, in observing the continuing optimism of the bulls drawing parallels between the Crash and the 1962 market nosedive, he proposes that "in 1962, it was morning in America. And now it's mourning in America." Among his listed New Year's resolutions 1-5 were "Never believe anything that comes out of Washington," "never ask Bernard Goetz for $5" and a prescient line that hurt to remember on Black Monday: "Never forget that portfolio insurance takes the risk out of equities for institutions or that junk bonds are no more hazardous than government obligations or that typhoid is not a communicable disease." The column, of course, is not all fun and pun. Abelson devotes the hind end of it to specific stocks, usually those being hyped by management, and Wall Streeters scan this with some care as there is frequently a reaction on Monday mourn.

Robert Bleiberg's full page editorial comments still seem of daunting length, as they have for decades, but those involved in the government or Wall Street debates he is targeting get their money's worth. His elephant memory and elephant files are mined weekly for quotes, forecasts and arguments made long ago by those he is skewering at the moment. One need not agree with him to admire his smoldering passion for argumentation, backed by this documented authoritativeness. We especially liked "Greenspan's Brief Honeymoon," 8-24, that raged at the new Fed chairman's past gaffes and confusion about what he really knows about the job. "If all this spells peace and quiet for Volcker's successor, we'd hate to see turmoil."

The small editorial staff produces three or four lengthy business features each week, the distaffers showing up most often on our scope. Diana Henriques produced competent, well-tailored business stories almost week after week. Shirley Hobbs Scheibla has been a mainstay in the Washington office for decades and continues to do careful pieces on regulatory and bureaucratic snafus, but is also up to handling regional business pieces and editorial commentary. Maggie Mahar had one of the best of the year with her cover story on the college teachers' pension fund, "Campus Rebellion: Professors Are Up in Arms," 8-17. Freelancers are used with frequency, Benjamin Stein being among the best who writes regularly for the weekly from Los Angeles, mainly about the movie business.

72

Like an old shoe, *Barron's* doesn't seem to get better year after year, just more comfortable. It has been good enough as long as we can remember, in a weekend class by itself.

Editor: Alan Abelson

Address: 200 Liberty Street
           New York, N.Y. 10281
           (212) 416-2000

Circulation: 295,113

BusinessWeek

We wrote last year that "there is no publication in American journalism that improved as much in 1986." In 1987, however, *BusinessWeek* slipped back, as it has from time to time, becoming once again a fast-food magazine. Readers could still get a good overview of what had gone on in the business world during the previous week, but would have to look elsewhere to make sense of the bigger trends. The magazine's weekly schedule, compared with biweekly for *Forbes* and *Fortune*, is both its greatest competitive strength and a possible source of weakness. There is a tendency to overreact to last week's news, and perhaps to tolerate some mediocre material simply to fill pages.

BusinessWeek's coverage of the ups and downs of the stock market illustrates a chronic tendency to exaggerate, and to extend the latest trends into the future. After the Dow Jones stock index dipped to 2254 in late April, *BusinessWeek*'s 5-11 issue was full of decidedly premature stories about the end of the bull market and imminent recession. Howard Gleckman and Blanca Riemer wrote that "the economy seems poised either to slide into recession or undergo a new round of inflation." Growth of real output instead averaged 3.6 percent for the first three quarters, inflation moderated, and the stock market surged another 500 points. *BusinessWeek* quickly changed its tune. "The Good Times Roll On," said the 7-6 issue; "on tap for the rest of 1987: lower inflation, stable interest rates — and plenty of money-making opportunities." One day before stock prices began to fall, Jeffrey Laderman was explaining "Why The Bull Is Such A Long-Distance Runner," 8-24, hinting that a 3000 Dow was around the corner. After the October 19 crash, *BusinessWeek* did another belated about face, with the hysterical cover story "Wake Up America," 11-16, advocating belt-tightening austerity and "Say Hello to the Lean Years." The magazine that had encouraged investors to sell stocks in May before they rose, and to buy in late August before they fell, now screamed that it knew all along that the real problem was too much prosperity. Cover stories alternated between such blatant sensationalism and fabricated, rather boring stories. Did anyone really want to read nine pages on "No Smoking Sweeps America," 7-27? Potentially interesting cover themes, such as "Quality," 6-8, didn't really break new ground.

BusinessWeek fared much better on stories about government officials, such as the insiders' insights in Lee Walczak's "Howard Baker's Long Hot Summer," 8-3, and Blanca Riemer's "What's in Store At The Fed," 6-15 ("Greenspan's appointment marks the triumph of the GOP's old guard"). Coverage of foreign economies, typically a weak spot in the U.S. press, was also better than usual, with Edith Terry reporting on the Canadian boom, 7-27, and one of the best cover stories of the year on "Japan: Remaking A Nation," 7-13, where we learned that the "hollow corporation" (manufacturing overseas) is really a Japanese problem. For those who like to read about the big wheeler-dealers, *BusinessWeek* offered typically competent stories about Bill Bricker of Diamond Shamrock, 2-16; Bill Gates of Microsoft, 4-13; Donald Trump, 7-20; and Carlo De Bendetti of Olivetti, 8-24. Reporter Anthony Bianco, whom we identified as extraordinarily talented in such people-oriented stories, scored only one big hit this year with "The Decline of The Superstar" on Wall Street, 8-17.

Our feeling about *BusinessWeek* this year was that nobody seemed to be in charge. Editor Bill Wolman was making lots of TV appearances, calling for expansionary policies at times his magazine was preaching austerity, or urging easy money after *BusinessWeek* had spent most of the year worrying about inflation. Many articles on economic policy seemed to be little more than raw opinion, a series of editorials misplaced in the news section. Glaring statistical errors were common, suggesting nobody is checking. Byline inflation ran amok. It took four people to write one page on "Why Americans Aren't Likely to Start Buying American," 11-23, and nearly all of the examples weren't imports at all, but Japanese products made in America, like Honda, Sony and Mitsubishi.

The regular features continue to demand at least a quick look, such as the pages of business and statistical statistics, curiously placed at opposite ends of the magazine. The "Economic Diary" by Gene Koretz has become a rather undiscriminating collection of what anyone says about the economy, the "Outlook" by William Franklin and James Cooper was relatively unimaginative and repetitive this year (how many times can we hear that it all depends on the consumer?). On balance, this was a distinctly disappointing year for *BusinessWeek* readers.

Editor-in-Chief: Stephen Shepard

Address: 1221 Avenue of the Americas
             New York, N.Y. 10020
             (212) 512-2000

Circulation: 852,367 (national)
             97,293 (international)

The Christian Science Monitor

In our earlier *MediaGuides* we did not give a thorough review to the *Monitor*, only because of limited resources. We've always recognized out of the corner of our eye that even though it is published in Boston, and usually seems an afterthought in Washington and New York, it is genuinely a national newspaper with an international flavor. Seeing it regularly during the year, we found it to be solid and dependable, a '63 Plymouth made of cast metal in a world of fiberglass hotrods. The *Monitor* stresses reliability, which has a cost in terms of both depth and flavor. The *Monitor* correspondents as a class seem bland, giving us the facts, ma'am, and avoiding analytical threads. A pinch of salt often seems to be the only spice permitted in the reports. This is its niche, though, and after we accepted this seemingly conscious formula we were pleased, if not excited, to see the slender tabloid arrive.

The *Monitor*'s main strength is its foreign coverage. Brave Carnegie fellow Robin Wright went to Teheran for some innovative and interesting stories that cut against the tone of the rest of the paper, as did most of their Persian Gulf coverage, courtesy of Baharain-based Warren Richey. We cite Ned Temko of the Johannesburg bureau this year as a four-star reporter. He will be missed in '88, leaving the *Monitor* in late '87 for British television. *Glasnost*, Paul Quinn-Judge's turf, was competently handled and a parallel issue, arms control, was mostly covered by veteran Elizabeth Pond out of Bonn, who generally produced clear pieces. William Echikson's reports from Paris were among the best we saw during the year, although he was stretched thin, running around Eastern and Central Europe where he also did fine reporting.

Julian Baum shifted from China to London, his material losing the bite we'd seen in '86, perhaps because of logistical distractions. His reporting on Deng's shifting back and forth on reforms seemed uncertain. The new China couple, Ann and James Tyson, have been getting on top of political events, but don't yet have a sure feel for the dynamic economic front. South America coverage sufficed for the *Monitor*'s general audience, picture postcards that focus on economic and political *conditions*, largely leaving matters of policy to the major newspapers. Carla Germani sent some impressive dispatches from Haiti, before the late year turmoil, that reminded us about how impoverished this backyard neighbor really is. The Philippine reporting, primarily done by Clayton Jones, was competitive. Also worth noting is Kristin Helmore and Sara Terry's heartrending series "Children in Darkness," July, a broad look at the use of child labor worldwide, both legal and illegal, that is a 10-best selection this year.

The *Monitor* has only a handful of foreign bureaus, but makes effective use of stringers around the world. Tyler Bridges, who also appears in the *Financial Times* and *Wall Street Journal*, had an off-the-beaten-path tack in "Bolivia Tries To Rebound," 8-6, on the country's attempts to revitalize the economy including such statistics as half its $1.2 billion export income is generated from cocaine, certainly nothing to sneeze at. From Brazil, Mac Margolis had two solid reports: "Brazil's New Finance Minister Inherits An Economy On The Brink," 4-30, on Finance Minister Pereira and the economic mess he inherited; and "Brazil's Leader Shaken By Economic And Political Crises," 5-13, tightly packed, with the urgency of Sarney's woes accurately conveyed. Other stringers, like Vyvyan Tenorio, appear regularly in the *Monitor*, giving us a broader sense of the places they cover. Stringer Hal Langfur had two innovative pieces on Brazil: "Tension Rises in Brazil Over Economic Woes," 8-14, where treacherous undercurrents in the slums are being ignored by the government's economic planners; and "Weak Support for Key Strike that May Spell Trouble for Brazil Labor," 8-21, detailing a poorly-honored strike, boding ill for unionization.

The *Monitor* is lighter on Washington, except in areas of foreign affairs and policy. National coverage is pretty routine. John Dillin, the national political correspondent, had his hands full with the intricacies of the presidential campaign and we were rarely impressed with his profiles or analytical pieces, and at times seemed to stretch material to score newsbeats. He had his moments, though, one on the inconvenience of the farmbelt recovery, "Upturn in the Heartland Undercuts Democrats Strategy for '88," 8-27. Charlotte Saikowski, Washington bureau chief, is competent, but unexciting and a bit of a peacenik, which was especially evident in her coverage of the Washington end of arms control. Godfrey Sperling, Jr., the senior Washington columnist, provided responsible, at times inventive, commentary on the flow of news through the capital. The coverage of the Iran-Contra hearings on the whole was pedestrian. The facts, ma'am.

The mushy op-ed pages really should be spiced. The editors seem much too concerned with being nice to everybody, as if their largely Christian Scientist readership is unable to handle any but the lowest common denominator. The pages are also annoyingly confusing, spread out over different columns over different pages over different columnists over different days. Melvin Maddocks appears Wednesday and Friday on the "Ideas" page and John Hughes appears on the "Opinion" page, while Joseph Harsch's "Pattern of Diplomacy" columns appear on the "International" pages — but they do have a regular paddock of sturdy columnists. In addition to the above, we read editor in chief Earl W. Foell and Rushworth M. Kidder. They span a wide scope of topics, with Kidder and Maddocks doing lighter, more social commentary, and Foell, Hughes and Harsch handling politics, but the columns could be much stronger. The best of them, John Hughes, a Pulitzer winner, can usually keep his views out of the blender. On the business page, where coverage is necessarily light, idiosyncratic, we read the occasional columns by David R. Francis who has definite views on matters economic.

The *Monitor* is the only newspaper that can reach its audience on the day of publication through the U.S. mails, which makes it a valuable supplement to those population pockets around the U.S. that are confined to a parochial press. Stronger, better organized opinion pages and sharper editorials would make the newspaper more attractive to readers beyond the church, and the Christian Scientists we've known over the years seem no less entertained by wit and controversy than anyone else.

Editor in Chief: Earl W. Foell

Address: 1 Norway Street
             Boston, MA 02115
             (617) 450-2000

Circulation: 165,000 Daily
             40,000 Weekly and Worldwide

Commentary

Once a month, without fail, we are treated to at least one, sometimes two, three or more, "must-read" articles here — the kind of serious reading for which you have to make available a chunk of uninterrupted time. We noticed that with other monthlies we could occasionally put off reading them, because when we did catch up, we learned we often hadn't missed anything critical. Not so with *Commentary*. On the cutting edge of policy debate in a host of areas, it frequently produces contenders for definitive treatment of a subject.

Maintaining critical attention on Central America in 1987, the editors opened the year with a powerful presentation. "Another 'Low Dishonest Decade' on the Left," 1-87, by ex-New leftists (and favorite targets of leftist venom) Peter Collier and David Horowitz, laid bare the post-Vietnam Left's ability to effectively delude people about its collusion with totalitarianism, particularly successful with its "techniques of dissimulation and disinformation" on the Sandinistas. The articles "How 'La Prensa' Was Silenced," 1-87, by its former editor Jaime Chamorro, and "Can the Sandinistas Be Stopped?" 7-87, by *Time*'s former South American bureau chief George Russell, plus the "Observations" column from Mark Falcoff, "Why Europeans Support the Sandinistas," 8-87, also were required readings on the issue.

Commentary, which had the best single article anywhere last year on the Strategic Defense Initiative ("How SDI Is Being Undone from Within," 5-86), again presented the best intervention into the issue, the same author, Angelo Codevilla, examining "How Eminent Physicists Have Lent Their Name to a Politicized Report on Strategic Defense," 9-27. "Why the Soviets Want an Arms-Control Agreement And Why They Want It Now," 2-87, by Eugene V. Rostow, Donald Kagan's "World War I, World War II, and World War III," 3-87, were excellent contributions on strategic debate. From another angle, "The Latest Myths About the Soviet Union," 5-87, by Nick Eberstadt, was of merit and had to be read, though we weren't fully persuaded by the analysis.

Outstanding lead articles, "The Guns of Watergate," 4-87 by Leonard Garment and "Crime, the Constitution & the Iran-Contra Affair," 10-87 by *WSJ* assistant editorial page editor L. Gordon Crovitz, were superior analytics, the historical bakground and tight presentation superbly done. And out of the massive coverage nationally on AIDS, Michael Fumento's "AIDS: Are Heterosexuals at Risk?" 11-87, attracted our attention.

Some of the best material anywhere on the cultural-intellectual front appears in *Commentary*. Ruth Wisse's "The New York (Jewish) Intellectuals," 11-87, Anne Roche Muggeridge's "Reclaiming the Catholic Heritage," 9-87, and "The Importance of Sidney Hook," 8-87, by *The New Criterion* eitor Hilton Kramer, were notable, provocative exegeses. Regular contributors Fernanda Eberstadt, Carol Iannone, and Terry Teachout made strong impressions with the depth of their essays in 1987, and a newcomer, James Nuechterlein has us hoping he'll be a regular, his "The Feminization of the American Left," 9-87, richly insightful.

Commentary's "Books in Review" section is always rigorous, the magazine able to call upon a host of reviewers who know their subject backward and forward, but it is its "Letters to the Editor" that's most revealing. The exchanges taking place there are as crucial as the featured articles presented. Immediately apparent are the high standards of its readership, an audience that demands rigorous analysis and presentation, which sustains the magazine's quality.

Advancing strongly in 1987, *Commentary* simply lapped the field among the monthlies, crossing the finish line long before others had even reached the starting gate. Editor Norman Podhoretz and staff earn hearty commendation for putting together such a powerful production month after month.

Editor: Norman Podhoretz

Address: 165 East 56th Street
              New York, N.Y. 10022
              (212) 751-4000

Circulation: 47,800

Defense News

If, at the outset of 1986, anyone at the Times Journal Company placed a wager on the success of yet another defense magazine/newsletter, he would have gotten some fairly long odds. First, the defense "community" is made up of people who don't have time to read (officials), or are only interested in parochial concerns (officials, contractors), or are overloaded with specialized journals, magazines, and newsletters (officials, contractors, scholars). Second, the editorial challenges facing any defense publication are formidable, including finding a niche, maintaining independence from the "Military-Industrial Complex," and presenting readable product in a field notorious for incomprehensible jargon. Third, there is the minor point of covering astronomical production costs and turning a profit.

Well, at the close of 1987, that bet appears to be a shrewd one, as *Defense News*, the Times Journal Co.'s weekly monitor of the defense and foreign policy firmament, has surpassed the expectations of its audience and caused some heartburn at some erstwhile competitors. *Defense News* has been a commercial success due to its comprehensive coverage of government regulations, legislative moves, and industry happenings that make it vital reading (and hence, vital advertising space) for anyone in the defense business. More importantly, the weekly is an editorial winner, both in terms of immediate events and broader perspectives. It has a wider appeal than service-oriented publications (*Army, Air Force*) or the authoritative, but highly technical, *Aviation Week*, and is far more mainstream than the breezy though eccentric *Armed Forces Journal*. *Defense News* is directly targeted at people who work in defense-related fields in some capacity, but its articles, editorials, and interviews are accessible to an intelligent lay reader. Refreshingly, it has few axes to grind, and its editorials are supportive of a strong defense without being shills for the Pentagon or the defense industry.

The core of the tabloid-style newspaper is a solid stable of talented and overworked reporters (plus overseas stringers), whose overlapping beats include anything under the defense sun: congressional hearings, contract awards, weapons test results, hirings and firings, technological breakthroughs and mishaps. SDI and technological security were the two big stories of '87. The average story is about the size of a *Washington Post* op-ed piece, presented in an attractive layout which utilized 4-color graphics and smaller news tidbits. Each issue covers breaking stories, e.g., McDonnell Douglas, 6-8, beating out Lockheed for an SDI contract, international news "Moscow Wants Pact by Next Fall," 3-9, and broader themes such as the state of NATO or tech transfer (Toshiba story got big play in summer).

Another staple is the "one-on-one" interviews, which are succinct summaries of views by U.S. officials Gen. Abrahamson of SDIO, arms control experts Jonathan Dean of the Arms Control Association, congressman Les Aspin, and allied and foreign defense bigwig UK Defense Minister George Younger. The mix of personality stories, e.g., "Kloske Plucks Another Pentagon Plum — Zakheim's Job," 4-6, with numbers crunching pieces is a nice blend, and the weekly roundup of new jobs filled and conference/convention schedules are comparable to the *National Journal*'s update on people and events. Every few weeks, a "Special Report" section covers some defense topic in depth, such as "Trainers & Simulators," 8-3, or an excellent 11-16 report on "Light Armor." We would like to have seen more on Central America, U.S. military forces there, a region given surprisingly little coverage; more, too, on the Afghan War.

Defense News carries a "Commentary" section, with one or two editorials, a letters column, and a small group of semi-regular op-ed contributors. The editorials are slightly right of center, delivered with workmanlike efficiency — if the editorial writers were a service, they would be more Army than Air Force. The editorials came down hard on Japan and Toshiba for breach in technological security, but upheld allied collaboration in defense programs, 6-15, Although supportive of some weapons systems, 11-9, boost for the MILAN II anti-tank weapon, the editors are not mindless boosters, "Use Good Judgment in Handling Covert Action," 1-26, scoring interservice rivalry and promoting reform measures resisted by the Pentagon. Of the regular op-ed writers, Robert Hunter CSIS and formerly of the Carter NSC is the worst, with a Milquetoast style to go along with his raging moderation in substance. Much better is Harry Summers, whose syndicated column runs occasionally, and guest writers such as strategy maven Colin Gray. It's still difficult to imagine busy assistant secretaries of defense, or corporate v.p.'s reading it cover to cover each week, but the layout is such that one can quickly turn to segments of interest — it can even be read from back-to-front, sports-page style, since some of the best interview pieces are located in the rear. In all, *Defense News*, in less than two years, has become a must-read for defense pros that is an easy-to-read for interested amateurs.

Editor: Richard C. Barnard

Address: 6883 Commercial Drive
             Springfield, VA 22159-0400
             (703) 642-7300

Circulation: Paid   9,729
             Qualified 9,231

The Economist

London's unique weekly is much more than the name implies. The emphasis is on business and economics, but the editorial objective is nothing less than a comprehensive report on the world political economy. There is a significant section on Books and Arts, and another on Science and Technology. What other non-technical journal would offer a rigorous "Schools Brief," 6-20, explaining artificial intelligence to laymen? Periodic, fact-filled surveys cover politics and culture, as well as economics in Mexico, 9-5, Brazil, 4-25, or even the entire world economy, 9-26. In the entire English-language press, only the *Financial Times* comes close to keeping track of the whole world.

A distinguishing feature of *The Economist* is its editorial arrogance. Like a Oxford-educated nanny, it always knows exactly what's best for everyone and ladles out its bitter medicine with spoonfuls of sugar. There is rarely a byline in the magazine, which is written with a singular tone of voice, sassy, know-it-all, off-putting to many. The editorials begin the magazine, or "newspaper," as it calls itself, and these are the most valuable opinion pages we read coming out of Europe — pretending as they do, to speak for all of Europe whether anyone likes it or not. Because of the haughtiness of tone, it takes an American some years of reading these pages to realize they ain't as smart as they always seem to be.

The Economist likes nothing more than to criticize the economic policies of other countries, often with a touch of wry British wit. The criticism is often warranted, particularly the repeated well-argued attacks on the dangers of American protectionism and German deflation, but the exercise can seem rather arrogant to the non-British reader. From all the harping about U.S.

budget and trade deficits, a reader would never guess that Britain's general budget deficits have been at least as high as America's in the late 1980s. *The Economist*'s lofty perspective on economic policy the world over is pure, undiluted Keynesian demand-management. There has not been a single interesting new idea on economic growth for the Third World in these pages in decades, and 1987 was no exception.

Criticism of the U.S. is as inconsistent as it is persistent. The inconsistencies probably reflect the annoying absence of bylines, so different editors can air different complaints without concern about consistency with each other, or about accountability when they are wrong. In the 9-12 issue, "America has been living beyond its means," but is supposedly also experiencing (without evidence) a "faltering growth in the standard of living." That is, Americans live too well and too poorly. A few pages later, in the same issue, "consumer spending has slowed sharply," yet the U.S. somehow needs "a tax increase...to check domestic overspending." Americans spend too much and too little? By 11-14, however, there was some sensible irony about "waiting for American investors' confidence to be restored by having to pay heavier taxes." A scary monster on the cover warns of "The Return of Inflation," 8-1, and inside the "figures point to an inflationary boom." By 10-31, though, "worries about higher inflation now look silly," and "the immediate task is a Keynesian one: to support demand."

The best criticism of foreign economies is not in the editorial analyses, but in the descriptive surveys, where theory is not always allowed to get in the way of reality. The 9-12 survey on the Netherlands provided an excellent case study on how to impoverish a country. By putting theory aside, we discover no "twin deficits" in the Netherlands, which routinely runs truly massive budget deficits along with trade *surpluses*. "This meant," *The Economist* explains, "that Dutch investors were transferring resources to the rest of the world because they felt they could get a better return there." The unintended lesson is that such creditor countries are not to be envied. They are cutting their own future output by exporting their capital to other countries, such as the U.S. and U.K. Why are investment opportunities so dim in Holland? Apparently, because work incentives are dismal, raising labor costs and cutting worker morale: "Many Dutch businessmen suspect that the lack of incentive because of high taxes has turned many bright youngsters off higher education, because they do better bumming around on welfare."

Despite the disarray of criticism levied at the U.S. and other economies, *The Economist* nonetheless does have a viewpoint, or ideology. Two American economists, Martin Feldstein of Harvard and David Hale of Kemper Financial, appear to be the leading gurus here, as they are at the *Financial Times*. Dissent is minimal. Feldstein is perhaps best known for his assertion in 1983-84 that the U.S. budget deficit made the dollar go up. "Mr. Feldstein, an economist of the highest academic standing, was obviously right," claims *The Economist*, 9-26. When the dollar went down, that too was attributed to the budget deficit: "Every day that passes without some credible action to reduce America's budget deficit adds to the pressure on the dollar," 11-7.

We continue to read the "newspaper" regularly, but not because it has anything useful to tell us about why markets or currencies rise or fall, or why economies fail or succeed. There is a wealth of world news in *The Economist*, but surprisingly little coherent economics.

Editor: Rupert Pennant-Rea

Address: 25 St. James's Street
                  London, SW1A 1HG
                  England
                  (212) 541-5730

Circulation: 124,717 North America
                  316,479 Worldwide

Financial Times

A remarkable paper, without equal in some respects, the *Financial Times* is surely the best single source of daily business and financial news about the entire world, excepting the United States. This exception, of course, makes all the difference. The *FT* surveys the world from London, which used to be the loftiest vantage point, but now has to strain to compete with *The Wall Street Journal* and *The New York Times* from its lower perch. Having been at the center of the world economy for two centuries gives London some remaining advantages, those being networks and experience. We doubt the New York newspapers will be able to assemble the experienced manpower to match the *FT* in covering global geopolitics within the next decade, although it surely will happen eventually.

There is a half page almost daily devoted to "American" news, but the U.S. shares space here with the rest of North America and all of Latin America. The New York and Washington bureaus are capable but too small to do much more than rewrite the U.S. papers and turn out occasional essays for the editorial page. What little of this space granted to the U.S. is conventional, often devoted to ritualistic scolding about budget deficits, which are somehow more objectionable than the larger deficits of Her Majesty's government. In short, the *Financial Times* is where the astute reader turns for wisdom about other countries, and a briefing about the United States.

FT's "Survey," a several-page special section that provides a comprehensive examination of individual countries or issues, appears frequently. Often it's just the kind of item to pull out and file for quick reference. The seven-page "Privatisation" survey, 9-16, for example, was an excellent look at the progress and setbacks of that development with a global perspective.

The paper did take a major loss, at least short term, during the year. The Tokyo bureau had been the jewel in the crown, as far as we were concerned, with bureau chief Jurek Martin and his four-star business/economic writer Carla Rapoport. Martin returned to London as foreign editor at the start of the year, a splendid long-term move for the *FT* as he is one of the best global thinkers and writers we've seen over the years, his credentials gilt-edged. With Japan being a central source of financial, economic and political news during the year, his loss was painful for the short-term, and Rapoport's output and contribution was considerably off her glittering '86.

The rest of the foreign service, though, enjoyed offsetting improvements. Patrick Cockburn in Moscow had a wonderful year, almost single-handedly keeping up with, plus supplementing, the work of the *NYT* bureau. Similarly, we came to rely on David Marsh in Bonn for the very best reporting out of West Germany, which was only a step behind Japan during the year at center stage. David Housego left the Paris bureau in the spring, where he'd been one of our favorites, but Paul Betts, who stayed on, made us forget Housego's loss. The Rome bureau is better than any other, actually covering the Italian economy and political scene. Leslie Colitt is just fine in Eastern Europe, as is Tony Walker in Egypt. Anthony Robinson produced another fine portfolio out of South Africa.

The *FT*'s Asian coverage not only weakened in Japan, but also in China, where Robert Thomson seemed early on to go along with the pack in deciding the reforms had run into a ditch, and thereafter seemed disoriented, reporting after the fact. We preferred the *NYT* to Chris Sherwell in Southeast Asia. In the New World, the *FT* remains of secondary importance to us, not only in North America, but also throughout Mexico, Central and South America.

The editorial pages were palpably superior to those of the previous year. The most important change was the naming of Edward Mortimer as foreign affairs columnist, a great improvement over the commentary of Ian Davidson, who was dispatched to the Paris bureau. Mortimer writes with a quiet, penetrating authority on the great subjects of the epoch and the moment. His "The Parts That Glasnost Fail to Reach," 9-22, was one of the ten best commentary pieces of the year. On economic and financial comment and opinion, we were attracted again and again to the writings of John Plender and Michael Prowse, pushing analytics of global debt, taxation or capital flows without a sense of rigid dogma in their framework, a rare trait in older British journalists of the Keynesian era. Similarly, the dean of British financial journalists and commentators, Samuel Brittan, finally threw off the baggage of monetarist dogma that had slowed him down through the 1980s and, thus liberated, produced some of the most adventurous writing on economics that we saw in any newspaper.

Editor: Geoffrey Owen

Address: Bracken House
            10 Cannon Street
            London
            EC4P 4BY
            England
            011-441-248-8000

Circulation: International 316,967

Forbes

Forbes continues to be one of the most informative, absorbing and integrated publications on our shelf, the very best business periodical for investors. The magazine distinguishes itself by going far beyond presenting isolated stories to its readership. Consistently, *Forbes* reveals the philosophical underpinnings of successful business in its people and idea-centered pieces. On a micro-scale, *Forbes* can analyze an event, the progress or failure of a company, or a trend in a particular market, inside out. The aggregate effect on a macro-level is to powerfully convey the energy of the American and world markets — something no other business publication has achieved at such a high level this year.

Editor James W. Michaels, one of the best in the business, is said to be a hard taskmaster, and the constant churning on the masthead suggests a lively effort and reward system. But the key to the kind of boldness we continue to see in *Forbes* is Michaels' courage. He has the fortitude to back his reporters by running with material no other publication would touch, as long as he's decided the material is solid, that all the questions have been asked, all the rigorous analysis completed. A perfect example of this, "Is Leslie Wexner Riding For a Fall," 4-6, by Steve Weiner, an audacious cover story that for all practical purposes predicts, correctly, the decline of the high-flying giant retailing chain, The Limited, Inc. Again and again we see journalists given their head at *Forbes*, digging out material and having it displayed where other publications would be wringing their hands, larding in qualifications, and shoving risky stuff to the back of the book if at all. Weiner, now a high-flyer himself at the magazine, can't relax, because if he does and gets sloppy, he'll be riding for a fall with Michaels doing the pushing.

Then again we have the case of Ashby Bladen, the doomsday columnist who for seven years, through one of the greatest bull markets in history, predicted collapse in almost every issue. Michaels patience finally gave out in '87 and Bladen was furloughed, but told he could come back when disaster struck. In "Johnny One-Note Sings Again," 11-16, Bladen is back, telling this I-told-you-so story and noting that Michaels had called him back the day after the Crash.

Another journalist pushed out the door by Michaels, 7-22, was longtime popular business psychology columnist Srully Blotnick. This, after the *New York Daily News* published a story, 7-19, saying Blotnick "built his career on sand." His doctorate came from an unaccredited correspondence school, and his claim to have researched the careers of 5,000 Americans over a span of many years was largely untrue. Blotnick called the allegations "clearly unfounded," but his column was dropped after he refused to provide the magazine with the names of the people he has been interviewing. Dean Rotbart, editor of a newsletter, *The Journalist & Financial Reporting*, criticized *Forbes* for not divulging details of the episode. Since there were no allegations of a public trust being violated, as in the R. Foster Winans "Heard on the Street" column at the *WSJ* (which Rotbart, incidentally, wrote after Winans was fired), *Forbes* to us seemed justified in maintaining its silence.

The revolving door aside, the magazine had a spectacular year by comparison with *BusinessWeek*, which, in the '87 guide we had "coming on with a rush." *Forbes'* confidence in its own world view made the difference, we thought, as *BW* was blown by the winds, after the Crash showing every sign of Ashby Bladenism, while *Forbes*, keeping its cool, was giving us "Post-Crash Investment Strategies," its "Picking Up the Pieces" cover of 11-16. Even at the outset of the year, though, *Forbes* was breaking away from its competitors, its "39th Annual Report on American Industry," 1-12, a far better overview of many more industries than *BW* provided, the writing tighter, better numbers on profitability and growth. One of our new *Forbes* readers reported at year's end: "One has the growing impression that one knows more of what is happening in business around the world, and that, perhaps even more importantly, it all fits, it all makes sense in a larger context, and you begin to absorb a sense of why things are going the way they are. Events become more predictable. There's a continuity between issues that enables you to have insights into trends and identify with observations. This seems attributable to superior minds, doing superior reporting, guided by superior management."

It's not all roses, though. Last year we noted the relative weakness of *Forbes'* cover stories and we thought there was not much improvement this year. There were great ones, including Steve Weiner's. The marvelous 70th Anniversary issue, 7-13, led with "Creative Destruction," by William Baldwin, a reprise on Schumpeter. But then came the lists: The original "richest people in America," the *Forbes* "400" issue, 10-26, has spawned "The 797 Most Powerful Men and the Three Most Powerful Women in Corporate America," 6-15; "Japan's Billionaires," 7-27; "America's Richest Entertainers," 9-21; and finally, "The Richest Man in the World and 95 Also-Rans," 10-5. Okay, okay. Then there was "The McKinsey Mystique," 10-19, superficial and flattering on the arrogant, overpriced management consultants. And while we've liked Peter Brimelow, his "Are We Spending Too Much For Education?" 12-29-86, and "Judicial Imperialism," 6-1, read like right-wing screeds, over the line into editorial country.

The Forbes' themselves have a certain *noblesse oblige* about them that could leave a bad taste in some mouths, and there are still sporadic comments from readers about an elitist tone slipping into the editorial content. On the whole, their influence on the publication exemplifies the best attributes of an American aristocracy — superbly informed, enormously well-traveled, witty, confident, compassionate, bold and brave. The magazine is, in a sense, an embodiment of the Forbes dynasty itself. There seems little chance the dynasty will weaken in this generation. Malcolm Forbes, Jr., 40, has none of the flair of his motorcycling father, but he is an exemplary businessman and journalist who has somehow maintained the outlook of an entrepreneur. His regular column, "Facts and Comment II," is always our first reading, consistently simple, well-shaped observations on global business, politics and finance that go to the margin. We complained in the '87 *Guide* that he was slipping, spending more time running around on behalf of Radio Free Europe and the Voice of America. He's better than ever this year.

One small step we especially appreciated *Forbes* taking during the year was to identify its writers in the table of contents, following the longtime practice at *Fortune*. This leaves only *BusinessWeek* as a holdout, but until the weekly moves away from its multiple byline policy, there's no sense in it converting the table of contents. We have our favorite writers, and find it much easier to make our selections by going for the byline as much as the topic. Thank you, Mr. Michaels.

Editor:	James W. Michaels
Address:	Forbes Building 60 Fifth Avenue New York, N.Y. 10011 (212) 620-2200
Circulation:	728,459

Foreign Affairs

Ever so gradually, this publication of the Council on Foreign Relations continues to improve. We had noted last year that after a long period in which *FA* simply gathered dust, unopened, editor William G. Hyland had begun to turn things around. There's still an unevenness, winning articles shuffled in with losers, but enough of the former that we read every issue.

Analyses of post-Reykjavik policy, arms control, and the concept of containment were frequent, regularly treated themes this year. Additionally, essays on topical issues of foreign policy were folded in. The issue of containment, the "greatest of American foreign policy problems," was a main feature of the Spring issue: a reprint of the famous "The Sources of Soviet Conduct," by X [George F. Kennan]; excerpts from the rebuttal of it from 40 years ago by Walter Lippmann, "The Cold War;" a reflection on the concept from today's vantage point, "Containment Then and Now," by George F. Kennan; and an examination of the lessons of Soviet policy in the forty years since the Marshall Plan and the Truman Doctrine, "On Ending the Cold War," by W.W. Rostow. The package of thoughts — old and new — underscored the need to develop what Kennan called a "wider concept" of containment, one "more closely linked to the totality of Western civilization at this juncture in world history...more responsive to the problems of our own times."

Rostow's essay took up a common theme in foreign policy analysis today — the relative decline of American power and the cyclical character of U.S.-Soviet relationships. Rostow views the Soviet bid for strategic hegemony as not at all unique, but rather along the lines of other "latecomers" in the past, Germany and Japan, for example. "Collective memory," and "impulses of fear and ambition" are introduced to support the view that the Soviet case is not unique, but on this point, Rostow's case is unconvincing, there still being a body of evidence to suggest that Soviet policy has always represented a dramatic break with the past, not its continuation.

The containment issue appeared also in "America and the World 1986," issue, *The Wall Street Journal* correspondent Clifford Krauss, arguing the case that the policy has been successful in Central America, "Revolution in Central America?" The Sandinistas are presented as merely a "wart," not a cancer, and the contra cause as hopeless if not undesirable. In a Panglossian analysis, Krauss advises the "domino theory" simply doesn't hold water, since Catholicism and conservatism are barriers to communism in Central America.

In the same issue, "Realism and Vision in Foreign Policy," by James H. Billington, mixed serious analytics with chiliastic preaching. Citing the danger of a "growing tendency to permit weapons to become the measure of everything else in foreign policy, and the arms control process the main public measure of superpower behavior," Billington advises that policy ought to be informed on the forces in the world that give a new relevance to the American experience and the concept of the "West." He strays somewhat in his attempt to refashion a view of how the U.S. should relate to a changing world, indulging in preaching about the American notoriety for consuming too much. The latter canard enjoyed wide treatment in *FA* this year.

The twin deficits bogey was advanced by Leonard Silk, "The U.S. and the World Economy," in that same issue, and was taken up again by Martin Feldstein and C. Fred Bergsten, "Correcting the Trade Deficit," and "Economic Imbalances," respectively, Spring issue. *FA*'s contributions on global economy were the weakest materials it presented this year, all suffering from an obsolete and self-contradictory model. Bergsten, a monetary protectionist who has been urging constant devaluations of the dollar for 20 years, has been a regular in *FA*'s pages, and one suspects even Hyland doesn't understand the implications of having a neo-isolationist as the quarterly's big thinker on the global economy. It necessarily skews all non-economic treatments of the world political economy. Pedro-Pablo Kuczynski's "The Outlook For Latin American Debt," Fall, reviews the failure of debt containment strategies and offers some perspectives on long-term solutions. But there's little fresh here, privatization and liberalization advanced as domestic initiatives that are required, but no indication anywhere of what fiscal and monetary structural reforms are also needed.

FA's contributions on Soviet foreign policy were its highlights this year. These articles most held our attention with new angles of perception, new questions to weigh. Dimitri K. Simes' "Gorbachev: A New Foreign Policy?" in the "America and the World" issue was provocative, challenging assertions there's been any "turning inward" or scaling down of Soviet global ambitions to concentrate on economic modernization. He acknowledges Gorbachev's difference from his predecessors in the handling of arms control, but primarily in terms of his "tactical flexibility." The General Secretary, he advises, still views U.S.-Soviet relations from a zero-sum model of global politics. "Europe's Security Dilemmas" by Christopher Bertram, "Gorbachev and Eastern Europe" by Charles Gati, and "The U.S. and Eastern Europe" by William H. Luers, all in the Summer issue, each contained critical observations on the new relationship of forces emerging there. Gati's essay was the best of the three, with fresh information and analysis. "Reagan-Gorbachev III," Fall, by editor William G. Hyland, was reasoned assessment of what's ahead in the newly-emerging stage of U.S.-Soviet relationships, with Hyland examining shiftings in Europe, China, and the Third World.

FA tried to cover the globe comprehensively, adding a focus on various major themes of timely concern for American foreign policy. Among the latter, "Assad and His Allies," Fall, by Christopher Dickey, attracted our attention, the most thorough assessment on this relationship of the Mideast scene. "Gandhi At Midterm," Summer, by Paul H. Kreisberg, however, was less satisfying; the economic picture there was only cursorily examined, leaving his assessment inadequate.

On the whole it was a better year for the journal's readers, and we think editor Hyland is getting closer to — not some of the key answers, but some of the key questions on foreign policy.

Editor: William G. Hyland

Address: 58 East 68th Street
            New York, NY 10021
            (212) 734-0400

Circulation: 91,323

Foreign Policy

Editor Charles W. Maynes gets credit for presenting Seweryn Bialer's "Gorbachev's Move," in the journal's fall issue, *FP*'s best feature for 1987. Among the many essays appearing in policy journals, Bialer's came closest to providing some reading on the economic transformations Mikhail Gorbachev seeks. In Bialer's model, the USSR faces two technological and economic revolutions simultaneously — the revolution of mass consumption and the revolution of mass information and communication. After addressing them, he examines the difficulty the Soviets face with the rapid growth of global interdependence in the economic sphere and in culture and science. While there was plenty of room for differences on Bialer's broader thesis (Nick Eberstadt's critique in *Commentary* the best we saw), *Foreign Policy* at least made an attempt to fill the big gap in reporting and analysis on *perestroika* and *glasnost* in the media.

Also in the fall issue, Maynes himself presented the case for the West's adoption of "pragmatic but vigorous cooperation with the Soviets," in "America's Chance." Noting the new Soviet policy of seeking normal participation in the international community, he advised dramatic shifts in the USSR's foreign policy are forthcoming. The West will lose "support among their own citizens, if they fail to be as bold as the Soviets themselves," he added. In general, among the foreign policy journals, the quarterly of the Carnegie Endowment for International Peace goes the furthest in an inclination — albeit cautiously — to see the Soviet's course under Gorbachev as an opportunity for the West rather than a threat.

Foreign Policy provided several essays during 1987 dealing with the state of the western alliance. "Europe's Drift" was a constant theme. "The Superpower Squeeze," Winter 1986-87, by West German journalist and political analyst Peter Bender advanced the perspective that "The European countries now need safeguards not only against Moscow and Washington but also against the tension that arises between the superpowers." Seeing the basis upon which the Atlantic Alliance was founded now dramatically changed, Bender reduced the East-West conflict to a "competition of superpowers," the Europeans caught in the middle. "The Third Way," by Professor Jolyon Howorth, Winter 1986-87, added to the "Euroconsciousness" analyses, asserting that "detente from below is now a booming industry in both parts of Europe, thanks largely to the inadequacies of detente from above." "Alliances in Flux" in the Summer issue, continued the discussions on the same theme with "Atlanticism Without NATO," by Christopher Layne and "Hidden Committments," by Terry L. Deibel.

In "Lost Illusions," Spring, by Simon Serafty, Reagan's foreign policy was held accountable for the eroding of an Atlantic consensus. "Not only have the past 6 years yielded fewer achievements than the Carter Administration...but they also point to even more crises for the future," he argued. Reagan's "Gaullism *a l'americaine*" was unrealistic, and *FP* consistently gives little or no support to the Reagan Doctrine. Serafty acknowledges a world less hostile to American values because of Reagan, but is merciless on the President's overall foreign policy record. Serafty expresses the general viewpoint of *FP* — America must redefine a more restrained role for its power, interests and purpose.

"Positive Containment In Nicaragua," Fall, by Viron P. Vaky, a senior associate of the Carnegie Endowment, provided a concrete argument on behalf of the "restrained role." It presented very well the strategic conceptions of this camp in the foreign policy arena. Again directing an attack on the Reagan Doctrine, it comes very close to accepting the order of things that existed when the Brezhnev Doctrine was unchallenged, vague on policy for change within Nicaragua, focusing essentially on containing the Sandinistas.

Among the other contributions to *FP* in 1987, we noted "A Canadian Opportunity," Spring, by C. Michael Aho and *Dun's Business Month* senior editor Marc Levinson, outlining the great potentials for a U.S.-Canada free-trade accord and a new model for the GATT talks. "Israel's Dangerous Fundamentalists," Fall, by Ian S. Lustick wasn't totally unconvincing, especially when compared to the treatment on the same issue that appeared in *Global Affairs*, "The Search for an Israeli Ethos," Summer, by Mordechai Nisan. "Yellow Rain: The Story Collapses," by Julian Robinson, Jeanne Guillemin and Matthew Meselson, Fall, revisits the debate over defecating bees vs. toxic warfare, making a persuasive case for busy *apis mellifera*.

Demonstrably, 1987 was a banner year for "black hole" economic features in most of the print media, dense matter from which no light issues forth. *FP*'s contribution to this was a pitch black effort by Lester C. Thurow and Laura D'Andrea Tyson, "The Economic Black Hole," Summer. Just as the entire structure and behavior of matter changes in a black hole, so does economics in theirs.

Foreign Policy is a vanguard journal in the attempts to redefine post-Reagan U.S. foreign policy, reflecting the strategic views of a large section of the political community. As this becomes a center of debate in 1988, *FP* will continue to be important reading.

Editor: Charles William Maynes

Address: 11 Dupont Circle, NW
Washington, DC 20036
(201) 797-6420

Circulation: 26,631

Fortune

The best we can say about Marshall Loeb's first full year as editor of *Fortune* is that we almost always find one rewarding piece somewhere in each issue. We're spending more time with it. After leaving a successful tenure as editor of *Money* in June of 1986, Loeb's step up to Time Inc.'s prestige flagship naturally invited speculation that he would convert the troubled *Fortune*, whose slip had been showing for years, into a slightly more sedate version of the magazine he'd left. He still might, but there continues to be so much to-ing and fro-ing under the Loeb aegis that it's not clear what kind of character it will have when matters crystallize.

Clearly it has become "the most painfully yuppie-oriented" of the business magazines, as one of our readers puts it. Another of our "news gourmets," a genuine Wall Street yuppie, had this line in his year-end summary: "Many of the articles are pleasant, pleasing stories that almost seem as if the *Fortune* writers are reporting on their fellow fraternity brothers, which most often strikes me that way when they're writing about *Fortune* 500 chiefs, RR, Secretary Baker, or Alan Greenspan." This isn't a hard-and-fast rule, by any means. Peter Nulty's sharp look at Allied-Signal's Edward Hennessy, 12-7, had the rough and tumble flavor we've come to expect in *Forbes*. We also appreciate Alex Taylor III, profiling Chrysler's Richard Dauch, 6-22, not Lee Iacocca. There is nothing wrong with admiring portraits at this pinnacle of American business. We look for the business profiles of Stratford P. Sherman and Peter Petre, big canvases for captains of industry, but they are too few and far between, even with Loeb's penchant for putting a face on almost every cover.

Too often we get "The Year's Most Fascinating Business People," 1-5, an entire issue of yup that we had to whip our readers to look into, with three out of four of the sketches flat as pancakes. We had to go to the whip again with "The World's 50 Biggest Industrial CEOs," 8-3, producing this snippet from the *most positive* of the critiques: "A spicy, spare-no-feeling, human-interest feature on the big boys. No depth, but lots of fun." Still another of our readers, not quoted in any of the above, on the 6-22 cover, "The Biggest Banker's Bold Stroke," on Citicorp's John Reed: "An old, tired story of what already happened at Citi, not, like the *Forbes* piece, focused on what we need to know now. Rehash of daily press by an obvious power worshipper."

Loeb has also had three memorable cover stories in 18 months that he'd like to forget. First there was "What Managers Can Learn from Manager Reagan," 9-15-86, two months before the Iranamok scandal broke, quoting RR's advice: "Surround yourself with the best people you can find, delegate authority, and don't interfere." Before the Crash, *Fortune* put George Soros, world's greatest investor on a breathless onward and upward cover, 9-28 (Soros lost zillions), and then had the luck to spread Alan Greenspan's avuncular mug over the 10-26 cover, on why the new Fed chief is BULLISH! Because of the practice of dating a magazine two weeks up, it actually was circulating before Black Monday, October 19, and by airing Greenspan's view that he thought the dollar would continue to decline, it almost certainly contributed to the Crash. It's no criticism of the magazine that it did not predict the Crash. Few saw it coming with such force, but the kind of general anxiety about the markets that became widespread on Wall Street after Labor Day did not reach the *Fortune* high command.

Loeb himself does not appear to have a world view, as his predecessor, William S. Rukeyser, also a former editor of *Money,* did not. The world is rather a collection of interesting bits and pieces of political, financial and commercial activities, stitched together. It seems to matter little to Loeb that this journalist or that is put on an assignment, as long as they can produce lively, coherent material that is not out of the conventional mainstream. The notion that a constantly devaluing dollar aids U.S. commercial interests is woven through even the very best *Fortune* pieces on the world economy, unquestioned, although monetary devaluation is, by definition, trade protectionism (making foreign goods too expensive to import). Because the trade, currency issues were vital to so many stories in *Fortune* this year, the devaluation quirk threw a wrinkle or a warp into all of them. It's central to the writings of Sylvia Nasar, Richard

Kirkland, and all others in the economic unit that we see. It's silliness was at a zenith in "Crawling Out of the Trade Tunnel," 12-21, with Vivian Brownstein explaining why the 40% decline of the dollar didn't improve the trade balance: "It was the infamous J curve," which argues that the deficit gets worse before it gets better, but because the dollar keeps devaluing, this produces "more J curves, one after the other." The J curve, a great hoax perpetrated by a handful of economists on the financial press, masks the idea of currency debasement that is alien to the world view at *Forbes*, as it was to the editors at *Fortune* prior to the 1970s.

This neutralism on Loeb's part to the great global economic debate certainly colors the pattern of the magazine's movement. It's safer at the micro level of business, where the cosmic forces for the most part wash out from one company to the next in a given industry. On that turf, though, it runs up against the expertise and audacity of *Forbes*, a biweekly, and the swiftness of *BusinessWeek*, a weekly. In between, there's a little of everything, and too often we have the feeling we've seen the material weeks or months before. *Fortune* was the last to catch up with the superconductivity story, for example, although we must acknowledge "Superconductors Get Into Business," 6-6, was a solid contribution to the unfolding story.

One of the best articles about *Fortune* appeared in the February 1987 *Manhattan, inc.*, "Turn of *Fortune*," by Judith Adler Hennessee, who raises the question of Loeb's style of journalism: "Some of the old guard actively despise it, seeing the demise of standards, the loss of prestige — the end, in fact, of *Fortune* as they knew it. 'The point about Marshall,' says a former staffer, 'is that he is the first ME of *Fortune* ever who thinks of it not as a sacred trust and himself as a keeper of the flame, but as a business, a profit center, like the businesses we write about...There is a lot of cultural sea change.'"

This isn't quite the way we see *Fortune* going under Loeb's stewardship. He is not a businessman, but a lifelong journalist, who understands the communication process as well as any editor around. In understanding the nature of the target audience at *Money*, he was able to strengthen the product to get its circulation to 1.4 million from 865,000 in four years. He knows the target audience at *Fortune* is a wholly different one and is not so dense as to try and sell iceboxes to Eskimos. When he got the assignment in '86, he spent days leafing through the editions of yesteryear, the glory days, as if trying to tap their power. But 18 months isn't enough time to turn the flagship around, even if Loeb had the clear vision and the supporting staff. The best we can say of it is that we are reading more of it as he experiments with story lines and personnel and a world outlook. And that is not nothing.

Managing Editor: Marshall Loeb

Address: Time-Life Building
                           Rockefeller Center
                           New York, N.Y. 10020
                           (212) 586-1212

Circulation: 771,988

Harper's

We knew *Harper's* was in trouble when the first thing we turned to — by habit — was the cutesy "Harper's Index," which emblematically the magazine advertises as one of its strengths. *Harper's*, once a solid journal of serious opinion, satiric wit, and critical thought, continued to deliquesce in 1987. We don't fully subscribe to the impression that journals have a necessary organic life cycle, each having eventually to submit to the laws of entropy. Rather, like any successful marriage, a magazine simply requires good, hard work consistently to prevent its devolution.

We still find Editor Lewis Lapham's talented wordsmithery losing none of its polish. The Administration's "misadventure in the international arms trade," he observes in "Sending in the Clowns," 2-87, "plays as *opera bouffe*. It isn't hard to imagine President Reagan's privy counselors dressed up in preposterous military uniforms, wielding papier mache swords and singing the music of Offenbach." However, where Lapham's writings once flashed with wry and witty exchange, the rapier's thrust-and-parry, the iconoclast's puncturing of elite "wisdom's" bloated pomposities, we now find them swollen with a bloated elitism of his own. His visceral reaction to "the testimony and derring-do of Colonel North" in "Landscape with Trolls," 9-87, reveals a contempt for the American public. "Eager and boyish in his adventurer's uniform of woodland green, the colonel sounded like Peter Pan telling Wendy and her little brothers about his marvelous exploits in Never Never Land." His success, he continues, "testified to the ignorance of a credulous American public increasingly in thrall to the fairy tales told by the mass media."

Harper's may aspire to be the "judicious eccentric" of literate journals — and that is wholesome — able to step outside the conventional perceptual framework, to find a new angle or perspective from which to peer over the world's shoulder. Its accomplishments haven't measured up to its aspirations and ambitions. Rather than the delight of a "glittering play of wind-soft thought," *Harper's* passes on to us cosmic flatus. There is, as many of its readers have communicated to the magazine, a random, unserious, oblique quality to its purpose and intent, quirky rather than erudite.

We select for illustration the May issue — though most any other one would have easily served the same purpose. The lead essay, "The Next Panic," by contributing editor L.J. Davis, purports to examine "fear and trembling on Wall Street." But it's merely *Harper's* contribution to the "woe is us" litany, Davis seeking to deny the success of Ronald Reagan's economic expansion. In this gullible paean to Indian cultist Ravi Batra, Davis can't make sense of the stock market and concludes it must be irrational. Full of misleading statistics and contradictions — "the rich drove the market....[but] the great bull market was marked from the very beginning by the presence of the general public" — it was completely within the conventional mold.

"The Endless Summer of Love," a report on Goa, the "wildlife preserve for the endangered hippie," by David Black, reveals the author's ability to, Winnie-the-Pooh-like, recapture the enchanted innocence of those former acid-tripping, dope-doing, inebriated years of the counter-culture sixties.

"Miscellany" from executive editor Michael Pollan, who in "Cultivating Virtue," believes he's addressing the mundane and the sublime — "compost and its moral imperatives." Not only do we get a description of the stuff itself, but Pollan goes on in an attempt to "grasp" the very "metaphysics of compost" itself.

At least with William Pfaff, the syndicated columnist whose literate journalism often appears in *The New Yorker,* there was an effort to challenge the conventional — not from the exotic or bizarre viewpoint — but from some original rethinking of assumptions. "Perils of Policy" makes the point that the "Marshall Plan only worked once," and that aid-assists-democracy is an easy-way-out convention.

There does exist a substantial readership for whom the magazine's first person voice titillates and touches a shared vision of "what it's all about." After all, *sale* copies of the magazine are up substantially since *Harper's* editorial and methodological redesign almost four years ago. Yet there's a threshold for how much ooze can be absorbed. *Harper's* 1987 productions strained close to the limits.

Editor: Lewis Lapham

Address: 666 Broadway
            New York, N.Y. 10012
            (212) 614-6500

Circulation: 184,941

Human Events

Required reading for the conservative movement, *Human Events* is the "combat" publication for the troops. And with the Reagan Revolution as well as the President besieged in 1987, the vitality we found lacking at *HE* in RR's peak years was back again as the weekly rushed to the front lines. In close hand-to-hand combat, the Marines could not have done better.

As productive as ever, Capitol Hill editor Allan Ryskind's front-page efforts were rigorous, informed, strategically focused all year. Among them we particularly noted: "Is President Reagan Out of the Woods?" 12-27-86; "'Iranscam' Masking Crucial Foreign Policy Problems," 3-7; "White House Should Come Out Swinging in Its Own defense," 5-23; and "Media Owe Reagan A Full Apology," 7-25. Each was written from a field commander's perspective, assessing the weak points in the offense's deployment, the margins for retaking the high ground, the critical question of morale and signs of fatigue or accommodation addressed. Did they have an impact on policy? Not the one hoped for, but had *HE* not been in the foxholes around the White House, and clippings of *HE* articles in the President's pockets, more ground would have been lost.

Its excellent work on the anti-Sandinista resitance and Nicaragua policy in 1986 was repeated again this year, fighting the battle for the contras block-by-block, street-by-street: "New Strategy Needed To Win In Nicaragua," 1-3; "Reagan's Nicaragua Policy Threatens To Unravel," 2-28; "Bold New Program Needed to Oust Sandinistas," 3-21; "Arias Plan Considered 'Disaster' By U.S. Officials," 8-22; "Ortega Reveals Why Peace Plan Is A Pipe Dream," 9-12.

Supportive material on other fronts in this arena was presented as well. Well-done were Allan C. Brownfeld's review of *Against All Hope*, by Armando Vallardes, 2-7; J. Michael Waller's "U.S. Leftists in Nicaragua Are Armed and Fighting," 6-13; and "ARENA: Strong Second Party Emerging in El Salvador," by Deroy Murdock, 8-22. This was the only report we saw *anywhere* in all of 1987 on the democratic opposition in El Salvador.

There's little middle-ground passion for *HE*; it's either passionately loved, or passionately despised. Congressional aides who will take calls from the Communist Party's publications hang up on *HE*. But they don't ignore it. The opposition to Judge Bork kept close watch on *HE*, spreading the word that it was over for him when "*even* the national conservative weekly, *Human Events*" says "Bork Nomination too Close to Call," 10-17. *HE* was ahead of the curve with its warnings, 7-11, that fierce opposition was mounting to Bork's nomination, and that the Administration's strategy of a test-run to get the Hill's reaction would let the opposition control the battlefield.

"Buchanan for President?" 1-24, an excellent examination of the question, influenced the former White House Communications Director's decision not to run, clearly affecting the GOP's presidential race. "Looking to '88: Kemp and the Conservatives," 1-31, by M. Stanton Evans impressed us as weak, not really rigorous enough for its front-page placement. But the best interview we saw anywhere with Pete DuPont appeared in *HE*, 7-4. "'Mandatory Mike' Aims for the White House," 2-14, by former *Boston Herald* editorial writer John A. Barnes, was a probing examination of Gov. Dukakis' record in Massachusetts, Barnes finding evidence he still opposes tax cuts.

Good work on a host of foreign policy issues, particularly keen attention on southern Africa. While most of the press ignored the testimony of former ANCers on its Moscow connections and strategy of terrorism, Allan Brownfeld got the news out in an 8-1 article. The interview with Alan Keyes, 11-7, provided the best sense of what his departure from the State Department is all about.

HE used interviews to intervene on policy to great effect: Sen. Malcolm Wallop (R-WY), 4-18, and Rep. Jim Courter (R-NJ), 6-27, on inertia and unclarity in the Administration's defense policies. The exclusive with Secretary of Education William Bennett, 9-19, on the "3 C's" — character, content and choice — was also an excellent feature.

One of the few publications maintaining a steady watch on SDI, contributing editor M. Stanton Evans covered that subject and defense-tech transfer issues all year, *HE* adding a timely SDI story by Gregory Fossedal and Lewis Lehrman, 3-28. Warren Brookes appears more frequently now, his well-done columns the mainstay of *HE*'s coverage on the economy. Other conservative columnists appear regularly. Among them, we found the contribution by Jon Basil Utley, associate editor of *The Times of the Americas*, "What 'Misery Nations' Can Learn from the Far East," 6-20, especially noteworthy for its factual material and sharp insights.

The "Inside Washington" pages frequently produce amazing items, as for example "Arthur Liman's Interesting Thesis," 7-18, a story initially broken by Rachel Flick of the *New York Post*. Examining Liman's undergrad thesis at Harvard, *HE* reported it ironically was an attack on select committees and their dangerous proclivity toward pillory and demagoguery. "Focus on the Media" by Cliff Kincaid appears more regularly this year than last, watchdogging the media's egregious sins of commission and omission, but also giving credit where due, as in its acknowledgment of *The Washington Post*'s much-improved Central American reporting this year.

A very good year for *Human Events* under its three-star generals, editors Thomas Winter and Allan Ryskind.

Editor: Thomas S. Winter

Address: 422 First Street, SE
            Washington, D.C. 20003
            (202) 546-0856

Circulation: 40,000

Insight

In its second full year of publication, the ambitious newsweekly of the Unification Church and The Washington Times Corp. continued to reach for the high standards of journalism it has set for itself. The publishers assume its one million readers are upscale and at least as intelligent and probably a cut above the readers of the three leading newsweeklies. The model is one of erudition, eschewing any hint of Impact!, sensationalism or smarm and making the assumption that its readers have already digested the basic news of the week from other sources. If the faculty of the University of Missouri School of Journalism set out to design an ideal newsweekly for such an audience, *Insight* would be it. Of course, design isn't everything, which is why Editor Kirk Oberfeld and his staff continue to reach, struggling with the material that goes into it. In trying to do more and better in '87 with its youthful staff, they achieved a bit less than we'd come to expect, but the magazine remained an important component of our essential reading.

An even larger struggle is going on to get *Insight* onto a financial footing, its proprietors hoping to get it into the black by 1990, or at least to the point where the Rev. Sun Myung Moon's church does not have to reach so far into its deep pockets to keep it afloat. The press run of 1 million achieved at the end of 1986 was simply *given* to people identified as upscale, with the aim of eventually weaning them from the free list to paid subscribers. At 1987's end, we're told, there were about 300,000 forking over the modest $25.50 a year, a target of 500,000 by spring and the whole million by 1989. The move also continues to get the advertisers — now a slim 11 1/2 pages a week — to pay full rates, which one supposes gets easier when the folks getting *Insight* are paying for it. One way or another, it certainly seems the magazine is going to be around for a long time.

The cover stories we raved about in the *1987 MediaGuide* are still being cranked out with little or no regard for the week's news. But this year the dazzlers were fewer and further apart. Two were produced by Charlotte Low, a lawyer/journalist. "The Law and the Land," 9-26, was perhaps the least likely cover story of any newsweekly during the year, promising a deep snooze, but it turned out to be a comprehensive, lucid, review of property rights in a matrix of legal philosophy. Ms. Low was much closer to the news with the first deep look at Robert Bork and his judicial theories, "A Philosopher of Restraint for a Once Activist Court," 7-20, appended to the lead cover piece by David Brock, "Fighting Words: Reagan Says Bork." Henrik Bering-Jensen's "Soviet Leader Mikhail Gorbachev: Who Is He? What Does He Want?" 3-30, provided a superior, deep analytical report on the politics of Gorbachev's reforms. The cover on philosopher Allan Bloom, "The Book of the Year," 5-11, by David Brock, had the most lasting impact, elevating Bloom, his book and education theories into the national debate on these matters. The George Bush cover story, 10-19, by Don McLeod, was among the best portraits we've ever seen of the Veep.

The foreign cover stories were the big disappointments of the year. In 1986 we devoured the foreign covers, finding information and insights packaged with crisp analytics we were not getting anywhere else. But the Brazil (8-17), Mexico (10-5), Korea (10-12), and Pinochet and Chile (11-16) cover spreads of 1987 were routine at best, occasional nuggets in material that seemed repackaged, and at worst, the "exclusive interview with Pinochet," a waste of time, a few mumbles from the old man pumped with air to fill a dozen pages. Part of the problem may be the new emphasis on economic backgrounding in these pieces, the *Insight* editors discovering that's what their businessman editors want. But some of the reporters don't seem up to digging as deeply into an economy as the daily financial press can get, and this weakness winds up diluting the otherwise sound political and cultural reporting. The magazine missed Adam Platt, who can get around this horn, he taking the year off to work on a book. And Bering-Jensen, another stalwart who can burrow well beneath the surface of a national economy, did not undertake as many major efforts this year.

The inside material held up well, often pushing beyond standard boundaries and usually good reading, more tightly edited. We especially liked Glenn Garvin's "Heading Back," 7-13, on what's really happening with the Sandinistas and "Two Rebel Groups Become One," 2-2, detailing the agreement between UNO (United Nicaraguan Opposition) and SOB (Southern Opposition Bloc), Bill Whalen's "The House of Questionable Repute," 9-14, tough on the new Speaker of the House and Democratic scandal, and Peter Younghusband's "Cornfields Among the Minefields," 4-13, or the farmers in hell, targeted by the South Africa's ANC for terrorist attacks.

One healthy sign at *Insight* was the turnover, a number of good people being plucked away by the bigger kids on the block. Robb Deigh and John Podhoretz were hired away by *U.S.News* and Malcolm Gladwell went to *The Washington Post* business page. The hothouse atmosphere at *Insight* will develop talent rapidly, making the magazine prey to publications that will pay bigger bucks and have bigger audiences. This is healthy because *Insight* is identified with the Unification Church, which signals to talented young journalists that it can be a stepping stone. And Oberfeld continues to build staff: Christopher Elias, Richard Starr, Carolyn Lochhead, Danielle Pletka, Holman Jenkins and Maxine Pollack all coming aboard within the last year or so, helping to keep the magazine fresh. Maxine Pollack, for example, excelled with several pieces she could not have done as a rookie with *Time* or *Newsweek*: "Pious Plans Under An Official Knell," 6-1; "Thousands of Citizens Sent to Uncertain East Bloc Future," 7-27; "Signs That Moscow Is Tiring of War," 8-3.

Last year we noted *Insight* as one of the most important press developments of '86, calling it "one of the most interesting happenings in print news in years," because of its energy and high quality. The problems it had in '87 did not seem to cut against this judgment in any fundamental way. We mark them down to growing pains.

Editor-in-Chief: Arnaud de Borchgrave

Address: 3600 New York Avenue, NE
             Washington, D.C. 20002
             (202) 636-8800

Circulation: 230,000

The Journal of Commerce

Against the mighty resources and circulations of the *WSJ* and *NYT*, the tiny *Journal of Commerce* seems in a hopeless competition, except it really doesn't act quite like a competitor. Like the shipping trade that has been its chief audience for 161 years, the newspaper is comfortable with the idea of peaceful coexistence of tugboats and supertankers. The niche it has secured depends on keeping a closer watch, than the big circulation papers, on the rocks and shoals, swirls and eddies, that could disrupt or facilitate world commerce.

The scope of international news in *The Journal of Commerce* is surprisingly satisfying at this close-in level, its small staff and foreign service bolstered by freelance contributors in the major commercial centers. But forget about keeping up with developments in the Communist bloc through this paper. Or, for that matter, with sub-Sahara Africa, the Asian subcontinent, or the most impoverished parts of the western hemisphere. Where trade is at a trivial level, so is coverage by *The Journal of Commerce*. For those interested, there are pages regularly devoted to energy, insurance, chemicals and transportation, and an occasional whole section devoted to a single industry or country. The special trade and investment survey of Japan, 6-29, was an impressive collection of material on the continuing restructuring of that nation's economy. Since the paper is owned by Knight-Ridder, the news services fill any gaps in its own reports. The format changed on April 27, switching from two sections to three, with a section on steamship schedules.

The Journal of Commerce changed editors early in the year, the retiring Albert Kraus turning the rudder over to Stan Erickson. The paper's editorials have improved with this fresh eye on the horizon, lengthening, but at the same time layering in factual information we might not notice in news reports. "A Dangerous Path," 10-30, about pending U.S. trade legislation, observed that "the least publicized yet potentially most damaging paragraphs make technical changes in the laws concerning imports deemed to be 'unfair,' " and then went on to give eye-opening examples. (Curiously, the newspaper's publisher, Don Becker, is an ardent protectionist.) "The Buying of America," 7-9, reveals that Japanese firms own only about 6% of the foreign-owned manufacturing in the U.S., with recent acquisitions smaller than Ireland or Sweden. In "Untangling the Skies," 6-1, an innovative proposal is put forward to end airport congestion, but at the same time we get a clearer picture of what's going on in all that traffic. Like the editorial pages of *The Wall Street Journal*, there is often more hard information in such brief editorials than can be found in news features on the same subjects.

Foreign news goes beyond mere factual reporting to a typically deep look into the politics and economics of many countries. Coverage is particularly strong in Asia, with A.E. Cullison consistently among the top two or three reporters on Japan, and P.T. Bangsberg out of Hong Kong often just as original on other Asian countries. News about policy shifts that could affect commerce out of Europe, Mexico, Brazil and Israel is also on the margin. *The Journal of Commerce* uncovered several fascinating case studies on creeping capitalism this year, such as the tax-cutting, deregulation and privatization in New Zealand, 5-15, Israel, 5-4, and Jamaica, 1-16. The newspaper provides sharper detail on trade-related issues in Washington, with Keith Rockwell usually ahead of the competition in bird-dogging developments on trade legislation.

With the U.S. trade deficit and trade legislation, so important to world financial markets, before the Congress in 1988, Wall Streeters would do well to keep an eye on this agile little tug.

Editor: Stanford Erickson

Address: 110 Wall Street
New York, N.Y. 10005
(212) 425-1616

Circulation: 22,614

Los Angeles Times

We added the *Los Angeles Times* to our regular reading pile this year, having already been attracted enough by the reporting of some of the daily's journalists to include them in the last two *MediaGuide*s. We observed in last year's *MediaGuide* that "several of the big circulation dailies that act as if they were national — with big Washington outlets and a foreign corps — must still be considered regional. *The Chicago Tribune*, the *Philadelphia Inquirer*, the *Denver Post*, for example, 'think regional,' as they should. The *Los Angeles Times* more than any other regional paper strains to radiate a national attitude, with an excellent far-flung foreign service and a beefy Washington bureau." We expand our entries for the *LAT* this year, though most are for the publication's foreign correspondents. The *LAT* now has 25 foreign bureaus, the latest one opening in Managua midyear, and its foreign coverage is one of the strengths of the paper. It serves to distinguish the *LAT* from other dailies which still have a regional focus, and this was the area we most closely focused on in reading the paper this year.

The *LAT* is particularly competitive with its Central American reporting, Marjorie Miller in El Salvador doing a better job than her counterpart at the *NYT* and often pulling ahead of *The Washington Post*. Richard Boudreaux, the head of the new Managua bureau, got off to a fine start, also helping to advance the paper as a source on this region that cannot be neglected. Another strong bureau is Jerusalem, where Dan Fisher was energetic all year, examining and reporting the shifts on the margin among Israel's Arab populations. Coverage of South America weakened this year, but that was a consequence of personnel changes, former Rio bureau chief Juan de Onis leaving for *U.S.News*, William Montalbano's vacancy in Buenos Aires unfilled after his switch to the Rome bureau, with William Long trying to fill all the holes single-handedly. Its Asia coverage is certainly competitive, China and the Philippines strong, Japan adequate, though weaker on the subcontinent.

Europe suffers because, as with most postings to Bonn and Paris (excepting the *Financial Times*), we get more treatment of East-West issues, little of the political economies of France and West Germany. The *LAT* seemed to still be feeling its way in the USSR, although it had a better grip on Eastern Europe. We didn't sense the bureau pushing hard enough against the constraints and digging deeply for the story of *perestroika* and *glasnost*, although we don't dismiss as unnotable the work that was done. Michael Parks came across as a little too eager to draw conclusions where the evidence seemed inconclusive, but on the whole kept the *LAT* very competitive on South Africa.

The paper's beefy Washington bureau contains some of the hardest-working journalists around. We've watched Tom Redburn burn the candle at both ends for a number of years, noting how much better he is when he backs off from the daily assignments to do broader analytics. Another hardworker, political writer Robert Shogan strives to give more than a horse-race account of political campaigns, and Barry Berack, a national reporter and Miami bureau chief, caught our attention with an impressive and comprehensive profile of Vice President George Bush, "Team Player Bush: A Yearning to Serve," 11-22. We noticed also that DC staff reporters David G. Savage and David Lauter's professional reporting on Judge Bork's nomination steered clear of the rancorous tones that sometimes crept into others' coverage.

Both Robert Toth and John Broder, covering national security and defense respectively, rose above the routine to make their way into our entries and ratings of journalists in that category.

Business/finance and the economy is a mixed bag. *LAT* has a "Board of Economists" who regularly contribute commentary on the economy. We sometimes read them, sometimes skip them, but the effort is novel among the dailies, somewhat similar to *BusinessWeek*'s guest columns. A little more variety and rotation among these voices often seems warranted. Some of the freshest thinking we saw anywhere for new angles on economic issues was produced by DC staff reporter Oswald Johnston. Columnist James Flanigan's prodigious efforts kept us watching, and he has the potential of producing one of the better, regular business columns anywhere. We noted that Flanigan and Redburn teamed up to examine the sea changes now underway on the competitiveness issue in a notable contribution to the *LAT*'s series on the subject, 1-25.

The best coverage of the early stages of the Iran-Contra affair was from *LAT*, their eight-page pull-out of 12-26-86, comprehensive and balanced. Several other survey-like features were well-done, "AIDS," 8-9, and a series on Gorbachev's reforms running through the fall, "Remaking the Revolution." Though not part of their AIDS survey, Barry Siegel, a national department staff reporter in the LA bureau provided one of the year's ten-best stories on the issue.

Though the paper seeks to become a serious voice commenting on and affecting public policy nationally, it buries its daily editorial page in the "Metro" section. It was the weakest section of the paper this year. There's a very predictable knee-jerk liberal content to the editorials that simply doesn't carry the weight or impact of the more carefully thought-out editorials of the *NYT* or *Washington Post*, for example. Its Sunday editorial and op-ed page is relatively lifeless in comparison, none of the vibrancy and diversity of voices one finds in the *Post* or the aggressiveness that distinguishes the *NYT*. Syndicated columnists appear, Jeane Kirkpatrick or William Schneider (now with the *LAT* syndicate as well as the *NJ*), but the only voice identified as a *LAT*'s own, Ernest Conine, lacked resonance and depth this year. Commentaries by academics and professionals are more heavily employed on these pages, but in getting the sound of the paper's voice, we end up with a whole less than its parts.

We skip the magazine, which is totally regional in content and outlook, though it gets credit for running a version of *Manhattan, inc.*'s profile of Mike Milken by Edward Jay Epstein. Its cultural pages, while not competitive with the Big Four's, contain an occasional delight, Richard Eder's book reviews foremost among them.

The daily *LAT* sometimes seems to outweigh the Sunday *NYT*, copies of which, with all its pages of advertising geared to the LA market, are airlifted to Washington, DC, and made available in coinboxes on the street. We and our Morristown, N.J. mailman would love to see a stripped-down *LAT* for national consumption. The *Post* has been successful with a weekly national edition, running the best of its daily reports and features, but that option seems over the horizon for the *LAT*.

Editor: William F. Thomas

Address: Times Mirror Square
                Los Angeles, CA 90053
                (213) 237-5000

Circulation: 1,384,857 Sunday
                 1,113,459 Daily

Manhattan, inc.

Among the new city business publications that have appeared in the last few years, the slick, glossy *Manhattan, inc.* appears to have been one of the more successful ventures. Now in its second year, the monthly had an impressive performance in 1987, and looks as if it'll be around for quite a while now. There was a major staff change early in the year, when editor Jane Amsterdam departed in March, differences over editorial independence and a clash over management styles with publisher and owner D. Herbert Lipson unresolved. Managing editor Duncan Stalker and art director Nancy Butkus joined Amsterdam in resigning, and Lipson brought Clay Felker aboard as new editor.

Edward Jay Epstein's "Wall Street Babylon" column is the first section we always turn to. Epstein attracted widespread notice with his "Free the Kidder 2!" 4-87, locating a struggle on Wall Street between corporate America and the new upstarts, defending the risk arbitragers and shooting holes in the government's case against them. Epstein's "Inside the Secret World of Mike Milken," 9-87, an intimate portrait of the head of Drexel Burnham Lambert Inc.'s junk-bond operations, was a blockbuster, widely read and discussed. "Greed and fraud" in the centers of wealth was a frequent topic, the lead sections of the April issue devoting five separate articles to the issue. Case studies on "energetic lawbreakers" prefaced by Ron Rosenbaum's observation that "there are similarities between crack dealers and Perrier-drinking Martin Siegel clones," the point of the Epstein column seemed lost upon the editors who put that issue together.

Manhattan, inc., provided some of the best features on the Fourth Estate, Judith Adler Hennessee's "Manhattan Ink" columns including serious profiles of Marshall Loeb's *Fortune*, 2-87, and a review of *Financial Times*' successful foray into the U.S., 5-87. Jonathan Alter and Bill Powell, senior writers at *Newsweek* were stupendous with their exploration of the balance sheet at CBS after one year under Larry Tisch, "The Soul of CBS's New Money Machine," 11-87. "Shorts' Sheet," 6-87, by Charles C. Mann, a look at *Barron's*, "America's most glorified tip sheet," was an extensive feature, but still a disappointment. Errors of fact and judgments were too frequent.

The magazine expanded its field this year, broadening its focus, though "always through the lens of Manhattan." Philip Weiss in "The Choices of a New Generation," 7-86, did a remarkable job covering the search of Wall Street's young Democratic millionaires for the right candidate. In it we learn how they pulled the rug out from under Gary Hart. John Seabrook's profile of Chase chairman Willard Butcher and his perspective for rescuing the American Enterprise Institute from financial disaster, "Capital Gain," 3-87, was interesting for as far as it went on Butcher's perceptions of the rift between free enterprise and government. Unfortunately, he didn't take up on the chairman's remark that "we as a bank are in the middle of trying to decide whether to remain a bank or whether to give up our banking charter."

Manhattan, inc. also provided readers with a chapter from *The Prosecutors*, by *The Wall Street Journal* reporter James B. Stewart, "Eyeball-to-Eyeball: Giuliani Takes on His Boss," 8-87, the featured cover story, though it wasn't apparent this was not an original article until you got inside to the piece. A short story by Tom Wolfe, "Anatomy of a Dinner Party," 10-87, was the featured attraction. Editor Clay Felker indicates that "literary journalism, with its reporting about the way people really live and what they actually do," might become a regular staple of the magazine in the future.

After two years, it's risky to say the magazine has "made it," but from its efforts this year we'd say the odds point that way.

Editor: Clay Felker

Address: 420 Lexington Avenue
New York, N.Y. 10170
(212) 697-2100

Circulation: 85,000

Mother Jones

Named after the orator, union organizer and general hell-raiser, Mary Harris "Mother" Jones (1830-1930), this monthly maintains her hell-raising tradition with high spirits. The most widely-read leftist periodical in the U.S., *Mother Jones* enjoys an advantage over its competitors by qualifying as a non-profit publication of the Foundation for National Progress. Our first year reviewing the San Francisco-based magazine, we found it sometimes flaky, sometimes academic, but on the whole provocative, even refreshing at times. *MoJo*'s radical-progressive politics are more "mellow" in comparison to the harder-line *The Nation*, (and we leave it up to them as to whether that's a compliment or not).

Its cover stories have had wide impact on occasion. "The Soviets Take Over the U.S.," 1-87, for example, provided ammunition for the campaign against ABC's "Amerika" miniseries, quoted and relied upon to make the case that it feeds war hysteria in the U.S. Miriam Pawel's "Nine Great Myths About MARIO CUOMO," 2/3-87, was filed away for quick reference by many in the leftist political community who wanted reasons not to support a presidential bid by the NY governor. *MoJo* takes Jesse Jackson's candidacy very seriously, focusing on the content rather than his style. We learned a lot from the cover story by editor Doug Foster, "Jesse Jackson, What Does He Really Want?" 10-87, the first really serious interview we saw with the candidate. While Andrew Kopkind's feature on Michael Dukakis in *The Nation* revealed a lot about the candidate, we think Foster did a bit better in his interview with the governor, "Tough Questions He Hates to Answer," 12-87, revealing what comes from the gut and what comes from the more calculating mind.

Other cover stories of note were the excerpted chapters from books by *The Wall Street Journal*'s Jonathan Kwitny and the *San Francisco Chronicle*'s Randy Shilts — *Vile Patriots: Spies, Dope and Dirty Money*, 8/9-87 and *And the Band Played On: People, Politics, and the AIDS Epidemic*, 11-87, respectively. Less satisfying was "The Greatest Story Never Told," 6/7-87, by former Students for a Democratic Society organizer Todd Gitlin. He raises legitimate concern that the media too often serve as megaphones for the Establishment on defense questions, but his case breaks down when he tries to convince us that Reagan's SDI has gotten a free ride from the press. There's an "us vs them" framework here that just doesn't work, and we cite this example because it's a drawback of *MoJo*. We note at *The Nation*, for example, a better appreciation for the critical nuances of policy differences among the Establishment thinkers and doers. For a publication that seeks to build a movement that can influence policy, lacking that discriminatory sense is a liability.

MoJo isn't just all cover stories. Its "Frontline" column contains juicy tidbits of information, sometimes very amusing, sometimes just right-bashing, but always worth a look. All the issues of the "movement" are addressed in its "features" section, where sizable essays from various contributors appear. They have an "expose" flavor frequently, as in "Dead Men Tell No Tales," 4-87, by Joel Millman, which examined the possible roles in "the administration's dirty little war against Nicaragua" of seven dead Contragate players.

Central America is a constant focus, sympathies for the guerrillas in El Salvador and scorn for U.S. policies always upfront, as in "El Salvador. Pushing the Limits," 10-87, by Janet

Shenk, but amid the rhetoric and bias, there's often a perception or two that's genuinely free from ideological cant, as in "Guatemala. Who Calls the Shots?" 10-87, by Elizabeth Farnsworth. An "unholy" alliance between Israel's orthodox "zealots" and "reactionary" Christian fundamentalists was discovered in "Terror on Sacred Ground," 8/9-87, by Robert I. Friedman, but here, as with so many other features, a specific incident serves for a broader indictment of the administration, or conservatives, or U.S. policy, or Reagan himself, that simply isn't warranted.

Adam Hochschild passed the editor's hell-raising pitchfork midyear to writer Doug Foster with some evident pride. *MoJo*'s impact can be assessed somewhat by the numerous reprints of its articles that appear in other "movement" press. New editor Foster has an impressive resume, having produced Emmy winning television documentaries, investigated stories for "60 Minutes," and done segments for "MacNeil/Lehrer NewsHour." The last few issues of 1987 were promising and we look forward to seeing what Mr. Foster can do now with *Mother Jones*.

Editor: Douglas Foster

Address: 1663 Mission Street
             San Francisco, CA 94103
             (415) 358-8881

Circulation: 186,341

The Nation

Founded in 1865, this weekly has gone through many twists and turns. Its pre-World War I circulation, under the scholarly and philosophy inclined editor Paul E. More, was around 6,000, yet the circulation of the magazine's ideas among intellectuals was far more pervasive than those figures would suggest. During the 1930s and '40s its circulation expanded, its influence in the U.S. socialist movement growing. In the post-war years, it skidded toward oblivion, circulation and influence dropping, the magazine becoming more sectarian as the leftist movement itself receded. Under the tenure of Hamilton Fish III, the magazine's circulation went from 20,000 in 1977 to 85,000 today. *The Nation* is still outside the mainstream of political magazines in the U.S., but, along with *Mother Jones*, takes its place as the leading publication of the leftist political community. Fish departed this year turning the job over to Arthur L. Carter, a former investment banker who is also a major owner of the weekly.

Nicaragua, economic policy, the cold war, feminism and Israel continue to be major issues covered in the weekly — Israel because "U.S.-Israeli relations form the prime zone of mystification and censorship in the U.S. media...[contaminating] the political culture...[and compromising] efforts to establish left politics."

The skilled technicians under editor Victor Navasky (there are no geniuses there) devoted more effort this year to reworking old ideas. A serious attempt was undertaken by *Nation* columnists Alexander Cockburn and Robert Pollin to provide its readers with "more than a denunciation of mainstream ideas," by opening up a discussion 2-28 on "concrete" proposals for economic policy. *The Nation* was alert in seeing the utility of work by economists Barry Bluestone and Bennett Harrison for challenging "market logic with socialist logic," though there is still a tension in the magazine over the issue. I.F. Stone, for example, in the post-Crash front page "Binge. End of a Profligate Era," 10-31, seemed shop-worn, visions of 1930's soup lines and mass unemployment the staples of his articles on the economy. Nothing to compare with Cockburn's more politically honed sense: "As the bulls fought back, progressives and liberal Democrats joined a chorus alternately panic-stricken and gleeful, urging joint Congressional and presidential action to curb the deficit, balance the budget, raise taxes — in short, do everything humanly possible to insure the onset of a major depression," 10-31.

Along with Cockburn's "Beat the Devil" column, there's Christopher Hitchens' "Minority Report" column, which always requires a few tons of salt, as with his report, 7-4, that there is evidence Reagan's campaign team promised Teheran weapons if release of U.S. embassy hostages would be delayed until after the November elections. Jefferson Morley, recruited from *The New Republic* as Washington Editor, often teams up with correspondent David Corn, their "Beltway Bandits" columns often throwing us items neglected elsewhere, as for example, their discussion with Jonathan Bush on his brother George's stand on abortion, 10-3. "I just say that he supports the right to an abortion and then back off the topic...When you're raising money there is no time for politics."

Stephen Cohen's "Sovieticus" column was sanguine all year on prospects for Gorbachev's reforms, as was the collection of articles on the subject in the 6-13 issue. Andrew Kopkind's coverage of the presidential candidates seems to be verging toward a cheering section for Jesse Jackson, his critical investigations of Gephardt and Dukakis quickly ruling them out.

Editorially, we noted a sharper political sense this year on occasion. "The Baker Regency," 3-14, saw the change in the Administration toward "damage control" and a shelving of the Reagan Revolution. "Medium Gains," 10-3, was very alert in sensing an opportunity for detente via Sen. Sam Nunn (D-Ga), whose "tactic of linking treaty ratification to continued progress in the disarmament dialogue could help keep the Administration on the peace track."

The feminist movement continued to be the issue that seemed to provoke the widest and most heated exchanges at the weekly. "The Strange Case of Baby M," by Kathy Pollitt, 5-23, an argument for the movement taking up defense of Baby M's mother as a feminist cause, was a provocative feature, but the really hot debates occurred around the issue of pornography and feminism, and whether "heterosexuality is a crime" or not, Maureen Mullarkey's "Hard Cop, Soft Cop," 5-30, generating one of the hottest collection of outraged letters to the editor.

"Internation," an innovation providing investigative features utilizing a pool of journalists here and abroad premiered, hitting for example, "The Heritage Foundation Abroad," 6-7. Features from various contributors range over a wide assortment of issues. Among them we noted "The Defiling of Writers. The F.B.I. and American Lit," 10-10, by Natalie Robins, investigative work into the bureau's collection of files on American authors. Jonathan Kwitny also made an appearance, though his "Money, Drugs, and the *Contras*," 8-29, was mostly an update on his book, *The Crimes of Patriots*.

Despite some progress, there's still a lot of the "wasted space" in *The Nation* that Cockburn chafed about to editor Navasky, as the weekly wrestles with the formidable task of maintaining a voice for the socialist persuasion. "The right defines the politics and ideology, the liberals limit themselves to technical or legalistic questions, and the left doesn't exist," *The Nation* editorialized, 6-7. But hope springs eternal, the April 25 mobilization against U.S. policy on Central America and South Africa seen as a victory for rebuilding a mass movement on the left. At last, "The left-out had a chance to look at each other as they marched," *The Nation* observed, 5-9.

Editor: Victor Navasky

Address: 72 Fifth Avenue
               New York, N.Y. 10011
               (212) 242-8400

Circulation: 90,000

The National Interest

Heading into its third year of publication, this foreign policy quarterly is at last beginning to hold our attention. We are attracted by occasional analyses generally not seen elsewhere.

Some cut against the grain of conventional foreign policy analysis and some offer new angles from which to view problems of strategic and foreign policy. *TNI* hasn't effected a full-fledged transformation of the terms and content of foreign policy debate, on the whole representing just "another side" of the discussion.

It assesses the Administration's foreign policy as one that has functioned without the "conceptualizing and orchestrating [of] a strategically coherent policy." Yet, this critique is not so far removed from similar ones that might be found in *Commentary* or *Policy Review*, or for that matter, even in *Foreign Affairs* or *Foreign Policy*. The perception is hardly novel, nor is the conclusion that the President suffers a policy problem, not a management one. *TNI*, however, aspires to transcend the conventional assumptions in foreign policy commentary and analysis, and go beyond being merely a "conservative" point of view in policy circles. We still did not see much evidence of that, however.

Summitry and arms control were both subjected to treatment this year. *TNI* opened the year with an examination of the 1986 Reykjavik summit — "a near disaster...not a near triumph." In "Summits and Troughs," Winter, co-editor Owen Harries argued that "Reykjavik has done what conservatives have always feared summit conferences would do: it has raised unrealistic and dangerous expectations concerning the imminent possibility of a general settlement." The U.S. had surrendered the agenda, letting arms control totally dominate it, and, Owens editorialized, the next summit could find the President with less grounds to resist a bad agreement.

More satisfying on arms control was the challenge to the conventional set of assumptions that appeared in "The Sarajevo Fallacy: The Historical and Intellectual Origins of Arms Control Theology," by Patrick Glynn, Fall. Contrary to the paradigm that "the arms race caused the [first world] war," Glynn reviews the historical record to demonstrate that only "by assuring that deterrence and defensive alliances remained unambiguously strong" could states be prevented from unleashing war. "Power politics was — and is — a permanent feature of the human condition."

We also noted, as an insightful contribution to the analysis of the Iran-Contra affair, "Executive Power & Our Security," by Carnes Lord, Spring. "The Iran operation pointed to...the inability of the White House to ensure effective implementation of its policies by the bureaucracy...Congress, the media, the courts, and the bureaucracy have all proven more promising vehicles for the advancement of liberal policies." The presidency has increasingly run up against "Congress and the media in alliance with elements within the federal bureaucracy...particularly the case in the national security area."

One of the better efforts at an examination of the USSR under Gorbachev to appear in policy journals, "What's Happening In Moscow?" Summer, provided some fresh material, both analytically and in terms of detail and data. A symposium of views, however, the effort was mixed, ideologically fixed positions amid efforts to think through what might be different about Gorbachev's Russia from the previous one. In the same issue, "Swords Without Shields," by Albert Wohlsetter, perhaps the greatest strategic theoretician of our time, was an engrossing examination of defense strategies, and the issue of strategic nuclear defense was addressed with the contributions to "How To Proceed With SDI," Spring. The "Deploy Now," case was stated by Rep. Jack Kemp (R-NY) with William J. Perry, Brent Snowcroft, Joseph S. Nye, Jr., and James A. Schear presenting the case for continued research and opposition to any U.S. strategy to "go it alone."

Among the analytical features on U.S.-Soviet relations, one of the best anywhere on the two powers' strategic interests in the Third World was "Patterns of Intervention: America & the Soviets in the Third World," Spring, by Samuel P. Huntington. Huntington sorted through their various interests, from the tangential to the critical, and noted a historical pattern: "Soviet surges into the Third World have tended to coincide with tendencies toward detente in Soviet-American relations. When those relations have become more antagonistic, the Soviets have tended to pull back and to make a point of avoiding 'adventurism' in the the Third World.''

Unlike *Foreign Affairs* and *Foreign Policy*, *The National Interest* did not feature a major analytic on economic policy and global strategy. Although we appreciate not having to subject ourselves to "black hole" and "twin deficit" jibber-jabber again, we did expect *TNI* would develop into a journal that would make new attempts at a comprehensive examination of foreign economic policy — a few plowshares along with the swords.

Editors: Owen Harries
             Robert W. Tucker

Address: 1627 Connecticut Ave., NW
             Washington, DC 20009
             (202) 483-0630

Circulations: 3,700

National Journal

The *NJ* is without a doubt the nation's most influential publication relative to its subscription base, a mere 5,600 who pay $575 a year for 50 weekly issues (skipping weeks in July and December). In fact, it's probably more influential than we had believed a year ago. In the *1987 MediaGuide* we said it was "a weekly chronicle of official Washington...probably never seen by the President, members of Congress, or the most senior bureaucrats... but must-reading for a mid-management layer inside Washington that slices across Capitol Hill, the federal bureaucracy, the Administration, the lobbyists, and the heavier guns of the national press corps.''

Since then, we've heard from fans of *NJ* in Congress and in the top layers of the bureaucracy who tell us they do too see it, some of them getting it at home. As a result, we spent more time and resources on *NJ* in '87, having every issue go through several hands. Indeed, one of our readers, a career federal bureaucrat, considers *NJ* "the benchmark of legitimate reporting," although the consensus was not quite as strong. It is consistently thorough, accurate, and non-partisan in its coverage of politics and government. It runs to about 60 pages, with several full-page ads from high-tech defense industries who like to keep their names before the folks who are responsible for doling out contracts for defense and space. The journalistic standards are so scrupulous that when subscribers in September were sent a brochure on General Motors' high-tech capabilities, almost immediately a letter of apology came from the publisher, John Fox Sullivan, citing impropriety and complaints from staff and readers.

The strength of the weekly has always been its broad overviews of public-policy matters, comprehensive reporting and focused perspectives. Each issue leads with four "Reports," on "Foreign Policy," or "Trade," or "Campaign," or "Defense," etc., long, detailed articles far beyond the needs of even the average "informed" citizen. It is more readable than its chief competitor in Washington, *Congressional Quarterly*, Capitol Hill's trade magazine, which is for the most part confined to the nuts and bolts of the legislative process. One superb example was Bruce Stokes' "Foreign Owners," 9-19, with wonderful detail, statistics and analysis of the impact foreign ownership of U.S. business and industry is having on the lobbying process, with special-interest trade associations being neutralized.

The "trade focus" was an important one for *NJ* in '87, reflecting the intensity of the issue in Washington, but we expected more detail from it on the 1,000 pages in both the Senate and House versions of the trade bill. It did have the best analysis we saw on the "Plant Closing Law's Political Dynamics," 8-15, by Jonathan Rauch. And Ronald Brownstein's "Tangling Over Trade," 9-19, on the political parties switching sides on the trade issue was an analytical standout.

Brownstein, the magazine's star political reporter in 1986, moved to California in '87 to write a book, producing occasional pieces as *NJ*'s West Coast correspondent. His replacement, James A. Barnes, produced a few memorable pieces on Jack Kemp, 2-27, and George Bush, 6-6, but the falloff in quality was noticeable. Dick Kirschten's White House column was also a disappointment, after favorably catching our eye in '86. But two other political columns, William Schneider's lofty view and Germond & Witcover's view from the trenches, gave *NJ* a net plus in political coverage for the year. Schneider especially is an attraction, having become one of the most important political analysts in the Capital.

We were moderately critical of *NJ*'s coverage of defense issues in '86 and found no improvement in '87. David C. Morrison is consistently useful in his reports on tactical issues, but still seems to draw on too narrow a range of sources on strategic issues. We were not disappointed in Carol Matlack's coverage of science and space.

Other features we genuinely appreciate are the "People" column, which keeps tabs on Washington's musical chairs, and "At a Glance," a checklist of major issues, which remains the best in the business. *NJ* has been a Times-Mirror magazine since 1986.

Editor: Richard S. Frank

Address: 1730 M Street, NW
            Washington, D.C. 20036
            (202) 857-1400

Circulation: 5,600

National Review

National Review gets a new publisher for the new year, 39-year-old Wick Allison of *Art & Antiques* replacing the retiring William Rusher. William Buckley, sole owner of the magazine, may eventually turn over ownership to Mr. Allison if the arrangement works, wanting to keep the same conservative spirit alive in the periodical. We hope so — *National Review* regained a lot of its verve this year, keeping us apprised of its view of the conservative agenda in columns and articles.

"The Week" columns are consistently lively and entertaining, foaming at the mouth like crazy. The 5-8 issue began with: "They fell for it. The Soviets believed that the dummy building in Moscow they were bugging was our *real* embassy, and that the male models they treated to the slinky Russian beauties were *real* Marines. Why, they even think the fellow we sent over to talk about missile reductions is our *real* Secretary of State." Wonderful. In another "Week," we were surprised and gratified to see Kemp endorsed by *National Review* as the conservative candidate of choice so early on in the race "Kemp for President?" 8-14: "The Republican field now assembled is a good one. The best man in it is Jack Kemp." John McLaughlin gives it to us "From Washington Straight" in his columns. A new feature this year: "SDI Watch," appearing in alternate issues, unbylined hard analysis of the technical end of the Strategic Defense Initiative using "technical advisors" and "scientists" as sources, "Notes & Asides," 5-22. The "Books, Arts & Manners" section is one of the best of its kind around — articulate, intellectual, funny. And we enjoy the "help!!!" cartoon and quip section: "Press Another Button, Please," 2-27, by W.H. von Dreele, a little bit of whimsy that was somewhat prophetic:

"See the dollar falling
   Like a plunging rock.
Its descent's designed
   to get us out of hock.
Imports ought to shrivel
   exports ought to grow,

Turning business rosy.
Is it working? No.''

Brian Crozier handles foreign policy issues in ''The Protracted Conflict'' column, while Erik v. Kuehnelt-Leddihn deals with similar themes ''From the Continent'' and Anthony Lejeune writes home ''Letters from London.'' Jeffrey Hart appears occasionally, making us laugh. Sporadic pieces by managing editor Richard Brookhiser are always a treat. And even though editor-in-chief Bill Buckley always looks like he's slept in his clothing when he appears on television, his columns, reprinted by Universal Press Syndicate, are snazzy, bright and biting.

National Review had important cover stories this year, deep and inviting. William Tucker's vast ''Where Do the Homeless Come From?'' 9-25, goes deep beneath the surface figures, exploring demographic patterns and different environmental factors to explain the increase in the vast numbers of homeless Americans, and makes a startling, but well-supported and documented conclusion: the chief culprit is not the Reagan administration or its ''callous'' policies, but rent control. Earlier in the year, Peter Weber did a related and absorbing piece on empty building squatters in NY's Lower East Side, ''Scenes From the Squatting Life,'' 2-27. Max Singer asked ''Can the Contras Win?'' 2-13, evaluating the history of the contra war and concocting different strategic scenarios, if the administration can come up with a ''coherent plan for victory.'' James McGuire had a scathing indictment of Catholic Relief Services for their bureaucratic foul-ups and ripoffs at the expense of starving and dying Ethiopians, ''Scandals in Catholic Relief,'' 7-3. Articles editor Richard Vigilante put ''Big, Bad Bork,'' on the 8-28 cover, a respectful treatment of Bork, the Constitution and the relationship between the two. Joseph Sobran and J. Michael Walker let loose, revealing ''Congress' Red Army,'' 7-31, sharply worded, but illuminating. And a bevy of experts, including Richard Nixon, Henry Kissinger, Les Aspin and William Hyland, contributed to the 5-22 cover ''Reagan's Suicide Pact,'' offering insight on arms control.

The other feature stories that appeared this year were often enlightening, and often-handled hot topics. Secretary of Education William Bennett aired some very frank opinions on sex ed in schools, ''Why Johnny Can't Abstain,'' 7-3. Jeffrey Hart had the first-ever (as far as we know) review of a college (Dartmouth) ''Safe Sex Kit,'' panning it as being absent of ''the manners and substance of civilization,'' '''Safe Sex' and the Presence of the Absence,'' 5-8. In ''Cory Aquino and the Philosophy of Bubbles,'' 8-14, Max Singer wonders about Philippine election-fixing and corruption even under the ''People Power'' president, and the dangers of a coup, two weeks before one occurred. George Gilder argued the trade problem in the computer industry ''Don't Let the Grinch Steal Christmas,'' 4-24 saying ''what matters in international economics is not the exchanges of particular goods but the entire fabric of international intercourse in goods, services, ideas, people and money. The chief danger to the world economy today is...that global trade volume will be sacrificed in an effort to achieve national trade balance.''

We salute William Rusher on his retirement, going out on a banner year at *National Review*, and we look forward to Allison's staying the course under Buckley's tutelage. We're even more looking forward to *National Review* once again becoming *the* place where conservative intellectuals can find a forum for ideas — and they're well on their way.

Editor: William F. Buckley, Jr.

Address: 150 East 35th Street
            New York, NY 10016
            (212) 679-7330

Circulation: 122,034

The New Republic

TNR continues to be the nation's most important political journal. The slim weekly is close enough to the mainstream to serve as a forum for the great policy debates and just far enough from it to be on the margin, where change occurs. And it does so with a longer perspective than the editorial pages of the major newspapers can provide. It was a true journal of the left when American liberalism was mainstream, but it has remained vibrant and vital by shifting with the perimeters of the ongoing political debate.

To Charles Peters of the neoliberal *The Washington Monthly*, *TNR*'s editor Michael Kinsley is a "neoconservative," but that's with tongue-in-cheek. There are plenty of neo-con currents in the magazine, but Kinsley is not one, valiantly keeping his oar to port, his "TRB" column paddling against the contras, corporate greed, Judge Bork, and the Reagan Administration in general. But Kinsley's mission is to reinvigorate the Democratic party's liberals, to shape them up to the point where they might once again present serious White House challenges, to redefine liberalism so that it once again is palatable to the electorate. So he might seem a neo-con for spending so much time directing his magazine against foolishness, incompetence and irrelevance in his own ranks.

"TRB" of 6-1, for example, writes of "Nice Young Man," Senator Gore, who Beltway liberals have been elevating as a possible white hope amidst chatter of "Gore Chic." Kinsley kills him with kindness, piling on the praise, "thoughtful," "sincere," "responsible to a fault," "high gloss," "resume," "an old person's idea of a young person," "admissible, admirable, admissible," and we get it that Gore ain't the white hope, but the white bread candidate. "TRB" of 6-22 yearns for Senator Bill Bradley to get into it, attempting to shame him into the race.

Indeed, we come to think of the magazine under Kinsley as a sheepdog, constantly trying to keep the flock together and headed in a promising direction, but also nipping or barking at the wolves and mavericks. The 10-10 issue is a perfect example, with an editorial on "The Closing of the Democratic Mind," on the sorry state of the presidential field, Henry Fairlie writing on "Hamalot," a savage critique of Senator Kennedy, partly for his vivid slurs against Judge Bork, and Andrew Sullivan's "The Bork Show," disdainful observations on Senator Biden & Co. All the while, mind you, Kinsley is in *high-minded* opposition to the Bork nomination and puts the magazine firmly in opposition to him. This is how publisher Martin Peretz keeps *TNR* the hot political magazine it has been through the conservative Reagan years, giving his editors leeway to range about and put their own imprint on the book. For his own part, Peretz is as pro-Israel as one can find in the ranks of American publishers, but he is in the same way a harsh critic of errant Israeli policies and posturings. The "Israelamok" editorial, 3-30, sees the Iran-arms affair and the Pollard spy affair as only the most outrageous instances of a policy run amok.

So, too, with the magazine's handling of blacks and issues touching on black Americans, who are also part of the Kinsley's flock in the Democratic Party. "On the Beach," 2-23, an editorial in the wake of the Howard Beach trauma is a sharp paddling of Jesse Jackson's exploitation of the incident. "The search of Jackson's appeal is that he uses the rhetoric of unity to divide." In the "Closing of the Democratic Mind" editorial, we're told the one certainty is that Jesse Jackson will not be the Democratic nominee, not because of racism at all. "Ask yourself: What if Jesse Jackson were white? The truth is he'd be a laughingstock. As it is, he's gotten a free ride and the simulacrum of respect. That is due to a residual, patronizing racism that refuses to hold a black candidate to even the abysmally low standards to which we hold white candidates." In "The Imperial Mayor," 10-26, Juan Williams, a black reporter for *The Washington Post*, writes a devastating critique of Mayor Marion Barry of the District of Columbia, one of several critical assessments he's done of self-serving black politicos, which he probably could not get into the *Post*. One of the best articles of the year in *TNR* was "The Case Against Compassion," 12-15-86, by Mickey Kaus, now of *Newsweek*, arguing that the Democrats' appeal to compassion will not and has not ever worked, only self interest and the general interest will.

The more conservative regulars of *TNR* were hired not by neoconservative Peretz, but by liberal Kinsley. Fred Barnes, who writes the traditional "White House Watch" column, like Kinsley, is a four-star journalist in this year's *MediaGuide*. Like columnists Evans & Novak, we have little doubt about his general political taste, but never know what he's going to serve us, always hard analysis that follows hard reporting, with never a crutch of conventional wisdom — which by its nature is already out of date. He's no Dole fan, but gives us "Dole Moment," 1-26, seeing the Senator as the candidate of the artificial moment, whose fortunes soar by default — but will this moment be sustained? His "Shevardnaze Schmooze," 10-19, covers RR's happy talk with the Soviet Foreign Minister, but is also very sharp analysis of Reagan's patience of six years paying off with a zero-option INF offer. Where other liberals talk themselves into thinking of Reagan as a senile nitwit, *TNR* finds ways to remind them that there may be more to him than meets the eye.

The other more or less conservative regular, Charles Krauthammer (there are no "right-wingers" at *TNR*), does the foreign policy analytics. Morton Kondracke, like Kinsley and Barnes, a fairly regular guest on TV's political talk show, "The McLaughlin Group," is yet another drawing card at the magazine, polishing his byline after a few years behind a *Newsweek* desk. Other bylines that always catch our attention are those of James K. Glassman, John Judis, and Leon Wieseltier, with Jeff Pasley up and coming.

Kinsley has had his widest audience with a monthly column in *The Wall Street Journal*, many of them skewering the *WSJ* for inconsistent or illogical editorial positions, as he sees it. In 1988, he'll have an even broader audience, leaving the *Journal* for a monthly essay page in *Time*. But his principal energies will continue to go into keeping *TNR* the hottest property on the block. Especially in one of the most interesting and unusual presidential election years of our time.

Editor: Michael Kinsley

Address: 1220 19th Street, NW
              Washington, D.C. 20036
              (202) 331-7494

Circulation: 92,500

Newsweek

The trendiest of the weeklies, *Newsweek* further developed its liberal "social conscience" as it explored the frontiers of "Impact!" journalism. As we noted last year, "*Newsweek* proved in '86 that the print media can compete with TV news in providing drama, in chucking serious news coverage since it might bore, in not worrying about what its coverage actually says, but more about how it says it." And so it was in '87. Targeting the OINK and DINK population with a Madison Avenue vengeance has allowed the "Impact!" mentality to further smudge the magazine's integrity. (For those not in the know, that's "one income-no kids," and "double income-no kids," as coined by Bill Powell in "TV: The Vanishing Viewer," 5-18.)

A spate of fashionable, but social consciousness-raising covers were produced to accent the exclamation point. Absolutely painful cover stories included "Every Parent's Nightmare," 3-16, one reporter's excruciating personal account of a child born with a birth defect, and "The Face of AIDS: A Year in the Epidemic," 8-10, a stark black-and-white photo montage of dead AIDS victims, reminiscent of the classic Vietnam era cover. Notably absent was last year's "Impact!" story, "The Drug Crisis," which *Newsweek* was going to cover as intensely as that aforementioned war, evidently out of vogue this year, with only one piece that we saw ("Urban Murders: On the Rise," 2-9).

Other particularly faddish cover subjects followed the "Impact!" credo: Two of Jim and Tammy Bakker ("Holy Wars," 4-6; "Heaven Can Wait," 6-8); marriage ("How to Stay Married," 8-24, a perverse follow-up to last year's 6-2 cover "The Marriage Crunch," which told us most women after a certain age would probably not get married); Max Headroom ("Mad About Max," 4-20); "The Untouchables" ("Mob Hit," 6-22); "Les Miserables" ("Show of Shows," 3-30); and Vanna White ("Game Shows," 2-9). It's true that all three weeklies focus an occasional human interest story on the cover, but none quite has the same jangled feel to it as *Newsweek*.

Having adopted the Yupper West Siders as the target audience, social issues were also prominent on the covers: "Depression," 5-4; "A Celebration of Heroes," 7-6 (Vietnam veterans); "Mothers for Hire," 1-19; "Brothers: A Vivid Portrait of Black Men in America," 3-23; and two AIDS covers ("Kids with AIDS," 9-7, cited by executive editor Steve Smith as one of the pieces he is most proud of, and the aforementioned "Face of AIDS"). AIDS also was prominent inside the magazine, understandably so. Coverage was sometimes heartless: an Aric Press piece on AIDS-infected prostitutes and others who spread the virus knowingly ended with the admonition "Caveat emptor" ("The Charge: AIDS Assault," 6-22). But more often than not, on the up side of "Impact!," *Newsweek* stepped in where other weeklies feared to tread. In "A New Panic Over AIDS," 3-30, a doctor is quoted as saying that with an AIDS patient, suicide is always a possibility. A related story was the wonderfully extensive Gregg Easterbrook cover of 1-26, "A Revolution in Medicine," telling you all you need to know about health care today.

The Washington bureau, under its first year with Evan Thomas as bureau chief, produced several Watergate-like covers on the Iran-Contra affair, screaming "Coverup," 3-2 (in vivid white on black, no less); "Reagan's Failure," 3-9; "The Pressure Builds," 2-23; and "Oliver North, Star Witness," 7-13, relentlessly sniffing for the smoking gun. Coverage of the unfolding presidential campaigns has been more demure. With the fall of Gary Hart, a team including Margaret Garrard Warner, Howard Fineman, Erik Calonius and "bureau reports" got the poop to senior writer Tom Morgenthau, who assembled the "Sex, Politics and the Press" cover of 5-18. The finished product, "The Sudden Fall of Gary Hart," offered such political tidbits as Donna Rice "posing with one breast exposed for a poster...more recently, to judge by her publicity photos, she has apparently had cosmetic surgery to enlarge her bust." As evidence, the enterprising story was accompanied by a photo of Ms. Rice in a bathing suit, revealing ample portions of what quite possibly could be a cosmetically altered bust. With the return of Eleanor Clift, the advent of Evan Thomas, and the addition of Mickey Kaus, formerly of *The New Republic*, we expected more splash in 1987, more impact. Still, we await 1988's presidential coverage with high hopes.

The business pages of *Newsweek* we find the most interesting of the three newsweeklies, with Bill Powell and Rich Thomas the power hitters, easily holding their own. Powell's "Citizen Trump" cover, 9-28, was a gem. Annetta Miller caught our eye as well and we even felt a bit more comfortable with Jane Byrant Quinn than in earlier years. She offers financial advice, alternating on the business commentary page with Robert Samuelson, who has the best socio-economic column going, also more palatable, relevant and timely than it seemed last year.

We drubbed the foreign reporting last year for the floweriness of the writing. This year the language has been straightforward, but the coverage, particularly in Central America, has been irregular, and sometimes unacceptable. On the up side, Andrew Nagorski shone in "The Rebirth of an Idea," 3-30, on the reunification of Europe, nicely treated. But deputy foreign editor Rod Nordland continued to disappoint. Both "A Do-or-Die Offensive," 5-11, and "The New Contras," 6-1, written after a month of research in Nicaragua, were tilted toward the Marxist government — even more than we expected from this new, fashionable *Newsweek*.

We always read George Will and Meg Greenfield as they alternate weeks on the back-page commentary, pleased with the mellower George. A new feature we find useful, and fun, is the "Perspectives" page of cartoons and quips, placed strategically at the beginning of the magazine as a lure.

Editor-in-Chief: Richard M. Smith

Address: 444 Madison Avenue
             New York, N.Y. 10022
             (212) 350-4000

Circulation: 3,050,000

The New York Review of Books

A bright, young freelancer, Scott Lahti, writing in *National Review*, "The Fourteenth Colony," 12-31-86, provided an insight into the consequence of the left-liberal ideological monopoly at *The New York Review of Books* — "*TNYRB* reads as if it were centrally planned by John Kenneth Galbraith and Irving Howe." Despite the heavy unevenness this produces, the biweekly still contains sparkling gems here and there. In fact, "The Political Impasse," 3-26, by *The Washington Post*'s political writer Thomas B. Edsall, a dazzling political essay *cum* book review, was among the year's top ten articles in that category.

Editors Robert B. Silvers and Barbara Epstein used "regulars" on the various major stories of 1987. The Iran-Contra affair was Theodore Draper's baby, though Stanley Hoffman also filled in. Draper decided not to look at the minutiae of the affair, but at its implications for the institutions and structure of our government. Somehow he discovered "The Reagan Junta," 1-29, going on later to describe "The Fall of Reagan's Junta," 10-22. There's "something new about the Reaganite phenomenon...A would-be imperial president has prepared the way for a would-be presidential junta," he wrote. He took on Irving Kristol, Norman Podhoretz, Pat Buchanan and Charles Krauthammer for complicity in defending or rationalizing the affair. The "junta," however, was a strawman all year, battered around until there was simply no chaff left, as there was no junta to begin with. More meritorious was his foreign policy analysis, "Reckless America," 7-16. A critique of "American Hubris from Truman to the Persian Gulf," it was properly passionate, consistent with *TNYRB*'s voice. Hoffman's "Reagan's Underworld," 5-7, was less compelling.

Ian Baruma, cultural editor of the very fine *Far Eastern Economic Review*, seemed to have the East Asia "franchise," most prolific on the region. His main feature, "Korea: Shame and Chauvinism," 1-29, was a very skillful and revealing study of Kim Dae Jung — "One searches in vain for Kim's definition of democracy beyond moral platitudes." In contrast, Timothy Garton Ash, whose Central European reportage is almost without peer, simply wasn't utilized sufficiently this year, his "Who Was Churchill?" 5-7, not what we hoped he would be focusing on. Michael Massing, who writes on foreign affairs for *The Atlantic, TNR, The Nation*, etc., was impressive with his profile of Mangosuthu Buthelezi, "The Chief," 2-12. Massing's "Hatred in Haiti," 12-3, also attracted our attention.

Lord Zuckerman was completely predictable again, "Nuclear Blundering," 4-23, and "Nuclear Hope," 5-7, among his articles against SDI: "Until that golden day dawns when the lion and the lamb lie down together, when swords are beaten into plowshares, all that is needed is for the West — and the East — to remain possessed of no more than the sufficient nuclear strength to underwrite the environment of deterrence in which we have learned to live."

Ronald Dworkin's legal reflections in "Renata Adler & the Case of 'Reckless Disregard,' " 2-26, were unexciting. His most widely read article, however, was the snarling, frothing harangue against Judge Robert Bork's "right-wing" and "reactionary" views, "Bork the Radical," 8-13. He made the reasonable point that Bork wants to "too concretely" apply the "original interest" principles of the Framers, but that wasn't enough of a spine for the essay to stand as a whole.

Joan Didion was powerful all year, "Miami: La Lucha," 6-11, great — and thought-provoking — journalism. We noted the release (and order to emigrate) of Anatoly Koryagin shortly after David Satter's "A Test Case," 2-12, made the case for his freedom if Gorbachev is to be taken seriously about human rights in the USSR. Peter Reddaway always has to be read seriously, and we appreciated his "Gorbachev the Bold," 5-28, though not fully persuaded by his analysis.

John Kenneth Galbraith, passe now, and Robert Heilbroner, who can still polish a mean, sophisticated sentence, were used less prominently by Silvers and Epstein. Instead, the major economic features were handled by Felix Rohatyn. In "The Blight on Wall Street," 3-12, "a cancer has been spreading in our industry...greed," he wrote, calling for a limit on tax deductibility of interest by highly leveraged companies and a tax on the profits on securities transactions of currently tax-free institutions, among other things. (Michael Kinsley directed an interesting query to him after this article: tell us, dear Felix, how you made your millions without any taint of greed.) Better was Rohatyn's "On the Brink," 6-11, in which at least — unlike other aspirants for Democrat Administration postings — he seriously addresses approaches to stable monetary policy.

TNYRB was very engaged with the issues of 1987, and though we found it less engaging than we'd hoped, we're noting among the talent there, a fresher and slightly wider-ranging voice.

Editors: Robert B. Silvers
             Barbara Epstein

Address: 250 West 57th Street
             New York, N.Y. 10107
             (212) 757-8070

Circulation: 79,666

Policy Review

The quarterly of The Heritage Foundation, *Policy Review* is one of the most influential journals of conservative debate on the major issues of the moment. It proceeds from the conviction that the conservative revolution is not over, and it has an agenda for the movement. One measure of its success has been the quarterly's ability to alter and shape the framework and content of policy debate in this country. There's an intellectual rigor that comes with its commitment to a "revolutionary" conservative world view. *Policy Review* seeks no less than hegemony for its perspectives in the conservative movement and fundamental transformations of the existing order. It will not, for example, settle for peaceful coexistence with the welfare state.

Contributions from both economic and social conservatives are combined in its pages. There is a "Young Turk" quality to the work by its editors, tough, but never tendentious or truculent. Editor Adam Meyerson, a former *Wall Street Journal* editorialist, does a fine job of successfully running the publication as a forum for the conservative debates, restraining any tendency for *PR*'s transformation into a podium for exhortation.

We saw this year some excellent work on strategic policy. Rev. Pat Robertson's "Dictatorships And Single Standards," Winter, and Rep. Henry Hyde's (R-Ill) "Apologists For Soviet Treaty Violations," Spring, plus Rep. Jim Courter's (R-NJ) Churchillian "The Gathering Storm," Fall, were very timely critical perspectives. Combined with them were essays on the science and politics of the Strategic Defense Initiative. Edward Teller's "Open Letter to Hans Bethe," Winter, examines the political opposition to SDI from some layers of the scientific community.

"Emasculating America's Deterrent," Summer, by Robert Jastrow and James Frelk details the increased vulnerability of the U.S. to Soviet ICBMs as SDI is continually moved to the back burner.

Additional material, on America's foreign policy, cohered with the direction of the discussion on strategic policy. There is a view held by some conservatives, Melvyn Krauss and Irving Kristol, for example, that the West would be strengthened by a phased withdrawal of U.S. ground troops and the U.S. nuclear umbrella from Western Europe, Japan, and Korea. "How NATO Strengthens The West," Spring, by Adam Meyerson, was a well-argued challenge to that thesis. "Insurgents Against Moscow," Summer, by Alvin H. Berstein and "The Road To Managua," Winter, by Timothy Ashby, were both cogent arguments on behalf of the Reagan Doctrine. Assistant editor Michael Johns, however, was less sanguine, assessing at this stage the failure of the Reagan Administration to uproot the culture of appeasement that warps U.S. foreign policy. "The central failure of American conservativism over the past 10 years," Johns argued in "Peace In Our Time," Summer, "has been its inability to delegitimize the Soviet Union in the same way the left has delegitimized South Africa."

On social policy, "A Conservative Vision Of Welfare," Spring, by Stuart M. Butler, was outstanding. Butler goes beyond the critique of present-day welfare systems to address what conservatives have been less than forceful on — what'll you replace them with? "The Campus Cost Explosion," Spring, examines whether college tuitions are unnecessarily high, concluding they are, and that need-based aid allows tuition increases without limit. We also noted as refreshingly astute observations "The Bible Belt Is America's Safety Belt," Fall, by Rabbi Joshua O. Haberman; "The Counter-Revolution In Legal Thought," Summer, by Michael McConnell; former managing editor Dinesh D'Souza's essay on the political education of the Christian right, Summer; and the efforts of former assistant editor Cait Murphy to locate what works and what doesn't in the nation's anti-drug policies, "High Times In America," Winter.

"All Supply-Siders Now," Summer, by managing editor Gordon Jackson, was an important contribution to the history of this movement. Jackson concludes that although supply-side holds the theoretical high ground, "the forces of statism zero-sum thinking gather daily like dark clouds over Washington....but the idea that growth should be at the center of economic policy has unquestionably taken root..." Alvin Rabushka's "Great Leap Forward," Summer, on the spread of capitalism to the Third World, was very well-done. Attentive to the dynamics of tax rate reforms in these countries, Rabushka elevated the discussion beyond the traditionally limited conservative view that privatization *per se* is the key to growth there. "The Tax Capitalization Hypothesis," by Warren Brookes, Winter, in which Boston (low tax rates and booming) and Detroit (high tax rates and stagnating) are compared, was a healthy correction to the disinformation on the issue.

Policy Review continued to successfully alter the terms of debate. Only *The New Republic* is successful along these lines among the liberal political community's publications, otherwise they don't quite have a publication that's comparable to *Policy Review*. We keep looking for one among the journals of that community's various think-tanks, foundations and institutions, but none of them impressed us strongly enough for inclusion in the *MediaGuide*.

Editor: Adam Meyerson

Address: 214 Massachusetts Avenue, NE
           Washington, D.C. 20002
           (202) 546-4400

Circulation: 9,500

Time

A changing of the guard in December as Henry Grunwald stepped down and Jason McManus took over as Editor-in-Chief for Time Inc., and Henry Muller taking McManus' old post of *Time* Managing Editor. *Time*smen all, we doubt there will be much editorial change, especially since McManus spent six months or so with Henry learning the ropes after spending a paltry 30 years at Time Inc. Still, it's new blood at the top, and this cannot help but to freshen the magazine even further.

Snappy coverage this year, focusing on the hard core news beat overseas, but lighter at home. They're still doing the multiple byline shuffle, but in a regular time step, usually using one writer and one or two reporters, depending on the beat. The foreign coverage seemed to hit harder this year, steady as it goes. John Greenwald (reported by Johannesburg-based Bruce Nelan) had a profile of Cyril Ramphosa, black lawyer and general secretary of the then-striking National Union of Mineworkers that was intriguing, leaving us hungry for more. Nelan did a credible job in a single byline appearance that turned out to be one of the best profiles we saw all year on black U.S. Ambassador to South Africa Edward Perkins, "New Man in the Townships," 2-23. Roger Rosenblatt's essay/cover story on Russia was fabulous in "Enter This House and Let the Ice Melt," 10-26, but Moscow staffer James O. Jackson's coverage of Russia was disappointing, leaving us almost empty. In "Gateway to the Gulag," 4-20, he's short on the story of Magadan, formerly a Stalinist hell for political prisoners, giving us vague stats instead of a comprehensive picture, all the more disappointing because the government permitted him to actually go there. But also worth noting: the traditional "Man of the Year" cover appearing the first week of each year became "Woman of the Year" with Pico Iyer's stunning cover story on Cory Aquino, dignified and hopeful in January, then embattled (and covered, unfortunately, only sporadically) later in the year. In Mexico, John Moody noted rather vividly "Pollution is so bad in Mexico City (pop. 18 million) that birds regularly drop dead from the soot-filled sky" in a report on the economy, but missed the December 1986 stock market surge and capital inflow.

Like *Newsweek, Time* went a little berserk on the Iran-contra hearings. Rather darkly, the 3-9 cover queried "Can He Recover?" picturing an unsmiling Ronald Reagan in a dark suit against a dark background holding a darkly covered copy of the *Report of the President's Special Review Board*, contrasting with all-smiles-I-can-fix-it "New Chief of Staff [Howard] Baker" in the upper right-hand corner. Walter Isaacson's preachy "Passing the Buck," 7-27, turned over every stone in Washington to find a smoking gun, and not finding one, said it didn't matter anyway: more troubling is the "larger" pattern, a runaway foreign policy based on lies and deceptions to function outside the law. George Church got on the bandwagon early, portraying Reagan as senior space cadet, "so far out of touch, he's lost the ability to govern," "Is He More Out of Touch Than Ever?" 1-26. Church also produced the cover story "Ollie's Turn," 7-13 (reported by Michael Duffy, Jay Peterzell, and Barrett Seaman), that was an absolute travesty, smearing everybody, raising CIA connection to Lebanese terrorists who blew up 80 people in March 1985 and implicates North, going on to imply the administration was running wild with covert operations, never naming one besides the Iran-Contra initiative. One covert initiative does not running amok make. Better was Church's "Tower of Judgement," 3-2, crisp and credible journalism.

Domestically, their "Campaign Portrait" series, following prospective presidential candidates on the road, was a wonderful idea, but turned out conventional, telling us little, bordering on the boring. Bob Dole's, for example, was routine, slow-starting with a focus on his withered arm instead of digging into his record or personality (Jack E. White, "Survivor on the Track," 3-23). Walter Shapiro's "The Duke of Economic Uplift," 7-27, on Mike Dukakis, was equally ho-hum, never giving a good picture of his vision. Other political reports were nothing to holler about either. Lawrence Barrett's 1-19 "Rushing to an Early Kickoff" was evidently too early, superficial and flawed: Jesse Jackson was pictured, listed third in the presidential poll results requisite for this type of article, but mentioned only once in the text and then as a Baptist minister. We found nothing redeeming about Washington bureau chief Strobe Talbott's coverage of national security affairs which was biased, dry, and misinformed. Coverage of Robert Bork's confirmation hearings was mixed. In looking at his judicial history Richard Lacayo gives us a muddy analysis of Bork's legal philosophy, noting his stands on public obscenity: "Opponents say it is the intellectual expediency of a man more provoked by the sight of obscene words than by signs reading WHITES ONLY," "The Law According to Bork," 9-21. In the same issue, David Beckwith, though, had a shimmering cover story, "A Long and Winding Odyssey," that focused carefully on Bork's metamorphosis — wonderful. But we never miss a Hugh Sidey "Presidency" column, though he seems to have been disheartened this year by Ronald Reagan's troubles. And Richard Stengel had a fine wrap-up of why Mario wouldn't run, "Letting the Cup Pass," 3-2.

The covers of 1987 were a mixed bag. *Time* had the first cover, "Air Travel: How Safe Is It?" 1-12, on air travel safety, months before it was a trendy issue after the crash of the Northwest jet in Detroit. Hip covers included "You Bette!" 3-2, on Bette Midler; "U2: Rock's Hottest Ticket," 4-27; "Whatever Happened to Ethics," 5-25; "Who's Bringing Up Baby?" 6-22; "Steve Martin: He's Off the Wall," 8-24; "Are Women Fed Up?" 10-12, detailing Shere Hite's latest report; the inescapable Jim and Tammy Bakker ("Unholy Row," 4-6; and "God and Money," 8-3); and "Cosby, Inc.," 9-28. For the most part, these items were covered according to their news value, as opposed to their trendiness quotient. A false note: a cover story on "Africa," 2-23, seemed like it got into *Time* by mistake, belonging more to *National Geographic*, with its photographs of the wilderness and beasts of the jungle and tribal drums. What about *Africa*?!?

Odds and ends that we liked: Jon D. Hull's nightmarish "Slow Descent into Hell," 2-2, gave us a real feel for the plight of the homeless in Philadelphia, not surprisingly since he took up residence with them to do the story. The "American," "World," and "Business Notes" columns are useful and informative, filled with quips and fun little abstractions. A special item of note: "A Poet's View of *Glasnost*," 2-9, by Yevgeni Yevtushenko, interestingly done.

This year, *Time* receives the award for most nauseating color photograph accompanying "The Coup that Failed," 9-7, p. 25, of a Philippine citizen killed in an aborted coup attempt, 8-28, bullet holes are clearly visible, *countable*, in lurid color. A close and ironic also-ran was the picture of photographers snapping away at bodies left rotting in the sun from the war in Nicaragua, accompanying a press article on the difficulties of covering the contras ("The War That No One Can Cover," 2-16, p. 60). Blame photo editor Arnold H. Drapkin and photographers Noli Yamsuan of Picture Group ("The Coup...") and Mr. Franklin of Magnum. *Newsweek*'s "Impact!" mindset must have seeped in a little.

Still the most reliable weekly for cocktail party banter, *Time* is good as far as it goes. Lightly skimming all it covers, *Time* is hors d'oeuvres, but not a main meal. Let's see what McManus and Muller can whip up for '88.

Editor-in-Chief: Jason McManus

Address: Time-Life Building
             Rockefeller Center
             New York, N.Y. 10020-1393
             (212) 586-1212

Circulation: 4,698,325

USA Today

Why argue with success? Since being launched in September 1982, *USA Today* has grown to become the nation's second largest paper, with a circulation of 1.55 million, mostly from newsstands and vending machines. In May, the Arlington, Virginia publisher, Gannett Co., even announced that the paper turned its first monthly profit, after losing $458 million in '86. Advertising space rose 24% in the first 8 months of the year, and ad revenues were expected to be up 40% for the year as a whole. We're not sure the newspaper has settled into the black, however. The Gannett organization is so vast that it would be child's play to submerge *USA Today*'s red ink in the other parts of the empire, with creative accounting. But it will be nice if we wouldn't even have to imagine that going on, as many of its employees do.

Critics called it fast-food "McNews," easy to swallow, but without much quality or substance. Gannett chairman Allen Neuharth didn't mind. He even commissioned a book published in '87, *The Making of McPaper*, by cover-story editor Peter Prichard. *USA Today* is not out to impress the elite, but merely to fill a niche. For those in a hurry, particularly those who live where there is no decent morning paper, it's a quick and easy read. Hotels and airlines give away a quarter of a million copies around the country, where no local or big-city paper could really serve as well. Travelers can find some tidbit of news from back home, as well as the national weather. For similar reasons, there are 35,000 sold in Europe, the Middle East and Asia. Foreigners would surely look elsewhere to find out what is going on in this country.

Obvious strong points include the splashy use of color photos and graphs, keeping stories on a single page rather than making the reader flip to page 37D, and providing separate sections on Sports, Money and "Life" (people and entertainment). Each section, like the news section, has its own quick roundup section along the left column, even though the whole section often amounts to less than four pages. Some of these advantages have disadvantages. Keeping all stories (except the cover story) on a single page means no subject gets more than a few words, and the style gets as clipped as a telegraph.

The editorial page suffers a similar fate, with a cartoon and interview taking up so much of the page that four articles on a single topic end up being ridiculously short. Serious national issues can't really be developed logically in fewer than 400 words. Standard op-ed length in *The New York Times* is 750. We still believe Neuharth should consider *USA Today* Gannett's flagship, which would mean creating a bona fide editorial page with a top-drawer editor and staff that would define the paper's intellectual character.

There is a great deal more space devoted to sports news than to all issues of national or international importance. Sixty percent of the readers are male, with a median age of 38, and they like sports. And money. The Money section is quite good, crammed with charts and statistics. But the financial news is as myopic as the editpage's, limited to what happened yesterday. Severe space limitations make it impossible for writers to really show their stuff. *USA Today* has lost several promising financial journalists, most notably Mike McNamee, who went to *BusinessWeek*. Among survivors, Anne Kates shows originality, as in "Tax Selling Sets Market Up For A Fall," 11-27. In 1986, *USA Today* did a creditable job in explaining the evolving tax reform law, but nothing really stood out this year in that way. But then, we don't really compare *USA Today* with other newspapers. It's in a class by itself and we wish it solid financial success.

Editor: John C. Quinn

Address: 1000 Wilson Boulevard
            Arlington, VA 22209
            (703) 276-3400

Circulation: 1,324,223

U.S.News & World Report

After drubbing the weekly in the last two *MediaGuide*s, we were pleased to note modest changes for the better at the magazine. Relatively and absolutely, *U.S.News & World Report* had its best year in several.

The most important development was the addition of two stars to the roster. There are movers and shakers who had not cracked open *U.S.News* for years who are now taking a peek. Former defense department assistant secretary Richard Perle, on everyone's list of the smartest people in Washington, is now a regular columnist. Even more important was the wooing of Michael Kramer from *New York* magazine as a weekly columnist on foreign policy and domestic politics. Publisher Mortimer Zuckerman still makes poor use of the magazine's back page by giving us his own parboiled views on the world around him, but he is at least strengthening the magazine's voice on public policy inside the book. *U.S.News*'s timbre has changed with the two weighty additions, and it's at least poised to become a respected competitor among publications with serious influence on policy. There is additional talent appearing regularly as well, including Daniel Boorstin, Richard C. Darman, John Keegan, and John Podhoretz.

There were other notieeable improvements at *U.S.News*. It's still handicapped *vis a vis* its competitors on the breaking, hard-news reporting, an earlier weekend deadline than *Time* or *Newsweek* a liability. (The "scoop" of printing excerpts of Bob Woodward's *Veil* really doesn't count, enough reason to suspect *Newsweek* and the *Post* maybe preferred some advance hype from elsewhere than their pages.) With that constraint, there's always the worry that a "Newsweakly" imitation might emerge. There have been plenty of hands hired away from the trendy *Newsweek* these last few years. But it didn't and looks like it won't. *U.S.News* can handle trends without being trendy, and its news reporting improved this year. There was much less of the thin summary of last week's events or the coverage of what this or that official had to offer of hindsight.

Its new layout works well, playing on its strengths by emphasizing the "News You Can Use" sections. The new tone and style of its voices this year are well-balanced and the straight reporting is just that. Also improved, "Washington Whispers," which had nowhere to go but up, the "gossip" fresher. We expect this feature to improve further as the network of key contacts available to Perle, Kramer and the others can be tapped.

U.S.News, it seemed, held the edge for the number of its cover stories that were picked up and reported on by others — "In a story that appears in *U.S.News* this week...," an often heard preface to the electronic media's news coverage this year. Its cover story on airline gridlock at the end of last year, with the news that things were going to get worse, was shrewdly timed, practically selling out at airport terminals where stranded passengers whiled the time away reading it. What you need to know about "AIDS," 1-12, contained enough new information for it to be treated as news itself by the rest of the media. Among other solid productions of note: "Help Wanted," 9-7, where the jobs are; "America's Best Colleges," 10-26, everything you needed to know on what they offer and what it takes to get in, including what you may not have wanted to know about the costs involved for some; "Alcoholism," 11-30, excellent, no trendy "impact" orientation whatsoever; a hard-news story that focused on the medical breakthroughs occurring with this condition. "Narcotics: Terror's New Ally," 5-4, was a hot piece that circulated among the political and intelligence communities, *U.S.News* exploring this dimension of the drug plague more deeply than others. The cover that Zuckerman can bronze with justifiable pride, "The Bull Market: Time to Get Out?" 8-31, by Jack Egan and Daniel Weiner, appeared in readers' hands at almost precisely the peak on Wall Street, 8-25. It was a gutsy move.

Foreign reporting isn't a strength of the weeklies, given the lag time compared to the dailies (though the *Far Eastern Economic Review* has found a way to be very competitive with daily publications). Among the U.S. weeklies, *Time* holds the lead on foreign coverage overall.

However, we think *U.S.News* just barely edged them out on Asia this year, as Mary Lord and Walter Taylor were more satisfying than their competitors at *Time* and *Newsweek*. The European coverage improved this year, Robin Knight doing just fine as new, senior European editor, and Jeff Trimble in Moscow is more fleet-footed than his predecessor. John Barnes holds up well in the Middle East, and both Bernard Simon in Canada and Jim Jones in Johannesburg are assets, who, with more direction and assignments from editors, could set the pace among the weeklies there. Among the contributing editors rounded up by Zuckerman, Simon Jenkins adds great strength on foreign matters, particularly South Africa. A new foreign editor, hired from *The Economist,* we hear is on the way.

U.S.News has all the makings for out-distancing *Time* and *Newsweek* on national security and defense. With Richard Perle doing regular columns, and frequent material from contributing editor Col. Henry Summers, Jr., it's a serious contender now. We think the atmosphere's changing there as a consequence, Henry Trewitt and Robert Kaylor both attracting our attention more so this year.

To add to these gains, Zuckerman's team of editors have to decide more concretely whether to move further in the direction of individualistic reports or stick with the kind of news digesting that it has relied on in the old newsweekly style, collective journalism and multiple bylines. The top of the masthead, underneath Zuckerman and David Gergen, looks stronger than ever, with Mike Ruby, Peter Bernstein and Christopher Ma, a talented trio. With growing confidence they might take a few more risks, take some flyers. The bear market at *U.S.News* might be ending.

Editor: David R. Gergen

Address: 2400 N Street NW
             Washington, D.C. 20037-1196
             (202) 955-2111

Circulation: 2,223,000

The Washingtonian

Owned by Philip Merrill, who also owns the Annapolis daily, *Capital*, and *Baltimore* magazine, *The Washingtonian* was established in 1965. Under the editorship of John A. Lippert since 1969, the monthly's circulation has grown from under 20,000 to more than 145,000 paid. Averaging over 300 pages per month (442 in November) there's always a good to very, very good feature or article to be found here.

Amazingly fresh for a monthly, "Capital Comment," edited by John Sansing, contains tidbits of new information on the Beltway scene we just didn't see anywhere else. Staff writers Rudy Maxa's and Diana McLellan's articles are light, entertaining, primarily for the DC crowd, but often worth a skim. For example, from McLellan's zodiacal search for the next president, "The Stars of '88," 11-87: Bob Dole — "Hey, he's the mother we all wish we'd had — he has four planets in Cancer! He's tender, protective, loving, humorous, but always the boss." Maxa waxes along in a similar style, though "The Book on Bradlee," 5-7, his profile on *The Washington Post* executive editor was a cut above.

Among the notable occasional writers, we always look for the bylines of James K. Glassman, Vic Gold, and Owen Ullman. From Vic Gold's "It Was A Mistake!" 1-87, two selections from his "Top 'Second-Guessers'" list: Robert McNamara, "the whiz-kid Secretary of Defense who predicted victory in Vietnam by the end of 1966. Since leaving government he spends most of his time telling Presidents and Defense Secretaries where they've gone wrong;" and Ralph Nader — "if it breathes, second-guess it; if it moves, sue it." Ullman's "Who's In Charge?" 8-87, was solid on the political establishment's love-in with new chief of staff Howard Baker.

"As much as the establishment loathed Regan, the outsider, it loves Baker, 61, the quintessential insider," though disappointed their boy had yet to "moderate Reagan's right-wing instincts." An early reading on the new Administration, Ullman even raised speculation that Baker was too "laid back," and that maybe aides Tom Griscom or Ken Duberstein were running things. An attempt to tell the Paul Volcker-Fed story by *Chicago Tribune* economics correspondent Bill Neikirk, "The Importance of Being Volcker," 3-87, impressed us with its effort, though it was still unsatisfying.

Fred Barnes of *The New Republic* frequently appears in *The Washingtonian*. One of *The Washingtonian*'s best features (and Barnes') was surely "The Post vs. The Times: Which Is Better?" 5-87. We were flattered and impressed by the coherence of his superb critical vignettes on the editors and journalists with those of our own *MediaGuide*. Former *Washington Journalism Review* editor Barbara Matusow moved from contributor to regular staff writer. Among the best in the business on the media front, with several fine articles for the magazine in 1987, her "The Incredible Shrinking Anchor," 6-87, was outstanding work on the ups and downs at CBS News.

If one single *Washingtonian* article comes to mind from 1987 it can only be "The Ollie We Knew," 7-87, by David Halevy and Neil Livingstone. Halevy, a military-affairs correspondent for *Time* magazine, teamed up with Livingstone, a consultant on terrorism and low-intensity warfare, to produce one of the 10 best stories of the year from the print media. What North really did, and why, unadorned by any myth, every aspect of the remarkable Colonel's character and being is richly presented in this virtuoso piece. Bravo to them for producing it, and bravo to *The Washingtonian* for featuring it.

Editor: John A. Limpert

Address: 1828 L Street NW
               Washington, D.C. 20036
               (202) 296-3600

Circulation: 149,323

The Washington Monthly

Compiling the biographical data of the many U.S. journalists of the major periodicals for our "Biographics" section, we were reminded of how many cut their teeth at Charles Peters' delightful monthly. Some great talent was nurtured there before moving on to editorships, columns, or reporting elsewhere. Of course, great quality is still at *The Washington Monthly*.

The magazine's philosophy is *neoliberal* — a term coined actually by *TWM* itself — and nowhere does it show up better than in Peters' "Tilting At Windmills" column. Chivalrously jousting sometimes, or just plain old bashing at others, the editor-in-chief deploys his lance primarily against the mentality and activities of Jurassic-age bureaucratism, with horny-membraned conservatives, and the "neo-conservative" [sic] colleagues of Michael Kinsley the recipients of his barbs as well. But nutty new-age libs and jellyfish liberalism don't escape either. With a sort of "'nuff said?" observation he cuts them all down to size. For example, from his 4-87 column, "if you wondered why California voters threw such a nice liberal as Rose Bird out of office" consider her court's decision to overturn Bernard Lee Hamilton's murder conviction. "The Bird court found that his 'intent' to kill...[Eleanore Frances Buchanan] was not clear. Although he stabbed her, hacked off her hands, and cut off her head, the court held that 'the victim might have been accidentally killed.'"

The Washington Monthly had one of the great covers for 1987 — a grim-faced Maxwell Smart, calling headquarters on his shoe telephone, a gun pointed to his head, under which the headline for a feature story, 3-87: "Would You Believe...Iranian Moderates?" The article itself, however, by Marci McDonald, Washington bureau chief for the Canadian newsweekly

Macleans, wasn't so great. Challenging the CIA's record under Bill Casey, she laid out the charges that he specifically tailored the agency's intelligence "to fit the administration's passions about Nicaragua" and that in general he used "intelligence as a tool to justify a foreign policy." While noting some defenses of Casey against the charges, they were begrudged, reinforcing our impression that her conclusion was assembled before her evidence.

We loved Art Levine's and Kathleen Currie's "Whip Me, Beat Me and While You're at It Cancel My NOW Membership," 6-87: "Spurred by the growing acceptance of the anti-porn campaign, fueled by the Meese Commission Report....the Great Sex Wars engage the best and the brightest of radical feminists in an intellectual's version of mud-wrestling." Reviewing the feminists' civil war over porn, the authors introduce readers to the great debates over what is "politically correct erotica" and whether or not enjoyment of sex with the male enemy is "collaboration."

There was a steady barrage on Pentagon positions from *TWM* trenches in 1987. "The Dark Secret of the Black Budget," 5-87, by Tim Weiner of the *Philadelphia Inquirer*, opened fire on the rapid growth of spending on secret weapons and programs, asserting that the "black budget" projects have "become a hiding place not just for weapons and operations that should be kept secret but for those that are poorly managed or conceived." Robert Coran, *Atlanta* contributing editor, authored "The Case Against the Air Force," 7/8-87, strafing the initiative to convert frontline fighter planes into carriers of smart bombs behind enemy lines. "All at the expense of providing close-air support to U.S. troops in battle," he argued.

Editors Steven Waldman and Paul Glastris are regularly productive. Glastris' "The Powers That Shouldn't Be," 10-87, presented the case against five Washington insiders the next Democratic president shouldn't hire. Among them, Jimmy Carter's Assistant Secretary of Education Mary Frances Berry who wrote in 1982 that black Americans faced in the 1960s "the threat of genocide...roughly comparable to the threat faced by Jews in the 1930s" and Carter's NSC director Zbigniew Brzezinski, "now...just about in sync with the right wing of the *Republican* Party....[and] the master of counseling bold action even when reality dictated another course." While the business-financial magazines produce their versions of the "Best and Worst" companies, CEOs, etc., Waldman produced a clever "The Best and the Worst Unions," 7/8-87. Yet after outlining the criteria for a "good" union, he unconvincingly anointed the United Auto Workers as one of the "good," the International Brotherhood of Teamsters one of the "bad." Since former President Douglas Fraser's appointment to the Chrysler board in 1980, the UAW thinks of the common good, he asserted, never mentioning its championing of protectionism or the union's distance from the pro-growth perspectives of Walter Reuther. Moreover, the IBT serves its members badly, he argued, presenting the Justice Department's case via the dubious charges of the leftist Teamsters for a Democratic Union.

TWM runs a "Political Booknotes" and an "On Political Books" section. The former are generally crisp and incisive reviews by staff and outsiders that meet the standards one expects in a "book review." The latter, however, resemble the kinds of book "reviews" one sometimes comes across in *The New York Review of Books* — i.e., instead of anchored, critical treatment of the book, a flying exegesis on its subject matter. Because *TWM*, however, separates this section from its "book reviews," it's not disturbing or objectionable, and in fact has been very rewarding (or disappointing), depending on the writer's competence.

Overall, *The Washington Monthly* was a treat in 1987. We know Charles Peters will never run out of windmills with which to tilt, and we look forward to *TWM*'s tournaments next year.

Editor: Charles Peters

Address: 1171 Connecticut Avenue, NW
            Washington, D.C. 20009
            (202) 462-0128

Circulation: 27,898

World Press Review

What does *L'Osservatore Romano* have to say about U.S. policies, international affairs, the major political, economic, social, cultural events of our times — or for that matter, *The Times of India, Der Spiegel, Yomiuri Shimbun, Le Monde, South China Morning Post, Izvestia, Jornal do Brasil*, etc?

World Press Review, which started out as *Atlas* magazine in 1961, provides a selection of news and views from publications around the world, monitoring in one form or another at least 250 publications outside the U.S. *WPR* reports what these publications are reporting or editorializing and reproduces the text of important articles on major issues. Many of the articles have to be translated into English, with *WPR* handling 24 different languages currently. The work is impressive, the selections balanced, the variety of views well-represented generally. We found the monthly increasingly indispensible.

The variety of content — from a cover story on detente and disarmament to a feature on the lifestyle of European yuppies or just a good read like the evocative return to Waterloo's battlefield — is always rich. We get "Early Warning" reports — quick summaries of key news items in various nations' press on economic, political, technological, environmental developments in their countries. For example, *Pagina/12* reports Paraguay's President Gen. Alfredo Stroessner may be planning to sidestep the February 1988 elections and eventually install his son as president. "Viewpoints" rounds up press views on current major issues. On the Persian Gulf, *WPR* reproduced the reactions from press in Teheran, Baghdad, Amman and Riyadh, as well as from Europe and South Africa, 11-87, for example. Both columns contain very useful material for filling in holes missed by U.S. press accounts.

"Regional Reports," organized into Asia/Pacific, the Soviet Union, Latin America, Africa, and the Middle East categories, selects from those areas' publications that month's significant reports. We learn of strains between civilians and the military in the USSR from the reviews of *Komsomolskaya Pravada* and *Literaturnaya Gazeta*, 8-87, and of reactions to President Alan Garcia's nationalization of Peru's banks, 10-87. *La Jornada* and *Excelsior* of Mexico City are critical, the latter observing "State absolutism is bringing economic ruin to the poor nations." *El Commercio* of Lima features Mario Vargas Llosa's challenge to Garcia's plan, while *La Republica* of Lima defends him. There is always important information here that we find nowhere else.

The "Business" and "Technology" reports are also must reading. We learned from *Business Day* of Johannesburg, 11-87, of serious strains on South Africa's mining groups, as marginal shafts that closed during the strike stay closed, job losses mounted, and national production capacity may permanently be diminished.

We are not as satisfyingly rewarded with *WPR*'s cover stories. The editors attempt to balance the viewpoints reflected there on major issues, combining reproductions of editorials with efforts by individual journalists, but the selection process is questionable at times. For example, *WPR* presented views from Australian, British, and Argentine press on "The Japan Problem," 8-87, but aside from *Asahi Shimbun*'s view of "Toshiba vs. the U.S." no commentaries from Asian periodicals were included. Generally, however, *WPR* will at least include "Other Comment on the Affair," excerpts from a roundup of articles and editorials beyond the ones reproduced in the cover story. Its handling of the Iran-Contra hearings, 9-87, was a good example, presenting a Communist, Indian, British, Italian, and German "view" as well as press reactions from Beijing to Paris to Tel Aviv. There is a problem, however, that in selecting items to "represent" a view, the occasionally unique, unconventional points of view end up not covered in the feature story — though *WPR* generally will mention them in one of its department columns.

We're pleased that *WPR* has restored its temporarily abandoned policy of using political labels ("independent," "pro-government," "leftist," "semi-official," etc.) to describe the foreign publications from which it excerpts. The issue was a matter of wide debate among the magazine's readers, with enough of them finding the designations appropriate and necessary. Unfortunately, *WPR* hasn't responded to its readers' pleas that it indicate the date of publication of the articles it reproduces.

WPR underwent some design changes in 1987, the result being a more readable product. The monthly functions as a *review*, not a *digest*, so the design is critical. After all, it has to take the many, many voices represented and organize them contextually without submerging their distinctions. It continues to improve in this effort, and we find ourselves increasingly appreciating the existence of this unique magazine.

Editor: R. Edward Jackson

Address: 230 Park Avenue
            New York, N.Y. 10169
            (212) 697-6162

Circulation: 60,000

THE RATING GUIDE

In this third year of the *MediaGuide* we have retained the standards applied in last year's edition. The number of rated journalists has expanded by more than a fifth mainly because of additional attention to foreign correspondence and business reporting. We consider all journalists as being at the top of the profession, the big leagues of print journalism. All ratings are based on 1987 work, although in order not to lose material because of *MediaGuide* production deadlines, work of the previous December is also taken into account. Quantity of output means almost nothing; as a rule we review at least three major pieces for each entry, usually many, many more for the upper tiers. The bulk of a reporter's work in a year is routine and could be adequately handled by thousands of other reporters not listed in this guide; as in the Michelin dining guide, caloric output doesn't count. A single (★) rating indicates the journalist has been selected above the routine and ordinary. The reader may notice journalists with the same rating may have accompanying positive or negative remarks, but this invariably indicates the one has moved up to that rating and the other down.

We find the system biased toward the center. It's harder to lose ground at the very top because we tend to read most of the output there for the rewards of doing so. It's also harder for those at the bottom to move up, we find, especially if their trend direction has been down, because we tend to pass over them and miss good material. Past reputations thus have this shadowing effect, which has parallels in all kinds of human experience, including team dynamics in the sporting world. We are well aware that a great many journalists who should be included in the guide are not, owing to the resources at our disposal. But those worth inclusion, we believe, eventually force themselves to our attention by the quality of their work. Dozens of journalists have been dropped from this edition. Some because they have moved up as editors, others because of retirement, still others because we saw no need to continue commenting negatively on their work.

The criteria for reporters are the three basic criteria of the wire services, fairness, accuracy, and balance (objectivity), plus three additional that elevate work toward excellence: depth of reporting, writing skills, and consistency. For columnists and commentators, the basic criteria are content reliability and a minimum level of interesting material presented on a regular basis, plus three additional: depth of insight and information, presentation, and consistency. In order to give a single rating rather than address each criterion, we merge the weightings during discussions and reviews.

(−) Failing in the basic criteria on one or more counts.

(½★) Failing the secondary criteria on one or more counts.

(★) Good. Reporters: Professional. Columnists: Worth trying.

(★½) Good/Very Good. Very Good inconsistently.

(★★) Very Good. In reporters, above average level of reporting and writing, average analytical skills. In columnists, generally interesting content and presentation.

(★★½) Very Good/Excellent. Above average in consistency.

(★★★) Excellent. In reporters, superior reporting and writing, above average in analytical skills. In columnists, superior content and presentation, frequent important insights and information.

(★★★½) Excellent/Exceptional. Approaching the very best.

(★★★★) Exceptional. In reporters, loftily objective, pacesetters for the profession in reporting and writing, penetrating analytical skills, always worth reading. In columnists, pacesetters for the profession in journalistic integrity and independence, must reading for insights and information, a consistently well-shaped point of view.

(NR) Not rated. Insufficient sampling. Material cited has promise.

THE HIGHEST RATED JOURNALISTS OF 1987

Barnes, Fred	*The New Republic*	Commentary	★ ★ ★ ★
Broder, David	*The Washington Post*	Domestic Reports	★ ★ ★ ★
Brooke, James	*The New York Times*	Foreign Dispatch	★ ★ ★ ★
Brookes, Warren	*The Detroit News*	Financial Reports	★ ★ ★ ★
Evans & Novak	*Chicago Sun-Times*	Commentary	★ ★ ★ ★
Grenier, Richard	*The Washington Times*	Commentary	★ ★ ★ ★
Kinsley, Michael	*The New Republic*	Commentary	★ ★ ★ ★
Lewis, Anthony	*The New York Times*	Commentary	★ ★ ★ ★
Raines, Howell	*The New York Times*	Foreign Dispatch	★ ★ ★ ★
Sanger, David E.	*The New York Times*	Financial Reports	★ ★ ★ ★
Schneider, William	*National Journal*	Commentary	★ ★ ★ ★
Temko, Ned	*The Christian Science Monitor*	Foreign Dispatch	★ ★ ★ ★
Truell, Peter	*The Wall Street Journal*	Financial Reports	★ ★ ★ ★
Cullison, A.E.	*The Journal of Commerce*	Foreign Dispatch	★ ★ ★ ½
Darlin, Damon	*The Wall Street Journal*	Foreign Dispatch	★ ★ ★ ½
Echikson, William	*The Christian Science Monitor*	Foreign Dispatch	★ ★ ★ ½
Edsall, Thomas B.	*The Washington Post*	Domestic Reports	★ ★ ★ ½
Fields, Suzanne	*The Washington Times*	Commentary	★ ★ ★ ½
Fung, Vigor	*The Asian Wall Street Journal*	Foreign Dispatch	★ ★ ★ ½
Glassman, James K.	*The New Republic*	Financial Reports	★ ★ ★ ½
Gleick, James	*The New York Times*	Financial Reports	★ ★ ★ ½
Kotlowitz, Alex	*The Wall Street Journal*	Financial Reports	★ ★ ★ ½
Mansfield, Stephanie	*The Washington Post*	Domestic Reports	★ ★ ★ ½
Robinson, Anthony	*Financial Times*	Foreign Dispatch	★ ★ ★ ½
Rosenbaum, David	*The New York Times*	Domestic Reports	★ ★ ★ ½
Rosett, Claudia	*The Asian Wall Street Journal*	Foreign Dispatch	★ ★ ★ ½
Safire, William	*The New York Times*	Commentary	★ ★ ★ ½
Weiner, Steve	*Forbes*	Financial Reports	★ ★ ★ ½
Abelson, Alan	*Barron's*	Financial Reports	★ ★ ★
Alsop, Ronald	*The Wall Street Journal*	Financial Reports	★ ★ ★
Asman, David	*The Wall Street Journal*	Foreign Dispatch	★ ★ ★
Bangsberg, P.T.	*The Journal of Commerce*	Foreign Dispatch	★ ★ ★
Bennett, Robert A.	*The New York Times*	Financial Reports	★ ★ ★
Bering-Jensen, Henrik	*Insight*	Foreign Dispatch	★ ★ ★
Birnbaum, Jeffrey	*The Wall Street Journal*	Financial Reports	★ ★ ★
Blumenthal, Sidney	*The Washington Post*	Domestic Reports	★ ★ ★
Boroweic, Andrew	*The Washington Times*	Foreign Dispatch	★ ★ ★
Branigan, William	*The Washington Post*	Foreign Dispatch	★ ★ ★

Brittan, Samuel	*Financial Times*	Financial Reports	★ ★ ★
Brownstein, Ronald	*National Journal*	Domestic Reports	★ ★ ★
Buell, Barbara	*BusinessWeek*	Foreign Dispatch	★ ★ ★
Burns, John F.	*The New York Times*	Foreign Dispatch	★ ★ ★
Chira, Susan	*The New York Times*	Foreign Dispatch	★ ★ ★
Christian, Shirley	*The New York Times*	Foreign Dispatch	★ ★ ★
Clines, Francis X.	*The New York Times*	Foreign Dispatch	★ ★ ★
Cockburn, Alexander	*The Nation*	Commentary	★ ★ ★
Cockburn, Patrick	*Financial Times*	Foreign Dispatch	★ ★ ★
Cohen, Richard	*The Washington Post*	Commentary	★ ★ ★
Colitt, Leslie	*Financial Times*	Foreign Dispatch	★ ★ ★
Corry, John	*The New York Times*	Domestic Reports	★ ★ ★
Crossette, Barbara	*The New York Times*	Foreign Dispatch	★ ★ ★
Diehl, Jackson	*The Washington Post*	Foreign Dispatch	★ ★ ★
Dionne, E.J. Jr.	*The New York Times*	Domestic Reports	★ ★ ★
Donohoe, Cathryn	*The Washington Times*	Domestic Reports	★ ★ ★
Elliott, John	*Financial Times*	Foreign Dispatch	★ ★ ★
Forbes, Malcolm Jr.	*Forbes*	Financial Reports	★ ★ ★
Forsyth, Randall	*Barron's*	Financial Reports	★ ★ ★
Friedman, Thomas L.	*The New York Times*	Foreign Dispatch	★ ★ ★
Gannes, Stuart	*Fortune*	Financial Reports	★ ★ ★
Gertz, Bill	*The Washington Times*	Diplomatic Reports	★ ★ ★
Gilmartin, Trish	*Defense News*	Diplomatic Reports	★ ★ ★
Ibrahim, Youssef	*The New York Times*	Foreign Dispatch	★ ★ ★
Kamen, Al	*The Washington Post*	Domestic Reports	★ ★ ★
Kamm, Henry	*The New York Times*	Foreign Dispatch	★ ★ ★
Keller, Bill	*The New York Times*	Foreign Dispatch	★ ★ ★
Kristof, Nicholas	*The New York Times*	Foreign Dispatch	★ ★ ★
Lee, Susan	*Forbes*	Financial Reports	★ ★ ★
Low, Charlotte	*Insight*	Domestic Reports	★ ★ ★
Marsh, David	*Financial Times*	Foreign Dispatch	★ ★ ★
Martin, Richard	*Insight*	Domestic Reports	★ ★ ★
McGrory, Mary	*The Washington Post*	Commentary	★ ★ ★
Miller, Marjorie	*Los Angeles Times*	Foreign Dispatch	★ ★ ★
Mortimer, Edward	*Financial Times*	Diplomatic Reports	★ ★ ★
Norman, James R.	*BusinessWeek*	Financial Reports	★ ★ ★
Orme, William	*Freelance*	Foreign Dispatch	★ ★ ★
Pollack, Andrew	*The New York Times*	Financial Reports	★ ★ ★
Preston, Julia	*The Washington Post*	Foreign Dispatch	★ ★ ★
Quinn-Judge, Paul	*The Christian Science Monitor*	Foreign Dispatch	★ ★ ★
Rapoport, Carla	*Financial Times*	Foreign Dispatch	★ ★ ★
Rockwell, Keith M.	*The Journal of Commerce*	Financial Reports	★ ★ ★
Rosenthal, A.M.	*The New York Times*	Commentary	★ ★ ★
Schiffman, James	*The Asian Wall Street Journal*	Foreign Dispatch	★ ★ ★
Seib, Gerald	*The Wall Street Journal*	Domestic Reports	★ ★ ★
Seligman, Daniel	*Fortune*	Commentary	★ ★ ★

Shales, Tom	*The Washington Post*	Domestic Reports	★★★
Sherman, Stratford P.	*Fortune*	Financial Reports	★★★
Shields, Mark	*The Washington Post*	Commentary	★★★
Shribman, David	*The Wall Street Journal*	Domestic Reports	★★★
Sieff, Martin	*The Washington Times*	Foreign Dispatch	★★★
Sloan, Allan	*Forbes*	Financial Reports	★★★
Taubman, Philip	*The New York Times*	Foreign Dispatch	★★★
Taylor, Alex III	*Fortune*	Financial Reports	★★★
Trainor, Bernard	*The New York Times*	Diplomatic Reports	★★★
Walker, Tony	*Financial Times*	Foreign Dispatch	★★★
Walsh, Mary Williams	*The Wall Street Journal*	Foreign Dispatch	★★★
Welles, Chris	*BusinessWeek*	Financial Reports	★★★
Wilson, George	*The Washington Post*	Diplomatic Reports	★★★
Yoder, Stephen K.	*The Asian Wall Street Journal*	Foreign Dispatch	★★★

JOURNALISTS

FINANCIAL REPORTERS & COLUMNISTS

Abelson, Alan. *Barron's.* (★ ★ ★)
Editor. One of the best read and certainly the most entertaining of all financial columnists, Abelson's rambling, witty front-page "Up & Down Wall Street" has become an institution. A review of it is like going over the bull's temperature chart for the year. He properly claims membership in the "Royal Order of Worrywarts," 11-16. Among his wry New Year's resolutions, 1-3, were "never believe anything that comes out of Washington, never ask Bernard Goetz for $5, and never forget that portfolio insurance takes the risk out of equities for institutions." After the appointment of Howard Baker, "who is strongly addicted to compromise," Abelson, on 3-16, was one of the first to worry that "a weakened President will have difficulty fending off the hounds of the Hill as they howl for tariffs and quotas." The downfall of Gary Hart left Presidential politics wildly unpredictable, he reasoned, so "our domestic politics...might make for very nervous currency markets," 5-11. He fretted about the bull for most of the year, but at the peak seemed to tire of fighting the tape. Institutions, he said "have laid in ample stores of cash against the day the market would collapse...and that cash has become, instead of a comforting rainy day reserve, embarrassing evidence of lost opportunity." His column of 10-19, normally read by most the two days before, was priceless, after the Dow's 108-point plunge of 10-16: "Anyone who manages to keep his head while all about him others are losing theirs is never going to get our money to manage. The lesson writ large in the gruesome slaughter of the Wall Street Innocents is this: Avoid at all costs brokers who smoke pipes. Put your trust always in borderline hysterics. For they and they alone appreciate the importance, in any rounded investment approach, of an uncontrollable impulse to panic."

Alsop, Ronald. *The Wall Street Journal.* (★ ★ ★)
New York. Marketing columnist, always fresh and interesting, packaging his material well. The column seemed to get stronger during the year. "Firms Create Unique Names," 4-2, is a heavily reported, data-stuffed piece on corporate brand-name making. They come up with "Hyundai Rhymes with Sunday." In "More Prime-Time TV Shows Plug Airlines, Hotels in Scripts," 5-28, Bill Cosby plugs Hyatt in exchange for free rooms for 50 show staffers. Hertz and Eastern Airlines are doing swaps, too. The piece could have had more from traditionalists. "Can Honda Ads Get Any More Offbeat Than This?" 6-4, is full of interesting ideas and angles we hadn't seen before, about quirky ads appealing to left-field thinkers. "There are times when you have to stop asking questions and do something." Then there's "Don Rickles and Devilish Kid Bring Dull Carpet Ads to Life," 7-9, an instructive look at a carpet company boosting its ad budget to $50 million from $5 million in a $15 billion industry, entertainingly written. His "Tartar Control Toothpaste War," 8-20, is lively on the battle between Colgate and Crest, but he could have said a few words about the new technology. In "Busters May Replace Boomers As the Darling of Advertisers," 11-12, for the first time we hear about the post baby-boom cohort, the "afterboomers" born from '65 to '74. Best line: "For the coffee industry...the busters are an inviting but difficult market to crack since many of them have already adopted soft drinks as their breakfast beverage."

Anders, George. *The Wall Street Journal.* (★ ★ ½)
One of the *Journal's* heavy hitters on the Street, Anders either improved this year or the material we saw in '86 just wasn't representative. "Cloudy Cases: Insider Trading Law Leads to an Array of Interpretations," 2-19, was a rather pedestrian start, leaving us murky on stock tips and "chains" of information, but he didn't disappoint after that. "By the Numbers — Using Rote and Math, Wells Fargo Succeeds as a Money Manager," 3-23, an excellent front-pager on the atypical way the largest investor in the market makes its investment decisions, buying index funds, keeping costs way down, doing great with the bulls, but how about with bears? Anders tackles "Institutional Holders Irked by 'Poison Pill,'" 3-10, a well done account of the debate, a tough subject because of the strong arguments made on both sides. He scores high with "Has Japan Paid its Dues," 9-18, breezy observations on whether or not Japan will soon assume world financial leadership, giving a good historical context and a keystone quote: "It takes more than money to be No. 1." In "Gerald Tsai Finds Patience Pays Off," 5-28, with David B. Hilder, Anders profiles the visionary chairman of Primeamerica, who had just plucked Smith Barney Inc. for $750 million. Some colorful touches include Tsai wanting to name his company "with several Xs in it, because he thought that sounded futuristic." In a joint interview with John Orb, SB's CEO, Tsai allows as how Smith Barney is soon going to start selling insurance through its retail brokerage firms. Says Orb: "We've been selling insurance products for quite some time." So much for Tsai's fabled vision.

Ansberry, Clare. *The Wall Street Journal.* (★ ½)
Pittsburgh. A smart, thorough reporter who writes well and seems able to handle a wide variety of assignments. "Uphill Battle. Eastman Kodak Co. Has Arduous Struggle to Regain Lost Edge," 4-2, a front-pager on an age-old company getting fat and complacent, but very well told and thoroughly researched. "The Expense of Playing Host To The Pope," 8-31, has the details on the $20 million cost of the 10-day papal tour, with critics of course saying the Pontiff should stay home and the money be spent on the poor. Her compassion frames another front-page leader, "Fear and Loathing: AIDS, Stirring Panic and Prejudice, Tests The Nation's Character," 11-13. The heart of the story: "Plagues and epidemics like AIDS bring out the best and worst of society," says philosopher Jonathan Moreno, who teaches biomedical ethics at George Washington University in Washington, D.C. "Face to face with disaster and death, people are stripped down to their basic human character, to good and evil. AIDS can be a litmus test of humanity."

Auerbach, Stuart. *The Washington Post.* (★ ½)
A reliable veteran Capitol Hill reporter on government/business matters and trade who rarely has an analytical surprise and did not burrow hard enough in reporting the trade legislation. "Japanese Plan Latin American Loan Project," 4-23, was an adequate report on a $30 billion scheme to cut the trade surplus, but with little guidance on its credibility. A nice job on "Free Trade Losing Its Supporters," 5-3, quoting Rep. Bill Frenzel, "The so-called free-trade coalition has been ground down to a rock," and Consumers For Free Trade: "The majority of Democrats are not open traders any more." But little analytical depth. In "Mink Farmers Fear End of Import Ban," 5-24, we learn the House trade bill would lift a 1951 ban on mink pelts from the USSR, informative, but no attempt to get Fred the Furrier's view on price effects. "Trade Bill Sweeps By Senate," 7-22, notes the majority was large enough to override any veto, but some Republicans said they voted for it in hopes it would be softened in Congress. We needed better evaluations of the political spin, since the fate of a veto would be decided in the Senate. "Conferees Tackle Job of Meshing Trade Bills," 8-8, straightforward. The most illuminating piece we saw from him was "Commerce Nominee Calls on Chairman of Key Senate Panel," 8-12, in which we learn more than we knew about the connections of William Verity, Jr., to Howard Baker, Jr. A report on "Japan Balks at Accepting Bids From Foreign Firms on Projects," 10-31, tells us the incoming Prime Minister "is known to have close ties to the construction industry."

Banks, Howard. *Forbes.* (★ ★ ½)
Banks, the Washington bureau chief, "What's Ahead for Business" editor, and prolific writer, does good research and mines some gold. From "The Tax Cut Voodoo Lives On," 7-27: the rich really are paying more, and revenues really are higher from lower tax rates and economic recovery. In "Revisionist Thoughts on Savings," 9-7, Banks stands virtually alone in using academic research to debunk the statistical illusion that U.S. savings have fallen and are way below those of other countries. He jumped on the nationalistic bandwagon for "fair" trade in one piece, "No More Mr. Nice Guy," 2-9, which was a good statement of the point of view that some improvements in foreign treatment of U.S. goods are needed, although rabid protectionism is not. Aside from economic issues, Banks specializes in the aerospace industry. He wrote an incisive, compressed analysis of Airbus Industries and its relations with U.S. aircraft manufacturers, "Airbus Comes of Age," 2-23; "Achieve or Leave," 7-13, profiles United Technologies' new chairman Daniell as a no-nonsense gutsy guy who's giving a needed shaping up to UT, with a less hopeful 11-16 followup on key UT division Pratt & Whitney. In the military area, Banks turned out a good strategic analysis of the U.S. Air Force's Advanced Tactical Fighter project, including the possible future implications of prospective contractors building four "demonstrator" ATFs.

Bartlett, Sarah. *BusinessWeek.* (★ ½)
Money and banking editor, she continues to turn out issues-oriented banking stories with zest, but when it counted after the Crash, she ran with the *BW* pack in general pandemonium. Earlier, though, she built up some points. In the commentary, "Owning a Bank Isn't for Just Anybody," 6-22, she questions sweeping financial deregulation that would allow nonfinancial companies to own commercial banks. A lead writer for the cover, "The Home Equity Gold Rush," 2-9, a well-balanced, timely article on the effects of second mortgages on the personal finance landscape. "The Turnaround Trauma at Manufacturers Hanover," 8-24, was a punchy, informative analysis of recent culture and strategic changes at Manny Hanny as it struggles to meet global competitive challenges. In the 10-19 commentary, "Why the Bowery Deal Wasn't a Ripoff," Bartlett defends the FDIC bailout and cheap sale of Bowery Savings to an investor group, even after the investors' later resale made them a big profit. Among the better of the post-Crash *BW* offerings was Bartlett's 11-9 interview, "Taking Stock: A Talk with John Reed," who sniffs the situation and expects no further unwinding, lower interest rates, increased anti-protectionism, and more cooperation from Europe. "We've seen a loss...of $1 trillion of value in the U.S...And we can't find any blood." Causes? "I think the stage was set in April when interest rates started rising," and the equity and bond markets became incompatible. Alas, her writing on the broader economy, her introductions to two *BW* post-Crash covers on the markets, was woeful. Either she was over her head or writing up a bad line from higher-ups, 11-2 and 11-9. While warning about the dangers of quick fixes, the 11-9 piece "Starting Over" describes post-Crash America as now a "dependent nation."

Behar, Richard. *Forbes.* (★ ★)
Top specialist in company/industry analysis, with many pleasantly offbeat subjects. In his best of the year, he gets behind the blue jeans struggle between Jordache and Guess, a major developing scandal that has involved the IRS, "Does Guess Have a Friend at the IRS?" 11-16, two families engaged in a vicious blood feud. The surprise cover of 8-10, "Spreading the Wealth," is a fascinating piece on the PGA Tour, professional golf's rich "union," and its creative commissioner Deane Beman. But all is not well in Paradise, as Behar lets us listen in on top golf pros and commentators criticizing PGA "egalitarianism" whereby "today you can make a good living without winning." Or as Ray Floyd says, they've "essentially turned a capitalistic system into a socialistic one." "We'll Get Back to You on That," 4-6, is an excellent short piece on how two different acquirers of Ziff-Davis magazines treated the publications, and why one succeeded and one stumbled. On the sports front again, "Take That, Peter Ueberroth," 2-9, Behar reveals the resurgence of minor league baseball franchises, which have

"become a license to print money." Very good stuff, although we wish Behar had written more about the nitty-gritty working relationships of the minor league farm clubs with their major league "sponsors."

Bennett, Amanda. *The Wall Street Journal.* (★ ★)
New York, management beat. The transfer from Beijing to the Big A in '86 slowed Bennett down, but as we suspected the talent was only submerged by unfamiliarity with her new assignment. "How to Make Business History," 3-20, led the special section on Executive Style, a survey of CEOs on their management heroes (Lee Iacocca wins hands down), a discussion of what gets a businessman into the history books ("rascality and notoriety," is one answer, predicting our era will be known as "the Boesky era,") and predictions from some experts that the best-remembered business leaders of the era will be Japanese, Akio Morita of Sony and Konosuke Matsushita. A clever exercise we liked in spite of ourselves. Bennett's front-page profile of "Management Guru Peter Drucker," 7-28, had too much froth, but we got a solid hard core too, a smattering of Druckerisms, i.e., "The first and most important component of management is training." She does the nuts and bolts of her beat with competence, but with little enthusiasm. "What happens to unsecured pensions and pay when an employer is taken over or goes to bankruptcy court?" was her lead 5-21, then plodded through the detail. "The Job Hunt: Despite Downturn, Executives Find Spots of Demand," 8-3, was a routine roundup of that job market. A P.1 leader on how "Bell & Howell Takes Stock Crash in Stride," 10-27, with Michael J. McCarthy, doesn't persuade us the story may be typical, which would increase its importance, but still okay. Her best was a commentary on her old beat, "China's Hollow Ideology," 1-25, arguing Deng Xiao-peng will emerge stronger in the succession struggle by replacing Hu Yaobang, who he regretted as his choice for successor. And she was right.

Bennett, Robert A. *The New York Times.* (★ ★ ★)
The Sunday business section's pro on the banking beat, Bennett maintains a three-star rating for the third straight year with smart, clear, careful reporting that is always scrupulously objective. "Now, the Age of Fast Buck Banking," 12-14-86, looks like slanted hype, with a picture of a country fair hawker attracting customers to a bank, but that's the editors fault; the piece itself is a solid, fair summary of banking deregulation. "Pan Am's Disappearing Act," 1-18, a superb, careful look from every angle, but what would a takeover management do that Edward Acker isn't? "The Man Who Wears the Star," 2-22 is less satisfying on Texaco's James W. Kinnear, a nice fellow and all that, but what can he do? Bennett gives us an excellent profile on John S. Reed, "Citicorp's Defiant Leader," 5-21, after nominal acceptance of a $3 billion quarterly loss on the bank's Third World loan portfolio. It's vivid in evoking Reed's personality, and clear, if somewhat incomplete, in discussing the significance of the action, which is basically meaningless unless the IRS recognizes the loss for tax purposes. Still, "Mr. Reed's move...made it dramatically clear that Citicorp is his institution playing to his tune." In Farm Aid: Drawbacks Seen," 9-3, he finds government props under bankrupt farmers are preventing successful farmers from expanding; smart, good material and reporting. After the Crash, his "Banks Learning a Hard Lesson," 11-3, is also sharp, commercial banks rethinking moves into investment banking as a result of the Crash, seeing the immense losses suffered in securities with British Petroleum going public and realizing there are different kinds of risks, mindsets. One of the few bright spots of the Sunday business page, Bennett seemed to get less space and weaker assignments than in earlier years.

Berg, Eric N. *The New York Times.* (★ ★ ½)
Still in his 20s, but sporting a Stanford MBA, Berg continued to impress us on the daily banking beat, getting more information, clearly presented, in even routine stories than we are used to seeing. A memorable piece was "Many Bankers Upset By Talk of 'Superbanks,'" 6-10, which fans a 6-7 front-page scoop into a controversy and debate, building on a loose-lipped Treasury official's tilt toward superbanking. In "Humanizing Bank Machines," 9-9, we found ourselves reading every word about the state of the art on automated tellers, his impressive

flow of detail flowing so smoothly. He's uncharacteristically weak on analysis in "A Dow-Dollar Link is Seen by Experts," 1-26, leaving us as unpersuaded as Lee Cooperman of Goldman Sachs, who he quotes late in the piece: "It has nothing to do — zero — with the dollar's decline." His sidebars and features throughout the October Crash were consistently sharp. "Funds Lag a Dismal Market," 10-31, charts the mutual funds getting slaughtered, but Oppenheimer's Ninety-Ten actually gaining 7.98% as it saw the cracks coming. We scored him high on "Dark Cloud of Acrimony Over World Debt Crisis," 5-21, for sharp analysis of Citicorp's loan-loss move: "Having taken its lumps, Citicorp is in a better position than ever to be patient in future debt talks." We were disappointed that Berg did not delve into the Third World development debate, the source of the problem, but nobody else on the banking beat did much either.

Berger, Joan. *BusinessWeek.* (★ ½)
New York. A better performance for Berger, after we noted her "economics" articles of '86 seemed amateurish, often relying on the crutch of creating a phantom consensus of "most economists." Her news analysis in "Why the Fed May Zero in on the Money Targets," 7-13, was far better than the headline, layering in the evidence and the arguments presented on the several sides of the issue, quoting economists by name, and really allowing the reader to make use of this quality information instead of making an editorial point. Her article on "Productivity: Why It's the No. 1 Underachiever," 4-20, was less rigorous, devoting only a fleeting comment to one economist who questions the reliability of the numbers she uses to make her case, dismissing his point breezily with "It's more than a measurement problem." If she had dug into this issue, even if it meant the blow-up of her preconceived story, she could have presented an impressive no-stone-unturned piece. Her commentary column, "Tariffs Aren't Great, But Quotas Are Worse," 3-16, lays out the arguments with persuasive logic, but doesn't mention one of the biggest: With tariffs, at least goods can get into the country and be available to consumers, but not with quotas. In "How the Bull Market Has Enriched the Economy," 8-10, with Norman Jonas, she presents all the wealth-effect arguments, but says a bull-market drawback is that it has "exacerbated the recent decline in personal saving to record low rates," without mentioning the counter argument that individuals can save less when the value of their past savings rises.

Bernstein, Aaron. *BusinessWeek.* (★ ½)
Not a big year for labor relations in the news; labor editor Bernstein turned out assorted readable, but not memorable, items. "Detroit vs. the UAW: At Odds Over Teamwork," 8-24, reviews the possible Japanization of production procedures in the U.S. auto industry, namely, a management-sought shift to production teams. A cover story (with others) on the developing U.S. labor shortage, "Help Wanted," 8-10, although not very in-depth, touches on some consequences to ponder — whether corporate remedial education programs will pick up an increasing burden from the failing public school system, and whether labor shortages will lead to liberalization of the new immigration law. Naturally, since professional sports are a serious business, Bernstein wrote a nice post-strike commentary for businessperson sports fans, "NFL Owners May Have Fumbled Away Their Victory," 11-2. He discusses the potential troubles owners face from the union's antitrust suit and gets varied quotes on what the plaintiff's chances of winning are.

Berry, John. *The Washington Post.* (★)
A smart, veteran financial reporter who is sometimes able to keep his personal views on how government policy should be conducted from his dispatches. In "Volcker Reveals Fed Tightened Credit," 5-1, he does so, and we get a better-than-average report on the event. In "Conable Warns of 'Deep Recession,'" 7-11, we get a nice, concise report on the World Bank president's views. Berry, an adversary of Reaganomics throughout, writes "Unusual Expansion Just Keeps Rolling Along," 7-19, has plenty of statistics, data, opinions and quotes, okay, but not a word on the fact that the expansion has coincided with a dramatic tax reform, and even pooh-poohs that the two may have been related. In "Stakes Rise As Hill Tackles '88 Budget Reductions,"

5-3, Berry tells us flatly that financial markets are "in a tizzy lately" out of "fear there has been so little progress on reducing the federal budget deficit," with no mention of the continuing decline of the deficit through economic expansion. In "Budget Deficit's Size Deceptive," 11-1, Berry strains to demonstrate that the $73 billion decline in the federal deficit from '86 to '87 was gimmicky and the Crash really did turn on the red ink, although he does put contrary views high in the piece.

Bianco, Anthony. *BusinessWeek.* (★ ★ ½)
Whither, Tony Bianco? The consistent extraordinary quality of last year's superstar thinned to vexing unevenness in 1987, and we got some overcooked hamburger and light souffles along with the toothsome sirloin we were used to. To mention the worst first, it was Bianco's part in the 11-9 *BW* cover on the stock market crash (one of several of *BW*'s unbalanced, hysterical, weakly supported doom-and-gloom covers after October 19). His commentary, "Must the Panic Get Worse to Spark Reform?" resurrects his and *BW*'s old "Casino Society" cover bomb from 9-85 as the inspiration for explaining 1987 problems, and concludes that the demon "speculative excess" must be stamped out by new financial-market regulation. More heat than light on the subject of over-leveraging, and the consideration of economic fundamentals was conspicuously absent. As we noted last year, broad market analysis is not Bianco's forte. He was better with his investment bank coverage, although overall it was not as shining or assertive as last year's. A month after Lewis Ranieri's abrupt departure from Salomon, Bianco wrote a cover, "Decline of the Superstar," 8-17, which was a solid, thorough analysis of the strategic management reorientations on Wall Street that competition is causing. This was a huge improvement over an early response to the firing, "Salomon Brothers Parts with a Son," 7-27, — a disappointing tidbit, especially compared with *The Wall Street Journal*'s outstanding on-the-minute coverage. In the forward-looking "Can Salomon Grow by Shrinking?" 10-26, Bianco posits the firm's exit from the municipal and short-term markets as the most startling development to date in an eventful year. He shows the hard look at costs and profit margins behind the decision. "The Biggest Bomb Landed Smack in the Street," 11-2, pictured firms hit hard by trading losses in the Crash and facing further layoffs in the struggle for cost control begun months earlier. Here Bianco produces a provocative insight/prediction concerning Glass-Steagall: "If a big investment bank finds itself in financial straits, look for Citicorp or another big commercial bank to try to circumvent Glass-Steagall by offering to come to the rescue." An earlier Bianco work included a couple of good human interest pieces on women in finance, 2-23.

Birnbaum, Jeffrey. *The Wall Street Journal.* (★ ★ ★)
The Washington bureau's ace tax reporter through '86, Birnbaum moved to deficits and the budget in '87 and not only kept up with the red ink but delivered interesting features and analytics around the beat. His first front-pager, "Congress Pokes Again At Perennial Problem, The Budgetary System," 2-26, has not much new for old hands, and we wondered why it got top billing, but then he was off and away. "Some Lawmakers Go Homeless For a Night, Don't Like It Much," 3-5, was among the *WSJ*'s best A-heds of the year, the P.1, column 4 feature on "The Grate American Sleep-Out!" Best line: "A few homeless people were themselves distressed by the sleep-out. Their usual spots on the grates were crammed to overflowing with movie stars and camera crews." In "Democrats Find New Responsibility on Deficit Exacts Heavy Price," 3-19, he observes the Dems, boxed in by Gramm-Rudman, searching for GOP allies on tax hikes, and hoping for a RR accommodation. Birnbaum sees "a rare opportunity" for the Democrats: "In a significant change, polls show that Democrats are drawing even with Republicans on the question of which party is better at keeping government spending under control." We also get a timely report, "Congress Shifts Focus From Excise Taxes to Increasing Tax Burden On Wealthy," 5-28, that shows up in the tax bills passed in the fall. Generally remaining above the partisan debate, he provided the steadiest reports of the post-Crash budget summit. "Budget Negotiations Run Into a Snag as GOP Has Doubts on Tentative Pact," 11-13, is just such a comprehensive, satisfying account.

Bishop, Jerry E. *The Wall Street Journal.* (★ ★ ½)

New York. The *Journal*'s veteran science reporter and technology columnist, Bishop was strongest on health science, but did well to stay in sight of *The New York Times*' young heaters, Sanger, Gleick and Pollack on high tech. "Doctors Widen Cholesterol War, Setting Stricter Patient Guidelines," 2-24, has almost everything we want to know about cholesterol, heart disease, new drugs, etc. But the piece isn't clear that different types of cholesterol (HDL, LDL) have to be determined in ratios to set risk. "Case of The Mother's Day Brunch," 4-24, is a surprisingly readable feature on the tracking of a microbe with muscle, *enteritis*. Having fallen behind the *Times* on the superconductivity story, Bishop pooh-poohs the story, 5-5, reporting that research is running into fundamental limits, a distinctly downbeat piece. He does a rather breathless P.1 feature on a "Silicon Successor," 5-29, "a new raw material" for semiconductors, gallium arsenide, which has been in use since the mid-1960s. The piece seems really about ballistic transistors that do not necessarily have to use gallium ansenide at all. In June, Bishop has the first *WSJ* piece to bring something new to the superconductivity story, 6-19, an elegantly clear explanation of the phenomenon and the history of its emergence, but there was still no one doing the business, venture capital angles. On 8-3, he delivers an interesting and insightful article on the discovery and development of a chemical that revives tissues after loss of oxygen in heart attacks and strokes. His tech column, 8-7, is unusually fresh in describing an experimental way of generating methane, illuminating both the promise and problems of a "hydrogen economy." On 8-25, he discusses GE's prospects in medical markets without a word on the long-range significance of GE's decision to eschew consumer products. His 11-13 column on magnetic refrigeration was clear, intriguing, ahead of the pack.

Bladen, Ashby. *Forbes.* (-)

The doomsday columnist exulted after the Crash with his most entertaining missive of all, "Johnny One-Note Sings Again," 11-16: "Regular *Forbes* readers will remember that for more than seven years this column has been sounding the alarm...You also recall that Editor Jim Michaels decided I was becoming a Johnny-One-Note, and that my column should be suspended until the disaster I had so long predicted began to happen...I have been waiting ever since to discover what Michaels' idea of a disaster is. When he called me the morning after Black Monday, I found out." Alas, the writing of poor Bladen does not improve with time, and his burdens have not lightened, despite the recent sabbatical. He has one burden and one theme: that the United States has to "stop borrowing and start repaying" or else "we will bequeath to our children an impoverished and over-indebted nation." Dire dangers of the budget deficit dominate his thoughts in both an up market, "Beyond Our Means," 7-27, and a down market, "Going Down with the Ship," 11-30. If one is feeling masochistic and looking for a dose of disaster, this is the column to read. Next, Editor Michaels, whips and chains.

Bleiberg, Robert M. *Barron's.* (★ ★)

Publisher and editorial director. Like Abelson's front-page column, Bleiberg's "Editorial Commentary" page is also a *Barron's* institution, written in dead seriousness, no sign of tongue-in-cheek. They did strike us as livelier during the year, and they have to be, as they are by far the longest "editorials" in the business. At times, this is an advantage. His far-sighted "Greenspan's Brief Honeymoon," 8-24, written at the top of the bull market, was razor sharp in cutting the Fed chairman down to size, and he used every inch of the column to advantage. But who wants to read an article-length opinion, 1-19, on why credit cards are a good thing? Bleiberg does a nice job reminding us that some of the "underground economy" had come above-ground after tax rates came down, 1-12, so that 1984 revenues from the top tax bracket came in 24% higher than otherwise. He also offered a gutsy defense of Chile's swing toward freer trade, 6-22, and offended some investment bankers by advocating "the more financial deregulation the better," 9-28. Some Bleiberg columns are about the last samples we see of good old right-wing polemics. "Union Militancy," 6-8, he worries that unemployment is getting too low, so that "market forces are starting to tilt labor's way." In "Red China vs. Taiwan," 2-9, we get the expected lecture on the failings of Marxism. He's less predictable in "No Northern

Peso," 2-2, where prospects in Canada are looking up "despite Tory misgovernment." Bleiberg also uses "editorials" to give investment advice (buy municipal bonds, 11-9, don't pay too much for stock in privatized government firms, 8-31.) He reprinted uniquely optimistic forecasts from 1982-83 that look quite prescient in retrospect, 10-12. His celebration, "Good For George Bush," 10-19, on the Veep's call for a cut in the capital gains tax, was comprehensive on the subject, the best we saw.

Blustein, Paul. *The Washington Post.* (★)
Economics writer. A promising young talent as an economics writer in *The Wall Street Journal*'s Washington bureau, Blustein had an unhappy year. After being passed over for bigger assignments he left for a juicy portfolio at the *Post.* His work was disappointing for most of the year, not surprisingly. A piece on Vice Chairman Manuel "Johnson's Actions at Fed Frustrate Supply-Siders," 3-30, was pretty thin stuff built on a few weak quotes — and not much on Johnson's criteria for judgement. Blustein delivers a very zippy piece, though, on "Protectionist Views Win Respect, Friends for John Culbertson," 4-1, quoting MIT's Paul Krugman: It's like "someone talking about the psychic power of plants getting the same attention as people doing the research on re-combinant DNA." In "Shrinking Trade Gap May Be Painful," 7-6, he trots out all the usual zero-sum doleful deficit colors. "The risks of an economic collapse are heightened...if the U.S. doesn't cut the budget deficit...the U.S. will find itself lacking the resources necessary to finance domestic economic growth if and when the foreign money flowing into the country dries up." Routine austerity clatter. Blustein's last months at the *WSJ* were spent on an LDC debt series, but it may have disappeared for good. He hit the *Post*'s P.1 a few times late in the year with interesting material, one on how Treasury Secretary "Baker Fought For Accord on Budget Deficit," 11-23. We expect a more productive '88.

Bork, Robert, Jr. *U.S.News & World Report.* (NR)
On a leave of absence midyear, Bork impressed us otherwise with some solid reports. "'New Protectionism' to Fit the Times," 4-6, was a good review of the protectionist methods different countries use to keep each other's goods out. A piece on the trade bill, "A Trade Bill Gets A Bum's Rush," with James M. Hildreth, 7-6, gives us the scoop on some of the provisions in the Gephardt Amendment, and the Senate and House trade bills, with Robert Litan of the Brookings Institute calling the provisions "land mines."

Boyd, John. *The Journal of Commerce.* (★)
Boyd's "Economic Beat" is brief, written in punchy newsletter style, but perhaps too frequent to be done properly. It ends up void of any analysis or evidence, and usually just records other people's anxieties about budgets and the Fed. Boyd often seems torn between the risk of an overheating, 10-9, and the risk of recession, 9-11. When he rounds up his very familiar list of sources (the usual suspects of conventional wisdom such as Martin Feldstein, Lawrence Kudlow, Herbert Stein), it doesn't work as well. We've all heard them before. Boyd is better on his own. The market crash, he writes, 10-30, "may ruin the Republicans' chance to ride a prosperity theme into another term at the White House, [and] may have transformed a populist trade bill into a major threat to world commerce." That may all be wrong, but a columnist's opinion is what makes a column different from a survey of what other people think.

Brimelow, Peter. *Forbes.* (★ ½)
A former Dow-Joneser, originally from Canada, Brimelow has been getting some big assignments covering broad public-policy topics, but not living up to his potential during his second year at *Forbes.* His cover story "Are We Spending Too Much For Education?" 12-29-86, fails because he makes his case entirely on falling SAT scores, connecting them with rising spending and drawing a partial-equilibrium conclusion. Another major piece, "Judicial Imperialism," 6-1, is a conservative screed disguised as a cover story, without the benefit even of a liberal strawman. His profile of Thomas Sowell, the conservative black economist, "A

Man Alone," 8-24, seemed two dimensional, but there were some good quotes on Sowell's philosophy: "Compassion: The use of tax money to buy votes. Insensitivity: Objection to the use of tax money to buy votes." He's better with straight financial and investment topics, as in "The Saving of America," 4-30, a well-balanced airing of one economist's view that thrift is coming back into fashion. His best piece, another cover, "Why South Africa Shrugs at Sanctions," 3-9, could have deteriorated into a screed, but Brimelow held it to rigorous analysis to make it a worthwhile contribution.

Brittan, Samuel. *Financial Times.* (★ ★ ★)
The dean of British financial journalism, Brittan's increasingly convoluted columns of recent years finally zipped again after he ditched the crusty monetarist framework that held him back. Thus, he climbed atop global economic developments during the year with unusually thoughtful and innovative commentary, exploring new ideas. In "Washington Payments Jitters Worse Than 'Benign Neglect,'" 2-22, he favors "suppressing all statistics" about the balance of trade, arguing that the U.S. current account deficit is exaggerated by as much as $80 billion, and the eventual cost of servicing U.S. foreign debts is a "statistician's problem" that would amount to "perhaps 1/2% of the American GNP." "Having made such a fuss about the balance of payments, [Treasury Secretary] Baker is now hoist with his own petard." In "Time to Tackle the Euro Malaise," 6-22, Brittan writes of "the tension between the unreconstructed Keynesianism of most working forecasters who still think of demand management in real terms, and the unreflective financial orthodoxy of their political masters." The insistence by the Bank for International Settlements that "stimulus" should consist of budget deficits "reads too much like the central bankers' trade union passing the buck to governments." Brittan notes that the problem with the Louvre exchange-rate accord "is that it lacks an anchor," 7-23, so "it would be worth trying to stabilize...some index of world commodity prices...When it comes to international currency units such as the SDR or the Ecu, one might go further and advocate a definite commodity standard." He went further in "An Anchor for World Money," 10-5, arguing that "it is time the English-speaking economic establishment abandoned the hubris of dismissing gold as a barbaric relic and looked instead at the evidence...The ultimate objective should [be]...to link world currencies to something more real than the promise to exchange one piece of paper against another." Right or wrong, he's probing the frontier again, which makes for an exciting column.

Brookes, Warren. *The Detroit News,* Heritage Features Syndicate. (★ ★ ★ ★)
So few business journalists seem to be able to question economic statistics they get from their favorite political sources that Brookes, one of the rare ones, is practically a national asset. His columns, dominating the Commentary section of *The Washington Times*, should be preserved for the archeologists so they might be able to figure out what really was going on in 1987. Brookes was persistent in challenging the AFL-CIO hoax that the Reagan economic expansion produced only low-paying McJobs, "Sorry, Wrong Numbers on Jobs," 4-20. He debunks the hoax that Mass. Gov. Dukakis has been a tight-fisted liberal, "Not As Cheap As Image," 9-20. He debunks the major longtime hoax that the U.S. savings rate is dangerously low, "How We Undercount Our Savings," 6-11. He debunks the hoax that the U.S. has become a hat-in-hand debtor nation, "Black Cloud or Silver Lining," 10-19, demonstrating that the trade gap results from the desire of the rest of the world to invest in the U.S. He debunks the hoax that U.S. indebtedness has soared in the Reagan years, "Windfall From Reagan's Bull Market," 3-5, on the surpluses of state, local and private pension funds plus the value of corporate equity, $1.7 trillion in new wealth added since 1980. In "Mistaking Cause for Effect," 5-11, he shows how the U.S. trade deficit is mainly due to the Third World debt crisis, not Japanese exports. In "Urban League's Failed Vision," 2-2, and "The Rev. Jesse Jackson's War on the Poor," 8-26, he presents unorthodox arguments on the advance of black America in recent years. He debunks the hoax that the textile industry is in trouble and needs import protection, "Textile Tycoons Try to Pick Our Pockets," 5-18. And he challenges the hoax that the budget deficit caused the Crash, "Luring Securities Dealers Into Line?" 11-3. Brookes'

weakness is monetary policy, writing 8-12, that because money growth has been slow, it's been tight, and writing 10-6, because the gold price has climbed $100 since mid '86 and the dollar has fallen, it's clear money has been easy. But nobody's perfect.

Bulkeley, William M. *The Wall Street Journal.* (★ ★)
Boston. Still among the best in seeing trends in computer software and their investment implications, but with a few bumps in '87. "Digital Feuds With Smaller Companies," 1-26, was sharp in eyeing a risky strategy: "Digital's new get-tough policy is risky. While it may boost sales short-term, the strategy could hurt sales long-term by turning allies into enemies." In the Technology column, "The Right Mix: New Software Makes the Choice Much Easier," 3-27, a good piece on software that helps deal with tricky product pricing: "the mix problem involves opportunities for reducing costs that aren't intuitive and you wouldn't even know you were missing. If you're making a profit, you don't know if it's all the profit you could be making." A front-page "Two Computer Firms With Clashing Styles," 7-6, on the struggle between Apollo and Sun for the advanced computer workstation market is all froth, a counterpoint between the sunny Cal culture of Sun (jeans, jokes and beer) and the stuffy New England chill of Apollo (business suits and "scheduled meetings.") With this fluffy focus, the piece misses a good story on this new dimension of the computer market, invented and entirely dominated by American firms. Also missed by Bulkeley, but reported in the industry press, was that Sun, during the previous week, had won an estimated $280M contract with the National Security Agency, beating out both Apollo and the IBM RT for the sale of some 3,500 workstations. This changed the real story into how Sun had already won the battle. In "Software Makers Gird For an Assault On the Goliath of Spreadsheets," 9-25, he is crisp and informative on Lotus and the spreadsheet battles. "Toshiba Official Finds Giving Work to Firms In U.S. Can Be Tricky," 3-20, is very skimpy. Mr. Tanaka says this, Mr. Tanaka says that, hardly worth P.1.

Bylinsky, Gene. *Fortune.* (★ ★ ½)
Bylinsky is a master in his reporting niche of high-tech industry, with specialization in sector overviews. Although the general excitement over Star Wars' R2D2 and C3PO has long passed, Bylinsky informs us in "Invasion of the Service Robots," 9-14, that this market rather than the manufacturing market may be the robot wave of the future. He gives us a fascinating look at some of the applications under development, such as a housecleaning robot, a military flying spy robot, and a space-station assembly robot. "Japan's Robot King Wins Again," 5-25, is a concise sketch of Fanuc, the world's awesomely dominant producer of industrial robots and computerized numerical controls, although the piece could have been clearer on how Fanuc achieved lowest cost and highest quality where others, such as General Electric and General Motors, failed (and ended up in joint ventures with Fanuc). On the biology front, "Here Come the Bionic Piglets," 10-26, is an excellent overview of the biotech market. And "Coming: Star Wars Medicine," 4-27, is a thorough review of a potential rival to genetic engineering products: mass-produced monoclonal antibodies. The article smoothly reports on the major applications and the leading companies in the field.

Carley, William M. *The Wall Street Journal.* (★ ★ ½)
New York. A thorough-going professional of the old school covering airlines, lofty in objectivity, he doesn't waste words or our time, just delivering the facts. "A Pan Am Merger Could Benefit Fliers," 1-19, is just such material, comprehensive, with a dozen fresh items on interesting developments at Pan Am and the industry as a whole. His "Fatal Flight," 7-1, seems definitive on the 1986 plane crash that killed Mozambique's president, well-presented evidence that lends no support to the Soviet-Mozambican theory that the crash was a South African assassination. The Soviet crew simply committed one mistake after another. "Meanwhile, [the new Mozambique president] has evidently reached his own conclusions: He doesn't fly on Soviet planes." Carley's attention to detail also helps on a story not usual for him, "How the FBI, Tipped by a Russian, Tracked an Intelligence Leak," 3-17, about Ronald Pelton's journey

from NSC drone to Russian spy. Nice detail: Yurchenko thinking Pelton wanted to be paid in chicken soup. But does this merit a front-page leader? However, "Terror Aloft: Anatomy of Hijacking," 6-15, is superior drama, worth its P.1 slot.

Castro, Janice. *Time.* **(NR)**
We were especially impressed by "Charge of the Plastic Brigade," 3-23, a piece on the new 13.5% interest Amex Optima Card that beat the *WSJ* to the punch by two days. Also nicely done was "In Fashion, Bigger Is Now Beautiful," with Cheryl Crooks and Janice Horowitz, 5-4, which tactfully explored fashions for the size 14 + , and how the rag trade is accommodating them.

Cauley, Leslie. *The Washington Times.* **(★ ½)**
The only business reporter at the *Times* who really had to be read consistently to keep up with her subject, telecommunications and the federal government's dithering over "the largest — and most expensive — contract ever offered in the history of telecommunications," as her lead ran in "Government Phones Will Cost the GSA at Least $10 Billion," 5-8. The "FTS-2000" contract for a new telephone system for the government was closely watched as it put AT&T, which has run the government phones from its monopoly days, at risk, and Cauley's day-by-day, blow-by-blow coverage of the maneuverings over these megabucks kept her paper on the margin. Her "Brooks Blasts GSA Over Phone System," 5-18, was the first early sign that powerful Texas Rep. Jack Brooks, head of the House Government Operations Committee, would eventually disrupt the process. Almost daily through late May and June, there's a Cauley update on AT&T's victories in delaying the contract. The best overall reconnaissance of the struggle between AT&T and Martin Marietta, "Billions on Line as Titans Wait for Bell," 6-29, has fine detail and quotes: "FTS 2000 presents the opportunity to be the technical leader in the industry." And a Boeing spokesman, "There will never be another FTS 2000." When Rep. Brooks demands procurement alterations, "Marietta Hangs Up On Phone Changes," 8-6. Finally, victory for AT&T, which pushed for delays: "GSA to Delay Decision on FTS 2000," 9-17.

Chase, Marilyn. *The Wall Street Journal.* **(★ ½)**
San Francisco. Health, medical beat. Better than average presentations of her material. "FDA Rule Changes May Rush New Drugs to Very Sick Patients," 10-5, a front-page leader, could have been dry, but instead seemed thorough, well organized and definitive. "Asking AIDS Victims to Name Past Partners Stirs Debate on Privacy," 1-29, practically tells the story in the headline, okay, but should have been a sidebar to a larger AIDS story, not a front-page leader. Her fine P.1 leader, "In Lives and Dollars, The Epidemic's Toll Is Growing Inexorably," 5-18, zeroes in on San Francisco's experience, finding "MIAs," for "medically-indigent adults," and debate on whether to build an AIDS hospital, which would draw victims from everywhere and impose a crushing tax burden on the city. Her "Wider Use Seen For Heart Drug, But Side Effects Pose a Challenge," 3-23, effectively lays out the TDP technical story.

Coll, Steve. *The Washington Post.* **(★ ½)**
New York. Covering Wall Street's ups and downs, the scandals and investigations, financial innovations, etc., with competence, often teamed with David A. Vise, a Wall Streeter turned newsman. He was on his own with "Ex-Lawyer Convicted of Insider Trading," 8-19, on Israel Grossman, 34, who helped his family members gain $1.5 million on inside takeover tips, a fine account. In "Aggressive Strategies Questioned," 11-15, he's fairly lucid and concise in going over Wall Street's problems with bridge loans, with Goldman Sachs and Salomon Inc. stuck with $100 million on the Southland Co. postponing of its junk-bond offering, with some background we hadn't seen before. He writes "Inside Milken's Empire," 3-8, with Vise, a long, long interesting piece on one of Drexel's clients who took Drexel to court, but they uncover little that is new on the central story, and we felt a bit teased. It's not "Inside Milken's Empire," maybe inside his reception room at best. They are also together with "Boesky Case: One Year

Later,'' 11-8, bringing us up to date on it all, with the most interesting item tucked at the end: "Much of Boesky's time these days is spent as a student at the Jewish Theological Seminary,'' according to Rabbi Wolfe Kelman...focusing his efforts on mastering the Hebrew language..."I know he does his homework...He is not sullen. He gets tremendous satisfaction out of passing a test or doing well.''

Commins, Kevin. *The Journal of Commerce.* (★ ½)
A regular feature on exchange rates, complete with forecasts from five leading banks, he usually covers the field well. He tends to be forward-looking, in contrast with typical stories about what happened yesterday. Commins also provided excellent post-Crash stories explaining why "Portfolio Insurance Will Survive the Crash,'' 11-20 & 11-22, "As more and more plans adopted the technique [amounting to $60 billion], they began to bunch similar trades at the same time, a development that strained the capacity of the futures markets.''

Cook, James. *Forbes.* (★ ★)
Cook seems to have spent the year concentrating on an intriguing subject, the interface of government and private business. One of his most interesting articles was "Priming the Urban Pump,'' 3-23, about an organization (LISC) that puts together imaginative combinations of private and public financing for housing and renewal projects in blighted areas, planned in conjunction with neighborhood groups. A trip to Poland to see socialism in action produced "There Are No Garage Sales Here,'' 2-23, which concludes with a warning to Mikhail Gorbachev that there is no way to "reconcile socialism with economic efficiency.'' The subject is certainly not new, but the story is lively and well written. Great quote from a Westerner, referring to all the Western electronic equipment sold shamelessly by government stores for hard currency: "How do you run an idealogical society when everybody is out there watching *Rambo* on his VCR?'' "Losing Jobs by Trying to Save Them,'' 6-1, is an information-packed case study of how the years-long attempt by the International Longshoremen's Association to cushion the impact of containerization on its New York membership was a major factor in driving shippers to other ports — with Port and government action on behalf of competitiveness absurdly late. In "Power to the People,'' 10-19, Cook reviews the move by public power producers to jump in on a proposal for opening power generation to competitive bidding. The story provides some information, but not enough to do justice to a controversial, complicated topic.

Coyle, Dominick. *Financial Times.* (★ ½)
His reports on stock markets rarely stand out, but "Still Seeking A Sense of Balance,'' 11-14, was a representative exception, showing Coyle's sense of perspective. A table showed how all the world's markets had behaved since the crash, and observed (as others did not) that "London and Wall Street...were both still ahead of their levels twelve months ago...But Germany and France are a different story.''

Crossen, Cynthia. *The Wall Street Journal.* (★ ½)
Stock market reporter with a sense of humor that often buoys otherwise dry material. In "Remaining a Bear Isn't Easy,'' 1-19, she has a nifty and timely feature identifying the remaining bears, nailing John Mendelson of Dean Witter for a memorable quote: "The music stopped playing last summer, but the dancers are still dancing.'' Post Black Monday, "Market Timers Get a Boost From Wall Street Gyrations,'' 11-13, she surveys the folks who believe in jumping among stocks, bonds or cash to pick the winners: "Not long ago, admitting you were a 'market timer' wasn't much different from admitting you stuck pins in voodoo dolls. But lately, some money management experts have changed their minds.''

De-Witt, Philip Elmer. *Time.* (NR)
A consumer technology writer, De-Witt did two pieces in April that we noted and especially enjoyed. "Can a System Keep a Secret?'' 4-6, looked at new computer security spawned by

the retrieval of Ollie's notes. He's handy with anecdotes, which keeps his material light, but should have had something on the development of computer "bugs" that pick up transmissions, which would add depth to his report. "Driving by the Glow of a Screen," 4-20, told us of a new gadget for car aficionados: the computerized road map. Already in limited use in California, and possibly targeted as a dealer option for the 1990's, two current companies are marketing the devices.

Dobrzynski, Judith. *BusinessWeek.* (★ ★)
A sharp analyst who can plumb, with conciseness and style, the essence of a subject, especially financial dealmaking. She shows snappy style with good quotes 11-16 in "Who's Afraid of the Big Bad Bear? Not the Dealmakers." Punchy lead, quoting Lee Iacocca in a post-Crash reaction, "Now the raiders are dead, thank God," and her opening rejoinder, "Don't bet on it, Lee." After presenting the views of a number of prominent players, she predicts more corporate acquisitions than leveraged buyouts in the future, with more capital put up by the acquirer. Her 7-20 "Why Nothing Seems to Make a Dent in the Dealmaking" hits all the cardinal points in the capitalist dynamic reshaping American industry — presenting a strong defense of mergers and acquisitions as a positive response to market forces unleashed by deregulation.

Dowd, Ann Reilly. *Fortune.* (★)
D.C.-based Dowd is a jack-of-all-trades, writing on topics from presidential candidates' fund-raising to private arms dealers. "Who's Ahead in the '88 Money Race," 6-8, was a workmanlike, timely summary of campaign fund-raising and the status of the top contenders; barely a mention of those controversial political action committees. "How U.S. Arms Dealers Are Making a Killing," 2-16, is interesting to the point of meeting some of the varied personalities who conduct this byzantine business, but just doesn't get across the dark side of it — as a defense company executive puts it, "In a well-executed arms deal, someone cheats everyone...it's very nasty." In any case, are we given a reason for caring about it, one way or other? No. "Learning from Reagan's Debacle," 4-30, is a sophomoric exercise saying that Reagan's management principles are still valid but that executives can take some lessons from his mistakes as well. Apparently this is the second part of a twice-yearly exercise, a more negative followup to Dowd's 9-15-86 cover "What Managers Can Learn from Ronald Reagan." She should have stopped there. After the Crash, her "Where Does the U.S. Go From Here?" 11-23, seems sophomoric, but we blame the editors for having her go on and on: "Washington must show the stock markets...To prove their mettle, Congress and the President should set their...Congress must also challenge...Congress should aim for..."

Duke, Paul, Jr. *The Wall Street Journal.* (★ ½)
Dallas. A young up-and-comer whose "Washington Week in Review" TV Father preceded him at the *WSJ*. He does well on technology stories. "Powerful '386' PC's Show Promise, But Software Drags," 1-19, is an adequate update, although we somehow expected newer material. "Improved Voice-Directed Products Are Poised to Enter Mass Market," 3-17, is more satisfying, providing clear, smooth writing in a highly informative article on the scope of voice technology, limited but expanding. Still, it needed more cost-benefit probing. The best we saw from him, 7-6, offered a succinct and intelligent speculation on a Compaq computer press conference scheduled for that day. A genuinely interesting and newsworthy event, the session would bring together Bill Gates of Microsoft and other leading software magnates to declare that the new Microsoft operating system #2 — and other programs scheduled for next year for IBM's new PC system — will play just as well or better on Compaq machines. A good job by Duke, which should not have been buried.

Fabrikant, Geraldine. *The New York Times.* (★ ½)
Covering the entertainment industry, movieland, she seemed to push a bit more past the routine in '87 and we found some real sparklers. Her "Campaign Propels 'La Bamba,'" 8-13, was one such. The odds against 'La Bamba' becoming a hit were overwhelming; creative advertising

overcame the odds. "Coca-Cola's Movie Mystery," 9-24, is analytically clever on Coke's purchase of Columbia Pictures. There's less to recommend in "Cannon Loses Some Luster," 1-26, on how overextended Hollywood's Cannon Group has become, with too many films, too few hits, but without much clue on why the bombs. In "His Toughest Challenge Yet," 3-15, we get to know Sumner Redstone, 63, one of the richest men in the U.S., who buys Viacom International, although he knows little about entertainment, but we would have liked more depth and fewer bumps in the writing.

Farnsworth, Clyde. *The New York Times.* (★ ★)
The dean of the global trade beat, Farnsworth could have gotten back the third star he lost in the '87 *MediaGuide* if he'd have stayed away from lofty economic analysis and stuck to reporting. In "Trying to Shield Injured American Workers," 1-18, we get a good roundup on the RR administration's cumulative protection — $80 billion of $360 billion imported goods covered by some form of protection, 22% compared to 12% in 1980. In the Sunday week in review, 6-21, he presents an unusually lucid analysis of the proposed trade bills and their shifting rationales. The proposals seem based on mostly obsolete concepts (trade balance), deceptive novelties ("adversarial trade"), and trumped up foreign offenses ("dumping"). Farnsworth offers a clear view of the new jargon of protectionism. He's excellent in "World Bank's Staff Upheaval," 9-24, observing World Bank pres. Barber Conable making an omelet by breaking lots and lots of eggs. Great line: "Business schools will study this case for a long time as how not to conduct a reorganization." Clyde bombs with "The Risks of an Unchecked Trade Deficit," 5-3. It seems "Americans have not earned enough from the sale of their goods overseas to cover the cost of imports since the early 1980s. They already owe foreign creditors a sum nearly as big as the combined debts of Brazil and Mexico," a situation which, according to C.F., threatens a depression. This is single-entry bookkeeping.

Flanigan, James. *Los Angeles Times.* (★ ½)
A prolific columnist who invariably has fresh material, if not analysis. Few others noticed that "films, TV shows, video recordings and musical records and tapes produce a $4.9 billion trade surplus — second only to Boeing jet planes as an export earner," 9-9. His best thoughts at times need better writing. For example, 10-25, "if new taxes slowed the U.S. economy and caused it to take fewer imports from Japan and Europe before they got their economies growing enough to absorb more of their own goods, the world might quickly fall into the recession that already threatens it." An otherwise very good column, "Other Nations Can Do More To Help Out," 10-4, stumbles over some dubious figures from economist Frank Levy, comparing incomes between 1973 (when price controls exaggerated real wages) and 1984 (only two years after the recession). And Flanigan swallows the most fashionable fallacy of the year, that "the Federal Reserve must boost interest rates in order to persuade foreign savers to invest in U.S. securities." On the contrary, if the interest rates goes up, the price of U.S. bonds goes down, so foreigners lose money. Flanigan is consistently better with material about specific firms. One of his best: "A Gutsy Move by McDonnell Was Smart, Too," 1-2, about the new MD-11 airplane.

Flint, Jerry. *Forbes.* (★ ½)
The slam-banging business reporter of the old school had a bagful of big, talked-about pieces in '86, but he slumped this year with too many slapdash pieces that pulled him way down. He did hit par with "Fiddling With Figures While Sales Drop," 8-24: "Unless GM can check its decline in market share or slash capacity, the company is in fundamental trouble." Good, snappy material and a cutting interview with Roger Smith. With "Too Much Ain't Enough," 7-13, he scores with material that suggests the middle class standard of living isn't slipping so much after all, but lesser stuff follows. "Who Gets the Parachutes," 1-12, sympathizes with blue-collar and middle manager layoffs done to improve efficiency, just okay, not from an anti-business position. "Can They Keep It Up?" 2-9, argues TRW is in a super position, but he's not persuasive in explaining why its PE is only 13. His "Into the Valley of Death,"

10-19, describes the corner A&S department stores find themselves in, in terms of expansion, their move to Herald Square an act of desperation, but it's dull stuff. His piece on Honda Motor Co., also 10-19, contrasts Honda's marketing and investment strategies with its competitors and concludes it's acting boldly, but this too seems stale. We looked for sparkle in his Chrysler Corp. piece, "Any More Rabbits in the Hat, Lee?" 11-30, though he spends most of his time on the hat and never really explains why Jeep may be the next rabbit. The writing was a bit better, though.

Fly, Richard. *BusinessWeek.* (★)
Washington. Perhaps it's the lack of excitement in the Presidential campaign during 1987, but Fly's political coverage has lacked excitement as well. "Six Candidates in Search of an Issue," 10-19, (coauthored with Douglas Harbrecht) and "The Democrats Are Playing 'Front-runner for a Day,'" 8-10, offer little that has not already been said ad infinitum on those subjects. Similarly, "Escape from Iranscam," 8-17, is boring commentary on a boring Bush campaign. More interesting is "Why the Reagan Era Won't End in 1989," 7-13 (with Paula Dwyer and Dave Griffiths), which asserts that Reagan policies are so imbedded in such areas as spending, taxes, and the Supreme Court that they would even bind a Democrat successor. The 1-26 advance on Reagan's state of the union address ("For Reagan, It Will Be a State of the Presidency Address") warns that a cosmetic approach may not help "rescue Reagan from the crisis that still grips his Presidency."

Forbes, Malcolm S., Jr. *Forbes.* (★ ★ ★)
There are two "Fact and Comment" columns in *Forbes.* Malcolm Sr.'s, which we do not rate, is always fun, but reads as if he composed it while motorcycling from his hot-air balloon to his yacht. Malcolm Jr., "Steve," is all business, though, never more so than in '87. His prose is simple and unadorned. He's been thinking about the world economy and American business and banking since he was in short pants, has a clear vision of how it all fits together, and almost never writes a throwaway column. In "Major Problem With the American Economy: Hypochondria," 3-9, he clears away in one sweep the "caterwauling" among economists "that manufacturing is dead, that new jobs are all at the minimum wage, that we are on a spending binge, that we are too much in debt, and that Japan and the rest of the world will soon own all our assets," taking on these points one by one with hard numbers and logic. In "Brazil," 4-20, he discusses the deadlock in the Brazilian debt crisis, rejects the IMF austerity solution, and urges tax reforms a la postwar Germany and Japan. He follows this with cheers for Citicorp's John Reed, 6-15, for his bold decision to reserve $3 billion for potential loan losses, Brazil foremost among debtor nations, but advising a follow up to spur growth in the debtor nations. In "Depleting Asset," 7-13, he discusses Ben Wattenberg's new book, *Birth Dearth*, the implications of the declining fertility rates in the western nations. And post-Crash, in both "1929? Or 1962?" 11-16, and "The Dollar," 11-30, he presents acute analysis that cuts against the Treasury's weak dollar policy. Forbes warned way back, 2-9, that "for the Bundesbank to be worried about inflation under these circumstances is similar to an anorexic worrying about overeating." He may not always be right, but he's always close, which is why he's about the best economic forecaster in journalism.

Forsyth, Randall. *Barron's.* (★ ★ ★)
When it comes to tracking interest rates, the "Current Yield" column really has no rivals. The weekly schedule and added space gives Forsyth an inherent edge over daily bond columns, which mainly rush to collect opinions about what happened the day before. Forsyth takes a longer perspective, and looks ahead. In "Real Support for the Dollar, Finally," 5-4, Forsyth explained why "the Fed tightening, far from hurting bond prices, pulled the market out of its tailspin." Another typically crisp verdict, at the peak of the market, 8-24: "The markets, rather than reacting to stale trade numbers, more likely are testing the resolve of the newly installed Fed chairman, Alan Greenspan, to maintain the purchasing power of the dollar." His "Skepticism About D.C. Orthodoxy," 10-5, observed that the bond market did badly

after the Gramm-Rudman budgetary fix, suggesting that the budget wasn't the real issue. Forsyth, instead, saw more potential in Treasury Secretary Baker's proposal to stabilize commodity prices, which he explained better than most. "Central banks would receive prompt warnings of inflation and deflation, so they could temper price swings. That would lead to greater coordination of policies and stability of exchange rates." His succinct "Trade Hysteria Sends Rates Higher, Again," 10-19, was read the weekend before Black Monday: "The fact is that all the markets now react to the monthly trade numbers in the same reflex manner they once used for money supply data...In any case, after the latest trade numbers hit the wires, the markets decided it was a problem that pointed to further declines in the dollar, rises in interest rates, protectionist legislation, or all of the above." At times lately, 4-6 for example, Forsyth has been getting a bit too technical, reflecting recent graduate studies in economics and finance. But he's usually very good at translating tough material into readable English, "Misleading Indicators?" 2-9, an example.

Francis, David R. *The Christian Science Monitor.* (★ ½)
A financial reporter of established competence, Francis still cranks out big scope, whither-the-economy pieces, and we still read them with care, but he often seems bored since the heyday of monetarism, which he championed. He finally swallowed hard two years ago, 2-11-86, and wrote that if his monetarist friends "are wrong again this year [about high inflation in '86], they will have to offer some good excuses to save their economic theory from disrespect." But he was back, without excuses, quoting the same bunch in '87 in "How Well Is the Fed Using Monetary Tools to Avert Recession?" 11-2. When the '86 inflation failed to arrive on schedule, the monetarists were now happy that "the Fed has injected the banking system with a huge slug of money." Francis gives us a "Falling Dollar Helps American Industries," 7-16, but a "Dollar Plunge Unsettles Allies," 1-16. While he has the competence to put all this together in challenging the central policy question of beggar-thy-neighbor monetarism, we didn't see it. Francis is also responsible for the *Monitor*'s coverage of Canada, with mixed results. "Canada's Conservatives are Losing Ground — and Wonder Why," 9-16, a good question but we were left wondering why, too. A report on the Commonwealth meeting in Vancouver, "Thatcher Dilutes Commonwealth Resolve on S. Africa Sanctions," 10-19, was crisp, comprehensive, the only place we saw Maggie describe the ANC as "a typical terrorist organization."

Frank, Allan Dodds. *Forbes.* (★ ★ ½)
A versatile free spirit at *Forbes*, Frank loves to deliver pieces on shady characters, swindles, gun-runners and fast money, but he knows high finance, too. Typical is "You Can't Keep a Smart Crook Down," 12-29-86, on the amazing John Peter Galanis, who gets caught again and again in high level scams and works still bigger fleeces. Better still, "Everyone Wants Us," 2-23, definitive on the current political/economic footing of Panama, "what Casablanca and Lisbon were during World War II: a neutral zone and home for agents with murky identities and murkier backgrounds," the Japanese and Soviets lurking. In "Malcolm McLean's Pirate Ships," 3-23, the collapse of U.S. Lines opens prospects of "killer ships" acquired at dirt-cheap prices, and Frank weaves in the lurking maritime unions with the smell of big money throughout. The *Forbes* cover story on the stinking rich in the entertainment industry is, of course, Frank's (with Jason Zweig). "The Fault is Not in Our Stars," 9-21, with Bill Cosby maybe making $100 million in the year, is basically junk, but Frank elevates it by casting "entertainment goods" as the No. 2 earner behind aircraft among U.S. exports, $4.9 billion in '86. He does a frothy little thing on "The Foam Finger," 5-4, the "No. 1" foam mitt that football fans wave around, which is beneath his talents. There's a once-over-lightly on the Jamaican economy, "The Locomotive Needs Help," 1-26, a waste of time. After the Crash came a snoozy interview with the incredibly overrated Robert Hormats of Goldman, Sachs, who jibber-jabbers as usual.

Franklin, William B. & Cooper, James C. *BusinessWeek.* (½ ★)
The "Business Outlook" column, we wrote last year, "has usually been the best available review of near-term developments in the U.S. economy." That was not true in 1987. The outlook column was mainly reduced to repeating, over and over again, that consumer spending determines production. "Consumer spending is the key to pace of the economy in 1987," 1-26. "Consumer caution puts the brakes on growth," 7-27. "Consumer spending is the sector where demand looks worrisomely weak," 8-10. "Prospects for consumer spending...are far less certain," 8-31. This got a little tiresome, week after week, while manufacturing, construction and business investment kept zooming ahead, with Franklin and Cooper trying to explain why each good statistic was an illusion. They did not explore the idea that incentives to produce provide the jobs, wealth and income to finance consumption — not the other way around. Finally surprised by 9 months of consistently wrong forecasts (manufacturing had risen 5.5% over the year), their whole story abruptly changed. Suddenly, "consumers are buying as if there were no tommorow," 10-5, and "the growing risk is that, as production picks up, consumers will continue to spend at too rapid a clip," 10-12. The market crashed the following week, and *BusinessWeek*'s solution, 11-16, was to raise taxes to "cool the party down," because "all agree that [consumer] spending must fall." Franklin and Cooper, however, had reverted to worrying, 11-2, that, "More than ever, consumers are the key to the business outlook."

Frazier, Steve. *The Wall Street Journal.* (NR)
Houston. His "Under a Cloud — Tesoro and Chairman Face a Host of Charges in a San Antonio Trial," 3-12, is a rip-roaring story, thoroughly reported and organized, with a brisk lead: "Finance ministers prefer blondes." But Frazier still leaves us wondering how the directors let the chairman (West) get away with so much. A few quotes from the directors, among them Irving Kristol, would have rounded this into one of the best business stories of the year. In "Housing-Market Bust In Houston Is Creating Rash of Instant Slums," 2-5, he asks "How could it all happen — and with such frightening speed?" The oil bust? "But many local housing experts insist that Houston's retrenchment economy can't begin to account for the level of home abandonments." The answer, he thinks, was the frenzy of overbuilding that continued even after the oil slump was evident. But why that? We aren't quite satisfied on the economics, but he gives us enough on the instant-slum phenomenon to make this worthwhile as sociology.

Freedman, Alix M. *The Wall Street Journal.* (★ ½)
New York. "Space-Age Savor: Flavor Specialist Strives For Microwave Foods," 7-28, on International Flavors and Fragrances Inc.'s test lab finding ways to improve microwave flavors had nice detail, examples, and was well put together. A P.1 leader, "Cigarette Smoking Is Growing Hazardous To Careers in Business," 4-23, tells us that "smoking has gone from being a socially acceptable practice to one that is increasingly seen as a character defect indicating weakness and a lack of self-discipline." Worthwhile for the corporate culture, but is soft, soft news that should be the column four A-Hed, not the paper's lead. In "Forsaking the Black Box: Designers Wrap Products in Visual Metaphors," 3-26, spots a move away from "minimalism" in design to "product semantics," a radio that looks like earphones, a tea kettle "with a plastic bird perched on its spout that whistles when the water boils." Imaginative feature.

Fuerbringer, Jonathan. *The New York Times.* (★ ½)
Another hard-working year on the budget beat, with Fuerbringer seeming less intense, less certain that he had to help bring down the deficit with his reporting, but he's still pretty bleak. "Budget Panel's Chairman Ready to Forget the Law's Deficit Goal," is a thorough, clear account of the disputes over Gramm-Rudman targets. In an update on Speaker Wright's proposal to raise taxes to cut the deficit, "Rostenkowski Backs Tax Rise Idea," 3-6, although the story makes it clear Rosty will support but not advocate. There is no mention of the dramatic decline of the deficit or Gramm-Rudman '87 target being met in "Deficit Cuts: Less of a Bite,"

9-25. But there was good coverage of the November budget summit, "Elusive Spirit of Compromise," 11-5, one of his best, with the two boxers in the fiscal fight still throwing punches. Also good on "Trade Bill Passes House Unit," 3-26, explaining the nature and basic details of the House bill "which will become the centerpiece of trade legislation" coming up later, a nice job sorting out the protectionist arguments. "Senate Approves Trade Bill, 71-27, Defying President," 7-22, is routine, bare bones, no drama, no comment on unanimous Democratic vote, or how firm it is. In "Reagan To Accept Limits on Budget But Vows to Fight," 9-27, he states as axiomatic, "This country's budget deficit is a factor in determining exchange rates between the dollar and other currencies and is a cause of the huge American trade deficit," although the issue is a central debate among economists. This kind of advocacy tends to creep into Fuerbringer's material, which makes even his superior reports a bit harder to take.

Fuhrman, Peter. *Forbes.* (★ ★ ½)
Transferred to Europe late in the year, an elevation from the reporter's pool where he showed superior talent, intelligence and breadth. In "The Securities Act of 1988," 3-9, we get a stunning quote from Kidder's Martin Siegel the previous summer, he wanting "to be a part of the reshaping of corporate America." A good review of the Securities Exchange Act of 1934 and its coming Supreme Court challenge. "Here We Go Again," 7-13, gives a first-rate perspective on the current merger wave, showing that measured in historical terms, it is the fourth such wave in U.S. history and by no means the largest or most convulsive. In "Playing Politics," 8-4, there's excellence and originality in a contrast of news and investment values, pivoting on the Korea Fund and Korean economy, with penetrating observations on the media's lack of understanding of world markets. In "Cleveland Cliffs," 10-5, there's high drama in the iron ore industry, related straightforwardly. A lot of complicated maneuvering by a number of players is skillfully outlined in a short piece and we see Fuhrman is obviously in control of his pen and his facts. One of the best interviews of the year in "As I See It, the Soviet Economy is in a Grave State," 10-19, with the economist who is most responsible for the reforms under *perestroika,* with incisive questions and eloquent, frank answers. Enterprising.

Gall, Norman. *Forbes.* (½ ★)
The *Forbes* editors have been fascinated with Gall's intellectual pretensions for some years, so we slog on, trying to get the message in his bigdome efforts. "The Ghost of 1929," 7-13, is an ambitious attempt to compare the economic conditions of mid-1987 with those prevailing before and during the Great Depression — written three months before the 1987 Crash. Gall gets an "A" for effort and for a number of scattered nuggets, but he's off the mark in determining causes of the Depression (limited to World War I debt and "collapse of inflated asset values") and incoherent in making connections between the U.S. and world economies. Also, in his historical narrative, he fails several times to give dates although it's obvious the year has changed (and who was his editor?). "Bungling in Brazil," 7-27, is a meager, unbalanced throwaway piece on why foreign capital is pulling out of Brazil. At the least, given the complex subject of foreign investment, one would have expected to learn why companies like IBM, General Motors, and Ford are staying — but they were given short shrift. In "The Japanese Strategy for Computer Supremacy," 2-9, Gall presents an alarmist interview with an MIT computer expert warning that Japan will soon dominate the semiconductor and computer industries worldwide and "undermine the entire U.S. industrial base." This could either be scary or — didn't somebody say that about steel, too?

Gannes, Stuart. *Fortune.* (★ ★ ★)
Technology reporter of the front rank, new to us this year with a fast-paced, no-nonsense style. His "Sun's Sizzling Race to the Top," 8-17, is *Fortune*'s best technology piece of the year, the first of a dozen efforts we saw that explained the dazzling rise of Sun Microsystems without the hokem of its laid back California style, beer blasts and blue jeans. The secret of going from zero to $500 million in sales in five years: providing "letchas" instead of a "gotcha" mentality, computers that can connect to all other systems and use standard components and

software. Sun CEO Scott McNealy oversimplifies a bit: "In the past, computer companies have been able to charge a premium for proprietary technology. In the future, they will have to offer a discount." His only weakness was in not exploring the promise and pitfalls of Sun's effort to create a new standard by designing a proprietary microprocessor and licensing it to competitors, including Fujitsu. Another sizzling rise is in "Merck Has Made Biotech Work," 1-19, "the flood of innovative prescription drugs from Merck's labs is the talk of the pharmaceutical industry." Why, a fanatical commitment to research when Wall Streeters were worrying about a research black hole: "Having sold its consumer products business — which made over-the-counter items like Sucrets throat lozenges and Calgon bubble bath — in the Seventies, Merck dumped chunks of its specialty chemicals division. Now more than 90% of revenues comes from drugs." His "Strong Medicine for Health Bills," 4-13, catches up with HMO "propaganda" and Gannes catches us up in a hurry on what's going on in company health-care costs and strategies.

Glaberson, William. *The New York Times.* (★ ½)
Sunday business reporter, new to the section, seemed to draw some of the soft assignments that could not penetrate our interest level. On 6-14, for example, he gave us *a la* Upton Sinclair's "The Jungle," a report on the working conditions in the U.S. meat-packing industry, but he has the talent to handle major stuff. In "A Falling Dollar is Said to Invite a Recession," 2-12, he covers his bases in looking at the negatives of dollar devaluation, but we noted the material was a bit behind the *Wall Street Journal*. Clearly his best effort of the year was "Life After Salomon Brothers," 10-11, getting behind the sensationalism of Wall Street myths to give us a perceptive and sympathetic look at the individuals who helped build Salomon into a power, but alas are no longer with the firm. Timely, given Salomon's restructuring and decision to lay off about 800 people.

Glassman, James K. *The New Republic.* (★ ★ ★ ½)
The "Money Culture" columnist. The only reason we do not give Glassman the highest rating, or create an even higher category for him, is that *he denies us*. He writes too seldom, when the spirit or desire for cash money moves him. We see him mostly in *TNR*, but he scatters his pearls before whatever swine will pay his minimum, even *Vanity Fair* at times. His review of two books on the 50-year anniversary of *Life* magazine, "One Life to Live," 2-9, was breathtaking, a stunning plunge into the soul of Henry Luce and of the philosophical margins of American photographic art. "The candid camera is no longer possible. It has made itself obsolete...The American population had learned the visual and emotional habits of a world on film." His "Money Culture" columns though are priceless gems, quiet excitements that leave us dizzy and speechless. "Free Gifts," 7-27, on how Dayton Hudson Corp. of Minneapolis buys the Minnesota legislature with charitable contributions, is the sweetest kind of muckraking. "Chartists," 4-6, is simply about stock-market chartists, *a la* Elliott Wavist Robert Prechter and his ilk, about 1200 words that are all you ever have to read about the Chartists of Wall Street, or the "Z theorists" that brood over the *Daily Racing Form*. Ah, Glassman. In "The Shrug Market," 1-5 & 12, he can't understand why Wall Street shrugged off Boesky so quickly, and believes Wall Street is wrong. He bets $1000 that the S&P index will fall below 231 in three months, or "I lose everything." Ah, Glassman, a loser! But in reality, this byline wins going away.

Gleick, James. *The New York Times.* (★ ★ ★ ½)
Another dazzling technology writer that has blossomed in the *Science Times* hothouse. Without question he deserves a Pulitzer for his pioneering story on superconductivity, 3-10, both for authoritatively breaking the major technical story of the decade and for staying in the lead for months against all his competition. His front-page story, "Discoveries Bring a 'Woodstock,'" 3-20, on the American Physical Society meeting, vindicated his scoop of ten days before and brought the breakthrough to the attention of the rest of the world. On 5-6, he reports IBM had already solved the lack of current capacity in superconductors in some

applications, and 5-23, again explains the new advances and their significance, detailing reports of operations near room temperature and breakthroughs in high current superconductivity. On 7-7, another intoxicating piece on superconductivity, suggesting the potential of human levitation. On 8-17, in the Sunday magazine, an intriguing piece on the possibility that Paul Chu's Houston team had deliberately misrepresented the material it had employed in its superconductor score, prompting wild goose chases around the world with ytterbium, not the yttrium Chu had actually used. No Jimmy-One-Note, on 6-1 he breaks a big story on the dynamics of running shoes, but fails to make shoe technology as clear and comprehensible as superconductivity. On 6-30, he explains the scientific interest in the feedback loops that results in additional cloud cover as the earth surface warms. The new contribution in this article is Gaia: a Godlike mother earth, consisting of flora and fauna that spontaneously correct for environmental damage and thus perpetuate life on the planet. On 7-14, we get an amazing tale of an unknown Indian mathematician born a century ago, whose theorems and insights, at last verifiable on computers, are now inspiring new discoveries in such frontier fields as superstring theory in physics and molecular dynamics.

Gray, Patricia Bellew. *The Wall Street Journal.* (★ ½)
Legal Affairs. A breezier touch in her writing, in what is mostly a dull grey world, lifted her material noticeably this year. She got our attention with "two voluptuous nude women in a bathtub with nary a bubble for cover," in "More Lawyers Reluctantly Adopt Strange New Practice — Marketing," 1-30, the ladies gracing a promotional brochure for Vetter & White of Providence, R.I. We're sure the piece was extremely well read by the many lawyers who subscribe, down to the closing twist: "'Marketing is largely a myth,' [says one consultant]. 'Law firms are finding that the most effective way to get new business is to hire lawyers who already have it.'" Another on "Law Firms Big Fee Hikes, etc.," 3-19, with $350 per hour for senior partners at Skadden, Arps, is well written, mildly informative, but we're still puzzled given the abundance of lawyers. Gray's "Some Firm Advice," 5-15, is offered to small businessmen on how to find the right lawyer, quite informative and useful: "Expect to interview several of them, and negotiate on fees. After all, with a glut of lawyers in the market, these are increasingly tough times for all but the biggest law firms. It's a buyer's market, so be courageous." One of her biggies of the year, a P.1 leader "Legal Nightmare," 8-3, on the multiple allegations of impropriety besetting the elite law firm of Sullivan & Cromwell, has a breezy start, which gets the story good position, but it really belonged inside.

Griffiths, Dave. *BusinessWeek.* (★ ½)
This is a politically-oriented reporter writing on "in the news" topics in national security and defense. "Sam Nunn Is Sticking to His Guns," 8-24, succinctly shows the Senator's power and policy on defense, which he would use to block the Democrats from going soft on the subject. In the 11-16 "The Pentagon Budget: Cuts Are Certain, But Where?" Griffiths gives a concise outline of the broad choices faced by Congress. Two are to cut new weapons systems still in development, or cut operations expenses. Seeing the latter as unlikely, he presents a third choice — to upgrade some current weapons instead of creating brand new products. "After Arms Control: What Does NATO Do Now?" 10-19, is a good summary of concerns that, once an intermediate-range nuclear-weapons treaty is in place, conventional forces in Europe may be insufficient to hold off a Soviet attack. Major opinions quoted in the article come primarily from Carter administration defense officials such as Harold Brown, leaving readers wondering where the Reagan administration stands on this question.

Gupta, Udayan. *The Wall Street Journal.* (NR)
New York. A nifty newsbeat for Gupta, 8-4, reaching and interviewing Chen while the *NYT* reporter on the story wrote that Chen was "unavailable," then writing an incisive story on his prospects for getting financed, treated by the same *NYT* as far-fetched, but which have since proven immense, not only for U.S. venture capitalists and the supercomputer users in the U.S. government, but also Japan. In "Raising Money the New Fangled Way," 9-18, the

Journal's special report offered this trenchant piece on the success of LSI Logic of Silicon Valley, raising some $200 million around the world to finance its foreign subsidiaries. U.S. startups have begun exploiting global capital markets in ingenious new ways. We see much of the U.S. high technology capital formation of recent years has been financed overseas, and as in the case of LSI Logic, the U.S. parent will reap the returns.

Gupte, Pranay. *Forbes.* (★ ★ ½)
A prolific former *Times*man who had been freelancing and bookwriting about his native India, Gupte signed on at *Forbes* early in the year as a contributing editor and writes a regular opinion column we see sporadically in *Newsweek International.* Much of his best writing is about the political economy of the subcontinent. He interviews Rajiv Gandhi in "We Don't Have the Bomb," 5-18, and the Aga Khan, "What a Legacy For Our Children!" 6-15, always pushing questions on economic policies that may promote growth. He's also been getting deeper into the world arms trade and got info in '87 we didn't see elsewhere, and wonder why. The best, "Rhetoric & Reality In the Iranian Arms Trade," 10-19, pins the tail on Sweden's late Prime Minister Olaf Palme, described in a subhead Gupte did not write as the "apostle of peace and friend of the poor countries, turns out to have been one of the world's top arms salesmen," with the piece itself wisely free of moralizing or drawing obvious comparisons with the U.S./Iranian arms deals. Informative and well reported, and we wonder where's the rest of the press corps on this. Another, more comprehensive piece with revealing graphics on the global arms industry, "Russia: Arms Merchant to the World," 11-2, makes the deeper point that as Congress makes it tougher for the U.S. to sell arms abroad, it gets easier for the Soviets, now the champs, reaping advantages in money and political influence.

Hamilton, Joan O'C. *BusinessWeek.* (★ ★)
San Francisco. We've become so discouraged with the myriad bylines that go into the *BW* stew, it's a delight to come upon Hamilton doing her solos, in Silicon Valley, the wine country or even L.A. Her vino report on "Paul Schlem Uncorks a Turnaround Plant," 9-28, is a simple one-pager on Vintners International Co. buying up Paul Masson, Taylor, and Great Western graperies, making it the nation's No. 3 wine producer. We sip her report with pleasure, especially a bell-ringing quote: "Television ads have always been good for the industry, but I've never seen them help any one brand," re the Masson "will sell no wine before its time." But what about Bartles & Jaymes? Hamilton zips with "It Has 400HP, Costs $40,000 — and Comes from Toyota?" 4-27, a zinger on the souped-up Supra, and she uses her available space to lay out the stats, which is what the buyers eye up, and a quote from a Beverly Hills dealer: "I think it could bring Porsche and Ferrari buyers into the Japanese market," Hamilton adding, straight-faced, "It could lure consumers who can't spare $200,000 for Porsche's new 450 hp 959 model." Two pieces on AIDS in San Francisco, 3-23, add just a bit to what we already know. She chips in with Alex Beam of the Boston bureau with "Camouflaged Drugs Make Enzon Stand Out," 4-27, on enzyme-based drugs, moderately informative, moderately confusing, and we wished she were doing the piece on her own.

Hamilton, Martha M. *The Washington Post.* (★ ½)
Airlines. A dependable business reporter worth noting, she approaches even routine stories with a little extra verve and her features usually pull us through even on busy days. One such, "Snails Pace the Path to Profits," 4-5, a light and delicious Sunday business feature about a California snail processing firm. "Airlines Tailor New Facilities to Hub Needs," 5-24, notes '86 passenger miles at 278.3 billion, double 1970, and while markets change quickly, major facility change takes years; useful although it could have been better organized. "High-Sky Balancing Act As Airlines Juggle Discounts," 5-17, has terrific graphics backing up her piece, showing high peak, low peak on American. "Airlines Betting on Value of Service," 9-22, is a smart piece on Continental's competitors as they try to outguess in balancing ticket price and service. In "Airlines Fight To Make Skies Friendly Again," 11-15, the Sunday lead starts with, "Some of the nation's airlines have discovered a simple way to improve their on-time

performance: They've started telling passengers the truth about flight times," i.e., American adds 39 minutes from its Dulles-LA flight 75. And good detail on "hot spares."

Hampton, William J. *BusinessWeek.* (★)
Detroit. Not so many ideas thrown out to readers this year as last. The more or less obvious auto-industry topics get covered competently, if not always excitingly. "Why Image Counts: A Tale of Two Industries," 6-8, reviews an old story — how U.S. industry will have to avoid making mistakes in design and manufacturing rather than rely on fixing them later. In "How IBM Wooed Ford Into a More Meaningful Relationship," 3-30, Hampton reveals that IBM is bending on its usual secrecy about future products in order to discourage Ford's shopping around. The 3-16 cover, "General Motors: What Went Wrong?" is a thorough, but not novel, examination of the big automaker's plight. Good photo comparison shows two GM look-alikes, a $26,000 Cadillac Seville and a $9,700 Olds Calais — the only obvious difference being the price. Most intriguing is Hampton's "General Motors' Little Engine That Could," 8-3, which previews Quad 4, a new engine designed from scratch that turns out 150 horsepower from 4 cylinders.

Harris, Anthony. *Financial Times.* (★ ½)
Usually solid, rarely startling, Harris is best at calming overblown anxieties, such as observing that British trade deficits and accelerating economy being two sides of the same coin. "We All Pay for the Debt Crisis," 2-28, bashes banks for trying to make up for bad foreign debts by overcharging on credit cards. "Time to Invent A Few New Taxes," 1-2, exposes a damning memo that proposes new British taxes on wealth, land, property and credit cards. "A Shortage Of Speculators," 5-30, notes that only central bankers are allowed to engage in stabilizing speculation in foreign exchange, because dealers don't carry open positions for long.

Hayes, Thomas C. *The New York Times.* (★ ½)
Western economic correspondent, doing rather well over a range of different kinds of business stories in '87. "Pickens All Set for New Game," 1-26, has a nice angle on the new flexibility at Mesa Petroleum to pursue takeovers. "Economist Or Mystic? Tune In, Around 1990, To Find Out," 8-30, is well done on Ravi Batra and the coming Great Depression. He does a reasonably good job, 7-1, analyzing the current position of Texas Instruments as the top U.S. competitor to the Japanese in microchips. He doesn't say what part of TI's share of recent chip profits come from a one-time-only $108 million DRAM patent settlement with six Asian rivals. While he points out TI has kept pace with Japan in DRAM technology, the bulk of TI's DRAMs are made in the company's Japan plants, raising interesting points ignored in the piece. Hayes covers another dramatically growing computer domain pioneered by American startups: the minisupercomputer, 7-8. He focused on Convex Computer Corporation, a venture of Sevin-Rosen Management, and the kind of explosive growth predicted for the industry.

Hays, Laurie. *The Wall Street Journal.* (★ ½)
Philadelphia. A solid business reporter who can bring us up to date, but should push harder on the future. Good reporting on a semi book review, "Book Maps U.S.A. Today," 7-14, on Peter Pritchard's *The Making of McPaper.* But it's not quite clear on the paper's current financial situation, which supposedly is in the black, but is it simply creative accounting by Gannett? Similarly, in "Bronfmans of Seagram Take Increasing Role in DuPont Co. Affairs," 7-17, is very imformative on this angle, but doesn't get very far beneath the surface on the financial impact. A P.1 leader, "Du Pont's Difficulties In Selling Kevlar," 9-29, offers a good, rich history of the development of this "tough fiber," 25 years and a $700 million investment (and news the President wears a Kevlar vest in public). But when's the payoff and how big can it be?

Helyar, John. *The Wall Street Journal.* (★ ★ ½)
Atlanta. A fine business reporter with super writing skills. "Sun Trust Leads U.S. Banks in

Earnings," 8-3, is an excellent deep look at a super-regional bank that is doing remarkably well. In "Altered Landscape: The Holiday Inns Trip: A Breeze for Decades, Bumpy Rides in the '80s," 2-11, a thoroughly absorbing piece with an arresting lead, "It was a perfectly miserable vacation that 1951 summer." The problem: "Mr. Wilson didn't have the managerial mindset of a conglomerateur, but rather the restless urgings of an entrepreneur."

Herman, Tom. *The Wall Street Journal.* (★ ½)
New York. After years of sharing a byline with Ed Foldessy, Herman is now on his own with the "Credit Markets" column (sometimes shared with Matthew Winkler). The column now draws from a more diverse set of sources, including people who actually manage money. For comments on Federal Reserve policy, though, Herman relies too heavily on three former Fed officials (who are obscure by training, and don't really have inside dope on the current Fed governors). Most of the space is still taken up with describing in laborious detail what happened the day before, with no coherent theme linking even two days together. A typical Herman theme, reflecting the ambiguity of his sources, was that the slightest tightening by the Fed would toss the economy into recession, while any easing would be wildly inflationary: "A credit-easing move would be awkward in the midst of the dollar's decline, as would a tightening in light of trade tensions," 3-30. A day later, in "Bond Prices Take Biggest Fall in 6 Months as Worry About Dollar Grows," 3-31, investors were said to be worried that the Fed *will* defend the dollar, even though falling bond prices were correctly attributed to the expectation that the Fed would *not* defend the dollar. A later drop in bond prices was blamed on "stronger economic growth and a huge trade deficit," 8-18, though there was really no new information about both familiar trends. The next day, 8-19, the column was instead worrying about "the weaker dollar and the perception that it will generate inflation." On the day of the crash, 10-19, Herman was behind the times, predicting that "further credit-tightening by foreign central banks appears likely." There are signs of experimentation in Herman's new solo column, which may bear fruit next year.

Hershey, Robert D. *The New York Times.* (★ ½)
A Washington bureau general assignment reporter with a byline-a-day on routine government economics, with enough experience to do heavier lifting. But most of 1987 seemed reliable and routine meat-and-potatoes, as in "Volcker Sees Slight '87 Gains," 2-17, a faithful report of the Fed chairman's testimony. "U.S. Oil Shortages Seen Unavoidable to Many Analysts," 2-17, seemed a one-sided scare story by Energy Secretary Hodel and oil "experts" who argue $18/bbl is not enough to invite U.S. exploration, giving control back to OPEC; no counter arguments were cited. "How the U.S. Economy Sustains Its Long Lacklustre Climb," 5-31, presents a Q&A on the subject with a good line, "Expansions do not die of old age," but otherwise, not terribly useful observations. "For Greenspan, No Dearth of Tests," 6-4, rounds up the usual suspects (Lawrence Kudlow of Bear Stearns being one) to quote two-dimensional views that change hourly anyway. He's smart enough to see news in "Fed Official Warns of Inflationary Acts," 7-30, a report on Fed Vice Chairman Manuel Johnson's remarks at a CATO conference: raising the minimum wage and protectionist legislation could spur inflationary forces, provoking the Fed to tighten credit. Quotes him as saying, "I don't see a need for any easing of credit at this time." Important points, not seen in the other papers.

Holusha, John. *The New York Times.* (★ ½)
A journeyman on the auto beat, highly respected in the industry for playing it straight. A solid '87 with several standout pieces. "Merger Motive for Chrysler," 3-12, is a timely column on Chrysler getting Jeeps immediately — by buying AMC — instead of investing $1 billion to develop competition. In "Likely Targets for Ford Cash," 7-28, he ponders Ford Motor's $11 billion cash hoard and looks around on how to spend it. On the labor front, "Union Stressing Job Security at GM," 6-3, the UAW's strategy is to make layoffs so expensive the company will seek other alternatives. "Auto Job Guarantees Sought," 7-7, has medium analytical depth on the new UAW drive for lifetime guarantees. A sturdier effort is "UAW

Proposes Ford Guarantee Jobs in New Pact," 9-9, with UAW's Owen Beiber asking job guarantees for the length of its new contract, arguing competition from plants Japanese are building here could provoke production cutbacks by the big three. A profile of GM's "Rising Star," 10-4, Elmer W. Johnson, one of four in line to succeed Roger Smith in 1990, is a bit too puffy, always a Holusha weakness around big wheels. His best lead of '87 is in "Chevy's Crucial New Models," 4-1: "A shark's fin glides through dark blue water and then a car emerges from the deep. The clear message from the television commercial is that the 1988 Chevrolet Beretta is as sleek and aggressive as a shark — and even more important, a break from the GM Corporation's recent run of indistinguishable look-alike cars."

Horowitz, Rose. *The Journal of Commerce.* (★ ½)
Author of some major features on the international economy in 1986, we saw fewer of them from her this year as she tackled less ambitious issues, such as "Asbestos Cases Soared in 1986," 6-11. "Viable Program Could Win Brazil New Funds," 2-24, relied too heavily on one American "expert," William Chase, and said nothing about what constitutes a "viable" program. "Debt Swap May Not Boost U.S. Exports," 5-28, found "no consensus that sustained economic growth in the developing countries will necessarily mean more U.S. exports to Latin America." No consensus? The U.S. would export just as much to depressed Latin American economies? "Management Korea-Style: It's All in the Family," 4-8, was novel and interesting. "Productivity is about the same at Samsung's U.S. plants as it is in the company's plants in Korea," but Korean workers are more "loyal."

Isikoff, Michael. *The Washington Post.* (★ ½)
A fair, accurate business reporter who we usually see on spot news and routine reports out of the federal bureaucracy, but he often teams with others for bigger stories. "The Costly Wait For a Space Station," 3-19, with Kathy Sawyer, on aerospace companies spending $100,000 a day while the White House makes a decision, a good piece ahead of the New York papers. "The Good Life at PTL," 5-22 and 5-23, with Art Harris, gives us mind-numbing detail on the financial excesses of Jim and Tammy Bakker, but Isikoff strains to be fair.

Johnson, Robert. *The Wall Street Journal.* (★ ★ ½)
Chicago. An extremely promising beat reporter who turned in one of the 10-best business stories of 1987, "General Mills Risks Millions Starting Chain of Italian Restaurants," 9-21, which the *WSJ* ran in its most prominent front-page spot. We get the lowdown on the Minneapolis-based company's Olive Garden restaurant chain, how the idea began, how the plans kicked around the corporate bureaucracy, the decisions to play to unsophisticated palates, offering "Italian Margaritas," a "Venetian" chicken simmered in Teriyaki sauce, and chocolate mousse. It's hilarious, but about as instructive on corporate decision making in mass marketing as we've ever seen. Johnson's wry sense of humor carries easily throughout. "Americans may think they like real Italian food, but General Mills knows better." Easy on the garlic. In a P.1 feature, "Low-Budget Bronson Wins All His Battles Except With Critics," 7-10, former footballer Fred Williamson has made 16 bad-guy movies @ $500,000 each. "He is the only black actor who regularly appears as a leading man in action films." A black film critic says "He gets by on a smirk, or — if he's really trying to be expressive — a smirk and a cigar clenched between his teeth." In "Chicago's HUD Chief Gives Mayor Washington A Fight Over Housing Program," 8-14, we get serious stuff, but with a light, sensitive touch as Gertrude Jordan, a black woman, fights City Hall patronage and the Chicago Housing Authority.

Johnston, Oswald. *Los Angeles Times.* (★ ½)
Most of Johnston's time seems to be taken up with necessary but unexciting reports on government statistics, but one lengthy feature revealed much greater potential. "Foreign Capital in U.S. Economy," 11-12, was a real eye-opener. It neatly blended sophisticated ideas, actual examples, and rare statistics (e.g., government debt accounted for only $80 billion of the $500 billion increase in foreign investment in the U.S. from 1981 to 1986). Experience at European-

owned plants in Spartanburg, South Carolina, "suggests that foreign investors — lured by the world's best opportunities to make money — may not only continue to invest in the United States but also to reinvest their profits here instead of taking them home with them." Rather than assume an accumulation of foreign debts with nothing to show for them, Johnston figured that foreign capital in the United States "could be laying the foundations for another historic surge of growth." A real heresy, quite convincingly argued.

Kaletsky, Anatole. *Financial Times.* (★)
Probably the most frankly opinionated economic journalist anywhere, which can be entertaining or just irritating. In "Unkind Cut for Wage Slaves Pursuing a Dream," 1-20, Kaletsky says, "American wage and salary earners have enjoyed no real improvement in living standards for nearly 20 years, now a misfortune which can be found in almost no other country outside Africa and Latin America." This gross error comes from measuring "living standards" by average real wage rates. This is a "blue collar" measure that, among other problems, excludes salaries and benefits, and includes a rising proportion of students working part-time. Instead of abusing bad statistics, Kaletsky usually settles for unsupported assertions. In "Inflationary Fears Revisited," 9-7, Kaletsky simply announces that "overexpansion, rather than recession, is the greater threat,...[so] unemployment is the indicator that Dr. Greenspan is likely to be watching most closely...[and] the falling dollar...will keep up the heady rise of stock prices." The whole, long article consisted of such scattered raw opinions. When not displaying his penchant for random America-bashing, Kaletsky can still get serious. In "US Concentrates on Conditions for Growth," 3-6, which was actually about growth in the Third World, he reports positively on "a gradual tilting of the balance in the US government's concern to the fostering of conditions for worldwide economic growth." "The Price of Job Security," 9-23, on the Ford-UAW contract was expertly done. He was much more consistent in 1986, following another weak year in 1985. Readers never know what to expect under this unreliable byline.

Karmin, Monroe. *U.S.News & World Report.* (½★)
"Economic Outlook" columnist. The consistent use of Alan Greenspan as a source finally paid off when Greenspan went on to become Fed chairman. Karmin is not as bleak as Ed Mervosh used to be, but the outlook is still mired in Keynesian thinking and is very tentative. In the "Fandango over the Budget," 1-12, Karmin, with Gloria Borger and Robert Morse, says that the budget deficit may get smaller — or it may not. "Inside the Federal Reserve," 4-13, was bad news all around: the dollar is falling, interest rates are rising, Japan is recessioning (or close to it) and even the good news is bad — the drop in unemployment is not because more people are employed, but because fewer people were looking for work. Next to Alfred Malabre, Jr. at the *Journal*, the most depressing columnist in the continental U.S.

Kestin, Hesh. *Forbes.* (NR)
Not enough this year from Kestin to allow a rating, but he's worth noting for his descriptive powers. In the opening of "The World's Greatest Middleman," 10-26, he tells us "By all odds, Shoul Eisenberg is the world's greatest middleman. Written on the far frontiers of 20th-century capitalism, his story reads like *The Merchant of Venice* grafted onto TV's *Dallas*, then transmogrified into some Far Eastern potboiler by James Clavell. Now 66 and entering the twilight of his career, Eisenberg has amassed little honor, many enemies and a fortune worth $500 million." We also enjoyed "High Marx, Low Marx," 1-26, informative on the products of Israel's kibbutzim, but we saw nothing in between.

Kilborn, Peter T. *The New York Times.* (★ ★ ½)
The most important financial reporter in the world, with an aggressive talent that keeps him close to the margin at all times. Kilborn's 1987 reports on the shifting policies of the U.S. Treasury and other world finance ministries and central banks will be important sources for future economic historians. He should and could be at (★ ★ ★ ★), but too often in '87 seemed a bull in a china shop, his impatience pushing the news instead of waiting for it to arrive.

In the year long fight at Treasury over whether to defend the dollar or let it sink, Kilborn in effect helped the latter forces with his avowed Keynesian slant instead of deepening his understanding of the global forces at work. His "Officials Say U.S. Seeks Bigger Drop For Weak Dollar," 1-14, rattled the markets and sank the dollar, but he quoted only "administration sources" who asked "that they not be identified by agency or function." Again, in the story that triggered Black Monday, "U.S. Said to Allow Decline of Dollar Against the Mark," 10-18, Kilborn did not quote Secretary Baker, presenting "insider" views that may have tipped the scales. His "Can the G-7 Learn to Waltz," 5-31, is an impressive effort on the Louvre accord on exchange rates, flawed by historical inaccuracies — "Currencies began floating again in the early 1970s when the nations rejected the belt-tightening policies required to stop inflation." His "Key Role for Gold In New Economic Order," 10-13, is well ahead of the pack in analyzing Baker's surprising IMF speech that elevates gold as part of a monetary target. Seemingly unable to thread his way out of the maze of the October Crash, he then seemed to fall apart, with "Where the Reagan Revolution Went Awry," 11-8, a surprisingly superficial and intemperate eulogy to an administration that has 14 months to go. And there he goes again with "Nations Letting Dollar Slide; U.S. Officials Welcome Fall," 10-10, with unattributed quotes that sent the dollar reeling, until the White House and President disavowed it.

Kleinfeld, N.R. *The New York Times.* (★ ½)
A snazzy writer on the business beat, he catches our attention a few times a year with clever features. We enjoyed "Across America Fish Are Jumpin'," 3-1, an especially "good read," although the material isn't all fresh. His "Pills and Peas — At the Pharmacy," 5-31, is another breezily written Sunday business feature on the economics of the local pharmacy as an angle on medical crosscurrents, doctors cutting into druggists' turf by selling pills. We suspect he can handle heavier stuff, though.

Klott, Gary. *The New York Times.* (★ ★)
After an exemplary 1986 as No. 2 man on the Washington bureau's tax beat, we thought we'd see bigger things for Klott in '87, but he didn't seem to be getting the big assignments. In "The Democrats Narrow Hunt," 3-24, he's on track with the Democrats' search for new revenues to cut the deficit, with Rostenkowski saying no new tax increases are possible without RR's support. It would have been interesting to see him turned loose on the budget/revenue debate, above the level of the trenches since nobody else was. Instead, we get "Sleep-In Yachts and Eat-In Lunches," 4-12, with the business world flowing toward new loopholes as old ones close up: "With the economy showing no major allergic reactions, Congress faces no urgent pressures to make significant changes with its monumental new system." "PTL's Ledgers: Missing Records and Rising Debt," 6-6, was a fascinating roundup on the "Praise The Lord" financial accounts. Nice work, but Klott is capable of bigger things. A "'Supply Side' Reappraisal," 11-10, is done with finesse, quoting opponents at length before his close: "...despite all the skepticism from mainstream economists, supply-side philosophy is now firmly etched into Federal tax policy. As a result of the Tax Reform Act of 1986, tax rates are at their lowest level in more than half a century, and Congress seems reluctant to raise them any time soon."

Kneale, Dennis. *The Wall Street Journal.* (★ ½)
Kneale continues to cover the business side of IBM, but loses a lot because he can't run with David Sanger of the *NYT*, who knows his business and is super on science. Kneale was thorough, though, on the Rev. Leon Sullivan's push to get U.S. companies out of South Africa, 6-4, and a front page "Leaving South Africa, IBM, Others Sell Units to Employe Trusts," 8-24. He can write on high-tech, of course, and we found the Technology column, 11-6, especially absorbing, "Computers Are Making Strides in Portraying Scientists' Ideas." But there wasn't much we had not seen in "Patent Disputes Could Affect Disk-Drive, Network Markets," 2-13, or in his "Computers" column of 6-12. He's much stronger with "IBM Tells Some Workers: Move, Retire or Quit," 4-8, with plenty of fresh information and angles on Big Blue ending

a tradition. He teamed with Michael W. Miller after the Crash with a front-pager, "Markets May Sink, But for the Yuppies It's Full Speed Ahead," 10-26, but they came up with little more than we got in the headline, except the testimonials. We thought we'd get parallel quotes from bullish investors following past panics, but there were none. Kneale seems better than his assignments.

Koepp, Stephen. *Time.* (★ ½)
A fine writer, Koepp is light on analysis and heavy on descriptions and examples. "The Insider Scandal Travels Abroad," 3-23, reported by Marlin Levin and Frank Melville, on London's scandal in Merrill Lynch wound up speculating on still wider conspiracies. "The Big Dip Is History," 8-3, with Richard Hornik and Gary Taylor, was chock full of stats, theory and numbers which actually form a cohesive whole, but does the Iran-Iraq war and corresponding tensions increase oil prices; it's not really touched on except to say Iran needs oil $s to keep financing war. The cover "For Sale: America," 9-14, with Scott Brown, Richard Hornik, and Frederick Ungeheuer, was fascinating on foreign buying, mostly a listing of bigger buyers and their purchases, but gets into pros and cons, fears, and light analysis three-fourths of the way through. His most prescient piece though, "How Ripe for a Crash?" 10-5, with Richard Hornik and Lawrence Malkin, asked, with reasoning not all that impressive, but scary in a prophesy of America "waking up to find frightening headlines in the morning paper in a year or two from now."

Koretz, Gene. *BusinessWeek.* (★ ½)
The "Economic Diary" usually mixes a few serious reports from academic economists, who are otherwise quoted no-where, along with many more light reflections from business economists who are already quoted everywhere (David Hale of Kemper appears so regularly, perhaps he should share the byline). The mix tilted toward the light side in 1987, at times reporting ill-supported opinions, such as Alan Greenspan predicting, 4-27, that the budget deficit would be vastly larger than $176 billion (it instead came in much lower). But the column nonetheless has to be mined for rare, sparkling surprises. "A major component of personal savings is employer contributions to private pension plans," Koretz discovered, 6-15, "and such contributions have slowed sharply since 1982 as soaring stock prices have boosted the value of pension fund assets." Where else would we learn that "personal" savings rise when corporations have to devote more profits to pension plans? A few Congressmen could also benefit from another study, 10-5, which revealed that "imports got a boost in recent months as overseas exporters and U.S. importers sought to build stock in anticipation of import-restricting trade legislation." Koretz obviously *reads* more than most economic journalists, which is how he finds his best material, but there is so much more to sift.

Koten, John. *The Wall Street Journal.* (★ ½)
Chicago. A careful, intelligent reporter who has handled important business stories in the Midwest with deftness and objectivity. In the *Journal*'s March series on the shattering middle class, Koten's "Upheaval in Middle-Class Market Forces Changes in Selling Strategies," 3-13, is the most informative piece on marketing dynamics we saw in all of 1987, a broad and deep report on how disdain for the average is polarizing the market. "Companies today even think twice before broadcasting that they sell the leading brand — an image many people might consider as a negative." In an earlier piece in the same series, though, "Steady Progress Disrupted by Turbulence in Economy," 3-11, Koten swallows the tempting statistics on growing wage inequality cooked up by socialist economist Barry Bluestone to support a theme that economic turbulence is contributing to the splintering of the middle class. Warren Brookes of *The Detroit News* devoted several columns thereafter decimating the Bluestone hypothesis; Koten should have been more critical, but that would have cracked the keystone of the series.

Kotlowitz, Alex. *The Wall Street Journal.* (★ ★ ★ ½)
Chicago. An enterprising reporter who seems to dog a story until it produces for him, and

for us. We didn't think we wanted to read his P.1, "Job of Shop Steward Has New Frustrations In Era of Payroll Cuts," 4-1, but he pulled us through by persuading us we would learn something about what's happening on the shop floor these days. And he can write: "'I felt betrayed,' says Mr. Moseley, pounding his kitchen table and sending a cluster of doughnuts dancing in the air." The same with "Finding Strikes Harder to Win, More Unions Turn to Slowdowns," 5-22, with a focus on the tactic at McDonnell Douglas. In "Weaker Dollar Isn't a Boon for Caterpillar," 2-20, we see he can handle business and finance, a report on the company, having sent many operations overseas during the rising-dollar days, now finding the falling dollar is a mixed blessing. In "Changes Among Families Prompt a Vanishing Sense of Community," 3-11, second of a series on "The Shattered Middle Class," his material is so well organized and presented, he pulls us through again in spite of ourselves. His crown jewel of '87, though, is "Day-to-Day Violence Takes a Terrible Toll On Inner-City Youth," 10-27, a fascinating and troubling reporter's notebook of three months in the life of Lafayette Walton, a 12-year-old black youth on Chicago's West Side, who lives with the daily sound of gunfire. "*Wednesday, June 24*: The summer sun highlights the hundreds of small shards of glass littering the asphalt. The debris is a reminder of the time two years ago when Lafayette threw a chunk of glass that accidentally put out a friend's eye. 'I got real mad at myself,' he mumbles. 'I thought of pulling my eye out.'" One of the best of the year, with the kind of Impact! that *Newsweek* tries for but does not reach.

Kriz, Margaret. *National Journal.* (★)
The congressional banking reporter produces numbing detail. *NJ* subscribers pay for this, but we hoped for clearer analysis or brighter imagery, or both. "Lobbying Hardballs at the Budget Office," 6-20, is a boring article about a boring person doing a boring job. A bit better with "Reshuffling the IOUs," 7-18, a long-winded review, with middling analysis of John Reed's Citicorp Third World debt maneuver on loan-loss reserves. It's worthwhile for the head-scratching quotes and viewpoints. Her "Band-Aid Banking Law?" 8-15, is a rigorous description of the S&L problem and critique of the banking bill "moratorium" approach to needed change.

Labich, Kenneth. *Fortune.* (★)
Labich seems to have written about many after-the-fact or widely reported-on subjects, which sometimes he barely covered, while others were adequate but without many new angles. The one-sided "Scandal of Killer Trucks," 3-30, used a somewhat sensationalist headline and rounded up the usual suspects. A graph on the number of truck accidents between 1980 and 1986 shows a startling upward leap at 1983, which the author does not see fit to explain. "How Dick Ferris Blew It," 7-6, is a highly-critical analysis of how the Allegis chairman lost his job. Is there not one person in the whole world to defend Dick Ferris? One would think not, after reading this. Also, for those versed in German, Labich is obligingly elitist in using the word *Schadenfreude* to describe a happy Wall Street reaction to Ferris' resignation. For those without German — a pity. "Why Air Traffic Is a Mess," 8-17, raises all the right questions, but doesn't offer much backup for the writer's answers, or explore interesting questions like future airport expansion. "Winners in the Air Wars," 5-11, is a gutsier, lengthier analysis of the five U.S. megacarriers, based on interviews with the heads of at least two of these airlines.

Laderman, Jeffrey. *BusinessWeek.* (★)
BW's markets and investments editor, whose understanding of the markets seems not much improved over last year. He continues to stress technicalities such as program trading as major motivators of market action and does not instill confidence with his rather superficial discussions of economic fundamentals. Program trading is the chief villain in "What's Making the Market Swing So Wildly," coauthored with John Franks, 2-9, but then in "Why the Bull Is Such a Long-Distance Runner," 8-24, he discounts those among the pros already sitting on cash and says the market is undervalued, in line with the optimistic cover story "The Good Times Roll On for Investors," 7-6. That brief overview is mainly a necklace of data and forecasts strung together without much of a design, or much backup of assertions. It nonetheless points

out some useful items, i.e., the fiscal deficit is expected to contract by about $20 billion in 1988. Similar themes continue in "The Bears May Be Taking the Wrong Trail," 10-19, published the week before the Crash, indicating that bond buyers' fears of increasing inflation and the trade deficit were exaggerated.

Landro, Laura. *The Wall Street Journal.* (★ ★)
Los Angeles. Covering movieland and its outskirts, impressing us with her restraint in laying out the personality conflicts that seem at the heart of most important stories in Hollywood. "David Puttnam Stirs Controversy as Chief of Columbia Pictures," 2-20, has a jazzy tension to it despite its understatement. The British producer of "Chariots of Fire," a "vociferous critic of Hollywood's bigspending ways," has "incensed" icons Warren Beatty and Dustin Hoffman, and they have thus refused to let him see their film "Ishtar," a $40 million Columbia film due to be released in May. Landro sets it up with: "If 'Ishtar' fails...it will provide the perfect fodder for Mr. Puttnam's criticisms of highly paid stars and big-budget films." The film bombed. Another personality feud, "The Ross-Siegel Battle Still Rocks Warner After A 3 1/2 Year Run," 7-18, pits two old friends, Steven J. Ross and Herb Siegel, as we learn about the struggles of Warner Communications Inc. "Who is this guy Herb Siegel?" asks Barbra Streisand. "Doesn't he run a boat company?" "As Cable-TV Industry Keeps Growing, Rivals Demand Reregulation," 9-17, gives a vivid impression of the conflicting interests and parties to the rivalry, but with not quite the depth or insight as in the Puttnam piece.

Lawrence, Richard. *The Journal of Commerce.* (★ ½)
Washington. Important reports on international trade issues. At his best where there is more fact than opinion, such as "Panel Vows Fast Action on Textile Quota Bill," 5-8, which noted that the bill would cost consumers $10 billion to protect an industry where output was up 10% and return on equity is high. "Pasta Wars Boil Over...Again," 7-31, updates the latest European retaliation (raising duties on U.S. walnuts and lemons) in a four-year dispute over $30 million in U.S. pasta imports. We learn that the official estimates of U.S. exports of services may be $47 billion too low, 9-2, according to the Office of Technology Assessment. "Reagan May Prefer Last Year's Trade Bill," 2-9, gave a good account of how the vetoed '86 bill gave the President more flexibility. But Lawrence seemed a voice for special interests on the editorial page with, "A Good Trade Bill After All?" 9-16, "thanks largely to the U.S. Chamber of Commerce" and "the top international officer at the National Association of Manufacturers." In "Mr. Baker Loses His Prudence," 10-28, Lawrence opines that even mentioning any role for gold in international monetary affairs "would smack of a certain abandon" and "seemed gratuitous," so he explains to the Treasury Secretary of the United States that what we really need is "a progressive new trade law" (as defined by NAM and the Chamber of Commerce?).

Lee, Susan. *Forbes.* (★ ★ ★)
Lee — senior editor and a money and investments columnist — continued to prove her potential as a leading business economic writer with more spirited, well-thought-out pieces. "Hi Ho, Silver," coauthored with Stuart Flack, 3-9, plumbs the subject of part-time, freelance, and "flexible" workers and raises it above the level of "amply covered" to a new understanding. Too bad this wasn't the cover story. In "The Protean Corporation," written with Christie Brown, 8-24, which was a cover, she offers a good, solid, classical economic overview of U.S. industry and provides lots of good statistics debunking the deindustrialization of America. The 11-30 Lee/Brown cover, "Why the Market Crash Won't Cause a Recession," starts off with the reassuring news that four of nine crashes in this century were followed by prosperity (which Jack Willoughby writes on in more detail) and ends with a warning against panicky government interference, like tax increases or overregulation of markets. In between? A critique of Keynesianism by rational-expectations theory, not — alas — filled in with Lee's theory on what "supply shocks" may have caused the '87 Crash. A couple of the prolific Lee's noteworthy columns were: "Beam Me Up, Scotty," 10-19, an excellent discussion of contrarians' interest in beaten-down utilities stocks, with a masterful capsule description of the outlook for this

industry; and "Flag-Waving Foreigners," 11-2, which tells us Lee's "heavy-duty" post-Crash phone survey turned up the news that foreign money managers are enthusiastically pumping more money into U.S. stocks — *cum* wonderful quote from one manager, that "Americans have too many mystic analysts and forecasters who are inborn pessimists. And too many economists who are pessimists 80% of the time and unclear the other 20%."

Loomis, Carol J. *Fortune.* (★)
A big prizewinning byline at the magazine for eons, but Loomis has not come through in recent years. Perhaps losing a step in the faster-paced, high-tech world, or perhaps because the competition has improved. In "The Biggest Private Fortune," 8-17, on Si & Don Newhouse and their $7.5 billion media empire, we get a two-dimensional profile with the boys not cooperating, timing "a bit off" they say. "The whole Newhouse establishment would cooperate in September, [Si] said, if the article were postponed. *Fortune* declined." *Fortune* should have accepted. She does get an interview with Carl Icahn, 5-11, and gets a dandy quote: "We had 175 people in one European city, and they said we couldn't cut. Okay, I said, we won't fly there. We stopped for two weeks. They said, 'Come over and talk.' We're down to 103 people." She has a run at the J. Walter Thompson story, which should be fun, "Et Tu, Brutus? This Time Caesar Won," 3-2. Boring. (See "Surviving a Palace Coup," 2-1, by Richard W. Stevenson, *The New York Times*, for fun.) Her "IBM's Big Blues: A Legend Tries to Remake Itself," 1-19, may have started the Big Blue badmouthing early in the year, but was very disappointing on the amount of new information here, especially given the length and quotes from top corporate people and from analysts. She doesn't talk to any customers but says IBM should have more and better salesmen. Hmmm. And no technology. Marshall?

Lowenstein, Roger. *The Wall Street Journal.* (★ ★ ½)
A talented reporter and lively writer, mostly on the commercial real estate beat, thorough in asking the right questions and covering all angles. "New Jersey Rides the Tide of an Economic Upswing," 8-6, the best we've seen on the burgeoning Garden State. In "Regional Mall Developers Try New Tactics as Market Shrinks," 9-2, we are amazed at what's coming up in entertainment malls, 9 million square feet with indoor roller coasters. His best of the year: "The Herald is Wooing Cuban Readers, But It Risks Loss of Anglos," 3-5, a P.1 leader, rich in detail, understanding of the painful tension between Anglo reporters and the community, Knight-Ridder waiting for assimilation. The Hispanic "El Herald" has two reporters, the rest of the staff translates. After the Crash, his Real Estate column asks "Will Investors Prefer Property Now That Stocks Are Down?" 10-28. He doesn't answer the question, but we get a lot of thoughtful pros and cons, the weight on the negatives, especially with the line "Historically, stock slides presage recession more than they do inflation."

Magnet, Myron. *Fortune.* (★ ★ ½)
The quality of Magnet's material advanced sharply during the year, the first signs we've seen of the big reputation he'd developed at the magazine. There hasn't been a resident philosopher at *Fortune* since Max Ways departed a dozen years ago, and Magnet has been auditioning, taking on some large, difficult topics — and producing some provocative, worthwhile evaluations. "The Money Society" cover, 7-6, though a bit whiney in spots, is a searching look at the "epidemic of money enchantment" besetting Americans of the '80s, written with an ironic, angry passion. He concludes that the money society is filling a vacuum left by the decline of traditional values, which were bled nearly to death by the negativism of the '60s. "America's Underclass: What to Do?" a 5-11 special report, is also a passionate, perhaps idealistic approach to an incessantly covered subject, offering specific directions for solutions. Magnet — bravo! — shows why the much ballyhooed, little criticized, Massachusetts workfare program is "dubious" ("all rights and no obligations") compared with the more effective California program. "Restructuring Really Works," 3-2, is an excellent case study of a number of corporate restructurings — a big step up from a 1986 Magnet article that dealt with other aspects of restructuring in a too-broad, shotgun fashion. "Think like a raider when you analyze

your company," Magnet says in distilling the principles for management restructuring of a diversified enterprise. After the Crash, his cover story lead essay, "1987 Need Not Become 1929," 11-23, was crisp and constructive, not the boilerplate we expected.

Mahar, Maggie. *Barron's.* (★ ★)
A standout financial reporter at the Dow Jones weekly, Mahar has a knack of developing topics that are potential snoozers and bringing them to life. Her cover story on the management of the huge college teachers' pension fund, TIAA-CREF, we knew was a sure bet as one of the ten best business stories of the year as soon as we read it. "Campus Rebellion: Professors Are Up in Arms About Their Retirement Fund," 8-17, was thorough, enterprising and illuminating, with an opening twist that gets the material on this "cool $63 billion" portfolio right off the ground. Most of the other Mahar work we noted during the year was less ambitious, but always competent. "No Thrills Drug Company," 1-19, was another unexciting topic, spruced up to convey thorough analytical work. "Variable Annuities; Their Sales Boom While Their Performance Lags," 2-2, is another assignment into dullsville, but her analysis seems authoritative. She offers a good perspective in "Speculative Heat," 3-2, on a new company that grows synthetic skin for burn victims.

Maidenberg, H.J. *The New York Times.* (NR)
Maidenberg was one of the first to emphasize commodity prices as an indicator of emerging inflation pressures, 5-4, and virtually the only reporter to explain how the threat of U.S. protectionism reduces foreign demand for U.S. bonds directly, as well as sinking the dollar, 4-30.

Malabre, Alfred L., Jr. *The Wall Street Journal.* (½ ★)
A veteran economics writer who contributes to the important Monday "Outlook" column, Malabre came out with one of the year's first doomsday books, *Beyond Our Means*, suggesting imminent horrors related to the federal deficit. This may have colored his judgment at times, as good news detracted from his thesis. (The best review of his book appeared in *Fortune*, 5-11, by David Henderson, an effective debunking of the Malabre's evidence.) The U.S. economy expanded at a brisk 3.7% pace in the first three quarters of the year, but Malabre refused to see it. "The rate of growth will prove disappointingly small," he wrote, 6-19, and "whatever growth occurs appears likely to be labored," 8-10. In an amazing flip-flop, Malabre even wrote that "a recession seems already to have started," 9-10, and then predicted, 9-14, "a period just ahead of appreciably brisker growth." But even faster growth doesn't cheer him up: "If the economy does in fact keep expanding through 1987," he wrote, 4-6, "inflation seems far more apt to intensify." Malabre is paranoid about debts, even when debts are matched by hard assets. "Between 1983 and 1986, consumers bought some 55 million new cars and light trucks," he complained, 3-10, "and much of this buying was through installment loans!!" And homeowners have mortgages!! With Lindley Clark, Jr., 2-2, he predicted the budget deficit in 1987 could be as high as $300 billion (it was $143 billion). Not that smaller deficits would cheer them, as "Gramm-Rudman could require spending cuts and/or tax increases that could throw the economy into recession." Malabre's other main theme was that real after-tax income per person dipped slightly for a couple of quarters, 3-30 and 9-10. But it was common knowledge that overwithholding and taxes on capital gains were temporarily lowering after-tax income (stock market gains aren't counted as income, but the tax on those gains is subtracted from income). The whole subject seems beyond the means of this chronic malcontent.

Matlack, Carol. *National Journal.* (★ ½)
A space, science reporter who doubles in covering the Washington lobbies, doing well at both. Her "Prox's Pox," 10-3, has fine detail and yet is crystal clear on Sen. Proxmire's cutting $1.2 billion on his appropriations subcommittee, wrecking NSF and NASA projects. "NASA Still Waiting For a Liftoff," 7-18, is a quick report on NASA's budgetary, morale and tech problems, clearly picturing an agency in trouble, mired in self-doubt and lethargy. We should have seen this months earlier, though. "Reviving an Industry Is No Chip Shot," 9-19, has

good pros and cons on the Gov't's financed "Sematech," the industry consortium on semiconductors, again impressing us with her clarity. "Mobilizing a Multitude," 10-17, suggests the small business lobby may have finally gotten its act together, spurred by a host of new pro-labor bills in the Democratic Congress.

McGinley, Laurie. *The Wall Street Journal.* (★)
Washington bureau, regulation. McGinley impressed us tremendously in 1985 when she seemed to be quickly mastering the politics and complexities of the Federal Reserve. Her shift to NASA and the space program in early '86 did not give her much time to learn the beat before the Challenger disaster, and she never seemed to catch up to the heaters at the *Times* and *Washington Post*. In "NASA's Recovery From the Challenger Disaster Is Slow and Painful," 1-26, she had the right theme, one that others got around to later in the year, but the material was routine, far too much on the micro impact, motel rooms going for $5 a day at Cocoa Beach, etc. Her efforts on airline regulation were far superior later in the year. "Federal Regulation Rises Anew in Matters That Worry the Public," 4-21, a P.1 leader, was the first of a series on "Regulatory Revival," this one quoting AEI's William Schneider, "The anti-government revolt of the 1970s is over." It was timely, cogent, with straws in the wind on possible re-regulation. "FAA Seeks More Airports to Lessen Congestion," 8-26, was a more comprehensive picture of the crowded airports and skies than we'd seen before.

Melloan, George. *The Wall Street Journal.* (★ ½)
His Tuesday "Business World" column is new in '87, but the deputy editorial page editor has been with the *WSJ* for 35 years. A fine reporter who has seen it all, Melloan's columns are the first he's done, and like Rosenthal of the *NYT*, he's experimenting with his voice. Most of his output in '87 was more in the nature of news features, as if he's still uncomfortable expressing his opinion under his byline. "Battle of the Auto Giants: People vs. Machines," 2-24, has lots of data on GM and Ford, but there's no focal point, and he meanders into the protectionist issue. "Californians and PURPA Power," 3-31, is all about public utilities being forced to buy expensive power alternatives, adding hugely to consumer costs. "Robots Talk Back to Product Designers," 5-26, chats with a robot consultant, an okay feature with a nice line, "The Japanese make a product flow like water." But he's too modest, frying such little fish. He should paint on a much bigger canvas, we realized in reading his column of 10-20, written with a hot word processor in the few hours after the market crash of the day before, "A Dollar Poker Game Aided the Market Plunge." It was the best commentary that we saw anywhere, print or electronic media, on that day, with an opening line that rumbled with chained passion: "As should be abundantly evident by now, Treasury Secretary James Baker's efforts to talk the stock and bond markets out of their melancholy last Thursday were less than a howling success." Melloan should be talking to bigwigs about the business world, not public utility infielders or robot consultants, and asserting himself. He's earned that much.

Miller, Annetta. *Newsweek.* (★)
Concentrating on marketing and advertising, Miller does mostly light, frothy pieces, but then again, sometimes that's what advertising is all about. "A Sizzling Food Fight," 4-20, asked To Beef, or Not to Beef? The ad campaign, nicely done, dealing with both the Beef for Real People ads and rebuttals, including an embarrassing "publicist's" gaffe, saying beef spokesperson Cybil Shepherd lists "cutting out fatty foods" and "staying away from red meat" as part of her beauty regimen. "Television: And Now The Naked Truth," 5-11, was a cutesy spoof leader on steamy Madison Avenue ads with a terrific quote from *Adweek* senior editor Barbara Uppert, about how scantily-clad females in commercials set off "the Emergency Feminist Broadcast System." "You Must Know Me," 8-17, on the American Express card ad campaign using famous faces caught us with the opening, "Tip O'Neill wiggling his tootsies in the sand," and follows through nicely with facts on the credit card war. But "Putting Faith In Trends," 6-15, on trend analysis consultant Faith Popcorn loses steam halfway through, beginning to sound like snake-oil with style.

Miller, Michael. *The Wall Street Journal.* (★ ★)
New York. A facile writer and reporter who seems able to keep up with the financial and technology aspects of modern Wall Street, LBO's, program trading, SuperDots and all that. We were very impressed with his report on "Insider Trading: The Scandal Spreads," 2-17, a very careful, balanced account of the impact on Wall Street of the arrest of Robert M. Freeman of Goldman, Sachs & Co., quoting one veteran trader: "A lot of these other guys are relative nobodies. Freeman is clearly a relative somebody." With fine detail here, a good picture of Freeman emerges. Miller is the lead writer, with Laurie P. Cohen, in "Corporate Raiders Predict Hard Times for Hostile Bids," 4-23, a well-presented roundup of the Curse of the Takeover Class and its reaction to the Supreme Court's decision upholding Indiana's anti-takeover law, plenty of good quotes from all sides. His "Seldom Seen Now, Boesky Nevertheless Leaves a Few Tracks," 6-19, is rather disappointing, with Miller coming up practically empty on Ivan's whereabouts and doings. (We had to wait until Steve Coll and David Vise of *The Washington Post* found Boesky studying Hebrew, 11-8.) Excellent, though, with "The Crash of '87: Were Computers a Help or a Hindrance?" 12-11, with a quote from a computer consultant that crystallizes it all: The securities industry "is the only one where the goods have no physical reality — they're nothing but an electronic message. So you can move the entire industry at the stroke of a key." In "High-Tech Alteration Of Sights and Sounds Divides the Art World," 9-1, Miller is away from the Street with this piece loaded with interesting examples of artistic infringement: "New technology is making the '80s a strange and lawless time to be a creative artist...questions that strain the modern boundaries of law, morality and aesthetics."

Mitchell, Constance. *The Wall Street Journal.* (★ ½)
An able and accurate business writer who can handle a broad range of topics with clarity, which gets her on the front page more than most. Her best of '87 was "A Growing Shortage Of Skilled Craftsmen," 9-14, quite timely as industry complaints swelled on this issue. This could have been a great piece if she'd been willing to bring in the high unemployment rate among urban blacks and relate it to her central theme. In "Prices of Small Items, Services Rise Rapidly, Hint of New Inflation," 4-24, she offers a P.1 leader on rapidly rising prices of "commonly used goods and services that shape consumer perceptions about inflation — things such as toothpaste, coffee, haircuts and taxi rides." But she loses us with some dubious economics, "The price surge in small items bodes ill for the overall outlook," she says, quoting Economist Lacy Hunt that "prices of small ticket items tend to lead inflation and tend to accelerate rather rapidly once you get into an inflationary mode." Which is an assertion to us, not persuasive. Again on the front page, "As Business Brokers Proliferate, So Do Clients' Complaints," 3-24, was informative, but we thought rather dull stuff for column 6 leader. Also well done and lucid, but overplayed, "Avoiding Tax on Social Security Is Harder For Some Under New Tax Law," 1-8. But we can't blame Mitchell for hitting P.1.

Moffett, Matt. *The Wall Street Journal.* (★ ½)
Houston. A capable reporter who can present facts as well as dig them up, Moffett worked the dismal oil patch and its troubled bankers, occasionally traipsing into Mexico. In "First City Bancorp. Limps On in Texas," 5-26, he draws stark lines, quoting Coastal Corp.'s chairman, "If the truth be known, there's not a solvent bank out there." And, "Once an unspeakable possibility, it's now conventional wisdom that an acquirer of First City probably would require the inducement of federal assistance." A front-pager on the maneuverings of Jack Stanley and his "bankrupt" Trans-American Natural Gas Corp., "Endurance Test," 7-30, with Charles F. McCoy, is thoroughly fascinating, Stanley not only keeping the company going while in Chapter 11 for nine years out of 12, but by wearing out creditors he has thrived, making it second only to Exxon Corp. among Texas natural-gas producers. His report on "Pennzoil Co. Balks At Giving Up Any Of Texaco Award," 3-20, has a smarty quote: "'I'm not in the habit of giving away $2 billion,' said Joe Jamail, Pennzoil's chief counsel; $2 billion here, $2 billion there — after a while it begins to add up." A P.1 A-hed, "Out of Mexico Flow People and Narcotics, Out of America VCRs," 7-23, highlights the smuggling trade into

Mexico, where tariffs and taxes add 50% to the cost of imported consumer electronics. His most impressive effort, "Labor Discontent Rocks Mexican Politics," 11-5, gets deeply into the strains emerging between the government and organized labor, contrasting the new young President-designate, Carlos Salinas de Gortari, 39, who designed the austerity program for Mexico, and Fidel Valesquez, the octogenarian leader of the labor unions. A promising reporter.

Morgenson, Gretchen. *Forbes.* (★ ½)
Another of the magazine's adroit corporate analysts, especially attuned to probing for weakness. Her most noticeable score of the year, "Fabulous Fads That Fizzled," 2-23, rummaged through bubbles of yore and then zeroed in on Home Shopping Network, puncturing it with the startling revelation that at $30 a share, its market capitalization of about $3.2 billion was about equal to that of CBS. A terrific short sale at that point, with HSN getting deep, deep down in the bargain basement, halfway off even before the Crash. In "Old Game, New Twist," 1-12, she funs *Fortune* for having Harry S. Patten, chairman of Patten Corp., listed as one of the most fascinating business people of '86, saying the only thing fascinating about the company is its accounting methods. Her "Municipal Garbage," 3-9, is great muckraking of an awful muni fund. "You thought munis were safe? Then you haven't bought any unit trusts from Miller & Schroeder of Minneapolis." Tough stuff. Her "Checklist For Stock Market Prognosticators," 4-4, came in handy around October 16: "What does a market top look like?..Many comparisons to 1929, 1972...position oneself against a major correction — build cash..."

Morris, Betsy. *The Wall Street Journal.* (★)
Atlanta. Sometimes lightweight reporting that, nevertheless, has a nice flavor to it. "As a Favored Pastime, Shopping Ranks High With Most Americans," 7-30, a P.1 leader, gave us all the latest poop on the national shopping epidemic, "orgy," presumably written for the many vendors who read the *WSJ*, but it should have been pitched that way as serious marketing analysis instead of as a frothy feature. "Coke's Strategy Is to Divide and Conquer," 10-8, the "49% Solution" a "hot new restructuring tool" that could reshape "the soft-drink giant into what may be the prototype post-1980s conglomerate — a company that goes back to basics but retains big stakes in diversified businesses while assuming little risk." So why only P.6? Her front-page, two-parter on the lack of community in the suburbs while the town governments deal with city problems was enough to make us want to go back to the city, but some of our readers loved every word of it. ("America's New Cities: Shallow Roots — New Suburbs Tackle City Ills While Lacking a Sense of Community," 3-26; "Young and Old Alike Can Lead Lonely Lives in New U.S. Suburbs," 3-27).

Mossberg, Walter S. *The Wall Street Journal.* (★)
A Washington bureau diplomatic correspondent shifted to Treasury early in the year, a very bright and talented writer who will need at least another year to learn the beat. We gave him high marks for his report on the Tower Commission, "White House, In Its Iran Affair Moves, Ignored the Intelligence Apparatus It Claimed It Rebuilt," 2-26, "a clear, useful summary of Iran-Contra events on the public record, with the biggest question on CIA's Casey," said one reader. But "Reagan Administration Hopes Summit Will Aid 3rd World Debt Strategy," 6-2, seemed "a rather confused report," said another reader. "Reagan Goes to Venice Hurt By U.S. Position as Top World Debtor," 6-4, a P.1 leader, is useful only in that it provides the views of several Keynesian economists who had high posts in the Carter Administration. Says Mossberg: "The U.S., aided by the weaker dollar, (must cut) its trade deficit by reducing imports and raising exports," a view the *Journal* disagrees with editorially. Mossberg teamed with Alan Murray on several major stories after the Crash, the citations of which can be found in Murray's entry.

Murray, Alan. *The Wall Street Journal.* (★ ½)
A Washington bureau utility reporter on the economics beat in 1986, Murray became a senior writer on the beat with the 1987 departures of Art Pine and Paul Blustein. He had his moments,

but there was more spinning of wheels and grinding of gears as he tried to keep up with the *NYT*. After the Crash, his major efforts were in tandem with Walter S. Mossberg, the new man on the Treasury beat, the two leaning on each other. "Stock-Price Collapse Is Confronting Fed With Policy Dilemma," 10-29, a P.1 leader, sees runaway inflation if Fed does this, deep recession if Fed does that, but what if Fed does nothing? They get an exclusive interview with Secretary Baker, "Treasury View," 11-5, with Baker *seeming* to tell them he doesn't care if the dollar falls as long as the Fed doesn't have to raise interest rates, a position reported earlier in the week by the *NYT*. But without direct quotes, we weren't sure what Baker's precise views were on the matter. In "Monetary Policy Holding Steady, Fed Aides Say," 11-11, we are told the Fed is doing nothing, thereby avoiding the dilemma posed 10-29. Murray's best pieces appeared early in '87, under less pressure. "Is Fed's Money Policy Pointing to a Return of 70's-Type Inflation?" 2-19, is a fair, balanced, even sophisticated leader on the day of Volcker's Senate testimony on the money-supply targets. "Lobbyists for Business Are Deeply Divided, Reducing Their Clout," 3-25, is shrewd, incisive analysis with a focus on the shake-up at the Business Roundtable. But he's silly with a P.1 Outlook column, "Recession May Be Trade Gap's Only Cure," 9-21, unleashing a Keynesian beaut of single-entry bookkeeping. In "Supply-Siders Suffer Decline in Demand For Their Policy Ideas," 10-18, he fails to ask if they have any policy ideas to cure the trade gap that does not require a recession. He'll do better in '88.

Nasar, Sylvia. *Fortune.* (★)
The editors continue to assign Nasar, a young economist, stories having to do with macroeconomics, which means the magazine tilts in the direction of her narrow model. At best she muddles through monetary/fiscal topics. When she is credible, it is usually on "other," more nitty-gritty subjects that have little to do with grand policy design. "Why Greenspan Is Bullish," the 10-26 cover dated after the 10-19 Crash is a fluffy piece that perhaps could have made *People* magazine, featuring such gems as "Fed Chairman Arthur Burns...told Alan that inflation was a threat to capitalism, and it was his patriotic duty to fight it" (when Greenspan was chairman of the Council of Economic Advisors). "Competitiveness: Getting It Back," 4-30, misses the mark, given that U.S. industry — despite common perceptions — is alive and getting better. The 9-14 cover, "Do We Live as Well as We Used To?" is a decent, well-researched piece that answers with a definite "yes." The graphs are splendid with their snapshot comparisons of 1956 and 1986 measures, and Nasar also reminds us of a change in expectations in quoting a retired Californian: "Kids nowadays want more than we did when we were their age...They're impatient. TV was out four or five years before we bought it."

Nash, Nathaniel C. *The New York Times.* (★ ★ ½)
The Washington bureau regulatory reporter has another fine year, even his routine filings seeming crisper than we need expect. He especially excelled in covering the contentious banking deregulation legislation. "Treasury Now Favors Creation of Huge Banks," 6-7, was a front-pager that made waves and had Treasury pleading innocence and the primary reason behind the Greenspan appointment emerged, a rationale for an end to bank regulation. Nash was ahead of the field on "How the White House Lost Its Big Bank Battle," 7-12, super reporting on Volcker's revenge. "Final Battles Shape Up On Major Banking Bill," 7-27, has RR thinking veto while Volcker says override, sharp political analysis here. A column, "Horse Trading For Bankers," 11-12, is an excellent, cogent summary of Treasury's failed divide-and-conquer strategy in winning for the nation's 14,000 commercial banks, permission to enter three previously forbidden industries — securities underwriting, insurance and real estate.

Norman, James R. *BusinessWeek.* (★ ★ ★)
New York. A business writer who can deliver important stories on finance, corporate strategies or personalities with intelligence, accuracy and clarity. In Houston for part of the year before moving to headquarters as a senior writer, Norman was thorough in exploring the horizon for pros and cons in "Bankruptcy Court For Texaco: The Lesser Evil — Barely," 4-27, the best reconnaissance we saw from this angle. An earlier piece on "Mastering the New Potential

of Limited Partnerships," 12-29-86, also provided lucid state-of-the-art analysis. Norman tried valiantly with "Donald Trump: What's Behind the Hype?" 7-20, with Marc Frons, a crisp wrap-up of Trump's maneuvers, his destructive feud with Mayor Ed Koch, moves into greenmailing and Atlantic City and potential over-extension, suggesting egotism could cost him dearly. In the end, we finished thinking of the Wizard of Oz behind the hype and wondered who *is* Trump? A less ambitious "Bob Wright's Surprising Script for NBC: Grow, Grow, Grow," 3-9, was more successful in pitting CEO Wright against NBC's bosses at General Electric Co., who would milk the cash cow unless he milks it himself. Norman is at his best in "Diary of a Decision: A Week in the Life of Amex," 11-9, following around CEO Allan Born as he decides to buy back Amex stock as it plunges in the Crash. A good idea, well executed. A feature on "Yale B-School Struggles to Make the Grade," 11-23, was interesting enough, but the assignment seemed beneath Norman's prowess.

Norton, Robert E. *Fortune.* (★ ★ ½)
This is a reporter who can make a bank story an adventure. He knows the banking industry and goes for the guts of a situation, talking with a broad array of people to bring varied perspectives into the write-up. He is also adept at pithy, pictorial phrases that can quickly communicate ideas. In "Citibank Wows the Consumers," 6-8, Norton does an impressive job presenting Citicorp's impressive consumer banking division, as it dares to make mistakes to be number one. Others have written on the subject, but this is the best we've seen. In another good story, "Upheaval Ahead on Wall Street," 9-14, he writes a prescient pre-Crash primer, with good data and analysis, on how times will be tough for Wall Street's high rollers and fat-cat young Turks if the market heads south. "Deep in the Hole in Texas," 5-11, is an illuminating look at the Texas savings and loan debacle and House Speaker Jim Wright's role on the speculators' side. In "A Muddled Future for Mellon Bank," 3-30, Norton turns a pitiless gaze on recent performance problems at the Pittsburgh bank, whose condition has altered from secure status as "a Mercedes-Benz among financial institutions" to "strategic schizophrenia." Too bad Mellon's senior executives wouldn't talk to Norton to allow the article that "horse's mouth" balance provided by a key source.

Nulty, Peter. *Fortune.* (★ ½)
"Small Payoffs From Big Deals," 12-7, an unflattering profile of Allied-Signal Chairman Ed Hennessy, who sells off "money losers" and "dogs" that soon flourish in other hands and buys winners that don't pan out. After the Crash, Hennessy went on a buying spree of Allied stock, "mopping up 13 million shares. That may have kept the price from sagging lower, and it may reduce the Street's fear that Hennessy will use Allied's cash to make a big new acquisition." Still, there's balance, letting Hennessy have his say on Allied's expensive R&D program that could, after all, pay off. His quick profile of Mad Ave's Jerry Della Femina, "An Aging Boy Wonder Shakes Up the Ad Business," 4-13, is a disappointment, a two dimensional focus on bathroom humor and the "f---" word, instead of reaching for whatever new insight the boy wonder has up his sleeve. Another snapshot, of Union Pacific's Drew Lewis, 1-5, is also flat, and we wonder if Nulty shouldn't stick to straight business. A piece on the economics of natural gas was a bit disjointed, "Guess Which Fuel Is Looking Hot," 6-8, but it seemed smart and timely nevertheless, especially interesting on NG-powered autos.

O'Reilly, Brian. *Fortune.* (★ ★)
People-profiler O'Reilly does well with some edgy, below-the-surface portraits of executives who aren't household names. "How Jimmy Treybig Turned Tough," 5-25, is a thrilling corporate novella of a boss' transformation from cheerleader to demanding manager at Tandem Computers — clearly showing cause and effect, but somewhat lacking in psychological handles on how this man changed his personality/behavior nearly overnight. "How Tom Mitchell Lays Out the Competition," 3-30, is a hair-raising story about the gung-ho president of Seagate Technology, whose ex-wife told a divorce judge, "Tom is 99% work, 1% jogging." "A

Billionaire for the Common Man,'' 1-5, is a superficial, only slightly flattened puff piece on the legendary H. Ross Perot; just not in the class of O'Reilly's other pieces.

Pauly, David. *Newsweek.* (★)
Pauly is a thorough writer who is good at pulling together material from a variety of sources, but usually seems to lack a point of view that would be useful in carrying us through. He caught our eye early in the year with "New Arrests on Wall Street," with Bill Powell, Carolyn Friday and Rich Thomas, 2-23, a good look at what happened on the Street, and what may come of all of it. He gave us an update in "Wall Street's Prime-Time Crime Drama," 4-6, with nice detail on Charles Atkins' tax-avoidance schemes and a good hook: "Welcome to 'Wall Street's Indictment of the Week.' Here's your host...Rudolph Giuliani.'' But we got old news in "A Scourge of Video Pirates," with Carolyn Friday and Jennifer Foote, 7-27, telling us about the bootlegging bad boys of the video world, and in "Travel Scams: A Costly Trip," with Erik Calonius, 4-27, Pauly gave us examples and stories of travel ripoffs through the mail and on the phone and how "You win!" turns into "Gotcha!" but not much otherwise.

Pennar, Karen. *BusinessWeek.* (½ ★)
A dismal year for Pennar, of the *BW* economics staff, supplying a mixed bag of reportage and interpretation. "Why Manufacturing Will Revive," 1-12, a cover story, makes some good points but is mostly nonpremium vanilla ice cream — wordy, cautious, consensus-based analysis. "The Fed Sees Trouble if the Deficits Diverge," 3-30, is worse than superficial. No Fed officials are quoted, even anonymously. The best of the article was its fretting that the trade deficit will fall faster than the budget deficit. At least one nugget in "Jitter! Unsettling Economic Signs Hang Americans on Edge," 5-11: "Yet a determined Fed nudging rates higher now may be exactly what's needed to stabilize the dollar and bring an end to the jitters." Otherwise, not much new. Pennar was lead writer in two stories that were part of post-Crash covers. Both were subpar efforts. The 11-2 "That Rumble You Hear Is Called 'Recession'" (with other writers) was full of platitudes, at best, and, at worst, its pessimistic assertions were supported by air. Sample: "The odds that a recession will occur in 1988 have risen dramatically thanks to the market crash," period (unless budget and trade imbalances are righted, she added). At least she points out that inflationary expectations in the bond market declined with the Crash and that rising interest rates in spring '87 were a factor in the Crash. The second cover effort, 11-16, "The New Economy: Say Hello to the Lean Years," was awful, unbelievably awful, so awful that it would be camp if you didn't think somebody (*BW* editors if not Pennar) really meant it. As the subhead summed it up for post-Crash America, "Sacrifice, hard work, and frugality will be the new ethic as living standards decline." R.I.P.

Petre, Peter. *Fortune.* (★ ★ ½)
Petre produced one of the 10-best business pieces of 1986, a profile of Digital Equipment's Ken Olsen, 10-27-86, and of Jack Welch of GE, 7-7-86. But there were no comparable captain-of-industry portraits in '87, a big disappointment. Although he is back with "The Man Who Brought GE to Life," 1-5, another shot at Welch for *Fortune's* "50 Most Fascinating Business People" issue, and he may be getting tired of painting the same face. Petre has a talent for getting us deep into company strategies and we see it in "AT&T's Epic Push in Computers," 5-25, a review of the shifting strategies in the short, sordid history of AT&T's venture into computers — which may, or may not, turn around under the aegis of its third computer chief in four years. "GE's Gamble on American-Made TVs," 7-6, offers a strong lead, good focus, good information on GE's great adventure; although a bit skimpy in explaining why the Japanese can't play the same game. "A Liberal Gets Rich Yet Keeps the Faith," 8-31, is an incredible puff piece on Ira Magaziner, 39, a liberal activist turned consultant, whom Petre apparently met while doing the GE article, as Magaziner did consulting work for GE on its TV project and others.

Petzinger, Thomas Jr. *The Wall Street Journal.* **(NR)**
One of the most talked-about *WSJ* stories of the year was Petzinger's front-pager, "Quality of Justice: Texaco Case Spotlights Questions of Integrity Of the Courts in Texas," 11-4, with Caleb Solomon. The team divulged that in Texas, one of nine states where Supreme Court justices are still elected through partisan campaigning, "Lawyers representing Pennzoil contributed, from 1984 to early this year, more than $355,000 to the nine Supreme Court justices sitting today, according to a tally by this newspaper. One of those lawyers for Pennzoil had contributed $10,000 to the lower-court judge who later presided at the start of the state-court trial in Houston...the shadow that big-money politics has cast over the entire state judiciary in Texas has, in the minds of many, tainted Pennzoil's unbroken string of victories in the Texas state courts." Pennzoil lashed back with newspaper ads in 35 cities, complaining the *Journal* rejected an ad it wanted to place disputing the story. The *Journal* came back with an editorial, "Texas Trials and Tribulations," 11-27, asserting its position and raking over the story again. It was indeed a sensational and troubling report that must lead to reforms in Texas if major corporations are going to feel comfortable doing business in the state. But we were astonished that no other newspaper had this story a year earlier. The Texas press, as a unit, should stand in the corner under a tall pointy hat.

Platt, Gordon. *The Journal of Commerce.* **(★)**
Financial editor. Platt mostly reports routinely on what the markets did yesterday, but sometimes gives credibility to silly ideas: The "debt explosion" supposedly created liquidity, according to one source, and "because this liquidity is not needed in an economy which is growing only slowly and fitfully, it finds a home" in stocks, 4-8. Investors supposedly have a lot of cash, because they borrowed it, and can't find anything to do with all that money (and debt) except to buy stocks which implies that if the economy were booming the stock market would go *down*? He can also be better than average, as in "Citicorp Plans To Swap, Sell Its LDC Debt," 5-21, which explained the issue well.

Plender, John. *Financial Times.* **(★ ★ ½)**
Provocative financial commentary, nearly always with an unpredictable twist, which is neither left or right. "Who's Afraid of Re-Entering Bretton Woods," 7-13, noted that "a ferocious lobbying campaign by the American Coalition for flexible exchange rates," is backed by institutions that derive "substantial profits" from exchange rates gyrations. "One thing we do know for certain," wrote Plender, "is that the most rapid period of economic growth the world has ever known...took place within the framework of fixed exchange rates." He shows remarkable understanding of the problems for Japan in finding creditworthy uses of capital outflows in "And Now for the Credit Crisis," 4-14, such as "the inability of the world's capital markets to import enough Japanese capital," and "whether the rest of the world is prepared to pay Japanese pensions in the 21st century." How's this for illumination?: "Japan is now the world's biggest creditor with external assets of more than $200 billion. Over three quarters of the outflow has, however, been going to the U.S., which is now — albeit slowly — cutting back its twin deficits and inflicting losses on foreign investors by devaluing the dollar. [!!] The rest of the world, meantime suffers from a shortage of creditworthy borrowers and risktakers."

Pollack, Andrew. *The New York Times.* **(★ ★ ★)**
San Francisco. Almost David Sanger's equal as a technology reporter, not letting too much slip past him in Silicon Valley. "Gene Splicing Payoff Is Near," 6-10, offers a comprehensive survey of the bioengineering field, but we didn't get an appraisal of the FDA's obstruction of Genentech's TPA (tissue plasminogen activator) which dissolves blood clots in heart attack victims. He shows his competence in the semiconductor domain on a collaboration between TI and Intel on custom circuits, 7-8, clear and intelligible in explaining the technologies. On 7-15, he provides the first clear explanation we've seen in the press on the different categories of semiconductor memory: chiefly differentiating static from dynamic random access devices.

A wonderful piece that should have been displayed better was "Chips That Emulate Functions of Brain," 8-26, with Pollack discovering Carver Mead of Caltech, one of the most creative figures in U.S. electronics since WWII. Now the awesome task: developing "machine vision" with computers, a new wave of specialized chips that mimic the brain. In "Putting 250,000 Pages On a CD," 3-4, Pollack is conscientious in covering Microsoft's CD-ROM technology, but relegates to the last paragraph the big story of the conference, a revolutionary RCA chip that represents a 100-fold advance in the efficiency of encoding video images, which could obsolesce the VCR, once improved recording and erasing techniques are perfected. "Can Steve Jobs Do It Again?" 11-8, the lead Sunday business item on Jobs' Next Inc. Pollack is carefully skeptical about this idea of sophisticated computer simulations that "will allow students to walk through Athens with Plato," especially after Jobs starts the project by spending $100,000 to design the company logo.

Powell, Bill. *Newsweek.* (★ ★ ½)
One of the few *Newsweek*ers whose talent shines through the fast-food gloss, consistently producing concise and clear articles, he shone in '87 with good personality profiles. His "Citizen Trump" cover, with Peter McKillop, 9-28, on Manhattan's Mr. T. could have been one of the ten-best business pieces if it had just a little bit more substance and a little less lifestyle of the rich and famous, but *Newsweek* is *Newsweek*. He scored also with "Cable's Biggest Leaguer," with Elisa Williams, 6-1, on John Malone of TCI Cable in Colorado, the "Darth Vader" of the industry. His "Tips for the Hands-on CEO," also with Williams, 3-16, was inspired by RR's management non-style and the release of *The Tower Commission Report*: "Look at it this way: It's one less management book you'll have to read. There will be no 'Ronald Reagan's Guide to Executive Leadership' after the President leaves office." The same jaunty tone appears in "Coping With The Markets," 4-27, on the confusion in the economic community caused by the falling dollar: "If you are wise enough to know when a market is *pretending* to panic — as opposed to panicking for real — feel reassured. If you're not, pass the Valium." But his best quote of the year came from "TV: The Vanishing Viewer," 5-18: "OINK" or "one income, no kids," a new demographic term that, thankfully, came and went quickly.

Prowse, Michael. *Financial Times.* (★ ★ ½)
Like John Plender, Prowse develops fascinating angles on global financial issues by throwing away the book and mulling things over with a fresh start. It helps that London has been contemplating global capital flows for centuries, which is why U.S. commentators sometimes seem like they are in knickers by comparison. In "Looking on the Bright Side of Debt," 3-21, he presents a case for optimism in the LDCs — "and it is only optimism for the longer term — that the cold shower of the debt crisis has prompted what amounts to a revolutionary change in attitudes towards development in both the rich North and the poor South...Ideological baggage carried proudly since the early 1950s is being unceremoniously junked. World Bank officials declare themselves amazed at the speed with which market-oriented policies have been embraced in parts of Africa and South America. The shock of the debt crisis is accomplishing an intellectual revolution that might otherwise have taken decades." In "Third Term Tax Priorities," 7-3, Prowse contemplates Margaret Thatcher's proposed poll tax, and suggests that while "President Reagan's income tax cuts may send cold shivers down the spines of socialists, but as an attack on egalitarianism, they are feeble stuff...the US income tax code will retain some progressivity...The Thatcher poll tax, by comparison, is as unfair as any of the bitterly opposed levies of feudal times...The Tories are planning to cap this idiocy with a tax that bears equally on the Duke of Westminster and a streetcleaner in a bedsit."

Quinn, Jane Bryant. *Newsweek.* (★ ½)
A good effort this year with her personal investment column. Quinn seemed to be more on top of things. "Winning the ARM's Race," 1-19, was a nice explanation of adjustable-rate mortgages vs. fixed rate ones. "Stocks: The Inside Story," 3-16, gave some interesting tidbits

on insider buying and selling, but only that. The dying of FSLIC was detailed in "How Safe Is Your Money?" 4-13, with good reporting, advice and suggestions on how to tell if your S&L is sound, and what is happening to crush the FSLIC and banks in trouble. "No Place To Hide," 5-11, was a sound debunking of mutual funds. Her best for the year was "AIDS: Testing Insurance," 6-8, the bottom line being who will pay for AIDS? Is antibody-testing by insurance companies legitimate? If so, then is automatic rejection of HIV patients? She does not argue for or against anything, but simply presents, and is brave in asking such questions.

Quint Michael. *The New York Times.* (★ ½)
New York. "Credit Markets" column. We had given the edge in recent years to Quint over his rival bond columnists in the *WSJ*, for being more original. Still solidly professional, Quint was less inventive this year. His colleagues got the jump on him at important times during the year. H.J. Maidenberg caught the real scoop, 4-30, "Trade Vote Deals Blow to Bonds," while Quint turned in a lesser piece on municipal bonds. Maidenberg did it again with "Commodity Price Rise Suggests New Inflation," 5-4, while Quint simultaneously thought "the rise in interest rates is based more on paranoia." Quint rarely mentioned commodity prices as an influence on inflation or interest rates, despite the fact that several Federal Reserve Governors did. At the peak of the stock market, 8-26, Quint properly noticed that a stronger "Dollar Pushes Bonds Higher." That was only half the story. It was Kenneth Gilpin, the same day, who explained that the dollar was "buoyed by supportive comments from Japanese, West German and United States officials." Bond prices later rose as stock prices crashed, 10-20, and Quint did make that connection as well as anyone. He noted "the steep drop in rates for Treasury bills — a traditional safe haven for investors in times of uncertainty," and figured that this scramble for liquidity and "prospects for a weaker economy" reduced expected inflation. Too many Quint columns were inconclusive, such as "One group of analysts sees continued healthy economic growth with rising inflation pressures and rising interest rates. Another sees slower growth, little increase in inflation...and falling interest rates," 8-6. The reader at least gets two conclusions, but needs some help from Quint with facts and analysis.

Rachid, Rosalind. *The Journal of Commerce.* (★ ½)
New York. Based here, but she covers a wide variety of world issues. Unlike many journalists, Rachid uses statistics to great advantage, showing "South America: Economy At A Glance," 6-12, and noting, 5-26, that, "Since it joined the [European] community in January 1986, Portugal's exports to fellow EC members have climbed 16.6%, inflation has fallen to 11.9% from 19.3% in 1984, real wages have improved by 4%." An otherwise neglected aspect of the weakness of U.S. investment in the Philippines was attributed to the absence of an investment treaty with the United States, 7-8. Rachid also wrote stories about import industries that even gave the reader a taste for smoked fish, 6-22. One of the best: "Free Traders Claim A Victory," 5-1, describes specific complaints about the trade bill, and identifies some powerful lobbyists *against* protectionism: Caterpillar, Cargill, Boeing, Bank of America, J.C. Penney, IBM, NCR, K-Mart and Lockheed.

Ramirez, Anthony. *Fortune.* (★)
An up-and-comer who has been getting more space for competent reporting and writing, with another few years of seasoning all that may be needed to produce deeper material. *Fortune* was the last of the relevant magazines to get around to the "Superconductors Get Into Business" story, 6-22, but Ramirez was first in getting the story essentially right, with appropriate focus on IBM's dual successes with high currents and with thin films. A profile of "Revlon's Striking Makeover Man," Ron Perelman, 1-5, is not bad, at least a good surface look: "[He] has a penchant for contrasts: a tangy personal life and the practice of Judaism, fancy restaurants and junk food, earsplitting rock music aboard his corporate jet and long, pensive walks around Manhattan." A flattering profile of Donald Kingsborough of Worlds of Wonder, "Top Gun in the Toy Business," 3-2, catches him at the top, with no clue that WOW was even then hitting

the slippery slope. Instead, a glittery *non sequitur,* "Kingsborough's Midas touch with toys is ironic: He had few as a child."

Rasky, Susan F. *The New York Times.* (★ ½)
Greatly improved in '87 by generally steering clear of economic theorizing, leaving that bog to Leonard Silk and others, sticking to her trade beat. Very early in '87, for example, in "What's New in Economic Circles," 1-18, there is nothing new. But "U.S. Seen Easing Stance on Toshiba," 7-20, one of several on the Toshiba affair, is a good running account by Rasky. "Import Reliant Port Wary of Trade Bill," 7-21, shows the other side of the Gephardt sword by talking to Baltimore port officials: "This bill is not going to generate one pound of exports," says one. In "Trade Debate Takes a Role in Campaign," 7-27, she gives a brief picture of each Democratic candidate's stand on the issue and we see Rep. Gephardt's is hardly the most extreme of those considered protectionist. "Battle Over Plant Closings," 8-27, tests labor's power in the Democratic Senate and observes some businessmen defecting from protectionist ranks over the issue. "Groping For a New Order on Trade," 8-30, is a useful summary on the pros and cons of GATT's effectiveness. "Top U.S. Corporations Lobbying Against Curb," 9-14, is an arresting P.1 piece from Washington, Rasky seeing the U.S. and Japanese economies, particularly in electronics, now so intertwined that U.S. punitive trade action is inevitably self-destructive. Which is why IBM, Apple, Motorola, GE, etc., are lobbying against the proposed import ban against Toshiba products. Illuminating.

Rauch, Jonathan. *National Journal.* (★ ½)
A talented up-and-comer with his first year on the economic beat, with hits and misses. "Plant Closing Law's Political Dynamics," 8-15, is handled easily, the best detail and explanation on this provision of the trade bill. "Where's That Dragon," 7-11, presents a comprehensive overview of the state of the supply-side movement, here and there and all over the place, but good on direction, new faces. "Riding the Low Dollar," 8-15, strings together a lot of quotes from this expert and that, but not very useful and we suspect Rauch is a bit over his head on international money. "Election-Day Economy," 10-24, goes in circles trying to tell us something interesting about the stock market crash, the state of the economy in '88, and which party will be favored based on past statistical correlations, with no mention of candidates or issues, like trying to predict the winner of the Kentucky Derby by describing the condition of Churchill Downs. "Comeuppance," 10-31, fails as rambling observations on the Wall Street crash.

Redburn, Tom. *Los Angeles Times.* (★ ★ ½)
Washington. Few journalists inside the Beltway challenge the prevailing economic fads at all, but Redburn has the audacity to do so with logic and evidence. A lengthy feature, "Bids to Bolster U.S. Competitiveness," 1-25, was one of the first to question the notion that the U.S. had a weak manufacturing industry, with "new jobs" paying poverty wages. "New jobs invariably pay below-average incomes," wrote Redburn, "because younger workers entering the job market must accept lower wages than older, established employees." Besides, manufacturing output was up 30% since '82, not down. "U.S. Becoming a Tax Haven," 12-22-86, was completely unique. Using persuasive foreign quotes, Redburn notes that Canadians are worried about losing their best hockey players to U.S. teams, and that Australians and Europeans are worried about a general exodus of talent, skill and capital. "The crowning irony of this round of international tax-rate reductions is that the United States appears to be forcing many countries to conform more closely to an American model when [Lester Thurow and Martin Feldstein] have been arguing that this nation should have been moving in the direction of the...tax systems popular in Europe." Redburn simply did a superior job of reporting in "U.S. Seeks Role for Gold in World Monetary System," 10-1, catching a key quote from James Baker that other reporters missed, and noting (as most reporters did not) that "Baker told reporters that the proposal to use commodity prices to help guide policy

decisions was supported by Federal Reserve Chairman Alan Greenspan.'' A generally informative Q & A, "Making Sense Out of The Dollar's Fall," 11-13, noted that "practically every country has a budget deficit and if budget deficits led automatically to trade deficits, every nation would run a trade deficit, which is impossible." Redburn isn't always right, of course. He went along with "overwhelming numbers" of economists who thought "the new tax law [would] cause an economic slowdown" in the first half of 1987. But he almost always presents the varied sides to such issues, making his readers think.

Reed, Julia. *U.S.News & World Report.* (★ ½)
Doing breezy business profiles and reports, she ventured now and then into politics. "'The Last Southern Gentleman,'" 3-16, was a profile of Walter Percy, an author yet to gain wide recognition, insightful, well-written, but was skimpy on background (you find out in the last paragraph, briefly, he went to med school and is a "physician"). "'Spin Control' on Wall Street," 4-20, told us of the advertising of Drexel Burnham, but the lead-in analogy of PR problems to J&J's Tylenol crisis is in poor taste: "When the news of Wall Street's first insider-trading scandal broke last fall, it was like the first drop of cyanide in the Tylenol bottle." "Battle Royal on the Old Boardwalk," 4-27, was light analysis of the problematic development of Atlantic City and its gambling casinos, with facts and figures, and silly bits like Donald Trump plays casino tournament softball, claiming the problem is other corporations have "zero personalities." Reed branches out in "The Hot New Politics of AIDS," with James Hildreth and Kathleen McAuliffe, 3-30, with a wonderful line in the second paragraph: "AIDS, and the question of how best to control its spread, has long pitted gays against straights, conservatives against liberals, the religious right against public health experts and, most recently, the President's advisers against each other."

Reinhold, Robert. *The New York Times.* (★ ★)
Dallas. A dependable reporter whose business features are always lively and who also makes his words count. "Houston in Lead for Democrats in '88," 1-26, is just such an efficiently written feature on the politics of picking a convention city. In "U.S. Drug Searches Snarl Border Traffic and Vex Businesses," 2-16, we get a crisp, thorough picture of trucks lined up for miles as the feds unload a cargo of hot asphalt searching for cocaine. A business feature on cellular telephones, "Car Phones Transforming U.S. Highways," 8-21, is vivid: "It is 4 p.m. in Southern California and the freeways have become one big moving telephone booth." And "The Cowboy...Alive and Well in Northern Texas," 4-1, is a neat look at the life of the modern cowpoke, "The universal definition of a good cowboy remains eternal: he has the sixth sense about livestock that tells him when a cow is fixin' to break from the herd and gallops over before she does."

Riley, Barry. *Financial Times.* (★ ★)
Financial Editor. We're seeing Riley regularly now in "The Long View" column of the weekend *FT*. He doesn't write as smoothly as Anthony Harris, who had been writing the column, but his material is superior, even if you have to dig for it. Among his best was "Bond Markets Pose an Enigma," 9-12, which has the intriguing premise that with bonds down everywhere and stocks climbing, and, "on the basis that changes in monetary conditions tend to lead the ups and downs of the real economy, the bond markets could have a worrying message." The excellent analysis is inconclusive, but here Riley is thinking thoughts most others didn't think until after Black Monday. In "Spare a Thought for Shareholders," 9-5, we get to the good stuff at the tail end, Riley making the point that with the growth of index funds and foreign ownership of shares, there's a loss of shareholder influence on management. "If indexing becomes widespread, the ability of the stock market to value individual shares sensibly will be undermined." He presents a rather good snapshot of the U.S. and world economies on the eve of the Crash, "U.S. Economy a Key Problem," 9-28, repeating his earlier theme of the worrisome signals from the bond markets. After the Crash he's doing on-the-one-hand, etc., with "A Speck Appears on the Horizon," 12-5, hinting inflation may come back, but

maybe it won't, and "Take Cover When the Bears Growl," 12-12, hinting the equity markets may fall again, but maybe they won't. Still, we read his inconclusive thinking out loud because he thinks so well.

Riley, Karen. *The Washington Times.* (★)
Capitol Hill. We keep an eye on Riley's material because in her wide-ranging routine filings on monetary and fiscal policies there are often snippets of information we don't see elsewhere. We're rather surprised she hasn't undertaken more ambitious projects, but perhaps she's overloaded on the small business staff. She's still weak on monetary policy, too. "Money Growth Alarms US Economy Watchers," 2-18, presented only one view, quoting officials that money growth is "running amok." "Volcker Says Fed Charts Slower Monetary Growth," 2-20, was an adequate report on his speech to Congress, with Volcker reaffirming tentative growth targets for broad new aggregates 5.5% to 8.5%. "Citicorp Writes Off $3 Billion In Loans To The Third World," 5-20, was mainly descriptive, with consideration of the effects left to Donald May. Her "Senate Wants Labels On Imported Foods," 7-1, was much better, reporting on one of the amendments to the trade bill, noting the cost of about $100 million per year to require labels that list all imported ingredients, i.e., this or that concentrated orange juice uses Florida, Brazilian, and Israeli oranges. We didn't see this elsewhere.

Rockwell, Keith M. *The Journal of Commerce.* (★ ★ ★)
Washington. A newcomer to the *MediaGuide*, but a *JOC* veteran, with some of the best reporting on the trade bill seen anywhere. "Trade Legislation Heads for Conference Debate," 7-22, offered a remarkably concise comparison of the House and Senate bills. "Trade Bill Conferees Face Major Task," 7-23, followed with an equally tight summary of the areas of disagreement with the Administration. Later pieces, 9-25 and 10-8, dug deeply into the politics of delaying the bill: "The relationship between Rep. Rostenkowski and Speaker Wright has been frosty at times. Questions have been raised over whether the speaker's decision to spread conference participation around wasn't a conscious effort to put a few roadblocks in the path of the Illinois Congressman." In "Market Shift May Stymie Push Toward Protectionism," 10-26, we find Senator Lloyd Bentsen and others beginning to worry about repeating the trade wars of the 1930s. A slick look into "Tokyo's Motivation on Bilateral Loans," 6-11, finds lobbying and commercial strings tied to foreign aid. Weaker with "Gephardt Push for Oil Fee Draws Fire," 9-2, which seemed to tilt toward the candidate, offering only a paraphrased sentence to rival Mike Dukakis. He quotes Gephardt uncritically, "It would help Mexico because it would serve to get the worldwide price of oil up" (the *world* price has to go *down* with lower U.S. oil imports). Rockwell's opinion piece, "No Quick Fix for U.S. Trade Deficit," 8-21, echoed a rather muddled version of conventional belt-tightening "cures." In all, his uncertain grasp of economics was rarely allowed to infect his powerful, informative news reports.

Ross, Philip E. *The New York Times.* (★)
A new talent emerging in science writing at the *Times*. In "The Long Struggle to Harness Ceramics," 9-16, Ross provides a lucid analysis of the state of play in the use of ceramics in diesel motors. Deftly hooking the story to the problems of manipulating the new ceramic superconductors, he describes the frustrations of engineers working on ceramics in auto engines. He reports the expert view that the Japanese "are ahead of us in all aspects of the use of ceramics," except as superconductors, he might have added. In "Honda Expansion: U.S. Exports a Goal," 9-18, he reveals Honda's current plans to become America's largest automobile exporter and third largest producer. It is now as cheap to produce in America as to produce in Japan and ship to the U.S.! He also notes that "Honda's workers have twice rejected organizing efforts by the United Auto Workers."

Rowen, Hobart. *The Washington Post.* (★ ★)
Economics editor. At 70 in 1988, Rowen still hasn't slowed a step, producing a wide and deep stream of stories and columns on the unfolding world economy. He wobbled a bit on trade

at midyear and also after the Crash, trying to write history on the run. His 2-23 report, "Finance Heads Agree to Stop Dollar's Fall," is a solid account of the G-5 meeting pact "to cooperate closely to foster stability of exchange rates around current levels." In "Sen. Bentsen Walks Tightrope on Trade Bill," 3-8, a great summary: "He must shepherd a trade bill through the Senate that will sound tough enough to Japan and Europe, but not so protectionist as to spark a veto from President Reagan." His "Japan Is Keeping Its Cool," 4-23, is timely and illuminating on "The Japanese press — in what some say reflects a private compact among publishers — has not attempted to whip up anti-American sentiment." He blasts the administration for its "Chip Shot at Japan," 3-31, warning of the bigger danger that the public will be led to believe the trade deficit can be wiped out. He has a good angle in "What's Wrong With the Gephardt Amendment," 5-28, but advances the illogical idea that "bad as the final product is likely to be...it would be worse not to have any [trade] bill." This has us wondering if Rowen is a wolf in sheep's clothing, especially followed by "Jim Baker and the Veto Bait," 8-6: "If out of all this Baker can get a trade bill that the president can sign — perhaps while holding his nose — he can claim a legislative miracle." In "Figures Blurring Trade Reality," 8-23, he's uncharacteristically sloppy, asserting that C. Fred Bergsten, a manic devaluationist, speaks "for all economists." After the Crash, in "Behind Baker's Policy Shift," 11-8, he follows the Bergsten line "with the benefit of hindsight, it becomes clear that the famous Louvre Accord — designed to stabilize the dollar's exchange rate — is a key cause of the crash of financial markets," never explaining why the crash came *after* Secretary Baker revealed he was prepared to cut loose from the Louvre Accord! Tsk, tsk.

Rudnitsky, Howard. *Forbes.* (★★)
Potentially a big hitter in business reporting, but he does whiff now and then. Extra bases with "Play It Again, Sam," 8-10, a nice short piece on Wal-Mart's Sam Walton and his expansion plans. But with "Teddy Ruxpin Stumbles," 8-24, he's late on Worlds of Wonder nosediving, with no clue where it's headed and little on where this fits into the larger picture of where the toy market is heading. There's strong reporting in his piece on Echo Bay Mines, 10-5, what seems to be a promising investment, including all the bottom line information with interesting twists of verbiage. Maybe he likes gold stories, with another winner "There's Gold in Them Thar Hills," 11-30, not just a replay on his Echo Bay piece, but a much expanded and more thoroughly researched piece. He teams with Richard L. Stern with a 1-26 bold effort on "Commercial Real Estate — the Worst Is Yet to Come."

Salpukas, Agis. *The New York Times.* (★½)
A journeyman on the airline beat, mostly serving dependable meat and potatoes, but more adventurous fare that we note from time to time. "The 2-Tier Wage System Is Found to Be 2-Edged Sword By Industry," 7-21, an excellent description of a host of problems associated with the money-saving 2-tier approach, although he asserts it won't disappear. "Climbing Air Fares Stir Wide Concern," 9-9, makes the front page with unusually skimpy support for the assertion, Salpukas somehow swallowing the very idea of an 8-company oligopoly.

Sanger, David E. *The New York Times.* (★★★★)
Only 27 and already the best technology analyst in the press corps, with an awesome catalog of superb reports in '87. At the Int'l Solid States Circuit Conference, 2-26, he's the only reporter who sees the full significance of IBM's fully manufacturable 4 megabit dynamic random access memory (DRAM). "A Peek at IBM's Trump Card," 3-8, on IBM's Burlington, VT. semiconductor production facility, the world's largest, shows his unparalleled feel for technology issues and hints at the awesome power IBM can unleash on the electronics industry — at a time when much of the business press is engaged in rampant IBM bashing. His report on IBM's new PC series, 4-3, is crisp, knowledgeable, but fails to note the limitations of the new machines compared to advanced clones at lower prices. He gives us a sophisticated look, 4-28, at the important new business relationship in software between Lotus and IBM, Lotus beginning to design programs for mainframes. His pithy summary, 6-21, of the Toshiba-Kongsberg export

scandal makes clear the impossibility of keeping most strategic technologies from the Soviet Union. One of his best, a lucid, insightful P.1 scoop on a major National Security Agency supercomputer project in parallel processing, 8-13, beating the industry press as well as his usual rivals. The story is a shocker, the U.S. Gov't., without any plausible pretext, barging in to make an advanced computer that is being targeted by scores of private companies. A brilliant P.1 report on GE's epochal trade of its consumer electronics business to Thomson of France, 8-24, correctly focuses on GE's relinquishment of the world's largest electronic market. In "A Crucial Test for Thiokol," 8-26, we get great detail on last-minute preparations for the test of the spare shuttle boosters, and 8-28, describing the experiment's failure. In "NASA's Staggering Bills," 9-6, he shows off his flair for provocative prose, describing NASA as "often acting more like a troubled freight hauler than a pioneer shooting for Mars," and quoting an Air Force official: "No one could design a more expensive way to get things in space even if they tried."

Saporito, Bill. *Fortune.* (★ ½)
Marketing. Saporito clearly has the talent to do the big *Fortune* pieces that could restore its prestige, a good writer with a nice eye for vivid quotes and angles. He has to wrestle a bit more with his material, though, too often leaving us vaguely unsatisfied with the total effort. "Just How Good Is the Great A&P?" 3-16, runs through the numbers and chats with CEO James Wood, but we are no closer to an answer to the headline question after we've reached the end. In "The Life of a $725,000 Scab," 10-26, we get far more than we've ever wanted to know about the finances of Mark Gastineau of the New York Jets in this "Labor" column, backing in to a shallow review of the NFL strike. "Discounters in the Dumps," 8-3, is a better review of the headaches among electronics retailers. "Last year the record began to warp," but we'd have rather read this when the warp began. The most satisfying marketing piece he delivered was "The Most Feared Family in Retailing," 6-22, about Herbert and Robert Haft of the Dart Group, unconventional in every respect, vivid insightful quotes. Best of all: "'What the hell do we need a computer for,' explains Haft, standing in a store a rifle shot away from an army base. 'If we sold two Virginia Woolf's in this particular store the computer would go ahead and order three more. The manager knows better.'"

Scheibla, Shirley Hobbs. *Barron's.* (★ ★)
Washington bureau. A Beltway veteran for the financial weekly, Scheibla still writes with youthful enthusiasm on many topics, delivering several novel and important stories during the year. A timely 1-5 interview with the new Senate Finance Committee chairman, Lloyd Bentsen, gave the earliest and best review of what he expected to accomplish, particularly regarding trade legislation. After the stock market crash, 10-26, Scheibla alone reported on the financial health of a little-noticed agency, the Securities Investor Protection Corp, that is supposed to aid stockholders if brokerage firms go bankrupt, which was a major anxiety at the time. A bold, fact-filled comment, "Anti-Apartheid or Pro-Soviet," 8-3, documented the enormous U.S. dependence on the Soviet Union for many critical materials once imported from South Africa, such as antimony for bullets and ferosilicon manganese for ships and tanks. "U.S. imports of chrome ore from the Soviets surged to a whopping 6,440 gross tons per month...compared with a mere 479 gross tons during...1981 through 1985. Chrome, of course, is essential to the manufacture of stainless steel and superalloys; hence it is vitally important in the aerospace, chemical, defense, power-generation and transportation."

Scherer, Ron. *The Christian Science Monitor.* (★ ★)
A capable financial writer who seems to look for material and angles we don't see elsewhere, finding enough to keep us watching his byline. A Scherer piece presented the difficulties of trying to restrict imports from specific countries in "Fraud Soars as Exporters Try to Ship More to U.S.," 4-10: "East German steel is stamped as a product of West Germany to receive lower tariffs. Sweaters woven in the People's Republic of China are relabeled 'Made in Japan' to bypass textile quotas." At a time when most of the financial press was still waiting for the

weak first quarter that almost all economists had forecast for '87, he gave us "Economy Leaves Winter Behind," 3-12, which left other reporters behind in spotting the emerging strength of the first quarter. A real novelty, "Developing Countries Cut Income Tax to Fight Evaders, Promote Growth," 7-7, leaked IMF figures on supply-side tax reforms in eight developing nations. We saw nothing similar even attempted in the major dailies. Scherer presents a balanced piece, quoting an official who was skeptical about lower tax rates doing any good in Jamaica. We may have missed a Scherer follow-up, but by year's end, Jamaican officials were worried about their economy overheating. In trying to sort through trade and capital flows, "Living Beyond Its Means," 12-1, he is out of his depth, though, producing economic slaw.

Schlender, Brenton. *The Wall Street Journal.* (★ ★)
San Francisco. Technology reporter, probably the best at the *WSJ* on the computer beat, at times scoring over the heavy hitters at the *NYT*. He covered the Intel-TI agreement, 7-8, more fully and knowledgeably than the *Times*, including the establishment of a new design standard around IBM design tools. On the same page, Schlender also showed his growing assurance in a story on Sun Microsystems and their new workstation, the Sun 4, based on a microprocessor designed by Sun, manufactured by Fujitsu, and licensed for production also to Cypress and Bipolar Technology, two microchip startups of the new generation. Full of chewy news instead of Sun fluff. But when on page one with a leader on Apple Computer, 7-16, he's fluffier, reducing the conflict at Apple to "company culture" as it shifted from Steve Job's one-man product-development policy team to a more collective motif. He almost ignores Job's unforgiveable error, the problems of incompatibility between generations of Apples, not his leadership style. The piece also misses the provocative story reported in the *NYT* of the day before, 7-15, on Apple's urgent testimony to the House trade committee against the proposed ban on Toshiba imports, "devastating" because of Apple's dependence on Toshiba desktop printers. Another leader, "Microsoft's Gates Uses Products and Pressure to Gain Power in PCs," 9-25, is marred by factual errors, telling us Microsoft "sells two financial spreadsheet programs for IBM compatible personal computers," when one is for the incompatible Apple MacIntosh, and reports that "Ashton Tate's dBase III is the biggest-selling spreadsheet program for IBM compatible PCs" when it is not a spreadsheet program at all. Better with "Personal Computers Lead Strong Rebound From Industry Slump," 4-24, a solid, snappy P.1 update on the business side of the industry, IBM, Apple, Tandy and Compaq accounting for three-fourths of PC sales in first quarter.

Schlesinger, Jacob M. *The Wall Street Journal.* (★ ★ ½)
Detroit. A standout in covering the auto industry's difficult labor negotiations in '87, plus intelligent strategic observations on labor-management developments. A bread and butter *WSJ* leader, "Plant-Level Talks Rise Quickly in Importance, 3-16, is a very useful trend piece on union/management talks "going local," to accommodate "the incredible diversity of economic pressures across firms and plants and across industries." In "Job-Guarantee Contracts Are Becoming More Common," 6-29, he covers all the bases on an idea that has picked up speed recently. In "UAW Faces Dilemma in Coming Talks," 7-21, he gets deeper into the complexities arising out of job security demands, seeing the union's solidarity cracking over it — as the traditional union principle of similar pact provisions for all workers runs into market forces that "in the next three years promise to be particularly brutal for the auto industry." In "Auto Firms and UAW Find That Cooperation Can Get Complicated," 8-25, Schlesinger sees a "costly friendship" in the formal experiments aimed at increasing productivity, instead yielding new bureaucratic waste, some scams and a patronage advantage for the UAW. Within the union they debate whether shared responsibilities really save jobs or just blur the overall union mission. Schlesinger really shines in "GM Looks For Contract Loopholes," 10-2, a superb review of the muddled Ford/GM contract picture, with an appropriate metaphor that cuts through the complexities: "The UAW likes to say the Ford contract 'takes a snapshot' of current employment

levels and tries to preserve it. But GM officials say that comparative pictures of bloated GM and trim Ford would be like 'before and after' photos from a weight-loss clinic.''

Schneider, Keith. *The New York Times.* (★)
Agriculture. A young liberal whose bias pops up too often amidst his otherwise professional reports, an easy prey for almost any special interest lobby on the left. ''A Liberal Group Makes Waves,'' 7-20, gives a lot of shameless waves to the port-side Christic Institute for its ''investigations'' of the Nicaragua contras. Then we get ''New Product on Farmers in Midwest: Hunger,'' 9-29, front-page nonsense that is being promoted by Harvard libs, with Schneider dutifully going out and finding a farm family with an empty refrigerator, or at least, ''the refrigerator and cupboards are often bare.'' Boo. Editors? He's on the front page again with ''Tearful Scientist Halts Gene Test,'' 9-4, a weeping Dr. Gary Strobel cutting down 14 elm trees to comply with federal regulations. It's a good story, but Schneider's byline makes us wonder where it came from. ''The Subsidy 'Addiction' On the Farms,'' 9-13, was about the best we saw from him, more on subsidies, lots of numbers and no way out. Best line from a farmer: ''It's insane to spend $12 billion to subsidize less than $4 billion in exports...It would be cheaper to dump corn in the ocean.'' Schneider also tried his hand at a business technology column, 6-3, on the use of organic thin films in chip manufacture, commendable in his ambition, but hopelessly confusing to the uninitiated.

Schwadel, Francine. *The Wall Street Journal.* **(NR)**
Chicago. We liked her ''Marietta Forges Into New Space Field,'' 3-24, a lively, informative piece on Martin Marietta's seeming advantage over General Dynamics, as the Air Force chooses the McDonnell Douglas Delta rocket, quoting an MM executive, Caleb Hurtt: ''We're in an active marketing mode...We don't have anybody telling us, 'Go away, we hate you guys.''' Another Schwadel piece we saw, ''Philadelphian Focuses On Raising City's Spirit As Well as Its Buildings,'' 7-10, on Willard G. Rouse III, ''the developer who dared to break with tradition and build the city's first skyscraper'' was as colorful and exciting as the city.

Sherman, Stratford P. *Fortune.* (★ ★ ★)
One of several light-fingered wordsmiths at the magazine, Sherman continues in 1987 as a compelling and colorful writer and audacious reporter. In the '87 guide, colleague Peter Petre's Ken Olsen cover edged out Sherman's Ted Turner profile in a ten-best selection. There's no doubt this year with Sherman's ''The Gambler Who Refused $2 Billion,'' 5-11, on Pennzoil's Hugh Liedke. ''Asked by *Fortune* whether he is the greediest man in the world or simply in need of psychiatric help, Pennzoil's barrel-bellied chief executive chuckled and replied in a voice so gravelly and deep you practically had to drill for it, 'Maybe both.''' Rich in color, detail, analysis. [See 10 Best] In the pungent ''CEO's Take On Their Investment Bankers,'' 3-27, Sherman shows how the insider-trading scandal could lead to lower fees on Wall Street, providing some great quotes in the process. ''Drexel Sweats the SEC Probe,'' 3-16, is a very good overview of Drexel and the SEC's insider-trading investigation. A reprise on his Ted Turner etching, ''TV's Boldest Gambler Bets the Plantation,'' 1-5, is surprisingly fresh, Sherman able to go back to the well for even deeper water. He is, though, capable of an occasional ordinary piece, as in ''The Trio That Humbled Allegis,'' 7-20, on Coniston Partners. But not many.

Silk, Leonard. *The New York Times.* (★ ★)
After a fertile 1986, when he won us back to regular, thorough reading of his column, we expected a better year from the dean of economic journalists than we got. It should have been a great year for economic analysis, the best since 1929, but he detoured into a *cul de sac* early in the year and there he stayed. Okay with ''Fury in the Markets,'' 1-25, defining Treasury Secretary Baker's strategy of using the threat of futher dollar devaluation to extract greater

cooperation from Germany and Japan in expanding their economies. But is this right? Silk doesn't say. In October, the Crash is triggered by this Baker "strategy," yet Silk ties a small market rally to the dollar's decline, and in December, his *Times* colleague Peter T. Kilborn is still writing, "The Dollar Gamble," 12-3, "By allowing the dollar to fall since the middle of October, the Reagan Administration...is betting that it can force major changes on the economic policies of other governments." Earlier, from Silk, we also got, "Jim Baker's Cagey Global Strategy," 2-1: "Last month, Mr. Baker and his team engineered a new burst of dollar devaluation." Hmmm. And in "Why Markets Are Confident," 3-18, it's because, unlike 1929 when the U.S. was on a gold standard, it can now inflate (i.e., devalue the dollar) out of a deflation. "In Global Financial Circles Everyone Is Growing Frantic," 4-5, he observes the Dow running up 69 points on 4-3 and opines: "Ironic as it may be, by the end of the week the markets were finding good news in the evident pains of the readjustment process." In "Trade Deficit: Strains Show," 4-15, the dollar is still overvalued, but in falling, it may force Germany and Japan to act!!! In "World System Seeks Stability," 11-13, he finds confusion "over whether the United States intends to defend the dollar or not." Never once do we find Dr. Silk, a free trader, questioning the wisdom of dollar devaluation, i.e., monetary protectionism. Most of the year in a *cul de sac*, but we still never miss his column.

Sims, Calvin. *The New York Times.* (★ ½)
Up and coming on the telecommunications beat, business in general, accurate as far as he goes but we sometimes sense he could push deeper into a story. He covered the Compaq computer conference, 7-7, but seemed to get less out of it than the *Wall Street Journal* reporter, but neither probed a significant point: Without government help, IBM is not far enough ahead of the field to avoid substantial problems with the next transition in the PC industry, and such help would hobble its US competitors, like Compaq and Apple. Sims gives us a deeper look at the learning-curve gains of cellular phones, 9-23, adding 30,000 a month and by 6-87 up to 800,000 in the U.S. He could have explored the extent to which the technology is made in Japan. His best of the year we saw was an important story on the limits of U.S. patent law regarding industrial processes, 5-13. U.S. patent holders can act against domestic but not foreign rivals that copy manufacturing techniques. Excellent detail.

Sloan, Allan. *Forbes.* (★ ★ ★)
The most important reporter at *Forbes*, a Wall Street veteran who writes with confidence and authority in a way that gives backbone to the constant turnover in the reporting pool. His piece on the relationship between Ivan Boesky and Drexel Burnham, "An Extra Slice of the Pie," 2-9, was one of the smartest conjectures we saw on what was driving Boesky. He has "A Chat With Michael Milken," 7-13, getting the wizard of Beverly Hills to open up with an impassioned defense of his financial revolution, some wisdom on the U.S. economy, third-world debt and junk bonds, and the personal priorities that really matter in life. We come away thinking, if the SEC shuts this guy down, it's a replay of Galileo and the Church. In "What Color Is Your Mail," 10-19, Sloan takes an interesting flip-flop at Salomon, with valuable reporting that alerts investors on what's going on beneath the surface. ("Why did Salomon pay an above-market price for its own stock and then sell preferred at below market?") In "Apres Moi...," 10-5, Sloan bashes the S&L system, succinctly pinpointing the problems with recapitalization; colorful, incisive, and witty as usual. He seems a bit behind the curve with "Biting Half the Bullet," 7-27, which is evidence of *Forbes'* balanced reporting after several very pro-bank, mostly Citicorp, articles. But *The Economist* had the story on the remaining exposure two months earlier, when the banks made their first move.

Stern, Richard L. *Forbes.* (★ ★ ½)
Another in a lengthening string of satisfying years for this solid reporter on markets and investments. There's "Bye-Bye Bob Brennan," 12-29-86, clear and interesting on the financials Brennan is shoving around in an attempt to sell First Jersey Securities. There's fresh, bold reporting in "Commercial Real Estate — the Worst Is Yet to Come," 1-26, with Howard

Rudnitsky, the research done and conclusions stated without a barrage of qualifications. Direct, fast-paced writing here, which suggests Stern's partner, though. A memorable cover story, "Land of the Rising Stocks," 5-18, with Rudnitsky and Peter Fuhrman, makes some headway in explaining the huge but thin Tokyo stock market. He's working with Allen Sloan in "The Day the Brokers Picked Their Own Pockets," 11-16, but the stylish writing suggests Sloan is the lead man on this nice post-Crash piece. But Stern's solo with "Deja Vu All Over Again," 11-30, is a very zippy piece about mythmaking on the wonders of electronic marketmaking: "In the frenzy of the all-but-forgotten 1962 crash, the partners of one large over-the-counter brokerage house figured a simple way to minimize their losses. They turned out the lights. In those days, the bid and asked prices were chalked on a wall-sized blackboard for the traders. No lights, no market...Global electronic trading and powerful computers were to have transformed securities transactions...But when stocks crashed this time, some marketmakers quickly found another way to cut their losses: They stopped answering the telephones."

Sterngold, James. *The New York Times.* (★ ★ ½)
Financial markets, mergers and acquisitions. A solid young reporter who got his start with Dow-Jones, seeming to ripen in his fourth year with the *Times*. We especially appreciated his coverage of the fallout and continuing investigations of the Wall Street scandals, as in "Inquiry Said to Focus on Invoice From Drexel," 2-6. Although later in reporting this than the *WSJ*, to his credit it's far more cautious in describing the suspected illegalities. In "Bache Braves a New World," 7-3, we get rather interesting bits and pieces as Pru-Bache tries to build an investment banking business against tough odds. He has the Sunday magazine as his platform for "Hardball on Wall Street," 8-16, but doesn't do much with it. His best business piece of the year was "Shaking Billions From Beatrice," 9-6, the Sunday business lead, a fascinating account of the Beatrice leveraged buyout, which could have been in the running for our 10-best selection but for the early focus on the big fees garnered, which only slowed it down. After the Wall Street Crash, his front page "The Events That Changed the World of Wall Street," 10-26, was the best single wrap-up we saw within the first week.

Stevenson, Richard W. *The New York Times.* (★ ★)
Los Angeles. Out of *Ad Week*, he covered the ad industry early in '87 before moving to the Coast, now ranging all over the business page with impressive results. In "Red, White and Blue Is Out," 3-16, he spots trends in advertising going from flag waving to ads "more biting, a little tougher, a little more cynical," spotlighting the successful Isuzu ads and Coke's Max Headroom. A memorable last line in "Surviving a Palace Coup at JWT," 2-1, on continuing troubles at J. Walter Thompson: "And 13 years after taking the helm, Don Johnston still must prove that he knows how to run an advertising agency." Boyd L. Jeffries confesses to stock manipulation in the Boesky scandal and Stevenson drafts a sympathetic profile, almost a eulogy, "A Broker Who Went Too Far," 3-20: "Mr. Jeffries had become almost legendary in the industry as a workaholic and a maverick." We appreciated the thoroughness and organization of "Texaco Fighting Pennzoil Attack, Asks Bankruptcy," 4-13. Even the routine, "Bidding For the Stars," 7-20, on the stakes of the space station contract, is notable for its clarity on the "team efforts." His "Alien Law Causing Shortages of Labor in Some Industries," 6-6, is timely on an interesting development, but unsatisfactorily explained, too many questions left. He's very sharp on Japanese car upscaling, taking a luxury slice from the Europeans, "Japanese Cars For Cadillac Tastes," 10-4. "Bringing the Movies to Life," 11-4, is extremely interesting, on Showscan's 65mm movie film, so lifelike it would draw big crowds, its developers say: "People are looking for something they can't get in the living room."

Stewart, James B. *The Wall Street Journal.* (★ ★ ½)
New York. A four-star reporter in the '87 *MediaGuide*, the *Journal*'s ace on mergers and acquisitions could easily have repeated this year, but he pushed a little too hard for our tastes, seeming as if he wanted to hasten indictments in the dealmaker scandals. A lawyer who was executive editor of *American Lawyer* magazine before joining the *WSJ* in 1983, Stewart has

been the reporter to beat on Wall Street's frantic M&A beat, with a keen eye, great sources, and a sidekick legman, Daniel Hertzberg, whose byline often appears below Stewart's. "The Wall Street Career of Martin Siegel Was a Dream Gone Wrong," 2-17, was among the best we've ever seen from Stewart, a colossal effort that squeezed a book of information and drama into a fascinating news account. He's authoritative with "Death of a Theory? Supreme Court May Revamp Insider Trading Law," 9-30, arguing the Court is likely to do so in a review of the R. Foster Winans conviction. But on his coverage of Drexel Burnham and Michael Milken, we became increasingly distressed with his scoops, as the following entries from our readers indicate: "Boesky and Drexel Aides Joined in Illicit Scheme, Records Suggest," 2-4, "a clear and insightful piece on Boesky and Drexel 'parking stock' with each other, but these are extremely serious allegations not to have a source that they can name." And "U.S. Accumulates Evidence Supporting Case Against Milken, Sources Say," 4-28, "excellent piece with a clear description of the possible wrongdoings, a good analysis of what the case will hinge on, but there is no source quoted by name." Then, "Boesky Ex-Aide Could Provide Data on Milken," 9-24, "is Stewart becoming an arm of the Justice Department? He seems to be fanning embers here: 'Yesterday's announcement seems likely to dispel impressions on Wall Street that the government's investigation of Drexel...is floundering.'" Finally, "After the Fall," 11-19, "very serious accusations are made here about the subject's personal life and style. Perhaps more quotes would have been helpful from people who know him." Author of a new book, *The Prosecutors*, Stewart seemed to be going to trial by press, a breach of journalistic standards that he shares with his editors.

Stipp, David. *The Wall Street Journal.* (★ ½)
Boston. A promising technology reporter who tries hard to present financial implications of new technologies. In "Genetic Engineers Seek Ways to Improve Food Processing," 1-23, carrots are made crunchier, celery crispier through biotechnology, a clear account with a few firms mentioned in the lead. "Japan's Top Engineers & Scientists Receive Extra Training at MIT," 1-23, has a nice line, the Japanese are "looking for the goose, not the golden egg," but the piece doesn't seem worth the top front page display. The closing graphs on Japanese students at MIT defecting to U.S. companies seems more like P.1 material. His technology column, 7-9, is down on superconductivity, Stipp presenting a new list of possible obstacles while the *NYT* is writing about new applications. It is well written and knowledgeable, but the kinds of problems it describes (brittleness, expense, lack of markets, strong competition from other technologies) were also cited by IBM when it dropped its Josephson Junction superconductivity project a few years ago; nobody said it would be easy. "Venture Capitalists Are Plugging Into Superconductors," 7-29, is also a good effort on the wary side, telling us "An awful lot of money is going to be lost by a lot of people trying to invest in this." We don't even see a vague outline of how this will come out. A more positive "New Superconductor Research," 10-2, reveals new IBM experiments show superconductive ceramics can transmit 100 times faster than fiber optics, but the news is buried; James Gleick of the *NYT* has it on P.1 the same day in a more informative story. "New Findings About Alzheimer's May Offer Insights Into Its Cause," 2-20, is lucid on "genetic markers" that "tell scientists approximately where to look in the maze of genetic material for the gene or genes that cause inherited Alzheimer's."

Stokes, Bruce. *National Journal.* (★ ★)
One of the better Capitol Hill reporters on international trade, although plain awful when he decides to write lofty commentary on the world situation. His "Foreign Owners," 9-19, analyzing the impact of foreign ownership of U.S. plants on congressional lobbying just missed being one of the 10-best political pieces of the year, on the journalistic frontier, with far-reaching implications for integrated economies and continued free trade. "Setting the Stage," 1-17, a useful report on the issue of competitiveness, projecting a trade bill that will take care of some of the problems, but saying little will be done until 1989, after the issue dominates the '88 campaign. "Although exit polls last November continued to show that voters did not see trade and competitiveness as major issues, politicians sense that may change." In "Bentsen's

Benchmark,'' 7-25, there is glowing treatment of Senator Bentsen and his expert maneuvering on the trade bill, but not much analysis amidst the flattery. In "Derailed Deal?" 9-12, we get a status report, but don't learn much about why going is so slow on both sides. "Our Ideology," 6-6, is a supercilious call for a debate on our competition with Japan. And in "Moral Leadership," 1-24, we get "The U.S. today lacks the values of a competitive economy," and Oh, no, not quoting Pogo? Yes: "We have met the enemy and he is us!"

Sullivan, Allana. *The Wall Street Journal.* (★)
New York. We find her reporting adequate day-to-day on routine petroleum industry news, but she needs some help with the heavy lifting. She obviously spent lots of time on "Mobil's New Chairman Acts Quickly to Reduce Debt," 1-29, and the *Journal* put it in its top P.1 position (perhaps because of Mobil's continuing advertising and news boycott of the *WSJ*). But it turned out to be a ho-hum personality piece on Alan Murray, the new CEO, with very little of use on the company. "Texaco and Pennzoil Lock Horns Again," 10-5, reported on an important development in the case, but we had to read it twice to get it straight. Murkier than it needed to be.

Swardson, Anne. *The Washington Post.* (★ ½)
Tax beat, foreign debt issues. Straightforward reporting, nothing fancy from Swardson, but little new ground broken that we saw. Her reports on Citicorp were a cut above routine, "Citicorp Will Lose $2.5 Billion," 5-20, and "Citicorp Raises Debt Stakes," 5-21, cautious in trying to plumb too much meaning into John Reed's maneuver, but sound. Her "Panel Issues Warning On Foreign Debt," 8-11, has the interesting thought that "As the new money [from the trade deficit] came into the country, the value of the dollar in relation to foreign currencies went up," which doesn't explain why the dollar more recently had gone down while the trade deficit went still higher; she needs to talk to different economists. The same problem in reporting "Tax Rate Is Higher For Poor, Lower For Rich Than in 1977," a report on a CBO study, which doesn't ask why use the 1977 base year, since the '81 tax cuts were designed to offset inflationary bracket-creep that occurred throughout the '70s. In "The Literary Tax Lobby," 8-18, she reports on authors banding together to revive the tax deduction they lost in the '86 Tax Reform Act, well done, first seen here. The most informative, timeliest piece we saw from her was "Hill Finds Raising Taxes an Especially Unsavory Prospect This Year," 5-28, which was definitive at the time.

Swartz, Steve. *The Wall Street Journal.* (NR)
New York. "Loose Bull," 7-27, is prescient on how the Crash will be interpreted, seeing the incredible tensions between high growth on a long leash and managerial controls on Wall Street. This is an important, comprehensive overview of Wall Street on a roll and the dangers of overextension. He's one to watch.

Tanner, James. *The Wall Street Journal.* (★ ★)
Houston. With Youssef Ibrahim moving over to the *NYT* in '87, Tanner is once again the *Journal*'s top gun on the world oil beat. In 1973, when the "energy crisis" unfurled, he often seemed the only U.S. oil reporter who made sense, with a sure grasp of petroleum politics and economics. He left the paper for several years to write a newsletter, returning in 1986. He can turn out gems, as "Lean Exxon Tiger, Still a Giant, Has a Smaller Appetite," 3-17, a crisp, expert account of Exxon in liquidation, buying its own shares — which means buying oil at $2.42/bbl. In "Cartel's Comeback," 8-21, Tanner predicts that OPEC in a few years is likely to reassert control over world oil markets. The output of non-OPEC oil nations is flat as aging fields dry up and demand increases. The political implications are enormous, so even while the piece is not persuasive on out-year economics, it is a useful leader, loaded with numbers on the near and mid-term. In "Saudis Vow to Maintain Price of Oil," 11-11, he interviews Saudi oil minister Hisham Nazer in Chicago for an advance look at the winter OPEC meeting.

Taylor, Alex III. *Fortune.* (★ ★ ★)
An excellent writer who can mesh fact and imagery in delightful ways, getting us the otherwise dry statistical essentials of a business story with style. Mainly covering autos, his "Who's Ahead in the World Auto War," 11-9, is immensely satisfying for this reason (plus wonderful graphics). "For carmakers, unlike consumers, the golden age is likely to be fleeting. Last year some 488 million vehicles roamed the earth." He tackles this enormous subject almost casually, and it works, a dandy piece of analysis, too. Taylor's profile of Jack Telnack, "The Stylist Who Put Ford Out in Front," 1-5, breezes us through the fellow who designed the Taurus and Sable, topped with a great quote: "With Ford striving to give all its products better aerodynamics, will they wind up looking the same? Answers Telnack: 'All birds are aerodynamically designed, but you can still tell a canary from a buzzard.'" Another on Richard Dauch, "Lee Iacocca's Production Whiz," 6-22, has great stats and Dauch thinking the Japanese "overrated." In "Why the Bounce at Rubbermaid," 4-13, we learn why a company that sells humdrum products in a mature market has a P/E of 28, with no stone unturned in a brisk two-pager about ice trays, desk organizers, file boxes, management, marketing and design. Plus: "Foreign competition isn't an appreciable threat because there is no profit in shipping 20-gallon garbage cans long distances." Taylor's weakest was "Why Car Rentals Drive You Nuts," 8-31, a solid core about the industry, wrapped in consumerism fluff that belongs in *Money*. "There's one piece of good news in all this. You can still find good deals...You just have to work at it." It closes with more consumer poop that we never thought we'd see in *Fortune*. This can't be Taylor's fault.

Terry, Edith. *Business Week.* (★ ★ ½)
Acting Toronto bureau chief, Terry has taken hold over the past year as a perceptive analyst of Canadian developments. The 7-27 story, "Industry's Surprising Revival North of the Border," is the best piece on Canada's economy we saw during 1987. "If the free-trade talks succeed, some Canadians argue, the lowering of barriers could make Toronto the industrial capital of the American Midwest as well as Canada." In "From Working Stiff to Political Hero," 3-30, Terry's subject is Robert White of the Canadian Auto Workers, who was against Prime Minister Mulroney's free-trade plan and who could be the next head of the Canadian Socialist Party. Lots of good information on trade and union tensions across the border. Large asset sales by the Bronfman family holding company, carried out to pay off younger family members cashing in their Seagram shares, prompted Terry to question whether Charles and Edgar could or would maintain control of Seagram, "Can the Bronfmans Keep Seagram in the Family?" 6-1. On any little company profile she turns out we learn a bit more than we expected about the Canadian economy in general and its relationship to the U.S. A perfect example in "Canada's Labatt Has Just One Way to Grow: South," 11-9, about the constraints on the big brewery, enough about chairman Peter Widdrington to color up the main message, but also the impact the new trade deal had on him, with Labatt launching a "preemptive strike" by buying Latrobe Brewing Co. and its Rolling Rock brand.

Thomas, Paulette. *The Wall Street Journal.* (★ ★)
Houston. Thomas had her hands full in '87 covering Texas Air Corp. and Frank Lorenzo, but she did stray long enough to do an arresting front-pager on the miserable state of education in the Pelican state, "Subpar Schools Deepen Louisiana's Troubles," 2-26, with Hilton having to interview 12,000 applicants to find 500 employees, then train them twice as long as elsewhere; some companies refuse to relocate to Louisiana! The powerful piece surely shook things up. The same day she had "Texas Air's Rapid Growth Spurs Surge in Complaints About Service," tough, thorough reporting on TA's growing pains, but careful to say high up that "industry analysts generally accept the company's view that service problems will be short lived." In "Bumpy Ride: Pilots Feel the Stress Of Turmoil in the Airline Industry," 4-24, she buys the arguments of the pilots' union that the hustle-bustle of competition gets on their nerves, and "We can't just pull over for a cup of coffee when things get too tense." Airline executives dismiss the complaints, but we remembered the piece in November when a Continental flight

out of Denver crashed, taking off in a snowstorm. Another related Thomas story, "Texas Air Asks Its Employes to Go On Offensive Against Firm's Critics," 5-15, quoting a memo to employes from Continental president Thomas Plaskett complaining of "Continental bashing" in Congress and the media and warning "Unless we do something about all of this," the future of the airline and its employes "could be gravely threatened."

Thomas, Rich. *Newsweek*. (★ ★)
Chief economic correspondent. We dropped Thomas by a full star this year, because we didn't see enough of him on a single byline, and working in tandem has diluted his power. What's there is okay, but he really should solo. "Reagan's 1988 Wish List: Already 'D.O.A.'" 1-12, was a nicely done sidebar on Reagan's 1988 budget proposals: it would have made a good full piece. "How to Solve the Trade Problem," 1-12, was a super piece on potential trade legislation — a new nonprotectionist tariff system. Also good was "The King of the S&L's," 3-30, on Preston Martin "bottom fishing" in the troubled S&L industry, an inspired subject, with good quotes. "How Tough Is Greenspan?" with Penelope Wang, 6-15, was probably his best work in a pair, a worthwhile assessment of Greenspan's probable courses of action, letting the experts do the talking, pulling quotes together only with quick bridges and facts and figures. But "The Wright Man To See," with David Pauly, 6-29, was a passable report on Jim Wright's negotiating on behalf of Texas S&Ls that was structured to imply unethicalness if not illegality. Paired with Susan Dentzer, now a senior editor for economics at *U.S.News*, Thomas was off in "Nearing Full Employment, But Will It Spur Inflation?" 7-20, the "Phillips curve" appeared as though stagflation (high inflation and high unemployment) had never happened, one-sided and sensationalist. Better with "Forecasting's Dim Prognosis," 7-27, detailing management troubles at Townsend-Greenspan since Greenspan was leaving to go to the Fed.

Trachtenberg, Jeffrey A. *Forbes*. (★ ½)
Marketing editor. With a light, easy touch, Trachtenberg is more anecdotal than insightful. He's most often editing material of other *Forbes* writers. "Here's One Tough Cowboy," 2-9, was one of his better efforts, on the power of the product image, using the very successful Marlboro Man as an example, "In an era when consumer tastes swing on small differences — as often as not, differences of image rather than product — Marlboro is a pure marketing success. The product has associated itself with an image of almost universal appeal: the cowboy in his red flannel shirt and suede vest on horseback, looking serious and professional; a couple of guys breaking horses or awaking in the bunkhouse or just enjoying their solitude. No special effects, and no fancy dialog — the Marlboro man never talks." "I Am Betting My Destiny," 3-9, was also sharp on the Canon vs. Minolta camera wars, but mostly he tells us things we already know. "The Sweet Smell of Success," 8-10, concludes that if you make a good product, develop loyalty, and sell it at the right price, you'll be successful, just like Old Spice cologne. "Listening the Old-Fashioned Way," 10-5, was a so-so piece on the latest Madison Avenue trend of using focus groups. "Beyond the Hidden Persuaders," 3-23, a quick read on how advertisers sell soap, shoes, and Renaults.

Truell, Peter. *The Wall Street Journal*. (★ ★ ★ ★)
The *Journal*'s ace on the geopolitical banking beat, brought from London to New York at the start of 1987, a smart move that put Truell in position to cover the Brazil and other Third World debt stories centered in NYC. "Latin Debtors Seek Way to Link...Debt to Rise in Exports," 1-26, was the best update at this point on Mexico, Third World debt, and U.S. debt planning, with Truell in Mexico City. His best, "Citicorp's Reed Takes Firm Stance on Third-World Debt," 2-4, is an important, rare interview with John Reed, great quotes illuminating Reed's fears and his motives for resisting discounts for debtors. His "Manila Offers Bankers Option on Interest Rates," 3-9, written from NYC, can't match the *NYT* account from Manila, Nicholas Kristoff reporting. Also among his best was a front-page leader "Borrowing Trouble: Banks' Reserve Action May Make Debt Crisis Even More Vexatious,"

7-2, an update of the fuss Reed caused in May with his $3 billion loan loss. "Commercial Banks Isolation of Brazil Contributed to Finance Chief's Departure," 4-28, is a sparkling account of the international financial and political squeeze on Funaro. In "Financing For Exports Grows Harder to Find For All But Big Firms," 4-14, we get a good collection of examples and economic arguments on why this is happening, although he could have developed tax roadblocks mentioned in the closing graphs. "Bankers View Brazil Debt Plan As Unacceptable," 9-4, from Vienna; as in other Truell pieces on the Brazil debt throughout the year, it was superior to the competition, authoritative and crystal clear. We're hoping he can get out to a few big debtor nations in '88; his 10-1-85 piece on Mexico was definitive.

Uchitelle, Louis. *The New York Times.* (★ ½)
The deputy Sunday business editor until the top job shifted at the start of '87, and before that the business editor at Associated Press, Uchitelle now runs around with pencil and notebook. We first noted "Bonds in Slump As Dollar Stirs Fear of Inflation," 4-23, unusually coherent in handling several variables, although we wonder why he questions as "too rosy" the government '87 GNP forecast of 3.2% on the day the first quarter came in at 4.3%. His roundup of "Greenspan's Special Talents," 6-8, has pros and cons, but not enough of either. His "America's Army of Non-Workers," 9-27, was one of the most panned of the year by our readers. ("The 'hard-core' unemployables turn out to be folks who won't work unless they are paid more than they are worth." "A non-story supported by non-facts, playing the employment boom upside down." "An utterly shameless broadside..." "We get pages of anecdotes and Barry Bluestone quotes without a mention of the presumably relevant fact that this so-called army of non-workers comprises a smaller share of America's population than ever before in history.") On the other hand, Uchitelle's "Economic Scene" column, 7-1, is scattered with stars. ("A useful corrective to scores of editorials, news stories and op-ed ululations on the U.S. position as a net debtor." "He shows a commendable command of double-entry analysis, pointing out the U.S. overseas debt is only 6% of GNP." "He goes against the conventional wisdom, showing net foreign investment did flow into capital formation.") For all his ups and downs, he did rather well.

Vise, David A. *The Washington Post.* (★ ½)
A Wall Streeter who escaped from Yuppiedom for a press card, Vise teamed with Steve Coll for some fairly good efforts on the financial scandals. On his own, he seemed to be tightening up, better organized than what we saw in '86. "Wall Street's Scandal Goes Upstairs," as Martin A. Siegel, "One of the Market's Best and Brightest is Caught," 3-2 (Weekly), a respectable rundown with thoughts on what the investigation may provoke on Wall Street via Congress. In "Court Backs State Law on Takeovers," 4-22, Vise gets good backup quotes, one from T. Boone Pickens, "It is a sad day for shareholders and for the free-market system." He has an enterprising piece on Pickens' takeover advances on Newmont Mining developed out of confidential board meeting notes made public in November in a Delaware lawsuit involving Pickens and Newmont, "Board Room Battle Notes: 'Finish Him'," 11-15, an interesting inside look at anti-takeover strategy being cooked.

Waldholz, Michael. *The Wall Street Journal.* (★ ★)
A capable science reporter covering the pharmaceutical industry. "Healthy Grant: New Cholesterol Drug Enhances Merck's Role As Leader in Research," 12-23-86, is fairly typical, thorough, well written. "A Psychiatrist's Work Leads to a U.S. Study of Alzheimer's Drug," 8-4, is able treatment of a complex, difficult subject, the THA drug described. "Squibb's Fortunes Rise as Hypertension Drug Is a Hit With Doctors," 5-28, excels in telling us all about Capoten, but not enough about the potential competition from Merck's Vasotec, only a few passing comments near the end of the piece. "Doctors' Orders: Cholesterol Study Calls for Broad Treatment Change," 10-5, is a weaker piece, reporting on a study that implies 20% to 25% of American adults will be found in need of therapy! The material doesn't give us enough to know whether this is serious stuff. He mentions supplementary LDL tests near the

end of the piece, but offers no sense of how these tests could reduce therapy needs in the broader category. With Brenton Schlender, 6-16, he barged into the breach with a great story on the FDA, Genentech, and the activase ruling. Vivid, informative, probing the failure of Genentech to follow the twists and turns of the FDA policy as the biological division struggled with the more prestigious drugs division for control over the revolutionary substance.

Walsh, Sharon Warren. *The Washington Post.* (★)
A general assignment reporter on the business page, Walsh covers local business and industry, but steps out occasionally with features of broader interest. One such worth noting: "As Corporations Tighten Belts, Economists Feel the Squeeze," 12-10-86. With economic forecasting unreliable, corporate cost-cutters ask: "What is it these guys do for us anyway? The answer is they don't produce money, they just cost." There's good assembly of information here and a nice quote from Chase Econometrics Lawrence Chimerine, "We have to admit that in many cases, we haven't really focused on...making economic analysis useful." She manages "Condom Sales Take a Turn," 2-15, on increased prophylatic sales due to the fear of AIDS, without so much as a smirk.

Watson, Ripley Jr. *The Journal of Commerce.* (★)
Adequate credit market commentary, often as wrong as most such efforts to explain interest rates. "A weaker U.S. economy, less inflationary pressure and a watchful Federal Reserve add up to an improved picture for the credit markets," he wrote on 5-26, when none of those things proved true. Nothing wrong with being wrong, but there should be some good reasons. Watson also covers some statistical releases, such as "Survey Finds Capital Spending Bright," 4-10, which seemed to conflict with his 5-26 description of a "weaker economy."

Wayne, Leslie. *The New York Times.* (★ ½)
A Business Day reporter who tackles big pieces and subjects with verve, but often doesn't iron out the kinks. "Drexel's Municipal Bond Tie," 12-8-86, has the scoop on Drexel's cornering yet another market, but we could not puzzle through her explanation of how the system — using Guaranteed Investment Contracts — works. "Why the Dollar Ought to Drop," 4-28, interviews MIT's Paul R. Krugman, who argues unless the dollar comes down by another 20%, the trade deficit can't be balanced and the U.S. runs the risk of recession. Her questions allow too much, although she does ask about inflation. In "Five-Year Stock Rally: The Far-Reaching Impact," 8-3, offers a buffet of ideas and opinions on the bull market, opinions and counter opinions, then a classic "critics say..." We were not sure what to make of it all. Her best of '87, "Wall Street's Newest Magic Show," 9-13, one of the best Sunday business leads in months, although big fees again drives the story — Drexel's Mike Milken looking at ways to cash in on $400 billion of Latin debt. The alchemy of junta bonds?

Weiner, Steve. *Forbes.* (★ ★ ★ ½)
Midwestern bureau manager, one of the sharpest business journalists we read during the year, a confident and authoritative analyst of companies big and small as well as unfailingly interesting, clear and informative. We really began following his byline after his colossal cover story, "Is Leslie Wexner Riding For a Fall?" 4-6, an audacious forecast of big trouble ahead for the high-flying retailing chain, The Limited, Inc., built around first-rate marketing analysis and a telling interview with the boss. A classic worthy of both business and journalism school reading, one of our 10-best of the year. But they roll on, an "Up & Comers" column on Frank Purcell and the Walnut Lumber Co., 8-24, is a heartwarming entrepreneurial fable, oddly appealing in its simplicy, complete with a moral lesson for all businessmen. In "Hyundai Motor Co.," 10-5, Weiner again demonstrates his facility with key marketing concerns and strategy, focusing on Hyundai's success and examining its future in light of the crowded, low cost subcompact market. "National Car Rental," 10-19, another little gem, balanced and fact-filled. Then again, "Electrifying," 11-30, a zippy piece on the power surge at Rayovac Corp., the battery and flashlight maker, juiced with wonderfully awful puns throughout. He's so good

we even hate to see him foul one off, as in "Trading Machine," 11-30, on Tom Dittmer and the powerful Refco Group, the nation's largest futures and options brokerage. Not bad anyway, but we get no sizzling insights. And after all, he has yet a third piece in the same issue. We are Weiner fans.

Weiss, Gary. *Business Week.* (★ ½)
An able finance writer who we see pushing more than most in getting to the margin of analysis. He and Christopher Power (with Stan Crock) wrote "Insider Trading: Business as Usual," 8-24. It is based on a *BW*-commissioned study of pre-bid trading in takeover stocks over the past year, which found price run-ups in 70% of the targets. The story suggests that, scandals or no, insider trading will not be controlled. In the same issue, a Weiss commentary, "The SEC Isn't Clearing Up Anything," is a clear, concise critique showing weaknesses in the SEC's *de facto* definition of insider trading and the connection with the U.S. Supreme Court's Winans-case review, then pending. A short review, "Was Program Trading to Blame," 11-2, suggests that program trading was a convenient fall guy after the Crash, not a basic cause, and that the liquidity difficulties in market-making during a crisis are a more serious problem.

Welles, Chris. *Business Week.* (★ ★ ★)
Welles continues as an astute and classy observer of the equity markets, impressing us greatly as he swam against the tide of hysteria that cascaded from *BusiWeek* after the Crash. Earlier, one of his best was the 8-10 "The Case Against Drexel: Will the Government Come Up Short?" — one of the more balanced pieces in print on what Drexel may or may not have done that was illegal. Solid analysis, based on the reporter's "extensive inquiry" into specific Drexel/Michael Milken deals. "Ivan Boesky's Secret 'Parking Lot,'" 6-22, was less successful, being heavy on speculation. In the post-Crash scene, Welles kept his head better than some other *BW* reporters, not only avoiding foolishness but contributing useful insights. In "Did Specialists Do Their Jobs?" 11-2, he defends Big Board specialists for attempting to maintain their markets under the most difficult of circumstances. "The Markets: Some 'Heavy Tinkering' Ahead," 11-9, says the importance of program trading in the Crash was exaggerated, with a more serious issue being the inadequacy of market-makers facing institutional-trade volume that the system wasn't designed for; no broad reregulation foreseen, though. "Why All the Fuss? Maybe Stocks Were Just Too High," 11-16, is a welcome humorous, skeptical antidote to *BW*'s end-of-the-world-is-near cover stories on the Crash, even though he makes too much of the Crash as the bursting of a purely speculative bubble unconnected to larger economic events. Welles switches gears with an interesting corporate portrait on the Advo direct mail concern, 11-2, showing the depth of challenge it represents for newspapers' advertising revenues.

Willoughby, Jack. *Forbes.* (★ ★)
Willoughby paints deft company portraits, packing a lot of essential information into a small space. Two good examples are "High-Octane Banking," 9-21, on Boston Safe Deposit, "the nation's fastest-growing lender to the rich and near-rich," which took an old-fashioned idea about service and ran with it; and "This Gorilla Can Putt," 10-19, about the recent strategic shift by North Carolina's First Union Corp. In the absorbing companion pieces, "Endgame Strategy" and "The Last Iceman," 7-13, Willoughby delves into the seemingly offbeat subject of "smart managers making money in declining industries," from vacuum tubes to harpoons, wooden propellers, and, yes, buggy whips. He asks us to think about future implications for the appliance, chemical, and auto industries. In "The Stock Market Is a Lousy Economic Forecaster," 11-30, he gives superficial histories of the other eight market crashes in this century, starting with 1929. Although lean on analysis and sometimes confusing in not defining generalities like "strong economy," the piece is useful in showing that the economy's behavior after the market breaks was very mixed (one Depression, three short downturns, four strong advances). But cause-and-effect relationships are left unclear. The conclusion for 1987?

Worthy, Ford S. *Fortune.* (★ ★)
Chicago. Best when dealing with investment matters, Worthy did a few of the better pieces we saw on junk bonds during the year. The cover story, "The Coming Defaults in Junk Bonds," 3-16, was superior to the misleading headline and accompanying exaggerated graphics, suggesting Worthy's admirable research and analysis, developing the risks and rewards associated with junks, didn't fit the editor's preconception. Again, the head, "Trying Times for Junk Bonds," 12-7, misleads, Worthy instead pointing out that on Black Monday, "managers feared that their shareholders would bail out en masse, so they scrambled to sell bonds in order to be ready to redeem shares. For the most part, the stampede never came. The shareholders apparently were less rattled by the crash than the fund managers." And, "Devotees of junk say the large spread guarantees that...high-yield bonds should outperform government bonds even in the event that the most extreme predictions of defaults come true." In "You're Probably Working Too Hard," 4-27, we're told execs are toiling longer, but often it's just "face time." Better than we expected, some depth of analysis here. He does the "Where America is Booming" cover, 8-17, light snapshots of six boom areas, no attempt at analysis or something to link them together, but mildly interesting. He does not pull off "Accounting Bores You? Wake Up," 10-12, a look at basic and some advanced accounting techniques, with no central point, except that many companies are inefficiently run, and "most large companies recognize that their cost systems are not responsive to today's competitive environment," but haven't done anything about it. Yawn. Back to sleep.

Yemma, John. *The Christian Science Monitor.* (★ ½)
Yemma's firm grasp of international commercial and financial linkages shows up in "With Barriers Down, Stock Rises Ripple Through World Markets," 1-8, and "Despite US-Iran Rumblings, Energy Supply Looks Secure," 8-9. A prescient sample, from "Falling Dollar, Act II," 1-22: "If a sagging dollar leads to a rise in interest rates, the [U.S.] stock market rally could stall...[Stock markets in] Hong Kong, Singapore, South Korea and Taiwan benefit greatly as the strong yen makes Japanese companies less competitive. In London, investors expect rising oil prices to benefit the British economy. Higher gold prices (a consequence of the falling dollar) have helped the Canadian stock market. Stronger commodity prices have given Australia a boost."

FOREIGN CORRESPONDENTS

Almond, Peter. *The Washington Times.* (★)
Moving from London back to the U.S. midyear, Almond's reports were mostly lightweight, perhaps in anticipation of the move. "British Policemen Turning Reluctant to Arm Themselves," 1-26, was very informative on the non-pistol-packing bobbies: "In the whole country, the police fired only seven shots during the whole of 1985, and two of them went into innocent victims." A not very informative blurb, "London Laughs At 'Loony Left,' But Establishment Not Amused," 2-25, was a mere fringe item on the front page. "Debt-Wrecked Zimbabwe Buys Top-Of-Line Soviet Jets," 4-13, was recycled from a *Sunday Telegraph* report on the 10 MIG-290s purchased by Zimbabwe. But the worst was "Royal Duo In Royal Trouble," 6-27, a *People* magazine-like report on sensational London press accounts, gossiping about Charles and Di. Almond was accurate about the press reports, but guilty of the same tactics, using the "hook" approach to sensationalize, telling us at the very end of story that they still call each other darling and kiss in public.

Anderson, Harry. *Newsweek.* (★)
One of the newsweekly's prizewinning writers, Anderson just seems to be coasting these days, leaving the hard news to the other bigwigs on the foreign desk, like Rod Nordland, who then make mincemeat out of it. Part of the problem may be the institutionalization of the multiple byline: Anderson is listed as a senior writer, rarely dealing with domestic or economic issues. He comes up with a passable summary of the Argentinean military rebellion and President Alfonsin's subsequent difficulties, but he skims the top of the issue and only really gets his teeth into it towards the last paragraphs in "Aftershocks of the Dirty War," with Martin Andersen, 4-27. Later, contrariness seems to be his middle name concerning Alfonsin's control of his country, asserting the "showdown actually proved how *little* control he has over his men in uniform" and citing evidence that would support the opposite claim, "Argentina's Mixed Blessing," with Alma Guillermoprieto, 5-4. Better with "Settling In for a Long Stay," with John Barry, Ronald Henkoff and Anne Underwood, 9-28, a look at U.S. policy in the Persian Gulf which noted that in Washington "the resignation to a long stay is growing."

Asman, David. *The Wall Street Journal.* (★ ★ ★)
"Americas" column editor. A much better year, scooping everyone on important fiscal and tax policy breakthroughs in Latin America, among them Bolivia's tax rate reform. Primary attention on Mexico, "Has the Mexican Government Rigged the Oil Business?" 2-6, was a very detailed and focused examination of the economic devastation PEMEX has wrought. He examines Villa Hermosa, where the oil boom produced a population surge from 30,000 to 300,000 but where the boom has gone bust. The crisis in this capital of Tabasco reveals PEMEX's damage to the economy. With oil rig gluts, closing of efficient private enterprises, and on the verge of bankruptcy, unionized workers there still must be paid despite work stoppages. With "The PRI's 'Cure' in Southern Mexico," 3-3, he examines the rise of the left-wing PSUM as the significant minority party in the Oxaca and Chiapas, amid the background of poverty, backwardness and tension. Here, he reports, the PRI is wedded to a system of social-economic inequality. In "Spiritual Capital Is About All Brazil Has Left," 5-15, he gives us a sense of how "confidence in the Brazilian spirit" is about all that stands in the way of abject resignation to economic woes. An excellent interview with Miguel de la Madrid, "Is This Recovery for Real?" 9-10, informs us on the persepctive for "de-Echeverriazing" the Mexican economy.

Bangsberg, P.T. *The Journal of Commerce.* (★ ★ ★)
Hong Kong. Probably the best business reporter on the Asian NICs in the United States, Bangsberg is relentless in getting us pure, unvarnished information on matters vital to commerce and trade. In "Hong Kong Team Shows Optimism On New Trade Legislation in US," 2-10,

for example, he interviews Hamish MacLeod, Hong Kong's trade director, just back from talks in Washington full of gossip on the outlook for protectionism. "China Liberals Rebel Against Western Ideals," 2-14, reports the tension with creeping capitalism that almost every other reporter was dispatching, but quotes the minister of light industry on a "major reform" that will give factory managers "free reign." We're kept abreast with detailed explanations of statistics in such articles as "Hong Kong Boom Slows," 5-28. With all the fuss about Japanese semiconductors, it was interesting to learn that Malaysia is number three in this business, 5-22, yet facing "keen competition" from India. An important analytical piece, 4-8, with Edwin Unsworth, reports that "Europeans and Asians both fear that President Reagan's Irangate problems may have weakened his ability to fight protectionist legislation." One of the best this year: "South Korean Reform Welcomed By Investors," 7-1. The Korean stock market roared ahead after Roh Tae Woo's announcement of democratic reforms.

Barchard, David. *Financial Times.* (★ ★ ½)
Turkey. Interesting things going on in Turkey, which has been the fastest-growing, tax-slashing economy in Europe. In "Mr. Ozal Takes The High Ground," 9-14, readers must be persuaded that the Prime Minister "can claim to have removed an undemocratic shadow over Turkey's ambition to join the European Community while being assured, at the same time, that popular support for the pre-coup leaders is limited." An equally clear, balanced and authoritative article, 9-5, had already previewed the 9-6 referendum on political freedoms.

Barnard, Bruce. *The Journal of Commerce.* (★ ★)
London. Solid coverage of the whole European scene, with occasionally brilliant insights and facts on Britain. In "UK Readies Sanctions Against Japanese," 4-3, trade war against Japanese financial firms threatens to backfire, driving the whole business to Paris and Frankfurt. In "UK Poised to Retaliate Against Japan," 3-1, the UK again can't live with 'em, or without 'em. "Omens for Labor Are Grim," 6-16, reported that since Mrs. Thatcher took office, "the percentage of British families owning homes has increased from 52% to 66%, the percentage of people who own stock has risen from 7% to 19%, [and] the proportion of workers belonging to trade unions has declined from 30% to 23%...Labor is perceived as a party of losers."

Barnathan, Joyce. *Newsweek.* (NR)
Moscow bureau. She was very impressive in '86, with a vivid portrait of the "dissident" issue. Unfortunately, her byline is so often beneath someone else's in *Newsweek* that we can't rate her on individual efforts. We noted, however, her interview with Andrei Sakharov and Yelena Bonner shortly after his return from internal exile, "Vowing to Fight On," 1-5. Among the observations she elicited from Sakharov: "There is more *glasnost*, more and more openness in the press, in artistic works....This is very important...success...is possible only if glasnost exists. But glasnost alone is not enough. We have to wait and see how events develop." Also of worth, "Shcherbitsky: The Politburo's Untouchable," 5-18, a tight, timely profile on an Old Guard oppositionist to Gorbachev.

Barnes, Hillary. *Financial Times.* (★ ½)
Denmark. To understand Denmark (or Holland, or Belgium) is to begin to understand why European economies (except the U.K. and Turkey) are always stuck in the mud; Barnes sometimes provides a shovel. "High Cost of the Good Life," 3-20, notes that the government employs 30% of the labor force, and "today's high living standards are built on a net foreign debt equal to about 40 per cent of the gross domestic product" (for comparison, the fashionable nightmare of a trillion dollar U.S. foreign debt in 1992 would then only amount to 16% of GNP). In "Danish Love of Cosiness Overrides Poll Razzmatazz," 9-7, Barnes isn't quite convincing, arguing that "the distance between the political extremes in Denmark is slight." She thought the Danish stock market would fall if the Schlueter coalition lost, 9-8, and therefore had no explanation why the market instead fell 11.5% when the coalition won, 9-10. Perhaps the answer was hidden in the well-crafted "Danish Plan Aims to Sharpen Exports," 9-11, where the government appears mercantilist, pushing exports at the expense of domestic prosperity.

Barnes, John. *U.S.News & World Report.* (★ ★)
Middle East. Barnes digs beyond the headlines and comes up with some unusual angles. "One Dagger Not Aimed at America," 4-27, was a breezy one-pager about the relationship between the U.S. and Oman, and the role it plays in the Persian Gulf, with a fascinating mini-profile of Oman's "benevolent dictator," Sultan Qaboos. He can be tough as well in "Kuwait Rolls the Dice for High Stakes," 8-3, Barnes takes us precisely through the strategic ins and outs of reflagging from the Kuwaiti side. He had a good lead in "A 'Sea Change' in Arab Attitudes?" 11-23, on the Middle East summit: "It was billed as an emergency summit, a gathering of Arab League leaders desperate to begin reuniting an Arab world so fragmented that they had not even been able to meet for five years. Hemmed in by hatreds old and new and above all by the intensifying pressures of the Iran-Iraq War, last week's meeting in Amman was a monumental gamble for the forces in moderation. At the end of the four days of talks, those who risked the most won the day." Supporting evidence followed.

Barringer, Felicity. *The New York Times.* (★ ★)
Moscow. An especially fine feature writer, Barringer is very observant in catching signs of progress or unfulfillment on the promises of *glasnost*. She measures the rhetorical and substantive changes in Soviet human rights policies with "No Easing of Exit-Visa Battles for Many in Soviet," 1-11, finding little changed for Soviet Jews; they are still "chasing evanescent assurances" on migration, yet the number permitted to leave in 1986 may have actually dropped by 20%. A vivid picture of alienation among restless Soviet youth, "Suddenly, A Soviet Veil Is Lifted, Revealing Scenes of Bitter Youth," 2-16, illuminates with sociological insight; quoting a Soviet social scientist: "A young man may well see the situation as hopeless...[he] may work well, but there is a line beyond which there will be no reward for extra work." Very interesting on Pushkin's esteem in the USSR with "Soviet Vigils Held Widely for Pushkin," 2-15, but she left us wondering why — though we found the idea provocative. A fine reading on palpable signs of press *glasnost* with "Moscow Magazine Is Leader in New Openness," 3-22, reporting on the Soviet weekly *Ogonyok*. "Other newspapers have become increasingly provocative, but *Ogonyok* lives closest to the limits of the permissible." With a circulation of 1.5 million, it's on sale 9:00 am Saturday and sold out an hour later. Looking through *glasnost* to the darkness on the other side with "Despite Gorbachev Changes Punitive Psychiatry Lingers," 10-21; even while the Soviet press criticizes it, the barbaric practice continues.

Battersby, John D. *The New York Times.* (★ ½)
Johannesburg. The *Times* had planned to move former Moscow bureau chief Serge Schmemann to Johannesburg in 1987. Burned by the ragged performance of 1986 bureau chief Alan Cowell, however, the RSA wouldn't admit Schmemann. Battersby's reporting has restored the *Times* South Africa coverage to respectable standards. Though he's a South African himself, we attribute the improvement to professional standards, not nationality. A slow start with "7 Black Youths Killed in South Africa," 3-18, was police blotter level, without details on the striker demands, and we wondered why it was a front-pager. Much improved with "Botha Is Welcomed in Black Township," 6-5, he reported the enthusiastic welcome by hundreds of cheering Sharpesville blacks (the AP wire reports omitting it) and covered mayor Esau Mahlatsi's warning to Botha on his national council proposal: "an exercise in futility" if it doesn't lead to parliamentary participation of blacks and whites "on a par." Appropriately restrained analytically in "Pretoria Frees A Black Leader Jailed 23 Years," 11-6, he raises the right questions (is it a gesture to the ANC by Pretoria?) and provided enough material for us to suspect it was. On the massacres at Homoine, he interviewed survivors, and while referring to "Renamo's acts of terror against civilians," did at least acknowledge Renamo's denial of any involvement, "Mozambique Massacre Is Recounted," 7-24. We wonder, however, why he (and so many other journalists) haven't gotten around to reporting from Renamo-held territory in Mozambique.

Baum, Julian. *The Christian Science Monitor.* (★ ★ ½)
London. For most of '87 Baum reported from Beijing, his dispatches again astute on critical

political shifts and developments. But his treatment of economic news from China was skimpy, updates more than deep digging into the '87 dynamic, reducing a bit his previous three-star rating. "Whither Deng Xiaoping's reform policies?" was the big question early in the year, after Hu Yaobang's dismissal as Party Secretary. His January dispatches (1-14, 15, 20), covering the crackdown on Party intellectuals and the leadership shuffle were well abreast of the new developments, locating the failure to engineer an ideological and political framework for Deng's modernization thrust. "China's New Reformist Premier Fends Off Conservative Party Critics," 4-6, provided a solid picture of Zhao Ziyang's skill, redressing a conventional consensus that Deng's reforms were being shelved. He advanced the assessment that Deng had restored the shaken confidence of intellectuals and professionals regarding further reform initiatives, with the issue scheduled for top priority at the 13th Party Congress, 5-29. "In China's Heartland, Concern Is Over Prosperity, Not Politics," 7-28, perceptive, but he missed the opportunity to expand on the economic news, and a 7-15 report on the changes in rural China was too much of an update, no new ground turned on the economic picture. "China's Leaders Grease the Wheels for New Economic Reforms," 9-8, was an important description of the next phase of economic reform, and "U.S., China Struggle To Sew Up Textile Accord," 8-11, was a timely reading on China's move toward competitiveness, viewed from its push on textile exports vs. burgeoning US protectionism. But there wasn't nearly enough of this coverage.

Bering-Jensen, Henrik. *Insight.* (★ ★ ★)
One of the magazine's most reliable home-run hitters, Bering-Jensen seemed to vanish for much of the year, taking it easier after all the globetrotting he did in '86. He reviewed the situation in "Chirac's Political Challenge: Fighting Policy in the Streets," 2-2, detailing the setbacks to the "bulldozer" and the vulnerabilities of "cohabitation," working in ominous parallels to the 1968 unrest in France, but concluding the "show is still largely Chirac's." "Gorbachev: Who Is He, What Does He Want?" 3-30, was everything we wanted to know about Gorbachev, but couldn't seem to find out: it is a 10-best selection for the year. Bering-Jensen had another good cover story late in the year, "The Iron Lady's England," 12-14, a three-part panorama of the Margaret Thatcher era in the Commonwealth, giving us the scoop on her politics, economics, agenda, desire for social change and even her opposition, and, despite her warts, he's obviously admiring of Maggie: "Margaret Thatcher has become something of a mythic figure. With a 101-seat majority in Parliament and a string of three election victories, she has touched a record set by Lord Liverpool in the early 19th century. Indeed, early next year, she will become the longest-reigning British prime minister of the 20th century...In conversation, a civil servant recently referred to the prime minister as 'her majesty,' which somehow seems an understandable slip."

Bernstein, Richard. *The New York Times.* (★ ½)
Former Paris bureau chief, reassigned to the U.S., he made no headway over last year, still doing decent, sometimes good work, but rarely anything great. He presented rather a thin account of the race for France's Presidency in "A Shrewd Mitterand Rises Above The Fray," 7-5, as he flagged Francois Leotard, present Minister of Culture, for Pres. In Mozambique, again quite shallowly, he gave a rundown of the drought and civil war portraying only a two-dimensional view, "Outlook For Mozambique," 8-30. Bernstein, though, did have a front-pager, "AIDS Hits Western Europe," 3-9, in which he gave us a pretty good rundown on how AIDS is spreading and what demographic patterns it is following. He's gritty and unforgiving in "France Sentences Terrorist to Life," 3-1, giving verbatim the presiding judge's hard and fast, short and to the point ruling: "'No,' he said. 'There are no extenuating circumstances. Consequently, Georges Ibrahim Abdallah is sentenced to imprisonment for life.'"

Berthelsen, John. *The Asian Wall Street Journal.* (★ ★)
Reduced to dribs and drabs in *The Wall Street Journal*, we found him to be less of a resource, both because we didn't see as much of him, and because what we did see was of slightly lesser quality than last year. "Hong Kong's Posh Royal Jockey Club Has Inside Track for Scandal

Record," 6-23, was a light, breathless review of race-fixing in the Orient. In "Australian Beer Baron's Property Binge In Hong Kong Arouses Some Skepticism," 6-15, he gives us the dirt on Alan Bond, the America's cup winner and real estate wheeler-dealer, equally breathless, but with more solid information: "As for the glass-facade office complex on which the Australian tycoon has hung his name calling it Bond Center they say he may have paid too much money for the two towers, currently under construction. So, while Mr. Bond's admirers view him as a financial genius, his detractors say he has overextended his empire through dubious purchases that now must be paid off at a time of higher interest rates." He also did credible, bare-boned stories on the difficulties that the Singapore markets and economy had, both before and after the Crash of '87: "Singapore Institutes New Rules Today to Perk Up Trading in Sesdaq System," 8-3; "Ex-Broker Pleads Guilty to 1 Count In Singapore Case," 9-18; "...While Singaporeans Wonder If Tokyo Is Exporting Trade Woes," 10-7; and "Singapore Suffered Asia's Sharpest Drop, But Lessons of Past Help Market Survive," 11-4.

Betts, Paul. *Financial Times.* (★ ★ ½)
Taking Housego's desk in the Paris bureau, Betts settled further into the French scene. "A Question Of Political Subjectivity," 6-24, was light on pre-election ramblings on the health of the French economy, with a few quotes from Raymond Barre, but nothing much else. "Postcard Prince," 3-16, was business-like on Prince Rainier sprucing up Monaco, H.R.Highness stating: "I certainly don't want to see in Monaco some of the things I saw in Las Vegas. It was very depressing to see people in wheelchairs under the slot machines." Ah, royalty. "Ministry of Competitiveness," 6-15, was enlightening on structural changes in the French economy with this report on Industry Minister Alain Madelin's thrust toward risk-taking. This is not a rapid rupture with *dirigisme*, but in the details Betts uncovers, we get the clearest sense of the cultural revolution taking place in the country's business and industrial attitudes. "Letdown Fears Subside," 10-13, explains the contrast between supportive French and more hostile British views on the Channel Tunnel, the beneficial economic impact well-outlined here. "A Change of Mood But Not of Prospects," 9-21, moves from France to survey Angola's bid for IMF membership, in the process giving us further readings on the country's convoluted economic "reforms." With "France Takes Long View of Its Growing Links with Angola," 9-30, he draws out the picture of President Dos Santos' ability to rack up a Western stake in the country's economy.

Blum, Patrick. *Financial Times.* (★ ★)
Eastern Europe. Well-organized examinations of Austria, Yugoslavia and Romania this year, weaving statistics, quotes, details and analysis into a solid texture. "Yugoslavia," a *FT* survey, 6-10, was comprehensive on the economic crisis there; "Economy on a Bumpy Track," and "Bitter Medicine Proves Difficult for the Patient to Swallow" were very detailed, both abounding with relevant stats. Another survey, this one on "Vienna," 6-9, applies the same rigorous detailing, and we end up with a sense of the tensions in Austria as a whole, between deep conservatism and municipal socialism, particularly well-posited in "City Where the Past Lives On," 6-1.

Bohlen, Celestine. *The Washington Post.* (★ ★)
Moscow bureau. Very steady and productive in the number two spot here, her features were colorful, generally rich in detail, perceptive vignettes on life in the USSR. A particularly striking piece was that on individualism in the Soviet Union, "Soviets Get Right to Sell Services," 5-1, then a nice touch in "Gorbachev Challenged By Romania," 5-28, with the 5000 party officials rising 15 times on cue while cheering President Ceaucescu, telling us "the repetitions were so extended that an unsmiling Gorbachev at one point hesitated, not knowing whether to stand or sit." Her August series on "Gorbachev's Impact In The Provinces," was interesting, although slow at the outset, with the outstanding piece coming at the end where she wrote a spirited feature on the Baikal-Amur line's project history in "Soviet Rail Line Pushes Ahead At The Speed Of Bureaucracy," 8-19.

Boroweic, Andrew. *The Washington Times.* (★ ★ ★)
Chief roving foreign correspondent. A veteran foreign reporter, winner of several journalistic awards and author of two books, Boroweic is one of the few members of the old school who is still working like a cub. Munich, Geneva, Bonn, Amman, Cairo, and Paris were among Boroweic's '87 datelines, and he seems to be well versed in local sources in each city. "Europe Wary of Gorbachev's Charm," 2-19, was early on the West European Kremlin watchers' cautions on Gorbachev's reforms. "Swiss Intelligence Defenseless Against Huge KGB Intrusion," 3-17, was a description of KGB infiltration of Switzerland: "there were...700 Soviet agents and at least twice as many locally recruited Swiss 'moles' or 'sleepers' whose tasks include possible cooperation with special Soviet troops known as 'Spetsnaz.' Such troops prepared the ground for the Soviet invasion of Afghanistan in 1979." In "New PLO Program Placates Radicals, Chills Peace Efforts," 4-27, he reports that despite earlier PLO reports, Muhammad Abu Abbas was re-elected to the organization's Executive Committee. "'Venezia '87' Platitudes Leave World Little Changed," 6-11, began with a downer: "There were no winners or losers in the 'Venezia '87' summit, which ended yesterday with a mix of diplomatic platitudes, cosmetic agreements, confusion and pledges in which few believe," but the rest is competent and solid. On the Soviet front, Boroweic again showed flair by reporting on the Shultz-Shevardnadze huddle, 11-25, one day after a Munich story about how Radio Free Europe analysts are looking at the challenges to Gorbachev. He captured true, as opposed to declaratory, the feelings of the NATO allies about the INF Treaty in 8-31's "NATO's Experts Cautious on Expectations for Nuclear Pact," and poured some cold analytical water on those who hope for better Western European cooperation on defense with a 11-16 report on problems in Franco-W.German armed cooperation. He's very valuable in his current slot.

Boudreaux, Richard. *Los Angeles Times.* (★ ★)
Managua bureau. An impressive start in the *LA Times*' newest foreign bureau, handling Nicaragua with aplomb and Panama with a perceptive touch. "A War Fuels 'Crazy' Nicaraguan Inflation," 9-20, focused sufficiently on Sandinista mismanagement, was detailed and factual, Boudreaux doing real reporting on this. He provided new information on the shift of sentiment and support for the contras within Nicaragua's Jinotega province in "Secret Rural Network Helps Sustain Contras," 11-5, finding evidence to support the following: "Before, if you collaborated, someone would inform on you. Now, everyone is collaborating, and the Sandinistas know there is nothing they can do." Informative on Panama, he reported the strike-breaking strategy aimed against the Civic Crusade, "Panama Opposition Stages Rally, Strike," 8-18, threats by the government to allow looting of businesses and shops that shut down. "Panama's Domestic Strife Spilling Over into Canal," 9-7, was quick on implications there: "The day they [the opposition] sense the U.S. is not actively opposing Noriega...they will shut down the canal." One of his best, "Panama Turmoil Leaves Noriega Still Entrenched," 9-21, analytics and reporting well-balanced.

Boustany, Nora. *The Washington Post.* (★ ★ ½)
Beirut bureau. An intrepid reporter, whose reports from Lebanon are never fatigued or drained, she provided a graphic chronicle all year of this country's continued dissolution. She had some neat little tidbits with "Failure To Make Deal Riled Waite's Captors," 2-5, on how Terry Waite was himself tricked into being taken as hostage. Boustany had an amazing story of life inside the Burj al Barajinah camp, with the only way in and out being "the Passage of Death,' a 200-yd stretch of land besieged by Shiite Moslem Amal fighters "trying to contain Palestinian guerrillas who also live inside." We made "Braving 'The Passage Of Death,'" 4-5, a 10-best pick for the year in foreign reporting. She also gave us an ominous look at the Iranian influence in Lebanon, "Iran Uses Void In Lebanon To Expand Network Of Ties," 7-19, that was complete and frightening.

Branigan, William. *The Washington Post.* (★ ★ ★)
Managua. Moving from Manila to Managua, Branigan's strong reporting skills excelled in

1987, and he became the journalist we most relied upon in covering Nicaragua. Alert, rigorous, tenacious, he pushed against every constraint to keep up. "Inflation Leaps, Output Falls in Nicaragua," 8-18, provided timely, critical data on the economic deterioration. "Graffiti Foot Soldiers Unrelenting," 5-25, sifts the crucial detail out of the morass, in a revealing picture of Sandinista elementary education. "Opposition Newspaper Again in Row With Sandinistas," 5-15, well-organized, with relevant quotes and background provided. His best, "Pattern of Abuses Laid to Sandinistas," 5-18, was a thorough, rigorously documented report on the Sandinista violations of human rights in Nicaragua. We hope the *Post* keeps him in Managua — but will Ortega, Borge and Co. tolerate him much longer?

Breen, Tom. *The Washington Times.* (★ ★)
Replaced midyear by Marc Lerner, Breen returned to DC as a political writer. The dispatches he sent from Manila as Southeast Asia bureau chief were somewhat improved this year, but still came up short in spots. "Peasants Find Quest for Peace Too Costly," 2-20, was a roundup of eyewitness reports on the 2-10 Lupao massacre, now being called the My Lai of the Philippines. His "Ramos Begins Shake-up of Filipino Troops," 3-2, was comprehensive on the complexities: RAM (Reform the Armed Forces Movement) and the Guardians Brotherhood disbanded; GB strong Marcos supporters. RAM wants Enrile in Malacanang Palace; and Defense Minister Ileto acknowledges the armed forces are unprofessional, lacking in morale and in need of reform. "Coup Rumors Rumble Through Philippines Capital Again," 3-18, reports on the Nueva Ecija province incident and Ramos' indication that he's growing weary of the job. In "Marxist-Led Rebels Insist They Really Aren't Communist," 4-23, Breen's off-center with the National People's Army company for nine days, reporting "we are nationalists." His "Priest Takes Reins In Tribal Region," 6-10, was confusing on a priest who turned communist head of a regional interior administration in the Philippines. "New Philippines Senate President Opposes U.S. Bases," 7-1, gave us some detail on Jovito Salongo, but not enough to satisfy.

Bridges, Tyler. Freelance. (★ ★)
A hardworking stringer whose dispatches often appear in *The Washington Post*, working the Latin American beat, he added more economic detail this year to his reporting. He gave us a crisp account of the Bolivian government being torn by big-buck temptations appearing in *The Washington Post* with "Corruption Hampers Bolivian Outriding Effort," 8-15. Covering Chile in *The Wall Street Journal*, he came up with a voting analysis piece telling us that only 2 million out of the 8 million voters have registered for the September 1988 election. "Voter Apathy Is Good News For The General," 9-11, showed that the opposition is badly divided on key issues, all to the advantage of Pinochet.

Brooke, James. *The New York Times.* (★ ★ ★ ★)
Africa correspondent. There's a large portion of the globe the media unfortunately notices only when earthquakes, other natural disasters, famines or coups occur there. James Brooke is therefore precious, almost single-handedly overcoming this deficiency, at least for Africa. His crisscrossing the continent left us panting to keep up with his prodigious efforts all year — so many outstanding dispatches that we're hard-pressed on which to cite. "Senegal Hails Vendors Home from 5th Avenue," 1-2, very informative, an absorbing piece exemplifying his resourceful knack for new angles. "Cuba's Strange Mission in Angola," 2-1 (Sunday magazine), comprehensive. Solid reports on the situation in Ethiopia — politics, economics, religion, crucial history covered 3-9, 3-15, 3-22, with anecdotal relish thrown in: Col. Mengitsu orders postage stamps with his likeness, but they fall off envelopes. The problem, the secret police report is that "Ethiopians are spitting on the wrong side." "AIDS Danger: Africa Seems of Two Minds," 1-4, early into this aspect, followed up with "AIDS Is Now Spreading to Populous West Africa," 4-15. Strategic geopolitical savvy with "In African Diplomacy, Israel Gains a Toehold," 7-27. On white cabinet ministers in Black Africa, 8-20, an "oddity" nowhere else reported. "Old Scourge Loses Ground in West Africa," 9-3, on the eradication of black

flies that cause river blindness, the "old man's" disease. "Francs and Fromage," 10-7, on the French responding to President Lansana's appeals for help in post Sekou Toure's Guinea, where "Conakry...[remains] much the colonial capital of 30 years ago — without 30 years of maintenance." The touch of a professional, almost insider's sense, in "Burkina Faso Coup Poorly Received," 10-26, reporting from Ouagadougou on the tenuous, unconsolidated hold of Capt. Blaise Campaore after the slaying of former head of state Capt. Thomas Sankara.

Brookes, Geraldine. *The Asian Wall Street Journal.* (★)
Australia. Strictly a feature writer, if trimmed a bit, her articles could fill the A-hed spot regularly. But the quirky, cutesy, amusing A-hed style detracts from what we need to know about down under. "Foreign Banks' Euphoria Turns to Gloom in Australia," 2-5, observed a "soft economy, [with] tough competition [that will] force newcomers to lower sights." "Politician Who Seeks to Lead Australians Isn't Easy to Follow," 3-13, a profile of Sir Johannes Bjelke-Petersen, Queensland's premier, who ran on the NP ticket for Prime Minister. It seems begrudging, citing that the rural vote outweighs the urban, with bizarre-like acts and the opposition's charge he's mentally incompetent and "close to the bottom of the range for brain-damaged speakers." In "Aussie Workplace: Theatre of the Absurd," 4-6, was a frivolous, featurish piece on some outrageous demands of Australian unions, such as the request for "tea money" by the workers building an entertainment center because "the appetizing aromas wafting from the nearby restaurants were 'creating hardship in the gastronomical expectations of the employees.' (The claim was later dropped.)" We had to dig for the insights on weak and remote management amid the unbusinesslike presentation. Her piece on the upcoming Parliamentary elections, "Australian Election Pits Man Against Distance," 7-10, was silly, giving us how the Aussies get to the polls, and not what they do, or might do, once they get there. What about the election?

Browning, E.S. *The Wall Street Journal.* (★ ★)
Paris bureau. A good portfolio from Browning, but not quite enough to satisfy our taste for comprehensiveness. His stronger feats came at the beginning of the year in covering the French rail strikes. Comparing the threat of French strikers to the anti-inflation policy of Chirac, he cited *Liberation*'s analogy to the situation of Reagan and PATCO and that of Thatcher and the National Coal Board, "Strikes Present Make or Break Situation for Conservative French Prime Minister," 1-6. He follows it up with the loss of face for Chirac and the gains for Mitterand and Barre in "Strikes Recede in France Leaving Chirac with Battered Image and Stronger Foes," 1-12. Later pieces were less reporting and more portrait pieces such as the charming "France's 'August Bachelors' Seek Love," 8-25, and "After Stumble, French Quick-Photo Whiz Plans Fast Comeback With New Products," 9-2, presenting Serge Crasnianski of Kis France, S.A. in good detail.

Bruce, James. *The Journal of Commerce.* (★)
Sao Paulo. Brazil gets decent coverage in the major newspapers, so the competition is tough. "Brazil's Industry Wary of Debt Moratorium," 2-24, didn't match *The New York Times* on details. "Brasilia Launches Economic Program," 6-15, was timely, but the interpretation was ambiguous. We have to read between the lines to figure out that stock in the state oil company rose 16.6% because of an expected cut in subsidies to fuel alcohol, and that "bars and restaurants are marking their prices up 20% at a time" in anticipation of devaluation and a price freeze.

Bruce, Peter. *Financial Times.* (★ ★)
Bonn. Above-average depth on German economic policy. Grasps a difficult story, in "Doubts Over Bundesbank Moves," 1-23, that confused even his colleagues, Andrew Fisher and Stewart Fleming, on the same day. Bruce quotes a noted German economist saying the German central bank's moves were "contradictory" cutting the discount rate, but also buying-up German marks to tighten their supply. U.S. journalists, were instead baffled about why the illusory German "easing" didn't strengthen the dollar. In "Bonn Tax Reform Proposals Fail to Elicit More

Than Faint Praise," 3-3, we get an early warning of Finance Minister Stoltenberg backing away from lower tax rates, proposing to raise consumer taxes. "Economists Predict Sharp Rise in W. German Public Borrowing," 4-14, shows five influential economic institutes nonetheless crossing their fingers, hoping that "tax reform planned for 1990 will be brought forward," and "that the Bundesbank will be liberal."

Buell, Barbara. *BusinessWeek.* (★ ★ ★)
Tokyo. No. 2 in the bureau, with Larry Armstrong the chief, Buell is who we look to for close reports on the unfolding Japanese political economy, generally close to the power curve. In "The Political Rivals Jockeying for Japan's Top Job," 4-20, she does as well as any in surveying the struggle at the top of the LDP, and the impact of the trade and exchange-rate crisis on the political outcome. Her commentary in "Japan Just Can't Believe It's a Superstar," 7-13, is illuminating: "From schoolchildren to pensioners, the Japanese still repeat in creed-like fashion: 'We are a small island nation with few natural resources.' This perception of vulnerability shapes the national mind-set," with a quote that the Japanese have both a superiority and an inferiority complex. Her stock-market reports, before and after the Crash, were always smart and useful, "Why the Japanese Bull is Having a Feast," 3-23, noting the 250 p/e ratio at Nippon T&T Corp., 2-9, but also "Many steelmakers, banks and railroads are carrying properties on their books at as little as 1% of their current market values." In "Bloody Monday Didn't Bloody the Tokyo Exchange Much," 11-16, her report conveys a calm as the exchange moves further toward deregulation even as "the rest of the world lurches back toward regaining some control over financial activity." With Armstrong, her "Rise and Rise of the Japanese Yuppie," 2-16, is fun and absorbing on the flush young spenders. "Strong Silent Japan Starts to Speak Up," 11-30, is very timely, as the Crash has Japanese leaders out of character in "letting fly with blunt public statements about the U.S.'s ability to manage its economy." Good stats on the feverish housing boom, 1.8 million units in the summer quarter.

Burgess, John. *The Washington Post.* (★ ★ ½)
Tokyo. Almost three stars, but after three years reporting from Japan he didn't quite make the breakthroughs we'd hoped for on economic news. "Japanese Brace for U.S. Steps," 3-27, was an excellent report on Tokyo's shock "at the depth's of Washington's anger over trade in semi-conductors." Burgess's dispatches bring some needed perspective to the zero-sum competitiveness model, catching their disposition toward the private sector and eschewal of the xenophobia exhibited by Americans. "The Sound Not Heard Around the World," 4-13, reports voluntary restrictions by Japan of digital tape recorders in the U.S. (Their quality is so good, they fear U.S. recording companies will convince Congress to restrict them.) He was getting close to grasping the economic dynamics, as in "Japan Preparing New Economic Policy," 4-4, with good detail presented. But "U.S.-Japan Relationship," 8-3, was surprisingly weak, on the level of the *Weekly Reader.* Ending his three years as NE Asia correspondent with a zippy "Japan's White Collar Clones," 8-23, a day in the life of the "salaryman" — the "industrial warrior." His "Sun Never Sets on the World's Linked Markets," 11-1, was a primer, hardly worth the lead of the Sunday business section.

Burns, John F. *The New York Times.* (★ ★ ★)
Toronto. We cited Burns in both the 1986 and '87 *MediaGuide*s with four stars as the best foreign correspondent around, but in '87 he moved to the Canadian outback after several stunning years in Moscow and Beijing, and his production coasted. He's still marvelous at everything he does, but there was one big story we wanted to read out of Canada in 1987 and Burns did not come through for us: Why is Prime Minister Brian Mulroney and his Tories so unpopular and how did the NDP get on top in the polls? Burns flirted with the story in "As Trudeau Ends Silence, Storm Begins," 6-1, a solid outline of the reemerging threat to federalism in Mulroney's Meech Lake accord, giving Quebec more political flexibility. Closer still with "For Canada's Chief, 3-Year Old Victory Turns Sour," 8-23, was the best we saw on Mulroney's decline, again loosely linking this to his concessions to *Quebecois*' demands

for special status. "Rising Canadian Party Scores at Polls," 7-22, was sharp on the volatile political state of the Dominion as the New Democrats emerge as contenders for power. We sensed the shadow of the story in his account of Rene Levesque's funeral, "Under the Fleur-de-Lis, All Canada Hails Levesque," 11-6, a beautifully written piece with the tension of Pierre Trudeau who opposed Meech Lake showing up at the wake, but skipping the funeral. "Why Canada Walked Out of the Trade Talks," 9-27, was timely, welcome reporting, highlighting Canada's refusal to give up domestic protectionism and subsidies. A classic feature, "Across the Ice in a 26-Wheel Rig," 2-17, is a colorful account of Canada's intrepid truckers who supply gold miners on the country's last frontier. "Canada Waits on the Back Burner," 3-29, a routine wrap-up on Reagan's scheduled trip, done well. "Canada's West Feeling Neglected," 5-31, brisk, informative. His last material from China appeared in "A Reporter's Odyssey in Unseen China," 2-8 (Sunday magazine), finding a lot of tolerance for making money, very insightful anecdotes in fresh reports from areas of China inaccessible to foreigners since the 1930s.

Butler, Steven B. *Financial Times.* (★ ½)
London. Back from Southeast Asia at the close of '87, his reports were generally good spot accounts, but with little depth. A more comprehensive report, "Vietnam Sweeps Away The Old Guard," 2-18, gives us the Vietnamese version of the cabinet shuffle, 13 ministers dismissed, 18 new appointments announced, with a partial resolution of the power struggle going on since the Congress convened in December. The shake-up reported was prompted by grass roots pressure due to the economic crisis (about 60 people per day die from starvation in Vietnam), and the changes represented a clear victory for new party Secretary General Nguyen Van Linh. More typical were "A Painful Transition." 5-7, which saw the reforms of Vietnam's "new leaders" as the beginning of the radical alteration of the structure of the economy, overdoing it and lacking depth on what sort of phenomenon is operating in Vietnam, and "Hanoi Wants To Welcome Washington Back," 6-16, on Vietnam's eagerness for the U.S. to come back in order to "wean" it from its dependence on Moscow.

Chesnoff, Richard. *U.S.News & World Report.* (★ ½)
Senior correspondent for Western Europe, Chesnoff combines competent reporting with a clean writing style, and the result is crisp and sharp dispatches. Although he doesn't dig deeply, he will sometimes come up with something not seen elsewhere. "Liechtenstein: A Mouse that Roars," 6-22, gave us a peek at a country laughing all the way to the bank, or, a country that according to a Zurich banker "where the Swiss go when *they* hide money." In "Qadhafi Magic: Turning Defeat to Verbal Victory," 4-13, Chesnoff detailed Muammar's struggles and his resilience and his retreat from the war in Chad, with a nice quote at the end from Fathi Omar: "America is stupid if it thinks it will solve its problems by killing Qadhafi...the secret of his power is that there are 3 million Qadhafis." His best and most compelling piece was "France Brings Barbie And Itself To Trial," 5-18, which gently drew us in with "Some say he was there himself that spring morning when they came for the children of Izieu. If so, he watched with his hawklike eyes lest one small 'enemy of the Reich' escape, keeping count as they were torn from their protectors and tossed like parcels onto the truck that took them to the ovens of Auschwitz."

Chira, Susan. *The New York Times.* (★ ★ ★)
Tokyo correspondent. She keeps her three-star rating, producing some of the year's best reporting on the economic side of the Japanese (and Korean) scene. "A Job Crunch Jolts Japan," 1-18, the best account on the $26 billion cost of 900,000 surplus workers, was written as if she were covering "local" developments, jam packed with information. "Japan Weighing Steps to Ease Trade Dispute," 4-1, was a timely, well-organized wrap-up on the issue. Very good job examining the Japanese consensus on "food security," with "And in the 14th Generation Will Farming Perish?" 6-5, quoting economist Kenichi Ohme: "It's not the lack of land that forces poor living and residential conditions....[it's] that we have a lack of prosperity as a whole." In "Nakasone Asserts Toshiba Betrayed Japan with Sales," 7-15, she reports

his *mea culpa* speech before the Diet, and signs of a growing blacklash, many Japanese not sharing his view on culpability. She gives us good numbers, details on economic disparities in Korea, "Thousands Gather in Seoul to Mark Democratic Gains," 8-16, and gets into the stiff tests of the government's democratic commitments with "Seoul, In Switch, Moves to Resolve Hyundai Dispute," 8-19.

Christian, Shirley. *The New York Times.* (★ ★ ★)
Buenos Aires bureau chief. Rarely does a news story come across with the crisp drama of a good short story, but she produced one with "Visit by Alfonsin Peacefully Ends Argentine Mutiny," 4-20, capturing the intensity, the suspense and relief at the successful facing down of mutinous troops by a leader and whole nation. On the margin reporting with "Argentine Officers Resisted General," 4-24, flagging an emerging, new high-command structure more responsive to the concerns of the mutineers than to Pres. Alfonsin. The best of the foreign correspondents on Chile in 1987, she alerted us on 3-23 to the growing disillusion of the non-violent opposition with the extreme left as the methods of the Chilean Communist Party and allies were revealed. "Chile After the Pope: A Mood of Accommodation," 4-13 was a dramatic account of the difference Chileans notice in Pinochet after his 42 minutes with Pope John Paul II. From Bolivia, 7-27, a good update with new information on the effort to combat cocaine exports, reports strong opposition to US-Bolivian efforts by the Federation of Peasants of the Tropics. "Bolivia's Struggle to Revive Economy," 8-6, was useful, noting more taxes being paid there now, though she missed the tax reform in her report (but so did everyone else except the *WSJ*'s David Asman). She also brought new information into her wrap-up on the Peronists' comeback in the September elections, reporting 9-8 "the other political forces that gained ground were various smaller parties advocating free-market ideas and a rapid reduction in the role of the state in the economy."

Claiborne, William. *The Washington Post.* (½ ★)
Johannesburg. Moving from Jerusalem to Johannesburg last year, his initial dispatches suggested that the *Post*'s southern Africa coverage would stay competitive, and some of Claiborne's reports were above routine. "The Other Side of Disinvestment," (*Weekly*), 12-22-86, did a good job noting the receding of "social responsiblity" programs with U.S. corporate disinvestment. "South African Black Tells Informer's Tale," 3-10, was one of his best reports, confirming the East Bloc training of ANCers as well as existence of ANC prison camps in Angola. But he's too frequently routine. On the elections, "Botha Is Gambling on Foes' Quarrels," 1-2, was a step above the wires. A bit better, on the constitutional convention in Natal, "Down But Not Out in Natal," 6-1, a useful update. But his sin wasn't mere routinism. Claiborne's ideological model intruded far too much all year. "S. African Jews on a Tightrope," 3-21, was superficial reporting, debilitated by dubious assertions (Taiwan attracted to tribal homelands because of low wages and lack of unions). His ideological model becomes obvious in "Waiting Is Angola's Pastime," 7-26, blaming the devastated economy on colonialism. "With the help from...the Soviet Union, Cuba, Bulgaria, East Germany, China and Vietnam, however, Angola is groping toward a more efficient system." Unfortunately, there was too much of that all year, diminishing the *Post*'s credibility on Southern Africa coverage.

Clines, Francis X. *The New York Times.* (★ ★ ★)
London bureau. A well-earned boost in this talented journalist's rating, he delighted us with superbly constructed features, light, warm, yet keenly perceptive readings from London to Moscow. In "Dutch Fear: AIDS Cases' Last Stop," 4-15, Clines spared us nothing in reporting the painful detail of the Netherlands' fear of an increase in immigration of foreign AIDS patients, from the U.S. and around the world, because of liberal attitudes towards euthanasia. In a lively, happier feature, "C. Parkinson Now Grateful To Fill Time," 9-25, he told us of a new principle: "The chief product of a hugely automated society is a widespread and deepening sense of boredom." Frankie's Law? Sometimes reduced to reporting on tragedies, Clines helps to make us care: "Memories of Sudden Terror," 3-8, on the overturned ferry boat; and

"Poignant Death on the Border Opens Hearts in All of Ireland," 12-7, which said "By the normal pace of Irish atrocity, the story of Miss Wilson's demise might have slipped from general sight by now into the local annals of Irish fratricide that darken the border crossroads. But the circumstances of her death in reassuringly squeezing the hand of her father, Gordon, who lay stricken alongside under the rubble, and then expressing her farewell to life are still being recounted well beyond, apparently affecting in particular to the politics of Dublin." In Moscow, we learned that "Moonshine Is Undermining Moscow's Temperance," 11-16, sounding breezily featurish, but well-stocked with information.

Cockburn, Patrick. *Financial Times.* (★ ★ ★)
Moscow. An indefatigable correspondent who seemed able to keep pace with the three-man *NYT* bureau in tracking *perestroika* and *glasnost*, and at times get a step ahead of it. Gorbachev provided an endless story for Moscow reporters, and Cockburn seized the opportunity. In "Why the Mould is Breaking Up," 3-27, he notes that "the shift of people from the villages to the cities, the spread of higher education...and a generation which has known neither famine nor war all mark a break with the past greater in its effect on the lives of ordinary people than the perestroika (restructuring) and glasnost (openness)....Social and economic development of the country has already tipped the balance between society and state in favour of the former." Nobody unraveled the story of *perestroika* this year, but few came as close as Cockburn to getting us inside. Cockburn quotes skeptical Soviet economists with good effect in "Gorbachev and the Committee," 6-24, which we cite as one of the 10-best foreign dispatches of the year. If the price system isn't allowed to work, says one, "then all the other reforms are useless." If the price system were allowed to work, the bureaucracy would be useless, so they fight real reform. Another article, 10-8, leaves "one question in people's minds: 'Is the leadership planning to solve all the problems of the economy by lowering the people's living standards?'"

Cody, Edward. *The Washington Post.* (★ ½)
Paris bureau. Frequently off to the Iran/Iraq front, it was *adieu* too frequently for the French political economic scene, an editor's decision that hurt. Cody chipped in with his AIDS piece while in Belgium as African seropositives were being expelled and cries of racism were echoing, "Belgium AIDS Tests Trigger Protests," 3-21. Later in the year, from Teheran, Cody did rather ordinary work. "Iran Says It Mines the Gulf," 8-21, was a straight report, telling us just that, and why: "to protect Iranian coastal installations...not inflict damage to oil tankers recently struck by mines in the Sea of Oman and on the Arab side of the Gulf." His piece on Islam in Iran as the *Komiteh*'s power increased told us nothing new of the intense religious zeal within the war-torn country, "A Growing Islamic Fervor Is Transforming Iran," 8-25. Even reporting from Paris, his dispatches often dealt with issues well removed from France. "Cambodian Opposition Figures Plan Talks," 12-5, datelined Paris, dealt with the announcement of an agreement between Prince and rebel leader Norodom Sihanouk and Cambodian Prime Minister Hun Sen to "work for a political solution to Cambodia's long and bloody conflict." Also from Paris, Cody reported that Yegor Ligachev was quoted as saying he and Gorbachev are "on the same wavelength" on reforms in *Le Monde*, "High Soviet Official Sees Kremlin Unity," 12-4. He did have periodic reports on France, or French politics, such as "France Decides to Build Own Advanced Warplane," 6-21, but not enough to keep us up.

Cohen, Roger. *The Wall Street Journal.* (★ ★ ½)
Rio de Janeiro bureau. We'd suggested last year that he be sent from the Miami bureau to South America; he seemed to moving ahead of the press corps with an appetite for taking on economics along with political reporting. The *WSJ* set him up in a Rio bureau, a good move that will pay off, we think. He's still best at the politics of the region, but did not make much headway on the dizzy economics of Brazil, drawn too often to describing the net result of poverty and maldistribution of income, the easy route. A consistently vivid writer, Cohen's most prominent pieces included the brisk and impressive contrast of Brazil and Mexico, where

he psychoanalyzed the two nations, "Brazil Stays Buoyant, Mexico is Dispirited In The Face of Troubles," 3-24, that rang true, the Brazilians believing they have a destiny of greatness. When the long struggle over the finance ministry brought forth a new chief, Luis Carlos Bresser Pereira, Cohen gave us a quickie profile "Brazilians Name A Finance Minister Who Is Likely to Seek Debt Compromises," 4-29, that warned us about the new man simply by stating some of his known views. Cohen puts his best foot forward in analyzing the Brazilian Democratic Movement Party, quoting and detailing Presidential candidates and their promised reforms, noting that the survival of the PMDB depends on the "Bresser" economic plan, "Brazil's Ruling Party Headed For Breakup," 7-21. He also came up with a gripping story of twins stolen by an Argentinean police officer, "Custody Battle: Fight Over Twin Boys Illustrates Grim Legacy Of Argentina's Junta," 8-27. A major front-page wrap-up effort, "Republic at Risk," 11-18, disappoints, yet another eyewitness account of deprivation.

Colitt, Leslie. *Financial Times.* (★ ★ ★)
Central/Eastern Europe. Some really fine work this year, broadening our knowledge of what's stirring and quavering in the East Bloc as *glasnost* winds move westward. Czechoslovakia was his main beat, but Colitt spotted and covered shifts in Hungary and East Germany as well. "Czechoslovakia and E.Germany Blow Cool on Gorbachev Reforms," 2-12, was the first report to provide serious detail on the cold shoulder Gorbachev's reforms were receiving from Party leaders there. Colitt can also condense and tightly present fresh economic news, as in "Setback for East Bloc Countries," 4-7, their economies strained. "The Pollution Threat from East to West," 2-13, we'd seen done elsewhere, but all with an outside-looking-in approach, while Colitt reported the acknowledgment throughout the East Bloc that its industries were indeed spreading filth. Excellent detail on the winds of change in Czechoslovakia during the spring: "Springtime Jitters for Mr. Husak," 4-4, unveils the uneasy situation facing the Czech party on the eve of Gorbachev's visit, as officials remind him that "some people" who talk up his reforms are really cloaking their "anti-socialist" activities. In a "A Mild Prague Spring," 4-21, he examines the prospects for reform, despite seeing an increasing awareness that the country has reached the end of its economic rope, with most economists not confident about the outlook for reform. Great detail in "Prague Has Another Try at Economic Freedom," 9-22, he explores the signs of some central economic decentralization in "The Necessity of Reform," 10-9. Despite low key, but successful, attempts at reform in agriculture and small private enterprise, he reports the strong hold the state keeps on these initiatives, quoting Finance Minister Jaromir Zak: "The state will make sure no one gets rich on this." "Senior Hungarian Official Assails Austerity Policy," 10-2, reports the widespread sentiment among party members for spokesmen who denounce the lack of alternatives to austerity. "E. Berlin Rejects Reform," 10-30, was an important dispatch on resistance there, reporting the party's chief ideologist Kurt Hager's admonition that the country cannot introduce reforms because it's on the "sensitive dividing line" between capitalism and communism.

Contreras, Joseph. *Newsweek.* (★)
Mexico City bureau. Adequate on the politics of Mexico, less so with El Salvador, but with a weaker grasp of their economies. "The Fickle Finger of a President," 1-12, gave us a routine profile of contenders for de la Madrid's successor in Mexico, giving the edge to Bartlett and del Mazo, but alert enough on Salinas' "infighting skills," to advise he "should not be underestimated." He was confused in El Salvador, not being able to come to grips with why the economy was in a shambles, "Duarte's Unkept Promises," 3-2. "A Political Spilt in Mexico," 7-6, introduces the Cardenas card, but overall is analytically bland. Better with detail, "The Far East Goes South," (with Joseph Schwartz), 6-22, updating the *maquiladoras* operation with a report on Japan's entry there.

Coone, Tim. *Financial Times.* (★ ★)
Buenos Aires bureau. His economic reports more descriptive than analytic, he still has a critical enough eye for the important nuance to produce fresh information. In "Sluggish Argentine

Economy Handicaps Pact,'' 2-6, we get as much economic detail on Brazil as Argentina here, as Coone examines the differences between their economies (as different as "the tango and the samba") that beset hopes of an integration plan. "Argentina Pins Fiscal Hope on Tax Amnesty," 2-16, gave a bit of extra detail, noting that a mere 29,000 Argentines out of 1.6 million tax creditors pay 84% of the government's total revenue from personal taxation. "People Unite to Save Alfonsin at Darkest Hour," 4-21 covers the abortive Easter Week rebellion adequately, but perhaps caught up in the euphoria, optimistically concludes that "Argentines have finally managed to shake off a tradition of military involvement in the country's politics and to stand up to their threats." (The next day another insurrection took place). "Argentina's 'Black' Economy Becomes a Fact of Life," 10-13, a great report, full of details on what keeps the country's economy from grinding to a halt. People simply ignore taxation and employment regulations, and only 39% of the active workforce over 14 years of age works in the formal economy. "Uruguay Army Comes Under Debate," 10-16, Coone examines the strains and tensions that are mounting in the country's fragile democracy as a referendum to overturn amnesty for armed forces activities during the period of military rule gets on the ballot.

Cowell, Alan. *The New York Times.* (★)
Athens bureau chief. In 1987, fortunately for him and for the *Times* credibility as "paper of record," Cowell was shifted from Johannesburg to Athens. "A Farewell to South Africa," 1-25 (Sunday magazine), were ruminations on his experience as the former bureau chief and did nothing to dispel our conviction that he belonged elsewhere. His fiery unrestraint of 1986 was replaced by a tendency for the blahs this year. Some feature-like material, "Greeks Mark a Rite Born in Paganism," 3-3 on their "clean Monday" ritual and "Linguist Pleads for a Glory That Was Greek," 4-19 on the impoverishment of the language since teaching classical Greek was abolished in 1976, were both with points of interest — but certainly not worthy of the front page. Better work with "The Bulldozer's Progress," 3-24, profiling the conservative mayor of Athens, a prime contender for leadership of the New Democracy opposition. Reports on the Iran-Iraq war tended to be roundups of various analysts' and diplomats' perceptions, as in "Quandary in Teheran," 7-24, and on the Kurds and Shiite underground in "Iraqis Are Facing a Growing War From Within," 9-22. This can be useful, but quoting an Iraqi "analyst" that "Even the [Iraqi] Shia cannot accept the idea of an Islamic Republic dependent on Iran" begged for some verification. "Slim Vote Ends Turkish Political Ban," 9-8, a routine wrap-up on the referendum to restore political freedoms to former politicians.

Crossette, Barbara. *The New York Times.* (★ ★ ★)
Bangkok bureau chief. Impressive in 1987, providing fresh, critical material from throughout Southeast Asia, starting with a very skillful interview with Singapore's PM Lee Kuan Yew, 12-22-86, discussing China's economic reforms and its improving relationship with the Pacific Rim nations. New material on Indonesia: "A Shift in Indonesia's Attitude," 1-26, on the growing disposition for privatization, and "In Indonesia, the Moslems Are Changing," 2-5, very sharp on Indonesian Islam as a model. "Thais Tense as Officers Demonstrate," 2-5, has all the necessary detail, background, context and perspective on the Chavalit Younchaiyudh — Kukrit Pramoj tensions. On Vietnam, she has some of the best reporting outside of the *Far Eastern Economic Review.* "Grass-Roots Politics Forced Hanoi Shakeup," 2-4, has 60 Vietnamese starving to death each day; "Youth Unrest Said to Stir in Vietnam," 7-9, "Young people fleeing Vietnam...fear forced farm labor in what are called new economic zones because of the harsh conditions;" in "Pragmatism and Dogma Vie as Vietnam's Regional Rivals," 8-23 — "Communism is not being challenged here...[though] Vietnamese say openly the party has lost the public's confidence;" "Where Tet Meant Death," 8-26 — "Sometimes the Vietnamese seemed to be blaming Americans less for what happened here than the Americans blame themselves." Good economic details in "Vietnam Seeking Capital, Eases Rules," 8-31; more readings on the factional jockeying in "Is a Newspaper for the Mandarins, or the Masses?" 9-8. Solid reports from the Philippines, far superior to what bureau chief Seth Mydans had

been doing all year — fine analytics in "Many Philippine Officers Agree with Rebels' Views," 9-4, and a superior report "Key Aquino Advisor Questioned by Legislator," 9-9.

Cullison, A.E. *The Journal of Commerce.* (★ ★ ★ ½)
Tokyo. With a new Tokyo team at the *Financial Times*, Cullison had the edge in Japan in providing coverage of the emerging tax debates. "Tax May Shake Japan's LDP," 3-4, revealed the political implications of "a massive nationwide rally against introduction of the 5% sales tax...in exchange for meager savings in their income tax payments." By 9-11, "what began as a grand radical tax reform project in Japan is ending up as little more than a minor income tax revision of small consequence." Cullison always selects his sources to reveal how the Japanese are thinking. In "Clouds Hover Over Economy," 6-29, he quotes a Japanese economics editor, "Most important of all, business leaders seem unable to achieve the kind of broad consensus on economic policy that has been the hallmark of this country's business elite since the early postwar period." In one of the best articles of the year, "Japanese Lack The Good Life," 5-20, he quotes an economics professor, "Are we saving to finance merely higher standards of living in countries already more affluent than our own?" He reports on a Tokyo lecture by MIT's Lester Thurow, 8-6, who advises "I would argue that your quitting lending money to us would be the best thing you could do for us," as this would force Washington to raise taxes. "Whoever becomes the next president of the United States most probably will raise taxes to correct the deficit problem," he added, "unless it is Rep. Jack Kemp, R-N.Y., a staunch advocate of supply-side economics." In "Broker Says Japan Will Sharply Boost Foreign Production," 10-29, we get a report that Japan in the 1990's will produce as much overseas as it exports, and with typically sophisticated analysis he reminds us that "Japan today is in much the same position as the United States was during the first half of the 1960s, with a massive annual trade surplus and a deficit in the balance in capital accounts."

Curtius, Mary. *The Christian Science Monitor.* (★ ★)
Middle East. No longer with the *Monitor*, her reporting from Amman, Cairo and Jerusalem ranged from adequate to very good. Her better efforts came out of Jordan where she scored an important scoop with "US-Jordanian Military Exercises Indicate Ties Stay Strong," 7-31, revealing that King Hussein kept operation Shadow Hawk/Eager Light secret from Jordanians while making overtures to the USSR and Syria. In "Undeterred by Lack of Firm Date, Jordanians Gear Up for Elections," 8-10, she handled very well Hussein's dilemma of creating "institutions that allow Jordanians a greater say in governing that kingdom without destabilizing it." A useful tangent on the Iran-Iraq war — an Egyptian role as protector of the smaller governments in the region — was opened up in her 1-22 examination of potential diplomatic gains for Egypt. "The Walls Fell, But the Barriers Remain," 5-27, on Palestinian-versus-Israeli attitudes over the fate of Jerusalem, was in the "adequate" realm of reporting, well-written and respectably covering old ground, but without adding new information. Her serious shortcoming, however, was evidenced in her 1-20 report on the views of Shamir's new economic advisor, Amos Rubin — Israel's defense requirements demand high taxation and more U.S. aid, with Rubin adding that any cuts in aid would necessitate resorting to a nuclear defense policy. Here was one of THE major Israel stories for 1987 that begged for further investigation and treatment, but she did not pursue it.

D'Anastasio, Mark. *The Wall Street Journal.* (★ ★ ½)
Moscow bureau chief. First full year on the job, doing good, not great work at first, with a burst later in the year that impressed. Early pieces came late, such as the shake-up of Gorbachev's officials, "Gorbachev Fails to Win Changes of Party Bosses," 1-29, others speculated on figures and theories that were not quite credible or backed up, "Soviets Are Said to Practice Deception to Show Their Economy is Improving," 3-10. Little evidence is used to back up his theme in discussing Soviet admission of "inflation," although the piece did contain careful detail, "Soviet Media Admit Inflation's Existence," 5-22. Outstanding pieces

toward the end of the year detailed the inadequacies in the Soviet health system, outlining perspectives for overhaul, "Red Medicine. Soviet Health System, Despite Early Claims Is Riddled By Failures," 8-18, and the KGB's immunity from *glasnost*, "KGB So Far Escapes Gorbachev's Effort...," 10-3. His useful analysis on "Gorbachev's Waffling on Summit Raises Speculation on Kremlin Power Struggle," 10-29, cuts against early thoughts that Mikhail miscalculated on RR's political strength, but oddly does not admit the possibility that varied forces, including the Wall Street Crash, were at work in the flip-flop.

Darlin, Damon. *The Wall Street Journal.* (★ ★ ★ ½)
Tokyo bureau. Great promise as the journalist on this beat who can comprehensively weave political and economic detail into a satisfying whole. His writing is full and interesting with his piece on opposition to Nakasone's tax reform and the Premier's way in dealing with it, "Tax Uproar Threatens Japanese Premier," 3-19. Discussing the Liberal Democratic Party's setbacks that threaten Nakasone's stimulative package, Darlin lacks detail but still comes through with a distressing report better than elsewhere, "Japan's Election Results Endanger Nakasone's Plan to Spur Economy," 4-13. Darlin checked in with an excellent page-one piece stressing the Japanese lack of concern for national security under the U.S. umbrella and the temptations of the Soviet market, paying five times more, "The Toshiba Case," 8-4. In his profile of Noboru Takeshita, Darlin suggests that this man could be Japan's Nixon, as in the case of China, and worsening U.S.-Japan relations as he has more pull with the LDP than Nakasone, "The Adjuster. Man Likely To Become Japan's Next Leader Lives To Comprise," 10-8. His "Japan Turns Corner on Its Trade Surplus," 11-10, is marvelous in providing statistical detail we've rarely seen before in a foreign dispatch: "Housing starts... are surging. Automobile registrations rose at a seasonally adjusted rate of 11% in the third quarter after growing 5% in the first quarter. Sales at major department stores rose 6.9% in September from the year before, the second-sharpest surge since 1981. A tax cut of 1.54 trillion yen ($11.4 billion) in December should continue to strengthen the consumer-spending boom." Our only quibble: What kind of tax cuts?

Dawnay, Ivo. *Financial Times.* (★)
Rio de Janiero. A rather unique, competent source of information on the Brazilian economy. "Brazil Helicopter Contract Puts Manufacturers in a Spin," 2-12, reports the intense competition among Brazilian manufacturers over the $1 billion joint venture with the U.S., but notes hesitation from the economic ministries who say "There are better ways to lose money." We get good new data in "Fears Grow That Brazil Is Headed for Recession," 2-11, where he reports indications the economy's on a downturn, unemployment and interest rates up (annualized rates on certificates of bank deposits soaring to over 630%), with Pres. Sarney unable to achieve a consensus on economic policy. He keeps us up to date with "Brazil Jobless Total Increases Dramatically," 7-1, reporting the doubling of unemployment and loss of a million jobs in five months resulted in the scrapping of a 30% consumption tax on cars. "Behind the deteriorating economic outlook lie fears that social unrest will force the government to reverse the new austerity program." Whose fears? If it *is* broke, why not fix it? He's weaker with "Trade War Threat Sparks Row in Brazil," 10-15, telling us there's a fierce row among the country's ministers over how to defuse the U.S. threat of retaliatory tariffs, but not reporting their differences.

Dean, Macabee. *The Journal of Commerce.* (NR)
Tel Aviv. Very few articles have appeared anywhere on the dramatic economic reforms going on in Israel, which brought inflation down from 445% to about 20%, and turned the economy around. One article alone makes up for the shortage of news, "Israel's Economy Strengthens," 5-4. The shekel was pegged to the dollar, the top tax rate cut from 60% to 48%, and "the government is still pushing ahead with its attempts to sell the government companies." Given the strategic importance of Israel, we hope to see much more of this high-calibre reporting.

Debes, Cheryl. *BusinessWeek.* (★ ½)
Singapore. Swinging around Southeast Asia and Australia, Debes has developed a taste for sunken treasure, on land and on sea. She delivered an aquatic sunken treasure piece, 11-3-86, that we thought clever. In "A Yellow Submarine Pops Up From Down Under," 9-28, we read of a tiny C'Cat, 26 pounds, selling for $5,000 that can roam the ocean floor taking photos, checking fish traps and ship hulls, "like a model airplane for underwater recreation." Then we get "Bill Simon Goes Treasure-Hunting in the Pacific," 3-9, well handled on the former Treasury Secretary checking the troubled hulks of Pacific basin S&Ls. A sidebar on his Aussie partner, "Bruce Judge: Simon's Kindred Spirit From Down Under," 3-9, turned up another treasure hunter, "Judge's knack for pouncing on undervalued assets, turning them around, and selling them." After the Crash, "The Raiders Down Under May be Down and Out," 11-9, sheds a tear over beer barons Alan Bond and John Elliott and financier Robert Holmes a Court, another trio of treasure hunters, but what about Simon and Judge? Debes seemed to be the lead reporter in "*Glasnost* Takes a Slow Boat to Vietnam," 9-28, which we appreciated for its timeliness, Hanoi struggling to repair its economy, "ruined by doctrinaire Marxist management," but its 140,000 troops in Cambodia discouraging outside investors, including Japan.

Delaney, Paul. *The New York Times.* (★ ½)
Madrid. Replacing Ed Schumacher here, Delaney didn't improve on the shortcomings of the *Times*' Iberian coverage. We looked for, but never found, sufficient news on the economies of the peninsula. Merely acknowledging rates of 20% unemployment or more in parts of Spain, for example, isn't enough. With "The Runaway Winner in Portugal," 7-21, he informatively profiles Anibal Cavaco Silva, telling us that under his coalition Portugal's economy experienced near boom conditions, but the many, many unanswered questions provoked here were never treated sufficiently. Good feature on the cultural front of the Basque-Spanish difficulties with "In the Schools, A Quieter Basque War," 6-1. "Palestinian Group Takes Harder Line," 4-23, was an important dispatch, reporting the Palestinian National Council's discussion of hardline resolutions on ties to Egypt and rejection of U.N. Resolution 242. Very good reporting in "Spain Rejects U.S. Deal on Bases, Foreshadowing the Treaty's End," 11-5, a well-organized and comprehensive treatment.

Denton, Herbert H. *The Washington Post.* (★)
Vancouver bureau. He's a good cut above the wire services, but just didn't tackle the big story here this year. "Illegal Aliens Flee U.S. For Refuge in Canada," 2-23, was a broad look at the influx of illegals leaving the U.S. for Canada before the new U.S. immigration law takes effect. A "Style" section piece gave us Lincoln Alexander, host of Andy and Fergie in Canada, "Her Majesty's Man in Toronto," 7-15. Denton gave us some detail of the economic dilemma of the Canadian rail workers' strike telling how there are no layoffs after four years of service despite a decline in rail traffic, "Rail Strikes In Canada Paralyze Service," 8-25. But it was back to the woods in "Cultures Clash Over Game Hunts in Arctic," 12-7, letting us know of the battle between animal rights groups and native Eskimo customs. All well and good, but what about the political and economic scene? Enough with the Canadian tourist bureau stuff.

De Onis, Juan. *U.S.News & World Report.* (NR)
Chile, special correspondent. Former Buenos Aires bureau chief for the *Los Angeles Times*, we just didn't see enough from him at his new post to give a rating. "Fitting Justice to Reality," 1-26, was an okay overview on Alfonsin's balancing act between human-rights activists and the Argentine military, calling immediate amnesty out of the question, but how lenient can the government be without undermining justice?

DeYoung, Karen. *The Washington Post.* (★ ★)
London. DeYoung tends to go for the feature, rather than the gusto, although she often manages

to stifle the impulse. In "Ireland Set to Go to the Polls," 2-15, she got close on economics but put her best material at the end: In Ireland where unemployment's at 20%, the average Irishman pays 60% in taxes. "In Britain, Concern Grows That Reagan Is Weakened," 2-8, she caught the dependence on George Shultz to carry the narrow interpretation of the ABM Treaty into the White House. "Britain's Two Davids Take on Goliath," 5-24, is a satisfying feature on the Alliance Twins, Davids Owen and Steele. Also with Benazir Bhutto's giggling during the interview on her arranged marriage, "The Making of a Marriage," 8-18, a nice revelation on the Pakistani opposition leader. Her election coverage was good, giving us a feel for the politics: "Propects Rise for Britain's Non-White Candidates," 6-10, on the increased number of non-whites running for Parliament who are expected to take seats; "Thatcher Tops U.K. Pre-Election Poll," 6-11, where Neil Kinnock is still "exuding confidence after what is widely considered to have been the best campaign performance of the race, [and] insisted that Britain was seeing 'the last days of Thatcherism;'" "Thatcher Reelected in Landslide," 6-12; "Thatcher Basks in Huge Win," 6-13; and then "Thatcher Unveils Program," 6-26, which gave us the dope on Maggie's plans. Her features range from mildly engrossing to good, though we expect more than features from this important foreign bureau. We sometimes we get it, but not often enough.

Dickey, Christopher. *Newsweek.* (★)
Cairo bureau. A better year, with his best work an analytical one in *Foreign Affairs*. A bizarre piece was introduced as he discussed the shaving of beards in Beirut, not to distinguish, but to assimilate, "The Battle for Beirut: A Close Shave," 3-16. He asserted the Persian Gulf situation, stating that Washington needs a clear, coherent policy *before* venturing into hot waters, "Guerilla War On The Water," 6-15. His *Foreign Affairs* article analyzed well Assad's byzantine relations with the Arab world and the Soviets, addressing implications for U.S. foreign policy and noting that the long-term course of Syria tends toward the ending of its alliance with Iran, "Assad And His Allies: Irreconcilable Differences?" Fall.

Diehl, Jackson. *The Washington Post.* (★ ★ ★)
Warsaw-based Eastern Europe correspondent. The best and the brightest in the *Post*'s otherwise mediocre year for the European corps, Diehl superbly illuminated the changing Central-East European scene for us. We credit him with one of the 10-best foreign dispatches of the year, his "Hungary Leads in Reform," 4-6, the best of the *Post*'s noteworthy five-part series, giving us a deep sense of the intellectual forces at work instead of simply scanning the marketplace. Diehl came up with some careful detail in the account of Poland's centralized heating system's problems, "Warsaw's Winter Bursts Pipe Dream of Centralized Heating," 2-2. His wonderful piece on Poland's news program gives an enlightened view of the 15-minute straight-talk, no-excess baggage, "Tele-Express" which doesn't advance public information but is fast-food *glasnost* reporting, "Glasnost Arrives With A Splash On Polish TV," 4-22. A month later, Diehl was again found waving the flag for *glasnost*, this time in the Soviet Union's leaders and their reaction to Poles, "Dissident Asks Poles To Test Gorbachev," 5-22 and later in the year, sharply analyzed Gorbachev's possible reactions to nationalist demonstrations of Tartars and Latvians, presenting economics of ethnic regions *vis-a-vis* Moscow, "Resurgent Nationalism Puts Soviets' Glasnost To The Test," 8-9.

Doerner, William. *Time.* (★ ½)
Associate editor. Doerner is most often seen atop a double byline on foreign stories. His best writing for *Time* was "Suddenly, A New Day," with S. Chang and Barry Hillenbrand, 7-13, where surely the Korean word for *chutzpah* must be Roh Tae Woo: "Roh seems convinced that his best chance is to run as the man who put aside partisanship and found a way out of a national political crisis." A week later, Doerner catalogued sadly "The Struggle Gains Its Martyr," also with Chang and Hillenbrand, 7-20, on the death of a student protestor in Korea. "The Perils of Power Sharing," with Jordan Bonafonte, 4-6, was lighter, celebrating the first anniversary of a sometimes rocky marriage *francais* between Chirac and Mitterand.

198

Breezy in "Troubles of a Tongue *en Crise*," with William Rademaekers, 9-14, on the French struggle to keep the *franglais* out. Doerner can be gritty though, as in "The High Cost of Non-Nationhood," with Peter Hawthorne, 10-12, on the economic disaster that the South African townships have become, in addition to the social travesty they have always been.

Done, Kevin. *Financial Times.* (★ ★)
Nordic correspondent. Each of the five countries of this group pursued different courses and faced different challenges this year. Done kept his focus particular, while covering the region as a whole. "The Pacesetters Falter," in the "Nordic Banking" survey, 1-16, provides the general and specific conditions behind the ebbing of growth among Iceland, Norway, Denmark, Sweden and Finland in this impressive report. "Iceland Prepares for an Uncertain Future," 4-25, the country's complicated electoral politics (8 parties among 171,000 voters) are examined. High economic growth last year (6.3%) and its once raging inflation (160%) tamed, but there's uncertainty about the future with the breakdown of the coalition government that presided over the economic reforms. In "End of Age of Innocence," 5-22, he notes: "Economically, doubts about the Swedish model may have set in long ago, but it is now other certainties and values that are under attack..." as Swedes question "the middle way to paradise," national mythology. In "Deregulation Gathers Pace," 10-2, we learn that new Prime Minister Harri Holkeri, the first conservative PM since 1940, plans continued privatization, deregulation and a massive tax reform for Finland, and enjoys support from the Social Democrats, especially with his "hard currency cabinet."

Drozdiak, William. *The Washington Post.* (NR)
Editor for foreign news. We only saw a bit of reporting from him since his elevation from Bonn bureau chief to foreign editor last year, and it was very disappointing. An example of this we found in "Pace of Reform Falters in China as Opposition Campaign Advances," 3-8, where a half-baked analysis was unsatisfying with no evidence of real reporting.

Eaton, William. *Los Angeles Times.* (★ ½)
Moscow bureau. He's competent on covering what bubbles up to the surface, less successful plumbing beneath that froth. "New Entrepreneurs Rush to Supply Consumers in Estonia, Latvia," 5-10, was informative on competitive enterprises being permitted alongside state-run outfits. A decent look at a bit of Baltic *perestroika*, but his dependence on official sources left it inconclusive. He provides good background in "Soviet Protests Urge Freedom for Baltic States," 8-24, with a proper sense of the important national-religious blend of the demonstrations. He tries to be comprehensive in "An Unpopular War: Soviets Seek Way Out," 11-5, and does a good job surveying opinion on the Afghan war. But it's primarily a round-up on the "debate" within the Soviet press, so it leaves us very uncertain on conclusions. "Gorbachev — 'Pragmatic Visionary' With Amazing Energy Confidence," 11-1, had too much the feel of outside-peering-in, little testing or probing of the portrait he paints. Eaton settles a little too much for the easy, general picture, and we just don't know if it's accurate on what's behind the scenes.

Echikson, William. *The Christian Science Monitor.* (★ ★ ★ ½)
Paris. The best we saw out of Paris in '87, the big dailies playing musical chairs with this bureau. His 1-13 report on the subsidizing of the strikes in France was a skilled assessment of the political toll for Jacques Chirac, capturing the picture with a perceptive quote: "The trains will run again, but society will be blocked." In "How France Links Iran to Terror," 7-31, he's impressive in backgrounding the rupture of Franco-Iranian relations, examining the conclusions of the top secret dossiers of the French "FBI" (DST). His sharp eyes and skilled hands extend beyond France, giving us excellent reports from Scandanavia, Finland and Central Europe. On Czechoslovakia, the east European country to watch as the barometer of East Bloc *perestroika*, "Winds of Reform Rustle Through Prague," 10-2, was smart, emphatically authoritative, the best we saw on the pressures squeezing the Brezhnevian Gustav Husak. Other East Bloc reports:

a vivid description of a Czech school kids' tour of the Secret Police Museum, 5-5; informative on Poland's "Freedom and Peace" group, a youth movement protesting the role of the Polish Army in crushing dissent and Poland's unequal alliance with the USSR, with Echikson noting the spread of alienated youth's focus from pacifism to ecology, 12-30-86; savvy on how Ceausescu's economic problems reduce Romania's options as the Soviets most unpredictable ally, predicting it'll be the country most likely drawn back into Soviet orbit, 5-27; and the lagging of reform in the East Bloc's formerly reformist vanguard as the policy to cut Hungary's living standards advances, 9-23. A series of very fine reports during September on Finland, Sweden, and the non-EC neutrals, with "US-Style Tax Reform Spreads to Tax-Strapped Scandanavia," 9-4, particularly outstanding. Good quotes in a report on European frustration at being blamed for the stock market crash, 10-23, with smart sense for critical detail — W. Germany's ready to cut tax rates if the U.S. does a budget move.

Elliott, Dorinda. *Newsweek.* (NR)
Beijing bureau. Some good work this year, with solid features on the continuing economic and social transformations in China. In evaluating the bold economic experiments in the city of Shenyang she explained the present failings, giving a quick, but well-organized picture, "The Shenyang Experiment," 3-30. In a story of Guar Guargruei, the Chinese capitalist entrepreneur, she details government resentment towards him with an important story examining the real extent that China was taking with economic reforms, "Cabbages and Capitalists," 7-20.

Elliott, John. *Financial Times.* (★ ★ ★)
New Delhi. He still reigns as first choice for the closest to comprehensive on coverage of India. "Gandhi Pledges to Liberalise Economy," 2-12, was an important early reading on Rajiv's intent to continue liberalization of the economy, tax reform kept on the agenda by Gandhi at this stage. "Heroin and Hired Guns Fuel Ethnic Strife in Karachi," 2-5, gave us some interesting political economy here on Pakistan, a breakdown of government authority in Karachi as ethnic tensions, gun and drug trade become intertwined. "The Idol Is Fallen," 4-30, said it all, sparing nothing: "...Gandhi has had to turn to the very men whom he used to shun, the power brokers of Congress I." "Riding The Tiger With Many Heads," 7-3, was a fine analytical report on India's separatist movements and Rajiv Gandhi's on-the-job training, but left us wanting more on reasons why states "all want...more devolution of economic and other power." V.P. Singh trys to topple Rajiv, and Rajiv conducts tax raids on the *Indian Express* newspaper, which leads the campaign against him, coming out in "Gandhi Opponent Sets Out To Extend Influence," 9-7. "Only On My Terms," 9-14, interviewed V.P. Singh, ousted Finance Minister and potential rival to Rajiv Gandhi, who stressed democratization of the Congress Party. "Learning The Ways Of Mother India," 9-29, gave us wonderful detail on Xerox building copiers in Rangpur: "About 40 percent of last year's sales figure of Rs 645M was spent on taxes and duties."

Fallows, James. *The Atlantic.* (★ ½)
East Asia correspondent. A mix of history, culture, politics in his reports, he sometimes comes across as more of a social anthropologist. Japan was his main focus and in "The Rice Plot," 1-87, he examines the cultural hold small private farming has in Japan's national mythology. There's detail and data there, but Fallows also weaves in a touch of "inscrutability." This shows up even more in "Playing by Different Rules," 9-87. A sweeping overview of Japan's problem with imports, he notes how this adversely affects their economy, but incorporates his not necessarily correct observations about deep cultural differences between Japan and the U.S. One comes away from his essays with a view of Japan as a country fundamentally alien to the ways of the West. More cultural anthropology in "A Damaged Culture," 11-87, with Fallows superficially concluding that "In the Philippines, the national ambition is to change one's nationality."

Fineman, Mark B. *Los Angeles Times.* (★ ★)
Manila bureau. A palpable improvement this year for Fineman, whose dispatches were more timely and detailed on the political scene, where he's always alert. Though weaker on economics, he made new efforts there this year. He kept on top of the political tensions, "Aquino Triumph Dimmed by Lack of Unity and Stability," 2-4, "Filipino Workers Assail Aquino Administration," 5-2, and "Aquino Asks Filipinos to Unite Behind Military," 9-11, each a well-organized, fresh report, just when it was needed. "Philippines Military, Under Critical Fire, Still Misses Key Targets," 2-23, was sharply informative on the picture two weeks after armistice, with quotes from key players very well-used. His best workmanship, "Philippines: New Crisis in Education," 9-21, comprehensive on this major problem. In "Philippines Finds Much to Cheer in New Debt Package," 3-31, we saw him struggling to get inside the country's economy, a "C" for substance, "A" for effort. His Korea material was rather disappointing, "S.Korea Party's Draft Charter Would Bar Candidacy of Kim Dae Jung," 7-21 and "Seoul to Crackdown on 'Radical Leftists,'" 8-28, for example, merely routine.

Fisher, Andrew. *Financial Times.* (★ ★)
Frankfurt. Almost rivals David Marsh from Bonn, with whom he sometimes shares a byline, as one of the best reporters on the German economy. The two broke an important story, "Bundesbank Plays Down Money Supply," 4-2, noting that "the West German central bank is instead giving priority to trying to stabilize the exchange rate," and revealing that "some within the Bundesbank believe the 1988 tax cuts should have been brought forward to this year." In "Lambsdorf Attacks US Over West German Economy," 9-29, the maverick economic spokesman for the junior party of the coalition government criticizes U.S. officials for being too polite about the German refusal to cut tax rates. Revealing signs of Bundesbank head Karl Otto Poehl beginning to bend a little, with exchange rates taking the lead over "money supplies" before the Venice summit, in "Poehl Paints the Economy in Brighter Colors," 6-5.

Fisher, Dan. *Los Angeles Times.* (★ ★)
Jerusalem bureau. Fisher is good on the country's factional politics, and very, very good with lifting the veils on the underlying political-social transformations, particularly in Israel's Arab communities. A grand contextual picture with "Six Day War: The Legacy of Conflict," 5-31, the first of a sweeping three-part series that also included "West Bank: More Prosperous but Bitter," 6-1, and "Gaza: A Mideast 'Orphan' Isolated by War, Politics," 6-2. We also noted analytical depth in "Rise of Islamic Militants Worries Israeli Officials," 9-14. "Israel Exists Without a Constitution," 8-16, was one of the best we saw on that dilemma. In "Sharon Defends Invasion Role," 8-12, he's sloppy, maybe a bias intervening, giving more input to Sharon's opponent than coverage to the former Defense Minister's remarks. In Moscow during the fall, he contributed to the *LAT*'s series on the USSR. "Glasnost — Soviets Try to Open Up," 10-29, was a semi-impressive survey, the analytics mixed; too narrow on *glasnost*'s internal use, but sharp on its foreign motive: "to foster a more benign image of the Soviet Union...making it easier to import the necessary foreign equipment and technology to modernize its economy." A little too glowing on *glasnost*'s accomplishments there, he compensated with "Moscow Moving Forward and Backward on Rights," 11-3.

Ford, Maggie. *Financial Times.* (★ ★)
Butler's successor in Korea, Ford just barely managed to hold her own in the political vortex. "Torture Case Spoils Korean Leader's Credibility," 1-23, was an okay report on the quick reuniting of the opposition New Korea Democratic Party as the police torture scandal rocked the country, with Ford noting that President Chun's hopes for a speedy resolution of the negotiations on constitutional reform are now dashed. "U.S. Cigarettes Fail to Draw S. Korean Smokers," 2-18, assessing Seoul's efforts to open its markets to imports, used the example of cigarettes to show agreements to allow products into the country don't lead to real sales,

because numerous barriers are left intact. "The Strains of Success," 5-14, contained good juxtaposition of the higher standards of living and the unsatisfied craving for greater political freedom. In "Widening Gap Adds to Tension," 5-14, Ford details the threat from Kim Il Sung's North Korea as still very real, but for some in the South, "the threat of the North is receding as an issue....As the people's thoughts turn more and more to democratic reform, so their gratitude for the U.S. contribution towards the country's security gets entangled in resentment that the U.S. is not doing enough to promote change." Ford's "Divided Partners," 10-1, reports on the rivalry within the opposition camp as the presidential race gets underway in S. Korea, but as with most other reports on this, we still don't get a picture of the programatic differences between the two Kims.

Ford, Peter. *The Christian Science Monitor.* (★ ½)
Managua. Okay dispatches, but he isn't straining against the limits that hem this bureau. Making a serious effort to draw a picture of the contras "under siege," he examined from 1-21 through 1-26, the pressures on the anti-Sandinista resistance from all sides in Washington, their political and strategic military debates, allegations of rights abuses, the efforts to recruit support among the Moskitos. Ford followed the back-and-forth responses of the Sandinistas between the Contadora and Arias peace plans, reporting 6-8 on Ortega's resistance to the initial (Central American) Arias plan. Several September dispatches covered the progress of the later Arias proposal, rounding up reactions in the region on its prospects. "Nicaragua Looks to Latin America as Soviets Appear to Limit Aid," 6-8, could have been a breakthrough report on the Sandinista's economic nightmares. Though it provided some detail on their disastrous mismanagement, it exemplified his tendency to hold back. Sparse coverage on El Salvador, 7-15, noting students spearheading a militant opposition as discontent mounted, yet failing to consistently explore. Honduras got short shrift, generally sticking to its relationship to the contra-Sandinista struggles, his 9-15 report an example. Better on Panama, examining 6-19, what drives its economic elite to take to the streets. One of his best, "Despite Close Ties with Moscow, Havana Balks at Pursuing *Glasnost*," 6-22, reporting that Cubans can read about Gorbachev's reforms only in *Moscow News*. Castro's "reforms" are focused instead on tightened central control and exhortations for harder work and revolutionary moral stamina.

Frankel, Glenn. *The Washington Post.* (★ ★)
Jerusalem bureau. Moving from South Africa to Israel toward the end of last year, Frankel delved right into his new posting. He selects his material well, catches the important detail, and does very good work with broader analytical pieces. In March he presented an analytical story on the Pollard spy conviction suggesting, correctly, that it had created a battle among American Jews, "A Spy's Shadow Darkens A Special Relationship," 3-20. Later in the year he detailed only one incidence, of tourists being harassed in Israel, although authorities had stated there were more than fifty, "Some Arab-American Tourists Charge Harassment By Israel," 7-16, skimming the issues in a light report. His notable series, "Israel and the Palestinians: 20 Years After the Six-Day War," included examination the country's altered society in the wake of deflated dreams, "War's Legacy Strains Jewish State," 5-31; a review of the prolonged struggle between Arab and Jew in the occupied territories, "Souls on Fire on the West bank," 6-1; and the religious conflicts that particularly intensify in the Holy City, "Golden Jerusalem: The Grand Prize," 6-2.

Friedman, Alan. *Financial Times.* (★ ★ ½)
Italy. Friedman knows what to look for here, the most productive reporter all year covering Italy's shifting economic contours. "Italian Banking Slips Its Chains," 2-10, showed us how Italy ended fifty years of tight restrictions on commercial banking after five years of parliamentary debates. Friedman gives all the critical details and projections on this key step forward for the modernization of the country's financial market. He notes that Mediobanca, the supreme arbiter of Italy's corporate finance, will end up with a much diminished role as a consequence. "Italy Widens Its Inner Circle," 10-13, was an excellent report on the

privatization of Mediobanca, locating what it represents on the margin for the power structure of Italy's Old Guard capitalists. The closed, exclusive nature of this operation functioned to the advantage of a small circle of leading industrialists. Friedman traces the webs of power and networks it represented, all of which are now cut loose, opening the way for new capitalist players in Italy. "Mafia Charges Flay Politicians," 4-23, covered the historic "maxi-trials" of alleged mafiosi in Sicily, "a procedural nightmare," with 468 defendants, more than 200 inside specially constructed cages within the courtroom. One positive outcome, there were only 80 Mafia-conducted murders in Palermo last year. He reports on the flack Christian Democratic party leader Giulio Andreotti is getting from alleged connections to the society. Andreotti's supporter in Sicily, CD member Salvo Limi: "I am perhaps part of the evil here, but at least I get things done." His "Year of Consolidation," 4-23, was a short, concise assessment of the economic recovery in Italy. While it's heading for continued growth, no action has been taken on the public sector deficit or finances. "Clouds on the Horizon," 11-17, comprehensive on the content of this year's economic "renaissance," putting in a close look at the runaway public spending that threatens it all.

Friedman, Thomas L. *The New York Times* (★ ★ ★)
Jerusalem bureau chief. Obligated by his editors to cover every aspect of Israel, he sometimes stretches, "The Focus on Israel," 2-1, offering some new material but not enough for the Sunday magazine. Otherwise, consistently important. "An Islamic Revival Is Quickly Gaining Ground," 4-30, was a masterful sweep of the phenomenon within Israel. In "One West Bank Plan," 6-2, the first we saw on Mayor Ron Nachman's plan to build Ariel into a 100,000 resident city (with a perspective of improving relations with West Bank Arabs!). Rabbi Meir Kahane's proposal on Judea and Samaria doesn't exist in a vacuum, the plan no longer isolated as other senior officials propose resettling Arabs in Jordan, "Israeli Proposes Ouster of Arabs," 7-31. "Road to Power," 8-4, a very insightful examination of the intellectual's debate: "Has Israel already become a Jewish-Arab state in all but name?" Illuminating on the trial of Israelis for having dinner with PLOers and smiling, 3-22. Quick and sharp on the concern Yasir Arafat's return from oblivion is causing, "Israelis on PLO Talks," 4-24. Comprehensive on the national religious power struggle, "Fight for Religious Power Builds in Israel," 6-29. "Israel Faces Reality," 9-2, one of his best, combining a fine historical framework with analytic depth on the pragmatist vs. visionary as the cabinet votes 12-to-1 to scrap the Lavi jet. "A country in Meltdown," 2-8, on Lebanon not as a news story but a nightmare: "What readers wanted to know most was not what... Gemayel said to...Karami, but rather, how does a society unravel." Some disappointments: a one-dimensional look at the Lebanon War debate and Ariel Sharon's politics, 8-13; "Lesson's in Israel's Recovery," 8-9, jibber-jabber on how Israel tamed inflation, but at least there was some data.

Fung, Vigor. *The Asian Wall Street Journal.* (★ ★ ★ ½)
Beijing bureau. He gets us closer to the grass-roots China than anyone on this beat, and we couldn't have done without his reporting this year. Earlier pieces were not too promising except for the analysis of Shanghai airlines, "China's National Airline Gets Competition," 1-2, which was a great story on "de-reg" and China's first independent airline since 1949. He arrived at a different way of expressing worn news with, "China's Media Coverage Of Three Dengs Acts As A Barometer Of Political Climate," 3-30, concerning contenders for Hu Yaolang's post. Fung got us closer to the real China in "Cooling Off With Hot Pot," 7-24, a wonderful piece that describes the inhuman temperatures and perspiration as the ambling folk sit down to a plate of hot, spicy food "As the sun blares down they are devouring some of the spiciest food imaginable." "Chinese Workers' Enthusiasm for Stock Prompts Peking to Expand Experiment," 2-20, gave a behind-the-scenes glimpse of the reaction to capitalization: "Pang Ruiyong brightens at the prospect of receiving her first dividends from 50 shares in the state-owned Guangzhou Silk & Flax Mill where she works. 'I love this place,' she says. 'Now I begin to feel that I really am the master of the factory.'" But his pieces appear too few and far between in the U.S. edition of the *Journal*. Editors!

Gardner, David. *Financial Times.* (★ ★)
Mexico. Gardner manages to handle both politics and economics passably well, but the political side is definitely better. "Youth and Ability Win Day for Salinas," 10-6, was the best profile of the new president-select. While most others sounded like dressed-up official bios, Gardner's piece was laden with real info on his thinking and activity. Salinas has a mind that de la Madrid "positively drools over." "The Problem Cash Cannot Solve," 3-20, was routine, from Mexico City: "The cautious economic strategy that has served Mexico well over the past year could prove an early casualty of the presidential transition." Gardner's best effort went into the special section on Mexico, 12-10, "On the Brink of Hyperinflation," which had the best detail we'd seen on the economic policy approaches likely under the president-designate. Although a bit murky on analysis, it included an explanation of the "heterodox shock" theory of disinflation that we gave up on after three readings. In the same section, Gardner had a thorough review of the crash of the *bolsa*, the stock market that had climbed 329% in dollar terms in the first three quarters of '87, "Meteor's Inevitable Crash-Landing."

Gargan, Edward A. *The New York Times.* (★ ½)
Beijing bureau chief. China reporting, by the press as a whole, was less satisfying this year than last. Gargan, a new kid on the block, didn't help. We got an early warning of Gargan's difficulties with his treatment of Hu Yaobang's dismissal in "Clues Clarifying Shifts in Beijing Remain Elusive," 1-18, which means "I don't know what's happening, boss." New to the assignment, he was having trouble with sources, hence a reliance on "analysts." In "China Watchers Say Turmoil Cut Deng's Power," 2-25, there are supporting bits of evidence, but from Hong Kong, not Beijing, rather inconclusive. The editors played it in on P.10, suggesting they weren't sure of the reading. Also murky, "China Sees Long War on Western Ideas," 3-15, and "Is Deng Still Supreme?" 3-16, too cursory. A major spread in the Sunday magazine, "China's Cultural Crackdown," 7-12, was simply too shallow. No government officials are directly quoted, complaints of several artists are reported (but even they say they haven't been affected except by the undercurrents), and we were left wondering if the campaign was the one step backward that follows the two steps forward. Later in the year we saw some breakthroughs on pure politics from him. "China Party Congress Meets Today," 10-25, was a fairly good report on the state of reforms and likely leadership changes. Maybe his best, "Beijing Is Gliding Ever More Westward," 11-1, had good detail of the Communist cadres who insist on being "bought off" if they're to relinquish control. Even so, we suspect his range is too narrow.

Garvin, Glenn. *The Washington Times.* (★ ★ ½)
Central America. Relentless in his coverage of the region, Garvin cuts through the jungles to get to the heart of the matter. "Cruz Finally Quits Contra Triumvirate," 3-9/10, was a beefy report on contra politics on eve of the moratorium vote in the House. Chamorro and Robelo don't know why he left, but Garvin saw two reasons: Cruz wanted a "worldwide election" among Nicaraguan exiles and rebel forces put under his political supporter, an engineer. "Prices Soar As Nicaragua Faces Oil Shortage," 6-11, was a well-done analysis of Nicaraguan belt-tightening after the Soviets pulled the plug on the oil supplies. Yet, "Sandinista Revolution Bogs Down In Despair," 6-18, was a mind-boggling portrait of suffering in Nicaragua, vivid, horrifying, but showing a dignified people. Garvin puts it on the line: "Anywhere you look in Managua, modern civilization is crumbling away," and then he goes on to prove it.

Germani, Clara. *The Christian Science Monitor.* (★ ★ ½)
Miami-based, covering South America and Haiti. Her Brazil reports sparse, Chile better, her real strength is the Argentine political scene. Early she flagged Antonio Cafiero, leader of the important *renovadores* faction of the Peronists, noting his chances to win the governorship of Buenos Aires Province, and 9-4, alerted us on his serious potential as a 1989 presidential candidate. On 9-8, Germani reported the Peronists no longer felt bound to negotiate with

President Alfonsin, the prospect of imposing their policies tempting after their electoral victories. Importantly, she located in their win a gain for political stability — with two strong parties now, coup scenarios are somewhat reduced. She also kept a rein on the tumultuous passions of Argentina's politics, assessing the Peronists' image problems (disunity and general belief their turbulent reign provoked the 1976 military takeover), soberly reporting on 9-18 that their wins came from protest over economic woes more than new-found affection for Peronism. Her 9-28 report on Soviet Foreign Minister's Eduard Schevardnadze's 10-day Latin American tour, revealing Argentina's almost total dependence on the Soviets for export income, is about as close as she gets to the country's economy. Very good on the political scene, she did, however, no serious examination of the monetary and fiscal policies of Pinochet's or Alfonsin's governments. Reporting from Haiti during the summer, "Business Goes Bust in Haiti as Unrest Grinds On," 8-3, was loaded with detail, one of the best reports on the country's economic woes. The best anywhere on Haiti's ecological disaster was her powerfully done "Drought and Famine Add to Haiti's Woes," 7-29, a 10-best selection. Two years into a drought there's cheap food for sale, but no one with money and no means to earn it. Instead, people rip up trees to sell as charcoal — or for bark to eat.

Getler, Michael. *The Washington Post.* **(NR)**
Foreign editor. Getler is mostly deskbound, but he produced two pieces in February on a trip to South Africa that are worth noting: "Races Search For Survival," 2-10, a lengthy, comprehensive overview of RSA problems and politics; "Scenes of Irony Abound in a Land Defined by Race," 2-11, a detailed, poignant description of life in the townships with fascinating, tragic bits of detail.

Gillette, Robert. *Los Angeles Times.* **(★ ★)**
Moscow bureau. A former domestic reporter handling energy and environment, Gillette was sent into Moscow the latter part of the year. We noted "4.4 Billion Sought for Largest Atom Smasher," 1-31, which outlined plans for building the super-collider and the debate over its financing. Gillette reported that despite criticism involving its "practicality" given its costs, advances in theoretical physics have taken scientists close to "an understanding of the common links between the four basic forces in nature." His reporting from Moscow was more than just peeps through random windows, "Perestroika: Bold Shift in Economy," 10-24, a serious effort to present the grand picture of the new system. "Soviet Factory Readies for Greater Autonomy," 10-24, catches the contradictions the new policy evokes, reporting from Novosibirsk that "In addition to new wage pressures on workers to achieve higher quality and greater efficiency, plant managers face the challenge of explaining why a factory's newly-retained profits should be invested in improved machinery rather than in new housing for workers..." Further information on why the reforms are so slow appeared in "Entrepreneurs Find a Place in Soviet Union," 10-27: "Mindful perhaps of the Russian proverb that 'the tallest flower gets cut down first,' relatively few would-be entrepreneurs have stood up so far and volunteered to organize cooperatives, open family shops or take on the risks of family farming."

Gourlay, Richard. *The Journal of Commerce, Financial Times.* **(★)**
Manila. What is reported is well done, but it's what's not reported that disappoints. There is little specific information on how the economy is doing, except "recovering strongly," 7-3. An interesting tax reform, instituted with quiet guidance from an IMF specialist, was never mentioned. "Executives Say Philippines Improves," 7-9, actually provided some data on falling Japanese and American investment. "Philippines Lags in Privatization Movement," 7-7, was superior, explaining who is blocking the sale of 121 government-owned white elephants, and why, and quoted a gutsy official, "The government should send a strong signal to existing and future investors that it has no intention of competing in their markets." In the *FT*, he gave routine, wire service reports all year, as in "Investors Turn an Inquiring Eye on Manila," 3-16, which was okay on the Philippine economy turning up, creating a calmer climate for venture capital. "Slow Start To Philippines Privatisation Programme," 6-25, was a good update,

but Gourlay admits puzzlement on the delays. Couldn't he dig deeper? But, "New Team, Old Problem," was the best analysis we saw on Cory sifting through her cabinet, bouncing Joker Arroyo and Jaime Ongpin.

Gowers, Andrew. *Financial Times.* (★ ★ ½)
Middle East editor. We were very impressed by his reports, several of which demonstrate an ability to successfully probe the muddy waters in the region and find what's ready to surface, as with "Ritual Dance of the Gulf Gathers Pace," 4-10, on the U.S.- Kuwaiti relationship. "Waiting for the Superpowers," 4-21, examined recent moves in the Mideast peace process. He noted, but didn't fixate on, the disillusionment of King Hussein over the U.S. gambit with Iran, going on to freshly assess the long-standing divisions and obstacles there. Interviewing Yasir Arafat, he cuts through the PLO leader's rhetoric to assert that in some form, Arafat accepts Israel as an irreversible fact, and the leader comes up with some semblance of belief that negotiation is possible, "No Way Round," 9-7. From Dubai, he reports that, despite belief that the Gulf is a confrontation with the U.S. waiting to happen, increasingly more incidents are being defused than ignited by the U.S. Navy's message to Iran's revolutionary gunboats, "This Is Your Last and Final Warning," 10-5. In assessing Perez de Cuellar's Gulf peace mission, he sees "A Hope, if Only a Slim One," 9-10, the breakthrough coming more from a Soviet-U.S. understanding than the offices of the U.N. itself. His contributions to the "Survey" on the "Gulf Co-operation Council," 7-24, provided us more detail on the financial and economic changes taking place there than we saw elsewhere.

Graham, Bradley. *The Washington Post.* (★ ½)
Buenos Aires bureau. We kept waiting for some breakthrough reporting this year on the swirling economies down there, and though "*manana*" finally came, the results just weren't worth the waiting. "Police, Protesters Battle During Papal Mass in Chile," 4-4, calmly reported chaos during a Papal mass, leaving the emotional flavor of the riots unwritten. "Study Disputes Claim Of Chile's Resurgence," 5-24, outlined the statistical battle between government and opposition on whether the economy has improved or worsened in Pinochet's 13 years, but it's unsatisfying, Graham never getting to the bottom of the debate. "Pinochet Balks At U.S. Nudges," 8-25, had little new on the opposition wanting the U.S. to put more pressure on Pinochet, but notes at the end that moves against Pinochet are "the product of a small State Department team." His "Hopes For The Future In Pinochet's Chile," 8-30, was sticky, sweet nostalgia for old-golden days. "Argentina Tries To Kick Beef Habit In Effort To Keep Economy Afloat," 8-30, with the old maxim, "Cheap meat, happy people..." but continued high domestic demand means less meat for export. Alfonsin reportedly wants to reduce consumption to boost exports, but Graham's too close to the government perspective here in reporting. Surely other impediments to beef exports exist other than rates of domestic consumption.

Graham, George. *Financial Times.* (★ ★)
Paris bureau. After Paul Betts, we turn to Graham to flesh out the French scene, particularly the financial contours. A bang-up job on France's "Big Bang" in "A Late Run for the Winning Post," 4-7. This was the most comprehensive treatment we saw anywhere on Paris' ambitious plans for becoming the premier financial center of Europe, and we found rich layers of financial information not seen elsewhere. Graham can handle the politics adroitly enough as well, "Mitterrand Steps into Pacific Islands Row," 8-27, and "Setbacks Compel Le Pen's Party to Take Harder Line," 10-13, both solid examples of that. Quickly, but not cursorily, he gave a reading on the reaction in French political and financial circles after Black Monday, "French Small Shareholders Urged to Sit Tight," 10-20. With Paris share prices already collapsing in the weeks before "*Le Krach*," government ministers and the chairman of the stock exchange were out on the barricades urging small shareholders to keep their *sang froid*, which unnerved some big institutional investors. Minister of Justice Albin Chalandon had been proposing reform of French criminal law procedures, planning a revolutionary restructuring of an institution

that's existed since Napoleon. "Legal 'Revolution' Threatens Investigating Magistrates," 10-2, was a comprehensive treatment of that and the fierce opposition it's provoked.

Graham, Robert. *Financial Times.* (★ ½)
Latin American editor. His focus appeared more on the Caribbean countries, leaving the rest of the continent to Tim Coone. On the eve of the Pontiff's trip to South America "Where Christ Is the Guerilla," 3-21, examined the problems the Pope faces with the liberation theologists. Graham quotes a remark from John Paul during his July, 1986, trip to Colombia — "We must recognize the usefulness and necessity of liberation theology" — to give a picture of stronger support for the Medellin perspective from the Papacy than he ought. While good on liberation theology's appeal in the area, he ventured too close to seeing a Vatican endorsement of the new model. Handling the lead in the survey, "Puerto Rico: A Very Special Relationship," 3-27, he produced prosaic banalities, and little else: "For all Puerto Rico's autonomy, the island remains in a quasi-colonial relationship with the US." Certainly better, from the survey on "Venezuela," 10-13, "Careful Eye on Progress," and "High Inflation Dampens Forecasts," both detailed readings on attempts to move from complacency to economic self-sufficiency in the wake of oil price collapses. Graham's lead in the Mexico survey, "An Air of Expectation," 12-10, has a nice patina, the country awaiting the July '88 change of presidents, "an atmosphere of expectation that Mexico soon might have its own version of glasnost." But too many silly asides, "That the bubble has burst is no bad thing," and "In political terms, Mexico needs to return to growth as soon as possible," yet "pressing for growth of 3 percent next year is scarcely compatible with holding back inflation."

Greenhouse, Steven. *The New York Times.* (★ ★)
Moving from the Chicago business beat to Paris during the summer, the change in scenery did Greenhouse good. "Revving Up the American Factory," 1-11, wasn't lofty enough, with nothing on narrowing the costs of capital between the U.S. and Japan, but gave us useful anecdotes about GE, Cummins Engine, and IBM Proprinter. "Airbus's Offensive Threat," 5-28, was a great piece, putting together the politics and economics of jetliner competition between private Boeing and McDonnell Douglas and European Airbus Industries, striking a fine balance and hitting all the pros and cons. His early dispatches from France were promising. "In France, Economic Malaise," 7-29, told us that most French citizens, 70% of those polled, view the nation's economy in a state of decline, that Chirac's political rivals are doing their best to exploit these concerns, and gave us a good overall picture on the economy: "...French manufacturers make few of the items...that French consumers crave." His "Comparing Wealth As Money Fluctuates," 8-23, was beefy, with lots of numbers on exchange rates and comparative living standards, the first such information we'd seen. A disappointing "Economic Anemia In Europe," 9-8, Greenhouse showing only the obvious facts of U.S. growth and Eurosclerosis, noting that economies growing fast (Britain and Italy) have trade deficits with slow-growing countries (West Germany and France), but there's not even a suggestion that a trade deficit can often be an indication of economic strength and should not be fought by government.

Gumbel, Peter. *The Wall Street Journal.* (★ ★)
Now back in New York, Gumbel gave us crisp, meaty reporting, among the best we saw on West Germany's elections when he was overseas. "Germany Plans Emergency Tax Cuts Later if '87 Economy Starts to Falter," 1-15, reported the shift in Bonn's thinking about the economy, quoting Economics Minister Martin Bangemann and outlining the possiblities: advance the '88 tax cut to 1987 and invoke law to allow Finance Minister Gerhard Stoltenberg to propose an extra round of tax cuts this year. "Smug Germans Favor Kohl..." 1-20, was the best account up to that point on the election climate from CDU viewpoint: "This is our rally, and they'll have to play by our rules" and Kohl's "conservative colleagues, sensing victory are giving no ground to critics, foreign or domestic." His "Green's Gains Shake Up German Politics," 1-27, was old hat, telling us little that we hadn't heard already. "Japan Stock Market Overtakes

The U.S. As World's Largest," 4-13, was back on track, putting changing values in perspective, saying Japanese P/E ratios "aren't watched as closely in Japan as in the US, with many companies sitting on huge assets that justify their high stock prices." In "Moscow Enigma," 7-17, on the Soviet plan to let in foreign firms proving frustrating in practice, the turf battles and bureaucracy thwarting joint ventures, he concludes Gorbachev's reforms came so fast, the bureaucracy hasn't had time to change the way it thinks and works. "Who Gets These Jobs Anyway?" 9-18, was an entertaining piece on types landing big Wall Street portfolio slots: "There is a chronic shortage of talented securities analysts, traders and portfolio managers with knowledge of equity and bond markets around the world," and with a little more work could have been a P.1 leader instead of a special section insert.

Haberman, Clyde. *The New York Times.* (★ ★ ½)
Tokyo bureau chief. On the bottom line, he's always solid, reliable, and very hard-working, but more importantly he doesn't settle for just the bottom line, pushing hard again to get ahead of the changes in Japan's political economy this year and staying on top of the Korean elections. "U.S. Prods Seoul Rivals to Settle Rift," 2-16, was a credible update on internal political maneuvering in Korea, new U.S. Ambassador James R. Lilley meeting with Kim Young Sam. "Political Crisis Deepening for Nakasone," 3-12, was solid on the public outcry against Nakasone's tax reform, and the new 5% sales tax, but needed deeper economic detail: "Repeatedly, he has denied having lied in a national election campaign last summer when he promised not to press for a 'large-scale indirect tax.'" In "Japan Plans to Deny Visas to Aliens with AIDS Virus," 4-1, he details a different kind of protectionist legislation proposed to deny entry to AIDS carriers "likely to spread the disease," and the debate on testing foreigners currently in Japan. "Japan Acts To Spur Economy Mildly," 8-1, had some detail on the government's proposed tax reform, but the opposition may kill a plan to put 20% tax on small savings accounts. "Cheers For Korean Opposition Leader," 9-9, on Kim Dae Jung's homecoming to Kwangju, absent since '72, was disappointing though, turning out to be a puffy report on his bodyguard's book, citing "autocratic behavior," but no probing of his character or ideas. Haberman's December reports on the last days of the Korean presidential campaigns gave much better closeups. In "Is South Korea Ripe for Democracy or More Repression," 12-13, we learn the two Kims "leave no doubt that [if Roh Tae Woo wins] they will accuse him of wholesale cheating, and then devote themselves to a struggle to overthrow him."

Harden, Blaine. *The Washington Post.* (★ ★ ½)
Nairobi-based Africa correspondent. The dazzling pace and work that earned him a 3-star rating last year wasn't there this year. A little too much cultural anthropology and not enough political economy, his Africa at times tended toward the remote and curious. Jetting into Washington, DC, to do Dinka anthropology in "Manute Bol's Shortcut Out of Africa," 5-4, for example, suggests the problem was his editors. "Feud Over Corpse Dramatizes Friction in Modern Africa," 2-12, the first of two, was a fascinating article about a family squabble over a body and tribal custom that personifies the cultural schizophrenia in Africa, followed up by "Tribalism Slows Nation-Building," 2-13, an exploration of tribalism in Africa. The tribe got the body. "Tribal Customs Worsen Spread Of AIDS In Africa," 7-3, was an eye-opener on how the "cleansing" tradition and other customs are contributing to the spread of AIDS in Africa, where a political leader was quoted as saying "it was wrong for anyone to forsake culture for AIDS." Cleansing is the custom of a surviving spouse sleeping with an in-law to dispel the deceased spouse's spirit. Caught in the cycle, as more die of AIDS, more will "cleanse" with infected relatives, a different angle on an important story on his beat. "Two Years Alter Retirement, Nyerere Sparks Debate," 7-11, was mildly interesting, informative on Tanzania's Nyerere, retiring as President, but retaining power as party chairman, and his flip-flops on retiring from the party chair "to help speed the demolition of the socialist system he built" to rebuild Tanzania's economy. "Peace Corps Enters Middle Age," 8-2, was the best piece we'd seen on the subject, from Burundi, a fine news feature on what's happening

here. "Drought Renews Threat Of Famine," 9-22, was excellent, on Ethiopia hammered because part of the cure is part of the disease: "a large proportion of the estimated 1 million deaths in Ethiopia during the last famine occurred in famine shelters, which were breeding grounds for infectious diseases."

Hawkins, Tony. *Financial Times.* (★ ½)
Africa correspondent. He seems to share the same bias and model as his editor, Michael Holman, but he keeps a better check on it, rendering his reports more reliable. Thanks to him alone, the story of a World Bank success in Mauritius' economic recovery and expansion was properly told. "Mauritius Proves Textbooks Wrong," 8-11, not only links the unleashing of real economic growth there to the country's supply-side monetary and tax reforms, but also disproves the argument that the experience of the Pacific Rim's "Four Tigers" cannot be duplicated by a majority of the developing world. In "A Launch Pad for Expansion," 3-2, he falls short of a satisfactory, comprehensive treatment of Nigeria's economic reforms, his assessments too restricted by his model and bias. Deregulation and privatization, alongside currency devaluation and tight fiscal policies, are emphasized as conditions for growth, and there is an examination of the infrastructural problems that complicate it all. Yet barriers to internal investment aren't really examined in depth, and attention to the tax rate changes in Nigeria are left out of this account. In "Deflationary Forces at Work," 3-2, he does mention the tax changes in the 1987 budget — a slight cut of individual rates and a 5% reduction in corporate taxes, but no detail on thresholds, marginal rates.

Hazarika, Sanjoy. *The New York Times.* (★ ½)
New Delhi. We didn't see his byline that frequently, but some reports stood out. "Legislators in an Indian State Contest Role of Gandhi Party," 7-22 provided good detail on the precarious state of Gandhi's political forces in Uttar Pradesh state as former supporters peel away in opposition. Hazarika alerted us that Rajiv would resurrect his mother's language in the campaigns and refer to "unnamed" foreign countries undermining India. "Crisis for Bombay Exchange," 7-27 lagged *The Economist* by a month, but was a bit better on particulars: "A key element behind the crisis...was the failure of Mr. Gandhi's budget...to reduce taxes, which brought on a bearish trend in the stock market." Though it was "second-hand" reporting, he caught the important news on the margin in "Dalai Lama Urges Peaceful Protests," 10-8, noting the spiritual leader's restraint on independence for Tibet: "For the future, my stand is open. There are many options."

Hiatt, Fred. *The Washington Post.* (★ ★)
East Asia correspondent. Hiatt centered his reports in '87 on the Korean elections, and the social changes therein. At times, though, he seemed to concentrate on peripheral people issues, where he ought to have been thinking about hard-core politics. "At Seoul Camp Teenagers Meet The Motherland," 7-17, was mildly interesting on teens going back to Korea to be instructed in the culture, but not important enough for the first page, especially with all the wrangling over the constitution. "Clamor For Liberties Grows In Korea," 7-18, on impatient Koreans keeping the pressure on the government, was better but still too featurish. "Those Left Behind: Prisoners Illustrate Korea's Divisions," 7-20, was a powerful look at political prisoners still in South Korea's jails, with a simple, but gripping opening: "Soh Loon Shik's term in a South Korean jail was supposed to end in 1978." It's liberal-based to the end, never supposing these people might be guilty of the crimes for which they are in prison, but nobody deserves treatment as it's described here. Hiatt's people-oriented skills were appreciated in "South Korea Awaits Decision: Will Kim Dae Jung Run?" 9-13, a portrait of a complex and contradictory man, handling the gossipy book issue well: "A bestselling memoir by a former bodyguard, rich with gossip of bargirls and political payoffs, enlivened the summer and, whatever its mixture of truth and slander, reminded Korea of Kim's two faces. Not only a deeply religious fighter for democracy and survivor of persecution that might have killed a

lesser man, Kim is also a machine boss attended at times by sycophants, a wily politician who has outmaneuvered his rivals more times than they care to count.'' Changes in the social climate were documented in the article ''In a Political Sea-Change, Kimchi Remains,'' 12-9, as well as giving us some election mudslinging, like accusations the Unification Church has donated substantial amounts to opposition candidate Kim Young Sam.

Hijazi, Ihsan A. *The New York Times.* (★)
Beirut bureau. He kept ahead of the wires on this beat with decent spot reporting, but no great flashes of insight, his analyses were only a degree above tepid. ''Waite Kidnapping Linked to U.S.-Iran Arms Deal,'' was a mere roundup of speculation, with no key information on issue. A little bit deeper, ''Syria Said to Warn Party of God on Captives,'' 3-27, gave us a lot of unnamed sources, but some snippets of information as well. ''P.L.O. and Lebanese Shiites Agree to End Fighting,'' 9-12, was short and to the point, but again, little depth. There's a different angle in ''Chaos in Lebanon Hampering UNICEF's Work,'' 10-25, with plenty of examples to support the thesis, but obvious: isn't it difficult to work in chaos anywhere?

Hoagland, Jim. *The Washington Post.* (★ ½)
Chief foreign correspondent. Running around Europe like there's no tomorrow, Hoagland manages to do fairly well covering diverse events, although he did hit some false notes. ''Allies Show Growing Unease Over U.S. Stance on Missiles,'' 3-8, had no evidence presented to support his ''growing unease'' assertion on the zero option. ''Questions for Shultz,'' 3-27, was deplorable, on George Shultz asking Congress to restore State Department budget cuts: ''Why doesn't Shultz simply turn to the sultan of Brunei, or those other oil-rich covert spendthrifts, the Saudis, and ask them to pitch in a couple of hundred million to bolster foreign aid and save the seven U.S. consulates Shultz is closing this year for lack of money?'' ''A Horse Race In France,'' 4-3, gave us Raymond Barre on the sidelines, the ''Thatcher of France,'' a better column than usual, but still rather uninformative, classifying Barre as ''something of a scold, a personal quality you would think a country in economic trouble would turn away from until you remember England's natural nanny, Margaret Thatcher.'' On the Venice Summit we had ''The Politics Of AIDS,'' 5-22: ''Like an oil slick, the fear of AIDS is spreading across the globe, forcing governments to begin to respond to a health problem that is rapidly becoming one of the world's most volatile political issues,'' complete with the obligatory blast at the right wing. Better with ''Gorbachev Seen Fashioning More Flexible Foreign Policy,'' 8-5, replete with good quotes, analysis: Gorbachev knows the Soviets overplayed their hand with the weakened Nixon post-Watergate, leading to a U.S. resurgence.

Holley, David. *Los Angeles Times.* (★ ★)
Beijing bureau. Replacing Jim Mann here midyear, we didn't see pessimism on the course of reforms in his mainland coverage so much as caution, as he's still feeling his way, it seems. His caution served well, though, in ''China Teaching Students Life Is More Than Books,'' 8-11, where instead of putting the ''back to Maoism'' spin on the ''work-study'' programs there, he cut through the rhetoric to establish as superficial the resemblance to the practices of the Cultural revolution. More confident on Taiwan, ''Opposition in Taiwan Welcomes Openness,'' 8-22, was solid reporting, comprehensive and satisfying on the new political directions, his best for the year. Weaving historical background and context into an informative ''Tibet — Old China Ties Still Chafe,'' 10-15, he gives some idea of what the Dalai Lama's perspectives are — some sort of special arrangement similar to what Beijing offered Taiwan and Hong Kong. ''China's New Economic Plan,'' 10-26, gets the direction right, basing the assessments around Zhao Ziyang's injunction: ''Whatever is conducive to this growth is in keeping with the fundamental interests of the people and is therefore needed and allowed to exist by socialism.''

Holman, Michael. *Financial Times.* (★)
Africa editor. The *FT* is still the single-most important source of current news on the political

economies of black Africa. There is a serious and recurrent problem, however, that continually distorts the reporting, and it flows from Holman's tendency to serve, at times, as a shill for an obsolete IMF/World Bank economic model. The case of Nigeria is instructive. In "A Blueprint for Economic Recovery," 3-2, Holman reports the country's recent radical structural readjustments set the basis for reversal of economic decline. Austerity (per capita incomes down 25% amid high unemployment and industry operating at less than 30% capacity), a 66%-to-75% devaluation of the naira, bans on imports of rice and wheat, and privatization win approval, supposedly making the country more attractive for foreign investment. "Not a sector of the economy has been left untouched," he writes. Yet nowhere is their any examination of the country's tax structure and its role in smothering internal investment. There's a Malthusian bias that too often intrudes, as in "Explosive Growth Must Be Checked," 3-2, which sees too many Nigerians as a problem. His reporting is again skewed by the demands of his economic dogma, as in his report on the economic boom in Mauritius, where he totally misses the significance of this World Bank success story. Supply-side monetary and tax reforms were the central new dynamic there, but in "Everything Is Up But Inflation," 8-6, Holman can only report "austerity measures have paid off."

House, Karen Elliot. *The Wall Street Journal.* (★ ★ ½)
Foreign editor. Less shooting from the hip this year, she's thinking through her strategic assessments, coming up with some masterful geopolitical analytics, particularly strong on the Middle East. Early in the year, House hit on the same theme again and again, that U.S. arms sales to Iran have destroyed U.S. credibility and destabilized the entire region: "Iraqi Minister Predicts a Basra Victory Will Limit Iranian Offensives for 1987," 1-14; "Iran's Assault on Basra Takes Psychological Toll on Iraq," 1-21; "Our Disillusioned Arab Friends," 1-21. "U.S. Needs Patience In Korea," 6-9, was a credible defense of Roh as a competent candidate for the transition to democracy, and she's hard on the Kims for the lack of any policy other than a lust for power, urging U.S. caution: "The ultimate paradox is that Washington probably has a greater ability to destabilize South Korea than does Pyongyang." She had an interview with the General in "Jaruzelski Seeks Major Economic Reform," 7-30, with Robert Keating and Barry Newman. "Mosque And State," 8-7, was perceptive, paying attention to the particulars: "At a time when Marxism is so debilitated it is being shored up by capitalism, when Christianity lacks much of the missionary fire that once drove it, when Maoism is all but entombed with its founder and when democracy sounds only a muted appeal to much of the world, Islamic fundamentalism stands out as the movement on the march." "Arabs Look Again To Old Unreliable," 10-8, was a hard evaluation on the mark: in the Middle East "The usually well-meaning but unreliable old Uncle Sam is back for a brief visit and everyone is happy to see him" but while the U.S.'s credibility is still weak, the Persian Gulf endeavor could be redemption. A sparkling year.

Ibrahim, Youssef M. *The New York Times.* (★ ★ ★)
Paris. For several years *The Wall Street Journal*'s ace oil reporter, with great sources inside OPEC, Ibrahim moved to *The New York Times* this year, with dispatches that demonstrate his feel for the politics of the global oil patch. Before leaving the *Journal*, he did some good work in the Middle East, giving us some vivid slices of life. "Causeway Luring Saudis to Bahrain for Pleasures Denied Them at Home," 2-20, on the $1.2 billion causeway that links not only two countries, but two cultures. "Revolutionary Islam of Iran is Neutralized by Policies of Bahrain," 8-11, and "As Moslem Zeal Rises, Egypt Under Mubarak Avoids Confrontation," 8-10, gave us a feel for fundamentalism in other Arab states, fascinating and informative. For *The New York Times*, he stayed much on the same beat: "Mixed Feeling About US Role In The Gulf," 10-4, an overview of various attitudes among Arab states, concluding there's no consensus among Arabs in their view toward Iran. "Iran Strike Disconcerts A Range Of Enemies," 10-25, was superb reporting and analysis as Iran complicates U.S. strategy by hitting oil facilities instead of tankers. His report on an Arab League summit in Amman, "Arabs Smooth Way to Resume Ties With Egypt," 11-12, is sure-footed in guiding us through the

significance of the shifting sands, pointing out that Algeria and Syria, which had backed Teheran, joined the other states in opposing Iran. "It marked a sea change in Arab politics and the ascension of a center-moderate camp that appeared to take charge of Arab decision-making." In Vienna, "Iran and Arabs Clash In OPEC on Oil Policy," 12-10, Ibrahim is authoritative in dismissing Iranian threats to double its oil output.

Ignatius, Adi. *The Asian Wall Street Journal.* (★ ½)
Beijing bureau. Slower starting than his co-workers here, his material tends to be inconclusive. "Chinese Leaders Do Business At The Beach," 7-29, was weak, making us look halfway through this long piece, on what seems to be about a vacation resort, for the real story, the examination of the succession question and possible candidates as the major issue. "Black Market For Jobs Blossoms In Beijing," 9-23, was only a mildly interesting feature on the spot labor market, anecdotal. "Socialist Inhibitions About Speculation Put Damper On Stock Trading In China," 8-18, was better, telling us "The main problem is the question of ownership [Liu Funian, chief of financial control at the People's Bank of China and proponent of stock market experimentation]. Selling shares to the public transfers state property into private hands — China hasn't yet decided whether or not that's acceptable."

Jackson, James O. *Time.* (★)
Moscow bureau. Most often seen under someone else's byline, though when he does appear singly, Jackson is usually disappointing. "Gateway to the Gulag," 4-20, was especially so, much too short on the development of Magadan, formerly a Stalinist hell for Russian political prisoners. He leaves you wanting more visual pictures of life now, and of life then, instead of vague statistics, all the more disappointing because Jackson was there, one of the first foreign press visitors in years: what did he see and think?? Shortly thereafter, we got "Tales from a Time of Terror," 4-27, a pseudo book review *cum* report on *Children of the Arbat*, Rybakov's novel of Stalinist Russia, finally being published after nearly 20 years. What's there is interesting, but there's not enough on the political motivation for publishing, except to say "the book obviously has high level support." Is publication a byproduct of *glasnost*? What about future publications of banned novels? Jackson doesn't touch on this.

James, Canute. *The Journal of Commerce.* (★ ½)
Kingston. A better bead on the Jamaican economy than we saw elsewhere, starting with "Jamaica Gets $132 Million From IMF," 1-16, despite Prime Minister Seaga's refusal to comply with IMF plans to debauch the currency. James belatedly noticed that corporate tax rates had been cut from 45% to 30% in 1986, and import duties gradually cut from 200% to 30%, but he neglected to mention that individual tax rates were also slashed from 58% to 33%. It worked so well, conservatives began to worry about "overheating," in "Jamaica Buoyancy A Cause of Worry," 10-28, simply because unemployment fell from 27% to 22% and the economy grew by 5.5%. Other developing countries should have such "worries." Coverage of other Caribbean countries was a bit sparse, though "Caribbean Clothiers Fret Over Proposed US Cap," 8-6, warned of unexpected victims from the proposed U.S. trade bill. James also strings for the *Financial Times* where we saw "Surinam Rebels Pledge to Continue Struggle," 4-30, a thorough report on the government pledge of elections Nov. 25 in response to intense pressures from the U.S., Holland, local unions and foreign business, but rebels say it's a sham and will fight on, although hurt by cutbacks in arms supplies and other materials.

Jameson, Sam. *Los Angeles Times.* (★ ★)
Tokyo bureau. Working the Tokyo-Seoul shuttle all year, he kept atop the big changes in both places, but was part of the conventional pack on the key turn in Japan. "Nakasone Foresees $5-Billion Trade Surplus Reduction," 5-30, was a timely pre-Venice summit picture of Japan's efforts to fulfill promises to stimulate domestic growth. "Japan to Tax Interest on Savings Accounts," 9-21, was short but concise, noting that despite Nakasone's use of American pressure as a rationale, the government sees it as an avenue for more tax revenue. There was also

"Nakasone's Legacy: A New Japan," 11-7, a thorough retrospective on the transformations he effected: "The institutions with the power to implement reform in Japan...have remained aloof. Nakasone's greatest successes came when he was able to subvert them, or bypass them." He caught Nakasone's uniqueness, but didn't hold onto it in "Takeshita Elected Japan's Prime Minister," 11-7, a little too inclined to assume no major changes in policy would occur. His reporting from Korea was above routine, but without the zip that could have provided fresher assessments and news. "Opposition in Seoul Splitting Over Candidate," 9-30, covered the basics, good quotes from both the Kims, but just not strong enough with what could distinguish the two.

Jenkins, Loren. *The Washington Post.* (★ ½)
Rome bureau chief. Unfortunately the post serves primarily, it seems, as an airport for trips elsewhere. Another of the *Post*'s "parachute" journalists for the Iran/Iraq front, he managed coverage of Italy's elections, but otherwise was bland as a pot of *polenta* on the country this year. Outside Italy he was occasionally better. "U.S. Arms Cited in Iran. Major Role Seen in Basra Offensive," 1-27, was just shoddy, though, "analysts here" say, etc., much too serious an issue to be strung together the way Jenkins does it. "Iran Has American Journalist," 2-2, was better constructed, an inside look at the Seib detention, with inside detail. "The Power Struggle Inside Iran Is Escalating," from *The Washington Post Weekly*, 2-16, gave insights into the factional battles, saying Rafsanjani is the leading advocate of a battlefield victory over Iraq and therefore his interest in a U.S.-Iranian arrangement for arms. A side note on Hashemi's arrest and confession, describing it as a power move by Rafsanjani against Montazeri. "Mecca Riot Is Aspect Of Broader Struggle," 8-10, had fair depth of news analysis: Khomeini seeking Shiite ascendancy, while Sunni sheikdoms are alarmed that Iran may throw all caution to the wind.

Jones, Clayton. *The Christian Science Monitor.* (★ ½)
Manila. A promising and prolific talent who needs to tighten up his material. He suggested the Pol Pot nature of the communist NPA, but we had to wade through a cutesy lead on a guerrilla wedding, 2-11, and piece it to details in a 1-21 report on life under the NPA in Samar Province. "Aquino's New Tactics to End Rebellion," 3-19, was chewy — amnesty for the communists, prison for armed vigilantes who resist them. Insufficient reporting on the economy, acknowledging a 6.5% rate of growth, noting a new tax code and Finance Minister Jaime Ongpin's credit arrangements as stimuli in a 3-31 report, but otherwise avoiding it for the year. On the proposed land reform, some details 7-1, but to President Aquino's voluntary perspective, he posited U.S. advisor Roy Prosterman's arguments for confiscation. Good instincts on the widening of hairline cracks of dissent into wide political crevices after the "Cory" legislative sweep, "A New Filipino Opposition," 5-21. Mixed attempts to cover the transformations in Vietnam, a little too uncritical, 4-6, on the choice-of-candidates policy there while party "purification" takes place. A 9-16 interview with Foreign Minister Nguyen Co Thach was sharp, revealing Vietnam's view that it's but a pawn in the Sino-Soviet dispute, its relations with China able to change overnight. Too passive, however, with Justice Minister Min Phan Hien, 11-2, on the end of the "Bamboo Gulag," the minister assuring him detention without trial in "reeducation" camps is unlawful now that a policy of "laws — not edicts" is underway. A insightful report, 11-3, on Vietnam's first commercial bank, with richer enterprises favored for loans over socialist egalitarianism, quotes an official: "Business is business." Outstanding, his very well-done feature on the incredible trek to freedom of three Cambodian families, "Out of Asia's Daily Dramas, a Tale of Rare Courage," 9-16.

Jones, Jim. *U.S.News & World Report.* (★ ★)
Special correspondent for South Africa, Jones is a reliable reporter who also appears in the *Financial Times*. A tendency, albeit slight, to see major change occurring in the political fabric faster than events can confirm, he's still credible in his reporting on the bid by Botha for a white mandate and the tensions that exacerbated in the country, as with "Botha Defies the Tides, Gets Tougher," 2-16, and "South Africa: Subtle Stakes," 5-11. His best, however,

was "The Horatio Algers of South Africa," 7-20: "These South Africans have little in common with well-to-do blacks who developed their fortunes through cozy relationships with the white central government." His profiles of these businessmen, whose "sheer drive and persistence," paid off revealed a side of affairs rarely reported from South Africa. "South Africa's Whites Face a New Reality," 8-24, is a decent dish of meat-and-potatoes updating on the gold miners strike and labor's increasing muscle. From Zimbabwe, an excellent report that is full of information and analysis, "Outsiders in the Sunshine," *FT*, 4-25, asks and comprehensively answers "What ever happened to the white Rhodesians?"

Kamm, Henry. *The New York Times.* (★ ★ ★)
Budapest. The *Times* was smart in opening this bureau and even smarter deploying a pro like Kamm from Greece to Hungary. Fresh material on central Europe and the Balkans all year, starting with Ceausescu's economic disasters in "Cold Days Are Back in Rumania," 1-4, reporting a 5% cut of the armed forces amid severe shortages and rationing. A bird's-eye view of the emerging "social" ills, as Hungarians work double workweeks to purchase better cars and homes — more "freedoms," less "equality" in "Keeping Up With the Laszlos," 3-12. Attentive on signs "Kadarism" has exhausted its possibilities, giving us good readings on the austerity proposals in Karoly Grosz's designs to reduce consumption; "Lean Times in Hungary," 8-5, was crisp, comprehensive on Hungary's declining political economy: "A western-style value-added tax and new income-tax law...revenue-raising measures are intended to reduce the chronic budget deficit and to slow down inflation by soaking up excess cash." One of the best reports anywhere on Yugoslavia with "Yugoslavia May Cut Off Aid to State Companies," 6-26, masterful on the political, economic, and ethnic tensions in that "paralyzed system going toward atrophy." Some fine investigation of the current situation in Indochina, his best "From Cambodia, Still Misery and War," 7-7, where even surgeons are called from operating tables to attend lectures on Marxism, and the dominant reality is still pervasive economic deprivation. Critical details and keen analytics in a timely "Far Reaching Economic Changes Stir in Bulgaria," 10-7 on Todor Zhikov's moves to break the centralized bureaucratic stranglehold. "The most changed nation in the Eastern Bloc could be one result."

Kaufman, Michael T. *The New York Times.* (★ ★)
Warsaw bureau chief, covering Poland and Czechoslovakia. Good hitting again this year, though with few of the triples or home runs we saw from the competition, but resourceful and hard-working, we anticipate better scoring next year. He has a knack for revealing the Kafkaesque nature of life in central Europe. "5 Jazz Fans Are Convicted in Prague," 3-12, provided satisfying detail on the trial, noting the judge's commendation of the officers of the jazz organization — even as he sentences them to jail. He covers well the developments of intellectual circles, never treating them as mere froth above the surface, but we would have liked comprehensive pictures on the deeper workings in Poland and Czechoslovakia. His "Serenading the Lost Lambs of the Counterculture," in the Sunday *Magazine* 2-5, was timely and informative on the "Sons of Communism," interviewing the sons of purged Slansky and Rajik and reporting that behind the governments' "national reconciliation" overtures to writers and artists remains the hard-line on "political" intellectuals. "Restore Rural Solidarity, Pope Says," 6-1, thorough on the Pontiff's message to his flock, pushing the regime to honor its agreements with Poland's farmers. Additionally well-treated, the complex, critical issue of Ukrainian Catholicism's peculiar situation and the Pope's role as protector, "Trip by Pope Stirring Issue of Ukrainians," 6-5. "Gorbachev on a Prague Stroll," 4-10, capturing the excitement of cheering Czechs who have aspirations of *glasnost* potentials, was a flavorful treat. Among his best, "Glasnost Upsetting to Soviet Allies," 4-5, plumbing the old guard's wariness — "They have spent their entire careers trying to prevent the sort of changes that Mr. Gorbachev is now trying to accomplish in the Soviet Union."

Keller, Bill. *The New York Times.* (★ ★ ★)
Moscow. On the *glasnost* beat. Sent to USSR in late '86 after successive *Times* stints on the

labor and Pentagon beats. To his credit, he learned the language before diving in here and kept his head well above water most of the year. We got more out of him on *glasnost* than anyone else. His Sunday *Magazine* piece, "Russia's Restless Youth," 7-26, gave us extraordinary glimpses of the coming generation in a dormant society, disbelieving Gorbachev. "It is hard to feel sanguine about Gorbachev's prospects...the generation now coming of age shows every inclination to abstain." One reader noted: "Wonderful interviews, quotes, broad and deep reporting, overwhelmingly excellent." In "Atheist Preaches Glasnost, So a Priest Has Hope," 6-8, on the Rev. Gleb Yokumin's view of Gorbachev's reforms: "He's an atheist, but a reformer." He shows good initiative in interviewing a leading reform economist, "Soviet Planning Big Labor Shift Out of Industry," 7-4, with scary plans for an end to food and housing subsidies. A "Searching for Outer Limit of 'Glasnost,'" 8-13, sees it evolving and maturing from sanctioned criticism of the last regime's shortcomings to the beginning of a political debate over the future of the Soviet system. Next step will be who controls the debate. "Moscow Welcomes Offer on Missiles; Hints Pact Is Near," 8-28, was a rehash of Gennadi Gerasimov (the Cardinal Richelieu of Soviet propaganda) bashing a Reagan speech on U.S.-Soviet relations. A think-piece, "West in a Quandary," 4-16, pointed out the skill with which Gorbachev plays on Western hopes of detente, but quotes from Tom Downey do not reflect sufficient breadth of commentary. On the plus side were his professional, if slightly generous, coverage of the 27th CPSU Conference in February, a piece on KGB infiltration of the Russian Church, 6-21, and a report on Gorbachev's 70th Anniversary speech, 11-3, digging up new sources (writer Burlatsky, anti-Stalinist historian Samsonov) to complement old warhorse Roy Medvedev. Keller's post-summit news analysis, "The Test of Gorbachev's Talents Has Just Begun," 12-13, is very sharp, pointing out that his big test begins January 1 when the new economic law takes effect. A fine rookie year.

Kifner, John. *The New York Times.* (★ ★)
Cairo. The tug of the Persian Gulf War intruded on all Mideast correspondents, but Kifner managed to stay on top of the news in Egypt, though his furrowing wasn't as deep as it ought to have been. "Over Strong Coffee, Talk of a Shiite Fifth Column," 2-3, was passable on alarmed reaction in Kuwait over arrest of Kuwaiti citizens engaged in terrorist bombings. "Shiite Radicals Rising Wrath Jars the Mideast," 3-22, was a wide review, historical background; new information not outstanding, giving us some perspective on the challenge to Syria now. "They Dance For Mubarak," 10-6, gave us vignettes on Hosni Mubarak's victory, winning a second six-year term in a one-candidate election with fewer than five percent of the voters turning out.

Kinzer, Stephen. *The New York Times.* (★ ★)
Managua. He seemed a little slower this year — and a little sloppier — but overall his day-to-day coverage was good enough to hold our confidence. "On the Airways, Contras Gain Ground," 3-12, was a fine account of the "news and salsa" mix on the CIA-financed contra radio, where politicized soap opera draws big audiences for Radio Liberation. In "Contras Raid Civilian Targets," 3-10, he reported that the contras shot a pregnant woman in the stomach, bayoneted a baby, and shot elderly women to death in Chontales province. But there wasn't the evidence for his characterizing this as the norm for contra tactics and their human rights record. We got straight reporting in "Managua Cracks Down on Group That Presses for Prisoners' Rights," 4-4, and on the government attacks on critics in "Nicaraguans Call for More Protests," 8-21, though he indulged his tendency to see a split between a "hardline" Tomas Borge and "reasonable" Daniel Ortega on policy. This indulgence was chronic all year, reporting 9-15, for example, that Borge appeared opposed to the Central America peace accord — despite Borge's unequivocal endorsement of the plan, 8-26. Very timely with "Rebels Are Now a Force Within Nicaragua," 5-10, and good on Moscow's dismay with Sandinista economic mismanagement in "For Nicaragua, Soviet Frugality Starts to Pinch," 8-20, but late behind Branigan of *The Washington Post.* "Kirkpatrick Is Cheered in Managua," 10-13, was a solid account of the amazing reception contra champion Jeane Kirkpatrick received everywhere *in*

Nicaragua — ovations and adulation from Nicaraguan citizens — while mere mention of Sen. Dodd's name provoked boos and hisses from the same crowds.

Kirkland, Richard I., Jr. *Fortune.* (★ ★ ½)
European editor. We've had our ups and downs with Kirkland's material over the years, scoring him high on micro-economics, especially his work on service industries, and low on macro, especially on international money and capital. He still sneaks in plugs for dollar devaluations here and there, but otherwise handled macro gingerly this year and produced a string of winners. An example: "The Bright Future of Service Exports," 6-8, a cover story reconnaissance that sees U.S. service exports, including the golden McArch, paying the interest on U.S. foreign debt. A great job, jammed with interesting angles and data, one of the year's 10-best business pieces. Kirkland warmed up to this with "We're All in This Together," 2-2, also on service exports. In the same issue, "What Maggie Has Wrought," 6-8, he gives us the best, brief review of the Thatcher record we saw at election eve: "A foreigner is constantly struck by how many Britons, even among those who say they plan to vote for her, volunteer their dislike for Thatcher's arrogance." His "Where Gorbanomics is Leading," 9-28, is another very sharp, compact report on *perestroika*, but needed more space, an old-fashioned *Fortune* major take-out instead of a brief. (Although giving Gorby a "C" in economics seems excessive.) In the mag's "50 Most Fascinating Business People," 1-5, his short profile of Fiat's Cesare Romiti was tantalizing, but stopped well short of fascination. "Britain's Own Boesky Case," 2-16, on the Guinness Affair, a fair wrap-up. After the Crash, "Global Traders Head For Home," 12-7, with Louis Kraar in Asia, with Kraar getting the better stuff. A good picture of Nigel Lawson, though, complaining there was no reason for the European markets to have followed Wall Street off the cliff, that Europe's economic houses are in far better order than Washington's. Oh, yeah?

Knight, Robin. *U.S.News & World Report.* (★ ★)
Senior European editor. A much better year, providing among other reports, one of the few look-sees into Albania to appear in the press and the first interview by East Germany's Eric Honecker with a U.S. publication since 1972. In "'Ample Opportunities' for Arms Pact," 1-12, which concentrated mostly on prospects for arms control, we learned Honecker's hungry for a most-favored-nation trade status with the U.S., an arrangement they already enjoy with Canada. In "Albania Peeks Out, Never Forgetting That Life is Earnest," 5-11, we're in a land "that bans private cars, frowns on long fingernails for women...produces so few consumer goods that many people rise at 4 a.m. just to make sure they buy a bottle of milk." He gives us a tightly done picture of what has and hasn't changed there. Though he never interviewed the "1 out of 1,830,653 voters [who] cast a ballot against the official candidate," he finds evidence the outside world is slowly chipping at the edges of rigidity here. "Angola: Trapped in the Cross Fire," 2-16, notes that "as a colony, Angola exported food...Today half the food is imported." He doesn't just attribute this to the civil war, citing the role of Marxist economic mismanagement. "It's not all beer and skittles," he reports in "The Long Reign of Britain's 'Maggie III'," 6-22; "her cost-conscious cutting...stands in the way of any major government-financed attack on unemployment..." Beyond that, though, he didn't explore the contradictions of the economy here, a little too inclined to take as given the current signs of improvement.

Kraar, Louis. *Fortune.* (★)
Asian editor. His stories are long on facts, which, although sometimes enlightening in themselves, doesn't make up for an irritating shortage of analysis at key junctures. "Aquino Needs a New Miracle," 9-14, offers scattered bits and pieces about the Philippine economy that probably could have been strung together in New York, while some of the more interesting items — like the post-Marcos pump-up of Manila stocks by over 700% — were not pursued and explained. Similarly, in "Korea's Big Push Has Just Begun," 3-16, one would have liked to get an assessment (for instance) on whether the huge capacity resulting from the new Posco steelworks will actually be used — "if we actually produce that much steel," said the company

president, "we will be No. 2" in the world. "The China Bubble Bursts," 7-6, was a year-old story with new anecdotes, obsolete as a new bubble had already begun. Post Crash, Kraar teamed with Richard I. Kirkland, Jr., on the exodus of U.S. investors from European and Asian stock markets, 12-7, with Kraar's material on Hong Kong worth noting.

Kraft, Scott. *Los Angeles Times.* (★ ★)
Nairobi bureau. A talented writer who, even when he trails others here, gives us totally absorbing reports. "Bananas — Staff of Life in Rwanda," 7-1, was a nifty feature in which Kraft illuminates on the country's economy with a focus on this staple of its production and consumption. "Beira: Improved Route May Cut Dependence of Neighbors on S. Africa," 8-23, is a story told many-times over, but Kraft gave it some added value for retelling, informative updates on Western involvement, and noting a creeping realization that "the biggest obstacle to economic independence from South Africa, however, is not the transportation network, but rather the sad state of domestic economies of southern Africa." His "S. African Multiracial Regional Body Formed," 11-4, was timely on "a significant first in South Africa," the meeting between President Pieter W. Botha and Zulu chief Mangosuthu Buthelezi to launch a multiracial advisory body for Natal province. We see so little on what's happening in South Africa's "homelands," so "S. Africa's 'Nations' Prove Political, Financial Drain," 11-2, was appreciated. Corruption scandals rampant, unemployment as high as 50% in some districts, despite modest economic growth, even the "model" states have become a financial drain on the RSA, and the debate of widely-ranging views on their future is taking place in and outside of the homelands.

Krauss, Clifford. *The Wall Street Journal.* (★ ½)
In the Miami bureau until August '87, is there a preconceived view here that debilitates his reporting from Central America? It seems to structure his selection of materials and the conclusions he draws, and we couldn't help but notice how it doesn't hold up to what all others were reporting this year. "Nicaragua Committees' Woes Epitomize Domestic Resistance to Sandinista Plans," 1-29, reports the reversal of fortunes for the Sandinista Defense Committees which, combined with other tactical retreats, have reduced Sandinista control of the country and cites various reasons why. "Salvador Regime Fails to Build Consensus," 3-27, we learn right-wing parties are "boycotting the national assembly to protest Christian Democratic austerity measures and alleged attempts to control the national elections commission." But Krauss gets into advocacy: "The U.S. Embassy has failed in efforts to urge President Duarte to devalue El Salvador's currency faster..." But "If The Contras Collapse, U.S. Faces Bigger Task In Containing Marxism," 5-18, was four-star work, laying out the real geopolitical stakes involved, and escaping the bog of cliches passing for debate concerning the region. "Contras Find A Haven Inside Nicaragua," 8-3, was quite a scoop, portraying the Chontales province as unique with special circumstances that make it an anti-Sandinista bastion, "...less than two hours drive from Managua, in the center of the country, the Contras have won the active support of the peasantry." "Nicaragua Is Getting Little Foreign Aid In Righting Economic Mess It Created," 8-4, was improved work on this beat, on Managua's incompetence exacerbating the Sandinistas' Achilles' heel, the economic crisis.

Kristof, Nicholas. *The New York Times.* (★ ★ ★)
Hong Kong. We applauded when the *Times* moved this young business reporter from the LA bureau to this post late in 1986. Our expectations were quickly rewarded with "Taiwan's Embarrassment of Riches," 12-21-86, dazzling on the ROC's "cash crisis" and strategic financial-policy debates. Sparkling with "Australians Shift Their Sights to Asia," 1-11, on Aussie youngsters studying Chinese, Japanese and Asian "business negotiation" to command $350,000 salaries, and "Digging a Bucketful of Diamonds a Day," 4-5, was a brilliant business feature. He was the first to *finally* give us a satisfying profile of Queensland Premier Johannes Bjelke that focused on his economic perspectives (set a 25% top tax rate!), 4-29. Slight blemishes with his Philippines coverage, "Signs of Life in the Philippines," 3-23, startling data on the

sense of impending boom, though missing 1987 projections and overlooking the 6-86 tax reform. Flawless, however, with China: "Capitalism Lifts Bank of China," 3-24, and "Debate in China Over Stock Trading," 4-27, both finding the trend toward reform continuing where others were reporting a reversal of Deng's policies. Super-productive on China, (three bylined stories on one day!) with "Japan Winning Race in China," 4-29, a polished analysis of Nippon's strategy: go for market share and worry about profit later. There were a few bumps in portions of his four-part April series, "The Crucial Moment," and "Anti-Americanism Grows in S. Korea," 7-12, simply drew too many unconvincing conclusions. However, he was splendid with "Koreans Testing Democracy's Limits," 7-11, the analytics sharp, and his interview with a "moderate" student official, 8-2, effectively communicated the strains of anti-U.S. feelings. Excellent in every respect, "China: Hong Kong's Factory," 9-4, on 1 million Chinese subcontracting at 30 cents an hour for the H.K. "storefront." Send this man to Beijing.

Larmer, Brook. *The Christian Science Monitor* (★)
Mexico City. Adequate reports, but just settling into this beat, there wasn't great depth in his 1987 efforts. "Despite Growing Isolation, Panama's Ruler Retains Upper Hand," 8-5, assessed the opposition's perspective as a long, but "irresivible" effort to oust General Antonio Noriega, and "Can Either Side Afford Unrest?" 8-5, was a cursory look at the current economic dislocation. On his main beat, Mexico, he produced a three-part series, 9-28 through 9-30, examining the growing apathy among Mexico's voters, the PRI's control of resources, its crisis of legitimacy, and the demographic changes producing pressure for an open political process. Again, not much new, although adequately presented. Likewise — adequate, but lacking depth — "Mexico Unveils Presidential Successor," 10-5, profiling Carlos Salinas' inexperience. His potential's there, however. A well-done "Landless Mexicans Hang in Legal Limbo," 9-23, did provide new information on the suspended state of Mexico's 70-year-old land reform — a new strategy for rural survival emphasizing national production goals but cuts in aid and credit to peasants. "Cerezo Gains in Guatemala Tax War," 10-21, was the first we saw of President Marco Cerezo's tax hike while the economy was growing at a 2 to 3% rate, provoking a three-day strike by businessmen.

Lee, Gary. *The Washington Post.* (★ ½)
Moscow bureau chief. No longer wading in the shallow end of the pool, Lee got some strokes in this year, but still no deep diving. "Reforms in Afghanistan Confront Tradition. Najibulla Adopts Gorbachev's Liberal Lifestyle," 1-27, delivered the image-polishing tone and the limited intention of reforms, still planning 5-year industrial growth of 38%, and a blanket exclusion on amnesty. Lee finds dumb observers who say "the analogy between U.S. involvement in the Vietnam war and Soviet involvement applies as much to the attempts at *cultural reconciliation* as to the terms of war." His "Soviet Law Would Free Up Collectives," 2-8, left us wanting more detail on economic experimentation in the industrial sector, like elected managers, salaries, direct ties with capitalist firms, and groups of private citizens starting up and managing a factory or enterprise, a really unprecedented loosening of centralization. Lee sat at his TV for the report "Soviets Extend 'Glasnost' To Airwaves," 5-4, a thin look at Americans appearing on Soviet TV, some in place of Soviets, and the public pros and cons. "Russian Nationalism Spreads," 5-24, was ahead of *NYT*'s Taubman by four days, but weak presentation pushed this to page A25 where Taubman was P.1. "Chernobyl Trial Opens," 7-8, was light from Chernobyl on the trial for criminal negligence involving last year's explosion and nuclear fallout, with some analysis, some snips of info, but should have been more in-depth as this is *important* for Gorbachev's *glasnost* (as he mentions briefly): why isn't there more here? "Gorbachev Offers Concession On Medium-Range Missiles," 7-23, was just a report from a report on an interview in an Indonesian paper, a broad overview, but still third-hand.

LeMoyne, James. *The New York Times.* (★ ½)
San Salvador bureau chief. Not at all up to his previous years' work, LeMoyne slipped a long way. We sensed all year that his selection of material suggested a bending to editors' priorities.

218

Covering the contras since 1983, he's carved out a niche as "the contra correspondent," hence his "Can the Contras Go On?" 10-4, a Sunday *Magazine* cover story, carried some weight. Additional reports throughout the year added new information, the general theme being an increased shift in sentiment by Nicaraguans to the anti-Sandinista resistance, as in "Along Honduran Border, Peasants Rally to the Contras," 3-4, and "In Nicaragua, Peasants Face Hard Crisis," 6-3. *The Washington Times* had more meat on the Arturo Cruz resignation than his "Top Contra Aid Quits, Saying Changes Were Blocked," 3-10, but "New Arms Haven't Changed Contra Ways," 6-1, was insightful on the resistance's political and tactical mistakes, especially their tendency to defend fixed positions. It's on El Salvador that he slipped the most. LeMoyne has yet to report beyond the cursory on anything the democratic opposition there has to say. We get ample reports from his travels with the guerrillas on the revolutionary left's activities, as for example, "Just Miles From Ruined Army Base, Salvador Rebels Defy Army," 4-7. But in "After Parades and Promises, Duarte Flounders in El Salvador," 2-16, he lathers and foams about irregularities, the growing disparities between rich and poor, and the serious economic decline, without a word from the political opposition. His front-pager, "Duarte Accuses a Rightist Leader in Killing of Archbishop in 1980," 11-24, was a judge-jury-and-executioner presentation of the case against ARENA's Roberto D'Aubuisson, without balance, scrutiny, or objectivity, his editors culpable for this black spot as well.

Lerner, Marc. *The Washington Times.* **(NR)**
Lerner took over the Southeast Asia beat from Tom Breen midyear, coming from a national desk job, and what we saw in the last couple of months in the year looked okay, all things considered. One story of interest: "'Sparrows' Bloody Return Shatters City's Brief Calm," 9-1, on vigilante justice in the Philippines, specifically Alsa Masa in Davao, sounding just like the wild East, with nice detail, snips of information making the story readable and informative.

Lescaze, Lee. *The Wall Street Journal.* **(★ ★)**
Stationed in New York, there's certainly potential here, though it will take better assignments to produce it. Mixed in with routine reporting, he showed occasional, bright flashes of reportial ingenuity. "Angola's Inept, Indifferent Marxist Elite Run a Nation Where 'Nothing Gets Done,'" 2-19, was a typical picture of Marxist stagnation, but little sense of internal politics. "Manila's Mood," 10-29, was also standard, with little new, and, surprisingly, some tendency to editorialize: "Government leaders always have represented the interests of the wealthy," quoting a Catholic priest at the end, "...radical social change is needed...Nothing in the last 70 years has brought the average Filipino much benefit." "Manila's War Against Communist Army Hard To Find," 10-13, was terrific and entrepreneurial, Lescaze going in search of war 250 miles from Manila, and finding kids playing basketball.

Lewis, Flora. *The New York Times.* **(½ ★)**
"Foreign Affairs" columnist. She provided more PR than analysis or critical judgment too often this year, though there was an occasional flash of insight in her reworking of old news. Her reporting from Mozambique, where she met with President Chissano, verged on uncritical retailing of FRELIMO's PR push to present the Soviet client state as "changed," as in "The Ordeal of Maputo," 1-20. In "Hannah's Distant Cousins," 1-30, she reports what she has not verified, characterizing the anti-Marxist resistance RENAMO as "a rag-tag group of mercenaries, ethnic malcontents, hungry youths" who are "bent on disrupting the economy, preventing development, substituting banditry for labor." Nothing we don't already get from FRELIMO press releases. Old news in "Cuba Slides Downhill," 3-2, but at least she caught the reversion to "moral incentives" there. A little more thought in "South Africa Is Budging," 3-18, finding fissures produced by pressure from the outside. "Moscow Still Believes," 4-10, wasn't without some perception on Gorbachev's "wounded pride," although she was merely reporting on the interview with Aleksandr N. Yakolev that appeared in *New Perspectives Quarterly*. She was traveling old ground frequently this year, as with "The Long Seventh Day," 7-10, recalling her 1968 trip to Israel's West Bank where "everyday life flourishes, but without

hope,'' and finding two decades later that "the last 20 years have been nothing more than the seventh day of the six-day war.'' But this is really the stuff of memoirs, we think.

Liu, Melinda. *Newsweek.* (½ ★)
Asia regional editor. Occasionally journalists get a juicy scoop, a big break like an interview with the head of an unsuccessful coup d'etat. Liu's clandestine interview with Col. Gregorio (Gringo) Honasan of the Philippines would have seemed such an opportunity. "I Am Not the Second Gift of God,'' 9-21, excerpts from Liu's [and CBS' Diane Sawyer's] interview, however, was pretty insipid stuff, almost innocuous chit-chat with a character who'd just tried to depose Cory Aquino with bullets. "Inside the Rebel Camp,'' 9-21, comes out better, and Liu adds to the report news on the shake-ups in Cory's cabinet. Her attempt to embellish the article with drama has her reporting what she didn't really see — Cory Aquino's "face tight with rage'' as the President demanded resignations by all her cabinet members. We aren't getting reporting from her as much as misguided social work sentiment, as in "Resistance on the Right,'' 8-10: "If Filipinos want to close the gap between rich and poor, land reform is essential.'' Not up to her better work of '86.

Lohr, Steve. *The New York Times.* (★ ★)
London bureau. Lohr has improved his coverage of the City of London, and with Howell Raines, giving the *NYT* the strongest bureau there. Lohr's mini-pictures are freshly done, but attempts at multisided, big pictures were not always satisfying, too many key questions never posed or pursued. "New Doubt on Tunnel in Channel,'' 2-23, was late, but with enough fresh news to hold our attention throughout, giving us Alastair Morton, the new Brit chairman with a sharp tongue, "Morton's fork.'' In "A Chillier Climate For the Left in Finland,'' 3-22, he gives us a sharp political snapshot. "Communism…is a spent force in Finland,'' he writes, with CP leader Arvo Aarto sounding "more like Peter Drucker and other gurus of business management than Karl Marx.'' In the Sunday Business section, "The Best Of Times In British Business,'' 4-5, he goes a bit overboard on the U.K.'s economy, "The nation may finally have found a cure for 'British disease,''' but he doesn't get to the high unemployment numbers. "Nissan's Revolution In Britain,'' 6-2, informed on the 50 Japanese companies in the U.K., neck-and-neck with W. Germany as the European nation of choice for Japan enterprises, as there's no time clock, the quality's up and no union grievances. Hmmm! "In August, Swedes Go A Little Wild With Louisiana Crayfish,'' 8-24, was a sprightly feature on the end of August Swedish bacchanal. "The Rank And File Buy Shares In Thatcherism,'' 9-13, was focused and detailed on union members drifting toward the Tory party and its policies. Most typical: "Amstrad Plots A U.S. Invasion,'' 9-26, on Alan Sugar, British computer entrepreneur, thinking he can peddle in the U.S., a smart, lively business feature, that's not quite authoritative: "From now on, analysts say, Amstrad's growth…should average 20 percent annually for the next several years.''

Long, William R. *Los Angeles Times.* (★ ★)
Rio de Janiero bureau. Very hard-working, having to cover the southern cone as well after Montalbano's departure from Buenos Aires, his reporting is always timely, well-organized and focused, with colorful, informative features thrown in. "Rio Cultists: Good Looks At The Beach,'' 8-15, a feature on Brazil's corporeal preoccupation and the body cult that's becoming a "calling card'' in business and social contacts. "Drug Lords Rule Over Rio's Slums,'' 10-16, absorbing feature on the social fabric of Brazil's slums, where drug chieftains are acknowledged by law enforcement officials to exercise parallel power with the government in the *favelas*. "Amid Protests, GIs Train Drug Fighters In Bolivia,'' 8-11, on the disinformation campaign against U.S. soldiers and DEA agents accused of abusing the local populace was mostly an account of an unidentified US official's claim that things are improving in the anti-cocaine project, but it was a good update nonetheless. "Election Setback May Jeopardize Alfonsin Plans,'' 9-8, was a basic election report, noting the importance of Antonio Cafiero, Peronist party victory in the Buenos Aires province governor's election and that Alfonsin is now a lame duck.

Lord, Mary. *U.S.News & World Report.* (★ ★)
Asia correspondent. A honed sense for which way the balance was tipping during critical times in China and Korea, she was the best of the weeklies' bunch covering northeast Asia this year. The fall of Chinese Communist Party leader Hu Yaobang early in the year had all the press trying to digest its implication for the course of Deng's reforms. Lord took a bite with "China's Reforms Consumes One of Its Creators," 1-26, without swallowing the conventional view. Deng hadn't fallen off the tightrope and, despite the resurgence of orthodox opponents, knows his economic reforms will stall without further political liberalization, she observed. The astute assessment held up through the year. "Chun's Option: To Crush or Concede," 6-29, steered clear of analogies with the Philippines experience, an excess that crept into others' reports at the time, and was as good as the analytical wrapups that appeared in the dailies. "Political Poker Game, Japanese Style," 7-20, provided mini-profiles of potential Nakasone successors, projecting Noburo Takeshita as most likely, though calling attention to his role as co-architect of the 1985 agreement that sent the dollar down and the yen skyrocketing. In a terse picture of a different Japanese political scene ahead, she points out that "The next Prime Minister must cope, too, with rising unemployment, an aging society and a new generation that works less, plays harder and demands much more from the government than rabbit-hutch housing and crowded commuter trains."

MacDougall, Colina. *Financial Times.* (★ ★ ½)
China. Looking into 1987, she produced one of the best analytics on the perspectives for Deng's reforms, "Deng's Reforms Exorcise Mao," 12-18-86 in which the succession question is seen as Deng's biggest problem to come. The private economy played a key role in diminishing unemployment, defusing a previously explosive issue. But without political reform, economic reform will falter because managers and experts need freedom to make decisions. How to give factory managers more power without sending economy off the rails was a good assessment of the tasks and perspectives for 1987. "China Reminds Army Of Lessons Of Lei Fang," 3-25, was almost as impressive, with signs of revived "Learn for Lei Fang" movement significant in sections of army for toughening of "anti-bourgeois liberal" campaign, beating up of rival factions aiming for post-Deng power. "The Spark Which Lit a Tibetan Fire," 10-6, provides necessary background on the eruptions there, noting that "Buddhism is like the Catholic Church in Poland." A good year.

Manguno, Joseph. *The Asian Wall Street Journal.* (★ ★)
Covering the Korean scene, we noted his admirable persistence in keeping political and economic reporting meshed. His analytics, however, were mixed, in need of a little more honing in some cases. "Seoul's Heir Apparent Must Prove His Political Agility," 6-9, a backgrounder on Roh Tae Woo, for example, was okay, but not as sharp as others we'd already seen elsewhere. "Chronic Frictions Between Korea, U.S., Take on Uglier Tone," 9-23, needed more than mostly anonymous quotes to be persuasive. He was quick, beating everyone with the important story on the government's edict to 26 *choebol* (trusts) for divestiture within 3 years. We got very good coverage on the labor strikes in the ROK, "South Korea Acts to Resolve Hyundai Strike," 8-19, focusing on the role deputy labor minister Han Jim Lee in defusing the clash by meeting company and police officials and then boldly meeting the hostile strikers. "Worker's Death in Korea Clouds Strike Outlook," 8-24, added further to the picture on the "new era" in which both workers and management were feeling their way along. On Kim Dae Jung's pondering a presidential run, he was the best of the press in providing detail and analysis, in "Korean Opposition Leader Faces Agonizing Dilemma," 9-11.

Mann, Jim. *Los Angeles Times.* (★ ★)
Domestic reporter, former Beijing bureau chief. A reliable source of information last year and this, although he seemed off the track at times, holding too strongly to the view that the anti-Dengist orthodox Marxists were widening their control over China. He importantly notes in "Chinese Reports From America Reflect Negative Propaganda Campaign," 2-5, China's official press on an anti-America binge, the change coming shortly after student demonstrations

there in favor of Western-style democracy. An excellent report on the new Soviet courtship of China, "Kremlin Envoys Selling New Look in China," 5-5, one of his best. "Those who advocate change in China and the Soviet Union are studying each others policies...Economically, the Soviet Union is hoping to take advantage of China's trade problems with the West and Japan." His "China's Conservatives Act to Mold Education, Culture," 5-29, examines the trend toward orthodoxy's resurgence in the ideology, education and intellectual life of the country, but unconvincingly gives the trend more strength than it warrants. Most of his dispatches during this period gave an emphasis to a hard-line China in domestic and foreign relations, as in "China Tells Japan Reporter to Leave as Tension Mounts," 5-9; "China-India Border Dispute Smoldering," 5-8; "China Moves To Limit Self-Rule In Hong Kong," 5-11; "China's Censors Announce Policy of Strict New Curbs On What Public Can Read," 5-16. Back in the U.S., Mann still follows events on the mainland. "U.S. Double Standard Seen on China Rights," 11-23, looks at the various factors shaping U.S. responses to human rights violations in the USSR vs. those in China, highlighted by the different reactions from the State Department and Congress on China's actions in Tibet.

Markham, James M. *The New York Times* (★ ★)
Paris bureau chief, his sixth foreign bureau after spending much of 1987 as chief in Bonn. Less prolific than in past years, he chose his topics carefully, hitting points missed by others. One example was his 2-19 report on subtle Soviet negotiating moves with a key personnel change at the Soviet foreign ministry in Geneva. Markham hit P.1 with his newsbeat on Soviet concessions on verification, although the issue subsequently became murkier. "The Uneasy West Germans: Yearnings Despite Prosperity," 8-2, was excellent on the "soft" state of West Germany — pessimism, declining birth rates, the temptations enticing them east. He displays his skill for precision readings on the Euro-pulse with "NATO, Wary of Soviet Inroads, Considers a Post-Summit Meeting," 10-22, reporting on the real effects of Soviet propaganda, psy-war in the Western Alliance — a story that will make bigger waves in 1988. Successfully repeating his 1986 story of terrorism's quiescence after the U.S. strike on Libya, he demonstrates how allies have come around to firm signals from Washington in "European Policy in the Gulf," 9-16. The report on Germany's investigation of atomic smuggling to Pakistan, 5-5, could have been better lobbed to colleague Sciolino who's been long on top of this, but he really hit the long ball with "Reports on French Hostages Bring Angry Denial From Chirac," 8-2, a revelation on Chirac's outraged fulminations on the disclosure of his secret communiques with the mullahs over hostages. There's an unaccountable world-weariness that sometimes creeps over him that we hope is gone before next spring's French presidential elections. Sadly lacking were any serious investigation and fresh news on Germany's fiscal and monetary policies — unforgivable in a year when that country played such a critical role in global economy and yet he seemed frantic after the October global market Crash.

Marsh, David. *Financial Times.* (★ ★ ★)
Bonn. Excellent, timely reports, greatly improved over 1986. "West Germany Pays The Price for D-Mark Policy," 1-8, provided early clues on the deflating economy, and the internal and foreign pressures on Germany to carry more of the load in lifting the world from stagnation. "Both the OECD and the Bank for International Settlements believe West Germany could bring forward the 1990 fiscal package without endangering budgetary balance," 7-2, but the government instead intends to dilute and delay the tax cut. Perhaps the best of many, "Wunder Turns to Whimper," 11-4, surveys the longer-term performance of the German economy. Economic growth has dropped "very likely permanently below the average of the industrialised world," the employment situation showed "worse deterioration than any other major country apart from Spain and the U.K.," and "capital formation as a proportion of gross national product has almost halved" in this decade. Marsh makes a sophisticated point that most economists missed in "Bundesbank Marches Into The Front Line," 11-25, namely, that "dampening short-term currency inflows [by lowering interest rates] could act to contract, rather than expand, banking liquidity [and the money supply]."

Marshall, Tyler. *Los Angeles Times.* (★ ½)
London bureau chief. The Loch Ness deeps may have held secrets, but none as important as those of the U.K.'s economic contradictions this year. Neither surfaced on his watch this year. Marshall does have a flourish for features that do throw light on the UK scene, however. "Time Erodes Tough Corners in London East End," 11-1, was his best of that genre, a bittersweet account of redevelopment in London's fabled East End, heart of the Cockney community. The "vast stretch of urban decay half the size of Manhattan is the center of the world's biggest inner-city renewal project — about $15 billion of high-rise office space, high-tech industry and 25,000 upscale residential housing units," all of which rends the native East End community, as DINKYs (dual income, no kids yet) pay up to $500,000 for a riverview and "mug a yuppie" graffiti appears. We could have done without "Loch Ness Monster Search Will Try More High Tech," 10-4, though we confess to reading it, simply because Marshall's writing style is so engaging. "After Massacre, Britons Take Aim at Guns and TV," 10-12, goes way beyond the routine to weave in insightful observations on the changing national consciousness underway. "Quiet Talks in Rustic Settings Help Solve World's Ills," 10-11, takes us on a trip far from the madding crowd to Wilton and Ditchley Parks, where diplomats from East and West exchange views and play croquet, and praise the arrangement as perfect for candid exchanges outside the public view. Says one, "More than half the value is what you learn at 5 o'clock in the morning over a glass of Guinness."

Martin, Paul. *The Washington Times.* (NR)
A stringer who appears sporadically in the *WT*, his dispatches were so good they left us wondering why the *Times* or somebody else doesn't snatch him up. Two of note: "Labor Unrest Wreaks Havoc In Australia," 6-9, a well-reported piece on the Union strikes and the politics that sparked it, that had none of the *WSJ*'s human interest nonsense; and "U.S., Australia To Push For Closer Defense Cooperation," 6-19, an analysis of Pacific defense and the strategic importance of Australia, replete with interesting, concise nuggets. Get the man on staff.

McCartney, Robert J. *The Washington Post.* (★)
Bonn bureau chief. He paid attention to political developments within Germany as much as to East-West issues and NATO, but the events were often refracted through a focus on arms control. In "Germany's Once-Radical Greens Now an Established Party with Impact," 1-20, he reports on the niche the Greens have established, concern over the environment along with calls for unilateral withdrawal of U.S. medium range missiles attracting votes. "W. Germans Reelect Kohl's Coalition," 1-26, was reported as "an advance for detente-oriented policies" of the Free Democrats. Escaping any mention, however, were the FD's forceful tax reform proposals during the campaign. An overview of the steps being taken to prevent the spread of AIDS in West Europe, "A Silent Killer Heard 'Round the World," in *The Washington Post Weekly*, 3-30, was okay as a roundup, but off to Teheran, for "Meanwhile in the Capital of Iran...," *Weekly* 5-4, his coverge of Rafsanjani's disclosures about the arms deal with the U.S. could have been written from press comuniques back in the Federal Republic just as easily. "The Shadows Austria Can't Escape," *Weekly* 4-24, got into Chancellor Franz Vranitzky's perspectives for redressing the country's adverse image abroad because of President Kurt Waldheim's WWII activities in Hitler's army. An analytic on the May state elections examined defense worries as the cause of Kohl's setbacks in Germany, reporting his murky announcement on the acceptance of a U.S.-Soviet agreement as hurting the Christian Democrats, "German Voters Were Up in Arms," 6-1. He stays clear of economic issues, with no significant probing there all year.

Meisels, Andrew. *The Washington Times.* (NR)
Middle East, based in Israel. A stringer for the *Times* and the *New York Daily News*, Meisels does credible work, but his pieces are often few and far between. In "Settlers Blame Peres For Outbreak Of Terror On West Bank," 4-13, the Judea and Samaria Settlements Council reacts. "Shultz Aide Hears Shamir Inveigh Against Conference," 8-11, reports P.M. Yitzhak

Shamir's position in meeting with Charles Hill, personal assistant to Secretary of State George Shultz. Hill, he reports, didn't push for an international conference, but brought it up as one of several options.

Meisler, Stanley. *Los Angeles Times.* (★ ½)
Paris bureau chief. He keeps up with the political news, a decent hand with feature material also, and was energetic on a temporary Moscow assignment. "Mitterrand, Chirac Clash Over Racial Conflict in Distant New Caledonia," 8-29, gives a good picture of this festering political conflict in France, plus background on the Kanak-European tensions in the territory, but South African-like images weren't appropriate. In his feature, "As 200th Anniversary Nears, French Still Fret Over Revolution," 10-13, he examines the signs of divided sentiment among Frenchmen over their revolution, but puts the most significant material at the end: "As more and more French intellectuals turned their backs on the Soviet Union in the last two decades, scholars felt free to study the French Revolution closely without any ideological need to justify it." Reporting from Moscow, he contributed to *LAT*'s series, "Remaking the Revolution," with "Changes Bring Both Hope, Fear," 11-1, and "Few Can Agree on Where Soviet Reforms Will Lead," 11-5. They both showed a lot of work, Meisler interviewing numerous citizens and officials to add to our picture of the events taking place there. Certainly not as deep or with the sensitivity to key nuances someone there all year might show, but overall enough to satisfy. Off to North Africa for a strictly routine "Tunisia Calm as Bourgiba Is Replaced," 11-8, there's not much there he couldn't have as easily rounded up from analysts and TV reports in France.

Melcher, Richard A. *BusinessWeek.* (★ ★)
London bureau manager. With *The New York Times* London bureau jumping to the head of the pack early in the year, Melcher's material seemed to have a relative decline. But *BW* readers still got his steady, cogent political reports, with Melcher holding an edge on the stock exchange. His "Instant Relic: The New Exchange Floor," 1-12, was one such, the "spanking new $5 million trading floor is about to become the Big Bang's latest victim," as traders flee to their computerized dealing rooms. In "Thatcher, After the Crash," 11-16, Melcher gives us a snapshot of where things stand, all the relevant stats on the economy and budget, but the analytical component seemed tepid: "More bad news for Britain is almost certainly on the way" is too strong a statement given the evidence he presents. Another post-Crash report on "How the Highest Rollers Overseas Made Out," 11-9, was thankfully more than just a scorecard of winners and losers, saved by quotes from Big Winner Sir James Goldsmith, who tells Sir Gordon White, "We're the only two around with plenty of money." The two, writes Melcher, are among the super-rich who smelled something wrong in the market and cashed out...[Goldsmith] is on the sidelines for now. 'I don't know how deep this is going to go.'" One of his better analytical pieces was a book review, "A Bitter Obituary for a Once-Proud Country," 7-13, reviewing Britain's post-WWII industrial slumber.

Miller, Marjorie. *Los Angeles Times.* (★ ★ ★)
San Salvador bureau chief. She makes the *LAT* a must-read on Central America, up there with *The Washington Post* and ahead of the *NYT*. Skilled at knowing what to look for, there's a conclusive tone to her reporting. She caught our attention with "Fiery Leader Quits Nicaragua To Embrace Contra Cause," 5-24, a straightforward report, the essentials without a spin. She knows how to discriminate between key and secondary matters, displaying that in her coverage of the Central American peace talks, as in "Duarte Offers to Meet with Guerrillas," 8-14, which gave a clear picture of both sides' perspectives. She notes Reuben Zamora of the Revolutionary Democratic Front ready to "take advantage of the political space the [Central American peace] plan offers," but doesn't leave out the fact that "The guerrillas of El Salvador's Faribundo Marti National Liberation Front receive logistical and military assistance from Nicaragua as well as Cuba and the Soviet Union," in "Contra, Salvador Rebels Leaders May Go Home to Join Legal Opposition," 8-21. She catches the importance of the Contadora foreign

ministers' inclusion in the commission to monitor the peace plan, reporting in "Officials to Monitor Latin Accord Named," 8-23, that Nicaragua needs them as "an instrument of pressure on the five Central American countries." The discriminating eye again in Panama, catching the first serious split between Noriega and his functionaries in "Thousands Stage Panama Protest," 8-7, when Pres. Delvalle countermanded the ban on demonstrations ordered by Noriega's cousin and mayor of Panama City. She secured an important interview with Delvalle, 8-14, which revealed how little power he has, his confusion at the "mixed signals" coming from the U.S., and his assertion that a cutoff of U.S. aid will increase pressure to turn to the Soviets. One of the *LAT*'s best foreign correspondents.

Miller, Matt. *The Asian Wall Street Journal.* (★ ★ ½)
New Delhi bureau. Finally someone besides the *Financial Times*' Elliott is producing steady streams of details and analysis on the changing political economy here. "Gandhi Shifts Controversial Finance Minister," 2-2, on the shifting of Vishwavath Pratap Singh from Finance to Defense and how the business community is dissatisfied with his performance, initial euphoria turning to alienation, especially by old-guard businessmen who flourished under the protectionist environment. "Glow Fading From Rajiv Gandhi's Halo," 3-24, has an adequate picture of Gandhi losing his grip: "The prime minister's image has changed quickly from that of a young, dynamic statesman to an immature, often ill-informed and sometimes petulant politician," although he continues to reign supreme in both his party and the country. "Philippines' Latest Coup Attempt Underscores Aquino's Weaknesses," 8-31, was one of the few press accounts that continued to report projection of 6.5% GNP growth in the Philippines, but had none of the details of the program outlined to achieve it. A roundup of criticism of Cory's past softness was nothing new, although he reports that "After the first bid to seize power in July 1986...Ramos ordered 30 push-ups for the rebel soldiers." A marvelous "High Tech World Sees IBM Case As Way Out Of The Copyright Maze," 9-18, which was clear on the legal/technical issue, as a substitute for a court battle, showing promise for all of the global computer industry.

Montalbano, William D. *Los Angeles Times.* (★ ★)
Rome bureau chief. A strong reporter on the South American beat, he moved from Buenos Aires to Italy during the year, leaving a hole *LAT* has yet to fill. He gets high marks for his South American reporting. We aren't getting the kind of solid material on Italy his predecessor Don A. Schanche used to pour out, however. Next year, we hope. His best from Argentina, "Selling Dream of Reform, Alfonsin Tours Heartland," 8-14, gives us a portrait of Alfonsin and his circumstances, "the man whose plans exceed his grasp." While the rule of law has returned to Argentina, official venality endures in a suffocating bureaucracy, he reported, and the President still hasn't subordinated the armed forces to civilian control. Though we didn't get enough of an analytic, he did outline Alfonsin's intentions of scrapping a U.S.-style of government in favor of a parliamentary system. We found his detailed report on lifestyles of U.S. businessmen and diplomats in Colombia and Peru thoroughly absorbing. Targets for kidnappers and terrorists, he reported in "Expatriates 'Hostage' to Safety Fears," 8-5, it's "No jogging, no golf, no bike rides, no picnics...The world is one big no." From Italy, he keeps abreast but not out ahead, still a little too routine, as in "Bush Meets Italian Leaders At Start Of European Trip," 9-26; "Catholic Bishops Gather to Consider Role of Laity," 10-2; and "Pope Promises Action in Upgrading Laity," 10-31: Nothing there we couldn't get from the wires. His feature on the product of prosperity, "Rome Copes With Eternal Woe: Traffic," 11-5, was fine in and of itself, but was there really anyone who didn't already know that?

Moody, John. *Time.* (★)
Mexico City bureau. Well-organized reports from Mexico and Guatemala, he gets credit for trying to cover the brutal economic conditions there. "A Swelling Tide of Troubles," 2-23, on the Mexican economy had no mention of the stock market surge in December '86, or the

capital inflow, but left us with an image we cannot forget: "Pollution is so bad in Mexico City (pop. 18 million) that birds regularly drop dead from the soot-filled sky." "Giving Democracy a Chance," 4-20, a sort-of profile of Guatemalan President Cerezo, and his efforts for peace in Central America. His luck, in simply staying in office, "having survived two coup attempts," sounds extraordinary.

Morgan, Jeremy. *The Journal of Commerce.* (★)
Buenos Aires. Not quite up to the high standard of other country reports from this paper, or to his own work last year. Very few facts, except about inflation. Too often he sounds like an uncritical press secretary for the finance minister, who "will insist on substantial cuts in interest rates when he meets senior international bankers," 4-8, and "unveiled a complex set of measures aimed at battling inflation," 7-23, and "has also taken the plunge toward full-scale deregulation of Argentina's state-dominated oil industry," 7-22. There was a provocative teaser about Brazil and Argentina adopting a common currency, 7-16, "as a solid first step toward creating a Latin American economic and political alliance similar to the European Community."

Mydans, Seth. *The New York Times.* (½★)
Manila bureau chief. A few timely, informative reports from India and Bangladesh, but unproductive again this year on his major beat, the Philippines. We're still getting soggy impressions instead of hard analysis or reporting that digs deeply. "In Truce, Filipino Rebels Press a Political Point," 1-18, romanticizes the communists, a husband-and-wife team as oh-so-lovely, but almost no probing on motivations in the Aquino era. "As Truce Ends, Rebel Leader Tries a Taste of Normal Life," 2-8, was a waste, telling us about Victoria Justiniani, NPA peace negotiator, who takes advantage of the truce to put on borrowed perfume, high heels, earrings and go out for an evening. "Aquino Demands Military Victory Over Insurgents," 3-23, a straight report on armed actions, not reform as an answer to terrorism and the escalation of communist attacks, was better. "A Sign Of War In Philippines: The Refugees," 4-8, was intriguing on the government's new aggressive policy toward communists, the soldiers eager to fight, now feeling less restrained by Aquino. "Aquino Decrees A Compromise On Land Reform," 7-23, was thin on details: "Ms. Aquino appeared to have been most sensitive to the pressures of large landowners," leaving questions of timetable, maximum legal holding and priorities for redistribution of different types of croplands in the hands of the legislature rather than rewriting the decree. "In The Big Manila Land Plan, Steps Are Small," 10-18, was gullible reporting, taking arguments at face value, quoting a communist leader who says they "would have had a problem if Ms. Aquino had implemented liberal democratic reforms such as land reform," and "Through much of the country, extreme poverty is the result of the land shortage and the imbalance in ownership." His reports from other areas were better. "India Signs Pact With Sri Lanka To End Turmoil," 7-30, gave details on the widespread rioting, the most disputed element of the agreement is the creation of a single semi-autonomous administrative unit for the Northern and Eastern province. "A Bank Battles Poverty," 7-12, had the potential for a four-star magazine piece, but was sliced to fit in "The Week in Review," on Grameen Bank in Bangladesh lending tiny amounts to the poor at 16% interest, with a 98% rate of repayment.

Nagorski, Andrew. *Newsweek.* (★)
Bonn bureau chief. Nagorski gets a bit deeper than some of his compatriots in the weekly business, immersing himself in the story. "The Rebirth of an Idea," 3-30, on *Mitteleuropa*, or the reunification of Europe, was finely tuned, nicely treated, going further than the standard weekly fare: it "ought to be an anti-xenophobic idea." His "Too Long at the Table," 4-6, was a nice overview on Willy Brandt's resignation as chairman of the SDP. "Germany: East Meets West," 9-14, he wonders if ever again East really will meet West: is reunification of Germany really an issue? But in a year of political and economic ferment in and around his

beat, he either didn't produce the big, deep material we know he can, or the magazine didn't want it.

Neilan, Edward. *The Washington Times.* (★ ★)
Tokyo bureau chief. The descriptive Neilan brings a good sense of the politics of the region to his dispatches, as well as a view of the people. With so much ground for him to cover in a busy, busy year, there weren't as many deeper analytical pieces from him as we'd come to expect in earlier years. "Military Risk Seen in N. Korean Olympics Frustration," 2-19, showed there's no hint of compromise in North Korea's call for a bigger share of the Olympic schedule, compounded by the fear that if North Korea is deserted by its allies in this stance, unbearable humiliation could lead to serious military provocation. His reporting of the Korean protests was vivid. In "Seoul Fears Protests, Rounds Up Hundreds," 6-10, South Korea's first steps down the slippery slope seemed on the surface to be quite different from Cory's people-power. "Thousands Protest Chun's Successor," 6-11, told of how "Police and protestors kicked and punched each other while the lobby string orchestra played a Viennese waltz." Then, in "South Koreans Ecstatic Over Reform Vows," 6-30, we find that "Taxi drivers refused payment for rides. Pedestrians excitedly discussed prospects for a new electoral system and a downtown Seoul tea house put up a sign reading, 'Free tea service on this delightful day'" in celebration of promises made. "Korean Kims' Accord Judged Fragile," 7-2, gave us very good detail on the politics and background of the two Kims. Neilan's December dispatches from Seoul on the election campaigns were competitive, frequently with touches and detail we did not see elsewhere.

Nelan, Bruce W. *Time.* (★)
Johannesburg correspondent. Usually under someone else's byline, Nelan, when he pops up on his own, produces concise, credible pieces, a good cut above wire service quality. "New Man in the Townships," 2-23, on the comings and goings of the first black ambassador to South Africa, Edward Perkins was the best we'd seen: "A resolution of S.A.'s troubles will take a long time, he says, Americans are too impatient for quick fixes and should learn to plan and work for the long haul." His "306 Solutions to a Baffling Problem," 3-23, was an interesting exploration of the scenario set forth by, and reaction to *South Africa: The Solution*, a non-fiction bestseller in South Africa. It described a political system allowing differing forms of government under the umbrella of a national two-house parliament, only capable of policing essential national interests, such as defense, finance and foreign relations, and allowing the cantons each to have their own parliament, constitution and form of government. "Digging Out To Avoid A Cave-In," 9-7, was straight, cut-and-dried reporting with adequate information on the union settlements in South Africa.

Newman, Barry. *The Wall Street Journal.* (★ ½)
London. He had promising material all year from all over Eastern Europe, but insufficiently worked, it was slow rising and unleavened. "Budapest Embraces a Democratic Device: The Survey of Opinion," 1-8, gave us Hungary and the use of pollsters, but Newman doesn't say to what end. "Quiet Crusade," 6-1, had no new information on the Church's strategy in Poland, as John Paul prepared to visit his homeland again, just "steady, subtle steps toward making totalitarianism less total." His "Solidarity's Legacy," 7-23, contained good raw research, a real sense of the progress the democrats are making since martial law was imposed, but Newman thinks all this activity in the underground somehow has something to do with *glasnost*, or at least he implies it. He does, though, mention the appearance of the new conservative monthly *Res Publica*, telling us the state doesn't own it, the church doesn't protect it, but no other details: it's "a private, critical publication." But "Red Greenbacks: The Dollar Is Strong In Poland, at Least, and Greatly Prized," 2-5, was an exception, strongly done: "While their Soviet mentors look upon alien currency as a corrupt influence, the Polish authorities not only let a dollar economy thrive alongside their own they operate it."

Nordland, Rod. *Newsweek.* (−)
Roving foreign correspondent and deputy foreign editor. Still biased, inflammatory and dramatic, but so prolific we couldn't discount him. Caution is the watchword with all his reports. In "Is There a Contra Drug Connection?" 1-26, he interviewed two convicted drug traffickers who claimed the DEA and CIA knew about drug and weapons operations and contra involvement, but presents no other sources. "A Pakistan Bombshell," 3-16, was fine, but opens a whole new story in the last sentence that's left unexplored: "If the nuclear club really has a new member, the subcontinent may be in for a frightening new arms race." A related issue was lightly treated in "A Rock And A Hard Place," with David Newell, 7-27, on the Pakistanis and the development of a nuclear bomb, and the to-aid-or-not-to-aid dilemma of Congress. "Nicaragua: Radical Flick," 4-20, was confusing, and cutely structured (it reads like a script) on Alex Cox's film on William Walker, who took over Nicaragua in 1856 and ruled for two years. There's a point in here somewhere, about the political implications of the film and the government, which assigned to it a "national producer," but muddled. "A Do-Or-Die Offensive," 5-11, and "The New Contras?" 6-1, the product of three weeks with a contra unit gave us, respectively, semi-profiles of four contras, and a portrait of a poorly run, undirected contra resistance from a reporter who ran then with *the Sandinistas*, that was slanted and ideological in the Sandinistas' favor. He tells us "The conduct of the Sandinistas made a striking contrast with the contras...We never saw the Sandinistas impress campesinos as guides or make them walk in front of the troops. Peasants we talked to from both sides all agreed that only contras do that" and concludes in agreement with a Nicaraguan citizen that the war has degenerated "into banditry" on the part of the contras. Absolutely biased and inexcusable, Nordland would make a better editorial writer than a reporter. Get him a column where he can express his opinion openly instead of clandestinely.

Norman, Peter. *The Wall Street Journal.* (★ ★ ½)
London. A first rate correspondent whose byline has our instant respect, but who never really knocks us out. He came closest, early in the year, with "British Tories' Fortunes Are Renewed By Labor's Mistakes, Changed Attitudes," 1-2, observing the Tories' advance is sluggish on tax reform, but Labour gets no edge because it's so estranged from the electorate. Norman sees new relationships emerging as traditional labor voters move slowly under Thatcher toward a more market-oriented world, but with no real dynamic yet for a self-sustaining enterprise culture. A report on "Lawson Unveils Cautious British Budget," 3-18, presents details on the cut in the basic income-tax rate to 27% from 29%, but with nothing on the impact on economic debate. Norman's "Europe Debates the Mark's Leading Role," 9-8, is helpful to us in getting a glimpse of detail on these discussions, analysis okay, but we think, what? It's flat. Can nothing be done to prevent occasional devaluations? There's a Deutschemark deflationary bias hereabouts, we suspect. His "British Stock Slide Puzzles Government," 10-28, has all the numbers we want to see, but Nigel Lawson is not depicted in full fury as we have heard from other sources, on his dismay in seeing London follow Wall Street over the cliff, especially after London has been so responsible. We somehow think Norman is capable of greater adventures.

Norton, Chris. *In These Times.* (★)
El Salvador corespondent for *ITT*, he frequently appears in *The Christian Science Monitor* as well. Norton certainly has a set of biases and an ideological model that often intrudes, but his investigative zeal produced new information less fully explored by others on this beat. "Salvador War Tax Causes Political Stir," *CSM*, 1-9, was one of the better press accounts of President Jose N. Duarte's imposition of a new tax on net worth coupled with steep hikes in rates for higher brackets. Norton gave a balanced report on the "right" and labor opposition against this harsh austerity amidst conditions where 60% of the economically active population is already under- or unemployed. In "Salvador Poor Skeptical of New Draft Law," *CSM*, 1-20, he uncovered the forced recruiting of young men from poor communities as the new

law for obligatory military service for men and women was put into effect. "Salvadorean Hopes for a New Era Fade," *CSM*, 7-9, was less satisfying, a little too much "diplomats and political analysts say." Similarly, "A Comeback for the Death Squads," *ITT*, 7-22, rounds up a variety of sources, the credibility of some very questionable, to report a resurgence of death squad activity. His quote from Herbert Anaya of the Human Rights Commission is unconvincing on what is taking place: "There will be an increase in repression, simply because the causes of dissent are still there. There is still hunger, misery, lack of housing and political demagoguery that promises a lot but delivers nothing." The material in "Christian Democrats Gripped by Corruption," *ITT*, 8-19, was handled a little better, a wider range of sources employed.

O'Boyle, Thomas. *The Wall Street Journal.* (★ ★)
Bonn. Attentive and timely on the politics and economics of West Germany, he was still sluggish when it came to peeling away the layers for the missing detail. "Cautious W. German Monetary Policy..." 1-8, told us *no one at the Fed* expects much change at the Bundesbank after the January 25 elections, with Helmut Schlesinger arguing for tightening to stay within 6% money-supply growth, but nothing on pro-growth arguments to dispel the layers of gloom. "Rau Campaigns Less to Win Than to Avert a Disaster for the Social Democrats," 1-20, gave us the divided social dems — Rau opposed the Social Democrat-Green coalition; the Greens are picking up gains on the left and the Social Democrats are leaderless and fragmented, but there's not a lot here. "German Central Bank Chief Believes Dollar Decline Has Gone Far Enough," 1-26, was better, a timely interview with Karl Otto Poehl that asked the right questions. "Slow W. German Growth Saps Europe and Dims U.S. Hopes on Trade Deficit," 3-23, was again timely, but little on the internal debate or the prospects for policy change, and there was nothing really to support his claim of the "sapping" of Europe. Better later in the year with "German Neutrality Is Gaining Ground Among Right Wing Upset By Arms Talks," 6-2, which managed to take a large and important story and present it in a concise way that leaves us, not just with the evidence, but with a good feel for the meaning and significance of the evidence. "Support For More Stimulative Measures Wanes Within Germany's Government," 8-7, reports signs that the government is having second thoughts about the already promised tax cuts and is closing ranks in opposition to more stimulative measures. The *Financial Times* was way ahead on this, but O'Boyle gives us a nice update.

Oka, Takashi. *The Christian Science Monitor.* (★ ★)
Tokyo. Chief Far Eastern correspondent. His report on a Japanese view of their educational system, 1-15, was better than *USN&WR*'s cover story on the subject. A good political-economic report, "Japanese Worry That US Ready to Wage War on Trade Surplus," 1-20, revealed the "crisis atmosphere" in Tokyo as the yen soared on foreign exchange markets, squeezing the Japanese economy — exports down in quantity and soon in terms of dollars. Also fine, 3-10 on the 25% work-force loss in steel with cost-saving cuts and the shattering of "Japan is steel" national mythology. He played the interview with U.S. Ambassador Mike Mansfield all wrong, 5-21, putting what should have been the lead at the end — Mansfield's proposal to create a free trade agreement with Japan, using it as a vanguard to pull all the Pacific Basin along. Nakasone's tasks and troubles were adequately addressed, 4-14 and 4-29, yet his trip to Washington and Japan's elections begged for deeper treatment. Oka was good on the Korean scene, noting Chun's deferral on constitutional change and widespread support for direct presidential elections in "The Dilemma of Transition," 4-14. "South Korea Unions: A Potent Voice Shaping Democracy Debate," 9-21, provided sociological insights on the coming restructuring of Korean society. Not a lot of new material on the various candidates, though he was alert on Roh Tae Woo's singular qualities, 6-22, and reported, 7-29, the radicals' perspective to heighten labor unrest, angered over Roh's ability to outflank them. We expected better from him than "no one knows" how the military, students, unions and candidates will interact in shaping the new democracy, 9-22. He got his feet wet in the ROC with "New Breed of Leaders Comes to Fore in Taiwan," 9-16, but sunk with a routine "Japan's New Premier to Push Old-Style Consensus," 10-20.

Orme, William A. Freelance. (★ ★ ★)
Mexico. A stringer whose reports appear in *The Washington Post* and *The Journal of Commerce*, Orme has a serious focus on the Mexican economy, though his political reporting holds up well, also. Very capable at describing the current conditions, digging up a mass of details we don't see elsewhere, he gets very close to a comprehensive picture, but leaves uninvestigated the country's onerous tax, tariff and regulatory structures. "Strike Closes Key Mexican University," *WAPO*, 1-30, gave us a close-up look at the student strike over the entrenchment of the bureaucracy at National Autonomous University in Mexico, which may possibly affect the '88 elections. "Mexico May Be Forced to Follow (Brazil)," *JOC*, 2-24, told us of the political pressures that may push Mexico into a debt moratorium, pointing out "Mexico has yet to receive a penny from the crucial $7.7 billion commercial component of the rescue package." In *The Nation*, we had "Mexico," 4-11, a broad analysis of how the UNAM strike of January was unlike the 1968 Tatelolco massacre, in that there was no explicit leftist focus on broad social change; it was more on alterations in academic policy, saying the PRI caved in to student demands lest the protest spill over into other issues. Now the students, we find, are reaching out to bigger constituencies, in a somewhat Pyrrhic victory; the elite trend is away from UNAM. Not much incentive to fix the economy, according to "Mexico Clinches Loan With Negative Growth," 5-18, since "negative 3% growth...has made Mexico eligible for $500 million...under a World Bank guarantee program." In "U.S. Affiliates Help Mexico Boost Sales," 6-26, the biggest Mexican exporters of manufactured goods are U.S. companies, like Chrysler, Ford and IBM, which worry about U.S. protectionism. "End Of Mexico's Oil-Boom Era Has Meant Hardship For Citizens," 8-16, had good closeups of the citizenry and statistical relationships. Orme never lets his own point of view intrude, and we appreciate it.

Parks, Michael. *Los Angeles Times.* (★ ★)
Johannesburg bureau chief. We didn't see the kind of work this year that won him a Pulitzer for his 1986 reporting, and there was a tendency this year to stick to a fixed view in political coverage. A short but concise reading on Pretoria's perspectives for the year with "S. Africa to Resist U.S. Pressure for Talks With Blacks, Foreign Minister Says," 2-4, quotes Roelof F. (Pik) Botha's angry message to the U.S. that Congress' "sanctions...have discouraged black moderates from coming forward to negotiate...and have encouraged the radicals in their violence." The government's intentions remain negotiation from strength, which means continued effort to restore law and order. Very rigid in his post-election analysis, "Botha's Vote Victory Sharpens Lines of Conflict," 5-10, he discounts it as a boost to Botha's efforts at gradual reform, but instead concludes that "South Africa now appears to be moving toward direct political, and probably armed, conflict on an even broader scale than before..." "S. Africa Trial Becomes Political Forum," 8-8, gives us wide coverage to the testimony of UDF general secretary Popo Molefe during his trial for treason, but without any assessment. The charge that the government's step-by-step efforts at reform are "simply attempts to prolong white rule" is left unexamined. "'Orderly Urbanization' — S. Africa Eases Resettlement," 11-19, was more along the lines of his previous year's work. South Africa's "influx laws" and the country's enormous housing crisis are illuminated in this feature, and here we find signs of progress and change. Especially well done, "Angola Sacrifices a Bit of Ideology to Boost Economy," 8-8, reporting the abandonment of plans for a big state farm because the government "didn't have anyone who could manage 200 dairy cows and operate a big farm."

Pollack, Maxine. *Insight.* (★ ★)
Pollack joined the weekly in April, a welcome addition to their cadre of fine correspondents. "Pious Plans Under An Official Knell," 6-1, told us that Lithuania's last bastion of nationalist thinking is the church, *glasnost* having produced few positive changes there. Soviets are making special efforts to deny that the church is the chief defender of Lithuania's cultural heritage and its real interests, although June marked 600 years of Christianity in the country. "Thousands Of Citizens Sent To Uncertain East Bloc Future," 7-27, on the 60,000 Vietnamese "guest

workers'' in the USSR and the East Bloc, had revealing information on these circumstances; we hadn't seen the subject treated as well anywhere else. ''Signs That Moscow Is Tiring Of War,'' 8-3, was a thorough update on Afghanistan, detailing impressive victories from the resistance's summer offensive, like the column of 5,500 Soviet troops, including Spetsnaz special forces, that were turned back after hand-to-hand combat in June and heavy desertions from the Afghan army. She also reports of better coordination via the U.S.-backed Afghan alliance and of the decisive role of stingers and British Blowpipes. An impressive start.

Pond, Elizabeth. *The Christian Science Monitor.* (★ ½)
Veteran Bonn bureau chief, who also spent time in Moscow and often files from Washington. Pond partially plugged the hole we noted in her reporting last year, delivering several stories on the German economy, and Bonn's view of U.S. economic moves, with pieces such as 11-23's ''West Germany Gives Thumbs Up to US Deficit-reduction Plan.'' On the whole, however, she stuck with defense and arms control issues, and there her record was mixed: solid on German politico-military developments, unbalanced and off the mark on U.S.-Soviet arms control and SDI, which she repeatedly, and to our minds annoyingly, referred to as President Reagan's ''pet.'' Her most disappointing story of the year was ''Soviets Push Reagan to Reexamine What SDI Is Worth to Him,'' 10-26, which went to great lengths rationalizing for Gorbachev's short-lived back-tracking on the summit, complete with the anti-SDI quotes inserted as ''analysis.'' Ditto on 9-30, with a veiled promotion for Paul Nitze's hidden-hand campaign to negotiate SDI testing limits. In the ''oh, really?'' category was 7-6's ''West Germany Welcomes Elimination of Medium-range Missiles,'' focusing on the zero option, which certainly contradicts much of the off-the-record comments from Europeans before and since. On the plus side was a thorough series on East German strongman Erich Honecker's visit to West Germany, 9-4, 9-8, 9-9, 9-11. Pond also produced a subtle, informative piece on the split in the West German Green Party, 11-24. She was very early on the INF breakthrough, ''Soviet Said To Offer New 'Zero Option,''' 4-2, but couldn't resist opening with ''In one of his shrewdest tactical moves to date on arms control, Soviet leader Mikhail Gorbachev...''; she was sold the story on short-range missiles by Bonn officials recently in Moscow. There was disputed significance of Pershing 1's in an 8-24 ''sideshow'' story, which demonstrated the arms-bad, treaty-good mindset that has seeped into the *Monitor*'s reporting.

Porter, Janet. *The Journal of Commerce.* (★ ★)
London. The European bureau chief scored with ''Signs Point to June Election,'' 5-15, where the Labour Party seems to be a collection of feuding minority interests with irrelevant values, which has ''suffered from the government's hugely successful privatization program that has made millions of people shareholders for the first time.'' Yet ''Suddenly, Thatcher Runs Scared,'' 6-2, has Labour's Neil Kinnock winning a poll as the best campaigner, with his party revitalized around the National Health issue. A little-noticed danger of declining international lending, 5-27, due to investor concerns ''about future exchange rate and interest rate trends...[which] may result in a switch toward national markets, and especially government paper.''

Powers, Charles T. *Los Angeles Times.* (★ ★)
Warsaw bureau chief. A stalwart of *LAT*'s foreign corps, the former Nairobi bureau chief settled right into his Polish assignment this year, handling especially well the course of the regime's attempts at economic and political reordering. One of his best, ''Poland Chews on the True Cost of Meat,'' 11-17, was an excellent feature on an issue that has historically provoked social upheavals in the country. ''Western TV Shows Still Aren't for Everyone in Poland,'' 11-14, was lighter, but also revealing on the limits to logical, wonderful ideas (using a round dish antenna to provide better TV reception for an entire apartment block). Gen. Jaruzelski's political reforms remained vague, but Powers gives us crystal clear pictures of the economic reforms in ''Warsaw Uses Hard Sell to Urge Poles to Approve Reforms,'' 11-28. His roundup on ''what may be a unique experiment in democracy in post-war Eastern Europe,'' the

referendum on political and economic reform, was comprehensive and detailed, one of the best overall. He produced several very strong features with his solid reporting this year. "Polish Grave Site Reopens War Wounds," 9-28, combined the best of both his strengths.

Preston, Julia. *The Washington Post.* (★ ★ ★)
Salvador bureau chief. Commendable work all year, Preston was one of the foreign desk's brighter lights, contributing to the *Post*'s superior Central American coverage. "Ortega Signs Nicaragua Charter, Quickly Suspends Many Rights," 1-10, gave us the scoop on the new constitution, the powers it gives the president to rule without it, the opposition's refusal to endorse it, and Ortega's suspension of rights. "Nicaraguan Medical Care Crimped By Shortages," 1-27, detailed the seriously deteriorating situation in medical services there, but we wonder why she repeats, without questioning, the Sandinista claim that it increased life expectancy by three years with its health campaigns after 1979. She is careful to report the U.S. embargo specifically exempts medical supplies and quotes Health Minister Dorin Tellez that there's no evidence U.S. customs are blocking shipment of medical spare parts to Nicaragua. "Contras Burn Clinic During Raid on Village," 3-7, was only so-so on the contras alienating their supporters, but at least it's balanced, giving several sides. "Contras Active In Rural Nicaragua," 8-1, was also well-balanced, and timely on this important development.

Quinn-Judge, Paul. *The Christian Science Monitor.* (★ ★ ★)
Moscow. Strong on covering the "battle of ideas" at the higher levels of Soviet society, his attention to their translation into practice at the lower levels was weaker. But so timely and keyed in on the critical shifts on the margin in the leadership, he was essential on Gorbachev's reforms all year. "Gorbachev Proposes Changes That Would Challenge the Elite," 1-28, crisp assessment of the speech before the Central Committee and the very bold perspectives outlined. "Gorbachev's Task," 1-30, was perceptive on the stage of battle between Gorbachev and the local party "mafia" — "In the world of ideas, *perestroika* is doing very well. Now we need to start seeing its effects in the shops." Comprehensive on the unprecedented degree of proposed structural changes, 3-10, and despite Soviet criticism for reporting on resistance to Gorbachev, he provided continued insights into the factional line-ups, as with the study of Yegor Ligachev, 5-22, and the reporting on Boris Yeltsin's "frustration" at the slow pace of reform, 11-2. Additionally, "Gorbachev Shakes Up Military," 6-1, on Defense Minister Sokolov's replacement, Gen. Dimitri Yazov. Crisp, informative material throughout the year, as in "Moscow Trip Strengthens Thatcher," 4-2, with Maggie besting Soviet journalists on TV, lunching with Sakharov and boosting Gorbachev's reforms; also "Soviet Afghan Vet on Life at the Front," 10-7, was sparse, but informative, the first interview we saw with a genuine Afghan vet. Less sanguine than the *NYT* with his "Soviet Leader Fails to Boost Bold Reform," 11-3 assessing Gorbachev's speech on the 70th anniversary of the revolution. He reports frustration, disappointment among the reformers, seeing a shift toward the middle, Gorbachev "spinning his wheels."

Raines, Howell. *The New York Times.* (★ ★ ★ ★)
London bureau chief. A satisfying year, his first at the post, Raines was relentless in delivering brilliant analytical insights and rich, economical reporting that made us feel right at home across the British isles. "British Politics: One Eye on a Third Force," 2-9, Howell's first from London, was well-focused, asking can the Liberal and Social Democratic Party gain enough seats in the coming election to deny Maggie a majority? The breakthrough piece was "Key to Irish Election: Reagan-Thatcher Economics," 2-15, which gave us the economic detail of the Irish political debate that we were looking for. After that everything seemed to fall into place. "Labor Chief Fighting Thatcher, Tries to Calm Party Storms," 3-15, was short and sweet, not wasting a word, on Neil Kinnock going backwards, struggling against the "loony London left" and worried about Maggie's coming tax cuts on income with a new "jobs package." Raines draws a parallel with the '84 Mondale race, which he covered for the *Times*, "In Britain, Battle Is On For Compassion Votes," 5-25. A Sunday *Magazine* cover, "Thatcher's

Capitalist Revolution," 5-31, did a fine job of telling us what's behind Maggie's remarkable transformation of Britain from "sick man of Europe" to a property-owning democracy with brilliant insights, notes, observations, reportage, one of the 10-best foreign pieces of the year. "Thatcher Keeping Her Head In Polls," 6-7, was a satisfying account of "the most Americanized campaign even in Britain because of its emphases on personality and staging," with Maggie still seven points up. A banner year for Raines.

Rapoport, Carla. *Financial Times.* (★ ★ ★)
Tokyo correspondent. There was no encore to her four-star work of last year, perhaps a change in *FT*'s Tokyo bureau this year a factor. We noted that her longer pieces were often double-bylined with several other *FT* correspondents during the year, but we still got healthy production from her solo efforts. Attentive on budget and tax policy movement, she noted that "VAT is the glue holding together...[Nakasone's] budget and his plans to cut taxes," but with the opposition regarding "like AIDS, something that could kill the whole country," a defeat on it could end any plans for extension of Nakasone's tenure, "Japanese Up in Arms About VAT," 2-11. "Tokyo Approves Framework to Boost Domestic Economy," 4-8, was sketchier on details of the LDP's pump-priming recommendations, though she reports 80% of the government's public works projects are front-loaded into the first half of the year. More detailed, "Why Tokyo's $35bn Boost Should Impress," 4-14, finds the government still tight-lipped on the hows and whens of implementation, but committed to "expansion of domestic demand" via pump-priming. "Tokyo Admits to Flaws in US-Japan Chip Pact," 2-12, reported MITI's attempts to come up with a solution satisfactory to the U.S. "Japan Cuts Chips Output in Bid to Save US Pact," 2-19, further elaborates, reporting the orders to cut production by as much as 20% and the steps to enhance market access for foreign chipmakers in Japan. She shifted gears quickly, catching the change in attitude with "Japan Condemns 'Unfair Play' of US in Chip Negotiation," 4-13, and "Tokyo Mulls Retaliatory Move on US Imports," 4-14. One of her best, an assessment of the likely impact of the trade sanctions, "Japanese Lose Face, But Not Much Business," 4-21, with all the signs of a humiliated and angered Japan reported.

Raun, Laura. *Financial Times.* (★ ★)
Amsterdam. The Netherlands provides one of the best examples of "Eurosclerosis," particularly in the 11-23 "Survey" on that country, with several very fine pieces from different angles by Raun. "Unfortunately, most discussion centers on how to ensure that slowly expanding wealth is fairly shared out and less on how to create more wealth, and therein lies the biggest risk for the future...Combined taxes and welfare premiums are so progressive that salary increases and overtime work sometimes leave the worker with less take-home pay...Joblessness has not fallen below 14 percent in six years, partly because unemployment, disability and welfare benefits are so high and permanent." A glimmer of hope in "Support Grows for Dutch Tax Reductions," 3-13, due to "worries over high Dutch taxes and the floor they put under wage and manufacturing costs."

Reiss, Spencer. *Newsweek.* (★)
Johannesburg. Concise, firmly packaged writing gives Reiss' dispatches a taut feel. "South Africa's Fault Lines," 5-11, was a credible summary of South African electoral politics and policies, followed up by more on the actual elections in "A Stunning Roar For Apartheid," 5-18. But "Botha In The Lion's Den," 6-15, missed the emotional impact of Botha's visit to Sharpville, giving us the sparks but no fire. "Children On The Front Line," 7-27, was the best we saw of his for the year, a terrifying look at what events in South Africa are doing to the psyche of her children.

Revzin, Philip. *The Wall Street Journal.* (★ ★)
Paris bureau. When he keeps a rein on a tendency to overwrite, he produces just what we want — the basic picture and critical details, all crisp, short and sweet. In "Joblessness Threatens

Algeria's Stability,'' 2-25, we find Algeria's growth halted by the oil price decline, and their determination to pay debts, but there's too little detail on policy. "Chirac's Middle East Policy Is Tested By France's Diplomatic Row With Iran,'' 7-20, told us the bold stroke by Chirac has the backing from politicians of both the right and the left. "North Africa's Rulers Seeking To Stem Fundamentalism,'' 8-12, had good material on Islam. "Who Gets the Blame for the French Strikes?'' 1-14, was wonderfully analytical, asking can Chirac muster the courage and patience to alter long-term consequences; the inflation bogey isn't working and the forthcoming elections are hemming him in. "France Economic Outlook,'' 9-11, was exactly what was needed, good detail on policy, stats, to the point directly.

Richburg, Keith B. *The Washington Post.* (★ ½)
Manila bureau. Richburg's Philippines reporting was good on economic and political detail, focus and analysis, but he was swept off his feet in Indochina, his impressionable reporting there upside down. On the up side, his "Enrile Campaigns Against Aquino Dictatorship.'' 1-10, was thorough, the best detail we saw at that point. "Filipinos Criticize Aquino Over Shooting,'' 1-26, reported the pressure on Cory from the church to advance land reform, quoting Jaime Cardinal Sin: the government's failure to implement meaningful land reform "in great measure'' is responsible for the recent shooting deaths and the government's "credibility'' depends on "its sincerity and readiness to act in this area.'' "Philippines Cease-Fire to Expire,'' 2-8, gave us the whole frustrating picture: the blunt rejection of a return to the negotiating table, the rejected plebiscite-approved constitution, and the reports of state disarray in the CPP and NPA over how to handle Aquino's government. "Philippine Senate Smite Enrile With His Past,'' 8-18, was a terrific account of Juan Ponce Enrile's debut in the Senate, all decorum gone in the packed house. The three bylined pieces on the Philippines coup attempt, 8-30, were the best we've seen on Cory's tightrope act, still confused on the particulars but crystal clear on one point: the military just doesn't like Cory. "Guerrillas Kill 21 In Philippines,'' 9-4, had information beyond the body-count headline, with the NPA announcing plans to intensify their activity following the coup attempt, taking advantage of disarray in military. The coverage from elsewhere in the region was more like cheerleading than reporting. "Phnom Penh Recovering From Pol Pot's Rule,'' 4-4, on the new Phnom Penh, was so-so: "a portrait of a city neither fully at peace, nor fully at war.'' "'Wind Of Change Blowing' In Vietnam,'' 7-14, was an overly optimistic overview of new freedoms in Vietnam, as was "In South Of Vietnam, It's Business As Usual,'' 7-15, on socio-capitalism in Vietnam. More hard-hitting was "Hanoi Keeps War Memory Alive To Fuel Demand For US Aid,'' 7-16, giving both sides of the Vietnam aid requests. But there's still too much rah-rah, given the evidence presented.

Richey, Warren. *The Christian Science Monitor.* (★)
Bahrain. Richey provides adequate coverage of the Iran-Iraq war, almost from the front lines, but he too often played second fiddle to Robin Wright's tough dispatches from Teheran. At the height of the reflagging debate and the tanker war, Richey was most prolific, appearing on the front page almost daily. "Iran Exploits Gulf Lull To Put Squeeze On Iraq,'' 7-28, reported Iranian Parliament Speaker Rafsanjani's threat to spread the war directly to the other Gulf states: "A new policy of retaliation,'' in which Iran will "hit industrial or other coastal targets in any country which should back Iraq'' if Iraq resumed air attacks against Iranian oil facilities. "Some Gulf Muslims Are Receptive To Iran Claims On Mecca Tragedy,'' 8-5, was too generalized, thin; based on a conversation with one teen in a Bahrain cafe, Richey theorizes on the extent of anti-American feeling due to the Mecca slaughter. "US Discounts Threat Of Iranian Submarine,'' 8-6, was a sub update, concluding that only their defense department knows for sure. "Unescorted Ships Face Heightened Risks In Gulf,'' 8-11, was dramatic, florid on increasing tensions in the Persian Gulf, but not terribly informative. Later we got insights like "Among Shiites In Iraqi Front-Line City, There's Little Sympathy For Iran,'' 9-21, quoting a Shiite Iraqi sergeant: "...Shia and Sunni don't like Khomeini because Khomeini is bombing them.'' "Gulf Tanker War Gives Region's Shipyards A Booming

Business," 8-19, was much better, giving us a silver-lining type angle on the Gulf war story that we didn't see elsewhere.

Riding, Alan. *The New York Times.* (★ ★ ½)
Rio de Janiero bureau chief. Good on the politics of the region, he's only fair on its economics, but he gets higher marks this year because of his serious efforts to grapple with Brazil's complex economic workings. Sometimes late where he should have been timely, as with Peru's bank nationalizations. In "Crisis in Ecuador: Democracy Is Loser," 1-28, on Fevres Cordero under heavy criticism for freeing Lieutenant General Vargas Pazzos, with signs of his isolation evident in deep rifts in the Armed Forces and Congress turning against him; Riding explains all this by reviewing events that preceded the Taura Air Force base incident outside Guayaguil, 1-16, giving good background on the emerging crisis here. "Brazil Economy: Faith Turns to Fear," 2-9, told us the 600% inflation rate is back and the government has lost control of the economy, but not much else. "Brazil Keen on Starting New Talks," 2-23, was an improvement, a Monday morning biz lead after the debt halt, with calming details. "Stern Brazilian Idealist on Economic Mission," 3-2, told us Finance Minister Dilson Funaro was resisting the austerity route, not negotiating as a pragmatist looking for a deal, but as a moralist defending a principle. "Brazilians Struggle Against Gloom And Economic Disarray," 9-13, was an okay update, on a crumbling economy. There was good information, analytics in "Brazilian Debate: A President or A Premier," 7-1. In other parts of South America, Riding also made headway. "Peru's Leader Under Fire As Rebels Make Gains," 4-23, had a somber update on Garcia's wavering between combatting the "shining path" through military action and through investment in the impoverished areas, creating mounting criticism of his government as terrorist violence is now seen as his most serious problem. "It's Official, It's Cheap, It's Smuggled," 7-11, told us how Paraguay works, with pyramids of smugglers with franchises dealt out by President Stoessner: "The system works logically. The navy operates the river borders with Argentina, the army runs the land borders with Brazil and the air force has the airports." And he had two eye-opening pieces on Colombia: "Colombia Effort Against Drugs Hits Dead End," 8-16, with good detail; and "Colombia's Drugs And Violent Politics Make Murder A Way Of Life," 8-23, telling us their murder rate is four times that of the U.S, and with important numbers and analysis, we find: "This may be the only country where an offense is automatically answered with a bullet."

Riemer, Blanca. *BusinessWeek.* (★ ★ ½)
Paris. A midyear transfer to the Paris bureau took Riemer away from Washington, where she had provided expert coverage of monetary policy and international finance, particularly of Paul Volcker and the Federal Reserve. On the Volcker front, there were three notable stories. In "Are We Ready for Life After Volcker?" 1-26, Riemer is on the mark, the first to suggest that the world could survive Beryl Sprinkel as Fed chairman. The Volcker cover, "Will He Stay?" 3-30, is comprehensive and accurate, but she takes Alan Greenspan's standing at face value without independent checking. Another cover, "What's in Store at the Fed," 6-15 (with Sarah Bartlett, Frank Comes, and John Templeman), was the best synopsis of the moment in all the press. On the Paris front, the jury is still out. A survey on how the U.S. Crash affected Europe, "Trouble from Tokyo to Timbuktu," 11-9, caught her up in the general frenzy that afflicted the entire magazine, indicating much European criticism of their government leaders in the wake of the Crash, and the possible threats to privatization moves. It seemed too early to accept the article's premise of economic contraction or the conclusions that followed.

Robbins, Carla Anne. *U.S.News & World Report.* (½ ★)
Latin America correspondent. Still plugging along, Robbins doesn't seem to be able to get beyond adequate summaries of what's going on. "Colombia to Drug Lords: Enough Is Enough," 1-19, was a decent summary of Colombia's efforts to clean up the drug mafia that left us wanting more detail. "The Pontiff's Even Hand: Blessing for All in Chile," 4-13, gave

us little new information on John Paul's visit to Chile, telling us how sad that it takes a Papal presence to allow some small forms of civil freedom. "Contras Can't Live Off Land," 8-24, was very light: "What the Contras seem unable to do is take to the hills and fight on their own a real option for rebels elsewhere. After five years of war the Contras get only limited help from sympathetic peasants." What exactly are real options for rebels anywhere? Is there a handbook?

Robinson, Anthony. *Financial Times.* (★ ★ ★ ½)
Johannesburg bureau. Another great year of strong reporting on the shifts, changes, setbacks and advances in South Africa, and with superb analytics of the reality beneath the swirling parts here. "Botha Seeks Mandate from White Electorate for an Unidentified Agenda," 1-2, on the NP's strategy, which made the top priority undercutting growing support for right-wing political and paramilitary organizations, with Botha's government offering only "evolutionary" reform coercion and co-optation. "What's Left of a Tribal Laager," 3-3, was an excellent analytic on Botha calling the election to head off the challenge from his right, and having to face a more serious challenge from the "left." "Economy Fails to Stir White Voters," 5-5, told us that color, not class, is the South African obsession and that's why the NP will still form the government after the elections despite a record of mismanagement. "A Giant Lurch to the Right," 5-8, showed in this post-election roundup how Botha's strategy was vindicated, but at great political risk. "Inside, Doubt Takes Root," 6-16, was terrific, telling us disinvestment has not built anti-apartheid pressures; instead new white management are withdrawing from the Sullivan principles and black unions are caught in the middle. "Pretoria's Tough AIDS Curbs Will Affect Thousands," 9-5, had the government sending victims back to where there are no treatment facilities, only abetting the spread of the disease. He had us a tad confused, though, with a front-page story "Prisoner Release Could Help Set Mandela Free," 9-7, and a same day, P.3, "Prisoner Exchange Unlikely To Entail Release of Mandela."

Rodger, Ian. *Financial Times.* (★ ½)
Tokyo correspondent. He appreciates Japan as "the free world's second most important country," and worked hard to cover the shifting political economy there this year. "Toward a Season of Domestic Horsetrading," 2-16, examined the changing climate for Japan's financial institutions, reporting on the rapid regulatory changes taking place. "The High Price of Success," 7-15, was an informative survey of the country's economic decline this year, with an added picture of the country "seizing up" in reaction to the growing crisis in its international relations. He reported little signs of anxiety among Japanese companies most affected by US tariffs in "Shadow Falls Over Japanese Tariff Hopes," 8-27; "the main reason for this calm attitude is that they have accelerated their plans to manufacture products in the US, in order to get around the tariffs." An interview with Finance Minister Kiichi Miyazawa, "Looking West from the Limelight," 9-16, was okay, the Minister reaffirming that he harbors no anti-American sentiment contrary to a recurring rumor, but Rodger didn't push deeper into the Minister's perspective on several issues for more details. "Buggin's Turn and Turn Again," 10-16, a profile of the three main contenders to succeed Nakasone was unsatisfying, and tilted toward misinformation: "Whatever the outcome, no one expects any change in the thrust of Japan's main foreign and domestic policies...as long as...market opening and domestic demand stimulation are pursued vigorously, the country may avoid...foreign relations crises."

Rohter, Larry. *The New York Times.* (★ ★)
Mexico City bureau chief. We weren't wrong when we cited his great promise here in last year's *MediaGuide*. Never superficial in his reporting, he probed and peeled to find the dynamics at work in the mind, culture, politics and economy of Mexico all year. Less expansive in treatment, his reports from Panama were still astute and timely. "Ruling Party in Mexico Does Battle with Son of Founder," 3-15, had Cardenas speaking out for more democracy, anti-austerity, and being threatened with expulsion from PRI. "Plants In Mexico Help Japan Sell

To U.S.'' 5-26, was the first we saw of the Japanese companies in Mexico not subject to computer chip sanctions: "A growing awareness that investment in Mexico can be a way to get around trade restrictions." In "They Trickle Back, Those Who Left With Hope," 4-21, he describes the new immigration law's effect on the Mexican workingman, giving us an idea of how it affects his mind, not just his behavior, the best account we saw. "Inside The Operating Room: A Day Of Bold Brain Surgery," 7-21, was a stunning "Science Times" account from Mexico City on new experimental surgery on Parkinson's disease. "Intransigence In Panama," 7-30, had Noriega adamant despite calls for his ouster, welcoming on one level tensions with the U.S. since they allow him to play the martyr and defy the gringos. "Anxiety In Mexico: Elections Are Near," 8-19, described the "Year of Hidalgo," a time when both government spending and corruption rise in anticipation of presidential elections. Rohter's two pieces on Carlos Salinas de Gortari, the PRI's designated President, were among the better profiles of him, "A Mexican On The Fast Track," 10-5, and "Hurdles Await Mexico's Next Leader," 10-7. After the Crash, "Mexico's Hard Economic Struggle," 12-16, is an interesting snapshot of fact and rumor, but seems helpless in trying to present coherent economics.

Rosett, Claudia. *The Asian Wall Street Journal.* (★ ★ ★ ½)
Editorial page editor. She leaves the reporters on this beat in the dust, turning out superb analytics that are laden with detail and new information we don't see anywhere else. Despite one miscall, she was super all year. "The Philippines' Dangerous Land Reform," 4-13, was the first thoroughly detailed report on the scope of the land reform plans contemplated by the government, one of the 10-best foreign dispatches of the year. "'Rogernomics' Transforms New Zealand," 7-21, was rich in detail, analytical, covering the subject widely and deeply, and was the best overall picture on the radical changes in that country's economy. "Korea's Roh Tae-Woo Places His Bet," 7-27, a super interview and profile of Roh, and in it we discover for sure that the guy's a *democrat.* "President Aquino Risks Frittering Away Philippine Democracy," 9-28, was an adequate update, with a good presentation of what is needed to know about the current stage of Philippine politics and economy, with Finance Minister Jaime Ongpin's reforms stalled, and Aquino under pressure from left to check them. This set the basis for asserting that Aquino is frittering away her mandate and the situation can only deteriorate unless she demonstrates resolve. Her one misfire: "Japan: So Much Yen, So Little Else," from the op-ed page of 4-29, which warrants an "A" for effort in her attempt to understand the financial markets there, but the economics seemed hopelessly confused and contradictory.

Ross, Michael. *Los Angeles Times.* (NR)
Cairo bureau chief. We didn't see enough throughout the year to rate him, but we did come across generally satisfactory work. "Fear of Iran Growing in Emirate," 8-24, was late, though Ross gave it a more comprehensive treatment than we saw in the earlier reports of others. "Saudis Indicate New Toughness in Iran Policy," 8-29, was weaker, Ross relying too much on one "well-placed" unidentified Saudi source, and he can only test it against what diplomats say. This tendency to report what analysts say runs a little too freely in his dispatches, as in "Iran Waging Terrorist Sea War to Undermine U.S. Role, Analysts Say," 10-5. "Iran Threat Driving Arabs to Restore Egyptian Ties," 11-5, does a good job reporting this shift, but he weakened it with his lead, "according to diplomats and other officials."

Rule, Sheila. *The New York Times.* (★ ★)
Nairobi bureau chief. We saw her struggle all year with the economies of East Africa, vividly reporting on conditions, but with only fair depth of analysis. In "Zambia, IMF Fallout Mirrors Third-World Woes," 6-8, Rule tried to present all the views on this, obviously bewildered as to what might be done or what other options there may be, but the piece was still an important and timely review of the conventional views on both sides. "OAU Parley Marked By Division," 8-1, reported on the division in OAU, with no new substantive approaches to Africa's $200 billion debt. "Uganda Tries Bold Steps To Revive Its Economy," 8-19, was nice in detailing

the loan agreements between the IMF and the government of President Yoweri Museveni in Uganda. It included tightening money, a 75% currency devaluation, a new shilling introduced, a 30% tax on all money converted to new (in an attempt to reduce money supply), increases of up to 500% in prices paid to farmers (to revive agricultural production), salary increases for civil servants, $310 million in aid over the next year, and a rescheduling of debt payments. "Burundi's President Is Ousted By Army," 9-4, on leftist President Jean-Baptiste Bagaza's overthrow and new leader Major Pierre Buyoya, telling us in recent months "the authorities revealed a deep sense of insecurity by sharpening a campaign to destroy Burundi's Catholic Church," with some background on Tutsi-Hurtu ethnic divisions, but otherwise disappointing, a straight report from an official government communique. A front-page report on the latest Ethiopian drought, 11-12, has some nice quotes from the U.S. Ambassador critical of the Addis Ababa government's policies that keep it "a perpetual beggar nation," but at the tail end.

Rupert, James. *The Washington Post.* (★ ★)
Untethered for most of the year, roaming the globe, Rupert lost much of his pinpoint-sharp sense of reporting, as the issues he covered varied so greatly. He opened the year covering an anti-American demonstration in Washington by Iranians, because of the American arms sales to Iran, in "Iranians Protest in Lafayette Park Against Khomeini, Arms Sale Decision," 2-7. He moved on to Haiti, detailing the general mood there. "Haiti Quiet as Troops Are Kept Off Streets," 7-7, giving us a vivid picture of the weeklong protest strike: "The mood of slum dwellers who form a large part of Haiti's urban population remained volatile today, reflecting anger at killings of civilians by soldiers and at the government's recent effort to take direct control of the coming local elections." In a poverty postcard, "Rural Haiti Unchanged," 7-30, we get another vivid, well-presented picture, but little we didn't already know. Dateline Jerusalem gave us "Film Showings Revive Debate Among Israelis," 8-22, which described well the deepening divisions and rising tensions between the orthodox and reform Jews. An impressive "Iran, Iraq Step Up Raids In Gulf," 9-3, on the front page, convinced us that Rupert belongs in the hot spot, and needs to stay there to live up to his potential.

Ryan, Leo. *The Journal of Commerce.* (★)
Montreal. Improved reporting from Canada's bureau chief. "Long, Hot Summer of Talks," 6-10, provided early details on the U.S.-Canadian free trade negotiations, albeit inconclusive. A related article, 5-27, covered Quebec's stake in ending "near-total protectionism" (the Jones Act) of U.S. shipping. "Canada Targets Farm Trade War As Top Priority," 5-26, likewise noted that "Canada has felt the brunt of several U.S. restrictive trade measures in the past year," and worries about the backlash from U.S.-European tensions over farm subsidies.

Schiffman, James. *The Asian Wall Street Journal.* (★ ★ ★)
Beijing bureau. With Vigor Fung working the grass roots, Schiffman takes on the peaks, covering the political economy of the state and party, and as a team they were unsurpassed on China reporting. "Chinese Students Speak Out on Communism's Failings," 1-8, showed his hard work in Peking man-on-the-street interviews, getting good credible quotes and a desire for a free "private" press expressed. He had the definitive work on the succession question: "Deng's Protege's Demise as Party Leader Hints at Contest for Succession in China," 1-19, gave us the picture of factions and spokesmen, and things to watch for in the future. "China Slows Its Free Market Experiments," 2-23, beating Gargan of the *NYT* by two days, with an excellent source in Peking, Zue Muqiao, a leading architect of reform, to put it all in perspective: "I think that once we have solved the problem of the economy running out of control, we will go back to the policy of reducing the scope of the planned economy and further opening market forces." "Premier Zhao Says Chinese Reforms Will Be Continued," 3-26, was well reported, Zhao offering something for both economic reformers and conservative Marxists, managing to pacify the orthodox party members but still pursuing economic

experiments. "China Tightens Rebels On Stock And Bond Issues," 4-8, told of the setback for disputed reform, a victory for conservatives and was very astute on the "drift" toward socialist orthodoxy, reporting it as a particular blow to Zhao Ziyang, since the old guard was more upset by stocks than bonds because the notion of stocks challenges the concept of state control of the economy. "Chinese Peasants Spend More On Tombs As Their Wealth Blossoms," 5-22, took initiative, showed imagination, telling us about a $1,600 wedding party for a rich farmer, and concluding: "With prosperity has come a rebirth of tradition." "Using Western Management Techniques Chinese Students Find Factories 'Faults,'" 8-3, described successful innovations: reduction of bureaucratic layers, organizational flowcharts, standardized production, focus on sales and profits, balance sheets and income statements, etc. Between the two reporters, we got a full, rich picture of life in China.

Schmemann, Serge. *The New York Times.* (★ ★)
Bonn bureau chief. A brief stint in Mozambique, then taking over in Bonn when James Markham moved to Paris, his byline was in abeyance for part of the year after South Africa nixed this former Moscow bureau chief's posting in Johannesburg. "Black Nations' Trade Route Seeks to Bypass South Africa," 2-3, was a post-*WSJ* Thurow piece, but Schmemann does a fuller picture, especially on the Beira corridor and the boom-like conditions around it. "Mozambique Rethinking Its Dreams," 2-19, gave details on the country's IMF-sponsored austerity: new taxes, devaluation, increases in costs of housing, electricity, fuel, coupled with a 50% wage increase and loosening of price controls on farm produce in search of development aid, but Schmemann uses the piece to get a dig in against Renamo. He was more regular once he settled in Germany. "Bonn's Coalition Agrees To Endorse Missiles' Removal," 6-2, was a roundup of the agreement to accept the "double zero" solution on warheads. "Rallying Cries Of East Berliners: Gorbachev!" 6-10, was interesting, but he just spooned out the bare essentials on the East German youths' skirmish with police for three nights; they had been barred from eavesdropping on a Genesis concert taking place on the other side of wall, chanting "The Wall must go!" and "Gorbachev! Gorbachev!" In two stories, Schmemann was credible in exploring the basic missile debates, "Bonn Would Scrap A-Missiles In Reply To U.S.-Soviet Pact," 8-27; and Helmut's subsequent little bomb on scrapping the Pershings, "Kohl's Coup On Missiles," 8-28.

Sherrid, Pamela. *U.S.News & World Report.* (NR)
United Kingdom correspondent. A competent writer on the business-economics desk, "The Gnomes Behind the Dollar's Fall," 2-16, was well-written, focusing on institutional detail, and had a good sense of the problems of exchange-rate fluctuations. We'd hoped to see more of her on this issue, but she's now on the foreign correspondence beat, reporting from London. "Why Irish Eyes Frown at U.S. Help," 8-24, was a nice mixture of reporting and analysis on the MacBride principle campaign in northern Ireland. We anticipate impressive work from this new posting in '88.

Sherwell, Chris. *Financial Times.* (★ ½)
Southeast Asia correspondent. Sometimes preachy, he's not above weaving his own prognosis into what ought to be straight reporting. "The Debate Intensifies," 3-30, was comprehensive on the efforts for tax reform in Australia, reporting every faction's perspectives and complaints about their opponent's proposals. Here, we could overlook Sherwell's unsubstantiated claim that Prime Minister Hawke's failure to impose a consumption tax was his "single biggest missed opportunity." With "Australia Prepares for Painful Adjustments," 11-27, however, we didn't get enough info on PM Hawke's policy perspective, and we just couldn't tell where Hawke left off and Sherwell took over with "Australians have continued to live beyond their means," and "that is likely to mean further belt-tightening" is necessary. A nifty feature in the "Tasmania" survey, "Island of the Bold," 11- 19, was very detailed, informative on everything

you'd want to know. Not the case with "Sir Joh Refuses to Resign After Party Revolt," 11-27, summarizing the week's drama over Bjelke-Petersen's refusal to step down as Queensland state premier, he had no clear focus of the issues involved.

Sieff, Martin. *The Washington Times.* (★ ★ ★)
Assistant foreign desk editor, and editor for Soviet, Middle East and Central European affairs, Sieff's reports have an intellectual flavor to them that is rarely seen, his analytics credible and sometimes original. "Peres-Shamir Scrap Strains Israeli Unity," 3-4, was an intelligent look at Israeli political difficulties. "Gorbachev's New Look," a three-part series, 2-17/18/19, was a comprehensive look at *glasnost* and *perestroika*, detailing the foes and supporters of Gorbachev's reforms and the dangers therein, both inside and outside the Soviet Union. "'*Mitteleuropa*' Concept Stirs Again; Specifics Vary Widely," 4-13, a good overview and broad analysis, noted "eastern Europeans welcome the *Mitteleuropa* concept as a chance to build bridges to the West, the Kremlin has also proved skillful at promoting it as an attraction to seduce Western Europeans from the NATO Alliance." His "Military-Party Conflict Possible, Could Be Worst Since Khrushchev," 6-18, was a complicated news analysis that seemed to pivot on the principle the Russians are no good, but this time they're fighting each other in the Politburo. "Jordan Bows Out of the US Sphere of Influence," 7-21, took another important step in America's strategic retreat into the light as Jordan has given up on U.S. friendship and is playing footsie with the Soviets, playing on all the facts and angles. "Mubarak Puts Emphasis On Private Investment," 8-5, on Egypt's recognition of socialism's failure, setting 50% five year plan goals (1987-92) to be realized through private investment, and quoting Yussef Butros Ghali, Mubarak's chief economic adviser, that Egypt's plan is like Reagan's "supply-side economy" concept of strengthening business. "How Iran-Soviet Ties Are Being Forged," 9-4, seems logical, clear on Iranian-Soviet ties both current and developing.

Smith, William E. *Time.* (★ ½)
Senior writer handling some of the foreign coverage, Smith's able to capture situations without misleading, often because there's so little analysis, which keeps us reading. "Sounds of Freedom," with Ken Olsen, 2-23, was a good job, reporting on the Soviet "prisoner of conscience" release. "Campaign of the Iron Fist," with Bruce W. Nelan, 4-27, described the South African crackdown on those protesting the detention without charge of South African citizenry that's graphic, but light on the political side. "Running The Gauntlet," with Michael Duffy and David Jackson, 8-3, a colorful report on the actual sailing on a tanker in the Persian Gulf, including a quoted sub-piece by Duffy from aboard the USS Fox, was well-organized, but, again, light on the analytics. "Massacre Deep In The African Bush," with Peter Hawthorne, 8-3, contained no new information, but presented the history and the human side of the Mozambique situation, moderating the tone on Renamo.

Sneider, Daniel. *The Christian Science Monitor.* (★ ★)
Tokyo. A major news-front all year, Sneider handled the Japanese scene competently, with good coverage of events in South Korea as well. "Tax Reform Hands Japan's Ruling Party a Telltale Defeat," 3-10, was a focused account of the upset Socialist victory after 25 years in a conservative stronghold; Nakasone's proposed sales tax was the margin for defeat, and the end to his ambitions for staying on as LDP leader after this year. The analysis is extended in "Nakasone Gets Flak From All Fronts," 3-31, with an examination of the economic problems undermining his leadership. He's attentive on the emerging mix of defense frictions with trade tensions in U.S.-Japanese relations, 3-31, on the FSX flap, and solid presentations 5-21, and 9-11, on the Toshiba Machine Company case. "Japanese Move to Head Off US Retaliation Over Chips," 3-31, was very professional, capturing the heavy sense of shock in Japan over the threat to US-Japan relations, the anger at being bound to an "agreement that was unenforceable from the beginning," and the quick slide into "unnecessary friction." From Seoul, "In S. Korea, a Waft of Compromise Amid Tear Gas," 6-23, sensing the "new mood of cautious optimism," he found positive indications for a successful parley between the

opposition and the government of President Chun Doo Hwan. "What Led to Government Concessions?" 6-30, is smartly examined, quoting Democratic Justice Party chairman Roh Tae Woo, "The people are the masters of the country and the people's will must come before everything else."

Southerland, Daniel. *The Washington Post.* (★ ★)
The *Post* held its own on China with Southerland doing good reporting, still catching detail or angles missed by the much swifter competition, but we know he can run on higher octane. "China's New Party Leader Is Pragmatist and Reformer," 1-17, is still another profile of Premier Zhao Ziyang, but reminded us it was Zhao who initiated the agricultural reforms in Szechuan that have become the model for the nation, raising living standards for peasant farmers, and quoted one as saying: "If you want to eat, look for Zhao Ziyang." His "Party Chief's Ouster Raises Uncertainty Over China's Plans," 1-19, left the unanswered questions unanswered, but Southerland gives some details about a possible candidate for the premiership, Vice Premier Li Peng, cast as a central planner and possible pointman for opposition to Deng-Zhao. There was good detail and persuasive analysis in "Deng Pushes Political Reform Plan," 3-20, on Deng Xiao-Ping stirring the reform pot once more, promising change at the 13th Communist Party Congress. "Despite Years Of Controls, China Fears New Baby Boom," 5-24, tells us rural prosperity means farmers can pay penalties for a second child. "After 38 Years, Taiwan Lifts Martial Law; Prisoners Freed," 7-15, gave us a few details on new national security laws, but more on what Western observers are speculating. "China Stresses New Party Chief's Role as Ideological Guide," 11-6, had an important angle, seen only here, that Zhao Ziyang has "the primary stage of socialism" [i.e., capitalism] lasting until the 2050s.

Spaeth, Anthony. *The Asian Wall Street Journal.* (★ ★)
Manila bureau. Steady workmanship, though not prolific, though he did give us the year's best account of the communist NPA. A flurry of articles on the lifestyles of the NPA cadres appeared during the Aquino armistice, most of which tended to portray them as not-so-bad-folks. Spaeth's "'Killing Fields' Uncovered in Philippines," *WSJ*, 5-29, put back into perspective the unabashedly Pol Pot nature of this organization. "Operation clean [the internal purge resulting in hundreds of murders] has also confirmed the worst fears of those sympathetic to the cause: that the party is capable of wholesale slaughter." With "Disunity Dims Promise of Aquino's Revolution," *AWSJ*, 2-23, we got our first full-flavored picture of the irreconcilable factional differences in President Aquino's cabinet. We get detailed reporting on the saga of the San Miguel Corporation, the venerable blue chip outfit the Philippine Government and the Soriano family battled over, in "Soriano's Tenuous Hold on San Miguel Under Attack From Manila Commission," *AWSJ*, 3-30, and "San Miguel Board Clears Soriano's Buyback Plan," *AWSJ*, 4-6. A departure from his otherwise objective reporting, "Marcos Palaces: A Guided Tour of Glitzy Monuments to Greed," 7-6, indulges a charge that has never been proven — that Marcos "fabricated a war record as a guerilla fighter against the Japanese." Spaeth produced about the best we saw on the hardships of India's drought, "Harshest Drought in Decades Devastates India's Crops, Slows Economic Growth," 8-19.

Sparks, Allister. *The Washington Post.* (★ ★)
Johannesburg. Sparks set off no fires with his reporting, but the embers glowed brightly all year when he covered the ANC. In "S. African Rebels Seek Wider Base," 1-19, on the ANC policy shift emphasizing appeal to whites, he was somewhat speculative, quoting Tom Lodge, political scientist, who sees battle weariness in the ANC, and refers to the ANC's "message of conciliation," but gives no evidence or treatment of contradictory information. "S. Africa Spawns a New Underground for Second Child," 5-24, was much too slow at the start. "Afrikaners Find Accord With ANC," 7-13, on the white Afrikaners and black nationalists meeting in Senegal, leaning surprisingly to the liberal, hopeful, lets-fix-everything tack. In "Afrikaners Given Warm Welcome In Black Africa," 7-20, on the same subject, Sparks reports on the Afrikaner tour, headed by the former leader of S.A.'s liberal Progressive Federal Party,

Frederick van Zyl Slabbert, who was "astonished then delighted at the warmth of their reception..." But he mostly tells of organized trips here and there without an account of the substance of discussions. It was the ANC delegates' defense of the commitment to the principle of multiracialism that removed the Afrikaners' initial skepticism, he reports. Currently on sabbatical.

Sterba, James P. *The Wall Street Journal.* **(NR)**
Senior editor. Oceania's "out of sight, out of the limelight" island countries were a frequent focus of his reporting, some of which was feature material, some a little more rigorously treated. Not unimportant, but we wonder why this priority for a senior editor. Among them, "Tiny Pacific Islands," *WSJ*, 7-20, informs us on the crisis in Nauru (pop. 8,000), where the per capital income of $20,000 per annum is threatened by a decrease in guano and a loss of topsoil. He contributed to the *WSJ*'s series "Mosque and State," with a treatment of Indonesia's brand of Islam in "Coexistence of Islam, Secular Authority Gets Trial in Indonesia," 8-13, reviewing its teaching as political ethics, rather than its use as a political system.

Stewart, William. *Time.* **(★ ½)**
Hong Kong bureau. Sometimes a once-over-lightly touch, sometimes late behind others' reporting, but also very well-organized and detailed, with informative follow-ups that always attract our attention. "Slowly Turning the Corner," 4-27, gave us the first steps toward economic recovery in the Philippines, but it didn't deal enough with land reform and the problems involved, though at least he hit all the bases. "Rise Of The Vigilantes," with Michael Serrill, 5-11, was *late* by a couple of months on this phenomenon in the Philippines, noting: "A year ago Davao city and its 1.4 million people were so firmly in the control of the insurgents that Manila officials called the city a communist 'urban laboratory.' But in the last eight months the NPA has fled into the hills, and the city has been transformed into a government stronghold."

Strasser, Steven. *Newsweek.* **(★)**
Moscow bureau. We seem to see more of Strasser than his comrade Joyce Barnathan in single bylines, covering lighter issues than Barnathan. "Where Old Ways Die Hard," 6-22, was oddly colorless on the restructuring of Uzbekistan or the attempt at it by Gorbachev. "In Chernobyl's Grim Shadow," 6-29, was still lighter, skimming the process of recovery at Chernobyl, relying on Chernobyl spokesmen and the Soviet magazine *Yunost* for most of the story. "A Surprise At The Pushkin," 9-14, had us applauding *glasnost* in art with the Chagall exhibit at the Pushkin, *Sovietskaya kultura* calling it "depicting 'deliverance of the human spirit from the bondage of a stagnant, narrow-minded world.'" It only goes so far though; "Revolution" is not on exhibit, and Chagall was "recently castigated" for this painting of October, 1914.

Sullivan, Scott. *Newsweek.* **(NR)**
European regional editor, worth noting for a piece that was a cut above. "Europe Faces Its Nazi Past," 4-20, on the then-upcoming trial of the butcher of Lyons, Klaus Barbie, with an interesting analysis of the implications and self-retribution in Europe, cautious and intriguing. He gives us a genuine feel for the struggles of Europeans, striving to remember, and at the same time, to forget.

Suro, Roberto. *The New York Times.* **(★ ★)**
Rome bureau chief. His coverage of the Vatican and the Pontiff's journeys abroad were very well done, but on Italy he's a little too "dolce," giving us only the frosting, not enough of what's underneath. Covering Iran early in the year, he had a sloppy "Iranian Justifies Beirut Abductions," 1-29, reporting the remarks of the Speaker of the Iranian Parliament on the seizure of hostages, with some information on a more restrained tone towards the U.S. He improves with "Iran's Unpredictable Behavior Reflects Rivalries in Regime," 2-4, where all

opposition outside its ranks is subdued while the regime suffers from increasingly volatile internal rivalries, Khomeini the arbiter and center of gravity. "Milan Communist Runs As Capitalist," 5-30, was good on Guido Rossi, the Italian Communist Party's candidate for the Senate from Milan who defines himself as "a Massachusetts liberal," and gave a clear picture of the CP's new outlook. "'Aw Shucks' Premier For Italy," 7-30, a so-so profile of Giovanni Giuseppi Goria, "an accountant who is also a politician," cited as the CD's most authoritative voice on economic matters, but we get no picture of his perspective in that regard. On the John Paul road show, Suro did his best work. "Pinochet Assures Pope He Is Seeking Stability," 4-1, the message aimed at all Chileans. "Jews And Pope Discuss Concerns; No Real Shifts, But Discord Eases," 9-2, summarizes his meeting with Jewish leaders, who indicate their anger over the Waldheim issue. "At Vatican, Extraordinary Preparation For Crucial Papal Trip," 9-8, was a good preview of what the Vatican and John Paul hope to focus on in the U.S., with terrific quotes from Archbishop Rigali: "The idea that there is tension between Rome and the church in the United States was promoted by a tiny group of American Catholics...and it has been artifically manipulated and nurtured with a lot of help from the media;" and Joseph Cardinal Ratzinger: "In a world like the West, where money and wealth are the measure of all things, and where the model of the free market imposes its implacable laws on every aspect of life, authentic Catholic ethics now appear to many like an alien body from times long past."

Symonds, William. *BusinessWeek.* (★ ★)
Rome. The Pittsburgh bureau chief who gave us one of the 10 best business pieces of '86 on the troubles at Allegheny International, 8-11-86, has just about gotten his feet on the ground in Italy. His byline is almost always submerged in the soup with several others, but occasionally they let him step out on his own. His cover story on "Dealmaker [Carlo] De Benedetti," 8-24, is entertaining about the boy wonder who now, at age 51, has been almost completely vindicated by his management of Olivetti since '78, after quitting Fiat three months into his stay. We looked for analysis of the AT&T/Olivetti partnership, in giving AT&T a future in personal computers, but it wasn't here. Symonds has De Benedetti ploughing ahead despite fear about the economy, quoting him at the precise peak of the bull market: "I am very pessimistic about the future...I see the risk, which in my mind is a very high risk, of a big recession coming, and consequently, a very bleak period for the whole world." In "Tooling Into the Luxury Market in a Lamborghini," 5-4, Symonds runs through the Chrysler mating with style, and we're startled with the thought that "the personality is defined above all by the motor," quoting a Lamb'i designer. His "Italy Gets Set to Vote on Its Future," 6-8, is rich in detail on the economy, but analytically weak, Symonds unable to figure out why things are so good. We learn a very important fact: the voting in the Italian Parliament is by secret ballot! Then, in "Will Italy Be Able to Regain the High Ground?" 8-10, we get a quick look at Giovanni Goria, 44, youngest prime minister in Italy's history, but not much space for analytical depth.

Tagliabue, John. *The New York Times.* (★ ½)
Warsaw. Tagliabue, working out of Bonn in '86 on the global oil beat, was bounced around when the *Times* snatched Youssef Ibrahim from the *WSJ*, as the oil reporter. When South Africa refused to admit Serge Schmemann as the *Times* correspondent in Johannesburg, Schmemann was posted to Bonn. Tagliabue's byline popped up in Rome, "Italians Boycott Group of 7," 2-23, which doesn't even hint at the domestic politics being played by Bettino Craxi in the maneuver. A nice business feature on "Fiat Hopes to Use Alfa to Cut American Niche," 3-16, with a fetching lead on how the people of Arese tell "how Henry Ford always tipped his hat when an Alfa drove by." He's back in Bonn with a Sunday feature on the German armament industry, "trying to shed the burden of history and bid for new clients," 3-29. Then Warsaw, in time for the first referendum in Poland since 1946, when the Communists last rigged one. "Poland Will Raise Prices 40 percent; Shoppers in Panic," 11-15, starts it off, when the government, counseled by the International Monetary Fund (who else?), decided to go for the Big Austerity; it asked the "voters" approval, throwing in a second question of whether the "voters" want a "deepening democracy." In "Polish Vote Seen Backing

Austerity," 11-30, we get a Polish joke along with good details on the procedure, the voters asked to cross out the word "yes" if they disapproved and "no" if they were in favor. "It was like asking people to scratch the left ear with the right hand," admitted a government spokesman. Then, in "Poland Will Raise Prices 27 Percent," 12-16, the government decided the 55% austerity approval rate wasn't high enough to support the 40% boost. Tagliabue needs to get deeper into the mechanisms of the economy once he settles down.

Tanzer, Andrew. *Forbes.* (★ ★)

Tokyo. A very sharp business correspondent, he's stronger with economic analysis than with character profiles. He grabbed us first with a catchy headline, "James Baker, Meet the Dokushin Kizoku," 4-30. As Washington decries Japan's excessive savings, the "single aristocrats" are doing their best to keep the economy moving, creating a retailing fortune for Marui Co.'s Tadao Aoi. His splashiest of the year, "Land of the Rising Billionaires," 7-27, uses the unusual proliferation of billionaires as a starting point, but quickly moves on to a more interesting topic: What are the underlying political and economic factors that have made this possible? It's light, fast-paced, and revealing for those with little knowledge of the social and political obstacles to change in Japan, but otherwise a bit thin and repetitive. In "Kumagai Gumi," with Marc Beauchamp, 11-30, he delivers astounding figures, describing the true daring of one of Japan's big six consruction companies, breathtaking because of the subject itself. His most important contribution of the year was "Korea Grows Up," 11-16, a clear concise picture of where the Korean economy is going, both timely and excellent on a topic uppermost in investor's minds as they watch the civil unrest rippling with political change. His attempt as a profile, "Taiwan's Billionaire Sea Lord," 8-24, is flat, a "who cares?" piece, with little redeeming value.

Taubman, Philip. *The New York Times.* (★ ★ ★)

Moscow bureau chief. A great time to be reporting from the USSR, and Taubman worked hard on the big picture, attentive to the context and perspectives of the transformations underway. With Patrick Cockburn of the *FT*, he came the closest to providing a satisfactorily comprehensive account. Strong reporting out of Afghanistan early in the year, with "Afghan Visit Shows Damage of a Continuing War," 1-22, and "Russians Hold Key to Power, But Not to Afghanistan's Soul," 1-26, describing the power politics and the continuing Sovietization of the country, though the resistance prevents it from being the 16th republic. "Dismantling the Stalin Myth: New Effort Under Gorbachev," 3-15, was sharp on the fine line the General Secretary walks on this issue, and we got a further picture of the obstacles he faces from the Old Guard in "Gorbachev Push to Win Control in Ukraine Seen," 3-22. "Why Glasnost Drags," 5-28, reported signs that Yegor K. Ligachev is supportive of the resistance to current thrusts for literary and artistic freedom. One of the better accounts on the plans for *perestroika* was "Gorbachev Orders 'Radical' Changes to Spur the Economy," 6-26, followed by a solid "Gorbachev's Gamble," 7-19, a Sunday *Magazine* feature that was meaty on the politics involved, though more slender on economics. He was very attentive to the shifting geopolitics in the area, noting the increased Soviet commercial and trade penetration into Iran with "Iran and Soviet Draft Big Projects, Including Pipelines and Railworks," 8-5, and "Odd Couple: A Marxist Soviet and an Islamic Iran," 8-7. "In Soviet East, New Rapport With Chinese," 9-25, gave us interesting anecdotal evidence of a warming relationship. "Without Gorbachev, Glastnost Pauses," 10-4, was superlative on Gorbachev's importance and the lack of economic improvement: "Until benefits start to appear, all Mr. Gorbachev has to offer is a more interesting intellectual climate."

Taylor, Walter A. *U.S.News & World Report.* (★ ★)

Asia correspondent. One of this weekly's best on the foreign beat, he's a strong reporter who has a fine sense for assessing trends in this region. "Rebirth of a Rebel Army," 9-28, was timely on the intensification of NPA activity after the end of Aquino's armistice. Though he reports no evidence of direct government help from outside the Philippines for the communist insurgents, he quotes an analyst's reminder that "if need be, the world's largest stockpiles of used M-16 rifles are only 700 miles away in Vietnam." As an overview, "Aquino Hands Over Power and Problems," 8-3, he covered all the bases more than adequately, although there were some thin spots, especially on the economy. We didn't get as much as we wanted from him on what's happening in Burma, but his "A Detour on Burma's Road to Socialism," 9-21, was a detailed, informative update.

Temko, Ned. *The Christian Science Monitor* (★ ★ ★ ★)
Johannesburg. An assignment that reveals the best and worst qualities of journalists, with government press restrictions testing their mettle for pushing beyond the limits of constraint. The complexity of this country demands superior reporting skills, and the marked temptation here, as nowhere else, is to indulge in advocacy journalism. Temko passed all these tests. In one excellent report after another, he was the best in telling us what was new in South Africa, always alert for the shift on the margin, never omitting the necessary detail. See, for example, "S. Africa Election," 1-5; "S. Africa White Politics in Flux," 3-19; "S. Africa White Voters Restive" and "If Blacks Could Vote, However," 5-4. Excellent again with his coverage on the "second-breath" for Magosuthu Buthelezi's multi-racial *Indaba* plan, 5-6, his focus not limited merely to the key political events. "In Search of the Real Soweto, By Bus," 3-10, a picture of the "place where blacks seethe, fester in poverty, and battle with the police" as something much more — rich with revelations that overturn conventional assumptions. An example of solid analytics, "Shultz Meeting with ANC Chief Lends Validity to S. Africa Rebels," 1-26, was balanced in presentation and adept on perspective — although we think his sympathetic side-bar profile of the ANC's Oliver Tambo was off-base (noteworthy because it was the only instance all year where we balked on Temko). Approaching the war in Angola as a superpower struggle 10-6, he sorted fact from fiction, verifying the hands-on involvement of the Soviets (with 30,000 Cubans for back-up) against Jonas Savimbi's UNITA. His best, "Untangling a Web of Conflict," 5-18, an in-depth feature on the Guguletu battle that provides critical insight into South Africa's convulsions. Leaving *CSM* in '88 for television work, his byline will be missed.

Tempest, Rone. *Los Angeles Times.* (★)
New Delhi bureau chief. Too slender on the economy of the subcontinent all year, the adequate coverage of the heated political conflicts wasn't enough to satisfy the need to know more. We'd already seen Anthony Spaeth's report on the Indian drought when Tempest's "India Faces No Food Shortage Despite Drought," 8-30, appeared. We did find it very well done, but it was late and didn't add much new to what we'd already learned. Tempest was timely on Sri Lanka coverage, providing new information. "Sri Lanka Fears Infiltration by Outlawed Group," 8-22, was very informative on the shifts in the Marxist-Leninist Peoples' Liberation Front, from an emphasis on class struggle to the Sinhalese race war against the Tamils. The confrontation between India's largest newspaper chain, the Express Group, and the Indian government, was handled well. "India Raids Offices of Anti-Gandhi Newspaper," 9-2, provided solid background and context on the issue.

Tenorio, Vyvyan. *The Christian Science Monitor.* (★)
New Delhi-based stringer. She's adept with the politics of the subcontinent, but she hasn't found her way yet into the economies of those countries. Her reporting on Punjab paid close attention to Gandhi's policy, noting how it was basically stalled and vague all year, as with "India's Gandhi 'Tougher Action' on Punjab," 1-21, and "Indians Urge Gandhi to Add Carrot to Security Stick in Punjab," 7-14, both solid pictures of the operational policy drift. She stayed atop Gandhi's continuing political headaches, covering the fallout from Defense Minister V.P. Singh's resignation, as in "India's Gandhi Besieged by Critics in Wake of Aide's Resignation," 4-14. "India Faces Rising Pressure for Arms Race With Pakistan," 3-9, was less satisfying, relying too heavily on "analysts" and quoting no Pakistani sources. One of her best, "Shaping a Dream in Sri Lanka," 9-8, was a well-organized and detailed report on

Sri Lanka's housing program, a fairly important issue in that troubled country, reported best here.

Thomson, Robert. *Financial Times.* (★ ½)
Beijing. A fine reporter, but his digging wasn't intense this year, and too many events got by him. Disoriented early on the course of Deng's reforms, he had troubles getting his bearings, settling for after-the-fact analysis. He began cautiously after Hu Yaobang's dismissal with "Peking Turmoil Trickles Down to Factory Floor," 2-4, noting importantly that the resurgent hard-liners "are certainly not Maoists." However, he let go of that insight with "Mao's Words Return With a Lesson for China's Modernizers," 2-23, relying too much on "some diplomats say" for the assessment that "the renewed emphasis on Mao's teachings is a sign of the political turmoil that...has set back the country's development several years..." We didn't get much investigation into the course of economic reform during this period, his focus instead on "The Arts in China Turn Into a Political Battlefield," 4-24. "It Looks Like a Tactical Retreat," 8-27, was better, Thomson noting that the conservatives have had little success in their attacks on economic reform, the main reason being the success of the reformers' economic policies. His reports during the 13th Party Congress, were competent wrap-ups, but without much spontaneity or new additional information, as in "China Prepares for Next Decade," 10-24, "Deng Triumphs Over Old Guard Critics of Reform," 11-2, and "China to Push Ahead with Political and Economic Reforms," 11-3.

Thurow, Roger. *The Wall Street Journal.* (★ ★)
Johannesburg bureau. A knack for the anecdotal illustration, and while he's often inconclusive, he always provides an interesting feature. "Bitter Legacy: Leaving South Africa, U.S. Companies Anger and Disappoint Blacks," 12-23-86, was the first thorough story on this, good quotes. "Pretoria Again Resorts to 'U.S. Bashing' In Announcing a Whites Only Election," 1-2, was too heavy on the NP's rallying of voters against U.S. pressure to strengthen its hold on the government, but the real story is what the NP would do with a mandate-size vote. "African Front-Line States Resist Pretoria," 1-22, told us that as neighboring countries strive to become more self-reliant, the front-line states are finding that their dependence on South Africa is actually increasing; the goal here is to go beyond getting the U.S. to disinvest and to relocate operations in their countries. "South African Blacks Start Their Own People's School," 6-25, was a well-done, feature on a school run by blacks to educate black children for post-apartheid life. "South Africa's Black Unions Take Anti-Apartheid Lead," 7-22, told us COSATU is firmly positioned at the front of the black opposition movement in South Africa, going from a traditional labor union to a committed political organization, replacing the schools and street of the black townships as the flashpoints of confrontation. "A White Company's Unusual Contacts Help Promote Peace In Southern Africa," 7-28, profiled Beira Corridor Group, Ltd., a private company run by whites working for the benefit of black nationalist Zimbabwe and Mozambique. "Miners In South Africa End Strike But Will Press Demands Next Year," 8-31, is reported as a setback for the black union movement, though the unions already have thrown down the gauntlet for next year. "Plight Of S. Africa Sugar Industry Shows Sanctions Fall Heavily On Blacks," 10-2, is annoyingly anecdotal, with little analysis, but interesting as a feature.

Treaster, Joseph B. *The New York Times.* (★)
Miami bureau, covering the Caribbean. Some improvement this year, but he still tends toward being a police reporter when we need a foreign correspondent. "Ecuador General Denies Role in Taking President Hostage," 1-20, for example, was police blotter stuff, with no presentation of the issues in conflict between Congress and President Cordero. He has a talent for feature writing, as in "Portrait of a Disaster: Panic Amid Flames at Hotel," 1-10, the best report anywhere covering the disaster at San Juan's Dupont Plaza Hotel. "Castro Recoils at Hint of Wealth," 2-8, was one of his better efforts early in the year, reporting Castro's reactions to even miniscule signs of inequality, but he didn't develop a sense of the course of the political

crackdowns associated with that attitude. Haiti was his main beat, where his year was mixed. "Calls Grow, Amid Violence for Ouster of Haiti's Rulers," 7-4, was a spot news account, but he improved with "Turmoil in Haiti Stalls Political Progress," 7-12, giving a fairly clear picture of the political unrest there, though it still needed better detail. "Duvalier Candidate and a Killing Blunt Optimism of Haiti Voters," 10-20, began getting the dope on the unlikelihood of free elections, despite the $5 million the U.S. provided for them. Treaster seemed taken in by Haiti President Namphy early in the year, mistaking him for a true-blue democrat, and this may have skewed his reporting on the election turmoil.

Tuohy, William. *Los Angeles Times.* (★)
Bonn bureau chief. He provides more than the wire services in his Germany coverage, but not much deeper probing this year. From Moscow, he reported on the reaction in Soviet circles to *PAMYAT*, the Russophile organization, in "New Moscow Movement Viewed as Anti-Semitic," 5-24, but his report was confined primarily to an article crtitical of *PAMYAT* appearing in *Komsomolskaya Pravda.* "Premier of West German States Quits Amid Scandal," 9-26, reports on the resignation of Schleswig-Holstein's Christian Democrat Premier, Uwe Barschel. Again, the reporting seem constricted, limited here to a roundup of official communiques. "West German Scandal Tests Faith in Politics," 11-2, on the soul-searching that took place after Barschel's suicide, was better. Scandal was also the focus of an informative "No Longer Untarnished, Swedes Find," 11-11, on how the country's sense of moral superiority was challenged by disclosures of corruption within the government. "Inflation's Specter Haunts Germany's Fiscal Planning," 11-17, was disappointing. A roundup of observations on Germany's obsession with near-zero inflation, the material was inconclusive.

Tyler, Patrick E. *The Washington Post.* (★ ★)
Cairo. We think he'd rather be doing geopolitical analyses, a constant staple of his wide-ranging deployment this year, and he probably could have handled the Post's Iran/Iraq coverage all by himself. "Why Are the Saudis Buying All that Sophisticated Weaponry?" *Weekly*, 3-2, tells us analysts say their military buildup is aimed at Israel. "Egyptian Food Crisis Feared As Waters Of Nile Drop," 3-25, was much later than the *Financial Times'* account, an okay update, but nothing new on the self-sufficiency in food production that was the case as recently as two decades ago and the current crisis. "In Egyptian Lab, Cobra Takes A Bite Out Of Cancer," 3-20, was totally absorbing, on how the spitting cobra's venom has a devastating affect on membranes of common cancer cells and how the discovery came about. "US Aborted 1983 Trap Set For Libyan Forces," 7-12, on John Le Carre-type spy-stuff exposed by leaks that's interesting, but it really inadvertanly makes a case for why covert actions ought to stay *covert.* "Kuwait May Offer Support Facilities," 7-21, gave a pretty detailed descriptive of a Kuwaiti Sheik's news conference, a broad, clear picture. "Reflagged Tanker Hits Gulf Mine," 7-25, was concise, no-nonsense reporting, with good detail in spots, but bland. "American, Kuwaiti Convoy Concerns Differ," 7-28, relayed the business vs. safety concerns in the Gulf. "Iran's Threats Alarm Arab Gulf Sheikdoms," 7-29, was comprehensive on the cause and effect of threats, with analysis that touched all the bases.

Wain, Barry. *The Asian Wall Street Journal.* (★ ½)
Asia bureau. We didn't see a lot, but his reporting from Vietnam was notable. "A Deeply Dissatisfied Populace Is Prodding Vietnam's Leaders Down the Road to Reform," 6-1, reports the Vietnamese Communist Party "concluded that it would forfeit its moral authority if it continued to impose bankrupt policies on a resentful populace." Wain provides historical background on the failed attempts at centralized planning, the economic havoc this produced, and the desperation the leadership feels as Vietnam is now one of the poorest countries in the world. "A triumph of economics over ideology" is the theme of "Vietnam Is Setting the Wheels in Motion For Pragmatic Overhaul of Economy," 6-8. He details the changes taking place there, the increased reliance on the South for spearheading economic development, its residual capitalist expertise now encouraged. At the same time, he's restrained enough to note

that "all this amounts to mere private-sector froth on a seriously defective and stagnant economy." A gutsy trip to Ha Giang resulted in "Vietnam-China Border Conflict Drones Into Ninth Year," *WSJ*, 6-23; Chinese artillery and mortar fire rain down constantly there, and Chinese troops are reported to occupy positions inside the Vietnamese frontier.

Walker, Tony. *Financial Times.* (★ ★ ★)
Cairo. The best correspondent in Egypt, Walker was also very productive on the front between the Levant and the Maghreb. A report rich with details and analysis, "Mubarak Moves Back into Mainstream of Arab Politics," 2-6, covers all aspects of Egypt's movement into the Middle East power vacuum, noting it's not simply a political-diplomatic move, but a serious bid to open up Arab investment flows into the country. "Egypt Fights for Children's Lives," 2-11, truly informs on the country's health program to reduce high rates of infant mortality, still as high as 96 per 1,000. The challenge from Egypt's fundamentalists is sharply assessed in "Islamic Values Put to Polls Test," 4-6. An excellent analytic, "Dead Ends in a Game of Bluff," 4-25, examines the many reverses for Colonel Qaddafi in the twelve months since the U.S. strike. The triumphant upturn in the career of PLO leader Yassar Arafat was well-covered in "Arafat Presides Over PLO Reconciliation," 4-25. "Jordan Fends for Itself Against Economic Presssure," 8-27, was the best on the strains the country feels now as Gulf neighbors fail to fulfill promises of assistance. On Iraq's extensive pipeline developments, "Baghdad Restores the Oil Flow," 9-30, provided more detail than did others. An adept feature, "Babylon Rises From The Swamp After 2,000 Years," 10-15, surveys the scene as Nebuchadnezzar's ancient capital is rebuilt. We got fresh information on Egypt's sliding economy in "Mubarak Gains Endorsement But Faces Challenge," 10-7. With GDP growth down to 2%, the essentials of the IMF's "root canal" strategy were reported: credit restrictions, import curbs, budget cuts, and currency devaluation, with a floating of the Egyptian pound.

Wallace, Charles P. *Los Angeles Times.* (★)
Nicosia bureau. A pedestrian year, a little too much of "analysts say" formed the spine of his reporting. Some of those reports were able to stand on their own, though, as in "Soviets Seek More Clout in Mideast," 4-27, which was timely and authoritative on the improved standing of the USSR in the region. "Iran Says U.S. Seeks to Renew Diplomatic Ties," 8-30, was limited to a review of official communiques. "Analysts Puzzled by U.S. Clash, Say Tehran Has Tried to Avoid Confrontation," 10-10, should have never gotten by the editors, the entire report based on unidentified Western observers, the Iranian press agency IRNA and UN Ambassador Said Rajaie-Khorasani. Better on the Arab heads of state summit in Jordan, with "Arab World's Prospects Called Bleak on Eve of Summit," 11-8, reporting widespread sentiment for the rehabilitation of Egypt. "Arab Summit Condemns Iran, OKs Ties With Egypt," 11-12, was an okay roundup.

Walsh, Mary Williams. *The Wall Street Journal.* (★ ★ ★)
Mexico City. Great instincts on knowing what to look for as she peels away the layers that surround the workings of this country and its people, Walsh found gems all year. "Stoic Masses: Poor People of Mexico, Afraid of Protesting, Endure Much Injustice," 12-29-86, was excellent on the Mexican people and why they tolerate the PRI. "U.S. Retirees Again Flocking to Mexico," 3-10, had a lot of good detail on living costs and changes over recent years to expatriates, telling us one needs $800 to $1000 a month to live well. But "Mexico Shows Signs of Economic Upturns," 3-19, misfired, fine as an interesting snapshot of sudden optimism, but she has no clue as to what's going on economically, making no mention of a December tax cut. "Proposed Mexican Anti-Inflation Plan Raises Concern About Effect On Economy," 7-20, was light on detail, the idea being to slow the monthly devaluation rate to 4-5% to fight inflation, but not much more. "Mexico Fights Inflation With Measures On Trade, But Currency Move Is Diluted," 7-30, had the scoop on businessmen wanting to slow the pace of currency devaluation, but free traders pushing hard for tariff reductions, fearing that de la Madrid's successor may be less supportive of the reforms. "Mexican Business Warms To Government,"

8-20, was upbeat and illuminating. "Mexicans Debate State vs. Private Aid For Development," 10-8, was poignant on the Paisajits story and how state intevention worsened conditions of poor peasants. The PRI bureaucrats opposed to private initiatives, set up fish co-ops, but wouldn't listen to peasants when the prawn ponds were failing. Now peasants are heavily in debt, worse off than before. A wonderful account of how state capitalism smothers peasant aspirations and efficiency.

Weintraub, Richard M. *The Washington Post.* (★)
New Delhi bureau. He's acquiring veteran status here, but we have yet to see any serious attempt to report on the subcontinent's economic news. His reports from Afghanistan constituted his better work this year. "Afghan City Scarred by War," 5-6, and "Soviets Bolstering Afghan Ties," 5-13, was detailed on the vast network of trade, aid, and cultural relations, even more elaborate than its military presence, "but you can't colonize a country you can't control." In "Kabul Life Difficult for Russians," 5-13, the soldiers, we learn, stay in the camps. "India's Endless Web of Violence," *Weekly*, 7-27, reports on the Hindu-Sikh wrath that is putting the country's social cohesion to the test and weakening the fragile bonds between the people and the government. He provided a good reading on Pakistan's worries of a confrontation with the U.S. over the country's nuclear program and the risks of a volatile, new political equation in an already unstable region, "Pakistan Is Under Seige From All Sides Now," *Weekly*, 8-10. "Timeout for the Tamils," 8-17, covered all the bases on the political gamble India's Rajiv Gandhi and Sri Lanka's Junius Jayewardene were taking with their accord to bring peace to the country.

Weisman, Steven R. *The New York Times.* (★ ★)
New Delhi. He clearly refocused this year, his efforts on India's political scene serious, wide-ranging and fresh, but he dozed through Afghanistan and was meager on the subcontinent's economics. "In a City of Calamities, 300,000 Live on the Street," 3-18, told us there's poverty in Calcutta, but nothing about any policy debates over possible cures. "Pakistan Stiffens on Atom Program," 3-22, raised doubts about the reliability of Washington as a friend, a solid Sunday account of what's going on with the nuclear Afghan aid flap. "The Daunting Gandhis And A Dauntless Challenger," 4-24, profiled Ramakrishun Hedge, chief minister of Rajar Non as "so rude," "surrounded by a small coterie and yet cut off from everyone else." His "Ethnic Hatred," 4-26, was notably poor on the killings in Southern Asia, making it almost generic by omitting the fact that Tamil terrorists are Marxists out to destroy any moderate force. "Indians To Send Convoy To Sri Lanka," 6-2, was on track again, with alarming stuff as India infringes on Sri Lanka's sovereignty, covering the charges, counter-charges, motivations, etc. "New Worry For Sri Lanka: Threat To Pact By The Right," 8-21, told us of the People's Liberation Front, the largest and most powerful militant group opposed to the accord, with evidence some members have inflitrated the army and police. His "Sri Lanka: A Nation Disintegrates," 12-13, the Sunday *Magazine* cover, tries so hard to tell us why, but he doesn't quite do it; still, we appreciate the effort. "Turmoil And A Scandal Take A Toll On Gandhi," 8-24, reviewed Gandhi's standing in the polls, the suspicions he's involved in corruption, but not a lot new. "Is The Raja Ready For War, Or Losing His Steam?" 10-8, covers the meeting of the new People's Front established by Gandhi opponent Vishwanath Pratap Singh, the former Finance Minister who, under Gandhi, slashed government regulations and lowered taxes.

Williams, Dan. *Los Angeles Times.* (★)
Mexico City bureau. A better year on south of the border reporting, the politics competently treated, but, with so little idea of what the economy's all about, he lags far behind the competition. "Violence Halts Haiti's Political Campaigning," 8-10, was a competent roundup on the increased inability of electoral campaigning in the country. A quick overview of the candidates for PRI successor to Miguel de la Madrid, "Mexico's Candidates: Hoopla but, Except for No. 7, Mostly Generalities," 9-1, added little to the already known picture. "Mexico's Campaign Goes Topsy-Turvy," 9-25, was improved, reporting on the upstaging of the PRI

campaign by dissidents and opposition politicians "intent on breaking political rules of long standing." He covers the immediate economic news as with "15-Billion Windfall Presents Mexico With New Fiscal Headaches," 8-27, and we got a good presentation of the debate on what to do with the money. But he doesn't stray far from one-dimensional treatment, as with "Peso's Value Dives as Mexico's Central Bank Cuts Off Dollars," 11-19.

Williams, Nick B. Jr. *Los Angeles Times.* (★ ★)
Bangkok bureau chief. Williams moved throughout the region this year with a good feel for the critical developments. His sober reporting and assessment of the reality behind Vietnam's "new look" particularly stood out. He was alert in his Korea reporting, "Korea Ruling Party Agrees to Start Talks on Constitutional Revision, Direct Voting," 7-25, was a satisfactory account of the government's new perspective. "North Korea Urges Mutual Troop Cuts," 7-24, was an important dispatch, though dependent on official communiques. "S. Korean Workers Reach for Bigger Slice of the Pie," 8-22, examines government charges that the strikes were instigated by student radicals, finds no conclusive evidence of that, and presents a rounded picture of this critical social transformation. In an important interview with Hun Sen, "Cambodia Says It Holds MIA Remains," 9-26, the Cambodian President acknowledged that "we also have the bones of American MIAs. But no one has gotten in touch with us, so we have kept them. If the American goverment doesn't come, there is nothing we can do about that." There was a sharp blend of analysis and historical background in "Memories of Kwangju Haunt Korea," 11-3, the Korean city to which all candidates travel, with hopes of bending its history to their own purpose. Williams examines some indications that the reintegration of the Cholla provinces back into the Korean mainstream is not a closed question.

Witcher, S. Karene. *The Asian Wall Street Journal.* (★ ★)
Asia bureau. We were happy to see the appearance of this talented, hardworking journalist's byline in Australia. The *Journal*'s reporting from down under needs someone who can get it up to speed, and she's just the one to do it. "Australia Budget Proposes Cutting Deficit to Lowest Level in Years," 9-21, was comprehensive on Treaurer Paul Keating's new budget and the opposition to it, as good as anything we saw in *FT*. Another comprehensive sweep, "With 'God on My Side,' Coup Leader Attempts to Regain Fiji's Paradise Lost," 10-23, balanced detail and analysis in a sharp account of Lt. Co. Sitveni Rabuka's coup and what lies ahead for Fiji. We got very good business detail in "Holmes a Court Is Said to Rebuff Offers for Stakes," 11-17, on the plans of Australia's richest man for taking on his cash crisis.

Wright, Robin. Freelance. (★ ★)
Appearing occasionally in *The Christian Science Monitor*, we were impressed by her fearlessness in traipsing about the Iranian capital. She has a good grasp of the internal workings of Iran's politics and it shows in her dispatches. "8 Years of Khomeini Transform Iran," 1-30, had some interesting insights in this historical overview. But her most impressive work, like Warren Richey's, appeared at the height of the summer during the so-called tanker war. "Mecca Clash Has Deep Roots In Islamic Schism," 8-7, was light as opposed to the comparable series that ran in *WSJ*, but was still penetrating, examining several factors that helped to put the Shiites on the defensive, such as leadership roles, government. "Iran Wait-And-See Stance On US Gulf Moves," 8-17, gave intelligent projections on what might transpire next in the Gulf war and what is going on now. "Rhetoric Aside, Iranians Still Fascinated With US," 8-19, pricked our curiosity, thinking maybe we're not "The Great Satan" after all, but really proving the universal appeal of a certain blond "60 Minutes" correspondent: "A hotel clerk [in Iran] wants to send a note to CBS reporter Diane Sawyer," but doesn't explore the implications. "War-Torn Iran Still Affords Guns, Butter," 8-20, looked inside the Iranian shortages with neat little bits of information, like the government managing since 1979 to pay off the foreign debt

allowances and the current cost of meat and poultry, but is really human interest stuff, not going far enough in explaining or delving into the mechanisms of a dual economy. Her best was an intelligent analysis of Iranian politics, in a series: "Jockeying For Position In Post-Khomeini-Iran," 8-25, on the mating dance beginning as parliamentary elections approach; "Iran's Armed Forces: The Battle Within," 8-26, on the rumblings of discontent within the Iranian army; "Wily Speaker Excels At Iran's Political Game," 8-27, an excellent, profile of Rafsanjani, that's well-conceived, well-written, very comprehensive on background and politics, giving us lots to munch on.

Wyles, John. *Financial Times.* (★ ★ ½)
Italy. Very strong reporting on the political economy of Italy, he teamed up very well with Alan Friedman, and between them no one else covered the country as well. We got the basics on Italy's proposed changes in tax law with "Tax Plans Benefit Better-off in Italy," 1-23, which "bears more than a passing resemblance to the recent changes in U.S. tax legislation." "Underground Economy Gives Italy's GDP a Hefty Boost," 2-17, spells out the implications for healthier stats on deficit reduction and taxation as a percentage of national income. One of the best overall assessments on the Italian political economy was "Parties Back at War," 4-23, detailing the continuing economic vitality despite political uncertainty. We saw very well done interviews that illuminated on the structural changes in Italian finance and business, as in "Italy Moves to End Tradition of Controls," 10-2, on Foreign Trade Minister Renato Ruggiero's plans for new foreign exchange rules, and in "The Seven Years War," 10-12, on the push for privatization under IRI's president, Romano Prodi. "Concern Over the Budget Deficit," 11-17, has a mountain of information on the slackening of the economy as attempts are made to reduce the enormous budget deficits by, among other things, postponing adjustments to income tax rates and by increased indirect taxes.

Wysocki, Bernard Jr. *The Wall Street Journal.* (★ ★)
Tokyo bureau. Although wide-ranging, Wysocki broke little new ground, his spadework not as deep as *The Asian Wall Street Journal* diggers. "Prior Adjustment: Japanese Executives Going Overseas Take Anti-Shock Courses," 1-12, on Japanese business training courses, specifically those given by NEC Corporation, was interesting, but thin, never pulling together a big picture or relating it to American business plans or courses. "Big Dealer. Tough Japanese Firm Grows in Importance in Securities Markets," 4-1, was better, but Wysocki seems to give *all* the credit for Nomura Securities' success to the tough, competitive Japanese, not thinking about outside factors like the strong yen and the tremendous run-up in the Japanese stock market? "South Korean Election Isn't Only Politics," 7-31, gave us a feel for the cultural and political differences of the "mosaic of rival provinces" that may have an effect on the December elections, but he doesn't hypothesize how. A sad, pre-obituary in "Hirohito, Gravely Ill, Stirs Deep Emotions in Many Japanese," 10-30, had some nice lines on Hirohito's life and Japanese imperial protocol, like his hospitalization causing stock prices of paper companies to rise because of a need for new stationary with a new emperor's reign, but little else. Doing part of a series, he turned out a well-done, more analytical "South Korea: Troubled Transition — Korean Military Shows New Restraint, Old Restiveness," 9-15, which examined the police and military apparatus, their uses and misuses, and the hesitancy of the government to use them excessively during the 1987 unrest. He held his own in a new topic, in "Gene Squad: Japanese Now Target Another Field the U.S. Leads: Biotechnology," 12-17, on the emerging biotech race between Japan and the U.S.

Yoder, Stephen Kreider. *The Asian Wall Street Journal.* (★ ★ ★)
Tokyo bureau. The technology reporter here, there was no one in the entire press corps who was even remotely close to him in covering this scene. "Japan Is Racing to Commercialize

New Superconductors,'' with help from Jerry Bishop, 3-20, on the frantic research effort was timely and well organized. "Superconductivity Race Shows How Japan Inc. Works," 8-12, was well-done, typical of the workman-like job Yoder did, covering the superconductivity front in Japan. His most interesting piece, "Rush to Exploit New Superconductors Makes Japan Even More Patent-Crazy," 8-27, described a blizzard of some 2000 patent applications already swamping the Japanese patent office on ideas for superconducting materials and devices. The applications, many launched defensively, without any prototype, reflect a Japanese law that gives priority to the first applicant for protection rather than to the first documented source of an invention, as in the United States. The area of intellectual property is clearly a domain where we do not have to learn from Japan.

NATIONAL SECURITY/DEFENSE/DIPLOMATIC CORRESPONDENTS

Adams, Peter. *Defense News.* (★ ★)
Reporters for *Defense News* probably deserve a handicap in a rating of mass media journalists, their routine product generally far ahead of the dailies in terms of depth, perspective and sheer volume of information. Unlike some other "professional" defense journalists, though, Peter Adams spurns much of the acronym-mongering and jargon worship that detracts from effective communication on already complicated ideas. Adams tackled U.S.-Soviet relations, arms control politics and alliance politics with equal relish, churning out data without losing a sense of proportion. Perhaps the best interviewer on the staff, he scored a big with one with Ed Luttwak, the provocative strategic eminence in "Luttwak: Europe in Pre-Prewar Period," 5-11, and with a 5-25 piece on new SACEUR Gen. John Galvin, who worries about conventional defense of Europe after the INF treaty. Adams is weaker on the Soviet Union, relying on Jerry Hough and Stephen Cohen, the Kremlin's favorite Kremlinologists, for "Gorbachev Moving Quickly to Incorporate Dramatic Changes Throughout Soviet State," 11-9. He might have included Adam Ulam or Peter Reddaway, both prestigious experts not so enthused by Gorbachev. Ditto "Soviet Reform Offers Chance to Reduce Tension," 4-6. He's much better on European reactions to arms control, as in "NATO Defense Ministers Continue to Quarrel Over Zero-Zero Option," 5-18, where he knows much more. Another workhorse for one of the best new defense publications in recent years.

Beeston, Richard. *The Washington Times.* (★ ½)
Diplomatic Correspondent. One of the older hands in de Borchgrave's shop, Beeston is a polished stylist and is capable of first-rate material, but has a tendency to relax, which is quite apparent in this newspaper of over-achievers. Still, Beeston must be credited with one of the most important, and entertaining, stories of the year, "Traitor Philby Pops Up Again," 11-25, in which Beeston recounts his 1978 chance meeting with "Third Man" Kim Philby in Moscow and describes his sudden reappearance on Soviet television this year. Beeston describes his acquaintance with Philby in Beirut, and got some choice quotes from former British and American intelligence officials explaining his reemergence. More often, though, Beeston seemed content to produce boilerplate, as in "KGB Bugging of Embassy Backfired, Schlesinger Says," on the Moscow business, 7-2, or "Reflagging Announcement by U.S. Embarrasses British," which added little to an understanding of the Gulf situation (and, to be fair, was based in part on wire service reports). He did well in covering Pakistani proposals about Afghanistan in the U.N. in a 9-28 New York dateline, and added to the *Times*'s excellent coverage of Soviet disinformation efforts with a story on the Russian retraction of charges that AIDS was created by the Pentagon, 11-3. Beeston is an obvious talent and could be fired up a bit more by emulating some of his junior colleagues on the staff.

Brinkley, Joel. *The New York Times.* (★)
We rapped Brinkley last year for his erratic reporting. This year, he's still erratic, but the bad stuff isn't so awful and the good stuff is getting better. One of the best was "Say US Lacks The Resolve To Improve," 4-20, a review of intelligence officials and reports on counter-espionage security policy that he put together well. "Tower Study: Tension Rises," 2-19, was also nice, explaining why and how the computer backup files at the White House are going to cause trouble for officials there involved in the Iran affair, taking us through the mechanics of the electronic filing system. "Contra Arms Crews Said to Smuggle Drugs," 1-20, didn't fly, giving no evidence that North was involved — it appears to be a freelance operation, not for the benefit of contras, *but* "if the new charge proved true [that North stopped the FBI investigation], the White House could be accused of trying to stymie a drug-smuggling

253

investigation.'' In ''A Perplexed Reagan,'' 10-28, RR's aides say he doesn't understand calls for greater ''leadership'' in crisis; that he's the same man, missing the point that RR doesn't see decline in his ability to control Congress.

Broad, William J. *The New York Times.* (★ ★ ½)
Scientific hardware, with special concentration on military-technology issues in space. Broad has no peer in prestige in the press corps in terms of technical savvy, which is far ahead of his political sophistication. Still, his stories are always substantial, as in ''Space Weapon Idea Now Being Weighed Was Assailed in '82,'' 5-4, which pointed out the emerging split between the early deployment lobby and the ''research forever, deploy never'' establishment in the Pentagon. He also filed several dense pieces on America's vulnerable and declining satellite network, such as ''Pentagon Nursing an Aging Network of Key Satellites,'' 7-20, and 8-25 on private satellite nets, but did anyone read them? He was one American reporter allowed to tour the Krasnoyarsk radar complex with the famous liberal House pilgrims; unlike other absentee reporters who filed stories, though, Broad actually called a violation a violation. He also stated what should be obvious, i.e., traipsing through the facilities does not a full-fledged inspection make. His ''Pentagon Starts Project to Judge Anti-Missile Plan,'' 8-16, on SDI assessment project was also detailed, but slightly marred by his obligation to say the ''issue'' was whether it would be PR or real tests. The editors could buck some of Michael Gordon's assignments over to Broad with good effect, and we'd love to see a Broad series on Soviet SDI.

Broder, John. *Los Angeles Times.* (★)
Pentagon/defense reporter. A former *LAT* business writer, Broder got his feet wet on this new beat in 1987. Frequently reporting on Gulf War incidents involving the U.S., his organized presentations were competently rounded. In ''U.S. Copters Fire on Iranian Ship,'' 9-22, he reports the reactions of all the big players, including Soviet Foreign Minister Shevardnadze's response that this ''is why we are against any military presence in the gulf. The concentration of naval ships cannot lead to anything good. We know that this will lead to complications.'' He covered Cap Weinberger's interview with the *LAT* well enough in ''West to Increase Its Forces in Gulf,'' 8-26, extensively quoting the DoD secretary, but filling the necessary details on naval deployments in and around the area. ''Navy Begins to Face Age of Chemical Weapons,'' 11-8, provided material not seen elsewhere, though he had to use sources outside the Navy. Very limp, though, with ''Soviet Radar Site No ABM Violation, U.S. Visitors Say,'' 9-9, reporting the conclusion of a U.S. congressional delegation that the Krasnoyarsk radar station doesn't violate the 1972 treaty, and State Department spokesman Charles Redman's conviction that it does. Surely the issue could have been expanded upon with a more conclusive treatment, but we give him the benefit of a novice's first year.

Carrington, Tim. *The Wall Street Journal.* (★ ★ ½)
First-string defense correspondent, as we tended to see his by-line (alone or sometimes with a colleague) on the most important, interesting defense stories of the year. Up a notch this year due to his continued seasoning and wider range. He was not chained to the Pentagon, as stories from the USS Memphis, a Navy attack submarine, 6-24, and Parris Island Marine base, 7-2, demonstrated sure-handed field reportage. From his Beltway office, Carrington has developed a first class, forthcoming group of sources which reflect a maturing awareness of key issues and contexts. While most reporters on this beat spent much column space reinventing the nuclear proliferation wheel in Pakistan, Carrington delivered two ''other side'' numbers on India (2-24 with Robert Greenberger, 6-12 solo), treating the whole range of high tech exports that the pro-Moscow New Delhi regime was seeking. The two pieces not only covered the scene in India meticulously, but also managed to shed light on the fracas between Commerce and the Pentagon on export controls, a juicy theme explored further in ''Pentagon's Firm Control Over Export Licenses May Lessen in Face of Politics, Big Trade Gaps,'' 3-13, (with Greenberger). He occasionally penned a ''Foreign Insight'' think piece that was also new and different, such as ''Koreans Harbor Resentment of the U.S. Over Their Subordinate Role in

Defense," 7-28, which presented another side to the tangled U.S. role in promoting Korean democracy. At times his material seems more appropriate for *Defense News*, as in the detailed report, 7-13, on the awarding of Amraam missile contracts, and his Persian Gulf stories (e.g., 8-31, 9-1, 9-9, 10-20) lacked firepower, but his coverage of the SDI debate, particularly the legislative progress report, 9-22, was superb. A fine reporter, he's deserving of more challenges/opportunities.

Cushman, John H. Jr. *The New York Times.* (★ ★)
The second year on the Pentagon beat has seasoned Cushman somewhat, and his stories demonstrate more imagination than was evident in '86 (a one star review in the '87 guide). Still, for a *Defense Week* alumnus, we still saw a disturbing propensity to rehash his own material on military spending, defects in weapons systems, and procurement blues. He also has a tendency to promote the Democratic congressional caucus line on several controversial issues. Two of his pieces belong in the *New Republic*'s "notebook" section that juxtaposes conflicting headlines on like issues: "'Star Wars' Setup Likely by '94, Weinberger Says," a 2-25 account of Cap's meeting with the *Times* editorial royalty; and "Pentagon Secretly Prepares Plan for Missile Defense in Mid-1990's," 4-8, which "reveals" the true nature of the program through the staff report of two anti-SDI senators. He does file informative, hard-hitting stories, such as "Navy Warns of Crisis in Anti-Submarine Warfare," 3-19, an interview/story with top USCG expert on ASW; and "U.S. Has Fallen Years Behind on a Fleet for Clearing Mines," 7-29, a tough, fair account of how the minesweeper program got short shrift in the 1980s. He also filed from Teheran in August, with a solid piece on trial of cleric who first exposed the U.S. arms shipments to Iran, 8-17. More often than not, however, his material is old hat, as in "U.S. Fleet in Gulf: Mission Inscrutable," 5-19, or a tiresome review of the Packard Commission's first anniversary, "Pentagon Seen Changing Little in Arms-Buying," 7-15. Needs better assignments, and/or editing.

Davidson, Ian. *Financial Times.* (½ ★)
Paris correspondent. The "Foreign Affairs" columnist for eight years, Davidson had become addicted to commenting on the world at large, but there was less wisdom or detachment this year. "What the West Failed to Notice," 2-23, makes some reasonable observations on a Brookings Institute thesis that Soviet doctrine on nuclear weapons gives strategic priority to arms control, but Davidson thinks "red-blooded Reaganites" just can't see that. He takes a few swipes at SDI, but really let's loose against it in "Mr. Reagan's Dangerous Dream," 3-2; "Star Wars" is seen as the president's policy with "dream appeal" that can "make America forget the ignominy of forgetfulness and senility." He's better in "The Gap Between Headline and Text," 4-6, questioning whether anything "really earth shattering had happened in Moscow" with the Gorbachev-Thatcher meeting, and offering possible scenarios of what Gorbachev may have sought and gained. But back to his major focus for the year, "My Life with (Among Others) Mr Reagan," 6- 15: "President Reagan...has probably caused more damage to the European-American relationship in the Atlantic Alliance than any of his predecessors...No recent President has come to office so committed to ideological hatred of the Soviet Union, so hostile to arms control..." There was just too much of that kind of "analysis" from him all year, the once lofty and learned commentary of yore replaced by sour-bellied invective.

Donnelly, Tom. *Defense News.* (★ ★)
Another *Defense News* foot soldier, Donnelly usually has one long piece and a few shorts in each issue, focusing on weapons procurement and army doctrine. Editors shape much of the product at this weekly professional tabloid, so the reporters can be better judged on their hustle and interview style. Donnelly was strong on Army stories, such as "U.S. Army Reconsiders Its Air Defense Plans," 2-23, a thorough collection of quotes on possible shift of gears, and "NATO Allies Settle on Deep-Strike Strategy to Counter Soviet Conventional Force Advantage," 6-29, which focused on a major doctrinal issue that will be a hot issue in 1988. *Defense News* staff covers Beltway think tanks closely, which is useful, but a story on Brookings Institution's

defense budget report could have benefited from a dissonant voice, 6-22. Donnelly showed some flair on 10-26 with a new twist on the stock market crash and how it "may have granted the U.S. Defense Department's 1988 budget request a stay of execution" from Gramm-Rudman, since an emergency budget deal would treat Pentagon spending better than the indiscriminate $11.5 billion G-R axe. He spotted, sooner than most, the waning power of now-departed Pentagon procurement czar Richard Godwin with "Services Fight for Procurement Authority," 7-6.

Dorsey, James M. *The Washington Times.* (★ ½)
Pentagon. The solid, productive journeyman journalist who produces standard daily reporting and an occasional analytical offering. Like all *Washington Times* reporters, Dorsey is constantly pounding the pavement in search of material, although his sources are not variegated as some others. He sometimes tries to make lemonade out of lemons, such as his 2-19 story on a Cato Institute debate between U.S. Ambassador to West Germany Richard Burt and Melvyn Krauss, author of a weak pull-the-troops from Europe tract, which worked; but the next day's report on Al Haig's lecture at the Heritage Foundation criticizing Reagan on arms control didn't. He had interesting story angles 6-23 and 8-31, the former on Japanese investigation of tech-transfer to North Korea, the latter on the Norwegian company Kongsberg Vaapenfabrik selling goods to the PRC. Both stories were relevant to the overall technological security scandal while shedding light on new twists. Dorsey also showed flair with "B-1B Has Friends on Base, Foes on Hill," 3-25, a report from the field which gave the pro-B-1 side which was missing in other reports. He scored a coup, 10-19, with report on Soviet acquisition of specs for U.S. Stinger missiles through a military espionage plot in Greece. Negatively, an otherwise informative piece on Europe after the INF Treaty was marred by Dorsey's reliance on two staffers from the Center of Defense Information, not exactly the most objective sources. He could show more consistency, but when he's on, he's very good.

Engelberg, Stephen. *The New York Times.* (★ ★ ½)
Washington. A young reporter in his second year on the major intelligence beat, Engelberg built his credibility by covering the sensitive Iran-Contra hearings with restraint and thoughtful analysis. He practically clears RR of a smoking gun in "Memo Details How a Frustrated Reagan Pondered Ways to Get Aid to the Contras," 7-11. In early April 1986, Col. North drafted a memo seeking RR's approval for Iran-Contra diversion. On May 2, RR is said to be seeking a way to finance the contras. "If Mr. Reagan knew of this question, it would seem unlikely he would be pressing Admiral Poindexter a month later for some other method of coming up with funding for the contras," writes Engelberg. Good job! We noted enterprise earlier with "Secord Restates Denial on Profits," 6-7, an interview with Gen. Secord. Also, a great effort with "Ex-CIA Chief: A Legacy of Doubt on His Role in the Iran-Contra Affair," 7-19, a comprehensive review of William Casey's role: "Bill didn't break the law, said one former advisor. That was not his style. Bill never went over the line. What he did was find a way to move the line." In "Behind the Gulf Buildup: The Unforeseen Occurs," (with Bernard Trainor) 8-23, a front-page backgrounder to the reflagging of Kuwaiti ships is masterful, a sweeping account that catches and organizes the significant nuances and turns that shaped this policy: "We're at the mercy of events...It's a day-to-day policy." He spent much of the year on the Marine/Embassy story, jumping the gun in "Two Marines Said to Allow Soviet Embassy Access," 3-26, on how much access Soviet intruders were allowed by Marine malefactors (damage in that case was less than thought). Embassy security stories were all the rage in the spring, but Engelberg's solid analyses "Behind Embassy Affair: Complacency on Spying," 4-8 and "Embassy Security: Story of Failure," 4-19, were overshadowed by the outstanding work of *The Washington Times* in this area, Bill Gertz in particular. Engelberg should be credited with a major scoop, 3-21, "Senator is Quoted as Saying U.S. Recruited Israeli Officer as Spy," an astonishing accusation/admission by Sen. David Durenberger (R-MN) compromising intelligence sources and methods. A very promising reporter.

Fialka, John J. *The Wall Street Journal.* (★ ½)
Fialka was spared daily reporting chores, but was handed occasional longer "Politics and Policy" leads and perspectives on important defense issues and personages. He did the best profile of the year in the national security arena, in any paper, 7-15: "Veteran 'Lone Ranger' Strategist Packs Firepower With Cold-Eyed Outlook on Soviet Nuclear Policy." It was a tour de force on Albert Wohlstetter, ageless guru of hardline defense analysts in which Fialka did extensive interview/spadework, getting people like Carter DoD official James Woolsey to opine, "It's not so much that he's caught the new trends...In a lot of cases, he's kind of created them." Moreover, Fialka knows the subject, as when he writes, "Rather than the apocalyptic conflict many nuclear planners and arms controllers talk about, Mr. Wohlstetter's theory envisions a short conventional missile attack that leaves both France and Britain with the option of either capitulating or of using their relatively small forces of nuclear tipped submarine missiles," a salient point. Fialka also followed our 1986 prediction (see review of Richard Halloran), in which we said more writers would cover the "low-intensity conflict" beat, with a piece, 3-17, on implementation of legislation on the special operations command, in which he showed good insight into the arcane battles within the Pentagon between conventional warriors and "snake eaters," as special operators are called. Another informative, though brief, report concerned the improved performance of U.S. Army units in Europe, "U.S. Army Units Win Battle Contests For the First Time," 7-6, showing the real upgrade in Army capabilities from the dark days of 1970s. Would like to see more product; what's there is choice.

Fink, Donald E. *Aviation Week & Space Technology* (★ ★ ½)
AW&ST's editor, lead editorial writer gains a notch this year due to the recognizable upgrade in the trade-oriented, info-jammed editorials this year. Fink produced some of the best essays on the Challenger's legacy, 1-26, the Atlas Aftermath, 4-13; and America's "Space Leadership Void," 7-27. Each pulled no punches on responsibility (NASA head Fletcher) and gave credit where credit was due (Air Force Secretary Pete Aldridge, who pushed to develop other lift vehicles). This is the kind of material *AW&ST*'s readers are used to. More interesting for the interested lay reader were Fink's report-editorial from Jerusalem, 6-8, covering items such as the Lavi jet fighter as well as broader issues associated with Israel's 40th anniversary. Also, we liked the tight editorial on Soviet space gains, 5-25, a neglected subject that should get more ink in '88. A piece on Airbus's threat to American aerospace firms, 8-3, and on the LHX helicopter, 3-16, were "inside baseball" editorials, but, after all, *AW&ST* is more of an industry journal than publications such as *Defense Week*. A decent rebound from an off-year, but our expectations are raised for the upcoming election year, in which space issues should be big news.

Gerth, Jeff. *The New York Times.* (★)
The Washington bureau's utility infielder on investigative reporting, peering into keyholes foreign and domestic, he came up in our esteem in 1987 after mangling, we thought, an '86 expose of Ferdinand Marcos' war record. He doesn't mishandle "Saudi Businessman in Iran Affair Tells of 'Playing Games' With U.S. Aides," 3-10, going to Paris to interview one of the few players in the Iran-Contra affair who had not yet been interviewed *ad nauseum*: Adnan Khashoggi, who describes with relish how he pulled the chains of the entire U.S. executive branch. In "Millions From Arms Sales Traced to Iran Group Aiding Kidnappers," 3-18, we get "associates of Mr. Ghorbanifar called the money 'ransom', while an American official described it as 'payment for services rendered.'" A useful report. In "Ginsburg Had Two Roles in a Court Case," 11-8, Gerth is robbed of a front-page scoop that would have pulled down Supreme Court nominee Douglas Ginsburg. Because Ginsburg quit on 11-7, the story was moved to p.36. Also on 11-8, Gerth chipped in the investigative side of a profile of Sen. Dole, "The Contradictions of Bob Dole," recording a few minor financial transactions.

Gertz, Bill. *The Washington Times.* (★ ★ ★)
National security correspondent, with particular emphasis on intelligence affairs. One of the

reasons the *Times* is being taken seriously these days, by friend and foe, is its defense and foreign policy coverage, which consistently outhustles and usually outproduces its rivals. Gertz has developed into the most resourceful daily defense scribe in Washington. Although his background seems skimpy, his three years in the Beltway have created a seasoned, informed, and above all, inexhaustible digger always looking for a new angle. Occasionally, he embarrasses the competition with scoops, such as "Soviet Commerce Chamber Identified as Front for KGB," 6-25, which revealed an unclassified CIA-State Dept. report on Soviet shenanigans *four months* before the *NYT*'s Clyde Farnsworth filed a similar piece, 10-28. He also beat the pack with two early year pieces on Afghanistan, 2-25 and 3-3, both of which presaged the numerous autumn stories on diplomatic maneuvers in Moscow and Kabul. Gertz's forte is the intelligence world, where he eclipsed the *Times*'s Stephen Engelberg by delving into the Soviet propaganda/disinformation complex, 2-9 and 6-29, detailing Soviet psywar on SDI. He departed from the crowd in the Moscow embassy spy scandal with two goodies on State Dept. efforts at suppressing a report critical of former Ambassador Hartman, 7-22 and 7-27. A 6-24 story of Richard Perle's testimony before House Committee on US-Soviet scientific exchange versus Western objectives (bridge-building), well done. In November, Gertz went to Moscow, reported on a new unofficial magazine, entitled *Glasnost*, published by a group of dissidents, which was a superb pre-Yeltsin affair dispatch on the coming crackdown in Moscow, 11-16. Gertz quotes the editor as saying, "The fact that different opinions are expressed in the mass media is very common for Western countries, but in our country it is a major sign of sharpening tension." He still has room, though, to broaden his topics and sources a bit.

Gilmartin, Trish. *Defense News.* (★ ★ ★)
Best of a very good bunch at *Defense News*, Gilmartin was one of a handful of correspondents in the defense news biz to produce two or three stories per week that were informed, objective and reliable. Her main focus was the SDI beat: including political fracas, a report on Hill opposition to a SDI "think tank," 5-11; "Republican SDI Advocates Circle the Wagons, Force Near-Term Deployment Decision" 3-30; industry gossip, "Competition for SDI Test Bed Program Enters Most Crucial Phase this Month," 4-20; and technological breakthroughs, "SDI Interceptor Tracks and Destroys Lance Missile in Test," 5-25. The material in her stories, as well as sources, frequently find their way into mainstream publications, but without the same eye for detail and nuance. Although reports such as "SDI Organization Begins Study of Midcourse Tier," 11-9, included much grist for contractor mills, and quotes people like Col. Jim Graham of the SDIO engineering and support office, they are quite accessible to anyone who can understand the basic *New York Times* news analysis (an oftimes daunting task, to be sure). Other issues covered by Gilmartin in 1987 were a waste-and-fraud story (a 6-29 report on the unfairly prosecuted, vindicated James Beggs, former NASA Administrator), and other space issues (NASA Space Station, 2-9, and ASAT weapon, 3-16). A thorough reporter with a firm grasp of issues and a fine journalistic style.

Gordon, Michael R. *The New York Times.* (★ ½)
Pentagon. The top banana on defense at the Paper of Record, judging by his frequent front-page bylines, regular "Washington Talk" features and Sunday thinkpieces. Gordon has the smarts and hustle of a good reporter, but carries his old arms control theologian's mantle too faithfully. Favorite subjects in '87 were SDI, internal administration bickering, and Pentagon classification of information. "Pentagon Curbing Public Data on 'Star Wars'," 1-26, and "How Public Remarks Became Classified Data," 2-20, illustrate latter proclivity for DoD bashing. He began to take on nuke proliferation issues, with solid "Norway Questions Israeli Use of Nuclear Material," 2-17, and "2 Charged in Plan on Pakistan Arms," 7-29. He was also first on Gorbachev's successful PR offensive with "Soviet Leads U.S. in Arms Cut Image," 6-7. Unfortunate that he still relies on his favorite unilateral disarmers William Arkin of IPS on nuke testing, 4-4, or Sidney Drell in "On Making a Better Warhead," 2-26. He can do better. Worst of all was SDI coverage, which seemed to have more Common Cause than common sense. See "Defense Department is Rebuffed on Soviet ABM Threat," 3-5, which disparages

Soviet Star Wars Program; "Advisers Questions Speeding Up Anti-Missile Plan," 7-29, which distorts a Defense Science Board report on SDI feasibility; and a priceless howler, "Cessna's Flight Adds an Element to the Debate Over 'Star Wars'," 6-1, in which intrepid Mathias Rust topples SDI with his Red Square landing. *Times* editors should begin cutting his load.

Goshko, John M. *The Washington Post.* (★)
Diplomatic correspondent, with focus on Middle East and Latin America. Old hand, could write in *Post* style in his sleep, which is part of his problem. Too many of his bylines seem to be knocked off without too much care or feeding. Moreover, other reporters (Moore, Smith) on the *Post* getting the jump on him, making some Goshko stories such as "Saudis Agree to Provide Aid to U.S. Gulf Forces," 8-22, or "Shultz, Latin Envoys Discuss Peace Initiative," 7-11, window dressing. Goshko also is ultimate "inside baseball" reporter, doing pieces on obscure GAO studies (9-11) or tangential meetings (8-29 on Arab delegation in DC to jaw about Iran-Iraq war.) Teamed up with Julia Preston for 5-30's "Defector Arrives for Debriefing; Cuba Plays Down Military Role," which was an interesting blip on former Cuban Gen. del Pino, although Castro later admitted that his defection hurt. One genuine scoop came on 10-28 with "Chile, Panama Provide Arms to Nicaragua," based on several unnamed U.S. sources, but an explosive story nonetheless. We see Goshko as part of the dwindling old guard, going against the grain of even the *Post*'s editorials (witness its call for the dismantling of the Krasnoyarsk radar on 9-11), plugging away without much verve. Consistently outdone by upstarts at *Washington Times*, and that message may be getting through.

Greenberger, Robert S. *The Wall Street Journal.* (★ ★)
In rating Greenberger last year we said that he was ready to move to first-string State Dept. coverage, and he did. He was given more "Washington Insights," lead international pieces, and did quite nicely. He has a knack for the subtle gradations of meaning in diplomatic subject matter, the result being that his stuff did not replicate pack journalism. Even a banal topic, such as U.S. concern about allied defense spending, was compelling reading in Greenberger's script. A 6-30 back-pager on the new popularity of ally-bashing was good precisely because it probed new twists in the congressional anti-NATO/Japan faction. It found many isolationists are using the righteous indignation toward allied defense spending to promote protectionism, which presaged the full-throated Toshiba outrage. He also called the U.S. position on the Iran-Iraq Ceasefire resolution in the U.N., 7-13. He expressed the pusillanimity of Congress well with "Congress Afraid to Challenge Regan on Sensitive Foreign Arms-Sales Issue," 4-6, and covered the Elliot Abrams line on the Arias plan, 8-17, with a piece on the skepticism of U.S. to the Guatemala accords. Greenberger hustles, does his homework, and has semantic touch that is distinctive without being obtrusive. He should be cared and fed, perhaps even given a Moscow posting.

Grier, Peter. *The Christian Science Monitor.* (★ ★)
The *Monitor* has a somewhat over-rated reputation as an "objective" newspaper with greater "balance" in its news coverage than most other dailies. In reality, *CSM* is home to as many editorial and reportorial spin doctors as the *Washington Post* or *Times*, with its bent far closer to the former. Still, it does pay a great deal of attention to defense/national security topics, most of which are done by this versatile Pentagon beatman. He has his favorite arms controller sources (Michael Krepon of Carnegie, Jack Mendelsohn and James Rubin of the Arms Control Association, and the ubiquitous John Pike of the American Federation of Scientists), but he does reach for the "peace through strength" crowd with less distaste than some of his colleagues. He was on top of key INF negotiation points earlier than most with two March pieces, "Keeping Track of Scrapped Missiles," 3-3, and "Arms Agreement May Hinge on Converting Missiles," 3-25, which highlighted the sticky problem of what was to be done with the withdrawn/destroyed intermediate nuclear forces. Greier followed up with an interesting discussion, 9-30, on the same issue, which others were covering by that point. He has a decent knack for profiles, as in the two he did on Gen. Galvin, currently the top NATO commander and former head of

U.S. forces in Central America, 4-28 and 5-1. Both touched on key regional concerns, Salvador's counterinsurgency effort and NATO's military shape in the 1990s. His 8-21 story-profile on Frank Gaffney, Richard Perle's immediate successor at the Pentagon, was wrong in that Grier, relaying Gaffney's viewpoint, suggested that the U.S. and West Germany would "stand firm" on Pershing 1-A missiles, a stand that went soft one week later. Also dubious, wispy piece on new CIA chief Webster, 10-8, who "looks for 'risk takers, not risk seekers.'" Grier could have found a sizeable professional opposition to consummate bureaucrat Webster, in and out of the intelligence community. "ABM Deal Won't Slow '88 SDI Tests," 11-23, on the budget compromise, had the kind of smart-aleck lead that shows *CSM* bias: "Reagan administration officials have settled a bitter dispute with Congress over arms control by solemnly promising to not do something they had not planned on doing anyway." Grier's byline is a staple of the newspaper, generally full of reliable data and decent sources.

Gruson, Lindsey. *The New York Times.* (★ ½)
Washington bureau, covering foreign affairs. Focusing on Central America the latter half of the year, Gruson did even-handed work, though his analytics were on the shallow side. "Land for Salvador's Poor: To Many, Bitter Victory," 9-28, examined the failures of land reform since 1980, the survey balanced, but the effort to answer "why?" was inadequate. The intrinsic problems of the experiments were never addressed. One of the better efforts on telling the refugees' story was "For Nicaraguans, Signs of Hope After Years of War," 9-28, a feature on the reunion of Nicaraguan families in Honduras as the Sandinistas permit citizens to visit refugee families across the border. "'I will return,' said one refugee, who met with her sister for the first time in eaght years. 'I like the plan, but the question is will the Sandinistas comply?'" "Duarte Calls Cease Fire: Rebels Say No," 10-7, noted the implicit reorganization of guerrilla influence in El Salvador, using quotes from President Jose Duarte and Communist Party leader Shafik Handal to good effect. "For Contras in One Area, Growing Civilian Support," 11-5, covered territory already worked by the *WSJ* and *Washington Post* without adding much new. Earlier we noted as well done, "Privacy of AIDS Patients: Fear Infringes on Sanctity," 7-30, an examination of the ethical and legal dilemmas doctors face with informing families of AIDS patients.

Halloran, Richard. *The New York Times.* (★ ★ ½)
An old defense hand, with special emphasis on conventional arms, military budgets, and manpower. He spent some of '87 promoting his book on the U.S. defense establishment, but still produced an abundant crop of thorough, balanced stories that, while not sexy, should serve as a model for defense correspondents everywhere. He has access to top brass and civilian officials, but displays admirable hustle and perspective by going to the war colleges, bases, and outposts to get material from working level officers and non-coms. Examples include "Latin Guerrillas Joining Forces, U.S. Officers Say," 3-3, filed from Panama, an alarming piece on the coordination among leftist insurgents in the region; a second 3-3 byline, "Reserve Officers Warn Forces Are Unprepared," pointing out one of the missing links in the Reagan buildup; "Lasers and 'Red Force': Realism in War Games," 7-27, a piece from Fort Irwin on improvements in simulation training; and "New Breed of Sergeants: Less Spit, More Polish," 9-3 from Fort Bliss on NCO training. It's hard to imagine that authoritative pieces such as "Lacking Parts, Armed Forces Cannibalize Costly Warplanes," 7-16, or "Navy Says Shortage of Sailors May Take Ships Out of Fleet," 4-13, would appear anywhere else in the non-specialist press. He doesn't miss the big picture, however, "Steering an Uncharted Course," 3-2, on the reorganization of the JCS, or as "The Reagan Navy: $485 Billion but Still Questions," 8-17, makes clear. Also, scored with profile of Beltway Bandits, "A Thriving Industry to Do the Pentagon's Work," 7-14. There was a slight anti-Navy, pro-"military reform" tilt noticeable this year, but on the whole, fair and forthright.

Healy, Melissa. *Los Angeles Times.* (**NR**)
Staff writer. A young reporter, new to *LAT*, coming over from *U.S.News & World Report*

to work the defense/national security beat. We didn't see enough to rate her, but "'Star Wars' May Harm Economy, Research Group Says," 11-18, was foreboding. It reported that the New York-based Council for Economic Priorities concluded missile defense plans will cause "severe economic dislocation," and that Congress should knock $3.7 billion off the Administration's budget request. Insufficiently balanced, giving the SDI Office's counter only cursory acknowledgment, there was a disturbing spin there. Perhaps all she needs is a bit more seasoning.

Kempe, Frederick. The Wall Street Journal. (★ ★)
Diplomatic correspondent, Kempe's byline often appears affixed to the Journal's "Insight" column, which sometimes comes through with insight, and sometimes doesn't. He scored highly with "Three for the Seesaw," 2-4, an example of his ability to marshall critical evidence, persuasive on Beijing's warming up to Moscow, despite their differences over Afghan and Cambodian policies. "Washington Is Facing New Challenges in E. Asia Trade and Diplomacy," 3-23, was a strike-out, bits and pieces strung together, quotes from the "We have to do something" pundits urging U.S. pressures on Seoul for more democracy and currency deflations there and in Taiwan. He just couldn't stay away from promoting appreciation of the won, later in the year quoting Treasury Secretary Mulford's assertion that the won's too low and the NICs are excessively exporting, "Korean Business Fears Democracy's 'Disorderly Period,'" 12-3. Reported from Seoul, this article was otherwise informative on the economic perspectives of officials and the various candidates. He displayed sharper analytics in "Riots In Mecca Show Failure Of Saudi Policy," 8-4, on the threats to the monarchy as its efforts to remain isolated from the Gulf War broke down. At his best handling the complications arms control talks were creating in West German-U.S. relations, as in his 7-29 review of the various positions circulating on the fate of Germany's Pershing 1As. The sharpest, however, was "Gorbachev Going Over Kohl's Head to Woo New Generations of Germans," 8-3, analyzing potentials of a Gorby gambit for a neutral Germany. Less rigorous analytically, "As Tensions Build in Korea, U.S. Fears It Will Have to Referee Vote Aftermath," 12-4, was too heavy with scenarios. Still a hit-and-miss player, he needs to concentrate on his strengths more.

Lewis, Neil A. *The New York Times.* (★ ★)
National staff, covering foreign affairs. Competent work, mixing good analytics with solid reporting, Lewis was timely on several occasions. "Angola Rebels In Offer On Rail Link," 3-27, was an important report on Jonas Savimbi's offer to let the MPLA re-open the Benguela railroad for non-military transport. Lewis noted that the move weakens allegations that UNITA is dependent on South Africa and that it could maneuver the MPLA into negotiations with Savimbi. "Abortions Abroad Are New Focus Of Widening Battle Over Reagan's Policy," 6-1, did a good job covering the Administration's loss of key fights involving two main points on this policy, though it still needed fuller treatment. "Contra Aid a Key, U.S. Official Says," 8-19, reported the failure of the Guatemala Plan as the armed threat in the region was seen as still unchecked. Lewis also covered the announcement of U.S. Rep. Jack Kemp (R-NY) that he planned to work Congress for approval of $310 million in military aid for the next eighteen months. "Reagan Expected to Seek More Aid for the Contras," 11-5, was a balanced account of the President's likely next move on contra aid.

Lewis, Paul. *The New York Times.* (★ ★ ½)
UN bureau. Moving from the Paris beat to the UN after Elaine Sciolino's departure, Lewis had already made a strong impression with his "Food Surplus May Bankrupt European Bloc," 12-26-86. Mountains of food surpluses, swelled by CAP subsidies, had prices dropping and officials throwing up their hands, declaring "We can't go on." Lewis made the story urgent by drawing out the implications for U.S.-European trade strategies. Timely, but not as clear on what was up, "Rightist Split Deals a Blow to Chirac," 6-7, reported the problems in Chirac's coalition with a rebel who wouldn't shut up or resign. On his new beat, the wrap-up on the UN Conference on Trade and Development, "Economic Parley Termed a Success," 8-3, gave

us the details on the sentiment for free-market policies there. He was quick with "New Soviet Interest in UN Broadens," 9-25, noting they're finally going to pay their share of the peacekeeping missions. The article was timely, raising what has yet to be answered — is it propaganda or is it real? Sharp instincts and sharp mind, the experienced Lewis will work this new beat with ease.

Marcus, Daniel J. *Defense News.* (★ ★)
Army beat, although, like all *Defense News* scribblers, Marcus sometimes does double or triple duty, often covering Hill budget news as in the 11-9 report on $2 billion cut in command, control, and communications budget, or doing an interview, a fine "one-on-one" with Brent Scowcroft, 4-27. Marcus co-authored, with Peter Adams, 4-6, a scoop on private satellite images revealing Soviet radar at Krasnoyarsk to public view for first time. We only wished they took it a bit further to explore implications of privately-owned satellites for the intelligence/national security biz. Marcus was unexpectedly frivolous with "The Novel Side of David Aaron," 5-18, a weightless piece on the liberal Carter NSC aide Aaron that belonged in *The Washington Post* "Style" section. His pieces on Army systems, a quiet service during the years of squeakier wheels like the Navy's John Lehman, were quite solid, if a shade esoteric at times, "Army Extends ACCS Bid Time," 6-15, and "Lawmakers Fight JTC3A Relocation," 4-6. We wanted more in a 6-15 interview with former Carter DoD official Walter Slocombe, who said "Jack Kemp can say genuinely foolish things, such as that deterrence is immoral," an inexcusable parody that Marcus should have flagged.

Moore, Molly. *The Washington Post.* (★ ★)
In response to widespread criticism (even from, dare they admit it, the *MediaGuide*?), the *Post* brahmins decided to upgrade their coverage of the defense community by adding reporters, increasing assignments, and cutting back on some of their weaker scribblers. New kid on the block Molly Moore, not even reviewed in '86, files from the Pentagon with effective reportorial skills covering up for an observable lack of a detailed defense background. Moore had three areas of specialization in '87: procurement problems, the Stark/Persian Gulf escort situation, and the *sine qua non* story of the year, security lapses/spy stuff in the military. Material on the year of the spy was quite solid, including a 2-11 story on Pentagon clearances, a 5-1 piece with Helen Dewar on the Moscow embassy mess, and "High-Tech Security Failures Rise," 6-8, in which super-sensitive nuclear command codes "traveled cross-country over unsecure, commercial telephone links in a security breach that could have left critical secrets vulnerable to enemy surveillance." The other example of Moore coming close to a scoop was "Repairs to Navy's Phoenix Missile Cause New Defects," 5-30, an expose on the missile snafu that got worse when the Navy tried to fix it. Most of the other gold-plated, big ticket item stories were either copies of other stories or were from one or two of the same old military reform source network. Several stories on the B-1, the most unfairly maligned U.S. weapon system in years, fall into that category (2-24, 2-26, 7-19, 10-26), as does "Stealth Costs Exceeding Estimates," 5-2. Moore's Persian Gulf reporting was a mixed bag, with a very good "Navy's Webb Hits Allies for Lack of Aid in Gulf," 9-9, on SecNav showing unusual candor, mixed with a silly "U.S. Escorts Costing $1 Million a Day," 8-22, full of guesstimates and "administrative sources." Part of the problem may be that *Post* editors cannot bring themselves to think about more interesting defense issues for their reporters to cover. We think Moore is a welcome addition, who could get much better, but not without some more care and thought from 15th Street higher-ups.

Morrison, David. *National Journal.* (★ ½)
Defense, with an occasional foray into international affairs. Improved slightly from '86, his first year on a regular beat after several years at the Center from Defense Information, the liberal disarmament lobby — and he hasn't quite gotten over the ideological hangover from

CDI. This is readily apparent in his regular "Defense Focus" column, but he's better in the longer "reports," obliged to fish in a bigger quote pond. Favorite themes in '87 were the Pentagon's continuing war on "freedom of information," "Dancing in the Dark," 4-11; "For Our Eyes Only," 5-23; "Our Secrets Act?" 8-15. Also, whistleblowers, and the dreaded Mil-Industrial Complex with a profile on "Service Lobbies," 10-17, and "Made in America" on procurement protectionism, 11-28. He also re-ran his favorite anti-SDI pieces from last year, such as "Washington Update" on ASATs, 3-21, complete with quotes from liberal space guru Paul Stares and Rep. Les AuCoin. There was quality in a cover story on Frank Carlucci, 2-28, plus a fairly comprehensive look at the rising tide of NATO-bashing among those in the defense community and Congress, "Sharing NATO's Burden," 5-30. He showed good grasp of the Euro-jitters about the INF Treaty with "Trauma Over Treaty," 5-27, but less complete was his 5-9 cover story on the intelligence community after Iran-Contra. He seemed to take up the cause for the arms control association on the ABM Treaty interpretation issue, 7-4 and 9-12, which is at least arguable, and on Soviet Treaty violations, 3-28 which is not. Morrison saved his biggest polemical guns for the television series "Amerika," 2-14, (did anybody take that show seriously apart from professional anti-anticommunists?). He's expanded his contacts within the pro-defense world of officials and analysts, but needs to put some more thought into his choice of subjects and underlying premises. *Caveat emptor* for '88.

Mortimer, Edward. *Financial Times.* (★ ★ ★)
"Foreign Affairs" columnist. Assuming this new position midyear, his thoughtful analytical powers had already attracted our attention in "Jostling to Fill a Power Vacuum," 4-7. Looking ahead to an "Afghanistan After the Russians," he counts no chickens before they're hatched and projects a "Lebanonization" of the country if and when the Soviets do withdraw. The puzzles of a resurgent Islam are explored in a rewarding discussion with Ernest Gellner, "Scholar of the Holy War," 4-21. The first of his "Foreign Affairs" columns we saw, "Why Europe Is in Need of the Thatcher Touch," 6-23, speaks of the need for a greater capacity by Europe for action in its own interest. Thatcher, who ought to be the spokesperson for this, "has credentials for an international role, but lacks a long-term strategic view of what needs to be done." He's persuasive with his analytic on Honecker's trip to West Germany, the "unity" question and Gorbachev's motives in "That Old Obsessive Question," 9-8. He probes deeply into the new role of the Soviets at the UN, raising the right reservations, but not neglecting what may be positive in it, "The Soviets Come in From the Cold," 10-26. Most impressive all year, his analytics on Gorbachev's Russia. "A Captivating but Empty Anniversary," 11-3, avoids the all too facile analyses that rely on an "immutable definition of national character," and comes up with insights into the contradictions of a new Russia. "Parts That Glasnost Fails to Reach," 9-22, was state of the art on the extent and limit of debate in the USSR, one of the 10-best commentary pieces of the year.

Oberdorfer, Don. *The Washington Post.* (★ ★ ½)
National security, with a special tilt toward the politics of foreign policy/defense decision making. He roamed over the subject lot as his colleagues seem to do, but unlike some of them, he had a decent range of sources whose knowledge involved more than their most recent slight. His acumen showed with "Carlucci Reviewing Secret Operations," 2-26, picking out the most important, as opposed to the most sensational, nuggets from an editorial luncheon with a NSC adviser. It included dithering on an SDI deployment decision, new export control procedures, and a PRC consulate in L.A. He co-authored "State Dept. Acted to Block U.S.-Egypt Attack on Libya," 2-20, which made a big stir, but co-author was Bob Woodward, so we don't know how much was "reported" by BW and how much was dug up by Oberdorfer. Two reports on South Korea, 6-23 and 6-26 in hindsight appear alarmist, but he was talking to the right people. Caught in midsummer, he bashed Pakistan on nukes, relying too much on Hill dems and not reaching out to informed foggy bottomers. On the other hand, he covered all the bases

with "U.S. Quietly Reduces Ties to Panama," 7-23, and in an occasional piece on the Philippines, he was well-plugged in, 9-11; an old hand, with some bookish inclinations as well, he's one of the better *Post* defense beatmen, and should be given more space, slack.

Ottaway, David B. *The Washington Post.* (★ ½)
Roving defense correspondent, Columbia Ph.D., and former Middle East correspondent whose most detailed work still focuses on that region. With a slight Arabist flavor to his writing, he emphasizes the reasonableness of "moderate" Arabs in contrast with hard-nosed, fire-breathing Israelis. He covered Prime Minister Shamir's visit to U.S. in February and the Iran-Iraq War through the summer, with an occasional foray into the over-exposed embassy security biz or the equally overboard *Post* coverage of Iran-Contra. Ottaway filed two slightly different stories, one month apart, using the same map, "U.S. Expects Pact With Saudis Soon," 6-19, and "Arab Cooperation with U.S. Grows," 7-21, both of which dealt with AWACS coverage of the Gulf, but presented completely different patrol routes on the two maps. There was generally unobjectionable, if unexceptional, reporting, of the comings and goings of various personages and reports around DC. A couple of fine pieces were written on Stinger missiles in Afghanistan and their effect on the war, 2-8 and 7-19, but were still no match for the *Times* defense honchos on that score (New York's Trainor, Washington's Gertz). New ground was broken with "U.S. Policymakers Split on Philippines," 4-28, an unusual report from a Boston conference on counter-insurgency in which a Pentagon man laid out the case against the State Dept. and the Aquino govt. in its half-hearted attempt to defeat the guerrillas in the Philippines. Creative, non-doctrinaire reporting was not a mainstay for Ottaway, though; more common were pieces such as "U.S. Tried to Bug Soviets Here in '79," 4-9, a man-bites-dog story using a building architect as its only source; a 2-25 filing on Pakistan's nuclear testing potential; and he outdid himself with "U.S. Can't Verify Pakistan Not Building A-Bomb," 10-23, based on a single State Dept. source. Not a bad reporter, for a Columbia Ph.D., but underwhelming even by *Post* standards.

Pincus, Walter. *The Washington Post.* (★)
Iran-Contra beat, mostly. Pincus was on a slight upcurve, mostly due to his teaming up with Dan Morgan and Don Oberdorfer more than with Lou Cannon. While Bob Woodward presumably kept all of the Bill Casey/CIA goodies to himself and his publisher, somebody had to do the daily dirt on CIA covert action. Still, it does provide a retrospective chuckle to read "Casey's Ill Health Leaves Big Gap in Iran Probe," 3-25, wondering how many "gaps" colleague Woodward could have filled. Actually, Pincus was generally fair and straightforward on his Iran-Contra stories, such as two February stories on the amount of Iran diversion and the internal CIA probe on extent of covert ops in favor of contras, 2-11. We counted at least 15 dual bylines with Dan Morgan on the Congressional Iran hearings, basic reports on the daily revelations before the Inouye panel. Three standouts were "Memory Blank on '85 Shipments," 7-20; on convenient lapses by central figures, "Reagan Sought to Hide Iran Details," 7-26; which showed Reagan more engaged in the mess, and an incredible 7-30 filing on secret plans to continue shipments of arms to Teheran after the cover was blown. Pincus can be energetic, as when he has the ammo against a favorite whipping boyproper spin trail, such as "Administration Upset By Adviser's ABM Letter," 3-17, picking on State Dept. counsellor Abe Sofaer. On the whole, though, Pincus had slowed down, or had had his wings clipped, which may help the *Post*.

Sciolino, Elaine. *The New York Times.* (★ ★)
Moving from the U.N. to Washington in '87, she covered a mixed bag of U.S. diplomatic stories, primarily Central America and the Middle East. Her stories on Central America, which occupied her in the early part of the year, focused on politics of contra aid (dual entries on contra aid and unity, 2-11) and early peace-plan maneuverings in "U.S. Officials Split Over Costa Rican Peace Plan," 3-19. Generally undistinguished on issues, she was not as informed as Shirley Christian could have been in the same beat. Her forte appears to be Northwest Asia,

Iran-Pakistan-Persian Gulf, where it seems that her work at the U.N. paid off in contacts with various Washington envoys from the region. Laudable spade work a piece on the Pakistani request for U.S. radar planes, 4-28, and her "U.S. Officials Called Bitterly Split Over Continuing Trade With Iran," 6-22, a shocking story which went beyond the usual Beltway backbiting with aggressive probing. A 5-5 filing on Asst. Secretary of State Richard Murphy's latest trip to Arab capitals was strictly in the "It's a dirty job, but..." department. She had the weekend talk shows buzzing with "A Soviet Overture to Iran Reported," 6-30, which is the ultimate sign of a serious scoop these days. She joins the *Times* platoon covering the U.S. escort of Kuwaiti tankers overkill with "Convoy Starts Amid Fear of Reprisal," 10-20, following up non-descript coverage of the Congressional Dem attempt to halt convoy policy on 6-26. She's demonstrated skills, made no major *faux pas*, and could be a star in the right foreign post.

Shipler, David K. *The New York Times.* (★ ½)
If the *Times* were the State Department, Shipler would be working in the "Politico-Military Affairs Bureau." His amorphous beat careens from Middle Eastern political shenanigans to US-Soviet arms control and back again, a minister without portfolio but with general interests in diplomacy abroad and disarmament at home. All reporting done from powertown, Shipler's output was down in '87, perhaps resting on laurels and book tours from his acclaimed opus on the Middle East, *Arab and Jew: Wounded Spirits in a Promised Land.* His pieces also tended to reflect reportorial *ennui*, since he tended to repeat himself, as in "U.S. Role in Gulf Seen as a Way to Regain Arabs' Favor," 7-12, which replays "U.S., Hurt by Iran Affair, Is Courting Arabs Anew," 2-13. A solid job on U.S. Embassy mess, 4-6, getting the dope from all the usual suspects, but his general output on Washington-Moscow was disappointing, as a 5-5 story on U.S. strategic arms proposals demonstrates. Most tenuous was his 9-9 puff-piece on Krasnoyarsk radar, which rehashed Michael Gordon and William Broad on the same topic. He can recycle leaks with the best of them, as in "Three Compete for Arms-Control Post," 9-4, on the ACDA job, though he is capable of a first-rate scoop from the Levant (e.g., his reporting on the *Stark* aftermath in "Fahd Agrees to Wider U.S. Air Patrol," 6-20, or on the Israeli rebuff of Soviet overture for diplomatic relations, 10-2). We suspect that he hasn't been given enough juicy assignments, perhaps due to young turk competition, but it seems clear Shipler was bored and underutilized in '87. A change of scenery, *a la* Jim Wooten, may be good for this seasoned vet.

Smith, R. Jeffrey. *The Washington Post.* (★ ½)
Another newcomer to the *Post*, Smith takes the Arms Control Association Chair in Defense Reporting at the *WP*. A fairly decent stylist, who makes the least out of working in a town full of people who know something about the issues he covers. He spent much of 1987 writing stories on SDI, the "insignificance" of Soviet offenses and defenses, and the INF treaty talks. Typical of Smith's portfolio was "Reagan Seen Complicating Arms Talks," 4-11, a specious treatment of two "decisions," sticking to broad interpretation of ABM Treaty and a refusal to lock U.S. into the treaty for a number of years, that were allegedly protested by Shultz and meant that "any resulting agreement would take far more than a year to put into treaty language and be reviewed by the Senate." Of course, we saw no retraction when the treaty was concluded six months later. By the way, we are still looking for a *Post* headline, "Gorbachev Seen Holding Up Arms Talks," but that's not Smith's job. He also dropped the ball on two important issues, Soviet compliance with the ABM Treaty, 2-25, in which it is asserted that the Soviets were removing missile defense radars when in fact they were simply relocating them, and "Short Range Missiles a Central Obstacle to Treaty Progress," 3-30, a piece on Euromissiles that ignored the conventional military significance of Soviet short range missiles. "SDI Plan Draws Military Critics," 6-28, implied that uniformed opposition to SDI springs from disinterested analysis as opposed to parochial budgetary priorities. A 10-28 story on MX missile problems shows the talents of Les Aspin's staff in selling their line to reporters. Credit is due for a 6-3 piece on intelligence community resistance to on-site inspection, and mid-summer coverage of Geneva negotiations on the INF was basically on target. Also, a good 9-16 entry

on history of U.S.-Soviet "risk reduction centers," detailing the long and winding road to a basically insignificant treaty. Expect more, and one hopes, better, bylines from Smith in '88.

Strobel, Warren. *The Washington Times.* (★ ½)
Defense, with an emphasis on SDI and the politics of national defense on Capitol Hill. A young workhorse, Strobel has come on fast as a defense correspondent, only three years removed from statehouse reporting in Missouri. He had more than his share of two byline days, and, while still a tad green, is rapidly gaining perspective and sources. No spectacular scoops, but simple and readable filings from inside and outside the Beltway. Most of his assignments dealt with technological aspects of the SDI program, such as 6-3 on "hit capability" of kinetic weapons, "SDI Facing a Crucial Review and Rumble of Skeptics," 6-30, on the Defense Acquisition Board's report; and a report on "Army Speeds up Research on Particle Beam," 9-29. He also travelled to Huntsville Air Force Base for a tight series on how the SDI program is faring on the working level. Strobel worked on the story of Paul Nitze's possible involvement in negotiations between Soviet and U.S. scientists on how to craft the Soviet negotiating stance on SDI, a major scandal if it breaks (Greg Fossedal also plugging away at that one). His reports on technical issues are clear and jargon-free, a plus, though he does rely on a limited group of "experts" such as John Pike. He saw the political nature of Union of Concerned Scientists in "Former 'Star Wars' Researcher Claims System Vulnerable," 6-5, about a SDI "defector" who was hustled to Washington by the UCS to trumpet his complaints. Sometimes he has difficulty separating wheat from chaff, as in an 8-17 story about the Congressional Research Service report on smaller nations acquiring missiles, or in a press release-style "Contracts Awarded on SDI," 6-4. Like his effort, worth watching in the future.

Summers, Col. H.G. (Harry). *U.S.News & World Report, Los Angeles Times* Syndicate. (★ ½)
A retired career officer, Summers caught our eye last year in *U.S.News*, his opinion columns having a certain spit and polish. In "Gen. Rogers vs. Reagan: A Crisis Of Conscience," 7-6, *Defense News*, he's up on former NATO Commander Gen. Bernard Rogers public criticism of the Administration's rush for the INF treaty: "With the hasty and ill-conceived arms control proposals made at the Reykjavik summit as evidence that the White House is dominated by imagemakers rather than strategists, and with the Iran-contra hearings as further evidence that the administration's decisionmaking process is almost unbelievably inept, Rogers has good reason for concern." Summers is not an Oliver North fan and suggests, at the height of Olliemania, "A Dream Ticket for '88 — Ollie and Jane [Fonda]," 8-23, *LAT*: "It'd be a dream ticket. They've both proved that if you're attractive enough, brazen enough and a good enough actor...you can get away with anything." He's ardent in defending besieged Captain Brindel of the U.S.S. Stark in "Stark Tragedy: U.S. Policy Invites Disaster," 5-24, *LAT*, calling the U.S. policy in the gulf too vague to be useful, citing flaws in the operation as primarily responsible for the tragedy opposed to flaws in the Captain or crew. Summers smartly addressed the key question of "Why advocate the use of a weapons system that puts *you* at an inherent disadvantage?" in "For Once We're Bargaining Away a Disadvantage," 10-1, *LAT*, a treatment of the INF agreement that stated "on nuclear issues professional military officers are much more sane than either the protesters or the 'experts.'" He then makes his case.

Talbott, Strobe. *Time.* (-)
In an absolutely abominable year from the magazine's Washington bureau chief, we kept finding an unacceptable bias in his reports. The list is endless. "A Shield Against Arms Control," 2-2, took sides in the covert struggle in the Administration that was supposedly taking place: Shultz (use SDI as leverage for arms control) vs. Weinberger (use SDI to sink arms control). "What the ABM Treaty Means," 3-23, was stridently anti-SDI, anti-administration interpretation with two paragraphs devoted to the Reagan side of the argument, and nine to the Nunn side, saying in effect the Senate knew what it was doing in '72, and was right in doing it. "Slouching Toward an Arms Agreement," 4-27, was filled with insidious little opinion jibes, so subtle it's hard to catch, but witness the two paragraphs describing the Nitze-Kvitsinsky

"walk in the woods" seemingly touted as the solution to all ills, and then "was rejected in both capitals." His best for the year was his least dangerous, a straight report *cum* profile of Tom Watson's nostalgia trip, only innocuous because he was so dry and unimaginative in "From Moscow To The Bering Sea," 8-3.

Thatcher, Gary. *The Christian Science Monitor.* (★ ½)
Diplomatic correspondent who occasionally dabbles in "human interest" profiles or defense politics (who's up, who's down). A former television correspondent who punched his *CSM* ticket in South Africa and Moscow, Thatcher has the tools to be a first-rate feature writer. He lacks the detailed knowledge of the players in the national security games and therefore has limited quotable sources on both left and right. He got on board the INF bandwagon in the fall, along with everyone on the staff save the sportswriter, so we got predictable, watered down, here's the dope from the "pragmatists," or "hardliners." In a sense, his penchant for personality pieces, which served him well with 9-8 job on Matvey Finkel, recent Soviet emigre, came up short on national security topics. Sure, personalities make a difference, but controversies also entail substantive concerns. Hence, two stories on NSC adviser/SecDef Frank Carlucci, 10-27 and 11-5, focus inordinately on Carlucci's qualities, not enough on the real reason the administration/GOP is split: conventional defense of Europe after INF and whither SDI. Also highly questionable was an 11-24 piece indicating that a "weaker" Gorbachev would be coming to the Washington summit, which was based on two sources and is contradicted by a State Dept. official quoted in the *NYT* as saying, "we really don't know what is going on over there." He was better on the Iran-Contra Report in mid-November, an excellent reading of the Reagan tea leaves in "Reagan Change on Contras," 10-8, detailing the alteration of the Administration's view of the Arias peace plan. Inconsistently good.

Toth, Robert C. *Los Angeles Times.* (★ ★)
National security reporter. A seasoned pro who handles his material carefully. In "Soviets May Lead U.S. in 'Star Wars,'" 1-2, he gives us a solid review of expert consensus on Soviet advantages over the U.S. in strategic defense research: "...the Soviets match or lead the United States in the basic technology of lasers and particle beams — and perhaps even in converting the exotic technology into weapons," while noting "...they remain significantly behind in computers, sensors and other supporting equipment vital to constructing an effective space based missile defense system." The Soviets insist they have no SDI program of their own, but in "Soviet Beam Devices to Aim at Mars Moon," 4-2, he reports the disclosures of U.S. arms control advisor Paul Nitze that the USSR's plans to test a laser and a particle beam device against the Martian moon Phobos. In the shadows of the INF agreements, he notes progress toward a chemical weapons ban with "U.S., Soviets Move Toward Pact to Ban Chemical Weapons," 11-17, Gorbachev's initiative making it a likely agenda item next year, despite all the good reasons for U.S. hesitation. He sees the breakthrough coming in "Accord Believed Near on Missile Plant Inspection," 11-19, singling out as significant Soviet movement on the on-site inspection proposal "because of the precedent it will set for verifying compliance with any future agreements reducing intercontinental weapons."

Trainor, Bernard E. *The New York Times.* (★ ★ ★)
Apparently looking for a permanent successor to the Drew Middleton Strategy Chair, the *Times* reached out to the career military and came up with Bernard Trainor, who along with *U.S. News*'s Harry Summers demonstrates that our armed forces can produce strategic thinkers and writers of clear prose. Trainor has adapted quite well to the newspaper game, and has brought with him the vigor and professionalism of the old (young) Middleton. His "Military Analysis" articles delve beneath the headlines, such as his 2-4 analysis of potential air strikes on terrorist bases, and "A Missile Free Europe: Little Impact on a War," 5-1, which dispelled some of the prevailing arms control euphoria by pointing to the troubling disparities in conventional forces. Perhaps as a counterweight to the Dem-Disarm crowd favored by Michael Gordon, Trainor makes extensive use of administration types, and, more interestingly, serious

defense analysts such as Norman Polmar (quoted in a 3-15 piece on Iranian anti-ship missiles, a real scoop). Other top drawer items include "Russians in Vietnam: U.S. Sees A Threat," 2-25, which draws appropriate geopolitical connections between Soviet bases and creeping pacifism in Australia and New Zealand; a tight 7-7 outline on the use of Stinger missiles in Afghanistan by the resistance; and "U.S. Fears Soviet Use of New Nicaraguan Airfield," 7-25, on the Punta Huete 10,000 foot runway "being built even though the Sandinista Government has no aircraft that need a runway that long." Overall, a welcome complement to Halloran, Trainor can be counted on to understand military events as they are taking place with a historical perspective missing in many defense reporters.

van Voorst, Bruce. *Time.* (★)
A CIA political analyst-turned-journalist, van Voorst gives us the spook's viewpoint. "From Star Wars to Smart Rocks," 2-23, on smart rock technology, was noticeably tilted away from SDI with quotes from John Pike and Spurgeon Keeny of the Arms Control Association, but had some detail on SBKKVs or Space-Based Kinetic Kill Vehicles. "George Shultz's Feisty Lawyer," 4-6, reported on the flap over Abraham Sofaer's position, as State Department legal advisor, on the ABM treaty that turns into a nicely done mini-profile at the end, calling Sofaer the quintessential "NY lawyer." In "How Many Fingers on the Button?" 4-20, van Voorst gave us a semi-review of *State Scarlet*, the scenario concocted by former NSC staffer David Aaron. He doesn't really give us as much of the nuts and bolts of arms control as we think the readers could take.

Walcott, John. *The Wall Street Journal.* (★ ½)
Defense/Diplomacy, with continuing coverage of Iran-Contra. Tough to grade this year as his most important pieces were team efforts. His solo flights targeted arms control, Mideast, Iran, and his favorite hobby-horse from '86, Libya. "Reagan Administration Won't Increase Pressure in Campaign Against Gadhafi," 4-10, a one-year-after the Tripoli bombing story, was a fine, tight backgrounder on Gadhafi's quiescence since the attack and his own problems with Chad. Walcott hit the right notes with "Arms Control Shouldn't Blind the West to Other Ways of Easing Nuclear Risk," 4-20, quoting a decent array of experts and pointing out Soviet interests in arms control as propaganda. He also filed a prescient post-hearing "Washington Insight" on the Iran-Contra hearings, correctly predicting the short shelf life of Ollie-induced pro-contra polls. In covering the Shultz Middle East trip in the fall, he filed "Arab and Israeli Officials Tell Shultz U.S. Should Stage Counterattack on Iran," 10-19, an overview that demonstrated Walcott's ability at quote-seeking. He developed the point that Israel has belatedly recognized, in the words of one diplomat, "There are no moderates in Iran," and raised the possibility of future Israeli-Iraqi relations. Of co-authored pieces, most notable were a 2-13 scoop (with Rogers) on the shadowy world of arms trade, detailing how the DoD buys Soviet weapons from Poland to give to anti-communist insurgents, and a Walcott-Kempe analysis of Syria clamping down on Abu Nidal, 6-19. A rather safe than sorry story with Carrington on "warring defense aides" 2-12, didn't add much to an already tired refrain, and most Iran-Contra stories lacked pizazz. He hooked up with David Shribman to present a tidy 11-17 report on the GOP presidential candidates' opposition to detente II, although there's more to the criticism of Reagan's INF deal than they suggested. But why lure Walcott away from *Newsweek* if *WSJ* editors keep lumping him with co-authors? Either they're not giving him enough rope or they are disappointed with this young veteran.

Wilson, George C. *The Washington Post.* (★ ★ ★)
National defense, with a specialized bent toward Pentagon Dwellers (OSD, Joint Chiefs, Services), Wilson is the *Post*'s premier expert on "the Building." With 21 years of award-winning national security reporting, Wilson has stellar sources and credibility. He doesn't roam much, but his DoD filings represent exemplary awareness and gravitas. Unlike the usual, simplistic stories about the latest turf battle, Wilson demonstrates refreshing originality in stories

about substantive policy differences. "Contras Need a Success Soon, Crowe Says," 2-13, a piece on doctrinal cleavage between the Joint Chiefs (Crowe) and the former Commander-in-Chief of U.S. forces in Panama (Gen. Gorman), on how to train Nicaraguan opposition, was a prime example of *important* internal administration splits. Likewise, Wilson filed his best stories of '87 on John Lehman, the flamboyant and controversial Secretary of Navy who outhustled other Service Chiefs for funds and ruled his roost with unsurpassed ruthlessness (a 3-3 story on Lehman causing an "admirals revolt" on promotions, and a superb interview/report recapping Lehman's 6-year tenure). He hit a peak in June with an expose on the absence of high-level naval brass from Washington during the *Stark* crisis, and two 6-26 stunners, "Norway Criticizes Canada's Decision to Redeploy Troops," on the disturbing repositioning of the Canadian brigade, and the explosive "Top Marine Sees Loss of Moral Fiber," in which outgoing Marine Commandant P.X. Kelley blamed working women and secular schooling for America's decline. Wilson isn't a Johnny one-note on personalities, however, as 7-1 piece on Soviet satellites and 7-17 update on new Soviet submarines will attest. The long history of the All-Volunteer Force, "Nixon Gamble Paying Off for Today's Army," 9-1, was slightly on the rosy side, but a masterful overview of the structural changes in the Army brought about by Nixon's abandonment of conscription. Wilson certainly is the best of the lot in a shop that has improved, but still has a ways to go.

SOCIAL/POLITICAL REPORTERS

Adler, Jerry. *Newsweek.* (★ ½)
Author of the perfectly excruciating cover story "Every Parent's Nightmare," 3-16, on children with birth defects, all the more painful because it's a *personal* account. Still, we have to give him credit. It could not have been an easy piece to write. Lighter and much more cheery was "You Call This a Party?" 10-5, a half tongue-in-cheek review of Tish Baldridge's *Complete Guide to a Great Social Life*, which recalls one memorable cocktail hour where commandos drilled — as the entertainment. A very fine "The Genius Of The People," 5-25, a poetically written, no-nonsense celebration of the enduring legacy of the US Constitution that does not attempt to overblow or overstate, remarking flatly "the framers fell short of perfection," in terms of the rights of blacks and women. "Yet here we are, 200 years later, still faithfully running our government as if Rhode Island and Wyoming had a common interest to protect against the tyranny of Pennsylvania and California."

Alter, Jonathan. *Newsweek.* (★ ★ ½)
Intelligent in his coverage of the media, Alter gets inside the story and more often than not beats par. He branched out a bit this year, examining issues as well as events. "When Sources Get Immunity," 1-19, outlined the difficulties of finking on a source, and what Alter calls "the access trap," personified in the case of Ollie North. "Death of a Conservative," 1-12, wasted Alter's talent on an obituary for Terry Dolan and was out of his realm in "Sex and the Presidency," 5-4, but still enjoyable: "the question is not whether a presidential candidate has ever been unfaithful to his wife, but whether he makes a consistent, destructive habit of womanizing" that would be relevant to his job performance. Succession stories abounded, both at *The New Yorker*, "The Squawk of the Town," 1-26, and at *Time*, "A New Chieftain for Time, Inc.," 4-27, handled nicely. "Rethinking TV News in the Age of Limits," 3-16, was well-focused and detailed without beating around the bush or wasting words. His best for the year: "America's Q & A Man," (with Renee Michael, Michael Lerner), 6-15, a fascinating cover story and portrait of "Nightline's" Ted Koppel, extremely comprehensive, giving thoughts, views and background; and "A Close-Up Look At Glasnost," 6-29, an excellent review of CBS' much advertised Soviet documentary "Seven Days In May," calling it a product of the "parachutist style of documentary making," or dropping in out of nowhere and letting it rip.

Altman, Lawrence K. *The New York Times.* (★ ★ ½)
A steady flow of careful reports on the continuing AIDS story, getting our attention first with "Fact, Theory and Myth on the Spread of AIDS," 2-15, a front-page Q&A worth special mention. In "U.S. Study Examines Prostitutes and AIDS virus," 3-27, we get a thoroughly reported piece on an important AIDS study, but the last two graphs should have come earlier: "The researchers said it was only reasonable to presume that men could contract the AIDS virus from infected prostitutes on the basis of data from studies in the United States of sexual partners of intravenous drug users and hemophiliacs, and studies of prostitutes and AIDS in Africa." Another well-reported piece, "U.S. and France End Rift on AIDS," 4-1, on who discovered the virus, *les francais* or the Americans. Among the best we saw in '87, "AIDS Expert Sees No Sign of Heterosexual Outbreak," 6-5, at a time of hype in the other direction: "The principal victims of AIDS in this country remain homosexual men and intravenous drug users, who together account for 9 out of 10 cases. Federal officials believe that about 4 percent of the nation's AIDS cases were acquired through heterosexual intercourse, in many cases by the sexual partners of drug addicts."

Apple, R.W., Jr. *The New York Times.* (★ ★)
The *Times*' chief Washington correspondent is expected to produce the long-headed, deep, deep insights on the unfolding Beltway beat, often leading the Sunday week in review section

271

with his arms around everything. His '87 was an average of big hits and big misses. At his best with "In a Spirit of Contrition," 3-5, a fine analytical piece in which he summons up the past, recalls what was done before when the White House got some twit caught in a wringer, reminds us that the President hasn't said "I'm sorry," and places the Iran-Contra affair in historical perspective with a marvelous economy of words. "RX For Recovery," 3-22, wraps up RR's week with undeep insight, telling us he's convalescing politically, but the prognosis is unknown. His experience showed in "Changing Morality: Press and Politics," 5-6, on the heels of Hart & Rice, a great piece on how press coverage of political character has changed over the decades. "Stalemate in Venice," 6-10, is a satisfying news analysis of the economic summit: "Fearful that President Reagan would be portrayed as the big loser, because he came to Venice with the most clearly defined set of goals, American officials spent most of the afternoon working out a strategy for presenting the results in the best possible light." He bombs, for the most part, in his articles on the Iran-Contra hearings. "Fighting the Good Fight," 7-9, offers a convoluted psychological analysis of Oliver North that suggests Apple doesn't quite know what's going on. In "Of History and Honor: Shultz's Story," 7-24, all we learn is that Apple takes a shine to the Secretary of State. Better in "Foreign Policy Challenging President's Staying Power," 8-16, with RR having "an Everest of a mountain to climb," although he says nothing about the bull market, just a week away from its peak.

Applebome, Peter. *The New York Times.* (★ ½)
He covered the Southwest with a nice touch on feature stories. We noted a dozen fresh such pieces in '87, among them "The Wildcatter's Tale," 3-1, in which we find Duke Rudman, 77, drilling for oil again, with the oil price down by 50 percent, but so are costs. "If you find enough oil, price doesn't matter," says Rudman. A timely piece, an interesting way to review the oil-patch deflation among the independent operators, although he could have deepened it beyond anecdotes by checking with the industry pulsetakers. In "Executions Rise as Legal Barriers Fall," 8-9, he covers more serious ground with a very well done survey on the death penalty, with 18 executions so far in '87 against the high of 21 in '84, since the Supreme Court reinstatement in 1976.

Archibald, George. *The Washington Times.* (★ ★)
Solid, dependable, a staple at the *Times*, Archibald handles the hot stuff with finesse. Potent in "Butcher Fraud Case Widens; Congressman Ford Indicted," 4-27, on the 19-count indictment of Rep. Harold Ford (D-TN), along with one of the Tennessee Butcher brothers for bank, mail and tax fraud. He scored the same day with "Justice Department Probes Hansen Arrest," on former Rep. George Hansen's alleged parole violations after serving six months of a prison sentence and paying a fine of $50,000 for filing incomplete financial disclosures as a House member: "unshaven and thin in the face after a seven-day hunger strike to protest his treatment, was brought to the meeting in handcuffs, waist chain and leg irons." Good in "New Top G-Man Wins Respect As Tough Guy," 6-27, a colorful profile of U.S. District Judge William S. Sessions, RR's new FBI chief, a "strict disciplinarian," to the point one must wear coats in his courtroom. He's always understated, reliable, even when his editors give him silly headlines: "Wedtech Top Leaders Accused of Scheming," 9-10, was a no-nonsense report on the latest developments in the Wedtech scandal.

Barnes, James A. *National Journal.* (★ ★)
The new political correspondent, he didn't quite fill Ron Brownstein's shoes, but he's clearly on his way to being a bigfoot. Not afraid of issues, he gave us "Old Pitches for the '88 Season," 6-27, concluding, after a meticulous search of the Democrats and their issues, that the elevator does not go to the top floor. New ideas all require bigger government, and only Teddy the K wishes to push that envelope, and he can't run. Similarly, "The Issues Issue," 6-20, offers a solid, low-key essay on the role issues play in presidential campaigns; nothing new for the junkie, but a good perspective for the fans. "Looking for Credibility," 4-25, is a balanced,

competent look at the Jackson and Robertson campaigns in relation to their parties. "Jackson's Chance," 5-23, asks if Jesse can appeal to the white voter, good background, but not much beyond. There's a dutiful "Party in Waiting" piece, 9-19, the old story that the GOP can't crack Dixie's statehouses and courthouses, but without much juice. The best we saw were "Kemp's Slow Start," 2-27, an impressive feature that touched all the bases, high on objectivity and analysis, and "Out on His Own," 6-6, a cover story on the Veep, with nice detail on the front-runner's campaign. Best line from his pollster, Robert Teeter: "There's just something about television that filters out Bush's qualities."

Barnes, John A. *The Detroit News.* (★ ★)
Deputy editorial page editor. Former editorial writer for *The Boston Herald*, Barnes moved to Detroit to fill the vacancy created when Tony Snow moved to *The Washington Times*. We see his material in the conservative print media, often in *Human Events*. There's a "basher" bent in his articles, but he does the hard work of digging up evidence that lends weight to his cudgel. He caught our attention with "'Mandatory Mike' Aims for the White House," *HE*, 2-14, finding evidence to temper any notion that Dukakis is a tax-cutter. "Political Careerists Recruited for Top Media Posts," *HE*, 8-15, raises questions about the thin wall that exists between practicing politics and practicing journalism within the profession and the dual standards of reaction according to the politics of the violator. "Competitive Urges," *TAS*, 6-87, goes out on a limb, predicting trade protection fever will abate by fall. He crams a lot of info into "Reviewing the Account of Europe's Aid to Nicaragua," *WSJ*, 5-19, and catches the shift toward a "pro-business" image with "The New Face of British Trade Unionism," *WSJ*, 10-1. A nice piece of reporting, "Sasso: Before the Fall," *HE*, 10-31, delves into the history, function and role of the man who could "take care of things" for the Governor. In the fine tradition of muckraking, he goes after the ethanol subsidy business as corporate welfare, with a persuasive critique in "Anatomy of a Rip-Off," *NR*, 11-2.

Barrett, Laurence I. *Time.* (★)
National political correspondent. A mediocre year, at times interesting, but mostly sloppy, messy writing and reporting. "Rushing to an Early Kickoff," 1-19, was *too* early, a superficial overview of the different prospective presidential candidates in which Jesse Jackson is pictured, listed third in the poll, but then is only mentioned once in the text, and that as a Baptist minister on the Democratic left. Bush's "voodoo economics" quote from '80 is touted as correct without any support. Equally light on Al Haig beginning his campaign, noting cynically: "even if he makes little progress, the publicity can only fatten his bookings on the lecture tour," "A Quixotic Four-Star Foray," 4-6. "Tackling Further to the Right," 3-2, told of Rep. Jack Kemp stirring up C-PAC with a call for Shultz's resignation, but otherwise barely skin deep. Better late in the year with "Where are the Wingers?" 10-26, at least absorbing, even if scattered with silly analogies. Barrett notes, for example, that the differences between Bush and Dole "are as scarce as heavy metal bands at Republican rallies." Really?

Battiata, Mary. *The Washington Post.* (★ ★)
A *Post* "Style" reporter, she does better with profiles than with issues. "Arthur Liman And The Contragate Crucible," 7-7, was a delightful, satisfying picture of Arthur Liman, both in and out of the courtroom and the Iran-Contra hearings: Does he really occasionally shower with his shoes on? Equally satisfying in portraits of Kris Kristofferson, "Kristofferson and the Business of 'Amerika,'" 2-18, and Susan Estrich, "Susan Estrich and the Marathon Call," 10-16, on the new manager of the Dukakis campaign, but Battiata can't seem to get a handle on the broader stories. "The Physician and the Angry Charge of Rape," 11-13, okay when talking to the people directly involved in a specific case, but gets caught up in stats, becoming disjointed. "The Hucksters and the Hearings," 8-8, was disappointing on the ways advertisers were using the Iran-Contra affair and have used other political events, a great idea that was only half realized.

Belcher, Mary. *The Washington Times.* (★)
An often bland political writer who usually has many of the ingredients of a good story, but without the spice. "Pat Robertson's Political Journey," 3-11, is a fairly comprehensive but colorless profile of the Rev. Pat, and we suspect she's straining to be neutral toward her subject, instead of letting loose. "Hall Altered, Shredded Key Papers From North's Office," 6-9, is a detailed accounting of Fawn's altering of NSC documents that was nice, but uninteresting. "Ex-NSC Aide Ledeen Says Advice Ignored on Arms-for-Hostages," 9-29, hit a little harder.

Belsie, Laurent. *The Christian Science Monitor.* (★)
Chicago. Belsie turns in affable, likeable, but sometimes run-of-the-mill reports. "Have Computers Made a Difference in American Business?" 1-22, was ultimately disappointing on computers and company productivity: "'It wasn't just the computers that made the change,' says Mr. Scott of Federal Kemper Life. 'We had to change our whole way of doing business.'" His series on child psychiatric services was interesting, obviously well-researched, timely, "Helping Children - Or Controlling Them?" 5-13; "Psychiatric Services For Children Grow," 5-14; "One Judge's Community Approach," 5-15. "Drawing On '84 Run Jackson May Be Democrat's Front-Runner," 5-18, was brisk and well-balanced, hypothesizing Jesse as the front-runner in the Dem race. Folksy, but still professional in "Florida Citrus Growers Slowly Recover from Devastating Freezes," 11-6: "The transformation is starkly laid out along Route 19, a meandering north-south highway that bisects Lake County and connects towns like Eustis, Tavares, and Howey In the Hills. In places, dead orange trees raise bare, black branches to the sky. But in other spots, leafy young specimens have taken root."

Berger, Joseph. *The New York Times.* (½★)
Religion writer. We always get an unacceptable spin in his reporting. "Being Catholic in America," 8-23, a Sunday magazine cover story was wafer-thin, superficial. Berger gives a one-dimensional peep of Catholicism in America on the eve of the Pope's U.S. visit: "...the ferment among articulate Catholics steeped in the logic and habits of democracy poses one of the most profound dilemmas the Vatican faces. How can the Vatican hold the allegiance of the church's wealthiest and perhaps most influential nationality, and yet retain respect for its historic primacy in determining church policy?" Instead of reporting on a complex dialogue between the Pontiff and his flock, he covers the "confrontation," a very skewed, and in fact partisan misrepresentation of what took place this year. "The Healing of a Breach," 9-2, indulges the simplistic view of "two sides" in turmoil and conflict, and "For Catholics, A Chance to Raise Issues With Pope," 9-9, elevates Catholicism's fringe dissidents as representative of the "articulate" Catholics in the U.S. He can, of course, hold sympathies with the latter's criticisms of their church's traditions and practices, but letting that bias slop over into his reporting was inexcusable.

Blumenthal, Sidney. *The Washington Post.* (★ ★ ★)
Not a prolific year for Blumenthal, but still choice. A very talented young political writer and liberal intellectual, he spends almost all his time covering personalities and trends in the conservative movement. He spent much of '87 working on a three-parter on "Richard Perle, Disarmed but Undeterred," 11-23, 24, 25, good, not great. He's normally loathed by the right, and they hated him for his report "Thunder on the Right," 10-19, on the so-called "Second Thoughts Conference," where "ex-radicals could expiate their sins and be blessed by such elders of neoconservatism as Norman Podhoretz and Irving Kristol, who had made the same passage. Thus purified, the newly converted would assume their stations." In one very funny passage, one "second thoughter" arises to announce he has had "third thoughts" about the contras, doesn't think they can win, and that "he was now a lobbyist for the People's Republic of Mozambique. 'Boo!' shouted Reed Irvine, the conservative press critic. 'Boo!' shouted Arnold Beichman, the anti-Soviet specialist at the Hoover Institution. And Norman Podhoretz, the neoconservative editor of *Commentary*, could not stop shaking his head." But they liked

"North And the Charge of the Right Brigade," 8-5, a masterful overview of the impact the Iran-Contra hearings had on movement conservatives. "Overnight they were transformed from the battle weary to the battle ready." In "Standing Below the Fray," 7-26, he sees the Democrats ignoring issues the public cares about and warns they must deal with Ollie North as more than a "media epiphenomenon." His "Dawn of The New-Age Democrats," 5-19, is a nice try to capture all the young Democrat presidential candidates at once, but he doesn't quite make it. His best, "The Candidate From Kansas," 11-9, is a classic profile of Senator Bob Dole, going to his childhood roots and plumbing his antipathy to debt. "'As I travel around the country,' says Dole, 'people are willing to take the bitter medicine, but nobody wants to hold the spoon.'"

Boyd, Gerald. *The New York Times.* (★)
White House No. 2 man behind Bernard Weinraub, Boyd is a competent meat-and-potatoes pro with rarely a surprise, up or down. Mostly following the Veep around in '87, "Bush Quietly Sets Stage for Drive," 4-19, well done, citing "character" and Bush's role in Iran-Contra as key issues. "Bush Presidential Campaign is Nagged by Demos," 4-27, reviews image problems using polls, aides' views, an okay update. "Bush Taking Some Positions at Odds With White House," 8-13, really stretches to find supporting evidence. In "Reagan Urges Abstinence for Young to Avoid AIDS," 4-2, Boyd's report is a bit confusing, identifying the audience both as "schoolchildren" and the "College of Physicians in Philadelphia," but with adequate reporting of RR's first extended comments on AIDS. We appreciated his revealing interview with the departing (by invitation) White House counsel Peter Wallison, "Reagan Counsel Recounts Chaos Over Iran Affair," 3-13, in which Wallison reveals that the NSC head told him to get lost when he tried to find out what had been going on: "You have no role in this." So what's a White House counsel for?

Brandt, Thomas D. *The Washington Times.* (★)
With 1988 fast approaching, Brandt did better with the nitpicky details of an election rather than viewing the grand scheme. He provides the ingredients and we have to add water and spices, stir and cook. "Gephardt Rips Aid to Contras as Iowa Audience Applauds," 3-11, was chock-full with little stats, but we got little perspective. "Democrats Who Led Centrist Shift Fear Activist Rebound in Primaries," 3-26, was an improvement, interesting, with analysis of the possible results of the primaries as result of the shift to the middle by the leadership of Democratic Party and strategies to insure, as Chuck Robb says the "narrow interest voters are overwhelmed by the general interest voters." In an *Insight* feature, he pulled us through on Bruce Babbitt, "Babbitt Tries to Sharpen His Profile," 3-2, a floating vignette.

Brock, David. *Insight.* (★ ½)
Brock ranged broadly in '87, producing at least a few standout, memorable features. "The Pollard Case: Opening Wounds In U.S.-Israeli Affairs," 3-30, was a useful overview of the fallout: citing Sharon as involved, finding the State and Defense departments facing off on Israel, a useful picture. A shimmering cover on philosopher Allan Bloom, "The Book of the Year," 5-11, was an important contribution by the magazine to the emerging national debate on higher education, with lasting impact, elevating Bloom, his book and education theories. "The Marines' King Of The Hill Stirs Ground Swell Of Support," 7-27, looked at policy implications, not narrowing his treatment of North to a mere stylistic phenomenon. His "Korea: Learning The Steps To The Democracy Dance," 10-12 cover story, was so-so, covering familiar ground, little sense of the policy distinctions between the Kims and Roh Tae Woo. But one fine quote from a Samsung exec: "The banking system is 50 years behind where it should be. We are still primarily a cash economy. The judicial system is a remnant of Japanese colonialism. Trade unions are not allowed. If Chun had begun to update those institutions, he would not have lost support." His "Fighting Words: Reagan Says 'Bork,'" 7-20, another cover, was adequate, outshone by the Chrarlotte Low piece immediately following.

Brown, Patricia Leigh. *The New York Times.* **(NR)**
We happened to bump into her only once in '87, on the "Style" page's "For Brides, All Roads Lead to Kleinfeld's" and "The Perfect Wedding," both 4-4, taking the entire page with stellar feature writing. Kleinfeld's in Bay Ridge, Brooklyn, dominates the wedding dress business, pulling in anxious brides and mommas from Mexico, Nigeria, even Manhattan, who seek the advice of Miss Flo and Miss Irene. Funny and bright without being mean. The second feature has more edge as Brown profiles WASP deity Martha Stewart, who writes "perfect" books about "perfect" dinner parties. Her latest book is "a wedding voyeur's dream." Impressive for a "Style" feature in that it's so tightly written, funny without being insufferable, and held to non-jump length as the story is allowed to be the star rather than the writer.

Brownstein, Ronald. *National Journal.* **(★ ★ ★)**
A fine young political reporter who was often a pacesetter in '86 on the White House/political beat. He's now "West Coast Correspondent," a part time job while he writes a book, but he still shines. "And Now, Heeeere's Mario," 2-7, finds Cuomo coming to California and turning down liberal chic parties, quoting one LA lib: "I think there is a sense that Cuomo is not particularly accessible." He does an excellent piece on the California budget, "Eyeing New Spending," 5-23, ten years after Prop 13, pressures building to reduce its restrictions. In "Running on His Record," 7-18, he looks at Mass. Gov. Mike Dukakis, a comprehensive analysis of his economic record and personality, with views right, left and center. Brownstein's experience in banking and finance is a great strength in his political work, as we see in the marvelous "Tangling Over Trade," 9-19, with the two political parties switching sides on the trade issue. "Many strategists in both parties believe it will be hard to convince a majority of voters that they are miserable in an era of falling unemployment and steady growth and with interest rates and inflation significantly lower than when Reagan took office."

Chaze, William. *U.S.News & World Report.* **(★)**
More meat this year from a usually bare bones reporter. "A Holy Row from a Visit to a Holy City," 1-12, was a nice overview of NY's John Cardinal O'Connor's latest *faux pas*, this time an international one, including a brief summary of some of the other goofs he's made in the name of Catholicism. Much more descriptive in handling hard news adequately in "What It Was Like to Fear 'A Knock on the Door,'" 1-19, a day in the life of an illegal alien, who hopes through the new law to become legal; "The Anglo Empire Shows Its Other Face," 9-7, on South African mine strikes; and "Who Arms Iran? Almost Everyone," 8-31. But still not chewy enough.

Church, George J. *Time.* **(½ ★)**
Senior writer. Church spits out bits of information, but too often it's colored confetti. "Is He More Out of Touch than Ever?" 1-26, rehashed the issue of Reagan's detachment as again "a sensitive" issue, with RR's almost bizarre indifference to the world outside the White House windows: "Sense of drift," "so far out of touch, he's lost ability to govern." It was the theme all that particular week, with everybody else doing it better (see Fred Barnes' "Brain Dead," *TNR*, for example). The cover story "Ollie's Turn," 7-13, was a confetti smear. He's marginally better with "The Art of High-Tech Snooping," 4-20, a mind-boggling summary of different kinds of bugs, and possibilities for future technological advances, and "Tower of Judgment," 3-2, neatly written and credible. "Now, Super Zero?" 4-27, was not as technically detailed as a parallel *Newsweek* story in terms of stats and numbers, but there was more analysis and opinion from people like Henry Kissinger, Volker Ruhe and Bernard Rogers. Church was back to disorganizing in "The Work Ethic Lives!" 9-7, discovering that in the Reagan years Americans are working harder and at more jobs than ever and ascribes it all to the income effect, i.e., poverty, debt, and declining hourly wages. Not a word about substitution effects from the obvious tax cuts: the more you make, the more you *keep*.

Clift, Eleanor. *Newsweek.* (★)
Back to her old desk after a stint at the *Los Angeles Times*, it seemed she spent more of the year doing the legwork on multiple bylines than the writing. One we liked was "So Why Is the A Team Sitting on the Bench?" 4-27, a field of reasons why the Dem field is so devoid of A players, listing Nunn, Cuomo, Robb, Bradley, Bumpers as examples, done with a light, deft touch. Equally skillful in "Scrutinizing 'Simon Pure,'" 11-30, but still not very deep. Paired with Jennet Conant, she did a credible job on Democratic wives on the stump for their husbands and in their own right, "First Ladies in Waiting," 8-17. Lighter though on another double byline in "Coming Soon: The Odd Couple," 2-2, with Timothy Noah, about the pairing of Senators Claiborne Pell (D-RI) and Jesse Helms (R-NC) as Chairman and ranking Republican, respectively, on the Senate Foreign Relations Committee. But so what? Clift is stronger on TV as a liberal foil to conservative Robert Novak on "The McLaughlin Group" talk show.

Cohen, Richard E. *National Journal.* (★ ½)
A stolid congressional reporter who is attentive to detail and accuracy, but writes with a heavy pen, rarely a word image to break the flow of facts. He tells us in "New Visibility," 2-27, that Sen. Jay Rockefeller (D-WV) is trying to make himself an expert on competitiveness, but what is he learning? "Baker's Limits," 3-7, offers an okay quick focus on Howard's themeless competence. The same with "Quick-Starting Speaker," 5-30, on Jim Wright, straight reporting, sleepy writing. "The Insider Steps Out," 6-27, on Bob Dole, suggests a lack of strategy in the Dole campaign, but with nothing new for the politically informed. "Living With a Lame Duck," 8-1, has RR bouncing back with an accurate, albeit tedious review of his potential. Cohen was at his most effective with "Byrd on the Spot," 10-3, analyzing the Bork struggle by focusing on Senator Byrd. With Burt Solomon, he gave us a series of very well done quick profiles of 13 junior House members, "Congress' Rising Stars," 1-24. A cover on "Long Distance Runner Richard A. Gephardt," 10-31, runs on and on and on.

Corry, John. *The New York Times.* (★ ★ ★)
The *Times*' public affairs television critic, a job created in 1984 by former executive editor A.M. Rosenthal to report on TV's coverage of national and global news. Corry's reports are always elegantly done, gently twitting the networks when they drift too far into the breathless liberalism that defines their culture. He also applauds vigorously when they do it right. "Iran Contra Hearing as Television Drama," 7-9, he sees two trials, one in the Senate caucus room, one on the TV screen, with a scorecard on how the commentators are inclined to view Ollie. "Gripping, emotional, exciting." We get a good review of a powerful statement in "Battle for Afghanistan," 7-29, on the "CBS Reports" documentary, that the Soviet objective is to either annex Afghanistan or depopulate it. In "Even Revolutionaries Smile for the Cameras," 10-4, he reports on the new phenomenon of foreign leaders using American television to propagandize, and that our "Television correspondents are respectful to foreign leaders, more so than they are to domestic politicians." Corry zings Ted Koppel of ABC's "Nightline" for his chat with the Iranian president: "Mr. Koppel provided no adversarial presence and assiduously stayed in neutral." His best of the year, "A Week of 'Donahue' Taped in Soviet Union," 2-12, has Blabby Phil chatting with a Soviet woman: "International hostility, he said, is caused by the 'small percentage of people in both countries — yours and mine — who remain hard-line and militaristic.' In fact, Mr. Donahue was at the core of his programmatic philosophy: There is a moral and political symmetry between East and West; only a few madmen disturb it.'"

Coulson, Crocker. *The New Republic.* (★ ★)
He's marvelous at debunking that which needs it, especially adept in the area of the expose. "The $37,000 Show," 1-19, was an excellent and comprehensive indictment of NYC's system for housing the homeless, offering proposals for approaching the problem nationally, with

a good assembly of details on the NYC mess. In "Geezer Sleaze," 4-20, he exposes the ultimate interest group, James Roosevelt's National Committee to Preserve Social Security and Medicare, a creation of the direct-mail industry.

Davidson, Joe. *The Wall Street Journal.* (★)
Washington bureau. A general assignment reporter who can harvest facts but too often bogs down when cooking the meal. "States Turn Out a Flood of AIDS Related Bills As Issue Remains in Talking Stages in Washington," 8-20, with the article as unfocused as the headline. We find, after sifting, that the material is here, but all over the place. A profile of Sen. Paul Simon as a presidential candidate also has plenty of facts, but we don't get much true sense of Simon or his campaign out of this catalog and bio.

deCordoba, Jose. *The Wall Street Journal.* (★ ½)
A solid, straightforward reporter who showed the right stuff in "White-Collar Inmates Find That Tennis And Good Food Do Not A Prison Unmake," 6-9, on minimum security prison life for bankers and embezzlers. "Beating The Bank," 7-9, was a great populist story on an elderly woman who beat the bank on credit card problems. Reporting from Miami, he outlined the competition for the Hispanic audience in the bilingual city in "Rivalry Intensifies Within Spanish-Language Television," 3-11, interesting and informative. One to watch in 1988.

Deigh, Robb. *Insight.* (★)
A reporter who left *Insight* for *U.S.News* late in '87, we saw less and less of him as the year progressed. He was articulate and organized in "The Very Major General in a Colonel's Secret Army," 1-12, on the relationship between Messrs. North and Secord, paralleling their careers to give a rudimentary sense of how they could get where they were, and interesting on the moving of the baby boomers from home to home in "Population on the Road Again, Relocating American Dreams," 5-25. Informative in "Welfare Joins the Age of Automation," 7-27, he tells us of Automatic Teller Machines and a welfare recipients program in MN, which allows "recipients [to] get their money the same way other bank customers do" out of an ATM account, saving the bank the time and aggravation of a deluge of clients on the first of the month. Too much of his work is pedestrian, interesting enough for a sidebar, but not a lead story. Still, we'll be looking for him on his new beat.

Dewar, Helen. *The Washington Post.* (★ ½)
Congressional correspondent. We've noted in the past a liberal tilt in Dewar's reporting, but none of our readers flagged her in '87, and her skills are still professional. In "Reagan-Congress 'French-War' Stalls Work on Hill," 7-14, she reports on pre-recess gridlock on everything, nothing getting done, using sources on all sides. In "A Byrd in the Paw, Or, A Parable for the Reflagging," 7-17, we get a neat insider look at the silly things that are sometimes said in Congress, with a terrific dialogue between Sen. Byrd and Rep. Hopkins. In "Senate Belatedly Suggests Alternatives to Reflagging," 7-22, she reports on the debate raging after the fact, with a nice (but wordy) lead: "The Senate wound up two months of fretting over the Reagan administration's plan to put Kuwaiti oil tankers under the protection of the U.S. flag in the Persian Gulf and finally passed a resolution urging 'alternatives to the reflagging' — just after Old Glory was hoisted over two Kuwaiti ships." She sees "Judge Kennedy Off to Smooth Start," 11-13, even quoting Sen. Jesse Helms near the top as being pleased after meeting him, thinking "he'd make a fine member of the Supreme Court," after earlier threatening opposition "in hopes of winning the nomination for a more conservative jurist."

Diamond, Edwin. *New York.* (★ ★)
Media critic. Always well-written, we find ourselves agreeing with much of the interpretation of the material he presents. "And Now, 'Impactweek,'" 5-11, detailed *Newsweek*'s new strategy to overtake the other weeklies. Diamond outlined the print media's fascination with AIDS, and how to handle it on paper in "Sexual Hysteria," 6-22, but really didn't tell us anything

we didn't already know. Same with "The 'Times' Of Frankel," 10-10. He's best when dealing with just the facts, straight up-and-up reporting: "The Empire Strikes Back," 4-13, on Citizen Hearst; "Now The New York 'Observer,'" 7-13, businessman Arthur Carter's NYC startup; and "Puck's Bad Boys," 7-27, on the irrepressible editors of *Spy*, and their irrepressible publication. Occasionally venturing into TV dispatch as well, Diamond did an informative piece on the new A.C. Nielsen rating system, or as he called it "Attack of the People Meters," 8-24.

Dickenson, James R. *The Washington Post.* (★ ½)
A seasoned political correspondent who handles spot news around the federal government during slow political seasons, but gets out on the campaign trail when necessary, keeping up with most of the kids. A hearty sense of humor comes in handy in "Friendly Advice From Predictors Anonymous," 2-2, on the silliness already afoot on the early predictions in Washington on the '88 race, a nice piece. And he has a great lead in a new rule laid down by the government ethics folks, "Bureaucrats Cannot Accept Free Meals," 10-3: "It may be the end of Western civilization as many in Washington have known it." His report "Baker Courts Critics," 3-7, is very well done on indications that Howard Baker, Jr. is seriously reassuring conservatives that the Reagan agenda is also his, quoting cheers from Richard Viguerie as proof. But in "Howard Baker Appears As Prime Minister to Reagan," 3-8, there are only flat observations, no insights worth the trouble. In "Reagan: AIDS Is 'Health Enemy No. 1,'" 4-2, he's short and to the point in reporting RR's address to the College of Physicians. Dickenson seemed to be getting more campaign chores late in the year, shuttling to Iowa with candidates preparing for the important caucus event.

Diegmuller, Karen. *Insight.* (★ ½)
Quiet, usually conventional pieces from this *Insight* writer. "Vintage Rivalry for U.S. Market," 11-30, was a perky bit on competition in the wine industry and challengers to the old standard French and Italian vinos. Earlier in the year, Diegmuller had a amicable portrait of HUD's Samuel Pierce, Jr.: "Ever dapper, never flamboyant, Pierce's persona and image do not always jibe. His desk, credenza and conference table are cluttered...Yet Pierce seems remarkably uncluttered and self-effacing; he laughs readily, often at his own expense." "Alternatives to the Juvenile Courts," 3-2, is just what it purports to be, clean and crisp, but is still skimming a bit: surely there are more alternatives than can be covered in two brief pages. Her byline appearing in *The Washington Times*, "Atlantic City Faces Big Gamble," 6-28, told of a city moving away from day-trippers to conventioneers as its target, but didn't tell us much besides.

Dillin, John. *The Christian Science Monitor.* (★)
Politics, served with no garnish, often cold and unsatisfying. He was late with Gary Hart in "Hart Meets Moral Issue Head On," 5-6, handled without sensationalizing, waiting for Hart's rebuttal to go to print, but a day behind everybody else. "Laxalt Bows Out Of Republican Race," 8-28, was conventional analysis, a day late (Laxalt withdrew on Wed., story appeared in Friday paper). Better and on-time with "Cuomo's Challenge: Shed His Eastern Liberal Label," 1-14, reporting on "The Cuomo Factor," the Marist Institute book examining factors behind the Gov's immense popularity, and "Despite Bush Lead, Iowa Contest Still 'Fluid' For GOP Hopefuls," 6-2, noting that some GOPers are now worried more about a strong show for Rev. Pat Robertson than the party-weakening Dole-Bush clashes in Iowa. "Upturn In Heartland Undercuts Democrats Strategy For '88," 8-27, the second of two related articles was probably his best, the inconvenient recovery in the farmbelt helping to force Democratic candidates to find new issues for 1988. Too often, though nothing is developed or revealed: "GOP Right Courts Buchanan," 1-14 and "Kemp Tries To Rally A Right Wing Looking For Champion," 4-6, old stuff, with quotes. "It's Looking Up In The US Heartland," 8-26 (the first of two "Upturn in Heartland..."), skim economics, he doesn't have any idea of *why* states recovered; and "Robertson's Bid Taken Seriously," 10-2, was shallow analysis but an okay snapshot of Pat.

Dionne, E.J., Jr. *The New York Times.* (★ ★ ★)
In his first full year as national political correspondent after two sterling years as Rome bureau chief, Dionne has a fine portfolio to his credit, but a bit below our lofty expectations of him. He seemed to do his best early in the year, dragging the miles piled up on the campaign trail. A few home runs in '87: "Iran Affair Raises Democrats' Hopes and Caution on '88," 1-18, had fresh insights, with the higher value of the nomination slowing down the race as the pros "reassess their hopes and interests"; "Labor to Seek Consensus on Supporting '88 Presidential Candidates," 2-19, covers all the bases in a richly detailed report on organized labor's thinking, with widespread indecision on who's best. He has a good look at some subtle strengths and weaknesses of Jack Kemp in "New Hampshire Tries to Understand Kemp," 1-22, and we get a superior account in "Gephardt Opens Campaign," 2-24. A Sunday magazine cover story, "The Elusive Front-Runner," 4-3, was a subtly supportive piece on Gary Hart that helped us understand the rumors surrounding him and contained Hart's challenge to "put a tail on him." In "The Hart Legacy: He Broke Democrats' Link With Politics of New Deal," 5-12, we get a new angle. Pieces on Pete DuPont, 6-2, and Paul Simon, 8-7, are more than adequate. In "Democrats Clash on Foreign Policy," 10-8, he sees Senator Gore emerging as "tougher on defense" than the competition. His best of the second half, "Primary Upsets Hint Shift in Votes," 11-3, has great insights on "the trend toward last-minute voting decisions reflect[ing] the extent to which voters were repelled by, and impatient with, the demands of politics."

Donohoe, Cathryn. *The Washington Times.* (★ ★ ★)
A "Capital Life" and now "Life!" reporter, Donohoe is one of the best portraitists around. She can handle people and issues well, not being intimidated by either. "Doctors And AIDS," 6-10, painted a stark, expansive landscape of the doctors who treat AIDS as a career choice that was well done, not hysterical or overblown. "Domination by Stunning," 1-29, was a superlative Polaroid of the "Prince of Darkness" of the "McLaughlin Group" and News America Syndicate, Bob Novak, the first paragraphs grabbing us with an anecdote we'd not heard before, and then keeping us entertained with Novak's peccadilloes. There were fascinating angles in "In Iowa, Peace Groups Are Political Mainstream," 11-18, on peaceniks in Iowa, and "Stennis," 1-6, colorful on this profile of Senator John Stennis, the oldest Senator in Congress.

Dowd, Maureen. *The New York Times.* (★ ★ ½)
Among the best writers on the campaign trail, Dowd paints picturesque features from oblique angles. Her front-page newsbeat on Joe Biden cribbing from Neil Kinnock, putting Biden on the slippery slope, gives her a small footnote in political history. "Schroeder: At Ease With Femininity and Issues," 8-23, is a delight: "Ms. Schroeder has a tendency to call programs she does not like 'icky,' sign her Congressional mail with a smile face, and punctuate thoughts with eye-rolling declamations like 'golly'and 'doggonit!' and 'yippy-skippy' — not the perfect candidate that women hoped for, in the view of some." A cutesy "Liberals Peek Out and See Spring," 1-19, spies the reemergence of "liberal chic." A Sunday magazine look at "The New Flirt," 3-2, has this delicious line: "It will be considered captivating once more to be on a chaise lounge, pass a lacy handkerchief across the eyelids, and complain of a case of springtime giddiness." A semi-profile of the Surgeon General, "Dr. Koop Defends His Crusades," 4-6,is unusually deft on this right-wing hero, "smiling behind his Captain Ahab beard," suddenly a hero to the left on AIDS/sex education. In "Official Still Seethes About Deal," 8-1, she has this great summation line on Caspar Weinberger's testimony before the Iran-Contra hearing: "Like children with a favorite bedtime story, the members wanted to hear Secretary Weinberger say — over and over again — that it was not right to trade arms for hostages and lie to Congress and shred documents and deceive allies and use international businessmen as 'negotiators' and have the United States open to blackmail."

Drew, Elizabeth. *The New Yorker.* (★ ½)
The "Letter from Washington" columnist wasn't as steady and observant this year, with more argumentative editorializing than objective reportage showing up. She was far too irate in her 2-16 "Letter," mixing in her biases freely: "The Iran-Contra affair appears to be another example — along with...SDI and the whopping budget deficit as a result of Reagan's refusal to raise taxes — of an obsession on the part of the President which his aides could not deflect or even encouraged." But she takes heart with "the gradual cracking of the Reagan myth." A little better in her 3-30 "Letter," portraying Reagan as a bystander at his own presidency: "[Howard] Baker was cooked up by others and served to him." She quotes Rep. Dick Cheney (R-WY) on the consequences; whatever center of gravity existed previously, it was gone after his first term, the apparent sense of indecisiveness in foreign policy allowing Congress to move in. Also better, her 5-4 "Letter" noting "something odd about the Reagan Administration's apparent eagerness to reach an agreement with the Soviets on...INF, since arms control policy is still dominated by those who oppose arms control." Pre-Ollie North, she declared the search for the "smoking gun" a diversion from the real issues of the Iran-Contra affair, and in her 6-22 "Letter" she focuses on the constitutional issues. But her partisanship shows, as she includes uncritically the unsupported Edwin Wilson "connection." However, she does provide some details of how the absence of strategic thinking by the Administration on the hearings seemed to push it deeper and deeper into the morass.

Easterbrook, Gregg. *Newsweek.* (★ ★ ½)
A new contributing editor this year, Easterbrook had the longest piece in newsweekly journalism in '87. "The Revolution in Medicine," 1-26, was way overlong, but thoroughly comprehensive, covering nearly everything you'd need to know before seeing a doctor or going into the hospital. Coupled with Larry Martz in "Lost in Space," 8-17, on the stalled space program and NASA's problems, it spurred a spate of articles in other publications, getting the issue to the surface, although the piece was hardly definitive despite its great length. On a related note, but not so high up, Easterbrook vigorously debunked the idea that deregulation is the cause of the airline industry's current difficulties, "The Sky Isn't Falling," *The New Republic*, 11-30. But his feet are firmly on the ground.

Edsall, Thomas B. *The Washington Post.* (★ ★ ★ ½)
Political reporter. Among the best of the *Post*'s big political team, assigned to the Dole campaign, with special responsibilities in handling the South and Super Tuesday. He's also the resident expert on campaign financing, his analytics in this area the best anywhere. Edsall's jewel of 1987 was "The Political Impasse," 3-26, in the *New York Review of Books*, a sweeping reconnaissance of the broad national picture confronting the two parties. [See 10 Best section]. There were few better pieces on Dole than his "Dole's Transformations: Ideological Blur Characterizes Career," 3-9, the best early profile with a good sense of the Kansas senator: "The core of Dole's philosophy remains closely tied to a midwestern conservatism...The one issue that brings forth a passionate, animated reaction from Dole is the deficit. The deficit is 'going to engulf this country one of these days. That may be gloom and doom, but it's a fact.'" In "The Early Contests of 1988: A Paradox is Found," 8-14, good material is developed around the theme, Iowa is more liberal, New Hampshire more conservative, but we expected more on the distinction between caucus and primary voting. He reported the "Dole Makes It Official," 10-10 news story with crisp thoroughness, following it the next day with fine news analysis, "Dole Defying Both Parties' Assumptions," 11-11, seeing Dole, in running against the budget deficit, going against "the collective wisdom drawn from Walter F. Mondale's failed bid for the presidency in 1984 and the strategy adopted by the New Right wing of the Republican Party: that calling for sacrifice does not win elections." Edsall also notes this has begun to "constrict another core element of his political strategy: his commitment to presenting himself as a Republican who will care for the elderly, the sick and the needy."

Farney, Dennis. *The Wall Street Journal.* (★ ★)
A dependable veteran of the Washington bureau, his experience always shows in careful reporting and writing. "Missouri's Rep. Gephardt Announces Presidential Campaign, Cites Trade Issue," 2-24, is a quick and cogent summation of Gephardt's platform. Also spare is a profile of Arkansas Gov. Bill Clinton, 4-28: "Ambition and its consequences, six and a half turbulent years as governor, have made him 'the oldest 40-year old man in America,'" he says. A 9-21 back page profile of Gephardt held us throughout, about as good as we've seen, but did not quite catch him. His profile of Pete du Pont, 10-22, was the best we saw on "the Duper" in '87, a rich, three-dimensional portrait. Best line: "He once had a blind date with Jane Fonda, but can't remember what they did." A P.1 leader on "The New West," 10-28, reports on the economic gloom in Wyoming and Montana at a low point in the boom-bust natural resource/commodity cycle and is worth a look. Very professional. We expect to see a lot of him on '88 campaign trail.

Fineman, Howard. *Newsweek.* (★)
Political reporter who usually does thoroughly unlikeable, and sometimes unreliable, work. He's better this year, taking out the snide commentary, and leaving us straight reports, often giving us little bits we didn't see elsewhere. "Gary Hart: A Candidate in Search of Himself," 4-13, was a thorough profile of Gary, complicated and driven, involving and informative in terms of the man, more so than in terms of the candidate, containing a prescient line, quoting John McEvoy, an '84 advisor: "He's always in jeopardy of having the sex issue raised if he can't keep his pants on." Fineman should be able to produce regularly at this level, but doesn't. Standard stuff for the rest of the year: "The Democrats Prep For An '88 Free-For-All," 5-18; "The Vox Pop Hit Parade," 8-10; "Memo To Sam: It's Going To Be Tough," 8-31; "A Tennessee Stalking Horse," 9-14; all conventional on the Democrats. But "The Pat Robertson Effect," 9-28, was a little more intriguing, betting that Pat won't win, but could turn the GOP convention in New Orleans into "a right wing rhetorical spectacle with religious overtones."

Fleming, Stewart. *Financial Times.* (★ ½)
Washington bureau chief. In his first full year in the job, Fleming is still adjusting. At the end of last year, "Democrats Tread Softly in Search of Victory," 12-22-86, was an insightful picture of how Reagan has changed the political environment and the effect that has had on Democratic attempts to retake the political lead. "Handles On The Election Trial," 6-16, was just a catalog of pitfalls, not very useful: "The other key components of the economy have been disturbingly weak, however. Consumer demand fell in each of the last two quarters, a rare development when there is no recession." "Commerce Not Welcome At The Bank," 8-28, was well-written, but quite one-sided, editorializing against financial deregulation in this report on the U.S. financial services industry. Quite good back-to-back profiles of the IMF's Michael Camdessus and the Fed's Greenspan from Stewart, 9-28.

Fumento, Michael. Freelance. (★ ★)
Late of *The Washington Times* as a legal affairs reporter, Fumento is off to a great start as a freelancer. "AIDS: Are Heterosexuals at Risk?" appearing in November's *Commentary*, was the definitive piece on the subject, shattering the myth of the heterosexual epidemic, citing redefinition of carriers and victims as part of the myth and concluding "Every dollar spent, every commercial made, every promiscuous anal intercourse and needle-sharing as the overwhelming risk factors in the transmission of AIDS is a lie, a waste of funds and energy, and a cruel diversion." His work for the *Times*, though, was less impressive: "Effort To Put Creation Science In Schools Appears Doomed," 6-22, noted the decision against creationism "looked at the motives behind the legislation — and not just at the legislation itself — analysts said it would be very difficult for any sort of law mandating the teaching of creation science to ever pass muster;" and "Bork Battle Looms As One For The Book," 6-27, was carefully drawn with coalitions lining up left and right, but not much attempt at analysis.

Gest, Ted. *U.S.News & World Report.* (★)
Supreme Court and Justice. A competent, reliable reporter, Gest handles the law and order end of things, as opposed to the intellectual, Bork-like ideological questions. He details frightening examples opposing the 'Make my day' laws, citing statistics supporting the laws, on the other side, but is somewhat disorganized about it, leaving the then-pending landmark Goetz case until the end of the piece in "'Make My Day' Laws — The Impact," 4-20. "Dissidents, Old Allies, Shake NRA," 4-27, was filled with really awful puns — "pot shots," "shooting match," "firings" — but had some good tidbits of information on the inside and outside problems of the National Rifle Association. "Teaching Convicts Real Street Smarts," 5-18, was a fairly good account of the prison population at a staggering 549,659 leading to innovations in rehabilitation. But Gest let his anti-Bork bias show in "Did Robert Bork Bend The Rules In A 1984 Case?" 7-20: "It's not certain that Bork did breach the rules, but critics see his conduct as proof that he is an ideologically rigid judge with fixed conservative opinions on most key issues."

Grabowski, Gene. *The Washington Times.* (★)
A utility political reporter, Grabowski strikes us as competent, organizing and reporting well. On the up-and-up in "Reform of Federal Election Laws Forecast as Annual Ritual Begins," 3-5, tight and insightful on the possibility of passage of federal election law reform. A great lead in "Democrats Plan To Coerce Reagan To Accept Tax Rise," 6-8, a nice summation of Dem maneuverings on the budget: "Democratic congressional leaders plan to hold as hostage changes in the budget process desired by the administration in an effort to force President Reagan to agree to raise taxes for 1988, Capitol Hill sources said." Solid in "Senate Is in Filibuster Over 'Star Wars' Plan," 5-18, with detail, but standard and obvious in "U.S. Aid Cuts Seen Opening Door to Soviets," 3-11, a recitation of conventional wisdom.

Greenhouse, Linda. *The New York Times.* (★ ★ ½)
Taking over the Senate beat in '86 after years covering the Supreme Court, Greenhouse was in perfect position to cover the Bork confirmation fight and we came to depend on her steady reporting throughout. In "Ideology as Court Issue," 7-3, she sizes up the battle, assessing the political risks to Democrats with sensitive shadings: "It becomes a referendum on the very issues that make senators most uncomfortable. Abortion, affirmative action, questions of church and state, all the legislative glories that the Reagan revolution let out of the bottle in the early 1980s and that the Senate, in the interest of getting on with its work, has more or less managed to bottle up once again." There are good pieces on Democratic strategy, "Foes on the Left Strive for Unity," 7-9, and "Byrd Warns Against a Partisan Battle," 7-29, and a good picture on the developing strategies on both sides, "No Grass is Growing Under Judge Bork's Feet," 8-4. We see her expertise in "Legal Establishment Divided Over Bork," 9-26, and in "Bork Rejects Seeking Withdrawal of Nomination," 10-5, with Sen. Howell Heflin (D-AL) now leaning toward opposition, buying the view that Bork is an extremist, not a conservative. She's weaker on the grand political backdrop of the battle, "What Went Wrong," 10-7, seeing Judge Bork as a victim of a particular moment in history, forgetting that her 7-3 scenario of a referendum on the social issues was never played out as the opposition made it one of civil rights and privacy, the White House bungling. Her work on the Senate battles over contra funding was also deft. See "Redrawing Battle Lines to the Contras," 2-26, "The politics of the issue are wondrously complex," and an excellent account, "Latin Peace Plan is Put Forth by Administration," 8-5. An admirable year.

Griffith, Thomas. *Time.* (★ ★)
"Newswatch" columnist dealing with both the print and the tube. His columns are short, a strange fusion of fact and anecdote, but often insightful, with insider goodies we don't see in comparable columns. Two worthwhile reports in 1987 commended Scotty Reston on an admirable career and much-deserved retirement, "The Best Journalist of His Time," 8-31,

and the advent of Abe Rosenthal to the *Times*' Op-Ed page, "Short-Notice Wisdom," 2-9, which suggested other columnists he might pattern himself after, Safire, Will, Buckley, etc: "There is another *Times* model Rosenthal might consider...Russell Baker...has now widened his range to take on the entire culture...to call him a humorist does not contain him...When the story of our times is written, historians may find it best defined not by conventional Washington experts but by Baker's down-home wisdom." He's conventional, standing with the rest of the press in "Sex, Privacy and Journalism," 6-8, really only a summary of what other journalists thought, but well put: "there are two kinds of news, the important and the interesting." He handles journalism, too, but sometimes misses the point: in "Better Slow Than Sorry," 5-4, he advises caution in print, noting "correspondents would rather be considered slow than wrong;" and in "Offsetting the True Believers," 10-5, he details the maverick stance of the *Wall Street Journal*'s editorial pages, using "aggressive reporting to offset bellicose editorials," but skips noting the long-standing feud between the Washington and editorial bureaus.

Gross, Jane. *The New York Times.* (NR)
A metro reporter who caught our eye with her excellent reports on AIDS. "The Devastation of AIDS: Many Dead, More Dying," 3-16, was a brief, over-emotional overview of series of articles to follow, one of which was also authored by Gross: "An Ever-Widening Epidemic Tears at the City's Life and Spirit," 3-16, collected interviews with victims and friends of the afflicted that paints a vividly comprehensive picture of the ways people cope with AIDS in New York. Gross also did a frightening portrait of gay teens in Manhattan, some of whom are on the streets, turning tricks to survive, and how they deal with a developing sexuality and the spectre of AIDS, "AIDS Threat Brings New Turmoil for Gay Teenagers," 10-21, a intimate examination that no one else could bring themselves to do.

Haas, Lawrence J. *National Journal.* (NR)
Joining *NJ* midyear, we didn't feel we could evaluate Haas only having seen a half-year's work, but what we saw was promising. A noteworthy piece: "Big-Ticket Restrictions," 9-26, the best we saw on Social Security politics, but still a little short of what we need on economic analysis of the growing S.S. surplus.

Hallow, Ralph Z. *The Washington Times.* (★ ★)
Still breezier than we'd like, Hallow at least seemed more sure of himself on the political beat and chalked up a respectable year. Late in 1986, he had one of the first reports on conservative rethinking on the new NSC appointment in "Carlucci Reaches Out to Stroke Hill Conservatives," 12-4-86, more appreciative now. "Dole Bars Media Advice, 'Vision' Idea," 3-5, detailed Dole's plans and interoffice squabbles, quoting him: "...the press is not going to set my agenda." A fine roundup of views in "Bush Ducks Speech, Risks Ire of Right," 2-16, on the Veep's decision not to address C-PAC, and very fair, quoting Rep. Dornan (a Bushie) at length. Sharp, early analysis in "Confirmation Row May Benefit GOP," 7-3, Ronald Reagan trapping liberals on Bork, quoting prominent Democrats. Good reporting in "Supply-Siders Unsure of Greenspan," 6-4, noting Art Laffer, comfortable with the old guard, thinks things just might work out. Hallow's just cheerleading in "Kemp Win: Straw In The Wind?" 8-18, Kemp coming in first in a poll where 75% of the people at a barbeque are party regulars.

Hey, Robert P. *The Christian Science Monitor.* (★ ½)
Competent and reliable, but because he moves from issue to issue, Hey tends to just skim the top of a story. "Welfare Reform Gains Fresh Impetus In Senate, White House," 5-27, is nicely done, but could have been much tighter, more in-depth. "Family Incomes Rise As US Moves Further Away From Poverty," 7-31, is better, a straight report acknowledging the rise of single-parent families and their plight without the canard that RR's policies are the cause. Hey ventures into business in "AIDS Presents A Number of New Challenges For US Employers," 8-17, further proof that AIDS is going to be a major policy issue in the '88 elections

with management expert Orion recommending a "bailout" since half AIDS cases are people "at the fringes of society" and other managers for corporate insurance, for example, seem to feel the federal government ought to be handling this. A fun, quirky note: "Post Office Of Future To Be More Automated," 8-25, with some weird, but still neat little statistics on the modernization of the Post Office — like all the mail from 1986, if had been mailed in regular business envelopes and laid out end-to-end, would go to the moon and back over 40 times.

Hoffman, David. *The Washington Post.* (★ ½)
White House. The No. 2 man behind Lou Cannon at the WH, Hoffman turned out steady spot news and some interesting features, but either we weren't watching closely enough or he didn't produce anything as impressive as his 10-28-86 profile of the Veep. An extremely busy time around the White House produced almost 250 Hoffman bylines during the year, however. There was "A State of the Union Short on Substance," 1-29, collecting Beltway opinions of various "high-ranking administration policymaker[s]" and "senior assistants," but this was fluff. There was some nice inside stuff on "Reagan's 'Worst' Speech," 7-20, the story of RR's ineffective 11-13-86 Iran-Contra TV address, blaming everyone but the writer. A timely piece, "President Will Limit Response to Congressional Hearings," 8-2, was timely, thorough and professional. His "'88 Candidates Have No Deficit of New Spending Plans," 11-16, is mildly interesting, a rundown of all the big-ticket promises being made on the stump by candidates who are supposedly aghast at the Reagan deficits, including Bob Dole who "launched his campaign last week with a vow to 'tackle the runaway federal deficit.'" But even this read like a catalog, his notebook poured into a word processor. We know he's better.

Hornblower, Margot. *The Washington Post.* (NR)
Formerly New York bureau chief for the *Post.* Two pieces she produced back to back in August are worth noting: "South Bronx, 10 Years After Fame," 8-25, is better than most looks at the area than we get from the *NYT*, skimpy on analysis, but satisfying in cataloging history and surface decay; "City in The Spotlight Casts Corrupt Shadows," 8-26, is a better rundown of the scandals in the Koch administration than we've seen prominently displayed in the *Times*, an admirable effort. It occurs to us the *Times* should rent *Post* reporters like Hornblower to do major pieces on the rot in the Big Apple for the Sunday magazine, where never is heard a discouraging word.

Hume, Ellen. *The Wall Street Journal.* (★)
Washington bureau general assignment, writing up the *Journal*'s public-opinion panels, helping out around the White House and making a better impression on us than in '86. A feature on the new press secretary, Marlin Fitzwater, 4-2, was okay puffery, but with needless jabs at the departed Larry Speakes. A P.1 leader, "Voters Seek a Leader Who Is Both Strong and Straightforward," 5-22, we think is largely a waste of time, a panel of voters quizzed, but this isn't her idea. Another front-pager tells us, no kidding, "Survey Shows Concern Over Economy Rising After Market's Crash," 10-30. More interesting is "Poll Says More Americans Oppose Bork Than Back Him for Supreme Court Seat," 9-25, although it seems implausible that 76% of those polled had an opinion, and there seemed to be no questions on how they had arrived at their opinions. Hume's byline appeared on a very important story, "Administration Seems Increasingly Paralyzed In Wake of Bork Fight," 10-16, part of the gathering storm that sent Wall Street crashing three days later, but co-author Gerald F. Seib, with his name on top, probably did the lion's share of it. Everyone in Washington read "The Rise and Fall of Don Regan," in January's *Regardie's*, with Jane Mayer; sparse with giving credit and excessive with detraction, but the Chief of Staff's own remarks made it all worthwhile.

Ingwerson, Marshall. *The Christian Science Monitor.* (★ ½)
Political beat, covering mostly the Democrats and the South. In "South: Region In Search Of A Candidate," 4-14, he categorizes Super Tuesday as "a race but no face," quoting Pat

Caddell: "As a national party, the Democrats are a minority party." Ingwerson shot straight from the hip on the blurring of party lines in favor of the issues in "Southern Voters Put Issues Ahead Of Party In Presidential Race," 8-20, also noting again the "Character" factor, but it's all so conventional. Equally so with "Southern Blacks Show Clout on Bork," 10-13, noted unanimous opposition to Bork, but gave no analysis on why Southern Blacks feel that Bork would "roll back two decades of civil-rights gains." Better with "Gore Stakes Out Right On Defense," 10-7, a solid report on Sen. Gore's turf claim. Still better was "Saving Favorite Programs Tops America's Budget Priorities," 10-29, right on with deficit-mania not being able to rally the troops.

Innerst, Carol. *The Washington Times.* (★ ½)
Covering health, education and welfare, Innerst naturally segued into the AIDS debate. "Koop Suggests Abortion as Option for AIDS Carriers," 3-25, detailed the strong, almost fanatic, remarks of the Surgeon General to the National Press Club, with an interesting citation of study by Michigan State which documents occurrence of intercourse (and discussion thereof) between unmarried partners on TV and in film which are witnessed by young adults, to support Koop's argument. "NEA Leader Laments Decline in Share of Federal Spending," 5-28, was loaded with statistics on the drop in education spending, with NEA President Mary Futrell pining for more dollars and Secretary of Education William Bennett chiding her and the NEA for its "cash register mentality," a carefully balanced report between the two. The subjects of AIDS and Secretary Bennett were linked in "Bennett's Own Guide on AIDS Distributed," 10-7: the guide urges sexual restraint, highlighting the debate on condoms between Bennett and Koop and within the administration itself.

Jacoby, Tamar. *Newsweek.* (★)
Coming off *The New York Times'* editorial pages to work in the DC bureau of *Newsweek*, Jacoby had an irregular first year. "William Casey: Silent Witness," 5-18, was full of innuendos and conjecture about the Iran-Contra Affair. "The Stalwarts Retreat" (with Robert Parry), 6-22, was a decent summary of the first phase of the Iran-Contra hearings, with a somewhat anti-Reagan sentimentality. "Nunn's View: A Chance To 'Educate' Europe," 5-4, was a short interview with Sam Nunn, that was still useful despite its brevity. "A Cult Of 'Covert Ops,'" 7-20, was again, slanted against North, but made some valid points about the pros and cons of covert actions, and used history (Vietnam, Bay of Pigs) to back it up: "North sees no reason for America to tie its hands with the scruples that, he feels come with careful oversight. The only reason has to do with the democratic values America seeks to defend, which argue for both restraint and accountability." "Reagan's Kingpin," 8-24, was off on Baker and how he irons out the rough spots despite RR's stubbornness. Give her another year to get the bias out.

Johns, Michael. *Policy Review.* (★ ★)
Assistant editor. A hard hard-liner, he often employs a sledgehammer instead of a journalist's pen or typewriter. His best, "The Lesson Of Afghanistan," Spring, is a savvy geopolitical analytic in which Johns examines why the country's resistance enjoys almost universal bipartisan support while no such consensus applies to Angola, Mozambique and Nicaragua. "Not since Pol Pot's Cambodia have such heinous atrocities been inflicted on one people and one land," Johns charged, and a reprinted version of the essay in *The Washington Times*, 4-8, prompted the following reply from the Afghan embassy: "...what is happening in Afghanistan is a brave struggle to transform an underdeveloped country into a modern and progressive nation." Johns views "Gorbachev's Soviet Union...[as] less bloody than Lenin's and Stalin's, but in almost every respect his nation is still the house that Lenin built." In "Seventy Years of Evil," Fall, he chronicles Soviet crimes from Lenin to Gorbachev, to convincingly make the point that we still face "an evil empire." There's no quarter either with "Tributes to Totalitarianism," Winter, in which he lists examples of egregious misinformation provided by the media on the Sandinistas since 1978. In "Peace in Our Time," Summer, he finds the "culture of appeasement" metasticizing through the culture and values of the West.

Jones, Alex S. *The New York Times.* (★ ★)
Covering the newspaper industry as a business along with the foibles of the press, Jones may be burdened by more than the usual amount of institutional restraints at the *Times*, but manages to keep things lively and even produce prize-winning material. We loved his "Fairness Stressed by Nation's Press," 12-5-86, on the press' love for a good scandal, with good, colorful quotes. "The USA Today Story," 7-3, is a book review, more or less, on "The Making of McPaper," with good detail on its horrendous losses, less clear on a prognosis for the paper. He has the Sunday business lead with "Busting Into the Big Leagues," 9-20, on William Dean Singleton's purchase of the *Denver* and *Houston Post*, a fairly interesting profile livened up with some good quotes: "I want to die and at the funeral have a lot of people stand around and say, 'Dean Singleton' built a hell of a newspaper company."

Judis, John. *In These Times.* (★ ★)
Senior editor. One of the left's most promising journalists, who, along with their Salvador correspondent Chris Norton, is the reason why we read this socialist weekly. Judis often appears in *The New Republic* where he uses his pen the way Lizzie Borden used her axe. Patrick Buchanan was hacked to bits in "White House Vigilante," *TNR*, 1-26, although the Buchanan butchered was more of Judis' construction than the genuine article. Reagan revolutionaries are his favorite targets, lesser foes on the right unchallenging as serious threats to his leftist perspectives. In "The Mouse That Roars," *TNR*, 8-3, he wields his axe again with vicious blows on Gary Bauer, marking him for the left's attention as "the New Right voice in the White House." Liberals who goof-up are excoriated in his *ITT* articles, as in "Bork Foes on the Defensive Thanks to Biden's Blunders," 8-19. Thanks to his "tenuous grasp of constitutional issues," the Bork confirmation would be harder to prevent, a point the White House strategists never absorbed. In "A Conservative Backlash on Reagan's Contra Policy," 9-2, he's alert on the new reality of the Reagan-Wright plan, advising the movement that "Reagan unwittingly gave the green light to Central American leaders to adopt a plan that would scuttle the contras." He succumbs to the lower depths with "Behind the House Trade Bill," 5-6, endorsing trade sanctions against Japan and the Gephardt amendment with a hodgepodge of spurious arguments. But he rockets back up to the top with the brilliant "Apocalypse Now and Then," *TNR*, 8-13, one of the year's 10-best commentaries.

Kamen, Al. *The Washington Post.* (★ ★ ★)
Supreme Court. Of all the SCOTUS reporters, Kamen has the best political instincts. His "Time Running Out for Reagan to Reshape Court," 1-22-86, was way out ahead of everyone else in seeing the horizon that awaited Bork and Ginsburg. He had one of the very best Court pieces of '87, "Scalia Making Conservatives Nervous," 3-8, observing that Justice Scalia has been voting with Rehnquist only 75% of the time — and writing the opinion on a police search with "the Constitution sometimes insulates the criminality of a few in order to protect the privacy of us all." Kamen notes, "Brennan couldn't have said it any better, and clearly understands the difference between a populist conservative, Scalia, and an elitist (statist) conservative, Rehnquist. In "Justice O'Connor to Brief GOP Donors at High Court," 5-1, Kamen has the scoop on Rep. Newt Gingrich's GOPAC forum, a political event, the piece forcing Justice O'Connor to bow out. He didn't break the Ginsburg story, but his "Ginsburg Acknowledges He Smoked Marijuana," 11-6, atop the *Post*'s front page, laid out all the elements, letting the reader put two and two together instead of doing it for them. With Dale Russakoff, Kamen did a fine two-part series on Bork, 7-26 and 7-27. [See Russakoff, Dale.]

Kastor, Elizabeth. *The Washington Post.* (NR)
Style section. A nifty writer who serves up long features we usually swallow whole. Her long, long "The Cautious Closet of the Gay Conservatives," 5-11, was very well handled and illuminating, following the death and funeral of Terry Dolan, NCPAC's founder, who died of AIDS. "Julien Barnes' Big Questions," 5-18, is impressive too, a snappy interview with the British novelist.

Kaus, Mickey. *Newsweek.* (★ ★)
A new and important addition to the Washington bureau, stolen away from *The New Republic*, Kaus did good work, most often heading up a multiple byline. "Nobody's Perfect," 5-25, was an essayish, semi-tongue-in-cheek look at the oddities of the Constitution, defining categories therein as: "least necessary provision;" "most badly drafted language;" "weirdest clause;" "biggest breeder of pointless litigation;" "biggest accident waiting to happen;" and "best argument against changing any of the above," with hilarious supports for all of them. "Here Comes Gary, Again," (with Margaret Garrard Warner and Peter McKillop) 6-29, was the sad story of a man without a purpose, told without the "I-told-you-so" attitude other press accounts had. "Far Too Much Ado About Little Iowa," (with John McCormick and Howard Fineman) 7-6, was well done, bringing up some good points, but a snippy review of the Iowa caucus process: "Is there anything wrong with turning over presidential selection to a bunch of conscientious Midwesterners who look like Bartles and Jaymes but talk like MacNeil and Lehrer?" and "If you run in Iowa and don't finish in the top three in your party, it's generally believed you might as well book a cruise on the Monkey Business." Better in "Gunplay On The Freeway," 8-10, razor sharp writing on the LA freeway shootings and "Biden's Belly Flop," (with Eleanor Clift, Howard Fineman, John McCormick) 9-28, an insightful explanation on hype over Biden's "over-exuberant" errors and then on to other Democratic candidates saying the reporters jump on an "incident they could interpret in light of their pre-existing doubts."

King, Wayne. *The New York Times.* (★ ½)
A utility reporter who catches our eye with offbeat angles to familiar stories. In "Dilemma For Democrats in Jackson's Statement on Vice Presidency," 5-30, he tweaks the conventional view that candidates who announce their willingness to settle for VP could take themselves out of serious consideration for No. 1, but this doesn't apply to Jesse, whose announcement may even enhance his candidacy. In "Cards and Calls (And Cash) Pour in For North," 7-11, we get some quirky quotes, from Norman Lear and others. His debate coach is best: "It's a mixture of righteous indignation and courage and honesty and anger. It comes through visually." But, "It does not mean that the audience approves of his behavior when they think about the issues." For the record book, he gives us "The Latin Peace Plan According to Wright," 8-11, recounting that former Rep. Tom Loeffler visited Speaker Jim Wright's home with "a pizza and a peace plan for Nicaragua."

Knobelsdorff, Kerry Elizabeth. *The Christian Science Monitor.* (★)
Human interest stuff in the business arena, Knobelsdorff comes up with some quirky, eye-catching material that often doesn't live up to its promise. "AIDS In Workplace Forces Companies To Address Employee Concerns," 8-17, looked at different tactics of management actually in the workplace setting: it's all been said before, but it's well put together. "IBM's Four-Month-Old PS/2 Has Put Computer World On Hold," 8-19, was better, outlining the pros and cons of IBM's PS/2 on the market, asking will it succeed but leaving the question of IBM's possible overextension by only producing one model of the 1st generation untouched, and skimming over actual business applications. In "Stricter Regulation Sought Over Labs Using Animals in Research," 1-8, she does an adequate job of covering the growing animal rights movement. Better in "Motels Pin Growth to Upscale Frills, Usual Economy," 11-3, on the addition of hot tubs and other amenities to the proverbial No-tell Motel.

Kosterlitz, Julie. *National Journal.* (★)
NJ's health reporter, she spends her days covering the drug industry, health insurance corporations, etc., but her reporting is dry and unexciting. AIDS was a major issue this year on her beat, but she couldn't seem to catch the emotional flavor of the crisis: she's dispassionate in "AIDS Vaccine's Ethical, Legal Thicket," 3-21; downright cold in "The AIDS Schism," 7-4; but there is more feeling and good info in "AIDS Strains the System," 6-27. Her "Bowen's Quiet Strength," 2-7, on HHS Secretary Otis Bowen takes forever to get going, and "In Person:

Arthur S. Flemming,'' 5-9, was colorless, telling us what he's done by age 85, not giving us much on what he thinks or who he is. A disappointing year.

Kurtz, Howard. *The Washington Post.* (★ ★ ½)
New York. A high-spirited roving reporter who one of our readers has come to identify as the *Post*'s "pit bulldog." In "Amid Many Failures, Meese Makes a Mark," 7-13, Kurtz offers a tentative evaluation of where Meese's "legacy" is going, concentrating on the failures of course, but not bad at all. In "Congress Is A Convenient Place to Stockpile Campaign Aides," 7-13, he gets his teeth into the incredible abuse of congressional payrolls for political staffs and does a great service. Anyone who has tried to get into, no less work or live in, New York City lately, will appreciate "Worming One's Way Back Into the Big Apple," 7-13. His "Policy of Hospitalizing N.Y. Homeless Set Back," 11-13, is priceless, simply reporting on a state judge's release of Joyce Brown, the first person hospitalized under Mayor Koch's new policy of taking mentally ill people off the street, because she is "rational, logical, coherent" and, Kurtz writes, "free to return to her life on a hot-air vent on Second Avenue...Brown, a 40-year-old former secretary from New Jersey, had captivated a court hearing at Bellevue with lucid, witty testimony about her life as a 'professional' street person. She said she occasionally tears up money and curses people who try to help her because she resents having dollars tossed at her when she has panhandled enough for the day." And on and on, a classic. *The New York Times* account the same day, top of page one, tells us none of this and is clearly furious with the judge, as is Mayor Koch, for not keeping Brown ensconced in a $600-per-day unit at Bellevue instead of the $7 a day she says is all she needs to panhandle to live.

Langley, Monica. *The Wall Street Journal.* (★)
Washington bureau. A steady reporter who sometimes surprises us with important material, but usually doesn't get beyond the second dimension. Among the surprises, "Freer Finance: U.S. Regulators Move to Let Banks Enter Several New Businesses," 12-29-86, the big banks threatening to drop their charters in order to force regulators to ease. We also liked "Rostenkowski Leans Toward Increasing Tax on Gasoline," 3-23, a good picture of Rosty's unenthusiasm about weighty tax proposals. Her coverage of the trade issue on Capitol Hill seemed uniformly light, hitting only the high spots. "W.Va. Senators Hold Divergent Views of U.S. Trade Problem," 3-23, a front-page leader on Jay Rockefeller and Bob Byrd, free trader and protectionist, is personality fluff. "Gephardt, Taking Aim at The White House, Pushes a Trade Measure That Has Divided His Own Party," 4-29, reviews the Gephardt amendment, quotes a few Democrats who oppose it, but really says very little new. We thought we'd finally get a definitive analysis of the trade bill's prospects in "Trade Bill Is Loaded With Import Curbs Aiding Local Interests," 11-12, another column 6 leader, but there is only anecdotal material on lamb, sugar and steel mesh interests — three little pieces of a vast puzzle, with no attempt to assess the power of the combined interests to override a veto if one is forthcoming. This year, Langley will cover the media as it covers politics and the presidential campaigns.

Lardner, George. *The Washington Post.* (★ ½)
A watchdog for fraud in government, Lardner has been trained in the snoop school of journalism and often hits paydirt if he digs enough. "Pinochet Linked to Murder Cover-Up," 2-5, was a comprehensive look at the 1976 Letelier murder in Washington that evidently was plotted and then covered up by Chile's Pinochet government, intriguing, nice detail and organization. "Large Amounts of Air Force Material Unaccounted for, GAO Chief Says," 2-19, detailed the latest chapter in the $640 hammer saga, a supported and documented account of hearings on government financial management (or mismanagement) — poor John Glenn is "incredulous." Sinking his teeth into the Iran-Contra affair, Lardner reported the goings-on with glee in "Investigators Trip Over Each Other, Independent Counsel's Client Probed," 2-21; "North Given Gift of Home Security: A $2000 Gate," 3-17; an other boondoggle in "Donovan Fraud Case Goes to Jury, Defendant Masselli in Hospital Gown," 5-21; "Hill Unit

Backs Special Counsel Bill," 6-23; and "Renewal of Special Counsel Law Advances," 11-21, on the strengthening of a bill to make the independent counsel law permanent; "Wedtech Aid Offered 'Gift,' Hill Told," 9-30, on the Wedtech quagmire. His happiness at the perfidy of government seems to be a hindrance in his writing.

Lemann, Nicholas. *The Atlantic.* **(NR)**
Not enough material this year from *The Atlantic*'s national correspondent to warrant a rating, but the two pieces we saw were worth noting. "Fake Masks," November, on African masks and ritual objets d'art; and "Magnetic Attraction," which appeared in *The New Republic*, 4-13, on the failure of the Magnet School: "What kept Magnet Schools from ending up with a lot of other attractive ideas in the graveyard of educational vogues was that they acquired powerful allies: federal judges. As the great migration of blacks to the cities drew to a close, it became clear that the overwhelming problem of urban public schools over the next generation was going to be racial integration. Magnet schools offered a way to integrate school systems without busing. The glamour of a high school of the performing arts or the health professions would keep white students from defecting to private, parochial or suburban schools; meanwhile, through the use of racial quotas, the magnet schools could be racially balanced."

Low, Charlotte. *Insight.* (★ ★ ★)
Law reporter, who turns dry briefs and issues into meaty meals. "A Philosopher of Restraint for a Once Activist Court," 7-20, was *the* article on Robert Bork, outlining his credentials and philosophy without all the confusion or monotony of pure recitation. In a post-Bork follow-up, "Lobbyists Hustle the High Court," 11-16, Low details the tactics of the anti-Bork factions, all of which were "good, legitimate politics," quoth Senator Gordon Humphrey (R-NH) and Bork supporter. "The Pro-Life Movement In Disarray," in *The American Spectator*, 10-87, gave us fine detail on the splintering of pro-life forces. Also, she had two terrific cover stories, "The Law and the Land," 9-28, on property rights, and "Quotas: A New Equation for Equality," 4-27, on the ever-changing face of affirmative action, rounded out an impressive year.

Mackenzie, Richard. *Insight.* (★ ★ ½)
One of the most versatile reporters at the weekly, Mackenzie goes from the Middle East to Congress to Australia and back again, with ease and panache. "The Hearing of Hyde Begun Anew," 8-31, was vivid on Rep. Hyde and his battle against federally-funded abortions, and "The 'Deep North's' Premier Unabashedly on the Hustings," 5-25, equally rich, on Sir Johannes Bjelke-Petersen: "If nothing else, Sir Joh is good for a quote. So good, in fact, that several books of his disjointed sayings have been published in paperback." He ventures into the world of 007 in "The Case of a Colonel with Camera," 4-13, delving into Middle East intrigue, complete with the abrupt booting of military attaches from embassies and shootings of liasion officers under mysterious circumstances. Mackenzie gives a gentler touch to "When It All Comes Tumbling Down," 3-30, on the passing of an era in Texas: the death of the Texas billionaire as a breed because of collapsed oil prices. He was too light in cover "Egypt: The Writing Is On the Wall," 1-12 cover, just skimming the top of the economy and going barely a hair deeper on the spread of Islamic fundamentalism.

Madison, Christopher. *National Journal.* (★ ½)
New to the congressional foreign policy beat in '87, Madison, a thoughtful reporter who doesn't miss many tricks, just about has his feet on the ground. His reports on the Iran-Contra hearings were better than most. In "Was Von Clauswitz a Contra, Too?" 5-30, he observes only two weeks after they started the Iranscam hearings, that they were generating support for the contras. "Goodbye Contras?" 6-27, is a fine essay on congressional zigs and zags on foreign policy, including the Persian Gulf, Central America and trade and arms control. In "North Attacks a Hill Held by the Enemy," 7-11, we get Ollie's covert operation defense, told in a "yeah, yeah, yeah, sure," fashion. He's better with "Did Panels Lose a Battle — Or a War?" 7-18, an accurate portrayal of North's week. In "Another Hero," 7-25, he does a puffy, deserved

profile of Rep. Lee Hamilton (D-IN), House chairman of the hearings, the only place we saw his impressive performance so noted.

Magnuson, Ed. *Time.* (½ ★)
Senior writer dealing with State Department and national security issues. He writes well, which moves his material along, but with more of an editorial tone than we can stomach in news columns. Just so with his coverage of the Iran-Contra affair. "The 'Fall Guy' Fights Back," a 7-20 cover story, reported by Michael Duffy, Hays Gorey and Barrett Seaman, was outrageous, snide and manipulative. "An Edge of Anger," 8-3, reported by Hays Gorey, gave us George Shultz the martyr bit, with a few qualifiers, "some presidential aides thought Shultz had been self-serving," but really just wanting us to see George as the good fellow they know he is. Better earlier in the year with "Soviets in San Diego?" 3-23, reported by Bruce van Voorst, reporting on on-site inspection plans for deployed missiles. "Crawling with Bugs," 4-20, reported by James O. Jackson, Bruce van Voorst, gave us more balanced coverage of the infested embassy in Moscow, with good coverage of both sides of the Marine scandal, concluding the "key issue...[is] not whether the Soviets had broken some unwritten rule of civilized snooping or what American agents had done to them. A more relevant question was just why American Marines and State Department officials had permitted the Soviets to compromise U.S. security so thoroughly — and so easily."

Mansfield, Stephanie. *The Washington Post.* (★ ★ ★ ½)
Down a half-star from her '86 rating, we felt that Stephanie didn't quite achieve the same pinnacle as last year. Her profiles are still tremendous, one, "Arianna's Grand Arrival," 2-17, is a ten best selection, but they often left us with a sense that the whole person wasn't quite there, maybe because she's been relegated at times to the Rona Barrett beat. For example, "Diane Keaton, Up From 'Heaven,'" 4-22, is just a quickie portrait: "She is amazingly anonymous, able to shop and eat and walk without interruption," and gets to go walking with Kevin Costner of "No Way Out" and "The Untouchables," producing a light "Costner in the Wry," 8-14, that somehow fell short of her potential. "A Good Look: Shear Excitement For The Hearings," 7-13, was a sweet, funny idea, making over the Iran-Contra supporting players for Hollywood, but it didn't seem fully developed although it did contain the best description seen *ever* of Arthur Liman's hair "which is growing more fettucine-like every day." She's back to her old form in "Dead Men Tell Tales," 11-8, about Pulitzer Prize-winning police reporter Edna Buchanan of *The Miami Herald*: "There's a breathless urgency to her, as if she's on some perpetual deadline. 'I want to know what the heck happened. I hate secrets. Besides,' she says, further explaining her obsession, 'Corpses are a heck of a lot easier to get *along* with.'" Stephanie then explores Buchanan's style of journalism, evidently equally breathless: "Her sentences are short. Pithy. Like a police report. The 'Dragnet' school of journalism." Take her off the Hollywood beat and back into the real world!!

Martin, Richard. *Insight.* (★ ★ ★)
Almost every bit as thorough as in '86, Martin is not afraid of hot topics. "Caught Looking for His Pot of Gold," 8-10, offered a bizarre tale of conspiracy and sting operations involving former Philippine President Marcos, raising questions about both Marcos' intentions and the U.S. handling of the deposed dictator, with a great lead: "By now, the U.S. government undoubtedly wishes Ferdinand Marcos would take up a nice, safe hobby like golf rather than toy with the idea of making a triumphant return to Manila." Hard-hitting in "A Fragile Democracy Held Hostage," 3-9, on Ecuador's political troubles, and "France's Headache in South Pacific," 2-16, about French isolationism in the region. A frothy change of pace in "Adventurers Face Shortage of Firsts," 5-11, on the few things one can do for the first time, where no man has gone before. But he misfired badly in "Brazil: Where Tomorrow Never Comes," a 4-part cover, 8-17, which could have been one of the most important cover stories of the year for the magazine, given the intense interest in the LDC debt issue and the time Martin spent there. Yes, there was plenty of political and economic background, but was

disappointing on knowledgeable quotes and economic analysis and Martin ended up pushing the usual hoary nostrums of the World Bank and State Department, privitization and land reform, with little or no support.

Massing, Michael. Freelance. (★ ★ ½)
An up-and-coming bright star on the left-liberal side, Massing was dazzling in "Trotsky's Orphans," *TNR*, 6-22. He gives a concise education on the splintering of the old socialists and the emergence of neocons and social democrats. We suspect that Mangosuthu Buthelezi really isn't his cup of tea, but he was balanced in his profile and interview in "The Chief," *TNYRB*, 2-12, giving us the best vantage for learning how and what the Zulu leader thinks. We know his biases and see them openly expressed in "While Haiti Burns," *TNR*, 11-16, where he advises the Democratic Party's National Democratic Institute for International Affairs on an agenda for its workshops in Haiti: "Land for the peasants...mobilizing the masses...general strikes...soak the rich," etc. But he assembles the evidence to show how myopic was the view that the army wouldn't clash with efforts to begin the process of democratization there, digging far deeper below the surface than anyone else. A much broader report, "Hatred in Haiti," *TNYRB*, 12-3, examines the anti-Americanism spreading there as a consequence of that myopia.

Mathews, Jay. *The Washington Post.* West Coast. (★ ½)
We applauded Mathews last year with two stars for his admirably crisp news reports and fast-flowing features, never padded. So now we notice padding, at least now and then. In "IQ Tests Restricted by Race," 7-6, he has all sides fairly represented and varying perspectives described on a touchy subject. But he's alternatively wordy and spare, good quotes but thinly spread through the lengthy piece, which could have had solid impact if it had been written sharply after stating the overall dilemma up front. In "Highway Robbery In California," 7-26, he's the fellow we remembered, wall-to-wall information on the politics of growing pains as traffic congestion in Orange County leads to pressure for toll roads. "California Veto a Blow to Bi-Lingual Education," 8-2, is a balanced explanation of Gov. Deukmajian's veto and the reasoning of educators pro and con. There's good, no-nonsense reporting here, explaining the reasoning of educators, Secretary Bennett, and others who discourage bilingual in favor of English immersion. "Yuletide Treasure Thrives Despite Northwest's Dry Spell," 11-8, tells in the first few paragraphs about how, luckily, 10 million Christmas trees won't be affected by the drought, followed by 20 graphs of padding, taking up half of page three. Maybe it just depends on the editor of the day.

May, Clifford D. *The New York Times.* (★ ½)
A utility infielder who can play almost any base, with impressive credentials as a science writer, foreign correspondent and political reporter. Assigned to track the Kemp campaign, he was in Corpus Christi for "Kemp Lone Republican at Hispanic Conference," 6-27, a perceptive piece, given the relative absence of Hispanics in the early primary states. Then, 6-29, he's reporting from London as Angola frees a U.S. pilot in a "gesture" to the U.S. "Kemp's '88 Strategy Focuses on Iowa," notes Kemp's fund-raising strains, his "run for Iowa state office approach," and his strategy of seeking a respectable third place finish. Then to Central America, as "Kemp, In Honduras, Assails Latin Peace Plan," 9-9, with President Jose Azcona Hoyo telling Kemp he didn't believe Congress needed to end contra aid to comply with the plan, continuing aid until Nicaragua fulfills its pledge to democratize. Elsewhere, "Mincing No Words, Or Pictures, On Birth Control," 7-29, a solid account of Planned Parenthood's campaign against the administration's anti-abortion policy for foreign aid. "Where the Opposition Makes War on Bork," 9-25, a useful, impartial feature on the folks in the Senate Judiciary war room.

McDowell, Edwin. *The New York Times.* (NR)
We follow McDowell with respect on the New York cultural scene and book beat, but he rarely edges into public policy. We can't resist citing "'His Eminence and Hizzoner' to Write a Book," 8-23, as NYC Mayor Ed Koch and Cardinal O'Connor plan a joint book on social issues.

"Mr. Koch said the book would 'tell it like it is,' but is not gonna be a 'kissy-huggy book.' His co-author, wincing exaggeratedly, quipped, 'I can see the headline now on this story: No Kissy-Huggy Book.'"

McLeod, Don. *Insight.* (★ ★)
McLeod had one of the 10 best political pieces for 1987, his definitive cover portrait "George Bush, Front Runner," 10-19, but the remainder of the year was mixed. He was comprehensive in "Mayors Work for a Common Cause," 8-10, on the joining of forces by mayors across the country in order to put federal aid on the agenda for '88. A strong cover story of, "Everybody Comes to Iowa," 7-27, a colorful picture of the Dems and the Iowa caucuses: "The object is to do 'well,' whatever that means." But "The 'Doc' Is Out, Is Democracy In?" 4-6, a Haiti report, was spongy and slow, a chance for solid stuff blown. He misses completely in "A Meeting of the Parties: Toward a Compromise Agenda," 3-23, pinning conservative hopes on Howard Baker, when it is Baker who engineered the moderate shift in the agenda.

Moffett, George D., III. *The Christian Science Monitor.* (★)
Okay in his reporting of foreign affairs, sometimes giving us an angle not seen elsewhere. "US Leery of Soviet-Afghan Peace Flurry," 1-16, was a nice summary of the trials and tribulations of a possible peace in Afghanistan. "Measure In Congress Would Pressure Romania On Human Rights," 5-20, a report on a measure restricting trade to Romania because of human rights abuses and an alleged Palestinian training ground, was not specific on abuses or on lobbyists and Congressmen who wrote and supported the bill. Teamed with Warren Richey in Amman, Jordan, "Arab Leaders Seek Elusive Unity Against Iran in First Summit on Gulf," 11-6, was an organized, efficient treatment of the summit.

Morgan, Dan. *The Washington Post.* (NR)
Paired with Walter Pincus for much of the Iran-Contra coverage, Morgan is an old hand, bringing Pincus up to snuff. He's worth noting separately for "Falwell, Bakker and the Fundamentals," 3-29, a "10 Best" selection on evangelicals, and "The Iran-Contra Report: Iran Report Accuses Administration 'Disdain for Law,'" 11-19, which was tough, but fair, on the release of *the* report.

Noah, Timothy. *Newsweek.* (★)
Generally light and tepid within the confines of the *Newsweek* Washington bureau, we found we liked Noah better when we saw him elsewhere. "War Powers Inaction," *TNR*, 7-6, was a strong slam-dunk of the War Powers Act and Congressional use and misuse, with some splendid lines: "Thus the true function of the War Powers Act: it allows jittery members of Congress to avoid responsibility for risky military actions, while at the same time avoiding responsibility for the consequences of *not* taking action" and "the favorite war power of Congress is the power to complain that it isn't being consulted." His material for the weekly he works for is a tad too breezy. "Gore Chic," 2-16, reads like paid advertisement for Senator Gore, 38: "Will Gore chic blossom into a Gore presidential bid? Gore's answer is typically shrewd, gracious and measured: 'I sincerely believe that the best approach is to concentrate fully and completely on the responsibilities at hand and let the future take care of itself.'" "Corporate Watchdog," 4-20, was better, an okay profile of Rep. John Dingell, not as sycophantic. "The Business Ethics Debate," 5-25, was just silly: a muddled, confusing, poorly organized piece on ethics courses, where are they required? Should they be? "Rather than examining past ethical dilemmas or attempting to guess what scandals may lie ahead, ethics teachers would do better to get students into the habit of seeing an ethical dimension to every business situation they come across." "A Warning For Workers," 8-24, was short, deciding on the obvious: the chances of buyouts of troubled companies are pretty slim if they will not cooperate by opening their books.

MediaGuide

Nordheimer, Jon. *The New York Times.* (★ ★ ½)
Miami bureau. Consistently well-written, thorough news reports and features from the Southeast that Nordheimer lifts above the parochial. The headline is a bit misleading on "Puerto Rico's Economy Finally on Upswing," 1-28, with emphasis on the key economic issues facing Gov. Raphael Hernandez Colon. He's under pressure to bring down tax rates, with unemployment still at 17%; useful, fresh information and analysis we found to be accurate. "Bacardi's Glass is Half Empty," 2-15, is a superb business feature. We learn a great deal about the business in a single article, including changing tastes, lifestyles and demographics. In "Nicaraguan Exiles Find a Place in the Sun: Miami," 7-29, we get a great quote in an old story unfolding on the streets of Miami: "Miami is a paradise for us. You can come here with one suitcase, sleep on the floor and start reaching up for the sky the next day." Very nice, too, with "U.S. Officials Criticized on Efforts to Curb AIDS Among Minorities," 8-10, scathing against the lumbering bureaucracy, insightful on challenges facing minority leaders in combatting AIDS and social ills in tandem. He takes a roving photographer kind of look at viewpoints in Arcadia, Fla., on the Ray children, infected with AIDS, "To Neighbors of Shunned Family, AIDS Fear Outweighs Sympathy," 8-31. His bias shows, but the piece is powerful, nevertheless.

O'Leary, Jeremiah. *The Washington Times.* (★ ½)
A solid year from one of the patriarchs of the Washington press corps. In "Carlucci to Size Up Contra Prospects," 1-29, he gave us some details on Reagan's NSC message to Congress, also reporting Carlucci's denial of remarks attributed to him that the contras couldn't win. A well-done interview piece with Howard Baker revealed some of Baker's style, managing things "more with a velvet glove than an iron fist," in "Amiable Baker Uses Velvet Glove to Guard Access to the President," 5-21. He's concise and no nonsense in "Reagan Bars Imports From Iran, Limits Exports," 10-27, with facts and figures throughout. Lighter in "Reagan's Spirit Raised by Reception in Missouri," 3-27; we know he was there because what we get is verbatim comments of Reagan to the MO show-me schoolchildren. This is typical, though, of what we too often get from O'Leary: recycled Presidential quotes, nice sometimes because he puts them into some sort of context, but mostly it's just quips strung together by connecting sentences, with no attempt to analyze.

O'Rourke, P.J. Freelance. (NR)
Appearing sporadically in *The American Spectator* and *The New Republic*, we count P.J. as notable for his belly-laugh quotient, even though we only saw two pieces by him in the mainstream press. In August's *TAS*, he had the last laugh on Jimmy and Rosalynn Carter in a scathing review of their book *Everything To Gain*, running rings around them: "So now what are we going to do with him, him and his nitwit wife? We can't go on letting them write books. It's too embarrassing. This is an industrialized, Western nation. We can't have things like this in our bookstores." In *TNR*, 11-2, O'Rourke does a breathless number on the Age of Aquarius, beginning: "Everything. You name it and I believed it. I believed love was all you need...I believed Mao was cute...I believed Yoko Ono was an artist. I believed Bob Dylan was a musician...I believed the I Ching said to cut classes and take over the dean's office. I believed wearing my hair long would end poverty and injustice...With the exception of anything my parents said, I believed everything," going on to give a hilarious account of one particular segment of his own '60s experience. Cosmic, man.

Ostling, Richard. *Time.* (★ ★)
Covering all kinds of religion, Ostling is knowledgeable, never preachy. "Israel's New Conversion Crisis," (reported by Martin Levin) 1-19, sensitively outlined the agonizing arguments in Israel prompted by the emigration of an American convert and her desire for citizenship, asking when is a Jew not a Jew? "Is It Wrong to Cut Off Feeding?" 2-23, examined the Catholic debate in the removal of feeding tubes from comatose or terminal patients. "Technology and the Womb," (reported by Cathy Booth, Michael P. Harris) 3-23, was a comprehensive look at the content of and reaction to the Catholic issuance of guidelines of

294

methods of conception. His coverage of the Televangelist flap in "TV's Holy Row" (reported by Barbara Dolan, B. Russell Leavitt, and Charlotte and Michael Riley) 4-6, and "Enterprising Evangelism" (reported by Barbara Dolan and Michael Riley) 8-3, held nothing back, but was not unduly unkind or nasty, no mean feat considering some of the information revealed. A pair of splendid articles on Pope John Paul: "John Paul's Fiesty Flock," (reported by Sam Allis, Barbara Dolan, and Michael Riley) 9-7, a comprehensive look at Catholic dissent in the U.S.; "John Paul Draws The Line," (with Sam Allis and James Willworth) 9-28, presented reality while describing surface things like small crowds and "wooden" deliveries and the physical energy of the man who is Pope, deeper concerns of American Catholics are pointed out. These people are required to make adjustments to the changing world which don't match up with the unchanging authority from Rome.

Otten, Alan. *The Wall Street Journal.* (★ ½)
A *WSJ* veteran in the Washington bureau, once the paper's top political reporter, bureau chief and all, now preoccupied with life and death issues. "Birth Dearth: Some Thinkers Expect Population to Drop And Trouble to Result," 6-18, "Like some modern Paul Revere, Ben J. Wattenberg is about to get on his horse and gallop across the country warning, 'The birth dearth is coming. The birth dearth is coming.'" An offbeat P.1 demographic story with interesting detail, but we wondered why Otten doesn't connect it to the pro-life movement. In a pro and con piece on "Debate Rages Over AIDS-Test Policy," 6-18, Otten reports the negative (Gerald F. Seib reports the pro-test side). He travels to Amsterdam for a provocative piece, "In the Netherlands, The Very Ill Have Option of Euthanasia," 8-21, finding it practiced "voluntarily." That is, "Officially illegal but nonetheless countenanced under strict conditions, it accounts for anywhere from 1,000 to 7,000 deaths a year. The Netherlands is pioneering in an area that in the coming decade is likely to be a focus of medical, legal, ethical — and intensely emotional — debate in many industrialized countries."

Pear, Robert. *The New York Times.* (★ ★)
Washington bureau general assignment with wide-ranging capabilities but special expertise on health/welfare issues. Another prolific year, but not as many splashes as we counted in '86. He surprised us with his easy handling of "Plan Offered for Vast Atom Smasher," 1-19, a heavy piece on a $6 billion, 52 mile around subatomic particle accelerator, but we didn't quite know how serious to take it. His "Reagan Expected to Back Proposal on Major Illness," 2-10, gets the front page lead, an excellent summary and news account of a controversial issue, catastrophic insurance. "U.S. to Pursue Proposal to Bar Aliens With AIDS," 3-27, informs on an unusual form of protectionist legislation while a few other countries are throwing out foreigners with the disease. We had problems, though, with "Poverty Rate Dips As The Median Family Income Rises," 7-31, quoting a Census Bureau official who says income inequality is greater now, but Pear says the administration denies its policies contributed to this while Democrats say they did, thus the census report has vast political implications. The census official mentions as factors contributing to "inequality": increase in female-headed households, increase in two-income married couples, large numbers of baby boomers entering the labor force, etc. The material could have been handled better.

Peirce, Neil R. *National Journal.* (★)
A specialist in state and local government, Peirce's reporting has always been useful in providing snapshots of what's going on around the statehouses and courthouses. His framework is almost entirely cultural, with sparse attention to how national, state and local economic policies mesh to produce different regional results. "Tide's Up, Newark's Down," 8-15, earns our favor simply by giving a long look at Newark, N.J. (Where is *The New York Times*?) But the picture is muddled. He quotes an urban professor, "A rising tide lifts all boats except the scrapwood like Newark," but there's enough detail that hints Newark is being lifted, too. He should talk to more shopkeepers and fewer social workers. In "Rural Education That Stifles American Youth," 9-12, he gives us a characteristically informative, uncharacteristically lively report

on his subject. We noted a report on "Public Pension Funds With 1980s Know-How," 6-6, with approval.

Perry, James M. *The Wall Street Journal.* (★ ½)
A veteran political writer pulled back from the London bureau in midyear to help staff the presidential campaign. His strength is his writing, always entertaining, a practiced cynical amusement. His back-page profile of Bob Dole, 9-25, had nothing new, but some wry comments: "He doesn't care for people who grew up with inherited wealth (Vice President George Bush, for example) or people with theories who write books (Jack Kemp, especially)." His piece on "Jesse Jackson's Campaign...Is Taken Very Seriously This Time," 10-8, could have been among the best political pieces of the year, capturing the sense of "mission" in the campaign, but Perry's cynicism peeps through, and we see he really doesn't take Jackson seriously at all and expects something to come up to ditch this dwarf. Some of his best work from London early in the year also had this edge. "British Voters Distrust Reagan," 6-3, a front-page report on a *WSJ* panel of 32 Brits talking about RR, amuses, "I find it quite astonishing that a B-grade actor could become President," says one. "I don't think people like Reagan should be considered for that job," says another. "He comes across like a dimwit," yet another. But this is froth dressed up to seem like a serious piece on the British elections and run on P.1. But he is a pro, "Controversial as Ever, Mrs. Thatcher Begins Drive for Third Term," 5-12, is a respectable curtain raiser, closing with a nutshell quote from a professor: "She hasn't been dealt a very good hand, but she's a skilled player and the rest of the people around the table are such poor players they allow her to win."

Petzinger, Thomas Jr. *The Wall Street Journal.* (NR)
One of the most talked-about *WSJ* stories of the year was Petzinger's front-pager, "Quality of Justice: Texaco Case Spotlights Questions of Integrity Of the Courts in Texas," 11-4, with Caleb Solomon. The team divulged that in Texas, one of nine states where Supreme Court justices are still elected through partisan campaigning, "Lawyers representing Pennzoil contributed, from 1984 to early this year, more than $355,000 to the nine Supreme Court justices sitting today, according to a tally by this newspaper. One of those lawyers for Pennzoil had contributed $10,000 to the lower-court judge who later presided at the start of the state-court trial in Houston...the shadow that big-money politics has cast over the entire state judiciary in Texas has, in the minds of many, tainted Pennzoil's unbroken string of victories in the Texas state courts." Pennzoil lashed back with newspaper ads in 35 cities, complaining the *Journal* rejected an ad it wanted to place disputing the story. The *Journal* came back with an editorial, "Texas Trials and Tribulations," 11-27, asserting its position and raking over the story again. It was indeed a sensational and troubling report that must lead to reforms in Texas if major corporations are going to feel comfortable doing business in the state. But we were astonished that no other newspaper had this story a year earlier. The Texas press, as a unit, should stand in the corner under a tall pointy hat.

Pichirallo, Joe. *The Washington Post.* (½ ★)
Iran-Contra. It seems that everyone except the sportswriters on the *Post* filed something on the scandal in the vain hope of retrieving past glories. This time, the stuff generally fell flat, as *The New York Times* had better "concept" pieces and *The Washington Times* featured more innovative daily news items. Newcomer Pichirallo focused exclusively on the story, with the result being occasionally humorous pegs such as "Contras' Small Cut of Iran Funds Puzzles Aspin," 7-21, or "Abrams Chastised by Panel Members," a real eye-opener. He also was on shaky ground by playing up Christic Institute, a pro-Sandinista church group, whose accusations about contra drug smuggling were given too much credibility in 6-29 story on Gen. Secord. He co-authored a 9-22 piece on a contra critic who was deemed a "terrorist threat" by the FBI, which, after one reads the article, doesn't seem too farfetched. Contributed to "North Hoped to Sway '86 Election, Hill Told," 6-5, a story about Ollie's immunity that had nothing to do with the midterm elections. Now that the scandal mongering has died down, we wonder

what Pichirallo will do next. Maybe some real grown-up reporting, with corroboration and all that stuff.

Platt, Adam. *Insight*. **(NR)**
A three-star foreign correspondent in the *1987 MediaGuide*, Platt spent most of '87 on leave, assisting with the memoirs of Joseph Alsop. His one major contribution to the magazine is worth noting, the three-part cover story on "The New Democracies of Central America," 5-18, a reconnaissance of El Salvador, Guatemala and Nicaragua, a fair effort worth a look for a general feel for what's going on. We hoped he'd give us more on the mechanics of government in the region, but there's almost none of that. A brief mention, for example, of the Salvador business community going on strike when President Duarte imposed an "austerity tax," thus losing what popularity he had, but that's it. Why the tax, what kind, what does the U.S. embassy think about Duarte's economic management, are these measures debated in the assembly, what is the composition of the budget, spending, revenues, and export/import policies? All these questions bear on the economic health of the region and we'd like to hear about them, but got very little in this presentation.

Press, Aric. *Newsweek*. **(★)**
Competent reporting, but often the snideness that seems to permeate the offices of *Newsweek* comes out. In "The Charge: AIDS Assault," (with Lynda Wright) 6-22, on the legality of whether homosexual sex in the army that may or may not be construed as assault, since one of the partners had AIDS, and knew it: it's okay when dealing with what might be the beginning of an onslaught of prosecutions involving AIDS transmission, citing cases of NY/Miami prostitutes, ending with *Caveat emptor* — inappropriate — this is not funny. He's not so subtly slanted against North's lawyer Brendan Sullivan for his "ventriloquism" and "hair trigger" while Nield and Liman "performed in an unusual combination of fire and ice" in "I'm Not A Potted Plant," 7-20. Better with a serious and scary "Gridlock On Death Row," 5-4, detailing the grinding halt as the inmates wait in line. We had to give him extra points for this one: he's the writer on a byline with more reporters listed than attended Reagan's press conferences for his tenure. His best for 1987: "The Grilling Of Judge Bork," (with Ann McDaniel) 7-28, a very balanced, fair, accurate account of Bork's confirmation proceedings to date.

Price, Joyce. *The Washington Times*. **(★ ½)**
Responsible for the *Times*' coverage of AIDS, Price did some good work here, steady, competent reporting, often hitting an angle or quote we missed elsewhere. "AIDS Experts Fear Epidemic Among Teens," 3-11, was the first we saw on this, months before Jane Gross at the other *Times* took a close-up look: the possibility and logic (time of experimentation with sex and drugs) of its spread among teens. Price followed up the story with an enterprising "Students Haven't Changed Behavior Despite AIDS Fear," 9-3, broadening her base in an informal survey of local college students, who are still carrying on like college students. She was also early on debunking the heterosexual epidemic in a 3-5/6 series, "AIDS Among Heterosexuals," getting a bead on the research and on the stats. "Leading AIDS Scientist Sees No Cure in 'Anyone's Lifetime,'" 3-26, gave us frightening words from Dr. Gallo, the U.S. scientist who isolated the virus. "Researchers Suggest 'Manhattan Project' To Fight AIDS Virus," 9-2, noted the call for better coordination on AIDS research, some recommending more for treatment than for a vaccine. Not so hot with "Area Volunteers May Be Used in First Test of AIDS Vaccine," 3-23, the head raising false expectations of a vaccine, the limitations of which we don't find until the sixth graph.

Randolph, Eleanor. *The Washington Post*. **(★ ★)**
Covering the news media for the *Post*, print and TV, Randolph provides a steady flow of interesting media gossip, never bratty, and can do the big story too. Her 1986 series on the *NYT*, 1-7 to 1-9-86 was classic. "Network News Confronts Era of Limits," 2-9, is a complete look at the struggles and evolution of the network news broadcasts, with changes of tone and

technology, well done. "Bitter NBC Strike Reflects Hard Times at Networks," 8-9, is a timely update on GE playing hardball, with 700 people filling 3500 jobs since June 29. Her rundown is the best we saw on how Senator Biden's problems in lifting a Neil Kinnock speech surfaced in the *NYT*, "Routine Exchange...Out of Control for Dukakis Aides," 10-3. Her Sunday "Outlook" lead, "How Newshounds Blew The Iran-Contra Story," 11-15, excellent in rubbing their noses in the scoop by "'that rag in Beirut,' as President Reagan called the Lebanese weekly Ash Shiraa." Her profile of "William Safire, Right to the Core," 8-24, was among our Randolph favorites in '87, thorough and well-tuned on the *Times* columnist, on the publication of his epic novel *Freedom*. She starts with "William Safire, his voice uncommonly soft for a newspaper columnist..." And when she finishes we know him. "In fact, what has happened to Safire in some ways argues against the old code that only a lifetime journalist can be a good journalist. The years in public relations and the White House seem to have given him an ear for sour notes on both sides — among those in power in government and those in power in the press." Generous.

Reid, T.R. *The Washington Post.* (★ ½)
Political reporter. Reid handles his spot assignments professionally, producing good profiles and sketches now and then. "Candidates of All Stripes Urge Curbs on Defense Budget," 8-3, is a good round-up, but by not mentioning candidates Bush or Kemp, the story is weakened a bit. His "Schroeder Talking Tough," 8-4, gives us a solid line on Rep. Pat Schroeder having a hard time raising money or hiring staff, which suggests she won't run, and was on target.

Rich, Spencer. *The Washington Post.* (★)
A veteran utility reporter around the federal establishment, getting on angles now and then. We noted especially "Social Security Lobby Group Is Said to Mislead Aged," 3-11, reporting on a House Ways & Means hearing, with witnesses accusing James Roosevelt, chairman of the National Committee to Preserve Social Security, of terrifying the elderly with a direct mail fund campaign warning of Social Security's possible collapse. Well done. His "Census Bureau Looks to 1990 As Lawsuits Over 1980 Linger," 8-19, gives us interesting early detail on census planning.

Ricklefs, Roger. *The Wall Street Journal.* (★ ★)
New York. A *Journal* veteran back from a stint in the Paris bureau, Ricklefs was most impressive with his AIDS coverage. "Plague Years: AIDS Has Been Cruel to Greenwich Village and Its Homosexuals," 3-13, paired with Ellen Graham, a requiem for a once thriving New York neighborhood, was sad and telling: "A young job applicant frets about having told a prospective employer that he has AIDS. He gets the job. It turns out the employer has AIDS, too." "Expert Advice: Out of a Crisis A Legal Specialty Emerges," 10-7, was concise on the legal profession's reaction to AIDS, and a companion piece, equally well-done, "AIDS Cases Prompt a Host of Lawsuits." His best for the year was the front-page leader, "Wiped Out: AIDS Victims Find That a Death Sentence Leads First to Poverty," 8-5, a shattering realization of the cost of the virus in human terms, not just the bare statistics. Ricklefs also did a range of frothy feature stories that we weren't thrilled with, as "What a Darling Baby! Let's Push Rewind and See Her Again," 1-24, on video children and pets for those who don't otherwise have the time or the patience, and "Sentenced to the Jury Room," 6-5, a bubbly look at jury duty. "Personal Taxes: Planning for '87," 2-27, was much better, more serious, and gave us some good angles, and "The Bowery Today: A Skid Row Area Invaded by Yuppies," 11-13, gave us an accurate picture of the gentrification of the Bowery.

Roberts, Steven. *The New York Times.* (★ ★ ½)
Congressional correspondent in '86, the White House in '87 for a respectable year. His most important story, from the Western White House, was "Reagan's Advisers See Shift in Focus," 8-23, a front-pager that signaled Howard Baker, Jr.'s decision to compromise with Congress instead of drawing lines; the stock market hit its peak two days later. "Baker is Finding His

Niche, as a Counselor-Compromiser," 3-17, is revealing, especially the last line: "'The real question,' said an aide to Senate Democratic leaders, 'is whether Baker can get the President to compromise.'" He doesn't say "on taxes." Another revealing comment later in the year, in "Baker Seems to Be Vindicated," 11-12: "From the day he took his current job last February, Mr. Baker has been quietly preparing the President to abandon his long-standing opposition to new taxes. Almost daily he has nudged the President along by suggesting different kinds of taxes, and then gauging Mr. Reagan's reactions." Less insightful, "Baker Counts the Right — and Influences Policy," 5-31, obligatory puff. Better with "President Admits Error in Rejecting Warnings on Iran," 3-15, seeing RR refusing to admit a fundamental mistake and would "do it again." In "White House Rethinking Its Outlook," 7-12, a remarkable piece, he captures the world passing by RR, noting RR needs the warmth of public acceptance to stay healthy, that he is losing his self-esteem. Moreover, it notes RR's admiration for Lincoln in acting without Congressional support. In "Reagan's Veto Strategy Not Getting Rave Reviews in Congress," 8-3, he sees Democrats wanting to extract retribution for frustrations of the last two years. Roberts is weaker handling the Bork fight, showing less distance than we'd like. In "White House Tries to Combat Idea of Bork Tipping the Court's Balance," 7-9, he goes too far with "Almost overnight the legal darling of the right has been converted into a raging pragmatist."

Rogers, David. *The Wall Street Journal.* (★ ½)
Washington. A political reporter who spent much of the year assigned to the Iran-Contra affair. He produced respectable matter-of-fact coverage, dictated by the smaller news hole allotted to the story by the *WSJ* compared to the other majors. In a front-page curtain raiser to the resumption of the hearings, "The Interrogators: Getting Ready for Col. North," 7-6, Rogers slips in an editorial: "Impeachment isn't in the air, but neither is acquittal. The record of lies and lawlessness in the government is too great, and few any longer believe that the only issue is what Mr. Reagan's aides told him of arms profits diverted to the Contras." Tsk, tsk. But he's generally straight in "Shultz Says Iran Arms Sales Provoked 'Battle Royal' in Reagan Administration," 7-24, citing documents indicating Meese knew more of 1985 arms sales to Iran through Israel than he admitted. "Meese Says 'Pure Accident' Led to Lack of Notes," 7-30, mentions contradictions with North's testimony, a better account than in the *NYT*. While his review of the hearings testimony was solid, "Iran Hearings Show Conflict," 8-3, it does not seem as thorough as the account by Rosenbaum of the *Times* the same day. A wrap-up the following day, "Iran-Contra Hearings End in Rhetoric," 8-4, had a bit more. In "Newly Released Poindexter Testimony Shows White House Obsessed By Secrecy," 9-11, with Andy Paztor, the focus seems misplaced; there's no mention that Poindexter told investigators in May that he never told RR about the diversion of funds.

Romano, Lois. *The Washington Post.* (★ ★ ½)
"Style" section, another of the several distaffers that enliven, Romano having an especially good political feel in her portraits and sketches. Her "Leading the Charge on Bork," 9-15, was a breezy, colorful profile of Ralph Neas, director of the Leadership Council on Civil Rights, a bit controversial, too, as Romano reported that Neas began mobilizing his liberal coalition of special interests against Bork as soon as he heard Justice Powell had resigned, *before* he knew who the nominee would be. The article was cited in a *Wall Street Journal* editorial as proof that the liberals had arranged a "lynching" for any Reagan appointee. Her "The Rankling Puzzle of Pat Caddell," 11-18, was the talk of the town when it appeared, sizzling the aging political wonderboy to a crisp, giving us a sweeping replay of his years on top, and wonderfully malicious, but leaving him the last hopeful word. All we could want in this kind of piece, a 10-best political selection.

Rosenbaum, David. *The New York Times.* (★ ★ ★ ½)
The Washington bureau's lead tax reporter in previous years, Rosenbaum moved to a lead slot on the Iran-Contra investigations and hearings. After a bumpy start we were always glad

to see his byline, appreciating his knack of separating wheat from chaff. At first, though, in "Many in GOP Hoping Reagan Will Apologize," 1-15, is questionable as "some" show up in the lead, others opposing apology show up near the end. In "Senators Charge a Web of Deceit," 1-30, he puts a bad spin on a report asserting RR was primarily interested in swapping arms for hostages, using third hand "evidence": "According to Meese, the President, according to North..." But Rosenbaum quickly settled down to impartiality. "Iran-Contra Pause," 6-10, is very important, a crisp, balanced front-page wrap-up at the end of the first stage of the congressional investigation. Nor is there a spin in "The Iran Contra Thicket," 8-3: "No evidence has been developed to contradict President Reagan's assertion that he did not know." He gives us less to chew on than we expect in "North Popularity Won't Curb Panel," 7-12, but at least interesting questions are raised. In "Data is Issued on Poindexter Showing His Early Testimony," 9-11, we get key information, extremely well assembled. Poindexter in May told congressional staff investigators he had not told RR about his decision to use Irans arms funds for contra aid. "If the staff lawyers had revealed what they knew in May it might have cut the hearings short." And while hearings began May 5, Poindexter's and North's appearances were delayed at the request of Lawrence E. Walsh, the special prosecutor, "to give him time to gather evidence against the two officers."

Russakoff, Dale. *The Washington Post.* (★ ½)
A general assignment reporter who is best at covering people and politics, not so hot when the issues are complex or technical. The *Post* was late in covering superconductivity and finally did a five-parter in June, with Russakoff handling, "U.S. Marshalling Free Market Forces," 5-20, a rather manic-depressive mode of competitive analysis, with a quote, "Superconductivity has become the test case of whether the United States has a technological future" and locates the key problem as the "yawning federal deficit." The piece was valuable in displaying the general jingoism and ignorance of politicos and bureaucrats on technical subjects, summed up through an Energy official explaining a foreign ban to a superconductivity journal: "We're not going to play Uncle Sap." Her two-part series on Robert Bork (with Al Kamen) was about the best we saw on his life and personality. "A Trip Across The Political Spectrum," 7-26, was balanced, respectful, illuminating on Bork's early life, ending with a positive note: "A year later, in 1962, Bork left his $40,000-a- year law partnership and joined the Yale University law faculty for a salary of less than $15,000." Part II, "The Shaping of Robert Bork," 7-27, presents the chronology and philosophical detail of his odyssey from left to libertarian to Alex Bickel and neoconservatism. [See Kamen, Al.]

Saikowski, Charlotte. *The Christian Science Monitor.* (★)
Washington. An economics writer who regularly delves into the mysteries of summitry and arms control, generally to fight the good fight. Typical lead found in 10-28's "Arms control still hinges on 'star wars:'" "President Reagan's top aides helped bring him around on the issue of tax increases. Can they do the same on 'star wars?'" So, taxes are good and SDI is bad, and the President only needs to be brought around. A front-pager "Next on Arms Talks," 9-21, could be a Tass press release, so laden is it with quotes from Soviet military officials and political hacks, leavened with perspective from Brookings softliner John Steinbruner. We saw a slight bright spot with 9-14 story on Sam Nunn, and "White House Looks to Reagan Impact in '88," 9-16, had some useful polling data matched with historical references. She was deft with two November pieces linking the Wall Street jolt and the protectionist specter. In her arms control material, though, the enthusiasm for one side and hectoring of the other are too palpable in the news coverage, inappropriate to journalistic standards of balance and distance.

Sanoff, Alvin P. *U.S.News & World Report.* (★)
Senior editor for social trends, Sanoff's reports are breezy, sometimes eccentric, but usually interesting. "The Way It Is for the Network News," with Deborah Kalb and Michael Kimmelman 3-16, was lightweight in information and organization, but nice on some points

in detail such as the number of crews in Beirut. "The Foul Ball That Shook Baseball's Front Office," 4-20, was competent on the lack of blacks in upper management, and the stink over Al Campanis of the Dodgers' reasoning: "Why are...black people not good swimmers? Because they don't have the buoyancy". Interesting sideline from Ernie Banks who says "friendships, not ability, determine who gets hired." So what's so different about baseball's management? "Who Wrote The First Five Books of the Bible?" 8-24, offered no conclusion on the author of the Pentateuch, but was comprehensive and authoritative on the options. "Hollywood Takes a Gamble on Movies with a Message," 11-16, gave a taste of changing times in Tinseltown, going for the message, not the medium, at least temporarily. Most enjoyable though, are his "Conversation" bylines, with, for example, singer Paul Simon, "A Songwriter's South African Odyssey," 3-2; violinist Yehudi Menuhin, "Music: The Universal Language," 4-13; and author Paul Johnson, "The Age of Media Democracy," 6-22.

Sawyer, Kathy. *The Washington Post.* (★ ★ ½)
Space. The best mass media reporter we see on the space beat, keeping up and generally ahead of the boys. We cited a cluster in August as examples: "U.S. Shuns Commercial Rocket Liability," 8-11, seems expert, assured reporting on complex aerospace-finance-insurance questions. Her "Study Urges Missions to Moon, Mars," 8-18, was worth its P.1 slot, the *NYT* burying its piece the same day. In "White House Accused of Failing to Give NASA Source of Mission," 8-17, provided an excellent survey of the space effort, far less breathless than the *Newsweek* "Lost in Space" cover of 8-17. Sawyer teamed with Michael Isikoff with "The Costly Wait For A Space Station," 3-19, and clearly had the best continuing coverage of the bureaucratic and budget wrangling over the Space Station all year.

Scardino, Albert. *The New York Times.* (NR)
Worth commending for his "Building a Manhattan Empire," 4-18. A 10-best selection this year, we learned of other real estate magnets besides Mr. Trump, the big Olympia & York, or the second buying of Manhattan island, this time fetching considerably more than $24 in trinkets.

Seib, Gerald R. *The Wall Street Journal.* (★ ★ ★)
Washington. "Among the best foreign correspondents in the U.S. press," we noted in the *1987 MediaGuide.* On assignment in Teheran, 1-31, he was arrested and jailed and lived to write about it, "Four Days in Iran Jail Leaves Reporter Seib Baffled as to Reasons," 2-10. In April he was reposted to Washington to assist on the Iran-Contra story. His talent still shows on his old diplomatic beat, but he seems hemmed in by the bureau's teamwork approach to covering breaking news or the bigger picture. While he was still abroad, we noted his superior analytical nuances to the *NYT*'s Roberto Suro, in "Iran's Rafsanjani Courts, Scorns U.S., and Shows His Power Isn't Diminished," 1-29. An earlier "Teheran Days," 1-26, contained interesting vignettes of life in the city to a first-time visitor, normal life but crowded cemeteries. In "Iran Aims to Be Superpower of Gulf," 3-12, we get sharp analysis of Iran's intentions, problems for Israel if Arab vs. Israel becomes Islam vs. Israel. His "Egypt Seeks Easier Terms on Debt With U.S.," 1-19, has Mubarak sounding like he prefers something like debt forgiveness. Great detail on the internal politics of Egypt leading to the 4-6 elections, in "Egyptian Leader Seeks Stronger Mandate," 3-23, with Mubarak the democrat and opponents grumbling over the new election laws, but he doesn't spell out programmatic content. Seib's work in DC was professional, but had a bit less vitality. A timely piece on RR trying the rebound, "Visibly Aged and Hurt by Hearings," 8-12, with Ellen Hume, was better than the headline. And his analytics in "Summit Path," 8-27, seemed much crisper than the *NYT*'s on the same subject. Also timely and useful, his front-page "Risky Strategy," 10-20, with Tim Carrington, the pros and cons of the U.S. strike against the Iranian offshore military platform, and, with Robert S. Greenberger, 11-24, an assessment of RR's legacy on foreign policy. Very informative with "The White Hats of Black Monday," 11-10, the roster of Wall Streeters Howard Baker, Jr. is in touch with, pointedly noting the absence of Paul Volcker.

Shales, Tom. *The Washington Post.* (★ ★ ★)
TV Critic and "Style" writer, Shales is among the most consistently entertaining columnists around, not handling substance as deftly as Corry of the *NYT*, but far breezier. His review of "'Amerika,' the Viewable," 2-15, went against the grain, "Citizens for This and the Committee for That have rushed to denounce it for supposed Cold War mongering...that the mini-series imagines a WWIII fought without nuclear weapons has ticked off some of the peace groups making war on it." His "Roseanne Barr: Kvetch as Kvetch Can," 3-7, gives great profile, quoting Barr: "Feminists are a bunch of white ladies in limousines who give each other awards." In "The High Drama Of a Duel," 7-8, he sees immediately that Ollie North rolled the Iran-Contra committee, no ifs, ands or buts. "He'd Rather Be Rather," 8-12, reports on CBS, worried about being No. 3 on the evening news, trying to get Dan to be laid back, but he doesn't like the Valium result. Why No. 3? Shales ponders in an excellent report. "Score One For Donohue," 11-6, goes on and on about the 20 years of Phil Donohue, but we read on like eating peanuts, getting to a nutty close: "For now, he's the proverbial pig in slop. 'I can't can't imagine living in a time when there are more issues than there are today,' Phil exults. No rest for the blabby. Is the caller there?"

Shapiro, Robert J. *U.S.News & World Report.* (★)
"Tomorrow" columnist. An innocuous little column, it's mostly light reading, rarely giving us anything newsy from inside the Beltway. It's well-written and quirky in its presentation, and that makes it more interesting than it might otherwise be. In "Congress and Administration to Pitch for Workers' Favor," with Ted Gest 1-19, Shapiro is optimistic, discussing minimum wage, human-rights policy, drug testing and Federal highway funding. "Is the Pentagon Taking Charge of the Space Program," 4-13, was late on much of the race to the stars, Mars and pesticides (*NYT* had the Mars information a couple of weeks earlier). "A Donnybrook Over the Fairness Doctrine," with Robert H. Bork Jr. and Charles Fenyvesi 8-17, was fine on fairness and the FCC, more pesticides and the 100th anniversary of the Eiffel Tower.

Shapiro, Walter. *Time.* (★)
Defecting from *Newsweek* to join the political writing cadre at *Time*, Shapiro's pieces are standard, adequate, but rarely anything special. "The Loneliest Long-Distance Runner," with Laurence Barrett, 4-27, was still another run-of-the-mill profile of Gary Hart. Better on Gary in "Just What is He Up To?" 9-21, as Hart tries to figure out a way to fit back into the political process: "As he moves from disgrace toward dignity, Hart may come to relish the joy of speaking his mind with the perfect freedom of a man who has nothing left to lose." "The Duke Of Economic Uplift," 7-27, a profile of Mass. Gov. Michael Dukakis, was disappointing, very thin on ideas, the issues in his race with Ed King aren't addressed and we never get a good picture of his vision. We had to hunt for the good stuff in "The Unreal Campaign," 9-14, with Laurence Barrett, on the absence of hot issues and lead candidates for '88 in both parties. On-target in the facetious introduction: it is the press and those in the know whom the candidates have been trying to impress as much as the voters.

Shogan, Robert. *Los Angeles Times.* (★ ½)
Political reporter. This tireless veteran spreads himself everywhere and has a deserved reputation as one of the hardest workers on the political beat, though you'll never get a bird's eye view of the political scene from him. "Dole Campaign Stresses an All-American Image," 11-15, is straight reporting on the candidate's belief that "the old-fashioned script" can play well in Peoria and everywhere else, but we get no flashes of insight that add to what we already knew about that. Better, "Presidential Candidates Gephardt, Kemp Debate Trade," 7-21, where he gave a sense of Gephardt's strategy of saddling Kemp with a defense of administration trade policy. He covers the broad field of responses from the candidates in "Stock Market Forcing Candidates to Reshape Strategies," 11-8, but doesn't provide enough evidence to support his conclusion that Dole is the best situated to benefit from the changed environment, although he may be right. A nice job, however, in getting both sides of Jesse Jackson's boosts

and bumps with "Democrats May Get Points but It's Jackson's Game at Black Caucus," 9-27, and "Jackson Gets Reminders of Anti-Semitism Issue in N.Y." 10-31.

Shribman, David. *The Wall Street Journal.* (★ ★ ★)
The Washington bureau's political bigfoot, he mixed it up nicely in '87 with lofty strategic pieces on partisan strategies and issues and close-ups of the campaign trail. "Puzzled Party: Taxes and Trade Are the Toughest Issues Facing the Democrats," 6-29, puts a front-page, magnified focus on the party's dilemma over these two dangerous issues. Says Republican Kemp, "The Democrats are in a political and intellectual *cul de sac.*" In "Divided Right," 4-29, Shribman is thorough, but a bit bland, in setting out the tensions among social and economic conservatives as the post-Reagan era approaches, "between those who were drawn to the movement by economic self-interest and those who were drawn to it by ideology." He got important attention at a critical moment with an opinion round-up, "Out of Control: As Reagan's Problems Grow, Many Now Say Damage Is Irreparable," 2-25, summarizing the Beltway mood at the terminus of the Donald Regan period, with the drumbeat that produced Howard Baker, Jr. There are more elegant insights, analysis and detail in "Back to School: Education Emerges As Hot Political Issue and the GOP Seizes It," 9-11. Shribman's roving eye caught "Wyoming's Wallop Veers to Right," 1-20, the first notice we've seen of the Senator's rising star among conservatives, although it misses his powerful intellect. His profile of Sen. Sam Nunn as a presidential possibility, 2-6, is about the best we saw on the Georgian, fine detail but sufficiently detached to note that he "has no experience in national political campaigns and hasn't yet demonstrated any broad political vision." His coverage of Jack Kemp's entry, 4-7, had a wider range of quotes and a fuller picture of his program than the competition provided. A piece sifting through Gov. Dukakis' economic record, 7-21, gets the pros and cons on the record; Warren Brookes, columnist in *The Washington Times*, had been hammering Dukakis on this.

Simpson, Christopher. *The Washington Times.* (★)
On the campaign trail for the year, Simpson follows the Democrats, giving us bread-and-butter sustenance. "Morality Becoming a Major '88 Issue," 6-11, was a semi-consensus of candidates, experts and voters on the legitimacy of the morality issue in campaign, but he is murky on what this all means or even what kind of morality he's talking about — are we dealing with Watergate or Ricegate? "Kirk Brings Order Out Of Democratic Chaos," 6-30, allows Democratic National Committee Chairman Paul Kirk to have his say. "Hart Drops Strong Hint He Will Re-Enter Run For President," 9-3, was a mere report on Hart's interview with Danielle Gardner, where he's still blaming the press for reporting on his overactive hormones instead of himself for letting them percolate so indiscriminately, just a rehash of old news. "Reflective Dukakis Presses On," 9-8, was better, more complete, but still left us wondering about the Duke, who he is, and what kind of a president he thinks he would be.

Soloman, Burt. *National Journal.* (★ ½)
Northeast correspondent. A good, sturdy reporter who manages to get some life into his material. "Our Facts, Their Facts," 6-6, is a sly rundown on the economic and special "studies" that special interests commission to support their pleadings, those commissioned walking a fine line between pleasing their clients and protecting their reputations. In "Where America is At," 9-26, he previews the New Hampshire primary, what it's like, the demographics, in an illuminating style. "Congress' Rising Stars," 1-24, with Richard E. Cohen, is a very well done set of profiles on 13 junior House members.

Specter, Michael. *The Washington Post.* (★ ½)
Science reporter, who in 1987 found himself flip-flopping between AIDS and, of all things, superconductivity. "U.S., France Settle AIDS Study Feud," 4-1, was straight forward and well written as to which country discovered the virus, but wasn't as thorough as we would have liked. "Hospital AIDS Measures Debated," 7-28, raised serious questions in the medical

profession, like the segregation of AIDS and non-AIDS patients; health-care safety guidelines; increased testing, but contained no analysis. A follow-up, "Many Health-Care Workers Doubt Value Of Proposed AIDS Guidelines," 7-29, sounded like controlled panic in the profession, but doesn't mention the guidelines for handling of AIDS patients and AIDS-infected blood products, just the confusion and debate over them. "AIDS Researchers Shift Focus: Vaccine Setbacks Bring Call for Emphasis on Drugs for Those Infected," 9-1, was on-target, giving us a look at change in research direction away from the mass population not at risk for AIDS and towards the already infected. His superconductivity reports, while rather late, were only clear as far as they went, but he shied away from deeper science reporting. "Superconductor Progress: Some Materials Evince Property at About 65 Degrees," 6-23, had a lead that reflected the excitement within the profession: "Two groups of physicists reported today that they have developed materials showing tantalizing signs of being superconductors of electricity near room temperature," although other groups have been unable to duplicate their test results or figure out how they got them.

Stanley, Alessandra. *Time.* (★)
Political beat, Stanley handles brief candidate profiles and lighter issue pieces, for example, "Let Us Entertain You," 1-12, on the cities' fight over the 1988 conventions and convention revenues. Her "AIDS Becomes a Political Issue," 3-23, capturing the sense of emotion in how the candidates want to deal with AIDS, timely, informative, but somewhat muddy, quoting Kemp campaign staffer Jeff Bell: "Anyone advocating the ACLU line on AIDS will not be acceptable in the Republican nomination fight," but she doesn't say what the ACLU line is. "Run, Pat Run!" 8-3, was an okay, brief profile and assessment of Rep. Pat Schroeder and the possibility of her running for the Democratic presidential nomination. We got a better sense of Pete du Pont in "A Blueblood With Bold Ideas," 9-4, as an intensely private person, but we didn't find out much about his ideas or views. "Secretary Dole Meet Mrs. Dole," 9-21, was a feminist, sort of silly as a pseudo-portrait of Liddy Dole and an explanation of why she resigned to help her Bob's campaign, never seriously considering she may have done so because she loves her husband.

Stengel, Richard. *Time.* (★)
Stengel caught our eye with a fine wrap-up of Mario Cuomo, "Letting the Cup Pass," 3-2. "Congress Shows Its Impatience," 3-23, with Barrett Seaman and Michael Duffy, was a nice round-up of the latest battle in aid for the contras. "At Issue: Freedom For The Irrational," 9-14, with Wayne Svoboda, was a competent, haunting picture of the homeless mentally ill in the U.S., adequately covering the arguments in the debate, but makes no conclusions. We were disappointed by "True Belief Unhampered By Doubt," 7-13, with Jeanne McDowell and Alessandra Stanley, a smear-job profile of Ollie North with descriptions like "the desire to please superiors," "somewhere...he went off the track," "did not know when to stop," presenting him as determined man with serious character flaws. Stengel seemed to string together material to fit a pre-conceived impression.

Swan, Christopher. *The Christian Science Monitor.* (★ ★ ½)
Media reporter, his articles are interesting, timely and useful with tidbits we don't find elsewhere. Swan is intriguing on Daniel Boorstin, in "Man of Books Opens a New Chapter," 3-18, on Boorstins' retirement as keeper of the Library of Congress, showing us the man, scholar and author who thinks "to be associated with a great institution is a kind of immortality." "Kalb To Lead Exploration Into The Media's Impact On Public Policy," 4-30, was well-done, giving us analysis of NBC's Marvin Kalb's appointment to head the Joan Shorenstein Barone Center on Press, Politics and Public Policy at JFK's School of Government at Harvard: "some fairly acute observers insist that Kalb has a leg up on creating an epicenter of activity and ideas that will have some real impact on the way government and media people understand each other." "And Now A Word From William Safire," 8-28, was respectful and unpartisan, focusing on his accomplishments in journalism and on his new novel on the Civil War, *Freedom*. His best

for the year: "Whirlwind Waltz on the Campaign Trail," 10-23, a snazzy three-dimensional feature on the boys (and girls) on the Presidential campaign bus.

Taylor, Paul. *The Washington Post.* (★ ★ ½)
Political correspondent, second to Broder in the pecking order, suddenly famed in '87 for asking the press conference "A" question that tipped Gary Hart out of the '88 race and brought Hester Prynne into it. Another very good, but not great year for Taylor. Among his best: "'88 Race Shaping Up as 'Short and Intense,'" 1-14, a round-up of the way each contest is shaping up in a very fluid race, that will remain so until the voters get into it in February 1988. His "Will Hart's Denial Give Us the Late, Late Mario Scenario?" 5-24, was the best we saw of the genre, "Someone in will get big, or someone big will get in," with the thought: Carter in '76 "shot out of a field as headless as the one the Democrats now confront." Sharp analysis, too, with "A New Front Runner Crowned By Brickbats," 8-24, Dukakis now the target of the other dwarfs. His Sunday magazine piece, "Playing With Fire," 7-12, is a sad, rather wistful story of Hart's last week as a candidate from the reporter who asked him point-blank if he ever committed adultery, told through the eyes of staffers, not sensationalized. He was only middle deep on the issue mesh with the campaigns, "Democrats Revive Old Tune As GOP Gropes to Write One," 5-1, is an okay early line on issues. "The Way We Choose Presidents Is Crazy And Getting Crazier," 3-29, tells it all, the state of the art on the quadrennial horserace turning into a zany steeplechase, backed up with "Iowa Marathon Wears Down Gephardt," 11-11, including his vocal cords. "Election '88: Sullen Voters And the Cult of Personality," 10-18, gropes for meaning in the "sudden wrecks" he has encountered on the campaign trail, a cross between "a demolition derby and a game of Trivial Pursuit," but comes up without much.

Taylor, Stuart, Jr. *The New York Times.* (★ ★)
Supreme Court. A full-time job in '87 and Taylor was resourceful and reliable in covering the nominees. Earlier in the year, "Conservatives Assert Legal Presence," 2-1, a curious report on the Federalist Society, 500 conservatives meeting in DC, some insisting Dixie had a right to secede. "Newest Judicial Activists Come From the Right," 2-1, speaks of "free market libertarians" who feel a kinship with liberal activism, Judge Bork later cast in this mold by opponents as a "radical." In "Scalia Proposes Major Overhaul of U.S. Courts," 2-16, he reports "a much greater tone of urgency" than in previous appeals by Chief Justice Burger. In a 5-31 report, he finds the Court, in 19 of 27 recent cases, siding with the prosecution over the defense, supposedly a trend. In a Bork profile, "A Committed Conservative," 7-2, his lead is rather alarmist, saying Bork "has accused the Supreme Court of usurping the power of elected officials." [That makes him conservative *per se*?] "Powell and His Approach," 7-12, is a remarkable 3-hour interview with Justice Lewis F. Powell, Jr., with insights into the workings of the Court. In "Bork at Yale," 7-27, Taylor is enterprising, interviewing the nominee's former colleagues and Bork's integrity comes through even from those who oppose his nomination. We were troubled by "Judge Bork: Restraint vs. Activism," 9-13, the curtain raiser, a bit tilted against Bork: "In contrast to his arguments that the Supreme Court may not thwart the legislative will by recognizing individual rights that are not clearly spelled out by the Constitution, he has cited the vague separation of powers principles implicit in the 'structure' of the Constitution as a mandate for judges to strike down restrictions on the executive branch." A pretty weak *non sequitur*. In his balanced "Politics in the Bork Battle," 9-28, there's a timely quote from Lloyd Cutler: "We're getting perilously close to electing a Supreme Court Justice."

Thomas, Evan. *Newsweek.* (½ ★)
Brought over from *Time* last year to head up the Washington bureau after Morton Kondracke gave up the job, Thomas seemed the perfect yuppiefied candidate for the job. We were not surprised to get more impact! out of Washington than any other individual bureau, but his own writing is partisan and biased. "Dick Darman Calls It Quits," 4-13, on Dick Darman

leaving the Treasury Dept., made Darman look like a jerk, "the last Brahmin sold out," focusing on his personality drawbacks and not his potential in the private sectre. "New Navy Boss: Poet and Warrior," 5-4, profiling the new Secretary of the Navy James Webb, more warrior than poet, a desktop Rambo, making him sound like he's some kind of nut, using examples of Lehman decisions he reversed, his war record, the plots of his novels, and wording like "warrior," "ferocious." "The Lady Has A Midas Touch," 6-15, on fundraising at the home of Pamela Harriman was especially disappointing, with a "People" magazine quality profile, dropping names, names, names, oozing charm and pate. Obviously, this lady is no slouch in the brains department, but Thomas glosses over her views in favor of her menus.

Tolchin, Martin. *The New York Times.* (★ ½)
A savvy veteran on the political beat who is comfortable and adept at investigative reporting, and not without a sense of humor in that dark line of work. For much of '87 he seemed tied up in obligatory reports that were outside our interest, but we did appreciate a Cape Cod round of golf he had with "Ex-Speaker O'Neill: A Salty Par For the Course," 8-28, with colorful quotes from Tip's book, running down President Reagan: "It was sinful that Ronald Reagan became President." He teamed with another *Times* investigative reporter, Jeff Gerth, on a Sunday magazine spread, "The Contradictions of Bob Dole," 11-8, a rather damaging piece on the Senator with its even-handed bottom line: "He has a meanness of spirit but a capacity for compassion." There are rather unimportant financial shuffles raked over, but the worst is: "If Mr. Dole's early experience with poverty and his wounding in the war bred a deeply felt compassion, they also engendered a bitterness that has plagued his political career. It first surfaced during his initial campaign for Congress, in 1960. Mr. Dole's Republican primary race was marred by a whispering campaign alleging that his opponent, Keith Sebelius, had a drinking problem...the whispering campaign engendered a lifelong enmity between the Sebelius family and Mr. Dole, who was pointedly not invited back to the home after attending Mr. Sebelius's 1982 funeral."

Toner, Robin. *The New York Times.* (★ ½)
A sophomore in the Washington bureau, she does well handling odds and ends on the political beat and will no doubt get bigger assignments down the line. "'88 Contenders Battle Jackson For Black Vote," 4-27, makes the point that none of the Demo candidates is a Mondale, with a national base of black support, so Jesse has a big lead. In "Gephardt Looking Beyond Trade Issue," 6-3, she observes him winning unionists with his trade sanctions, but getting a less popular reaction in the rest of the country. An image precedes him now: A politician seeking to protect the country from competition rather than leading it bravely into the fray. "Democrats and Women: Party Shifts Approach," 7-11, is a bit sketchy on feminist complaints they are being neglected by the candidates. A good story with "Biden, Once the Field's Hot Democrat, Is Being Overtaken by Cooler Rivals," 8-31, seeing his campaign sputtering, but also not enough questions raised. "Iowans Unswayed By Dukakis Visit," 10-5, dwells on the backlash over the Biden affair, a well-handled report.

Walsh, Edward. *The Washington Post.* (★ ★)
Political correspondent. Not one of the *Post*'s heavy artillery, but Walsh could be the political bigfoot at most other newspapers. In "Hart: Still Fascinated With World of Ideas," 1-20, he managed to get mid-deep into Hart's record and reputation in a profile that just missed. "Freshman on the Spot," 4-2, was well done on Sen. Terry Sanford (D-NC) agonizing over the highway bill veto over-ride vote. Walsh's "Court Change Elevates Biden's Profile," 7-12, includes Biden's explanation of his pro-Bork remarks of 11-86, that "can and will be used against him." The best we saw in '87 was "Will Laxalt's Style Play in New Hampshire," 8-25, a sturdy, prescient analysis of the Nevada Republican's style and problems as a potential presidential candidate.

Walsh, Kenneth T. *U.S.News & World Report.* (★)
Political beat, Walsh covered Congress, the White House, and now he's on the campaign bus with the rest of the crew. But he's pretty much at the back of the bus. "Can 'Operation Comeback' Work?" 1-26, was so-so on Ronald Reagan's age and the detachment issues already raised before and decided upon by voters; the main thrust of his "comeback" will be political basics. "Bushwacking the 'Wimp Factor,'" 3-30, was a competent report on Bush retooling his image and a summary of the problems he faces that seemed to rely a bit on the Diane Sawyer "60 Minutes" interview. "Gary Hart's Ticking Debt Bomb," 4-6, was an interesting foray into Hart's 1984 campaign debt with good quotes and some documentation, with Hart even owing money to Pat Caddell, his pollster. Also on Hart, "The Same Old Questions About a New Candidacy," 4-20, was conventional, with little insight into the man or the candidate.

Weinraub, Bernard. *The New York Times.* (★ ★)
Chief White House correspondent in '86, Weinraub moved to the political beat, preparing for the '88 elections and covered the Dole campaign like a blanket. "Sizing Up Dole, His Style and Chances for '88," 2-25, is cogent, a smart outline of Dole's pros and cons, ending on a "one-man band" negative. In "Bush's Rivals Resent His Advantages," 6-10, he quotes Lee Atwater, the Veep's campaign mgr: "These charges are very unfortunate because I think he [Dole] has done a good job of hiding his mean streak so far in this campaign. However, I always felt it would emerge sooner or later." Dole, though, had to be happy with the dozens of *Times* stories that appeared, practically a campaign diary. "Dole Focuses '88 Campaign on Bork and Nicaragua Chief," 9-11, a strategy designed to broaden his appeal to conservatives, but ephemeral. Early in '88, Weinraub was adequate on the purging of Donald Regan, "Regan Says Days Were Numbered After Clash With First Lady," 3-1, although there is not a word of Stuart Spencer's role in fomenting dissent. "Nancy Reagan's Power is Considered at Peak," 3-3, reporting how the First Lady's plans focus on an arms control agreement to restore her husband's place in history, the Edith Wilson image coming through as RR's age and health are cited. In "Walter Mondale or Not Saying 'I Told You So,'" 3-4, is a good interview as Fritz feels vindication, blaming Mrs. Ferraro (but did the voters want higher taxes?). "AIDS Emerging as a Key Issue for Campaign in '88," 4-2, interesting on difficulties of dealing with the issue. Good quotes. A Kemp aide: "Everyone's trying to avoid this issue because it combines homosexuality, sexual disease and death, matters in which most of us wish to be unenlightened."

Wermiel, Stephen. *The Wall Street Journal.* (★ ★ ½)
Supreme Court. Wermiel has not been as politically astute as Al Kamen, his counterpart at *The Washington Post*, or as readable as Stuart Taylor of the *NYT*, but he was clearest and most accurate in his accounts of the Supreme Court nominees and the legal issues surrounding the confirmation battles. His front page: "The Right Stuff?: Robert Bork Faces a Confirmation Battle," 7-2, the day following RR's nomination of Judge Bork, seemed a very nice job at the time. But, reading it again four months later we realized what a powerful piece it really was, setting the stage with great precision: "...the president has picked a rare judicial — rather than a political — conservative, a judge committed to a narrow role for the courts rather than to the Reagan administration's political agenda." His was the best account of "ABA Panel Opposes Limits on Damages," 1-12, on the ABA commission rejecting arbitrary caps on the size of damage awards, a good assembly of information. "Two Centuries Later, There is Hot Debate Over 'Original Intent,'" 5-26, was a good, broad piece that no doubt helped prepare Wermiel for the Bork debate. He could have been livelier in his account of "Justice Scalia Calls For Special System of Federal Courts to Pare Case Backlog," 2-17, handled with more verve in the *Times*. We docked him points here and there for missing nuances on issues we thought he should have seen, but there are no quibbles with "The Right Stuff?" It was.

Whalen, Bill. *Insight.* (★ ★ ½)
One of the youngsters on the *Insight* crew, Whalen is also one of the most talented. "Hart Starts into '88 Campaign as Creditors Dog Him for '84," 5-11, was informative on the debt issue, promises, promises: "The fact is, Hart's rivals do not need to try to keep the debt issue alive; the Hart organization has been doing fine by itself. In 1985, Bill Dixon, former administrative assistant to the senator and now his campaign manager, assured all concerned the debt would be retired in time for the World Series that year. Kansas City defeated St. Louis in seven games, but the debt retirement campaign went into extra innings." "The Super Strategy Strains as Democrats Play to Dixie," 8-24, took us through the intricacies of Super Tuesday planning. "The House Of Questionable Repute." 9-14, was very tough on Speaker Jim Wright, pointing to Democratic scandals in the House. Also, incisive on "The Candidacy that Would Not Be," 10-19, giving us the scoop on what kind of candidate Pat Schroeder might have been, her policies, her views, not just her sex.

SOCIAL/POLITICAL COMMENTATORS

Baker, Russell. *The New York Times.* (★ ★ ½)
Regaining his mirth in 1987, Russell now provides a genuine chuckle free of charge in almost every column, no mean feat in an unfunny year. His topics vary wildly: from televangelists, "The Forgotten Camel," 3-28; to shopping malls, "Heaven in Asphalt," 3-17; to the misery of summer doldrums and driving on "Helldriver's Boulevard," i.e., the Beltway, "At Wit's End," 8-12. He's bitter about Baby M and the "piffling sum" on "babymaking as business" in "Bring Back the Stork," 4-3, noting that somebody paid $8 million to save Oral, but Stern only spent $17,500. He's especially good when he has outrageous material to work with. In "All Shall Be Disclosed," 5-12, he suggests an unorthodox, but hilarious way for George Bush to offset the wimp factor: "Polled people are showing a lot of volatility towards candidates with low adultery incidence. You could read the figures several ways, but one of the most worrisome interpretations could mean the public equates a low adultery incidence with a low energy level." His strongest this year: "A Ship On His Shoulder," 7-21, on Kuwaiti reflagging, Khomeini's response, and RR's. "What the US is doing is putting a Kuwaiti tanker on its shoulder and daring the Ayatollah to knock it off if he thinks he's tough enough... A President who is thinking of dealing with the world's Irans with surgical strikes is like a person whose doorbell is being rung by a friend with a kitten. In either case, you had better have a firm policy prepared in advance. Or you are in for trouble."

Bandow, Douglas. Copley News Service. (★)
Once a youthful policy analyst for President Reagan, Bandow writes more or less from a Reaganaut angle. "The Perils of Postcard Economics," 7-23, was a strong pull against protectionism. "Break Relations with South Africa," 2-27, pulled against RR policy but seemed quirky, urging the U.S. to acknowledge failure of economic sanctions and substituting "diplomatic sanctions" to "send an overdue message to South African blacks." His arguments were more persuasive in "It's Time To Drop Draft Registration," 7-23, and in arguing against limiting credit card interest rates in the name of competition, citing drawbacks in states that have done so, in "Government's Helping Hand Is Hurting Consumers," 7-30. We see his work when it appears in *The Washington Times*, the best being on Barber Conable's left-field appointment of Robert McNamara to the official steering committee to oversee the World Bank's reorganization, quoting an official who admitted near the end of McNamara's World Bank presidency: "We're like a Soviet factory. The push is to maximize lending..."

Barnes, Fred. *The New Republic.* (★ ★ ★ ★)
Quite a year for *TNR*'s senior editor. So consistently fresh and luminescent in his White House column and other writings that we could not deny him, for the first time, the top rating. There was no one better in chronicling the Reagan Administration's decline, from "Brain Dead," 12-22-86 ("The *de facto* end of the Reagan Presidency came at the precise moment — noon, November 25 — the White House disclosed that proceeds from the arms sales had been laundered and funneled to the contras."), to "Washington Rules" in the May *American Spectator*, on how Donald Regan lost in a power play by the Washington establishment, to "The Ford Years," 5-25, citing the President as a new Jerry Ford, a "eunuch." His "Out of Control," 5-4, catches Alexander Haig's quirkiness, "a man possessed." All the GOP contenders for 1988 get a look in "The Summer Line," 7-6, very well done. "Jesse Goes Country," 8-3, limns the torment of Jackson's split personality in his presidential bid, about the best of the year on the Rev. J.J. "Peaced Off," 8-31, provides useful chronology on the Reagan-Jim Wright Nicaraguan peace plan. "Bork Talk," 9-7, struggles a bit with analysis on why the Judge is likely to be confirmed. "Shevardnaze Schmooze," 10-19, is smart analysis on Reagan's six-year patience paying off on his zero-option INF offer on arms control. Barnes, one of the "McLaughlin Group" TV talk-show regulars, is always boyishly pleasant, never supercilious, and greatly respected in the political press corps for his savvy.

Beichman, Arnold. Freelance. (★ ½)
Appearing regularly in *The Washington Times*, this grizzled cold warrior remains credible and combative on Soviet-East bloc issues, relentlessly scrutinizing Gorbachev and his Warsaw bloc counterparts with unalloyed skepticism. His "Candor Creeps Into Soviet Journals," 2-19, thus meant something more, on published articles detailing the gap in living standards between the "lower depths" and the *nomenklatura*. But he basically sticks to his persistent theme that Marxism-Leninism can never be compatible with the West. In "Concern About Sakharov," 3-20, he questions Andrei Sakharov's speeches at an international forum in Moscow: "Mr. Sakharov envisions the convergence of socialism with modern capitalism as not only possible but also desirable. Unfortunately for Mr. Sakharov's thesis, Marxism-Leninism does not offer the slightest hope of convergence," the laws of communism precluding "any fundamental changes in the Soviet political or economic structure." In "Look Who's Learning Our Drug Strategy," 4-14, he makes the case against sharing DEA training with Eastern bloc police as lunatic since the Soviets and clients have an interest in spreading drug culture in the West, citing published testimony as evidence. His alert on some interesting political possibilities north of the border, "A Leftward Lurch Coming in Canada," 8-11, was the best we saw of him.

Bethell, Tom. *The American Spectator.* (★ ★ ½)
The Washington columnist only due to locale, not to content. A British-born Oxford grad and a relentlessly conservative Roman Catholic, he relishes taking humanistic Catholics to task, as in November's "Humanists and Heretics." "A Stroll With Sidney Hook," May, is delightful, so vividly recreated you want to argue either with Bethell or Hook himself, depending on which side of the religious debate you're on, but the debate is definitely the focus. He does venture into Washington politics once in a blue moon, as in "Conservative Bird, Liberal Bush," August, a ruthlessly accurate depiction of the failings of the Reagan administration in advancing the conservative cause. A powerful observation: "The Democrats established a new role for government as a player that was supposed to join on the losing side, the idea being to equalize the score. Unable to counter this shift, the Republicans found themselves stuck with the villain's role: siding with the winners. Until they can find the courage to believe in the neutrality of government, Republicans will continue to slink along guiltily in the shadows." In "Play The Sea-Lanes Game, Pass Go, Save Assets, Collect Choke Points," 6-28, *LAT*, he has a clever strategy for hitting two birds with one stone, Khomeini and Gorbachev, but as journalism, just a little too collegiate. But superb in "Festive Foolery," April, on National Condom Week at Stanford: "AIDS is perceived as a greater threat to the sexual revolution than to the health of America," and "If the GOP Is Ripe for a Takeover, Will It Be Pat Robertson in the Promised Land?" 9-30, *LAT*, getting a bead on Republican realignment.

Broder, David. *The Washington Post.* (★ ★ ★ ★)
Dean of the political press corps on the sunny side of 60, Broder loped along the campaign trail with a marvelously prolific '87. By discarding extraneous ideological baggage, he still grows, hip to the ideological workings of campaigns in ways the younger hotshots have yet to experience. He's in his favored element, covering the beginnings of the wide-open presidential race, punching out features and columns and not above filing simple news blurbs. In "These Front-Runners Look Shaky," 5-24, his experience really shows; assessing the presidential field, he couldn't be much better: "The outlines of the 1988 contest are not yet visible." "The Night They All Laughed," 4-1, notable for Broder's gentle tone, appreciation for Reagan's sense of humor at Gridiron dinner, contrasting him with LBJ, Nixon and Carter: "Not all Presidents have understood the value of a laugh." In a fine piece, "The Democrats Nobody Knows," 7-22, he leans on informal polling and historical precedent to suggest, "Later, if not now, the Democrats are almost certain to pay a price for offering a skeptical nation a stranger as President." Broder's profile of Richard Gephardt, "Gephardt's 'Greening': An Eye On The Center," 8-31, is one of our selections for the 10-best political reports of 1987. Also among his best: "Democrats Cultivate Patch of Left-Leaning Grass Roots," 8-2, spotting the Demo field on the political spectrum. A winning opening line: "It was the kind of gathering where

Bruce Babbitt could draw boos for saying Marxism is a dying ideology.'' A quote from Rep. Pat Schroeder takes the cake: "Schroeder also suggested that President Reagan has done the nation a disservice because he 'redefined Americans as winners. People who met failure or disappointment in their lives were ashamed and didn't even feel like Americans, and it's increased the suicide rate and driven people to drugs.'"

Brookhiser, Richard. *National Review.* (★ ★)
Strengthening in 1987, Brookhiser snaps and crackles, championing the conservative cause. He did a sparkling profile of Bill Bradley in "Born-Again Bradley," 9-25, and in "Democracy in South Africa," 7-31, he gets moving with this description of P.T. Botha: "In person, he had a bald head, a bull neck, and a drop-dead-and-go-to-hell-smirk on his face. I liked him." Agile outside politics as well, he's gentler and poignant in "Bobby Short's Cafe Carlyle," in May's *American Spectator*, a sweet salute to the last bastion of urbanity in Manhattan, and "My New York, My New York," 2-13, *NR*, persuading us of New York's citified superiority to Washington: "Washington may be defined as the city in which George Will causes a sensation by wearing a bow tie. In New York, he'd have to try wearing green hair...Politically, Washington is where things are *prevented* from happening...political ideas...get made or broken beyond the Beltway...Supply-side economics was whooped in the *Wall Street Journal*, not the *Washington Post*. Inside the Beltway lives the mass of men who do not understand the true insignificance of Donald Regan."

Bovard, James. Freelance. (★ ★)
We see Bovard most often in *The Wall Street Journal*, writing from the maxim that government agencies were born to be bashed, and he bashes well. "The Slow Death of Eastern Europe," 2-26, gives it from both sides: looming ecological catastrophe, offering detail on incidents, consequences, reasons, combining this with failure to boost living standards to conclude East Europe is "economically doomed." "USDA's 'Swampbuster' Policy Is All Wet," 4-6, explodes the idea of unintended government subsidies for wetland conversion: "Unfortunately, our agriculture programs will likely continue to be measured by the usual test: If Congress throws money up in the air and some of it lands in farmer's pockets, the prosperous are a success." In "A Country At War With Its People," 9-4, *The Washington Times*, he says the U.S. ought to go one way or another with Ethiopia since the government there is engaged in the systematic destruction of its people through its resettlement and collectivization programs: "Giving Col. Mengista more aid in the hope that he would treat his people better would be like giving Hitler aid so he could improve conditions in concentration camps. We can either be accomplices in the murder of the Ethiopian people — or in the overthrow of the Ethiopian government. Or we can stay out of Ethiopia completely, which would be better than the status quo." His best for 1987: "American History: Pass A Tariff, Start A War," 7-20 (*WSJ*), a retrospective on protectionist assaults in America since 1750.

Buckley, William F., Jr. Universal Press Syndicate. (★ ★)
The editor of *National Review* was much improved in 1987, his column regaining some of its old fire. We had been complaining that he'd lost his cutting edge, that he diluted his energies writing those mystery books we never read, his columns knocked out on portable word processors in taxicabs between Park Avenue and La Guardia. We don't think we imagined it, but the Buck seemed to be back, his columns almost always showing more than a morsel of effort, which is all this talented fellow needs to exert. He at least had the best line we saw all year on Jim Bakker in "Beyond Bakker," 7-3, putting his finger on the root of all evil: "It is one thing at the witching hour to fall into the coils of lust. Quite something else to live studiedly as Bakker and his wife did, begging dollars from the poor, and using them to finance a lifestyle that would embarrass a Rolling Stone." In "George Will Commits Crimes Against Truth," 1-22, WFB calls his old friend George to account for abusive commentary and rhetorical abuses of Cardinal O'Connor and the Vatican. He charges at liberal media bias, taking a CBS news broadcast at random and shredding the text in a sulfurous "Good Night, Dan Rather,"

5-5. Perhaps Reagan's difficulties had some lubricating effect on Buckley's vital juices, a thought that crossed our mind in reading "Reagan, RIP?" 2-13: "no one — not Pericles, not Erasmus, not JFK — could be a President capable of discharging all the duties imposed upon him by the one hundred Congresses since the launching of our Republic. Reagan's skill is peculiar to his temperament...He made a major mistake in deciding to traffic with Iran, and the bureaucratic resiliency of his office was insufficient to handle the ensuing strains. But — caution! Do not go further than that in counting him out." We count Buckley back in.

Cannon, Lou. *The Washington Post.* (★)
Another acceptable year for this old-school White House correspondent and "Reagan columnist" who does his best work when he sticks to simple political stuff, gets into trouble when he thinks big and wheels out his psychiatrist's couch. "Bork and the True Believers," 7-6, is very nice, straightforward, sensible on Supreme Court justices who turned out differently than expected. So too, "A Doer Departs," 4-6, a dignified profile and assessment of Richard Darman's departure from Treasury, which doesn't judge Darman's character as *Newsweek* does. Sharp analysis in "Writing Reagan's Final Scenes," 7-27, with RR versus Howard Baker, Jr., on how to play the last 18 months, tough or conciliatory, with RR — at that moment, at least, winning. But we get a bellyache with his pseudo-Freudian analysis of Reagan in "The High Cost of Secrecy," 7-20, which suggests RR has a loony obsession: "Reagan brought with him into the White House a mistrust of the news media that had many other sources. He resented Hollywood coverage of the breakup of his first marriage...." In "Reagan's Warring Impulses," 8-3, RR's "good instincts" to help people versus "worst impulses have always been his tendency to oversimplify and overdelegate. He governs by reducing complex issues to simplicities of lower taxes and anticommunism and relying on others to carry out the policies embodied by the slogans." Rather sappy oversimplification of a complex President. Cannon was also part of the feeding frenzy that drove Donald Regan from the White House, heavy on "well-informed" sources for rumor and speculation in "Chief of Staff in Worsening Bind," 2-18.

Carter, Hodding III. *The Wall Street Journal.* (½ ★)
His monthly column presents occasionally interesting opinions. But nothing important surfaced in his writing in '87. "And the Winner Is...Iran," 1-29, was overdone and overwrought, calling the U.S. impotent and deciding U.S. sending arms to Iran may have tipped the balance in the fight with Iraq. He lacks cogency in "Democrats Decry Potholes in Reagan's Policies," 4-2, confused on who is to blame for the collision over the highway bill, then drifting into the Social Security issue. He heads a TV production firm, but seems sappy in a plea that anchormen take pay cuts to make more jobs for cheaper help in "Salary Cuts Could Help Television Newsroom Woes," 2-12. In "Economic Success Story Has Its Costs," 8-27, Carter notes economic indicators are positive *but* "...something unhealthy and in the long run destructive is also at work in the economy," because workers are not inspired enough by management and environment to give decent service, seen as an inevitable side of mergermania. His best and strongest column, "The False Spring of RR," 3-12, on the Iran-Contra affair relished the "months of dirty revelations yet to come...for the Reagan presidency."

Chamberlain, John. King Features Syndicate. (★ ½)
One of the *MediaGuide*'s oldest gentlemen rated, born in 1903 and still going strong, zipping merrily along with a curious zest for the future. His equanimity, optimism and charity to his intellectual adversaries, all rare in conservative columnists, brings a perspective and perceptivity that only a sage man could possess. "Press Conference Corrida," 4-2, was a thoughtful, careful, *fair* critique of Sam Donaldson's reportorial technique. Reporting *cum* reviewing of speeches before the Annual Conservative Political Action Conference, Chamberlain found "Jack Kemp, in making a direct pitch for the party's nomination, really outdid all the rest" in "A Strong Pitch by Jack Kemp," 3-4. It is Chamberlain, appropriately, who asks persuasively "Must Social Security Remain Unmentionable?" 5-11, in outlining different options to deal with the demographic problems of the program. And "Putting an Idea to Work," 5-20, is one of the

few pieces that appeared in the press on the spreading impact of the enterprise-zone concept, stuck in Congress but picked up regionally and successfully with 20 states planning to renovate "the decaying downtown areas in 182 communities in a few years time."

Cockburn, Alexander. *The Nation.* (★ ★ ★)
"Beat the Devil" columnist. Still our favorite Marxist, Cockburn is the sharpest and most ferocious of the left's journalists. He's as charming as a spitting cobra in his columns for *The Nation*, but he's an unrestrained pit bull on the op-ed page of *The Wall Street Journal*. He snarls at Sen. John F. Kerry (D-MA) for gutlessness in "U.S.-Israel Quarrel Gives Truth a Fighting Chance," 1-15, *WSJ*: "It's one thing to beat up on contras and quite another to take on the U.S.-Israel lobby." He sinks his teeth into the *Journal*'s condemnations of Sandinista violations of human rights, with a biting critique of their record of silence on Antonio Somoza and Chile's Augusto Pinochet, "U.S. Doesn't Know What It Wants in Nicaragua," 8-13, *WSJ*. Behind the rhetorical jargon, he's often a voice of substance for the frustrated "left-outs" as in "Reagan Reversals Uplift the Left in the Northwest," 2-26, *WSJ*: "About half this country's political spectrum, from the middle out to the left, is systematically excluded from what passes for public dialogue." "'Amerika' Isn't Tuned In to New Soviet Challenge," 2-5, *WSJ*, impressed us as wild with its "The USSR is now a great deal more serious than the US about reducing the threat of nuclear war," but others far to his right have asserted no less. Pure venom in "The March of Power," 5-2, *TN*, he spits at *TNR* columnist Charles Krauthammer as an accessory to U.S.-backed "war crimes" in Nicaragua. Among pro-Sandinista columnists, Cockburn has no equal on the hard-line defense, the hooded throat threateningly fanning even against co-workers, as in "Playing to the Crowd," 5-2, *TN*, when Christopher Hitchens dared suggest the Sandinistas ought to let *La Prensa* roll again.

Cohen, Richard. *The Washington Post.* (★ ★ ★)
Still our favorite "liberal" columnist in the *Post*, but Cohen seemed a bit off his feed in 1987 when he should have had a heyday, given all the unpleasantness around the White House. But he had some fine columns in his twice-weekly op-ed space and his "Critic at Large" column in the otherwise abominable Sunday magazine. "...Even With Cheerleaders," 1-30, was an acidly pointed, wonderfully written review of the State of the Union address. Biden and Cuomo played their own delightful versions of Hamlet in "The Presidential Procrastination Society," 2-10. Cohen's perceptive in "Greedgate, Irangate, Godgate," 3-27, "Bakker and his flock - indeed, many of the evangelical ministers are like rigid buildings in a high wind. They have no give, and so they snap. They acknowledge confounding relativity." In "...And The New Jesse Jackson," 5-19, he coolly demolishes Jesse Jackson's credentials: "...The political community has responded with surgery of its own — a laboratory. The rhetoric of Jackson's last campaign has apparently been forgotten." "Judge Bork: Fancy Footwork," 7-31, is an effective argument: "It's impossible to know which comes first — the theoretical egg or the actual chicken. As lawyers (and columnists) know, it's possible to work backward — to arrive at a conclusion, and then, by selective argument and with quotations, make it appear that the conclusion was the inevitable product of rigorous reasoning." But he's uncharacteristically soft in: "It's Autumn For The Administration," 8-18, merely a string of assertions that could have been better argued. "More Mindless Anticommunism," 4-23, used weak logic, some detail on Karl Linnas in cheering his deportation, Oxbow fury, "The same people who champion the death penalty in this country — Buchanan, William F. Buckley, Jr. — blanch at its use by a communist country." Among his best, "A New Generation and Its Leaders," 9-30, in which he holds the Democratic presidential field to his special standard and consigns them all to oblivion.

Crozier, Brian. *National Review.* (★)
Writing from London, "The Protracted Conflict" columnist, Crozier's focus is the Atlantic geopolitical pivot and related Cold War issues, but not always on the news and with less verve than Beichman. In "The Fragile Polity," 1-30, he discusses which has the better system of

government, France, England or the U.S., giving his own proposals for "a strong and stable democratic system that would preserve the essential liberties while avoiding some of the absurdities of the present systems" noting also "the trouble with democracy is that, like terrorism, it is probably invincible." He goes a step further in "The Democracy Syndrome, Con't.," 6-19, noting that with all the turmoil in democratic governments, Iranscam, the dangers of returning the Labour Party to power in the British elections, etc., "the only beneficiaries of the democratic syndrome as exemplified today on both sides of the Atlantic are Mr. Gorbachev and his colleagues." In "Red Star Blazes On," 8-14, he's wary of Gorbachev and Maskisovka, but nice, almost admiring, before he gets to the darker side of arms control: Gorby's "an intelligent man, he is well aware that the Soviet system doesn't work. He also knows that he cannot propose to jettison the ruling ideology, if he is to stay in power. So he tries to borrow the principle of the economic market without restoring the bourgeois class that was liquidated in the name of History."

Evans, Harold. *U.S.News & World Report.* (★)
More willing to take a stand on one side of an issue this year, but going from *U.S.News'* Editorial Director to Contributing Editor left less column space of him to stand, with still too much pontification from this platform. Okay on the Constitution in "Does the Constitution Need Reform?" 4-27, chewing on flaws he sees. "The Missouri Standard," 10-12, sounds the alarm on the slow destruction of the ozone layer by CFCs (chlorofluorocarbons), but without much persuasion. His best work was a vigorous, strongly focused piece, "Getting Away With Murder," 3-23, slamming Pinochet on his human rights record and the tolerance of the U.S. State Department: "There are two causes of U.S. wobblies...Chile's economic progress...if Pinochet goes, Communism will follow...It is right to be concerned about the Communist threat in Chile. It is probably growing — but it is growing because of Pinochet and his excesses. He is polarizing the country." But it still seemed too secondhand, huffing and puffing.

Evans, M. Stanton. *Human Events.* (★ ½)
Strategic defense and national security questions his primary focus, he gets good marks for being the most abreast of SDI's political side. He argues on behalf of a policy perspective more than he reports on the subject, though he's never estranged from the current developments. His exploration of the case for deployment, "SDI Should Be Reagan's No. 1 Objective," 2-7, was forceful and cogent, one of his best. "Toshiba Case: Tech Transfer Bombshell," 7-4, makes a case against Commerce for watering down security controls on high-tech exports, noting trade bill provisions for expanded East-West trade that will abet the leakage. Not totally convincing, but it can't be dismissed. Less satisfying, "Looking to '88: Kemp and the Conservatives," 1-21, asked and answered questions in a tautological mold.

Evans, Rowland & Novak, Robert. *Chicago Sun-Times*, News America Syndicate. (★ ★ ★ ★)
Still the best, most influential political column in the world. All the more amazing in that the dynamic duo, whose average age is over 60, have their own weekly TV show and Novak is the star of several others. Their tilt is definitely conservative, but the secret of their success is a rigid commitment to the highest standards of their profession, which means nobody stays mad at them for very long. In "Don Regan Nearing His Goal of Dumping Fed's Volcker," 1-12, their scoop derailed plans to move Beryl Sprinkel into the job and helped send Regan down the chute. They are characteristically blunt in "SDI: Shultz Backs Off," 1-28, describing the Secretary of State's retreat from the "pro-defense GOP gang of 5." They're after Shultz again in "Another Threat to the Contras," 8-7, noting contra Adolfo Calero met with Shultz the day after the RR-Jim Wright initiative was cooked up and heard not a word about it. "So Long, Contras," 8-14, is terrific on the behind-the-scenes maneuverings, especially the Shultz backing of the Arias plan. "Dole Flares Up," 7-15, sees the return of Bob Dole and how the opposition camps missed him, among the best political columns of 1987. The most prescient is "Reagan's Surrender," 3-2, on his selection of Howard Baker, Jr., as chief of staff, a capitulation to the Old Guard.

Ferguson, Andrew. *The American Spectator.* (★)
The "Washington Spectator" columnist, Ferguson chortles lightly through DC, and bounds around other cities as well, with easy-to-read observations but little that sticks to your ribs. In the May issue, he reviews Ronald Reagan's performance at "*the* most important press conference of the President's career,'' describing his speaking style as "the rudiments of intelligibility; but before long a clause will pop up unbidden and wander toward uncharted territory, where it tumbles into wide patches of syntactical quicksand." He's just as frothy in November on Judge Bork, and in August on modern art in Washington. On the road, at least he was outrageous in San Francisco with hilarious personal recollections, "The Golden Gate Spectator: A Bridge Too Far," July, and also in Chicago with comments aplenty on the mayoral primaries and Jane Byrne: "In her gayer moments she still makes Rosalynn Carter look like a drunken dancehall girl," "The Chicago Spectator: 'Black Roots','' April. But there were sour, sour grapes from him in a long September feature "Can Buy Me Love: The Mooning of Conservative Washington," a hatchet job on a conservative competitor, *The Washington Times*, no doubt commissioned by his boss, who loathes the *Times*. Ferguson clearly has potential, though.

Fields, Suzanne. *The Washington Times.* (★ ★ ★ ½)
Gritty, often electric in dealing with feminist issues and the ever-raging battle of the sexes, we keep expecting her to run out of things to captivate us with, but there's always more and better, witty and irreverent. In "Rediscovering Their Intuition," 3-26, she defines men as "hard-headed, ornery cusses....who may be 'explosive, silent, controlling, withholding, self-centered, arrogant,' but who can also be 'sensitive, helpful, charming, talented, or funny.' The trick is to get one set of adjectives without the other." She's scathing on scandalous DC in "Brokering Naked Power," 9-15, on a stupefying lack of discretion in Joan Braden's autobiography, asking if Joan expects her "children to find it amusing to read that their mother took a shower with Nelson Rockefeller" and "only teased Bobby Kennedy with a few kisses on the bed," comparing Braden to Gary Hart and ending with a simple "Welcome to Washington." On "Dwarfettes In Search Of A Role Model," 7-30, she points out the incongruence of Eleanor Roosevelt as heroine for radical feminists and failures of aspiring Democratic first ladies to take Bess as a model: "The Truman marriage was much more a partnership of love and work than that of the Roosevelts." In "The Cruelest Lie of All," 6-9, Fields advocates mandatory AIDS testing for marriage licenses, noting "women have always been susceptible to men who lie, but lies in the past rarely came with a death sentence."

Foell, Earl W. *The Christian Science Monitor.* (★)
Editor of the *Monitor*, Foell seemed a bit rusty after his sabbatical, his weekly column low on strength or conviction. "Sherlock Holmes and the Case of Youth Unrest in Marxland," 1-21, details the rumblings of discontent in Communist Russia and especially China, with a Baskerville bark metaphor that doesn't quite work. In "Iran-U.S. Situation Minus The Distortion," 8-11, he outlines an interesting premise, tries to go deep for the long ball, but doesn't quite make it. A better argument in "Birth Dearth Is Worth Skepticism," 8-18, a critical reaction to Ben Wattenberg's book, with Foell going for the demographic flow as family size is linked causally to opportunity.

Fossedal, Gregory. Copley News Service. (★ ★)
Trying to cover the world from Palo Alto whilst writing books, Foss slipped a full star from last year. He is still one of the most knowledgeable columnists around on SDI, producing columns and occasional newsbeats we see in *The Washington Times*. A page-one scoop, "Nitze, Scientists Craft SDI Curbs for the Soviets," 11-9, got our attention. But at times there was less rigor in the material, more shortcutting. "What The President Never Said," 6-4, was much too cutesy on Reagan in his "history phase." Another was "The Nicaragua Scandal: Policygate," 6-12, which headlined each point with "**ITEM**." Yet his raw talent showed in classifying *glasnost* as "an important shift in the way communism works on the margin" in

"It May Be a Charade, But Glasnost Bears Watching," 5-18, and when comparing a Bush presidency with "the style and substance of the 1987 Reagan administration" in "Getting the Drift of a Bush Presidency," 4-28, both without the nonsense gimmickry. His best: "Spiritual Bouquets' Counter Gay Attacks On Pope Visit," 8-13, on Mother Teresa's teaching "it's little things done with great love that matter" — Bernie and Sue Biynak counter planned anti-Pope activities in San Francisco with fasting and prayer — a spiritual bouquet and the idea spread, to 10,000 participants, a lyrical retelling.

Gergen, David. *U.S.News & World Report.* (★ ½)
The magazine's editor and strongest of the three back-page mainstays in *U.S.News*, Gergen, a former White House Communications Director, is always sober in delivering Beltway experience and perception. At times we get true civil-servant boilerplate, as when he calls for better quality people to serve in government, outlining options (yes, including better pay) to entice people to government as a line of work in "Somebody Has to Do It," 6-29. But he can also arouse himself against the tide, as in "Prevailing In the Gulf," 9-14, in support of U.S. military presence in the Persian Gulf, making some persuasive arguments for "staying power." And in "On Christian Understanding," 4-6, he has a rather bold thought for a DC denizen, supporting the Christian movement's right to exist as both a religious and political entity. It's nicely formulated, using statistical evidence and reason to point out that Christians as such are not necessarily backward, nor dangerous politically, a way-out idea we've rarely encountered in the mass media. "Staying on Top," 10-26, entertains us with arguments for more money for colleges, coincidentally accompanying a cover story on higher education. However, running a magazine doesn't leave too much energy for way-out ideas, and there is too much boilerplate to warrant higher marks.

Germond, Jack & Witcover, Jules. *National Journal.* (★ ★ ½)
Hard-working veterans on the national political beat, G&W report from the trenches without lofty or fancy strategic insights, and with a moderately Democratic New Deal tilt. For the first time in years, we saw them weekly in the *NJ* and found their political handicapping useful. They still shy from issues, stressing the mechanics of politics and the personality of politicians, but their angles are often acute. In "1988 Could Be the Year That a Late Starter Wins," 2-7, they observe Gary Hart was almost broke in 1984 when he won New Hampshire, and Senator Bradley could thus start late and win. "Size of Vote May Hold Key to Iowa Victory," 4-25, offers some good historical comparisons with the 1980 GOP caucus. "New Hampshire No Longer Stands Alone," 1-24, questions whether early organizing counts for much anymore in NH, after Iowa and national TV expense, but it's not clear what they really think. "Bush's 'Imperial' Ways Antagonize Opponents," 6-6, gossipy, but not much more. Their "Inside Politics" column, 10-10, has Dukakis "kept afloat" by a quick apology for his staff's role in embarrassing Senator Biden, but surprisingly no word on the impact of his campaign manager's departure. They find a "Wide Open Democratic Contest in Iowa," 10-17, but correctly tip us on a Paul Simon surprise. At a difficult time in covering political complexities, their experience counts for a lot.

Geyer, Georgie Anne. Universal Press Syndicate. (★ ★)
Going 'round the globe and back again, Geyer still finds time for an occasional stop at "This Week With David Brinkley" to talk about the world. She visited with Singapore's Lee Kuan Yew, bringing back accolades in "Nation With A Niche," 4-13, and Turkey's "free-marketer prime minister" Turgut Ozal in "Turks Respond to Free Market Ideas," 7-6, detailing the Ozal-engineered economic turnaround while acknowledging the problems (too-high inflation, political struggle, military discontent, and "Khomeini-style fundamentalists"). And late last year we noted "Carlucci's Successful Ways in Portugal," 12-29-86, a vivid anecdote of Carlucci as Ambassador to Portugal in 1975-76, facing down Communists, backing Mario Soares. Geyer is perceptive in "Afghan Guerrillas Are Winning the War," 7-31, in which she details Rep. Charles Wilson, the mover and shaker for Mujahidin aid in Congress, and developments in

Afghanistan to prove the point: "it is time to take Soviet leader Mikhail Gorbachev's recent talk about the Russians leaving Afghanistan seriously." But her material can also be pretty thin, as in the obvious "Hostage-Takers Don't Use Reason," 2-19, saying we don't understand the Iranians, but they understand us, and that's why they continue to get the best of us.

Goodman, Ellen. *The Boston Globe, Washington Post* Writers Group. (★)
Last year we cited her "occasionally insightful commentary buoyed by a subtle humor." But there seemed fewer insights and less subtlety in 1987 as she mainly deals with social issues concerning women. Now stuck in a 1950s time warp, she yearns for the ideals of bygone days, which we would not mind except for the self-righteous whine that goes with it. In "The Neighborhood Mom," 1-31, Goodman explores the trials and tribulations of being the stay-at-home-mom when all the other moms are out there having it all: a significant and relevant topic in terms of shifting social conditions, but so fishwifey you find yourself on the side of the working mother, which is not her intent. Better, strangely, on Oliver North in "The Good, the Bad and the Boffo," 7-11, less carping, more substance, rebutting North's arguments in defense of the Contras and neutralizing his use of murdered Natasha Simpson as an icon: "More than a thousand civilians, 'living, breathing human beings' — including 210 under 12 — have been killed by the war we created in Nicaragua. North helped make these things happen. So did his lies to Congress." But she's better with subtle humor.

Greenberg, Paul. Freelance Syndicate. (★ ★)
We see Greenberg in *The Washington Times* where he was a strong and versatile, writing soup to nuts with predictably conservative flavoring. He adds another hilariously written verse to "The Ballad of Boogaloo Bill," 6-27, on Rep. Bill Alexander (D-AR) and his publication of three and a half years of Boland Amendment debates in one volume, and he's striking on "The Boland Specter," 5-27, which tells of the Reagan administration resting on "63 words, the key paragraph of the Boland Amendment," the original intent of which was "to hogtie the president of the United States." In "Destructive Engagement," 11-9, he takes on South Africa sanctions, calling them a means by which nothing is done "to speed apartheid's downfall," but allows those doing the sanctioning to go home "feeling righteous." He praises Maggie Thatcher for her objections to them "with nothing more than spunk and sense to back her up." And he's poignant on Australia in "Still Off Limits to History," 4-15, Australia being the only one of 17 countries, including the U.S., who voted "no objection" to the opening of the U.N.'s War Crimes Commission files: "It only takes one voice ever demanding that men must look and see, and eventually they must...the power of what is unearthed may be enough to overcome all the flimsy evasions. It takes only one nation, like Australia, to speak out, and the world is shamed by its silence."

Greenfield, Meg. *Newsweek, The Washington Post.* (★ ½)
The editor of the *Post*'s editorials, Meg's columns seemed to be hitting the same D&D notes in column after column, Disillusionment and Disappointment, reading like a two-column sigh emanating from Deep in the Diaphragm. She had plenty to work with in '87. On Gary Hart, in "Private Lives, Public Values," 5-18: "It was about the way a 50-year old man who would be president chooses to live, about his relationship with and respect for other people, about his honesty, about whether he feels contempt or consideration for the sensibilities and values of those he aspires to lead, about achieving a right relationship between what one professes to be and what one actually is." In "The Illusion of 'Security'," 4-20, she despairs of real safety from crime, accidents, and acts of God. And in "When Right Isn't Right," 5-12, she observes that even the right-wing has its D&D problems: she observes that the right is never publicly happy with their heroes once they take office, but she doesn't really know why. "How We Shred the Past," 10-5, conjured up images of Orwell's *1984* with Washington overtones, detailing the "expedient" writing of history. She spent the year out with her lantern, looking for an honest man. Maybe in 1988!

Grenier, Richard. *The Washington Times.* (★ ★ ★ ★)
The powers that be at the *Times* sent one of the best columnists in the English language traipsing all over the world in '87 and he returned with malaria, amoebic dysentery and a portfolio of solid gold. The only living U.S. journalist we can think of who would fit in at the old Algonquin Roundtable, a cross between Harpo Marx and H.G. Wells, Grenier is always light on his feet. "In Angolan Struggle, U.S. Plays Both Sides," 3-11, looks on the two faces of American policy in Angola, supporting both Savimbi and the government, including such wisdom for the U.S. as "This is worth considering as a way of life: No grandstanding. Avoid unnecessary somersaults." In "Decay Amidst the Slogans," 9-4, we get a vivid portrait of Marxist Maputo. Without stopping to feel the heat, he remains as always a ladies man, cheeky in his hilarious treatment of Amy Carter, "Let Us Give Thanks for Little Amy," 3-30, and proclaiming his love for Zinzi Mandela, "A Strange Attraction to Zinzi, Of Course," 4-6. On the home front, Grenier, an Annapolis man to boot, was livid over the Stark affair in "How Ready For Action Is Our Navy?" 6-17. Watching the Iran-Contra hearings, "How Many Men Can Rise To Such Heights?" 7-29, he weighs George Shultz's performance: "Being in the presence of Mr. Shultz is like being in the presence of an almost dead oak tree. Somewhere, you realize, just a little bit of sap must be flowing." His lead on "A Little Glasnost at CBS," 6-29, is priceless: "I am so mad. Ever since last week when CBS did its 'Seven Days in May,' investigating *glasnost* in the Soviet Union, I've been hearing people castigate poor Dan Rather for his obsequious, sycophantic, toadying smile when dealing with Soviet officials. This is deeply unfair. What they were seeing on Dan Rather's face was the warmth and natural love he feels for all humankind." Please, editors, keep this man at home in 1988, on the presidential campaign trail!

Harsch, Joseph. *The Christian Science Monitor.* (★ ½)
We gave his column more attention in 1987 and found an occasional feast along with the usual pleasant fare. He's best on diplomatic issues, bland on politics, leaden on economics. In "The USS Stark and the Price of Empire," 5-28, he's eloquent in raising the question and turning it over for us, even though leaving it unanswered. "Words of Caution for Those Who Live By the Sword," 1-16, recites recent aggressive military blunders, well written. "Sandinista Peace Concessions Due to Pressure From Friend and Foe," 8-21, is smart and useful on RR's foreign policy. Also, "Why What Didn't Happen Last Week Is Important to U.S.-Soviet Ties," 7-31, noting RR dropped criticism of Gorbachev from a prepared text: "He seems to be headed for an exercise in East-West detente on a set time schedule, which violates one of the main rules for dealing with the Soviets." But "The Battle of the Scandals," 5-7, which is more about the battle of presidential hopefuls, is oddly without fever, rather light, conventional analysis. The most elitist column of the year, "Citizens or Congress: Who Shall Elect the President?" 5-21, would never sell in Peoria. "The 'Let Reagan Be Reagan' Days Are Over," 8-11, much better, accurately seeing RR as being hemmed in by his advisors.

Hart, Jeffrey. *National Review.* (★)
A Dartmouth professor most of the time, "The Ivory Foxhole" columnist weekly, Hart keeps us apprised of the goings-on in the academic world. He fights the liberals, communists and assorted campus radicals with a snide humor, keeping the Ivory Tower safe for conservatives. In "Oh, If I Could Only Be a Communist," 6-19, Hart argues that "any opinion, including Communism, may legitimately exist within the university" but, only half tongue-in-cheek, that the rights conferred by the Constitution, such as free speech within the university, are only applicable to those who believe in it and not to those dedicated to its overthrow. "Ethnophobia, Heterophobia, & Liberal Fascism," 2-13, presents a poor freshman and the "transvaluation of values" he confronts. "'Safe Sex' and the Presence of the Absence," 5-8, was the first ever review of a "Safe Sex" kit, slamming Dartmouth for "what is **not** present in the Dartmouth 'safe sex' kit — and no doubt in this it resembles others — is the manners and substance of civilization," outlines what you find in the kit, and the accompanying brochure which never

mentions "the fewer partners one has, the lower the risk one incurs." His best line: "I myself had never heard of some of these sexual practices, and I have lived in Paris."

Hempstone, Smith. *The Washington Times*, The Hempstone Syndicate. (★)
An armchair pundit whose writing talent often pulls us through frequently tired material. In "Ganging Up on Abrams," 7-10, he defends Asst. Secy. of State Elliott Abrams' appearance before Iran-Contra hearings: "When he has spoken in error, he has corrected himself, when his behavior before a congressional committee has been more than unusually outrageous, he has apologized with his normal ill-grace." He's fresh with "Are We Ready to Go the Distance?" 7-29, arguing we have to play hardball with Khomeini because he's been asking for it, even if this risks cementing Iran into the Soviet sphere. In "Prodding the Tiger," 9-2, he potshots the IOC for granting some Olympic events to Pyongyang, calling North Korea "politically weird even by Communist standards," but the material seems unfocused, weird even by Hempstone standards. In "The Odds Keep Going Up," 9-11, his thesis is that Cory Aquino is in over her head, but God bless her for getting this far sort of thing. Things are bleak, but maybe if she makes more concessions to the Army to quell dissent! His ruminations on "Waning Hopes in Post-Duvalier Haiti," 2-20, are equally dire, and he suggests land reform!

Hentoff, Nat. *The Washington Post, The Village Voice.* (★ ★)
A competent jazz critic, among other things, it was Hentoff's music commentary that first caught our eye. "The Chief Would Be Proud," 2-6 in *The Wall Street Journal*, was a touching and skilled assessment of how Count Basie's band keeps the founder's spirit going, evoking memories of Birdland. Another jazz critique that was respectful, yet focused and sharp, was "The Gentleman of Jazz," 4-6, *WSJ*, on Benny Carter, who acknowledges fantastic endowment of talent with young performers today, but finds them sacrificing emotional content for technique. He's credible outside the music world as well. In "AIDS: Mandatory Testing Would Help," 5-30, *WAPO*, Hentoff motivates the argument against ACLU's opposition to testing, noting that testing could help prevent babies with AIDS. He points out in "Amy and Abbie vs. Free Speech," 5-9, *WAPO*, that while in the "peace forces" celebrating the Abbie Hoffman-Amy Carter acquittal, that "forgotten during all the toasts are the 12 students who wanted to hear the recruiter on campus. Their First Amendment right, at a public university, to receive information has found few champions." He further theorized that in a free exchange between U Mass students and a CIA recruiter, the students "could have demolished him with the facts," but he never made it onto campus: "That is not 'doing democracy.' That is doing in democracy."

Hitchens, Christopher. *The Nation.* (★)
"Minority Report" columnist. If you're on a low sodium diet, you'll never survive his columns, all of which have to be ingested with heavy doses of salt. He gets blood pressures pounding over the limit with his 2-14 column. "The Holy See was one of the patrons of fascism," he writes, drawing an identity between the movement and Catholicism, and slandering Cardinal John O'Connor of New York and Cardinal Manuel Obando y Bravo of Managua as well. Too often, his material in *The Nation* is of these depths. A blithe disregard for real evidence keeps his enthusiasm untempered, as with his columns of 6-20 and 7-4/11, suggesting the Reagan campaign in 1980 may have cut a deal with the mullahs to hold up release of U.S. hostages until after the election in exchange for arms later (an allegation *In These Times* "scooped" *TN* on). Occasionally he's genuinely perceptive as in "Thatcher's Regime Has Already Begun to Take on a Gaullist Tinge," 6-6, criticizing her "every man for himself" philosophy and, without naming it, exposing the Phillips Curve road to low inflation via high unemployment. Outside *The Nation*, he's far more palatable. "Blabscam," 3-87, *Harper's*, was a tasty critique of TV's "rigged" political talk shows. However, "It Dare Not Speak Its Name," 8-87, *Harper's*, was sulfuric acid straight up with a splash of bitters, with Hitchens foaming about the coterie of closet gays in "Reagan's bizarre network of lucre, guns, and *contras*." Hitchens was, though, balanced in his profile of a repeated target of *The Nation*'s barbs, Michael Kinsley of *The*

New Republic, "The Kinsley Report," 9-87, *Vanity Fair*, a tasty morsel on political journalism's *enfant terrible*.

Hughes, John. *Los Angeles Times* Syndicate. (★ ★)
Appearing in *The Christian Science Monitor*, he draws our attention by regularly coming up with oblique perspectives that are even useful when he misfires, as in "Nicaraguan Peace," 8-7, an interesting scenario that breaks down when he suggests the Soviets could use their economic power to topple the Sandinistas. He's solid on "Glasnost Redux," 8-28, asserting "the aim is to make the USSR a better and stronger nation under Communism." We first think "The Press on Trial," 5-6, is about the Hart-Rice thing, instead find a nicely done review of press coverage of Iran-Contra, future and past. He turns in some zippy lines now and then. In "What They Think Reagan Should Say," 1-21, he uses various voices (Qaddafi, Regan, Hart, etc.) making suggestions for the State of the Union. George Bush: "If you could slip in a line boosting Pat Buchanan for President, that would be good. The more political blood-letting there is among right-wing conservatives, the better my own chances. And you know how dedicated I am to continuing Reaganism." In "Tears in Politics," 10-2, on Pat Schroeder crying her way out of the campaign: "Margaret Thatcher...is more likely to reduce reporters to tears than break into tears herself."

Johnson, Haynes. *The Washington Post.* (★)
An old-time liberal who, given all the difficulties of the Reagan administration, ought to have had a great year, having something to push against. Not a great year, but better. He was fresh and jaunty in "Hypocrisy Sweepstakes," 2-11, zapping the television networks for airing "sexual themes highlighted in abundance", but refusing to air condom ads: "The networks can make a simple contribution by doing what they already know how to do best: make a profit by selling something associated with sex." In "North Revelation of Casey Brainchild Triggers Bitter Debate," 7-11, he was articulate, on the arguments within the select committee on North and Liman's questioning, but not very deep. Also on the hearings, "North's Dramatic Distracting Impact," 7-14, was well written, but told us nothing we couldn't see for ourselves. "Goals Of The Best And The Brightest," 4-22, was mindless, quoting high IQ kids who are being forced to study serious subjects if they want financial security, concluding "and this from an era that was supposed to produce a rekindling of American values." And he's just wild about George in "Shultz: Compelling and Bracingly Blunt," 7-24, on the Secretary of State's appearance before the Iran-Contra committee "It was a grim story [Shultz told], but one with a positive side." Hmmm.

Kidder, Rushworth M. *The Christian Science Monitor.* (★)
"Perspectives" columnist for the *Monitor*, Kidder appears each Monday, producing a light, common-sense column. "Resolving Ethical Issues With All Deliberate Speed," 5-18, was nicely done, exploring the ethical problem of expediency. Kidder gained strength as the year went on. He was timely in "Developing 'Character' Again At American Universities," 7-27, quoting Harvard's President Derek Bok on a crusade to reawaken commitment to ethical standards on campuses. He scored with "An Annoying, Fascinating Look at Mid-1980s America," 8-10, on Louis Harris' *Inside America*: "the danger of polling, after all, is that it's nothing more than the study of mere opinion. It's sometimes the societal equivalent of a cyclotron, in which tiny opinions are whirled about a closed track until they attain the atom-smashing force of apparent truth."

Kinsley, Michael. *The New Republic.* (★ ★ ★ ★)
Editor and "TRB" columnist has another sparkling year, with razor-sharp, never mean-spirited analytics from the new, young left, often against the grain. His commentary on Albert Gore, "Nice Young Man," 5-1, was one of the 10-best columns of the year. His monthly *Wall Street Journal* column (he switches to *Time* in 1988) is often directed against *Journal* editorial policy, infuriating the flock. One such, "The New Conservative Sophistication," 8-20, hammers *WSJ*

editorials for being permissive on white-collar crime: "It used to be there was nothing conservatives hated worse than criminals getting off on technicalities." In "Down the Memory Hole With the Contras," 3-26, *WSJ,* tough and incisive in skewering the administration's cuts and turns in making the contra case: "Maybe an honest case can be made, but the administration has not tried to make it." His "Nazis and Communists," 5-11, is to the point in arguing what was wrong in turning Karl Linnas over to the USSR. "Companies as Citizens: Should They Have a Conscience?" 2-19, *WSJ,* superb, surgical dissection of two new books about the corporation, zapping Boone Pickens along the way. He's weak, though, on "The Time is Right to Finally Destroy OPEC," 3-5, *WSJ,* cockamamie scheme No. 912 for the final, utter destruction of OPEC by taxing U.S. consumers. His worst of the year, "Plumbing the Leakers to Serve the Truth," 7-30, *WSJ,* an incredible defense of *Newsweek* for breaking its promise of confidentiality to Col. Oliver North, on the relativist theory that there is no need to keep promises we make to people it turns out we don't like (which explains a lot of modern divorces). But we love his highwire act, even when he falls.

Kirkpatrick, Jeane. *Los Angeles Times* Syndicate. (★ ½)
A former U.N. Ambassador and scholar turned columnist appearing in the *Post,* Jeane adds another feather in her most distinguished cap. "Crimes Against Humanity," 7-13, was an eloquent and well-informed discussion of the nature of human rights violations and justice's treatment of them under different regimes. "Abrams And the Strange Workings of a Divided Government," 7-6, was stinging on the Iran-Contra hearings, with a terrific lead: "It is not easy to explain to foreign friends, or even to ourselves, what the Iran-Contra hearings are all about: All those lawmakers, all those lawyers, all that testimony, all that investigation. So far there have been arms sales, crazy cakes, Swiss bank accounts, a beautiful woman — but not nearly enough spies or sex or corruption to explain the enormous expenditure of public money, time, newsprint and American reputation." No nonsense in "Democrats, What Would You Do?" 7-20, telling the Dems to either put up or shut up on Iran-Contra, angry, one-sided, but she had a *good* point: What exactly would they do? "The Sinister Oliver Tambo," 2-2, is on the mark, detailing ANC's terrorism continuing bloodshed that's not akin to American revolutionary forces — rather Robespierre, Ortega, Lenin. But a too-high percentage of her columns are ho-hum, as in "Just As Hamilton Predicted," 8-3, our forefathers turning in their graves over Congressional encroachment of executive power in foreign policy.

Kirschten, Dick. *National Journal.* (★)
We were much impressed with what we saw of his "White House Notebook" in 1986, this piece "sparkling with insights," that one filled with "peppery quotes." But we had to drop him a full (★) this year, wondering what happened to the insights and the pepper. His "After 6 Years of Firebrands...RR Turns to Pragmatists," 2-7, sees "one small flicker" in Gary Bauer at the White House Office of Policy Development, is an okay personnel review, but does not see the larger clash of forces at work. "Kicking Off a New Road Show," 6-20, is a thin and conventional angle on an evening news view of the White House. "The President's Counselor," 5-23, has Howard Baker Jr. chuckling amiably through a long, long boring piece that we could spice up with a dash of oatmeal. His column "After All His Years in Politics, Reagan's Still Touchy About Race," 10-17, has an odd focus to analyze the Bork struggle, and it's all ho-hum. One wonders if Kirschten is a chameleon who takes on the color of the White House chief of staff.

Kondracke, Morton. *The New Republic.* (★ ★)
Happily back with his byline after spending most of '86 flunking a *Newsweek* desk job, but now clearly third banana after Kinsley and Barnes. A good, seasoned reporter who enjoys doing complex analysis and often succeeds, but his commentaries seem more intense and humorless than we'd remembered from the old days. In two parts on "A Visit to Salvador," 8-10/17, he defends the Nicaragua contras: "...under U.S. influence the *contras* are promising democracy, just as under U.S. influence El Salvador is creating it." But he has no sense of

factors behind economic distress. "Gephardt's Inside Moves," 6-1, profiles Rep. Dick Gephardt while drooling over Sen. Bill Bradley; colorless, but that may be more Gephardt's fault than Kondracke's. He digs well in "Cool Hand Duke," an 8-31 cover on Mass. Gov. Mike Dukakis, asking "Can an earnest technocrat sell Kennedy School liberalism in Texas?" and makes a good case that the Duke's policy initiatives had little to do with the state's remarkable economic turnaround of recent years. "Where's the Beef?" 7-6, is a lively questioning of GOP candidates' ideas and proposals. His worst, "The Case Against Glee," 1-26, a whiny "Reagan's-magic-has-worn-off" piece that blames Donald Regan's character and management flaws. Soppy, sob-sister stuff. "Father, how could you?!!"

Kramer, Michael. *U.S.News & World Report.* (★ ★)
One of our favorite political reporters when he was at *New York* magazine, Kramer is now the "opener" for us at *U.S.News.* But as a rookie weekly columnist, he is a shade less effective. His first, "The Self Destruction of Gary Hart," 5-18, resurrects quotes and telling anecdotes from Hart's earlier years. No fresh analysis, but useful and we read it all. His "Parade of the Seven Pygmies," 7-13, is smart on the Democratic Firing Line debate, especially Senator Gore standing out from the pack with a strong stand on the Persian Gulf. But why the first person quotes? His "Covert Operations: Play By the Rules," 7-20, is a vigorously argued critique of Ollie North, who "didn't lie to save lives; he lied to save his ass." He has "no regrets, because he sincerely believed that a White House-directed covert operation was mandated by Congress' failure to appreciate the threat." Good stuff, but a bit too angry to be fully effective. We read his Central America columns with attentiveness. He sees no alternative to aiding the contras, but in "Contras: Ending the Pipe Dreams," 8-3, finds "The contras are doing poorly because they aren't attractive to the average Nicaraguans," and frets about their human rights problems, reported atrocities, etc. A bit preachy, unsupported, but he can't be dismissed. "A Central American Yalta?" 8-24, sees the White House outmaneuvered by Central American leaders, with Arias' plan mostly unworkable. He's serious-minded, walking around the problem carefully, which we appreciate, but we expect fresher analysis from him. A Bork cover, "The Brief on Judge Bork," 9-14, was a curtain-raiser, excellent on legal issues, albeit late in the game. With some seasoning, he's going to be a jewel at *U.S.News.*

Krauthammer, Charles. *The New Republic, Washington Post* Writers Group. (★ ★ ½)
A tough-minded neoliberal with a Pulitzer prize for his work in 1986, but we found his writing in 1987 a bit more impressive. "A Strange Tag Team," 3-6, *WAPO*, was his hottest column, Gorbachev agreeing to RR's zero-zero option on INF and Kraut asking RR: "Will you take yes for an answer?" and predicting a treaty. The column shook conservatives who never expected a "Yes." He chides "Sam Nunn and the Imperial Senate," 10-6, *WAPO* on the ABM treaty interpretation, another effective column. In "Spare Us The Sixties," 5-1, *WAPO*, he notes "You cannot have it both ways. A society cannot lionize entrepreneurship and then look down its nose at those who switch from liberal arts to business. It cannot deplore the fact that we turn out lawyers and sociologists while the Japanese turn out engineers and managers, and then consider our young engineers and managers to be sellouts." "Boland VI," 8-14, *WAPO*, was crisp, sharply critical analysis of Reagan-Wright segue into the Arias Plan, calling for elections in Nicaragua in 1990: "By then the contras will have been dead for three years, and free elections will be a less pressing matter for Managua." "Gorbachev's Retreat: Khrushchev Would Have Gagged," 11-6, *WAPO*, was the best critique of a Gorbachev speech that we saw, made effective by directly comparing it with a 1956 Khrushchev anti-Stalin speech. But he sometimes is reduced to huffs and puffs as in "Spectacle," 5-22, *WAPO*, making the mass media responsible for the Iran-Contra orgy.

Kristol, Irving. *The Wall Street Journal.* (★ ★ ½)
The erudite John M. Olin professor of Social Thought at NYU Grad School of Business, Kristol's columns sparkled optimism and good vibes, even after the October Crash. In "Look at 1962, Not 1929," 10-28, Kristol outlines what he sees as the explanation and implications

of the Crash, logically moving from one thing to another, concluding: "if any one thing is clear, is that the decline in the stock market had nothing whatsoever to do with the budget deficit. If there had been a connection, the dollar would be collapsing right along with stocks, and it hasn't. Besides, how can the American budget deficit explain the collapse of all major stock markets — British, Japanese, German, French, Italian, even Hong Kong? Clearly, there is a global factor at work," ending with a reassuring "it [the Crash] may temporarily slow down economic growth, but nothing more." Kristol also did a half-facetious "Ethics, Anyone? or Morals?" 9-15, asking "why are those professors teaching ethics, rather than, say, morals?" noting the difference between the two (ethics are value-free, morals are not) and opining the dangers of teaching ethics over morals in schools. "The Missing Social Agenda," 1-26, chastised the Administration for responding to bad social policy initiatives with inertia. Kristol even makes a foray into Sunday Safire territory in "The War of the Words," 6-11, looking at the language and the use of language in the political arena, holding his own well: "Conservatives...are extraordinarily slow to realize its [language's] political, as distinct from its cultural, abuse. As a result, liberals and socialists have, over recent decades, made a highly successful takeover bid, so that the words we unthinkingly use end up being their words, with their connotations, insinuating the exclusive legitimacy of their way of looking at the world."

Ledeen, Michael. *The American Spectator.* (★ ½)
The *Spectator*'s media watchdog, fairly effective in his documentation, although he has his own ax to grind. He was involved up to his knickers in the Iran-Contra play as a government consultant. While obviously ideological, he is smart, and comes up with such interesting information that we can't discount him. "The Shame of It," May, took *The New York Times* to task for not checking a Seymour Hersh story that appeared in the Sunday *Magazine*. "Exposing the Disaster," July, was precise in chronicling the story of the Toshiba-Kongsberg technology sale to the Soviets, praising The Detroit News for breaking the story, and then for following it up in "Hot Times on the Potomac," October. In "Distortions, Omissions, Lies," November, Ledeen ran two stories on the *same* event, one from the *NYT*, the other from *The Washington Post*, dissecting each and then revealing interesting gaps on each side.

Lerner, Max. *New York Post, Los Angeles Times* Syndicate. (★ ★)
Like his octogenarian contemporary John Chamberlain, Lerner is still dispensing clear-eyed wisdom although hardly the liberal of yesteryear. He had a slew of solid columns on Bork: "One doesn't have to search for hidden motives to see why the liberals feel that more Reagan appointments to the court will spell a watershed judicial power disaster for them" in "Naked Power Fears Revealed," 6-27, *The Washington Times.* Then catching what it's all about in "Battling for the Conscience of the Court," 7-6, *WAT*: "It is an event in the historic contest between two modes of judicial decision that have — inherently — little to do with political ideologies...'judicial activeness' and 'judicial restraint.'" Lerner notes "an entire court of Justice Powells would make me reasonably happy" in "Divine Right and Wrong of Justices," 7-1, *WAT*. Combative and tough in "Papal Blunder," 6-29, *WAT*, on Pope John Paul II's reception of Kurt Waldheim, asking how the Pope will "heal the wound he has inflicted on both the Jews and his own moral authority." On target with "The Sacred ABM Shroud," 2-19, *WAT*, getting the prime story of RR's second term — SDI. Gentler but no less determined in "Shifting From Fear To Resolve," 6-22, *WAT*: "American society as a whole, white and black alike, will be psychologically healthier and more secure when any one of us can ride in a bus or subway car without having to change our seats because of panic and fear. That sense of constant danger has no place in the daily life of a society as a collective organism."

Lewis, Anthony. *The New York Times.* (★ ★ ★ ★)
The nation's most important liberal columnist, the most loathed by conservatives because he is so effective. The *Times* Supreme Court reporter from 1955-65, Lewis provided the "respectable" arguments against Judge Bork's confirmation, first defending "Bork and the Press," 8-30, on libel law, then in "Bork and Free Speech," 9-3, arguing that he is a "radical"

who wants to upset legal traditions established by Holmes and Brandeis. A wrap-up, "Question of Judgement," 9-27, stipulates that Bork is a helluva fellow, but "is he a wise person?" Furthermore, "There is something deeply troubling about a judge who seeks certainty in abstractions." He did the same on the Iran-Contra hearings, addressing legitimate areas of concern in "But Do We Believe?" 12-9-86, on the breach of constitutional constraints on the executive's role in foreign policy. With wicked timing, he takes aim at Reagan in "The Man Responsible," 2-24, while other liberals are still celebrating Donald Regan's scalp. "The Empty Chair," 2-27, calmly lays out a deadly focus: RR's inattention to detail is inappropriate to the office. In "The Avalanche Starts," 5-1, he's getting ready for a conspiracy to reach to Reagan. But he is not a good loser, and in "What Reagan Did," 8-9, he jumps up and down, fulminating because RR is clearly off the hook. In foreign affairs, he defends the far left African National Congress simply by stating that it is "the organization that for 75 years has worked for a non-racist South Africa" in "Realism in Africa," 1-26. One of his most effective columns, "A Profound Test," 3-10, looks Gorbachev in the eye and tells him to get out of Afghanistan. At least once a year his brew is unacceptably bitter, as in "To Speak Against Evil," 3-27, a dubious tale of torture in Chile. And he makes more than his share of factual mistakes, once being chastised publicly by Andrew Neil, Editor of *The Sunday Times* of London in a feisty letter to the editor, 11-19. But we must read him.

Lofton, John. *The Washington Times.* (★ ★)
Wicked to the point of viciousness in savaging liberals and the left wing. His salvation is his relentlessness as a reporter, backing up his blasts with damning quotes or facts. He gives no quarter, and his shots are usually pointed and well-directed. In a hilarious pseudo-review of Eleanor Smeal's "act," he calls her, among other things, "unhinged" in "Tuning in to Eleanor Smeal," 3-18. He has a rumbling sense of humor as seen in "Now for the 'Bad' Views," 9-16, in which we get with Michael Jackson's going from "Bad" to worse: "Michael Jackson may be many things, but 'bad' ain't one of them...Bad? Give me a break, unless, as I say, you are talking about his manners or demeanor." In "Preaching a Prosperity Gospel?" 6-17, post-Jim Bakker, he slams the notion of a "prosperity" gospel eloquently as "*human*-centered and focus [sic] on *human* potential for successful living, health and wealth rather than glorifying *God's* grace and providence." He's scalding when taking the press to task in coverage, 1933-1945, of the Holocaust in "What Did the Press Know and When?" 7-6, with special emphasis on the *NYT* for ignoring the story or burying it. In one of the oddities of the year in "Soft on Natural Rights," 7-8, he attacked the Bork nomination on the grounds that the Judge was not a true conservative, but it didn't seem to help Bork a bit.

Maddocks, Melvin. *The Christian Science Monitor.* (★ ½)
Relentless this year on journalism practices and ethics, and other areas as well, always stylishly penned. In "A Few Scruples on the Ethical Revolution," 5-27, he muses that "these days news is a moralist's orgy...The trap with ethics is that just to talk about it leaves the illusion that you're doing something about it." Later, in "Declaring a Timeout on Legend-making," 8-21, he outlines an irreverent 10-point plan of restraint in coping with the mortal anniversaries of Marilyn and Elvis, such as "All editors will lose their two-hour lunch privileges if they assign writers to such non-stories as 'Who Will Be the Next Elvis (or Marilyn)?'" Then, on capital punishment, he quotes Dostoevsky on death row and comments "if Dostoevsky's reaction [to execution] seems extreme and uncompromising, consider the extreme and uncompromising punishment he so narrowly escaped" in "Capital Punishment: What Dostoevsky Knew," 5-1. And he doesn't hesitate to venture into the boardroom in "Conversations in the Executive Suite," 8-7.

McCarthy, Colman. *The Washington Post.* (★)
A harmless, wandering flower child who is given shelter by Ben Bradlee because he is a better than average scribbler, spending most his time ranting and raving about the madness of the world, hysterical on Bork, Reagan, AIDS, Catholicism, and you name it. "The Undermining

Truth of the Reagan Presidency,'' 3-8, venomous on how Reagan "peopled his government with Oliver North-like zealots. They saluted God and country and then proceeded in their own agencies, to spit on poor people, students, minorities, the unemployed, human rights, privacy, the first amendment, refugees, disarmament, the environment and anything else on the list of Reagan undesirables.'' His "Of Condoms and Condemnation,'' 3-1, first mangles Catholic teaching on sexuality, then advises AIDS is a health crisis, not an area for meddlesome church teaching. Then it's his dirtiest job, but somebody has to do it, so McCarthy defends Bishop McGann for crapping on Bill Casey during Casey's funeral in "A Bishop's Refreshing Candor,'' 5-16. His best pieces were forceful, caustic blowups: "What Robert Bork Says,'' 7-12, on Bork's references, qualifications, ideas and politics, noting "The 'one man, one vote' reappointment ruling in 1965, acceptable to everyone except some pit bull terriers to the extreme right, has no constitutional basis, according to Bork.'' And so it goes.

McGrory, Mary. *The Washington Post.* (★ ★ ★)
Mother McGrory won back her third star this year, stirring the Iran-Contra cauldrons and exorcising the perfidy of the Reagan Administration. It should have been a sensational year for liberal columnists, but she was among the few who worked at it instead of celebrating. The lady took strong punches at the State of the Union address, categorizing RR as "a teacher who has lost control of his class," "Spinning His Wheels," 1-29, and had a finely written, wry column on the battle over the highway bill and the education of Terry Sanford in "Present for the Curtain Calls," 4-2. In "Still In The Game," 7-23, Ma is ruthless against her boys, "The Democrats, holding all the cards but one, lost the Iran-Contra hearing." In "Shultz: Stoic Loyalist," 7-26, she loves George, but has it exactly right: "Shultz obviously thinks that Ronald Reagan has to be carefully monitored, to be shielded against his own worst instincts and his evil comparisons." She's got Meese's number: "Edwin Meese III, bulky, fair-haired, intermittently affable, was born to be a henchman" in "Mediocrity Beyond Doubt," 7-30. She adores Mario Cuomo, swooning in "At the Top of His Game," 2-5; he's "impressive," "soothing," "masterly," "gracious," "provocative," "commanding," "potent." In "Who'll Break The Colonel's Spell," 7-12, she has a self-righteous debunking of Col. North's testimony, ending with: "One man can break the spell. It is of course...Daniel Inouye of Hawaii...who knows what democracy is all about." Back on track with "Hill To Reagan: All Is Forgiven," 8-4, giving the liberal spin on Iran-Contra: "Congress, like a battered wife, will take back the abusive husband. He fell among evil companions, that's all. She will give him another chance. Divorce, like impeachment, can be so messy."

McLaughlin, John. *National Review.* (★ ½)
The mastermind behind the best political "talk" show on television, "The McLaughlin Group," his marvelous must-read column of pre-TV days may be gone for good. But what we get is still okay. "Reagan's No-Risk Regimen," 11-6, is impeccable in arguing that the Reagan administration began heading downhill when Howard Baker and the First Lady decided to placate the opposition and Congress. Yes, yes. But in November this is history. Where were these observations in August? "Tackling Toshiba," 8-14, has reasonable points and arguments on why RR will veto the sanctions, but they are all over the place. In "Covert No More?" 8-28, he posits that the Iran-Contra hearings will revive the CIA as a covert agency, an interesting thought that could have been better developed. "AIDS in '88," 5-8, skimmed the debate, noting "the AIDS issue will be the more politically unmanageable if special interests politicize it." Some good analysis and scenario construction in "Super Tuesday, Super Mistake," 4-24, but it's still just conventional wisdom. Wonderful, though, 2-27 on "Detroit Powerhouse" John Dingell, "an imperious SOB. Power hungry. A blue-collar rep. Tough, but fair. A man of his word."

Meyer, Cord. News America Syndicate. (★ ★)
Specializing in foreign affairs, Meyer writes with U.S. policy options in mind and doesn't often fall flat. Late last year "More than Holding Their Own...," 12-26-86, *The Washington Times*,

caught our attention as an excellent update and analysis, a "Commentary" lead on the Afghan rebels and Gorby's strategy shift, cutting supply lines across Pakistan. "Tugging at the Leader Under Savimbi," 2-20, *WAT*, was detailed on MPLA-Cuban-Soviet relations and strategies and how U.S. weaponry has helped remove the danger of a Soviet-directed offensive on UNITA's main southern bases. Persuasive on "Why U.S. Fails To Make Headway In Angola Talks," 7-23, *WAT*, outlining reasons: President Eduardo dos Santos is not a strong enough leader to "take risks for peace;" Castro is a determined opponent of any withdrawal of his 37,000 Cuban troops (and Soviets who've provided $1B in arms to MPLA are equally committed to Cuban force); MPLA offensive *finally* is beginning to move against Savimbi's bases; serious negotiations have to wait until offensive runs its course. Light on "Can Cory Overcome The Forces Of Political Gravity?" 9-11, *WAT*, just touching on land reform, focusing instead on the needs of the military, and suggesting the U.S. take a more active stance in maintaining Aquino presidency, a "long-term commitment."

Novak, Michael. *National Review.* **(NR)**
We gave a star and a half last year to the "Tomorrow and Tomorrow" columnist, now a contributing editor, but we saw too little of him to evaluate him fairly. Two pieces of note: "Spellbound by Her Life of Silence," 2-20, poignant on St. Therese Martin and the film about her; and "The New Science," 7-17, on the cultural and philosophical unity of the framers of the Constitution.

Pfaff, William. *Los Angeles Times* Syndicate. **(★)**
Of an older school of journalism, the graceful, literary style of his commentary is always appreciated. The Paris-based Pfaff is a frequent contributor to *The New Yorker*'s "Reflections" column. "On Nationalism," 5-25, was an absorbing retrospect on the phenomenon in the late 19th century, with Pfaff attempting to locate the repeated and disabling conflicts with radical national movements today as results of unsatisfied nationalism. Another broad analytic, "Perils of Policy, 5-87, *Harper's*, a retrospective on the Marshall Plan and why its aid-promotes-democracy promise won't hold today. He's best at the longer commentaries, more thought going into them. His shorter syndicated columns, however, seemed less thoughtful. "Reagan's Foreign Policy a Washout," 1-12, was definitely old-school reaction from the hip — the President's low marks could be boosted by the State Dept. professionals, especially if George Shultz can convince him to be "idealistic." The title says it all in "Fascist Mentality Surfaces in American Policy," 3-9, Pfaff simply foaming over the activist style of new radical conservative politics.

Podhoretz, Norman. *Commentary,* News America Syndicate. **(★ ½)**
Turning down the fire-breathing act in 1987, Podhoretz produced consistent, credible but still uncompromising columns that were always readable. "A Subliminal Endorsement of Suicide," 3-11, *The Washington Post*, was compassionate but firm on why his buddy Sidney Hook is wrong to advocate euthanasia. He devises an outlandish scenario in "Cuomo's War," 2-11, *WAPO*, that has President Mario sending in troops to Nicaragua in 1989 because President Ronald and his Congress waffled on Contra support in 1987. "...No, It's Not to Blame," 11-17, *WAPO*, was a tender, but one-sided defense of a battle-weary Israel, long worn from "siege, surrounded by enemies sworn to destroy it and by a wider world that has never fully accepted its legitimacy...Now, frustrated by their inability to call off this 40-year war against them, the Israelis have begun blaming one another. In truth, however, they are all equally the victims of a relentless and murderous aggression," saying, fairly enough, that's it's up to Israel's own to decide her politics and her fate. "What Reagan Knew and When," 3-5, *WAPO*, is tough on Reagan and Israel for giving into terrorists in the Iran-Contra Affair: "The overriding reason Ronald Reagan sold arms to the Khomeini regime was that he wanted to free the American hostages who were being held in Lebanon by terrorists under Iranian control...In all this, Reagan was abetted by the Israelis and their expert in counterterrorism whose expertise seemed to consist in figuring out new ways of paying terrorists off...Israel

can no longer be counted upon to set an example for the rest of the world on how to deal firmly with terrorism.''

Price, Raymond. *New York Times* Syndication Sales. (★ ½)
Robust on politics, the former Nixon speechwriter that we see in *The Washington Times* ventured into other territory with "Why Is It So Easy To Gloat?" 4-2, on the transgressions of Jim and Tammy Faye Bakker: their transgressions were minor stuff in their downfall, but their gross exploitation of faith is outrageous. "Were The Iran-Contra Hearings Worth It?" 8-7, makes a point: "If there was a genuine chance for an opening to Iran — and there probably was — these hearings have almost certainly blown it," observing Congress has to learn difference between opposition and obstruction. But "Hidden By The Euphemists," 9-3, seemed a bit naive on changing the atmosphere in the slums. Okay when he stuck to basics: "If we're going to save our cities, the first requirement is to append the perverted structure of values that infests the slum and foster a climate of crime and violence." He suggests Michael Jackson's latest video might be the start of the campaign to do this: "its going to take people with roots themselves in the ghetto community and who have the guts, the character and the celebrity to carry the message back: Bad is bad, and those who pretend otherwise ain't no heroes." How about *Jesse* Jackson instead of Michael Jackson?

Pruden, Wesley. *The Washington Times.* (★ ★ ½)
Managing editor. We urged Pruden in the *1986 MediaGuide* to drop his Reaganesque "Pruden on Politics" column and devote his energies to editing, and are now glad he ignored us. The column has become one of the consistent treats of the *Times*, smart, colorful, informed, often electric in its audacity. In "All the President's Loyal Lieutenants," 6-27, he zaps Cap Weinberger and George Shultz for opposing the Iran-Contra deal without moving their lips, a funny, stinging piece without being vicious: Shultz "had to use two towels the next morning to dry himself from all those slobbery kisses in the *Post* and *The New York Times*." In his "Rootin' for Ollie, From Coast to Coast," 7-10, he has a great line: "Arthur Liman, whose dissection of Ollie North was supposed to be an audition for attorney general in the Democratic Administration that was supposed to be ordained by these proceedings, performed yesterday as if he might have been the mouthpiece for the likes of John Zaccaro, Robert Vesco or Carl Icahn — which, in fact, he was." Describing the immediate reaction to Reagan's Tower Commission speech in "The Gipper's Back (ain't it awful?)" 3-6, he noted Sam Donaldson's dismay: He "wanted a full grovel, in the nude." There's hilarity, too, in "There's One Behind Every Great Man," 6-17, an irreverent, wisecracking look at Pierrette le Pen's appearance in European *Playboy*: "She is, you might say, conducting a full-frontal assault on her husband's celebrated vanity." Often on the margin, but at times a bit too caustic for many tastes.

Rabinowitz, Dorothy. News America Syndicate. (★)
Watching the tube and the media for any indiscretions, she catches them a good portion of the time. "Braving the Media Spotlight," 3-9, *The Washington Times*, was a surprisingly muted column on the stars going out to the homeless and spending the night on the streets: "Just what earthly good this overnight encampment of stars was going to do for the homeless was a question not just the host of 'Nightwatch' was asking." In "A Crimp in TV's Sex Life," 3-23, *WAT*, she evaluated the "new" attitudes of television. "The new conservatism, far from being upon us just yet, resembles more our old liberality, wearing precautions." Mighty when reviewing PBS' "Lesbian Mothers" in "Their Real Message: Our Way Is Better," 8-10, *WAT*, concluding that the message of such documentaries exploring deviance doesn't merely claim that their life style is as good as any other, but that they're superior. "Murder, She Wrote, Is Murder," 9-15, *WAT*, slams Rupert Murdoch's "A Current Affair" in the airing of a segment on teen killer (his parents, a 7-11 clerk) Sean, now a death row poet for perpetuating the "Save the Artist! school of social thought" a la Jack Abbott: "...not two days have passed in the last 20 years, it's a safe bet, without some authority on a talk show or other media format

coming forward to complain that the government has abandoned efforts at criminal 'rehabilitation.'"

Raspberry, William. *The Washington Post.* (★ ★ ½)
The *Post*'s preeminent black columnist, Raspberry produces consistently solid and rewarding writing. "We Contradict Ourselves," 2-2, was an eloquent argument for what might be termed as contradictions to the rules in terms of policy, sounding like Orwellian Doublethink, but frighteningly simpler. Powerful and fresh on "Sanctions Backfired," 1-28, concluding Congress was flat out wrong: "The only people who can be cheered by events in South Africa...are those who believe that bloody revolution is the only solution and that sanctions, by making conditions completely intolerable for blacks, will bring on the revolution. Is that what we really want?" Good job in "What About The Miami Herald?" 5-11, first thinks the stakeout sleazy, but after careful reading of accounts decides the *Herald* acted with journalistic responsibility. Raspberry turns the flip side of Bork's nomination in "Fighting Bork's Philosophy," 7-3, quoting Mary Berry: "It is perfectly clear that the president can nominate for any reason whatever. But it is also clear that the Senate can give its advice and consent on any basis and for any reason. They are equal." But not much new in "Who Is The New Front Runner?" 5-13, the one big complaint being that Jesse J. isn't being treated as front-runner. His best of the year, "The Civil Rights Movement Is Over," 2-25, "for the same reason World War II is over: we won it."

Rosenblatt, Roger. *Time.* (★ ★)
The essayist at *Time*, a philosopher wordsmith, Rosenblatt doesn't always delight us, but his "Enter This House and Let the Ice Melt," 10-26, a long, deep essay on life in the Soviet Union, was beautifully executed, a glimpse of another forbidden foreign place that most will never enter. His other essays were lighter. "Baby M. — Emotions for Sale," 4-6, was a somewhat bland accounting of the difficulties of the Baby M. case in terms of the bargain made and then broken: "Instead of a simple deal, he [Stern] has swung a deal whose complications are infinite, and infinitely surprising," ending "whatever Stern and Whitehead thought their pact was about, they were trafficking in goods too elusive to package and too universal for personal property. What you do not own, you cannot sell." Light and lyric on Shallus, the man who "wrote" the Constitution, going from "the quill age to the space age" in "Words on Pieces of Paper," 7-6, and poignant on "The Aged Mother," 6-1, whom we all know and love.

Rosenfeld, Stephen. *The Washington Post.* (★ ★ ½)
An editorial writer who is allowed a weekly column of his own, had a good year as usual, in foreign affairs. "Encourage Soviet Reform," 1-16, was a thoughtful piece noting there's been no systematic official review or broad public discussion of potentially vast implications of the Soviet initiative, raising the issue: Is it to U.S. interests to encourage reform or not? He goes beneath the surface of the trial of former nuclear technician Mordechai Vanunu in "Israel's Nuclear Crusade," 1-2, to address the fading of ambiguity and deniability surrounding Israel's nuclear program and ties in "Amerika" the program to America the country in "'Amerika' Is About Our Temper," 2-19. "A Not-So-Feeble Foreign Policy," 5-1, recognized "Events...are refusing to respect Reagan's political disabilities." Rosenfeld echoed Kirkland's reservations about the rally for peace and justice in Central America and Southern Africa, "A Mobilization Against Democracy," 4-24, and had sound analysis on why RR opted for the Central America initiative: "The material pressure that Ronald Reagan had more than six years to bring to bear was demonstrably insufficient to do the job," "A Good Choice," 8-14. But he seemed muddled in "Letting Go In Eastern Europe?" 5-29, Gorbachev trying to replace the still-reigning Brezhnevs of Eastern Europe to bring the region's Gorbachevs to power: What does it mean? He's unclear.

Rosenthal, A.M. *The New York Times.* (★ ★ ★)
In his first year as a *Times* columnist after 20 as its editor, Abe did very well after a lethargic trial and error start. His "On My Mind" column finally got moving with "A Question for

Cuomo,'' 2-26, both profound and irate that the New York governor had dropped out of the presidential race, that it was Cuomo's *obligation* to run: ''I am not so 'understanding' about Mario Cuomo deciding that there were other things more important than trying to lead this nation. He had gone too far — not in the campaign, but in what he had said the country meant to him.'' His first commentary on *The Miami Herald* snoop of Gary Hart was also irate: ''There is no such thing as The American Press. It is exactly what it should be — free individuals making free decisions under First Amendment rights...But because a story is important does not justify disreputable conduct in gathering it.'' A good line in ''The Mother and the Judge,'' 4-5: ''The Baby M case was a tragedy without villains until the very end, and then the judge stepped forward.'' He presented ''The U.S. Case Against the Estonian,'' 4-24, on Karl Linnas and Soviet evidence, a crisp windup. In ''Their Spies, Our Spies,'' 4-16: ''Espionage is carried out by a system of government. The superpowers are not alike and if that matters so does who wins and who loses the big ones.'' Then a great AIDS column, ''Eight Steps for Life,'' 5-31, ''Some of these points are unpleasant to read or write, particularly those that may touch on civil liberties. Better now and minimally, rather than late, when, with fear, disregard for liberties may grow even faster than the spread of the disease.'' In ''Streets Of Seoul,'' 7-23, he disparaged conventional wisdom: ''the idea that a nation is 'not ready' economically for freedom is a condescension and an arrogance.'' If he would do just a little bit more reporting and get some new information into his columns, the punditry would soar.

Royko, Mike. Tribune Media Services. (★ ★ ½)
Sprightly, often pointed, social commentary that we only got to enjoy while passing through Chicago until he began appearing this year in *The Washington Times.* In ''Skirting the Issue in a Thigh-Minded Fashion,'' 6-10, he dwells on the reappearance of the miniskirt and all those nasty double standards. If ''high-spirited'' men react, ''with a whistle...the thigh-flashing female is offended. They can't have it both ways: engaging in semi-nudity and being mortified when they get the predictable reaction.'' He's cheeky again in arguing for truly full disclosure in ''If They Want to Get Personal...,'' 6-22, prompted by *The New York Times*' demand to see political candidates medical records and FBI files: ''I called and asked about the marital status and divorces of its top editors. These are very powerful guys. Their stories, editorials and columns have shaped and swayed the government's foreign and domestic policies, caused legislation to be defeated or passed, caused candidates to lose or be elected. In other words, *The New York Times* has on many occasions influenced the course of history. That's very heavy stuff. So it seems only fair that we should have some insight into the character and judgement and stability of these people.''

Rusher, William A. *National Review,* Newspaper Enterprise Association. (★ ½)
Planning to retire in early 1988 from his post at *NR*, his often dark, sonorously conservative column glowers from the pages of *The Washington Times.* With grimacing wit in ''Fumes From the Swamp,'' 4-14, on the Iran-Contra affair, he advises: ''The orchestra is tuning up. Prepare to spend a large part of your spring in front of your television set, watching (carefully selected) excerpts from the testimony of the victims of this political feeding frenzy.'' In ''A Spectacular Example Of Dishonest Journalism,'' 8-1, he climbs into a tower of rage over *TNR*'s Michael Kinsley's 7-6 ''TRB'' column on the failings of the President: ''a masterpiece of deliberate deception, which counts heavily on the reader's ignorance or stupidity.'' He celebrates the conservative movement in ''Cleaning The Stables Without Hercules,'' 9-1, citing patriarchally encouraging examples on its non-death. He has a political insight we don't always see elsewhere, as in ''Not For The Same Reasons,'' 9-3, pinning Sen. Sam Nunn's refusal to run for president on the ''conventional wisdom, which holds that, in the absence of very special circumstances, the payoff in American presidential politics is on the economic front.'' Or, voters will not change horses in midstream and will stick with the GOP.

Rutherford, Malcolm. *Financial Times.* (★ ½)
The ''Politics Today'' columnist continues to impress us with his persuasive analysis on British politics, but all too often we have to await several clearings of the throat before he gets down

to business. In "Lawson: The Best Chancellor They Have," 3-20, we found it heavy-going to mine this long piece for nuggets, but eventually came up with just Nigel Lawson wanting "license to get on with tax reform" and enter the EMS. He's also very good in "Lessons To Be Learned All Round," 6-13, mulling Maggie Thatcher's victory in the U.K. elections, but it's also a slow starter that at last gets into fairly deep and satisfying territory: "The unions are learning to live with the Tory devil they know rather than with the Labour god who never appears." A "Not Such A Quickie Divorce," 7-3, was pleasant chit-chat-over-the-garden-fence commentary on the squabbles and philanderings within the SDP and its hesitancy to get it together (constitutionally) once and for all with the Liberals — who don't seem too bothered either way. Rutherford jibes at David Owen's contradictions which bring resentment from other SDP members, his best line: "The SDP leader thinks that many of the Liberals are 'wet' and now uses the same term about some of his own colleagues."

Safire, William. *The New York Times.* (★ ★ ★ ½)
A wonderful year for the *Times'* resident conservative, after two years treading water. Now we know he had been working on his Lincoln novel, and has now returned to giving his column the benefit of all his powers. Petulance gave way to the cutting good-humored Safire of yore. He's one of Reagan's best defenders, as the wolves close in, often chiding RR's allies for causing the problem. In "The First Lady Stages a Coup," 3-2, he has Nancy "an incipient Edith Wilson, unelected and unaccountable" in her power play against Donald Regan. Then a defiant apology to her in "113 Days is Enough," 3-12, defending the harsh words he leveled at her for shielding her husband from the press. A great closing line, a smoking fastball across the plate: "As for Gentleman's Quarterly, here's what to wear to a White House dinner: no man's collar — and no woman's either." In "Howard Baker's Folly," 8-16, he offers fine detail and analysis on Baker/Shultz blunders in Central America: "What a tragedy of errors. As the saying goes, none of this would have happened if Ronald Reagan were alive." His "Myths About the Reagan Decade" in the Sunday magazine, 3-22, was the best roundup and assessment we saw at that point. Also big hits on Israel's Iran-Iraq strategy, "Appease or Oppose," 2-26, a persuasive case against mandatory AIDS testing, "Failing the Tests," 6-4, and a generous review of the Bob Woodward book, saying it's worth reading, minus the Bill Casey deathbed hype, "In From the Cold," 10-4. He is weakest when traipsing into economic policy.

Samuelson, Robert J. *Newsweek, Washington Post* Writers Group. (★ ½)
Economics for the untutored. Generally upbeat and charming, his columns are breezy, but sometimes light on substance. In a commentary on the markets and what makes them work, "I'm as befuddled as anyone" in "The Biggest Bull Market," 4-20. He zings the doom and gloomers in "Cassandra Economics," 5-18, arguing for perspective in economics: no great catastrophes a la the Crash of '29, but no bed of roses either. A promoter of what might be called pragmatic economics, Samuelson relies mainly on common sense: "what government can do is create a favorable climate for economic growth and then hope for the best" in "Competitive Confusion," 1-26. Nice on the retirement of Fed Chairman Paul Volcker in "The Age of Volcker," 6-15, giving him a 21-dollar salute that was well-intentioned and well-deserved. "Progress And Poverty," 8-24, gives us plenty of stats on economic growth and the poor who are left behind, telling us what we all know — education is the key: "Children need to acquire better basic skills," but he isn't really sure if this would work though "even if the public were willing to pay for them." His best for the year, "The American Job Machine," 2-23: "Contrary to what you may hear, it isn't producing only low-skilled and low-paying unemployment." Sensible commentary, for crazy times.

Schneider, William. *National Journal, Los Angeles Times* Syndicate. (★ ★ ★ ★)
His weekly "Political Pulse" is one of the loftiest of all the political columns reviewed, surprisingly crisp and lucid and at the same time professorial, non-partisan. "With Cuomo Out, Hart Has Lost His Target," 2-28, was superbly on target: "Until Cuomo said NO, the race was shaping up as a fire-and-ice competition...Now, Hart's problem is, he has no one

to run against." (Except, as it turned out, himself.) He was first, in detail, on "Robertson Struggling to Hold Political Base," 5-30, after the Bakker scandal. By 9-26, "Early Robertson Success a Sign of Restive Right," sees the Rev. Pat as "the candidate who comes closest to what conservatives really feel — disillusionment and absentment," and sees Senate rejection of Judge Bork as a trigger to a broader Robertson appeal. In "Putting Politics Ahead of Nuclear Arms Strategy," 9-19, he presents perhaps the best political analysis of the INF treaty, seeing European and U.S. leaders "unable to resist the chance to support the first agreement in history that would actually reduce, and not just control, nuclear weapons. As for the strategic implications of such an agreement — they'll worry about that later." Also superb, "Olliology is at the Root of the Iran-Contra Affair," 7-18, arguing North was right, as far as it goes, but in defining the chasm between covert operations and covert foreign policy, he sees North and the NSC engaged in the latter. Very persuasive, powerfully structured. In "Congress Openly Defies Public Opinion on SDI," 5-23, he observes Democrats maneuvering to keep SDI from becoming political reality before Reagan leaves office in 1989. Two lengthy political essays in *The Atlantic* fix him in the four-star firmament: "The New Shape of American Politics," January, a superb synthesizing essay on political realignment, seeing the '60s, not the '80s as the crucial realignment period; and "The Republicans in '88," July, with bold, incisive commentaries on all the candidates, set against the Zeitgeist.

Schmertz, Herb. Heritage Features Syndicate. (★ ½)
A media basher, but with kid gloves, Mobil Oil's well-known Superflack is politically androgynous, swooning over Teddy K. and charmed by Bob Dole. We see his whimsical stuff in *The Washington Times*, where he always has some media-related point to make. In "The Mania To Bash Japan Is Misguided," 8-10, a theme repeated in 1987, he zaps the press for abetting the yellow peril, citing Ian Baruma's 4-12 *NYT* Sunday magazine feature as an example. "Anchors Away on the Surrogate Sea," 1-26, was a frothy follow-up on his idea that TV network anchormen be elected by national ballot (some folks take him seriously). "Newsman Mudd, Always a Bridesmaid," 2-6, twits Roger for a career that confuses newsmaker with newsman. "Modern Media's Insideness Disease," 6-9, was a nice semi-review of David Broder's *Behind The Front Page*, but light, not asking too many questions. He makes his point with a nice example, chiding Dan Rather for his huffy disappearing act on the evening news, "When Anchors Go Away," 9-29, comparing him to Wally Pipp, who "held down a great job for 10 years, until one day he didn't feel like working: so he told the boss he had a headache... Lou Gehrig, beginning that afternoon, played first base for the Yankees for 2,130 straight games — Wally Pipp never got his job back."

Seligman, Daniel. *Fortune.* (★ ★ ★)
Fortunately, Seligman, the keeper of the "Keeping Up" column, doesn't change much from year to year in his irreverence, wit, and ability to dig behind the obvious. A proponent of modern computer weapons, he does battle through the Nexis data base and Lotus 1-2-3 spreadsheets. He manages to weave his favorite sports, as well as computers, into pieces of column, such as "A Software Sale," 7-6, where he announces his invention of The Seven Dwarfs Sweepstakes, a computer-software Democratic candidate horse race; and "Strange News from the Diamond Market," 5-25, in which he uses spreadsheets to figure out how much of the difference in baseball players' salaries can be explained by performance data. (Only about half.) In "Wall Street Poker," 3-30 (referencing another favorite sport), he takes on those with "elevated IQs" who are attacking insider trading, which Seligman describes as "more of a solution than a problem." His reportorial talents show up in "Don't Bet Against Cigarette Makers," 8-17, where he makes a convincing case that, despite many enemies, lawsuits, and increasing excise taxes, the cigarette business — an "awesome money machine" — has a profitable future ahead. "Turmoil Time in the Casino Business," 3-2, is a balanced, comprehensive analysis of this interesting industry, based on apparently extensive on-site research, and includes the differing business strategies of leading casinos and the outlook for the business.

Shields, Mark. *The Washington Post.* (★ ★ ★)
A Boston Irish politico (with a Notre Dame philosophy degree), Shields turned to journalism, and both professions benefited. He relied a bit less on charm and wit to carry his column, but we were happier with the extra weight and analytical depth and suspect he still has not realized his potential. There are good, rich thoughts in "The Most Important Primary State," 9-4, applauding New Hampshire: "There is a serious reason for having a small state hold the first primary. Here candidates must campaign 'retail' — personal campaigning that requires them to answer real questions from real voters...In a small state, money does not inevitably determine the winner." His "Losers From the Hart Exit," 5-19, is inventive, witty and informative: "Biden, who has noned a good 25-minute speech, tried unsuccessfuly to hone it into ten: 'As Martin Luther King said, I have a dream...and so forth.'" He's bold in "For Dukakis, the Start of a Long Goodbye?" 10-3, arguing the loss of his campaign manager could prove fatal to Dukakis. He has a strong column, 5-1, on public campaign financing: "...the Senate is not working. One reason is campaign money, its feverish pursuit and its unchecked growth." Better still a pungent "'Volunteers' For America," 8-4, on the aloof attitude toward the Persian Gulf crisis: "It's a sure bet that any Washington dinner party guest — conservative or liberal — does not personally know a single one of the nearly 2 million enlisted Americans currently in our armed forces, but that the same guest does personally know at least one of the 20,000 Americans who have died of AIDS." This is classless America? Nifty.

Sidey, Hugh. *Time.* (★ ★)
The weekly Presidency column had less verve, more damp lyricism than in the previous Reagan years, but it wasn't such a hot year for RR either. Sidey, a marvelous writer, is best at sketching the joys and splendid miseries of the Oval Office. "The Presidency: Gulliver's Travails," 1-12, the disheartening of an American President, is beautifully written and concerned. "The Bottom Line on Reagan," 3-16, is a poetic summation of the Reagan record. "For longer than many people thought possible, he inspired and instructed his countrymen to do a lot of things they never dreamed they could or would do." In "A Trouper Plays America Again," 4-6, RR visits Missouri and a jellybean White House built by schoolchildren. In defense of RR, there's an unusually hard edge to a piece on the Tower panel, "Even Reagan Was Somber," 2-23, and a bleak defense of RR in "The Circuits are Overloaded," 3-9. "Can he cope with the job? This is a twilight time." He bombs with "Never Give Up," 8-24, a 40-minute interview with RR that is *Time*'s lead piece, the subject of well-deserved ridicule in the TRB column of *The New Republic*, 9-7.

Sitomer, Curtis J. *The Christian Science Monitor.* (★)
Thursday's "Justice" columnist, Sitomer deals with moral or social justice more than judicial issues *per se*, only occasionally venturing onto that turf. "Society Needs Clear, Positive 'Signals' on Racism," 1-15, argues that "signals" aren't enough to solve the underlying problems, but it's a start and everything's got to start somewhere in the wake of the Howard Beach fiasco. His "Protecting Our Children," 5-7, was an effective report on censorship for the children's sake, occasioned by book censorship and FCC dirty word ruling. But he doesn't really touch on parental responsibility, except to note that "cleaning up one's own act is usually the best solution. Censorship is probably the worst." "Advocates Of Prayer In School Watch High Court Case Testing 'Minute of Silence,'" 10-7, was professionally reported. "Tie-Breaker Seat Empty As Term Begins," 10-5, was a review of Supreme Court term without Powell with fair detail and depth of analysis. He could give us a bit more to chew on, with all the material that's floating around.

Sobran, Joseph. *National Review,* Universal Press Syndicate. (★ ½)
A die-hard conservative, incisive and unforgiving. In "A Pope's World War II Secrets," 1-29, Sobran takes on the myths and distortions of the role of Papacy and Pius XII on Jews during WWII. He's particularly combative in "How Not to Fight Aids," 3-19: "I really don't see why abstaining from casual sex is supposed to be such an effort. After all, you have to make

a rather complex effort to indulge in it" and to be blunt, one can "relieve a desire that could more conveniently be exercised, shall we say, without leaving home." A pro-Bork piece is well written, "Biden Makes The Litmus Test Official," 7-2, but with few new thoughts on the nomination. In "Given a Panel of His Own," 7-3, he's searing on Rep. George Crockett of Detroit, who now chairs the House Subcommittee on Western Hemisphere Affairs, "after a lifetime of fellow traveling with American communists" and scathing on Maria Shriver and her NBC special "God Is Not Elected" in "Preparing US For The Pope's Visit," 9-1. His "Coal Miner's Son From Delaware," 9-17, column was amusing on Joe Biden's speech that was Neil Kinnock's, and prescient as well: "If you think Gary Hart blew it, watch Sen. Joseph Biden...Not exactly a world-class scandal, but these are the sorts of things that erode respect for a man among the people who are paying close attention. And Mr. Biden wants a lot of attention. If he's not careful he may get it." In "Congress' Red Army," 7-31, a lengthy indictment of lefty Representatives, with J. Michael Walker, is very strong stuff, but he has a fundamental critique.

Sperling, Godfrey, Jr. *The Christian Science Monitor.* (★)
Sperling seemed to have the blahs this year, caught up in the *ennui* of RR's lame duck status. "Bush vs. Dole," 1-13, was mediocre on the wisdom of prospective presidential candidates kicking the incumbent when he's down, deciding neither Bush or Dole is the winner. A nice testimonial to Bush in "George Bush — A Strong Candidate?" 5-5, but we are not convinced: Sperling switches from refuting the wimp factor to touting Bush's resume too soon, and overdoing it on Bush later in the year, applauding his support of RR, and concluding unpersuasively that Reagan's star arising post-hearing will boost Bush in "Cheers for George," 7-28. He echoes Meg Greenfield (even quoting her directly) in "Candidates And Character," 5-19, about the meteoric fall of Gary Hart that still stands nicely on its own: "the personal relationships of candidates insofar as they may disclose what kind of a president he will be." Sperling is hopeful despite somewhat dreary outlook on RR's "bill of political health" in "Reagan And The 'Forgiveness' Factor," 5-26, and later is realistic, picturing RR as determined, "An Active President," 8-18. "Punishment — Or Presidential Pardon?" 8-11, is an eloquent exploration of reasons and arguments on the possibility of pardons for Secord, Ollie and John, but relies too much on comparison to Watergate and gives us no conclusions.

Thomas, Cal. *Los Angeles Times* Syndicate. (★)
A meat and potatoes columnist, lots of nutrition, but few frills. In "Campaign '88 And The Adultery Issue," 6-15, Thomas argues for the bottom line — it is not disclosure of the affair that does the damage but the affair itself: "if the candidate will not live up to a promise to his spouse, why should the candidate be believed when he makes promises about the economy or defense?" His commentary on freedom and conviction, and the fact that conviction today in government is seen as "extremism," asked what happened to the strength Jefferson and Washington had in "A Less Certain Future," 9-17. Better in "A Rare Vote For Common Sense," 7-29, on the House vote to restrict travel to Nicaragua, which was filled with interesting quotes and fairly sharp analysis.

Tyrrell, R. Emmett, Jr. *The American Spectator*, King Features Syndicate. (★)
With his syndicated columns appearing less than once a month in *The Washington Post*, Tyrrell's discontent became more and more evident as the year went on. Smug in "The Doddering Decline of the Democrats," 1-21: "Like a beauty fingered by time, the Democratic Party resorts evermore to cosmetics to conceal its doddering decline into purposelessness." He's sad and respectful in "Bill Casey's Reading...," 5-13, much gentler than we'd ever seen him in this eulogy. Good in "A Conservative Crack-Up?" 3-27, tough, but a little too disgruntled: "The Conservatives have not adapted to an era that is moving beyond the problems of the early 1980s. They have not even thought of maintaining enduring institutions comparable to those of the liberals. There is something decidedly shaky and ephemeral about all their think tanks, their magazines, their activist groups." The columns that do appear in the *Post* are worthy

enough. His "The Continuing Crisis" columns, however, in *The American Spectator* are becoming too often mean funny, at times ugly, with Tyrrell writing the most tasteless line of 1987 (see *TAS* review) after we awarded him the funniest line of 1986 in last year's *MediaGuide*. There's a fine line between the two.

Wade, Lawrence. The Lawrence Wade Column. (★ ★ ½)
A conservative young black columnist syndicating himself for the first time, still appearing regularly in *The Washington Times*, which has a sizeable black audience. A fairly steady, solid year for Wade, who generally has well-conceived and well-drawn subjects, breaking ground by always risking his reputation in the black community. In "The Moaning After," 6-19, for example, he argues strenuously in defense of the Goetz verdict: "In defense of your life — or, against what you think is lifethreatening — any force is justifiable. Fighting crime isn't the Celtics vs. the Lakers. It's the decent vs. the indecent" asking "what kind of society holds victims of crimes to rules of law and order while excusing — simply because their skin is black — hoodlums who mug or murder?" Equally so in "Case Dismissed For Lack Of Evidence: A Demurrer To Marshall's Plea," 9-14, Wade defends Reagan's civil rights record, slamming Justice Thurgood Marshall for ranking him near the bottom of U.S. presidents on civil rights: "Justice Marshall has hit bottom. Somebody should show him the door." Wade makes a useful point on Jimmy Carter's confession: "Jimmy Carter says that Americans are all racists...he's obviously projecting *his* feelings" in "Is Carter Spreading His Guilt," 2-20. In another defense of "a 204% presidency" he asks "Will the Whiners Let Him Lead?" 3-6, citing the bull market and economic expansion as evidence.

Wattenberg, Ben. Newspaper Enterprise Association. (★ ½)
Syndicated, now appearing occasionally in *The Washington Times*, Ben received more attention in 1987 for his book *The Birth Dearth*, than for his column-writing. He's incensed on the abrupt dismissal of Les Aspin as chair of the House Armed Services Committee, citing the then-upcoming vote for a new chairman as being a watershed for the Democrats, either soft or solid on defense, "The Aspin Test," 1-15. In "Military Takes High Ground in American People's Trust," 1-8, he draws the lessons for the major drop in confidence by American peoples' confidence in the church: "people want religion, not politics, coming from the pulpit — sacraments, not Sandinistas; worship, not weapons' divinity, not divestiture." Wattenberg is right at home in *Birth Dearth* territory in "Yuppie Disease of the '80s?" 4-16, debunking the idea that female infertility is becoming a major national problem. He gives us a peek into the psyche of Gen. Pinochet of Chile in "Add Pinochet to the CIA Bashers," 4-30, reading more like a report than a column, Pinochet talking "about his long, private conversations with the pope. He said he liked him a great deal, in part because he is 'as anti-communist as I am.'" In "Democrats Face Three Little Words," 8-13, Wattenberg pins the future of Central America on Congress and the Democrats, arguing persuasively "if the Democrats press the issues of democratization, it can have real effect. If they ask tough questions and get wrong answers, the Sandinistas must worry that the peace process may stall and that some Democrats, convinced of communist insincerity, will vote for contra aid. If the Congress united on this issue, the Sandinistas would be finished, and they know it." The three little words? "Blame America First."

Wicker, Tom. *The New York Times.* (★ ★)
A bit less blatantly partisan in '87, Wicker was back in a comfortable groove as a soft-core liberal and scoring a bit higher with us. Not as sharp as his stablemate Tony Lewis, he was at least early in advancing the idea that it's okay for Senators to vote against Judge Bork on ideological grounds in "Judging Robert Bork," 7-2: "...might his accession to the Supreme Court pose an unrelenting threat to the values and beliefs of millions of Americans...?" Hmmm. In "Star Wars Stampede," 1-25, his old arguments don't move the debate, but in "Moving to Mobility," 12-28-86, he sees an opening for "survivable deterrent forces" as a wedge against SDI, praising RR's decision to produce the Midgetman. "Teflon and Power," 2-25, reminds

"Reagan fans" that RR is still a powerful man, suggesting "if all his efforts fail to overthrow the Sandinista regime... (he) could still order American troops to do it." But in "Don't Count on Ollie," 7-22, he concludes that "the hard fact is that Ronald Reagan doesn't scare anybody anymore." A timely, sharp analysis of the Demo presidential field, "Godot Isn't Coming," 9-3, concludes that we might as well get used to the seven dwarfs, that's all we're getting. Wicker for years has been warning Democrats against backing higher taxes. In "A New Political Picture," 10-22, after the Wall Street crash, he warns anew "if voters are facing leaner times, they will not be happy with a party that causes them to hand over more to the tax collector... If taxes have to be raised, the leadership ought to be provided and the political onus taken by the President who primarily caused the problem." Wicker had one of the 10 best columns of the year on Thanksgiving Day, "A No Trump Game," 11-26.

Will, George. *Newsweek, Washington Post* Writers Group. (★ ★ ½)
The man with the bow tie and John Lennon glasses is also one of the best conservative pundits around, but we had to complain that his columns of recent years were subpar. We were thrilled and delighted that they sprang back, better than we've seen in years. He not only worked at them, but also seemed to cross a threshold, seeming more relaxed with himself, less self-important. In *Newsweek*, "The Sickening Soviet Reality," 1-19, debunks the Soviet myth, asserting conditions in the USSR are on a par with sections of India, making a strong case. "The Networks' Evening Blues," 3-30, was thoughtful and interesting throughout: "On normal days, the evening newscasts, in their current format, are of declining importance." "The Fuse That Lit the Fire," 4-13, was a refreshing change for George, a sweet, poignant remembrance of Jackie Robinson, "an alloy of fire and ice, a fierce competitor....he became the perfect model for black Americans, and for white Americans, too." His *Post* Supreme Court and Bork coverage was good: "You'd Think It Was The Warren Court," 4-2, was hard reporting and careful analysis of the SCOTUS reverse discrimination case, "...the court acted as brazenly legislatively as ever the Warren Court did;" "Biden vs. Bork," 7-2, gave good arguments on why Bork should be confirmed over Biden's objections and splendid on Joe, who will have to oppose Bork on "naked political grounds," as someone "whose mood swings carry him from Hamlet to hysteria;" and "Bork Up Against A Stall Defense," 8-2, making a plea for reasonable debate, and puts those who would factionalize the issue (on both sides) in their rightful place, including Biden and Dole. He still, now and then, lapses into wholesale abuse, mean-spirited and malicious. Two examples from the *Post*: "The Cardinal's Alibi," 1-15, on John Cardinal O'Connor, "he was only obeying orders;" and "Hey — Man — Like — Warhol," 2-27, tasteless and nasty, an art critic he isn't. If he could stamp this out, he could easily be ★ ★ ★ ★.

Yoder, Edwin Jr. *Washington Post* Writers Group. (½ ★)
A prize-winning editorialist for the now defunct *Washington Star*, Yoder has not been able to make a successful transition to columnist, and we watch him struggle year after year. His old guard GOP "we're-going-to-hell-in-a-hand-basket" mindset has been out of sync in the Reagan years. But even that would be okay if he would try to persuade, instead of simply pronounce with editorial pomposity. In "ABM: The Amateurs vs. Sam Nunn," 4-2, *WAPO*, he advises us that Senator Nunn is smart and that his fellow columnists Evans & Novak write "drivel" when they say Nunn is seeking to transform himself into a presidential candidate acceptable to the dominant anti-defense Democratic left by supporting its position on the ABM treaty. Says Yoder: "Nunn's position is conservative in the best sense." Hmmm. "Totalitarian Journalism," 5-4, is simply a tirade against *The Miami Herald* for its coverage of the Gary Hart/Donna Rice imbroglio. Still in his early 50s, he could have plenty of good years and columns ahead of him if he would do a bit more reporting and a lot less dictating.

Zuckerman, Mortimer. *U.S.News & World Report.* (★)
For the first half of the year, the Big Boss and only zillionaire columnist in the press corps was evidently too wrapped up in his *Atlantic Monthly* lawsuit to be interesting reading, but

after settling there was modest improvement. He's muddled on the Russians in "Gorbachev's Tomatoes," 4-20, and "The Winds of Change," 4-27; simplistic on AIDS, "AIDS: A Crisis Ignored," 1-12; and bearish on America's economy, "When Does the Party End?" 1-26. His best lines are buried at the end in "Letter from Moscow," 11-16, saying "There is more intellectual ferment in the Soviet Union today than there has been for some six decades...Still, his [Gorbachev's] reforms, for all their boldness, do not go far enough — particularly in the direction of market forces — to alter the fundamentals of the Soviet system. He and his colleagues may well be in the quandary described by Matthew Arnold: 'Wandering between two worlds, one dead, the other powerless to be born.'" In "A Tale of Two Cities," 11-9, he simply shouts at Washington, D.C. to cut the deficit or the market will fall another trillion dollars in NYC. Mort should relax, like zillionaire Murdoch, and hire talent to fill his space.

BIOGRAPHICS

Abelson, Alan. *Barron's.* Editor. B. 1925, NYC. CCNY, 1946, BS-English & Chemistry; U. of IA, 1947, MA-Creative Writing. Freelance, to 1949. *New York Journal-American*, copyboy, metro reporter, financial desk to 1956. *Barron's*, reporter to 1965; Managing Editor, 1966; "Up & Down Wall Street" columnist, current, 1981; Editor, current. NBC-TV, "News at Sunrise" business commentator, current.

Abrams, Pamela. *Harper's.* Associate Editor. B. 1957, Ithaca, NY. SUNY, Purchase, 1981, English & Political Economy. *Nuclear Times*, to 1983. *Harper's*, Assoc Editor, current, 1984. NYU, Center for War, Peace & News Media, current, Assoc.

Adams, Nathan Miller. *Reader's Digest.* Senior Editor. B. 1934, NYC. Colby College, 1958, Art. US Air Force, 1960-63. *New York Journal-American*, "Logbook of Crime" columnist, feature writer, to 1965. Time, Inc, London stringer, to 1968. *Sunday Times*, London, 1967. *Reader's Digest*, Senior Editor, special assignments, Europe & Middle East, current, 1968. Author *The Fifth Horseman*, 1967.

Ali, Salamat. *Far Eastern Economic Review.* Delhi Bureau Chief. B. 1934, India. Government College (Lahore, Pakistan), 1953 BSc-Chemistry & Zoology. *Pakistan Times,* reporter, 1957-60; political correspondent, 1963-78. *Civil & Military Gazette* (Lahore), potical correspondent, 1960-63. *Far Eastern Economic Review,* Pakistan correspondent, 1978-79; Delhi Bureau Chief, current, 1980.

Almond, Peter J. *The Washington Times.* Domestic Correspondent. B. 1946, Northampton, UK. Nieman Fellow, 1981. *Northern Echo* (Darlington, UK), 1964. *Yorkshire Evening Press*, to 1969. *Cleveland Press*, reporter, to 1979; investigative, to 1982. *The Washington Times*, State Dept correspondent, to 1985; London correspondent, to 1987; domestic correspondent, current, 1987. Heywood Broun Award, 1979; Thomas L. Stokes Award, 1979; Charles Stewart Mott Award, 1976; Northeast OH Press Club, 1st Place Business Reporting, 1982; OH UPI 1st Place, Series, 1982.

Alter, Jonathan. *Newsweek.* Senior Writer & Media Critic. B. 1957, Chicago, IL. Harvard, 1979, History. Freelance, Washington, to 1980. *The Washington Monthly*, Editor, writer, to 1983. *Newsweek*, Assoc Editor, news media writer, to 1986; Senior Writer, media critic, current, 1986.

Altman, Lawrence K. *The New York Times.* Science Times Reporter & "Doctor's World" Columnist. B. 1937, Quincy, MA. Harvard, 1958, BA-Government, *cum laude*; Tufts School of Medicine, 1962, MD. U. of WA

Affiliated Hospitals, Seattle, resident, internal medicine, 1966-68; Senior Fellow, medical genetics. *The Lampoon*, advertising manager, treasurer. *The Quincy Patriot Ledger*, feature writer, to 1962. Mt. Zion Hospital, San Francisco, intern, to 1963. US Public Health Service, *Morbidity and Mortality Weekly Report*, Editor. World Health Organization, Chief, Epidemiology & Immunization Section's Foreign Quarantine Division, Washington. Freelance, current. NYU Medical School, clinical assoc prof. *The New York Times*, science times reporter, current, 1969; "Doctor's World" columnist, current. George Polk Award, Africa AIDS series, 1986.

Anderberg, Kenneth J. *American City & County.* Associate Publisher & Editor. U. of IL, 1966; Armstrong State College, 1971; U. of NH, 1977, BA-Political Science. US Army, 1968-69, Bronze Star. *Savannah News-Press*, sports writer, 1967; National News Editor, to 1971. *Manchester Union Leader*, Copy Editor, to 1976; National News Editor, to 1977. *Rural Georgia Magazine*, Managing Editor, to 1980; Editor, to 1983. *American City & County*, Assoc Publisher & Editor, current, 1983. Atomic Industrial Award, 1973; George Haggard Memorial Award, 1980.

Andersen, Kurt. *Spy,* Co-Editor. *Time*, Architecture & Design Writer. B. 1954, Omaha, NE. Harvard, 1976, Sociology. NBC, writer, to 1980. *Time*, politics & justice writer, to 1984; architecture & design writer, current, 1984. *Spy*, Co-Editor, current, 1986. Author *The Real Thing*, 1980: co-author *Tools Of Power*, 1980; *The Reagan Report*, 1984: co-Editor *Laughing Matters*, 1987. ABA Award, 1984; NY Newspaper Guild Page One Award, 1985.

Anderson, Jack. United Feature Syndicate. Columnist. B. 1922, Long Beach, CA. U. of UT, 1940-41; Georgetown, 1947-48; George Washington U., 1948. US Merchant Marine, 1944-45; US Army, 1946-47. *Salt Lake Tribune*, reporter, 1939-41. Church of Jesus Christ of Latter-Day Saints, missionary, to 1944. *Deseret News*, war correspondent, 1945. *Washington Merry-Go-Round*, reporter, 1947-65; partner, to 1969; owner, from 1969. *Parade*, Washington Editor, 1954-68; Washington Bureau Chief, from 1968. United Feature Syndicate, columnist, current. Author & co-author 12 books. Pulitzer Prize, National Reporting, 1972.

Andrews, Fred. *The New York Times.* Business & Financial Editor. B. 1938, Roanoke, VA. Duke, 1960, BA-Political Science, *magna cum laude*; Princeton, 1965, MA-Politics. *The Richmond News-Leader*, intern reporter, summers 1958, '60. Union Carbide, copywriter, 1962. Fair Campaign Practices Committee, Inc, NY, research assoc; Research Director, to 1965. U. of MD, Far East Division, Taiwan, instructor, 1966. *The New York Times* & Time-

Life News Service, correspondent, Taiwan, to 1968. *The Wall Street Journal*, reporter, "Tax Report" columnist, to 1976. *The New York Times*, reporter; "Taxes and Accounting" columnist; "Management" columnist; Deputy Editor, 1977-85; Business & Financial Editor, current, 1985. Author 3 books including *Tax Tips and Dodges*; co-Editor *The Equity Funding Papers: The Anatomy of a Fraud*.

Andrews, Walter E. Jr. *The Washington Times*. Pentagon Correspondent. B. 1933, Elizabeth, NJ. St. Peter's College, 1955, Chemistry. Reuters, Washington, to 1980. Bell Labs, Public Relations, to 1982. *Army Times*, to 1983. *The Washington Times*, Pentagon correspondent, current.

Apple, R.W. *The New York Times*. Chief Washington Correspondent. B. 1934, Akron, OH. Columbia, 1961, History, *magna cum laude*. *The Wall Street Journal*, reporter, to 1961. US Army, 1957-59. NBC News, writer & correspondent, to 1963. *The New York Times*, metro staff, to 1965, '68; Saigon Bureau Chief, to 1968; chief Africa correspondent, to 1969; national political correspondent; London Bureau Chief, 1976-85; Chief Washington Correspondent, current, 1985.

Archibald, George. *The Washington Times*. National Correspondent. B. 1944, Newmarket, Suffolk, UK. Old Dominion U., 1967, BA-Political Science & History. *The Arizona Republic*, editorial writer & columnist, to 1973. Administrative, Capitol Hill, to 1982. *The Washington Times*, national correspondent, current, 1982.

Arledge, Roone. ABC News & Sports. Group President. B. 1931, Forest Hills, NY. Columbia, 1952, BBA. Dumont TV, 1952-53. NBC, producer, director, 1955-60. ABC, network producer, to 1961; VP, sports, 1963-68. ABC News, President, to 1985. ABC Sports, Inc, 1977-85. ABC News & Sports, Group President, current, 1985. Emmy Award, 1958, 1966-74; 3 George Foster Peabody Awards; Broadcast Pioneers Award, 1968.

Armbrister, Trevor. *Reader's Digest*. Senior Editor — Washington. B. 1933, Norwalk, CT. Washington & Lee U., 1956, English. *Trailways Magazine*, Editor, 1958-61. *The Saturday Evening Post*, Asst Editor, to 1965; Contributing Editor, to 1965; Washington Bureau Editor, to 1969. Freelance, to 1976. *Reader's Digest*, Roving Editor, to 1979; Senior Editor, Washington, current, 1979. Author *A Matter Of Accountability*, 1970; *Act of Vengeance*, 1975: co-author (with Don Riegel) *O Congress*, 1972; (with Gerald R. Ford) *A Time to Heal: The Memoirs of Gerald R. Ford*.

Armstrong, Larry. *BusinessWeek*. Tokyo Bureau Manager. Northwestern, BA-Chemistry, MSJ. *Medical World News*, editorial trainee, 1970. *Electronics*, Washington correspondent, to 1972; Dallas Bureau Chief, 1972; Chicago Bureau Manager, to 1978. *BusinessWeek*, Chicago correspondent, to 1984; Tokyo Bureau Manager, current, 1984.

Armstrong, Richard Alford. *Fortune*. Executive Editor. B. 1929, D'Lo, MS. Studied U. of AL, 1946-47; U. of MO, 1950, BJ; Columbia, 1955, MA-English. US Army, 1951-52, Bronze Star. *Gadsden* (AL) *Times*, reporter, 1950-54. *Time*, Contributing Editor, 1956-61. *USA-1*, Managing Editor, to 1962. *The Saturday Evening Post*,

Contributing Editor, to 1969. *Fortune*, Assoc Editor, to 1971; Board of Editors member, to 1975; Asst Managing Editor, to 1977; Exec Editor, current, 1977.

Arnold, Robert. *BusinessWeek*. Senior Editor. U. of MO, BA, MAJ. *The Wall Street Journal*. *The Washington Post*. *BusinessWeek*, Labor Dept Staff Editor, 1978; Editor, to 1985; Senior Editor, current, 1985.

Asman, David. *The Wall Street Journal*. Editor — "Americas" Column. B. 1954, Hollis, NY. Marlboro College (VT), 1977, BA-Anthropology; postgrad Northwestern. *Prospect*, Editor, to 1980. *Manhattan Report on Economic Policy*, to 1982. Freelance, to 1983. *The Wall Street Journal*, Editor, "Americas" Column, current, 1983. Co-Editor *The Wall Street Journal on Management: The Best of Manager's Journal*.

Aubin, Stephen P. *Defense Media Review*. Managing Editor. B. 1958, Newport, RI. Georgetown, 1980, BA-Government; 1982, MA-National Security Studies. *Current News* (Pentagon, Foreign Media edition), writer; Editor, 1981-82. *Military Intelligence* (Ft. Huachuca, AZ), Editor, 1985-86. *Defense Media Review*, Managing Editor, current, 1987. National Assn of Government Communicators "Blue Pencil Award", 1986.

Auchincloss, Kenneth. *Newsweek*. Managing Editor & Editor — Overseas Editions. B. 1937, NYC. Harvard, 1959, History. *Newsweek*, Assoc Editor, 1966-72; Senior Editor, 1972; Exec Editor, to 1976; Managing Editor, current, 1976; Overseas Editions Editor, current, 1986.

Auerbach, Stuart. *The Washington Post*. Financial Correspondent. B. 1934, NYC. Williams College, 1957, BA-Political Science. *The Berkshire Eagle* (Pittsfield, MA), reporter, Suburban Bureau Chief, to 1960. *The Miami Herald*, reporter; columnist, to 1966. *The Washington Post*, reporter, to 1969; national medical & science reporter, campaign political correspondent, Latin America, to 1976; Middle East correspondent, Beirut, to 1977; legal correspondent, columnist, to 1979; South Asia correspondent, New Delhi, to 1982; financial correspondent, current, 1982.

Aynesworth, Hugh G. *The Washington Times*. National Correspondent. B. 1931, Clarksburg, WV. Salem College, 1950, Journalism. *Clarksburg* (WV) *Exponent*, part-time sportswriter, 1948-50. *Ft. Smith* (AR) *Times Record*, Sports Editor, to 1953; Managing Editor, 1954-56. *Arkansas Gazette*, sports columnist, 1953-54. *Wichita* (KS) *Eagle*, Aviation Editor, 1956-57. *Dallas Times Herald*, reporter, photographer, to 1959; investigative & State Editor, 1975-77; special correspondent, 1985-86. UPI, Denver reporter, 1959-60. *Dallas Morning News*, Aerospace & Science Editor, to 1967. *Newsweek*, Houston Bureau Chief, to 1974. ABC News, "20/20" Chief Investigative Reporter, 1979-81. KDFW-TV (Dallas), consultant, to 1984. CBS-TV, consultant, 1984. *The Washington Times*, national correspondent, current, 1986. Author *The Only Living Witness*, 1984. 75+ state & national awards, including Headliners & Special Achievement Awards.

Baig, Edward C. *Fortune*. Reporter/Researcher. B. NY. York College, BA-Political Science; Adelphi U., MBA. *Fortune*, cable desk; reporter/researcher, current, 1980.

Baker, Russell Wayne. *The New York Times.* "Observer" Columnist. B. 1925, Loudon County, VA. Johns Hopkins, 1947, BA-English Literature. US Navy, to 1945. *The Sun*, reporter; London staff; White House correspondent, to 1954. *The New York Times*, Washington staff, to 1962; "Observer" columnist, current, 1962. Author 9 books, including *The Rescue of Miss Yashell and Other Pipe Dreams,* 1983. Frank Sullivan Memorial Award, 1976; George Polk Award, Commentary, 1979; Pulitzer Prize, Distinguished Commentary, 1979; Pulitzer Prize, Biography, 1983.

Bakshian, Aram Jr. *National Review & The American Spectator.* Contributor. B. 1944, Washington, DC. Harvard Institute of Politics, Fellow, 1975. Deputy asst & director, speechwriting, to Ronald Reagan, 1981-83. *National Review, The American Spectator*, contributor, current. Author 5 books, including *The Candidates 1980*; co-author *The Future Under President Reagan; The Wargame.*

Baldacchino, Joseph F. Jr. *Human Events.* Associate Editor. B. 1948, Detroit, MI. Mt. St. Mary's College (MD), 1970, BA-History, *magna cum laude*; Catholic U., 1983, MA-Political Theory. *Dorchester News* (Cambridge, MD), to 1972. *Human Events*, Asst Editor, to 1972; Assoc Editor, current, 1975. Author *Economics and the Moral Order*, 1985.

Baldwin, William. *Forbes.* Assistant Managing Editor. Harvard, 1973, AB-Linguistics. *News Journal* (Wilmington, DE). *Forbes*, reporter; Houston Bureau Chief; Senior Editor, 1980-87; Assistant Managing Editor, current, 1987.

Bandow, Douglas. Copley News Service. Columnist. B. 1957, Washington, DC. FL State U., 1976, BS-Economics; Stanford Law, 1979, JD. Reagan for President Committee, Senior Policy Analyst, to 1980. Office of the President-Elect, Senior Policy Analyst, to 1981. Special Asst to the President for Policy Development, to 1982. *Inquiry Magazine*, Editor, to 1984. Copley News Service, columnist, current, 1983. Cato Institute, Senior Fellow, current, 1984. Editor *U.S. Aid To The Developing World: A Free Market Agenda*, 1985. Freedoms Foundation Citation, Journalistic Activities, 1979.

Bangsberg, P.T. *The Journal Of Commerce.* East Asia Correspondent. B. 1942, Syracuse, NY. TV/radio (Buffalo, NY), news writer, Sub-Editor, producer, 1959-60. UPI, Sub-Editor, Editor, to 1963. ABC Radio News (NY), Sub-Editor, to 1965. *The New York Times*, Sub-Editor, to 1966. *The Daily Telegraph* (London), Sub-Editor, to 1969. *The Times* (London), Asst Night Editor, to 1972. *The Birmingham Post* (UK), Asst Editor, Chief Sub-Editor, to 1974. *Birmingham Evening Mail* (UK), Managing Editor, to 1981. *South China Morning Post* (Hong Kong), Asst Editor, to 1983. *The Journal Of Commerce*, East Asia Correspondent, current, 1984.

Banks, Howard. *Forbes.* Washington Bureau Chief & "What's Ahead for Business" Columnist. B. 1938, Hatfield, Hertfordshire, UK. De Havilland Aeronautical Technical School. Aerospace industry & trade papers, to 1970. *The Economist*, Industrial Editor; "Business Britain" Editor; West Coast correspondent, to 1982. *Forbes*, Washington Bureau Chief, "What's Ahead for Business" columnist, current.

Barmash, Isadore. *The New York Times.* "Business Day" Reporter. B. 1921, Philadelphia, PA. Charles Morris Price School, 1941, Journalism. *Home Furnishings Daily*, Editor-in-Chief. *Woman's Wear Daily*, Managing Editor. Fairchild Publications, reporter, Bureau Chief; Editorial Copy Chief. *New York Herald Tribune*, financial & business feature writer, to 1965. *The New York Times*, "Business Day" reporter, current, 1965.

Barnard, Richard C. *Defense News.* Editor. B. 1943, Alabama. FL Atlantic U., BA-Political Science; American U., MA-Communications. *The Sun Sentinel* (Ft. Lauderdale, FL), reporter, 1967-69. Defense Intelligence Agency, to 1973. *The Times Journal Co*, writer, Pentagon correspondent, to 1980; Editor, 1984-85. *Defense Week*, Founding Editor, 1980-84. *Navy Times*, Editor, to 1985; *Defense News*, Editor, current, 1985. National Press Club Award; Education Writers Assn Award.

Barnes, Fred. *The New Republic.* Senior Editor. B. 1943, West Point, NY. U. of VA, 1965, BA-History. Nieman Fellow, 1977-78. *The Charlotte News & Courier*, reporter, to 1967. *The Washington Star*, reporter; Supreme Court reporter; White House correspondent, to 1979. *The Sun*, national political reporter, to 1985. *The New Republic*, Senior Editor, current, 1985. *The American Spectator*, contributor, current.

Barnes, James A. *National Journal.* Chief Political Reporter. American Enterprise Institute, policy analyst. *The Christian Science Monitor, The Washington Post*, contributor. Chief speechwriter, Treasury Secretary James Baker, to 1987. *National Journal*, Chief Political Reporter, current, 1987.

Barnes, John. *The Detroit News.* Deputy Editorial Page Editor. B. 1960, NYC. NYU, 1982, BAJ. *The Washington Times*, metro reporter, to 1984. Rowland Evans & Robert Novak's "Inside Report," national political reporter, to 1986. *The Boston Herald*, Chief Editorial Writer, to 1987. *The Detroit News*, Deputy Editorial Page Editor, current, 1987. Freelance, current.

Barnes, Robert A. *The Washington Post.* Metro Reporter. *Clearwater* (FL) *Sun*, Tallahassee Bureau Chief. AP, reporter. *St. Petersburg Times*, lead writer, state & national politics, 1981-87. *The Washington Post*, metro reporter, current, 1987.

Barol, Bill. *Newsweek.* Senior Writer. B. 1957, Philadelphia, PA. Harvard College, 1979, American History. WNBC-TV News (NY), election researcher, 1980. *City Limits* (Boston, MA), Editor, to 1982. Freelance, 1982. *Newsweek On Campus*, writer, to 1984. *Newsweek*, General Editor, to 1986; senior writer, current, 1987. Benjamin Fine Award, American Assoc of U. Professors Higher Education Writers Award, 1984; 1st Prize Education Writers Assoc National Awards, Education Reporting, 1984.

Barone, Michael. *The Washington Post.* Editorial Page Staff. B. 1944, Highland Park, MI. Harvard, 1966, AB-History; Yale, 1969, LLB. Law clerk, Judge Wade H. McCree, US Court of Appeals, to 1971. Peter D. Hart Research Assocs, VP, to 1982. *The Washington Post*, editorial page staff, current, 1982. Co-author *The Almanac of American Politics* (1972, current).

Barrett, Laurence I. *Time*. National Political Correspondent. B. 1935, NYC. NYU, 1956, History, Columbia, 1957, MSJ. *New York Herald Tribune*, local reporter 1958-62; national political reporter, to 1965. *Time*, writer, to 1970; Senior Editor, to 1975; NY Regional Bureau Chief, to 1978; White House correspondent, to 1979; roving senior correspondent, 1979; Reagan campaign reporter, 1980; senior White House correspondent, to 1985; national political correspondent, current, 1986. *Columbia Journalism Review*, contributor. Author *The Mayor Of New York*, 1965; *Gambling With History: Reagan In The White House*, 1983.

Barron, John. *Reader's Digest*. Senior Editor. B. 1930, Wichita Falls, TX. U. of MO, 1951, BAJ, 1952, MA. US Navy, to 1957. *The Washington Star*, to 1965. *Reader's Digest*, from 1965: Senior Editor, current, 1986. Author 3 books including *KGB Today*, 1983: co-author *Murder of a Gentle Land*, 1978. George Polk Memorial Award, 1964; Raymond Clapper Award, Distinguished DC Correspondence, 1964; DC Newspaper Guild Front Page Award & Grand Award, 1964; Sir James Goldsmith International Award, 1985.

Bartholomew, Douglas. *The American Spectator*. Chief Saloon Correspondent. B. 1949, Cleveland, OH. Northwestern, 1971, BAJ. *Peru* (IN) *Daily Tribune*, reporter, to 1971. *The News Herald* (OH), reporter, to 1973. Educational Testing Service, Editor, to 1977. Bank of America, Editor, to 1984. Freelance, to 1986. *The American Spectator*, Chief Saloon Correspondent, current, 1980. AP 1st Prize, Enterprise Reporting, 1972.

Bartlett, Sarah. *BusinessWeek*. Money & Banking Editor. B. 1955, Buffalo, NY. U. of Sussex (UK), 1977, BA-Political Science, 1979, MPhil-Development Studies. *Fortune*, reporter, to 1983. *BusinessWeek*, International Money Editor to 1983; Money & Banking Editor, current, 1986. Co-winner Overseas Press Club Award, Best Magazine Reporting Overseas, 1985.

Bartley, Robert L. *The Wall Street Journal*. Editor & Vice President. B. 1937, Marshall, MN. IA State U., BSJ; U. of WI, MS-Political Science. US Army, 1960. Grinnell (IA) *Herald-Register*, reporter, 1959-60. *Iowa State Daily*, Editor-in-Chief. *The Wall Street Journal*, reporter, 1962-64; editorial page staff, to 1972; Editor, Editorial Page, to 1979; Editor, current, 1979; VP, current. Overseas Press Club Citation, Excellence, 1977; Gerald Loeb Award, Editorials, 1979; Pulitzer Prize, Editorial Writing, 1980.

Bayles, Martha. *The Wall Street Journal*. TV Critic. B. 1948, Boston, MA. Harvard-Radcliffe, 1970, BA-Art History. *The New York Times*, book critic, 1981-83. *American Spectator*, film critic, to 1984. *The Wall Street Journal*, TV critic, current, 1984. Freelance, current. Joan Grey Untermeyer Poetry Award, Radcliffe, 1969, '70; American Academy of Poets Award, 1975; Arthur L. Andrews Fiction Award, 1976.

Bazell, Robert. NBC News. Science Correspondent. B. 1945, Pittsburgh, PA. U. of CA, Berkeley, 1967, BA, candidate in Philosophy, 1971; studied U. of Sussex, 1968-69. *Science*, writer, 1971-72. *New York Post*, reporter, to 1976. NBC News, science correspondent, current, 1976.

Beardsley, Tim. *Scientific American*. Washington Correspondent & Board of Editors Member. B. 1957, Chesterfield, UK. New College, Oxford, Zoology, PhD; U. of Oxford, 1984. *New Scientist* & *The Economist*, articles, from 1980. *Nature*, correspondent, 1983-84; Washington correspondent, to 1986. *Scientific American*, Washington correspondent & Board of Editors member, current, 1987.

Beatty, Jack. *The Atlantic*. Senior Editor. B. 1945, Cambridge, MA. Poynter Fellow, Yale, 1980. *The New Republic*, Literary Editor, 1978-83. *The Atlantic*, Senior Editor, current, 1983.

Becker, Don Crandall. *The Journal of Commerce*. Publisher & President. B. 1933, Sacramento. San Jose State U., 1957, BA. US Army, 1954-56. *Santa Cruz* (CA) *Sentinel*, reporter, 1957-58. UPI, reporter, Editor, San Francisco, to 1959; correspondent, Manager, Singapore, to 1962, Manila, to 1967, San Juan, PR, 1969-72, Miami, to 1973. National Professional Soccer League, NY & San Francisco, 1967-68. Knight-Ridder Newspapers, Corporate Relations Director, 1973-78. *Gary* (IN) *Post-Tribune*, Publisher & Chairman, to 1979. *Detroit Free Press*, President, to 1984. Detroit Symphony, Marketing VP, 1982-83. *The Journal of Commerce*, Publisher & President, current, 1985.

Behar, Richard. *Forbes*. Staff Writer. B. 1960, NYC. NYU, 1982, Journalism & History. *The New York Times*, stringer, researcher, education desk, to 1982. *The New York Times Selective Guide to Colleges*, writer, 1982. *Forbes*, staff writer — investigative business, current, 1982.

Behr, Edward. *Newsweek*. European Cultural Editor. B. 1926, Paris, France. Magdalene College, Cambridge, 1950, MA (Hons). Reuters, 1951-54. *Time*, 1957-63. *The Saturday Evening Post*, to 1965. *Newsweek*, from 1965; currently European Cultural Editor. Author 4 books including *The Last Emperor*, 1987; co-author *The Thirty Sixth Way*, 1968.

Behr, Peter. *The Washington Post*. Assistant Managing Editor — Business & Finance. *The Washington Post*, reporter; financial columnist, to 1987. Asst Managing Editor, business & finance, current, 1987. *The Washington Post Weekly*, Editor, 1987.

Beichman, Arnold. Freelance Writer. B. 1913. Columbia, 1934, BA, 1969, MA, 1973, PhD, all Political Science. Newspaper *PM*, City Editor. *Newsday*, reporter. AFL-CIO News, UN correspondent. Freelance, current. Author 4 books including *Herman Wouk: The Novelist As Social Historian*.

Belcher, Mary. *The Washington Times*. Capitol Hill Bureau Chief & White House Correspondent. B. 1951, Columbus, OH. U. of CO, 1981, Journalism. *Education Daily*, Congressional reporter, 1982-84. *The Washington Times*, education reporter, 1984; White House correspondent & Capitol Hill Bureau Chief, current, 1985.

Belkin, Lisa. *The New York Times*. Reporter. B. 1960, NYC. Princeton, 1982, Politics. *The New York Times*, clerk, to 1984; consumer reporter, to 1985; business reporter, to 1987; television & media reporter, current, 1987.

Belsie, Laurent. *The Christian Science Monitor.* Writer. B. 1959, Paris, France. Northwestern, 1980, Journalism. Reuters, intern, 1978. *Jackson* (MI) *Citizen-Patriot,* intern, 1979. *The Christian Science Monitor,* editing posts, 1981-83; writer, Chicago, current, 1983.

Benjamin, Evelyn. *Fortune.* Deputy Chief of Research. Bennington College, Economics. Time, Inc, 1957-60. *Fortune,* research assoc, to 1970; Assoc Editor; Deputy Chief of Research, current.

Bennett, Amanda. *The Wall Street Journal.* Management Reporter. Harvard, 1975, AB-English Literature. *The Wall Street Journal,* reporter, Toronto, to 1978; Detroit, to 1982; Washington, to 1983; Peking, to 1985; management reporter, current, 1985.

Bennett, Ralph Kinney. *Reader's Digest.* Senior Staff Editor. B. 1941, Latrobe, PA. Allegheny College, 1963, English. *The Greenburg* (PA) *Tribune-Review,* part-time reporter, 1960-63. *The New Haven Register,* writer, to 1964. *Philadelphia Inquirer,* writer, to 1966. *The National Observer,* writer, to 1968. *Reader's Digest,* Assoc Editor, Washington, to 1976; Washington Senior Editor, to 1986; Senior Staff Editor, current, 1986.

Bennett, Robert A. *The New York Times.* "Business Day" Reporter. B. 1941, Newark, NJ. Studied U. of Chicago. *The American Banker,* reporter, 1962-73. Econocast Services, CEO & Founder, to 1979. *The New York Times,* banking reporter, to 1985; "Business Day" reporter, current, 1985.

Berg, Eric. *The New York Times.* "Business Day" Reporter. B. 1958, NY. U. of PA, 1980, Economics; Stanford, MBA. *Chicago Tribune. Cleveland Plain Dealer,* reporter, to 1980. *Dallas Times Herald,* business & financial reporter, to 1982. *The New York Times,* "Business Day" reporter, current, 1984.

Bering-Jensen, Henrik. *Insight.* Writer. B. 1951, Copenhagen, Denmark. Oxford, MA-English Literature. Stanford, International Fellow, 1981-82. Danish newspapers, reviewer, 1977-85. *Insight,* writer, current, 1985.

Bernstein, Carl. Freelance Writer. B. 1944, Washington. Studied U. of MD, 1961-64. US Army, 1968. *The Washington Star,* copyboy to reporter, 1960-65. *Elizabeth* (NJ) *Journal,* reporter, to 1966. *The Washington Post,* reporter, to 1976. ABC, Washington Bureau Chief, to 1981. ABC News, correspondent, to 1984. Co-author (with Bob Woodward) *All the President's Men,* 1974; *The Final Days,* 1976. 1st Prize General Reporting, NJ Press Assn, 1966; 1st Prize Investigative Reporting, 1966; Drew Pearson Award Investigative Reporting, 1972; George Polk Memorial Award; Worth Bingham Prize; Heywood Broun Award; *Sigma Delta Chi* Distinguished Service Award; Sidney Hillman Award; Gold Medal, U. of MO School of Journalism: co-winner (with Bob Woodward) Pulitzer Prize, Watergate coverage, 1973.

Bernstein, Peter W. *U.S.News & World Report.* Managing Editor — Business, Personal Finance, Horizons & Special Projects. B. 1951, NYC. Brown, BA-American History; Christ's College Cambridge, MA-History. Samuel T. Arnold Fellowship, Brown, 1973. *The Argus Newspaper,* reporter, South Africa, 1973-84. *New York*

Daily News, reporter, 1976-77. *Fortune,* Assoc Editor, 1977-84; Washington Editor, 1983-85; elected to Board of Editors. *U.S.News & World Report,* Managing Editor, current, 1985. Editor *Arthur Young Tax Guide.* ABA Certificate of Merit, 1979.

Bernstein, Richard. *The New York Times.* Domestic Correspondent. B. 1944, NYC. U. of CT, 1962-66; Harvard, MA, 1970. *Time,* writer, 1973 to 1976; Hong Kong correspondent, to 1978; State Dept correspondent, to 1980; Peking Bureau Chief, to 1982. *The New York Times,* metro reporter, to 1983; UN correspondent, to 1984; foreign correspondent, Paris, to 1986; Paris Bureau Chief, to 1987; domestic correspondent, current, 1987. Author *From The Center of the Earth: The Search for the Truth About China,* 1982.

Berry, Richard. *Astronomy.* Editor-in-Chief. B. 1946, Greenwich, CT. U. of VA, 1968, BS-Astronomy; York U., 1972, MS. *Telescope Making,* Founder, 1978. *Astronomy,* Technical Editor, 1976-78; Editor, 1978-82; Editor-in-Chief, current, 1982. Clifford Holmes Award, 1982.

Bethell, Tom. *The American Spectator,* Contributing Editor & Washington Correspondent. *National Review,* Contributing Editor. B. London. Oxford, 1962, Philosophy & Psychology. Freelance, current. *The American Spectator,* Contributing Editor & Washington correspondent, current. *National Review,* Contributing Editor, current. 1st Prize, John Hancock Award; 1st Prize, Amos Tuck Award, both 1980.

Bianco, Anthony. *BusinessWeek.* Senior Writer. B. 1953, Oceanside, CA. U. of MN, 1976, BA-Humanities. *Minneapolis Tribune,* reporter, 1976. *Willamette Week* (Portland, OR), business writer, 1978-80. *BusinessWeek,* correspondent, San Francisco, to 1982; NY correspondent, senior writer, current. Amos Tuck Media Award, 1979.

Bird, Kai. *The Nation.* "Capitol Letter" Columnist. B. 1951, Eugene, OR. Carleton College, 1973, BA-History; Northwestern, 1975, MSJ. Thomas J. Watson Fellow, 1973-74; Alicia Patterson Fellow, 1984; John Simon Guggenheim Fellow, 1985; German Marshall Fellow, 1986-87. Freelance, Far East, to 1976. *Newsweek International,* Assoc Editor, to 1977. *The Nation,* Assoc Editor, to 1982; "Capitol Letter" columnist, current, 1982.

Bishop, Jerry E. *The Wall Street Journal.* Science & Medicine Reporter. B. Dalhart, TX. U. of TX, 1952, BAJ. *The Wall Street Journal,* copyreader, 1955-57; reporter, to 1959; Washington reporter, to 1960; science & medicine reporter, current, 1960.

Bissinger, H.G. III. *Philadelphia Inquirer.* Political Writer. B. 1954, NYC. U. of PA, 1976, English. Nieman Fellow, 1985-86. *Ledger-Star* (Norfolk, VA), 1976-78. *St. Paul Pioneer Press,* to 1981. *Philadelphia Inquirer,* Atlantic City, to 1982; investigative reporter, to 1985; political writer, current, 1987. Livingston Award, National Reporting, 1982; National Headliners Award, 1987; Silver Gavel Award, 1987; Pulitzer Prize, Investigative Reporting, 1987.

Blake, George. *The Cincinnati Enquirer.* Editor & Vice President. B. 1945, Chicago, IL. Wheeling College, 1967,

Economics. *Joliet Herald News,* reporter, Copy Editor, to 1973. *Times-Union* (Rochester, NY), Copy Editor, 1973. *Pacific Daily News* (Guam), Managing Editor, to 1976. Gannett News Service, Washington reporter, 1977. *Fort Myers News-Press,* Exec Editor, to 1980. *The Cincinnati Enquirer,* Editor & VP, current, 1980.

Bleiberg, Robert M. *Barron's.* Editorial Director & Publisher. B. 1924, Brooklyn, NY. Columbia, 1943, BA-Economics; NYU, 1950, MBA. *Barron's,* Assoc Editor, to 1954; Editor, to 1981; Editor & Publisher, to 1982; Editorial Director & Publisher, current, 1982. Dow Jones & Co, Inc, VP, Magazine Group, current, 1980. NY Financial Writers Assn's Elliot V. Bell Award, Significant Long-term Contribution to Financial Journalism, 1985.

Block, Alex Ben. *Forbes.* Associate Editor — Entertainment Industry. B. 1946, Syracuse, NY. Ithaca College, 1968, BA-Business Administration. *The Miami News,* Entertainment Editor, movie critic, 1970-76. *The Detroit News,* columnist, to 1979. *Los Angeles Herald Examiner,* Asst City Editor; business, entertainment columnist, to 1984. *Forbes,* reporter, 1968-70; Assoc Editor, entertainment industry, current, 1984. San Fernando Valley Press Club Best Spot News Story, 1982; LA Press Club Best Entertainment Story, 1984; Silver Angel Awards, 1983, '84; Hearst Awards, 1981, '82, '83, '84.

Blount, Roy Jr. Freelance Writer. B. 1941, Indianapolis, IN. Vanderbilt, 1963, English; Harvard, 1964, MA-English. *Atlanta Journal,* reporter, editorial writer, 1966-68. *Sports Illustrated,* writer, Assoc Editor, to 1975. Freelance, current, 1976. Author 7 books, including *Soupsongs/Webster's Ark,* 1987.

Blumenthal, Sidney. *The Washington Post.* Political Reporter. B. 1948, Chicago, IL. Brandeis, 1969. *The New Republic,* national political correspondent, to 1985. *The Washington Post,* political reporter, current, 1985. Author *The Permanent Campaign,* 1980 (2nd Ed, 1983); *The Rise of the Counter-Establishment,* 1986.

Blundell, William. *The Wall Street Journal.* National Correspondent. B. 1934, NJ. Syracuse, 1956, BS-Psychology; postgrad U. of KS, 1961, Journalism. *The Wall Street Journal,* Dallas reporter, to 1964; NY reporter, to 1965; "Page One" rewrite man, to 1968; LA Bureau Chief, to 1978; national correspondent, current, 1986 (editing duties added 1986). Author *Storytelling Step by Step: A Guide to Better Feature Writing,* 1986. Scripps-Howard Foundation Award, Public Service, 1974; American Society of Newspaper Editors Award, Best Non-deadline Feature Writing, 1982: co-winner Meyer Berger Award, Distinguished Metro Reporting, 1966.

Bock, Gordon. *Time.* Business Writer. B. 1955, NYC. Columbia, 1976, Political Science & Urban Studies; Columbia, 1977, MSJ. UPI, NY reporter, to 1981. *U.S.News & World Report,* NY correspondent, to 1984. *BusinessWeek,* Staff Editor, to 1987. *Time,* business writer, current, 1987. Columbia Grad School of Journalism, adjunct prof, current, 1987. Computer Press Assn, Best News Report, Non-computer Publication, 1986.

Boldt, David R. *Philadelphia Inquirer.* Editor. *The Washington Post. Philadelphia Inquirer,* Sunday

Magazine Editor, Deputy Editor, to 1987, Editor, current, 1987.

Bonafede, Dom. *National Journal.* Special Contributing Editor. B. 1933, Buffalo, NY. Rutgers, 1953, English, Journalism. Nieman Fellow, 1959-60. *Havana Herald,* reporter, Asst Editor, 1953. *Miami News,* reporter, to 1957. *The Miami Herald,* Chief Latin America Correspondent, to 1963. *New York Herald Tribune,* Washington correspondent, to 1966. *Newsweek,* Washington correspondent, Chief Latin American Correspondent, to 1969. *National Journal,* White House correspondent, to 1979; Chief Political Correspondent, to 1984; Special Contributing Editor, current, 1984. *Washington Journalism Review,* senior writer, 1978-82. *The Washingtonian,* Contributing Editor, current, 1974. American U., Asst Prof, Journalism, current, 1985. Contributor 3 books including *Studying The Presidency,* 1983. Overseas Press Club Citation, Cuba & Caribbean coverage, 1960; NY Reporters Assn Award, Congressional ethics series, 1965.

Borger, Gloria. *U.S.News & World Report.* Assistant Managing Editor — Special Reports, National Affairs. Colgate U. *The Washington Star,* MD & Washington political reporter, 1975-78. *Newsweek,* political & Capitol Hill reporter, to 1986. *U.S.News & World Report,* Asst Managing Editor, special projects, current, 1986.

Bork, Robert H. Jr. *U.S.News & World Report.* Associate Editor — Economy. B. 1955, NYC. Carleton College, 1977, History. Herbert J. Davenport Fellow, U. of MO, 1980. *Columbus Ledger-Enquirer,* police & court reporter, business writer, 1978-80. *Fort Worth Star-Telegram,* business writer, to 1982. *Detroit Free Press,* business writer, to 1983. *Forbes,* Southwest bureau writer, to 1986. *Regulation,* Managing Editor, to 1987. *U.S.News & World Report,* Assoc Editor, current, 1987.

Boroweic, Andrew. *The Washington Times.* Chief Foreign Correspondent. B. 1928, Poland. Alliance College, 1951, BA-Social Science; Columbia, 1952, MSJ. AP, rewrite man, reporter, foreign correspondent, chief, various bureaus, to 1966. *The Washington Star,* roving foreign correspondent, to 1975. Carnegie Endowment, senior assoc, to 1977. Freelance, to 1981. *Sun-Times,* foreign correspondent, Middle East, Europe, Africa, to 1984. *The Washington Times,* Chief Foreign Correspondent, current, 1984. Author *The Mediterranean Feud,* 1983; *Yugoslavia After Tito,* 1977. Overseas Press Club Best Reporting from Abroad Award, 1963, Citation same category, 1965; 1st Prize Front Page Awards, DC-Baltimore Guild, 1971.

Boudreaux, Richard. *Los Angeles Times.* Managua Bureau Chief. AP, from 1970: reporter, NY; News Editor, Argentina, 1979-82; from 1982: Mexico City, Chile Bureau Chief, Bolivia Bureau Chief. *Los Angeles Times,* Managua Bureau Chief, current, 1987.

Bourne, Eric. *The Christian Science Monitor.* Special Correspondent. B. UK. History & English Literature Degree. British Press Assn, Foreign Editor. *News Chronicle,* foreign room. Reuters, WWII correspondent; Chief Correspondent, Germany, to 1947. *Sunday Times,* to 1950. *The Christian Science Monitor,* special correspondent, Europe, current, 1950.

Bovard, James. Freelance Writer. B. 1956, Ames, IA. Virginia Tech, 1976-78, General Arts & Sciences. Cato Institute & Heritage Foundation, policy studies. *The Wall Street Journal, The New York Times, The New Republic, The Detroit News,* freelance contributor, current.

Bowring, Philip. *Far Eastern Economic Review.* Deputy Editor. B. 1942, UK. Cambridge, 1963, History; postgrad U. of Khartoum, 1964. Freelance, Africa, 1965, 1971-72. *Envoy* (UK), to 1967. *COI* (UK), to 1969. *Investors Chronicle* (UK), to 1971. *Finance Week* (Australia), 1972. Freelance, Australia, to 1973. *The Asian Wall Street Journal,* Investment Editor, 1978. *Financial Times,* SE Asia correspondent, to 1980. *Far Eastern Economic Review,* Business Editor, to 1977; Deputy Editor, current, 1980.

Boyer, Peter. *The New York Times.* Culture News Reporter. U. of MS, 1973; USC, 1976, Journalism. AP, reporter; columnist, LA, to 1981. *Los Angeles Times,* entertainment industry reporter, to 1984; Atlanta Bureau Chief, 1984. NPR, media critic, to 1985. CBS News, media critic, 1985. *The New York Times,* culture news reporter, current, 1985.

Bradlee, Benjamin Crowninshield. *The Washington Post.* Executive Editor. B. 1921, Boston. MA. Harvard, 1943, AB. US Naval Reserve, to 1945. *Sunday News* (Manchester), reporter, to 1946. *The Washington Post,* reporter, to 1951; press attache, Paris embassy, to 1953; Managing Editor, 1965-68; VP, Exec Editor, current, 1968. *Newsweek,* European correspondent, to 1957; Washington reporter, to 1961; Senior Editor, Bureau Chief, to 1965. Author *That Special Grace,* 1964; *Conversations With Kennedy,* 1975.

Bradley, Ed. CBS News. "60 Minutes" Correspondent. B. PA. Cheyney (PA) State College, 1964, BA-Education. WDAS radio (Philadelphia), news reporter, 1963-67. WCBS radio (NYC), news reporter, to 1971. CBS News, stringer, to 1973 (Paris, 1971; Saigon, 1972-74); Washington correspondent, to 1978; principal correspondent, 1978; "CBS Reports" principal correspondent, to 1981; "60 Minutes" correspondent, current, 1981. George Polk Award, 1980; Emmy Awards, 1979, '83.

Braestrup, Peter. *The Wilson Quarterly.* Founding Editor. B. 1929, NYC. Yale, 1951, BA-English. Nieman Fellow, 1960; Wilson Center Fellow, 1973-75. *Time,* writer, Midwest & South correspondent, 1953-57. *New York Herald-Tribune,* investigative reporter, to 1959. *The New York Times,* Washington staff, to 1962; Algiers to 1964; Paris, to 1966; SE Asia, to 1967. *The Washington Post,* Saigon Bureau Chief, 1969; Washington writer, to 1973, Vietnam, 1972. *The Wilson Quarterly,* Founding Editor, current, 1976. Author *Big Story,* 1977 (*Sigma Delta Chi* Research Prize, 1978); *Battle Lines* 1985.

Brandt, Thomas D. *The Washington Times.* National Political Writer. B. 1945, Pittsburgh, PA. Georgetown, 1980, Master, Liberal Studies. US Army, Editor, correspondent, 1968-70. *Coral Gables* (FL) *Times Guide,* city hall reporter, 1970. *The Miami News,* Asst City Editor, political writer, to 1975. *The Fort Lauderdale News,* Chief News Feature Writer, 1975. Miami Magazine, political columnist, to 1976. US House of Representatives, legislative staff, to 1982. *The Washington Times,* Capitol

Hill Bureau Chief, to 1986; national political writer, current, 1986. US Army, Editor, Best Unit Newspaper, 1970; Best Feature Story, FL Society of Newspaper Editors, 1970.

Bray, Nicholas. *The Wall Street Journal/*Europe. Paris Bureau Chief. Magdalen College, Oxford, Languages; SOAS, London, Social Anthropology. Reuters, Chief Correspondent, Belgium, Luxembourg, NATO & Common Market, 1972-82. *The Wall Street Journal/*Europe, Paris correspondent, to 1984; Paris Bureau Chief, current, 1984.

Bray, Thomas J. *The Detroit News.* Editorial Page Editor. B. 1941, NYC. Princeton, 1963, History. *San Antonio Evening News,* to 1964. US Army Reserves, 1964. *The Wall Street Journal,* reporter, national news desk, Bureau Chief, Assoc Editor — Editorial Page, to 1983. *The Detroit News,* Editorial Page Editor, current, 1983.

Breen, Thomas J. *The Washington Times.* Political Writer. B. 1946, MA. Temple, English. *Hartford Times,* Suburban Bureau Chief; Acting Asst Editor, 1968-72. *Courier Post* (Camden, NJ), reporter, political writer & columnist, Political Affairs Editor, to 1974. *Philadelphia Bulletin,* rewrite man, Acting Asst City Editor, to 1975. *The Washington Star,* sports desk, Night City Editor, to 1978. *U.S.News & World Report,* Washington News Desk Editor, to 1979. *Peninsula Times Tribune* (Palo Alto, CA), Sports Editor, City Editor, to 1980. *Arizona Republic,* Copy Editor, asst slot man, Scottsdale Bureau Chief, Deputy Sports Editor, to 1982. *The Washington Times,* City Editor; national political writer, Sports Editor & columnist; SE Asia Bureau Chief, Manila, to 1987; political writer, current, 1987. Best AP Story of the Month, 1972: co-winner Philadelphia Press Assoc Award, Best Investigative Story, 1974.

Breindel, Eric. *New York Post.* Editorial Page Editor. B. 1955, NYC. Harvard, 1977, Social Studies, *magna cum laude, Phi Beta Kappa*; London School of Economics, 1977-79; Harvard Law, 1982. Intelligence Committee staff, Sen. Moynihan, 1982-83. PBS-TV, "American Interests", Research Director, to 1984. Georgetown, Adjunct Prof, International Relations, to 1985. NYU, Adjunct Prof, International Relations, 1986. *New York Daily News,* Editorial Board, to 1986. *New York Post,* Editorial Page Editor, current, 1986.

Breslin, Jimmy. Universal Press Syndicate. Columnist. B. 1929, Jamaica, NY. Studied at Long Island U., 1947-50. Universal Press Syndicate, columnist, current. Author 6 books, including *Table Money,* 1983: co-author *Forty-four Caliber,* 1978. *Sigma Delta Chi* Award, National Reporting, 1964; Meyer Berger Award, Local Reporting, 1964; NY Reporters Assn Award, Reporting, 1964; Pulitzer Prize, Commentary, 1986.

Brimelow, Peter. *Forbes.* Senior Editor. B. 1947, UK. U. of Sussex, 1970, BA-History & Economics; Stanford, 1972, MBA-Finance & Economics. Richardson Securities of Canada, investment analyst, to 1973. *Financial Post,* Asst Editor to 1976; columnist, Contributing Editor, to 1980. *MacLean's,* Business Editor, to 1978. *The Wall Street Journal,* guest editorial writer, 1980. *Toronto Sun* Syndicate, columnist, to 1982. *Barron's,* Assoc Editor, to 1983; Contributing Editor, to 1987. *Fortune,* Assoc Editor, 1983-84. *Chief Executive Magazine,* Contributing

Editor, current, 1984. *Forbes*, Senior Editor, current, 1987. Author of *The Wall Street Gurus*, 1986; *The Frozen Crisis: Canada and the Canadian Question Revisited*, 1986.

Brinkley, David. ABC News. "This Week" Anchor. B. 1920, Wilmington, NC. *Wilmington Star-News*, reporter, 1938-41. UP, reporter, bureau manager, Southern cities, 1941-43. NBC Radio/TV, news writer, broadcaster, from 1943; Washington correspondent, 1951-81. ABC News, "This Week" anchor, current, 1981. DuPont Award; Peabody Award.

Brinkley, Joel. *The New York Times*. Washington Reporter. B. 1952, Washington, DC. U. of NC, 1975. AP, reporter, 1975. *Richmond News-Leader*, reporter, to 1978. *The Courier-Journal* (KY), reporter; Editor, to 1983. *The New York Times*, Washington reporter, current, 1983. Pulitzer Prize, International Reporting, 1980.

Brittan, Samuel. *Financial Times*. Principal Economic Commentator & Assistant Editor. B. 1933, London, UK. Jesus College, Cambridge, Economics. Nuffield College, Research Fellow, 1973-74; Visiting Fellow, to 1982. Chicago Law, visiting prof, 1978. *Financial Times*, to 1961. *The Observer*, Economics Editor, to 1964. Dept of Economic Affairs, advisor, 1965. *Financial Times*, principal economic commentator, current, 1966; Asst Editor, current, 1978. Author 9 books, including *Jobs, Pay, Unions and the Ownership of Capital*, 1984. Senior Wincott Award, Financial Journalists, 1971; George Orwell Prize, Political Journalism, 1981.

Broad, William J. *The New York Times*. Science Reporter. B. 1951, Milwaukee, WI. Webster College (St. Louis, MO), 1973; U. of WI, 1977, MA. U. of WI, Madison, U. Industry Research Program, reporter, to 1978; concurrently, teaching asst, History of Science Dept, research asst, Anesthesiology Dept, to 1978. *Science*, reporter, to 1982. *The New York Times*, science reporter, current, 1983. Science-in-Society Journalism Award, National Assn of Science Writers, 1981.

Broadwater, James E. *Washington Journalism Review*. Publisher. U. of FL, Journalism & Advertising. Young & Rubicam, Inc, account exec. *Texas Monthly*, Assoc Publisher. *Saturday Review*, President & Publisher. Baker Publications, Inc, Regional Publishing Director. Blue Water Press, Inc, Director. *Washington Journalism Review*, current, 1987.

Brock, David. *Insight*. Writer. B. 1962. U. of CA, Berkeley, 1985, History. *The Wall Street Journal*, intern, summer 1985. *Insight*, writer, current, 1986.

Broder, David S. *The Washington Post*. Reporter & Columnist. B. 1929, Chicago Heights, IL. U. of Chicago, 1947, BA-Political Science, MA, 1951. *The Pantagraph* (Bloomington, IL), reporter, 1953-55. *Congressional Quarterly*, reporter, to 1960. *The Washington Star*, reporter, to 1965. *The New York Times*, Washington reporter, to 1966. *The Washington Post*, reporter & columnist, current, 1966. Pulitzer Prize, 1973.

Broder, John. *Los Angeles Times*. Pentagon & Defense Correspondent. *Los Angeles Times*, business writer, to 1987; Pentagon & defense correspondent, current, 1987.

Brody, Michael. *Fortune*. Associate Editor. Harvard, 1970, *magna cum laude*; London School of Economics, MS-Economics. *Investor's Chronicle* (UK), Economics Editor. *Barron's*, Senior Editor. *Fortune*, Assoc Editor, current, 1984.

Brokaw, Thomas John. NBC News. "NBC Nightly News" Anchor. B. 1940, Webster, SD. U. of SD, 1962, BA-Political Science. KMTV (Omaha), Morning News Editor, 1962-65. WSB-TV (Atlanta), 11:00 News Editor, anchor, to 1966. KNBC-TV (LA, CA), reporter, correspondent, anchor, to 1973. NBC-TV, White House correspondent, to 1976; Saturday Night News, anchor, to 1973-76; "Today," host, to 1982; "NBC Nightly News," anchor, current, 1982.

Bronson, Gail. *Forbes*. Senior Editor. B. 1951, Washington, DC. Emory U., 1973, BA-Political Science, *magna cum laude*. *The Wall Street Journal*, intern, summer, 1973; reporter, 1974-81. *Money*, writer, 1982. *U.S.News & World Report*, Assoc Editor, to 1985. *Forbes*, Senior Editor, current, 1985.

Brooke, James B. *The New York Times*. Africa Correspondent. B. 1955, NYC. Yale, 1977, BA-Latin American Studies. *The Berkshire Eagle*, freelancer, reporter, to 1978. *The Washington Star*, reporter, 1980. Various publications, stringer, Brazil, to 1981. *The Miami Herald*, South America correspondent, to 1984. *The New York Times*, metro reporter, to 1986; Africa correspondent, Abidjan, current, 1986.

Brookes, Warren Timberlake. *The Detroit News*. Columnist. B. 1929, Summit, NJ. Harvard, 1952, BA-Economics. Heritage Distinguished Journalism Fellow, 1981-84. *The Boston Herald*, political economic columnist, to 1985. Heritage Features Syndicate, "The Economy in Mind" columnist, current, 1985. Hearst Features Syndicate, columnist, current, 1985. *The Detroit News*, columnist, current, 1985. Author *Economy In Mind*, 1982. Two 1st place USIC Editorial Awards, 1978, '79; UPI Editorials, MI, 1987.

Brookhiser, Richard. *National Review*. Managing Editor. B. 1955, Rochester, NY. Yale, 1977, English. *National Review*, Assoc, to 1979; Senior Editor, to 1985; Managing Editor, current, 1986. *The American Spectator*, contributor, current. Author *The Outside Story: How Democrats and Republicans Reelected Reagan*, 1986.

Brophy, Beth. *U.S.News & World Report*. Associate Editor — Personal Finance & Workplace. William Smith College (Geneva, NY); Northwestern, 1978, MSJ. CBS News. Capitol Publications. Medill News Service. Freelance. *Forbes*, government & public policy reporter, 1979-82. *USA Today*, business writer & columnist, to 1985. *U.S.News & World Report*, Assoc Editor, personal finance & workplace, current, 1985. Author *Everything College Didn't Teach You About Money: Money Management for the Young Professional*.

Brown, David M. *Oasis*. Assistant Editor. B. 1962, Rochester, NY. Cornell, 1984, History. *Fort Collins Enterprise*, Managing Editor, 1986. *Oasis*, Asst Editor, current, 1987. Freelance, current.

Brown, Peter. Scripps-Howard News Service. White House & Political Reporter. B. 1949, NYC. Syracuse,

1972, BS-Broadcast Journalism; 1974, MS-Newspapers. Nieman Fellow, 1981-82. UPI, Albany & Boston reporter, to 1976; Hartford Bureau Chief, to 1978; NE Political Editor, to 1979; political reporter, Washington, to 1980; health & human services reporter, 1981; Congress reporter, 1982. Scripps-Howard News Service, White House & political reporter, current, 1982.

Brownstein, Ronald. *National Journal.* West Coast Correspondent. B. 1958, NYC. SUNY, Binghamton, 1979, English Literature. Freelance, current. *National Journal*, finance & banking reporter, from 1983; political & White House correspondent, to 1987; West Coast correspondent, current, 1987.

Brownstein, Vivian. *Fortune.* Economist & Associate Editor. George Washington U.; studied NYU. Board of Governors, Federal Reserve System, Economist. Commission on Money & Credit of the Committee for Economic Development, Economist. *Fortune*, 1960-68; Economist & Assoc Editor, current, 1976.

Broyles, William Jr. *U.S.News & World Report.* Contributing Editor. B. 1944, Houston. Rice U., 1966, BA-History; Oxford 1968, MA-History. US Marines; Bronze Star. *Texas Monthly*, Founding Editor, 1972; Editor, to 1980. *California*, Editor-in-Chief, to 1982. *Newsweek*, Editor-in-Chief, to 1984. Freelance, current. *U.S.News & World Report*, Contributing Editor, current, 1986. Author *Brothers in Arms: A Journey from War to Peace*, 1986.

Brubach, Holly. *The Atlantic.* Staff Writer. B. 1953, Pittsburgh, PA. Duke, 1975, English & History. *Mademoiselle*, fashion copywriter, 1976-77. Freelance, 1978. *Vogue*, fashion copywriter & monthly dance columnist, 1978-82; Contributing Editor, current, 1984. *The Atlantic*, staff writer, current, 1982. National Magazine Award, Essays & Criticism, 1982.

Buchanan, Edna. *The Miami Herald.* Crime Reporter. B. 1940, Paterson, NJ. *The Miami Beach Daily Sun*, reporter, 1965-70. *The Miami Herald*, reporter, to 1971; criminal courts reporter, to 1972; police reporter, current, 1972. Author *Carr: Five Years of Rape and Murder*, 1979. Paul Hansell Award, Distinguished Journalism, FL Society of Newspaper Editors, 1979-80; Green Eye Shade Award, Deadline Reporting, *Sigma Delta Chi*, 1982; Pulitzer Prize, General Reporting, 1986.

Buchwald, Art. *Los Angeles Times* Syndicate. Columnist. B. 1925, Mt. Vernon, NY. USC. *New York Herald Tribune*, columnist. *Los Angeles Times* Syndicate, columnist, current. Author 26 books including *I Think I Don't Remember*, 1987. Pulitzer Prize, Outstanding Commentary, 1982. American Academy of Arts & Letters member, 1986.

Buckley, Priscilla Langford. *National Review.* Senior Editor. B. 1921, NYC. Smith College, 1943, BA. UP, copy girl, sportswriter, 1944; radio rewrite, to 1947; Paris correspondent, 1953-56. WACA (Camden, SC), News Editor, 1947-48. CIA, Reports Editor, to 1953. *National Review*, from 1956: Managing Editor, 1959-86; Senior Editor, current, 1986. One Woman's Voice Syndicate, columnist, 1976-80.

Buckley, William F. Jr. *National Review.* Founder, President & Editor. B. 1925, NYC. Studied U. of Mexico, 1943; Yale, 1950, BA-Political Science, Economics & History. *Sigma Delta Chi* Fellow, 1976. *Yale Daily News*, chairman. US Army 1944-46. Yale, asst instructor, Spanish, 1947-51. *American Mercury*, Assoc Editor, to 1955. Freelance, current, 1955. *National Review*, Founder, 1955; Editor, current. National Review, Inc, President, current. Universal Press Syndicate, "On the Right" columnist, current, 1962. PBS, "Firing Line" host, current, 1966. US Information Agency, Advisory Commission on Information member, 1969-72. Public member, US delegation, 28th General Assembly of UN, 1973. Author 24 books, including *Racing Through Paradise*, 1987: co-author *McCarthy and His Enemies* (with L. Brent Bozell), 1954. Best Columnist of the Year Award, 1967; USC's Distinguished Achievement Award in Journalism, 1968; Bellarmine Medal, 1977; NYU's Creative Leadership Award, 1981; Union League's Lincoln Literary Award, 1985.

Budiansky, Stephen. *U.S.News & World Report.* Associate Editor — Science. B. 1957, Boston. Yale, 1978, Chemistry. Office Of Technology Assessment, Congressional Fellow, 1985-86. *Environmental Science & Technology*, Assoc Editor, 1979-81. "Man And Molecules" (syndicated radio program), writer & producer, to 1982. *Nature*, Washington correspondent, Editor, to 1985. *U.S.News & World Report*, Assoc Editor, current, 1986.

Burns, Jimmy. *Financial Times.* Foreign Desk Page Editor — Latin America. B. 1953, Madrid, Spain. Stonyhurst College, University College (UK), BA-Latin American Studies; London School of Economics, MA-Politics. BBC Television, scriptwriter, 1975-77. Yorkshire Television, researcher, 1975-77. *Catholic Herald*, reporter, 1975-77. *The Christian Science Monitor*, Lisbon correspondent, to 1980; Buenos Aires correspondent, 1982-86. *Financial Times*, Lisbon correspondent, to 1980; International Desk Editor, to 1982; Buenos Aires correspondent, to 1986; Foreign Desk Page Editor, Latin America, current, 1986.

Burns, John. *The New York Times.* Toronto Bureau Chief. B. 1944, Nottingham, UK. McGill U.; Harvard, 1980-81, Russian; Cambridge, 1984, Chinese. *The Ottawa Citizen. The Toronto Globe and Mail*, reporter, to 1969; Parliamentary correspondent, to 1971; China correspondent, to 1975. *The New York Times*, metro reporter, 1975; South Africa correspondent, to 1981; Moscow Bureau Chief, to 1984; Peking Bureau Chief, expelled 1986; Toronto Bureau Chief, current, 1986. Co-winner George Polk Memorial Award, Foreign Correspondence, 1979.

Butler, Steven B. *Financial Times.* Southeast Asia Correspondent. B. 1951, Berlin, NH. Sarah Lawrence College, 1973, BA; Columbia, 1980, PhD-Political Science; field research, China, 1980; postdoctoral research, U. of MI, 1980-81, Center for Chinese Studies; Fellow, Institute of Current World Affairs for South Korea, 1983-86. Cornell, asst prof, Government, to 1980. NPR, consultant, special series on China & Japan, summer 1983. *The Christian Science Monitor*, contributor, to 1986. *Financial Times*, Seoul correspondent, to 1986; SE Asia correspondent, current, 1986.

Buxton, James. *Financial Times.* Scotland Correspondent. B. 1947, Norfolk, UK. Cambridge, MA-History. *Evening Echo* (Hemel Hempstead), reporter, 1969-72. *Financial Times*, London staff, to 1974; foreign desk, to 1977; Middle East correspondent, to 1980; Rome correspondent, to 1986; Scotland correspondent, current, 1986.

Byrne, John A. *BusinessWeek.* Department Editor — Management. William Patterson College (NJ), 1975, BA-Political Science. *Forbes*, Washington correspondent; Assoc Editor, 1981-84. *BusinessWeek*, Dept Editor, Management, current, 1984. Author *The Headhunters*, 1986.

Byron, Christopher. *Forbes.* Assistant Managing Editor. Yale; Columbia Law School. Citicorp Capitol Markets Training Program, 1984. *Time*, foreign correspondent, London, Bonn; Editor, NY, to 1983. Time, Inc, Senior Editor, *TV Cable Week*, 1983. *Forbes*, Asst Managing Editor, overseeing law, technology, & annual industry survey, current, 1985. Author *The Fanciest Dive*, 1984.

Cahan, Vicky. *BusinessWeek.* Washington Correspondent. Syracuse, BA. Bureau of National Affairs, Senior Editor, 1973-79. *BusinessWeek*, Washington correspondent, occupational safety & health, to 1986; Washington correspondent, financial regulation, current, 1986.

Calame, Byron. *The Wall Street Journal.* Senior Editor. U. of MO, 1961, BJ; U. of MD, 1967, MA-Political Science. *The Wall Street Journal*, reporter, 1965-74; Pittsburgh & LA Bureau Chief to 1987; Asst Managing Editor, LA, 1985-87; Senior Editor, current, 1987.

Caminiti, Susan. *Fortune.* Reporter. B. 1962, Brooklyn, NY. Fairleigh Dickinson U. (Teaneck, NJ), 1984, Communications & Economics. *The Record* (Bergen, NJ), part-time business writer, 1982-84. *Fortune*, reporter, current.

Campbell, Gail A. *The Washington Times.* Reporter. B. 1957, Washington, DC. Syracuse, 1979, Broadcast Journalism & International Relations. *The Washington Star*, dictationist, freelance reporter, 1979. *The Morning Sun*, reporter, to 1985. *The Washington Times*, reporter, current, 1985. School Bell Award, Easter Seals Society, 1982.

Canby, Vincent. *The New York Times.* Senior Film Critic. B. 1924, Chicago. Dartmouth, 1947, BA-English. *The Chicago Journal of Commerce*, reporter, asst to Drama Editor, to 1950. Public relations, 1951. *Motion Picture Herald*, reporter, to 1959. *Variety*, motion picture reporter & critic, to 1965. *The New York Times*, cultural news reporter, to 1969; senior film critic, current, 1969. Author *Living Quarters*, 1975; *Unnatural Scenery*, 1979: 3 plays.

Cannon, Lou. *The Washington Post.* White House Correspondent. B. NYC. Studied U. of NV, San Francisco State College. *Contra Costa Times* (Walnut Creek, CA), editorial. *San Jose Mercury News*, Editor, reporter. Ridder Newspapers, Washington correspondent. *The Washington Post*, political reporter, 1972-77; LA staff, to 1980; White House reporter, current, 1980. Author 4 books including

Reagan, 1982. American Political Science Assn Award, Distinguished Reporting of Public Affairs, 1969.

Carey, Peter Kevin. *San Jose Mercury News.* Investigative Reporter. B. 1940, San Francisco, CA. U. of CA, Berkeley, 1964, Professional Journalism Fellow, Stanford, 1983-84. *San Francisco Examiner*, reporter, 1964. *Livermore* (CA) *Independent*, Editor, reporter, 1966-67. *San Jose Mercury News*, aerospace writer, 1969-72; special assignments, 1972-78; investigative reporter, current, 1980. CA-NV AP "Mark Twain" Award, 1983; 2 San Francisco Press Club Awards, 1984; Investigative Reporters & Editors "Torchlight" Award, 1986; George Polk Award, International Reporting, 1986; Pulitzer Prize, International Reporting, 1986.

Carrington, Tim. *The Wall Street Journal.* Reporter. B. Baltimore, MD. U. of VA, 1973, BA. Information Institute, Washington representative, 1974. McGraw-Hill, Securities Week, from 1976; Managing Editor. *The Wall Street Journal*, reporter, 1980-83; Washington reporter, current, 1983. Author *The Year They Sold Wall Street.*

Carter, Hodding III. *The Wall Street Journal.* Op-Ed Contributor. B. 1935, New Orleans, LA. Princeton, 1957. Nieman Fellow, 1965-66. *Delta Democrat Times* (Greenville, MS), reporter, to 1962; Managing Editor, to 1966; Editor, Assoc Publisher, to 1977. Asst Secretary of State, Spokesman for President Carter, to 1980. *The Wall Street Journal*, Op-Ed contributor, current, 1981. PBS, "Capitol Journal" Editor-in-Chief, Chief Correspondent, current. ABC News, "This Week," discussion panelist, current. Author *The South Also Rises.* 4 Emmy awards; National *Sigma Delta Chi* Award, Editorial Writing, 1961; Edward R. Murrow Award, Overseas Press Club, 1983.

Carter, John Mack. *Good Housekeeping.* Editor-in-Chief & Director of Magazine Development. B. 1928, Murray, KY. U. of MO, 1948, BJ, 1949, MAJ. *Better Homes and Gardens*, Asst Editor, to 1951. *Household*, Managing Editor, to 1957. *Together*, Exec Editor, to 1959. *American Home*, Editor, to 1961. *McCall's*, Exec Editor, 1961; VP & Director, Editor, to 1965. *Ladies' Home Journal*, Editor-in-Chief, to 1974; Publisher, 1967-70. Downe Communications, Inc, President & CEO, 1972-73. *American Home* Publishing Co, President, to 1975. *Good Housekeeping*, Editor-in-Chief, current, 1975; Director, Magazine Development, current, 1977. Walter Williams Award, ◄Writing, 1949; U. of MO Medal of Honor, Distinguished Service to Journalism, 1970; Brandeis U. Publisher of the Year, 1977; Women in Communications Headliner of the Year, 1978.

Catto, Henry E. Jr. *Washington Journalism Review.* Contributing Editor. B. 1930, Dallas, TX. Williams College, 1952, BA-American History. Insurance, real estate, personal investing, to 1969. Deputy US Rep, Organization of American States, to 1971. US Ambassador, El Salvador, to 1973. Chief of Protocol, White House & State Dept. US Permanent Rep, UN European Office, to 1977 (rank of Ambassador, 1976-77). Washington Communications Corp, Founder & Chairman, current, 1979. Asst Secretary of Defense, Public Affairs, 1981-83. H & C Communications, vice-chairman, current. *San Antonio Light*, columnist, current. *Washington Journalism Review*, Contributing Editor, current. NPR, "All Things Considered," commentator, current.

Cave, Ray. *Time.* Editorial Director. St. John's College, 1949, BA. *The Sun*, Asst City Editor, reporter, 1952-59. *Sports Illustrated*, writer, to 1962; Senior Editor, to 1970; Asst Managing Editor, to 1974; Exec Editor, to 1975, 1976-77. Time, Inc, acting editorial director, 1975. *Time*, Managing Editor; Corporate Editor, to 1987; Editorial Director, current, 1987.

Chakravarty, Subrata Narayan. *Forbes.* Senior Editor. B. 1947, Calcutta, India. Yale, 1969, AB-Intensive Political Science; Harvard, 1971, MBA. Harvard Grad School of Business Administration, research asst, 1971-72. Goodyear India Ltd, New Delhi, India, Manager, Corporate Planning, to 1979. *Forbes*, reporter, to 1974; writer, to 1976; Assoc Editor, 1979-84; Senior Editor, current, 1984.

Chamberlain, John. King Features Syndicate. "These Days" Columnist. B. 1903, New Haven, CT. Yale, 1925, History. Advertising writer, 1925. *The New York Times*, reporter, to 1929; daily book columnist, 1933-36; contributing daily book columnist, 1941-44. *The New York Times Book Review*, Asst Editor, 1928-33. *Fortune*, writer, 1936-41. *Harper's*, Book Editor, 1939-47. Columbia, journalism lecturer, 1934-35; assoc prof, 1941-44. New School of Social Research, lecturer, 1935. Columbia Summer School, lecturer, 1937. *Life*, writer, 1944-50. *The Freeman*, Editor, to 1952. *Barron's*, writer, to 1960. *The Wall Street Journal*, writer, to 1960. Troy (AL) School of Journalism, Dean, 1972-77. King Features Syndicate, "These Days" columnist, current, 1961. Author 6 books, including *A Life With The Printed Word*, 1982.

Chancellor, John William. NBC News. "NBC Nightly News" Commentator. B. 1927, Chicago, IL. U. of IL. *Chicago Sun-Times*, reporter. NBC News, staff, from 1950: newswriter, reporter, 1953-58; Vienna correspondent, 1958, in London, to 1960; Moscow correspondent, to 1961; NY staff, to 1963; "Today," communicator, 1961-62; Brussels correspondent, 1963-65; network national affairs correspondent, current, 1967; "NBC Nightly News," anchor, 1970-81, commentator, current, 1981. Sol Toishoff Award, Excellence in Broadcasting, National Press Foundation, 1984.

Chapman, Stephen. *Chicago Tribune*, Editorial Writer & Tribune Media Services, Columnist. B. 1954, Brady, TX. Harvard, 1976, History. Freelance, to 1978. *The New Republic*, writer, Assoc Editor, to 1981. *Chicago Tribune*, editorial writer, columnist, current, 1981. Tribune Media Services, columnist, current, 1982.

Chavez, Lydia. *The New York Times*. Metro Reporter. U. of CA, Berkeley, 1974, BA-Comparative Literature; *Universite de France*, Montpellier, 1975; Columbia, 1977, MSJ. Contributor *The Albuquerque Times*, 1977; *Time*, to 1980; *New York*, to 1980. *Los Angeles Times*, energy & financial news reporter, to 1983. *The New York Times*, stringer, "Long Island Weekly" section, to 1980; San Salvador correspondent, 1983-84; foreign correspondent, Buenos Aires, to 1986; metro reporter, current, 1986.

Cheshire, William P. *Arizona Republic*. Editorial Page Editor. B. 1931, Durham, NC. U. of NC, 1958, BAJ. Heritage Foundation, Distinguished Journalism Fellow, 1987. *The Richmond News Leader*, reporter, Chief of Statehouse Staff, to 1961. *The Canton* (NC) *Enterprise*,

Assoc Editor, to 1963. *The Evening Post* (Charleston, SC), Assoc Editor, to 1968. *The State*, Assoc Editor, to 1972. Helms for Senate Committee, Director of Communications, 1972. Capitol Broadcasting Co (Raleigh, NC), Editorial Director, to 1975. *The Greensboro* (NC) *Record*, Editorial Page Editor, to 1978. *The Charleston Daily Mail*, Editor-in-Chief, to 1984. *The Washington Times*, Editor, Editorial Page, to 1987. *Arizona Republic*, Editorial Page Editor, current, 1987. George Washington Honor Medal, 1975; Council for the Defense of Freedom Award, 1978.

Chira, Susan. *The New York Times*. Tokyo Correspondent. B. NYC. Harvard, 1980, History & East Asian Studies, *summa cum laude, Phi Beta Kappa*; Inter-University Center for Japanese Language Studies (Tokyo); Middlebury College, Japanese. *The Harvard Crimson*, reporter; Editor; President to 1980. *The New York Times*, metro trainee, to 1982; reporter, to 1984; Tokyo correspondent, current, 1984.

Christensen, Bryce J. *The Family In America.* Editor. B. 1955, Mt. Pleasant, UT. Brigham Young U., 1978, BA-English Literature, 1980, MA; Marquette, 1984, PhD. *Chronicles*, editorial intern, 1982-83; Asst Editor, to 1985; Assoc Editor, to 1986. *The Family In America*, Editor, current, 1987.

Christian, Shirley. *The New York Times*. Buenos Aires Bureau Chief. B. 1938, Windsor, MO. Pittsburgh State U. (KS), 1960, Language & Literature; OH State U., 1966, MA. AP, UN correspondent; Foreign News Editor (NY); Bureau Chief, Santiago, Chile, to 1979. *The Miami Herald*, Central American correspondent, to 1984. *The New York Times*, Washington staff, to 1986; Buenos Aires Bureau Chief, current, 1986. Pulitzer Prize, International Reporting, 1981; George Polk Award, International Reporting under Perilous Circumstances, 1981; Maria Moors Cabot Award, 1985.

Chusmir, Janet. *The Miami Herald.* Executive Editor. *The Miami Herald*, reporter, columnist, Features Editor, "Living Today" Editor, Asst Managing Editor — features, 1968-82; Exec Editor, current, 1987. *Boulder* (CO) *Daily Camera*, President & Publisher, 1982-87.

Clad, James Clovis. *Far Eastern Economic Review.* Manila Bureau Chief. B. 1946, New Haven, CT. Victoria U. of Wellington (New Zealand), 1969, BA; Osgoode Hall Law School, Toronto; Auckland Law School (New Zealand), 1974, LLB with Honors. Center for International Affairs, Harvard Fellow, 1980-81. New Zealand Ministry of Foreign Affairs, diplomatic officer, 1975-83. *Far Eastern Economic Review*, Kuala Lumpur correspondent, to 1984; Kuala Lumpur Bureau Chief, 1985; Manila Bureau Chief, current, 1986. *International Herald Tribune*, Op-Ed contributor, current. BBC World Service, commentary, current. Co-author, Time-Life country series book on SE Asia, 1986.

Claiborne, William L. *The Washington Post.* Southern Africa Correspondent. B. 1936, NYC. Hobart College, 1960, English. *Democrat & Chronicle* (Rochester, NY), reporter, to 1966. *The Suffolk Sun*, City Editor, to 1969. *The Washington Post*, Night City Editor, to 1970; metro reporter, to 1972; national reporter, to 1974; correspondent, to 1977; Jerusalem correspondent, to 1982; New Delhi correspondent, to 1985; Jerusalem correspondent, to 1986; Southern Africa correspondent (Johannesburg-based), current, 1986.

Clark, Charles S. *National Journal.* Managing Editor. B. 1953, Washington, DC. McGill U., 1976, History. Time-Life Books, Chief Researcher, writer, administrator, 1976-82. *Congressional Quarterly*, senior researcher, writer, to 1985. *Worldwide Information Resources*, Assoc Editor, to 1986. *National Journal*, Senior Editor, 1986; Managing Editor, current, 1987. Freelance, current. An original Editor of *Mole*.

Clark, Evert. *BusinessWeek.* Senior Staff Writer — Science Policy. U. of NC. *The Durham Morning Herald* (NC), reporter, Asst City Editor, Aviation Editor, Feature Editor. *Newsweek*, science correspondent, Watergate reporter. *The New York Times*, science correspondent. *Aviation Week & Space Technology*, Space Technology Editor, Washington Bureau Chief. *BusinessWeek*, Technology News Editor; senior staff writer, science policy, current. Co-author *Contrabandista!*.

Clark, Lindley H. Jr. *The Wall Street Journal.* Economic News Editor. B. Indianapolis, IN. Earlham College (Richmond, IN), 1948, BA; U. of Chicago, 1949, MA. *The Wall Street Journal*, Copy Editor, 1949; reporter, rewriter, 1951-56; "Page One" Editor, to 1961; Editorial Writer, to 1965; Assoc Editor, to 1972; Economic News Editor, current, 1972; "Outlook" column writer, current; "Speaking of Business" columnist, current. Author *The Secret Tax*, 1976.

Clark, Timothy B. *Government Executive.* Editor. B. 1942, Washington, DC. Harvard, 1963, History. *Congressional Quarterly*, writer, Editor, to 1969. *Empire State Report*, Founder & Publisher, to 1977. *National Journal*, Co-Founder, 1969, to 1974; financial reporter, 1978-87; Contributing Editor, current, 1987. *Government Executive*, Editor, current, 1987.

Claus, Marty. *Detroit Free Press.* Managing Editor — Features & Business News. B. Detroit, MI. *San Bernadino Sun-Telegraph*, reporter, Copy Editor, Wire Editor, Features Editor, to 1977. *Detroit Free Press*, Copy Editor, to 1985; Asst Managing Editor, features, to 1987; Managing Editor, features & business news, current, 1987.

Clift, Eleanor. *Newsweek.* Washington Correspondent. B. 1940, Brooklyn, NY. Studied Hofstra College, Hunter College, Philosophy, English. *Newsweek*, researcher, NY, to 1965; Atlanta office manager, to 1972; Atlanta correspondent, to 1976; White House correspondent, to 1985; News Editor & Deputy Bureau Chief, 1985. *Los Angeles Times*, White House correspondent, to 1987. *Newsweek*, Washington correspondent, current, 1987. "The McLaughlin Group," panelist, current.

Clifton, Tony. *Newsweek.* London Bureau Chief. B. 1937, Melbourne, Australia. *Benalla Standard*, 1956-59. *The Herald* (Melbourne, Australia), to 1960. *Stratford Express* (UK), to 1963. *Daily Mail* (UK), to 1965. *Sunday Times* (UK), to 1970. *Newsweek*, Hong Kong correspondent, to 1975; Beirut correspondent, to 1978; London Bureau Chief, current. Author *God Cried*. Co-winner 3 Overseas Press Club awards.

Cody, Edward. *The Washington Post.* Foreign Correspondent. B. 1943, Portland, OR. Gonzaga U., 1965; U. of Paris Law, 1966-67; Columbia, 1968, Journalism. *The Charlotte* (NC) *Observer*, reporter, to 1969. AP, Editor, to 1973; correspondent, to 1978. *The Washington Post*, Editor, to 1979; Cairo correspondent, to 1980; Paris correspondent, 1981; Beirut correspondent, to 1982; Miami (for Central America/Caribbean) correspondent, to 1986; Mexico correspondent, to 1987; foreign correspondent, Europe, current, 1987. Overseas Press Club, Best Daily Newspaper or Wire Service Reporting from Abroad, 1976.

Cohen, Richard. *The Washington Post.* Columnist. B. 1941, NYC. NYU, 1967, Sociology; Columbia, 1968, MSJ. UPI, NY staff, 1967-68; education & MD legislative correspondent, to 1976. *The Washington Post*, *Washington Post* Writers Group, columnist, current, 1976. Freelance, current. "The McLaughlin Group," occasional panelist, current. Co-author (with Jules Witcover) *A Heartbeat Away — The Investigation and Resignation of Spiro T. Agnew*.

Cohen, Richard E. *National Journal.* Congressional Reporter. B. 1948, Northampton, MA. Brown, 1969, AB-History; Georgetown Law, 1972, JD. Legislative aide, Sen. Edward W. Brooke, 1969-72. *National Journal*, legal & regulatory reporter, to 1977; Congressional reporter, current, 1977. Author *Congressional Leadership: Seeking A New Role*, 1980.

Cohen, Roger. *The Wall Street Journal.* Miami Correspondent. Oxford, 1977, History & French. Reuters, London correspondent, to 1983. *The Wall Street Journal*/Europe, Rome Bureau Chief, to 1986. *The Wall Street Journal*, Miami correspondent, current, 1986.

Cohen, Stephen F. *The Nation.* "Sovieticus" Columnist. B. 1938, Indianapolis, IN. IN U., 1960, BA, 1962, MA; Columbia, 1969, PhD. Princeton, Prof, Soviet Relations & History, current, 1968. *The Nation*, "Sovieticus" columnist, current, 1982. Newspaper Guild Page One Award, Column Writing, 1985.

Cole, Robert. *The New York Times.* Financial & Business News Reporter. B. 1925, Woonsocket, RI. U. of TX, Austin, 1947, Journalism; Carson-Newman College (TN); Cornell. *The Mexico City Herald*, reporter, to 1950. *The New York Journal of Commerce*, Foreign Editor, to 1962. *The New York Times*, Financial Copy Desk Editor; "Personal Finance" columnist, to 1974; NYSE reporter, to 1976; Financial & Business News reporter, current, 1976. Award, U. of MO, 1971; Gerald Loeb Award, 1985.

Comarow, Avery. *U.S.News & World Report.* Assistant Managing Editor — Horizons. B. 1945, Macon, GA. U. of MD, 1969, English. *The Wall Street Journal*, copyreader, 1966-69. *Courier-Tribune*, reporter, 1970. *Times Herald-Record*, reporter, to 1972. *Money*, writer, to 1976; Washington correspondent, to 1979. *Consumer Reports*, Washington Managing Editor, to 1982. *Science '86*, Senior Editor, to 1985; Asst Managing Editor, to 1986. *U.S.News & World Report*, Asst Managing Editor, Horizons, current, 1986.

Como, William. *Dance.* Editor-in-Chief. B. 1925, Williamstown, MA. American Academy of Dramatic Arts, 1947. US Army, 1945-57. *Dance*, advertising manager, 1961; Editor-in-Chief, current, 1969. *After*

Dark, Founder, 1968; Editor-in-Chief, to 1979. Author several books including *Anatomy For The Dancer*.

Comstock, Robert. *The Record*. Executive Editor. B. 1927, NYC. Rutgers, 1952. *New Jersey News*, 1953. *The Record* (Bergen, NJ), reporter, Political Editor, News Editor, editorial writer, from 1953; Exec Editor, current. NJ State Director of Public Information, 1975-77.

Conason, Joe. *The Village Voice*. Correspondent. B. 1954, NYC. Brandeis, 1975, History. *East Boston Community News*, Editor, reporter, 1975-77. *The Real Paper* (Cambridge, MA), to 1978. *The Village Voice*, political correspondent, to 1986; Philippine elections correspondent, to 1987; Iran-contra coverage, current, 1986. Public Relations Society of America, 1978; Byline Award, NY Press Club, subway strike coverage, 1980.

Conine, Ernest. *Los Angeles Times*. Editorial Writer & Columnist. B. 1925, Dallas, TX. Southern Methodist U., 1948, Journalism. US Army Air Corps 1944-46. US Army, Psychological Warfare Division, 1951-52. UPI, Dallas, to 1948-51. *Dallas Times Herald*, Washington correspondent, to 1955. *BusinessWeek*, Washington staff, to 1960; Moscow staff, to 1961; Boston staff, to 1963. *Los Angeles Times*, Vienna staff, Eastern Europe, to 1964; editorial writer & columnist, current, 1964.

Cook, James. *Forbes*. Executive Editor. B. 1926, Schenectady, NY. Bowdoin College, 1947, AB; Columbia, 1948, AM. Yankton College, instructor, to 1949. OH U., instructor, to 1952. *Popular Publications*, Editor, to 1955. *Railroad*, Managing Editor, to 1955. *Forbes*, Assoc Editor, 1955-76; Reviewer Restaurant Guide, 1975-76; Arabic Editor, 1975-76; Exec Editor, current, 1976. Champion Tuck award, 1982.

Coone, Tim. *Financial Times*. Buenos Aires Correspondent. B. 1952, Aberdeen, MD. Newcastle U. (UK), 1978, BS-Agricultural Economics. Freelance, current, 1978. *Financial Times*, stringer, 1982-86; Buenos Aires correspondent, current, 1986. *The Christian Science Monitor*, contributor, current.

Cooper, Gloria. *Columbia Journalism Review*. Managing Editor. B. 1931, Oak Park, IL. Briarcliff College, 1970, BA-English, *summa cum laude*. Columbia, 1974, MA. *Columbia Journalism Review*, asst to Editor, to 1974; Asst Editor, to 1975; Editor, to 1976; Editor, writer, "Darts & Laurels" & "Briefings" columnist, current, 1976; Managing Editor, current, 1978. Editor *Squad Helps Dog Bite Victim*, 1980; *Red Tape Holds Up New Bridge*, 1987.

Corn, David. *The Nation*. Washington Correspondent. B. 1959, NYC. Brown, 1982, American History. Freelance, current. *The Nation*, Washington correspondent, current.

Corrigan, Richard. *National Journal*. Managing Editor. B. 1937, Glenridge, NJ. U. of FL, 1959, Journalism. *St. Petersburg Times*, to 1960. *The Washington Post*, 1962-69. *National Journal*, staff correspondent, to 1987; Managing Editor, current, 1987. President's Commission for a National Agenda for the '80's, member, 1980.

Corry, John. *The New York Times*. Cultural Reporter & Critic. B. 1933, NY. Hope College, 1954, Philosophy.

Nieman Fellow, 1965. *The New York Times*, sports dept, National News Editor, reporter, to 1968. *Harper's*, writer, to 1971. *The New York Times*, metro reporter; columnist; cultural reporter & critic, current, 1971. Author *TV News and the Dominant Culture*, 1986.

Cotliar, George J. *Los Angeles Times*. Managing Editor. B. 1932, Bronx, NY. LA State College (CA), 1961, BA-Journalism & History. *Los Angeles Examiner*, Copy Editor, 1956. *Culver City Star News*, reporter, to 1957. *Los Angeles Times*, editorial positions, to 1968; Exec News Editor, 1968; Asst Managing Editor, 1969; Managing Editor — Orange County, to 1972; Senior Asst Managing Editor, to 1978; Managing Editor, current, 1978. CA State LA Alumnus of the Year, 1984.

Covault, Craig P. *Aviation Space & Space Technology*. Senior Space Editor. B. 1949, Dayton, OH. Bowling Green State U., 1971, BSJ. *Urbana* (IL) *Citizen*, writer, to 1972. *Aviation Week & Space Technology*, Senior Space Editor, current, 1972. Freelance, current. Ball Memorial Trophy, Aviation & Space Writers Assn, 1982; National Space Club's Writing Award, 1984, '85; Jesse Neal Award, 1985.

Cowell, Alan. *The New York Times*. Athens Bureau Chief. B. 1947, Manchester, UK. St. Edmund Hall, Oxford, School of Modern Languages, 1968, BA. Reuters, foreign correspondent, to 1974; correspondent, Ankara, to 1981. *The New York Times*, foreign correspondent, Nairobi, to 1983; Johannesburg Bureau Chief, expelled 1986; Athens Bureau Chief, current, 1986.

Crock, Stan. *BusinessWeek*. News Editor — Washington. Columbia, BA-Political Science, JD-Law; Northwestern, MSJ. *The Palm Beach Post*, reporter. AP, reporter. *The Wall Street Journal*, regulatory agency reporter. *BusinessWeek*, Regulatory News Editor (McGraw-Hill World News), 1983; News Editor, Washington, current.

Crossette, Barbara. *The New York Times*. Bangkok Bureau Chief. B. 1939, Philadelphia, PA. Muhlenberg College, 1963, BA; U. of CO, 1965, MA; U. of London, Institute of Historical Research, research work, 1965. Fulbright Teaching Fellow, 1980. *The Teacher* (UK), Production Editor. *Philadelphia Bulletin*, Copy Editor, to 1970. *The Birmingham Post* (UK), Features Editor, political & features writer, to 1973. *The New York Times*, foreign desk, to 1977; Editor "Westchester Weekly" section, 1977; Asst Metro Editor, 1977; Asst News Editor, to 1979; Weekend News Editor, to 1981; foreign affairs reporter, Washington, to 1982; Asst Foreign Editor, to 1983; Deputy Foreign Editor, to 1984; Bangkok Bureau Chief, current, 1984. Columbia, member adjunct faculty, Journalism, current, 1975. Editor *America's Wonderful Little Hotels and Inns*, published annually.

Crovitz, L. Gordon. *The Wall Street Journal*. Assistant Editorial Page Editor & Editorial Board Member. B. 1958, Durham, NC. U. of Chicago, 1980, Politics, Economics, Rhetoric & Law; Wadham College, Oxford, Law, 1982 (Rhodes Scholar); Yale Law School, JD, 1986. *The Washington Post*, stringer, 1976-78. *Time*, stringer, to 1979. *Chicago Daily News*, stringer, to 1978. *The Chicago Journal*, Editor, to 1979. *The Wall Street Journal*, editorial page summer intern, to 1982. *The Wall Street Journal*/Europe, Editorial Page Editor, Brussels, to 1984; *The Wall Street Journal*, editorial writer, to 1986; Asst Editorial Page Editor, editorial board member, current, 1986. Finalist Gerald Loeb Award, 1987.

Crozier, Brian. *National Review.* Columnist & Contributing Editor. B. 1918, Kuridala, Queensland, Australia. U. of London, Trinity College of Music, 1935-36. Music & art critic, (UK), to 1939. UK Newspapers, reporter, to 1941. Aeronautics inspector, to 1943. Reuters (UK), to 1944. *News Chronicle,* (UK), Foreign Sub-Editor, to 1948. *Sydney Morning Herald* (Australia), Sub-Editor & writer, to 1951. Reuters-Australian AP, Day Editor, to 1952; foreign correspondent, SE Asia, 1952. *The New York Times,* stringer, to 1953. *Straits Times,* Features Editor, Singapore, to 1953. *The Economist's Foreign Report,* Editor, leader writer, correspondent, to 1964. BBC Overseas Services, commentator, 1954-65. Forum World Services (UK), Chairman to 1974. Institute for the Study of Conflict (UK), Director & Co-Founder, 1970-79. *Now!,* columnist, 1980-82. *The Times,* columnist, to 1983. *National Review,* columnist, Contributing Editor, current, 1978. Author 15 books, including *The Andropov Deception,* 1986: co-author *This War Called Peace,* 1984; *Socialism: The Grand Delusion,* 1986.

Crudele, John T. *New York.* "The Bottom Line" Columnist. B. 1953, Brooklyn, NY. Syracuse, 1974; NYU, 1979, MA. *Sports Illustrated,* reporter, to 1975. *Electronic News,* reporter to 1979. Reuters, financial reporter, to 1985. *The New York Times,* financial reporter, to 1987. *New York,* "The Bottom Line" columnist, current, 1987.

Cunningham, Miles. *Insight.* Writer. B. 1930, Rapid City, SD. U. of TN, 1955, Journalism. USMC Air Station, base newspaper, to 1957. *Times-Union* (Rochester, NY), political reporter, to 1963. Gannett News Service, Albany & Trenton politics reporter, to 1965. *Philadelphia Bulletin,* politics reporter, to 1982. Congressional staff, to 1983. *The Washington Times,* national, foreign & copy desks, to 1985. *Insight,* writer, current, 1985.

Curran, John J. *Fortune.* Associate Editor. Bard College, 1975, BA-Languages & Literature. Freelance, to 1977. *Wall Street Transcript,* weekly stock option columnist, to 1978. *Fortune,* reporter, researcher; Assoc Editor, current.

Curtis, C. Michael. *The Atlantic.* Senior Editor. B. 1934, NYC. Cornell, 1957, BA, postgrad, 1959-63. US Army, 1957. *The Atlantic,* Senior Editor, current 1963.

Danguilan-Vitug, Marites. Nieman Fellow. B. 1955, Solano, Nueva Vizcaya, Philippines. U. of Philippines, 1975, AB-Broadcast Communications; MA-Communications. Freelance, to 1978. *World Paper,* contributor, 1986. *The Christian Science Monitor,* correspondent, to 1986. *Business Day* (Philippines), reporter, current, 1979. *Newsday,* correspondent, current, 1984. Nieman Fellow, current, 1986.

Daniloff, Nicholas. *U.S.News & World Report.* Diplomatic Correspondent (On Leave). B. 1934, Paris, France. Harvard, 1956, BA; Oxford, 1959, BA, 1965, MA. UPI, foreign correspondent, to 1965; State Dept correspondent, 1966-80. *The Washington Post,* Foreign Editor, to 1966. *U.S.News & World Report,* Moscow correspondent, 1981-86; diplomatic correspondent, current, 1986, (on leave, 1987).

Davies, Derek. *Far Eastern Economic Review.* Editor. B. 1931, UK. Jesus College, Cambridge, UK, English Literature. Reuters, 1954-56. H.M. Foreign Office (Vice Consul, Hanoi, N. Vietnam; Third Secretary, Commercial, British Embassy, Vienna), to 1961. *Financial Times,* 1961. *Far Eastern Economic Review,* Editor, current, 1964.

Davis, Bob. *The Wall Street Journal.* Technology & Communication Correspondent. B. 1951, Brooklyn, NY. Queens College, 1972, Political Science. *Dealerscope II* (Waltham, NY), Editor & Founder, 1980-82. *The Wall Street Journal,* computer correspondent, Boston, to 1986; communications & technology correspondent, Washington, current, 1986.

Day, Anthony. *Los Angeles Times.* Editorial Page Editor. B. 1933, Miami, FL. Harvard, 1955, AB, *cum laude.* Nieman Fellow, 1966-67. *Philadelphia Bulletin,* 1957-60; Washington, to 1969; Washington Bureau Chief, 1969. *Los Angeles Times,* Chief Editorial Writer, to 1971; Editorial Page Editor, current, 1971.

deBorchgrave, Arnaud. *The Washington Times & Insight.* Editor-in-Chief. B. 1926, Brussels, Belgium. British Royal Navy, to 1946. Independent News Service, freelance, to 1947. UPI, telex operator, correspondent, to 1948; Brussels Bureau Chief, to 1950. *Newsweek,* Paris Bureau Chief, European correspondent, to 1954; Deputy Foreign Editor, to 1955; Foreign Editor, 1955; Senior Editor, to 1959; Chief European correspondent, to 1961; Foreign Editor & Managing Editor — International Editions, to 1963; Chief Roving Foreign Correspondent, to 1980. Center for Strategic & International Studies, Senior Assoc, to 1985. *The Washington Times & Insight* Editor-in-Chief, current, 1985. Co-author (with Robert Moss) *The Spike,* 1980; *Monimbo,* 1983. 2 Best Magazine Reporting from Abroad Awards; 3 NY Newspaper Guild Page One Awards; Best Magazine Interpretations of Foreign Affairs Award; George Washington Medal of Honor, Excellence in Published Works; High Frontier Outstanding Media Coverage Award, 1986.

Deigh, Robert. *U.S.News & World Report..* Reporter. B. 1952, Casablanca, Morocco. VA Commonwealth U., 1977, BSJ. American U., 1983, MS-Public Relations. US Army, reporter, photographer, Central America, 1974-75. *The Virginia Gazette,* political reporter, 1977-80. *Foreign Agriculture Magazine,* writer, Foreign Agricultural Service, US Dept of Agriculture, to 1985. *Insight,* reporter, politics & business, to 1987. *U.S.News & World Report,* reporter, current, 1987. 2 1st Place VA Press Assn Awards, Investigative Reporting, 1978.

Delfs, Robert A. *Far Eastern Economic Review.* Peking Bureau Chief. B. 1948, Long Beach, CA. Stanford, 1970, Chinese; Stanford, 1972; Princeton, 1976, MA-Asian Studies. *China Business Review,* writer, 1981. *Far Eastern Economic Review,* China economic correspondent, to 1986; Peking Bureau Chief, current, 1986.

DeMuth, Christopher. *The American Spectator.* Contributing Editor. B. Kenilworth, IL. Harvard, 1968, AB; U. of Chicago Law, 1973, JD. Staff Asst to the President, to 1970. Sidney & Austin, Chicago, Attorney, to 1976. Consolidated Rail Corp, Philadelphia, Assoc General Counsel, to 1977. Havard, Faculty Project on Regulation, Director, Lecturer, to 1981. Presidential Task Force on Regulatory Relief, Exec Director, to 1983. Office of Information & Regulatory Affairs, OMB, Administrator, to 1984. Freelance, current, 1971.

Regulation, Editor & Publisher, current. *The American Spectator*, Contributing Editor, current. American Enterprise Institute, President, current 1987.

Denby, David. *New York*. Film Critic. B. 1943, NYC. Columbia, 1965, BA-English. *The Atlantic*, film critic, to 1973. *The Boston Phoenix*, film cirtic, to 1978. *New York*, current, 1978.

Denton, Herbert H. *The Washington Post*. Canada Correspondent. B. 1943, Muncie, IN. Harvard, 1965, BA-History, cum laude. *The Washington Post*, metro staff, 1968-73; Suburban Editor, to 1976; City Editor, to 1980; national staff, to 1982; Beirut correspondent, to 1984; Canada correspondent, current, 1985.

Dentzer, Susan. B. *U.S.News & World Report*. Senior Editor — Economics. B. 1955, Philadelphia, PA. Dartmouth, 1977, BA-English Literature. Nieman Fellow, 1986-87. *The Southampton Press and Chronicle-News*, reporter to 1978. *Wall Street Transcript*, Editor, columnist, 1979. *Newsweek*, reporter & researcher, to 1981; business reporter, 1981; business news writer, to 1987; senior writer, 1987. *U.S.News & World Report*, Senior Editor, economics, current, 1987.

De Onis, Juan. *U.S.News & World Report*. Special Correspondent — Chile. B. 1927, NYC. BA-Economics, 1948; Williams College, MA; Columbia, 1952, MSJ. *Worchester Telegram* (MA), reporter, 1952, UPI, reporter, to 1957. *The New York Times*, correspondent, UN, Washington, Latin America, Middle East, to 1981. *Newsweek International*, columnist, to 1983. *International Herald Tribune*, Latin America correspondent, 1981-83. *Los Angeles Times*, Rio de Janeiro Bureau Chief, current, to 1987. *U.S.News & World Report*, special correspondent, Chile, current, 1987. Overseas Press Club Ed Stout Award; Maria Moors Cabot Award.

de Silva, Mervyn. *Financial Times & Newsweek*. Stringer. B. 1929, Colombo, Sri Lanka. Royal College Colombo, English. *Daily News*, Colombo, Parliamentary reporter, columnist, 1953-60; Editor, 1970. *Ceylon Observer*, Parliamentary Editor, to 1967; Deputy Editor, to 1970. BBC, stringer, current. *Associated Newspapers of Ceylon*, Editor-in-Chief, 1971-76. *Times of Ceylon*, Editor-in-Chief, to 1978. *Financial Times*, stringer, current, 1973. *Newsweek*, stringer, current, 1976. *Lanka Guardian*, Editor-in-Chief, Editor & Publisher, current, 1978. *Island, columnist, current.*

Desmond, Edward W. *Time*. Writer. B. 1958, Seattle, WA. Amherst College, 1980, BA-English; Fletcher School of Law & Diplomacy, 1982, MA Freelance, to 1984. *Time*, reporter & researcher, to 1985; writer, current, 1985.

Diamond, Edwin. *New York*. Media Columnist. B. 1925, Chicago, IL. U. of Chicago, 1949, BA-Political Science, MA, PhB. *Newsweek*, Senior Editor, to 1970; commentator, 1977. Washington TV commentator, to 1977. *New York Daily News*, Deputy Editor, to 1980. *Adweek*, Editorial Director, to 1984. MIT, faculty member, to 1984. *New York*, Contributing Editor, to 1977; media columnist, current, 1985. NYU, faculty member, current, 1984. News Study Group, founder. Co-author (with Bruce Mazlish) *Jimmy Carter*, 1980. Page One Newspaper Guild Awards from DC, Chicago.

Diaz, Tom. *The Washington Times*. Assistant Managing Editor. B. 1940, Ft. Olgethorpe, GA. U. of FL, 1963, BA-Political Science; Georgetown Law, 1972, JD; Law Journal. US Commerce & Defense Depts, staff, 1963-72. Law practice, to 1982. *Federal Times*, columnist, freelance, 1980-82. *The Washington Times*, "Barely Civil" columnist, Supreme Court correspondent, to 1985; national security reporter, to 1986; Asst National News Editor, 1986; Asst Managing Editor, current, 1986.

Dickenson, James R. *The Washington Post*. Political Correspondent. B. 1931, McDonald, KS. San Diego State U., 1953, BA-History; U. of IA, 1959, MAJ. US Marines, 1953-57. *Huntington Park* (CA) *Daily Signal*, 1959-60. UPI, San Francisco, 1960. *The National Observer*, national political correspondent, 1962-74. *The Washington Star*, national political correspondent, National Editor, political columnist, to 1981. *The Washington Post*, Asst National Editor, politics, to 1984; political correspondent, current, 1984.

Diegmueller, Karen. *Insight*. Writer. B. 1950, Cincinnati, OH. U. of Cincinnati, 1977, BA-Political Science, *summa cum laude*; U. of WI, 1979, MAJ. *Boone County* (KY) *Recorder*, reporter, 1980. *The Daily Journal* (Kankakee, IL), reporter, to 1981. *The Home News* (New Brunswick, NJ), reporter, County Bureau Chief, statehouse reporter, to 1985. *Insight*, writer, current, 1985. Co-author *Effective Feature Writing*, 1982.

Diehl, Jackson. *The Washington Post*. Eastern Europe Correspondent. B. 1956, San Antonio, TX. Yale, 1978, English. *The Washington Post*, metro reporter, to 1981; foreign desk, 1981; South America correspondent, to 1985; Eastern Europe correspondent, Warsaw, current, 1985. Inter-American Press Assn Award, 1984.

Dierdorff, John A. *BusinessWeek*. Managing Editor. B. 1928, Chicago, IL. Yale, 1949, English. *Yakima* (WA) *Morning Herald*, writer, 1950-52. *The Oregonian* (Portland, OR), writer, to 1956. *BusinessWeek*, Copy Editor, to 1960; Asst Editor, to 1961; Asst Managing Editor, to 1969; Senior Editor, to 1976; Asst Managing Editor, to 1977; Managing Editor, current, 1977.

Dionne, Eugene J. *The New York Times*. National Political Correspondent. B. 1952, Boston, MA. Harvard, 1973, BA; Oxford, 1982, PhD-Political Sociology (Rhodes Scholar). *The New York Times*, consultant, Sunday magazine, 1975-77; polling operations asst, 1976; reporter, to 1978; reporter, Albany, NY, to 1979; national desk reporter, to 1981; Albany Bureau Chief, to 1983; foreign correspondent, to 1984; Rome Bureau Chief, to 1986; national political correspondent, Washington, current, 1986.

Doan, Michael. *U.S.News & World Report*. Associate Editor. B. 1942, Oakland, CA. U. of CA, Berkeley, 1963, Journalism. *Delaware State News*, writer & Editor, 1963-65. *Pittsburgh Press*, Copy Editor, to 1966. AP, Portland, Las Vegas, San Francisco, to 1971; Washington writer, news desk supervisor, to 1979. *U.S.News World & Report*, Assoc Editor, features & business writer, current, 1979.

Dobbs, Michael. *The Washington Post*. On Leave. B. 1950, Belfast, UK. U. of York (UK), 1972, Economics. Reuters, correspondent, to 1975. Freelance, Africa, 1976.

The Washington Post, special correspondent, Yugoslavia, to 1980; Eastern Europe correspondent, to 1982; Paris correspondent, to 1987; on leave, to 1990. Co-author *Poland, Solidarity, Walesa*. Nicholas Tomalin Award, London *Sunday Times*, 1975; Overseas Press Club Citation, Excellence, 1981.

Dobell, Byron. *American Heritage*. Editor. B. 1927, Bronx, NY. Columbia, 1947, AB-History & Philosophy. Time-Life Books, Senior Editor, 1960-62; Asst Director of Planning, 1970-72. Esquire, Inc, Managing Editor, 1962-67; Editor, 1977. *Washington Post/Chicago Tribune Book World*, Editor, 1967-69. *New York*, Managing Editor, 1972-76. *Life*, Senior Editor, 1977-79. *American Heritage*, Editor, current, 1982. National Magazine Awards, Best Single Topic Issue, General Excellence, both 1985.

Dobrzynski, Judith H. *BusinessWeek*. Associate Editor. B. 1949, Rochester, NY. Syracuse, 1971, Journalism. Trade magazine & cable TV work, to 1976. *BusinessWeek*, Washington correspondent, to 1979; London correspondent, to 1983; Corporate Strategies Editor, to 1986; Assoc Editor, current, 1986. Deadline Club Award, 1987.

Doder, Dusko. *U.S.News & World Report*. Diplomatic Correspondent. B. 1937, Yugoslavia. Washington U. (MO), 1962, Philosophy & Political Science; Columbia, 1964, MSJ, 1965, MA. Wilson Fellow, 1976-77, 1985-86. AP, correspondent, to 1968. UPI, Moscow correspondent, to 1970. *The Washington Post*, Asst Foreign Editor, to 1972; State Dept correspondent, to 1973; foreign correspondent, to 1976. Moscow correspondent, 1978, 1980; Canada correspondent, to 1980; Asst Foreign Editor, to 1981. Moscow Bureau Chief, to 1985; national reporter, to 1987. *U.S.News & World Report*, Diplomatic correspondent, current, 1987. Author *The Yugoslavs*, 1978; *Shadows & Whispers*, 1986. Overseas Press Club Citation, Excellence, 1983; Weintal Prize, Diplomatic Reporting, 1984.

Doherty, Shawn Michelle. *Newsweek*. Boston Correspondent. B. 1959, Madison, WI. Yale, 1982, Comparative Lit. *Newsweek*, correspondent, Boston, current, 1983.

Donaldson, Samuel Andrew. ABC News. "World News Tonight" White House Correspondent. B. 1934, El Paso, TX. U. of TX, El Paso, 1955, BA; postgrad USC, 1955-56. US Army, to 1959. WTOP (Washington), radio & TV news reporter, anchor, 1961-67. ABC News, Capitol Hill correspondent, to 1977; "World News Tonight" White House correspondent, current, 1977. Author *Hold On, Mr. President*, 1987.

Donohoe, Cathryn. *The Washington Times*. Reporter. B. Bronx, NY. Middlebury College, 1958, BA-American Literature, *cum laude*; Columbia, Russian Literature; American U., Journalism. Radio Liberty, research & policy advisor, 1963-74. Freelance, to 1985. *The Washington Times*, feature reporter, current, 1985. Co-winner American Society of Magazine Editors' National Magazine Award, Public Service, 1985.

Donne, Michael. *Financial Times*. Aerospace Correspondent. B. 1928, London, UK. U. of London, Birbeck College. *Financial News of London*, 1945-46.

Military, to 1948. *Financial Times*, since 1946; aerospace correspondent, current, 1953; defense correspondent, 1956-83; broadcasting correspondent, 1961-75. TV/radio, frequent broadcaster, aerospace & defense, current. Author *Leader of the Skies*, 1981; *Per Ardua Ad Astra*, 1984. Appointed Officer of the Order of the British Empire, 1986.

Dorfman, Dan. *USA Today*. Columnist. B. 1931, Brooklyn, NY. Fairchild Publications, to 1964. *Herald Tribune*, to 1965. *World Journal Tribune*, to 1967. *The Wall Street Journal*, to 1973. *Wall Street Letter*, to 1974. *Esquire* magazine, to 1979. *Chicago Tribune* Syndicate, to 1984. *New York*, from 1976; "The Bottom Line" columnist, 1984-87. News America Syndicate, columnist, current, 1984. *USA Today*, columnist, current, 1987. CNN, "Moneyline" columnist, current.

Dougherty, Philip. *The New York Times*. "Advertising News" Columnist. B. 1923, Bronx, NY. Studied Columbia. US Military Police, 1942-46. *The New York Times*, copyboy, 1942; clerk, to 1950; society news staff, to 1963; news staff, to 1966; "Advertising News" columnist, current, 1966. WQXR (NY), "Advertising News" radio commentary, current.

Dowd, Ann Reilly. *Fortune*. Associate Editor. Smith College; Northwestern, MSJ. Press secretary, Sen. Larry Pressler (R-SD). *Dun's Business Monthly*, Senior Editor, to 1983. *Fortune*, Assoc Editor, Washington, current, 1983.

Dowd, Maureen. *The New York Times*. Washington Reporter. B. 1952, Washington, DC. Catholic U., 1973, English Literature. *The Washington Star*, editorial asst, sports columnist, metro reporter, feature writer, to 1981. *Time*, correspondent, writer, to 1983. *The New York Times*, metro reporter, to 1986; Washington reporter, current, 1986.

Dowling, Robert J. *BusinessWeek*. Senior Editor. Villanova U. *The Sun*, business & financial reporter. *American Banker*, banking & monetary affairs correspondent, to 1978. McGraw-Hill World News, correspondent, to 1980. *BusinessWeek*, Brussels Bureau Chief, to 1983; Senior Editor, international coverage, current, 1983.

Downie, Leonard Jr. *The Washington Post*. Managing Editor. B. 1942. OH State U., BA & MA-Journalism & Political Science. Alicia Patterson Foundation Fellow, 1971-72. *The Washington Post*, intern, summer 1964; investigative reporter, to 1971, 1973-74; Asst Managing Editor, metro news, to 1979; London correspondent, to 1982; National Editor, to 1984; Managing Editor, current, 1984. Author *Justice Denied*, 1971; *Mortgage on America*, 1974; *The New Muckrakers*, 1976. 2 DC-MD Newspaper Guild Front Page Awards; ABA Gavel Award, Legal Reporting; John Hancock Award, Business & Financial Writing.

Downs, Hugh Malcolm. ABC News. "20/20" Co-anchor. B. 1921, Akron, OH. Studied Bluffton (OH) College, 1938-39; Wayne State U., 1940-41; Columbia, 1955-56. WLOK (Lima, OH), radio staff announcer, 1939; program director, to 1940. WWJ (Detroit), radio staff announcer, to 1942. NBC, Chicago, to 1954; "Today," 1962-72. Radio/TV freelance broadcaster, from 1954:

"Home Show," to 1957; "Sid Caesar's Hour," 1956-57; "Concentration," to 1968; Jack Paar Show "Tonight," 1957-62, host. Raylin Productions, Inc, Chairman of the Board, current, 1960. UN, special counsel, Middle East refugee problems, 1961-64. ABC News, "20/20" co-anchor, current.

Doyle, Kevin. *Maclean's.* Editor. B. 1943, Fitzroy Harbour, Ontario, Canada. U. of Ottawa, 1965, BA-Politics & Economics; London School of Economics, 1972, MSc-Economics. *The Windsor Star*, reporter, 1965-67. *The Canadian Press*, Parliamentary reporter, Ottawa, to 1970; London correspondent for Europe, Asia, Africa & Middle East, to 1975; Washington staff, to 1976. *Maclean's*, Foreign & National Editor, to 1977; Managing Editor, to 1979; Deputy Editor, 1981-82; Editor, current, 1982. *The FP News Service*, Editor, 1979-80. *Newsweek*, General Editor, to 1981. *The Canadian Press*, Story of the Year, 1974, '75, '86.

Drogin, Bob. *Los Angeles Times.* National Correspondent. B. 1952, Jersey City, NJ. Oberlin, 1973, BA-Asian Studies; Columbia, 1976, MSJ. *Lorain Journal*, police reporter, 1973. UNICEF Assoc, Indonesia, to 1975. Freelance reporter & photographer, NY, Paris, 1976. *The Charlotte* (NC) *Observer,* police, investigative projects, to 1980. UNICEF officer, Thai/Cambodian border, 1980. *Philadelphia Inquirer,* reporter, to 1983. *Los Angeles Times,* national correspondent, NY, current, 1983. NC Press Assn Award, Investigative Reporting, 1978, & Spot Reporting, 1979: co-winner Pulitzer Prize, Meritorious Public Service, 1981; Robert F. Kennedy Journalism Award, Grand Prize & 1st Place, 1981; George Polk Award, Regional Reporting, 1981; Roy F. Howard Public Service Award, 1981; Villers Foundation Media Award, 1985.

D'Souza, Dinesh. Freelance Writer. B. 1961, Bombay, India. Dartmouth, 1983, BA-English Literature, *Phi Beta Kappa. The Dartmouth Review,* Editor, to 1983. *Prospect,* Editor, 1984. Freelance, current, 1985. *Policy Review,* Managing Editor, 1985-87. Author *Falwell: Before The Millennium,* 1984; co-author (with Gregory Fossedal) *My Dear Alex,* 1987. 1st Place, In-depth Reporting, Society of Professional Journalists, 1982.

DuBois, Peter C. *Barron's.* Foreign Editor. Princeton, 1952-56, English. RCA Records, writer. Union Carbide, technical writer. *The Journal of Commerce,* reporter. *BusinessWeek*, 1964-65. Securities analyst & salesman, 1967-73. *Barron's,* 1960-64, 1965-67; Assoc Editor, 1973-82; creator, "International Trader" column, 1978; Foreign Editor, current, 1982.

Duncan, Richard. *Time.* Assistant Managing Editor. B. 1935, Cincinnati, OH. Dartmouth, 1957, BA-English; Columbia, International Fellow, 1961, MSJ. Pulitzer Traveling Fellow, 1962. AP, to 1962. *Time*, correspondent, to 1966; Caribbean Bureau Chief, to 1968; Ottawa Bureau Chief, to 1970; Washington News Editor, to 1972; Western Regional Bureau Chief, to 1975; Deputy Chief of Correspondents, to 1978; Chief of Correspondents, to 1986; Asst Managing Editor, current, 1986.

Dunn, Donald. *BusinessWeek.* "Personal Business" Editor. U. of MO, Journalism. *Sales Management*, Asst Managing Editor. *Television Magazine*, Managing Editor,

Editorial Director, to 1967. *BusinessWeek*, Contributing Editor, to 1977; Media & Advertising Dept Editor, to 1980; "Personal Business" Editor, current, 1980. Author 3 books, including *Ripoff: The Corruption that Plagues America*, 1979; several musical books & lyrics: co-author (with Thomas F.X. Smith) *The Powerticians of New Jersey*.

Dyson, Ester. *Release 1.0.* Editor, Publisher & Owner. B. 1951, Switzerland. Harvard, 1971, Economics. *Forbes,* reporter, 1974-77; columnist, 1987. New Court Securities, securities analyst, 1977-80. Oppenheimer Co, securities analyst, to 1982. *Release 1.0,* Editor, 1982; Editor, Publisher, owner, current, 1983.

Easterbrook, Gregg. *The Atlantic,* National Correspondent. *Newsweek,* Contributing Editor. B. 1953, Buffalo, NY. CO College, 1976, Political Science. *Washington Monthly,* Editor, to 1981. *The Atlantic,* national correspondent, current, 1981. *Newsweek,* Contributing Editor, current, 1987. 2 Investigative Reporters & Editors Awards, 1980, '82; John Hancock Award, Business Writing, 1980; Livingston Award, National Reporting, 1986.

Eaton, William J. *Los Angeles Times.* Moscow Staff. B. 1930, Chicago. Northwestern, 1951, BSJ, 1952, MSJ. City News Bureau, Chicago, to 1953. UPI, to 1966. *Chicago Daily News,* to 1977. Knight-Ridder Newspapers, to 1978. *Los Angeles Times,* from 1978, Moscow staff, current. Pulitzer Prize, International Reporting, 1970.

Echikson, William.. *The Christian Science Monitor.* Foreign Correspondent. B. 1959. NYC. Yale, 1981, History. *Yale Daily News,* reporter, to 1980; News Editor, to 1981. *Newsday,* reporter. *Newsweek,* stringer, Europe. *The Christian Science Monitor,* stringer; foreign correspondent, current.

Eder, Richard. *Los Angeles Times.* Book Critic. B. 1932, Washington, DC. Harvard, 1954, History. *The New York Times,* reporter, 1954-62; S. America correspondent, to 1965; State Dept correspondent, to 1967; E. European correspondent, to 1968; Spain Correspondent, to 1972; England correspondent, to 1975; asst film critic, to 1977; drama critic, to 1979; cultural correspondent, to 1980; France Bureau Chief, to 1982. *Los Angeles Times,* book critic, current, 1982. Pulitzer Prize, Criticism, 1987; National Book Critics Circle Annual Citation, 1987.

Edsall, Thomas B. *The Washington Post.* Political Reporter. B. 1941, Cambridge, MA. Boston U., 1966, Political Science. *Providence* (RI) *Journal,* 1966-67. *The Evening Sun,* to 1974; *The Morning Sun,* Washington staff, to 1981. *The Washington Post,* political reporter, current, 1981. Freelance, current. Author *The Politics of Inequality,* 1984. DC-Baltimore Guild Grand Prize, 1982; Bill Pryor Memorial Award, 1982.

Ehrbar, Aloysius. *Fortune.* Board of Editors Member. Northwestern, BSJ, MSJ; U. of Rochester, MBA. City News Bureau, Chicago, reporter, Editor. *Democrat and Chronicle* (Rochester, NY), reporter, Financial Editor. *Fortune,* Assoc Editor, to 1978; Board of Editors member, current, 1978. John Hancock Award, Excellence, Business & Financial Writing; INGAA-U. of MO Award, Business Writing.

Elias, Christopher. *Insight.* New York Writer. B. 1929, NYC. Hartwick, 1952, English & History; Columbia, 1955, Journalism. *BusinessWeek,* to 1963. *The Wall Street Journal & New York Herald Tribune,* to 1966. *The Exchange* (NYSE), Editor, to 1970. Freelance, to 1976. Champion Intl Corp, corp speechwriter, to 1977. Editorial consultant, freelance, speechwriter, to 1983 (founded *Fact* magazine). *Investment Dealer's Digest,* Editor, to 1985. *Insight,* NY writer, current, 1986. Author *Fleecing the Lambs; The Dollar Barons.*

Elliott, John. *Financial Times.* South Asia Correspondent. B. 1939, UK. Christ's Hospital, UK. Building & architectural magazines, to 1966. *Financial Times,* to 1968; labor correspondent, to 1971; Labor Editor, to 1976; Management Editor, to 1978; Industrial Editor, to 1983; South Asia correspondent, New Delhi, current, 1983. Author *Conflict or Co-operation — The Growth of Industrial Democracy,* 1978. British Institute of Management Journalist & Author of the Year Awards, 1977, '79, '83.

Ellison, Katherine E. *San Jose Mercury News.* National Correspondent. B. 1957, Minneapolis, MN. Stanford, 1979, International Relations. *Los Angeles Times,* intern, 1978. *The Washington Post,* intern, 1979. *Newsweek,* intern, 1980. *San Jose Mercury News,* since 1980; national correspondent, current. Overseas Press Club Fellow, 1979; Investigative Reporters & Editors Award, 1986; George Polk Award, 1986; Pulitzer Prize, International Reporting, 1986.

Emery, Glenn D. *Insight.* General Editor — News. B. 1954, Akron, OH. U. of VT, Math. *The Washington Times,* reporter, 1982-85. *Insight,* writer, 1985; General Editor, news, current, 1986.

England, Robert. *Insight.* Business Writer. B. 1944, York, SC. Duke, 1967, English. *Hartford Times,* reporter, to 1969. *Washington Magazine,* Editor, to 1976. *Delaware Valley Business Magazine,* Editor, to 1978. *Metro Newark,* Editor, to 1985. *Oil & Gas Technology,* Editor, to 1985. *Insight,* business writer, current, 1985.

Epstein, Ari Wenkart. *Scientific American.* Board of Editors Member. B. 1962, Boston. Harvard, 1984, History & Science. *Concerto,* Assoc Editor, 1982-84. *Synthesis,* Board of Editors, 1983-84. *Scientific American,* Board of Editors member, current, 1984.

Epstein, Barbara. *The New York Review of Books.* Editor. B. 1929, Boston, MA. Radcliffe, 1949, BA. *The New York Review of Books,* Editor, current, 1963.

Erickson, Stanford. *The Journal of Commerce.* Editor. Transportation communications. Various publications, journalist, 15 years. *The Journal of Commerce,* Editorial Director, to 1986; Exec Editor, to 1987; Editor, current, 1987.

Erstein, Hap. *The Washington Times.* Theater Critic. B. 1948, Washington, DC. Rensselaer Polytechnic Institute, 1970, Literature. Patuxent Corp newspaper chain, theater critic & Theater Editor, 1977-82. *The Washington Times,* theater critic, current, 1982. WETA-TV, PBS, "Around Town", arts panelist, current, 1986.

Evans, Harold. *Traveler.* Editor-in-Chief. B. 1928, Manchester, UK. Durham U. (UK), 1952, Economics; U. of Chicago, Stanford, MA. Ashton-under-Lyne Group (Lancashire, UK), reporter, 1944. *Manchester Evening News* (UK), Sub-Editor, editorial & political writer, to 1956; Asst Editor, to 1961. *Manchester Guardian* (UK), reporter. *The Northern Echo* (UK), Editor, to 1966. *The Sunday Times* (UK), chief asst to Editor, 1966; Managing Editor, to 1967; Editor, to 1981. *The Times of London,* Editor, 1981. *U.S. News & World Report,* Editorial Director, writer, to 1986; Contributing Editor, current, 1987. *Traveler,* Editor-in-Chief, current, 1987. Conde-Nast Publications, consultant, current, 1986. Author 8 books including *Good Times, Bad Times:* co-author *Suffer The Children; We Learned to Ski.* European Gold Medal, Institute of Journalists; International Editor of the Year, *World Press Review,* 1976.

Evans, Katherine Winton. *Washington Journalism Review.* Editor (Retired). B. 1925, Spokane, WA. Vassar, 1946, American Civilization. *Minneapolis Times,* editorial writer, to 1948. Capitol Hill staff, Sen. Hubert Humphrey & Sen. Paul Douglas, to 1953. *New York Herald Tribune,* Washington columnist, "Women's Page," 1961-62. Freelance, to 1980. *Washington Journalism Review,* Managing Editor, to 1982; Editor, to 1987.

Evans, Medford Stanton. *Human Events.* Contributing Editor. B. 1934, Kingsville, TX. Yale, 1955, BA; postgrad, NYU, 1955. *Freeman,* Asst Editor, 1955. *National Review,* editorial staff, to 1956; Assoc Editor, 1960-68. *The Indianapolis News,* Chief Editorial Writer, 1959-60. *Human Events,* Managing Editor, 1956-59; Contributing Editor, current, 1968. Author several books including *Assassination of Joe McCarthy,* 1970. Freedoms Foundation Award, Editorial Writing, 1959, '60, '65, '66; National Headliners Club Award, Outstanding Editorial Pages, 1960.

Evans, Rowland Jr. News America Syndicate. "Inside Report" Columnist (with Robert Novak). B. 1921, White Marsh, PA. Studied Yale. US Marines. *Philadelphia Bulletin.* AP, Washington staff, to 1953; Senate reporter, to 1955. *New York Herald Tribune,* assorted national magazines, to 1962. News America Syndicate, "Inside Report" columnist (with Robert Novak), current, 1963. *Evans-Novak Political Report* (biweekly newsletter), co-author (with Robert Novak), current. *Evans-Novak Tax Report* (biweekly newsletter), co-author (with Robert Novak), current. *Reader's Digest,* Roving Editor (with Robert Novak), current. Freelance, current. CNN, co-host (with Robert Novak) "Evans & Novak" & "Insiders," current. Frequent appearances "Meet the Press," NBC; "Nightline," ABC. Co-author (with Robert Novak) 3 books including *The Reagan Revolution,* 1981.

Fallows, James. *The Atlantic,* Washington Editor. *U.S. News & World Report,* Contributing Editor. B. 1949, Philadelphia, PA. Harvard, 1970, BA, *magna cum laude*; Oxford, 1972, Economic Development (Rhodes Scholar). US-Japan Leadership Fellow, 1986-88. *The Washington Monthly,* Staff Editor, to 1974. Freelance, to 1976. *Texas Monthly,* Assoc Editor, to 1976. President Carter's chief speechwriter, to 1979. *The Atlantic,* Washington Editor, current, 1979 (reporting from Asia 1986-88). *U.S. News & World Report,* Contributing Editor, current. Author *National Defense,* 1981.

Fanning, Katharine. *The Christian Science Monitor.* Editor. B. 1927, Chicago, IL. Smith College, 1949, English Literature. *Anchorage Daily News*, Editor & Publisher, to 1983. *The Christian Science Monitor*, Editor, current, 1983. *Anchorage Daily News*, 1976 Pulitzer Prize Gold Medal, Public Service; Elijah Parish Lovejoy Award, 1979; Pulitzer Prize Board member, 1982-83.

Farnsworth, Clyde. *The New York Times.* Financial Reporter. B. 1931, OH. Yale, 1952, BA-English. UPI, to 1959. *New York Herald Tribune*, to 1962. *The New York Times*, financial reporter, current, 1962. Author *No Money Down*, 1962; *Out of This Nettle*, 1971. Overseas Press Club & *Sigma Delta Chi* Awards, Foreign Correspondence, 1968.

Feder, Don. *The Boston Herald* & Heritage Features Syndicate. Columnist. B. 1946, Troy, NY. Boston U., 1969, BA, 1972, JD-Law. Citizens for Limited Taxation (MA), Exec Director. Second Amendment Foundation (Seattle, WA), Exec Director. *On Principle* (newsletter), Editor, co-publisher. WEEI News Radio (Boston), editorial writer. *The Boston Herald*, columnist, current, 1983. Heritage Features Syndicate, columnist, current, 1986. Conservative Caucus Award.

Ferguson, Tim. *The Wall Street Journal.* Editorial Features Editor. B. 1955, Santa Ana, CA. Stanford, 1977, BA-Economics. *Orange County* (CA) *Register*, reporter; Asst Metro Editor; Editorial Page Editor, to 1983. *The Wall Street Journal*, Editorial Features Editor, current, 1983. Gerald Loeb Award, Business & Financial Journalism, 1980.

Fiefer, William Paul. *Bulletin Of The Atomic Scientists.* B. 1957, Aurora, IL. U. of IL, Urbana-Champaign, 1982, English Rhetoric. *Daily* (DeKalb) *Chronicle*, 1984-85. *The Progressive*, 1986. *Bulletin Of The Atomic Scientists*, current, 1987.

Fields, Suzanne. *The Washington Times.* Columnist. B. 1936, Washington, DC. George Washington U., 1957, BA-English Literature; 1964, MA; Catholic U., 1970, PhD. *World Week Magazine*, writer, 1957. Freelance, from 1965. *Innovations*, Editor, from 1971. *Vogue*, columnist, 1980-81. *The Washington Times*, columnist, current, 1984. Author *Like Father, Like Daughter*, 1983.

Fineman, Mark. *Los Angeles Times.* Manila Bureau Chief. B. 1952, Chicago, IL. Syracuse, 1974, BA-Journalism & Philosophy. *Sun-Times*, writer, to 1978. *Allentown Call-Chronicle*, writer, to 1980. *Philadelphia Inquirer*, Asia correspondent, to 1986. *Los Angeles Times*, Manila Bureau Chief, current, 1986. Amos Tuck Award, 1st prize, 1980; Overseas Press Club Citation, Excellence, 1985; George Polk Award, 1985.

Fink, Donald E., Jr. *Aviation Week & Space Technology.* Editor-in-Chief. B. 1935, Flint, MI. U. of MN, 1957, Technical Journalism. US Air Force, 1958-61. *Cedar Rapids* (IA) *Gazette*, police & aviation reporter, to 1962. *Aviation Week & Space Technology*, Engineering Editor, NY, to 1963; Space Technology Editor, to 1966; Asst European Editor, Geneva, to 1969; Paris Bureau Chief, to 1972; Management Editor, LA, to 1975; LA Bureau Chief, to 1978; Asst Managing Editor, NY, to 1981; Managing Editor, technical, to 1985; Editor-in-Chief, current, 1985. *Commercial Space*, current, 1985.

Finn, Edwin A. *Forbes.* Senior Editor. B. 1954, Whitinsville, MA. Tufts, 1976, BA-English & Political Science; Columbia, 1983, MA-International Banking & Finance. *Blackstone Valley Tribune*, Asst Managing Editor, to 1977. *Southbridge* (MA) *Evening News*, Managing Editor, to 1979. *The Wall Street Journal*, International Editor, to 1984; reporter, Dallas, to 1986. *Forbes*, Senior Editor, international business, banking & finance, current, 1986.

Fish, Hamilton III. *The Nation.* Publisher. B. 1951, Washington. Harvard, 1973, BA. "Memory for Justice" (film), co-producer, 1975-76. *The Nation*, Publisher, 1978-87.

Flanigan, James. *Los Angeles Times.* Business Columnist. B. 1936, NYC. Manhattan College, 1961, History, English. *New York Herald Tribune*, copy, editorial asst, Paris edition correspondent, Desk Editor, finance & business reporter, 1958-66. *Forbes*, writer; Bureau Chief: Washington, LA, London, Houston; Asst Managing Editor, to 1980, 1981-82, 1984-85. *Los Angeles Times*, writer; business columnist, 1980, 1983-84, NY, current, 1986. Co-winner Gerald Loeb Award.

Flanigan, William C. *Forbes.* Senior Editor. B. 1940. Brooklyn College, 1962, BA-English. *Bayonet* (US Army newspaper, Korea), Editor, to 1964. *Electrical World*, writer, reporter, Editor, to 1968. *BusinessWeek*, Editor, writer, personal business features, to 1976. *New York*, "Your Own Business" columnist, to 1978. *Esquire*, personal financial columnist, to 1979. *The Wall Street Journal*, "Your Money Matters" columnist, to 1980. *Forbes*, Senior Editor, current, 1980; originator "Personal Affairs" & "Careers" sections. CNN, "Moneyline" guest commentator, 1985. WABC Radio, "Bill Flanigan Show" host, current. Author 4 books, including *The Takers*, 1984.

Fleming, Thomas J. *Chronicles.* Editor. B. 1945, Superior, WI. Charleston College, 1967, BA-Greek; U. of NC, 1973, PhD-Classics. UNC, Miami U. of OH, Charleston College, Shaw U., Classics prof. *The Southern Partisan*, Founding Editor, 1979-83. *Chronicles*, Managing Editor, 1984-85; Editor, current, 1985. Freelance, current. The Ingersoll Prizes, exec secretary, current, 1985. Author *The Politics Of Human Nature*, 1987; co-author (with Paul Gottfried) *The American Conservative Movement Since 1945*, 1987.

Flint, Jerry. *Forbes.* Senior Editor. B. 1931, Detroit, MI. Wayne U., 1953, Journalism. *The Wall Street Journal*, reporter, to 1967. *The New York Times*, Detroit Bureau Chief; asst to National Editor, Business Editor; labor writer, to 1979. *Forbes*, Washington Bureau Chief; Asst Managing Editor, 1979-83; Senior Editor, current, 1983. Author *The Dream Machine*.

Fly, Richard. *BusinessWeek.* Washington Correspondent. U. of TX, Austin. *The Houston Chronicle*, legislative reporter, 1975-80. *The Dallas Times-Herald*, White House reporter, to 1985. *BusinessWeek*, Washington correspondent, White House & national politics, current, 1986.

Foell, Earl W. *The Christian Science Monitor.* Editor-in-Chief. B. 1929, Houston. Principia College, 1949, BA. *Los Angeles Times*, UN correspondent, 1968-70. *The Christian*

Science Monitor, reporter, editorial writer, foreign correspondent, 1953-68; Managing Editor, 1970-79; Editor, to 1983; Editor-in-Chief, current, 1983.

Foldessy, Edward P. *The Wall Street Journal*. Special Writer. B. NY. Iona College (New Rochelle, NY), 1963, BS-Physics. *The Wall Street Journal*, asst national news desk, "What's News," to 1964; news asst, "Bond Markets" & "Financial Business" columns, to 1966; reporter; "Credit Markets" columnist, to 1987; special writer, current.

Forbes, Malcolm S., Jr. *Forbes*. Deputy Editor-in-Chief & Editorial Writer. B. 1947, Morristown, NJ. Princeton, 1970, BA-History. *Business Today*, (Princeton business quarterly), Founder. Forbes, Inc, Director, 1971; VP, Secretary, 1973; President & Chief Exec Officer, current, 1980. *Forbes*, Assoc Editor, to 1978; Senior Editor, to 1982, Deputy Editor-in-Chief & editorial writer, current, 1982. Author *Fact & Comment*, 1974; "Some Call It Greed," 1977 (documentary). 4 Crystal Owls, US Steel Award.

Forbes, Malcolm S., Sr. *Forbes*. Chairman & Editor-in-Chief. B. 1919, NYC. Princeton, 1941, AB. *Fairfield Times* (Lancaster, OH), Owner, Publisher, 1941. *Lancaster Tribune*, founder, 1942. US Army, to 1945; Bronze Star, Purple Heart. *Forbes*, Assoc Publisher, to 1954; Publisher & Editor-in-Chief, current, 1957. NJ Senator, 1952-58. Forbes, Inc, President, to 1964; Chairman, current, 1980. 60 Fifth Avenue Corp, Chairman of the Board, current; Forbes Trinchera, Inc, President, current.

Forsyth, Randall W. *Barron's*. "Capital Markets" Editor & "Current Yield" Columnist. B. 1952, NYC. NYU, 1975, Economics, postgrad, Economics & Finance. *The New York Times*, financial news copyboy, 1970-72. *The Bond Buyer*, Asst Editor, to 1976. *Merrill Lynch Market Letter*, writer, to 1980. *Dow Jones Capital Markets Report*, reporter, to 1983. *Barron's*, "Capital Markets" Editor, "Current Yield" Columnist, current, 1983. NY Financial Writers Assn, President, 1987-88.

Fossedal, Gregory A. Copley News Service, Columnist. *Harper's* & *The American Spectator*, Contributing Editor. B. 1959. Dartmouth, 1981, BA-English Literature, *summa cum laude, Phi Beta Kappa*; U. of WI, Marxist Sociological Thought, 1977. Hoover Institute, Stanford, Media Fellow, current, 1986. *The Daily Dartmouth*, Editor-in-Chief, 1979-80. *The Dartmouth Review*, Founder & Editor, to 1981. *Dallas Morning News*, editorial columnist, to 1982. Charleston (NC) *Daily Mail*, editorial writer, 1982. *The Washington Times*, editorial page writer, to 1983. *The San Diego Union*, editorial page writer, 1983. *The Wall Street Journal*, editorial page writer, to 1986. *Harper's*, Contributing Editor, current, 1986. *The American Spectator*, Contributing Editor, current, 1986. Ernest M. Hopkins Institute, Dartmouth, member, Board of Directors, current, 1986. Copley News Service, columnist, current, 1986. Co-author 3 books, including (with Dinesh D'Souza) *My Dear Alex*, 1987.

Foster, Douglas. *Mother Jones*. Ediotr. U. of CA, Santa Cruz. San Francisco Center for Investigative Reporting, Editor. PBS Television, documentary Producer, 1985-87. *Mother Jones,* contributor, 1974-87; Editor, current, 1987.

Emmy Award; World Affairs Council of Northern California Award, 1985.

Frailey, Fred William. *Changing Times*. Editorial Staff. B. 1944, Arkansas City, KS. U. of KS, 1966, Journalism. *The Daily Kansan*, Managing Editor, 1966. *Sun-Times*, suburban reporter, Labor Editor, to 1971. *U.S. News & World Report*, Chicago Bureau Chief, to 1974, labor writer, Washington, to 1978; transportation writer, to 1979; Graphics Editor; Asst Managing Editor & "Business Briefing" columnist, to 1987. *Changing Times*, editorial staff, current, 1987. Author 2 books.

Francis, David R. *The Christian Science Monitor*. Canadian Correspondent & "Global Markets" Columnist. B. Newmarket, Ontario. Carleton U. (Ottawa), BJ, BA. *Winnipeg Free Press*, 1954-55. *Victoria Colonist*, to 1957. *Financial Post* (Toronto), to 1960. *The Christian Science Monitor*, business & financial correspondent, NY, to 1968; business correspondent, Washington, to 1972; Bonn correspondent, to 1974; Business & Financial Editor, to 1983; "Global Markets" columnist, current; Canadian correspondent, current, 1986. NE Education Writer's Award, 1961; Gerald Loeb Award, 1967, '75.

Frank, Allan Dodds. *Forbes*. Senior Editor. B. 1947, Pittsburgh, PA. Colgate, 1969, AB-History; Columbia, MSJ; Yale, 1981, MS-Law. *Anchorage Daily News*, reporter, Juneau Bureau Chief, Sports Editor, 1970-73. *The Washington Star*, national staff writer, to 1981. *Forbes*, Washington correspondent, to 1985; Assoc Editor, to 1987; Senior Editor, current, 1987. 1st Prize Award, Alaska Press Club; DC-MD Newspaper Guild Front Page Award, 1976.

Frank, Richard S. *National Journal*. Editor. B. 1931, Paterson, NJ. Syracuse, 1953, BA; U. of Chicago, 1956, MA. *Evening Record* (Bergen, NJ), local govt reporter, 1956-57. *Evening Sun*, statehouse & City Hall reporter, to 1964. Administrative Asst to Mayor of Baltimore, to 1965. *Philadelphia Bulletin*, state legislature, transportation, to 1968; Washington staff, to 1971. *National Journal*, legal affairs, economics, trade, to 1976; Editor, current, 1976.

Frankel, Glenn. *The Washington Post*. Israel Correspondent. B. 1949, NYC. Columbia, 1971, History. Professional Journalism Fellow, Stanford, 1982-83. *Richmond Mercury*, writer, to 1975. *The Record*, (Bergen, NJ), writer, to 1979. *The Washington Post*, writer, to 1982; Southern Africa correspondent, to 1986; Israel correspondent, current, 1986.

Frankel, Max. *The New York Times*. Executive Editor. B. 1930, Gera, Germany. Columbia, 1952, AB; 1953, MA-Political Science. *The Columbia Daily Spectator*, Editor-in-Chief. US Army, 1953-55. *The New York Times*, Columbia U. correspondent, to 1953; staff, NY, to 1956; foreign correspondent, Austria, to 1957; Moscow correspondent, to 1960; UN correspondent, 1961; Washington correspondent, to 1963; diplomatic correspondent, to 1966; White House correspondent, to 1968; Chief Washington Correspondent & Head of Washington staff, to 1972; Sunday Editor, to 1976; Editorial Page Editor, to 1986; Exec Editor, current, 1986. Overseas Press Club Award, Foreign Reporting, 1965; George Polk Memorial Award, Foreign Affairs, 1970; Pulitzer Prize, International Reporting, 1973.

Franklin, William B. *BusinessWeek*. Business Outlook Editor. Denver U.; Columbia, MA. *BusinessWeek*, 1950-63; Business Outlook Editor, current, 1965. Bureau of National Affairs & Conference Board, 1963-65. *The Economist*, special correspondent. FNN, commentator, current. NY Assn of Business Economists, former president.

Frazier, Steve. *The Wall Street Journal*. Reporter. U. of KS, 1978, BSJ. *The Daily Kansan*, reporter, Editorial Director, Editor. *The Miami Herald, The Wichita Eagle and Beacon, The Topeka State Journal, The Abilene Reflector-Chronicle*, intern, 1977-78. *The Wall Street Journal*, reporter, Dallas, to 1981; reporter, LA, to 1984; Mexico City Bureau Chief, to 1986; reporter, Houston, current, 1986.

Freed, John. *The New York Times*. Deputy Technology Editor. *Pasadena Star-News*, News Editor, Systems Editor. *The New York Times*, from 1983, National Desk Copy Editor, Asst to Technology Editor; Deputy Technology Editor, current, 1987.

Freedman, Jonathan. *The Tribune*, Editorial Writer. Copley News Service, Columnist. B. 1950, Rochester, MN. Columbia, 1972, Literature, *Phi Beta Kappa, cum laude*. Cornell Woolrich Writing Fellowship, 1973. US-Japan Journalists Exchange Program, 1985. AP, reporter, Sao Paulo & Rio de Janeiro, to 1975. Freelance, 1979-80. *The Tribune* (San Diego, CA), editorial writer, current, 1981. Copley News Service, columnist, 1986. Author *The Man Who'd Bounce The World*, 1979. 2 Distinguished Service Awards, National Society of Professional Journalists, 1985; Special Citation, Editorials, Columbia, 1985; Distinguished Writing Award, American Society of Newspaper Editors, 1986; Pulitzer Prize, Editorial Writing, 1987.

Friedman, Thomas L. *The New York Times*. Jerusalem Bureau Chief. B. 1953, Minneapolis, MN. Brandeis, 1975, BA-Middle East Studies; St. Antony's College, Oxford, 1978, MPhil. UPI, London & Beirut correspondent, to 1981. *The New York Times*, business reporter, to 1982; Beirut Bureau Chief, to 1984; Jerusalem Bureau Chief, current, 1984. Overseas Press Club Award, Business Reporting Abroad, 1980; Pulitzer Prize, International Reporting, 1982; George Polk Award, International Reporting, 1983; Livingston Award, Young Journalists, 1983.

Fritz, Michael. *Forbes*. Reporter. B. 1959, Harvard, IL. Purdue, 1981, Agronomy. ABC Publishing, to 1983. *Progress*, to 1985. *Forbes*, reporter, current, 1986.

Fritz, Sara. *Los Angeles Times*. Congressional Reporter. B. 1944, Pittsburgh, PA. Denison U., 1966, Writing. *The Pittsburgh Press*, copy desk, 1966. UPI, Harrisburg Bureau Chief, to 1973; Washington Weekend Editor, to 1975; national labor reporter, to 1978. *U.S.News & World Report*, labor reporter, to 1980; Chief White House Correspondent, to 1983. *Los Angeles Times*, Congressional reporter, current, 1983. Sidney Hillman Awards, judge; Reporter's Committee for Freedom of the Press, Exec Committee member.

Fromm, Joseph. *U.S.News & World Report*. Contributing Editor. B. 1920, South Bend, IN. U. of Chicago, Northwestern. *Mishawaka* (IN) *Enterprise*, reporter, to 1935. *South Bend News-Times*, reporter, to 1936. *South Bend Tribune*, reporter, to 1937. *Southtown Economist* (Chicago), reporter, to 1939. UPI, radio news writer, to 1940. AP, Radio News Bureau Chief, to 1941. *Chicago Sun* (air edition), Managing Editor, to 1942. *U.S.News & World Report*, foreign correspondent & Senior Editor, to 1974; Deputy Editor, Asst Editor, to 1985; Contributing Editor, current, 1985. US Committee, International Institute for Strategic Studies, Chairman, current.

Fuerbringer, Jonathan. *The New York Times*. National Economics Correspondent. B. 1945, NYC. Harvard, 1967, BA-American History; Columbia, 1968, MSJ. *The Boston Globe*, Copy Editor; reporter; statehouse reporter; financial reporter. *The Washington Star*, reporter, national economics correspondent, to 1981. *The New York Times*, national economics correspondent, current, 1981.

Fuller, Jack. *Chicago Tribune*. Editorial Page Editor. B. 1946, Chicago, IL. Northwestern, 1968, Journalism; Yale Law School, 1973. US Justice Dept, special asst to Attorney General, 1975-77. *Chicago Tribune*, legal writer, 1973-75; Washington correspondent, 1977-78; Editorial Board, to 1982; Editorial Page Editor, current, 1982. ABA Gavel Award, 1979; Pulitzer Prize, Editorial Writing, 1986.

Fumento, Michael A. Freelance Writer. B. 1960, Urbana, IL. U. of IL College of Law, 1985, Political Science (undergrad); Law (grad). *The Washington Times*, legal affairs reporter, 1987. Freelance, current.

Fung, Vigor. *The Asian Wall Street Journal*. Reporter. Chinese U. of Hong Kong, Journalism; Hong Kong U., MS-Political Science. *The South China Morning Post* (Hong Kong), intern. *The Asian Wall Street Journal*, reporter, current, 1980.

Gailey, Philip Lane. *St. Petersburg Times*. Washington Bureau Chief. B. 1944, Homer, GA. U. of GA, 1966, Journalism. *The Constitution*, reporter, to 1973; *The Miami Herald*, Washington correspondent, to 1978. *The Washington Star*, to 1982. *The New York Times*, Washington reporter, to 1987. *St. Petersburg Times*, Washington Bureau Chief, current, 1987.

Galloway, Joseph L. *U.S.News & World Report*. Senior Editor — International Section. B. 1941, Bryan, TX. Victoria College, Journalism. *The Victoria* (TX) *Advocate*, reporter, 1959-60. UPI, reporter, Kansas City, 1961; Topeka, KS Bureau Chief, to 1964; Asia Desk Editor, 1965; war correspondent, Saigon, to 1966; Asia Desk Editor, to 1968; Jakarta, Indonesia Bureau Chief, to 1973; Manager for S. Asia, New Delhi, to 1974; Singapore, to 1979; Los Angeles Bureau Chief, to 1982. *U.S.News & World Report*, West Coast Editor, to 1984; Assoc Editor, special projects, 1984; Senior Editor, Editor "Currents in the News," to 1987; Senior Editor, International section, current, 1987.

Gannon, James P. *The Des Moines Register*. Editor. B. 1939, Minneapolis, MN. Marquette, 1961, Journalism. *The Wall Street Journal*, reporter, Chicago, to 1966; labor reporter, Washington, to 1969; Pittsburgh Bureau Chief, to 1971; White House correspondent, to 1972; Treasury, FED, & economic policy correspondent, to 1976; national political correspondent, to 1978. *The Des Moines Register*, Exec Editor, to 1982; Editor, current, 1982.

Garcia, Beatrice E. *The Wall Street Journal.* Reporter & "Abreast of the Market" Columnist. Fairleigh Dickinson U. (Teaneck, NJ), 1978, English. *Shopper's Newspaper* (Fairlawn, NJ), reporter, 1977. Chase Manhattan Bank, NYC, public relations assoc, 1978. Munifacts News Wire, NY, reporter, 1980. *The Wall Street Journal*, Capitol Markets reporter, current, 1982; "Abreast of the Market" columnist, current, 1985.

Gardner, David. *Financial Times.* Mexico & Central America Correspondent. B. 1952, Brussels, Belgium. St. John's, Oxford, 1975, BA-English Literature. Freelance, Spain, to 1979. *Financial Times*, London, to 1983; Mexico & Central America correspondent, current, 1984.

Garment, Suzanne. American Enterprise Institute. Resident Scholar. B. Buffalo, NY. Radcliffe, 1967, BA; U. of Sussex (UK), 1968, MA; Harvard, 1973, PhD. Harvard, lecturer; John F. Kennedy Institute of Politics, Research Fellow. Yale, asst prof, Political Science, to 1978. Special asst to US Permanent Rep to UN, 1975. *The Wall Street Journal*, editorial writer, to 1979; Assoc Editor, editorial page, 1979-87; "Capitol Comment" columnist, 1981-87. American Enterprise Institute, resident scholar, current, 1987. Author *Decision to Prosecute: Organization and Public Policy in the Antitrust Division*, 1977; co-author (with Daniel P. Moynihan) *A Dangerous Place*, 1978.

Garvin, Glenn. *The Washington Times.* Latin American Correspondent. B. 1954, Ft. Campbell, KY. Stanford, 1975, Communications & Political Science. Eugene C. Pulliam Fellowship, 1975. *Delta Democrat Times* (Greenville, MS), political correspondent, 1975-76. *Austin (TX) American Statesman*, investigative reporter, to 1979. *The Miami Herald*, investigative reporter, 1979. *Inquiry*, Editor-in-Chief, to 1982. *The Washington Times*, news features, special projects, 1982-85; Latin American correspondent, current, 1985. 1st Place TX AP Managing Editors Award, News Writing, Feature Writing, 1979; Jane A. Harrah Award San Francisco Bar Assoc, 1981; DC Dateline Award, Sports Writing, 1983, Spot News, 1985; Mencken Awards, Investigative Reporting, 1985.

Gelb, Arthur. *The New York Times.* Managing Editor. B. NYC. NYU, 1948. *The New York Times*, copyboy, reporter, asst drama critic, to 1962; Chief Cultural Correspondent, to 1967; Metro Editor, to 1976; Asst Managing Editor, to 1977; Deputy Managing Editor, to 1986; Managing Editor, current, 1986. Co-author (with Barbara Gelb) *O'Neill.*

Gelb, Leslie. *The New York Times.* Deputy Editor, Editorial Page. B. 1937, New Rochelle, NY. Tufts, BA-Government & Philosophy; Harvard, 1961, MA, 1964, PhD. Wesleyan, asst prof, to 1966. Exec Asst, Sen. Jacob Javits, to 1967. US Defense Dept, Director of Policy Planning & Arms Control, International Security Affairs & Director Pentagon Papers project, to 1969. Brookings Institution, Senior Fellow, to 1973. State Dept, Asst Secretary of State (Director, Bureau of Politico-Military Affairs), 1977-79. Carnegie Endowment for International Peace, Senior Assoc, Security & Arms Control, to 1981. *The New York Times*, diplomatic correspondent, to 1977; national security correspondent, 1981-86; Deputy Editor, Editorial Page, current, 1986. *The New York Times*, "Washington Report," syndicated, commentator, current. ABC, Senior Consultant, producer, "Crisis Game"

(winner Emmy, DuPont, Hood Awards), 1983; Senior Editor, "45/85," 1985; Panelist, "Capitol Journal," educational TV. Co-author 4 books, including *Star Wars*, in progress. Pulitzer Prize, Explanatory Journalism, 1985.

Gergen, David R. *U.S.News & World Report.* Editor. B. 1942, Durham, NC. Yale; Harvard Law, 1967. John F. Kennedy Fellow, Harvard, 1984. *Los Angeles Times* Syndicate, columnist. American Enterprise Institute, Resident Fellow. White House staff, most recently Communications Director, 1981-83. *U.S.News & World Report*, contributing columnist, 1985; Managing Editor, to 1986; Editor, current, 1986.

German, William. *San Francisco Chronicle.* Executive Editor. B. 1919, Brooklyn, NY. Brooklyn College, 1939, Political Science & English; Columbia, 1940, MSJ. Nieman Fellow, 1949-50. *San Francisco Chronicle*, copyboy, reporter, Asst Foreign Editor, copy desk chief, to 1943; News Editor, Exec Foreign Editor, to 1977; Editor, *Chronicle*, Foreign Service; Managing Editor, to 1982; Exec Editor, current, 1982.

Germani, Clara. *The Christian Science Monitor.* South America Correspondent. B. 1956, El Centro, CA. USC, 1978, BAJ. City News Service, courts reporter, 1978. *Orange County* (CA) *Register*, police reporter & consumer affairs, to 1980. *The Christian Science Monitor*, NE writer, to 1983; San Francisco correspondent, to 1985; South America correspondent, current, 1985.

Gerstenzang, James. *Los Angeles Times.* White House Correspondent. AP, White House correspondent. *The Detroit News*, Lansing, MI, correspondent, to 1985. *Los Angeles Times*, Pentagon correspondent, to 1987; White House correspondent, current, 1987.

Gertz, William David. *The Washington Times.* National Security Correspondent. B. 1952, Glen Cove, NY. Studied Washington College, English Literature, George Washington U., Journalism. *New York News World*, Washington correspondent, 1979-80; State Dept correspondent, to 1981. Paragon House Publishers, Book Editor, to 1983. *New York City Tribune*, Washington correspondent, to 1984. *The Washington Times*, national security correspondent, current, 1985.

Gest, Kathryn Waters. Press Secretary, Sen. W. Cohen (R-ME). B. 1947, Boston, MA. Northwestern, 1969, BS; Columbia, 1970, MS. *The Patriot Ledger* (Quincy, MA), reporter, 1968. Voice of America, writer, Europe Desk (in Washington), 1969. *St. Louis Globe-Democrat*, reporter, to 1977. *Time*, St. Louis correspondent, 1975-77. *The Christian Science Monitor*, St. Louis correspondent, 1976-77. *Congressional Quarterly*, reporter, Washington, to 1978; News Editor, to 1980; Asst Managing Editor, to 1983; Managing Editor, to 1987. Press secretary, Sen. William Cohen (R-ME), current, 1987. Inland Daily Press Club Award, Investigative Reporting, 1977.

Gest, Ted. *U.S.News & World Report.* Legal Affairs Editor. B. 1946, St. Louis, MO. Oberlin College, 1968, Government; Columbia, 1969, MSJ. *St. Louis Post-Dispatch*, reporter & Editor, to 1977. *U.S.News & World Report*, White House correspondent, to 1980; Legal Affairs Editor, current, 1981.

Geyelin, Philip. *Washington Post* Writers Group. Foreign Affairs Columnist. B. Devon, PA. Yale, 1944, English Literature. *The Wall Street Journal*, Washington staff, 1947-56; Paris & London correspondent, covering Europe/Middle East, to 1960; diplomatic correspondent, to 1967. *The Washington Post*, Editorial Page Editor, to 1979. *Washington Post* Writers Group, foreign affairs columnist, current, 1980.

Geyer, Georgie Anne. Universal Press Syndicate. Columnist. Northwestern; Rhodes Scholar, Vienna. *Chicago Daily News*, society desk, reporter, 1959-64; Latin America correspondent, to 1967; roving foreign correspondent, columnist, to 1975. *Los Angeles Times* Syndicate, foreign affairs columnist, to 1980. Universal Press Syndicate, columnist, current, 1980. Author *Buying The Night Flight*; Fidel Castro biography, in progress.

Gibson, Paul. *Financial World*. Executive Editor. B. 1936, Leicester, England. Southam Journalist Fellow, U. of Toronto, 1969. *Financial Post* (Canada), stock market columnist. *Forbes*, Senior Editor. Philip Morris Cos. & Hill & Knowlton, public relations. *Financial World*, Exec Editor, current, 1986.

Giese, William. *USA Today*. Financial Reporter. B. 1946, Wayne, IL. Columbia, 1970, BA-English Literature; American U., 1983, MS-Business. *USA Today*, financial reporter, current, 1983.

Gillette, Robert. *Los Angeles Times*. Warsaw Bureau Chief. B. 1943, Rochester, NY. U. of CA, Berkeley, 1966, BA-Geology & Physical Sciences. Nieman Fellow, 1975-76. *The Blade* (Toledo, OH), science writer, to 1968. *San Francisco Examiner*, science writer, to 1971. *Science*, "News and Comment" section reporter, to 1976. *Los Angeles Times*, science writer, to 1980; Moscow Bureau Chief, to 1984; Warsaw Bureau Chief, current, 1984. Co-winner (both with Robert Rawitch) LA Press Club Award, Best Print News Story not under Deadline, 1979; Clarence Darrow Foundation Award, 1979.

Gilliam, Dorothy. *The Washington Post*. "Metro" Columnist. B. Memphis, TN. Lincoln U., BA; Columbia, MSJ. Tuskegee Institute (AL), Assoc Director of Information. *Jet*, Assoc Editor. WTTG-TV, Washington, "Panorama" special reporter. *The Washington Post*, reporter, from 1961; Asst "Style" Editor; "Metro" columnist, current. Author *Paul Robeson, All American*, 1976. Anne O'Hare McCormick Award; NY Newspaper Women's Club; Journalist of the Year & Achievement in Journalism Awards, Capital Press Club; Unity Award in Journalism, Lincoln U.; Columbia Alumni of the Year Award.

Gilmore, Kenneth O. *Reader's Digest*. Editor-in-Chief. B. 1930, Providence, RI. Brown, 1953. *Reader's Digest*, Washington staff, 1957-68; Washington Editor, to 1973; Asst Managing Editor, to 1975; Managing Editor, to 1982; The Reader's Digest Assn, Inc, Exec Editor, VP; Board of Directors & Exec Committee, member, current, 1984; Editor-in-Chief, current.

Girardet, Edward R. *The Christian Science Monitor*. Foreign Correspondent. B. 1951, White Plains, NY. Clifton College (Bristol, UK); U. of Nottingham; Free U. (West Berlin), 1973, German Literature. Journalists in Europe Fellow, 1977. English teacher, Paris. UPI,

reporter, 1974-76. NBC, radio correspondent, Geneva, to 1979. Freelance & radio reporter, Paris, to 1977, 1978-79; Afghanistan & Pakistan, 1979. *The Christian Science Monitor*, foreign correspondent, 1979; London-based foreign correspondent, current, 1986. US & European TV documentaries, reporter & producer, current. Author *Afghanistan: The Soviet War* (Overseas Press Club Citation, 1985). *Sigma Delta Chi* Award, Foreign Reporting, 1980.

Gladwell, Malcolm. *The Washington Post*, Business Columnist. *The American Spectator*, Contributor. B. 1963, Fareham, UK. Trinity College, U. of Toronto, 1984, History. Ethics & Public Policy Center, Asst Editor, 1985. *The American Spectator*, Asst Managing Editor, 1984-85; contributor, current, 1986. *Insight*, writer, to 1987. *The Washington Post*, business columnist, current, 1987.

Glasgall, William. *BusinessWeek*. International Money Editor. Boston U. Walter Bagehot Fellow. AP, energy reporter. *BusinessWeek*, Energy Editor, 1981-86; International Money Editor, current, 1986.

Glasser, Samuel. *The Journal Of Commerce*. Energy Editor. B. 1948, NYC. U. of Bridgeport, 1970, History. *Newark Star-Ledger*, Asst Sunday Editor, reporter, 1970-74. *The Journal Of Commerce*, chemical desk, to 1977; Energy Editor, current, 1977. NY Financial Writers Assoc, President, 1981-82.

Glassman, James K. *Roll Call*. Publisher. B. 1947, Washington, DC. Harvard, 1969, Government. *Boston Herald-Traveler*, reporter, to 1970. *Provincetown* (MA) *Advocate*, Editor & Publisher, to 1972. *Figaro* (New Orleans), Editor & Publisher, to 1978. *The Washingtonian*, Exec Editor, to 1981. *The New Republic*, Publisher, to 1984. *U.S.News & World Report*, Exec VP, to 1986. *The Atlantic*, President, to 1986. *The New Republic*, Contributing Editor, business columnist, to 1987. *The Washingtonian*, Financial Editor, to 1987. *Roll Call*, Publisher, current, 1987.

Glastris, Paul. *The Washington Monthly*. Editor. B. 1958, St. Louis, MO. Northwestern, 1981, History. *The Washington Monthly*, Editor, current.

Glazer, Nathan. *The Public Interest*. Editor. B. 1923, NYC. CCNY, 1944, BSS; U. of PA, 1944, MA; Columbia, 1962, PhD. Guggenheim Fellow, 1954, 1966; Joint Center Urban Studies Fellow, Harvard-MIT, 1960-61; study/travel, Japan, 1961-62. *Commentary*, editorial staff, 1945-53. Doubleday-Anchor Books, to 1955. U. of Chicago, Walgreen lecturer, 1955. Fund for Republic, Communism in American Life project, member, to 1957. U. of CA, Berkeley, lecturer, to 1958; prof, 1963-69. Bennington College, instructor, to 1959. Smith College, visiting assoc prof, to 1960. HHFA, urban sociologist, 1962-63. Harvard, education prof, 1968-69; education & social structure prof, current, 1969. *The Public Interest*, Editor, current, 1973. Author 6 books including *Ethnic Dilemmas*, 1983: co-author 3 books.

Gold, Philip. *Insight*. Writer. B. 1948, Pittsburgh, PA. Yale, 1970, BA-History; Georgetown, 1981, PhD-History. Freelance, current, 1982. Georgetown, prof lecturer, History, Social Sciences, current, 1982. *Insight*, writer, current, 1986. Author *Evasions: The American Way of*

Military Service, 1986; *Advertising, Politics, and American Culture: From Salesmanship to Therapy*, 1986.

Goodman, Ellen Holtz. *The Boston Globe.* Feature Writer, Columnist, & Associate Editor. *Washington Post* Writers Group, Columnist. B. 1941, Newton, MA. Radcliffe, 1963, BA, *cum laude*. Nieman Fellow, 1974. *Newsweek*, researcher, reporter, to 1965. *Detroit Free Press*, feature writer, to 1967. *The Boston Globe*, feature writer, columnist, current, 1967; Assoc Editor, current, 1987. *Washington Post* Writers Group, columnist, current, 1976. Author 3 books including *At Large*, 1981. NE Press Assn Columnist of the Year Award, 1975, & Newspaper Woman of the Year Award, 1978; Pulitzer Prize, Commentary, 1980; American Society Newspaper Editors Prize, Column Writing, 1980.

Gottlieb, Robert A. *The New Yorker.* Editor. B. 1931, NYC. Columbia, 1952, BA; Cambridge, 1954. Simon & Schuster, Editor-in-Chief, 1955-68. Alfred A. Knopf, Inc, Exec VP, 1968-73; Editor-in-Chief, current, 1968; President, current, 1973. *The New Yorker*, Editor, current, 1987.

Govoni, Stephen J. *Financial World.* Executive Editor. B. 1949, NYC. Syracuse, 1971, Journalism; Columbia, 1983. Walter Bagehot Fellow, 1983. Freelance, 1971-73; *The Advocate* (Stamford, CT), local government, courts, to 1976. *The Record* (Bergen, NJ), automotive & real estate correspondent, to 1979; business writer, to 1983. *Manhattan, Inc.*, writer, 1984. *Financial World*, Senior Editor, 1985; Exec Editor, current, 1985. Deadline Award, 1979; *Sigma Delta Chi* NJ Chapter, 1st Prize, Spot News, 1980; NJ Press Assoc, 1st prize, Business News, 1983; Saatchi & Saatchi Advertising Journalism Award, 1986.

Graham, Bradley. *The Washington Post.* Buenos Aires Bureau Chief. B. 1952, Chicago, IL. Yale, MA, 1974; Stanford, 1978, MBA. *Yale Daily News*, Managing Editor, to 1974. *St. Petersburg Times*, intern, summers 1972, '73. *The Trenton Times*, city & statehouse reporter, to 1976. *The Washington Post*, intern, summers 1974, '77; business writer, to 1979; Bonn Bureau Chief, to 1982; Warsaw Bureau Chief, to 1985; Buenos Aires Bureau Chief, current, 1985. American Society of Newspaper Editors Award, Deadline Writing, 1986.

Graham, Donald Edward. *The Washington Post.* Publisher. B. 1945, Baltimore, MD. Harvard, 1966, BA. US Army, to 1968. *The Washington Post*, from 1971; Asst Managing Editor, Sports, 1974-75; Asst General Manager, to 1976; Exec VP & General Manager, to 1979; Publisher, 1979, current.

Graham, Katharine. The Washington Post Company. Chairman & Chief Executive Officer. B. 1917, NYC. Vassar, U. of Chicago, 1938. *San Francisco News*, reporter. *The Washington Post*, editorial & circulation depts, to 1969; Publisher, to 1979. The Washington Post Co, President, to 1973; Chairman & Chief Exec Officer, current, 1973.

Granat, Diane. *The Washingtonian.* Metropolitan Editor. B. 1954, Chicago, IL. Northwestern, 1976, Journalism. Ford Foundation Fellow in Education Journalism, 1978. *Paddock Publications*, education & feature writer, 1976-79; Washington correspondent, to 1981. *The Washington Post*, freelance, to 1982. *Congressional*

Quarterly, reporter, to 1985. *The Washingtonian*, Metro Editor, current, 1986. Golden Hammer Award, 1982.

Gray, Patricia Bellew. *The Wall Street Journal.* Legal Affairs Reporter. B. 1956, Fairfield, CT. U. of CT, 1978, Economics. *The Bridgeport Post*, labor reporter, 1979; Business Editor, to 1980. *The Miami Herald*, business reporter, to 1984. *The Wall Street Journal*, San Francisco high-tech reporter, to 1986; legal affairs reporter, current, 1986.

Greeley, Brendan M., Jr. *Aviation Week & Space Technology.* Military Editor. B. 1939, Ft. Riley, KS. US Military Academy, 1961, Engineering. US Marines, Naval Aviator, designated 1963; A4 Series; Commander, Marine Attack Squadron 223. *Aviation Week & Space Technology*, Military Editor, current.

Greenberg, Paul. Freelance Syndicate, Columnist. *Pine Bluff Commercial*, Editorial Page Editor. B. 1937, Shreveport, LA. U. of MO, 1958, BAJ; 1959, MA-History; postgrad Columbia, American History, 1960-62. US Army, to 1960; discharged 1967. *Pine Bluff* (AR) *Commercial*, Editorial Page Editor, to 1966; current, 1967. *Chicago Daily News*, editorial writer, 1966-67. Freelance Syndicate, columnist, current, 1971. Grenville Clark Memorial Award, 1st Place, 1964; National Newspaper Assn Editorial Award, 1st Place, 1968; Pulitzer Prize, Editorial Writing, 1969; American Society of Newspaper Editors Distinguished Writing Award, Commentary, 1981; Walker Stone Award, Scripps-Howard News Service, 1st Place, 1986.

Greene, Bob. *Chicago Tribune* & Tribune Media Services, Columnist. *Esquire*, Contributing Editor & "American Beat" Columnist. B. 1947, Columbus, OH. Northwestern, 1969, BSJ. *Sun-Times*, reporter, to 1971; columnist, to 1978. *Chicago Tribune* & Tribune Media Services, columnist, current, 1978. *Esquire*, Contributing Editor, "American Beat" columnist, current, 1980. ABC News, "Nightline" contributing correspondent, current. Author 9 books including *Be True To Your School*, 1987. National Headliner Award; Peter Lisafor Award, Exemplary Journalism.

Greene, Richard. *Forbes.* Contributing Editor. B. 1947, West Haven, CT. Northwestern, 1977, BSJ. *Forbes*, reporter, researcher, to 1979; reporter, to 1981; writer, to 1982; Assoc Editor, to 1984; Contributing Editor, current, 1984. Freelance, current, 1984. Champion Media Awards, Economic Understanding, 1978.

Greenfield, James L. *The New York Times Magazine.* Editor. B. 1924, Cleveland, OH. Harvard, 1949, BA. *The Cleveland Press.* Voice of America. *Time*, Korea & Japan correspondent, 1951-55; New Delhi Bureau Chief, to 1957; Deputy London Bureau Chief, to 1961; Chief Diplomatic Correspondent *(Life & Time)*, to 1962. Deputy Asst Secretary of State for Public Affairs, to 1964; Asst Secretary of State for Public Affairs, to 1966. Continental Airlines, Asst VP for International Affairs. Westinghouse Broadcasting, 1968. *The New York Times,* Metro News Desk Editor, to 1968; Foreign Editor, 1969-76; Asst Managing Editor, to 1987. *The New York Times Magazine,* Editor, current, 1987.

Greenfield, Meg. *The Washington Post*, Editorial Page Editor. *Newsweek*, Columnist. B. 1930, Seattle, WA.

Smith, 1952, BA, *summa cum laude*; Fulbright Scholar, Newnham College, Cambridge, to 1953. *Reporter*, to 1965; Washington Editor, to 1968. *The Washington Post*, editorial writer, to 1970; Deputy Editorial Page Editor, to 1979; Editorial Page Editor, current, 1979. *Newsweek*, columnist, current, 1974. Pulitzer Prize, Editorial Writing, 1978.

Greenhouse, Linda. *The New York Times*. Chief Congressional Correspondent. B. 1947, NYC. Radcliffe, BA-Government, *magna cum laude*; Yale, 1978, MS-Law. Ford Foundation Fellow. *The New York Times*, clerk to James Reston, 1968; reporter, to 1970; Westchester Cty correspondent, to 1973; night rewrite staff, 1973; Albany correspondent, to 1976; Albany Bureau Chief, to 1978; Supreme Court reporter, to 1987; Chief Congressional Correspondent, current, 1987.

Greenhouse, Steven. *The New York Times*. Chicago Financial Correspondent. B. Long Island, NY. Wesleyan U., 1973; Columbia, 1975, Economics Reporting; NYU., 1982, JD, valedictorian. *The Chelsea Clinton News* (NYC), reporter. *The Westsider* (NYC), reporter. *The Record* (Bergen, NJ), labor & economics reporter, 1976. Law clerk, US District Court Judge Robert L. Carter, 1982-83. *The New York Times*, copyboy, 1973; reporter, 1983-84, financial correspondent, Chicago, current, 1984.

Greenwell, Gregory R. *Scientific American*. Editor. B. 1958, Caracas, Venezuela. Rice U., 1980, BA-Physics & Russian; MIT, 1985, SM. *Scientific American*, Editor, current, 1985.

Grenier, Richard. *The Washington Times*, Columnist. *The American Spectator*, Senior Editor. B. 1933, Cambridge, MA. US Naval Academy, Engineering. *Agence France Presse*, 1962, Paris. *Financial Times*, Paris, to 1969. Group W. Broadcasting, Paris, 1968-70. *Commentary*. *The New York Times*. *The American Spectator*, Senior Editor, current. *The Washington Times*, "Point Man" columnist, to 1987; columnist, current, 1987. Freelance, current. Author 3 books, including *The Marrakesh One-Two*, 1983.

Griffith, Thomas. *Time*. "Newswatch" Columnist. B. 1915, Tacoma, WA. U. of WA, Seattle, 1936, Journalism. Nieman Fellow, 1942-43. *Seattle Times*, reporter, Asst Editor, 1936-42. *Time*, writer, Contributing Editor, Assoc Editor, Senior Editor, Asst Managing Editor, 1943-63; Senior Staff Editor, to 1968; essayist; "Newswatch" columnist, current, 1976. *Life*, Editor, to 1972. *The Atlantic*, columnist. *Fortune*, writer. Author *The Waist-High Culture*, 1958; *How True, A Skeptic's Guide To Believing The News*, 1974.

Griffiths, David. *BusinessWeek*. Washington Correspondent. U. of VA, BA; U. of MO, MSJ. US Army. *The Kansas City Star*, reporter, 1973-77. *Aviation Week & Space Technology*, reporter, to 1981. *Defense Week*, reporter, to 1983. *BusinessWeek*, national security & defense reporter, Washington, current, 1983.

Grose, Peter. *Foreign Affairs*. Managing Editor. B. 1934, Waunton, IL. Yale, 1957, History; Oxford Pembroke College, 1959. Council on Foreign Relations, Senior Fellow, Director of Middle East Studies, 1982-84. AP, London & Africa, 1959-62. *The New York Times*, Paris & Vietnam, to 1965; Moscow Bureau Chief, to 1967;

Washington diplomatic correspondent, to 1970; Jerusalem Bureau Chief, to 1972; Editorial Board, to 1976; UN Bureau Chief, to 1977. State Dept, Deputy Director, Policy Planning Staff, to 1978. *Foreign Affairs*, Managing Editor, current, 1984. Author *Israel In The Mind Of America*, 1983; *A Changing Israel*, 1985.

Grossman, Lawrence K. NBC News. President. B. 1931, NYC. Columbia, 1952, BA; studied Harvard, 1953, Law. *Look*, Editor, 1953-56. CBS-TV, Advertising Exec, to 1962. NBC, Advertising VP, to 1966. Lawrence K. Grossman, Inc, President, to 1976. Forum Communications, Inc, President, 1969-76. PBS Television, Washington, President, to 1984. NBC News, President, current, 1984.

Grover, Ronald. *BusinessWeek*. Los Angeles Bureau Manager. George Washington U., BA-Political Science, MBA; Columbia, MSJ. *The Washington Star*, reporter, to 1979. McGraw-Hill World News, energy correspondent, Washington, to 1982. *BusinessWeek*, economic & political correspondent, Washington, to 1986; LA correspondent, to 1987; LA Bureau Manager, current, 1987.

Grunwald, Henry Anatole. Time, Inc. Editor-in-Chief (Retired 1987). B. 1922, Vienna, Austria. NYU, 1944, AB. *Time*, editorial writer, to 1945-51; Senior Editor, to 1961; Foreign Editor, to 1966; Asst Managing Editor, to 1968; Managing Editor, to 1977; Time, Inc, Corporate Editor, to 1979; Editor-in-Chief, retired 1987. Author 3 books, including *The Age of Elegance*, 1966.

Guillermoprieto, Alma. *Newsweek*. Rio de Janeiro Bureau Chief. B. 1949, Mexico City. Alicia Patterson Foundation Fellow, 1985. *The Guardian* (UK), Central America stringer, 1978-82. *Latin America Newsletters* (UK), Central America stringer, 1978-82. *The Washington Post*, Central America stringer, 1978-82; reporter, to 1985. *Newsweek*, Rio de Janeiro Bureau Chief, current, 1986.

Gupta, Udayan. *The Wall Street Journal*. Reporter. B. 1950, Patna, Bihar, India. Harvard, 1971, BA-Economics, *magna cum laude*; Boston U., 1976, MS-Film. Walter Bagehot Fellow, 1981-82. Boston U., film lecturer, 1974-76. NYU, Expository Writing instructor, 1980-82. *Black Enterprise, Hispanic Business*, contributor. *The Wall Street Journal*, reporter, current, 1985. Fund for Investigative Journalism Award, 1981.

Gupte, Pranay. Freelance Writer. B. 1948, Bombay, India. U. of Bombay; Brandeis, 1970, BA-Political Science & Economics; Columbia, 1971, MSJ. UN Travel Fellowship, 1982, '85. *The New York Times*, news clerk, business & national desks, summer 1968, '69, '70; personal asst to A.M. Rosenthal, to 1973; metro reporter, 1973, '78; suburban correspondent, to 1976; UN correspondent, 1977, '79; foreign correspondent, Africa & Middle East, to 1982. *International Herald Tribune*, editorial page columnist, current, 1982. Freelance, current, 1982. Author 3 books, including *Egypt A Population Study*, 1981. Publisher's Award, *The New York Times* series, 1977. Best Columnist, International Newspaper, Population Institute, 1984; Award, Highest Accomplishment in Journalism, National Federation of Asian Indian Organizations, 1986.

Guskind, Robert S. *National Journal*, Contributing Editor. B. 1958, Passaic, NJ. Georgetown, 1980, BA-

Government, *magna cum laude, Phi Beta Kappa*. WGTB-FM, news director, 1976-79. Freelance, current, 1980. *Washington Post* Writers Group, "The Neal Peirce Column" assoc, current, 1980. *National Journal*, contributor, 1982-84; Contributing Editor, current, 1984. *Planning*, Contributing Editor, current, 1987.

Guyon, Janet. *The Wall Street Journal*. Telecommunication Correspondent. B. 1955, Cleveland, OH. Duke, 1977, Economics & English. *News & Observer* (Raleigh, NC), general correspondent, to 1979. *The Wall Street Journal*, correspondent, Atlanta, to 1981; food correspondent, to 1983; telecommunications correspondent, current, 1984.

Gwertzman, Bernard M. *The New York Times*. Washington Diplomatic Correspondent. B. 1935, NYC. Harvard, 1957, BA, 1960, MA-Soviet Affairs. *The Evening Star*, diplomatic correspondent, to 1968. *The New York Times*, State Dept correspondent, to 1969; Moscow Bureau Chief, to 1971; Washington diplomatic correspondent, current, 1971. Co-author *Fulbright: The Dissenter*. Front Page Award, DC Newspaper Guild, 1966; Edward Weintal Award, Distinguished Diplomatic Reporting, 1984.

Haas, Lawrence J. *National Journal*. Staff Correspondent. B. 1956, Brooklyn, NY. U. of PA, 1978, American History; Princeton, 1980, MA-American History. *The Daily Register* (Shrewsbury, NJ), reporter, to 1982. *The Pittsburgh Post-Gazette*, statehouse correspondent, to 1983. UPI, Harrisburg Bureau Chief, to 1985. *The Bond Buyer*, Washington correspondent, to 1987. *National Journal*, staff correspondent, current, 1987.

Haberman, Clyde. *The New York Times*. Tokyo Bureau Chief. B. 1945, Bronx, NY. CCNY, 1966, BA. *The New York Times*, campus stringer, to 1966; "The Week in Review" Editor, 1976-78; reporter, to 1983; Tokyo Bureau Chief, current, 1983. *New York Post*, reporter, 1966-76.

Hadar, Mary. *The Washington Post*. Assistant Managing Editor — "Style." B. Brooklyn, NY. U. of PA, BA; Columbia, MSJ. *The Sun*. *The Jerusalem Post*, Foreign Editor. *The Washington Post*, "Style" Copy Editor, 1977-79; "Style" Night Editor, to 1981; "Style" Deputy Editor, to 1983; "Style" Asst Managing Editor, current, 1983.

Hale, Judson D. Sr. *Yankee & Old Farmer's Almanac*. Editor-in-Chief. B. 1933, Boston, MA. Dartmouth, 1955, English. *Yankee, Old Farmer's Almanac*, Asst Editor, 1958-61; Assoc Editor, to 1964; Managing Editor, to 1970; Editor-in-Chief, current, 1970. Author *Inside New England & The Education Of A Yankee*.

Hall, Alan. *BusinessWeek*. Senior Editor. Cornell, BSJ. *Plastics World*, Bureau Chief. *Modern Plastics*, Assoc Editor. *Chemical Week*, News Editor, to 1979. *BusinessWeek*, Research Editor, to 1985; Assoc Editor, Science & Technology, to 1986; Senior Editor, Science & Technology Section, current, 1986. Author *The Wildfood Trailguide; Wood Finishing and Refinishing*. AAAS/Westinghouse Award, Science Journalism; Deadline Club Award, Science Writing, NYC *Sigma Delta Chi*.

Hall, David. *The Denver Post*. Senior Vice President & Editor. B. 1943, Lebanon, TN. U. of TN, 1965, BSJ; 1966, MA-Economics. *Nashville Tennessean*, part-time reporter, to 1964. *Chicago Daily News*, financial reporter, Asst Financial Editor, Middle East correspondent, editorial writer, chief editorial writer, Asst Managing Editor, to 1978. *St. Paul Pioneer Press and Dispatch*, Managing Editor, to 1982; Exec Editor, to 1984. *The Denver Post*, Editor & VP, to 1986; Editor & Senior VP, current, 1986.

Hall, William. *Financial Times*. New York Correspondent. B. 1946, Birkenhead, UK. Cambridge, 1965-68, Economics. *The Banker*, Asst Editor, 1971-75. *Financial Times*, "LEX" column, to 1979; shipping correspondent, to 1981; banking correspondent, to 1983; NY correspondent, current, 1983.

Halloran, Richard. *The New York Times*. Military Affairs & Defense Correspondent. B. 1930, Washington, DC. Dartmouth, 1951, BA; U. of MI, 1957, MA-East Asian Studies; Ford Foundation Fellow, Advanced International Reporting, Columbia, 1964-65. *BusinessWeek*, writer; Asst Foreign Editor; Far East Bureau Chief, to 1964. *The Washington Post*, Northeast Asia correspondent; Asian specialist; economic correspondent, to 1969. *The New York Times*, reporter; diplomatic correspondent, to 1972; Tokyo Bureau Chief, to 1976; Washington reporter, to 1979; military & defense correspondent, current, 1979. Author *Japan: Images and Realities; Conflict and Compromise: The Dynamics of Foreign Policy*.

Hallow, Ralph Z. *The Washington Times*. Political Writer. B. 1938, Pittsburgh, PA. U. of Pittsburgh, 1960, AB, postgrad Law & History, U. of MO, Journalism. Ford Foundation Fellow, Northwestern. *The Pittsburgh Press*, Night City Editor, to 1969. *The Pittsburgh Post-Gazette*, editorial board member, to 1977. *Chicago Tribune*, Editorial Board, to 1982. *The Washington Times*, editorial writer, 1982; Deputy Editorial Page Editor, to 1984; financial writer, to 1985; political writer, current, 1985.

Hamill, Pete (William Peter). *The Village Voice*. Contributor. B. 1935, Brooklyn, NY. Studied Pratt Institute, 1952, Mexico City College, 1956-57. US Naval Reserves, 1952-54. Commercial artist, to 1960. *New York Post*, reporter, columnist, to 1974. *The Saturday Evening Post*, Contributing Editor, 1963-64. *New York Daily News*, columnist, 1965-67, 1969-79. *The Village Voice*, contributor, current, 1974. Meyer Berger Award, Columbia, 1962; Newspaper Reporters Assn Award, 1962.

Hannon, Kerry. *Forbes*. Reporter. B. 1960, Pittsburgh, PA. Duke, 1982, Comparative Literature. *The Washingtonian*, editorial asst, 1981. *Pittsburgh Magazine*, Contributing Editor, to 1985. *Pittsburgh Business Times*, Contributing Editor, 1983-85. *BusinessWeek*, correspondent, 1983-85. *Advertising Age*, regional correspondent, 1984-85. *Scripps-Howard's Business Journal*, Special Sections Editor, 1985. *Forbes*, reporter, current, 1985.

Harden, Blaine. *The Washington Post*. Africa Correspondent. B. 1952, Moses Lake, WA. Gonzaga U. (Spokane, WA), 1974, BA-Philosophy & Political Science; Syracuse, 1976, MAJ. *The Trenton* (NJ) *Times*, reporter, to 1977. *The Washington Post*, metro reporter, to 1980; Sunday magazine reporter, to 1982; metro reporter, to 1983; Africa correspondent, current, 1984. *The Washingtonian*, senior writer, 1983-84. Livingston Young Journalists Award, 1986.

Hargreaves, Ian. *Financial Times.* Features Editor. B. 1951, Lancashire, UK. Queen's College, Cambridge, English Literature. *Keighley News*, reporter, 1973-74. *Telegraph and Argus* (Bradford, UK), reporter; feature writer, to 1976. *Financial Times*, labor reporter; transport correspondent; NY correspondent; Social Policy Editor; Resources Editor; Features Editor, current.

Harries, Owen. *The National Interest.* Editor. B. Wales, UK. U. of Wales, 1950, Political Science; Oxford, 1952. U. of Sydney (Australia), faculty member, to 1965. U. of New South Wales (Australia), faculty member, to 1975. Senior Advisor to Australian Foreign Minister, to 1977; Head of Policy Planning, Dept of Foreign Affairs, to 1979; Senior Advisor to Prime Minister Malcolm Fraser, to 1981; Australian Ambassador, UNESCO, Paris, to 1983. Heritage Foundation Fellow, to 1984. *The National Interest*, Editor, current, 1985. Freelance, current. Editor *Liberty and Politics*.

Harris, Catherine L. *BusinessWeek.* Information Processing Department Editor. B. 1952, NYC. Trinity College (CT), 1974, American Studies. *Rowe Daily America*, to 1975. *Westchester Rockland Newspaper*, Gannett, to 1980. *Financial World*, to 1981. *BusinessWeek*, Info Processing Dept Editor, current, 1981. Co-winner (with Steven Prokesch, John Hoerr) John Hancock Award, 1983.

Harvey, Robert. *The Economist.* Assistant Editor. B. 1953, London, England. Oxford, 1974, Politics, Philosophy & Economics. *The Economist*, political correspondent & leader writer, from 1974: covered Spain, Portugal, Middle East, Afghanistan, Central America; Asst Editor, current, 1981.

Harwood, Richard. *The Washington Post.* Deputy Managing Editor. Vanderbilt U. Nieman Fellow, 1955. Carnegie Fellow in Journalism, Columbia, 1965. *The Courier-Journal. The Trenton* (NJ) *Times*, evening & Sunday editions, Editor, 1974-76. *The Washington Post*, national politics & public affairs reporter; Vietnam correspondent; National Editor; Asst Managing Editor, national news, 1966-74; Deputy Managing Editor, current, 1976.

Hayes, Thomas C. *The New York Times.* Western Economic Correspondent. B. 1950, Cincinnati, OH. Northwestern, 1973, BSJ; postgrad U. of MA, Amherst, & Xavier U. Walter Bagehot Fellow, 1978-79. *The Cincinnati Post*, sports reporter, summers 1968-70. *The Cincinnati Enquirer*, business reporter, to 1978. *The New York Times*, "Business Day" reporter, to 1981; Western economic correspondent, current, 1981.

Hector, Gary. *Fortune.* Associate Editor. Columbia, MSJ; NYU, MBA-Finance. *San Jose Mercury News*, reporter. *American Banker*, reporter. *Fortune*, writer, to 1982; Assoc Editor, Menlo Park, CA, current, 1982. Gerald Loeb Award, Distinguished Business & Financial Journalism, 1981.

Heins, John. *Forbes.* Los Angeles Staff Writer. B. 1960, Waverly, IA. U. of PA, Wharton, 1983, Accounting. *Forbes*, reporter, to 1985; staff writer, LA, current, 1985.

Helmore, Kristin. *The Christian Science Monitor.* Reporter. *The Christian Science Monitor*, reporter, current. Overseas Press Club Madeline Dane Ross Award.

Hempstone, Smith. The Hempstone Syndicate. "Our Time" Columnist. B. 1929, Washington, DC. U. of the South, (Sewanee, TN), 1950, BA-History. Nieman Fellow, 1964. *Louisville Times*, reporter, 1954. *National Geographic*, writer, 1955. *The Washington Star*, reporter, 1956; foreign correspondent, 1966-69; Assoc Editor, to 1975. Institute of Current World Affairs Fellow, to 1960. *Chicago Daily News*, foreign correspondent, to 1963; 1965. *The Washington Times*, Exec Editor, to 1983; Editor-in-Chief, to 1985. The Hempstone Syndicate, "Our Time" columnist, to 1981; current, 1986. Author 4 books, including *In the Midst of Lions*, 1968. Sigma Delta Chi, Foreign Correspondence, 1961; Overseas Press Club Foreign Correspondence, 1970, '75.

Henderson, Celia Nell. *The Washington Post.* Metro Correspondent. B. 1959, TX. Harvard, 1980, BA-Government, *cum laude*; London School of Economics, 1983, Economics. City News Service, LA, reporter, 1981. *Evening Outlook* (Santa Monica, CA), reporter, to 1982. *Los Angeles Times*, suburban reporter, 1983-84. *The Washington Post*, financial correspondent, 1984-86; transportation & metro correspondent, current, 1986.

Hendrickson, Paul. *The Washington Post.* On Leave. B. 1944, Fresno, CA. Seminary; St. Louis U., 1967, AB-English; Penn State, 1968, MA. Alicia Patterson Foundation Fellow, 1979-80; Lyndhurst Foundation Fellow, 1985-88. *Holiday* 1971-72. *Detroit Free Press*, to 1974. *The National Observer*, to 1977. *The Washington Post*, current, 1977 (on leave, 1986-87). Author *Seminary: A Search*, 1983. Penney-MO Best Single Story, 1985.

Henkel, Robert W. *Electronics.* Editor-in-Chief. B. 1930, Wayne, NE. U. of NE, 1956, BSJ. *The Wall Street Journal*, reporter, to 1958. *Electronic News*, reporter; LA Bureau Chief, to 1965. *BusinessWeek*, Technology Editor; Industrial Editor; Senior Editor, science, technology, 1971-85. *Electronics*, Washington Bureau Chief, 1965-71; Editor-in-Chief, current, 1985. Excellence in Business & Financial Journalism Award, 1978.

Henkoff, Ronald. *Newsweek.* European Economics Editor. B. 1954, Boston, MA. Carleton College, 1976, BA-History, *cum laude*; Columbia, 1977, MSJ; London School of Economics, 1984, MA-History. *Hudson Dispatch* (Union City, NJ), reporter, 1977-78. *Newsweek*, business reporter, to 1979; Houston correspondent, to 1981; London correspondent, to 1984; European Economics Editor (London), current, 1984. Overseas Press Club of America Best Magazine Story on Foreign Affairs, 1983; National Headliners 1st Prize, Magazines.

Hentoff, Nathan Irving. *The Village Voice*, Staff Writer. *The Washington Post*, Columnist. *The New Yorker*, Staff Writer. B. 1925, Boston, MA. Northeastern, 1945, BA, highest honors; postgrad Harvard, 1946. Fulbright Fellow, Sorbonne, 1950; Guggenheim Fellowship, 1972. WMEX radio producer, announcer, 1944-53. *Down Beat*, Assoc Editor, to 1957. CBS-TV, "The Jazz Review" Co-

Founder, Co-Editor, to 1960. Copley News Service, radio commentator, current. *The New Yorker*, staff writer, current, 1960. *The Village Voice*, staff writer, current. *The Washington Post*, columnist, current. *The Nation, Social Policy* & *The Wall Street Journal*, contributor. Several books including *The Day They Came To Arrest The Book*, 1982. ABA Silver Gavel Award, 1980; American Assoc John Phillip Immroth Award, 1983; People for the American Way Lifetime Achievement Award, 1986.

Herbers, John. *The New York Times*. National Correspondent (Retired 1987). Ferris Prof of Journalism, 1987; *Baltimore Sun* Distinguished Lecturer, U. of MD Journalism College, 1988 (1st lecturer named). *Greenwood* (MS) *Morning Star*. UPI. *The New York Times*, from 1963: Atlanta correspondent; Asst National News Editor; White House correspondent; Washington Bureau Chief; national correspondent, retired 1987.

Herman, R. Thomas. *The Wall Street Journal*. Reporter. B. NY. Yale, 1968, BA. *Yale Daily News*, reporter, Political Editor. *The Wall Street Journal*, intern, Washington, summer 1967; NY staff, to 1969, 1974-76; Atlanta staff, to 1974; Hong Kong (*The Asian Wall Street Journal*) reporter, 1976-77; reporter, NY, current, 1980; co-author "Credit Markets" column, current, 1980.

Hersh, Seymour. *The Atlantic*. Contributing Editor. B. 1937, Chicago, IL. U. of Chicago, 1958, BA-History. City News Bureau, police reporter, to 1960. UPI, correspondent, Pierre, SD, 1962-63. AP, Chicago & Washington correspondent, to 1967. Press secretary, Sen. Eugene McCarthy, MN (NH primary), 1968. *The New York Times*, Washington staff, 1972-75, 1979; NY staff, to 1978. *The Atlantic*, national correspondent, from 1983; currently Contributing Editor. Author 5 books including *"The Target Is Destroyed": What Really Happened to Flight 007 and What America Knew About It*, 1986. Worth Bingham Prize, 1970; *Sigma Delta Chi* Distinguished Service Award, 1970, '81; Pulitzer Prize, International Reporting, 1970; George Polk Memorial Award, 1970, '73, '75, '81; Scripps-Howard Public Service Award, 1973; Sidney Hillman Award, 1974; John Peter Zenger Freedom of the Press Award, 1975; Drew Pearson Prize.

Hershey, Robert D. Jr. *The New York Times*. Washington Reporter. B. 1939, Berlin, Germany. Gettysburg College, 1961, BA-Philosophy; NYU, American Civilization program. *The New York Times*, copyboy, 1962; news clerk, 1963; news asst, to 1966; financial dept copy desk, to 1967; financial reporter, to 1973; Asst Editor, Deputy Editor of Sunday financial section, to 1975; SEC & banking regulation reporter, to 1977; London business & economics correspondent, to 1980; Washington reporter, current, 1980.

Hertzberg, Hendrik. *The New Republic*, Contributing Editor. B. 1943, NYC. Harvard, 1965, Government. US Navy, 1965-69. Harvard Institute of Politics Fellow, 1981-86. US National Student Assn, Editorial Director, 1965-66. *Newsweek*, San Francisco correspondent, to 1967. *The New Yorker*, staff writer, 1969-77. White House staff, chief speechwriter, to 1981. *The New Republic*, Editor, to 1985; Contributing Editor, current, 1985. *TK Enterprises*, partner, current, 1986.

Hetzer, Barbara. *Fortune*. Reporter/Researcher. B. Brooklyn, NY. Queens College, 1984, BA. *Woman's Day*, editorial asst. *Cuisine*, editorial asst. *Fortune*, reporter/researcher, current, 1985; reporter, *Fortune* 500, 1986.

Hewitt, Don. CBS News. "60 Minutes" Executive Producer. B. 1922, NYC. Studied NYU, 1941. War Shipping Administration, special correspondent, WWII. 1st Kennedy-Nixon Debate, producer, 1960. Producer-director: A Conversation with President Kennedy, 1962; A Conversation with President Johnson, 1964. CBS News, coverage of Eisenhower in Europe & India, 1960-61, President Kennedy in Europe, 1962-63, political conventions, inaugurations, producer-director; "CBS Evening News with Walter Cronkite," Exec Producer, 1961-64; Cape Canaveral, Producer, 1960-65; "60 Minutes" Exec Producer, current, 1968.

Hiatt, Fred. *The Washington Post*. East Asia Correspondent. B. 1955, Washington, DC. Harvard, 1977, BA-History. US-Japan program, Harvard, 1986-87. *Journal and Constitution*, City Hall reporter, 1979-80. *The Washington Star*, VA reporter, 1981. *The Washington Post*, VA reporter, to 1983; Pentagon reporter, to 1986; East Asia correspondent, current, 1987.

Hicks, Jonathan P. *The New York Times*. Business & Financial News Staff. B. 1955, St. Louis, MO. U. of MO, 1979, BA-Political Science; U. of CA, Berkeley, Fellowship for minority journalists, 1980. *The Arizona Daily Star*, reporter, to 1982. *The Plain Dealer* (Cleveland, OH), business reporter, to 1985. *The New York Times*, business & financial reporter, current, 1986.

Hiebert, Murray. *Far Eastern Economic Review*. Indochina Correspondent. B. 1948, Canada. Goshen College, 1970, History. *Indochina Issues*, Editor, 5 years. *Far Eastern Economic Review*, Indochina correspondent, current.

Hildreth, James. *U.S.News & World Report*. Associate Editor. WVA U. US Marines. UPI. Newhouse Newspapers, to 1981. *U.S.News & World Report*, White House correspondent; Assoc Editor, Congress, current.

Hill, David. *Washington Journalism Review*. Writer. B. 1958, Oklahoma City. Colorado College, 1980, BA-English; Northwestern, 1984, MSJ. *The Colorado Springs Sun*, reporter, to 1986. *Washington Journalism Review*, writer, current, 1986.

Himmelfarb, Joel. *Human Events*. Associate Editor. B. 1959, Baltimore, MD. U. of MD, 1982, BA-Political Assignment. *Human Events*, Assoc Editor, current, 1982; "Conservative Forum" writer, current, 1982; writer, current, 1982.

Hitchens, Christopher. *The Nation*, Washington Columnist. *Harper's*, Washington Editor & Columnist. B. 1949, Portsmouth, Hampshire, UK. Balliol College, Oxford, 1970, Philosophy, Politics & Economics. *The Times* (UK) Higher Education Supplement, social science correspondent. "Weekend World," London TV, researcher, reporter. *The Daily Express*, foreign correspondent. *New Statesman*, writer, 1974-80. London *Times Literary Supplement*, "American Notes" columnist, current, 1982. *The Spectator* (UK), Washington columnist, 1981-86. *The Nation*, Washington columnist, current. *Harper's*, Washington Editor & columnist, current. *Newsday* (NY), book reviewer, current.

Hoagland, Jim. *The Washington Post.* Associate Editor & Chief Foreign Correspondent. B. 1940, Rock Hill, SC. U. of SC, 1961, Journalism. Ford Foundation Fellow, Columbia, International Affairs, 1968-69. *The New York Times* (International Edition), Copy Editor, Paris, 1964-66. *The Washington Post*, metro reporter, to 1968; Africa correspondent, 1969-72; Middle East correspondent, to 1975; Paris correspondent, to 1977; National Affairs reporter, to 1979; Foreign Editor, to 1981; Asst Managing Editor, Foreign News, to 1986; Assoc Editor & Chief Foreign correspondent, Paris, current, 1986. Author *South Africa: Civilizations in Conflict*, 1972. Pulitzer Prize, International Reporting, 1971; Bob Considine Award, Overseas Press Club, International Reporting, 1977.

Hochschild, Adam. *Mother Jones.* Writer & Co-Founder. B. 1942, NYC. Harvard, 1963, American History & Literature. *San Francisco Chronicle*, reporter 1965-66. *Ramparts*, reporter, Editor, 1966-68; 1973-74. *Mother Jones*, Co-Founder, 1974; Editor, to 1987; writer, current. NPR, "All Things Considered," commentator, 1982-83. Freelance, current. Author *Half the Way Home: A Memoir of Father and Son*, 1986. Overseas Press Club of America Certificate of Excellence, 1981; Eugene V. Debs Foundation Bryant Spann Award, 1984.

Hoeffel, Paul Heath. *Newsweek.* General Editor. B. 1947, Cambridge, MA. NYU, 1970, Literature. UN Office for Emergency Operation in Africa. *Africa Emergency Report*, Assoc Editor, 1986-87. *Newsweek*, General Editor, current, 1987. Outstanding Broadcast Service Award NY City Council of Churches, 1979; Overseas Press Club Award, 1980.

Hoffman, Ellen. *National Journal.* Contributing Editor. B. 1943, NY. U. of MN, 1964, BA-European History; Georgetown, 1966, MA. *The Washington Post*, reporter, to 1971. US Senate Subcommittee on Children & Youth, staff member, Director, to 1977. The Children's Defense Fund, Director of Governmental Affairs, to 1983. Freelance, current, 1983. Self-syndicated column, "The Resourceful Traveler," current, 1983. *National Journal*, Contributing Editor, current.

Hoge, Warren. *The New York Times.* Assistant Managing Editor. B. 1941, NYC. Yale, 1963, BA-English; George Washington U., Literature & Political Science. US Army Reserves, 1964. *The Washington Star*, police & courts reporter, to 1966. *New York Post*, Washington correspondent, to 1970; Night City Editor, City Editor, Metro Editor, to 1976. *The New York Times*, metro reporter, 1976; Asst Metro Editor, Deputy Metro Editor, to 1979; Rio de Janeiro Bureau Chief, to 1983; Foreign Editor, to 1986; Asst Managing Editor, current, 1986.

Holland, Max. *The Nation.* Contributing Editor. B. 1950, RI. Antioch College, 1972, Philosophy & Music. *Lincoln Star*, 1975-76. Voice Of America, 1976. *The Nation*, Contributing Editor, current, 1981.

Holley, David. *Los Angeles Times.* Beijing Bureau Chief. *Los Angeles Times*, metro writer, 1979-86; Tokyo & Hong Kong, intern, to 1987; Beijing Bureau Chief, current, 1987.

Hollie, Pamela G. Columbia University. Director, Knight-Bagehot Fellowship Program. B. 1948, Topeka, KS. Washburn U., 1970, BA; Columbia, 1971, MSJ. *Washburn Review*, Editor-in-Chief. Gannett Fellowship, U. of HI, 1976-77. *The Wall Street Journal*, reporter, 1969-75. *The Honolulu Advertiser*, special correspondent, Micronesia, to 1976. *The New York Times*, national business correspondent, LA, 1978-81; foreign correspondent, Manila, to 1983; "Business Day" reporter, to 1987. Knight-Bagehot Fellowship Program in Business & Economic Journalism, Columbia, Director, current, 1987.

Holman, Michael. *Financial Times.* Africa Editor. B. 1945, Penzance, UK. University College of Rhodesia, 1967, BA-English; U. of Edinburgh, 1971, MS-Politics. Freelance, Salisbury, Rhodesia (Harare, Zimbabwe), 1973-77. *The Financial Mail*, Rhodesia Editor, Johannesburg, South Africa, 1975-77. *Financial Times*, Africa correspondent, Lusaka, Zambia, to 1984; Africa Editor (London-based), current, 1984.

Holmes, John P. III. *Insight.* Science & Space Writer. B. 1955, Dalhart, TX. TX Tech U., 1977, Journalism. *The Corpus Christi Caller-Times*, reporter, to 1978. *The Lubbock* (TX) *Avalanche-Journal*, reporter, Regional Editor, to 1980. Press Secretary, Rep. Kent Hance (D-TX), to 1982. *The Washington Times*, "Capital Life" writer, to 1984; space, science & national news reporter, to 1985. *Insight*, science & space writer, current, 1985. *Texas Business Magazine*, Washington correspondent, current, 1982. *Home Team Sports* magazine, Editor, current, 1985. H.L. Mencken Award, Investigative Journalism (for work *DC Times*), 1985.

Holusha, John. *The New York Times.* Detroit Bureau Chief. Newark College of Engineering, 1965, BS-Chemical Engineering; postgrad George Washington U., 1976-78, Economics. Walter Bagehot Fellow, 1975-76. *The Daily Record* (Morristown, NJ), reporter. *The Advance* (Dover, NJ), reporter. *The Star Ledger* (Newark, NJ), reporter, Asst City Editor, Night City Editor, to 1970. *The Washington Star*, reporter, Asst National Editor, Asst Financial Editor, to 1979. *The New York Times*, asst to Financial Editor, to 1981; Editor, 1980 National & International Economic Surveys; Detroit Bureau Chief, current, 1982.

Holzman, David C. *Insight.* Medical Writer. B. 1953, Cambridge, MA. U. of CA, Berkeley, 1975, Zoology. Center for Science in the Public Interest, researcher, writer, to 1977. *People & Energy*, writer, to 1978; Editor, to 1980. Freelance, science, technology & medicine, to 1986. *Insight*, medical writer, current, 1986.

Hornik, Richard. *Time.* Peking Bureau Chief. B. 1948, NYC. Brown, 1970, Political Science. *National Journal*, researcher, to 1972. National Commission on Productivity, writer, Editor, to 1974. *Eastwest Markets*, Contributing Editor, 1975; Assoc Editor, to 1978. *Time*, Washington energy & economics correspondent, to 1980; Eastern Europe Bureau Chief, to 1983; Boston Bureau Chief, to 1984; Peking Bureau Chief, current, 1985.

Horowitz, Irving Louis. *Society.* Editor-in-Chief & President. B. 1929, NYC. CCNY, 1951, BSS; Columbia, 1952, MA; Buenos Aires U., 1957, PhD. Fellow, Brandeis, 1958-59. Buenos Aires U., assoc prof, 1955-58. Bard

College, asst prof, to 1960. Hobart & William Smith Colleges, sociology chairman, to 1963; Washington U., prof, to 1969. Livingston College, Rutgers, sociology chairman, to 1973; grad prof, current, 1969. *Society*, Editor-in-Chief & President, current. Author many books including *C. Wright Milles: An American Utopian*, 1983.

Horowitz, Rose. *The Journal of Commerce*. Foreign Trade Reporter. B. 1960, NYC. Queens College (NY), 1982, BA-English, *magna cum laude*; Columbia, 1984, MA-International Affairs. AP, Pittsburgh, PA; Charleston, WVA, 1984. *The Journal of Commerce*, foreign trade reporter, current, 1985.

Houck, James I. *The Sun*. Managing Editor. B. 1941, Bakersfield, CA. U. of CA, Berkeley, Journalism. *Bakersfield Californian*, reporter & Editor, 1960-62. *Daily Californian*, UCB, Managing Editor, 1963. San Francisco *Examiner*, Copy Editor, Telegraph Editor, News Editor, to 1981. *Dallas Morning News*, Sunday Editor, Assoc Managing Editor, 1971-72. *The Sun*, Managing Editor, current, 1982.

House, Karen Elliot. *The Wall Street Journal*. Foreign Editor. B. Matador, TX. U. of TX, Austin, 1970, Journalism. Institute of American Politics, Harvard, fall 1982. *The Daily Texan*, Managing Editor. *Newsweek*, stringer, to 1970. *Dallas News*, education reporter; political reporter, to 1974. *The Wall Street Journal*, regulatory agencies, energy, environment & agriculture reporter, to 1978; diplomatic correspondent, to 1983; Asst Foreign Editor, to 1984; Foreign Editor, current, 1984. Edward Weintal Award, 1980; Edwin M. Hood Award, Excellence in Diplomatic Reporting, 1982; USC's Journalism Alumni Assn Distinguished Achievement Award, 1983; Overseas Press Club Bob Considine Award, Best Daily Newspaper Interpretation of Foreign Affairs, 1984; Pulitzer Prize, Distinguished Reporting on International Affairs, 1984; U. of TX, Outstanding Young Alumna, 1986.

Housego, David. *Financial Times*. Paris Bureau Chief. B. 1940, Horsham, UK. Oxford, Politics, Philosophy, Economics. *Times Educational Supplement*, reporter, 1964-67. *Times*, Sub-Editor, to 1968; reporter, Teheran, to 1975. *The Economist*, reporter, Teheran, to 1975; Energy & Middle East writer, to 1976. *Financial Times*, reporter, Teheran, to 1975; Asia correspondent, 1976-81; Paris Bureau Chief, current, 1981.

Hueber, Graham. *Public Opinion*. Assistant Editor. B. 1959, Philadelphia, PA. U. of PA, 1981, Modern European History & 19th Century Russian History. American Enterprise Institute, Center for Middle East Studies, research asst, to 1984. *Public Opinion*, Asst Editor, current, 1984. Co-author (with Rus Chapin) *Uniform Rules Of Criminal Procedure*, 1983.

Huffman, Diana. Senate Judiciary Committee. Majority Staff Director. B. 1949, Louisville, KY. Northwestern, 1971, BA-Political Science; Columbia, 1972, MSJ; Georgetown Law, 1977, JD. WNET-TV (NYC), producer, reporter, to 1973. *Sentinel* (Montgomery Cty, MD), News Editor, to 1976. WJLA-TV (Washington), Asst Assignment Editor, 1976. Senate Judiciary Subcommittee on Administrative Practice & Procedure, counsel, to 1978. *Legal Times*, Asst Editor, reporter, to 1980; Editor, to 1983. *National Journal*, Managing Editor, to 1987. Senate

Judiciary Committee Majority Staff Director, current, 1987.

Hughes, John. *Los Angeles Times* Syndicate. Columnist. B. 1930, Neath, South Wales. Nieman Fellow, 1961-62. *The Christian Science Monitor*, Africa correspondent, to 1961; Asst Overseas News Editor, to 1964; Far East correspondent, to 1970; Managing Editor, 1970; Editor, to 1976; Editor, manager, to 1979. Hughes Newspaper Co, Founder & President, to 1981, 1985. USIA, Assoc Director, 1981. Voice of America, Director, 1982. Asst Secretary of State for Public Affairs, State Dept Spokesman, to 1985. *Los Angeles Times* Syndicate, columnist, current. TV commentator, current. Boston U., adjunct prof journalism, current, 1986. Author *The New Face Of Africa* & *Indonesian Upheaval*. Pulitzer Prize, International Reporting, 1967; Overseas Press Club Award, Best Daily Reporting from Abroad, 1971; *Sigma Delta Chi* Yankee Quill Award, 1977.

Hume, Alexander Britton. ABC News. Correspondent & "Weekend Report, Saturday" Anchor. B. 1943, Washington. U. of VA, 1965, BA. Washington Journalism Center Fellow, spring 1969. *Hartford Times*, reporter, to 1966. UPI, 1967. *The Evening Sun*, 1968. Freelance, Washington, 1969. Jack Anderson column, reporter, 1970-72. ABC News, consultant, Washington, to 1976; correspondent, current, 1976; "Weekend Report, Saturday," anchor, current, 1985. Author *Death and the Mines*, 1971; *Inside Story*, 1974.

Hume, Ellen. *The Wall Street Journal*. Special Writer. Radcliffe College, 1968, AB-American History & Literature. Kennedy Institute of Politics Fellow, 1981; Woodrow Wilson Traveling Fellow. *Somerville* (MA) *Journal*, 1969. *Santa Barbara News-Press*, reporter, 1970. KTMS, "Equal Time", 1970. *Ypsilanti* (MI) *Press*, to 1974. *Detroit Free Press*, business writer, to 1975. *Los Angeles Times*, reporter, to 1977; Washington staff, to 1983. *The Wall Street Journal*, NY reporter, 1983; Congressional reporter, 1984; special writer, Washington, current.

Hunt, Albert R. *The Wall Street Journal*. Washington Bureau Chief. B. Charlottesville, VA. Wake Forest U., 1965, BA-Political Science. *Philadelphia Bulletin*. *Winston-Salem Journal*. *The Wall Street Journal*, NY staff; Boston staff; Congressional correspondent; Washington Bureau Chief, current, 1983. Co-author 3 books, including *The American Election of 1984*. Raymond Clapper Award.

Iacocca, Lee A. *Los Angeles Times* Syndicate. Columnist. B. 1924, Allentown, PA. Lehigh, 1945, BS-Industrial Engineering; Princeton, 1946, MS-Mechanical Engineering. Ford Motor Co, management trainee; President; Chief Operating Officer, 1946-78. Chrysler Corp, President & Chief Operating Officer, board member, to 1979; Chairman, Board of Directors, current, 1979. *Los Angeles Times* Syndicate, columnist, current. Detroit Press Club Foundation member.

Ibrahim, Youssef M. *The New York Times*. Reporter. B. Cairo, Egypt. American U., Cairo, 1968, BA; Columbia, 1970, MAJ. *The New York Times*, foreign correspondent, to 1981. *Mideast Markets*, Assoc Editor. *The Wall Street Journal*, Energy Editor, 1981-87. *The New*

York Times, reporter, current, 1987. Overseas Press Club Citation, 1986.

Ignatius, David. *The Washington Post.* Associate Editor — "Outlook." B. 1950, Cambridge, MA. Harvard, to 1973; King's College, Cambridge, 1975, Economics. *Washington Monthly,* Editor, to 1976. *The Wall Street Journal,* steel correspondent, to 1978; Justice Dept & CIA correspondent, to 1979; Senate correspondent, to 1980; Middle East correspondent, to 1983; diplomatic correspondent, to 1985. *The Washington Post,* Assoc Editor, "Outlook," current, 1985. Author *Agents of Innocence,* 1987. Edward Weintal Prize Diplomatic Reporting, 1985.

Ingrassia, Lawrence. *The Wall Street Journal.* Boston Bureau Chief. B. Laurel, MS. U. of IL, Champaign-Urbana, 1974, BS-Communications. *Chicago Sun-Times,* reporter, to 1978. *The Wall Street Journal,* reporter, to 1979; reporter, Minneapolis, to 1983; News Editor, London, 1983; London Deputy Bureau Chief, to 1986; Boston Bureau Chief, current, 1986.

Ingrassia, Paul J. *The Wall Street Journal.* Detroit Bureau Chief. B. 1950, Laurel, MS. U. of IL, 1972, BSJ; U. of WI, 1973, MA. Lindsay-Schaub Newspapers, editorial writer, to 1976. *The Wall Street Journal,* reporter, Chicago, to 1980; News Editor, Chicago, to 1981; Cleveland Bureau Chief, to 1985; Detroit Bureau Chief, current, 1985.

Insolia, Anthony. *Newsday.* Editor & Senior Vice President (Retired 1987). B. 1926, Tuckahoe, NY. NYU, 1949, Journalism. *Yonkers Daily Times,* reporter, 1949. Park Row News Service (NYC), reporter, to 1951. *Stamford* (CT) *Advocate,* reporter, to 1955. *Newsday* (NY), reporter, 1955-59; Copy Editor, to 1960; Morning City Editor, to 1966; News Director, to 1969; Day Managing Editor, 1970; Managing Editor & VP, 1978-82; Editor & Senior VP, to 1987.

Irwin, Victoria. *The Christian Science Monitor.* New York Bureau Chief & Reporter. B. 1954, Seattle, WA. Principia College, 1975, BA-Sociology; Columbia, 1978, MSJ. *The Gresham* (OR) *Outlook,* reporter, 1976-77. *The Christian Science Monitor,* copy clerk, "Living Page" writer, National News Desk Editor, 1978-83; NY reporter, current, 1983; NY Bureau Chief, current.

Isgro, Anna Cifelli. *Fortune.* Associate Editor — Washington. Fairleigh Dickenson U.; Columbia, MA-International Affairs. UN Public Information Office. Population Institute, research director. *Fortune,* reporter/researcher; Assoc Editor, Washington, current.

Iyer, Pico. *Time.* Contributor. B. 1957, Oxford, UK. Oxford, 1978, BA-English Language, MA, 1982, Literature; Harvard, 1980, AM. *Santa Barbara News and Review,* profile writer, 1980. *The Movies,* contributor, 1983. Freelance, current, 1977. *Time,* "World Affairs" writer, reviewer, 1982-87; contributor, current, 1987.

Jackson, Brooks D. *The Wall Street Journal.* Washington Reporter. B. 1941, Seattle, WA. Northwestern, 1964, BS; Syracuse, 1967, MS. AP, reporter, NYC & Washington, to 1980. *The Wall Street Journal,* reporter, Washington, current, 1980. AP Reporting Performance Award, 1974; Raymond Clapper

Award, Washington Reporting, 1974; John Hancock Award, Business & Financial Reporting, 1978.

Jackson, Gordon S. *Policy Review.* Managing Editor. Duke; IN U., JD. *Amarillo Globe News,* editorial writer. Speechwriter & legislative asst, Rep. Beau Bolter (R-TX), to 1986. *St. Louis Globe-Democrat,* editorial writer, to 1987. *Policy Review,* Managing Editor, current, 1987.

Jackson, Robert D. *Los Angeles Times.* Investigative Reporter. B. 1935, St. Louis, MO. St. Louis U., 1956, AB, 1960, MA-Political Science. Fulbright Fellow, U. of Copenhagen, 1961-62. *St. Louis Globe-Democrat,* city desk staff, 1963-65. *Los Angeles Times,* city desk staff, to 1967; Washington investigative reporter, current, 1967. *Sigma Delta Chi* National Reporting Award, 1970.

Jacoby, Tamar. *Newsweek.* Senior Writer. B. 1954, NYC. Yale, 1976, English. *New York Review of Books,* asst to Editor, to 1981. *The New York Times,* Deputy Editor Op-Ed Page, to 1987. *Newsweek,* senior writer, current, 1987. Freelance, current.

Jameson, Sam. *Los Angeles Times.* Tokyo Bureau Chief. B. 1936, Pittsburgh, PA. Northwestern, 1958, BSJ, 1959, MSJ. US Army, *Pacific Stars & Stripes,* Tokyo, 1960-62. *Chicago Tribune,* Chicago, 1959-60; Tokyo Bureau Chief, 1963-71. *Los Angeles Times,* Tokyo Bureau Chief, current, 1971. Loeb Award.

Janensch, Paul. Gannett Westchester-Rockland Newspapers. Senior Managing Editor. B. 1938, Chicago, IL. Georgetown, 1960, BA-Philosophy; Columbia, 1964, MSJ. City News Bureau, Chicago, to 1962. UPI, radio newswire writer, to 1963. *Pollution Abstracts, Inc.,* Publisher, to 1975. *Philadelphia Daily News,* Managing Editor, to 1976. *The Courier-Journal,* reporter, City Editor, Washington staff, to 1968; Managing Editor, to 1979. *The Louisville Times,* Managing Editor, to 1978. *The Courier-Journal & The Louisville Times,* Exec Editor, to 1987. Gannett Westchester-Rockland newspapers, including *Nyack Journal-News,* Senior Managing Editor, current, 1987.

Janssen, Richard F. *BusinessWeek.* Senior Editor. B. 1933, St. Louis, MO. Washington U., 1954, Political Science. US Army, to 1956. *The Wall Street Journal,* reporter, Chicago, to 1963; Washington staff, economics correspondent, "Outlook" columnist, to 1972; London correspondent, European Bureau Chief, to 1978; financial & economic reporter, Editor, to 1981. *BusinessWeek,* Senior Editor, finance & personal business, current, 1981.

Jaroslovsky, Rich. *The Wall Street Journal.* Features Editor — Washington. B. Santa Rosa, CA. Stanford, 1975, BA-Political Science. *San Francisco Chronicle,* campus correspondent. *Stanford Daily,* Editor-in-Chief, 1974. *The Wall Street Journal,* intern, summer 1974; Cleveland reporter, 1975-76; Washington reporter, to 1981; White House correspondent, to 1985; Features Editor, Washington, current, 1985. Co-winner Aldo Beckman Memorial Award, 1983.

Javetski, William. *BusinessWeek.* State Department Correspondent. Hunter College; U. of CA, Berkeley, MA. USC Journalism School, business journalism teacher. *The Merced* (CA) *Sun-Star,* reporter. *The San Jose Mercury News,* writer. *The Berkeley Gazette,* reporter.

Business Week, LA correspondent; Toronto correspondent, to 1983; Toronto Bureau Chief, to 1986; State Dept correspondent, current, 1986.

Jenkins, Holman W. Jr. *Insight*. Writer. B. 1959, Philadelphia, PA. Hobart College, 1982, History; Medill School of Journalism, 1985. *Gas Daily*, Washington Editor, to 1986. *Fed Fortnightly*, writer, to 1987. *Insight*, writer, current, 1987.

Jenkins, Loren. *The Washington Post*. Rome Bureau Chief. B. New Orleans, LA. U. of CO, 1961, Political Science. Peace Corps, Freetown, Sierra Leone, to 1963. *Daily Item* (Port Chester, NY), reporter, to 1965. UPI, newsman, NYC, to 1966; correspondent, London, Paris, Madrid, to 1969. *Newsweek*, special correspondent, Madrid, to 1970; correspondent, Beirut Bureau Chief, to 1972; Bureau Chief, Hong Kong & Saigon, to 1975; Rome Bureau Chief, to 1980. *The Washington Post*, special correspondent, Madrid, 1969-70; special roving correspondent, Rome, 1980-85; Rome Bureau Chief, current, 1985. Overseas Press Club Award, Best News Magazine Foreign Reporting, 1976; Pulitzer Prize, Foreign Reporting, 1983.

Jennings, Peter Charles. ABC News. "World News Tonight" Anchor & Senior Editor. B. 1938, Toronto, Ontario. Studied Carlton U. (Ottawa, Ontario). CBC, Montreal. CJOH-TV, Ottawa. Canadian TV, Parliamentary correspondent, anchor. ABC News, from 1964, anchor, national correspondent: "World News Tonight," London anchor, to 1983; anchor, Senior Editor, current, 1985.

Jensen, Holger. *The Washington Times*. Foreign Editor. B. 1944, Shanghai, China. U. of Cape Town (South Africa), English Literature & Political Science. AP, foreign correspondent, to 1976. *Newsweek*, correspondent; Hong Kong Bureau Chief; Southern Africa Bureau Chief, to 1983. *The Washington Times*, Foreign Editor, current, 1986. APME Photo Award of the Year, 1972; Overseas Press Club Foreign Reporting from Abroad, 1974.

Johns, Michael. *Policy Review*. Assistant Editor. B. 1964, Allentown, PA. Cambridge, 1984, Economics; U. of Miami, 1986. *The Miami Tribune* (U. of Miami), Editor-in-Chief, 1983-84, 1985-86. Lyndon Baines Johnson Fellow, Rep. Don Ritter (R-PA), 1984. *The Miami Hurricane*, opinion columnist & reporter, 1982-83. *Human Events*, Capitol Hill reporter, 1983. *Liberty Report*, Contributing National Security Editor, current, 1987. *Policy Review*, Asst Editor, current, 1986. Iron Arrow Honor Society, U. of Miami; James Brady Press Award; Century III Leaders Scholarship, Shell Oil Co; US Achievement Academy National Award. Contributor *The Third Generation: Young Conservative Leaders Look To The Future*, 1987.

Johnson, Haynes. *The Washington Post*. National Affairs Columnist. B. NYC. U. of MO, BSJ; U. of WI, Madison, MA-American History. 2ce Ferris Prof of Journalism. *News Journal* (Wilmington, DE), reporter, 1956-57. *The Washington Star*, city reporter; Copy Editor; Night City Editor; national reporter, to 1969. *The Washington Post*, national reporter; Asst Managing Editor; national affairs columnist, current. Author 4 books, including *In The Absence of Power: Governing*

America, 1980: co-author 4 books, including *Lyndon*, 1973: Editor *The Fall of a President*, 1974. Pulitzer Prize, Reporting, 1966; *Sigma Delta Chi* Award, General Reporting.

Johnson, Tom. *Los Angeles Times*. Publisher & Chief Executive Officer. B. 1941, Macon, GA. U. of GA, 1963, ABJ; Harvard, 1965, MBA. White House Fellow, 1965-66. *The Macon* (GA) *Telegraph And News*, sports stringer, reporter & state desk, 1956-65. Asst White House Press Secretary, 1966-67. Deputy Press Secretary to the President, to 1968. Special Asst to President, to 1969. Exec Asst to President Johnson, to 1971. Texas Broadcasting Corp, Exec VP, to 1973. *Dallas Times Herald*, Exec Editor, to 1975; Publisher, to 1977. *Los Angeles Times*, President & Chief Operating Officer, to 1980; Publisher & Chief Exec Officer, to 1986; Times Mirror Company Group, VP, 1984-85; Senior VP, 1986; *Los Angeles Times*, Publisher & Chief Exec Officer, current, 1987; Times Mirror Company, Vice Chairman, current, 1987. Adweek US Publisher of the Year, 1984.

Johnston, George Sim. Freelance Writer. B. 1951, NYC. Harvard, 1973, English. Freelance, current, 1982. *The American Spectator, Harper's, Commentary, The Harvard Business Review*, contributor, current.

Jonas, Norman. *Business Week*. Economics Editor. CCNY, *magna cum laude*, Phi Beta Kappa. *The Wall Street Journal, The New York , 1973, English.*, *The New York Times*, business reporter. McGraw-Hill World News, senior economic correspondent, Washington. *Business Week*, senior economic correspondent, Washington; senior writer, to 1985; Economics Editor, current, 1985.

Jones, Alex S. *The New York Times*. Press Reporter. B. Greenville, TN. Washington & Lee U. *The Greenville* (TN) *Sun*, Editor, 1978-83. *The New York Times*, business reporter, to 1985; press reporter, current, 1985. Pulitzer Prize, Specialized Reporting, 1987.

Jones, Laurie Lynn. *New York*. Managing Editor. B. 1947, Kerrville, TX. U. of TX, 1969, BA. Columbia, asst to Director of College Admissions, 1969-70; asst to Director Office Alumni, to 1971. *Book World*, asst advertising manager, to 1972. *The Washington Post, Chicago Tribune*, 1971-72. *New York*, editorial asst, to 1974; Asst Editor, 1974; Senior Editor, to 1976; Managing Editor, current, 1976.

Jones, Tamara. *Los Angeles Times*. Denver Bureau Chief. San Diego State U., BSJ. *Los Angeles Times*, intern, 1978-79; Denver Bureau Chief, current, 1987. AP, NY, LA, San Diego, 1979-83; foreign correspondent, West Germany, to 1985; national correspondent, NY, to 1987.

Jurgensen, Karen. *USA Today*. Senior Editor. B. 1949, Durham, SC. U. of NC, 1971, BA-English. *The Charlotte News*, editorial & feature writer, columnist & Editorial Page Layout Editor, to 1975. U. of NC Sea Grant College Program, writer, Editor, to 1979. *The Miami News*, Asst Lifestyle Editor, 1979; Lifestyle Editor, to 1982; Asst City Editor, 1982. *USA Today*, Life Dept Topics Editor, 1982; Life Dept Special Projects Editor, to 1985; Life Dept Deputy Managing Editor, to 1986; Cover Stories Dept Managing Editor, to 1987; Senior Editor, current, 1987.

Kael, Pauline. *The New Yorker.* Film Critic. B. 1919, Sonoma County, CA. U. of CA, Berkeley, 1940, Philosophy. Guggenheim Fellow, 1964. Freelance, current. *The New Yorker,* film critic, current, 1968. Author 9 books, including *State of the Art,* 1985: contributed "Raising Kane" in *The Citizen Kane Book,* 1971. George Polk Award, Criticism, 1970; Front Page Awards, Best Magazine Column, 1974; Distinguished Journalism, 1983.

Kaiser, Robert G. *The Washington Post.* Assistant Managing Editor — National News. B. Washington, DC. Yale; London School of Economics, MS; Columbia, Certificate, International Reporting. Duke, Teaching Fellow, 1974-75. *The Washington Post,* intern, summer 1963; London correspondent, part-time, 1964-66; city reporter, to 1969; Saigon correspondent, to 1971; Moscow correspondent, to 1974; national news reporter, 1975-82; Assoc Editor, Editor "Outlook," to 1985; Asst Managing Editor, national news, current, 1985. Co-author 4 books.

Kamm, Henry. *The New York Times.* Budapest Correspondent. B. 1925, Breslau, Germany. NYU, 1949, BA, *Phi Beta Kappa.* US Army, 1943-46. *The New York Times,* editorial index dept member, Copy Editor, to 1960; Asst News Editor, *The Times International Edition,* Paris, to 1964; foreign correspondent, to 1967; Moscow Bureau Chief, to 1969; Asia correspondent, to 1971; roving correspondent, to 1982; Rome Bureau Chief, to 1984; Athens Bureau Chief, to 1986; Budapest correspondent, current, 1986. George Polk Memorial Award, Foreign Reporting, 1969; Pulitzer Prize, International Reporting, 1978: co-winner *Sigma Delta Chi* Distinguished Service Award, Outstanding Foreign Correspondence, 1968.

Kandebo, Stanley W. *Aviation Week & Space Technology.* Engineering Editor. B. 1958, Trenton, NJ. NJIT, 1980, BS-Chemical Engineering; U. of PA, 1982, MS-Chemical Engineering. McDonnell Douglas Astronautics Co, Design Engineer, 1982-85. *Aviation Week & Space Technology,* Engineering Editor, current, 1985.

Kann, Peter Robert. *The Wall Street Journal.* Associate Publisher. B. Princeton, NJ. Harvard, 1964, BA-Government. *The Harvard Crimson,* Political Editor, editorial board member. *The Wall Street Journal,* intern, summer, 1963; Pittsburgh staff, to 1966; LA staff, 1966; reporter, Vietnam, to 1968; roving Asia correspondent, Hong Kong, to 1976; 1st Publisher & Editor of *The Asian Wall Street Journal,* to 1979; Dow Jones corp rep, Asia, to 1979; asst to Chairman & Chief Exec, 1979; Assoc Publisher, current, 1979; VP, Dow Jones, Management Committee member, to 1985; Exec VP, Dow Jones, current, 1985; President, International & Magazine groups, current, 1985. Pulitzer Prize Board member, current, 1987. Pulitzer Prize, Distinguished Reporting, International Affairs, 1972.

Kaplan, Roger. *Reader's Digest.* Associate Editor. B. 1946, Neuilly, France. U. of Chicago, 1970, Literature & History, 1974, MA. Freelance, to 1984. *Commentary,* to 1986. *The American Spectator,* to 1986. *The Detroit News,* editorial writer, Op-ed Editor, to 1986. *New York Post,* editorial writer, Op-ed Editor, to 1986. *Reader's Digest,* Assoc Editor, current, 1986.

Kapstein, Jonathan. *BusinessWeek.* Regional Bureau Chief. B. 1939, RI. Brown, 1961, BA-English Literature;

Columbia, 1962, MS. *BusinessWeek,* Latin American Bureau Chief, Rio, 1969-72; Canada Bureau Chief, Toronto, to 1976; Italy Bureau Chief, Milan, to 1978; Africa Bureau Chief, Johannesburg, to 1983; Brussels Regional Bureau Chief, current, 1984. Overseas Press Club of America Award: co-winner Overseas Press Club Citation, Best Magazine Interpretation of Foreign Affairs.

Karmin, Monroe W. *U.S.News & World Report.* Senior Editor. B. 1929, Mineola, NY. U. of IL, 1950, Journalism; Columbia, 1953, MSJ. *The Wall Street Journal,* Washington staff, to 1974. House Banking Committee Member, to 1976. *Chicago Daily News,* Washington staff, 1977. Knight-Ridder Newspapers, Washington staff, to 1981. *U.S.News & World Report,* Senior Editor, economics, current, 1981. Co-winner *Sigma Delta Chi* Distinguished Service Award, 1966; Pulitzer Prize, National Reporting, 1967.

Katz, Susan. *Insight.* Writer. B. Riverside, CA. U. of CA, Davis, Medieval History. *Chattanooga Times,* reporter, 1978. *Dixon (CA) Tribune,* reporter, 1982; Editor, to 1985. *Insight,* reporter, to 1986; writer, current, 1986. Distinguished Achievement, Journalism Award, Air Force Assn, 1985; 1st Place, General Excellence Category, CA Newspaper Publishers Assn, 1985.

Kaufman, Michael. *The New York Times.* Warsaw Bureau Chief. B. 1938, Paris, France. CCNY, 1959, BA. *The New York Times,* copyboy, clerk, news asst, caption writer, radio script writer; metro staff, to 1975; foreign correspondent, Nairobi, to 1979; foreign correspondent, New Delhi, to 1982; Ottawa Bureau Chief, to 1984; Warsaw Bureau Chief, current, 1984. Author *In Their Own Good Time; Rooftops and Alleys: Adventures with a City Kid.* George Polk Memorial Award, International Reporting, 1979.

Kaus, Mickey. *Newsweek.* Senior Writer. B. 1951, Santa Monica, CA. Harvard, 1973, Social Studies. *Washington Monthly,* Editor, 1978-80. *American Lawyer,* Senior Editor, to 1982. *Harper's,* Politics Editor, to 1983. Speechwriter, Sen. Ernest F. Hollings, to 1984. *The New Republic,* West Coast correspondent, to 1987. *Newsweek,* senior writer, current, 1987. Freelance, current.

Kaylor, Robert. *U.S.News & World Report.* Associate Editor. *U.S.News & World Report,* Singapore Bureau Chief, to 1986; Assoc Editor, defense, current, 1986.

Keller, Bill. *The New York Times.* Moscow Correspondent. B. 1949. Pomona College, 1970. *The Oregonian* (Portland, OR), reporter, to 1979. *Congressional Quarterly,* lobbyist & interest groups reporter, to 1982. *Dallas Times-Herald,* reporter, to 1984. *The New York Times,* domestic correspondent, Washington, to 1986; Moscow correspondent, current, 1986.

Kelley, Wayne P. Jr. *Congressional Quarterly.* Publisher & Executive Vice President. B. 1933, Rochester, NY. Vanderbilt, 1955, BA. US Army, to 1957. Nieman Fellow, 1963-64. *The Augusta (GA) Chronicle,* City Editor, reporter, 1960-65. *The Journal,* Washington correspondent, reporter, to 1969. *Congressional Quarterly,* Assoc Editor, to 1972; Managing Editor, to 1974; Exec Editor, to 1980; Publisher, current, 1980; Exec VP, current, 1984.

Kempster, Norman. *Los Angeles Times.* State Department Correspondent. B. 1936, Sacramento, CA. CA State U., Sacramento, 1957, Language Arts. Professional Journalism Fellowship, Stanford, 1967-68; Joe Alex Memorial lecturer, Harvard, 1983, honorary Nieman Fellow. UPI, Sacramento, to 1961; Olympia, WA, Bureau Chief, to 1966; Deputy Bureau Chief, to 1968; Washington economics, White House correspondent, to 1973. *The Washington Star,* White House correspondent, to 1976. *Los Angeles Times,* Pentagon correspondent, to 1981; Jerusalem Bureau Chief, to 1984; State Dept correspondent, current, 1984.

Kestin, Hesh. *Forbes.* Contributing Editor. B. 1943, NYC. *New York Herald Tribune. Paterson* (NJ) *Call. Newsday. True,* Articles Editor. *Jerusalem Post,* Bureau Chief. *Newsview* (Tel Aviv), Editor-in-Chief. *Middle East Times* (Nicosia, Cyprus), Israel correspondent. *Present Tense,* Contributing Editor. *Forbes,* European correspondent, to 1987; Contributing Editor, current, 1987.

Kifner, John. *The New York Times.* Cairo Bureau Chief. B. 1941, Cornwall-on-Hudson, NY. Williams College, 1963, BA. Nieman Fellow, 1971-72. *The New York Times,* metro staff; national correspondent, 1969-78; covered Iranian revolution, 1979; Beirut Bureau Chief, to 1982; Warsaw Bureau Chief, to 1984; Beirut Bureau Chief, to 1985; Cairo Bureau Chief, current, 1985. Sidney Hillman Award, Reporting, 1971; Page One Award, NY Newspaper Guild, 1971, 1973; Award, Race Relations Reporting, Columbia, 1973; George Polk Memorial Award, Foreign Reporting, 1979.

Kilborn, Peter T. *The New York Times.* Economics Correspondent. B. 1939, Providence, RI. Trinity College, 1961, BA-English; Columbia 1962, MSJ-Economics. Providence *Journal-Bulletin,* reporter, to 1963. McGraw-Hill World News & *Business Week,* Paris correspondent, to 1968. *Business Week,* writer, Asst Tech Editor, to 1971; LA Bureau Chief, to 1973; Companies Editor, to 1974. *Newsweek,* Senior Editor, to 1978. *The New York Times,* financial reporter, to 1975, 1978; London economics correspondent, to 1977; Sunday Business Section Editor, to 1982; Economics Editor, Washington, to 1983; economics correspondent, Washington, current, 1983.

Kilpatrick, James Jackson. Universal Press Syndicate. Columnist. B. 1920, Oklahoma City, OK. U. of MO, 1941, BJ-History. *Richmond News Leader,* reporter, to 1949; Editorial Page Editor, to 1951; syndicated columnist, to 1965. *Washington Star* Syndicate, columnist, to 1981. Universal Press Syndicate, columnist, current, 1981. William Allen White Award, U. of KS; U. of MO Medal of Honor, Distinguished Service to Journalism; Carr Von Anda Award, OH U., 1987.

Kimelman, Donald B. *Philadelphia Inquirer.* Deputy Editor. *Philadelphia Inquirer,* Moscow correspondent, 1983-86; editorial board member, to 1987; Deputy Editor, current, 1987.

Kincaid, Cliff. *Human Events.* Contributing Editor. B. 1954, Kansas City, MO. U. of Toledo, Journalism. Accuracy in Media, former Asst to Chairman of the Board; radio commentary writer, commentator, current. *Human Events,* Assoc Editor, to 1987; "Focus on the Media" columnist, to 1987; Contributing Editor, current. CNN, "Crossfire" occasional co-host, current.

Kinnane-Roelofsma, Derk. *Insight.* Senior Writer. B. 1932, NYC. Columbia, 1955, BA-Humanities; Trinity College, Dublin, 1955-56; Tulane, Teaching Fellow, 1960, MA. U. of Baghdad, 1960-61. Freelance (London, Paris, Dublin), 1961-63. Reuters, European Editor, 1964; correspondent, 1965. *Agence France-Presse,* Editor, English Language Service, 1966, 1970. *The Irish Times* (Dublin), Paris correspondent, 1966-67. Societe Jegu, Account Exec for US Dept of Commerce, 1968. *Kayhan International* (Teheran), Editor, to 1971. BBC, stringer, 1970-71. *UNESCO Features* (Paris), Asst Editor, to 1980; Editor-in-Chief, to 1985. *Insight,* senior writer, current, 1985.

Kinsley, Michael. *The New Republic.* Editor & "TRB from Washington" Columnist. B. 1951, Detroit, MI. Harvard, 1972, Economics; Magdalen College; Oxford; Harvard Law. *The Washington Monthly,* Managing Editor, to 1975. *Harper's,* Editor, 1981-83. *The New Republic,* Managing Editor, to 1976; Editor, to 1979, current, 1983; "TRB from Washington" columnist, current, 1983. DC bar member.

Kinzer, Stephen. *The New York Times.* Managua Bureau Chief. B. 1951, NYC. NYU, 1969; BU, 1973, MA. Administrative Asst to Gov. Michael Dukakis (MA), 1975. Boston U., adjunct prof, journalism, to 1979. *The Boston Phoenix,* columnist, to 1979. *The Boston Globe,* reporter, to 1982. *The New York Times,* metro reporter, 1983; Managua Bureau Chief, current, 1984. Freelance, current. Author *Bitter Fruit,* 1982.

Kiplinger, Knight A. *Changing Times.* Editor-in-Chief. B. 1948, Washington, DC. Cornell, 1969, Government; Princeton, 1970, International Affairs. *Sentinel* (Rockville, MD), reporter, 1970. Griffin-Larrabee News Bureau, Washington reporter, to 1973; bureau manager, 1976-78. Ottaway Newspapers, Inc, Washington Bureau Chief, News Service Chief, to 1983. *Changing Times,* Editor-in-Chief, current, 1983. Co-author *Washington Now,* 1975.

Kirkland, Richard I. Jr. *Fortune.* Board of Editors Member & European Correspondent, London. Birmingham-Southern College, BA-English, *summa cum laude, Phi Beta Kappa;* Duke, AB-English, MA; NYU "Careers in Business" accelerated MBA program. *Fortune,* reporter/researcher, to 1981; Assoc Editor, Washington, to 1985; Board of Editors member, European correspondent, London, current, 1985.

Kirkpatrick, Jeane J. *Los Angeles Times* Syndicate. Columnist. B. 1926, Duncan, OK. Stephens College, 1946, AA-Political Science; Barnard, 1948, AB; Columbia, 1950, MA, 1967, PhD; postgrad French Govt Fellow, *U. Paris Institute de Science Politique,* 1952-53. State Dept, research analyst, 1951-53. George Washington U., research assoc, to 1956. Georgetown, assoc prof, Political Science, 1967-73; prof, to 1978; Thomas & Dorothy Leavey U., Georgetown, prof, current, 1978 (on leave 1981-85). American Enterprise Institute, Senior Fellow, 1977-81 (on leave 1981-85); Counselor to President. Cabinet Member, US Permanent Rep to UN, 1981-85. *Los Angeles Times* Syndicate, columnist, current. Contributor, journals, current. Author 9 books, including *The Reagan Phenomenon,* 1982. Presidential Medal of Freedom, 1985.

Klaw, Spencer. *Columbia Journalism Review.* Editor. B. 1920, NYC. Harvard, 1941, AB. *San Francisco Chronicle*, reporter, 1941. *Raleigh* (NC) *News and Observer*, Washington correspondent, to 1943. UPI, Washington correspondent, to 1941-43; reporter, NY, 1946. *The New Yorker*, 1947-52. *New York Herald Tribune*, asst to Sunday Editor, to 1954. *Fortune*, Assoc Editor, to 1960. Freelance, current, 1960. U. of CA, Berkeley, journalism lecturer, 1968-69. Columbia Grad School of Journalism, lecturer, current, 1970. *Columbia Journalism Review*, Editor, current, 1980. Author *The New Brahmins: Scientific Life in America, 1968; The Great American Medicine Show*, 1975.

Kleiman, Robert. *The New York Times.* Editorial Board Member. B. NYC. U. of MI, 1939, *Phi Beta Kappa. The Washington Post*, reporter, to 1941. *The New York Journal of Commerce*, White House correspondent, to 1943. Voice of America, White House correspondent, 1942. OWI Psychological Warfare Teams, Chief, 1943. *U.S.News & World Report*, Assoc Editor, to 1948; Central European Editor, Germany Bureau Chief, to 1951; Paris Bureau Chief, to 1962. CBS, commentator, Paris, to 1963. *The New York Times*, editorial board member, current, 1963 (on leave, 1986). Author *Atlantic Crisis-American Diplomacy Confronts a Resurgent Europe*, 1964.

Klein, Edward. *The New York Times Magazine.* B. 1936, Yonkers, NY. Columbia, 1960, BS, 1961, MSJ. *New York World-Telegram*, reporter, to 1960. *The Sun*, reporter, to 1960. *The Japan Times*, reporter, Editor, to 1962. UPI, Tokyo correspondent, to 1965. *Newsweek*, Assoc Editor, to 1969; Foreign Editor, to 1975; Asst Managing Editor, to 1977. *The New York Times Magazine*, Editor, to 1987. Author *The Parachutists*, 1981; co-author (with Richard Z. Chesnoff & Robert Littell) *If Israel Lost the War*, 1969.

Klein, Frederick C. *The Wall Street Journal.* "On Sports" Columnist. B. 1938, Chicago, IL. U. of IL, 1939, Political Science. *The Wall Street Journal*, Pittsburgh, NY & Chicago staffs, from 1963; "On Sports" columnist, current, 1977. Author *On Sports*, 1987.

Klingeman, Henry. *National Review.* Writer. B. 1964, NYC. Wharton, U. of PA, Economics. *National Review*, writer, current, 1986.

Klott, Gary. *The New York Times.* Business & Financial Reporter. B. 1949, Chicago, IL. U. of IL, 1971, Economics. UPI, national business & economic correspondent, to 1984. *The New York Times*, business & financial reporter, current, 1984. Author *The New York Times Complete Guide To Personal Investing*, 1987.

Knickerbocker, Brad. *The Christian Science Monitor.* National News Editor. B. 1942, MI. Hobart College, 1964, English. US Naval Aviator, to 1970. *Democrat and Chronicle* (Rochester, NY), reporter, to 1972. *The Christian Science Monitor*, City Hall reporter, to 1975; editorial writer, to 1976; San Francisco correspondent, to 1981; Washington Bureau Manager & Pentagon correspondent, to 1985; National News Editor, current, 1985.

Knight, Robin. *U.S.News & World Report.* Senior European Editor. B. 1943, Chalfout St. Giles, UK. Dublin U., 1966, Stanford, 1968, MA-Political Science (Hons). Rotary Foundation Fellowship, 1967-68. *U.S.News &*

World Report, London reporter, to 1974; London Bureau Chief, to 1976; Moscow Bureau Chief, to 1979; African Regional Editor, Johannesburg, to 1981; Mediterranean Regional Editor, Rome, to 1983; special assignments, Washington, to 1984; Senior European Editor, London, current, 1985. Foreign Correspondents Assn of Southern Africa, chairman, 1980-81.

Knowlton, Christopher. *Fortune.* Reporter/Researcher. Harvard, BA-English & American Literature, *cum laude.* Freelance, to 1985. *Fortune*, reporter/researcher, current, 1985. Author *The Real World*, 1984.

Knue, Paul F. *The Cincinnati Post.* Editor. B. 1947, Lawrenceburg, IN. Murray State U., 1969, Journalism & English. *The Evansville* (IN) *Courier*, reporter, Copy Editor, to 1970. *The Fort Wayne Journal-Gazette*, Copy Editor, 1970. *The Evansville Press*, Managing Editor, to 1979. *The Kentucky Post*, Editor, to 1983. *The Cincinnati Post*, Copy Editor, Night News Editor, Weekend Co-Editor, to 1975; Editor, current, 1983.

Kondracke, Morton. *The New Republic.* Senior Editor. Dartmouth, 1960. Nieman Fellow, 1973-74. *Chicago Sun-Times*, 1963-68; Washington staff, to 1973; White House correspondent, to 1977. NPR, "All Things Considered" & "Communique" commentator, 1979-82. WRC-AM, talk show host, 1981-83. United Feature Syndicate, columnist, 1983-85. *The New Republic*, Exec Editor, 1978-85; Senior Editor, current, 1986. *Newsweek*, Washington Bureau Chief, 1985-86. "The McLaughlin Group," commentator, current.

Koretz, Gene. *BusinessWeek.* "Economic Diary" Editor & Writer. B. 1931, NYC. U. of OK, BA-English Literature & Educational Psychology; U. of CT, MA; Columbia, MA. U. of CT, Robert College (Istanbul, Turkey), IN U., CCNY, English & Psychology teacher. Columbia Grad School of Journalism, Economic Journalism teacher. *International Economic Letter*, Citibank, Editor, writer. *Newsweek*, Editor, writer. *BusinessWeek*, "Economic Diary" Editor, writer, current.

Koselka, Rita. *Forbes.* Reporter. B. 1961, Adrian, MI. U. of Notre Dame, 1982, History & Modern Languages. Rotary Scholar, France, 1984. First Boston Corp, analyst, 1983. *Forbes*, reporter, current, 1985.

Kosner, Edward. *New York.* Editor & Publisher. B. 1937, NYC. CCNY, 1958, BA-English & History. *New York Post*, rewriteman, Asst City Editor, to 1963. *Newsweek*, "National Affairs" writer, to 1967; General Editor, to 1969; National Affairs Editor, to 1972; Asst Managing Editor, to 1972; Managing Editor, to 1975; Editor, to 1979. *New York*, Editor, to 1986; Editor & Publisher, current, 1986. Member, Exec Committee, American Society of Magazine Editors, 1977-86; President, 1984-86. Robert F. Kennedy Journalism Award, 1971; ABA Silver Gavel Award, 1971.

Kosterlitz, Julie. *National Journal.* Staff Correspondent. B. 1955, Chicago, IL. U. of CA, Santa Cruz, 1979, History. *Williamette Week* (Portland, OR), business reporter, to 1980. *Common Cause*, to 1985. *National Journal*, staff correspondent, health & income security, current, 1985. *The Washington Monthly* Journalism Award, 1983.

MediaGuide

Kotelly, George V. *Mini-Micro Systems.* Chief Editor. B. 1931, Boston, MA. Tufts, 1953, BS-Electronics Engineering. *Computer Design*, Technical Editor, 1977-79. *EDN*, Senior Editor, to 1983. *Mini-Micro Systems*, Chief Editor, current, 1983.

Koten, John F. *The Wall Street Journal.* Reporter, Chicago. B. Killeen, TX. Carleton College (Northfield, MN). AP-Dow Jones, 1977. *The Wall Street Journal*, Atlanta reporter, to 1980; Detroit reporter, to 1984; Second Front's Marketing columnist, 1984; Chicago reporter, current, 1984.

Kovach, Bill. *Journal and Constitution.* Editor. B. 1932, Greenville, TN. East TN State U., 1959, BS. *Johnson City* (TN) *Press-Chronicle*, reporter, to 1961. *The Nashville Tennessean*, reporter, to 1968. *The New York Times*, reporter, to 1969; Albany Bureau Chief, to 1970; NE Bureau Chief, to 1971; urban affairs reporter, Washington, to 1974; News Editor, Washington, to 1976; Deputy National Editor & Project Editor, to 1979; Washington Bureau Chief, to 1986. *Journal and Constitution*, Editor, current, 1986. Author *The Battle of Nashville*, 1964; contributor *Assignment America*, 1974.

Kozodoy, Neal. *Commentary.* Executive Editor. B. 1942, Boston, MA. Harvard, 1963, BA; Hebrew College, 1963; Columbia, 1966, MA. Woodrow Wilson Fellow, 1964-65; Danforth Fellow, 1965-67. *Commentary*, editorial staff member, current, 1966; Exec Editor, current, 1968. Library Jewish Studies, Editor, current, 1970.

Kraar, Louis. *Fortune.* Board of Editors Member & Asian Editor. B. 1934, Charlotte, NC. U. of NC, 1956, History. Edward R. Murrow Fellow, 1968-69. *The Wall Street Journal*, NY reporter, 1956-58; Pentagon correspondent, to 1962. *Time*, Pentagon correspondent, to 1963; New Delhi Bureau Chief, to 1965; Bangkok Bureau Chief, to 1968; Asia correspondent, Singapore, to 1971. *Fortune*, Assoc Editor, Singapore, 1972-74; Board of Editors member, current, 1975; Asian Editor, current, 1983. Overseas Press Club of America Citation, 1987.

Kraft, Scott. *Los Angeles Times.* Nairobi Bureau Chief. B. 1955, Kansas City, MO. KS State U., 1977, Journalism & Economics. AP, writer, Jefferson City MO, 1977; writer, Kansas City, to 1979; Wichita correspondent, to 1980; national writer, to 1984. *Los Angeles Times*, national correspondent, to 1986; Nairobi Bureau Chief, current, 1986. Top AP Reportorial Performance, AP Managing Editors Assoc, 1983; Peter Lisagor Award, Feature, Chicago Headline Club, 1985.

Kramer, Barry. *The Wall Street Journal.* Foreign Features Editor & Special Writer. Rutgers, 1962, BA-Biological Sciences & Journalism; Columbia, 1963, MAJ. US Army, 1964-65, 1969. WRSU, newsman, to 1962. *The New York Herald-Tribune*, campus correspondent, to 1962. AP, newsman, Newark, NJ, to 1964; AP-Wire Editor, NY, to 1964-67; Saigon correspondent, to 1968; World Service desk, 1969. *The Wall Street Journal*, reporter, to 1976; Asia correspondent, to 1981; Foreign Features Editor, special writer, current, 1981.

Kramer, Hilton. *The New Criterion.* Editor. B. 1928, Gloucester, MA. Syracuse, 1950, English & Philosophy. *Arts Magazine*, Managing Editor, Editor, 1954-61. *The Nation*, art critic, to 1963. *The New Leader*, art critic &

Assoc Editor, to 1965. *The New York Times*, Art News Editor, to 1973; Chief Art Critic, to 1982. *The New Criterion*, Editor, current, 1982. *Frankfurter Allgemeine Zeitung*, columnist, current, 1986. *The Wall Street Journal*, freelance book critic, current, 1985. CBC, "State of the Arts" (Toronto), frequent broadcaster, current, 1985. Author *The Age of the Avant-Garde*, 1973; *The Revenge of the Philistines*.

Kramer, Joel R. *Minneapolis Star and Tribune.* Executive Editor. B. 1948, Brooklyn, NY. Harvard, 1969, BA-History & Science. *The Harvard Crimson*, Editor. *Science*, reporter, to 1970. Freelance, to 1972. *Newsday* (NY), various posts to Asst Managing Editor, to 1980. *Buffalo Courier-Express*, Exec Editor, to 1982. *Minneapolis Star and Tribune*, Exec Editor, current, 1983. Co-winner Pulitzer Prize, Public Service, *Newsday*, 1973.

Kramer, Michael. *U.S.News & World Report.* Chief Political Correspondent. B. 1945, NYC. Amherst, 1967, Political Science; Columbia Law, 1970. *New York*, city political columnist, to 1976; Political Editor, 1979-87. *More*, Editor & Publisher, 1976-78. Berkeley Books, Publisher, 1978. *U.S.News & World Report*, Chief Political Correspondent, current, 1987. Co-author *The Ethnic Factor*, 1972; *"I Never Wanted To Be Vice-President of Anything,"* 1976. Overseas Press Club Award, Reporting from Central America, 1982.

Kraus, Albert L. *The Journal of Commerce.* Editor Emeritus. B. 1920, NYC. Queens College (NY), 1941, BA-History; Columbia, 1942, Journalism. Nieman Fellow, 1954-55. *Journal-Bulletin* (Providence, RI), business & financial reporter, to 1956. *The New York Times*, business, financial, banking; asst to Financial Editor; Asst Financial Editor, to 1972. *Bond Buyer*, Senior VP, to 1978. *The Journal of Commerce*, Editorial Director; Editor, to 1987; Editor Emeritus, current, 1987.

Krauthammer, Charles. *The New Republic*, Senior Editor. *Washington Post* Writers Group, Columnist. B. 1950, NYC. McGill U., 1970; Balliol College, Oxford, 1971, Political Science, Economics; Harvard Med, 1975, MD. MA General Hospital, Resident, Psychiatry, to 1977; Chief Resident, Psychiatric Consultation Services, to 1978. HEW, Director Division of Science Alcohol, Drug Abuse & Mental Health Administration, to 1980. Speechwriter, VP Walter Mondale, to 1981. *Time*, essayist, current, 1983. *The New Republic*, Senior Editor, current, 1981. *Washington Post* Writers Group, columnist, current, 1985. Author *Cutting Edges: Making Sense of the 80's*. Pulitzer Prize, Distinguished Commentary, 1987.

Kristof, Nicholas D. *The New York Times.* Hong Kong Bureau Chief. B. 1959, Chicago, IL. Harvard, 1981, Government; Magdalen College, Oxford, Law (Rhodes Scholar). *The New York Times*, economic writer, to 1984; LA financial correspondent, 1984-85; Hong Kong Bureau Chief, current, 1985.

Kristol, Irving. *The Public Interest.* Co-Editor. B. 1920, NYC. CCNY, 1940. US Army, to 1946. *Commentary*, Managing Editor, to 1952. *Encounter*, Co-Founder, Co-Editor, to 1958. *The Reporter*, Editor, to 1960. Basic Books, Inc., Exec VP, to 1969. *The Public Interest*, Co-Editor, current, 1965. NYU, faculty member, current, 1969; prof, Social Thought, Grad School of Business Administration, current, 1979. American Enterprise

Institute, Senior Fellow, current. Author 3 books including *Reflections of a Neoconservative*, 1983.

Kriz, Margaret E. *National Journal*. Staff Correspondent. *Chemical Regulation Reporter*, senior reporter, Copy Editor, to 1987. *National Journal*, staff correspondent, regulation & legal affairs, current, 1987.

Kronholz, June. *The Wall Street Journal*. Washington Deputy Bureau Chief. B. Pittsburgh, PA. OH U., 1969, BS; National Endowment for the Humanities, Professional Journalism Fellow, U. of MI, 1974-75. *The Miami Herald*, intern, 1968; reporter, to 1974. *The Wall Street Journal*, reporter, Dallas, to 1979; London reporter, to 1983; Boston Bureau Chief, to 1985; Hong Kong Bureau Chief, to 1987; Washington Deputy Bureau Chief, current, 1987.

Kucewicz, William. *The Wall Street Journal*. Editorial Writer & Editorial Board Member. B. Yonkers, NY. NYU, Economics, politics. NYU student newspaper, Editor-in-Chief. *The Public Interest*, Asst Editor, 1975-76. AP-Dow Jones, copyreader, 1975; reporter, London, to 1979. *The Wall Street Journal*, editorial writer, current, 1979; Editorial Board member, current, 1985. Overseas Press Club Citation, Excellence, 1981.

Kurtz, Howard. *The Washington Post*. New York Bureau Chief. B. 1953, Brooklyn, NY. SUNY, Buffalo, 1974, English. *The Record* (Bergen, NJ), reporter, 1975-77. Columnist Jack Anderson, reporter, to 1978. *The Washington Star*, reporter, to 1981. *The Washington Post*, Justice Dept reporter, 1981-86; NY Bureau Chief, current, 1987. Freelance, 1986. DC-Baltimore Newspaper Guild Front Page Awards, 1981, 1985; DC-MD Press Assn Award, 1st Prize, 1982.

Kuttner, Robert. *The New Republic*. Economics Correspondent. B. 1943, NYC. Oberlin, 1965, Government. Guggenheim Fellow, 1986-87. *The Village Voice*, Washington Editor, to 1973. *The Washington Post*, national writer, to 1975. US Senate Banking Committee, Investigator, to 1978. *Working Papers*, Editor-in-Chief, to 1982. *Boston Globe*, columnist, current, 1984. *BusinessWeek*, columnist, 1985-87. *The New Republic*, economic correspondent, current, 1982. Author *Revolt of the Haves*, 1980; *The Economic Illusion*, 1984.

Kwitny, Jonathan. *The Wall Street Journal*. Feature Writer. B. 1943, Indianapolis, IN. U. of MO, BJ; NYU, MA-History. *The Indianapolis Star*, reporter. *News Tribune* (Perth Amboy, NJ), reporter. *The New York Post*, reporter. *The Wall Street Journal*, feature writer, current, 1971. Freelance, current. "The Kwitny Report," host, current. Author 5 books including *Endless Enemies: The Making of an Unfriendly World*, 1985. Honor Medal, Career Achievement, U. of MO School of Journalism, 1982.

Ladd, Everett Carll. *Public Opinion*. Senior Editor. B. 1937, Saco, ME. Bates College, 1959, BA-Government; Cornell, 1964, PhD. Woodrow Wilson Fellow; Social Science Research Council Fellow; Ford Research Fellow, Social Sciences; Guggenheim Fellow; Visiting Fellow, The Hoover Institution; Rockefeller Foundation Fellow; Center for Advanced Study in the Behavioral Sciences, Fellow; American Enterprise Institute, adjunct scholar. Prof, political science, current, 1969. The Roper Center,

Exec Director & President, current, 1977. *Public Opinion*, Senior Editor, current. *U.S.News & World Report*, polling consultant, current. Author many books including *The American Polity*, 1985 (2nd ed. 1987): co-author (with S.M. Lipset) *The Divided Academy*, 1975; (with C.D. Hadley) *Transformations Of The American Party*, 1978.

Laderman, Jeffrey M. *BusinessWeek*. Markets & Investments Editor. Rutgers; Columbia, MAJ. NJ newspapers, writer. *The Detroit News*, reporter, writer, to 1982. *BusinessWeek*, Markets & Investments Staff Editor, to 1985; Markets & Investments Editor, current, 1985.

Lahti, Scott. *National Review*. Contributor. B. 1962, Lansing, MI. NYU, 1985, Economics. *National Review*, freelance contributor, Books, Arts & Manners Section, current, 1985. Greenwood Press (Westport, CT), royalty administrator, 10/86-7/87.

Laitin, Joseph. *The Washington Post*. Ombudsman. B. Brooklyn, NY. Deputy Press Secretary to President Johnson. Asst to the Director, OMB, Johnson & Nixon Administrations. Asst Secretary of Defense for Public Affairs, Asst FAA Administrator, Ford Administration. Asst Secretary of the Treasury for Public Affairs, Carter Administration. UPI, Reuters, correspondent. Writer & producer, network documentaries. Freelance, current. Government Relations Consultant, current. Hill & Knowlton, Washington Advisory Board member, current. *The Washington Post*, Ombudsman, current, 1986. Defense Dept Medal, Distinguished Public Service, 1975, upon being fired with Defense Secretary James Schlesinger by President Ford.

Lalli, Cele Goldsmith. *Modern Bride*. Editor-in-Chief. B. 1933, Scranton, PA. Vassar, 1955, Child Study. Ziff-Davis Publishing Co, science fiction division. *Amazing Science Fiction Stories*, Editor. *Modern Bride*, since 1970, Managing Editor; Exec Editor; currently Editor-in-Chief. TV & radio commentator, lecturer. Co-author *Modern Bride Guide to Your Wedding and Marriage*.

Lambro, Donald. United Press Syndicate, Columnist. *The Washington Times*, National Affairs Editor. B. Wellesley, MA. Boston U., Journalism. *The Boston Traveler*, reporter, to 1968. UPI, CT state legislature; Washington correspondent. United Press Syndicate, Washington columnist, current. *The Washington Times*, National Affairs Editor, current, 1987. AP Radio network & Mutual Broadcasting System, commentator, current. Author *Washington-City of Scandals; Fat City: How Washington Wastes Your Taxes*: "Star Spangled Spenders," PBS.

Landau, Peter Edward. *Institutional Investor*. Editor. B. 1933, NYC. Duke, 1955, AB; Columbia, 1959, MS-Economics. *Newsweek*, editorial asst, 1955-57; Asst Editor, to 1958-61; Assoc Editor, to 1967. Tiderock Corp, VP, 1967. *Institutional Investor*, Senior Editor, 1968; Managing Editor, to 1970; Editor, current, 1970.

Landro, Laura. *The Wall Street Journal*. Reporter. OH U., 1976, BSJ. McGraw-Hill World News, London, to 1977. McGraw-Hill Energy Newsletter Group, Asst Editor, to 1978. *BusinessWeek*, Staff Editor, to 1981. *The Wall Street Journal*, reporter, NY, covering entertainment, cable & publishing. Gerald Loeb Award, Deadline Reporting, 1986.

Lapham, Lewis Henry. *Harper's.* Editor. B. 1935, San Francisco, CA. Yale, 1956, BA; postgrad, Cambridge, 1956-57. *San Francisco Examiner*, VA reporter, 1957-60. *New York Herald Tribune*, to 1962. USA-1 (NYC), author, Editor, 1962. *The Saturday Evening Post*, 1963-67. *Life*, writer, to 1970. *Harper's*, writer, 1967-70; Managing Editor, to 1975; Editor, current, 1975. Author *Fortune's Child*, 1980; *High Technology and Human Freedom*, 1985.

Lappen, Alyssa A. *Forbes.* Staff Writer. B. 1952, New Haven, CT. Tulane, 1974, English. *Phi Beta Kappa. The Western*, Editor, 1974-75. *The New Haven Register*, reporter, to 1977. *The Journal Of Electronics Purchasing and Distribution*, Managing Editor, 1978; *Forbes*, reporter, researcher, to 1981; senior reporter, researcher, to 1985; reporter, to 1985; staff writer, current, 1985. Harvard Summer Poetry Prize, 1971.

Lardner, George Jr. *The Washington Post.* National Staff Reporter. B. 1934, Brooklyn, NY. Marquette, 1956, ABJ, 1962, MA. *The Worcester (MA) Telegram*, reporter, rewrite, night city desk, 1957-59. *The Miami Herald*, metro govt reporter, Ft Lauderdale, Miami, to 1963. *The Washington Post*, city staff, to 1964; local staff columnist, 1964-65; national staff reporter, current, 1966. *Sigma Delta Chi* National Reporting Award, Political Campaign Coverage, 1970; ABA Gavel Award Certificate of Merit, 1977; DC-Baltimore Newspaper Guild, Front Page Award, 1st Place, National Reporting, 1984.

Lau, Emily. *Far Eastern Economic Review.* Hong Kong Correspondent. B. 1952, Hong Kong. USC, 1976, BA-Broadcast Journalism; London School of Economics & Political Science, 1982, MS-International Relations. *South China Morning Post*, 1976-78. Hong Kong Television, news dept, to 1981; London correspondent, 1981-84. BBC, 1982-84. *Far Eastern Economic Review*, Hong Kong correspondent, current, 1984.

Lawrence, David Jr. *Detroit Free Press.* Publisher & Chairman. B. 1942, NYC. U. of FL, 1963, Journalism; Harvard Advanced Management Program, 1983. *St. Petersburg Times*, reporter, Copy Editor, Telegraph Editor, News Editor, to 1967. *The Washington Post*, Asst News Editor, "Style" News Editor, to 1969. *The Palm Beach Post*, Managing Editor, to 1971. *Philadelphia Daily News*, asst to Editor, Managing Editor, to 1975. Charlotte Observer, Exec Editor, Editor, to 1978. *Detroit Free Press*, Exec Editor, to 1985; Publisher & Chairman, current, 1985. Human Rights Award, Institute of Human Relations, American Jewish Committee, 1986. McNichols Award, U. of Detroit, Distinguished Achievement, 1987.

Lawrence, John F. *Los Angeles Times.* Assistant Managing Editor — Economic Affairs. Oberlin, 1956, BA. *Cleveland Plain Dealer*, correspondent, to 1956. *The Economist*, correspondent, to 1972. *The Wall Street Journal*, reporter, to 1961; Philadelphia Bureau Chief, to 1963; Pittsburgh Bureau Chief, to 1965; Asst Managing Editor, Pacific Coast Edition, to 1968. *Los Angeles Times*, Financial Editor, to 1972; Washington Bureau Chief, to 1975; Asst Managing Editor, current, 1975. Loeb Achievement Award, John Hancock Award, both 1971.

Lawrence, Steve. *Forbes.* Assistant Managing Editor. B. 1942, NYC. U. of CA, 1964, BA-Philosophy; Northwestern, 1966, MSJ. *New York Daily News*, special

projects, Asst Business Editor. *Dallas Times-Herald*, Exec Business Editor. *The New York Times*, Enterprise Editor, "Business Day," to 1984. Time, Inc, Senior Editor, Magazine Devlpmt, to 1986. *Forbes*, Senior Editor, to 1987; Asst Managing Editor, current, 1987.

Ledeen, Michael A. *The American Spectator.* Media Columnist. B. 1941, LA, CA. Pomona College, 1962, BA-History; U. of WI, 1969, PhD-Philosophy. Washington U., instructor & asst prof, history, 1967-73. U. of Rome, visiting prof, history, to 1977. *The New Republic*, Rome correspondent, 1975-77. *The Washington Quarterly*, Exec Editor, to 1981. *The American Spectator*, media columnist, 1980-81; & current, 1986.

Lee, Mary. *Far Eastern Economic Review.* Editorial Manager. B. 1948, Singapore. U. of Singapore, 1970, English. World Press Institute Fellow, 1974; Stanford Journalism Fellow, 1984. *Singapore Herald*, education reporter, to 1971. *New Nation* (Singapore), society columnist, Women's Page Editor, to 1974. *Sunday Nation* (Singapore), asst to the Editor, columnist, 1974-75. *The Guardian* (London), foreign news, Sub-Editor, to 1977. *Far Eastern Economic Review*, Hong Kong correspondent, to 1983; Peking correspondent, 1984-86; editorial manager, current, 1986.

Lee, Susan. *Forbes.* Senior Editor & "The Big Portfolios: Money & Investments" Columnist. Sarah Lawrence, 1965, BA; Columbia, 1969, MA, 1975, PhD. John Jay Fellow, Columbia, 1972; President's Fellow, 1974. Columbia, adjunct asst prof, Economics Dept, to 1980. *Fortune*, Assoc Editor, to 1981. *The Wall Street Journal*, editorial board member, to 1983. *BusinessWeek*, Senior Writer, columnist, to 1984. *Forbes*, Senior Editor, "The Big Portfolios: Money & Investments" columnist, current, 1984. ABC News, "Good Morning America" commentator, current. Author 3 books, including *Susan Lee's ABZ's of Economics*, 1986: co-author *A New Economic View of American History*, 1979. NCFE Award, Editorial Writing, 1982.

Lehrer, James Charles. PBS Television. "MacNeil/Lehrer NewsHour" Associate Editor & Co-anchor. B. 1934, Wichita, KS. Victoria College, 1954, AA; U. of MO, 1956, BJ. US Marine Corps, to 1959. *Dallas Morning News*, reporter, to 1961. *Dallas Times Herald*, reporter, columnist, City Editor, to 1970. KERA-TV (Dallas), Exec Producer, correspondent, to 1972. S. Methodist U., creative writing instructor, 1967-68. PBS, Public Affairs Coordinator, 1972-73; NPACT-WETA-TV (Washington), correspondent, from 1973; PBS, "MacNeil/Lehrer NewsHour" Assoc Editor, co-anchor, current. Author *Viva Max*, 1966; *We Were Dreamers*, 1975; "Chili Queen," 1987. Columbia-Dupont Award; George Polk Award; Peabody Award; Emmy Award.

Leinster, Colin. *Fortune.* Associate Editor. Polytechnic of North London, Journalism. Newspaper reporter, London. *Life*, Vietnam correspondent. Freelance, 1974-84. *Fortune*, Assoc Editor, current, 1984.

Lelyveld, Joseph. *The New York Times.* Foreign Editor. B. 1937, Cincinnati, OH. Harvard, 1958, BA-English History & Literature, *summa cum laude*, 1959, MA-American History; Columbia, 1960, MSJ. Fulbright Grant, 1960-61, Burma. *The New York Times*, copyboy, to 1963; financial writer, 1963; metro staff, to 1965;

foreign correspondent, Africa, to 1967; India Bureau Chief, to 1969; reporter, NY, to 1972; Hong Kong Bureau Chief, 1973-74; Washington reporter, columnist, to 1977; Deputy Foreign Editor, to 1980; South African correspondent, to 1983; writer, 1984; London Bureau Chief, to 1986; Foreign Editor, current, 1986. Author *Move Your Shadow* (Pulitzer Prize, 1986). Page One Award; George Polk Memorial Award; Byline Award.

Lemann, Nicholas. *The Atlantic.* National Correspondent. B. 1954, New Orleans, LA. Harvard, 1976, American History & Literature. *The Washington Monthly*, Managing Editor, to 1978. *Texas Monthly*, Assoc Editor, to 1979; Exec Editor, 1981-83. *The Washington Post*, reporter, to 1981. *The Atlantic*, national correspondent, current, 1983. Freelance, current.

LeMoyne, James. *The New York Times.* San Salvador Bureau Chief. B. 1951, Heidelberg, Germany. Harvard, 1975, Social Studies; Balliol College, Harvard, 1977, BA-Philosophy & Political Theory; London School of Economics, 1979, MA-20th Century European Diplomatic History. *The Washington Post*, stringer, London, to 1981. *Newsweek*, stringer, London, to 1981; Assoc Editor, Central American reporter, to 1983. *The New York Times*, metro reporter, to 1984; San Salvador Bureau Chief, current, 1984. Co-winner NY Newspaper Guild Page One Award, 1982.

Lerner, Marc. *The Washington Times.* Southeast Asia Correspondent. AP. *The Denver Post. The Washington Times*, National Editor, Business Editor, 1983-87; special projects, 1987; SE Asia correspondent, current, 1987.

Lerner, Max. *New York Post & Los Angeles Times* Syndicate. Columnist. B. 1902, Minsk, Russia. Yale, 1923, AB-Government; Washington U., 1925, AM; Robert Brookings Grad School of Economics & Government, 1927, PhD. Ford Foundation Grant, 1963-64. *Encyclopedia of Social Sciences*, Editor, Managing Editor, to 1932. Sarah Lawrence College, Social Science Faculty member, to 1935. Wellesley Summer Institute, Faculty Chairman, 1933-35. National Emergency Council, Director, Consumers Division, 1934. Harvard, Government Dept lecturer, to 1936; visiting prof, 1939-41. *The Nation*, Editor, to 1938. Williams College, Political Science prof, 1938-43. PM (NYC), Editorial Director, to 1948. *The New York Star*, columnist, to 1949. Brandeis, American Civilization prof, to 1973 (Dean, Grad School, 1954-56); Prof Emeritus, current, 1974. *New York Post*, columnist, current, 1949. *Los Angeles Times* Syndicate, columnist, current, 1949. US International U. (San Diego, CA), Distinguished Prof, Human Behavior, current, 1975. Notre Dame, Prof, American Studies, 1982-84. Author 14 books, including *Ted and the Kennedy Legend*, 1980.

Lerner, Michael Alan. *Newsweek.* Los Angeles Correspondent. B. 1958, NYC. Harvard, 1981, History & Literature. *The New Republic*, writer, to 1982. *Newsweek*, Assoc Editor, national affairs, to 1983; Paris-based correspondent, to 1986; LA correspondent, current, 1987. Page One Award, 1982.

Lescaze, Lee. *The Wall Street Journal.* Assistant Foreign Editor. Harvard, 1960, BA-General Studies. *The Washington Post*, copyboy, 1963; reporter, to 1967; Vietnam correspondent, to 1970; Hong Kong correspondent, to 1973; Foreign Editor, to 1975; National

Editor, to 1977; NY Bureau Chief, to 1980; White House correspondent, to 1982; Asst Managing Editor, "Style," to 1983. *The Wall Street Journal*, editing & writing, 1983; NY News Editor, 1984; Asst Foreign Editor, current, 1984.

Lewis, Anthony. *The New York Times.* "Abroad at Home" Columnist. B. 1927, NYC. Harvard, 1948. Nieman Fellow, 1956-57. *The Washington Daily News*, reporter, 1952-55. *The New York Times*, Sunday dept, 1948-52; Supreme Court reporter, 1955-64; London Bureau Chief, to 1972; "Abroad at Home" columnist, current, 1969. Harvard Law, lecturer. Author *Gideon's Trumpet; Portrait of A Decade*. Pulitzer Prize, 1955, '63; Elijah Parish Lovejoy Award, 1983.

Lewis, Ephraim A. *BusinessWeek.* Senior Editor. Studied U. of PA, NYU; graduated Brooklyn College. *BusinessWeek*, Asst Marketing Editor, 1962-67; Minneapolis Bureau Manager, 1967; Marketing Editor, to 1969; Assoc Editor, to 1976; senior correspondent, McGraw-Hill World News, 1976; Senior Editor, current, 1976, govt, energy, books, sports business, *BusinessWeek* Top 1000, other scoreboards, personal business supplement & *BusinessWeek*/Harris polls.

Lewis, Flora. *The New York Times.* "Foreign Affairs" Columnist. B. LA, CA. UCLA, 1941, BA-Political Science; Columbia, 1942, MSJ. *Los Angeles Times*, reporter, 1941. AP, to 1946. Freelance, to 1956. McGraw-Hill, Editor, 1955. *The Washington Post*, Bureau Chief (Bonn, London, Washington, NY), to 1966. *Newsday*, syndicated columnist, to 1972. *The New York Times*, Paris Bureau Chief, to 1976; European diplomatic correspondent & Bureau Chief, to 1980; "Foreign Affairs" columnist, current, 1980. Author 3 books including *One of Our H-Bombs Is Missing*, 1967. Columbia Journalism's School's 50th Anniversary Award, 1977; Aspen Institute's Award, Journalistic Excellence, 1977; Award, Distinguished Diplomatic Reporting, Georgetown School of Foreign Affairs, 1978; French Legion of Honor, 1981; 4th Estate Award, National Press Club, 1985; Matrix Award for Newspapers, NY Women in Communications, 1985.

Lewis, Paul M. *The New York Times.* United Nations Bureau Chief. B. 1937, London. Balliol College, Oxford, 1959-61. *Financial Times*, Common Market correspondent, to 1967; Paris correspondent, to 1971; Washington Bureau Chief, to 1976. *The New York Times*, economic correspondent, to 1987; UN Bureau Chief, current, 1987.

Levin, Doron P. *The Wall Street Journal.* Automotive Reporter (On Leave). B. 1950, Haifa, Israel. Cornell, 1972, History; Columbia, 1977, MSJ. *St. Petersburg Times*, police, business, reporter, 1977-80. *The Wall Street Journal*, automotive reporter, 1981, currently on leave.

Limpert, John A. *The Washingtonian.* Editor. B. 1934, Appleton, WI. U. of WI, 1959, BS. UPI, Minneapolis reporter, 1960; St. Louis regional exec, to 1962; Detroit regional exec, to 1964. *Warren* (MI) *Progress*, Editor, to 1965. *San Jose Sunpapers*, Managing Editor, to 1967. *D.C. Examiner*, Editor, 1967. Office, VP Hubert Humphrey, Congressional Fellow, 1968. *The Washingtonian*, Editor, current, 1969. Exec Committee of American Society of Magazine Editors, member, current, 1985; Treasurer, current, 1986. American Political

Science Assn Distinguished Reporting of Public Affairs Award, 1970. *Sigma Delta Chi* Award, Public Service, National Magazine Awards, Reporting, 1982; Public Interest, 1985; & Personal Service, 1985.

Lindberg, Tod. *Insight.* Executive Editor — News. B. 1960, Syracuse, NY. U. of Chicago, 1982, AB-Political Science. *The Public Interest,* Asst Editor, to 1983; Managing Editor, to 1985. *The National Interest,* Exec Editor, to 1986. *Insight,* Senior Editor, Asst Managing Editor, news, to 1987; Exec Editor, news, current, 1987.

Lindsey, Robert H. *The New York Times.* West Coast Operations Director. B. 1935, Glendale, CA. San Jose State College, 1956. *The San Jose Mercury News,* reporter, to 1968. *The New York Times,* transportation news dept, NY, to 1975; Western economic correspondent, to 1977; LA Bureau Chief, to 1985; West Coast Operations Director, current, 1985. Author *The Falcon and the Snowman: A True Story of Friendship and Espionage,* 1979; *The Flight of the Falcon,* 1983: co-author *Reagan: The Man, the Presidency,* 1980.

Lipman, Joanne. *The Wall Street Journal.* Advertising & Public Relations Reporter. B. 1961, New Brunswick, NJ. Yale, 1983, History. *The Wall Street Journal,* summer intern, 1982; real estate reporter, 1983-86, advertising & public relations reporter, current, 1986.

Lipsky, Seth. *The Wall Street Journal*/Europe. Editorial Page Editor, Editorial Director, International Editions. B. NYC. Harvard, 1968, BA-English Literature. US Army, 1969-70: *Army Digest,* Pentagon reporter; *Pacific Stars and Stripes,* Vietnam combat reporter. *Anniston* (AL) *Star,* reporter, 1968-69. *Far Eastern Economic Review,* Asst Editor, 1974-75. *The Wall Street Journal,* reporter, Detroit, to 1974; Asia correspondent, to 1976; founding reporter, *The Asian Wall Street Journal,* to 1978; Managing Editor *The Asian Wall Street Journal,* to 1980; Assoc Editor, Editorial Page, NY, to 1982; Foreign Editor, to 1984; Senior Editor, 1984; Editorial Page Editor, *The Wall Street Journal*/Europe, current; Editorial Director, International Editions, current, 1986.

Lochhead, Carolyn. *Insight.* Writer. B. 1955, St. Louis, MO. U. of CA, Berkeley, 1979, BA-Rhetoric *cum laude* & Economics; Columbia, 1983, MAJ. *St. Francisville* (LA) *Democrat,* Editor, 1979-81. *Paso Robles* (CA) *Daily Press,* reporter, 1982. *Chain Store Age Executive,* reporter, 1983. *Chase Economic Observer* (Chase Manhattan Bank), economic observer, Editor, to 1986. Goldman Sachs, Fischer Black's Editor, 1986. *Insight,* writer, current, 1987. LA Press Assn, 1981; CA Newspaper Publishers Assn, 1st Place Features, 1982.

Loeb, Marshall. *Fortune.* Managing Editor. B. 1929, Chicago, IL. U. of MO, 1950, BJ; postgrad, U. of Goettingen, W. Germany, 1951-52. Assoc Fellow, Yale; Berkeley College, current, 1977. *Garfield News & Austinite* (Chicago), reporter, 1944-45. *Garfieldian (Austin News),* reporter, columnist, to 1947. *Columbia Missourian,* reporter, to 1950. *Garfieldian,* reporter, columnist, to 1951. UPI, staff correspondent, Frankfurt, to 1954. *St. Louis Globe-Democrat,* reporter, to 1956. *Time,* Contributing Editor, to 1961; Assoc Editor, to 1965; Senior Editor, to 1980; Economics Editor, columnist, to 1980. *Money,* to 1986. *Fortune,* Managing Editor, current, 1986. CBS Radio Network, ABC-TV Money Tips,

commentator, current. Author *Marshall Loeb's Money Guide,* 1983; co-author *Plunging Into Politics* (with William Safire), 1962. Sherman Fairchild Foundation Honorable Mention, 1962; INGAA Award, U. of MO, 1966; Gerald M. Loeb Award, 1974; John Hancock Award, 1974; Citation Media Awards, Economic Understanding, 1978; *Sigma Delta Chi* of NY Citation, 1979. Dallas Press Club Award, 1978; Freedoms Foundation Award, 1978; Champion Media Award, 1981.

Lohr, Steve. *The New York Times.* London Economic Correspondent. Colgate, 1974; Columbia, MSJ. *Binghamton Press,* business & financial reporter. Gannett News Service, business & financial reporter. Freelance, current. *The New York Times,* Copy Editor, financial desk, reporter, to 1981; foreign correspondent, Tokyo, to 1984; Manila Bureau Chief, to 1985; economic correspondent, London, current, 1985.

Loomis, Carol Junge. *Fortune.* Board of Editors Member. U. of MO, Journalism. Maytag Co, Editor, house organ, to 1954. *Fortune,* research assoc, to 1958; Assoc Editor, asst to Chief of Research, to 1968; Board of Editors member, current, 1968. Gerald Loeb Award; John Hancock Award; Newspaper Guild of NY Page One Award.

Looney, Ralph. *Rocky Mountain News.* Editor. B. 1924, Lexington, KY. U. of KY, 1948, BA. *Lexington* (KY) *Herald,* office boy, to 1942. *Lexington* (KY) *Leader,* sports writer, proofreader, 1943; reporter, photographer, to 1950; reporter, to 1953. *Albuquerque Tribune,* reporter, 1955; City Editor, 1956-68; Asst Managing Editor, to 1973; Editor, to 1980. *St. Louis Globe-Democrat,* reporter, 1955; copyreader; Chief Copy Editor, to 1956. *Rocky Mountain News* (Denver, CO), Editor, current, 1980. Freelance, current. Author *Haunted Highways, The Ghost Towns of New Mexico,* 1969. NM Medal of Merit, 1968; George Washington Honor Medal, Freedoms Foundation, Editorial Writing, 1969. Robert F. Kennedy Journalism Award, 1970; 19 E.H. Shaffer 1st Place Awards, NM Press Assn, 1965-80.

Lopez, Laura. *Time.* Rio de Janiero Correspondent. B. 1957, Inglewood, CA. CA State U., Chico, 1979, Information & Communication Science. *Time,* stringer, Mexico City office manager, to 1983; writer, world section, 1984; correspondent, NY, to 1985; correspondent, Managua, to 1987; correspondent, Mexico City, 1987; Rio de Janeiro correspondent, current, 1987.

Love, Keith. *Los Angeles Times.* Political Writer. B. 1947, Burlington, NC. NYU, 1979, Political Science. *Richmond* (VA) *Times-Dispatch,* reporter, Asst State Editor, 1969-73; *The New York Times,* Copy Editor, to 1979. *Los Angeles Times,* Asst Metro Editor, 1979; reporter; political writer, current.

Low, Charlotte. *Insight.* Senior Editor — Law. B. 1943, Pasadena, CA. Stanford, 1965, English-Classics. *Los Angeles Daily Journal,* Law Editor, 1980-85. *Insight,* Senior Editor Law, current, 1987.

Lubenow, Gerald C. *Newsweek.* San Francisco Bureau Chief. B. 1939, Sheboygan, IL. Harvard, 1961, Geology. *Newsweek,* Detroit staff, 1965; Atlanta correspondent, 1965-69; San Francisco Bureau Chief, current, 1969; London Bureau Chief, scheduled Oct 1987. Page One

Award, News Feature Writing, 1977; Page One Award National Reporting, 1977; ABA — Gavel Award, 1978.

Lyon, Jeff. *Chicago Tribune.* Sunday Magazine Writer. B. 1943, Chicago, IL. Northwestern, 1965, Journalism. *The Miami Herald,* reporter, 1964-66. Chicago Today, reporter, to 1974. *Chicago Tribune,* reporter, political writer, to 1976; columnist, to 1980; feature writer, to 1984; Sunday magazine writer, current, 1984, medical & bioethical issues. Author *Playing God in the Nursery,* 1985. National Headliner Award, 1984; American Society of Newspaper Editors Writing Contest, 1985; Pulitzer Prize, 1987.

Ma, Christopher Yi-Wen. *U.S.News & World Report.* Deputy Managing Editor. Harvard, 1972; Boalt Hall School of Law, U. of CA. Michael Clark Rockefeller Traveling Fellow, China; Churchill Fellow, International Relations, Princeton. FCC, legal staff. Newsweek, Washington correspondent, to 1984; *Newsweek Access,* Senior Editor, to 1985. *U.S.News & World Report,* Asst Managing Editor, business, to 1986; Deputy Managing Editor, current, 1986. Co-author *Teleshock: How to Survive the Breakup of Ma Bell.*

Machalaba, Daniel. *The Wall Street Journal.* Transportation Reporter. B. NYC. NYU, 1971, BA, MA-English. *The Evening News* (Paterson, NJ), reporter, 1972. Fairchild Publications (NYC), reporter, to 1976; Managing Editor, textile staff, *Daily News Record,* 1976. *The Wall Street Journal,* reporter, Philadelphia, to 1979; publishing reporter, to 1983; transportation reporter, current, 1983.

Mackenzie, Richard. *Insight.* Senior Writer. B. 1946, Brisbane, Australia. El Centro, Dallas, 1974, Journalism & Criminal Science. Australian newspapers & TV, 1965-70. Mirror Newspapers (Toronto, Canada), Copy Editor, Layout Editor, to 1971. *Dallas Times Herald,* reporter, feature writer, to 1976. Freelance, to 1981. *Sydney Morning Herald* (Australia), NY North American Syn Manager, to 1985. *Insight,* senior writer, current, 1985.

MacNeil, Robert B.W. PBS Television. "MacNeil/Lehrer NewsHour" Exec Editor & Co-anchor. B. 1931, Montreal. Carleton U., 1955, BA. CBC (Halifax, Nova Scotia), radio actor, 1950-52; radio/TV announcer, 1954-55. CFRA (Ottawa), announcer; news writer, 1952-54. Reuters, Sub-Editor, 1955-60. NBC, London news correspondent, to 1963; Washington, to 1965; NY, to 1967. BBC, to 1971; 1973-75. National Public Affairs Center for TV, senior correspondent, 1971-73. PBS Television, "MacNeil/Lehrer Report," Exec Editor, co-anchorman, current, 1975; "MacNeil/Lehrer NewsHour," current, 1983. Author *The People Machine,* 1978; *The Right Place At The Right Time,* 1982. Dupont Award, 1977.

Madison, Christopher. *National Journal.* Foreign Policy Reporter. B. 1951, Brooklyn, NY. Northwestern, 1973, BA-English, 1974, MSJ. *Independent Register* (Libertyville, IL), reporter, to 1975. McGraw-Hill, Washington energy reporter, to 1978. *Legal Times,* Washington energy & environment reporter, to 1980. *National Journal,* energy reporter, to 1981; trade reporter, to 1984; foreign policy reporter, current, 1984.

Magnet, Myron. *Fortune.* Board of Editors Member. Columbia, BA, PhD; Cambridge, MA. Middlebury College (VT), teacher. Columbia, teacher, English & Political Theory. *Fortune,* freelance, 1980-82; Assoc Editor, to 1983; Board of Editors member, current, 1983.

Magnuson, Ed. *Time.* Senior Writer. B. St. Cloud, MN. U. of MN, 1950, Journalism. *Minneapolis Tribune,* reporter; Asst City Editor, to 1960. *Time,* correspondent, to 1961; senior writer, current, 1961.

Main, Jeremy. *Fortune.* Board of Editors Member. B. 1929, Buenos Aires, Argentina. Princeton, 1950, AB-Politics. Ford Foundation Fellow, 1971-72. US Army, 1951-53; *Pacific Stars & Stripes,* Tokyo & Korea. International News Service, Washington, 1950-51; Mexico City Bureau Chief, 1953-54; Madrid Bureau Chief, to 1956; West Berlin, to 1958. *Time,* defense & space correspondent, Washington, to 1961; Paris staff, to 1965. *Money,* writer, 1972-80. *Fortune,* Assoc Editor, 1966-71; Board of Editors member, current, 1980, management & productivity. U. of MO Business Journalism Award, 1982.

Malabre, Alfred Leopold. *The Wall Street Journal.* News Editor. B. 1931, NYC. Yale, 1952, BA. Poynter Fellow, 1976. *Hartford Courant,* Copy Editor, to 1958. *The Wall Street Journal,* reporter, Bonn Bureau Chief, Economics Editor, News Editor, & "Outlook" columnist, 1958-69; News Editor, current, 1969. Author 4 books including *Beyond Our Means,* 1987.

Mallin, Jay. *The Washington Times.* Metro Reporter. B. 1959, Havana, Cuba. U. of FL, English, postgrad, Electrical Engineering. Freelance, current. *The Washington Times,* Copy Editor, 1984; African correspondent, to 1985; Asst Foreign Editor, to 1986; metro reporter, current, 1986.

Mann, James. *Los Angeles Times.* Washington Writer. B. 1946, Albany, NY. Harvard, 1968, AB-Social Relations; U. of PA, nondegree program in International Economics & History of the Middle East, 1975. *Journal-Courier* (New Haven, CT), writer, to 1969. *The Washington Post,* writer, to 1972. *Philadelphia Inquirer,* reporter, to 1975. *The Sun,* Supreme Court & Justice reporter, to 1978. *Los Angeles Times,* Supreme Court reporter, to 1984; Peking Bureau Chief, to 1987; Washington writer, current, 1987. 1st Place Award, Humor, DC-Baltimore Newspaper Guild, 1970; Watergate articles contributed to *Post's* Pulitzer Prize, 1972.

Mann, Paul. *Aviation Week & Space Technology.* Senior Congressional Editor. B. Canandaigua, NY. US Congress, staff member, 1977-80. *Military Science and Technology,* Washington Editor, 1980. *Military Electronics,* Washington Editor, 1980. *Aviation Week & Space Technology,* Senior Congressional Editor, current.

Manning, Robert A. *U.S.News & World Report.* Diplomatic Correspondent. B. 1949, Bronx, NY. U. of CA, History, Anthropology. Freelance, policy analyst, current, 1972. *Africa,* US correspondent, 1979-84. *Far Eastern Economic Review,* Washington correspondent, 1980-85. *U.S.News & World Report,* diplomatic correspondent, current. NPR, BBC, CBC, contributor. PBS documentaries "Behind the Lines," 1981; "The Death of Henry Liu," 1985.

Mansfield, Stephanie. *The Washington Post.* "Style" Reporter. B. 1950, Philadelphia, PA. Trinity College

(Washington, DC), 1972, BA-English. *Daily Mail* (London), 1972-74. *Daily Telegraph* (London), 1974-76. *The Washington Post*, "Food" section, 1976-78; metro reporter, 1980; "Style" reporter, current, 1980.

Marcial, Gene G. *BusinessWeek.* "Inside Wall Street" Editor. Santo Tomas U. (Manila, Philippines); NYU, MA-Political Science; currently at NYU Law. *The Elyria* (OH) *Chronicle-Telegram,* writer. *The Hong Kong Standard,* writer. *The Wall Street Journal,* stock market writer, to 1981. *BusinessWeek,* "Inside Wall Street" Editor, current, 1981.

Marin, Richard. *The Washington Times.* Television Critic. U. of Toronto, MA-English; Columbia, MSJ. *Harper's,* Asst Editor, 1986-87. *The Washington Times,* television critic, current, 1987.

Marion, Larry. *Institutional Investor.* Writer & Editor. B. 1950, Philadelphia, PA. Drexel U., 1972, Science; Northwestern, 1974, Journalism. McGraw Hill, writer, to 1980. *Forbes,* writer, to 1981. *Financial World,* writer & Editor, to 1983. *Datamation,* Asst Managing Editor, to 1985. *Electronic Design,* Managing Editor, 1986. *Institutional Investor,* writer & Editor, current, 1986.

Markham, James. *The New York Times.* Paris Bureau Chief. B. 1943, Washington, DC. Princeton, 1965, European History; Balliol College, Oxford, 1967 (Rhodes Scholar). *Time,* 1966. AP, to 1970. *The New York Times,* NY, 1973; Saigon Bureau Chief, to 1975; Beirut Bureau Chief, to 1976; Madrid Bureau Chief, to 1982; Paris Bureau Chief, current, 1982.

Marquand, Robert. *The Christian Science Monitor.* Education Writer. B. 1957, FL. Principia College, 1980, English, Religion-Philosophy. *The Christian Science Monitor,* editorial asst, Literary & Fine Arts Page, 1982; Poetry Editor, to 1984; education writer, current, 1985. Benjamin Fine Journalism Award, 1986.

Marro, Anthony. *Newsday.* Editor & Senior President. B. Rutland, VT. *Rutland Herald,* reporter, to 1968. *Newsday, The New York Times, Newsweek,* Washington correspondent. *Newsday,* Washington Bureau Chief, 1979-81; Managing Editor, to 1986; Exec Editor & VP, 1986-87; Editor & Senior President, current, 1987.

Marsh, David. *Financial Times.* Bonn Correspondent. B. 1952, Shoreham, UK. Queen's College, Oxford, BA-Chemistry. Reuters, London, Frankfurt, Brussels, Bonn, 1974-78. *Financial Times,* economics staff, to 1982; correspondent, Paris, to 1986; Bonn correspondent, current, 1986.

Marshall, Tyler. *Los Angeles Times.* London Bureau Chief. B. 1941, Detroit, MI. Stanford, 1967, Political Science. *Sacramento Bee,* 1964-65. UPI, San Francisco, 1968. McGraw-Hill World News, San Francisco, to 1971; Bonn, to 1974; London, to 1979. *Los Angeles Times,* New Delhi, to 1983; Bonn, to 1985; London Bureau Chief, current, 1985.

Martin, Everett. *The Wall Street Journal.* Senior Special Writer (Retired 1986). B. IL. IN U., 1949, Journalism. City News Bureau, Chicago. *Elkhart* (IN) *Truth.* Insurance salesman, to 1953. *The Christian Science Monitor,* copyboy; NE News Editor; Detroit Bureau

Chief. *The Wall Street Journal,* industries reporter. *Time,* business writer. *Newsweek,* Deputy Foreign Editor, to 1965; Hong Kong Bureau Chief, 1965; Saigon Bureau Chief, to 1968; Hong Kong correspondent, to 1970. Fletcher School of Law & Diplomacy, journalist in residence, 1970. *The Wall Street Journal,* South American correspondent, to 1982; Senior Special Writer, retired March 1986. Overseas Press Club Award, Allende coup coverage, 1973; Maria Moors Cabot Prize, South American coverage, 1983.

Martin, Jurek. *Financial Times.* Foreign Editor & Assistant Editor. B. 1942, UK. Hertford College, Oxford, 1963, Modern History. Sabbatical, U. of SC, 1981-82. *Financial Times,* foreign desk, 1966-68; Washington correspondent, to 1970; NY Bureau Chief, to 1972; Foreign News Editor, London, to 1975; Washington Bureau Chief, to 1981; Tokyo Bureau Chief, 1982-86; Foreign Editor & Asst Editor, current, 1986. David Holden Award, British Press Awards, Best Resident Foreign Correspondent, 1984.

Martin, Richard. *Insight.* Writer. B. 1958, Jackson, MS. Yale, 1980, Literature. *Arkansas Times,* Assoc Editor, to 1983. *Globescan,* Contributing Editor, 1984. *Insight,* writer, current, 1985.

Martin, Richard. *The Wall Street Journal.* Chicago Bureau Chief. B. 1939, Salt Lake City, UT. U. of Denver, 1961, BA-History. *The Mountaineer* (Fort Carson, CO, US Army), reporter, photographer, Editor, to 1963. *The Wall Street Journal,* reporter, Dallas, 1961, 1964; reporter, Detroit, 1965; reporter, various editing assignments, NYC, to 1972; Asst NY Bureau Chief, 1972; Boston Bureau Chief, to 1976; Cleveland Bureau Chief, to 1977; Chicago Bureau Chief, current, 1977.

Marx, Claude. *The Washington Times.* National Staff Reporter. B. 1961, NYC. Washington U., 1983, BA-Political Science; postgrad Georgetown, 1984-85. Freelance, current, 1983. *The Washington Post,* news aide, 1984-85. *The Great American Video Game,* by Martin Schramm, chief researcher. *The Advertiser* (Montgomery, AL), reporter, 1985-86. *Nashua* (NH) *Telegraph,* political reporter, to 1987. *The Washington Times,* national staff reporter, current, 1987.

Mashek, John W. *Journal and Constitution.* Washington Correspondent. B. 1931, Sioux Falls, SD. U. of MN, 1953, Journalism & Political Science. *Dallas Morning News,* federal beat, courthouse, state & local politics, 1955-60; Washington staff, to 1964. *U.S.News & World Report,* Houston staff, to 1970; Congressional correspondent, to 1974; White House correspondent, to 1978; national political correspondent, to 1987. *Journal and Constitution,* Washington correspondent, current, 1987.

Mason, Todd. *BusinessWeek.* Dallas Bureau Manager. U. of WI, BA. *The Marshfield* (WI) *News Herald,* reporter. *The Midland* (MI) *Daily News,* reporter. *The Miami News,* business writer, to 1978. *The Fort Lauderdale News,* Business Editor, to 1980. *BusinessWeek,* stringer, correspondent (Ft. Lauderdale, FL), 1980-82; Dallas Bureau Manager, current, 1982.

Mathews, Jay. *The Washington Post.* Los Angeles Bureau Chief. B. 1945, Long Beach, CA. Harvard, 1967, Government, 1971, MA-East Asian Studies. AP, intern,

NY, 1966. US Army, to 1969. *The Washington Star*, intern, 1970. *The Washington Post*, metro reporter, to 1975; Asst Foreign Editor, to 1976; Hong Kong Bureau Chief, to 1979; Peking Bureau Chief, to 1980; LA Bureau Chief, current, 1981. Co-author (with Linda Mathews), *One Billion: A China Chronicle*, 1983. National Education Reporting Award, 1983.

Matlack, Carol. *National Journal.* Staff Correspondent. *Arkansas Gazette*, Washington correspondent; Washington Bureau Chief, to 1987. *National Journal*, staff correspondent, labor & technology, current, 1987.

Matusow, Barbara. *The Washingtonian.* Senior Writer. B. 1938, Philadelphia, PA. PA State, 1960, French. WRC-TV (Washington), trainee, assoc producer, 1968; producer, 1973. CBS News (NY), radio writer, producer, 1970. WNBC-TV (NY), writer, producer, 1971. WJLA-TV, Washington, producer, 1976. Freelance, 1978-85. *Washington Journalism Review*, Senior Editor, to 1987. *The Washingtonian*, senior writer, current, 1987. Author *The Evening Stars: The Making of the Network News Anchor*, 1983.

Maxa, Rudy. *The Washingtonian.* Senior Writer. B. 1949, Cleveland, OH. OH U., 1971, BSJ, *cum laude. The Washington Post*, Sunday magazine articles, investigative reporter, weekly people column, 1971-83. *The Washingtonian*, senior writer, feature writer, monthly people column, current, 1983. WRC Radio talk show host, current. Author *Dare To Be Great*, 1977; *Public Trust, Private Lust*, 1977.

May, Clifford. *The New York Times.* Political Correspondent. B. 1951, NYC. Sarah Lawrence, 1973, BA-Russian; Columbia, 1975, MSJ, 1975, MA-International Affairs. *The Record* (Bergen, NJ), reporter, 1975. *Newsweek*, Assoc Editor, to 1977. Hearst Newspapers, roving foreign correspondent, to 1978. *Geo Magazine*, Senior Editor, to 1980. *The New York Times*, Science Editor, Sunday Magazine, to 1983; Africa correspondent, to 1985; domestic correspondent, to 1987; political correspondent, Rep. Jack Kemp presidential campaign, current, 1987.

May, Todd Jr. *Fortune.* Chief Economist & Board of Editors Member. Northwestern. Econometric Institute, Economic Analyst, Department Head, to 1952. Union Carbide, Assoc Economist, Economist, 1960-69. Economic Advisory Board member, US Secretary of Commerce, 1967-68. *Fortune*, Assoc Editor, 1952-60; Assoc Economist, 1969; Board of Editors, current, 1972; Chief Economist, current, 1980.

Maynes, Charles William. *Foreign Policy.* Editor. B. 1938, Huron, SD. Harvard, 1960, History; Rhodes Scholar, 1960. Congressional Fellow, 1960. UN, Foreign Service Officer, Laos, USSR, 1962-70. Legislative asst, Congress, 1970-72. Carnegie Endowment for International Peace, Secretary, 1972-77. Asst Secretary of State for International Organizations, 1977-80. *Foreign Policy*, Editor, current, 1980. Syndication Sales, columnist, current, 1985. Olive Branch Award, Outstanding Magazine Coverage, 1983.

McArdle, Thomas. *Human Events.* Associate Editor. B. 1961, Bronx, NY. Trinity College, Dublin, 1985, English Literature & History Honors Degree. *Piranha* (student

magazine), Asst Editor, 1983-85. *Human Events*, Assoc Editor, current, 1986. "Conservative Forum," columnist & Managing Editor in absence of Robert Latham.

McAuliffe, Kathleen. *U.S.News & World Report.* Senior Writer & Editor. B. 1955, White Plains, NY. Trinity College, Dublin, 1977, Psychology, BA-Natural Science, MA-Natural Science, honors. *Scientific American*, researcher, proofreader, to 1978. *Omni*, science & medical correspondent, to 1983. *U.S.News & World Report*, senior writer & Editor, current, 1986. Freelance, current. Co-author *Life For Sale*, 1981.

McCartney, Robert J. *The Washington Post.* Central European Bureau Chief. B. 1953, Evanston, IL. Amherst College, 1975, American Studies, *magna cum laude. The Wall Street Journal*, reporter, Boston, to 1976. *The International Daily News*, Business Editor, Rome, to 1978. AP-Dow Jones News Service, staff correspondent, Rome, to 1980. AP, staff correspondent, Rome, to 1982. *The Washington Post*, Asst Foreign Editor, Washington, to 1983; Mexico City/Central America Bureau Chief, to 1986; Central European Bureau Chief, Bonn, current, 1986.

McCaslin, John. *The Washington Times.* Justice Department Correspondent. B. 1957, Alexandria, VA. Old Dominion U., 1980, Speech Communications & Journalism. KOFI radio (Kalispell, MT), News Director, to 1982. KJJR & KBBZ-FM (Kalispell), News Director, to 1984. UPI, correspondent, to 1984. *The Washington Times*, White House correspondent, to 1985; Justice Dept correspondent, current, 1985.

McCormick, John P. *Newsweek.* Chicago Deputy Bureau Chief. B. 1950, Dubuque, IA. Northwestern, 1972, Political Science & Journalism. *Chicago Daily News*, editorial asst, 1971. *Dubuque Telegraph Herald*, reporter & columnist, 1972-82. Freelance, current, 1975. *Newsweek*, Chicago correspondent, 1982-84; Chicago Deputy Bureau Chief, current, 1985.

McCoy, Charles. *The Wall Street Journal.* Miami Reporter. U. of TX, Austin, 1982; *Facultad de Filosofia Y Letras*, Spain, Spanish. *San Antonio Light*, reporting intern, summer 1981, '82. *Daily Texan*, sports reporter, 1982. *The Wall Street Journal*, Dallas reporter, to 1985; banking reporter, Chicago, to 1987; Miami reporter, current, 1987.

McCrary, Daniel D. *BusinessWeek.* Senior Editor. MI State U. *The Wall Street Journal*, reporter, to 1960. McGraw-Hill World News, Washington reporter, to 1964; Asst London Bureau Chief, to 1968; Asst News Editor, Washington, to 1972. *BusinessWeek*, General Editor, to 1976; Assoc Editor, to 1981; Senior Editor, late-breaking news coverage, current, 1981.

McDaniel, Ann. *Newsweek.* Justice Department Correspondent. B. 1955, Charlottesville, VA. Vanderbilt, 1977, Political Science; Yale Law, 1983, MS. *Dallas Times Herald*, 1977-83. *Newsweek*, Justice Dept correspondent, current, 1984.

McGinley, Laurie. *The Wall Street Journal.* Reporter. Syracuse, 1975, BA-Journalism & English. *Syracuse Post-Standard*, reporter, 1975-76. *Valley Monthly* (PA), reporter, to 1977. States News Service. *Anchorage Daily*

News, correspondent, to 1980. *The Washington Star*, reporter, to 1981. *The Wall Street Journal*, reporter, current, 1981.

McGrory, Mary. *The Washington Post*, Columnist. Universal Press Syndicate, Columnist. B. Boston, MA. Emmanuel College. Elijah Parish Lovejoy Fellow, 1985. *The Boston Herald*, 1947. *The Washington Star*, book reviewer, to 1954; national commentator, columnist, to 1981. Universal Press Syndicate, columnist, current, 1960. *The Washington Post*, columnist, current, 1981. George Polk Memorial Award, 1963; Pulitzer Prize, Commentary, 1975.

McGruder, Robert G. *Detroit Free Press.* Managing Editor — News. *Cleveland Plain Dealer*, reporter, City Editor, Managing Editor, 1946-86. *Detroit Free Press*, Deputy Managing Editor, to 1987; Managing Editor, news, current, 1987.

McGurn, William. *The Wall Street Journal*/Europe. Deputy Editorial Page Editor. B. 1958, Oceanside, CA. U. of Notre Dame, 1980, BA-Philosophy; Boston U., 1981, MSJ. *The American Spectator*, Asst Managing Editor, to 1983. *This World*, Managing Editor, to 1984. *The Wall Street Journal*/Europe, Editorial Features Editor, to 1986; Deputy Editorial Page Editor, current, 1986.

McIntyre, Douglas A. *Financial World.* President & Chief Executive Officer. B. 1955, Eric, PA. Harvard, 1977, Religion. *Time*, 1977-82. *Penthouse*, to 1983. *Financial World*, President & Chief Exec Officer, current, 1982.

McKillop, Peter. *Newsweek.* Acting New York Bureau Chief. B. 1957, Carthage, Tunisia. Wesleyan U., 1981, African Studies. *Paterson (NJ) News,* reporter, to 1984. *Newsweek*, correspondent, 1985; Acting New York Bureau Chief, current, 1987.

McLaughlin, John. *National Review.* Washington Editor. Boston College, 1951, BA, 1952, MA-Philosophy, 1961, MA-English; Stanford, 1963, Communications; Columbia, 1967, PhD-Communications. Fairfield U. (CT), Director of Communications & educator, 1960-63. *America*, Assoc Editor, 1967-70. ABC-TV (NYC), consultant, 1969. US Senate candidate, 1970. Special asst to the President, to 1974. McLaughlin & Co, Communications Consultants, President, to 1979. "The McLaughlin Group," moderator, current. "John McLaughlin's One on One," host & Producer, current. NPR, NBC Radio Network, commentator, current. *National Review*, Washington Editor, current. Excellence in Journalism Award, Catholic Press Assn, 1970.

McLeod, Don. *Insight.* Senior Writer. B. 1936, Memphis, TN. Memphis State, 1958, BA-Sociology, 1963, MA-History. AP, Memphis, to 1967; Nashville, to 1969; Washington, to 1983. *The Washington Times*, reporter, to 1984; National Editor, to 1985. *Insight*, Senior Writer, current, 1985.

McManus, Jason. Time, Inc. Editor-in-Chief. B. 1934, Mission, KS. Davidson College, 1956, BA; Princeton, 1958, MPA; postgrad Oxford, 1958-59 (Rhodes Scholar). *Time*, Common Market Bureau Chief, Paris, 1962-64; Assoc Editor, to 1968; Senior Editor, to 1975; Asst

Managing Editor, to 1978; Exec Editor, to 1983; Time, Inc., Corporate Editor, to 1985; *Time*, Managing Editor, to 1987; Time, Inc, Editor-in-Chief, current, 1987.

McWilliams, Rita. *The Washington Times.* National Desk Reporter. B. 1959, Washington, DC. Washington College (Chestertown, MD), 1980, BA-Political Science; Boston U., 1981, MAJ. *The Banner* (Cambridge, MD), reporter, to 1983. *The Daily Progress* (Charlottesville, VA), reporter, to 1984. *The Washington Times*, regional reporter, to 1986; national desk reporter, current, 1986.

Meacham, James. *The Economist.* Military Editor. B. 1930, Portsmouth. U. of MO, 1952, BSJ; George Washington U., MS-International Affairs; US Naval War College, 1967. US Navy, Line Officer, to 1973. *The Economist*, Military Editor, current, 1974. *Arab Defence Journal*, contributor, current.

Meier, Barry. *The Wall Street Journal.* Reporter. Studied Syracuse, 1969-73, U. of NM, 1975-76. *Eclipse Press* (NY), Assoc Editor, 1978-80. *Chemical Week*, Environment Editor, 1983-84. *The Wall Street Journal*, reporter, current, 1984.

Meisels, Andrew. *The Washington Times & New York Daily News.* Israel-based Correspondent. B. 1933, Budapest, Hungary. CCNY, 1955, English. AP, NJ & NY, newsman, to 1963. ABC News, Israel correspondent, to 1982. Satellite News Channel, Israel correspondent, to 1983. *New York Daily News*, Israel-based correspondent, current, 1985. *The Washington Times*, Israel-based correspondent, current, 1985. Author *Son of a Star; Six Other Days*: contributor *Lightning Out of Israel*. Overseas Press Club Award, Best Radio Spot News Reporting from Abroad, 1974.

Meisler, Stanley. *Los Angles Times.* Paris Bureau. B. 1931, NY. CCNY, 1952, English Literature; grad work, U. of CA, African Studies. AP, New Orleans, Washington, 1954-64. *Los Angeles Times*, from 1967, Nairobi, Mexico City, Madrid, Toronto bureaus; Paris bureau, current.

Melloan, George. *The Wall Street Journal.* Deputy Editorial Page Editor & "Business World" Columnist. B. Greenwood, IN. Butler U. (IN), BSJ. *The Wall Street Journal*, copyreader, 1952; reporter; "Page One" editing staff; Editor, "Business" column; Atlanta & Cleveland Bureau Manager; foreign correspondent, London, to 1970; Editorial writer, current, 1970; Deputy Editor, Editorial Page, current, 1973; "Business World" columnist, current, 1987. Co-author (with Joan Melloan) *The Carter Economy*, 1978. Gerald Loeb Award, Distinguished Business & Financial Journalism Commentary, 1982; Inter-American Press Assn Daily Gleaner Award, 1983, '87. National Conference of Editorial Writers, member.

Menand, Louis. *The New Republic.* B. 1952. Pomona College, 1973, BA; Columbia, 1980, PhD. *The New Republic*, Assoc Editor, current, 1986.

Mendes, Joshua. *Fortune.* Personal Investing Columnist. B. 1962, NYC. Dartmouth, 1984, English Literature. *Fortune*, personal investing columnist, current, 1984.

Meriwether, Heath. *Detroit Free Press.* Executive Editor. B. 1944, Columbia, MO. U. of MO, 1966, BA-Journalism & History; Harvard, 1967, MA-Teaching. *Columbia Daily Tribune,* sports writer, to 1970. *The Miami Herald,* reporter, 1970; education writer, 1971; Broward City Editor, 1972; Palm Beach Editor, to 1975; City Desk Assignments Editor, to 1977; Exec City Editor, to 1979; Asst Managing Editor, News, to 1981; Managing Editor, to 1981; Exec Editor, to 1987. *Detroit Free Press,* Exec Editor, current, 1987. *Herald* won 2 Pulitzer Prizes under editorship, 1986.

Merry, Robert. Congressional Quarterly, Inc. Managing Editor. *The Wall Street Journal,* political writer, to 1986. *Roll Call,* Exec Editor, to 1987. *Congressional Quarterly,* Senior Editor, 1987. Congressional Quarterly, Inc, Managing Editor, current, 1987.

Mervosh, Edward. *Business Month.* Senior Editor. Washington & Jefferson College, BA; Columbia, MA. *BusinessWeek,* Economics Editor, to 1985. *U.S.News & World Report,* Senior Economics Editor, "Economic Outlook" columnist, to 1987. *Business Month,* Senior Editor, current, 1987. Co-author *The Decline of America.*

Merwin, John. *Forbes.* Senior Editor. Trinity U. (San Antonio, TX), BAJ; U. of TX, MA-Survey Research; studied Southern Methodist U., Business, Law, & Government. *Dallas Morning News,* city reporter, 1971. KERA-TV (Dallas), reporter, documentary film producer, to 1974. *D Magazine,* co-Founder. *Forbes,* Assoc Editor, West Coast, to 1980; West Coast Bureau Chief, to 1983; Senior Editor, current, 1983.

Methvin, Eugene Hilburn. *Reader's Digest.* Senior Editor. B. 1934, Vienna, GA. U. of GA, 1955, BAJ, *cum laude.* US Air Force, 1955-58. *The Vienna* (GA) *News,* 1940-51. *Constitution,* reporter, 1952. *Washington Daily News,* reporter, 1958-60. *Reader's Digest,* Washington editorial office from 1960, writer, Assoc Editor; Senior Editor, current. Author *The Riot Makers, The Technology of Social Demolition,* 1970; *The Rise of Radicalism, The Social Psychology of Messianic Extremism,* 1973. *Sigma Delta Chi* Society of Professional Journalists National Award, Public Service, Magazine Reporting, 1965.

Meyer, Cord. News America Syndicate. Foreign Affairs Columnist. B. 1920. Yale, 1942, BA, *summa cum laude*; Harvard, Society of Fellows, 1946-47, 1949-51. US Marines, 1942-45, Bronze Star, Purple Heart, Presidential Unit Citation. Special asst to Harold Stassen as member US Delegation to Founding Conference of UN, 1945. United World Federalists, President, 1947-49. CIA, 1951-67; Asst Deputy Director for Plans, to 1973; Chief of Station, London, to 1976 (3 Times awarded Distinguished Intelligence Medal). News America Syndicate, foreign affairs columnist, current, 1978. Georgetown, lecturer, 1982-85. Author 3 books including *Facing Reality,* 1980. Special Weintal Award, Foreign Affairs Column, 1986.

Meyerson, Adam. *Policy Review,* Editor. *The American Spectator,* Senior Editor. B. 1953, Philadelphia, PA. Yale, 1974, History, Arts & Letters. *The American Spectator,* Managing Editor, to 1977; Senior Editor, current. *The Wall Street Journal,* editorial writer, to 1983. *Policy Review,* Editor, current, 1983. Co-Editor (with David

Asman) *The Wall Street Journal on Management: The Best of Manager's Journal.*

Michaels, James Walker. *Forbes.* Editor. B. 1921, Buffalo, NY. Harvard, 1943, Economics, *cum laude.* WWII, served India & Burma. State Dept. UPI, New Delhi Bureau Manager. *Buffalo Evening News. Forbes,* 1954-57; Managing Editor, to 1961; Editor, current, 1961.

Miller, Judith. *The New York Times.* Washington Deputy Bureau Chief. B. 1948, NYC. Barnard College, 1969, BA-Economics; Center for European Studies, U. of Brussels; Princeton, 1972, MA. NPR, foreign affairs, national security specialist. *The Progressive,* Washington correspondent, to 1977. Freelance, current. *The New York Times,* Washington reporter, to 1983; Cairo Bureau Chief, to 1985; Paris correspondent, to 1986; Washington Deputy Bureau Chief, current, 1986.

Miller, Julie Ann. *BioScience.* Editor. B. 1950, Chicago, IL. Harvard-Radcliffe, 1971, Biochemistry. Science Writing Fellow, Marine Bio Lab, Woods Hole, 1986. *Science News,* Life Sciences Editor, 1976-86. *BioScience,* Editor, current, 1981. Freelance, current.

Miller, Matt. *The Asian Wall Street Journal.* Reporter. Macalester College (St. Paul, MN), BA-Asian Studies; U. of Philippines. *Asia Travel Trade Magazine,* Deputy Editor. Freelance photographer, journalist. *The Asian Wall Street Journal,* reporter, Hong Kong, 1981-85; reporter, New Delhi, current, 1985. Journalist of the Year, Hong Kong Newspaper Society, 1984.

Miller, Michael W. *The Wall Street Journal.* Computer Correspondent. B. 1962, NYC. Harvard, 1984, English. *The Wall Street Journal,* intern, summer 1983; San Francisco computer industry correspondent, 1984-86; M NYC & A correspondent, to 1987; computer correspondent, current, 1987.

Miller, Norman C. *Los Angeles Times.* National Editor. B. 1934, Pittsburgh, PA. PA State U., 1956, Journalism. *The Wall Street Journal,* reporter, to 1964; Detroit Bureau Chief, to 1966; Congressional correspondent, political writer, to 1973; Washington Bureau Chief, to 1983. *Los Angeles Times,* National Editor, current, 1983. Pulitzer Prize, 1964; George Polk Award, 1964.

Minard, Lawrence. *Forbes.* Deputy Managing Editor. B. 1949, Seattle, WA. Trinity College, 1972, BA-Economics. *Forbes,* reporter, 1974; writer, 1976; special economic correspondent, Japan, to 1978; European Bureau Manager, to 1983; West Coast & Pacific Bureau Manager, to 1985; Asst Managing Editor, to 1985; Deputy Managing Editor, current, 1987. Co-winner (with David L. Warsh) Gerald Loeb Award, Distinguished Financial Reporting, 1976.

Mintz, Morton. *The Washington Post.* Reporter. B. 1922, Ann Arbor, MI. U. of MI, 1943, Economics. Nieman Fellow, 1963. *St. Louis Star Times,* 1946-50. *St. Louis Globe-Democrat,* to 1958. *The Washington Post,* from 1958; currently reporter, consumer issues. Heywood Broun Award, 1963; Raymond Clapper Award, 1963; George Polk Award, 1963; DC Newspaper Guild Public Service Award, 1963; Sidney Hillman Award, 1972; A.J. Liebling Award, 1974; Worth Bingham Award, 1977; Columbia

Journalism, 1983; DC-Baltimore Newspaper Guild Public Service Award, 1977, '86 & Grand Award, 1986.

Mitchell, Andrea L. NBC News. "NBC Nightly News" White House Correspondent. B. 1946, NYC. U. of PA, 1967, BA. KYW Newsradio (Philadelphia), reporter, 1967-76. KYW-TV, political correspondent, 1972-76. WTOP-TV (Washington), energy correspondent, to 1978. NBC News, Washington, to 1981; "NBC Nightly News" White House correspondent, current, 1981. *Sigma Delta Chi*, 1975; Women in Communications, Communicator of Year Award, 1976; AP Public Affairs Reporting Award, 1976; AP Broadcast Award, 1977.

Mohr, Charles. *The New York Times.* "Outdoors" Columnist. B. 1929, Loup City, NE. U. of NE, 1951, History & Journalism. *The Lincoln Star*, to 1951. UPI, Chicago, to 1953. *Time*, to 1963. *The New York Times*, Presidential campaign, 1964, '76; White House correspondent, to 1965, '77; Vietnam Bureau Chief, to 1966; SE Asia correspondent, to 1970; Africa correspondent, to 1975; Washington staff, 1978-87; "Outdoors" columnist, current, 1987.

Mohr, Major General Henry. Heritage Features Syndicate. Columnist. B. 1919, St. Louis County, MO. US Army Command & General Staff College, Military Tactics & Strategy. Heritage Foundation Journalism Fellow, 1984. US Army: decorated, Distinguished Service Medal; Meritorious Service Award, Director of Selective Service, 1987. Freelance, current. Heritage Features Syndicate, defense & national security columnist, current.

Molotsky, Irvin D. *The New York Times.* Consumer & Cultural Affairs Reporter. B. 1938, Camden, NJ. Temple, 1960, BS. *The Trentonian* (NJ), reporter, Editor. *Newsday* (NY), Editor, Nassau office; Editor, Suffolk office. *The New York Times*, Copy Editor, metro desk; Editor, "Long Island Weekly" section; Asst Metro Editor; Asst Family/Style Editor; Long Island Bureau Chief, 1967-79; Washington reporter; Night Editor; consumer news & cultural affairs reporter, Washington, current. SUNY at Stony Brook, NYU, Brooklyn College, American U., C.W. Post College, teacher.

Monaghan, Nancy C. *USA Today.* Managing Editor. City Newspapers, Rochester, NY, Metro Editor, 1973-75. *Democrat And Chronicle*, Rochester, NY, legal affairs reporter; Metro Editor, 1977-82. *USA Today*, National Editor, to 1983; Managing Editor, current, 1983. NY State Press Assoc Award, 1973, '74, '75; Women in Communications, Matrix Award, 1981; NY State AP Award, 1981, '82.

Monroe, Bill. *Washington Journalism Review.* Editor. B. 1920, New Orleans. Tulane, 1942, Philosophy. UPI, 1941-42. WNOE Radio (New Orleans), News Director, 1946-49. *New Orleans Item*, Assoc Editor, to 1956. WDSU-TV (New Orleans), news director, to 1961. NBC News, Bureau Chief, to 1969; "Today" Washington Editor, to 1976; "Meet The Press" Exec Producer & moderator, to 1986. *Washington Journalism Review*, Editor, current, 1987. Peabody Award, 1972; Paul White Award (RTNDA), 1976.

Montalbano, William D. *Los Angeles Times.* Rome Bureau Chief. B. 1940, NY. Rutgers, 1960, BA-English; Columbia, 1962, MSJ. *Star Ledger* (Newark, NJ),

reporter, to 1962. *Quincy* (MA) *Patriot-Ledger*, reporter-Editor, to 1963. *Buenos Aires Herald*, reporter, Editor, to 1965. UPI, Cables Desk, NY, to 1967. *The Miami Herald*, Latin America correspondent, senior correspondent, Projects Editor, Founding Peking Bureau Chief, Chief of Correspondents, to 1983. *Los Angeles Times*, Founding El Salvador Bureau Chief, to 1984; Buenos Aires Bureau Chief, to 1987; Rome Bureau Chief, current, 1987. Co-author 3 books. Cabot Prize, Ernie Pyle, Overseas Press Club.

Moody, John. *Time.* Central America Correspondent. B. 1953, Pittsburgh, PA. Cornell, 1975, Industrial & Labor Relations. UPI, Pittsburgh, NY, Moscow Bureau Chief, Paris Bureau Chief, to 1982. *Time*, Bonn, Eastern Europe Bureau Chief; NY writer; Central America correspondent, current, 1982. Co-author *The Priest And The Policeman*, 1987.

Morgenson, Gretchen. *Forbes.* Associate Editor. B. 1956, State College, PA. St. Olaf College, 1976, BA-English & History. Dean Witter Reynolds, stockbroker, 1981-84. *Money*, writer, to 1986. Freelance, current. *Vogue*, personal finance columnist. *Forbes*, Assoc Editor, current, 1987. Co-author *The Woman's Guide To The Stock Market,* 1981.

Morley, Jefferson. *The Nation.* Washington Editor. B. 1958, NYC. Yale, 1980, History. *Worthington* (MN) *Globe*, reporter, summer 1978. *Minneapolis Tribune*, reporter, summer 1979. *The Washington Post*, reporter, summer, 1981. *Foreign Policy*, editorial asst, 1981. Asst to Bruce Cameron, human rights lobbyist, to 1982. *Harper's,* Asst Editor, 1983. *The New Republic*, Assoc Editor, to 1987. *The Nation*, Washington Editor, current, 1987.

Morrison, David. *National Journal.* National Security Correspondent. B. 1953, Minneapolis, MN. Columbia, 1978, History, 1982, MSJ. Center for Defense Information, Senior Research Analyst, to 1985. Freelance, current, 1980. *National Journal*, national security correspondent, current, 1985. Olive Branch Award, 1987.

Morrison, James. *The Washington Times.* London-based Correspondent. *Alexandria Gazette. The Washington Star. The Washington Times*, foreign desk reporter, to 1987; London-based correspondent, current, 1987.

Morrison, Mark. *BusinessWeek.* Senior Editor. U. of TX. The Houston Post, reporter, to 1974. *BusinessWeek*, correspondent, Houston, to 1978; Chicago Bureau Manager; Senior Editor, current, corporate strategies, management, marketing, people.

Mortimer, Edward. *Financial Times.* Assistant Foreign Editor. B. 1943, Burford, UK. Balliol, Oxford, 1962, History. Fellow of All Souls, Oxford, 1965-72, 1984-86; Senior Carnegie Endowment, assoc, 1980-81. *The Times* (London), asst Paris correspondent, 1967-70; foreign specialist & leader writer, 1973-85. *Financial Times*, Asst Foreign Editor, current, 1987. Author *Faith And Power — The Politics Of Islam*, 1982; *The World That FDR Built*, 1988.

Mosher, Lawrence. *National Journal.* Contributing Editor. B. 1929, LA, CA. Stanford, 1951, History,

Journalism. *The Record* (Bergen, NJ), reporter, 1958-59. *New York World-Telegram & The Sun*, reporter, to 1962. Copley News Service, foreign correspondent, Hong Kong, Beirut, to 1967. *The National Observer*, reporter, to 1977. Georgetown, Center for Contemporary Arab Studies, writer-in-residence, to 1979. *National Journal*, writer; Contributing Editor, current, 1979. *The Water Reporter* (newsletter), Publisher & Editor, current, 1984. Co-author 3 books *World Resources 1987*, 1987. Copley Ring of Truth Award, Best Foreign Reporting, 1965; National Wildlife Federation Communicator of the Year Award, 1982. George Polk Award, Environmental Reporting, 1986.

Moss, Adam. *Esquire.* Deputy Editor. B. 1957, Brooklyn, NY. Oberlin College, 1979, English & Government. *Rolling Stone College Papers*, Assoc Editor. *Rolling Stone*, Projects Editor. *Esquire*, Managing Editor; Senior Editor; Deputy Editor, current, 1981.

Mossberg, Walter. *The Wall Street Journal.* Senior Washington Correspondent. *The Wall Street Journal*, reporter; Deputy Washington Bureau Chief, to 1987; senior Washington correspondent, current, 1987.

Moyers, Bill D. PBS Televison. Journalist. B. 1934, Hugo, OK. U. of TX, 1956, BJ, with honors; U. of Edinburgh, Scotland, 1957; SW Baptist Theological Seminary, 1959, BD, with honors. Aspen Institute, Arthur Morse Fellow. Sen. Lyndon Johnson's personal asst, 1960; special asst to President, 1963-67; press secretary, 1965-67. Peace Corps, Assoc Director, to 1962; Deputy Director, to 1963. *Newsday* (NY), Publisher, 1967-70. *Newsweek*, Editor, 1974-75. *Bill Moyers Journal*, Editor-in-Chief, to 1976; 1978-81. CBS-TV, "CBS Reports" Editor, Chief Correspondent, 1976-78; CBS News, Senior News Analyst, 1981-87. PBS Television, journalist, current, 1987. Author *Listening to America*, 1971. Dupont Award, 1979; George Polk Award, 1981; Emmy Award, 1983, '84, '85; National Academy of TV Arts & Sciences Award, 1974, '78; 1980-85.

Mudd, Roger H. PBS Television. "MacNeil/Lehrer NewsHour" Commentator. B. 1928, Washington. Washington & Lee U., 1950, AB; U. of NC, 1953, MA. Darlington School (Rome, GA), teacher, 1951-52. *Richmond News Leader*, reporter, 1953. WRNL (Richmond), News Director, to 1956. WTOP (Washington), reporter, to 1961. CBS, correspondent; Chief Washington Correspondent, to 1980. NBC News, broadcaster, to 1987. PBS Television, "MacNeil/Lehrer NewsHour" commentator, current, 1987.

Mufson, Steve. *BusinessWeek.* Stringer. B. NYC. Yale, 1980, BA. *Yale Daily News*, Editor-in-Chief. *Steady Work* (Yale periodical), Co-Editor, Co-Founder. *The Wall Street Journal*, intern, summer 1979; NY reporter, 1980-84; London reporter, to 1986. *BusinessWeek*, stringer, South Africa, current, 1987.

Mullin, Dennis. *U.S.News & World Report.* White House Correspondent. Edward R. Murrow Fellow, 1985-86. *U.S.News & World Report*, Middle East Bureau Chief, 1974-79; diplomatic correspondent, to 1985; White House correspondent, current, 1986.

Munro, Ross H. *Time.* South Asia Bureau Chief. B. 1941, Vancouver, Canada. U. of British Columbia, 1965, BA-

Political Science; postgrad Stanford. *The Globe & Mail* (Toronto, Canada), various beats & bureaus, 1967-71; Washington Bureau Chief, to 1975; Peking Bureau Chief, to 1977. *Time*, Pacific, Asia economic correspondent, to 1980; Hong Kong Bureau Chief, to 1982; national security correspondent, Washington, to 1985; South Asia Bureau Chief, current, 1985.

Murchison, William. *The Dallas Morning News* & Heritage Features Syndicate. Columnist. B. 1942, Corsicana, TX. U. of TX, 1963, BA-History; Stanford, 1964, MA. *Corsicana Daily Sun*, reporter, to 1966. *Dallas Times Herald*, reporter, editorial writer, to 1973. *Dallas Morning News*, editorial writer, Assoc Editor, to 1986; columnist, current, 1986. Heritage Features Syndicate, columnist, current. *National Review, Policy Review, Human Events, & The American Spectator*, contributor, current. Dallas Press Club Editorial Writing Award, 1972, '77, '84.

Murdoch, Keith Rupert. *New York Post.* Publisher. B. 1931, Melbourne, Australia. Worchester College, Oxford, 1953, MA. News American Publishing Inc, Chairman: *New York Post, New York Magazine, Village Voice*, current, 1977; *The Star, San Antonio Express and News*, current, 1974; *Boston Herald, Sun-Times*, 1983. News International Ltd Group, Chairman, London, current. News Ltd Group & Associated Companies, Chief Exec Managing Director, Australia, current, 1983.

Murray, Alan S. *The Wall Street Journal.* Washington Economics Reporter. B. 1954, Akron, OH. U. of NC, Chapel Hill, 1977, English, highest honors; London School of Economics, 1980, MS-Economics, with distinction. Morehead Scholar. U. of NC, 1973-77; Luce Scholar, Japan, 1981-82. *The Chattanooga Times*, Business & Economics Editor, 1977-79. *Congressional Quarterly*, international economics reporter, 1980-81, 1982-83. *Japan Economic Journal*, reporter, Tokyo, 1981-82. *The Wall Street Journal*, Washington economics reporter, current, 1983. Co-author (with Jeffrey Birnbaum) *Showdown At Gucci Gulch; Lawmakers, Lobbyists and the Unlikely Triumph of Tax Reform*, 1987.

Mydans, Seth. *The New York Times.* Manila Bureau Chief. B. 1946. Harvard, 1968. *The Boston Globe*, Copy Editor, 1971-73. AP, correspondent, Moscow, Bangkok, London, Boston, NY, to 1981. *Newsweek*, correspondent, Moscow, Bangkok, London, to 1983. *The New York Times*, metro reporter, to 1984; Moscow correspondent, to 1985; Manila Bureau Chief, current, 1985.

Mysak, Joe. *The Bond Buyer.* Assistant Managing Editor. B. 1957, Brooklyn, NY. Columbia, 1979, English. *More*, intern, 1975. Access Daily News Intelligence Service, Desk Editor, 1979-80. *The Bond Buyer*, from 1981: Copy Editor; reporter; Asst Managing Editor, current. *The American Spectator, National Review*, contributor. *The Bond Buyer* "Publisher's Award," 1983, '84.

Nagorski, Andrew. *Newsweek.* Bonn Bureau Chief. B. 1947, Edinburgh, Scotland. Amherst College, 1969, *Phi Beta Kappa*. *Newsweek*, writer, Assoc Editor, General Editor, to 1978 (*Newsweek International*); Asian Editor (International), Hong Kong Bureau Chief, to 1980; Moscow Bureau Chief, expelled 1982; Rome Bureau Chief, to 1985; Bonn Bureau Chief, current, 1985.

Freelance, current. Author *Reluctant Farewell: An American Reporter's Candid Look Inside The Soviet Union*, 1985: contributor *Africa and the United States*, 1978. Overseas Press Club Award, Best Business Reporting from Abroad, 1978: co-winner (with Peter Younghusband) Overseas Press Club Award, 1974.

Naj, Amal K. *The Wall Street Journal.* Auto Industry Reporter. B. 1951, Madras, India. Wilson College, Bombay, 1971, BS, The Queen's U., Belfast, 1975, Economics. *The Wall Street Journal*, 1978; auto industry reporter, Detroit, current, 1983.

Nasar, Sylvia. *Fortune.* Associate Editor. Antioch College, BA-Literature; NYU, MA-Economics. Institute for Economic Analysis, NYU, asst research scientist. Scientists' Institute for Public Information, Director of Energy Programs. Control Data Corp, Senior Economist. *Fortune*, Assoc Editor, current, 1983. Co-author (with Wassily Leontief, James Koo, Ira Sohn) *The Future of Nonfuel Minerals in the U.S. and World Economy*, 1983.

Navasky, Victor Saul. *The Nation.* Editor. B. 1932, NYC. Swarthmore College, 1954, AB, *Phi Beta Kappa.* Guggenheim Fellow, 1974-75. Russell Sage Foundation, visiting prof, to 1976. Ferris Prof of Journalism, to 1977. US Army, 1954-56. Special asst to Governor G. Mennen Williams (MI), 1959-60. *Monocle Magazine*, Editor & Publisher, to 1965. *The New York Times Magazine*, Editor, 1970-72. *The Nation*, Editor, current, 1978. Author *Kennedy Justice*, 1971; *Naming Names*, 1980.

Neff, Robert. *BusinessWeek.* Editor International Edition. B. 1947, St. Louis, MO. U. of MI, 1969, Political Science; U. of MO, 1974, Journalism. *Pacific Business News*, Honolulu News Editor, to 1976. *Kansas City Star*, reporter, to 1977. McGraw-Hill World News, Tokyo Bureau Chief, 1979-83. *International Management*, London Managing Editor, to 1986. *BusinessWeek*, LA correspondent, 1977-79; LA Bureau Chief, 1986-87; International Edition Editor, current, 1987. Inland Daily Press Assn, 1st Place Local Reporting, 1974.

Neher, Jacques. Freelance Writer. B. 1953, Cleveland, OH. U. of FL, 1975, BS-Journalism & Latin American Studies. *Tampa Times*, City Hall & Courts reporter, to 1977. *Rubber & Plastics News*, Managing Editor, to 1978. *Advertising Age*, reporter, to 1981. *Crain's Cleveland Business*, Editor, to 1985. Freelance, business & economics, current. Jesse Neale Award, 1981; *Sigma Delta Chi* Cleveland Press Club, 1st Place Editorial Writing, 1984.

Neikirk, William R. *Chicago Tribune.* Washington Economics Correspondent. B. 1938, Irvine, KY. U. of KY, 1960, BAJ. *The Kernal* (U. of KY), Editor, 1959-60. *Lexington* (KY) *Herald*, Asst State Editor, 1960. AP, 1961-70; economic reporter, to 1974; Chief Economics Correspondent, 1974. *Chicago Tribune*, economics correspondent, Washington, to 1977; White House correspondent, 1977; Washington economics correspondent, to 1983, current, 1984; Washington Bureau News Editor, 1983-84. Co-author *The Work Revolution*, 1983. *Chicago Tribune* Edward Scott Beck Award, 1975; U. of MO Business Writing Award, 1978, '79. John Hancock Business Writing Award, 1978, '79; Gerald Loeb Business Writing Award, 1978; Peter Lisagor Award,

1978, '84; Champion Media Award, Business Writing, 1979.

Neilan, Edward. *The Washington Times.* Tokyo Bureau Chief. B. 1932, Torrance, CA. USC, 1954, BA-Journalism & Political Science; U. of London, Institute for International Education Scholarship, postgrad, summer 1956. Thomas Jefferson Fellow in Communications, U. of HI, 1973. *The Daily Trojan*, USC, Managing Editor, to 1954. *Evening Star-News* (Culver City, CA), Sports Editor, reporter, 1950-54; City Editor, reporter, to 1957. Consultant, Ministry of Information, Republic of Korea, to 1960. *The Christian Science Monitor*, contract Tokyo correspondent, 1960-62. Copley News Service, Tokyo correspondent, SE Asia Bureau Chief, 1962-70; diplomatic & national correspondent, Washington, 1970-76. *The Asia Mail*, "American Perspectives on Asia & the Pacific," Editor, Founder, 1976-82. The Alexandria Gazette Corporation, President, Editor & Publisher; columnist; *The Alexandria Gazette, Springfield Independent, Burke Herald, Fairfax Tribune*, CEO, 1979-82. *The Washington Times*, Asst Foreign Editor, 1982; Foreign Editor, to 1986; Tokyo Bureau Chief, current, 1986. Overseas Press Club Award, Excellence, 1974; UPI Award, 1981. Co-author (with Charles M. Smith) *The Future of the China Market: Prospects for Sino-American Trade*, 1974.

Nelson, Anne. Freelance Writer. B. 1954, Fort Sill, OK. Yale, 1976, American Studies. *The New Yorker*, editorial staff, to 1977. Freelance writer & photographer, to 1983. *Maclean's*, Central America correspondent, 1980-83. Canadian Broadcasting Corporation, assoc producer, NY, "The Journal," to 1984. Independent writer & consultant, current, specializing in Latin America, 1984. Author *Murder Under Two Flags*, 1986.

Nelson, John H. (Jack). *Los Angeles Times.* Washington Bureau Chief. B. 1929, Talladega, AL. GA State U., Economics; Harvard, Politics, History, Public Administration. Nieman Fellow. *Daily Herald* (Biloxi, MS), reporter, to 1949. *Constitution*, writer, to 1965. *Los Angeles Times*, Atlanta Bureau Chief, to 1970; investigative reporter, Washington, to 1975; Washington Bureau Chief, current, 1975. PBS, "Washington Week in Review", current, frequent appearances. Author *Captive Voices - High School Journalism In America*: co-author 3 books. Pulitzer Prize, 1960; Drew Pearson Award, Investigative Reporting, 1975.

Newport John Paul Jr. *Fortune.* Associate Editor. B. 1954, Fort Worth, TX. Harvard, 1977, English, *cum laude. Fort Worth Star-Telegram*, reporter, to 1982. *Fortune*, reporter/researcher, to 1986; Assoc Editor, Wall Street, current, 1986. John Hancock Award, Business & Financial Journalism, 1981.

Newton, Maxwell. *New York Post.* Financial & Economic Columnist. *The Australian Financial Review*, Founding Editor (only national financial daily). *The Australian*, Founding Editor (only national daily). Financial & economic columnist, current, appearing in *New York Post, Sun-Times, Boston Herald, The Times* (London, UK) & 4 Australian papers. Author *The Fed.*

Nielsen, John. *Fortune.* Associate Editor. B. Highland Park, IL. US Naval Academy, Annapolis. *Newsweek*, General Editor. *Time*, Assoc Editor. *Fortune*, Assoc Editor, current, 1984.

Noah, Timothy. *Newsweek.* Congress Correspondent. B. 1958, NYC. Harvard, 1980, English. *The New Republic,* intern, 1980; writer, 1981-82. *The New York Times* Asst Op-Ed Page Editor, to 1983. *The Washington Monthly,* Editor, to 1985. Freelance, to 1986. *Newsweek,* Congress correspondent, current, 1986.

Noble, Kenneth B. *The New York Times.* Justice Department & Legal Correspondent. B. 1953, NYC. Yale, 1975, American Studies & Literature; U. of CA-Berkeley, 1978, Law Degree. *The New York Times,* from 1979: reporter, Wall Street; SEC & Labor correspondent, Washington; Justice Dept & legal correspondent, current.

Nordland, Rod. *Newsweek.* Deputy Foreign Editor, Senior Writer & Roving Foreign Correspondent. B. 1949, Philadelphia, PA. PA State, 1972, Journalism. *Philadelphia Inquirer,* investigative reporter, to 1978; Asia correspondent (Bangkok), to 1982; Central America correspondent, to 1984. *Newsweek,* Beirut & Cairo Bureau Chief, to 1986; Deputy Editor, senior writer & roving foreign correspondent, current, 1986. Author of *Names And Numbers: A Journalist's Guide To The Most Needed Information Sources And Contacts,* 1978: Editor, *The Watergate Files* 1973. Pulitzer Prize, Local Reporting, 1978; George Polk Award, 1982; Thomas L. Stokes & Edward J. Meeman awards, 1982.

Novak, Michael. *National Review.* "Tomorrow & Tomorrow" Columnist. B. 1933, Johnstown, PA. Stonehill College, 1956, AB; Harvard, 1965, MA; Gregorian U. (Rome); Catholic U. Harvard, Teaching Fellow. Stanford, asst prof of Humanities, to 1968. SUNY at Old Westbury, prof, to 1973. Rockefeller Foundation, Humanities Program, to 1976. Syracuse, Ledden-Watson Distinguished Prof of Religion, 1976. *Catholicism in Crisis & This World,* co-Founder. American Enterprise Institute, Resident Scholar, 1978-87; Director of social & political studies, current, 1987. Freelance, current. Syndicated Columnist, "Illusions & Realities," current. *National Review,* columnist, "Tomorrow & Tomorrow," current. Author 13 books, including *Will It Liberate: Questions about Liberation Theology,* 1986: co-author 2 books. George Washington Honor Medal, Freedoms Foundation, 1984; Award of Excellence, Religion in Media, 8th Annual Angel Awards, 1985; 1st US member Argentina National Academy of Sciences, Morals & Politics, 1985.

Novak, Robert D. News America Syndicate. "Inside Report" Columnist (with Rowland Evans). B. 1931, Joliet, IL. U. of IL, 1952. *Champaign-Urbana Courier,* reporter, 1952. US Army, to 1954. AP, Omaha, NE; Lincoln, NE; statehouse & political reporter, Indianapolis, to 1957; Capitol Hill reporter, to 1958. *The Wall Street Journal,* Senate correspondent & political reporter, to 1961; Chief Congressional Correspondent, to 1963. News America Syndicate, "Inside Report" columnist (with Rowland Evans), current, 1963. *Evans-Novak Political Report,* biweekly newsletter co-author (with Rowland Evans), current. *Evans-Novak Tax Report,* biweekly newsletter co-author (with Rowland Evans). *Reader's Digest,* Roving Editor (with Rowland Evans), current. Freelance. CNN, "Evans & Novak" "Insiders" co-host (with Rowland Evans), current. CNN, "Crossfire," & NBC, "Meet the Press," current. "The McLaughlin Group," panelist, current. Author *The Agony of the GOP,* 1965; co-author (with Rowland Evans) 3 books, including *The Reagan Revolution,* 1981.

Nulty, Peter. *Fortune.* Associate Editor. B. 1943, NYC. Wesleyan U.; 1965, Columbia, MA-International Affairs. *Middle East Monitor,* Editor & *Middle East Journal,* Asst Editor, 1970-75. *Fortune,* reporter/researcher; Assoc Editor, current, 1976.

Oakes, John B. *The New York Times.* Senior Editor (Retired). B. 1913, Elkins Park, PA. Princeton, 1934, AB, valedictorian, *Phi Beta Kappa*; U. of Dijon, France, 1935; Queen's College, Oxford, AB, AM, 1936 (Rhodes Scholar). US Army, 1941-46; Bronze Star, member of Order of British Empire (UK), *Croix de Guerre* (France). *State Gazette,* reporter. *Trenton* (NJ) *Times,* reporter, 1936-37. *The Washington Post,* reporter, special feature writer, to 1941. *The New York Times,* Sunday department, 1946; Editor of "Review of the Week," to 1949; Editorial Board member, to 1961; Editor, Editorial Page, to 1977; Senior Editor, 1977; now retired. Columbia-Catherwood Award, 1960; Collegiate School Award of Honor, 1963; George Polk Memorial Award, 1966; Thomas Jefferson Award of Unitarian Universalist District of NY, 1968; Silurian Society Award; Woodrow Wilson Award, 1970.

Oberdorfer, Don. *The Washington Post.* National Staff. B. Atlanta, GA. Princeton, BA-International Affairs. Ferris Prof of Journalism, 1977. *The Charlotte Observer,* Washington correspondent; local reporter. *The Saturday Evening Post,* Assoc Editor. Knight newspapers, national correspondent. *The Washington Post,* White House & diplomatic affairs correspondent, 1968-72; Tokyo correspondent, to 1975; national staff, current, 1977. Author *Tet!,* 1971.

Oberfeld, Kirk E. *Insight.* Managing Editor. B. 1945, Orange, NJ. Kalamazoo College (MI), 1967, BA-Political Science; OH State U., 1971, MAJ. UPI, writer, summers 1970, '71. *Battle Creek* (MI) *Enquirer and News,* Editorial Page Editor, to 1973; City Editor, to 1975. *Philadelphia Bulletin,* NJ News Editor, to 1976; "Focus" Editor, to 1977; Director of News Technology, to 1978. *The Washington Star,* Principal Asst Metro Editor, to 1980; Principal Asst Features Editor, to 1981. *The Washington Times,* Deputy Features Editor, to 1983; Asst Managing Editor, to 1985; National Edition Editor, 1985. *Insight,* Managing Editor, current, 1985. National Design Awards.

O'Brien, Conor Cruise. *The Atlantic.* Contributing Editor. Trinity College (Dublin), PhD-History. Irish Foreign Office, Asst Secretary-General & Deputy Chief, Irish delegation to UN. Personal representative, UN Secretary-General Dag Hammarskjold, the Congo, 1961. U. of Ghana, vice-chancellor. NYU, Albert Schweitzer Prof of Humanities. *The Atlantic,* Contributing Editor, current. Author many books, including *The Siege: Zionism and Israel,* 1986.

O'Connor, Clint. *Washington Journalism Review.* Associate Editor. B. 1958, Evanston, IL. Boston College, BA-English. WVNH Radio, News Director, 1982-84. *Washington Journalism Review,* writer, Asst Editor, to 1986; Assoc Editor, current, 1986.

Oka, Takashi. *The Christian Science Monitor.* Japan Correspondent. B. Japan. Postgrad Harvard, Fellow, Institute of Current World Affairs, 1964-66. *The New York Times,* Tokyo News Bureau Head, 1968-71. Set up Japanese edition, *Newsweek,* 1986. *The Christian Science Monitor,* copyboy, summer 1950; foreign correspondent, to 1964; opened Peking bureau, 1979; Chief Far Eastern Correspondent; Japan correspondent, current, 1986.

O'Leary, Jeremiah. *The Washington Times.* White House Correspondent. B. 1919, Washington, DC. George Washington U., 1941, English. *The Washington Star*, City Hall & State Dept reporter, nearly 45 years; Asst City Editor; Latin America; White House, to 1981. National Security Council, asst to William P. Clark, to 1982. *The Washington Times*, White House correspondent, current, to 1982. 1st Prize, National Reporting, DC Newspaper Guild, 1963, Kennedy assassination coverage; Maria Moors Cabot Gold Medal, 1980.

O'Leary, Timothy. *The Washington Times.* Business Writer. B. 1956, Alexandria, VA. George Washington U., 1980, BA-English Literature; Columbia, 1982, MSJ. *The Washington Star*, editorial asst, to 1981. *The Times-Picayune/States-Item* (New Orleans), reporter, to 1983. *The Washington Times*, reporter, to 1984; Latin America correspondent, 1984; Asst Foreign Editor, 1986-87; business writer, current, 1987.

Omestad, Thomas. *Foreign Policy.* Associate Editor. B. 1960, Minneapolis, MN. U. of MN, 1982, BS-Economics. *Foreign Policy*, editorial asst, Washington, 1984. AP, reporter (Pierre, SD), 1985. *Los Angeles Times*, reporter, to 1987. *Foreign Policy*, Assoc Editor, current, 1987.

Ostling, Richard. *Time.* Associate Editor & Writer. B. 1940, Endicott, NY. U. of MI, 1962, AB; Northwestern, 1963, MSJ; George Washington U., 1970, MA-Religion. *Morning News & Evening Journal* (Wilmington, DE), copyreader, reporter, to 1965. *Christianity Today*, Asst News Editor; News Editor, to 1969. *Time*, staff correspondent, to 1974; writer & Assoc Editor, current, 1975. CBS Radio, syndicated "Report on Religion," 1979.

O'Sullivan, John. *The Times* of London. Associate Editor. B. 1942, Liverpool, UK. London U., 1965, BA-Classics. Harvard, 1983, Fellow, Institute of Politics. Irish radio/TV, London correspondent, to 1972. *Daily Telegraph* (UK), "Parliamentary Sketch" writer, editorial writer, to 1977; Asst Editor, to 1979; Chief Asst Editor, to 1984, columnist, to 1986. *Policy Review*, Editor, to 1983. *The New York Post*, Editorial Page Editor, to 1986. *The American Spectator*, columnist, to 1986. *The Times* of London, columnist, to 1986; Assoc Editor, current, 1986.

Ottaway, David B. *The Washington Post.* Diplomatic & National Security Correspondent. B. 1939, New York. Harvard, 1962, History; Columbia, 1972, PhD-Political Science. UPI, Paris & Algiers correspondent, 1962-63. *Time & The New York Times*, Algeria correspondent, to 1966; Africa correspondent, 1974-79; Cairo Bureau Chief & Middle East correspondent, 1981-85. *The Washington Post*, diplomatic & national security correspondent, current, 1985. Co-author (with Marina Ottaway) 3 books including *Afrocommunism*, 1981. 2 Overseas Press Club Awards 1974, '82.

Page, Robert E. *Chicago Sun-Times.* President, Publisher & Chief Executive Officer. B. IL. Wesleyan U. *Illinois State Journal* from 1952. UPI, reporter & exec, 20 years; business manager, 1964-67; Asia wire service operations, 1972-80. *The Boston Herald*, President & Publisher, 1981. *San Antonio Express News*, General Manager, 1981. *Chicago Sun-Times*, President, Publisher & CEO, current, 1984. Board of Directors Newspaper Advertising Bureau, member, current. UPI Advisory Board, member, current. Outstanding Alumnus of the Year Award, 1979; Communicator of the Year Award, Jewish United Fund, 1987.

Paley, William S. CBS Television. Consultant. B. 1901, Chicago, IL. Studied U. of Chicago, 1918-19; U. of PA, 1922, BA. US Army, WWII, Dep. Chief Psychological Warfare Division. Congress Cigar Co, VP, secretary, to 1928. CBS Inc, President, to 1946; Chairman of the Board, to 1983; consultant, current, 1983. Whitcom Investment Co, Director, partner, current, 1983. Awards too numerous to list.

Parker, Laura. *The Washington Post.* Transportation Reporter. Nieman Fellow, 1986. *Seattle Post-Intelligencer*, reporter, 1979-86. *The Washington Post*, transportation reporter, current, 1987.

Parker, Maynard. *Newsweek.* Editor. B. 1940, LA, CA. Stanford, 1962, AB-History; Columbia, 1963, MSJ. *Life*, NYC reporter, to 1964; Hong Kong correspondent, to 1967. *Newsweek*, Hong Kong correspondent, to 1969; Saigon Bureau Chief, to 1970; Hong Kong Bureau Chief, to 1973; Managing Editor, (*Newsweek International*), to 1975; Senior Editor, National Affairs, to 1977; Asst Managing Editor, to 1980; Exec Editor, to 1982; Editor, current, 1982.

Parks, Michael. *Los Angeles Times.* Southern Africa Correspondent. B. 1943, Detroit, MI. U. of Windsor (Canada), 1965, English Literature & Classics. *The Detroit News*, reporter, 1962-65. Time-Life News Service, correspondent, to 1966. *The Suffolk* (NY) *Sun*, Asst City Editor, to 1968. *The Sun*, political reporter, to 1970; Saigon Bureau Chief, to 1972; Moscow Bureau Chief, to 1975; Middle East correspondent, to 1978; Hong Kong Bureau Chief, to 1979; Peking correspondent, to 1980. *Los Angeles Times*, Peking correspondent, to 1984; Southern Africa correspondent, current, 1984. Overseas Press Club citation, 1986; Pulitzer Prize, International Reporting, 1987.

Patterson, Jack. *BusinessWeek.* Editorial Page Editor (Retired 1987). Emory U.; postgrad, Columbia. *BusinessWeek*, Asst Marketing Editor, 1955-59; Atlanta Bureau Manager, to 1966; Cities Editor, to 1973; Assoc Editor; Senior Writer; Editor, Books Dept; Editorial Page Editor, retired 1987.

Pear, Robert. *The New York Times.* Washington Reporter. B. 1949, Washington. Harvard, 1971, BA-English, History & Literature, *magna cum laude, Phi Beta Kappa*; Henry Prize Fellow, Balliol College, Oxford, 1973; Master of Philosophy; Columbia, 1974, MSJ. Pulitzer Traveling Fellow, Henry Woodward Sackett Prize. *The Washington Star*, Harvard correspondent, to 1971; summer intern; reporter, 1974-79; Bureau Chief, to 1979. *The New York Times*, reporter, Washington, current, 1979.

Pearlstine, Norman. *The Wall Street Journal.* Managing Editor & Vice-President. Haverford College (PA), 1964; U. of PA Law, 1967. *The Wall Street Journal*, reporter, to 1973; Toyko Bureau Chief, to 1976; Managing Editor, *The Asian Wall Street Journal*, to 1978. *Forbes*, Exec

Editor, to 1980. *The Wall Street Journal*, National News Editor, to 1982; Editor & Publisher (*The Wall Street Journal*/Europe), to 1983; Managing Editor, NY, current, 1983; VP, current, 1983.

Peirce, Neal R. *National Journal.* Co-Founder & Contributing Editor. B. 1932, Philadelphia, PA. Princeton, 1954, History, *Phi Beta Kappa. Congressional Quarterly*, Political Editor, 1960-69. NBC News, consultant, commentator, national elections, to 1966. CBS News, consultant, commentator, national elections, to 1976. *Washington Post* Writer's Group, columnist, current, 1975. *National Journal*, co-Founder, 1969; Contributing Editor, current. Author *The People's President*, 1968; co-author (with Jerry Hagstrom) *The Book Of America: Inside 50 States Today*, 1983. American Political Science Assn Carey McWilliams Award, Political Reporting, 1986.

Peretz, Martin. *The New Republic.* Editor-in-Chief. B. 1939, NYC. Brandeis, 1959, BA; Harvard, 1965, MA, 1966, PhD; Bard College, 1982, PhD-Hebrew Literature. Woodrow Wilson Fellow, 1959-61. Harvard instructor, 1965-68; asst prof, to 1972; Social Studies lecturer, current, 1972. *The New Republic*, Editorial Board Chairman, 1974-75; Editor-in-Chief, current, 1975. U. of MO School of Journalism Medal of Excellence, 1982.

Perle, Richard N. *U.S.News & World Report.* Contributing Editor. B. 1941, NYC. USC, 1964, BA-International Relations; Princeton, 1967, MA-Politics. Senate Committees; Government Operations & Armed Services; Arms Control Subcommittee; personal staff of Senator Henry M. Jackson, 1969-80. Asst Secretary of Defense for International Security Policy, to 1987. American Enterprise Institute, resident scholar, current, 1987. *U.S.News & World Report*, Contributing Editor, current, 1987.

Perry, James. *The Wall Street Journal.* Washington Political Reporter. B. 1927, Elmira, NY. Trinity, 1950, English. *Leatherneck Magazine*, 1946. *Hartford Times*, reporter, 1950-52. *Philadelphia Bulletin*, general & rewrite, to 1962. *National Observer*, politics, to 1977. *The Wall Street Journal*, politics, Washington, to 1985; politics, London, to 1987; Washington political reporter, current, 1987.

Peters, Charles. *The Washington Monthly.* Editor-in-Chief. B. 1926, Charleston, WVA. Columbia, 1949, Humanities. Poynter Fellow, Yale, 1980. *The Washington Monthly*, Editor-in-Chief, current, 1969. Columbia Journalism Award, 1978.

Pfaff, William W. III. *The International Herald Tribune & Los Angeles Times* Syndicate, Political Columnist. *The New Yorker*, "Reflections" Contributor. B. 1928, Council Bluffs, IA. U. of Notre Dame, 1949, Philosophy of Literature. Rockefeller Grant, International Studies, Senior Fellow, Columbia Russian Institute. Infantry, Special Forces Unit, US Army, Korean War & after. *The Commonweal*, Assoc Editor, 1949-55. ABC News, 1955-57. Free Europe Organizations & Publications, Director of Research & Publications, to 1961. Hudson Institute, Senior Member, 1961-78. Hudson Research Europe, Ltd, Deputy Director, 1971-78. U. of CA, Regents Lecturer. *Los Angeles Times* Syndicate, political columnist, current. *The International Herald Tribune*,

political columnist, current. *The New Yorker*, contributor, "Reflections" column, current, 1971. Author *Condemned to Freedom*, 1971: co-author 3 books.

Phalon, Richard. *Forbes.* Contributing Editor. *New York Herald Tribune*, financial writer, 1954-64. *The New York Times*, metro reporter, to 1971; financial writer, to 1980. *Forbes*, from 1980; reported from Japan, 1983-84; opened Pacific bureau, Tokyo, 1985; Contributing Editor, current. Co-winner NY Newspaper Guild Award, Investigative Journalism; NY Newspaper Reporters Assn Award, Investigative Journalism.

Phillips, Kevin. *Los Angeles Times & The Christian Science Monitor.* Contributing Columnist. B. 1940, NYC. Colgate, 1961, AB, *magna cum laude, Phi Beta Kappa*; U. of Edinburgh, 1st Class Certificate in Economics; Harvard Law, 1964, JD. Administrative asst to Rep. Paul A. Fino, to 1968. Nixon for President Committee, asst to the Campaign Manager & chief political/voting analyst, 1968. Special asst to US Attorney General, to 1970. King Features Syndicate, columnist, to 1983. American Political Research Corporation, President, current. *The American Political Report*, Editor & Publisher, current. *Business and Public Affairs Fortnightly*, Editor & Publisher, current. CBS Spectrum & NPR, commentator, current. *Los Angeles Times*, contributing columnist, current. *The Christian Science Monitor*, contributing columnist, current. Author 5 books, including *Staying on Top: The Business Case for A National Industrial Strategy*, 1984.

Pike, Otis G. Newhouse News Service. Columnist. B. 1921, Riverhead, NY. Princeton, 1943, AB-Public Affairs; Columbia Law, 1948, LLD. US Congressman, 1961-79. *Newsday*, Columnist, to 1981. Newhouse News Service, columnist, current, 1981.

Pine, Art. *The International Economy.* Editor. *The Wall Street Journal*, Chief International Economics Correspondent, to 1987; agricultural reporter, 1987. *The International Economy*, Editor, current, 1987.

Pinkerton, Stewart. *The Wall Street Journal.* Deputy Managing Editor. B. 1942, Minneapolis, MN. Princeton, 1964, AB-English; NY Law School, 1982, JD. *The Wall Street Journal*, news asst, to 1965; Regional Copy Editor, to 1966; reporter, to 1971; "Page One" rewrite, NY, 1971; Managing Editor, Dow Jones Canada, to 1975; Asst NY Bureau Manager, 1975; NY Bureau Manager, to 1983; Asst Managing Editor, to 1985; Deputy Managing Editor, current, 1985.

Platt, Adam. *Insight.* Writer. B. 1958, Washington, DC. Georgetown School of Foreign Service, 1981, Humanities in International Affairs; Columbia School of Journalism, 1984. Business International-Asia Pacific, editorial asst, China desk, to 1983. *Insight*, writer, current, 1985.

Platt, Gordon. *The Journal of Commerce.* Financial Editor. B. 1949, Danbury, CT. Syracuse, 1971, Journalism & Psychology, Newhouse Scholarship, 1967-71. *The Bond Buyer, The Money Manager*, Munifacts News Wire, Assoc Editor, to 1980. *The Journal of Commerce*, Asst Managing Editor, to 1986; Financial Editor, current, 1986. Gannett Award, 1971.

Plender, John. Freelance. B. 1945, Cardiff, UK. Oxford, BA-Modern Languages (Hons). Deloitte & Co., chartered accountant, 1967-70. *Investors Chronicle*, to 1971. *The (London) Times*, to 1974. *The Economist*, Financial Editor, to 1979. British Foreign Office, policy planning staff, 1981-82. *Financial Times*, leader & feature writer, 1981-82; freelance, current, 1983. London Weekend TV & Channel Four TV (UK), Publisher, broadcaster, current affairs presenter, current. Author *That's The Way The Money Goes*, 1981; co-author *The Square Mile*, 1985.

Podhoretz, John. *U.S.News & World Report*. Contributing Editor. B. 1961, NYC. U. of Chicago, 1982, Political Science. *The American Spectator*, movie critic, to 1982; 1984-85. *Time*, reporter, researcher, to 1984. *The Washington Times*, Features Editor, to 1985; "Critic at Large" columnist, to 1987. *Insight*, Exec Editor, to 1987. *U.S.News & World Report*, Contributing Editor, current, 1987.

Podhoretz, Norman. *Commentary*, Editor. News America Syndicate, Columnist. B. 1930, Brooklyn, NY. Columbia, 1950; Cambridge, 1953, English. *Commentary*, Editor, current, 1960. Freelance, current. News America Syndicate, columnist, current, 1985. Author 6 books including *The Bloody Crossroads: Where Literature and Politics Meet*, 1986.

Pollan, Michael. *Harper's*. Executive Editor. B. 1955, Long Island, NY. Bennington, 1976, English; Columbia, 1981, MA. *Channels of Communications*, to 1983; Contributing Editor. *Harper's*, Exec Editor, current, 1983. Co-author: *The Harper's Index Book*.

Pond, Elizabeth. *The Christian Science Monitor*. European Correspondent. Principia College, BA-International Relations; Harvard, MA-Soviet Union Regional Studies. Alicia Patterson Fellow, 1969-70; National Endowment for the Humanities Fellow, U. of MI. *The Christian Science Monitor*, Sub-Editor, overseas news, to 1967; Saigon correspondent, 1967, '69; Tokyo correspondent, to 1974; Moscow correspondent, to 1976; European correspondent, current, 1977. *From the Yaroslavsky Station*, 1981 (rev, 1984, '85): co-author *Der Gefesselte Riese* 1981; *Indochina in Conflict*, 1972. UCLA Dumont Citation, 1969; Overseas Press Club Citation, 1982.

Powell, Sally. *BusinessWeek*. Senior Editor. B. Budapest, Hungary. *Theatre Arts*, Managing Editor. *Brooklyn Eagle*, Editor, Entertainment Page. *World Telegram*, Copy Editor. *Electronics*, Chief Copy Editor; Assoc Managing Editor, to 1970. *BusinessWeek*, creator, book review section, 1970; Senior Editor, current, 1980, marketing, legal affairs, media, advertising, corporate woman, social issues, & transportation.

Powers, Charles T. *Los Angeles Times*. Warsaw Bureau Chief. B. 1943, Neosho, MO. KS State U., 1966, BA-Journalism & English. Nieman Fellow, 1986-87. *Kansas State Collegian*, Editor, reporter, 1962-66. *The Kansas City Star*, intern, summers 1962, '63, '64; reporter, 1966-69. *Los Angeles Times*, writer, to 1971; "West Magazine" writer, to 1972; "View" writer, to 1975; writer, NYC, to 1980; Nairobi Bureau Chief, to 1986; Warsaw Bureau Chief, current, 1987. *Times* Editorial Award, 1973, '75 (co-winner, 1982).

Prewett, Virginia. Freelance Writer. B. Gordonsville, TN. Cumberlain U., NYU. *Sun-Times* Syndicate.

Washington Daily News, roving correspondent in Latin America. *The Washington Post*, columnist. *The Washington Times*, columnist, to 1983. *Human Events*, contributor, to 1986. *The Wall Street Journal*, contributor, to 1986. *The Hemisphere Hotline* (intelligence reports), Editor & Publisher, current, 1970. Freelance, current. Author 3 books. Maria Moors Cabot Medal; Citation, Center for Latin American Studies, U. of FL at Gainesville; Ed Stout Citation, Overseas Press Club.

Price, Joyce. *The Washington Times*. Medical Writer. B. 1945, Baltimore, MD. Towson State U., 1967, English. *News American* (Baltimore), Bureau Chief, to 1975; city desk edition reporter, to 1986. *The Washington Times*, metro reporter, 1986; medical writer, current, 1986.

Prina, L. Edgar. Copley News Service. Senior Correspondent (Retired 1987). B. 1917, West New York, NJ. Syracuse, 1938, AB-Political Science & Journalism, 1940, MA-Political Science. *Evening News* (Hornell, NY), Telegraph Editor, editorial writer, to 1941. *The New York Star*, Copy Editor, Asst Night City Editor, to 1948; Washington correspondent, to 1950. *The Evening Star* (Washington), national reporter, editorial writer, to 1966. Copley News Service, military affairs correspondent & Editor, to 1977; Bureau Chief, to 1984; senior correspondent, national security, retired 1987. Freelance, current. Washington Newspaper Guild Award, Best General News Story; 7 Copley Ring of Truth Awards, Enterprise, Spot News & Interpretive Articles.

Prokesch, Steven. *The New York Times*. "Business Day" Reporter. B. 1953, Geneva, NY. Yale, 1975. UPI, writer, to 1978. *BusinessWeek*, Pittsburgh correspondent, to 1980; Cleveland Bureau Chief, to 1982; Management Editor, to 1985. *The New York Times*, "Business Day" reporter, current, 1985.

Pruden, Wesley. *The Washington Times*. Managing Editor & "Pruden on Politics" Columnist. B. 1935, Jackson, MS. Little Rock (AR) Junior College, 1955, History. US Air Force, 1957. *Arkansas Gazette* (Little Rock, AR), writer, 1952-56. *The Commercial Appeal*, writer. *The National Observer*, writer, from 1963, (Vietnam, 1965-68, 1971; Middle East, 1969; London, 1970). Freelance, from 1976. *The Washington Times*, Managing Editor, "Pruden on Politics" columnist, current, 1985.

Putka, Gary. *The Wall Street Journal*. London Reporter. OH U., 1977, Journalism. *Journal Herald* (Dayton, OH), intern, summer 1975. AP, correspondent, intern, Israel, 1975-76. *Securities Week*, reporter, Chief Editor, 1977. *BusinessWeek*, reporter, Editor, 1980. *The Wall Street Journal*, senior special writer, "Heard on the Market," to 1984; reporter, London, current, 1984.

Quinn, Jane Bryant. *Newsweek*, Contributing Editor. *Washington Post* Writers Group, Financial Columnist. B. 1939, Niagara Falls, NY. Middlebury College, 1960, BA, *magna cum laude, Phi Beta Kappa*. *Insider's Newsletter*, Assoc Editor, 1962-65; Co-Editor, 1966-67. Cowles Book Co, Senior Editor, 1968. *Business Week Letter*, Editor-in-Chief, to 1973; General Manager, to 1974. *Washington Post* Writers Group, columnist, current, 1974. *Women's Day*, contributor, financial columnist, current, 1974. NBC News & Information Service, contributor, 1976-77. WCBS-TV (NYC), business correspondent, 1979; CBS-TV

News, current, 1980. *Newsweek*, Contributing Editor, current, 1978. Author *Everyone's Money Book*, 1979 (2nd ed, 1980). John Hancock Award, Excellence, Business & Financial Journalism, 1975; Janus Award, Excellence, TV Reporting, 1980; National Press Club Award, Consumer Journalism, 1980, '82, '83; Matrix Award, 1983; National Headliner Award, Consistently Outstanding Magazine Feature Column, 1986.

Quinn, John Collins. *USA Today*. Editor. B. 1925. Providence College, 1945, AB; Columbia, 1946, MSJ. *The Journal-Bulletin* (Providence, RI), copyboy, reporter, Asst City Editor, Washington correspondent, Asst Managing Editor, Day Managing Editor, 1943-66. Gannett Co, Inc, current, 1966: *Democrat and Chronicle & Times Union* (Rochester, NY), Exec Editor, to 1971; Gannett News Service, General Manager, 1967-80; VP, parent co, 1971-75; Senior VP, News & Information, to 1980; Senior VP Chief News Exec, parent co, 1980-83; President, current, 1980; Gannett Co, Exec VP, current; *USA Today*, Editor, current, 1983. Editor of the Year Award, National Press Foundation, 1986.

Quinn-Judge, Paul. *The Christian Science Monitor*. Moscow Correspondent. B. 1949, London. Cambridge, 1968-70, Slavonic Languages. American Friends Service Committee, aid worker, 1981. Freelance, SE Asia, 1981. *Far Eastern Economic Review*, Indochina correspondent, to 1986. *The Christian Science Monitor*, special correspondent, SE Asia, 1984; Moscow correspondent, current, 1984.

Quint, Michael. *The New York Times*. "Business Day" Reporter. Antioch College, 1973, BA. *American Banking Daily*, to 1980. *The New York Times*, "Business Day" reporter, current, 1980.

Rachid, Rosalind Kilkenny. *The Journal of Commerce*. Imports Editor. B. 1951, Georgetown, Guyana. CCNY, 1971, BA-French; U. of Madrid, 1971, Spanish Language & Literature Certificate; NYU, 1985, MAJ. English & French instructor, Uganda, 1973-74. English instructor, Zaire, to 1980. Bear Stearns & Co, Accounts Exec Asst, 1982-85. *Carib News*, freelance, 1982-85. *The Journal of Commerce*, international trade reporter, to 1987; Imports Editor, current, 1987.

Raines, Howell. *The New York Times*. London Bureau Chief. B. 1943, Birmingham, AL. Birmingham-Southern College, 1964, BA; U. of AL, 1973, MA-English. *The Birmingham Post-Herald*, to 1965. WBRC-TV (Birmingham), to 1968. *The Tuscaloosa* (AL) *News*, to 1970. *The Birmingham News*, reporter, 1971. *Constitution*, Political Editor. *The St. Petersburg Times*, Political Editor, to 1978. *The New York Times*, national correspondent, Atlanta, 1978; Chief Atlanta Correspondent, to 1982; White House correspondent, to 1985; Deputy Editor, Washington, to 1986; London Bureau Chief, current, 1986. Author *Whiskey Man*, 1977; *My Soul Is Rested*, 1977; contributor, *Campaign Money*, 1976.

Ram, Mohan. *NRC Handelsblad & The Indian Post*. Writer. B. 1933, Bangladore, India. Presidency College, Madras, MA-Economics. *The Indian Express*, 1960-65. *The* (Madras) *Mail*, to 1977. *The Christian Science Monitor*, to 1980. *Far Eastern Economic Review*, to 1986. *The* (London) *Guardian, Le Monde Diplomatique*,

contributor. Author several books on S. Asia. Harry Brittain Award, Journalism, 1976.

Randal, Jonathan C. *The Washington Post*. Roving Correspondent. B. 1933, Buffalo, NY. Harvard, 1955, Romance Languages. UPI, France, Algeria, London & Geneva 1957-60. *Agence France Press*, English language desk, Paris, 1957. *International Herald Tribune*, Paris & North Africa 1960-61. *Time*, N. Africa, Congo, W. Africa, Middle East, to 1966. *The New York Times*, Dominican Rep., Haiti, Vietnam, Laos, Cambodia, Warsaw, E. Europe, to 1969. *The Washington Post*, European Economic correspondent, to 1971; Paris correspondent, to 1975; roving correspondent, Middle East, N. Africa & Asia, current, 1975. Edward Weintal Prize.

Randolph, Eleanor R. *The Washington Post*. Media Writer. B. 1943, Pensacola, FL. Emory U., 1964, History. *Pensacola News Journal*, 1968-70. *St. Petersburg Times*, to 1973. *Sun-Times*, 1974. *Chicago Tribune*, to 1979. *Los Angeles Times*, politics, environment, to 1984. *The Washington Post*, media writer, current, 1984.

Range, Peter Ross. *U.S.News & World Report*. Diplomatic Correspondent. B. 1941, Tiffon, GA. U. of NC, 1964, German. Universitat Gottingen, Germany, Exchange Fellow, 1961-62; Woodrow Wilson Fellow, 1964-65. *Time* & NBC Radio, Berlin stringer, 1967-68. *Time*, Bonn correspondent, to 1970; Atlanta correspondent, to 1974; Saigon Bureau Chief, to 1975. Freelance, Paris, to 1976. *Playboy*, Chicago Senior Articles Editor, to 1977; Washington Contributing Editor, to 1985. *The Washington Post*, contract writer, to 1986. *U.S.News & World Report*, diplomatic correspondent, current, 1987.

Rappleye, Willard C. Jr. *Financier*. Founder & Editor. B. 1924, New Haven, CT. Yale, 1945, English. *Time*, Contributing Editor, 1947-50; Southwest Bureau Chief, 1952-57; national economic correspondent, to 1962. US AID Mission to Taiwan, public information officer, 1951. *American Banker*, Editor, 1962-75. *Financier*, Founder & Editor, current, 1976.

Raspberry, William J. *The Washington Post & Washington Post* Writers Group. Urban Affairs Columnist. B. Okolona, MS. Indiana Central College, BA-History. US Army, 1960-62. *Indianapolis Recorder*, reporter, photographer, Editor, 1956-60. *The Washington Post*, various positions; urban affairs columnist, current. *Washington Post* Writers Group, columnist, current. Capitol Press Club Journalist of the Year Award, 1965.

Rather, Dan. CBS News. "CBS Evening News with Dan Rather" Managing Editor & Anchor. B. 1931, Wharton, TX. Sam Houston State College, 1953, BAJ. Sam Houston State College, instructor, journalism, 1954. UPI, 1954. *Houston Chronicle*, 1954. KTRH (CBS), news writer; reporter; News Director, to 1958. KHOU-TV (CBS), Director of News & Public Affairs, to 1964; White House correspondent, 1964; London Bureau Chief, to 1966; 1966-74; Vietnam correspondent, 1966. CBS News, "CBS Reports" anchor & correspondent, to 1975; "Who's Who" Co-Editor, 1977; "60 Minutes" Co-Editor, to 1981; "CBS News with Dan Rather" anchor, Managing Editor, current, 1981. CBS Radio Network, "Dan Rather Reporting" anchor, current, 1977. Co-author *The Palace*

389

Guard, 1974; *The Camera Never Blinks*, 1977. 5 Emmy Awards.

Rauch, Jonathan C. *National Journal*. Economic Correspondent. B. 1960, Phoenix, AZ. Yale, 1982, History. *Winston-Salem Journal*. *National Journal*, staff correspondent, budget, to 1987; economic correspondent, current, 1987.

Reamy, Lois Madison. *Institutional Investor*. Contributing Editor. B. Fredericksburg, VA. Westhampton College, U. of Richmond, English. *The New York Times*, travel writer. *Glamour*, travel writer. *Destination America*, travel writer. *Institutional Investor*, Contributing Editor, current. Author *TravelAbility: A Guide For Physically Disabled Travelers In America*, 1978. American Library Assn Award, 1981; UN Year, Disabled Persons Award, 1981.

Reasoner, Harry. CBS News. "60 Minutes" Correspondent. B. 1923, Dakota City, IA. *Minneapolis Times*, reporter; drama critic, 1942-43, 1946-48. Northwest Airlines, Asst Publicity Director, to 1950. WCCO (Minneapolis), newswriter, to 1951. USIA, Manila, Editor, to 1954. KEYD-TV (Minneapolis), News Director, to 1956. CBS News, reporter, to 1970; "60 Minutes" correspondent, current, 1978. ABC News, 1970-78. Author 3 books, including Before *The Colors Fade*, 1981. Peabody Award, 1967; Emmy Award, 1968, '74.

Redburn, Tom. *Los Angeles Times*. Washington Reporter. B. 1950, LA, CA. Pomona College, 1972, Sociology & History. *The Washington Monthly*, Editor, writer, 1974-75. *Environmental Action*, Editor,writer, to 1976. *Washington Newsworks*, reporter, 1976. *Los Angeles Times*, business staff, to 1984; Washington reporter, current, 1984. Gerald Loeb Award, 1979; Greater LA Press Club Best Business Story, 1982.

Reed, Fred. Freelance Columnist. *Harper's*, Contributor. B. 1945, Bluefield, WVA. Hampden-Sydney College, 1970, History. *The Free Lance-Star* (Fredericksburg, VA), stringer, Israel, 1973. *Army Times*, stringer & staffer, Vietnam, to 1981. Freelance, to 1981. *Federal Times*, columnist, 1978-81. *Soldier of Fortune*, writer, 1980-81. *The Washingtonian*, writer, 1981. *The Washington Times*, military, science & op-ed columnist, to 1986. Freelance, current, 1986. *Harper's*, contributor, current, 1987.

Reed, Julia Evans. *U.S.News & World Report*. Associate Editor. American U., 1984, BA-Political Science. *Newsweek*, Washington staff. *Florida Kiplinger Letter*, reporter, 1984-86. *The Orlando Sentinel*, business reporter, to 1986. *U.S.News & World Report*, Assoc Editor, business, current, 1986.

Reston, James. *The New York Times*. Senior Columnist. Cincinnati Reds traveling secretary, to 1934. AP, sportswriter, to 1937; writer, London, to 1939. *The New York Times*, London, to 1945; national correspondent, Washington; diplomatic correspondent, to 1953; Washington Bureau Chief, correspondent, to 1964; Assoc Editor, to 1968; Exec Editor, News & Sunday Depts, to 1969; VP, 1969-74; Board of Directors member, 1973; "Washington" columnist, retired 1987; senior columnist, current, 1987. *The Vineyard Gazette* (Edgartown, MA), owner, current, 1968. Pulitzer Prize, 1945, '57.

Revzin, Philip. *The Wall Street Journal*. Paris Bureau Chief. B. Chicago, IL. Stanford, BA-English; Columbia, MA-English. *The Wall Street Journal*, intern, summer 1972; Cleveland reporter, 1974-77; London reporter, to 1980; Asst NY Bureau Chief, to 1983; London Bureau Chief, to 1986; senior correspondent, Paris, 1986; Paris Bureau Chief, current, 1986. Overseas Press Club Citation, Best Business News Reporting from Abroad, 1978.

Richman, Louis S. *Fortune*. Associate Editor — Frankfurt, West Germany. Dickenson College (Carlisle, PA), BA-History; Brandeis, MA-Modern & Contemporary History; MIT's Sloan School, MA-Management. *Sloan Management Review*, Editor. Brandeis & Hamilton College, History teacher. US Emergency Glass Co (Boston, MA), controller. Arlington, MA, Chamber of Commerce, Exec Director; Redevelopment Board member. *Fortune*, reporter, 1981; Assoc Editor, current, 1982; founded editorial office, Frankfurt, W. Germany.

Ricklefs, Roger. *The Wall Street Journal*. National Correspondent. B. 1940, San Rafael, CA. Harvard, 1961, AB-History. *The Wall Street Journal*, NY reporter, 1964-66; London reporter, to 1970; "Page One" rewrite staff, to 1972; feature writer, to 1981; Asst Editor, "Second Front," to 1983; Paris Bureau Chief, to 1986; national correspondent, current, 1986.

Riding, Alan. *The New York Times*. Rio de Janeiro Bureau Chief. B. 1943, Rio de Janeiro, Brazil. Bristol U., England, 1964, Economics; Gray's Inn, London, Law, 1964-66. BBC, 1966. Reuters, London, NY, Buenos Aires, to 1971. *The New York Times, Financial Times, The Economist*, freelance, to 1978. *The New York Times*, Mexico City Bureau Chief, to 1984; Rio de Janeiro Bureau Chief, current, 1984. Overseas Press Club Citation, Excellence, 1973; Maria Moors Cabot Prize, 1980.

Riemer, Blanca. *BusinessWeek*. Paris Economics Correspondent. B. Lima, Peru. Sorbonne, Paris, France, 1966, Literature diploma; *Institut d'Etudes Politiques*, Paris, 1968, International Relations diploma. Walter Bagehot Fellow, 1983. *Agence France-Presse*, financial reporter, Paris; economics correspondent, NY; economics correspondent, Washington. McGraw-Hill World News, correspondent, Bogota, Colombia, to 1983. *BusinessWeek*, Washington correspondent 1983-87; economics correspondent, Paris, current, 1987.

Rivard, Robert. *Newsweek*. Chief of Correspondents & Senior Editor. B. Petoskey, MI. *Brownsville Herald*, sports reporter, Desk Editor, 1977; city & county reporter, 1977. *Corpus Christi Caller*, investigative reporter, 1978. *Dallas Times Herald*, Mexico & SW USA correspondent, to 1980; Central American Bureau Founder, to 1984. *Newsweek*, San Salvador Bureau Founder, to 1985; Senior Editor, Chief of Correspondents, current, 1985. Star Reporter of Year, Texas Headliners Award, 1979, '81. *Sigma Delta Chi* Distinguished Service, 1982.

Robbins, William H. *The New York Times*. Kansas City Bureau Chief. B. 1924, Lumberton, NC. Wake Forest College, 1948, BA; 1949, MA. *The Wilmington* (NC) *Star*, reporter. *The Richmond Times-Dispatch*, reporter. *The Sun*, reporter. *Motor Magazine*, Managing Editor,

1957-58. *The New York Times*, Copy Editor, business news dept; national copy desk; Asst Real Estate Editor, to 1969; Asst News Editor, agriculture reporter, Washington; business reporter, Chicago, to 1980; Philadelphia Bureau Chief, to 1985; Kansas City Bureau Chief, current, 1985. Author *The American Food Scandal*, 1973.

Roberts, Steven V. *The New York Times.* White House Correspondent. B. 1943, Bayonne, NJ. Harvard, 1964, Government, *magna cum laude. The Harvard Crimson*, Editor. *The New York Times*, research asst to James Reston, to 1965; city reporter, to 1968; covered national political issues, 1968 campaign; LA Bureau Chief, to 1974; Athens Bureau Chief, to 1977; Washington reporter, to 1980; Congressional correspondent, to 1984; Chief Congressional Correspondent, to 1987; White House correspondent, current, 1987. Freelance, current. Author *Eureka*, 1974.

Robinson, Anthony Edward. *Financial Times.* Johannesburg Correspondent. B. 1942, Grimsby, Lincolnshire, UK. London School of Economics, BS-Economics. Reuters, London, Brussels, Milan, 1967-71. *Financial Times*, Rome correspondent, to 1976; London, 1977; East Europe correspondent, to 1982; Moscow correspondent, to 1983; Johannesburg correspondent, current, 1984.

Rogers, Ed. *The Washington Times.* National Reporter. B. 1917, Ashburn, GA. U. of GA, 1938, ABJ. US Naval Reserve, 1941-46. *The Atlanta Georgian*, to 1938. Insurance claims adjuster, to 1941. *The Nashville Banner*, 1941. UPI, reporter & desk, FL, Atlanta, Washington, 1946-82. *The Washington Times*, national reporter, current, 1982.

Rogers, Michael. *Fortune.* Associate Editor. B. NYC. Haverford College, BA; Northwestern, MSJ. *The Ledger* (Lakeland, FL), reporter, to 1983. *Fortune*, reporter, researcher, to 1987; Assoc Editor, current, 1987.

Rooney, Andrew A. CBS News, "60 Minutes" Commentator. Tribune Company Syndicate, Columnist. B. 1919, Albany, NY. Colgate, 1942. CBS-TV, writer, producer, from 1959; "60 Minutes" commentator, current, 1978. Tribune Co Syndicate, columnist, current, 1979. Author 7 books, including *Word For Word*, 1986; co-author, *Air Gunner*, 1944. Emmy Awards, 1968, '78, '81, '82.

Ropelewski, Robert R. *Aviation Week & Space Technology.* Managing Editor. B. 1942, Erie, PA. PA State U., 1965, Engineering, Journalism. *Aviation Week & Space Technology*, Engineering Editor, LA, 1972; Paris Bureau Chief to 1978; European Editor, 1978; LA Bureau Chief to 1984; Senior Military Editor, Washington, to 1985; Washington Bureau Chief, to 1987; Managing Editor, current, 1987. Writing Award, Aviation & Space Writers Assn, 1976, "Both Sides of the Suez" series.

Rosenbaum, David E. *The New York Times.* Washington Correspondent. B. 1942, Miami, FL. Dartmouth, 1963, AB; Columbia, 1965, MSJ. Borden Graduate Award, Pulitzer Traveling Fellow. *The St. Petersburg Times*, to 1966. *Ilford Recorder* (UK), 1966. *Congressional Quarterly*, to 1968. *The New York Times*, reporter, Editor, Washington, to 1981; Enterprise Editor,

NY, to 1984; correspondent, taxes, economic & domestic policy issues, Washington, current, 1984.

Rosenblatt, Robert A. *Los Angeles Times.* Washington Correspondent. B. 1943, NYC. CCNY, 1964, BA-Economics; Columbia, 1966, MSJ. *Broadcasting Magazine*, reporter, to 1965. *The Charlotte* (NC) *Observer*, reporter, 1966-69. *Los Angeles Times*, financial news reporter, to 1976; Washington correspondent, aging & the elderly, current, 1976. Gerald Loeb Financial Journalism Award, 1978.

Rosenfeld, Stephen. *The Washington Post.* Deputy Editorial Page Editor & Columnist. B. 1932, Pittsfield, MA. Harvard, 1953, BA-European History & Literature. US Marines, 1953-55. Columbia's Russian Institute, 1957-59. *The Berkshire Eagle*, 1955-57. *The Washington Post*, city staff, 1959-62; editorial writer, to 1964, 1966-82; Moscow correspondent, 1964-65; Deputy Editorial Page Editor, current, 1982; columnist, current. Author *The Time of Their Dying*, 1977: co-author (with Barbara Rosenfeld) *Return from Red Square*, 1967.

Rosenthal, Abraham Michael. *The New York Times.* Associate Editor & "On My Mind" Columnist. B. 1922, Saulte St. Marie, Ontario, Canada. CCNY, 1944, BS-Social Science. *The New York Times*, UN correspondent, to 1954; India-based, to 1958; Warsaw, to 1959; Geneva, to 1961; Tokyo, to 1963; Metro Editor, NY, to 1966; Asst Managing Editor, to 1968; Assoc Managing Editor, to 1969; Managing Editor, to 1977; Exec Editor, to 1986; Assoc Editor & "On My Mind" Columnist, current, 1986. Author *38 Witnesses:* co-author 3 books including *One More Victim.* Overseas Press Club Citation, 1956, '59; Pulitzer Prize, International Reporting, 1960; Number One Award, 1960; George Polk Memorial Award, 1960, '65; Page One Award, NY Newspaper Guild, 1960.

Rosenthal, Jack. *The New York Times.* Editorial Page Editor. B. 1935, Tel Aviv. Harvard, 1956, AB-History. *The Harvard Crimson*, Exec Editor. *The Oregonian* (Portland, OR), reporter, Editor. Press officer, State & Justice Depts, 1966-69. *The New York Times*, Asst Sunday Editor; editorial writer; Deputy Editor, Editorial Page, to 1986; Editorial Page Editor, current, 1986. Pulitzer Prize, Editorial Writing, 1982.

Rosett, Claudia. *The Asian Wall Street Journal.* Editorial Page Editor. B. 1955, New Haven, CT. Yale, 1976, Intensive English. Freelance, Chile, South America, 1981-82; New York, to 1984. *Policy Review*, 1984. *The Wall Street Journal*, Book Editor, to 1986. *The Asian Wall Street Journal*, Editorial Page Editor, current, 1986.

Rosewicz, Barbara. *The Wall Street Journal.* Middle East Correspondent. U. of KS, 1978, BAJ. UPI, reporter, Dallas; reporter (Topeka, KS); Topeka Bureau Chief, to 1981; Supreme Court reporter; Congressional reporter, to 1984. *The Wall Street Journal*, NY staff, to 1985; Middle East correspondent, Cairo, current, 1985.

Rothstein, Edward. *The New Republic.* Music Critic. B. 1953, Brooklyn, NY. Yale, 1973, Intensive Mathematics; postgrad Brandeis, 1974, Mathematics; Columbia, 1978, MA-English Literature. U. of Chicago, 1978-80, Humanities Fellow, Committee on Social Thought (residency completed for PhD). *The New York Times*, music critic, to 1984. *The New Republic*, music critic, current, 1984. Freelance, current, 1976. Macmillan, Inc, *The Free Press*, Senior Editor, current. Bennett Prize, Comparative Literature, Columbia, 1978; *The New York Times* Publisher's Award, 1981.

Rowe, James L. Jr. *The Washington Post.* Domestic & International Finance Economics Correspondent. B. 1948, Chicago, IL. Catholic U. of America, 1969, AB-Economics; postgrad U. of WI, 1969-70, Economics, Soviet Studies. *The Washington Post*, domestic economic reporter, to 1978; NY financial correspondent, to 1981; domestic & international finance economics correspondent, US banking & Latin American economics, current, 1982.

Rowe, Sandra Mims. *The Virginian-Pilot & The Ledger-Star.* Executive Editor. B. 1948, Charlotte, NC. East Carolina U., 1970, English. *The Ledger-Star*, reporter, to 1976; Asst City Editor, to 1977; "Daily Break" Editor, to 1978; Asst Managing Editor, to 1980; Managing Editor, to 1982. *The Virginian-Pilot & The Ledger-Star*, Managing Editor, to 1984; Exec Editor, current, 1984.

Rowen, Hobart. *The Washington Post.* Economics Editor & Columnist. B. 1918, Burlington, VT. CCNY, 1938, BSS-Government & Sociology, Honors. *The New York Journal of Commerce*, reporter, to 1942. *Newsweek*, Washington correspondent, "Business Trends" Editor, 1944-65. *The Washington Post*, Financial Editor, to 1969; Asst Managing Editor, to 1975; Economics Editor & columnist, current, 1975. *Washington Post* Writer's Group, columnist, current, 1975. PBS, "Washington Week in Review," panelist, current. Author *The Free Enterprisers: Kennedy, Johnson and the Business Establishment*, 1964: co-author *Bad Times and Beyond*, 1974; *The Fall of the President*, 1974. Sigma Delta Chi Distinguished Service Award, 1960; John Hancock Distinguished Service Award, 1966; Gerald Loeb Award, Business News Reporting, 1977; Journalist of the Year, National Economic Assn, 1984; *Washington Journalism Review*, Best in the Business, 1985.

Royko, Mike. *Chicago Tribune* & Tribune Media Services. Columnist. B. 1935, Chicago, IL. Wright Junior College, 1951-52. US Air Force, to 1956. Chicago Northside Newspapers, reporter, 1956. Chicago City News Bureau, reporter, Asst City Editor, to 1959. *Chicago Daily News*, columnist, to 1978; Assoc Editor, 1977-78. *Sun-Times*, columnist, to 1984. *Chicago Tribune*, columnist, current, 1984. Tribune Media Services, columnist, current. Author 4 books, including *Slats Grobnik and Other Friends*, 1973. Heywood Broun Award, 1968; Pulitzer Prize, Commentary, 1972; U. of MO School of Journalism Medal, Service, 1979.

Royster, Vermont. *The Wall Street Journal.* Editor Emeritus. B. 1914, Raleigh, NC. U. of NC, 1935, Classical Languages (Latin & Greek). *The Wall Street Journal*, Washington correspondent 1937-46; Washington Bureau Chief, to 1950; Assoc Editor, to 1958; Editor, to 1971; Public Affairs Columnist, to 1987; Editor Emeritus, current, 1987. William Rand Kenan Prof, Journalism & Public Affairs, 1971-81. CBS Radio/TV, commentator, 1972-77. Author 3 books, including *My Own, My Country's Time*, 1983. Pulitzer Prize, 1953, '84; 4th Estate Award, DC National Press Club, 1984; Distinguished Service Medal, Journalism, Sigma Delta Chi, 1958; Presidential Medal of Freedom, 1986.

Ruby, Michael. *U.S.News & World Report.* Executive Editor. U. of MO, BSJ. Nieman Fellow, 1974-75. *BusinessWeek*, correspondent, acting Chicago Bureau Chief, writer, 1966-71. *Newsweek*, business writer, to 1978; Senior Editor, business, to 1981; National Affairs Editor, to 1982; Managing Editor, international editions, to 1983; Chief of Correspondents; Asst Managing Editor, to 1986. *U.S.News & World Report*, Exec Editor, current, 1986.

Rudnitsky, Howard. *Forbes.* Senior Editor. CCNY, Baruch School, 1959, BBS. Moody's Investor Services. *Forbes*, Statistical Dept Head, 1961-69; writer; Assoc Editor, to 1978; Senior Editor, current, 1978. Co-winner (with Allan Sloan) Loeb Award, 1985.

Rule, Sheila. *The New York Times.* Nairobi Bureau Chief. B. 1950, St. Louis, MO. U. of MO at Columbia, 1972, Journalism. *St. Louis Post-Dispatch*, reporter, to 1977. *The New York Times*, metro reporter, to 1984; temporary assignment, Nairobi, to 1985; Nairobi Bureau Chief, current, 1985. Meyer Berger Award, 1985.

Rusher, William Allen. *National Review.* Publisher (Retired 1987). B. 1923, Chicago, IL. Princeton, 1943, AB; Harvard, 1948, JD. US Army Air Force, 1943-46. Shearman & Sterling & Wright, NYC, assoc, 1948-56. NY Senate Finance Committee, special counsel, 1955. US Senate, Internal Security Subcommittee, assoc counsel, 1956-57. *National Review*, Publisher, to 1987; National Review, Inc, Director, VP, to 1987. Universal Press Syndicate, columnist, 1973-82. Newspaper Enterprise Assn, "The Conservative Advocate" columnist, current, 1982. Author 4 books, including *The Rise of the Right*, 1984: co-author (with Mark Hatfield & Arlie Schardt) *Amnesty?*, 1973.

Ryskind, Allan H. *Human Events.* Capitol Hill Editor. B. 1934, NY. Pomona College, 1956, BA-Political Science; UCLA, 1959, MA. City News Service, Los Angeles, summer 1959. *Human Events*, Asst Editor, to 1967; Capitol Hill Editor, current, 1967; co-owner, current. Author *Hubert*, 1968.

Sackett, Victoria A. *Public Opinion.* Deputy Managing Editor. B. 1951, Portland, OR. Reed College, 1979, History. Office staff, Sen. Henry M. Jackson, 1971-76. *Public Opinion*, Assoc Editor, 1979-84; Deputy Managing Editor, current, 1984.

Sadler, Shelby. *Washington Journalism Review.* Managing Editor. B. 1961, NYC. Cornell, 1982, BA-English; American U., 1984, MAJ. *Washington Journalism Review*, news aide, Asst Editor, 1984; Assoc Editor, 1985; Managing Editor, current, 1986.

Safer, Morley. CBS News. "60 Minutes" Correspondent. B. 1931, Toronto. U. Western Ontario, 1952. Reuters, London, 1955. CBC, correspondent, to 1960; London correspondent, to 1964. BBC, correspondent, 1961. CBS News, Vietnam correspondent, 1964-71; "60 Minutes" correspondent, current, 1971. Sigma Delta Chi Award, 1965; Peabody Award, 1965; Overseas Press Club Award, 1965, '66; 4 Emmy Awards.

Safire, William. *The New York Times.* "Essay" & "On Language" Columnist. B. 1929, NYC. Studied Syracuse, 1947-49. *New York Herald Tribune* Syndicate, reporter, to 1951. WNBC-WNBT, Europe & Middle East correspondent, to 1951. US Army correspondent, to 1954. WNBC (NYC), radio & tv producer, to 1955. Tex McCrary Inc, VP, to 1960. Safire Public Relations, Inc, President, to 1968. Special asst to President Nixon, to 1973. *The New York Times*, "Essay" columnist, current, 1973; "On Language" columnist, (*The New York Times Magazine*), current, 1979. Author 9 books, including *Freedom*, 1987; co-author *Plunging Into Politics* (with Marshall Loeb), 1964; *What's The Good Word?* (with Leonard Safir), 1982. Pulitzer Prize, Distinguished Commentary, 1978.

Salamon, Julie. *The Wall Street Journal.* Film Critic. B. Seaman, OH. Tufts, 1975, BA; NYU, 1978, JD. *Tufts Observer.* *The Pittsburgh Press*, intern, 1976. *The New York Times*, freelance, 1978. *The Wall Street Journal*, intern, summer 1977; reporter, 1978-83; film critic, current, 1983. NY Newswomen's Club Front Page Award, Criticism, 1985.

Salpukas, Agis. *The New York Times.* Transportation Reporter. B. 1939, Kaunas, Lithuania. Long Island U., 1961, History. *The New York Times*, local staff, 1963-65; LI reporter, 1965-70; Detroit staff, 1970-76; "Business Day" reporter, to 1981; transportation reporter, current, 1981. *Sigma Delta Chi Award*, 1975.

Sanger, David E. *The New York Times.* Technology Reporter. B. 1960, White Plains, NY. Harvard, 1982, Government. *The New York Times*, college stringer, to 1982; news clerk, to 1983; technology reporter, current, 1983.

Sanoff, Alvin P. *U.S.News & World Report.* Senior Editor — Social Trends. B. 1941, NYC. Harvard, 1963, Sociology. NEH Fellow, U. of MI, 1974-75. *The Sun*, reporter, editorial writing, 1967-71. *Dayton* (OH) *Journal Herald*, Editorial Page Editor, 1971-77. *U.S.News & World Report*, Assoc Editor, 1977-83; Senior Editor, social trends, current, 1983. OH AP Award, Best Editorial Writing, 1974.

Santini, Maureen. *U.S.News & World Report.* State Department Correspondent. B. 1948, Hancock, MI. U. of WI, 1972, Political Science. American Political Science Assn. Congressional Fellow, 1974-75. *Wisconsin State Journal*, 1970-74. AP, Boston, to 1977; White House correspondent, to 1985; State Dept correspondent, 1985. *U.S.News & World Report*, State Dept correspondent, current, 1985.

Saporito, Bill. *Fortune.* Associate Editor. B. Harrison, NJ. Bucknell, BA-American Studies; Syracuse, MAJ. *New York Daily News*, 1978. *Chain Store Age Supermarkets* Magazine, Senior Editor. Freelance, 1982-84. *Fortune*, Assoc Editor, current, 1984; founded editorial office, Pittsburgh, PA.

Sawyer, L. Diane. CBS News. "60 Minutes" Correspondent. B. 1945, Glasgow, KY. Wellesley College, 1967, BA. WLKY-TV (Louisville), reporter, to 1970. White House, press office administrator, to 1974. Researcher, Richard Nixon's memoirs, to 1978. CBS News, State Dept correspondent, to 1981; "CBS Morning News" co-anchor; "60 Minutes" correspondent, current.

Scardino, Albert. *The New York Times.* Business & Financial Reporter. B. 1948, Baltimore, MD. Columbia College, 1970, American History. *The Georgia Gazette*, Editor, 1978-85; *The New York Times*, "The Week in Review" Editor, 1985; business & financial reporter, current, 1986. Pulitzer Prize, Editorial Writing, 1984.

Scharff, Edward E. *Institutional Investor.* Contributing Editor. B. 1946, St. Louis, MO. Princeton, 1968, English. *The Washington Star*, Capitol Hill; Washington & VA local politics; sociological & demographic trends; business, 1970-78. *Money*, personal finance, to 1980. *Time*, "Economy & Business," to 1982. *Institutional Investor*, Senior Editor, to 1987; Contributing Editor, current, 1987. Author *Worldly Power, The Making of The Wall Street Journal*, 1986. DC-Baltimore Newspaper Guild Front Page Award, 1974.

Schiebla, Shirley Hobbs. *Barron's.* Washington Editor. B. Newport News, VA. William & Mary, U. of NC, BA. *The Wall Street Journal*, Washington correspondent. Founded & ran own Washington news bureau. *Financial Times*, correspondent. *The Richmond News Leader*, correspondent. *Daily Press* (Newport News, VA), correspondent. *Barron's*, part-time writer, 1958-62; Assoc Editor, to 1967; Washington Editor, current, 1967. Author *Poverty Is Where the Money Is*, 1968.

Schiffren, Lisa. *The Detroit News.* Political Reporter. B. 1959, NYC. Bryn Mawr, 1982, AB-History. *The Washington Times*, reporter, 1984. *The Detroit News*, Editorial Writer, to 1987; political reporter, current, 1987. 1st Place MI AP Editorial Award, 1985; 1st Place UPI Editorial Award, 1986; 1st Place Detroit Press Club Foundation Editorial Award, 1986.

Schmemann, Serge. *The New York Times.* Bonn Bureau Chief. B. 1945, France. Harvard, 1967, BA-English; Columbia, 1971, MA-Slavic Studies. AP, to 1980. *The New York Times*, metro staff, to 1981; Moscow correspondent, to 1984; Moscow Bureau Chief, to 1987; Bonn Bureau Chief, current, 1987.

Schmertz, Herbert. Heritage Features Syndicate. "For the Record" Columnist. B. 1930, Yonkers, NY. Union College, 1952, AB; Columbia, 1955, LLB. American Arbitration Assn, member. Federal Mediation & Conciliation Service, general counsel, asst to Director, to 1966. Mobil Oil Corp, 1966; Director & VP, Public Affairs, current, 1979. Heritage Features Syndicate, "For the Record" columnist, current. Author *Good-bye to the Low Profile*: co-author *Takeover*.

Schmidt, Stanley. *Analog.* Editor. B. 1944, Cincinnati, OH. U. of Cincinnati, 1966, BS; Case Western Reserve U., 1969, PhD-Physics. Freelance, to 1978. Heidelberg College, asst prof, physics, to 1978. *Analog*, Editor, current, 1978.

Schneider, Keith. *The New York Times.* Washington Reporter. B. 1956, White Plains, NY. Haverford College, 1978. Freelance, to 1979. *Wilkes-Barre* (PA) *Times Leader*, reporter, 1979. The News and Courier (SC), reporter, to 1981. 2 independent news services, Editor, to 1985. *The New York Times*, reporter, Washington, current, 1985. George Polk Award, Investigative Reporting, 1984.

Schulz, William. *Reader's Digest.* Washington Editor & Bureau Chief. B. 1939, NYC. Antioch College, 1961, Political Science. Fulton Lewis Jr. King Features Syndicate, column ghostwriter, to 1966. *Reader's Digest,* Assoc Editor, to 1971; Senior Editor, to 1973; Washington Editor & Bureau Chief, current, 1973.

Sciolino, Elaine. *The New York Times.* Washington Correspondent. B. 1948, Buffalo, NY. Canisius College (Buffalo, NY), 1970; NYU, 1971, MA-History. Edward R. Murrow Press Fellow, 1982-83. *Newsweek,* reporter, from 1971; Paris correspondent, to 1980; Rome Bureau Chief, to 1982; roving international correspondent, 1983-84. *The New York Times,* metro reporter, to 1985; UN Bureau Chief, to 1987; Washington correspondent, current, 1987. Page One Award, 1978; Religious Public Relations Council Merit Award, 1979; Overseas Press Club Citation, Magazine Reporting from Abroad, 1983: co-winner National Headliners Award, Outstanding Major News Event Coverage, 1981.

Seib, Gerald F. *The Wall Street Journal.* Washington Correspondent. U. of KS, 1978, BSJ. *Daily Kansan,* Editor, fall 1977. Sears Foundation Congressional intern, office of US Rep. Gillis Long (LA), spring 1978. *The Wall Street Journal,* Dallas intern, summer 1977; Dallas reporter, 1978-80; Pentagon & State Dept reporter, to 1984; Middle East correspondent, to 1987; Washington correspondent, current, 1987.

Seiler, John. Freelance Writer. B. 1955, Detroit, MI. Hillsdale College, 1977, Political Economy. US Army, 1978-82. *Colorado Springs Gazette-Telegraph,* reporter, 1977-78. *University Bookman,* Asst Editor, 1982. *Conservative Digest,* Asst Editor, to 1983. *The American Sentinel* (newsletter), Editor, to 1985; Asst Editor, 1986. *The Washington Times,* editorial page writer, to 1987. Freelance, current.

Selic, Momcilo. *Chronicles.* Managing Editor. B. 1946, Belgrade, Yugoslavia. U. of Belgrade, Yugoslavia, 1971, Architectural Engineering. *Student, Vidici, Jez, & Knjizevna rec* (Yugoslavia), articles, 1968-83. *Casovnik* (Samizdat literary magazine), Co-Editor & contributor, 1979. Freelance, 1983. *Chronicles,* Managing Editor, current, 1983. Author *Zamor Materijala (Fatigue Of Materials),* 1979. "For The Artist In The World" (literary prize), "Fund Pour L'Imaginaire" of London, 1984.

Seligman, Daniel. *Fortune.* Associate Managing Editor. B. 1924, NYC. Rutgers; NYU, AB. *The New Leader,* 1946; labor columnist, 1949-50. *The American Mercury,* Asst Editor, 1946-50. *Fortune,* Assoc Editor, to 1959; Board of Editors member, to 1966; Asst Managing Editor, to 1969; Exec Editor, 1969-77; Assoc Managing Editor, current, 1977; "Keeping Up" columnist, current. Time, Inc, Senior Staff Editor, 1969.

Sellers, Patricia. *Fortune.* Reporter/Researcher. U. of Charlottesville (VA), BA-English, *Phi Beta Kappa.* *Washington Business Journal,* writer, to 1984. *Fortune,* reporter/researcher, current, 1984.

Semple, Robert B. Jr. *The New York Times.* Op-Ed Page Editor. B. 1936, St. Louis, MO. Yale, 1959; Berkeley, 1961, MA-History. *The New York Times,* reporter, political reporter, White House correspondent, to 1973; Deputy National Editor, to 1975; London Bureau

Chief, to 1977; Foreign Editor, to 1982; Editor, Op-Ed Page, current, 1982. NBC News, "Meet the Press," panelist, current.

Seneker, Harold. *Forbes.* Senior Editor. B. Philadelphia, PA. PA State U., 1967, BA-Biology. Value Line analyst, to 1970. Trade papers, to 1976. *Forbes,* Senior Editor, current. Developer, *Forbes 400.*

Shabecoff, Philip. *The New York Times.* Washington Reporter. B. 1934, Bronx, NY. Hunter College, BA; U. of Chicago, MA. *The New York Times,* newsroom stenographer, 1959-60; news asst, business & financial dept, to 1962; foreign trade reporter, to 1964; foreign correspondent, West Germany, to 1968; foreign correspondent, Tokyo, to 1970; Washington reporter, current, 1970, environment. Contributor *The Presidency Reappraised; American Government.*

Shapiro, Robert J. *U.S.News & World Report.* Associate Editor & "Tomorrow" Columnist. B. 1950, Baltimore, MD. U. of Chicago, 1970, AB-Committee on the Analysis of Ideas & Study of Method, high honors; London School of Economics, 1972, MS-Political Theory; Harvard, 1980, MA, PhD-Political Theory, Government. Institute of Policy Studies Fellow, 1972-73. Harvard Fellow, 1975-77. National Bureau of Economic Research Fellow, 1980-81. Legislative aide, Sen. Daniel Moynihan, to 1983; Legislative Director, Sen. Moynihan, to 1985. *U.S.News & World Report,* Assoc Editor, current, 1986; "Tomorrow" columnist, current, 1986.

Shapiro, Walter. *Time.* Senior Writer. B. 1947, NYC. U. of MI, 1970, BA-History, 1971, postgrad, European History. *Congressional Quarterly,* reporter, to 1970. *The Washington Monthly,* Editor, to 1976; Contributing Editor, current, 1976. Special asst, press secretary, to Secretary of Labor Ray Marshall, to 1978. Speechwriter to President Carter, 1979. *The Washington Post,* Sunday magazine writer, to 1983. *Newsweek,* General Editor, national affairs writer, to 1987. *Time,* senior writer, current, 1987.

Shaw, David. *Los Angeles Times.* Media Critic. B. 1943. UCLA, 1965, English Literature. *Huntingdon Park* (CA) *Signal,* reporter, 1963-66. *Long Beach Press Telegram,* reporter & Editor, to 1968. *Los Angeles Times,* reporter, to 1974; media critic, current, 1974. Author 4 books including *Press Watch,* 1984. 40+ Awards from ABA, American Political Science Assn, & LA Press Club; Award, Improving Journalism through Critical Evaluation (Mellett Fund for a Free & Responsible Press), 1983.

Shaw, Terri. *The Washington Post.* Foreign Correspondent. B. 1940, Washington, DC. Antioch College, 1963, BA; Columbia, 1965, MSJ. *Buffalo Courier-Express,* to 1964. AP, to 1970. Freelance, South America, 1966-67. *The Washington Post,* foreign correspondent, current, 1970.

Shawn, William. *The New Yorker.* Editor (Retired 1987). B. 1907, Chicago, IL. Studied U. of MI, 1925-27. *Las Vegas Optic,* reporter, 1928. *International Illustrated News,* Midwest Editor, Chicago, to 1933. *The New Yorker,* reporter, Assoc Editor, to 1939; Managing Editor, to 1952; Editor, to 1987.

Shenon, Philip. *The New York Times.* Washington Reporter. B. 1959. Brown, 1981, English, *magna cum laude. The Brown Daily Herald*, Editor-in-Chief, President. *The New York Times*, James Reston's clerk, to 1982; copyboy, financial desk, to 1983; metro reporter, to 1985; reporter, Washington, current, 1985.

Shepard, Stephen B. *BusinessWeek.* Editor-in-Chief. B. 1939, NYC. CCNY, 1961, BS-Engineering; Columbia, 1964, MS-Engineering. Columbia Grad School of Journalism, adjunct prof, 1970-75; Founder & Director, Walter Bagehot Fellowship Program in Economics & Business Journalism. *Newsweek*, Senior Editor, National Affairs, to 1980. *Saturday Review*, Editor, 1981-82. *BusinessWeek*, 1966-75; Exec Editor, 1982-84; Editor-in-Chief, current, 1984. Freelance, current. National Magazine Award; *Sigma Delta Chi* Headliners Award; U. of MO Award.

Sherman, Stratford P. *Fortune.* Associate Editor. B. 1952, CT. Harvard, 1974, English, *cum laude. The Harvard Lampoon*, writer. Netherlands Antilles, teacher. William Morrow Co, editorial asst, to 1977. *Fortune*, reporter, researcher, to 1982; Assoc Editor, current, 1982.

Shields, Mark. *The Washington Post.* Columnist. B. 1937, Weymouth, MA. U. of Notre Dame, 1959, Philosophy & History. Government asst, various positions. *The Washington Post*, editorial writer, 1979-81; columnist, current, 1979. Mutual Radio Network, commentary, 1984. CBS-TV, on-air analyst, 1984 Republican & Democratic conventions, campaign & election night. WMAL Radio (Washington), commentary, to 1986. Author *On the Campaign Trail*, 1985. Washington Dateline Award, Local Journalism, *Sigma Delta Chi*, 1985.

Shiner, Josette S. *The Washington Times*, Deputy Managing Editor. B. 1954, Orange, NJ. U. of CO, 1976, Communications. *The New York City Tribune*, National Desk Editor, 1976-77; Washington staff, 1977-82. *The Washington Times*, Features Editor, 1982-84; Asst Managing Editor, 1984-85; Deputy Managing Editor, current, 1985. National Press Club's Vivian Award & Meritorious Service Recognition, 1981; U. of GA Atrium Award, 1984.

Shipler, David K. *The New York Times.* Washington Foreign Affairs Correspondent. B. Chatham, NJ. Dartmouth. *The New York Times*, from 1966, news clerk; metro reporter; foreign correspondent, SE Asia, Eastern Europe, the Soviet Union, Middle East; foreign affairs correspondent, Washington, current. *Arab and Jew: Wounded Spirits in a Promised Land*, 1987 (Pulitzer Prize, General Non-Fiction).

Shlaes, Amity. *The Wall Street Journal*/Europe. Editorial Features Editor. B. 1960, Chicago, IL. Yale, 1982, English. Fellowship, W. Berlin, 1982-83. *The Wall Street Journal*, foreign desk, 1983-84; Cleveland reporter, 1984; Europe staff, 1985; Editorial Features Editor/Europe, current, 1985.

Shogan, Robert. *Los Angeles Times.* National Political Correspondent. B. 1930, NYC. Syracuse, 1951, Journalism & American Studies. *Detroit Free Press*, 1956-59. *Miami News*, Telegraph Editor to 1961. *The Wall Street Journal*, Asst Editor to 1965; Peace Corps, evaluation officer, 1966. *Newsweek*, correspondent to 1972. *Los Angeles Times*, national political correspondent, current, 1973. Author 3 books, including *None of the Above*, 1982: co-author (with Tom Craig) *Detroit Race Riot*. MI AP Sweepstakes, 1st Place Feature Writing, 1958.

Shribman, David M. *The Wall Street Journal.* National Political Reporter. Dartmouth, 1976, AB-History, *Phi Beta Kappa*; Cambridge, Graduate Fellow, to 1977. *Buffalo Evening News*, metro reporter, to 1979; Washington reporter, to 1980. *The Washington Star*, style & national reporter, to 1981. *The New York Times*, feature writer; Congressional correspondent; national politics reporter, to 1984. *The Wall Street Journal*, national political reporter, Washington, current, 1984.

Sides, W. Hampton. *The Washingtonian.* Writer. B. 1962, Memphis, TN. Yale, 1984, History. *Memphis*, Contributing Editor, 1984-86. *The Washingtonian*, writer, current, 1987. Rolling Stone College Journalism Award, Investigative Writing, 1984; City & Regional Magazine White Award, Writing (Gold) & Investigative Writing (Bronze), 1987.

Sidey, Hugh. *Time.* Washington Contributing Editor & "The Presidency" Essayist. B. 1927, Greenfield, IA. IA State U., 1950, BS. US Army, 1945-46. *Adair City* (IA) *Free Press*, reporter, 1950. *The Nonpariel* (Council Bluffs, IA), reporter, to 1951. *Omaha World-Herald*, reporter, to 1955. *Life*, correspondent to 1958. *Time*, correspondent, to 1966; columnist, to 1969; Chief, to 1978; Washington Contributing Editor, current, 1978; "The Presidency" essayist, current. Author 4 books, including *Portrait of a President*, 1975.

Sieff, Martin. *The Washington Times.* Assistant Foreign Desk Editor. B. 1950, Belfast, N. Ireland. Exeter College, Oxford, Modern History; postgrad London School of Economics. *Jerusalem Post*, researcher, Middle East affairs analyst, to 1979. *Belfast Telegraph*, Copy Editor, Production Editor, to 1984. *Belfast Newsletter*, Copy Editor, Foreign News Editor, to 1985. *The Washington Times*, Asst Foreign Desk Editor, Soviet & Middle East Affairs Editor, current, 1987; Central European Coverage Editor, current, 1987.

Siegal, Allan Marshall. *The New York Times.* Editor. B. 1940, NYC. NYU, 1962. *The New York Times*, from 1961: Pentagon Papers Editor, 1971; Asst Foreign Editor, to 1976; asst to Exec Editor in charge newsroom automation, to 1977; News Editor, current, 1977. Founding National Editor, 1980. NYU, 1966, & Columbia 1967-69, journalism teacher.

Silk, Leonard. *The New York Times.* "The Economic Scene" Columnist. B. 1918, Philadelphia, PA. U. of WI, 1940, AB; Duke, 1947, PhD, *Phi Beta Kappa*. Senior Fellow, Brookings Institution, 1969-70; Poynter Fellow, 1974-75. Duke, Economics instructor, 1941-42. US Army Air Forces, to 1945. U. of ME, economics instructor, to 1948. Simmons College, asst prof, Economics, to 1950. US Mission to NATO, Asst Economic Commissioner, 1952-54. *BusinessWeek*, Economics Editor, to 1964; Senior Editor, 1959-66; Vice-chairman & Economist, to 1967; Editorial Page Editor & Chairman of the Editorial Board, to 1969. *The New York Times*, Editorial Board member, to 1976; "The Economic Scene" columnist, current, 1976. Author 11 books, including *Economics in the Real World*, 1985: co-author 4 books. Loeb Award, Distinguished Business & Financial Journalism, 1961, '66, '67, '71, '72; Overseas Press Club Citation, Foreign Economic Reporting, 1967; Overseas Press Club Bache Award, Best Business Reporting from Abroad, 1972; Gerald Loeb Memorial Award, 1977; Elliot V. Bell Award, 1983.

Silvers, Robert B. *The New York Review of Books.* Editor. B. 1929, Mineola, NY. U. of Chicago, 1947, AB; *Ecole des Sciences Politiques*, Paris, 1956. US Army, 1952-53. Press Secretary, Gov. Bowles (CT), 1950. *Paris Review*, editorial board member, current, 1954. *Harper's*, Assoc Editor, 1959-63. *The New York Review of Books*, Editor, current, 1963. Teachers & Writers Collaborative, NYC, Director, current, 1966. Editor *Writing in America*, 1960: translator *La Gangrene*, 1961.

Simison, Robert L. *The Wall Street Journal*/Europe. "Page One" Editor. B. Waukon, IA. U. of KS, 1974, BSJ. *The Wall Street Journal*, reporter, Dallas, to 1978; reporter, Detroit, to 1984; special writer, Dallas, to 1985; Dallas Deputy Bureau Chief, to 1986; "Page One" Editor/Europe, current, 1986.

Simonds, John E. *Honolulu Star-Bulletin.* Executive Editor. B. 1935, Boston, MA. Bowdoin College (Brunswick, ME), 1957, English. *Daily Tribune* (Seymour, IN), reporter, to 1958. UPI, reporter, to 1960. *The Journal* (Providence, RI), reporter; Asst City Editor, to 1965. *Washington Evening Star*, reporter; Asst City Editor, to 1966. Gannett News Service, Washington correspondent, to 1975. *Honolulu Star-Bulletin*, Managing Editor, to 1980; Exec Editor, current, 1980.

Simons, Lewis M. *San Jose Mercury News*/Knight-Ridder Newspapers. Tokyo Bureau Chief. B. 1939, Paterson, NJ. NYU, 1962, English Literature; Columbia, 1964, MSJ. Edward R. Murrow Fellow, Council on Foreign Relations. US Marines, 1962-64. AP, Denver correspondent, to 1967; Saigon correspondent, to 1968; Malaysia & Singapore Bureau Chief, to 1970. *The Washington Post*, New Delhi Bureau Chief, to 1975; Bangkok Bureau Chief, to 1978; metro staff, to 1982. *San Jose Mercury News*/Knight-Ridder Newspapers, Tokyo Bureau Chief, current, 1982. American Newspaper Guild Investigative Reporting Award, 1981; American Newspaper Guild Grand Prize, 1981; Overseas Press Club Citation, 1983; Investigative Reporters & Editors Grand Prize, 1986; George Polk Award, International Reporting, 1986; Pulitzer Prize, International Reporting, 1985; Overseas Press Club Of America Award, 1986. Author *Worth Dying For*, 1987.

Simpson, Christopher. *The Washington Times.* National Political Reporter. B. 1955, Anderson, SC. Clemson, 1977, History & Psychology; postgrad, U. of SC, Journalism, 1979-80. *The Greensboro* (NC) *Record*, police reporter, 1979-80. *The Newport News* (VA) *Daily Press*, state govt & political reporter, to 1984. *The Washington Times*, Congressional reporter & political writer, to 1986; Capitol Hill Bureau Chief, 1986; national political reporter, current, 1987.

Singer, Daniel. *The Nation.* European Correspondent. B. 1926, Warsaw. *Bachelier es lettre* (Philosophy), BSc-Econs. *The Economist*, writer; Paris correspondent. *The Nation*, European correspondent, current. Author *Prelude To Revolution*, 1968; *The Road To Gdansk,* 1968.

Sitomer, Curtis J. *The Christian Science Monitor.* Senior Correspondent & "Justice" Columnist. B. 1932, NYC. Principia College, 1955, Political Science. *The Christian Science Monitor*, 1965; West Coast Bureau Chief, 1971-76; American News Editor, to 1982; Special Sections Editor, to 1983; senior correspondent, current, 1983; "Justice" columnist, current, 1983. National Headliner Award, Special Column of the Year, 1986.

Skrzycki, Cindy. *The Washington Post.* National Business Correspondent. American U., MA-Journalism & Public Affairs. *Buffalo Evening News*, reporter. Fairchild Publications, reporter. *Fort Worth Star-Telegram*, reporter. *U.S.News & World Report*, business writer, from 1983; Assoc Editor, 1983-87. *The Washington Post*, national business correspondent, current, 1987.

Sloan, Allan. *Forbes.* Senior Editor. Brooklyn College, 1966, BA-English; Columbia, 1967, MSJ. *Detroit Free Press*, business writer, 1972-79. *Forbes*, writer & Assoc Editor, to 1981. *Money*, writer, to 1984. *Forbes*, Senior Editor, current, 1984. Author *Three Plus One Equals Billions: The Bendix-Marietta War*, 1983. Gerald Loeb Award, 1975; co-winner (with Howard Rudnitsky) Loeb Award, 1985.

Slutsker, Gary. *Forbes.* Associate Editor. B. 1955, NYC. Middlebury College, 1977, AB-Political Science, Honors; Columbia, 1978, MSJ. *Electronic News*, reporter, to 1980. *Venture Magazine*, Assoc Editor, to 1982; Senior Editor, to 1984. *Forbes*, writer, to 1985; Assoc Editor, current, 1985; "Faces Behind the Figures" Editor.

Smilgis, Martha. *Time.* Associate Editor. B. 1946, Chicago, IL. U. of CA, Berkeley, 1968, Political Science. *Sports Illustrated*, reporter, 1975-77. *People*, senior writer, to 1980; LA Bureau Chief, 1983-86. *Time*, show business correspondent, LA, to 1983; Assoc Editor, current, 1986.

Smith, Geoffrey N. *Financial World.* Executive Editor. B. 1939, Cleveland, OH. Princeton, 1961, AB; NYU, 1970, MBA. US Army. Prentice-Hall, Harcourt Brace, Manuscript Editor, 1964. *Forbes*, writer, 1966-70; Asst Managing Editor, to 1976; European Bureau Chief, to 1978; Special Operations Editor, creator "Up & Comers" column, 1979; "The Numbers Game" column, 1980, & "Taxing Matters," to 1986. *Financial World*, Exec Editor, current, 1986. Author *Sweat Equity*, 1986.

Smith, Hedrick. *The New York Times.* Chief Washington Correspondent (On Leave). B. 1933, Kilmacolm, Scotland. Williams College, 1955, American History & Literature; Fulbright Scholar, Balliol College, Oxford, Political Science. Nieman Fellow, 1969. US Air Force, to 1959. UPI, to 1962. *The New York Times*, Washington correspondent; foreign correspondent, Saigon, Paris, Cairo; Moscow Bureau Chief, 1971-74; Deputy National Editor, to 1976; Washington Bureau Chief, to 1979; Chief Washington Correspondent, current, 1985. American Enterprise Institute, visiting journalist, current, 1985. Author *The Russians*: co-author *Reagan: The Man, The President* (with Leonard Silk *et al.*), 1981. Pulitzer Prize, Soviet Union coverage, 1974: co-winner Pulitzer Prize, 1972, Pentagon Papers series.

Smith, Lane Jeffrey. *Hot Rod.* Editor. B. 1954, Honolulu, HI. IA State U., 1978, Journalism & Mass Communications. *Car Craft*, Feature Editor, 1979-81; Technical Editor, to 1982; Senior Editor, to 1984; Editor, to 1987. *Hot Rod*, Editor, current, 1987.

Smith, Lee. *Fortune.* Board of Editors Member. Yale. NYC Dept of Consumer Affairs, Director of Research. *Black Enterprise*, Managing Editor. *Newsweek*, Assoc Editor. *Fortune*, Assoc Editor; Board of Editors, Tokyo (*Fortune International*); Board of Editors member, Washington, current.

Smith, R. Jeffrey. *The Washington Post.* National Security Correspondent. B. 1954, Chicago, IL. Duke, 1976, BA-Political Science & Public Policy Studies, William Randolph Hearst Foundation Scholarship; Columbia, 1977, MSJ. *Sarasota* (FL) *Herald-Tribune*, summer intern, 1973. *Des Moines Register*, Washington summer intern, 1974. *Milwaukee Journal*, summer intern, 1975. *Science*, Washington senior writer, news & comment section, 1977-86. *The Washington Post*, national security correspondent, current, 1986. National Assn Of Science Writer Science-in-Society Journalism Award, 1979 & 1982; Overseas Press Club Award Citation, Excellence, 1984; American Society of Magazine Editors National Magazine Award, Public Interest, 1986.

Smith, Randall. *The Wall Street Journal.* "Heard On The Street" Columnist. B. 1950, Montclair, NJ. Harvard, 1972, Social Relations. US Navy, 1972-76. MBA Communications, 1977. *New York Post*, city hall reporter, to 1980. *New York Daily News*, real estate reporter, to 1981. *The Wall Street Journal*, real estate reporter, to 1983; institutional investing reporter, to 1985; computer reporter, to 1986; "Heard On The Street" columnist, current, 1986.

Smith, Stephen. *Newsweek.* Executive Editor. B. 1949, NYC. U. of PA, 1971, BA-History. *Daily Hampshire Gazette*, city hall reporter, political writer, to 1973. *Albany Times-Union*, special reporter, to 1974. *Philadelphia Inquirer*, reporter, to 1975; Deputy Regional Editor, to 1976. *The Boston Globe*, Asst Business Editor, 1976; roving NE reporter, 1977; Asst Metro Editor, to 1978. *Horizon*, Senior Editor, 1978. *Time*, writer, to 1980; Senior Editor, 1981; "Nation" Editor, to 1985; acting Asst Managing Editor, to 1986. *Newsweek*, Exec Editor, current, 1986. Ernie Pyle Memorial Award, 1977.

Snow, Tony. *The Washington Times.* Editorial Page Editor. *Greensboro* (NC) *Record. The Virginian-Pilot. The Newport News Daily Press. The Detroit News*, Deputy Editorial Page Editor, to 1987. *The Washington Times*, Editorial Page Editor, current, 1987.

Solomon, Burt. *National Journal.* Staff Correspondent (On Leave). B. 1948, Baltimore, MD. Harvard, 1970, Social Studies. *Texas Observer*, freelance, 1971-72. *The Danvers* (MA) *Times*, reporter, to 1973. *The Real Paper* (Cambridge, MA), reporter, to 1975. *The Energy Daily*, Editor, to 1985. *National Journal*, staff correspondent, current (on leave, fall 1987).

Sowell, Thomas. Scripps-Howard News Service. Columnist. B. 1930. Harvard, 1958, AB-Economics; Columbia, 1959, AM-Economics; U. of Chicago, 1968, PhD. Center for Advanced Study in the Behavioral

Sciences Fellow, 1976-77. Hoover Institute Fellow, 1977. US Dept of Labor, economist, 1961-62. Rutgers, Douglass College, economics instructor, 1962-63; Howard U., economics lecturer, 1963-64. AT&T, economic analyst, to 1965. Cornell, asst prof, economics, to 1969. Brandeis, assoc prof, economics, to 1970. UCLA, assoc prof, economics, to 1974; economics prof, 1974-80. The Urban Institute, project director, 1972-74. Amherst College, visiting prof, economics, 1977. The Hoover Institute, Senior Fellow, current, 1980. Scripps-Howard News Service, columnist, current. Author several books, including *A Conflict Of Visions*, 1987.

Spaeth, Anthony P. *The Asian Wall Street Journal.* Manila Reporter. Williams College (MA), 1977. *The Asian Wall Street Journal*, reporter, to 1984; reporter, Manila, current, 1984.

Spevacek, Jennifer J. *The Washington Times.* Capitol Hill Reporter. B. 1961, Iowa City, IA. Wellesley College 1979-1981; U. of VA, 1983, BA-English. *The Washington Times*, VA capitol reporter, 1984-86; Capitol Hill reporter, current, 1986.

Stabler, Charles N. *The Wall Street Journal.* Assistant Managing Editor. B. 1925, Trenton, NJ. Swarthmore College, 1950, Economics. *Richmond Times-Dispatch*, reporter, to 1952. *The Wall Street Journal*, reporter, to 1955; established Southeastern bureau, 1955; Managing Editor, Pacific Coast edition, to 1964; Dow Jones Books, Director, to 1966; News Editor, *The Wall Street Journal*, Banking & Finance Editor, to 1981; Asst Managing Editor, current, 1981. Loeb Award, 1967.

Stahl, Leslie. CBS News. "Face the Nation" Moderator. B. 1941, Lynn, MA. Wheaton College (Norton, MA), 1963, BA, *cum laude*. Asst to speechwriter, NYC Mayor Lindsay, 1966-67. NBC News, "Huntley-Brinkley Report" NY election unit researcher, to 1969. WHDH-TV (Boston), Producer, reporter, to 1972. CBS News, Washington correspondent, from 1972; "Face the Nation" moderator, current, 1983. TX Headliners Award, 1973.

Stanfield, Rochelle L. *National Journal.* Staff Correspondent. B. 1940, Chicago, IL. Northwestern, 1962, BSJ, 1963, MSJ. The Council of State Governments, to 1966. Voice of America, news writer, 1966. National Governors' Assn, to 1970. US Advisory Commission on Intergovernmental Relations, information officer. US Conference of Mayors, to 1976. *National Journal*, staff correspondent, current, 1976.

Stark, Andrew. *The American Spectator.* Contributor. B. 1956, Vancouver, Canada. U. of British Columbia, 1978, BA-Political Science; London School of Economics, 1979, MS-Economics; Harvard, 1985, PhD-Government. Harvard, Teaching Fellow, Dept of Government, 1981-82. *The American Spectator*, Asst Managing Editor, 1980-81; Cambridge Editor, to 1985; contributor, current, 1985. Policy advisor, Prime Minister Brian Mulroney, Canada, current, 1985.

Steel, Ronald. *The New Republic.* Contributing Editor. B. 1931, Morris, IL. Northwestern, 1953; Harvard, 1955, Political Science. Scholastic Magazines, 1959-62. Freelance, current, 1962. *The New Republic*, Contributing Editor, current, 1980. Author 4 books, including *Walter Lippman And The American Century*. Sidney Hillman

Prize, 1968; Book Critics Circle Award, 1980; Bancroft Prize, American History, 1980; *Los Angeles Times* Book Award, 1980; *Sigma Delta Chi* Book Award, 1981; *The Washington Monthly* Book Award, 1981.

Steiger, Paul E. *The Wall Street Journal.* Deputy Managing Editor. Yale, 1964, BA-Economics. *Los Angeles Times*, writer, 1968-71; economic correspondent, Washington, to 1978; Business Editor, LA, to 1983. *The Wall Street Journal*, reporter, San Francisco, 1966-68; Asst Managing Editor, 1983-85; Deputy Managing Editor, current, 1985. Co-author *The 70's Crash.* 3 Gerald Loeb Awards, 2 John Hancock Awards, Economic & Business Coverage.

Stein, Benjamin J. *The American Spectator,* Contributing Editor. *The Los Angeles Herald-Examiner,* Columnist. B. 1944, Washington, DC. Columbia, 1966, BA-Economics; Yale Law, 1970, valedictorian. Speechwriter, President Nixon. *The Wall Street Journal*, columnist & editorial writer, 1974-76; freelance, current. *The New York Times, The Washington Post,* op-ed page writer, current. *The Los Angeles Herald-Examiner,* columnist, current. *The American Spectator,* Contributing Editor, current, 1972. Author 8 books, including *HER ONLY SIN*, 1986: co-author (with Herbert Stein) *On The Brink*, 1977; *Moneypower*, 1979. Freedoms Foundation Outstanding Essay Award, 1979.

Steinbreder, H. John. *Fortune.* Reporter. B. 1956, Connecticut. Franklin College, Switzerland, 1976, AA; U. of Nairobi, 1977; U. of Oregon, 1979, BAJ. *Burlington Free Press*, reporter (intern), 1981. *Fairfield Citizen-News*, reporter, 1982. Time, Inc, writer, reporter, to 1983. *Fortune*, reporter, current, 1983.

Stephens, Philip Francis. *Financial Times.* Economics Correspondent. B. 1953, London. Worcester College, Oxford, 1971-74, Modern History. Fulbright Fellow, Economic Journalism, *Los Angeles Times*, 1986. Europa publications, Asst Editor, to 1976. *Commerce International*, writer; Editor, to 1979. Reuters, London, Brussels correspondent, 1979-83. *Financial Times*, economics correspondent, current, 1983.

Sterba, James P. *The Wall Street Journal.* Assistant Foreign Editor. B. 1943, Detroit, MI. MI State U., 1966, BAJ. *The Evening Star*, Washington reporter, to 1967. *The New York Times*, asst to James Reston, to 1968; reporter, 1968; war correspondent, Saigon, to 1970; Bureau Chief, Jakarta, Indonesia & roving Asian correspondent, to 1973; Denver Bureau Chief, to 1975; Houston Bureau Chief, to 1977; economic development correspondent, 1978; Hong Kong Bureau Chief, to 1980; Peking Bureau Chief, 1981; Science writer, 1982. *The Wall Street Journal*, reporter & Editor, foreign desk, 1982; Asst Foreign Editor & special writer, current, 1983. Distinguished Alumni Award, 1970.

Stern, Richard L. *Forbes.* Senior Editor. B. 1941, NYC. Adelphi U., Psychology. AP, National Editor, 1970-74. *Securities Week*, Editor, to 1976. *Institutional Investor*, "Wall Street Letter" Managing Editor, to 1979. *New York Daily News*, business columnist, to 1980. *Forbes*, Senior Editor, current, 1980. Loeb Award, 1984.

Sterngold, James. *The New York Times.* "Business Day" Reporter. B. 1954, Detroit, MI. Middlebury College,

1977, BA-Philosophy. Columbia, 1980, MSJ. Time-Life Books, freelance, 1978-80. AP-Dow Jones Newswire, Hong Kong Bureau Founder, correspondent, to 1984. *The New York Times*, "Business Day" reporter, current, 1984. *The New York Times* Publishers' Award, 1987.

Stevens, Mark. *Newsweek & The New Republic.* Art Critic. B. 1951, NYC. Princeton, 1973, History. *Newsweek*, art critic, current, 1977. *The New Republic*, art critic, current, 1986.

Stewart, William Morgan. *Time.* Hong Kong Bureau Chief. B. 1937, Dundee, Scotland. Johns Hopkins, 1958, History. US Foreign Service (Washington, India, Vietnam), 1962-71. *Time*, New Delhi Bureau Chief, 1971-73; Beirut correspondent, 1974; Tokyo Bureau Chief, to 1977; NY Deputy Chief of Correspondents, 1978; NY Assoc Editor, 1979; Middle East Bureau Chief, Beirut, to 1984; Washington correspondent, 1984; Washington diplomatic correspondent, to 1986; Hong Kong Bureau Chief, current, 1986.

Stillman, Whit. *The American Spectator.* New York Editor. B. 1952, Washington, DC. Harvard, 1973, US History. *The Harvard Crimson*, News Editor, 1970-73. *The American Spectator*, contributor, to 1978; Publisher, to 1979; NY Editor, current, 1979. *Access*, Daily News Briefing, Exec Editor, 1979-80.

Stockton, William. *The New York Times.* New York Reporter. B. 1944, Raton, NM. NM Institute of Mining & Technology, 1966, BS-Chemistry. Nieman Fellow, 1972-75. AP, 1968-75. Physicians Radio Network, Exec Editor, to 1979. *The New York Times*, Director, science news & Editor, "Science Times," to 1982; asst to Exec Editor, to 1985; Mexico Bureau Chief, to 1986; NY reporter, current, 1986. Author *Final Approach*, 1977; *Altered Destinies*, 1979: co-author *Spaceliner* (with John Noble Wilford), 1981.

Stokes, Bruce. *National Journal.* International Economics Correspondent. B. 1948, Butler, PA. Georgetown, 1970, BSFS-International Affairs; Johns Hopkins, 1975, MA. Worldwatch Institute, Senior Researcher, to 1982. NPR, Producer, 1983. *National Journal*, international economics correspondent, current, 1984.

Stone, I.F. (Isidore Feinstein). Freelance Writer. B. 1907, Philadelphia. Studied U. of PA, 1924-27, BA, 1975. *The Progress*, Editor & Publisher, 1922. *The Haddonfield Press, Camden* (NJ) *Courier-Post, Philadelphia Inquirer*, reporter, 1922-33. *Philadelphia Record*, reporter, 1922-33; editorial writer, 1933. *New York Post*, editorial writer, 1933-39. *The Nation*, Assoc Editor, 1938-40; Washington Editor, to 1946. *New York Star, New York Daily Compass, PM, New York Post*, reporter, columnist, editorial writer, 1942-52. *I.F. Stone's Biweekly*, Editor & Publisher, 1953-71. American U., Distinguished Scholar in Residence, current, 1975. Freelance, current. Author 11 books including *Polemics and Prophesies*, 1972. George Polk Memorial Award, 1970; Columbia Journalism Award, 1971.

Strobel, Warren Paul. *The Washington Times.* National Desk Reporter. B. 1962, Camp Zama, Japan. U. of MO, at Columbia, 1984, Journalism. *Maneater*, U. of MO, Editor, 1983. *Missourian* (Columbia, MO), state capital

Biographics

reporter, spring 1984; city hall reporter, fall 1984. *The Washington Times*, intern, metro desk, summer 1984; metro reporter, to 1986; national desk reporter, current, 1986.

Stroud, Joe H. *Detroit Free Press*. Editor. B. 1936, AR. Hendrix College, BA-History & Political Science; Tulane, MA-History. Various newspapers, Pine Bluff & Little Rock, AR, reporter & editorial writer. *Winston-Salem Journal & The Sentinel*, Editor, Editorial Pages. *Detroit Free Press*, Assoc Editor, to 1973; Editor, current, 1973. William Allen White Awards, Editorial Excellence, 1973, '76, '77, '79, '80; Overseas Press Club Citation Reporting Excellence, 1974; Paul Tobenkin Memorial Award, 1976.

Struck, Myron. *Roll Call*. Managing Editor. B. 1953, NYC. Miami-Dade Community College, 1971-73; FL International U., 1973-75. *The Good Times*, newspaper, FL International U., founder, 1975. *The Miami Herald*, Sunday Features writer, Editor, 1974-75. Press asst to Michael Abrams, Chairman, Dade Cty Democratic Party, 1975. *Roll Call*, reporter, News Editor, to 1976, '79; Managing Editor, current, 1987. Press secretary, Rep. Phillip Burton (D-CA), 1977-79. States News Service, reporter, Desk Editor, to 1981. *The Washington Post*, reporter, "Federal Report" page, to 1985. *The Washington Times*, reporter, Asst National Editor, political coordinator, '86 elections, to 1987.

Sturm, Paul W. Jr. *BusinessWeek*. Assistant Managing Editor. Oberlin; Columbia, MSJ; Georgetown Law Center, JD. *Newsweek International*, writer. ESPN, "Business Times" Editor. *Forbes*, London, Washington, LA; Managing Editor. *BusinessWeek*, Asst Managing Editor, current, 1985; supervises annual issue of "Top 1000."

Sullivan, Allanna. *The Wall Street Journal*. Reporter. Queen's College (NY), 1971, BA-English; Columbia, 1977, MSJ. *Boating*, to 1975. *The Record* (Bergen, NJ), Copy Editor, 1977. *Nucleonics Week*, Wire Editor, to 1978. *Coal Age*, Asst Editor, Assoc Editor, to 1982. AP-Dow Jones, reporter, to 1984. *The Wall Street Journal*, reporter, current, 1984.

Sullivan, John Fox. *National Journal*. President & Publisher. B. 1943, Philadelphia. Yale, 1966, American Studies; Columbia, 1968. *Newsweek*, to 1975. *National Journal*, President & Publisher, current, 1975.

Sullivan, Scott. *Newsweek*. European Editor. B. 1937, Cleveland, OH. Yale, 1958; Cambridge, UK, 1960, English. *The Sun*, reporter, 1963-65; City Editor, to 1970; Paris correspondent, to 1973. *Newsweek*, Paris Bureau Chief, to 1975, 1978-83; Chief Diplomatic Correspondent, 1976-78; European Editor, current, 1983. NY Newspaper Guild Page One Award, 1977; Overseas Press Club Awards: Citation, Excellence, 1983; Mary Hemingway Award, 1982; Hallie & Whit Burnett Award, 1983; Ed Cunningham Award 1985.

Sulzberger, Arthur Ochs. *The New York Times*. President & Publisher. B. 1926, NYC. Columbia, 1951, BA. *The New York Times* Company, from 1951: asst treasurer, 1958-63; President & Publisher, current, 1963.

Summers, Colonel Harry G. Jr. *U.S.News & World Report*, Contributing Editor. *Los Angeles Times*

Syndicate, Military & Political Affairs Columnist. B. 1932, Covington, KY. U. of MD, 1957, BS-Military Science; US Army Command & General Staff College, 1968, MS-Military Arts & Science; Army War College, 1981. Military career: infantry squad leader, Korea; battalion & corps operations officer, Vietnam; negotiator with N. Vietnam on POW/MIA issues; negotiator, US withdrawal terms from Hanoi; General MacArthur Chair of Military Research, Army War College, 1947-85. Freelance, *Kansas City Star, Kansas City Times*, 1968-75; other publications, current, 1980. *U.S.News & World Report*, senior military correspondent, 1985-87; Contributing Editor, current, 1987. *Los Angeles Times* Syndicate, Military & Political Affairs columnist, current, 1987. Lecturer on Military Strategy & Military-Media Relations, current. Author *On Strategy: A Critical Analysis of the Vietnam War*, 1982 (Furness Award, OH State U.); "Vietnam War Almanac," (*Facts on File*), 1985.

Szulc, Tad. Freelance Writer. B. 1926, Warsaw, Poland. U. of Brazil, 1946, History. UPI, UN correspondent, 1949-53. *The New York Times*, correspondent, Washington, Latin America, Spain & Portugal, Eastern Europe, to 1973. Freelance, current. Author 15 books including *Illusion of Peace*, 1978; *Fidel: A Critical Portrait*, 1986. Maria Moors Cabot Gold Medal, Hemispheric Reporting, Columbia, 1959; Overseas Press Club Best Book on Foreign Affairs (*Illusion of Peace*), 1978; Knight of the Cross of the *Legion d'Honneur* (France), 1984.

Tagaza, Emilia. *Financial Times*. Canberra Correspondent. B. 1953, Manila, Philippines. U. of Philippines, 1975, AB-Mass Communication & Broadcast Communication. *Asian Business Magazine*, Asst Editor, Features Editor, to 1978. *Asia Banking Magazine*, Manila correspondent, 1982-85; Canberra correspondent, current, 1985. *The Christian Science Monitor*, Manila correspondent, 1983-85. *Financial Times*, freelance, Manila, to 1985; Canberra correspondent, current, 1985.

Tagliabue, John. *The New York Times*. Bonn Economics Correspondent. B. 1942, NJ. St. Peter's College; Catholic U. (Milan); U. of Bonn. *The Sun*, Bonn Bureau correspondent, to 1980. *The New York Times*, economics correspondent, Bonn, current, 1980.

Taki. *The Spectator & The American Spectator*. Contributing Editor. B. 1937, Athens, Greece. U. of VA, 1959, History. *Acropolis*, Chief Foreign Correspondent. *The Spectator*, columnist, current, 1977. *National Review*, contributor. *Esquire*, columnist, to 1984. *Interview*, columnist, current, 1984. *Spy*, columnist, current. *The American Spectator*, Contributing Editor, current.

Talbott, Strobe. *Time*. Washington Bureau Chief. B. 1946, Dayton, OH. Yale, 1968, BA; Oxford, 1971, MA (Rhodes Scholar). *Time*, Eastern European correspondent, to 1973; State Dept correspondent, to 1975; White House correspondent, to 1977; diplomatic correspondent, from 1977; Washington Bureau Chief, current, 1987. Author *Endgame: The Inside Story of SALT II*, 1979; *Deadly Gambits*. Edward Weintal Prize, Distinguished Diplomatic Reporting, 1980; Overseas Press Club Award, 1983.

Tamayo, Juan O. *The Miami Herald*. Middle East Correspondent. B. 1948, Guantanamo, Cuba. Marquette, 1971, Journalism. UPI, Hartford Bureau, to 1976; Foreign

399

Desk, NY, to 1979; Central America News Director, Mexico City, to 1982. *The Miami Herald*, Latin American Desk, to 1986; Middle East correspondent, Jerusalem, current, 1986.

Tanzer, Andrew. *Forbes.* Tokyo Bureau Chief. B. 1957, Washington, DC. Wesleyan U., 1979, BA-East Asian Studies, *magna cum laude*; Columbia, 1980, MSJ. Overseas Press Club Fellow. *Far Eastern Economic Review*, Taiwan reporter, to 1983; Hong Kong reporter, to 1984. *Forbes*, LA writer, to 1985; Tokyo Bureau Chief, current, 1985.

Tapscott, Mark. *The Washington Times.* Business Editor. US Office of Personnel Management, *Management*, to 1985. *The Washington Times*, national desk reporter; Asst Business Editor, to 1987; Business Editor, current, 1987.

Tarne, Eugene C. *Human Events.* Associate Editor. B. 1955, White Plains, NY. Georgetown, 1977, BA-Theology; George Washington U., 1979, MA-History of Religions. Press secretary, Rep. Bill Schuette (MI), 1986. *Human Events*, Assoc Editor, current, 1986.

Taubman, Philip. *The New York Times.* Moscow Bureau Chief. B. 1948, NYC. Stanford, 1970, Modern European History. *Time*, Boston staff, 1970-73; writer, NY, 1976; Washington staff, 1977. *Esquire*, Roving Editor, 1979. *The New York Times*, Washington staff, 1985; Moscow reporter, to 1986; Moscow Bureau Chief, current, 1986. Polk Award, National Reporting, 1982, Foreign Policy Reporting, 1984.

Taylor, Frederick. *The Wall Street Journal.* Executive Editor (Retired 1986). B. Portland, OR. U. of OR, Eugene, 1950, BS. US Air Force, 1955-57. *The Oregonian*, stringer, to 1950; sports writer, 1952-54. *Astoria* (OR) *Budget*, to 1952. *The Wall Street Journal*, copyreader, NY, 1955, 1957; reporter; "Page One" rewriteman; Detroit Bureau Chief, 1959-64; Washington "Labor Letter" originator, columnist (with John Grimes), to 1966; Pentagon correspondent, to 1968; Asst Managing Editor, West Coast operations, San Francisco, to 1970; Managing Editor, to 1977; Exec Editor, retired 1986.

Taylor, Paul. *The Washington Post.* Reporter. B. 1949, NYC. Yale, 1970, BA-American Studies. *Winston-Salem Sentinel*, reporter, to 1973. *Philadelphia Inquirer*, reporter & columnist, to 1981. *The Washington Post*, reporter, current, 1981.

Taylor, Stuart Jr. *The New York Times.* Supreme Court Correspondent. B. 1948, Philadelphia, PA. Princeton, 1970, *Phi Beta Kappa*; Harvard Law, 1977, 1st in class. *Harvard Law Review*, acting officer. Frederick Sheldon Traveling Fellow, Harvard, 1977-78. *The Sun/The Evening Sun*, reporter, 1971-74. Wilmer, Cutler & Pickering, Washington, attorney, 1977-80. *The New York Times*, legal correspondent, to 1985; Supreme Court correspondent, current, 1985.

Taylor, Walter. *U.S.News & World Report.* Singapore Bureau Chief. *U.S.News & World Report*, Asia correspondent, covering Tokyo & Peking, to 1986; Singapore Bureau Chief, current, 1986.

Teachout, Terry. *New York Daily News.* Editorial Page Editor. B. 1956, Cape Girardeau, MO. William Jewell

College, 1979, Music, Journalism. *Illini Review* (U. of IL), co-Founder (with Mike Fumento), 1984-85. *Harper's*, Asst Editor, to 1986; Assoc Editor, 1986; Senior Editor, to 1987. *New York Daily News*, editorial board, current, 1987. *The American Spectator, National Review*, contributor, current.

Temko, Edward James (Ned). *The Christian Science Monitor.* South Africa Correspondent. Williams College, 1974, Political Science, *magna cum laude*. AP, reporter, 1976. UPI, Brussels correspondent, to 1977; Beirut correspondent, to 1979. *The Christian Science Monitor*, Middle East correspondent, to 1981; Moscow Bureau Chief, to 1983; Middle East correspondent, to 1985; South Africa correspondent, Johannesburg, current, 1985.

Terry, Edith. *BusinessWeek.* Acting Toronto Bureau Chief. B. 1952, Montgomery, AL. Yale, 1974, BA-Asian History; Stanford, 1976, MA-East Asian Studies. Philippine Agency for National Minorities, researcher, to 1972. Library of Congress, Editor, Chinese section, to 1977. *The China Business Review*, Assoc Editor, to 1980. *BusinessWeek*, Staff Editor, to 1983; Toronto correspondent, to 1986; Acting Bureau Chief, current, 1986. Author *The China Traders*, 1986; *The Executive Guide To China*, 1984.

Thatcher, Gary L. *The Christian Science Monitor.* Diplomatic Correspondent. B. 1949, Beaumont, TX. C.W. Post College, Long Island U., 1972, BA-Communications, *summa cum laude*. WDAM-TV (Hattiesburg, MS), reporter, to 1974. WAPI-TV (Birmingham, AL), reporter, to 1974. *The Christian Science Monitor*, writer, to 1976; Atlanta correspondent, to 1978; Africa correspondent (Johannesburg-based), to 1981; National Editor, to 1983; Moscow correspondent, to 1986; diplomatic correspondent, current, 1986. Leelanau Center for Education, Glen Arbor, MI, lecturer, 1982, '83, '86. Clarion Award, Women in Communication, 1979; Certificate of Merit, ABA, 1979.

Thomas, Cal. *Los Angeles Times* Syndicate. Columnist. B. 1942, Washington, DC. American U., 1968, English Literature. KPRC-TV (Houston, TX), to 1969, 1973-77. NBC News, 1961-65, 1969-73. WTTG-TV, Washington commentator, current, 1985. NPR, commentator, current, 1985. *Los Angeles Times* Syndicate, columnist, current, 1984. AMY Writing Award, 1987; AP, UPI Spot News Awards, Headliners.

Thomas, Evan. *Newsweek.* Washington Bureau Chief. Harvard, 1973; U. of VA Law, 1977. *Time*, legal reporter, to 1979; Supreme Court & Justice Dept correspondent, to 1981; Congressional correspondent, to 1983; "Nation" writer, Assoc Editor, to 1986. *Newsweek*, Washington Bureau Chief, current, 1986.

Thomas, Helen. United Press International. White House Bureau Chief. B. 1920, Winchester, KY. Wayne U., 1942, BA. UPI, Washington wire service reporter, 1943-74; White House Bureau Chief, current, 1974. Author *Dateline White House.* 4th Estate Award, National Press Club, 1984.

Thomas, Rich. *Newsweek.* Chief Economic Correspondent. B. 1931, Detroit, MI. U. of MI, 1952, BA-English Literature; postgrad U. of Frankfurt, W. Germany, 1955, U. of MI, 1956-57. US Army, 1952-55.

U. of MI, Teaching Fellow, 1957. UPI, correspondent, Detroit, to 1959. McGraw-Hill, Public Affairs, to 1960. *New York Post*, Financial Editor, to 1962. *Newsweek*, writer, Editor, NY, to 1970; Chief Economic Correspondent, Washington, current, 1970. Gerald M. Loeb Award, 1970.

Thomas, William F. *Los Angeles Times*. Editor & Executive Vice President. B. 1924, Bay City, MI. Northwestern, 1950, BSJ, 1951, MSJ. *Buffalo Evening News*, Copy Editor, 1950-52; Asst Chief Copy Editor, to 1955. *Sierra Madre* (CA) *News*, Editor, to 1956. *Mirror-News*, copy reader, to 1957; reporter, to 1959; Asst City Editor, to 1961; City Editor, to 1962. *Los Angeles Times*, Asst Metropolitan Editor, to 1965; Metro Editor, to 1971; Exec Editor, 1971; Editor, to 1972; Editor & Exec VP, current, 1972. Harrington Award, Northwestern, 1951.

Thurow, Roger. *The Wall Street Journal*. South Africa Reporter. B. Elgin, IL. U. of IA, 1979, BA-Journalism & Political Science. *Daily Iowan*, to 1977. *The Wall Street Journal*, intern, summer 1979; Dallas reporter, 1980-81; Houston staff, to 1982; Bonn reporter (principal East-West reporter), to 1986; South Africa reporter (London-based), current, 1986.

Tinsley, Jack B. *Fort Worth Star-Telegram*. Vice President & Executive Editor. B. 1934, Angelina County, TX. Sam Houston State U., 1958, Speech & Journalism. *Fort Worth Star-Telegram*, reporter, education writer, Sunday Editor, Asst Managing Editor, asst to Editor, to 1975; Exec Editor, current, 1975; VP, current. 2 Pulitzer Prizes (Spot News Photography, 1981; Meritorious Public Service, 1985) under editorship.

Tolchin, Martin. *The New York Times*. Washington Reporter. B. 1928, NYC. ID State College, U. of UT; NY Law School, 1951. US Army, to 1953. Law clerk, NYC, to 1954. *The New York Times*, reporter, NY, to 1970; City Hall Bureau Chief, to 1973; Washington reporter, current, 1973: White House correspondent, 1978-79; regional reporter; currently covering Congress. Co-author (with Susan Tolchin) *To the Victor: Political Patronage from the Clubhouse to the White House; Clout: Womanpower & Politics*. The Women's Press Club, NY Reporters Assn, One Hundred Year Assn, NY Newspaper Guild, & Citizen's Budget Commission, 1966.

Tomlinson, Kenneth Y. *Reader's Digest*. Executive Editor & Vice President. B. 1944, Grayson County, VA. Randolph-Macon College, 1966, BA. *Richmond Times-Dispatch*, reporter, 1965-68. National Voluntary Service Advisory Commission, 1981-83. Voice of America, Director, 1982-84. *Reader's Digest*, correspondent, Senior Editor, 1968-82 (Paris-based European Editor, 1977-78); Managing Editor, 1984-85; Exec Editor, current, 1985; VP, current. Co-author *P.O.W.*, 1977. US National Commission on Libraries & Information Science, Chairman, 1986-87.

Tonelson, Alan. *Foreign Policy*. Associate Editor. B. 1953, Flushing, NY. Princeton, 1970, History. *The Inter Dependent*, Assoc Editor, to 1979. *The Wilson Quarterly*, Assoc Editor, to 1981. *Foreign Policy*, Assoc Editor, current, 1983. Freelance, current, 1982.

Toth, Robert C. *Los Angeles Times*. Washington Writer. B. 1928, Blakely, PA. Washington U., 1952, BS-Chemical

Engineering; Columbia, 1955, MSJ. Nieman Fellow, 1960-61; Pulitzer Traveling Scholar, 1955. US Marines, 1946-48; US Army, 1952-53. *Rubber World*, Assoc Editor, 1953-54. *The Journal* (Providence, RI), reporter, 1955-57. *New York Herald Tribune*, writer, to 1960; writer, Washington, to 1962. *The New York Times*, science writer, Washington, to 1963. *Los Angeles Times*, writer, Washington, science & Supreme Court, to 1965; London Bureau Chief, to 1970; State Dept correspondent, to 1972; White House correspondent, to 1974; Moscow Bureau Chief, to 1977; science writer, Washington, to 1979; writer, Washington, national security affairs, current, 1979. *Sigma Delta Chi* Award, Foreign Correspondence, 1978; Overseas Press Club Award, Foreign Correspondence, 1978; George Polk Award, Foreign Correspondence, 1978: co-winner *Times* Editorial Award, 1985; Edward Weintal Prize, Diplomatic Reporting, 1986.

Tower, Kenneth D. *Chicago Sun-Times*. Executive Editor & Vice President. Northwestvern. *Chicago Sun-Times*, copy clerk, reporter, editorial staff, to 1984; Managing Editor, to 1987; Exec Editor, VP, current, 1987.

Trachtenberg, Jeffrey. *Forbes*. Senior Writer & "Marketing" Editor. B. 1950, Mineola, NY. Franklin & Marshall College, 1972, BA-Literature. *Socio-Economic Publications*, labor reporter, 1974-77. Lebhar-Friedman Publications, business writer, to 1979. *Women's Wear Daily*, business reporter & 7th Ave reporter, Hollywood feature writer, 1978-84. *Forbes*, senior writer, "Marketing Editor," current, 1984.

Tracy, Eleanor Johnson. *Fortune*. Associate Editor. Wheaton College; studied Brown, Johns Hopkins, Columbia & NYU. *The Journal-Bulletin* (Providence, RI), feature writer, reporter. *The Sun*, feature writer, reporter. *San Francisco Chronicle*, feature writer, reporter. Time, Inc, researcher, 1956. *Time*, acting head researcher, 1956-57. *Fortune*, research assoc, from 1957; Assoc Editor, current.

Trainor, Bernard E. *The New York Times*. Military Correspondent. B. 1928, NYC. Holy Cross, 1951, History; U. of CO, 1963, MA. *The New York Times*, military correspondent, current, 1986.

Treaster, Joseph B. *The New York Times*. Caribbean Bureau Chief. B. 1941. U. of Miami, 1963, Journalism. *The Miami Herald*, reporter, to 1963. US Army newspapers, reporter, Vietnam, to 1965. *The New York Times*, reporter, to 1984; Caribbean Bureau Chief, current, 1984. Freelance, current. Co-author *Inside Report on the Hostage Crisis: No Hiding Place*. 3 Overseas Press Club Awards, 2 Page One Awards & Inter-American Press Assn Award.

Trewitt, Henry. *U.S.News & World Report*. Deputy Managing Editor — Foreign Affairs. Nieman Fellow. Santa Fe New Mexican, 1949-51. *Chattanooga Times*, to 1956. *The Sun*, to 1961; Bonn correspondent, to 1966; diplomatic correspondent, 1974-85. *Newsweek*, diplomatic & White House correspondent, to 1974. *U.S.News & World Report*, Deputy Managing Editor, Foreign Affairs, current, 1985. Author *McNamara: His Ordeal in the Pentagon*. Weintal Award, Diplomatic Correspondence, 1982.

Trillin, Calvin. *The New Yorker*, Staff Writer. King Features Syndicate, Columnist. B. 1935, Kansas City, MO. Yale, 1957, BA. *Time*, writer & reporter, to 1963. *The New Yorker*, staff writer, current, 1963. *The Nation*, contributor, current, 1978. King Features Syndicate, columnist, current, 1986. Author several books including *If You Can't Say Something Nice*, 1987.

Trimble, Jeff. *U.S.News & News Report*. Moscow Bureau Chief. *U.S.News & World Report*, Rome Bureau Chief, to 1986; Moscow Bureau Chief, current, 1986.

Truell, Peter. *The Wall Street Journal*. Reporter. Marlborough College (UK), 1973, Arts & Sciences; Pembroke College, Cambridge, 1977, MA-Modern History, (economics & business); St. Anthony's College, Oxford, 1979, MPhil. *Librarie Du Liban* (Beirut, Lebanon), Asst Editor, Dictionary dept, 1979. Orion Bank Ltd, London, junior exec, 1980. *Economist Financial Report*, London, Managing Editor, to 1982. *Middle East Economic Digest*, Deputy Editor, 1982. *The Wall Street Journal*/Europe, reporter, London, to 1987. *The Wall Street Journal*, reporter, NY, current, 1987.

Tucker, William. *The American Spectator*, New York Correspondent. B. 1942, Orange, NJ. Amherst College, 1964, BA-English & Economics. *Rockland Journal-News*, reporter, to 1973. *The Record* (Bergen, NJ), reporter, to 1975. *Rockland County Times*, writer-Editor, to 1976. *Harper's*, Contributing Editor, to 1982; current, 1983. *The American Spectator*, NY correspondent, current. Freelance, current, 1976. Author *Progress and Privilege: America in the Age of Environmentalism*, 1982; *Vigilante-The Backlash Against Crime in America*, 1985. John Hancock Award, Business Writing, 1977; Gerald Loeb Awards, 1978, '80; Amos Tuck Award, 1980.

Tumulty, Karen. *Los Angeles Times*. Washington Writer. B. 1955, San Antonio, TX. U. of TX, Austin, 1977, BJ, high honors; Harvard, 1981, MBA. *Daily Texan*, staff member. Long News Service, part-time reporter, 1976-77; *San Antonio Light*, intern, summer 1976; Business Editor, reporter, to 1979. *Los Angeles Times*, intern, summer 1980; energy writer, to 1983; Washington writer, current, 1983.

Tuohy, William. *Los Angeles Times*. Bonn Bureau Chief. B. 1926, Chicago, IL. Northwestern, 1951, English. *San Francisco Chronicle*, copyboy, reporter, Night City Editor, to 1959. *Newsweek*, back-of-book writer, Assoc Editor, Asst National Editor, national political correspondent, 1964; Saigon Bureau Chief, 1965. *Los Angeles Times*, Saigon Bureau Chief, to 1968; Beirut Bureau Chief, to 1971; Rome Bureau Chief, to 1977; London, to 1985; Bonn Bureau Chief, current, 1985. Headliners Award, 1965; Pulitzer Prize, 1969; Overseas Press Club, 1969.

Turner, David A. *Management*. Editor. B. 1947, Austin, TX. U. of TX, Austin, 1971, History. *Energy Reporter*, 1973-79. *Inside DOE*, 1979-81. *Management*, Editor, current. Outstanding Speechwriters, Washington, 1980, NAGC; Editor, Best Government Magazine "Blue Pencil Award," 1985.

Turner, Robert E. III. Turner Broadcasting System, Inc. Chairman of the Board. B. 1938. Brown U. Turner Broadcasting System, Inc, Chairman of the Board, current.

Tyler, Patrick E. *The Washington Post*. Middle East Correspondent. B. 1951, St. Louis, MO. U. of SC, 1974, Journalism. *The Hampton County* (SC) *Guardian*, Editor, 1974. *The Allandale County* (SC) *Citizen*, Editor, 1974. *Charlotte* (NC) *News*, reporter, 1975. *The St. Petersburg Times*, police & courts reporter, to 1978. *Congressional Quarterly*, 1978. PBS, WCET (Cincinnati, OH), host, "Congressional Outlook" documentary series, 1978. *The Washington Post*, metro, investigative, foreign staffs, to 1986; Middle East correspondent, current, 1986.

Tyrrell, R. Emmett Jr. *The American Spectator*. Founder & Editor. B. 1943, Chicago, IL. IN U., 1965, BA-History, 1967, MA. *The American Spectator* (originally *The Alternative)*, Founder, 1967; Editor, current, 1967. King Features Syndicate, "Public Nuisances" columnist, current.

Ungeheuer, Frederick. *Time*. Senior Correspondent. B. 1932, Frankfurt-am-Main, Germany. Harvard, 1956, Government (Theory). Reuters, correspondent, to 1963. Time-Life News Service, correspondent, West Africa Bureau Chief, to 1969. *Harper's*, Contributing Editor, to 1971. *Eastwest Markets/Mideast Markets*, Editor, to 1977. *Time*, UN Bureau Chief, to 1973; European economic correspondent, to 1980; financial correspondent, to 1982; senior correspondent, current, 1982.

Urquhart, John D. Dow Jones-Canada. Ottawa Bureau Chief. U. of Toronto, Liberal Arts. Reuters, Editor, London, 1960-63. *International Herald Tribune*, reporter, Paris, to 1967. AP-Dow Jones, reporter, London, to 1972. Dow Jones, reporter, to 1976. Dow Jones-Canada, Bureau Chief, Ottawa, current, 1976.

Utley, Clifton Garrick. NBC News. "NBC Nightly News" Correspondent & Occasional Anchor. B. 1939, Chicago. Carleton College, 1961, BA; postgrad Free U. of Berlin, 1961-62. NBC News, correspondent, Brussels, to 1964; Vietnam, to 1965; Chicago, 1966; NYC, 1966, 1971-73; Berlin, 1966-68; Paris Bureau Chief, to 1971; London correspondent, 1973-79; "NBC Nightly News" Chief Foreign Correspondent, current, 1980; occasional anchor, current.

Uttal, Bro. *Fortune*. Board of Editors Member. Harvard, *magna cum laude*; Harvard, MBA. Educational Management Assocs, Inc, consultant. *The Phoenix* (Cambridge, MA), columnist. *Boston After Dark*, columnist. *Fortune*, reporter, researcher, to 1982; Board of Editors, current, 1982, based Menlo Park, CA.

van England, Claude. *The Christian Science Monitor*. Foreign Correspondent. B. 1949, Brussels, Belgium. *Universite Libre de Bruxelles*, History. Nieman Fellow, 1981-82. RTBF (Belgian Public TV) staffer, 1971-77; Foreign News Editor, current, 1983. Freelance, Teheran, 1978-79. *Le Monde Diplomatique*, writer, 1979. *The Christian Science Monitor*, foreign correspondent, covering Middle East & Persian Gulf, current, 1983.

VanSlambrouck, Paul. *The Christian Science Monitor*. International News Editor. B. 1950, Teaneck, NJ. U. of CA, Santa Barbara, 1972, Anthropology. *San Francisco Business Magazine*, writer & photographer, to 1975; Assoc

Editor, to 1976. *The Christian Science Monitor*, NE reporter, to 1977; Asst Editor, Business Page, to 1979; magazine writer, Boston, 1979; domestic correspondent, to 1981; foreign correspondent, Johannesburg, to 1985; International News Editor, current, 1985.

Van Voorst, Bruce. *Time.* National Security Correspondent. U. of MI, 1955, MA-Soviet Studies. CIA, political analyst. Roving foreign correspondent, Europe & Latin America. *Time*, foreign correspondent; national security correspondent, current.

Vartan, Vartanig G. *The New York Times.* "Market Place" Columnist. B. Pasadena, CA. Yale. UPI, 1957-62. *The New York Herald Tribune*, 1957-62. *The Christian Science Monitor*, columnist, 1957-62. *The New York Times*, from 1963; "Market Place" columnist, current. Author *50 Wall Street; The Dinosaur Fund.*

Vaughn, Richard A. *Chronicles.* Publisher. B. 1954, Hinsdale, IL. Rockford College, 1976, Political Science. *Chronicles*, publisher, current, 1977. *This World*, publisher, current. *The Family In America*, publisher, current. *The Religion & Society Report*, publisher, current.

Vickery, Hugh. *The Washington Times.* Business Reporter. B. 1957, Yokuska, Japan. Hamilton College (Clinton, NY), 1980, Government. *National Geographic*, freelance, to 1983. *Washington Business Review*, reporter, to 1981. Association Management, Assoc Editor, to 1983. *The Washington Times*, business reporter, current, 1983.

Vigilante, Richard. *National Review.* Article Editor. B. 1956, Nassau County, NY. Yale, 1978, Philosophy. *Consumers Research*, Washington Editor, 1980-81. *Charleston Daily Mail*, editorial writer, 1982-83. White House Committee on Central America, speech writer, 1983. *The Washington Times*, editorial writer, to 1985. *National Review*, Article Editor, current, 1985. Freelance, current. TV documentaries, writer & producer, current, 1980. Author *Consumer Issues Of The '80s & Consumer's Research*, 1981: co-author (with Gregory Sanford) *Grenada: The Untold Story*, 1983.

Von Kuehnelt-Leddihn, Erik Ritter. *National Review.* European Correspondent. B. 1909, Tobelbad, Austria. U. of Budapest, Doctor of Economics & Political Science. *The Spectator*, London. Georgetown, teacher, 1937. St. Peter's College (NJ), Dept Head, History & Sociology. Fordham, Japanese instructor, 1942-43. Chestnut Hill College, (PA) faculty member, to 1947. Freelance, current. *National Review*, European correspondent, current. Author many books including *Leftism (From de Sade and Marx to Hitler and Pol Pot)*, in progress.

Wade, Lawrence. The Lawrence Wade Group. Columnist. B. 1948, Cleveland, OH. OH State U., 1977, Journalism. *The Wall Street Journal*, reporter, 1977. *The Miami Herald*, reporter, 1978. *The Journal Herald* (Dayton, OH), editorial writer, columnist, reporter, 1980. *The Orlando Sentinel*, editorial writer, 1982. US Commission on Civil Rights, Spokesman, Director of Press & Communications, 1984. *The Washington Times*, columnist, to 1987. The Lawrence Wade Group, columnist, current, 1987.

Walczak, Lee. *BusinessWeek.* Washington Bureau Manager. U. of MD; U. of MO, MAJ. McGraw-Hill World News, health, transportation reporter, Washington. *BusinessWeek*, NY; White House correspondent; Editor, "Washington Outlook;" Political News Editor; Washington Bureau Manager, current, 1985.

Waldholz, Michael R. *The Wall Street Journal.* Science Reporter. B. 1950, Newark, NJ. U. of Pittsburgh, 1972, BA-English Literature, 1973, MA-English Literature. *The Wall Street Journal*, science reporter, current, 1980. Co-winner National Assn of Science Writers' Science & Society Award, 1986.

Waldman, Steven. *The Washington Monthly.* Editor. B. 1962, NYC. Columbia, 1984, Political Science. States News Service, 1985. *The Washington Monthly*, Editor, current, 1986. Benjamin Fine Award, Education Journalism.

Wall, James M. *The Christian Century.* Editor. B. 1928, Monroe, GA. Emory U., 1949, 1955, Journalism; U. of Chicago, 1959, Theology. *Journal and Constitution*, sports writer, 1947-50. *Christian Advocate*, Managing Editor & Editor, 1960-72. *The Christian Century*, Editor, current, 1972.

Wallace, Christopher. NBC News. "NBC Nightly News" White House Correspondent & "Meet the Press" Host. B. 1947, Chicago. Harvard, 1969, BA. *The Boston Globe*, national reporter, to 1973. WBBM-TV, political reporter, to 1975. WNBC-TV, NY, investigative reporter, to 1978. NBC News, Washington, political reporter, to 1981; "Today" anchor, to 1982; "NBC Nightly News" White House correspondent, current, 1982; "Meet the Press" host, current, 1987. Documentary writer, including "Nancy Reagan, The First Lady," 1984. Peabody Award, 1978; Emmy Award, 1981; Overseas Press Club, 1981.

Wallace, Mike. CBS News. "60 Minutes" Co-Editor & Correspondent. B. 1918, Brookline, MA. U. of MI, 1939, AB. Radio, from 1939. CBS-TV, commentator, 1951-54; TV interviewer, reporter, current, 1951. CBS News, correspondent, from 1963; "60 Minutes" Co-Editor & correspondent, current. Author *Mike Wallace Asks*, 1958; *Close Encounters*, 1984. Emmy Award & Peabody Awards, 1963-71; DuPont Award, 1972.

Wallis, Claudia. *Time.* Associate Editor. B. 1954, Glen Cove, NY. Yale, 1976, Philosophy. *Time*, writer, 1979-84; Assoc Editor, current, 1984. Deadline Award 1982; William Harvey Award, 1983; NY Newspaper Guild Page One Award, 1984; National Magazine Award, 1984.

Wallraff, Barbara. *The Atlantic.* Associate Editor. B. 1953, Tucson, AZ. Antioch College, 1972, Political Science & Philosophy. *The Boston Phoenix*, Assoc Editor, Lifestyle Editor, 1978-83. *The Atlantic*, Assoc Editor, current, 1983.

Walsh, Edward. *The Washington Post.* National Staff Reporter. B. 1942, Chicago, IL. College of St. Thomas (St. Paul, MN), 1963, BA-Political Science & Journalism. Congressional Fellow, American Political Science Assn, 1970-71. Nieman Fellow, 1981-82. *The Catholic Messenger* (Davenport, IA), reporter, Asst Editor, 1965-67. *Houston Chronicle*, reporter, to 1970. *The Washington Post*, metro reporter, 1971-75; White House correspondent, to 1981; Jerusalem correspondent, to 1985; national staff reporter, current, 1985. Merriman Smith Memorial Award, White House Correspondents Assn, 1979.

Walsh, Kenneth. *U.S.News & World Report.* White House Correspondent. *U.S.News & World Report,* Congressional correspondent, to 1986; White House correspondent, current, 1986.

Walsh, Mary Williams. *The Wall Street Journal.* Mexico Bureau Chief. B. Wausau, WI. U. of WI, 1979, BA-French & English. Walter Bagehot Fellow, 1982, '83. Western Publishing, editorial asst, 1978. *The Progressive,* Assoc Editor, 1979. *The Wall Street Journal,* Philadelphia reporter, 1982-85; Mexico Bureau Chief, current, 1985.

Walsh, Michael A. *Time.* Associate Editor. B. 1949, Jacksonville, NC. Eastman School of Music, U. of NY, Rochester, 1971, Musicology. *Rochester Democrat & Chronicle,* reporter, to 1973; music critic, to 1977. *San Francisco Examiner,* music critic, to 1981. *Time,* writer, music critic, to 1983; Assoc Editor, current, 1983. NY State Publishers Assoc 1st Prize, Investigative Reporting, 1972; ASCAP Deems Taylor Award, Criticism, 1980.

Walters, Barbara. ABC News. "20/20" Co-Anchor. B. 1931. Sarah Lawrence College, 1953. WCBS-TV & WPIX, writer-Producer. NBC News, "Today," from 1961, regular panel member, 1963-74, co-host, to 1976. ABC News, "ABC Evening News" newscaster, from 1976; "20/20," co-Anchor, current; occasional "Barbara Walters Special" interview programs, current. *Reader's Digest,* contributor, current. Emmy Award, 1975; awards too numerous to list.

Wattenberg, Ben. United Features Syndicate. Columnist. B. 1933, NYC. Hobart College, 1955, BA. US Air Force, to 1958. Asst to President Johnson, 1966-68. Business consultant, Washington, to 1979. Aide to VP Washington Humphrey, 1970. Campaign adviser, Sen. Henry Jackson, 1972, '76. Mary Washington College, Eminent Scholar, Prof at Large, 1973-74. Presidential Advisory Board on 1972, '76 Ambassadorial Appointments, member, to 1980. US International U., Distinguished Visiting Prof, 1978, '79. International Broadcasting, Vice Chairman of the Board, 1981. Democracy Program, Vice Chairman of the Board, to 1983. Coalition for a Democratic Majority, co-Founder, Chairman, current, 1972. Reading Is Fundamental, Board of Directors member, current, 1977. Hudson Institute, trustee, current, 1976. American Enterprise Institute, Senior Fellow, current, 1977. United Features Syndicate, columnist, current, 1977. *Public Opinion,* Co-Editor, current, 1977. Author 4 books including *The Birth Dearth*: co-author 3 books.

Weber, Peter. Freelance Writer. B. 1957, NYC. Yale, 1980, Philosophy. Freelance, current, 1986.

Weberman, Ben. *Forbes.* Economics Editor. B. 1923, NYC. CCNY, 1943, BS-Mathematics; NYU, 1955, MBA. International Statistical Bureau, Assoc Economist, 1946-51. *The Journal of Commerce,* financial writer, to 1954; Financial Editor, to 1956. *New York Herald Tribune,* Bond Market columnist, to 1961; Financial Editor, to 1964; American Banker, Financial Editor, to 1975. *Forbes,* Senior Editor, current, 1976. *Reporting on Governments* (weekly bond & money market newsletter), Publisher & Editor, current. Author *Interest Rate Futures, Profits and Pitfalls,* 1979.

Weinraub, Bernard. *The New York Times.* Presidential Campaign Correspondent. B. 1937, NYC. CCNY, BA. US Army. *The New York Times,* copyboy, 1961; news clerk; news asst, UN Bureau; reporter, 1963-67; foreign correspondent, to 1968; metro staff, to 1970; London correspondent, to 1973, 1975-77; India correspondent, to 1975; Washington reporter, 1977-87; Sen. Robert Dole presidential campaign correspondent, current, 1987. Newspaper Guild Award.

Weisberg, Jacob. Freelance Writer. B. 1964, Chicago, IL. Yale, 1987, BA-Humanities. City News Bureau of Chicago, reporter, 1985. *The New Republic,* political reporter, researcher, to 1986. Freelance, current, 1986. John Hersey Prize, Journalism, Yale, 1985.

Weisman, Steven. *The New York Times.* New Delhi Bureau Chief. B. 1946, LA, CA. Yale, 1968, BA. *The New York Times,* metro reporter, 1970-74; politics & NYC's financial crisis, to 1976; Albany reporter, 1976; City Hall Bureau Chief, to 1978; Albany Bureau Chief, 1978; Washington reporter, to 1979; White House correspondent, to 1981; senior White House correspondent, to 1985; New Delhi Bureau Chief, current, 1985. Silurian Society Award, 1975.

Weiss, Gary. *BusinessWeek.* Staff Editor — Finance. B. 1954, NYC. CCNY, 1975, BA; Northwestern, 1976, MS. *The Hartford Courant,* reporter, to 1981. States News Service, reporter, 1981. Network News Inc, Business Editor, reporter, to 1983. *Barron's,* writer, to 1986. *BusinessWeek,* Staff Editor, finance, current, 1986.

Wellborn, Stanley N. Speechwriter. B. 1944, San Diego, CA. Washburn U., 1966, English. Washington Journalism Center Fellow, 1969; Ford Foundation Fellow in Education Writing, 1976. *Topeka* (KS) *Capitol-Journal,* 1962-66. Peace Corps member, Ghana, 1967-69. *Congressional Quarterly,* legislative & political writer, 1969-72. *U.S.News & World Report,* science, medicine, education, politics from 1972; Senior Editor, to 1987. Speechwriter, presidential candidate Sen. Robert Dole, current. Contributor *Dollar Politics.* Distinguished Achievement Award, Education Writers Assn, 1982; Space Pioneer Award, Challenger coverage, L5 Society, 1986.

Welles, Chris. *BusinessWeek.* Senior Writer. B. Boston. Princeton, 1959, honors. US Navy, 1959-62. *Life,* reporter, 1962; Business Editor, 1965-68. *Saturday Evening Post,* Business Editor, to 1969. *Esquire & Institutional Investor,* Contributing Editor, to 1983. *Los Angeles Times,* writer, to 1986. *BusinessWeek,* senior writer, current, 1986. Walter Bagehot Fellowship Program in Economics & Business Journalism, Director, 1977-85. Author *The Elusive Bonanza,* 1970, & *The Last Days of the Club,* 1975. National Magazine Award; Gerald Loeb, U. of MO & John Hancock Business Writing Awards.

Welling, Kathryn M. *Barron's.* Managing Editor. B. 1952, Fort Wayne, IN. Northwestern, 1974, Journalism, Urban Affairs. Dow Jones News Retrieval Service, copy reader, 1974. AP-Dow Jones, copy reader, 1975. *The Wall Street Journal,* Copy Editor, 1976. *Barron's,* Assoc Editor, to 1982; asst to Editor, to 1983; Managing Editor, current, 1983.

Wenner, Jann. *Rolling Stone.* Editor & Publisher. B. 1946, NYC. Studied U. of CA, Berkeley, 1964-66. *Rolling*

Stone, Editor & Publisher, current, 1966. *Outside Magazine*, Editor-in-Chief, 1977-78. *Look*, Editor & Publisher, 1979. *Record*, Editor & Publisher, 1981-86. Author *Lennon Remembers*, 1971; *Garcia*, 1972. National Magazine Award, 1970, '77, '86; USC Distinguished Achievement Award, School of Journalism & Alumni Assoc, 1976.

West, Diana. *The Washington Times.* Movie Critic. B. 1961, LA, CA. Yale, 1983, English. *The Public Interest*, Asst Editor, to 1984. *The Washington Times*, feature writer, to 1986; movie critic, current, 1987.

West, Woody. *Insight.* Associate Editor. B. 1934, Montana. St. John's College, American U., 1961, History. *Lincoln* (NE) *Star*, reporter, 1961. *Omaha World-Herald*, Copy Editor, to 1962. *The Washington Star*, Asst National Editor, Asst City Editor, reporter, to 1980; editorial writer, 1975-81. *The Milwaukee Journal*, editorial writer, Washington, to 1982. *The Washington Times*, editorial writer, 1983. *Insight*, Managing Editor, to 1986; Assoc Editor, current, 1986.

Whalen, Bill. *Insight.* Writer. B. 1960, Washington, DC. Washington & Lee U., 1982, BAJ. *Compass Publications*, Assoc Editor, 1983-85. *Insight*, writer, current, 1985.

White, George. *Detroit Free Press.* Columnist & Business Reporter. B. 1953, Detroit, MI. MI State U., 1975, BA-History & Journalism; 1981, MA-African History. *Minneapolis Tribune*, urban environment, Native American affairs, investigative, to 1979. *U.S.News & World Report*, midwest correspondent, to 1984. *Detroit Free Press*, columnist & business reporter, current 1984. Freelance, current.

Whitney, Craig R. *The New York Times.* Washington Bureau Chief. B. 1943, Milford, MA. Harvard, 1965, BA, *magna cum laude.* *The Worcester* (MA) *Telegram*, reporter, 1963-65. US Navy, to 1969. *The New York Times*, asst to James Reston, to 1966; metro news staff, 1969-1971; Saigon Bureau Chief, to 1973; Bonn Bureau Chief, to 1977; Moscow correspondent, to 1980; Deputy Foreign Editor, to 1982; Foreign Editor, to 1983; Asst Managing Editor, to 1986; Washington Bureau Chief, current, 1986.

Whitworth, William. *The Atlantic.* Editor. B. 1937, Hot Springs, AR. U. of OK, 1960, BA. *Arkansas Gazette* (Little Rock), reporter, 1960-63. *New York Herald Tribune*, reporter, to 1965. *The New Yorker*, staff writer, 1966-72; Assoc Editor, to 1980. *The Atlantic*, Editor, current, 1980.

Wicker, Thomas Grey. *The New York Times.* "In The Nation" Columnist. B. 1926, Hamlet, NC. U. of NC, 1948. Nieman Fellow, 1957-58. *Sandhill Citizen* (Aberdeen, NC), Editor. *The Daily Robesonia* (Lumberton, NC), Sports & Telegraph Editor. NC State Board of Public Welfare, Information Director. *The Winston-Salem Journal*, Copy Editor; Sports Editor, 1954-55; Editor, Sunday feature section, to 1957; editorial writer; city hall reporter, to 1959. US Naval Reserves, 1952-54. *The Tennessean* (Nashville, TN), Assoc Editor, to 1960. *The New York Times*, Washington reporter; White House correspondent, to 1964; Washington Bureau Chief, to 1966; "In the Nation" columnist, current, 1966.

Author 4 books, including *On Press*, 1978. John Peter Zenger Award, Freedom of the Press, U. of AZ, 1984.

Wiegner, Kathleen K. *Forbes.* West Coast Bureau Manager. B. 1938, Milwaukee, WI. U. of WI, 1960, BS-English & Journalism, 1962, MA-English & Comparative Literature, 1967, PhD-English & Comparative Literature. U. of WI, instructor, to 1967; asst prof, to 1974. *Forbes*, reporter, researcher, to 1975; reporter, to 1978; writer, to 1979; Assoc Editor, to 1984; Senior Editor, to 1985; West Coast Bureau Manager, current, 1985.

Wiggins, Philip. *The New York Times.* "Business Day" Reporter. B. 1942, East Orange, NJ. Rutgers. WINS News Radio, writer. *New Issue Outlook*, asst to Publisher; writer. *The New York Times*, copy reader; news asst; "Business Day" reporter, current. Author *Unorganized Violence.*

Wildstrom, Stephen H. *BusinessWeek.* Senior News Editor. U. of MI, *Phi Beta Kappa.* AP, Detroit staff, 1969-72. *BusinessWeek*, correspondent, Detroit, to 1974; correspondent, Washington (McGraw-Hill World News), to 1977; economic correspondent, to 1985; Senior News Editor, Washington, current, 1985.

Wilford, John Noble. *The New York Times.* Science Reporter. B. 1933. U. of TN, 1955, BSJ, *magna cum laude*; Syracuse, MS-Political Science. Ford Foundation Fellow, Columbia. US Army, Counter Intelligence Corps, 1957-59. *The Wall Street Journal*, reporter. *Time*, Contributing Editor, to 1965; science section writer, 1965. *The New York Times*, science reporter, to 1973; Asst National News Editor, to 1974; Science Director, to 1979; science reporter, current, 1979. Author *We Reach the Moon*, 1969; *The Mapmakers*, 1981: co-author 3 books, including (with William Stockton) *The Riddle Of The Dinosaur*, 1985. Gerald M. Loeb Achievement Award, 1972; National Space Club's Press Award, 1974; American Assn for the Advancement of Science/Westinghouse Science Writing Award, 1983; Pulitzer Prize, National Reporting, Science Writing, 1984: co-winner Pulitzer Prize, National Reporting, space shuttle disaster coverage, 1987.

Will, George. *Newsweek*, Contributing Editor. *Washington Post* Writers Group, Political Columnist. B. 1941, Champaign, IL. Attended Trinity College, Oxford; Princeton. Teacher, Politics, MI State U., U. of IL, U. of Toronto. Congressional aide, Sen. Allot (CO), to 1972. *National Review*, Washington Editor, 1972. *Washington Post* Writers Group, columnist, current, 1972. *Newsweek*, columnist, current. ABC, "This Week" commentary, current. Author 3 books, including *Statecraft as Soulcraft: What Government Does*, 1982. Pulitzer Prize, Commentary, 1977.

Williams, Dan. *Los Angeles Times.* Mexico City Bureau Chief. B. 1949, Pittsburgh, PA. Yale, 1971, BA-Political Science; Defense Language Institute, Cantonese. US Army, 1971-74. *The Miami News*, business writer, 1977-79. *The Miami Herald*, Latin American community reporter, Miami govt reporter, Peking Bureau Chief, Jerusalem Bureau Chief, to 1983. *Los Angeles Times*, San Salvador Bureau Chief, to 1985; Mexico City Bureau Chief, current, 1985.

Williams, Nick B. Jr. *Los Angeles Times*. Southeast Asia Bureau Chief. B. 1937, Santa Monica, CA. Claremont Men's College (CA), 1959, Business Administration. *San Diego Union*, metro reporter, Sunday desk, to 1964. *Sun-Times*, metro, financial & Sunday desks, to 1967. *Los Angeles Times*, Copy Editor, Metro News Editor, to 1972; Asst National Editor, to 1976; Asst & Deputy Foreign Editor, to 1985; SE Asia Bureau Chief, Bangkok, current, 1985.

Williams, Winston. *The New York Times*. Metro Reporter. Brown; Columbia, 1973, BA, 1974, MSJ. *BusinessWeek*, correspondent, to 1975; Pittsburgh Bureau Chief, to 1977. *The New York Times*, business & financial reporter, to 1987; metro reporter, current, 1987.

Willoughby, Jack. *Forbes*. Staff Writer. Carleton College (Ottawa, Canada), 1977, BAJ. Walter Bagehot Fellow, 1983-84. *Globe & Mail* (Canada), business writer, 1977-83. *Forbes*, staff writer, current, 1984. National Business Writing Award, Investigative Journalism (work at *Globe & Mail*).

Wilner, Judith. *The New York Times*. Technology Editor. *Norman* (OK) *Transcript*. Loveland (CO) *Daily Reporter-Herald*, News Editor. *Albuquerque Tribune*, City Editor. *The Denver Post*, Systems Editor, Copy Desk Chief. *The New York Times*, Deputy Technology Editor, 1984-87; Technology Editor, current, 1987.

Wilson, George C. *The Washington Post*. National Staff. B. Orange, NJ. Studied Georgia Tech; Bucknell; *Alliance Francaise* (Paris, France). *The Washington Post*, staff member since 1966; Pentagon reporter; Vietnam correspondent; national staff, military affairs, current. Co-author (with F. Carl Schumacher Jr.) *Bridge of No Return: The Ordeal of the U.S.S. Pueblo*. Mark Watson Memorial Award, Distinguished Military News Coverage, 1970.

Winder, David. *The Christian Science Monitor*. London Correspondent. B. South Africa. Fellowship, Columbia Grad School of Journalism. *The Natal Witness* (South Africa). *The Christian Science Monitor*, Boston, NY, LA bureaus, 1965-70; UN correspondent, to 1973; London staff, to 1978; Asst International News Editor, to 1983; roving Third World correspondent, to 1984; London correspondent, current, 1984. Population Action Council's Award, 1983.

Wines, Michael. *Los Angeles Times*. Washington Economic Correspondent. B. 1951, Louisville, KY. U. of KY, 1973, BA-Political Science & Journalism; Columbia, 1974, MSJ. *Lexington Herald*, reporter, 1974. *The Louisville Times*, reporter, to 1981. *National Journal*, Washington reporter, regulatory affairs, to 1984. *Los Angeles Times*, Washington economic correspondent, current, 1984.

Winter, Thomas Swanson. *Human Events*. Editor & Co-owner. B. 1937, Hackensack, NJ. Harvard, 1959, BA-Government, 1961, MBA. *Human Events*, Asst Editor, 1961-64; Editor, current, 1964.

Witcher, S. Karene. *The Wall Street Journal*. Reporter. B. Monroe, GA. Davidson College (NC), 1975, BA-English; U. of Montpellier, France; U. of MO, 1977, MSJ. *The Asian Wall Street Journal*, reporter, Hong Kong, to 1979; reporter, Singapore, to 1982. *The Wall Street Journal*, reporter, NY, current, 1982.

Woestendiek, John. *Philadelphia Inquirer*. Reporter. B. 1953, Winston-Salem, NC. U. of NC, 1975, Journalism. *Arizona Daily Star*, reporter, 1975-78. *Lexington Leader*, reporter, Asst City Editor, City Editor, to 1981. *Philadelphia Inquirer*, reporter, current, 1981. Various Star Press Awards, PA, KY & AZ; Paul Tobenkin Memorial Award, 1983; National Headliners Award, Investigative Reporting, 1987; Pulitzer Prize, Investigative Reporting, 1987.

Wolman, Clive R. *Financial Times*. Financial Services Correspondent. B. 1956, Sheffield, UK. Oxford, Philosophy, Politics & Economics, 1st Class Honors. *Reading Evening Post*, reporter, 1978-80. *Jerusalem Post*, Sub-Editor; economic & industry ministry correspondent, to 1981. *Financial Times*, company comments writer, to 1983; Personal Finance Editor, to 1985; financial services correspondent, current, 1985.

Wolman, William. *BusinessWeek*. Editor. B. Canada. McGill U.; Stanford, PhD-Economics. Citibank, VP, economic publications, 1969-71. Argus Research, economic trends forecaster, to 1974. ESPN, "Business Times," Exec Editor, 1983. *BusinessWeek*, economics staff, 1960-65; Economics Editor, to 1969; Senior Editor, Economics dept, 1974-79; Deputy Editor, to 1983; Editor, current, 1984. PBS, "Nightly Business Report" commentary, current. Author *The Beat Inflation Strategy; The Decline of U.S. Power*. U. of MO Journalism Award, 1978; National Magazine Award, 1981; Deadline Club Award, 1981; John Hancock Award, 1981; Champion-Tuck Award, 1984.

Woodbury, Richard C. *Time*. Houston Bureau Chief. B. 1933, NYC. St. Lawrence U., 1956, English. *Newsday*, sportswriter, summers 1954-56. Fairchild Publications, reporter, 1958-59. *Morning Sun* (Grand Junction, CO), reporter, 1960. *Daily Sentinel* (Grand Junction, CO), reporter, 1961. *The Denver Post*, reporter, Copy Editor, Bureau Chief, to 1965. *Life*, reporter, to 1972. *Time*, from 1972: correspondent; Denver Bureau Chief; Houston Bureau Chief, current.

Woodruff, Judy C. PBS Television. "MacNeil/Lehrer NewsHour" Correspondent. B. 1946, Tulsa. Studied Meredith College; Duke, 1968, BA. Benton Fellow, U. of Chicago. Knight Fellow, Stanford. WAGA-TV (Atlanta), reporter, 1970-75. NBC News, Atlanta news correspondent, to 1976; White House correspondent, to 1983. PBS, "MacNeil/Lehrer NewsHour" correspondent, current, 1983; "Frontline" anchor, current, 1983. Author *This Is Judy Woodruff At The White House*, 1982.

Woodward, Bob. *The Washington Post*. Assistant Managing Editor — Investigative. B. Geneva, IL. Yale, BA-English & History. US Navy, communications officer. *Montgomery County* (MD) *Sentinel*, investigative reporter, to 1971. *The Washington Post*, investigative reporter; Asst Managing Editor, investigative, current. Author *Wired; Veil: The Secret Wars of the CIA 1981-1987*, 1987: co-author (with Carl Bernstein) *All The President's Men*, 1974, *The Final Days*, 1976; (with Scott Armstrong) *The Brethren*, 1979. Drew Pearson Foundation Award; Heywood Broun Award; George Polk Memorial Award; *Sigma Delta Chi* Award: co-winner (with Carl Bernstein) Pulitzer Prize, Watergate coverage, 1973.

Wooster, Martin Morse. *The Wilson Quarterly.* Associate Editor. B. 1957, Washington, DC. Beloit College (WI), 1980, BA-History & Philosophy. *Harper's,* Asst Washington Editor, 1981; Washington Editor, 1983-87. Network News, staff writer, 1981-83. *The Wilson Quarterly,* Assoc Editor, current, 1987. Freelance, current.

Worsthorne, Peregrine. *Sunday Telegraph.* Editor. B. 1923, Chelsea, London, UK. Peterhouse, Cambridge; Magdalen College, Oxford, History. *The Times,* Washington correspondent, to 1952; leader writer, to 1955. *Daily Telegraph,* leader writer, 1955. *Sunday Telegraph,* Asst Editor, to 1986; Editor, current, 1986.

Woutat, Donald. *Los Angeles Times.* Energy Writer. B. 1944, Grand Forks, ND. U. of ND, 1969, English. *Daily News-Miner* (Fairbanks, AK), reporter, to 1970. *Minneapolis Star,* reporter, to 1974. *News Journal* (Wilmington, DE), police, Asst City Editor, to 1976. AP, reporter, to 1979. *Detroit Free Press,* auto writer, to 1981. *The Wall Street Journal,* Detroit staff, 1984. *Los Angeles Times,* Detroit Bureau Chief, to 1984; high technology writer, to 1986; energy writer, current, 1986.

Wright, Michael. *National Journal.* Executive Editor. B. 1942, Fort Benning, GA. U. of AL, 1964. US Navy, to 1968. *Constitution,* city hall reporter, editorial writer, federal courts reporter, to 1970. *U.S.News & World Report,* regional correspondent, Atlanta; Congressional correspondent, to 1976; White House reporter, to 1978. *The New York Times,* "The Week in Review" Editor, to 1986. *National Journal,* Exec Editor, current, 1986.

Wright, Robin B. *The Christian Science Monitor.* Contributor. Poynter Fellow, Yale, 1985. Carnegie Endowment for International Peace, senior assoc, 1986. *The Washington Post,* special correspondent, to 1977. CBS News, correspondent, Africa, to 1980; Rome, 1981. London *Sunday Times,* correspondent, Beirut, to 1985. Duke, visiting prof, 1985-86. *The Christian Science Monitor,* correspondent, 1972-73; Asst Foreign Editor, to 1974; special correspondent in Africa, to 1975; Teheran, contributor, current. Overseas Press Club, 1975, '76.

Wysocki, Bernard B. Jr. *The Wall Street Journal.* Tokyo Bureau Chief. B. Waterloo, IA. Dartmouth, 1971, AB-Liberal Arts. *Amherst* (MA) *Record,* reporter, 1972. *Daily Hampshire Gazette* (Northampton, MA), 1973. *Albany* (NY) *Times-Union,* business & economics reporter, 1975. *The Wall Street Journal,* reporter, Cleveland, to 1978; reporter, Chicago, to 1979; Philadelphia Bureau Chief, to 1982; News Editor, to 1983; NY News Editor, to 1985; Tokyo Bureau Chief, current, 1985.

Yardley, Jonathan. *The Washington Post.* Book Critic. B. 1939, Pittsburgh, PA. U. of NC, 1961, BA-English. Nieman Fellow, 1968-69. *The New York Times. Greensboro* (NC) *Daily News. The Miami Herald,* Book Editor, 1974-78. *Sports Illustrated,* Contributing Editor, 1974-81. *The Washington Post,* book critic, to 1981. Freelance, current. *The Washington Post,* book critic, current, 1981. Author *Ring: A Biography of Ring Lardner.* Pulitzer Prize, Distinguished Criticism, 1981.

Yoder, Edwin. *Washington Post* Writers Group. Columnist. B. 1934, Greensboro, NC. U. of NC, 1956, BA; Oxford, 1958. *Charlotte News,* editorial writer, to 1961. *Greensboro Daily News,* editorial writer, to 1964; Assoc Editor, to 1975. U. of NC, asst prof, history, 1964-65. *Washington Star,* Editorial Page Editor, to 1981. *Washington Post* Writers Group, columnist, current, 1981. NC Press Assn Award, Editorial Writing, 1958, '61, '66; Walker Stone Award, Scripps-Howard Foundation, 1978; Pulitzer Prize, Editorial Writing, 1979.

Young, Leah R. *The Journal of Commerce.* Reporter & Washington Insurance Editor. B. 1942, Brooklyn, NY. George Washington U., 1964, AB-Political Science; Columbia, 1965, MAJ. UPI, foreign desk, to 1966. *Baltimore News-American,* magazine writer, to 1966. Ghost writer, Sen. Harrison Williams, 1966. *The Journal of Commerce,* reporter, Washington Insurance Editor, insurance, law & banking issues, current, 1966.

Younghusband, Peter. *The Washington Times.* Special Correspondent, South Africa. B. 1931, Cape Town, South Africa. Educated in South Africa. *Northern Echo* (Darlington, UK), reporter, 1958. Reuters, London, desk rewriter, 1959. *Cape Times* (Cape Town), reporter, 1960. *Drum Magazine* (Johannesburg), feature writer, 1961. *London Daily Mail,* foreign correspondent (Africa, Middle East, Far East), to 1970; Washington Bureau Chief, White House correspondent, 1970. *Newsweek,* special correspondent, South Africa, to 1986. *The Washington Times,* special correspondent, South Africa, current, 1986. Co-winner (with Andrew Nagorski) Overseas Press Club award, 1974.

Zalaznick, Sheldon. *Forbes.* Managing Editor. B. 1928, NYC. University College, NYU, 1948, BA-English Literature; Columbia Teachers College, 1950, MA. High school English teacher, NYC, to 1952. *Newsweek,* copyboy, clip desk, researcher, sports, Editor, to 1956. Public Relations, NYC, to 1959. *New York Herald Tribune,* Founding Editor, "New York" (Sunday magazine), Sunday Editor, to 1966. General Learning Corp, writer. *Fortune,* Assoc Editor, to 1969; NY Editorial Director, to 1976. *Forbes,* Assoc Editor, Senior Editor, 1959-63; Managing Editor, current, 1976.

Zaslow, Jeffrey. *Chicago Sun-Times.* "All That Zazz" Columnist. Chicago. B. 1958, Philadelphia, PA. Carnegie-Mellon U., 1980, Creative Writing. *The Orlando Sentinel,* feature writer, to 1983. *The Wall Street Journal,* commodity reporter, features, Chicago, to 1987. *Chicago Sun-Times,* "All That Zazz" columnist, current, 1987.

Zonana, Victor F. *Los Angeles Times.* Financial Reporter. B. 1954, NYC. Dartmouth, 1975, AB-Economics, *summa cum laude, Phi Beta Kappa. The Wall Street Journal,* reporter, Philadelphia, San Francisco, to 1985. *Los Angeles Times,* opened 1st financial bureau, San Francisco; reporter, Northern CA business & economics, current, 1985.

Zucker, Seymour. *BusinessWeek.* Senior Editor, Economic News. Brooklyn College; New School for Social Research, PhD-Economics. Port Authority of NY & NJ, economist. NBC Planning Dept, staff economist. *BusinessWeek,* Economics Editor, 1974-80; Senior Editor, Economic News, economics, Wall Street, markets & investments, current, 1980.

Zuckerman, Mortimer B. *U.S.News & World Report*, Chairman, Editor-in-Chief & Editorial Writer. *The Atlantic*, Chairman. B. 1937, Canada. McGill U., 1957, Economics & Political Theory, 1961, Law; U. of PA, 1961, MBA; Harvard, 1962, Master of Law. Boston Properties, Chairman & Founder, current, 1970. *The Atlantic*, Chairman, current, 1980. *U.S.News & World Report*, Chairman, Editor-in-Chief & editorial writer, current, 1984.

Zumwalt, Admiral Elmo Russell Jr. *Los Angeles Times* Syndicate. "Zumwalt/Bagley Report" Columnist (with Worth Bagley). B. 1920, Tulare, CA. US Naval Academy, 1942, *cum laude*; Naval War College, 1953; National War College, 1962. Chief of Naval Operations, Member of Joint Chiefs of Staff, 1970-74. *Los Angeles Times* Syndicate, "Zumwalt/Bagley Report" writer (with Worth Bagley), current. Author *On Watch*, 1976. Co-author *My Father, My Son*.

Zweig, Jason. *Forbes*. Reporter. B. 1959, MA. Columbia College, 1981, Art History. *Africa Report*, editorial asst & Asst Editor, 1983-84. Freelance, W. Africa, 1985. *Time f.y.i.*, newsletter reporter, to 1986; "Economy & Business" reporter, researcher, to 1987. *Forbes*, reporter, current, 1987.

INDEX

A

A&P, 167
  see also James Wood
A&S, 137
  expansion, 137
  see also Herald Square
Aaron, David, 262, 268
Aarto, Arvo, 220
  see also Finland
ABA, 307
Abbas, Muhammad Abu, 186
Abbott, Jack, 327
Abelson, Alan , 71, 72, 73, **123**, 129
ABC-TV, 96
  "Nightline", 277
Abdallah, Georges Ibrahim, 184
  see also Terrorism
ABM Treaty, 1972, 36, 37, 54, 198,
  254, 258, 260, 263, 264, 265, 266, 268,
  322, 323, 335
  see also INF Treaty, Krasnoyarsk and
  Summit Meetings
Abortion, 98, 261, 283, 286, 290, 292
  Pro-Life, 290
Abrahamson, Gen., 77
Abrams, Elliott, 296, 319, 321
Abrams, Morris, 28
Abstinence, 19
  see also AIDS
ACLU, 319
A.C. Nielsen Rating System, 279
Accuracy in Media, 2
Acid Rain, 11
Acker, Edward, 126
  see also Pan Am
Activase, 41, 177
Adams, Nathan, 34
Adams, Peter, 36, **253**, 262
Adelman, Asher, 42
Adler, Jerry, **271**
Adler, Renata, 9, 106
Advertising, 123, 135, 149, 154, 158, 172
  TV ads, 143
  see also Jerry Della Femina
Advo, 178
Adweek, 154
Aerospace Industry, 125, 146, 257
Affirmative Action, 290
Afghanistan, 51, 186, 199, 218, 231, 232,
  244, 253, 258, 261, 263, 264, 268, 277,
  286, 293, 316, 317, 324, 326
AFL-CIO, 23, 131
Africa, 55, 57, 161, 187, 238, 240, 324
  AIDS, 18, 19, 20, 187, 208
  see also AIDS
  art, 290
  living standards, 147
  North Africa, 224, 234
  river blindness, 188

southern Africa, 89
sub-Saharan Africa, 1, 57
African National Congress, 324
Aga Khan, Karim, 143
Against All Hope, see Armando
  Vallardes
Aganbegyan, Abel G., 29
Agriculture, 22
  see also Farmers
Aho, C. Michael, 85
AIDS, 1, 6, **17-21**, 65, 70, 94, 105, 124, 133,
  164, 223, 233, 253, 260, 271, 275, 278,
  279, 280, 284, 285, 286, 287, 288, 294,
  295, 298, 303, 304, 307, 310, 319, 324,
  325, 329, 330, 332, 336
  anal intercourse, 282
  arthropod viral transmission, see arthropod viral transmission
  Africa, see Africa
  Arcadia, see Ray Family
  Belgium, see Belgium
  Catholic church, see Catholic Church
  children, 17, 20, 105
  civil liberties, 18
  Cuba, see Cuba
  economic complicatons, 17, 162
  hemophilia, see Hemophilia
  heterosexual transmission, 17, 18, 20, 21,
  271, 282, 297
  homosexuals, 19, 297, 298, 307
  Japan, see Japan
  Levi-Strauss employee program, see
  Levi-Strauss
  marriage licenses, see Marriage
  Licenses
  "medically-indigent adults", 133
  The Netherlands, see The Netherlands
  President's Commission, see President's
  Commission on AIDS
  prevention, 17, 19, 20, 102, 176, 286,
  310, 325
  prostitutes, 105
  Southern California, 70
  students, 18
  testing, 41, 315, 319, 330
  UK, see UK
  UN, see United Nations
  USSR, 20
  vaccine, 288, 297, 304 see also
  MicroGeneSys Company
  western Europe, 184
Airbus Industries, 125, 207
Aircraft Industry, 125, 138
Air Force, 77
  see also US Air Force
Airline Industry, 143, 150, 154, 166,
  175, 281
  see also American, Continental, Eastern
  and Federal Aviation Authority
Airport Congestion, 92

Air Travel, 110
  safety, 110
Albania, 216
Alcoholism, 112
Aldridge, Peter, 157
Alexander, Rep. Bill, 317
Alexander, Lincoln, 197
Alfa Romeo, 243
  see also Auto Industry
Alfonsin, Raul, 181, 191, 194, 197, 205,
  206, 220, 225
  see also Argentina
Alfred A. Knopf, 8
Algeria, 234
Algonquin Round Table, 318
Allegheny International, 243
Allegis, 150
  see also Dick Ferris
Allied-Signal, 86, 158
  see also Edward Hennessy
Allis, Sam, 295
Allison, Wick, 101, 102
Almond, Peter, 376, **181**
Al Shiraa, 30, 34, 298
  see also Iran-Contra Affair
Alsop, Joseph, 197
Alsop, Ronald, **123**
  see also *The Wall Street Journal* New
  York bureau
Alter, Jonathan, 5, 37, 95, **271**
Altman, Lawrence, 17, **271**
  see also *The New York Times*
  coverage of AIDS
Alzheimer's Disease, 172, 176
  THA, 176
AMC, 145
  Jeep, 145
  see also Auto Industry
American Airlines, 144
  see also Airline Industry
American Civil Liberties Commission, 304
American Enterprise Institute (AEI), 95,
  154
American Express, 133, 154
  Amex Optima Card, 133
American Federal of Scientists, 259
American Physical Society, 13, 39, 141
  "Woodstock" meeting at New York
  Hilton, 13, 141
  see also Superconductivity
The American Spectator, 2, **69-70**
'Amerika', 302, 313, 328
Amsterdam, Jane, 95
Amstrad, 220
  see also Alan Sugar
Anaya, Herbert, 229
  see also Human Rights Commission
Anders, George, **124**
  see also *The Wall Street Journal*
  coverage of Wall Street

Index

413

Don't Risk Losing Your Only Copy
Of *The 1988 MediaGuide!*

You know what will happen. Everyone will want to borrow your copy of *The MediaGuide* and eventually you'll lose track of it. But that doesn't have to happen. You can order additional copies for your colleagues...or have them order their own.

To order, fill out the coupon below and return it today. Any order for 10 books or more is eligible for a 40 percent discount.

The 1988 MediaGuide _____

Polyconomics, Inc.
86 Maple Avenue
Morristown, New Jersey 07960
(201) 267-2515

You're right; I don't want to lose my only copy. Please rush me _____ copies of *The 1988 MediaGuide.* I enclose $17.95 plus $2.00 for postage and handling for each book I order.

☐ I'm ordering more than 10 books and am taking your 40 percent discount.

Name _____

Address _____

Make checks payable to Polyconomics, Inc.

City _____ State_____ Zip_____

PLEASE PRINT